SCHIZOPHRENIA AND OTHER PSYCHOTIC DISORDERS (273)

295.xx   Schizophrenia
The following Classification of Longitudinal Course applies to all subtypes of Schizophrenia:
     Episodic With Interepisode Residual
     Symptoms *(specify if:* With Prominent

ABNORMAL PSYCHOLOGY

ABOUT the AUTHOR

David S. Holmes received his Ph.D. in clinical psychology from Northwestern University and did his clinical internship at the Harvard Medical School (Massachusetts Mental Health Center). He has been on the faculty at Northwestern University, the New School for Social Research, and the University of Kansas. He was also a Visiting Research Scholar in the Personality and Social Psychology "think tank" at the Educational Testing Service, Princeton.

Professor Holmes focuses most of his attention on the areas of psychopathology, personality, and health psychology. He has published more than 120 articles in leading scientific journals. Professor Holmes has received the Award for Distinguished Teaching in Psychology from the American Psychological Foundation. The citation for that award called attention to his "writing accessible textbooks with impeccable scholarship." He was also named the Outstanding Teacher in a Four-Year College or University by the Division of Teaching of the American Psychological Association, received the Standard Oil Foundation Award for Excellence in Teaching, and was named as one of the Outstanding Educators in America.

Within the American Psychological Association, Professor Holmes served on the Board of Scientific Affairs (chair), the Board of Educational Affairs, the Committee on Membership and Fellowship (chair), and the Board of Convention Affairs (chair). He has been elected a Fellow in the Divisions of Clinical Psychology, Personality and Social Psychology, Health Psychology, Teaching of Psychology, and General Psychology. He was also elected a Fellow of the American Psychopathological Association. For six years Professor Holmes served on the Advanced Psychology Test committee for the Graduate Record Examination.

ABNORMAL PSYCHOLOGY

THIRD EDITION

DAVID S. HOLMES

University of Kansas

 LONGMAN

An imprint of Addison Wesley Longman, Inc.

New York • Reading, Massachusetts • Menlo Park, California • Harlow, England
Don Mills, Ontario • Sydney • Mexico City • Madrid • Amsterdam

Acquisitions Editor: Catherine Woods
Developmental Editor: Marion B. Castellucci
Project Editor: Susan Goldfarb
Supplements Editors: Diane Wansing, Cyndy Taylor
Text and Cover Designer: Alice Fernandes-Brown
Chapter Opener Art: Edward A. Butler
Cover Illustration: Edward A. Butler
Art Studio: Burmar
Photo Researcher: Julie Tesser
Electronic Production Manager: Alexandra Odulak
Desktop Coordinator: Joanne Del Ben
Manufacturing Manager: Hilda Koparanian
Electronic Page Makeup: Joanne Del Ben
Printer and Binder: Courier/Kendallville
Cover Printer: Phoenix Color Corp.

About the Art: The pastel panels in this book were created especially for *Abnormal Psychology* by New York artist and graphic designer Edward A. Butler. A graduate of Philadelphia College of Art, Butler is the recipient of the Society of Illustrators Merit Award and the Philadelphia, Chicago, and New York Art Directors Clubs Awards. His work is held by several private collectors.

For permission to use copyrighted material, grateful acknowledgment is made to the copyright holders on p. 671, which is hereby made part of this copyright page.

Library of Congress Cataloging-in-Publication Data

Holmes, David S., (David Sheridan), 1939–
    Abnormal psychology / David S. Holmes. — 3rd ed.
        p.   cm.
    Includes bibliographical references and index.
    ISBN 0-673-98094-4
    1. Psychology, Pathological.   2. Psychology, Pathological—Case studies.   I. Title.
RC454.H62   1997   96-27907
616.89—dc20   CIP

ISBN 0-673-98094-4

1 2 3 4 5 6 7 8 9 10–CRK–99 98 97 96

CONTENTS in BRIEF

CONTENTS in DETAIL

CASE STUDIES

PREFACE

There have been a variety of interesting and important developments in the area of abnormal psychology since the second edition of *Abnormal Psychology* was published, and those developments are reflected in this new edition. In addition to including many new findings (there are hundreds of new references), I have added some new instructional features that make the presentation more efficient and will help students grasp the material. In the sections that follow, first I will describe the book in general for those readers who are not already familiar with it; then I will describe what is new in this edition; and finally I will describe the supplements that are available with the book.

GENERAL GOALS

My first goal in writing this book was to develop a text that would *teach* and *involve* students. Regardless of how up-to-date or sophisticated a book may be, if it cannot teach, it is virtually useless. To achieve that goal, I organized the material carefully (I'm a nut about organization), and I arranged it so ideas build systematically on one another. I also tried to convey a sense of excitement about the problems and progress in this area, and I used numerous case studies to illustrate symptoms, causes, and treatments.

My second goal was to present the *new and intriguing findings in the area of abnormal psychology that are not found in most of the other books in the area.* The "core" findings are here, but there is much more. This book is *not* what in the publishing industry is called a "me too" book.

My third goal was to present material in a context that encourages *critical evaluation.* Understanding what we know is important, but it is equally important for students to understand what we do not know. Furthermore, fostering critical evaluation is essential because throughout their lives students will be bombarded by reports of "new breakthroughs" in the area of mental health, and it is crucial that they be able to evaluate those findings effectively. We all hope that what we teach will last beyond the end of the semester, and the critical evaluation encouraged here should help achieve that goal.

EXPLANATIONS FOR ABNORMAL BEHAVIOR

All the major disorders discussed in this book are systematically examined from four perspectives: *psychodynamic, learning, cognitive,* and *physiological.* This approach provides balance, and it enables students to compare and evaluate the various explanations for a specific disorder. In presenting each explanation I have taken the position of an advocate of that position. However, the various explanations are not presented as mutually exclusive or necessarily competing. On the contrary, in many instances they are presented as complementing one another so that, when taken together, the four perspectives provide a more complete understanding of a disorder than any single perspective could. *The perspectives work together, and the whole is better than the sum of the parts.*

The trend in many books is to offer what is called an "integrated" approach, and in most cases this means that most disorders are described from one point of view, usually the cognitive point of view. I take a different position: specifically, I take the position that *different disorders can have different causes.* For example, phobias may result from classical conditioning, depression may stem from erroneous cognitions, and schizophrenia may be caused by physiological problems in the brain. Furthermore, *sometimes the same disorder may have different causes in different individuals.* For example, in some individuals depression may be due to erroneous cognitions, in others it may be due to stress that lowers the levels of a neurotransmitter, and in yet others depression may be due to genetically determined low levels of a neurotransmitter.

To use the "integrated" approach, in which all disorders are viewed explicitly or implicitly from one perspective, is analogous to arguing that cancer and diabetes have the same cause, and it is simply a modern version of the position taken 40 years ago, when all disorders were said to result from unconscious drives and conflicts. In this book, I have taken a broader perspective and I have incorporated into the discussion a number of different explanations. I believe that this more accurately reflects the state of our knowledge, and when the winds of data blow, I think we will be safer sitting on a four-legged stool than on a one-legged one.

ORGANIZATION

The overall organization of the book is fairly traditional in that the major parts are devoted to the following topics:

1. *Introduction* (history; descriptions of mental health professionals; introductions to the four perspectives; a discussion of stress; a summary of diagnostic techniques and research methods)
2. *Anxiety, somatoform, and dissociative disorders*
3. *Mood disorders*
4. *Schizophrenia and other psychotic disorders*
5. *Other disorders* (personality; infancy and childhood; eating, sleep, and psychophysiological; substance abuse; sexual; cognitive and retardation)
6. *Issues of law, patient care, and prevention*

For all practical purposes, these parts are freestanding and can be reordered to fit a variety of different course plans.

This book has more chapters than some other books because I split particularly large topics into several chapters. Students who used the book preferred and did better with the somewhat smaller units, and instructors appreciated the fact that if they wanted to reorder or eliminate topics, they could be more selective in doing so.

When discussing any one disorder, I used a consistent outline for presenting material:

A. Symptoms
  1. Mood
  2. Cognitive
  3. Somatic
  4. Motor
B. Issues
  1. History
  2. Prevalence
  3. Sociocultural factors
  4. Diagnostic problems
C. Explanations
  1. Psychodynamic
  2. Learning
  3. Cognitive
  4. Physiological
D. Treatments
  1. Psychodynamic
  2. Learning
  3. Cognitive
  4. Physiological

Students and instructors have liked the consistency and clarity of the organization. The outline provides them with a consistent template with which to organize material. The organization facilitates teaching, aids recall, and enhances the ability to compare ideas and disorders.

TREATMENTS

Rather than discussing all treatments in one chapter, as is done in many other books, *the treatment of a disorder is discussed immediately after the disorder is described and explained.* I did this because in most cases the treatment of a disorder directly relates to the cause of the disorder, and thus learning about treatment can be another way to learn about the disorder. Furthermore, discussing treatment in the context of the disorder also establishes a link between a disorder and its treatment, and that helps students understand why different treatments are used for different disorders. As the outline above shows, I conceptualize each disorder as a *package* that consists of symptoms, issues, explanations, and treatments.

I realize that instructors have widely differing views with regard to teaching about treatment (for example, some like to deal with treatment at the end of the course; others skip it because of insufficient time). The organization of this book permits a number of approaches. The instructor can deal with treatment as part of the discussion of each disorder; lump the sections on treatment together at the end of the course; have the students read about treatment but not lecture on it in class; or ignore treatment completely. Information and flexibility are built in; the choice of what to do is yours.

CASE MATERIAL

Case material is of crucial importance in a book on abnormal psychology, and I have used three types. First, there are *more than 60 case studies* that are set off from the explanatory material. A unique feature of many of these is that they are *first-person accounts* written by people who had experienced (or are experiencing) a particular disorder. For example, an undergraduate student describes the panic attack she had in class; a man suffering from a severe obsessive-compulsive disorder explains how his life is disrupted because he must do everything seven times; a mother discusses her postpartum depression; a student reviews his roller coaster life while suffering from the bipolar disorder; and a young professional woman describes the problems of living posed by her serious delusional disorder. These cases make the disorders more real and more personal.

Other cases involve well-known or particularly interesting persons such as Jane Fonda, who suffered from strategic anorexia and bulimia; John Madden, the CBS football announcer who suffers from phobias; Kenneth Bianchi, the "Hillside Strangler," who attempted to feign a multiple personality; the "three Christs of Ypsilanti," who tried to resolve the conflicts in their delusional identities; John Hinckley Jr., who tried to assassinate President Reagan; and "Billy Boggs," the woman who lived on the streets of New York and burned money. There are, of course, traditional case studies as well.

In addition to these case studies, each chapter is preceded by three or four brief vignettes that reflect the type of disorder or intervention that will be discussed in that chapter. These vignettes are used to catch the students' interest and alert them to relevant issues. Finally, there are many brief examples scattered throughout the text that are used to illustrate particular symptoms, concepts, issues, and problems. This mix of case studies, vignettes, and examples provides a rich foundation of clinical case material on which to build an academic understanding of causes and treatments.

LEVEL OF DIFFICULTY AND WRITING STYLE

In the publishing industry, books are traditionally labeled "upper-" or "lower-"level, depending on the type of school in which they will be used. We were pleased when the previous editions of this book were adopted at well over 500 colleges and universities *across the entire range of schools*. The reason for the wide range of adoptions was that the book contained the *substance demanded by scholars*, but was written in a style that made the material *accessible to a wide variety of students*.

I have done a number of things to make the book easy to read. For example, the material in each chapter follows a careful outline that is delineated with headings and subheadings. These headings correspond to the points in the outline that precedes the chapter. I also have been careful to use thesis sentences, simple declarative statements, boldface type to identify key terms, and italics to highlight important points. Furthermore, in discussing experiments I have included only details that are essential to understanding the what, why, or potential criticisms of the experiment. This makes reading easier without sacrificing sophistication.

Understanding is also facilitated by the use of *over 140 full-color graphs and diagrams*—more than five times as many as are found in most other textbooks. These graphic aids were designed to be easily readable, and

each is accompanied by a *caption* that summarizes the findings. In other words, the concept is discussed in the text, summarized in the caption, and displayed graphically in color, thus bringing the point home in three ways.

Readability is also enhanced by the elimination of nonessential names. For example, rather than saying, "In a recent experiment by Archer, Boring, Carter, and Dorg (1996), it was found that . . . ," I have said, "It was recently reported that . . . (Archer et al., 1996)." The emphasis is on the *ideas and findings*, not on individual investigators. This is a subtle change, but it greatly reduces "noise" and makes reading easier.

Finally, this book does not contain "boxes." Boxes serve to break up pages of text visually, but they also break up the flow and development of ideas. It is my view that if material is relevant, it should be integrated into the text; if it is irrelevant, it should not be included. The elimination of boxes also eliminates the questions "Is the stuff in the boxes important? Are we responsible for it?"

NEW IN THE THIRD EDITION

In preparing this edition, I did an extensive amount of rewriting to incorporate new information and make the material more accessible to students. In the sections that follow, I will briefly list some of the more notable additions and changes.

New Content

■ For each major disorder, a new section on *sociocultural factors* was included.

■ A new Chapter 16, titled "Eating, Sleep, and Psychophysiological Disorders," has been introduced, and all of the material on sleep disorders is new. Before discussing the sleep disorders, I spend some time discussing the basics of normal sleep and dreaming so that students have a foundation upon which to base their understanding of sleep problems.

■ In Chapter 19, "Cognitive Disorders and Mental Retardation," I introduce new material on cognitive disorders, organized around the concepts of dementia, delirium, and amnesia.

■ In the introductory chapter titled "Overview of Explanations," I include new findings concerning information processing that will help students understand the cognitive explanation for abnormal behavior. In addition, I provide a new discussion of brain structures in which the parts of the brain are organized in terms of levels and their influence on behavior.

■ The information in Part III on mood disorders and suicide was reorganized in a more efficient manner, thereby enabling me to reduce the number of chapters in that part from four to three.

■ One of the most popular and effective features of the earlier editions was the case studies, and a number of new case studies have been added to this edition. For example:

— *Case Study 3.1, "Research on Exercise and Depression: An Example of the Process."* In this case study I describe how a program of research on the effects of strenuous exercise was developed in my laboratory, and how that research had practical implications for treating depression. This provides a interesting illustration of the link between research and practice and the difference between "significant" and "meaningful" findings.

— *Case Study 5.1, "Erroneous Beliefs and the Development of a Panic Disorder."* This case illustrates how the misinterpretation of normal symptoms of arousal can lead to a panic attack.

— *Case Study 5.2, "The Man Whose Brain Tumor Led to an Obsessive-Compulsive Disorder."* This intriguing case illustrates how structural problems in the brain can lead to psychological disorders.

— *Case Study 6.5, "An Unexpected and Helpful Side Effect in the Treatment of Depression."* This is an interesting account of a student who suffered from both depression and a serious obsessive-compulsive disorder, and how the treatment of the depression led to a dramatic reduction of her obsessive-compulsive symptoms. The case has implications for understanding comorbidity and treatment.

— *Case Study 10.2, "'I Can't Sit Still!'"* In this case I offer a first-person account of a side effect (akathisia) of an antidepressant. Specifically, I describe how after taking Prozac as part of an experiment, I simply could not sit still. I did not suffer from mania or anxiety—I just could not sit still!

■ Particularly interesting new information includes, for example, data concerning the relationships between (a) diet and depression, (b) cholesterol and suicide, (c) serotonin and schizophrenia, and (d) neural migration and schizophrenia. There is also new information concerning (a) the process and effects of psychotherapy, (b) the treatment of somatoform and dissociative disorders, (c) the role of the respiratory control center in panic disorders, (d) alternatives to lithium for the treatment of the bipolar disorder, (e) side effects of medication, (f) cognitive and family therapy for schizophrenia, (g) new atypical neuroleptics, (h) the roles of serotonin and testosterone in the antisocial personality disorder, (i) Asperger's disorder, (j) the treatment of tic and Tourette's disorders, (k) sleep and sleep disorders, (l) new laws and recidivism of para-philias, (m) how nicotine leads to addiction, (n) brain stimulation and schizophrenia, (o) exposure with response prevention for the treatment of the obsessive-compulsive disorder, (p) how genetic factors lead to stress, (q) the role of classical conditioning in posttraumatic stress disorder, (r) cognitive therapy for anxiety disorders, and (s) how the absence of evidence for repression is raising a controversy over the existence of dissociative disorders.

New Features for Students

■ At the conclusion of most major sections I have added a discussion titled "What Can We Conclude Concerning . . .". In those discussions, I step back from the material to help the student integrate information and draw conclusions. These are more than summaries: they are syntheses, and students find them to be particularly helpful for developing conclusions after reading sections in which a lot of "conflicting" data are presented. In other words, these sections help students put the pieces together and form a picture of each major disorder.

■ Chapter summaries have been changed from a narrative style to a "bulleted list" style in which the main points of each section are highlighted in single sentences. This provides students with a different presentation of the information and an efficient means of reviewing.

SUPPLEMENTS FOR THE INSTRUCTOR

Test Bank

After students have worked hard in a course, there is nothing more disappointing and frustrating for them than having to take poor examinations that do not measure what they have learned. Similar frustrations are experienced by conscientious instructors who worry about whether their tests accurately reflect what the students have learned. Unfortunately, in many cases the preparation of a test bank is an afterthought, and the task is relegated to a person who was neither involved in writing the text nor skilled in writing test items. Because of my concern with this problem, I took primary responsibility for developing the test bank, and I think that you will find it to be an effective tool. The test bank is available in printed form and on diskettes for both IBM-compatible and Macintosh computers.

Instructor's Resource Manual

Completely revised for the third edition of the text, this resource, written by Thomas Joiner of the University of

Texas Medical Branch at Galveston, includes detailed chapter overviews and outlines; key terms, concepts, and names; lecture, discussion, and activity ideas; and suggested readings.

Videos

Two types of video supplements are available to qualified adopters.

■ Because I believe that there is no better way for a student to learn about disorders than from people who are affected by them, adopters of this textbook will receive *videos in which I interview patients diagnosed with various disorders,* from attention-deficit disorder to schizophrenia. These patients believe that speaking out about their disorders will remove much of the stigma that society places upon them. Some of those interviewed also appear as case studies in the text.

■ In addition, videos from *The World of Abnormal Psychology,* a telecourse produced by the Annenberg/CPB Project, in conjunction with Tovy Levine Communications, Alvin H. Perlmutter, and Addison Wesley Longman, are also available to qualified adopters. The videos are accompanied by literature on how to incorporate them into classroom lectures. Contact your local sales representative for details.

SUPPLEMENTS FOR THE STUDENT

The Textbook Companion for Students

Many students benefit from textbook support and additional guidance, and for them Marion Castellucci and I have prepared a very effective tool. Developed to partner the text, each chapter of *The Textbook Companion for Students* begins with a series of learning objectives, followed by "Guided Study." This new feature requires students to deal actively with text material, thus enhancing their storage, integration, and recall of the information. The *Companion* also includes sections called "Issues to Consider" that encourage students to take the topics beyond the covers of the book. Finally, we provide a wide variety of multiple-choice and fill-in questions that help students test their knowledge and prepare for exams. If *The Textbook Companion* is not assigned, individual students can order it by calling 1-800-828-6000.

SuperShell Student Software in DOS and Mac

Completely revised, this interactive software, written by Neil Lavender of Ocean County College, offers stu-

dents an additional opportunity to test their knowledge of the text content. For each chapter, SuperShell features a detailed outline and a series of multiple-choice, true-false, and short-answer questions, plus a complete text glossary.

ACKNOWLEDGMENTS

Writing and revising this book was a huge task, and its completion was made possible by the help of many individuals. First, recognition should go to the thousands of researchers whose work provided the basis for this book. Without their efforts, we would still think that abnormal behavior was caused by demons.

Second, it is important to acknowledge the contributions of the reviewers who carefully read the manuscript and offered helpful suggestions. Until now they have been an anonymous group, but now I would like to thank them all: Marilyn Blumenthal, State University of New York at Farmingdale; Thomas Bradbury, University of California, Los Angeles; Linda Bosmajian, Hood College; James F. Calhoun, University of Georgia; Michael Cline, J. Sargeant Reynolds Community College; Eric Cooley, Western Oregon State University; Robert D. Coursey, University of Maryland at College Park; William Curtis, Camden County College; Linda K. Davis, Mt. Hood Community College; Richard Downs, Boise State University; Stan Friedman, Southwest Texas State University; William Rick Fry, Youngstown State University; Steve Funk, Northern Arizona University at Flagstaff; Herb Goldberg, licensed psychologist, Los Angeles; Bernard S. Gorman, Nassau Community College; Stephen Hinshaw, University of California, Berkeley; William G. Iacono, University of Minnesota; Rick Ingram, San Diego State University; Boaz Kahana, Cleveland State University; Stephen R. Kahoe, El Paso Community College; Carolin Keutzer, University of Oregon; Alan King, University of North Dakota; Herbert H. Krauss, Hunter College; Stephen Lopez, University of California, Los Angeles; David Lowy, Oakland University; Janet R. Matthews, Loyola University; Paul Mazeroff, Catonsville Community College; Gary McClure, Georgia Southern University; Joseph Newman, University of Wisconsin–Madison; Dimitri Papageorgis, University of British Columbia; George W. Shardlow, City College of San Francisco; Stevens S. Smith, University of Wisconsin–Madison; Brian Stagner, Texas A&M University; Yolanda Suarez-Crowe, Jackson State University and Carol Thompson, Muskegon Community College.

Third, this revision would still be a pile of manuscript pages if it had not been for the staff at Longman.

Most notable in that group are Catherine Woods, psychology editor; Priscilla McGeehon, editor-in-chief; Marion Castellucci, development editor; Lisa Pinto, director of development; Susan Goldfarb, project editor; Alice Fernandes-Brown, design manager; Julie Tesser, photo editor; Diane Wansing and Cyndy Taylor, supplements editors; Mark Paluch, marketing manager; and Bruce Emmer, copy editor.

Fourth, and very important, is the large number of colleagues (especially LSW), students, friends, and family members (especially ESH) who provided information, advice, and support throughout this exciting but sometimes difficult period of revision. These people were invaluable; thanks!

Finally, thanks are due to my students, who kept asking tough questions, and to the clients who shared their painful experiences. Insofar as this book is dedicated to anyone, it is dedicated to my students and to the many individuals who suffer from mental disorders. I hope that this book will take us one step further in the process of understanding abnormal behavior.

CONTINUING SUPPORT AND FEEDBACK

Developing an understanding of abnormal behavior is an exciting but demanding task, and it can be helped by ongoing relationships between instructors, students, and author. *If there is anything I can do to help you, please let me know.* My mailing address is: Psychology Department, Fraser Hall, University of Kansas, Lawrence, KS 66045. My E-mail address is: DHolmes@eagle.cc.ukans.edu.

Many faculty members and students wrote to me in response to the first two editions of this book, and I will look forward to hearing from you concerning this edition. I am happy to answer questions, and I am always very interested in comments about what about the book succeeded in doing and what might be changed, added, or improved. Good luck with your courses—I will look forward to hearing from you!

David S. Holmes

ABNORMAL
PSYCHOLOGY

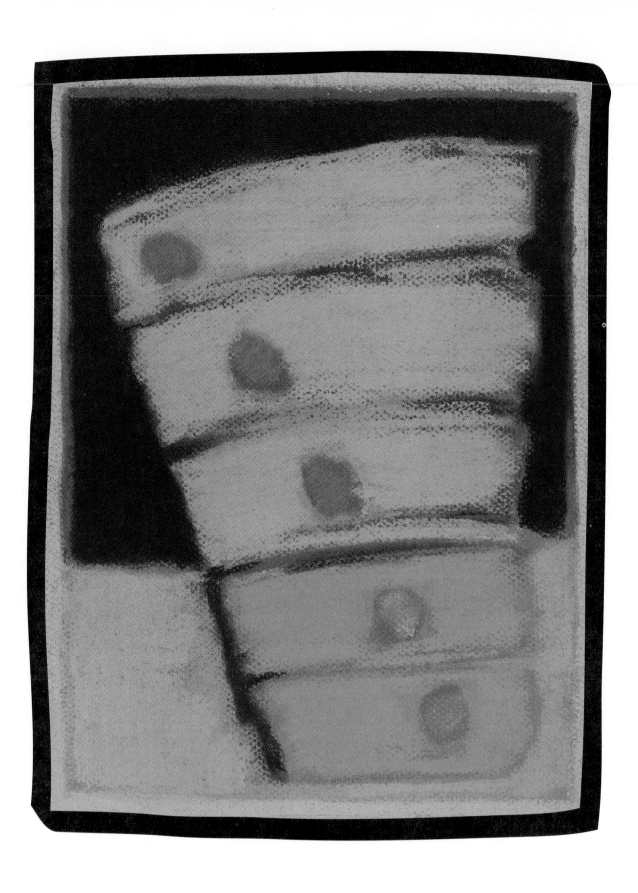

CHAPTER ONE
HISTORY
and
INTRODUCTION

OUTLINE

Mental disorders constitute one of the most serious and perplexing problems you will ever face. Consider the following facts:

■ More than 30% of Americans suffer from at least one major psychological disorder during their lifetimes.
■ About 15% of the population suffers from major depression, and the rate is increasing.
■ Valium and Prozac are used for the treatment of anxiety and depression, and they are among the most frequently prescribed drugs in the United States.
■ Alcoholism and alcohol abuse cost the U.S. economy about $125 billion a year.
■ Psychiatric disorders account for 14.2% of high school dropouts and 4.7% of college dropouts, and it is estimated that more than 7 million people terminate their educations prematurely because of these disorders every year (Kessler et al., 1995).

These figures are staggering, but they do not convey the intensely personal aspects of the problem:

■ The confusion and terror felt by an individual with schizophrenia when suddenly the world just does not make sense anymore
■ The agony and despair of the depressed individual who feels unreachable, in a deep, dark hole
■ The conflict of the individual with bulimia who binges and purges every day until her teeth and throat rot from the gastric acid
■ The shock of the mother whose unresponsive infant is labeled autistic
■ The terrible feeling of helplessness when the heavy door to the "closed ward" swings shut and locks behind you

This is not a book about the problems of someone else. Mental illness touches all of us at some time during our lives; if we are not the ones afflicted, then it will be a family member, loved one, or close friend. The problem of abnormal behavior is personally relevant and emotionally charged, but in this book we will explore the problem from an objective and scientific point of view. Although we must be dispassionate in our study of the problem, it is important that we keep in mind the importance and the intense personal ramifications of what we are studying.

We now know a great deal about the causes and treatment of abnormal behavior. However, there is still a gap between what we know and what we need to know. In this book, I will tell you about what we know, but I will also be honest in telling you about the gaps in our knowledge.

In this chapter, I will (a) describe how abnormal behavior was viewed in the past and how it is viewed today, (b) develop a definition of abnormal behavior, (c) examine the idea that mental illness is a myth, and (d) review the roles of the various professionals such as psychologists, psychiatrists, and social workers who work in the mental health field.

HISTORICAL BACKGROUND

Society has explained and treated abnormal behavior in different ways at different times. How a particular society reacts to abnormality depends on the society's values and assumptions about human life and behavior. For example, during the Middle Ages, when a religious point of view was predominant, abnormality was usually explained in terms of supernatural causes such as demons, and treatment involved prayers and various forms of exorcism. In contrast, in current Western society, to which science is important and in which people have a great deal of faith in the "miracles of modern medicine," abnormal behavior is considered evidence of "mental illness" and is often treated with drugs.

In the following sections, I will briefly review the history and evolution of our thinking concerning abnormal behavior. The information presented here should not be considered only as history because many of the old ideas still play important roles in our current thinking about abnormal behavior. That is, unlike many other sciences, when new ideas about abnormal behavior and treatment are developed, they do not necessarily replace older ideas. Instead, for better or worse, they are added to the existing group of explanations and treatments.

Demonology

Abnormal behavior was first thought to be caused by supernatural forces that take control of the mind or body. For example, papyrus scrolls, monuments, and the early books of the Bible indicate that the ancient Egyptians, Arabs, and Hebrews believed that abnormal behavior was the result of possession by supernatural forces such as angry gods, evil spirits, and demons. There was nothing unusual about attributing abnormal behavior to supernatural forces because in those cultures it was believed that many other phenomena, such as fires and floods, were also caused by supernatural forces.

The typical approach to treatment involved persuading the demons to leave through the use of incantations, prayers, or potions. In some instances, various forms of physical punishment, such as stoning or flogging, were used as a means of forcing the demons out of a possessed individual.

Introduction of Physiological Explanations

The first attempt to explain abnormal behavior in terms of natural rather than supernatural causes occurred during the Golden Age of Greece when **Hippocrates** (hip-POK-ruh-tēz; c. 460–c. 377 B.C.), the "father of modern medicine," taught that the brain is the organ responsible for mental disorders. More specifically, he suggested that behavior was governed by the levels of four **humors** (fluids) in the body: *black bile, yellow bile, phlegm,* and *blood.* For example, he believed that an excess of black bile caused depression; that too much yellow bile was associated with tension, anxiety, and personal instability; that high levels of phlegm resulted in a dull or sluggish ("phlegmatic") temperament; and that excess blood volume was related to rapid mood swings. Hippocrates lacked scientific techniques to verify his explanation, but his approach started us on the path toward seeing abnormal behavior as the result of a physiological malfunction or disease.

Treatment during this period involved attempts to restore the appropriate balance among humors, and that was usually done by draining off excess fluids from the body (e.g., bleeding the individual) or by altering diet, exercise, alcohol intake, or lifestyle in general. Because disturbed individuals were considered to be suffering from illnesses, they were cared for like other sick people.

Return to Demonology

During the Middle Ages (c. A.D. 500–1500), religion became the dominant force in virtually all aspects of European life, and the naturalistic approach of Hippocrates and his followers was essentially abandoned. Life was perceived as a struggle between the forces of good and evil, and the forces of evil were led by the Devil, who was thought to cause abnormal behaviors. In other words, the ancient idea of demonic possession was revived, and brutal exorcistic treatments were again used to drive the Devil out. For example, individuals who were thought to be possessed by the Devil would be stoned or tortured to get the Devil out. Worst of all, disturbed individuals might be accused of being agents of the Devil rather than merely his victims, and therefore labeled as *witches*. To aid with the task of identifying and destroying dangerous witches, a manual titled *Malleus Maleficarum* (The Witch Hammer) was published in 1486. Unfortunately for the mentally ill, the manual equated abnormal behavior with being a witch, and witches had to be killed, often burned alive. This practice spread to America, where witch-hunts reached their peak in the 1690s with the famous Salem witchcraft trials. Persecution of individuals as witches abated in some areas of Europe as early as 1610, and it was legally brought to a halt in America around 1700.

Introduction of Humane Care

Some fortunate individuals received **humane care** during earlier periods, but the 16th century marked the first time that it was widely recognized that disturbed individuals needed care, not exorcism or condemnation. In

During the Middle Ages, mental illness was thought to be the result of demonic possession. Various forms of exorcism were used to drive out the Devil.

1547, the hospital of Saint Mary of Bethlehem in London was dedicated to the care of disturbed people. However, the word *care* is hardly appropriate to describe how patients in these early hospitals were treated. In fact, the early hospitals were more like prisons than hospitals. Nothing was done for the inmates other than to confine them under horrible conditions. For example, patients were often chained to the wall, sometimes in a way that prevented them from lying down to sleep, or they might be chained to large iron balls that they had to drag with them whenever they moved. Furthermore, large numbers of extremely disturbed people were confined in close quarters, which resulted in dreadful chaos and confusion. Indeed, the word *bedlam*, which means "a place, scene, or state of uproar and confusion," was derived from the name of the Bethlehem hospital. The conditions in these early asylums were not a source of concern but instead were a source of amusement, and tickets to view the patients were actually sold to the public!

After disturbed individuals were recognized as patients, the next step in bringing about humane care involved improving the conditions in which the patients lived. The most famous effort in this regard has traditionally been ascribed to **Philippe Pinel** (fi-LĒP pē-NEL; 1745–1826) in 1792. He directed that the chains be removed from the patients in his hospital in Paris and that the hospital be renovated to make it more pleasant. In England at about the same time,

This painting shows patients being unchained at the Salpêtrière Hospital in Paris in 1792. The movement toward more humane treatment of mental patients marked an important turning point in society's attitude toward the mentally ill. However, it did not lead to significant improvement for most patients because effective treatments were not yet available.

William Tuke (tyo͞ok; 1732–1822) and the Quakers opened a "retreat" for patients on a country estate. Their approach was based on the notion that rest, fresh air, and exposure to nature had therapeutic value. In the United States, **Benjamin Rush** (1745–1813), the "father of American psychiatry," introduced humane treatment in the Pennsylvania Hospital in 1783. **Dorothea Dix** (1802–1887) was a New England schoolteacher who became concerned about the terrible living conditions and harsh treatments that were forced on patients, so between 1841 and 1881 she conducted an effective campaign to inform the public about the problem and raise money for new hospitals. She is cred-

ited with the establishment of 32 mental hospitals throughout the United States.

Freeing patients from their chains and building more and better hospitals undoubtedly made patients more comfortable, but the therapeutic effect of these changes has been greatly exaggerated. Written accounts and drawings of the time suggest that patients became tranquil and even normal when their chains were removed. That may have been true for a few patients, but in most cases it seems unlikely that the changes resulted in significant improvements. Indeed, if freedom and fresh air were sufficient to cure mental illness, mental illness would not be the serious problem it is today.

One early treatment consisted of spinning patients. Benjamin Rush, the "father of American psychiatry," is quoted as saying that "no well-regulated institution should be unprovided with the circulating swing."

During a visit to a Massachusetts jail in 1841, Dorothea Dix was shocked by the conditions there, especially by the mixing of criminals and mental patients. Her subsequent crusade resulted in the founding of state mental hospitals in many states.

Introduction of Psychological Explanations

The belief that abnormal behavior stems from psychological causes has been developing for about 200 years, and in that time numerous explanations have been suggested. Most of these explanations are linked to famous historical characters. Therefore, our discussion will be organized around the historical individuals and their ideas.

Mesmer and Suggestion. The first important individual in the development of the psychological explanations was a physician named **Franz Anton Mesmer** (MEZ-mur; 1734–1815) who practiced in Paris. Mesmer treated individuals who were suffering from a variety of physical complaints such as paralyses, and he believed that their problems were the result of an imbalance of "magnetic fluids" in the body. To correct the imbalance, Mesmer had groups of patients sit around a large tub filled with a "magnetic fluid," and while music played in the background, the patients would take iron rods from the tub and apply them to the parts of their bodies in which they were having symptoms. Mesmer would also touch the patients with his magnetized wand. As the treatment session progressed, some of the patients would start to tremble; their limbs would twitch convulsively; they would groan, choke, laugh, and scream; and finally some of them would dance wildly or faint. This "crisis" would continue for some time, but when it finally subsided, many of the patients were apparently "cured."

Mesmer's successes attracted considerable attention, and his patients included such notables as King Louis XVI, Queen Marie Antoinette, and the Marquis de Lafayette. Mesmer was apparently successful in relieving the symptoms of some of his patients, but his technique was seriously questioned by the scientific communities in Vienna and Paris. Because of the questions that were raised, a panel of experts was convened in 1784 to examine Mesmer's practices and issue a report. (The members of the panel included Benjamin Franklin, who was the United States' ambassador to France; Joseph Guillotin, who invented the decapitating machine; and Antoine-Laurent Lavoisier, who discovered oxygen.) The panel failed to find any support for the effects of magnetism on physical disorders and instead concluded: "That which has been proved through our examination of magnetism is that *man can affect man* . . . almost at will by stimulating his imagination" (Bromberg, 1959, p. 173). That is, the panel concluded that the effects of Mesmer's treatment were due to *suggestion*. Mesmer was labeled a charlatan and barred from further medical practice. Ironically, then, although Mesmer believed that abnormal behavior was due to a *physical* factor, his work led others to the conclusion that a *psychological* factor, suggestion, played an important role in many disorders. As a footnote to Mes-

This engraving shows one of Mesmer's treatment sessions.

mer's career, it should be noted that although he died in obscurity in Switzerland in 1815, he has had a lasting influence on psychology because he is considered the father of hypnotism, which was originally known as **mesmerism** (MEZ-mur-iz-um).

Charcot and Suggestion. The next well-known contributor to the development of the psychological explanations for abnormal behavior was **Jean-Martin Charcot** (shar-KŌ; 1825–1893), who was a neurologist and the head of the Salpêtrière Hospital in Paris. (This was the same hospital in which a century earlier Pinel had freed the patients from their chains.) Charcot was interested in patients who were suffering from physical symptoms such as paralysis, blindness, pain, seizures, and deafness for which no physical cause could be found. For example, an individual might have a paralyzed arm, but no muscle or nerve damage could be found to account for the paralysis. At that time, such problems were referred to as **hysterical disorders.**

Charcot believed that there was a link between hysterical disorders and hypnosis because patients with hysterical disorders could be hypnotized easily and because with hypnosis he could eliminate old symptoms and introduce new ones. Indeed, he became famous for demonstrations in which he hypnotized patients and then dramatically eliminated or induced symptoms. His explanation for the link between hysterical disorders and hypnosis was that both resulted from a neurological weakness. However, to his surprise, some of his students demonstrated that *normal* individuals could also be hypnotized and have symptoms induced. That demonstration led Charcot to revise his explanation and conclude that hysterical disorders and hypnosis were not a result of a neurological weakness (a physiological cause) but instead were the effects of *suggestion* (a psychological cause).

Freud, the Unconscious, and Psychoanalysis. **Sigmund Freud** (Froyd; 1856–1939) was a neurologist who, like Charcot, was interested in treating patients with hysterical disorders. Early in his career, Freud became friends with another neurologist, **Josef Breuer** (BROY-ur; 1842–1925), who told Freud about an interesting patient he had been treating, known as **Anna O.** Anna O. had been suffering from a variety of hysterical symptoms that included paralyses of her arms and legs, problems with her vision and speech, lapses in her memory, difficulty with eating, and a persistent cough. Two things about Anna O. were particularly interesting. The first was that her symptoms appeared to be related to stressful experiences that she had earlier in her life. For example, at times Anna O. was unable to drink water, but in talking with her one day, Breuer learned that some years earlier she had been disgusted by the fact that a friend had allowed her dog to drink out of a pitcher that she later used for herself. Anna O. had not made the connection between the earlier experience and her present symptom, but apparently the event had been so repulsive to her that she began to gag whenever she began to drink. The second interesting thing about Anna O. was that after she talked about her symptoms or the related earlier experiences, the symptoms disappeared temporarily. Breuer suggested that by talking about her problems, Anna O. was able to reduce tension and that the reduction of the tension led to the reduction of the symptoms. He labeled this process **catharsis** (kuh-THAR-sis), a term that is based on a Greek word meaning "to cleanse or purge."

The story of Anna O. led Freud to begin thinking about hysterical disorders in terms of psychological causes, and over time Freud developed the idea that abnormal behaviors are caused by *unconscious stresses that stem from early experiences.* Specifically, Freud suggested that if an experience was especially anxiety-provoking, the individual would banish the memory of the experience to an area of the mind that Freud called the **unconscious.** Doing that had two implications. First, after the memory was in the unconscious, the individual was no longer able to remember the experience, and therefore the experience would no longer cause the individual anxiety. Second, although the individual no longer remembered the experience, the experience would continue to influence the individual's behavior from the unconscious. For example, an unconscious concern about being abandoned might lead the individual to be depressed and cling to others "for no apparent reason." Freud likened the situation to an iceberg in which the mass of ice that is invisible below the surface of the water supports the relatively small amount of ice that is visible above the surface. In Freudian terms, the mass below the surface is our unconscious, and the ice above the surface is our current behavior.

Because Freud assumed that abnormal behaviors were caused by unconscious stressful experiences, he

Sigmund Freud developed one of the early psychological explanations for abnormal behavior. He is shown here with his daughter Anna Freud, who became a leader in the ego psychology movement.

developed a treatment strategy that was designed to help patients identify and then overcome the unconscious stresses. The treatment was based on the notion that *if the unconscious stresses were eliminated, the abnormal behaviors would be eliminated.* The treatment he designed is called **psychoanalysis,** and because psychoanalysis was the first major approach to psychological treatment and provided the basis for other treatments, it deserves some discussion here.

In psychoanalysis, the patient goes progressively back through his or her life experiences and examines each experience from a more mature and more objective standpoint. Freud likened the process to an archaeological dig in which the patient unearths layer after layer of his or her earlier life and in so doing gets a better understanding of the earlier experiences and how they are affecting him or her now. Of course, the problem is that the important early experiences are buried in the unconscious, so Freud had to develop techniques to get to the unconscious material. Four of those techniques deserve comment here:

1. *Free Association.* In a treatment session, the patient would lie comfortably on a couch and be encouraged to say whatever came to his or her mind without any restrictions or censorship. For example, at the beginning of a session a patient might comment that earlier in the day he had been cut off by a man driving another car. That might lead the patient to talk about earlier instances in which he had been frustrated or threatened by other men. The string of associations might ultimately lead to memories about feeling threatened by his father—experiences that might still be influencing him but of which he was unaware. The notion underlying **free association** was that if patients do not defensively censor what they are thinking and saying, important but otherwise unthought ideas will come to awareness. That is, one thought leads to another by association, thus providing a means of working back through a series of ideas, feelings, and experiences that are not ordinarily accessible.

2. *Dream Interpretation.* A second technique for getting to unconscious material was **dream interpretation** (Freud, 1900/1957). Freud believed that many experiences and feelings are so threatening that they cannot be expressed consciously even with the freedom provided by free association. However, such feelings and experiences may be expressed in dreams because during sleep the individual's control is relaxed, thus enabling the threatening content to slip through. Even then, some feelings and experiences may not be expressed directly and must be disguised and expressed in symbols. For example, in one case, Freud suggested that a man's overcoat was a symbol for a condom and that dreams about wearing an overcoat really reflected thoughts about sexual activities (Freud, 1900/1957). The fact that threatening content is often disguised in symbols was used to explain why at first dreams sometimes do not make sense. One of the tasks of psychoanalysis was to break the symbol code so that the dream could be interpreted.

3. *Resistance.* Often the flow of experiences and feelings in the process of psychoanalysis was blocked because the patient had encountered something particularly anxiety-provoking and did not want to deal with it. This blocking was called **resistance,** and it could involve talking about trivial issues rather than important ones, coming late for sessions, or even "forgetting" to come to a session. When resistance occurred, it was used as a sign that the patient had come to a particularly important issue, and then the problem was to overcome the resistance and discover the issue. For example, in the case of a patient who forgot to come to a session, the therapist would suggest that the patient did not forget the session but did not come because he or she did not want to remember the stressful experiences that would be uncovered in the session.

4. *Transference.* An important aspect of psychoanalysis was the relationship between the patient and the therapist, who is usually called an **analyst.** Because the analyst remained rather distant, aloof, and out of sight behind the patient, the analyst presented a generally neutral image to the patient. However, despite the analyst's neutral behavior, the patient often attributed characteristics to the analyst and responded to the analyst with feelings such as anger, dependence, seductiveness, or hostility. These reactions stemmed from the fact that the patient was responding as though the analyst were one of the significant individuals in the patient's emo-

tional life, such as a mother, father, sibling, or lover. This was referred to as **transference** because the patient *transferred* feelings about another person onto the analyst. Transference was important because it allowed the patient to see how he or she felt about others and because with transference the patient could relive problems that were associated with people who were not actually available in the therapy session. For example, a patient who expected to be rejected by an analyst may have come to realize that he or she inappropriately expected rejection from everyone and that those expectations were influencing his or her behavior.

In general, Freud viewed a patient as a traveler who earlier took a wrong turn and is now lost and anxious. In psychoanalysis, the patient-traveler tries to trace the path back to the point at which the wrong turn was taken, learn to read the road signs more accurately, and start over from there. Unfortunately, the road map for the early part of the trip is too faded to be read, and parts of it have been torn off. So the traveler, with the analyst as a companion, has to do a lot of backtracking and exploring to find the place of the original wrong turn. The analyst, who has had some experience on these roads, can make suggestions about where to look for signs and can point out things that the traveler missed along the way, but the analyst does not know exactly where they are going because the analyst joined the traveler long after the wrong turn. As the traveler returns to one town after another, long-forgotten experiences are recalled, and related feelings of joy and pain are felt once again. Sometimes the traveler slips and responds to the analyst as though the analyst were an individual whom the traveler knew and loved or hated in that town long ago. Once the crucial intersection is found and the traveler recognizes the errors that were made in reading road signs, the trip can be started over. Once the traveler is more experienced and knowledgeable, he or she is better equipped to find the intended destination and understand the situation, thereby eliminating the anxieties and confusion.

Psychoanalysis is still practiced today, but its popularity has waned drastically in the past 30 years. Indeed, many of the institutes in which analysts are trained no longer have enough applicants to fill their classes, and some have closed. This decline in interest stems from at least three factors. First, the Freudian theories on which psychoanalysis is based are less popular now than they once were. Second, questions have been raised about the effectiveness of psychoanalysis. Third, even if one accepts Freud's theory and believes that psychoanalysis is effective, for most people psychoanalysis is simply not a practical technique because it usually involves four sessions per week for a period of two or three years and can cost over $100,000! Psychoanalysis may be to more modern forms of therapy what the

1960 Cadillac is to present-day automobiles: It may get you from place to place, but it has been replaced by smaller, faster, more efficient, and less expensive models. For that reason, the discussion of psychoanalysis is in this chapter, on history, rather than in the later chapters on treatment. However, just as the Cadillac has contributed to modern cars, you will learn later that psychoanalysis has contributed to some modern forms of therapy.

Pavlov and Classical Conditioning. At the same time that Freud was treating his patients and developing his theory of behavior, a Russian physiologist named **Ivan Pavlov** (1849–1936) was working with dogs in his laboratory and making some very different discoveries about behavior. Pavlov discovered that if the sound of a bell was repeatedly paired with the presentation of meat that caused the dog to salivate, eventually simply ringing the bell would cause the dog to salivate. Today we call this process **classical conditioning,** and it is relevant for understanding behavior because it can be used to explain why an individual has an uncontrollable physiological or emotional response when exposed to a neutral stimulus such as an elevator—the elevator may have been paired with fear in the past.

Thorndike and Skinner and Operant Conditioning. While Pavlov was working with dogs in Russia, an American psychologist named **Edward L. Thorndike** (1874–1949) was studying how cats solved problems. He noticed that if a cat was given a reward (a bit of food) after turning a wheel to escape from a box, the

cat was more likely to use the wheel-turning behavior again in the future. In other words, Thorndike pointed out that behavior is governed by rewards and punishments, a process that he called **operant conditioning.** (The term *operant* comes from the fact that the animal acts or operates to get rewards or avoid punishments.) Animal trainers had been using the principles of operant conditioning for years (the old "carrot and stick" approach), but Thorndike refined the principles and made them scientifically respectable.

Some time later, the notion of operant conditioning received a considerable boost in visibility and credibility by the work of the famous American psychologist **B. F. Skinner** (1904–1992), who worked primarily with pigeons and white rats. By using rewards, Skinner taught pigeons to do everything from turning somersaults to guiding missiles! (The pigeons were taught to peck at a target on a screen in the nose cone of a missile, and their pecking would control the direction of the missile.) The point being made in the work of Thorndike and Skinner was that *behavior could be controlled by rewards and punishments.*

Watson, Behaviorism, and Behavior Modification. The early work of Pavlov and Thorndike introduced the notion that conditioning could influence behavior, but their work was limited to animals, and they were not interested in applications to human behavior. However, a brash young American psychologist named **John B. Watson** (1878–1958) seized the notion of conditioning and actively promoted the idea that it could be used to explain normal and abnormal behavior in humans. For example, Watson suggested that fears (phobias) are the result of classical conditioning rather than unconscious conflicts and that behaviors such as tantrums are operantly conditioned because they lead to rewards. Watson labeled this conditioning-based approach **behaviorism** because it was focused on observable behaviors rather than the unconscious and unobservable processes that were emphasized by Freud.

The notion that conditioning could be used to explain behaviors was quickly extended to the possibility that conditioning could be used to control or treat abnormal behaviors. For example, if an elevator phobia was due to the pairing of an elevator with fear (classical conditioning), then the phobia could be treated by repeatedly exposing the individual to elevators in a nonstressful way, thus breaking the link between elevators and fear. Similarly, if temper tantrums are due to the fact that they result in rewards (operant conditioning), then the tantrums could be treated by no longer rewarding the tantrums. This approach to treatment was called **behavior modification.** Behaviorism quickly became popular because of its objective and scientific basis, and behavior modification gained widespread acceptance because it provided a fast and inexpensive alternative to Freudian psychoanalysis.

B. F. Skinner was an influential advocate of behaviorism. His work in the area of operant conditioning paved the way for an explanation of abnormal behavior that is based on learning. Much of Skinner's work was based on research involving pigeons and rats.

Beck, Cognitions, and Cognitive Therapy. Behaviorism was widely accepted, but some psychologists believed that it was too limited because it ignored cognitive (thought) processes. That is, from the standpoint of behaviorism, the individual was seen as only responding to external factors such as rewards and punishments and was not seen as thinking. Indeed, one critic wryly pointed out that behaviorists saw the behavior of other people as due to rewards and punishments, but they saw their own behavior as motivated by a need to *understand.* The critics conceded that conditioning did occur and was important, but they suggested that *thoughts also played an important role in normal and abnormal behaviors.* For example, the thought "I am not a worthwhile person" could lead to depression, and the erroneous belief that "all snakes are dangerous" could lead to a phobia for snakes. Therefore, during the 1970s, interest increased in the influence of thought processes on human behavior. The movement gained additional momentum during the 1980s when psychologists discovered some of the ways in which humans process information. For example, it was learned that memories are linked together in networks and that stimulation of one memory can result in the recall of related memories in the network. That helped psychologists understand the "stream of consciousness." Also, it was discovered that strong selective processes occur in what we perceive and think about, and if we focus on certain information, such as our failures rather than our successes, we may develop the erroneous belief that we are no good, and that might lead to depression.

The treatment methods of Aaron Beck are based on correcting the patient's erroneous beliefs, which lead to abnormal behavior. Beck is shown at the Center for Cognitive Therapy at the University of Pennsylvania.

The research of many psychologists contributed to what has come to be known as the "cognitive revolution" in psychology, but it was a psychiatrist named **Aaron Beck** (born 1921) who used the findings to build a treatment approach called **cognitive therapy,** in which patients learn to *correct the erroneous beliefs that lead to abnormal behavior.* For example, individuals who are depressed because they erroneously believe that they are no good are taught to replace their erroneous beliefs about themselves with more realistic beliefs that they are good and their futures are not necessarily bleak.

In short, in the two centuries between Mesmer and Beck, the psychological explanations for abnormal behavior went from *suggestions* to *unconscious conflicts* to *conditioning* and finally to *erroneous beliefs.*

Renewed Interest in Physiological Explanations

By the middle of the 20th century, there were numerous speculations concerning the physiological basis of abnormal behavior ("never a twisted thought without a twisted neuron"), but there was very little evidence for the physiological explanations because scientists lacked the techniques that are necessary to study brain functioning. There were also numerous physiological treatments for abnormal behavior, but they were not particularly effective. For example, one treatment for schizophrenia was to strap the patient into a chair and spin the chair until the patient passed out. However, in the early 1950s, two French chemists discovered a drug that was effective for treating schizophrenia, and the fact that symptoms could be changed by changing brain chemistry stimulated new speculations about the physiological basis for abnormal behavior. Actually, the chemists were working to develop a new antihistamine for the treatment of allergies. One negative side effect of the antihistamine was its tendency to make normal individuals drowsy, but when the antihistamine was given to patients who were suffering from schizophrenia, they became calm, their cognitive confusion was reduced, and their behavior became much more normal. In other words, the calming that was a negative side effect for normal individuals was found to be helpful for individuals who were suffering from schizophrenia. You might say that the antihistamine cleared up the patients' heads in more ways than one.

More powerful forms of the antihistamine were quickly adapted for use as antipsychotic drugs, and they revolutionized the care and treatment of highly disturbed patients. Hospital wards were transformed from pits of confusion and chaos into places of relative calm. Furthermore, many patients who had previously needed to be locked up could now be given medication and released. Before the introduction of these drugs, it had been estimated that 750,000 hospital beds would be needed for psychiatric patients in the United States by 1971. In fact, fewer than half that many were actually required because the use of antipsychotic drugs greatly reduced the need for hospitalization.

A second important effect of the antipsychotic drugs was that they opened up a new way of studying the causes of abnormal behavior. If researchers could determine how the brain was affected by these drugs, it might be possible to determine what it was in the brain that caused the abnormal behavior.

Current Explanations for Abnormal Behavior

In the past 200 years, we have gone from demons to biochemistry in explaining abnormal behavior, but when new ideas have come along, we have not always abandoned previous explanations. Instead, we have accumulated explanations, and the resulting multiplicity of explanations is both good and bad. On the positive side, multiple explanations may be good because (a) different disorders may stem from different causes (e.g., anxiety might be due to psychological factors, whereas schizophrenia may be due to physiological factors), (b) any one disorder may result from more than one cause (anxiety may result from either psychological or physiological factors), or (c) different causes may combine to result in a disorder (physiological factors such as genetics may predispose an individual to a disorder that is then triggered by a psychological factor such as stress).

On the negative side, we have not abandoned some explanations and treatments that have no scientific support. For example, you may have been amused when you read that demons and the Devil were used to explain abnormal behavior and that torture was used to "cure" afflicted individuals as recently as 1700, but you should recognize that in some religious and cultural groups, psychological disturbances are still blamed on the Devil and exorcism is still used to treat disturbed individuals.

You should also recognize that although the inhumane treatment of disturbed individuals is usually seen as a thing of the past, that is not necessarily the case. In states facing budgetary cutbacks, patients who are in need of hospitalization may be refused admittance, and those who have been hospitalized may be discharged regardless of their conditions. Instead of being treated, those patients are relegated to the streets to fend for themselves, and they often exist in deplorable conditions. Also, among the general public, irrational fear of disturbed individuals persists. For example, in one city in New York, such fears led the residents to pass a law prohibiting disturbed individuals from living within the city limits. That is reminiscent of the banishment from medieval communities of individuals who were thought to be witches. (Fortunately, the New York law was overturned by the courts.)

Thus, it is clear that the present phase of understanding and treatment of abnormal behavior represents a melding of what has gone before, some of it worthwhile, some of it not. In subsequent chapters, I will carefully review and evaluate the currently accepted points of view concerning abnormal behavior so that you can develop an informed opinion about the causes and treatments of abnormal behavior.

DEFINING ABNORMAL BEHAVIOR

Arriving at a generally acceptable definition of abnormal behavior is difficult because some theorists define it from the point of view of the *individual whose behavior is being considered,* while other theorists define abnormal behavior from the point of view of the *culture in which the individual is living.* Both viewpoints have something to contribute to an overall definition, so both need to be considered.

When defining abnormal behavior from the point of view of the individual, attention is focused first on the individual's **distress.** Individuals are defined as abnormal when they are anxious, depressed, dissatisfied, or otherwise seriously upset.

Second, attention is focused on the individual's **disability.** Individuals are defined as abnormal when they are not able to function personally, socially, physiologically, or occupationally. From the personal point of view, then, abnormality is defined primarily in terms of the individual's *happiness* and *effectiveness,* and what others think about the individual is irrelevant.

When defining abnormal behavior from the cultural point of view, attention is focused on **deviance,** the degree to which an individual deviates from *cultural norms.* For example, an individual who hallucinates will be defined as abnormal because most people do not hallucinate. However, it is relevant to note that what is normal in one culture may be abnormal in another culture. For example, in some cultures hallucinations are taken as a sign of schizophrenia and the individual is hospitalized, but in other cultures hallucinations are thought to be the voice of a god and the individual is made a priest (Murphy, 1976). It should also be noted that only deviant behaviors that the culture considers "bad" are defined as abnormal. Having an IQ of 140 or being exceptionally well adjusted is also deviant, but such "good" deviance is not considered abnormal in the way the word *abnormal* is customarily used. From the cultural point of view, then, abnormality is defined in terms of cultural norms, and the feelings of the individual are disregarded.

From the preceding discussion, it is clear that distress, disability, and deviance (the "three Ds") can all play a role in defining abnormal behavior and that no one factor is sufficient to account for all

Marchers carried a mile-long rainbow banner up First Avenue in a gay pride parade in New York City in 1994. Demonstrations such as these are an indicator that both personal and cultural attitudes toward homosexuality have changed in recent years.

abnormal behavior. For example, if we ignore distress and rely only on deviance, the depressed individual will be ignored until he or she attempts suicide, whereas if we ignore deviance and rely only on distress, the happy but hallucinating individual will not be treated.

Sometimes the personal and cultural points of view concerning what is abnormal come into conflict. Such a conflict occurred in the case of homosexuality. The practice of homosexuality deviates from our cultural norm, and for many years homosexuality was labeled abnormal. However, in 1980 the panel of experts that prepares the diagnostic manual for mental disorders (see Chapter 3) reconsidered the issue and decided that homosexuality should not be considered abnormal unless the individual was unhappy about his or her sexual orientation (American Psychiatric Association, 1980). In other words, the cultural perspective was abandoned and attention was shifted to the personal point of view. The issue was considered again in 1987, when homosexuality was eliminated completely as an abnormal disorder (American Psychiatric Association, 1987). In the case of homosexuality, then, the rights of the individual were given precedence over cultural norms.

In summary, both personal and cultural aspects of behavior are taken into consideration in determining what is abnormal, and it is therefore possible for the definition of abnormality to differ from individual to individual, from culture to culture, and from time to

time. It is hazardous to attempt a specific definition, but it might be said that *abnormal behavior is behavior that is personally distressful or personally disabling or is culturally so deviant that other individuals judge the behavior to be inappropriate or maladaptive.*

THE "MYTH OF MENTAL ILLNESS"

In discussions of abnormal behavior, it is often assumed that the behavior is a reflection of an underlying "mental illness," and the concept of mental illness implies that there is something "wrong" to the point that the individual needs to be "treated." However, some critics argue that *mental illness is a myth;* in other words, there is no such thing as mental illness, and individuals do not need to be treated (Szasz, 1961, 1970). That is a radical departure from the usual point of view, and it deserves some comment before we go on.

The belief that mental illness is a myth is based on three notions. First, it is argued that abnormal behavior is simply *different* behavior and not necessarily a reflection of an illness. That is, individuals may have personality traits that deviate from what society wants, but that does not mean that the traits constitute an illness in the sense that a cancerous growth is an illness.

Second, an individual may have an unusual belief, but that does not mean that the individual is *wrong.* For example, we may not agree with an individual who believes that he or she is God, but that does not necessarily mean that the individual is not God. Indeed, many leaders and inventors were once thought to be "crazy." Furthermore, even if the individual is wrong, that does not mean that he or she is sick. For example, if you are wrong in your solution of a math problem, that does not mean that you are sick. Might an individual with a delusion simply be mistaken rather than sick?

Third, theorists who believe that mental illness is a myth argue that abnormal behavior is due to something that is wrong with *society* rather than something that is wrong with the *individual.* For example, if an individual breaks down in the face of an overwhelming environmental stress such as a war, the problem lies in the environment rather than in the individual. Furthermore, the critics argue that if the environment does not provide the individual with the support and resources to survive the stress, the problem is in the environment rather than in the individual. Withdrawing or becoming depressed may be a rational response to an irrational environment rather than a sickness. In summary, then, being different, being wrong, or responding to abnormal environments should not be the basis for labeling an individual as sick.

Proponents of this view also point out that the notion of mental illness can lead to unfortunate consequences. For example, if we label individuals as ill, we may implicitly encourage abnormal behavior because sick people behave in abnormal ways. Furthermore, by labeling individuals as ill, we may relieve them of responsibility for their behavior because sick people are not responsible for their conditions. Should an individual who commits murder be set free because at the time of the crime he or she was "insane"? Finally, if we attribute deviant behavior to illness, we may ignore the social factors, such as poverty and stress, that may cause abnormal behavior.

If the concept of mental illness is wrong, why is it such a popular explanation for behavior? Proponents of the myth point of view argue that the notion of mental illness is a convenient way for us to deal with people who disturb us. For example, if we label as "sick" people whose behavior we find disturbing, we can see them as different from us, which makes us feel better about ourselves. Also, if we label them as sick, we can justify locking them up so that they will no longer disturb us. As support for this, the proponents cite cases of individuals who were locked up for many years simply because they were annoying other people. The individuals may not have been "out of their minds," but by locking them up, we put the disturbing individuals out of *our* sight and out of *our* minds. Finally, by using mental illness as an explanation for deviant behavior, we avoid responsibility for the social problems that underlie the deviant behavior. That is, if we say that you are sick and should be changed, we do not have to undertake the difficult task of changing society.

Is mental illness a myth or a reality? The myth notion is a radical departure from the traditional point of view, but it does have merit. There are some serious forms of abnormal behavior that result from environmental factors rather than disease. For example, the *brief psychotic disorder* involves hallucinations, delusions, and a disruption of thought processes, but in many cases the disorder is thought to be a *reaction* to an overwhelming stress, and the symptoms will clear up when the stress is reduced regardless of whether the individual gets treatment (see Chapter 11). It is also the case that the definition of mental illness may have been stretched a bit. For example, if a child is having difficulty with arithmetic, he or she could be diagnosed as suffering from the *mathematics disorder* (see Chapter 15). Similarly, if you are unduly concerned about your physical appearance, you could be diagnosed as suffering from the *dysmorphic disorder* (see Chapter 7). Are those really psychiatric illnesses?

There is no doubt that sometimes the psychiatric system is abused or fails and individuals are mistakenly or unjustifiably incarcerated in hospitals. However, there are also individuals who experience serious symptoms in the absence of environmental stress and whose symptoms can be relieved only with some form of therapy. Furthermore, as the case studies in this book will

illustrate, some individuals suffer terribly from their bizarre symptoms, symptoms that cannot be written off simply as differences in personality or rational responses to an irrational society. The serious and debilitating symptoms from which these people suffer are not due to suggestion and are not under voluntary control. Clearly, *some individuals are ill.*

The notion that mental illness is a myth is less popular today than it was 20 years ago, a change that is probably a reflection of our increased understanding of abnormal behavior. Although it is now generally agreed that mental illness exists, it is important that we not ignore the voice of dissent on this issue. In considering abnormal behavior, we must be careful that we do not simply dismiss disagreeable behavior as due to illness, and we must not allow the system to be misused by accident or by intent. Mental illness is not a myth, but the possibility raises important issues that we must keep in mind.

MENTAL HEALTH PROFESSIONALS

Now that I have reviewed the history and definition of abnormal behavior, it might be helpful if I described the training and activities of the individuals who are most involved in the mental health profession. Questions like "What is the difference between a psychiatrist and a psychologist?" are often asked, and it is important that you understand the differences and overlaps.

Psychiatrists

Psychiatrists are individuals who after completing college go on to 4 years of *medical school,* where they obtain a general medical education, and then take a 1-year medical internship. On completion of the internship, they receive an **MD degree** (Doctor of Medicine) and are qualified to practice general medicine. They then enter a *residency in psychiatry,* which is a training program in psychiatry that usually takes about 3 years. The program is based in a hospital and is focused on the clinical practice of psychiatry (e.g., treatment of mentally ill individuals). At the end of that training, they take an examination; if they pass, they become board-certified psychiatrists and are qualified to practice psychiatry.

Clinical Psychologists

Traditionally, **clinical psychologists** are individuals who after graduating from college go on to *graduate school* for 4 to 6 years, during which they study abnormal behavior (e.g., diagnosis, treatment) and research techniques (e.g., design of experiments, statistics). During their time in graduate school, the students write a master's thesis and a doctoral dissertation, both of which involve original research. After completing their graduate studies, these individuals go on to a 1-year clinical psychology internship in which they refine their clinical skills. On completion of the internship, these individuals receive a **PhD degree.** *PhD* stands for Doctor of Philosophy, which reflects the scholarly and scientific heritage of clinical psychology rather than the more narrow training for practice. After earning the PhD degree, in most states the individuals who wish to practice as psychologists must take an examination to become licensed or certified.

Note that the training of psychiatrists is focused almost exclusively on clinical practice, whereas the training of clinical psychologists involves a blend of clinical practice and research. The training of psychologists is designed to produce *practitioners* who can work with disturbed individuals but who are also *scientists* who can conduct research that will advance our understanding of abnormal behavior. This approach to training is referred to as the **scientist-practitioner model** of training.

However, over the past 20 years, a second model of training for clinical psychologists has been developed in which the training in graduate school is focused almost exclusively on the development of clinical skills. That is, research training was essentially eliminated. This alternative model was developed because it was argued that many clinical psychologists spend their entire careers in clinical practice and do not do any research, and therefore the time they spent learning research methodology and conducting research in graduate school was not productive and could have been better spent developing their clinical skills. This graduate school program and the usual 1-year clinical psychology internship lead to the **PsyD degree** (Doctor of Psychology). Like the MD degree program, the PsyD degree program prepares individuals for clinical practice. Today, clinical psychologists may have either a PhD or a PsyD degree, and there is some controversy over which type of training is more appropriate. However, rather than arguing about which approach to training is best, when evaluating the qualifications of a psychologist it is more important to ask if the quality of his or her training is *sufficiently high* and if the training is *relevant to the work he or she is doing.*

The most notable difference in the professional activities of psychiatrists and clinical psychologists is the fact that psychiatrists can prescribe drugs and perform other medical procedures such as electroconvulsive therapy, whereas clinical psychologists cannot. That difference is a reflection of the differences in their training: Psychiatrists have gone to medical school, and psychologists have not. However, the difference between what psychiatrists and psychologists can do is becoming blurred because there is a movement afoot to grant clinical psychologists prescription privileges for psychiatric drugs (DeLeon & Wiggins, 1996; DeNelsky, 1996; Hayes & Heibly, 1996; Klein, 1996; Lorion, 1996; Pachman, 1996; Sammons et al., 1996). The argument is that the need for individuals who can prescribe drugs

far outstrips the number of psychiatrists who are available and that with some additional training, clinical psychologists could fill that need. Advocates for prescription privileges for psychologists also argue that there are already numerous nonphysician professionals, such as nurse-practitioners and dentists, who have limited prescription privileges, so there are precedents for extending the privileges to psychologists. Furthermore, for years psychologists in some hospitals have been prescribing drugs informally under the supervision of psychiatrists. To evaluate the ability of psychologists to prescribe psychiatric drugs, the National Institute of Mental Health is conducting an experiment in which a number of psychologists are receiving additional training in physiology, pharmacology, and the prescription of drugs, and their prescriptions are being monitored by a panel of experts. Some psychologists have already completed the program and are prescribing drugs within the military system. If this program is found to be generally successful, laws might be passed to extend prescription privileges to psychologists. However, even if the results of that experiment indicate that properly trained psychologists can effectively prescribe psychiatric drugs, the granting of prescription privileges is probably a long way off because such a move is strongly opposed by the American Medical Association, and there are even psychologists who argue that the traditional distinction between psychiatrists and psychologists should be maintained. The fact that the prescription privilege for psychologists is being seriously considered reflects a basic and important change, and it is a development to watch carefully. As a footnote to this discussion, it should be mentioned that originally the practice of psychotherapy was limited to psychiatrists. The change in prescription privileges may simply be a part of a general evolutionary process.

Other Professionals

Other professionals who work in the mental health area include *psychiatric nurses, social workers, occupational therapists, recreation therapists, art therapists,* and *music therapists.* In Chapter 21, I will discuss the specific roles that these individuals play, but in most cases their importance is related to the fact that they provide additional normal contacts and role models from whom disturbed individuals can receive feedback and guidance. That is, the messages that are conveyed in the context of sports, art, or music are probably more important than the sports, art, or music per se.

Evolution in Who Provides Treatment

Before concluding this section, it is important to note that over the past 40 years, important changes have taken place in terms of the types of professionals who provide treatment for individuals with psychiatric problems, and that evolution is continuing today

(Humphreys, 1996). For example, until the early 1950s, only psychiatrists provided psychotherapy; psychologists were limited to doing diagnostic testing, and social workers focused on helping the families of disturbed individuals. However, in the 1950s and 1960s, psychologists also began providing psychotherapy for patients, and in the past few years, growing numbers of social workers have begun providing psychotherapy. In other words, initially psychologists began supplanting psychiatrists, and now social workers are supplanting psychologists in providing psychotherapy. Earlier I pointed out also that some psychologists may begin prescribing medication, a role that was once limited to psychiatrists.

This evolution in who provides treatment is driven by three factors, the first of which is the *need for treatment*. As the number of patients needing treatment exceeds the availability of one professional group to treat them, other professional groups are brought in. A second and very important factor is the *cost of treatment*. As costs rise and resources dwindle, the insurance companies that pay for treatment seek out professional groups that are less expensive; psychologists are less expensive than psychiatrists, and social workers are less expensive than psychologists. The third factor is the *income of the professionals*. As any one professional group takes on more responsibilities, such as prescribing drugs or doing psychotherapy, it can demand somewhat higher fees, and that provides a strong incentive for the group to "infringe" on the territory of a better-paid group. This evolution can have positive effects, such as providing more treatment at less cost, but it is important that the professionals who begin providing treatment are appropriately trained and that a high standard of care is maintained.

Finally, a cautionary note should be sounded: Current laws regulate only the use of the labels of *psychiatrist, psychologist,* and *social worker;* that means that *anyone* can "hang out a shingle" and offer services as a *psychotherapist, counselor,* or any other title that implies expertise in the area of mental health. Therefore, in selecting someone for help, it is essential that you carefully check the individual's qualifications.

With this material as background, we can go on to Chapter 2, in which I will consider the various explanations that have been offered for abnormal behaviors and the related therapies that are used to treat abnormal behaviors.

SUMMARY

- ■ Western civilization has gone through six stages in the development of an understanding of the causes and treatments of abnormal behavior:
    1. *Demonology.* Initially it was believed that abnormal behavior was caused by spirits and demons, and treatment was focused on driving them out, often through torture.
    2. *Early physiological explanations.* Hippocrates introduced the notion that abnormal behavior was caused by the imbalance of humors (fluids) in the body, and treatment was focused on achieving a balance in the humors, for example, by bleeding the individual.
    3. *A return to demonology.* In the Middle Ages, it was again believed that spirits, particularly the Devil, caused abnormal behavior, and torture was again used.
    4. *The introduction of humane care.* Beginning in the 16th century, individuals such as Pinel, Tuke, Rush, and Dix worked to improve the conditions in which patients were confined and treated.
    5. *The introduction of psychological explanations.* Beginning about 200 years ago, a variety of psychological explanations and related treatments were introduced.
        a. Mesmer and Charcot brought attention to the role of suggestion, and hypnosis was sometimes used to relieve symptoms.
        b. Freud explored the influence of stressful early experiences, memories of which were stored in the unconscious, and developed psychoanalysis as a means of uncovering and dealing with them. The psychoanalytic process involves free association, dream interpretation, resistance, and transference.
        c. Pavlov, Thorndike, and Skinner demonstrated that the behavior of animals can be influenced by classical and operant conditioning, and Watson used those procedures to explain normal and abnormal behavior in humans, an approach called behaviorism. Furthermore, it was suggested that the principles of conditioning could be used to treat abnormal behavior, an approach called behavior modification.
        d. Many psychologists objected to the fact that behaviorism ignored the role of cognitions (thoughts), and in the 1970s, important breakthroughs

were made in understanding how we think and how our thoughts and beliefs influence our behavior. That information was used by Beck and others to develop cognitive therapy, in which erroneous beliefs that lead to abnormal behavior are replaced by more accurate beliefs.

6. *Renewed interest in physiological causes.* The accidental discovery that drugs can reduce abnormal behaviors led to increased interest in physiological explanations for abnormal behavior, and recent breakthroughs in medical technology have refined our understanding of how the brain works and how problems in the brain can lead to abnormal behavior. Physiological treatments for abnormal behavior often involve drugs that are used to correct problems in the brain.

◼ At present, we have many explanations for abnormal behavior, and it may be that different disorders stem from different causes, a given disorder may have more than one cause, and different causes may combine to result in a disorder.

◼ Abnormal behavior can be defined from the point of view of the individual or the culture in which the individual functions. When focusing on the individual, the crucial factors are distress and disability, whereas when focusing on the culture, deviance is the important factor.

◼ Some critics argue that mental illness is a myth, that rather than reflecting an illness, abnormal behavior is simply different behavior, wrong behavior, or behavior that reflects problems in society. They also argue that the illness model encourages abnormal behavior because it relieves individuals of responsibility and that it is a convenient justification for dismissing and locking up individuals who are different and disturbing to us.

◼ Psychiatrists differ from clinical psychologists in that they have gone to medical school and therefore can prescribe drugs and use other medical procedures. However, there is currently a movement to provide clinical psychologists with additional training so that they can prescribe drugs.

◼ Other mental health professionals include psychiatric nurses, social workers, occupational therapists, recreation therapists, art therapists, and music therapists.

◼ The roles of mental helth professionals are changing. For example, whereas once only psychiatrists were allowed to do psychotherapy, today many psychologists and social workers practice psychotherapy. This evolution is driven by increasing demand for treatment, the need for less expensive treatment, and the economic interests of the various professional groups.

KEY TERMS, CONCEPTS, AND NAMES

In reviewing and testing yourself on what you have learned from this chapter, you should be able to identify and discuss each of the following.

analyst (psychoanalyst)
Anna O.
Beck, Aaron
behavior modification
behaviorism
Breuer, Josef
catharsis
Charcot, Jean-Martin
classical conditioning
clinical psychologist
cognitive therapy
demonology
deviance from cultural norms (as a definition of abnormal behavior)
disability (as a definition of abnormal behavior)

distress (as a definition of abnormal behavior)
Dix, Dorothea
dream interpretation
free association
Freud, Sigmund
Hippocrates
humane care
humors (bodily fluids)
hysterical disorders
MD degree
Mesmer, Franz Anton
mesmerism
myth of mental illness
operant conditioning
Pavlov, Ivan

PhD degree
Pinel, Philippe
psychiatrist
PsyD degree
psychoanalysis
resistance
Rush, Benjamin
scientist-practitioner model
Skinner, B. F.
Thorndike, Edward L.
transference
Tuke, William
unconscious
Watson, John B.

CHAPTER TWO
OVERVIEW of EXPLANATIONS

OUTLINE

A major goal of this book is to provide you with an understanding of what causes abnormal behavior, and in subsequent chapters I will discuss the causes of a variety of disorders. However, to prepare you for those discussions, in this chapter I will give you a brief overview of the major explanations that are used in the area of abnormal behavior. This will provide you with an outline or template into which you can put the more detailed discussions that will follow.

INTRODUCTION

Different Causes for Different Disorders

At the outset, it is important to recognize that *a number of very different explanations have been developed for abnormal behavior.* For example, it has been suggested that abnormal behavior is the result of *stress,* that it is *learned,* that it results from *problems in the way we process information* (think), and that it is due to *physiological problems in the brain.* Each explanation has had its advocates, and there has been a hot and sometimes bitter debate over which explanation is correct.

That debate is still going on, but a resolution appears to be developing: It appears that *all the major explanations for abnormal behavior are correct—but no one explanation is correct for all disorders.* In other words, *different disorders may have different causes.* For example, anxiety may be caused by stress, whereas schizophrenia is caused by biochemical imbalances in the brain. Furthermore, *for some disorders, there may be more than one cause.* For example, in some cases anxiety may be caused by stress, in others it may be learned, and in still others it may result from biochemical problems.

The fact that more than one explanation can be correct means that you must not only understand the various explanations, but you must also understand *which explanations are best for which disorders.* This is a radical departure from the way abnormal behavior was approached in the past, but this approach is not unique to psychological disorders. For example, in the case of physical disorders, we recognize that colds and cancers are different disorders and that they have different causes. Indeed, it would be a serious mistake to assume that they had the same causes and to treat them in the same way. Regardless of whether the area is psychology or medicine, you should beware of the researcher, author, or clinician who claims to have come up with the one explanation and treatment for *all* disorders.

The exciting challenge in the area of abnormal behavior is to determine which cause or causes are responsible for which disorders. For me, each disorder is like a mystery, and my role is like that of a detective who puts the clues together to solve the case. Therefore, in the chapters in which I discuss different disorders, I will examine each of the possible explanations (suspects?) before attempting to draw conclusions concerning which explanation best fits the data for a particular disorder.

The fact that I will examine all of the explanations means that in some cases I will be considering explanations that have been discredited and abandoned. That may lead you to ask, why discuss discredited and abandoned explanations? The reason is that when those explanations were originally proposed, they seemed to make sense and were widely accepted until their flaws were recognized. It is therefore appropriate that we discuss those explanations along with their flaws so that when they come up again (as they always do), you will be able to evaluate them knowledgeably. With regard to the explanations for abnormal behavior, there is a lot of truth in the old saying "Those who do not understand history are doomed to relive it."

The Final Common Pathway

Disorders can be due to any one of a number of different causes, but it is essential to recognize that ultimately *all disorders are caused by physiological processes in the nervous system.* In other words, there are different starting points for abnormal behavior, but ultimately they are all funneled through physiology. That is illustrated in Figure 2.1.

More generally, it is interesting to note that all of your thoughts, feelings, and behaviors are based on physiological processes in your nervous system. For example, even thoughts about abstract concepts such as love, beauty, and truth are due to the firing of specific sets of neurons in your brain. Indeed, later you will learn that by using a very fine electrode to stimulate specific neurons in the brain, we can repeatedly call up specific thoughts, images, and feelings!

The fact that physiological processes are the last step in the pathway to abnormal behavior is important for two reasons. First, it enables us to understand how the various factors cause abnormal behaviors. That is, rather than just saying that stress leads to depression, by understanding the physiological processes we can understand why stress leads to depression. Second, recognizing the role of the physiological processes has implications for treatment because in some cases we may not be able to treat the real cause of the problem, so we must do the next best thing and intervene at the level of the physiological processes. For example, if an individual is seriously depressed because of an overwhelming stress that cannot be relieved immediately, it may be necessary

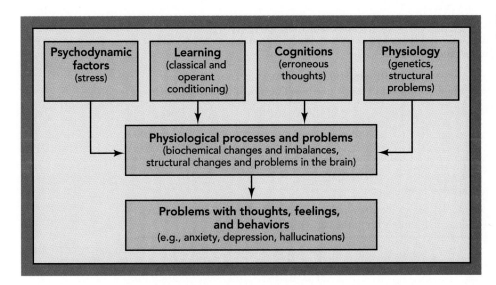

FIGURE 2.1 Pathways to abnormal behavior.

to use drugs to change the physiological processes until the stress can be brought under control. Alternatively, if a disorder is caused by a genetic problem, we may not be able to change the genes, but we may be able to change the physiological processes that are triggered by the genes.

With this material as background, let's review the major explanations for abnormal behavior.

PSYCHODYNAMIC EXPLANATIONS

The **psychodynamic explanations** suggest that *stress leads to abnormal behavior.* Specifically, psychological stress can cause a distortion or breaking of the personality, just as extreme physical stress can cause a steel girder to twist out of shape and break. That explanation is fairly straightforward, but there are wide differences among psychodynamic theorists over what causes the stress. In general, the theories fall into two groups. On the one hand, there is the traditional **psychoanalytic theory** developed by **Sigmund Freud,** in which he suggested that stress and abnormal behaviors were caused primarily by conflicts over the satisfaction of biological needs such as eating and sex. On the other hand, there are a variety of **neo-Freudian theories** that are similar to Freud's except that in those theories it is assumed that stress and abnormal behavior stem from personal problems such as feelings of inferiority or interpersonal conflict. (It might be noted that the term *psychodynamic* is based on *psycho,* "mind," and *dynamic* "force" or "energy," so generally speaking, the psychodynamic explanations refer to the interplay of forces or energies in the mind that can result in abnormal behaviors.)

Freudian (Psychoanalytic) Theory

The psychoanalytic theory was developed by Sigmund Freud, who suggested that *the most important cause of stress is conflicts between our biological needs and the restraints that are imposed on the satisfaction of those needs* (Fenichel, 1945; Freud, 1955). In other words, there is conflict between what we want to do and what our conscience or society tells us it is all right to do, and that results in stress, which leads to abnormal behaviors. According to Freud, the conflicts are originally encountered during early childhood, and the specific conflicts we encounter and how we resolve them will influence the development of our personality and can lead to abnormal behavior.

Psychosexual Stages, Conflicts, and Complexes. Freud suggested that we all go through a series of **stages of psychosexual development,** that most of those stages involve conflicts that must be overcome, and that the failure to overcome a conflict will result in a complex—that is, the continuance of the conflict will result in abnormal behaviors. The stages of psychosexual development and the related conflicts are listed in Table 2.1; here I will comment briefly on the anal and phallic stages.

During the **anal stage,** the child must go through toilet training, and how that is handled can lead to a number of conflicts and problems. For example, if a parent reacts with anxiety and disgust to the "mess" a child makes, the child may learn to be overly concerned about cleanliness and orderliness. (The many television advertisements for toilet bowl cleaners may be evidence of the traumatic and lasting effects of the American approach to toilet training.) Toilet training may also affect other aspects of personality. For

TABLE 2.1 Stages of Psychosexual Development

Stage	Issues and Conflicts
Oral	Pleasure associated with oral stimulation (sucking, eating). Infants learn whether others will satisfy needs willingly or whether one must fight for everything.
Anal	Toilet training is important, and attitudes toward cleanliness and control are developed.
Phallic	Conflicts over sexuality (the Oedipus complex). The superego develops through identification with parent.
Latency	Nothing much happens.
Genital	Individual achieves maturity and struggles with the conflicts that were not adequately dealt with in the earlier stages.

example, if the parent is strict and demanding in the process of toilet training (remember the toilet seat you were strapped into until you "performed"?), the child may retain the feces in retaliation. That behavior may generalize and result in the child's becoming a stingy or obstinate adult. By contrast, if the parent encourages the child and then praises the child when a bowel movement is produced, the child may grow up to be generous, productive, and creative.

Freud suggested that a child's experience with toilet training may lead to future conflicts and problems.

Freud attached a great deal of importance to the **phallic stage,** during which the child supposedly becomes sexually attracted to the parent of the opposite sex, thereby setting up a conflict with the parent of the same sex. For example, the little boy supposedly becomes attracted to his mother but then finds he must compete with his father for the mother's attention. During this conflict, the little boy notices or learns that some of his peers (little girls) do not have a penis, and he concludes that they have been castrated. That leads to the belief that if he continues to compete with his father, his father will castrate him, so he withdraws from the competition. However, he is still attracted to his mother, so he attempts to get her vicariously by *identifying* with his father; that is, he acts like his father and thus symbolically becomes his father and gets his mother vicariously. That resolves the conflict, and by acting like his father, the little boy takes on the culturally approved male role. If the little boy does not resolve the conflict by identifying with his father, he will not internalize the male role and, for example, may never develop a conscience (the culture's rules of right and wrong). Freud called this the **Oedipus** (ED-i-pus) **complex,** named for Oedipus, the character in Greek tragedy who unknowingly murdered his father and married his mother.

With regard to the little girl, Freud suggested that she becomes attracted to her father because of her "penis envy": if she can have her father, she will be more complete. However, to get her father, she must compete with her mother, and the little girl is threatened by what her mother might do (apparently her mother already castrated her). Therefore the little girl identifies with her mother so that she can have her father vicariously. By identifying with her mother, the little girl takes on the cultural role, standards, and mores of the society. Freud referred to this as the **Electra** (ē-LEK-tra) **complex.** It is interesting to note that

Freud suggested that it is women's continuing penis envy that leads to their feelings of inferiority and their dependent role!

Structure of Personality. As a way of conceptualizing the conflicts that go on within the personality, Freud offered his **structural approach to personality.** Specifically, he divided the personality into three components, the *id,* the *ego,* and the *superego.* The **id** is the *source of all of our innate biological needs (instincts),* and the id's goal is to *satisfy those needs as rapidly and as completely as possible.* Because the id seeks to satisfy biological needs and provide pleasure, it is governed by what Freud called the **pleasure principle;** in short, the id simply seeks immediate pleasure. However, the id is very ineffective in satisfying our needs. Indeed, rather than taking constructive actions, the id relies on what Freud called the **primary process,** which involves simply thinking or fantasizing about the satisfaction of a need. When we use daydreams instead of actions to satisfy our needs (e.g., thinking about food rather than going to the kitchen to prepare a meal), we are supposedly using the primary process to satisfy needs.

In sharp contrast to the id is the **superego,** which embodies the *restraints imposed on us by societal rules, taboos, and moral values.* We learn the dos and don'ts of society during the socialization process we go through as children. To the extent that socialization is effective, these restraints become part of us (the superego) rather than external forces. Of course, those restraints can result in conflicts with the id; for example, the id wants sex now, but the superego says you have to wait.

To resolve the conflicts between the id and the superego, Freud introduced the notion of the **ego,** which supposedly *mediates between the id and the superego.* To accomplish that task, the ego tries to find realistic and effective ways of satisfying the needs of the id while not violating the restraints established by the superego. For example, when we get hungry, our ego tries to find ways of getting food rather than leaving the id simply to fantasize about food. However, the method used to get the food must not conflict with the rules set out by the superego. If the ego is functioning properly, we work for our food; we do not steal it. Whereas our id operates on the primary process, the ego operates on the **secondary process,** which was Freud's term for thinking and problem solving.

In a variety of ways, the interactions of our id, ego, and superego can result in abnormal behavior. For example, if our ego does not effectively satisfy the needs of the id, the id will revert to the use of primary processes (fantasies) to satisfy its needs. Freud suggested that use of primary processes can result in childlike behavior, hallucinations, and delusions. In contrast, if our superego somehow gains most of the power, we may become constricted and rigid in our behavior. It is important to recognize that Freud did not suggest that the id, ego, and superego represented little people in our personality; rather they were concepts that he used to illustrate how conflicts developed and were resolved.

Levels of Consciousness. In addition to describing the personality in terms of the id, superego, and ego, Freud also described the personality in terms of levels of consciousness: the *conscious mind,* the *preconscious,* and the *unconscious.* At any point in time, you are aware of many things, such as feelings, friends, problems, and commitments. All of these things are in your **conscious mind.** There are also many things, such as friends from long ago or unimportant events, that you no longer keep in consciousness but you can recall if you try. This recallable material is in your **preconscious.** However, most important for Freudian theory is the **unconscious,** which is where you supposedly *store important but anxiety-provoking memories.* Because these memories are psychologically painful, you have locked them away in your unconscious, where you cannot remember them. However, although you cannot remember them, they continue to influence your behavior. Freud suggested that many "unexplainable" behaviors are motivated by unconscious memories, conflicts, and drives. For example, excessive cleanliness may be due to unconscious concerns about "messing" that were developed when you were a child. Similarly, individuals who always date people who are like their mothers or fathers may have an unconscious desire for them because the individuals did not adequately resolve their Oedipus or Electra complexes. Postulating an unconscious is a handy theoretical device because any behavior that cannot be explained with regard to observable factors can simply be attributed to unconscious factors.

Freud likened the personality to an iceberg: A small part of it appears above the surface (the conscious) and part of it occasionally bobs into view (the preconscious), but the major portion that supports the visible parts is below the surface and invisible (the unconscious). Just as the submerged portion of an iceberg can be dangerous for a ship at sea, supposedly the unconscious can be dangerous for you as you navigate life. As you will learn later, a major goal of psychoanalytic therapy is to bring unconscious material to consciousness so that the individual can be aware of it and respond to it in an appropriate way.

Anxiety and Defense Mechanisms. Earlier I pointed out that within the psychodynamic explanation, the notion is that conflict leads to stress and that the stress then leads to abnormal behaviors such as anxiety. In other words, the sequence is *conflict → stress → symptoms* such as anxiety. That is true, but in some instances the process is somewhat different because we may use **defense mechanisms** to reduce our anxiety, and *the* *defense mechanisms lead to abnormal behavior* (Vaillant, 1994). That is, the sequence is *conflict → stress → anxiety → defense → symptoms.* In Freudian theory, then, anxiety is considered to be both a *symptom* of a stress and a *signal* to use a defense mechanism.

Defense mechanisms are *psychological maneuvers by which we distort reality in ways that will help us avoid conflicts and reduce anxiety.* There are numerous defense mechanisms, the most important of which are discussed here (for a review, see Holmes, 1984a).

1. *Repression.* One way of dealing with anxiety-provoking conflicts or thoughts is to *force them from conscious awareness and into the unconscious.* This process is called **repression.** Repressed material is not lost like forgotten material; instead, it is *stored* in the unconscious, where it can continue to influence our behavior without our awareness. Freud suggests that we are unlikely to remember anything about our toilet training because we have repressed those "dirty" experiences, but they continue to influence our behavior through unconscious processes (e.g., that may be why some people are compulsively neat). Repression may be the most important defense in Freudian theory because it is through repression that material gets into the unconscious, and the unconscious plays a crucial role in explaining behavior.

2. *Suppression.* Another way to deal with anxiety-provoking material is to *intentionally avoid thinking about it.* This is called **suppression.** The most common method of suppressing material is to think about something else. For example, you may watch television to distract yourself from thinking about an examination you just failed.

3. *Denial.* **Denial** involves the *reinterpretation of the anxiety-provoking material to make it less threatening.* The failed examination may be reinterpreted as a valuable experience for learning about what you need to study.

4. *Projection.* **Projection** is the process whereby you *attribute your own personality characteristics to other people.* For example, if you are frightened, you might see other people as frightened. Projection can serve as a defense mechanism because if you have an unacceptable personality trait and you project it onto another person, your belief that the other person has the trait might reduce your concern about having the trait. For example, if you are hostile and see a respected friend as being hostile, you may be able to conclude that being hostile is not such a bad thing after all.

5. *Displacement.* There are two kinds of **displacement.** **Object displacement** occurs when you *express a feeling toward one individual that should be expressed toward someone else.* For example, a man may be angry with his boss but express his anger against his wife. He does this because it is less anxiety-provoking to be aggressive toward his wife than toward his boss. **Drive displacement** occurs when you *have one feeling (drive) that cannot be expressed, so the energy from that feeling is transferred to another feeling that can be expressed.* Freud suggests that sexual feelings may be displaced and expressed as aggression.

6. *Regression.* When facing conflict, stress, and particularly frustration, you may use **regression** to *return to an earlier stage of life in which you were more secure and successful.* Not only do we run home in the face of stress, but we may also go back to using previously successful strategies for solving problems.

7. *Identification.* When using **identification,** you *take on the personal characteristics of another individual* and thereby to some extent become the other individual. This may help you satisfy your needs vicariously. Dressing like someone you admire or envy is a form of identification. Alternatively, when you identify with someone of whom you are afraid, you might feel as though you have taken on some of that person's power, thereby reducing your fear. For example, some long-term prisoners in the Nazi concentration camps walked, dressed, and acted like their feared Gestapo captors.

8. *Rationalization.* **Rationalization** involves *giving a good reason for some behavior that is not the real reason.* In doing so, you can disguise actual but unacceptable motivations.

9. *Compensation.* If you feel threatened in some area, you may *work extra hard to overcome the real or imagined weakness,* and that is referred to as **compensation.** For example, some athletes may be compensating for their beliefs that they are weak.

10. *Intellectualization.* To avoid threatening emotions, you might *focus on the objective, nonemotional details of an otherwise emotional situation.* For example, a terminally ill individual may focus his or her attention on the technical aspects of a disease rather than the fact that he or she is facing death. That is called **intellectualization.**

11. *Reaction Formation.* **Reaction formation** is said to occur when you desire something or want to do something, but because of a conflict *you transform the desire or the behavior into the opposite.* For example, someone who is unconsciously aroused by pornography may defend against that by labeling pornography as disgusting and leading a fight against it.

The defense mechanisms I have mentioned here are only some of the defenses that have been identified. It is important to recognize that defense mechanisms help people avoid conflicts and reduce anxiety, but they usually do so at a cost. If you use a defense mechanism to avoid a conflict and reduce anxiety, you are unlikely to work on realistic ways of eliminating the conflict. For example, if you use denial to reduce the importance and anxiety associated with a future exam, you may not study for the exam and hence fail it. Also, defense mechanisms generally involve distortions of reality, and distortions of reality reduce our ability to function effectively. In these ways, defense mechanisms can lead to inappropriate and abnormal behavior.

Neo-Freudian Theories

Freud's ideas had a great impact on the thinking about behavior, but in time some of his followers began to disagree with him concerning some of his ideas, and one by one they broke with Freud and began building their own theories. Today, we refer to those individuals as *neo-Freudians*—"new Freudians." Their theories rely on many of Freud's ideas, but they differ in two important ways.

Importance of the Ego. First, neo-Freudians place *less emphasis on the id* and *more emphasis on the ego.* Whereas Freud believed that the biological needs of the id are the driving force in the personality and the ego is simply the mediator or compromiser between the id and the superego, the neo-Freudians believe that the ego is more powerful and is in control (Hartmann, 1958, 1964). In other words, rather than seeing humans as pushed in one way or another by the needs of the id and superego, the neo-Freudians see individuals as able to pick and choose consciously between the needs they want to satisfy.

Related to the role of the ego, the neo-Freudians also believe that the defense mechanisms that are used by the ego do not necessarily lead to abnormal behavior but can instead actually be *constructive.* For example, compensation can lead to extra effort and successes, as in the case of Jim Abbott, who worked hard to compensate for having only one hand and eventually became a pitcher with the New York Yankees! Because of the emphasis on the power of the ego, this approach is often called **ego psychology,** and one of the leaders of the movement was Freud's daughter, **Anna Freud.**

Sources of Stress and Anxiety. The second major departure the neo-Freudians introduced involves the source of stress and anxiety. Specifically, whereas Freud emphasized conflicts over biological needs, the neo-Freudians focus on *personal or interpersonal conflicts* as the source of stress and anxiety. For example, **Alfred Adler** suggested that **feelings of inferiority** create anxiety and that individuals spend much of their lives compensating for those early feelings (Adler, 1927; Ansbacher & Ansbacher, 1956). In his own case, Adler believed that he sought training as a physician in an attempt to overcome his concerns about his health that stemmed from a serious illness when he was a child.

Some neo-Freudians believe that anxiety stems from feelings of inferiority for which individuals then attempt to compensate. Pictured here is Jim Abbott, who became a major league pitcher despite the fact that he has only one hand.

Another neo-Freudian, **Karen Horney** (HORN-i), argued that stress and anxiety were due to *interpersonal conflicts* (e.g., problems with dominance, independence, inconsistencies in love) rather than sexuality (Horney, 1937, 1939, 1945). She went on to suggest that individuals attempt to overcome the conflicts by *moving toward people* (by seeking others, you can gain support), *moving against people* (by beating others, you can gain a sense of personal power), or *moving away from people* (by being self-sufficient, you can protect yourself from being hurt). Horney also reacted strongly against Freud's view of women and in doing so became one of psychology's first feminists (Horney, 1967). For example, she argued that if women feel inferior, it is because of the role given them by the culture, not because they have penis envy. She also suggested that men envy women's ability to give birth and may even have "breast envy." (Why else, Horney asked, would men spend so much time looking at breasts?)

Since the early theorists such as Adler and Horney broke from Freud, many others have joined their ranks and have identified numerous other sources of anxiety that range from sexual orientation to financial problems.

Stress

From the foregoing discussion it should be clear that opinions on what causes stress differ but there is widespread agreement that whatever its cause, *stress is a crucial link in the chain that leads to abnormal behavior.* Therefore, in this section, I will examine the notion of stress, how we respond to it, and how stress leads to abnormal behaviors.

Stressors and Stress. The word *stress* is often used to refer both to the *cause* of stress (e.g., a test is a stress) and to a *response* (e.g., you experience stress when you take a test). To be more precise in our usage, it is helpful to use the word **stressor** when talking about a cause of stress and the word **stress** when talking about the response to a stressor.

Having made that distinction, we must define what a stressor is. Actually, it is somewhat difficult to define stressors because what may be a stressor for one individual may not be a stressor for another individual. For example, standing in a cage with 10 hungry lions would undoubtedly be a stressor for many of us, but it is not a stressor for an experienced lion tamer. Rather than attempting to define stressors in terms of their physical characteristics, it is more effective to define them *operationally.* Defined operationally, stressors are *situations that require major adjustments that overtax us.* Facing the lions, you and I would be overtaxed by having to fight or run, but the lion tamer would simply go through a well-practiced routine. Both negative and positive situations can be stressful because they can both require major adjustments. Getting married may be a positive experience, but because it can require major adjustments, it can be a stressor.

Components of Stress. The stress response has two components, the *psychological* and the *physiological.* The psychological component of the stress response involves *emotions* such as anxiety and tension. Because of the unpleasant nature of these emotions, we are motivated to reduce them. The physiological component of the stress response involves *bodily changes* such as increased heart rate, blood pressure, and muscle tension. Those changes prepare us for physical action— *fight* or *flight.* They are also unpleasant, so we tend to want to reduce them.

An interesting question that arises is, which comes first, the psychological response or the physiological response? In other words, do your emotions lead to physiological responses, or do your physiological responses lead to emotions? On the one hand, it is widely assumed that stressors trigger *psychological responses (emotions) that in turn lead to physiological responses.* That is, if you become frightened, your heart rate increases. This is known as the **Cannon-Bard theory of emotion** because it was formulated by Walter Cannon and Philip Bard, two early investigators. On the other hand, it is also possible that *stressors trigger physiological responses that in turn lead to psychological responses:* That is, your heart rate increases, and therefore you begin experiencing fear. Evidence for that possibility comes

Extreme poverty can be a source of stress, which can lead to abnormal behavior.

from research in which college students were given drugs that increased their heart rates, and when that occurred, the students experienced fear despite the fact that they were in a nonfrightening situation (Schachter & Singer, 1962). This is known as the **James-Lange theory of emotion** because it was developed by William James and Carl Lange, two other early investigators.

Which explanation is correct? As with most things, it is probably not an either-or situation: Both explanations are probably correct. Stressors may stimulate both psychological and physiological responses, and once started, the psychological and physiological responses may stimulate each other, thereby heightening and maintaining the overall arousal.

Note that the physiological component of the stress response may not be appropriate for dealing with most modern-day stressors. For example, physiological responses that prepare you to fight or run away may help you deal with a hungry lion, but they will be of no value for helping you prepare for an examination in calculus or a demanding job, and those are the kinds of stressors with which most of us deal most often. Indeed, physiological arousal may be counterproductive in dealing with those stressors because the arousal may distract you from your cognitive problem solving.

From Stressors to Abnormal Behavior. Now that you have some understanding of the concept of stress, I can discuss the process that leads from stressors through stress to abnormal behavior. The steps in that process are discussed in the following paragraphs and summarized in Figure 2.2.

1. *Awareness and Appraisal.* After a potential stressor develops, the first step involves becoming *aware* of it and *appraising* the challenge it poses (Lazarus & Folkman, 1984). The individual who does not know that a tumor is developing in his or her body cannot take appropriate steps to have it treated, and an individual who does not know about an impending examination cannot begin studying. Sometimes there is some truth in the notion that if you are calm while all around you are losing their heads, you probably do not understand what is going on. Some individuals attempt to avoid or postpone stress by intentionally not looking for potential problems (e.g., they do not go to the physician for a physical or do not check syllabi for dates of exams). In contrast, other individuals are constantly seeking out problems and thereby increasing the likelihood of stress (Mathews et al., 1990). Clearly, awareness and appraisal are essential first steps leading to stress and abnormal behavior.

2. *Coping.* Once you are aware of the potential stressor, you can begin **coping**—solving the problem or adjust-

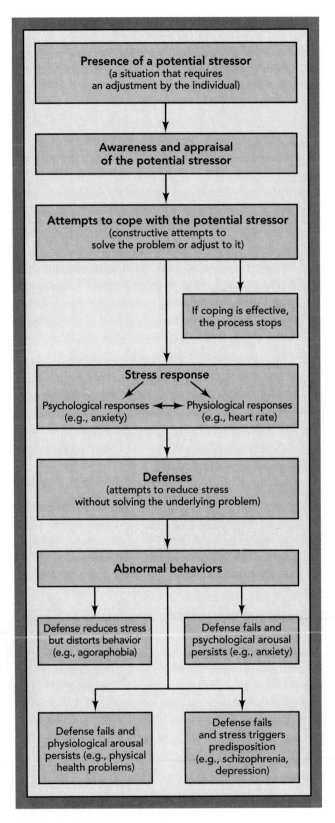

FIGURE 2.2 Steps in the process that can lead from stressors to abnormal behavior.

ing to it. The individual who discovers a tumor can go in for treatment, and the student facing an exam can reduce social activities and spend more time studying. In cases in which coping is effective for dealing with the stressor, the process stops.

3. *Stress and Defense.* If you are not able to cope with the situation and it overtaxes you, the stress response will be triggered, thereby resulting in the unpleasant effects of psychological and physiological arousal. Facing such a state of stress, you may begin using defense mechanisms to reduce the stress. Defense differs from coping in that coping involves *constructive problem solving,* whereas defense involves *reducing stress without solving the problem.* For example, one defensive strategy involves reappraising the stressor so that it is no longer viewed with alarm. This is generally called **denial** or **situation redefinition** (Bennett & Holmes, 1975; Holmes & Houston, 1974; Houston & Holmes, 1974). A tumor could be called a "bump," and the exam could be thought of as a "quiz." In one experiment, two groups of students were told that they were going to receive a series of painful shocks, but the students in one group were told to think of the shocks as "vibrating sensations" rather than painful shocks. The students who redefined the shocks as vibrating sensations subsequently had lower heart rates, perspired less, and reported less anxiety while waiting for the shocks than the students who did not use redefinition.

Another defensive strategy is **avoidant thinking,** which involves intentionally distracting oneself from thinking about upsetting things (Bloom et al., 1977). Dentists may use music to distract their patients from the stressful sound of the drill, and college students often watch television as a means of distracting themselves from unpleasant tasks on which they should be working. The students may not be interested in what is on the TV, but attention to the TV blocks thoughts about studying and tests. Other potential defenses were reviewed earlier in the section on defense mechanisms.

Three points should be noted concerning defenses. First, sometimes a defense requires so much effort that it results in as much arousal as the stress it was used to avoid (Houston, 1972; Manuck et al., 1978; Solomon et al., 1980). Indeed, sometimes it is more efficient to "take your lumps and get on with it" than it is to get involved in elaborate defenses.

Second, a defense may reduce stress in the short run, but if the defense postpones appropriate action, in the long run it can bring on more serious consequences and higher stress. For example, to avoid stress, some individuals avoid seeking medical attention for symptoms (e.g., persistent headaches, a lump in the breast), and by the time they are finally forced to get attention, it is too late for effective treatment.

Third, we now know that not all behaviors that were originally labeled defenses actually reduce stress.

Projection is a case in point. Many people project their undesirable traits onto other people, but there is no evidence that doing so reduces the stress associated with having the undesirable traits. In other words, projecting hostility onto others will not necessarily make an individual less anxious about being hostile (Holmes, 1978, 1981).

4. *Abnormal Behavior.* The final step in the process involves the emergence of abnormal behavior, and that can occur in four ways. First, the defenses may reduce stress, but *the behavior involved in the defenses may be abnormal.* For example, an individual who is afraid that something bad might happen if he or she goes out of the house might defend by staying in the house, but staying in the house for months at a time is abnormal (it is known as agoraphobia). Second, the defenses may not be effective, so *the psychological component of stress will persist,* resulting in anxiety or, if prolonged, possibly depression. Third, the defenses may not be effective, so *the physiological component of stress will persist,* and that high level of arousal can lead to physical problems such as coronary artery disease and headaches. Fourth, if the defenses are not effective, *the stress may trigger a predisposition* and result in disorders such as depression or schizophrenia (diathesis-stress). The ways in which stress may be related to specific disorders will be discussed throughout the rest of this book.

COMMENT

There is no doubt that Freud's ideas have played an important role in the thinking about the causes of abnormal behavior, and the concepts he introduced, such as id, superego, ego, castration anxiety, and the Oedipus complex, are widely recognized in Western culture. However, although Freud's ideas are still part of the popular culture, many of his ideas have been abandoned by the scientific community. There are four major reasons for that. First, in many cases Freud's ideas cannot be empirically tested. For example, if a patient has memories related to an Oedipus complex, that is taken as evidence for the existence of the Oedipus complex, but if the patient does not have those memories, that is also taken as evidence for the existence of Oedipal problems because it is assumed that the complex was so threatening that the patient repressed it. Similarly, if it is predicted that a patient will be angry but instead is loving, that is explained by suggesting that the patient changed the feelings through the process of drive displacement or reaction formation. Critics point out that a theory that explains all possible outcomes cannot be verified. Furthermore, if it can predict anything, it is useless from a practical standpoint.

Second, Freud's ideas were often abandoned because new and better explanations for abnormal behavior were developed. In that regard, it is interesting to note that in science, *ideas are abandoned because they are replaced by better ideas,* not because they are proved wrong. As you will learn in the subsequent sections of this chapter, new and better ideas have generally replaced Freud's original ideas. *like trends*

Third, it is now clear that some of the important case studies on which Freud based his theory were not accurately reported—indeed, Freud intentionally distorted them to make them fit the theory. For example, Freud reported that Anna O. was symptom-free after being treated, but in fact he knew that her symptoms persisted and that she spent much of her life in institutions (Gray, 1988). That is a very serious deception because the case of Anna O. provided the foundation for Freud's theory. In a more dramatic case, Freud asserted that a patient's nosebleeds were due to psychological conflicts, but when he learned that the bleeding was due to a physiological problem (indeed, a physician had accidentally left almost a yard of gauze in her nose after an operation!), Freud and his colleagues orchestrated a cover-up (Masson, 1984). Because Freud's theory is based on his case studies, the discovery of his distortions raised serious questions about the theory and Freud's credibility.

Fourth, recent evidence does not support Freud's important contention that childhood experiences have pervasive effects that last into adulthood and cause abnormal behavior (Seligman, 1994). Instead, the evidence now indicates that traumatic events do have effects, but the effects diminish over time such that within a few years, individuals who were exposed to traumas cannot be distinguished from those who were not. In view of that, it seems unlikely that the conflicts on which Freud focused can have the widespread effects he attributed to them.

The fact that Freud's original ideas have been generally abandoned does not mean that the entire psychodynamic approach has been abandoned. On the contrary, the notions of stress and the reactions to stress still play very important roles in our thinking about abnormal behavior. What has changed is what we see as the causes of stress (see the discussion of neo-Freudian theories).

With this material as background, I can go on to present some of the alternatives to the psychodynamic explanation. The first alternative is the learning explanation, which grew out of laboratory research with animals and was originally a reaction against Freud's ideas.

LEARNING EXPLANATIONS

The basic tenet of the **learning explanations** is that abnormal behavior is *learned.* At the outset, two general points should be noted with regard to the learning explanations. First, traditional learning theorists do not make any assumptions about internal processes such as thinking that cannot be observed directly. Instead, they take the position that our explanations for behaviors should be based only on *observable* variables, and therefore they limit their attention to external factors such as stimuli and rewards (reinforcements). In short, the individual is viewed as simply responding to external stimulation. This emphasis on observable variables reflects the learning theorists' reaction against what they thought was an unjustified and unscientific reliance on unobservable internal factors by psychoanalytic theorists. The second point is that the learning explanation encompasses two distinctly different types of learning, *classical conditioning* and *operant conditioning.* These two types of conditioning play different roles in the development of abnormal behavior, and in the following sections I will discuss each type of conditioning and how it leads to abnormal behavior.

Classical Conditioning

Classical conditioning was discovered accidentally by the Russian physiologist **Ivan Pavlov,** who was studying saliva from dogs. To collect saliva for analysis, Pavlov's assistant would ring a bell to get the dog's attention; Pavlov would immediately blow a small amount of powdered meat into the dog's mouth, which caused the dog to salivate; and the saliva would be collected with a tube fitted in the dog's mouth. As the story goes, one day Pavlov's assistant accidentally rang the bell before Pavlov was ready to blow the powdered meat into the dog's mouth. Much to Pavlov's surprise, when the bell was rung, the dog salivated. Because the bell and the powdered meat had been paired frequently in the past, the bell alone was enough to elicit a response that previously could be elicited only by the meat powder.

In general, classical conditioning occurs when a stimulus that elicits a particular response is consistently *paired* with a neutral stimulus that does not elicit the response, as when food that elicits salivation is paired with the sound of a bell. After the two stimuli are repeatedly paired, the previously neutral stimulus itself elicits the response—the sound of the bell results in salivation. The stimulus that originally elicited the response (e.g., the food) is called the **unconditioned stimulus,** and the neutral stimulus that takes on the ability to elicit the response (e.g., the sound of the bell) is called the **conditioned stimulus.**

Perhaps the most famous example of classical conditioning in humans is the case of **Little Albert,** a boy who was conditioned by **John B. Watson** and **Rosalie Rayner** in an attempt to demonstrate that fears are learned rather than innate (Watson & Rayner, 1920). Watson and Rayner first presented a white rat to Little

*Ivan Pavlov and his assistants acciden-
tally discovered classical conditioning
while collecting saliva from dogs.*

Albert, who showed no fear of the rat and enjoyed playing with it. When they next presented Little Albert with
the rat, they also rang a very loud gong that frightened
the child. This same procedure of pairing the rat with
the frightening gong was repeated a number of times
until later, when only the rat was presented, Albert
immediately became afraid. In this way, Watson and
Rayner used classical conditioning to make Albert fear
a stimulus that previously had not elicited fear. (The
procedures Watson and Rayner used have been criticized for a variety of technical reasons; Harris, 1979.
However, the principles suggested by this original
demonstration were subsequently confirmed by a substantial amount of well-controlled research; Hilgard &
Marquis, 1961.)

An instance of classical conditioning happened to
me one day when I was cleaning a pan I had used to
cook a meal. After scrubbing the pan with Comet
cleanser, I felt queasy, became nauseated, and had to
lie down. While lying there, I began thinking what
appeared to be random thoughts about a course in
experimental psychology that I had taken as an undergraduate student several years earlier. I thought about
the instructor, about some of the class projects, about
my experiences in the laboratory—and suddenly I realized why I was sick! It had been my job to clean the
monkey cages. That was a particularly unpleasant task
because I had to spend hours scraping and scrubbing
the feces-encrusted cages with Comet cleanser. While
doing this, I was often on the verge of getting sick to my
stomach. The repeated pairing of the neutral stimulus
of Comet cleanser with the sickening task of cleaning
the monkey cages had produced a classically conditioned nausea response to the stimulus of Comet
cleanser. Two years later, when I was confronted with

the stimulus, the nausea response was elicited again
and I became sick to my stomach.

Classical conditioning is relevant for our understanding of abnormal behavior because it provides the
basis for many inappropriate emotional and physiological responses, such as Little Albert's fear and my nausea. Little Albert's fear of the rat would certainly be
considered abnormal. Indeed, if he had been brought
to a clinic, Little Albert would probably have been diagnosed as suffering from a phobia (an irrational fear).
My getting sick to my stomach every time I used Comet
cleanser would be considered strange, if not abnormal.

Generalization of Responses. Through a process
called **generalization,** a classically conditioned response
may eventually be elicited by new stimuli that are *similar*
to the conditioned stimulus. For example, Little Albert
became fearful when he was shown a rabbit, a dog, and
even a ball of cotton. The degree to which generalization occurs is a function of the similarity between the
conditioned stimulus and the new stimulus; the greater
the similarity between a conditioned stimulus (e.g., a
white rat) and a new stimulus (e.g., a ball of cotton),
the more likely it is that the new stimulus will elicit the
conditioned response. Stimuli that are very dissimilar
will not elicit the conditioned response. For example,
Little Albert did not show an increase in fear in
response to a set of wooden blocks.

Generalization greatly increases the number of
stimuli that can elicit a particular conditioned
response, and generalization can also make it difficult
to understand someone's responses. For example, Little Albert's fear of cotton stemmed from his original
conditioning with the rat, but if we did not know about
his history of conditioning and the process of general-

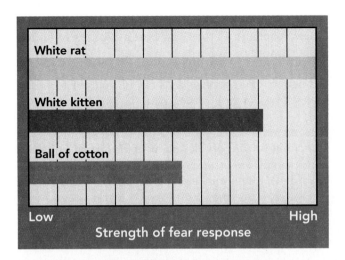

FIGURE 2.3 Generalization. Stimuli that are similar to the conditioned stimulus will elicit the conditioned response, but the response will be somewhat weaker than the response to the conditioned stimulus.

ization, his response to cotton would be very perplexing. The generalization of a conditioned response is illustrated in Figure 2.3.

Extinction and Endurance of Responses. Classically conditioned responses can be eliminated through a process known as **extinction,** whereby the conditioned stimulus is presented repeatedly *without being paired with the unconditioned stimulus.* For example, when Pavlov's dogs repeatedly heard the bell and did not get any powdered meat, eventually they stopped salivating in response to the bell.

Extinction may take a long time, and in many cases the conditioned response may reappear after it was assumed to be extinguished. For example, after extinction trials, Pavlov's dogs may have stopped salivating to the sound of the bell, but if a period of time went by and then the bell was presented again, the dogs would again salivate. That is known as **spontaneous recovery** of the extinguished response. The recovered response will be weaker than the original response, and over time it can be extinguished again. The cycle of extinction, spontaneous recovery, and extinction may have to be repeated a number of times until the response is completely extinguished. Spontaneous recovery can be discouraging to an individual who is trying to extinguish an inappropriate fear (a phobia) because the fear will keep coming back, though in a progressively weaker form.

It is important to remember that once a conditioned response is established, it may last indefinitely unless extinction procedures are introduced. For example, my conditioned response to the scrubbing with Comet lasted for over 2 years before it popped up

unexpectedly when I was again exposed to the cleanser. The endurance of conditioned responses was clearly illustrated in an experiment with sheep. In that experiment, a red light was paired with a shock to the hooves so that the sheep became classically conditioned to lift their front hooves when they saw a red light (J. Bescherat, personal communication, 1963). When the conditioning was completed, the sheep were turned out to pasture. Nine years later, the sheep were brought back into the laboratory and presented with the red light, and they immediately lifted their front hooves.

The endurance of classically conditioned responses is important for our understanding of abnormal behavior because inappropriate or abnormal emotional responses may be traced to much earlier instances of classical conditioning. As was the case with my response to Comet, the conditioned response may remain long after the situation in which it occurred is forgotten. You may have an irrational fear that stems from a conditioning experience you do not remember, and therefore you may erroneously attribute the fear to something else.

Involuntary Nature of Responses. One final and important point is that *classically conditioned responses are not under voluntary control.* Once the conditioning has been completed, the response occurs whenever the stimulus is presented, and the person or animal is unable to keep from giving the response. Pavlov's dogs had no choice but to salivate when the bell rang, Little Albert had no choice but to be fearful when he saw the rat, and I could not inhibit my feelings of nausea when I was confronted with the cleanser odor. The involuntary nature of classically conditioned responses makes the problem worse because it leads to feelings of being out of control. For example, if later in life Albert was given a ball of cotton, he would have no choice but to become very fearful, regardless of how irrational he realized it was and how hard he tried not to be afraid. Obviously, classical conditioning can lead to serious, prolonged, confusing, and uncontrollable abnormal behavior in a number of ways. We will return to the process of classical conditioning throughout this book as an explanation for abnormal behavior.

Operant Conditioning

Operant conditioning occurs when a response is *followed by a reward,* so that in the future you are more likely to use the response to get the reward (Skinner, 1953). Unlike classical conditioning, operant conditioning is due not to the simple pairing of two stimuli; instead it is due to the *pairing of a response with a reward.* (Traditional learning theorists do not use the term *reward* because its effects imply drive reduction, which is an unobservable internal process. Instead, they prefer the term *reinforcement*. However, for the sake of convenience, in this discussion I will take a more liberal position and use *reward*.)

A famous example of operant conditioning is **B. F. Skinner**'s experiments with white rats. In the simplest of these experiments, rats were placed in a cage with a lever that when pushed caused food to drop into a cup. The rats were hungry and quickly learned the response of pushing the lever to get the reward of food. In other experiments, the rats were placed in a cage with a lever that turned off a shock that came from a grid on the floor. The rats in these experiments learned to push the lever to turn off the shock and reduce their pain. In a variation on these experiments, a red light came on a few seconds before the shock, and the rats quickly learned that if they pushed the lever when the red light came on, they could avoid the shock. In all of these experiments, the rats learned the lever-pushing response because it resulted in a reward or because it resulted in the elimination or avoidance of something negative.

Although we like to think of ourselves as somewhat more sophisticated than rats pushing levers, much of our daily behavior can be understood in terms of attempts to gain rewards or avoid punishments. For example, you may be reading this book to obtain the reward of learning something new, to obtain the reward of getting a good grade, or to avoid the punishment associated with getting a bad grade. In each of these cases, your behavior is determined by the reward contingencies associated with reading the book.

Operant conditioning is relevant for our understanding of abnormal behavior because we often perform inappropriate behaviors to obtain rewards or avoid punishments. A child may have temper tantrums to gain attention, you may withdraw into your own fantasy world because it is more pleasant than the real world, or an individual who is claustrophobic may stay out of small rooms to avoid the anxiety engendered by being in a confined space.

Individual Differences in Rewards and Punishments.

There are large individual differences in terms of what is rewarding and what is punishing; to paraphrase an old saying, One person's reward is another person's punishment. In general, however, rewards are things that we will work to get, and punishments are things that we will work to reduce or avoid. Because individuals vary so greatly in what they find rewarding and punishing, it is crucial for us to analyze behavior in terms of what the individual involved considers rewarding or punishing and not in terms of what *we* think is rewarding or punishing. For example, some individuals find the aches, pains, sweat, and exhaustion associated with strenuous exercise rewarding, while others find it punishing. If those who find it punishing do not take the others' perspective, they may find it difficult to understand why others exercise.

Extinction of Responses.

When an operant response *no longer results in a reward,* it no longer has value for you, and you will stop using it. This process is referred to as *extinction*. Extinction of appropriate responses can contribute to the development of abnormal behavior. For example, if you are consistently ignored (not rewarded) when you make appropriate interpersonal responses, you may turn away from others who approach you and withdraw into a world of fantasy that is rewarding. Extinction can also be used to eliminate inappropriate behavior. For example, by ignoring the child who is having temper tantrums, we are refusing to reward the tantrums, and they will eventually be abandoned (extinguished).

Schedules of Rewards.

When you are learning a response, it is important that you receive a reward every time you make a correct response. The consistent use of rewards helps guide the early behavior and clearly links the response with the reward. However, once you have learned the response, the response will be more resistant to extinction if you are given rewards only *intermittently*, that is, only some of the times you use the response. The effect of an **intermittent schedule of reward** on operantly conditioned responses is clearly apparent in slot machine gambling. If a slot machine pays off 100% of the time, when it stops paying off, the gambler will realize that something has changed and will stop using the machine. But if the machine pays off only intermittently, the gambler keeps playing in the hope that the next response will result in a reward.

Understanding the effects of intermittent schedules of reward helps us understand why individuals continue to use certain behaviors even when those behav-

The intermittent schedule of reward used in slot machines keeps people responding even though they are seldom rewarded.

iors are rarely rewarded. It also points to the importance of being consistent about withholding rewards when our goal is to extinguish some particular behavior. For example, if a parent occasionally gives in to a child's temper tantrums, the parent will actually be strengthening the response with an intermittent schedule of reward rather than extinguishing it.

Voluntary Nature of Responses. Unlike classically conditioned responses, operantly conditioned responses are under *voluntary* control. Skinner's rats could have decided whether or not to press the lever to get the food, you could elect not to read this book in preparation for the examination, the child could voluntarily stop having a temper tantrum, and the gambler could decide to stop putting quarters in the slot machine. Operant responses are voluntary, but at some point the motivation to perform certain operant responses may reach such a high level that they effectively cease to be voluntary. For example, the starving rat may have little choice but to press the lever to get food, and the student with a classically conditioned fear of small spaces may have little option but to flee in terror when the instructor closes the door of a small classroom.

Vicarious Conditioning

In each of the examples of classical and operant conditioning that I have used, the learner was directly involved in the conditioning process. For example, Little Albert was exposed to the rat and the gong, and the child learned through trial and error that having temper tantrums resulted in rewarding attention. However, such direct involvement is not necessary for conditioning to take place. Indeed, another child who only watched when the rat and gong were presented to Little Albert could vicariously develop the conditioned fear of the rat, and a child who only watched another child get attention (reward) for a tantrum could learn to use tantrums to get attention. The old saying "Monkey see, monkey do" definitely applies to conditioning. This type of indirect conditioning is usually referred to as **vicarious** (vī-KER-ē-us) **conditioning,** but it is also sometimes called **observational learning** or **modeling** (Bandura, 1969; Bandura & Walters, 1963).

Because classical and operant conditioning can take place vicariously, we can develop conditioned responses without directly experiencing the conditioning process. We need not actually have a frightening experience with an elevator to develop an elevator phobia. Just hearing frightening things about elevators will do the trick. Because we do not need to experience the exposure directly, vicarious conditioning greatly expands the possibilities of developing inappropriate

conditioned responses. (Note that the occurrence of vicarious conditioning indicates that some internal processes, such as thinking, must be involved. This is contrary to the position of the traditional learning theorists, who believed that internal processes are not necessary to explain behavior.)

Combination of Classical and Operant Conditioning

It is noteworthy that classical and operant conditioning can combine to result in abnormal behavior. Classical conditioning can lead to fears, and then operant conditioning can lead to behaviors that are used to reduce the fears. Classical conditioning was responsible for Little Albert's fear, and through operant conditioning he could have learned to avoid white rats and balls of cotton.

Operant conditioning can also contribute to abnormal behavior by slowing the extinction of classically conditioned abnormal responses. For example, Little Albert's fear of rats was instilled through classical conditioning, but if he later avoided rats because doing so was rewarding (operant conditioning), he would never learn that they were no longer paired with the frightening gong and the fear would not be extinguished. Similarly, individuals who avoid high places because they were once frightened in a high place do not learn that high places are not necessarily frightening, and consequently their fear does not extinguish. The use of operant behaviors to avoid feared stimuli helps us understand why some classically conditioned fears are so persistent.

COMMENT

The principles underlying the learning explanations have been consistently supported by rigorous experimental research. However, you should not conclude that there is no controversy over the learning explanations for abnormal behavior. Critics do not question the validity of the principles of conditioning, but they do question whether those principles can account for the highly complex behaviors of disturbed individuals. In other words, the critics argue that the principles are true and may be able to account for some fears, but the principles may not be sufficient to explain more complex behaviors such as hallucinations and delusions. Whether the learning explanations are indeed too simple to account for the diverse and complex abnormal behavior observed in humans will be considered in greater detail later when we examine the various types of abnormal behavior.

Traditionally, conditioning has been thought to be an *automatic* process, or at least one that *does not involve thinking.* For example, in classical conditioning, if the neutral stimulus (e.g., a white rat) is simply paired with an unconditioned stimulus (e.g., a gong), after a number of pairings the previously neutral stimulus will "automatically" elicit the conditioned response (e.g., fear). However, in the past few years, it has been suggested that *thoughts may be involved;* the conditioned stimulus may serve as a signal that something is going to happen (e.g., the presence of the white rat signals that a gong will be rung), so the individual prepares for the expected event. That places conditioning in a very different light and has implications for treatment. For example, maybe we do not have to extinguish conditioned responses but instead only tell the individual that the stimulus no longer signals a coming event. I will discuss that possibility in the next section on the cognitive explanation.

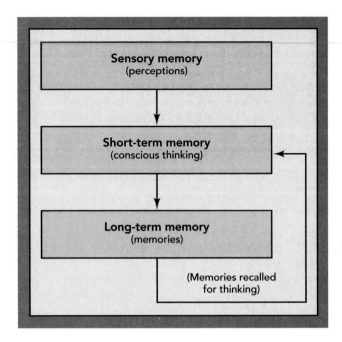

FIGURE 2.4 Stages of memory.

COGNITIVE EXPLANATIONS

The basic notion underlying the **cognitive explanations** is that abnormal behavior results from *erroneous beliefs* and from *disruptions of the thought processes.* That is, abnormal behaviors are due to problems with *what we think* and *how we think.* That makes intuitive sense, but to understand this explanation, you must understand how problems with erroneous beliefs and problems with thought processes develop.

In general, the erroneous beliefs that lead to abnormal behavior result from problems in the way we *perceive, store,* and *remember* information. If we make errors in what we see, store, and remember, that will greatly distort our views of the world and could result in abnormal behavior. How we perceive, store, and remember information is referred to as human **information processing.** In this section, I will explain how humans process information, and I will illustrate how that processing is related to abnormal behavior.

Stages of Memory Processing

In the cognitive explanations, the key factor in determining your behavior is your *memory;* after all, it is your memories of past experiences that you use as guides concerning how to behave and feel. For example, if you remember a lot of failures from your past, you may give up and be depressed. However, if those memories are incorrect, your behaviors and feelings may be incorrect. Therefore, I will begin this discussion with an overview of memory.

The most widely accepted explanation of memory is the **three-stage theory of memory.** Those stages involve (a) the entry of information through the *sensory memory,* (b) the passage of some of that information into the *short-term memory,* and (c) the processing of some of that information for storage in the *long-term memory.* The stages of memory processing are summarized in Figure 2.4 and discussed in the following sections.

Sensory Memory. Everything you perceive (e.g., see, hear, feel, smell) goes first to your **sensory memory.** It is like a photograph or a tape recording of everything that is happening. However, the sensory memory can only hold the information for a second or two at most, and after that it is as though the photograph fades or the tape wears out. Consequently, you must quickly select from your sensory memory the pieces of information that are most important and send them on to your short-term memory for processing. The remaining unselected information is lost.

The information selection process in the sensory memory is relevant for understanding behavior in two ways. First, in the selection process you may *focus too much attention on some things* and thereby get a distorted view of the world. For example, if you focused only on airplane crashes, you could develop an unrealistic view of how dangerous it is to fly, and thus you might develop a phobia for flying. Second, in the selection process you may *ignore things that are important.* For example, if you ignore your achievements, you may develop an unrealistic view of yourself that could lead to depression.

Short-Term Memory. Information that is selected from your sensory memory is then sent to your **short-term memory,** which is where you do your *thinking* and where you *process information for storage in the long-term memory.* The processing of information for storage in the long-term memory is crucial because if you do not process the information or you process it ineffectively, you will not be able to retrieve it later, and then for all practical purposes the information will be lost. Effective processing involves *actively thinking about how a piece of information is related to other pieces of information that are already in your memory.* In other words, to process information so that you can recall it later, you must put the information into a *network of memories* and link the information to as many other memories in the network as possible. Later, when the information is needed, you will be able to retrieve it by activating any of the memories to which the information is connected. If the information is not linked to other memories, later recall will be difficult or impossible, and you may not have access to needed information.

Long-Term Memory. Your **long-term memory** is where all of the processed information is *stored.* You are not conscious of the information that is stored in your long-term memory, but if it is needed, it can be activated and brought to the short-term memory and consciousness. There is a constant interplay between the short- and long-term memories in that information is continually being brought up from the long-term memory, used for thinking, and then sent back to the long-term memory.

The most important thing about the long-term memory is how the information is stored there, because how information is stored determines what information you will be able to recall. Therefore, in the following section I will explain how information is stored and retrieved.

Associative Networks and Recall

The most widely accepted explanation of how information is stored and recalled is called the **associative network theory** (Bower, 1981; Collins & Loftus, 1975; Estes, 1991; Ingram, 1984). In general, this theory suggests that *individual memories are linked together in networks, and activation of one memory will lead to the activation of other memories in the same network.* For example, if you have a network that contains depressing memories, and if you recall one depressing memory, you may suddenly recall many depressing memories. To understand this theory, you must consider three basic aspects of memories.

1. *Activation of one component of a memory will lead to the complete memory.* Each memory consists of a cluster of components such as images, feelings, and physiological responses, and the activation of any one of the components will lead to the activation of the other components and result in the memory. For example, your memory of a particular individual involves the individual's name, an image of the individual, your emotional response to the individual, a recollection of the scent of his aftershave or her perfume, and many other things. Activation of any one component will result in the memory of the individual. For example, an individual's name will bring the individual to mind, but so will his or her scent. (Women used to give men a handkerchief on which they had put some of their perfume, the notion being that the scent would keep active the memory of the woman while the couple was apart.)

2. *One memory can activate other memories in a network.* Individual memories that are related to one another are connected in networks, so the activation of any one memory can lead to the activation of the other memories in that network. For example, memories associated with school (e.g., other students, classes, parties, exams) may all be in one "school" network, and thinking about another student will cause you to recall other things about school. Have you ever noticed how when you go back to an old place, you are suddenly flooded with old memories? In that case, the physical stimuli have triggered the memory network. Similarly, memories that involve unpleasant events (e.g., failures, rejections, death of a loved one) may be linked in a network, and thinking about one unpleasant event will lead you to recall other unpleasant events. The sequential stimulation of memories in a network is the *thought process,* or the "stream of consciousness." With regard to abnormal behavior, the activation of one depressing memory could lead to the activation of an entire network of depressing memories, and recalling all of those could lead to depression.

3. *Activation of a memory primes it for future use.* Memories and connections that were used more recently or frequently are activated more easily and become stronger. For example, in a number of experiments, some individuals read happy passages while others read sad passages, and when they were then asked to recall experiences from earlier in their lives, the individuals who had read the happy passages were more likely to recall happy experiences than individuals who had read sad passages. That occurred because different networks had been activated by the reading of the different passages. This process is called **priming.** Of course, priming becomes circular in that a primed network is more likely to be used, and using it primes it for use again. For example, once you think a depressing thought such as something negative about yourself, you are likely to continue to think about that, and that can lead to depression. Furthermore, if you are not actively thinking about something else, a primed network will be activated automatically. That is, thought processes do not stop, and if one network is not stimulated, the most recently primed or strongest network is likely to be activated. This accounts for why you tend to drift back to a particular topic unless you are focusing your attention elsewhere. Using an analogy to a computer, a friend of mine who tends to be depressed described his depressing thoughts as his "default option." That is, whenever he is not thinking about something else, he begins thinking depressing thoughts. To avoid that default option, he tries to distract himself with television, radio, or reading.

A diagram of a simplified set of networks is presented in Figure 2.5. The overall network is made up of three networks, one involving negative memories (in blue), one involving memories of people (in red), and one involving positive memories (in black). There are strong associations or connections within networks (solid lines) and weaker associations or connections between networks (broken lines). An individual with this set of networks who experienced or thought about a failure would go on to recall other failures, rejections, missed opportunities, and possibly the death of a loved one. In contrast, an individual who experienced or thought about a successful experience would go on to recall praise from others, good relationships, and possibly a pleasant vacation. Because connections within networks are strong and used frequently, activation is likely to continue reverberating around a network, and therefore the individual would continue having those memories. If activation of the negative network is prolonged, the individual might become depressed.

Selective Attention and Selective Recall

By now, you may have realized that there is considerable selectivity in what we perceive, process, and recall. In other words, cognitive processes result in **selective attention** and **selective recall.** Specifically, (a) only a fraction of the information that enters the sensory memory is moved to the short-term memory, (b) only a limited amount of information that gets to the short-term memory is processed for storage in the long-term memory, (c) only the information in the long-term memory that has been processed effectively will be recalled, and (d) information in a primed or strong network is very likely to be recalled. This selectivity is not a random process; it is guided by what we

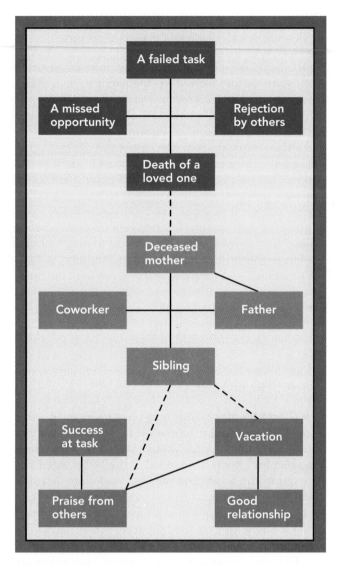

FIGURE 2.5 A hypothetical set of three connected memory networks. The overall network is made up of three networks, one involving negative memories (purple), one involving memories of people (rust), and one involving positive memories (blue). Strong associations are indicated with solid lines, and weaker associations are indicated with broken lines.

think is important and unimportant. We focus on what appears to be important and ignore what appears to be unimportant, and the process can become circular.

Selective attention and recall are important because they can lead to exaggerated or erroneous ideas, and those can lead to inappropriate or abnormal behavior. For example, if you believe that you are sickly, you will notice and remember every minor pain and interpret them all as signs of illness. Similarly, if you believe that you are socially inadequate, you will attend to and recall every minor social slight and blun-

Selective attention and recall can cause erroneous thoughts that may in turn lead to inappropriate or abnormal behavior. If you incorrectly think that others are rejecting you, you may in fact bring on that rejection by avoiding people or by behaving in a hostile way.

der. In some cases, selective attention can result in **self-fulfilling prophecies.** For example, if you incorrectly thought that others were rejecting you, you might begin avoiding them or behave in a hostile manner toward them, and those behaviors would bring on the rejection you had incorrectly thought was there earlier.

The process of selective attention and network building usually begins with early experiences. For example, if an individual is very sick as a child, unusual physical sensations (possible symptoms) and news about new illnesses may be viewed as important, so attention is focused on them and memories of them are stored for later retrieval.

To sum up, cognitive theorists suggest that (a) our early experiences lead to the initial development of cognitive networks, (b) the networks then lead to selective attention and recall, (c) the selective attention and recall influence what we think, and (d) our thoughts determine our behaviors (Basic Behavioral Science Task Force, 1996). In most cases, cognitive theories have focused on negative consequences; for example, selective attention to stressful things in the environment could lead to anxiety, and selective attention to depressing experiences could lead to depression. However, the flip side to that has also been proposed—that *selective attention to positive things could lead to illusions of well-being and mental health* (Taylor & Brown, 1988, 1994; see also criticism by Colvin & Block, 1994). In that case, problems are dismissed as inconsequential, poor abilities are seen as common, and positive traits are seen as special so the individual feels good and gets on with life. That explanation is a dramatic departure from the usual notion that good mental health involves being "in

contact with reality," but it is an interesting possibility that deserves attention.

Distortions of Memories and False Memories

So far I have focused on problems that arise because of not processing (not recalling) information or because of focusing too much attention on information. However, existing memories can also be *distorted,* and these distortions can influence behavior. In one experiment on **distortions of memories,** college students were shown a film of a traffic accident, and later one group was asked how fast the cars were going when they "contacted" each other, whereas another group was asked how fast the cars were going when they "smashed" (Loftus & Palmer, 1974). The students with whom the word *smashed* was used estimated the speed at almost 10 mph faster than the students with whom the word *contacted* was used. Clearly, memories can be distorted rather easily, and distorted memories might distort our behavior.

There is also evidence that entirely new **false memories** can be "implanted" and that once implanted, they are resistant to rejection. Specifically, if someone with credibility suggests that you had a particular experience, and if you do not have strong evidence to the contrary, you might accept the suggested experience as real. There is now a wide variety of evidence that completely false memories can be implanted. For example, in one such experiment, parental reports were used to identify college students who as children had *never stayed overnight in a hospital* (Hyman et al., 1995). Next the students participated in an interview in which they were asked to recall the details of a series of childhood experiences. Most of the experiences were events that really happened to the students (parents' reports were used to identify those), but one was a false event of staying overnight in a hospital. If a student did not recall a particular experience (true or false), additional cues were provided, but if recall still did not occur, the experimenter went on to the next experience. At the end of the interview, the students were encouraged to think more about the events and try to remember more details before the next interview, which occurred some days later. In the second interview, the students were again asked to recall the events (true and false). The results indicated that in the first interview, none of the students "recalled" the false event, but by the second interview, 20% of them did! In fact, not only did they "remember" it, but they elaborated on it and provided a variety of details concerning it. Furthermore, when at the end of the interview the students were told that one of the events they had been asked to describe was false and were then asked to indicate which one was false, most of the students who "recalled" the false event were unable to guess which event was false. A variety of other experiments have yielded similar findings, clearly indicating that false memories can be induced easily (e.g., Ceci et al., 1995; Hyman et al., 1995; Loftus, 1992; Loftus & Coan, 1995).

A more dramatic example of an implanted memory occurred in the case of a man who after prolonged questioning pleaded guilty to raping his daughters 18 years earlier (Ofshe & Watters, 1994). To test the possibility that the confession was due to a suggestion during the interrogation process, an experiment was conducted in which the man was told a *totally false* story that two of his other children had now accused him of forcing them to have sex while he watched. When he denied it, he was told to think about it, and then was returned to his jail cell. The next day the man reported "remembering" the event, and he added vivid details of what had happened. (It is noteworthy that the man had nothing to gain by his admission, and indeed because of it he could have faced an additional prison sentence.) Facing the overwhelming (but false) evidence of his children's testimony, and in the absence of proof to the contrary, he accepted the accusations as true and then embellished on the suggestion. Related to this, there is now a considerable body of evidence that some "confessions" given by alleged criminals in the course of interrogation are completely false (Bedau & Radelet, 1987; Kassin & Wrightsman, 1993). For example, in some cases it was later proved, much to the confessor's surprise, that he had been in a distant state when the crime was committed.

The overall conclusion to be drawn here is that our memories are subject to serious distortions and additions, and because our behaviors are guided in large

Paul R. Ingram (left) *confessed to molesting his daughters after he "recalled" false memories suggested by his interrogators. Here he is shown at his sentencing in Tacoma, Washington.

part by what we remember, our behaviors may be inappropriate and our explanations for our behaviors may be inaccurate.

Disrupted Cognitive Processes

It should now be clear that there are numerous ways in which what we think can be distorted and thereby lead to abnormal behavior. However, some forms of abnormal behavior appear to be due to **disrupted cognitive processes** rather than distortions in cognitive content. Consider the following example of a conversation between an interviewer and a patient suffering from schizophrenia:

Interviewer: Have you been nervous or tense lately?

Patient: No, I got a head of lettuce.

Interviewer: You got a head of lettuce? I don't understand.

Patient: Well, it's just a head of lettuce.

Interviewer: Tell me about lettuce. What do you mean?

Patient: Well, . . . lettuce is a transformation of a dead cougar that suffered a relapse on the lion's toe. And he swallowed the lion and something happened. The . . . see, the . . . Gloria and Tommy, they're two heads and they're not whales. But they escaped with herds of vomit, and things like that. (Neale & Oltmanns, 1980, p. 102)

Clearly, in this case the problem is not simply distorted ideas. It is one thing to be depressed because you consistently exaggerate the negative aspects of your life, but it is quite another thing to think and communicate like the patient in this example. The disruptions in cognitive processes like those shown by this patient are generally associated with more serious disorders such as schizophrenia.

Cognitive theorists believe that disruptions in cognitive processes are due to problems with *attention* and *associations*. The basic notion is that (a) individuals have lapses in attention, (b) during those lapses they are distracted by other thoughts, and (c) they then "spin off" on the new thoughts rather than following up their original thoughts. That is, instead of a patient's speech being complete gibberish as it initially appears, the speech actually consists of strings of thought fragments, no one of which is completely developed because the patient was distracted and went on to the next thought.

The thought fragments are not strung together randomly. Instead, through various associations, one thought fragment elicits the next thought fragment in the string, and so on. Researchers have identified a variety of types of associations that result in the intrusion of thoughts (Chapman et al., 1964, 1984; Maher, 1983). One of these types of disruptive associations occurs when words are used that have more than one meaning, such as *pen* ("writing instrument," "fenced enclosure," "jail"). When talking to another individual, an individual with schizophrenia may correctly use one meaning of a word with several meanings. However, as soon as the word has been used, it may give rise to another thought based on *another* meaning of the word, and then the individual may spin off onto the new thought without making the transition clear to the listener. For example, the individual may say, "Henry lent me his pen, which was full of criminals." In this example, the word *pen* was first used to refer to a writing instrument, but the use of the word gave rise to thoughts about a penitentiary. The speaker then spun off and finished the sentence with a phrase related to a penitentiary. Because a wide variety of associations can result in the intrusion of new thoughts, it can be very difficult to follow those associations and understand what is being communicated. We will consider other types of disruptive associations later.

Note that in the cognitive explanations, *the cognitive problems seen in disturbed individuals are considered extreme cases of the same types of problems experienced by normal individuals.* At one time or another, we have all behaved inappropriately because we have exaggerated the importance of some event, let our attention lapse, or made an associative error that led to a misunderstanding. Because it is true that the cognitive behaviors of disturbed individuals are only extreme instances of the types of cognitive behaviors seen in normal individuals,

much of our extensive knowledge about the cognitive behavior of normal individuals can be brought to bear on our understanding of abnormal behavior.

COMMENT

The cognitive explanations have considerable intuitive appeal, and they are supported by solid evidence from modern cognitive psychology. As a consequence, the cognitive explanations are currently very popular for explaining abnormal behavior. However, there are a number of questions and problems associated with the explanations that deserve attention.

The first question we must address is, *are erroneous beliefs a cause or an effect of abnormal behaviors?* The cognitive explanations assume that *erroneous beliefs cause abnormal behaviors;* for example, thinking "I'm a bad person and things will never get better" will cause depression. However, critics have pointed out that *abnormal behaviors can lead to erroneous beliefs.* For example, depressions that stem from a physiological cause may lead individuals to have erroneous beliefs. If you are depressed, you may look for an explanation for your bad mood and conclude that it stems from the fact that "the world is a terrible place and it's not going to get any better." Evidence supporting that possibility comes from experiments in which depressed individuals who had negative thoughts were given antidepressant drugs that eliminated their depressions, and when the depressions were eliminated, so were the negative thoughts. Does that mean that the cognitive explanation is wrong? No, it simply means that thoughts may not *always* be causes. In other words, the question should not be, are thoughts a cause *or* an effect? but rather, *when* are thoughts a cause and *when* are they an effect?

The second question revolves around the disrupted thought processes, as in problems with attention and associations that play a role in serious disorders such as schizophrenia. No one disputes the fact that individuals who suffer from schizophrenia have disrupted thought processes, but the question is, *why do they have disrupted thought processes?* Unfortunately, the cognitive explanations do not explain why the disruptions occur, and therefore these explanations are incomplete. (Later you will learn that the disruptions can be explained by excessively high levels of neurological arousal, so in this case cognitive and physiological explanations may work together.)

Finally, a comment must be made concerning the relationship between the learning and cognitive explanations. In recent years, there has been a movement to merge the learning and cognitive explanations. That movement is based on the notion that conditioning is not really an "automatic" process as it is often portrayed, but instead *conditioning is based on thoughts.* If that is the case, then conditioning becomes simply a part of the cognitive explanations. The question then is, is conditioning based on thoughts?

In the case of *operant* conditioning, in which rewards are used to change behaviors, there is evidence that conditioning only occurs when the individual *figures out* what behaviors lead to rewards and then *decides* to use those behaviors. For example, in a series of experiments, individuals made up sentences and the experimenter said "good" if a sentence contained a particular pronoun (e.g., *I* or *we*) but said nothing if the sentence did not contain the pronoun (Holmes, 1967). The results indicated that the only individuals who showed conditioning (an increase in the use of a particular pronoun) were those who made the connection between the use of the particular pronoun and the experimenter's saying "good" and who also decided to cooperate. That is, operant conditioning is not an automatic process but can be understood better in terms of *problem solving* and *cooperation*.

But what about *classical* conditioning? The traditional view of classical conditioning is that when a neutral stimulus (e.g., a bell) is consistently paired with a second stimulus that elicits a response (e.g., meat powder that results in salivation), the neutral stimulus and the response become *connected,* and thus when the neutral stimulus is presented, the response is *elicited automatically.* However, cognitive psychologists argue that the pairing of the stimuli is important only because it helps the individual figure out that the occurrence of one stimulus (e.g., a bell) *predicts the occurrence of an event* (e.g., the arrival of meat powder), and therefore when the stimulus occurs, the individual prepares for the event (e.g., salivates). In other words, cognitive psychologists argue that classical conditioning occurs because an individual realizes that there is a consistent relationship between a stimulus and an event, so when the stimulus occurs, the individual *expects* the event and prepares for it (Rescorla, 1988). For example, when you see a spider, you respond with fear because you expect the spider will hurt you, not because of some automatic process.

That expectancy explanation makes intuitive sense, and it is supported by some evidence (Jones et al., 1990, 1992; Kamin, 1969; Miller et al., 1995). For example, in the first part of an experiment, a *tone* was paired with a shock such that the individuals developed a classically conditioned fear response to the tone. Next, a *combination of the tone and a light* was paired with the shock. Finally, the tone and the light were presented separately, and the question was, would the individuals give the conditioned fear response to the tone and the light when they were presented separately? If the simple pairing of the stimuli with the shock is the crucial factor, then both the tone and the light should elicit the shock. However, the results indicated that *only the tone elicited the conditioned response.* That surprising finding was explained by suggesting that because originally the tone alone was effective for signaling the coming of the shock, the later addition of the light was irrelevant for the prediction, so the light was ignored. Therefore, despite the fact that the light had been paired with the shock, a conditioned response to the light was not established. This means that it was not simply the pairing of a stimulus with a response that led to conditioning; rather it was the *information value* provided by the pairing that led to the change in responding (conditioning). In the experiment I just described, the light did not add information, so it did not lead to the response.

Do these findings mean that we should completely abandon the classical conditioning explanation in favor of cognitive explanations? No, because we have recently learned that there are two pathways in the brain associated with classical conditioning of fear (Le Doux, 1992, 1994). One of those pathway begins at your sense organs, such as your eyes and ears; it then goes to a structure in your brain called the thalamus, where a rough identification of incoming stimuli is done; and finally it goes to a structure called the amygdala that generates emotion. That pathway does not involve much thinking. The second pathway also begins at your sense organs and then goes to your thalamus, but from there it goes to higher areas of your brain that are associated with thinking, and only then does it go to the amygdala. That pathway involves cognitive activity, and although it may take a while, it can override the other pathway. The existence of the two pathways explains why when you first see something that could be dangerous, such as a coiled object, you feel a sudden surge of fear—the coiled object could be a snake, and the first pathway has activated the amygdala. However, after you think about it briefly, you conclude that the coiled object is just a piece of rope, and the fear subsides; the second pathway has arrested the activity in the amygdala. Clearly, the classical conditioning of fear involves a relatively automatic process (the first pathway), as well as a cognitive process (the second pathway), so neither explanation should be abandoned.

In conclusion, there is no doubt that the cognitive explanations are useful for explaining and treating abnormal behaviors, but like the other explanations, the cognitive explanations may not be able to account for all disorders and therefore do not provide a complete explanation for abnormal behavior.

PHYSIOLOGICAL EXPLANATIONS

The basic assumption of the **physiological explanations** is that abnormal behavior is due to *problems with synaptic* *transmission* (i.e., the ways in which neurons in the brain communicate with each other) and to *problems with brain structures* (i.e., brain damage). The notion that abnormal behavior is due to problems in the brain is not new, but over the past 20 years it has been greatly expanded and strengthened by the development of new technologies that have led to a better understanding of how the brain works—and sometimes does not work. In the following sections, I will review the basic elements of the physiological explanations, and in later chapters in which I discuss specific disorders, I will elaborate on the details of these explanations.

The Brain

Layers of the Brain. In developing an understanding of the brain, it is important to recognize that as organisms became more complex in the process of evolution, layers were added to the brain. That evolutionary process explains how the brain is organized; specifically, *primitive functions such as breathing are controlled at a low level, emotions are generated at a middle level, and complex functions such as thinking are controlled at a higher level.*

In general, the brain can be divided into three levels, and each of those levels contains a number of structures that are responsible for different activities. At the first level we have the **brain stem;** it is located at the bottom of the brain, where it sits atop the spinal cord. The brain stem has two roles. First, some of its structures are responsible for controlling *basic physiological functions* such as breathing and heart rate. Second, other structures are responsible for *generating arousal* (electrical activity), which is then carried to higher levels of the brain to keep us awake and alert. The brain stem plays a role in only a few psychiatric disorders, but some drugs that influence behavior have their effects in the brain stem. For example, depressants such as morphine have a relaxing effect because they reduce activity in the brain stem, which then leads to a general reduction in neurological activity. The brain stem and the other layers of the brain are illustrated in Figure 2.6.

The second level of the brain is called the **midbrain,** and the structures in the midbrain have two major responsibilities. First, they maintain *homeostasis;* for example, they control the length of time we sleep, the amount of food we eat, and our level of sexual activity. Second, structures in the midbrain are responsible for *emotions,* and therefore problems in the midbrain can also lead to depression, mania, and anger. It is interesting to note that one structure in the midbrain, the *hypothalamus,* controls *both* homeostasis and emotions, and that explains why if you are depressed because of a problem in your hypothalamus, you may also have problems with sleeping, eating, and sex.

The third level of the brain is the **cerebrum**—more specifically, the **cortex,** which is a layer of neu-

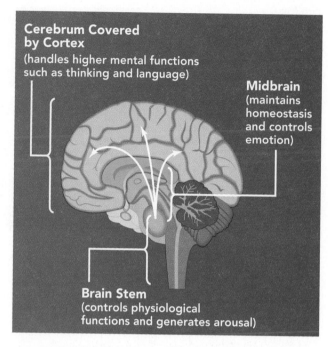

Cerebrum Covered by Cortex
(handles higher mental functions such as thinking and language)

Midbrain
(maintains homeostasis and controls emotion)

Brain Stem
(controls physiological functions and generates arousal)

FIGURE 2.6 Levels of the brain, structures in the levels, and nerve tracts that connect the levels and structures.

rons about an eighth of an inch thick that covers the cerebrum. Higher functions such as *thinking* and *language* are located in different parts of the cortex, and problems in the cortex can disrupt those functions. For example, individuals who have too much activity in the area of the cortex that is responsible for thinking will have problems with their thought processes; specifically, they will be easily distracted and confused, and those problems can lead to the diagnosis of schizophrenia.

It is important to recognize that nerve tracts connect the structures in the different layers of the brain. Some of those nerves *carry stimulation up from the lower areas to the higher areas,* and therefore they play an important role. For example, if at night too much stimulation is carried up from the brain stem to the cortex, you may be unable to get to sleep (i.e., you are too "wired" and alert), and you may develop a case of insomnia. Similarly, if high levels of stimulation are carried from your midbrain, where emotions are generated, up to your cortex, your thought processes may be disrupted, thereby resulting in the serious disorder known as schizophrenia. The nerve tracts connecting layers of the brain are illustrated in Figure 2.6.

Types of Problems in the Brain. In general, there are two types of problems in the brain, the first of which involves problems with the *structures* of the brain; that is, the structures may be malformed, may have deteriorated, or may be damaged. Of course, structural

FIGURE 2.7 A neuron (nerve cell).

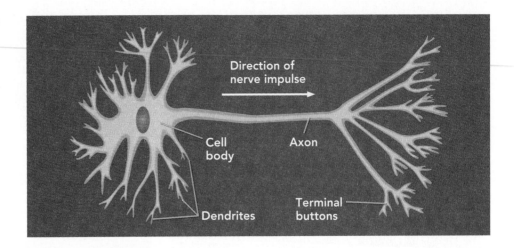

problems can influence behavior, and where the problems are will determine what behaviors are affected. For example, destruction of the area of the cortex that is responsible for the processing of words can lead to an inability to understand or produce language.

The second type of problem involves the *functioning* of the brain; in other words, the structures are fine, but for some reason they are not working properly. Problems with functioning usually stem from the fact that the neurons (cells) that make up the structures of the brain are either overactive or underactive. For example, if neurons in the hypothalamus in your midbrain are overactive, you will become manic, whereas if those neurons are underactive, you will become depressed. Most forms of abnormal behavior are due to problems in neuronal functioning, and in the next section I will explain how neurons function and what problems interfere with their functioning.

Neuroanatomy and Neuronal Functioning

The Neuron and the Nerve Impulse. The brain consists of between 10 and 12 billion cells called **neurons.** Strings or chains of neurons make up a **nerve fiber.** Depending on the function they serve, neurons differ greatly in size and shape, but they all share a number of structural and functional characteristics. As Figure 2.7 shows, each neuron consists of **dendrites,** a **cell body,** an **axon,** and **terminal buttons.** The important thing about neurons is that they can carry an *electrical* impulse called the **nerve impulse.** This impulse starts when one neuron stimulates the dendrite or cell body of another neuron. The nerve impulse then travels from the dendrite or cell body down the axon to the terminal buttons, where the impulse is transmitted to the next neuron.

Synaptic Transmission. Having traveled down the axon and out to the terminal buttons, the impulse

comes to the **synapse** (SIN-aps), which is a small gap separating one neuron from the next neuron in the chain. The first neuron is called the **presynaptic** (PRĒ-sin-AP-tik) **neuron,** and the second, the **postsynaptic** (PŌST-sin-AP-tik) **neuron.** The nerve impulse must then "jump" the synapse and stimulate the next neuron if the impulse is to continue down the chain. To make the jump, the impulse in the axon causes the terminal buttons on the presynaptic neuron to secrete a chemical called a **neurotransmitter.** The neurotransmitter then flows across the synapse and stimulates the next neuron. The neurotransmitter stimulates the postsynaptic neuron by entering **receptor sites** on the dendrites or cell bodies of the postsynaptic neuron. Figure 2.8 illustrates a neurotransmitter being released by a terminal button on the presynaptic neuron, flowing across the synapse, fitting into a receptor site on the postsynaptic neuron, and causing it to fire. Note the process by which the nerve impulse travels down the axon is *electrical*, whereas the process by which it crosses the synapse is *chemical*.

In most cases, neurons fire on what is known as the **all-or-none principle.** When a neuron is stimulated, it either does or does not fire, and if it does fire, it does so with a given amount of energy, regardless of the strength of the stimulation that provoked the firing. Because neurons always fire with the same amount of energy, the intensity of neuronal activity is not a function of the strength with which they fire but of the *frequency* with which they fire or the *number* of neurons that fire. When there is not enough of the neurotransmitter in an area of the brain, the neurons in that area will not fire at all or too few of them will fire to get the job done. In contrast, if there is too much of the neurotransmitter, there may be excessive neurological activity caused by neurons firing too many times or too many neurons firing. In either case, abnormal behavior may result. For example, insufficient levels of transmission

This photo of neurons illustrates the complex pattern of connections between neurons.

in the area of the brain that controls mood can result in depression, whereas excessive levels of transmission in that area can result in mania. Furthermore, excessive levels of transmission in certain areas of the brain can result in a disruption of thought processes like that seen in schizophrenia.

Neurotransmitters. The crucial factor in synaptic transmission is the presence of the neurotransmitter that carries the impulse across the synapse. There are many neurotransmitters, but at present only a few have been linked to abnormal behavior. Neurotransmitters belong to a general class of agents known as *biogenic amines* or simply **amines** (AM-mēnz). Because neurotransmitters are amines, explanations for abnormal behavior that involve problems with neurotransmitters

are sometimes referred to as **amine hypotheses.** We will consider particular neurotransmitters or amines in greater detail later when we examine the causes of specific disorders.

The fact that one neurotransmitter may operate in more than one area of the brain explains why we see combinations of otherwise unrelated sets of symptoms in some disorders. For example, the neurotransmitter that is responsible for some depressions also plays a role in appetite, and that is one of the reasons why depressed individuals show changes in appetite.

The influence of a neurotransmitter in more than one area of the brain also accounts for some of the side effects that occur when drugs are used to treat psychological disorders. For example, schizophrenia is thought to be due to high levels of a neurotransmitter called *dopamine* that operates in the areas of the brain that are responsible for thought processes. To correct that problem, individuals with schizophrenia are often given drugs that block the action of dopamine. However, dopamine also operates in the areas of the brain that are responsible for motor behavior. As a result, the drugs that are used to treat schizophrenia also influence motor behavior, and that can produce side effects such as a stiff-jointed walk or involuntary muscle contractions.

Factors That Influence Synaptic Transmission

Because synaptic transmission is so important to our understanding of abnormal behavior, we must give some attention to the various factors that influence it.

Neurotransmitter Levels. The level of a neurotransmitter present at the synapse is crucial because if it is

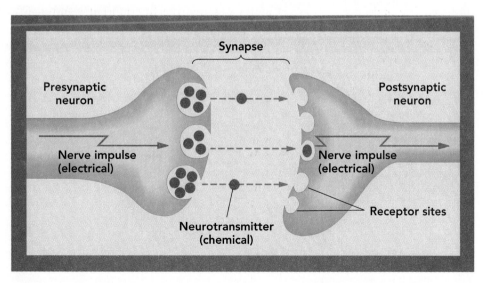

FIGURE 2.8
Neurotransmitters are released by the presynaptic neuron, cross the synapse, and stimulate the postsynaptic neuron.

too low, the next neuron will not receive enough stimulation to fire, and if it is too high, too much activity will be stimulated. Three processes influence the level of the neurotransmitter at the synapse:

 1. *Production.* The presynaptic neuron may produce too much or too little of the neurotransmitter.
 2. *Catabolism.* Substances called *enzymes* that are present in the area of the synapse destroy neurotransmitters in the area, and in some cases too much or too little of a neurotransmitter will be destroyed. This process is called **catabolism** (ka-TAB-ō-liz-em).
 3. *Reuptake.* The presynaptic neuron may reabsorb or take up the neurotransmitter before it can stimulate the next neuron. (It is like a sponge that reabsorbs liquid that was originally squeezed out of it.) That process is called **reuptake** (rē-UP-tak). Excessive reuptake reduces the level of the neurotransmitter below the level that is needed, whereas insufficient reuptake leaves too much of the neurotransmitter at the synapse.

A malfunction of any one of these processes can alter the level of a neurotransmitter and may thereby alter synaptic transmission and result in abnormal behavior. These processes are illustrated in Figure 2.9.

Blocking Agents. The neurotransmitter stimulates the postsynaptic neuron by fitting into receptor sites on the postsynaptic neuron much as a key fits into and opens a lock. However, other chemicals that are called **blocking agents** are structurally similar to the neurotransmitter and therefore can also fit into the receptor sites, but they do not cause the neuron to fire because they do not fit the receptor sites perfectly. When blocking agents are present, they block the neurotransmitter from getting into the receptor sites, thus preventing stimulation of the postsynaptic neuron. It is like putting the wrong key in a lock; that key does not open the lock, and it prevents you from putting the right key in the lock. Some drugs are blocking agents and are used to reduce excessive synaptic transmission. For example, the drugs that are used to treat schizophrenia block dopamine from entering the receptor sites, thus reducing the excessive levels of synaptic transmission and decreasing the disruption of thought processes. Blocking of receptor sites is illustrated in Figure 2.9.

Inhibitory Neurons. Another factor affecting synaptic transmission is the activity of **inhibitory neurons.** An inhibitory neuron is a neuron that makes connections with either the presynaptic or postsynaptic neurons and inhibits the transmission of the impulse between those neurons. On the one hand, when the inhibitory neuron releases its neurotransmitter and stimulates the presynaptic neuron, the presynaptic neuron releases less of its neurotransmitter, thereby reducing the likelihood that the postsynaptic neuron will be stimulated and fire. On the other hand, when the inhibitory neuron stimulates the postsynaptic neuron, that has the effect of decreasing the sensitivity of the postsynaptic neuron, and therefore it will be less likely to fire if it is stimulated by the presynaptic neuron. An inhibitory neuron is illustrated in Figure 2.10.

 Inhibitory neurons play important roles in a number of disorders. For example, some forms of anxiety occur because inhibitory neurons in some areas of the brain are not active enough; that leads to excessive synaptic transmission, which leads to what we experience as anxiety.

Neuron Sensitivity. A fourth factor influencing synaptic transmission is the level of sensitivity of the postsynaptic neuron; more sensitive neurons are more likely to fire when stimulated than those that are less sensitive. One explanation for depression is that the neu-

FIGURE 2.9
Neurotransmission is reduced by low production of transmitter substances, reuptake, catabolism, and blocking of the receptor sites.

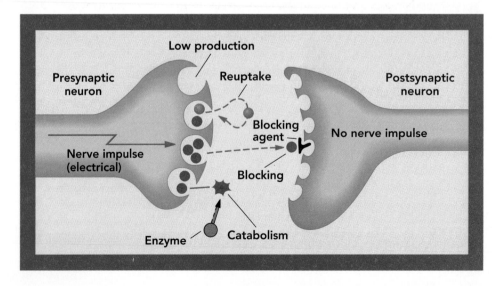

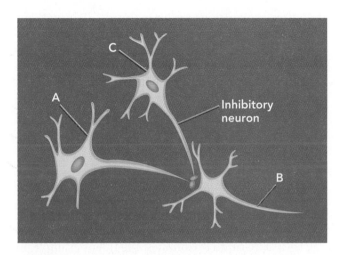

FIGURE 2.10 When an inhibitory neuron fires, it can inhibit synaptic transmission between other neurons.

rons that are associated with pleasure have become less sensitive so they are less likely to fire and therefore the individual is less likely to experience pleasure.

Number of Receptor Sites. Finally, the level of synaptic transmission can be influenced by the number of receptor sites on the postsynaptic neuron. Specifically, the likelihood of a neuron's being stimulated is increased if there are more receptor sites. With regard to abnormal behavior, it is believed that some individuals with schizophrenia have an excessively high number of receptor sites. Their high number of receptor sites leads to high levels of synaptic transmission, and that serves to disrupt their thought processes. It is interesting to note that the number of receptor sites declines with age, and so does the incidence of schizophrenia.

Hormones

Hormones are substances that glands secrete directly into the bloodstream, and once in the bloodstream the hormones serve to *stimulate* activity. (Indeed, the word *hormone* is derived from a Greek verb meaning "to stir up," based on a noun meaning "impulse" or "assault.") Abnormal levels of hormones are linked to disorders involving aberrant sexual behavior and aggression.

Genetic Factors

It is clear that problems with brain functioning can cause abnormal behavior, but the question now arises, what causes the problems in brain functioning? Two factors deserve attention, the first of which is **genetics.** Some years ago, it was generally agreed that genetics played an important role in physical characteristics such as height and in physical disorders such as heart disease, but eyebrows were raised when it was suggested that personality and abnormal behavior might also be inherited. That has changed dramatically, and today it is widely recognized that about 50% of the variability in normal personality traits is inherited and that many forms of abnormal behavior have a genetic basis (Carey & Di Lalla, 1994; Kendler, Neale et al., 1993a, 1993b, 1993c; Lander & Schork, 1994; Nigg & Goldsmith, 1994; Reiss et al., 1991; Rieder et al., 1994).

The fact that there is a genetic basis for traits and disorders does not mean that you inherit a specific trait or disorder; rather, you may inherit a high or a low level of a particular neurotransmitter, which will lead to the trait or disorder. For example, if you inherit a high level of the neurotransmitter dopamine, that can lead to high levels of neurological activity in areas of the brain where thinking occurs, and that high level of activity can disrupt your thought processes and lead to the symptoms of schizophrenia (e.g., confusion, hallucinations). Evidence for the role of genes in abnormal behavior comes from the finding that one of the best predictors of whether you will suffer from a particular disorder is whether you have biological relatives who suffer from that disorder. Indeed, in the case of schizophrenia, the biological children of individuals with schizophrenia show a high rate of schizophrenia even if the children are adopted at birth and raised by adoptive parents who do not suffer from schizophrenia.

Two qualifications should be noted with regard to the effects of the genes. First, in many cases, genes interact with environmental factors to result in disorders. For example, just as some individuals may carry the genes for freckles but do not develop freckles until they go out in the sun, so some individuals may carry genes that make them more sensitive to the effects of stress, but they will not develop a disorder until they are exposed to stress. Second, because most disorders probably occur because of a combination of genes, and because you do not get all of the genes of each of your parents, you may get all, some, or none of the genes from a parent that are necessary for a particular disorder. That means that you may get the disorder, you may get a milder form of the disorder, or you may not get the disorder. For example, in the case of schizophrenia, we know that the offspring of parents with that disorder may develop schizophrenia or may develop mild problems with thought processes that are not serious enough to qualify for the diagnosis of schizophrenia. In general, genes can contribute to the development of the physiological problems that provide the basis for abnormal behaviors, but genes cannot account for them entirely.

Biological Traumas

The second factor that can lead to problems in the brain and then to disorders are **biological traumas** such as physical injuries or diseases. For example, a mother's illness during pregnancy can influence the brain development of her unborn child, and those problems in brain development can lead to schizophrenia 20 years later. The point here is that physiological problems such as high levels of neurotransmitters and structural problems in the brain can lead to abnormal behaviors, and those physiological problems can be caused either by genetics or biological traumas.

COMMENT

There is a large and rapidly increasing body of evidence for the physiological explanations for abnormal behavior. Recognition of the growing importance of this explanation is reflected in the fact that the American Psychological Association requires that graduate students in clinical psychology take coursework that is specifically focused on the physiological explanations for abnormal behavior.

However, an important limitation of the physiological explanation is that it does not always explain why individuals develop the specific symptoms they do. For example, a high level of neurological activity in one area of the brain seems to be related to anxiety, but that does not explain why one individual develops a phobia for flying but another becomes fearful of snakes. It seems likely that the physiological perspective works *in combination* with other perspectives to explain abnormal behavior. That is, physiological factors may *predispose* individuals to general types of disorders, and then personal experiences give form to the disorders.

Finally, I should point out that although in many cases the physiological problems that lead to abnormal behavior are due to genetics or biological traumas, *in some cases the physiological problems are triggered by strictly environmental factors.* For example, prolonged stress can reduce the level of the neurotransmitter that is related to mood, and when that neurotransmitter is reduced, the individual will become depressed. Understanding these physiological links helps us understand why, for example, stress leads to depression.

OTHER EXPLANATIONS

The psychodynamic, learning, cognitive, and physiological explanations are the major ones in the area of abnormal behavior today, but three other explanations deserve mention here. These explanations can be important, but they have not been singled out for specific attention because they can be subsumed under the other explanations we have already discussed. For example, cultural factors certainly influence the development of abnormal behaviors, but cultural factors have their effects because they influence factors such as the level of stress and the behaviors that are taught in a particular culture. These explanations are discussed here so that you will understand how they fit in with the other explanations and so that you will be familiar with them if you encounter them elsewhere.

Sociocultural Explanation

The **sociocultural explanation** is focused on the fact that *social and cultural factors can play important roles in abnormal behavior* (Griffith & Gonzales, 1994). For example, in Asia there is a disorder known as **koro** that involves panic-like symptoms that stem from the belief that the genitalia are retracting into the abdomen and that the process will result in death. A less dramatic but possibly more important difference is reflected in the fact that schizophrenia is much more prevalent in the lower socioeconomic classes than the higher classes.

Sociocultural factors influence abnormal behavior in three ways. First, they can determine *what behaviors are labeled as abnormal.* For example, in most societies, hearing a voice that other people do not hear is defined as abnormal (i.e., a hallucination), but in some cultures it is assumed that the voice is the voice of God, and the individual is regarded a religious leader rather than a patient.

Second, sociocultural factors can influence the *level of abnormal behavior.* That is because in any one culture there may be more or less of a factor that contributes to abnormal behavior. For example, one culture or social class may be associated with more stress than another culture or class, and if stress leads to abnormal behavior, there may be a relationship between culture or class and the level of abnormal behavior. Also, in some cultures or classes, women receive less good medical care while they are pregnant, and that could lead to more problems in the prenatal development of their children, which could in turn lead to a variety of abnormal behaviors.

Third, sociocultural factors can influence the *nature of abnormal behavior.* In other words, cultural beliefs, standards, and role models can influence what symptoms develop. For example, in Malaysia and Africa there is a disorder called **amok** (a-MOK) in which after a humiliating experience, an individual (usually a male) broods for a brief period and then goes into what appears to be an uncontrolled frenzy and indiscriminately kills people and then usually kills himself. (This disorder is related to the phrase "running amok," which is used to describe an individual who is out of control and causing trouble.) Although amok is not approved of, in the Malaysian and African cultures it is a recognized and traditional means of responding to stress. With regard to amok, it is interesting to note that a similar pattern of behavior is now appearing in Western societies when, for example, a depressed former employee returns to his place of employment in a rage and begins randomly shooting people and then often kills himself (Gaw & Bernstein, 1992).

The effects of cultural standards on abnormal behaviors are also reflected in the changes in abnormal behaviors that occur when there are changes in cultural standards (Shorter, 1992; Spanos, 1994). For example, at one time, stress frequently led to paralyses of the arms and legs, but today such paralyses almost never occur. That change probably reflects the fact that with increasing medical sophistication, fewer people believe that stress can cause paralysis, and therefore they are less likely to use paralysis as a response to stress.

The effect of cultural factors is also reflected in the fact that there may be subtle variations in a disorder from culture to culture. For example, in many "primitive" cultures, some forms of abnormal behavior revolve around *spirit possession,* in which it is thought that the individual's body has been taken over by a spirit and therefore the individual is no longer in control. By contrast, in more developed cultures similar disorders exist but the possession is attributed to devices such as radio waves. In some respects, the multiple personality disorder may also be a Western form of a possession disorder; in that case, the individual is taken

over by another part of his or her personality rather than by a spirit. Finally, it is interesting to note that koro, which I described earlier, does not have a Western equivalent, but it can be treated effectively with a drug (clomipramine) that is effective for treating imagined bodily distortion in Western society. That suggests that koro may simply be a cultural variation of a more general disorder involving bodily distortion (Goetz & Price, 1994).

Clearly, sociocultural factors can play important roles in abnormal behavior, and we must be sensitive to those effects. However, it is essential to recognize that the sociocultural factors do not stand alone as explanations for abnormal behavior; instead, *they have their effects through the explanations we have already discussed.* That is, sociocultural factors influence abnormal behaviors because they influence (a) levels of stress, (b) what behaviors can be learned, (c) what beliefs can be developed, and (d) physiological factors. Looked at in another way, each of the explanations can be thought of as an equation that is used for predicting behavior, and sociocultural factors are values that we plug into those equations (e.g., high or low stress, models or no models for a particular behavior). For that reason, in this book I will not use a sociocultural explanation per se but rather, in discussing each of the other explanations for a disorder, I will explain the role that sociocultural factors play in that explanation.

In some cultures, spirit possession is thought to be a cause of abnormal behavior. In this photo, a Candomble priestess in Brazil holds a woman possessed by a saint in order to control the spirit.

Family System Explanation

The **family system explanation** focuses on *the role of the family in the development of abnormal behavior.* Specifically, within the family, the members can (a) influence each others' personal development, (b) generate conflict and stress for one another, and (c) provide models of abnormal behavior for one another. In those ways, the family can lead to abnormal behavior. In fact, from this position, the abnormal behavior of an individual is sometimes seen as only a symptom of an *abnormal family.* For that reason, psychologists who subscribe to the family system orientation do not treat a disturbed individual in isolation but instead treat the entire family and in so doing treat the individual.

The family system is important, but I will not discuss it as a separate explanation because the effects that family members have on one another, such as creating stress and providing role models, are dealt with by the other explanations. In other words, the family system does not provide a unique explanation for abnormal behavior; rather it provides a *context* (the family) in which other factors such as stress and learning can lead to the development of abnormal behavior.

Humanistic Explanation

The **humanistic explanation** for abnormal behavior is based on two notions: first, that the behavior of human beings is due to *conscious choices that are based on the individual's perception of the situation,* and second, that behavior is motivated by a desire to *achieve enhanced levels of personal fulfillment* rather than simply to avoid negative consequences.

The emphasis on the conscious control of behavior and the importance of one's view of the world for making decisions surfaced in the 1960s and early 1970s as a reaction against the psychodynamic, learning, and physiological explanations for behavior in which human beings are seen as simply the product of unconscious drives, conditioning, and physiology—as pawns of uncontrollable forces. The humanistic position was offered as an alternative view of humans, and at the time it was seen as somewhat radical. However, today the notion of conscious personal control and the importance of one's view of the world has been encompassed in the cognitive explanations for behavior, and therefore that element of the humanistic position has been largely usurped.

However, the humanistic notion that behavior is motivated by a desire for positive personal development and fulfillment remains unique. That is, in the psychodynamic and learning explanations, it is assumed that our behaviors are driven by a desire to reduce stress or gain rewards, and the cognitive and physiological explanations do not make any assumptions about what motivates us. However, theorists who hold the humanistic point of view assume that our behaviors are motivated by a positive striving for fulfillment and that it is that positive striving that makes us human.

The leading proponent of the humanistic position was **Abraham Maslow,** who suggested that we have five levels of needs that range from basic physiological needs to more human needs and that after we satisfy the needs at one level, we move on to the next level. The needs, from bottom to top, are *physiological needs, safety and security, love and belongingness, self-esteem,* and *self-actualization.* **Self-actualization** is the highest level of fulfillment, and people who achieve it are able to rise above their own needs and can freely experience and give of themselves.

From the humanistic perspective, anxiety and abnormal behavior occur when we are blocked in our attempt to move up the ladder of needs to fulfillment—that is, when there is a difference between where we are and where we think we ought to be. The problem becomes circular because the anxiety and tension block us from making further progress. In this explanation, psychotherapy is focused on helping the individual overcome obstacles and close the gap between the **current self** and the **ideal self.**

There are two reasons why the humanistic explanation is largely ignored today, the first of which is that many of its most important concepts, such as self-actualization, are poorly defined and impossible to measure. That makes the theory impossible to test, and an untestable theory is of little value.

The second problem is that the humanistic theorists have not developed a comprehensive theory of abnormal behavior. They have focused most of their attention on the mild anxiety and depression that relatively normal individuals experience, but they have not systematically addressed the many other, more serious disorders. However, it might be noted that in one attempt to explain schizophrenia, a leading proponent of the humanistic position suggested that schizophrenia was not a disorder but simply an alternative form of adjustment and that it was the "normal" individuals who suffered from a problem because they allowed themselves to be unduly restricted by cultural restraints (Laing, 1964). Obviously, that position is not widely accepted today.

You should be aware of the humanistic explanation because it provides an interesting contrast and counterpoint to the other explanations. However, because the humanistic explanation has not been applied to a broad range of abnormal behaviors and has not been subjected to many empirical tests, it will not be used systematically in this book.

WHAT CAN WE CONCLUDE CONCERNING THE EXPLANATIONS FOR ABNORMAL BEHAVIOR?

Three major conclusions can be drawn concerning the explanations for abnormal behavior. First, there are *four major categories of explanations:* (a) the psychodynamic explanations focus on the role of stress in abnormal behavior, (b) the learning explanations assume that abnormal behavior is due to classical and operant conditioning, (c) the cognitive explanations suggest that abnormal behaviors are due to erroneous beliefs, and (d) the physiological explanations attribute abnormal behaviors to physiological factors such as problems with neural transmission. Of course, it is important to recognize that each of these types of explanations works within a context. At the broadest level, they operate in a cultural context, so, for example, sociocultural factors can influence the level of stress, what we learn, and what beliefs we develop.

Second, it can be concluded that *different disorders are due to different causes* and that in some cases, *the same disorder can have different causes.* In other words, it is not that one explanation is correct and the others are incorrect; rather they are all correct, but they are correct for different disorders or for different individuals with the same disorder. Our task is to determine what explanation is correct for which disorder and for whom.

Third, it can be concluded that in some disorders, *different causes may work together to result in the abnormal behaviors.* For example, stress may trigger a disorder, but only in individuals who have a physiological predisposition to have a strong response to stress. Similarly, pairing a fear with a specific stimulus such as a spider can result in a classically conditioned phobia, but only in individuals who are physiologically aroused enough to develop the fear and the response. The fact that predispositions play a role in the development of disorders is referred to as **diathesis** (dī-ATH-uh-sis). (*Diathesis* means "a constitutional predisposition to a particular state.")

Therefore, you should not think of the various explanations for abnormal behavior as competing with one another, but rather as complementing one another. Just as each member of a team has a different role, so each type of explanation plays a role in helping us understand different disorders, and sometimes the explanations work together to help us understand a single disorder.

SUMMARY

- A variety of explanations for abnormal behavior have been offered, and there has been a debate over which is correct. Rather than one being correct, it appears that different disorders may be due to different factors, and some disorders may be due to more than one factor. The challenge is to determine which explanation is primarily responsible for which disorder.
- All disorders are ultimately caused by physiological processes in the brain (the final common pathway), but the physiological processes can be triggered by a variety of factors such as stress, learning, thoughts, and physiology.
- The psychodynamic explanation suggests that stress leads to abnormal behavior, but there are differences of opinion over what causes the stress.
- In his psychoanalytic theory, Freud suggested that stress stemmed from conflicts over the satisfaction of biological needs.
- Freud suggested that individuals go through five stages of psychosexual development (oral, anal, phallic, latency, genital), that each stage involves conflicts, and that if a conflict is not overcome, the individual will experience problems (complexes) later.
- Freud described the personality as having three components: (a) the *id,* which is the source of biological needs; (b) the *superego,* which is the moral arm of society; and (c) the *ego,* which meditates between the id and the superego. He also suggested that there are three levels of consciousness: (a) the *conscious mind* contains what you are aware at any one time, (b) the *preconscious* contains material you can recall when necessary, and (c) the *unconscious* contains material that is anxiety-provoking and cannot be recalled.

■ To defend against anxiety, individuals may use defense mechanisms such as repression, suppression, denial, projection, displacement, regression, identification, rationalization, compensation, intellectualization, and reaction formation. The defense mechanisms can reduce anxiety, but they can also lead to abnormal behavior.

■ Neo-Freudians accepted many of Freud's ideas but argued that the ego played a dominant role in personality functioning and that anxiety stemmed from personal and interpersonal problems (e.g., feelings of inferiority, interpersonal conflicts) rather than conflicts over biological needs.

■ A more contemporary psychodynamic approach revolves around the effects of stressors and stress. Stressors require adjustments that overtax us, thereby leading to stress, and there are wide individual differences in what people experience as stressors.

■ Stress has psychological (emotional) and physiological (bodily change) components. There is a question as to whether psychological responses lead to physiological responses (Cannon-Bard theory) or physiological responses lead to psychological responses (James-Lange theory); both explanations may be correct. The physiological component of the stress response may not be appropriate for many modern stressors.

■ The steps leading from a stressor to abnormal behavior include (a) awareness and appraisal of the stressor, (b) attempts to cope with the stressor, (c) stress that leads to defense mechanisms, and (d) abnormal behaviors that result from the defensive behaviors or the failure of the defense.

■ The learning explanations suggest that abnormal behavior is learned, and there are two processes by which the learning can occur: classical conditioning and operant conditioning.

■ Classical conditioning was developed by Pavlov, and it involves the pairing of a stimulus (the unconditioned stimulus) that elicits a particular response with a neutral stimulus that does not elicit the response. After the pairing, the neutral stimulus (not the conditioned stimulus) will elicit the response. Classical conditioning provides the basis for emotional and physiological responses (conditioned stimuli can elicit emotional responses); for example, a phobia for white rats was classically conditioned in Little Albert by pairing a frightening gong with a white rat.

■ Stimuli that are similar to the conditioned stimulus can also elicit the conditioned response, a process called generalization. If the conditioned stimulus is consistently presented without the unconditioned stimulus, the conditioned stimulus will cease to elicit the response, a process called extinction. Classically conditioned responses are not under voluntary control.

■ Operant conditioning was made well known by Skinner, and it involves the pairing of a response with a reward, as when a rat learns to push a lever to get food or a child learns to have a temper tantrum to get attention.

■ If an operantly conditioned response is no longer followed by a reward, the response will be given up (extinguished). Intermittent schedules for rewards make responses more resistant to extinction. Operantly conditioned responses are under voluntary control.

■ Classically and operantly conditioned responses can be developed when an individual simply watches another individual go through the conditioning process. That is called vicarious conditioning, observational learning, or modeling.

■ Questions have been raised over whether conditioning is sufficient to explain complex human behaviors and whether conditioning is an automatic process or whether it involves thinking (i.e., a stimulus is a signal to expect something or the individual makes a preparatory response).

■ The cognitive explanations suggest that abnormal behavior is caused by erroneous beliefs and disruptions of the thought processes.

■ Erroneous beliefs develop because of problems with information processing in the sensory memory, short-term memory, and long-term memory, where memories are stored in networks. Selective attention and selective recall influence what is put into and retrieved from memory. In addition to the distortion of memories, false memories can be implanted (suggested). Cognitive processes can be disrupted by problems with attention and associations.

■ Questions have been raised over whether erroneous beliefs are a cause or an effect of abnormal behavior; that is, does thinking you are a bad person lead to depression, or does depression lead you to think you are a bad person? Also, it is clear that problems with attention and associations can be used to describe disrupted cognitive processes, but the cognitive explanations do not account for why the problems with attention and associations occur.

■ There is now evidence that conditioning can be due to cognitive processes; that is, operant conditioning appears to involve problem solving and cooperation, and classical conditioning appears to be a response to the expectancy that a stimulus signals a coming event.

■ The physiological explanations suggest that abnormal behavior is due to problems with synaptic transmission and structural problems in the brain.

■ The brain consists of three layers. The brain stem controls basic physiological functions (breathing, heart rate) and generates arousal for other areas of the brain. The midbrain maintains homeostasis (controls the amount we eat, sleep, desire sex) and is responsible for emotion. The third level is the cortex, which is where higher mental functions such as thinking and language are located.

■ Problems with brain functioning can occur when the structures of the brain are malformed or damaged or when for other reasons the structures do not work properly (e.g., problems with synaptic transmission).

■ The brain is composed of neurons (cells) that generate electrical impulses when they are stimulated. An impulse travels to the end of a neuron's axon, where it stimulates the release of a neurotransmitter that flows across the synapse (gap) that separates the presynaptic neuron from the postsynaptic neuron. The neurotransmitter then enters a receptor site on the postsynaptic neuron, causing that neuron to fire. A neuron fires on the all-or-none principle (either it fires or it doesn't), so the intensity of activity is due to the frequency of firing or the number of neurons that fire.

■ Neurotransmission is crucial because too little or too much can lead to problems (e.g., depression or mania, respectively). Neurotransmission can be influenced by (a) levels of neurotransmitters (production, catabolism, reuptake), (b) blocking agents in the neurotransmitter receptor sites, (c) inhibitory neurons that reduce the release of neurotransmitters or decrease the sensitivity of neurons, (d) postsynaptic sensitivity, and (e) the number of postsynaptic receptor sites for neurotransmitters.

■ Genetics can influence factors such as the level of neurotransmitters, which can in turn influence behavior. In some cases, genetics interacts with environmental factors, as when genes establish a predisposition to a disorder that is triggered by stress.

■ Biological traumas such as injuries or disease can lead to abnormal behavior (e.g., a mother's illness during pregnancy can lead her child to develop schizophrenia years later).

■ The sociocultural explanation is focused on the fact that social and cultural factors can influence behavior because they can (a) determine what is labeled abnormal, (b) influence the level of abnormal behavior (e.g., one class or culture may have more stress), and (c) influence the nature of abnormal behavior (models may lead to different behaviors). However, sociocultural factors have their effects through processes that are embodied in other explanations; for example, they influence level of stress (psychodynamic), what behaviors are learned (learning), and what beliefs are developed (cognitive).

■ The family system explanation is focused on the role of the family in abnormal behavior. Family influences can be important, but they have their effects through processes that are central to other explanations; for example, families can increase stress (psychodynamic), teach abnormal behavior (learning), or foster erroneous beliefs (cognitive).

■ The humanistic explanation was developed as a reaction against the other explanations in which humans were seen as simply the products of drives, conditioning, and physiology. Behavior is seen as due to conscious choices that individuals make because of their view of the situation and a desire to achieve enhanced levels of personal fulfillment (self-actualization). However, the notion that conscious choices influence behavior has been taken over by the cognitive explanations. Apart from that, the humanistic explanation has been largely abandoned because many of its central concepts were not adequately defined or measurable and because it was never used to develop a comprehensive theory of abnormal behavior.

KEY TERMS, CONCEPTS, AND NAMES

In reviewing and testing yourself on what you have learned from this chapter, you should be able to identify and discuss each of the following.

Adler, Alfred
all-or-none principle
amine hypotheses
amines
amok
anal stage
associative network theory
avoidant thinking
axon
biological traumas
blocking agents
brain stem
Cannon-Bard theory of emotion
catabolism
cell body
cerebrum
classical conditioning
cognitive explanations
compensation
conditioned stimulus
conscious mind
coping
cortex
current self
defense mechanisms
dendrite
denial
diathesis

displacement
disrupted cognitive processes
distortions of memories
drive displacement
ego
ego psychology
Electra complex
extinction
false memories
family system explanation
feelings of inferiority
Freud, Anna
Freud, Sigmund
generalization
genetics
genital stage
hormones
Horney, Karen
humanistic explanation
id
ideal self
identification
information processing
inhibitory neurons
intellectualization
intermittent schedule of reward
James-Lange theory of emotion
koro

latency stage
learning explanations
Little Albert
long-term memory
Maslow, Abraham
midbrain
modeling
neo-Freudian theories
nerve fiber
nerve impulse
neuron
neurotransmitter
object displacement
observational learning
Oedipus complex
operant conditioning
oral stage
Pavlov, Ivan
phallic stage
physiological explanations
pleasure principle
postsynaptic neuron
preconscious
presynaptic neuron
primary process
priming
projection
psychoanalytic (Freudian) theory

psychodynamic explanations
rationalization
Rayner, Rosalie
reaction formation
receptor sites
regression
repression
reuptake
secondary process
selective attention
selective recall

self-actualization
self-fulfilling prophecies
sensory memory
short-term memory
situation redefinition
Skinner, B. F.
sociocultural explanation
spontaneous recovery
stages of psychosexual development
stress
stressor

structural approach to personality
superego
suppression
synapse
terminal button
three-stage theory of memory
    processing
unconditioned stimulus
unconscious
vicarious conditioning
Watson, John B.

CHAPTER THREE
DIAGNOSTIC TECHNIQUES and RESEARCH METHODS

OUTLINE

In this chapter, I am going to discuss two basic but separate topics. First, I will describe and comment on the techniques that are used to *diagnose* abnormal behaviors. Specifically, I will examine the systems we use for grouping symptoms into various disorders, and then I will describe the methods and tests we use to assess the symptoms. Obviously, how we group and assess symptoms is crucial for the understanding and treatment of abnormal behavior. In the second part of the chapter, I will describe the methods that we use for *studying* abnormal behavior. Those procedures are important because research provides the foundation for our understanding of abnormal behavior, and it is essential that you be able to interpret and evaluate the findings of research.

TOPIC 1
DIAGNOSTIC TECHNIQUES

Labeling an individual "abnormal" tells us very little because the label is too broad. We do not know whether the individual is anxious, depressed, having physical problems, hallucinating, delusional, addicted to drugs, or suffering from any of hundreds of other symptoms. The need for better descriptions led to the development of **diagnostic systems** that we use to group sets of symptoms into various disorders.

In general, a diagnostic system serves two major purposes. First, it enables us to *describe* individuals who suffer from abnormalities. For example, the diagnostic label "major depression" tells us much more about an individual's symptoms than the label "abnormal." Second, a diagnostic system helps us decide how to *treat* an individual. A diagnostic system itself does not lead to treatments, but once a set of symptoms (diagnosis) is linked to a particular cause or an effective treatment, the diagnosis helps us identify who should be treated in what way. In many respects, a diagnostic system provides the foundation for our understanding and treatment of abnormal behavior, and therefore it is important that you understand the current systems and how they work.

Two diagnostic systems are currently in use. The system used in the United States is presented in the fourth edition of the **Diagnostic and Statistical Manual of Mental Disorders,** generally referred to as **DSM-IV.** The system used throughout the rest of the world is set forth in the 10th edition of the **International Classification of Diseases,** and it is better known as **ICD-10.** The two systems are similar, but there are some differences (American Psychiatric Association, 1994, apps. G and H). Because it would be helpful if everyone used the same system, the two systems are in the process of being merged. In this book, DSM-IV will be used as the basis for identifying the symptoms that are necessary for a diagnosis.

DIAGNOSTIC SYSTEMS FOR ABNORMAL BEHAVIOR

Background

The *Diagnostic and Statistical Manual of Mental Disorders* was introduced by the American Psychiatric Association in 1952, and it has undergone extensive revisions since then. In its early forms, the manual consisted simply of brief descriptions of the symptoms of the various disorders along with discussions of what was thought to cause them. When making a diagnosis, a clinician tried to select the description or cause that best fit the patient.

Unfortunately, the early system suffered from two serious problems. First, the descriptions of the various disorders were rather vague. Second, there was no consistent basis for diagnoses because they could be based either on the patient's *symptoms* or on what was thought to *cause* the symptoms.

The vagueness of the descriptions and the inconsistent basis for making diagnoses led to two practical problems. First, the system was *unreliable*. (The **reliability** of a diagnostic system refers to the degree to which an individual with a given set of symptoms will receive the *same* diagnosis when examined by different clinicians.) For example, when using the original manual, there was often less than 50% agreement among clinicians who diagnosed the same patient (Beck et al., 1962; Ward et al., 1962; Zigler & Phillips, 1961). Second, the diagnoses arrived at with the manual were often *invalid*. (The **validity** of a diagnostic system refers to the degree to which an individual will receive the *correct* diagnosis.) The invalidity of the diagnoses stemmed from their unreliability; that is, because different clinicians came up with different diagnoses for the same patient, some of those diagnoses had to be wrong. Obviously, a system that yields so many unreliable and invalid diagnoses is not of much help, and consequently there was widespread dissatisfaction with it.

The Current System

Because of the problems with the original manual, in 1980 a completely new diagnostic system was introduced (DSM-III), and since then two further refinements have been published (DSM-III-Revised and DSM-

IV). These new versions involve four important advances that improved our diagnostic procedures:

1. *The symptoms for each diagnostic category are clearly listed.* Earlier manuals simply contained a short and vague description of each disorder, but in DSM-IV the precise symptoms of each disorder are listed, and it is specified how many symptoms must be present before the diagnosis can be made. For example, in Table 11.1 of Chapter 11, you will find a list of the symptoms that are necessary for a diagnosis of "schizophrenia."

In an attempt to make the system even more objective and uniform, the manual contains **decision trees** for making diagnoses. A decision tree for diagnosing mood disorders is presented in Figure 3.1. The decision trees lead the clinician through a series of branches as a function of what symptoms the patient has, and the branches will eventually lead to a diagnosis. With the necessary symptoms clearly listed and with the steps in the decision process outlined, the diagnostic process has become more objective and uniform and therefore more reliable. The only room for subjectivity comes in the decisions concerning whether or not the patient has a particular symptom.

2. *Assumptions about the suspected causes of disorders are not used in making diagnoses.* With the current system, diagnoses are based on *observable behaviors,* and suspected causes are generally ignored. The elimination of assumptions about causes resulted in the elimination of some popular diagnostic labels because the labels implicitly suggested an underlying cause. For example, for many years the term *neurotic* was used to refer to disorders involving the symptoms of anxiety, but because the term *neurotic* implies that anxiety stems from unconscious conflicts, it was eliminated. Instead, what were previously called *anxiety neuroses* are now called *anxiety disorders.* The new diagnostic label simply describes the symptoms and does not involve assumptions about their cause. In general, DSM-IV is atheoretical, that is, not based on any theory.

However, attention to the cause of symptoms has not been completely eliminated because *objective evidence* concerning certain causes can provide important information needed to make an accurate diagnosis. For example, if an individual is hearing the voice of John Kennedy (i.e., hallucinating) or believes that he or she is God (i.e., delusional), and if an examination reveals organic brain damage, the diagnosis would be changed from "schizophrenia" to "psychotic disorder due to a general medical condition." Similarly, if there is evidence that the individual recently took a hallucinogenic drug such as LSD, the diagnosis would be changed to a "substance-induced psychotic disorder." However, it should be recognized that the use of objective evidence about brain damage or previous drug use is very different from assumptions about ill-defined causes like "conflict with mother" that were used previously.

3. *The number of disorders was greatly increased over earlier editions.* For example, the first edition of the manual listed only four disorders of childhood, but DSM-IV lists more than 40. Some critics have suggested that too many problems are now listed as disorders and that we are overextending the boundaries of "abnormal." For example, a child who was having difficulty with arithmetic could be diagnosed as having a "mathematics disorder," and that may be pushing the limits a bit.

4. *Individuals are given diagnoses on five separate axes.* Until the publication of DSM-III, individuals were given one diagnostic label such as "depression" that described their major clinical problem. However, now individuals are given diagnoses on five *axes* (dimensions) so that their diagnoses contain more information. Those axes are as follows:

Axis I: Clinical Syndromes. This axis contains all of the *major serious disorders* such as anxiety, depression, schizophrenia, substance abuse, sexual disorders, sleep disorders, and eating disorders.

Axis II: Personality Disorders and Mental Retardation. This axis contains two categories, the first of which is *personality disorders,* which includes problems such as the obsessive-compulsive personality disorder, the dependent personality disorder, and the antisocial personality disorder (see Chapter 14). The second category on Axis II involves *mental retardation.* Individuals can have diagnoses on both Axes I and II. For example, an individual could suffer from a major depression (Axis I) and also show compulsive personality traits (Axis II).

Axis III: General Medical Conditions. This axis allows the diagnostician to indicate whether there are any medical conditions that are relevant to the understanding or treatment of the disorder. For example, evidence of organic brain damage may be relevant for understanding an individual with impaired cognitive abilities, and the presence of diabetes might influence how we would deal with an individual who was depressed.

Axis IV: Psychosocial and Environmental Problems. This axis provides the diagnostician with an opportunity to indicate whether there are any psychosocial or environmental problems that might affect the individual's diagnosis, treatment, or prognosis. Examples of potential problems include the loss of social support, death of a loved one, discrimination, educational problems, economic problems, legal problems, and other sources of stress.

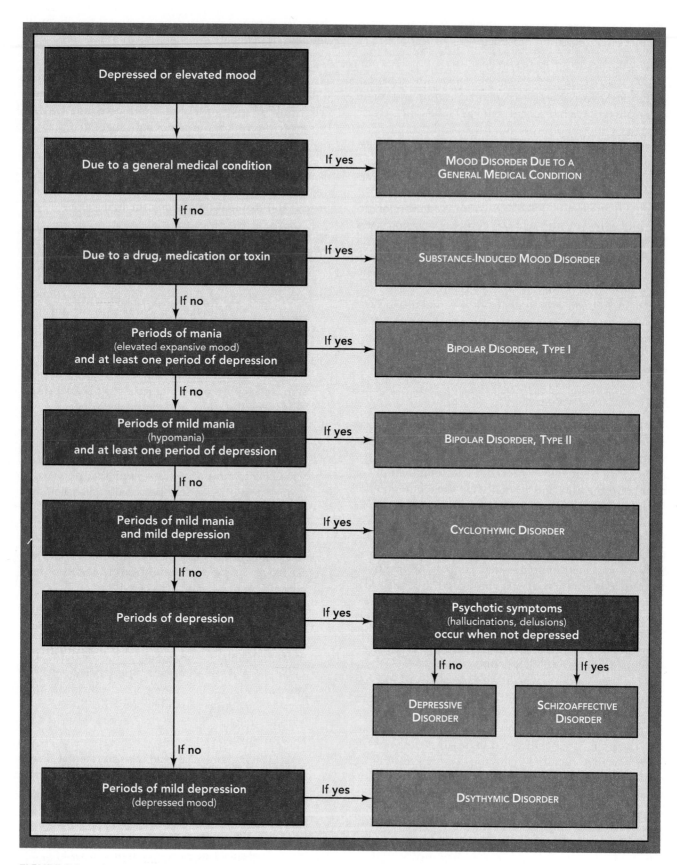

FIGURE 3.1 **A decision tree for diagnosing mood disorders.**
Source: Adapted from American Psychiatric Association (1994), pp. 696–697.

Axis V: Global Assessment of Functioning. This axis permits the diagnostician to indicate an <u>overall judgment</u> of the individual's psychological, social, and *occupational functioning at the present time* and the *highest level of functioning during the past year.* The rating of present functioning reflects the degree to which the individual needs treatment, and the rating of previous functioning is of value because it indicates the level of adjustment the individual can be expected to achieve after the disorder has been eliminated. For example, if the therapist knows that during the best of times the individual had only a marginal level of functioning, that would eliminate unrealistic expectations regarding treatment outcome. <u>Level of functioning is rated on a scale from 1 to 100</u>, with endpoints labeled "persistent inability to function" and "superior functioning."

The introduction of the multidimensional approach to diagnosis was quite revolutionary, and it greatly expanded the information provided by a diagnosis. For example, instead of simply labeling an individual "depressed," as was done before, we now might learn that the individual is depressed; tends to be obsessive-compulsive in personality style, which may make psychotherapy difficult; suffers from a serious heart disorder that limits activity and may contribute to the depression; and is experiencing moderate psychosocial stress (has recently changed careers), which may also contribute to the depression, but (e) has functioned very well within the past year, suggesting the potential to do well again.

The changes that were introduced in the DSM certainly improved the system and increased the reliability of diagnoses (Di Nardo et al., 1993). The validity of diagnoses has probably also been increased, but this is more difficult to assess because for most disorders there is no absolute standard against which we can compare our diagnoses. (With regard to validity, it should be noted that high reliability *is necessary* for high validity but that it *does not ensure* high validity. It is possible to do something consistently wrong so that you are reliable but invalid!)

Problems with Diagnostic Systems in General

The DSM and ICD systems are generally effective, but you should realize that there are three problems with any diagnostic system. The first problem is that whenever an individual is put into a category, some of that individual's <u>[1]uniqueness is lost,</u> and therefore we may miss something important about the individual. For example, all of the individuals who are diagnosed as suffering from depression are depressed, but there may be differences in the nature of their depression as well as other differences among the individuals such as social class, intelligence, interpersonal sensitivity, and attractiveness, all of which might be relevant. To some extent, in DSM an attempt is made to capture some of those differences with the various axes, but whenever we use a label or even a number of labels, we always lose something about the individual.

The second problem is that diagnoses can lead us to [2]<u>attribute characteristics to individuals that they do not possess.</u> For example, the diagnosis of "schizophrenia" is often associated with hallucinations and delusions, and therefore it is often assumed that a patient with schizophrenia will have hallucinations and delusions. However, the diagnosis of "schizophrenia" does not necessarily require that the individual have hallucinations or delusions because other symptoms can lead to the diagnosis. Unfortunately, the implicit link of hallucinations and delusions with schizophrenia often leads us erroneously to assume that individuals with schizophrenia have hallucinations and delusions, and if the individuals do not report having those symptoms, we assume that they are being defensive and denying or hiding the symptoms. What is worse is that assumptions about symptoms can lead us actually to create the symptoms in individuals through the process of suggestion. For example, if an authority figure such as a psychologist or a psychiatrist assumed that a patient with schizophrenia had hallucinations and repeatedly asked the patient about them, the patient might think that he or she *should* have them. Because the line between "thoughts" and "voices in my head" can become blurred, it is only a short jump for the patient to interpret thoughts as voices—and *voilà*, the patient has hallucinations!

The third problem with diagnoses is that <u>we often use them to refer to the *whole individual* when in fact they refer only to *one particular aspect of the individual.*</u> For example, sometimes we refer to individuals as "schizophrenics" rather than as "individuals with schizophrenia." This is like referring to an individual with cancer as "cancerous." Using the diagnostic label to refer to an entire individual is inappropriate because it implies that the disorder influences all aspects of the individual's life when in fact this may not be the case. For example, some individuals with serious disorders such as schizophrenia live normal and productive lives because their particular symptoms do not lead to inappropriate behaviors. To avoid attributing a disorder to the whole individual, DSM-IV does not use expressions such as "a schizophrenic" or "an alcoholic" and instead recommends phrases like "an individual with Schizophrenia" or "an individual with Alcohol Dependence." That is the approach I will follow in this book.

Checklists as an Alternative

Because of the problems associated with diagnostic labels, it has been suggested that we replace diagnoses with **checklists of symptoms.** The checklists would include items on which we would rate the degree to which the individual had hallucinations, delusions, depression, and anxiety, but the checklists would also include items on which we would rate the degree to which the individual was suicidal, verbally responsive, able to sleep, motivated to improve, able to interact effectively with others, bothered by feelings of guilt, physically active, able to organize, able to concentrate, reliable, and honest and the degree to which support was available to the individual from family and friends. With ratings on dimensions like these, we would know, for example, that an individual was depressed but also that he or she was suicidal, willing to talk (which is certainly important in dealing with suicidal individuals), and honest and that there is a social support system to care for the individual outside of the hospital.

In some respects, the use of checklists is the next step beyond the use of multiple axes for making diagnoses, but it has some differences. The checklist approach has many more dimensions, so we get much more information. Also, a checklist could be used by nurses, ward attendants, friends, and family members as well as psychologists and psychiatrists, and therefore we could get a broader perspective on the individual being rated. That might be very helpful because the traditional interview from which diagnostic impressions are obtained is brief and may not provide a representative picture of the person. The individual could even provide a self-rating, and the inconsistencies between that

report and those of others might help in understanding the individual. With multiple raters making judgments in multiple places, we could get a much better idea of the individual's problems as well as when and where the problems are most likely to occur. Checklists have been tried and found to be very effective (Derogatis, 1993; Wittenborn, 1951, 1962). However, probably because they involve a radical departure from the traditional way of thinking about and describing patients, they have not yet gained widespread acceptance.

With this material as background, in the next section I will discuss the techniques we use to assess the behaviors or symptoms that lead to diagnoses.

TECHNIQUES FOR DIAGNOSING ABNORMAL BEHAVIOR

In general, four different techniques are used to assess symptoms. They are *observation, interviews, psychological tests,* and *physiological tests.* More than one technique is usually used because the different techniques provide different types of information. Furthermore, the strengths of one technique can compensate for the weaknesses of another.

Observation

Observation of an individual in his or her natural environment can be very helpful because it enables us to assess behavior directly and to evaluate the effects of situational factors on behavior. However, direct observation usually plays a relatively minor role in the assess-

Psychologists use techniques such as observation to assess behavior in young children.

ment of abnormal behavior because of various practical and ethical problems associated with it. For example, it is simply not practical to have trained observers "in the field" recording the behavior of individuals. In addition, serious ethical questions are associated with observing individuals without informing them about the observation, and the behavior that can be observed with permission through one-way windows in a hospital is probably not typical behavior because the individual is aware of being observed. Although the unsystematic observations of friends and relatives are used, we must be cautious about such observations because the observers are not trained and may be biased; for example, friends may deny or ignore symptoms, or they may be influenced by cultural or sex-role stereotypes. Another source of unsystematic observations is the notes made by nurses and ward attendants on patients' charts; but a psychiatric ward may not be a good place to observe behavior because we cannot expect normal behavior in an abnormal environment.

In contrast to the case with adults, observations are frequently used with young children. For them, situations can be arranged in which they interact with peers or parents, and the children often ignore or are unaware of the observers. The fact that young children can be observed is important because unlike adults, they do not yet have the skills to report how they act or feel.

Interviews

It is often difficult or impossible to observe individuals in their natural environments, and therefore we use **interviews** in which the individuals report on how they

act and feel in various situations. In a **structured interview,** the interviewer rigidly follows a specific list of questions, whereas in an **unstructured interview,** the interviewer "goes with the flow," pursuing topics of interest and avoiding dead ends. Structured interviews have the advantage of ensuring that all relevant topics will be covered, at least superficially. Unstructured interviews may miss something that is relevant, but they allow for deeper probing when an important point is revealed. The best approach may be to do a structured interview followed by an unstructured interview in which important points are followed up.

Interviews also provide an opportunity to observe an individual's behavior. Indeed, an individual's style of responding may be more important than the content of what the individual says. In some interviews, the interviewer may actually behave in a particular way to see how the individual reacts. For example, in an interview designed to measure the aggressive and competitive personality style known as the *Type A behavior pattern*, the interviewer will occasionally pause and fumble briefly as if searching for the right word to use. What the interviewer is really doing is waiting to see if the individual will jump in and finish the sentence (Rosenman, 1978).

In other situations, the combination of content and style may be informative. For example, when asked about hallucinations, a patient might respond harshly, saying, "No! I don't hear voices! Only crazy people hear voices, and I'm not crazy!" In that case, the inappropriate vehemence of the patient's denial of the hallucinations may lead the interviewer to conclude that in fact the patient does suffer from hallucinations.

A diagnostic interview can reveal a lot about a person, both from what the person says and how the person behaves.

The interview is also important because it can yield valuable information about the individual's background and family. Increasing emphasis is being placed on family information because family interactions and genetic factors are now seen as playing important roles in the development of abnormal behavior. Not only do we want to know what problems there may have been in the family (e.g., family history of mental disorders, child abuse, infidelity), but we also want to know what, if anything, was effective in overcoming them.

In sum, the interview is of value because it provides both information about the individual and an opportunity to observe the individual. However, the interview does have a number of weaknesses. First, patients may not be good or honest reporters concerning their behavior. Second, sometimes the interviewer's interpretation of what a patient says or does may be based on an inference, and the inference may be wrong. For example, earlier I suggested that a patient's particularly vehement denial that he was hearing voices could be interpreted as suggesting that in fact he was hearing voices, but it is also possible that the vehemence of the denial was due to the fact that the patient was offended by the question, exasperated by being repeatedly asked about hallucinations, or just tired and cranky. Finally, the situation in which the interview occurs may not be particularly good for observing behavior because it is so limited and not representative of more relevant life situations. In other words, the way an individual responds in a formal interview in the office of a psychologist or psychiatrist may not be the way the individual responds in the "real world."

Psychological Tests

Psychological tests can be divided into four types: *objective personality tests, projective personality tests, intelligence tests,* and *neuropsychological tests.* In the following sections, I will consider each type in some detail.

Objective Personality Tests. In some respects, **objective personality tests** are an extension of the interview method of collecting information because the tests consist of lists of questions to which the individual responds. Numerous objective tests are used to measure a wide variety of abnormal behaviors, ranging from brief periods of anxiety to chronic schizophrenia.

The most widely used objective test of abnormal behavior is the **Minnesota Multiphasic Personality Inventory,** usually referred to as the **MMPI.** The MMPI was originally published in 1942, and a revision, the **MMPI-2,** was published in 1989. The MMPI-2 contains 567 questions grouped to form scales that measure nine types of abnormal behavior ranging from depression to schizophrenia. There is also one scale that mea-

TABLE 3.1 Items Like Those Found on MMPI Clinical Scales

Hypochondriasis (HS; Scale 1)
I have trouble with my bowel movements. (T)
I experience chest pains several times each week. (T)

Depression (D; Scale 2)
I generally feel that life is worth living. (F)
I do not sleep well. (T)

Conversion Hysteria (Hy; Scale 3)
Often I feel weak all over. (T)
It is easy for me to keep my balance when I walk. (F)

Psychopathic Deviate (PD; Scale 4)
I have many fewer fears than other people. (T)
In school, I was frequently in trouble for acting up. (T)

Masculinity-Femininity (Mf; Scale 5)
I enjoy raising house plants. (T)
I like to cook. (T)

Paranoia (Pa; Scale 6)
A lot of people have it in for me. (T)
I have frequently been punished for things that were not my fault. (T)

Psychasthenia (Pt; Scale 7)
I am anxious most of the time. (T)
I usually wake up feeling rested and fresh. (F)

Schizophrenia (Scale 8)
I cannot keep my attention focused on one thought. (T)
I hear strange things that others do not hear. (T)

Mania (Scale 9)
I am a very important person. (T)
I like to stir up activity. (T)

Social Introversion (Scale 0)
I like to talk to members of the opposite sex. (F)
At parties, I sit by myself or with one other person. (T)

sures masculinity-femininity. Each item is answered by checking "True," "False," or "Cannot Say." Table 3.1 contains items like those found on some of the scales. An individual gets a score on each scale, and the scores are plotted on a graph to yield a personality profile. Figure 3.2 contains an MMPI personality profile for an individual who has elevated scores on the Depression and Schizophrenia scales. It might be noted that the MMPI-2 yields comparable results for African-American and white individuals and that a Spanish-language version is available that works well (Lucio et al., 1994; Timbrook & Graham, 1994).

In addition to the *clinical* scales that measure problems like depression and schizophrenia, there are also three *control* scales that are used to identify individuals

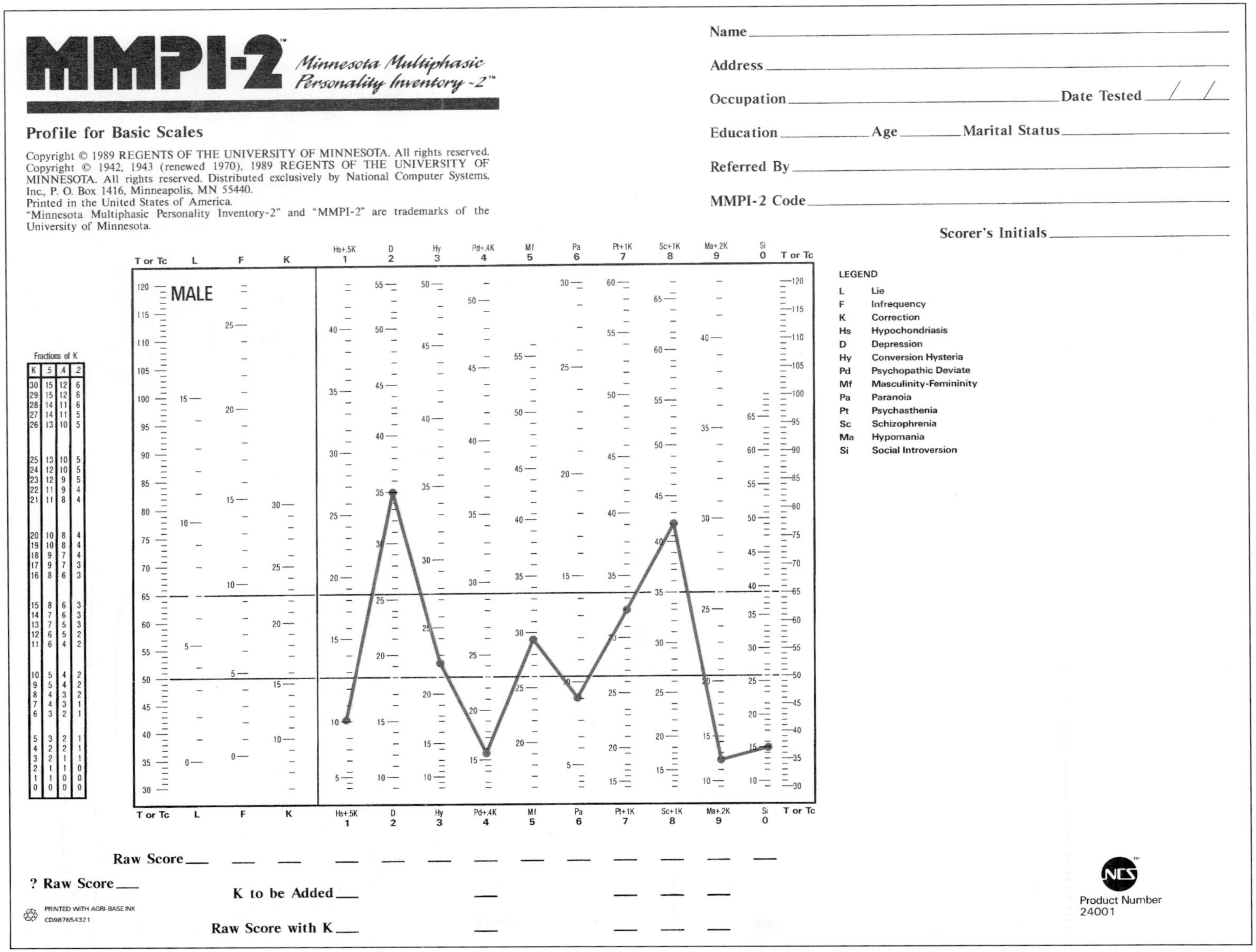

FIGURE 3.2 A Minnesota Multiphasic Personality Inventory (MMPI-2) profile for an individual with symptoms of depression and schizophrenia.
Source: Minnesota Multiphasic Personality Inventory-2 (MMPI-2) Profile for Basic Scales. Copyright © 1989 by the Regents of the University of Minnesota. All rights reserved. "MMPI-2" and "Minnesota Multiphasic Personality Inventory-2" are trademarks.

for whom the test scores may not be valid. For example, there is a Lie scale that identifies individuals who are trying to fake good scores. The Lie scale contains items like "I never put off until tomorrow things that should be done today." Because it is unlikely that many people could consistently mark "True" for items like that, if an individual does consistently mark "True" for those items, the assumption is that the individual is lying. That provides some potentially interesting information about the individual, but the other test results will be ignored as invalid (Wetter et al., 1994).

[handwritten margin note: Isn't this based on assumption?]

Interpretations of the MMPI can be based on simple inspection of a personality profile (see Figure 3.2), but it is now possible to use computer programs that will compare an individual's profile to that of thousands of other people about whom information is available and then print out a description of the individual (Bloom, 1992; Duckworth & Anderson, 1995; Matarazzo, 1986). The MMPI-2 can also be scored for a variety of new scales that measure characteristics such as dominance, social responsibility, college maladjustment, and posttraumatic stress disorder (Graham, 1990). With these new scales, a very comprehensive description of an individual can be developed.

Recently, a version of the MMPI was designed specifically for adolescents. This test is known as the **MMPI-A.** It has somewhat fewer items, the items are written at a lower reading level (6th grade), and the test also measures some topics such as family problems that are particularly relevant for understanding adolescents.

Objective tests are one of the most efficient and effective means of collecting data about individuals. However, the quality of the tests rests on the adequacy of the norms that were used in building the test. For example, when the test was developed, did the items on the Schizophrenia scale consistently differentiate between individuals who did and did not have schizophrenia? Unfortunately, many tests are published in which the items look good (i.e., they have *face validity*) but do not actually do what they are supposed to do (i.e., they do not have *empirical validity*). The MMPI is not a perfect measure, but as you will see later, it is one of the most helpful measures for describing and diagnosing individuals (Helmes & Reddon, 1993).

Projective Personality Tests. In psychology, the term **projection** refers to the fact that we often attribute our own personality characteristics and feelings to other people or to inanimate stimuli such as inkblots; that is, we project our traits much like a motion picture projector projects images on a screen. For example, an angry individual might see other people as angry or might interpret an inkblot as an ill-tempered monster. In addition, we may also project the *cause* of our feelings, and therefore a frightened individual may see others as frightening (i.e., hostile).

[handwritten margin note: me hard]

Based on those facts, **projective personality tests** were designed to assess what an individual projects onto others, the theory being that by knowing what the individual projects, we can know what the individual is like and how he or she sees the world. With projective tests, the individual is shown various stimuli such as inkblots or pictures of people and is then asked to tell what the inkblots look like or what is going on in the picture. Because the inkblots are really only inkblots and because the pictures do not tell a particular story, what the individual sees in the inkblots and pictures is supposedly due to the projection of the individual's own traits, needs, conflicts, and perceptions of the environment. It is also thought that because there are no clearly right or wrong answers, it would be difficult to fake answers on projective tests.

The best-known projective test is the **Rorschach (ROR-shok) test,** which was developed by Herman Rorschach after he noticed that his children saw different things when they looked at clouds (Rorschach, 1942). The Rorschach consists of 10 cards, each with one inkblot printed on it. An inkblot like that in the Rorschach is presented in Figure 3.3. Five of the cards have inkblots that are made with only black or gray ink, and five have inkblots that are made with different colored inks. The individual is given the cards one at a time, and with each card the individual is asked to tell the test administrator what he or she sees in the inkblot or what the inkblot might represent.

Responses to the Rorschach are scored in two ways. First, attention is given to the *content* of what the individual saw in the inkblot. For example, responses involving snarling monsters or squashed bugs might be interpreted as suggesting that the individual is hostile or sees the world as a hostile place, whereas responses

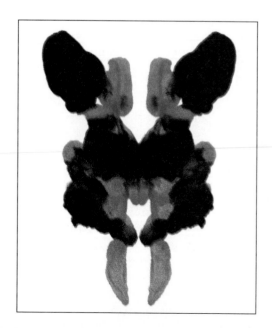

FIGURE 3.3 An inkblot like those on the Rorschach.

involving a smiling cat or flowers could be interpreted as suggesting that the individual is friendly and sees the world as a pleasant place.

Second, attention is given to what *aspect of the inkblot* led the individual to see what he or she saw. For example, does the actual shape of the inkblot justify what was seen? (Can you see a lobster in Figure 3.3?) If the shape justifies the response, that is considered to be an appropriate or healthy response and it is scored F+ (F stands for "form," or shape, of the object). However, if the response cannot be justified, that suggests that the individual does not perceive the world accurately and is not in touch with reality, and the response is scored F−. There are lists of acceptable responses for each card, but in most cases the judgment concerning whether a response can be justified is made by the test administrator; that is, if the test administrator can see what the client sees, the response is justified, but if the administrator cannot see what the client sees, the response is not justified. We do not expect any individual to give only F+ responses, but if the proportion of F+ responses falls below 60% or 70%, there is reason for concern over the degree to which the individual is in contact with reality.

The degree to which an individual uses colors in making responses is thought to be important because it supposedly reflects the amount of emotion the individual has. For example, an individual who sees brightly colored flowers in Figure 3.3 supposedly has more emotion than an individual who sees only the shape of flowers.

It is also thought that how the individual uses color reflects how the individual deals with emotion. For example, if an individual gives good responses (F+) to cards that are black and white but gives poor responses (F−) to cards that contain color, it is suspected that when confronted with emotions (color), the individual is overwhelmed and no longer functions well. Furthermore, if an individual takes longer to respond to a colored card or cannot think of a response for a colored card, that is called "color shock," and it is interpreted as meaning that the individual is overwhelmed by emotion and cannot function when faced with emotion. Numerous other factors are also taken into consideration when scoring responses to the Rorschach. For example, using the shades of gray in the inkblots supposedly reflects depression, and seeing motion such as "a person running" is interpreted as reflecting a rich fantasy life. (For more information on scoring, see Beck et al., 1961; Exner, 1993; Klopfer, 1962.)

The Rorschach is used widely, but very serious questions have been raised about its validity and value. The problem is that *the interpretations of the responses are based on assumptions that might not be true.* For example, it is assumed that the use of color reflects emotion, but there is very little evidence for that, and even if the use of color sometimes reflects emotion, insofar as it does not always reflect emotions, that assumption will lead to erroneous interpretations of the individual's responses.

FIGURE 3.4 A picture from the Thematic Apperception Test (TAT).
Source: Reprinted by permission of the publishers from the Thematic Apperception Test by Henry A. Murray, Cambridge, Massachusetts: Harvard University Press, © 1943 by the President and Fellows of Harvard College and © 1971 by Henry A. Murray.

The problem with using the Rorschach is clearly illustrated by the consistent finding that judgments about individuals that are based on demographic information (e.g., age, sex, social class, personal history) and Rorschach responses are usually less accurate than judgments that are based on only demographic information (see Garb, 1985). In other words, the Rorschach appears to introduce errors into the judgments, errors that apparently stem from the erroneous assumptions on which the scoring of the Rorschach is based.

Another widely used projective test is the **Thematic Apperception Test,** usually referred to simply as the **TAT** (Murray, 1943). The TAT differs from the Rorschach in that instead of giving responses to inkblots, individuals make up stories about pictures. Figure 3.4 contains a picture like those on the TAT. Theoretically, the stories the individual tells reflect the themes, problems, conflicts, and characters that are important in the individual's life.

As with the Rorschach, there are a number of problems with the TAT that undermine its usefulness. The most serious problem is that the TAT only measures traits that individuals *know they have,* and there is no evidence that individuals project traits of which they are unconscious (Holmes, 1968, 1981). For example, a hostile individual who believes that he or she is hostile will project that trait on the TAT, but a hostile individual who does not believe that he or she is hostile will not

A person taking the Thematic Apperception Test makes up stories that reflect underlying themes and problems from his or her life.

project that trait on the TAT at a rate greater than individuals who are not hostile. The fact that the TAT measures only conscious characteristics greatly limits its usefulness, and the results of a variety of investigations have revealed that simple self-reports are usually more effective than TAT stories for measuring personality (e.g., Holmes, 1971; Holmes & Tyler, 1968). For example, freshmen students' self-ratings of their levels of motivation were better predictors of their subsequent grades than were judges' rating of the students' levels of achievement motivation based on their TAT responses.

Another problem with the TAT is that individuals can *fake their responses* (Holmes, 1971). For example, in one investigation, students took the TAT twice, once responding honestly and once trying to hide their real personalities. Both sets of stories were then read by judges, and it was found that the judges came up with completely different personality interpretations for the two sets, and the judges could not identify which stories were the honest ones and which were the fakes!

Finally, even when an individual is not faking, there is a *problem with interpreting the stories* accurately because it is difficult to determine whether the traits that are being projected are the traits that the individual *possesses* or the *causes* of those traits. For example, if an individual describes people in the stories as hostile, it could mean that the individual is hostile, or it could mean that the individual is afraid because others are seen as hostile.

Another type of projective test is the **Incomplete Sentences Test** (Rotter & Rafferty, 1950), in which the individual is given a sheet with incomplete sentences like, "My mother . . . ," "What bothers me is that . . . ," and "Other people . . ." The individual then completes the sentence with whatever comes to mind first. In other projective tests, the individual is asked to draw a person (**Draw-A-Person Test;** Machover, 1949) or is asked to draw a house, a tree, and a person (**House-Tree-Person Test;** Buck, 1948). There is also a children's version of the TAT known as the CAT (**Children's Apperception Test;** Bellak, 1954). Most of these tests do not have formal scoring procedures. Instead, the interpretations are dependent on the subjective judgments and clinical intuition of the tester. In most cases, serious questions have been raised concerning the validity of these tests, but it is unclear whether the problem is with the principle on which the test is based, the test itself, or the skill of the tester.

For years, a hot debate has raged over the value of projective tests. On the one hand, the critics have argued that the objective research has revealed very little evidence that the tests help in making clinical judgments, and in fact that the tests may actually lead to errors (as I mentioned with regard to judgments based on the Rorschach). On the other hand, the advocates have argued that clinical experience with the tests suggests that they are revealing and helpful and that the lack of empirical evidence supporting their utility is the result of the insensitivity of the research methods that were used to assess them. In other cases, the users of the tests have agreed that the tests are without empirical support, but they continue to use them as a means of facilitating the interview process, much as "icebreakers" are used at parties. The debate over the value of projective tests has been going on for years, and although projective tests are still used widely, they are considered less important now than they were some years ago.

Intelligence Tests. Intelligence tests often play an important role in determining a diagnosis and developing a treatment plan because, for example, they can be used to help decide whether an individual's problems are due to mental retardation. Furthermore, the results of intelligence tests might also be used to determine what type of therapy might be most effective; for example, if testing revealed that the individual had poor reasoning skills, it might be concluded that psychotherapy would not be an effective treatment approach.

The intelligence tests used in clinical settings usually involve one-on-one interactions between an individual and an examiner during which the individual performs a series of tasks such as math problems and puzzles over the course of at least 2 hours. This type of testing allows for the assessment of various abilities and provides the examiner with an opportunity to watch the individual work so that the examiner can determine the reasons for poor performance and take them into consideration. For example, individuals who are excessively anxious or depressed may perform at levels below their actual ability, and that must be taken into consideration when interpreting the results of the test and predicting future performance.

Most of the individual intelligence tests contain subscales designed to measure **verbal intelligence** and **performance** **intelligence.** With the **Wechsler Adult Intelligence Scale (WAIS),** verbal intelligence is measured with six subtests:

1. Information (How far is it from New York to San Francisco?)
2. Comprehension (Why do we have laws?)
3. Arithmetic(A shirt that usually sells for $30 is reduced in price by 15% during a sale. What does the shirt cost during the sale?)
4. Similarities (How are a pound and an inch alike?)
5. Digit Span (Repeat the following list of numbers from memory: 2, 7, 9, 4, 8.)
6. Vocabulary (What does the word *overture* mean?)

Performance intelligence is measured with five subtests:

1. Picture Completion (looking at pictures of objects and determining what parts are missing)
2. Block Design (arranging blocks to form designs; see Figure 3.5)
3. Picture Arrangement (arranging a set of pictures to make a story)
4. Object Assembly (putting puzzles together)
5. Digit Symbol (learning to associate numbers with various symbols)

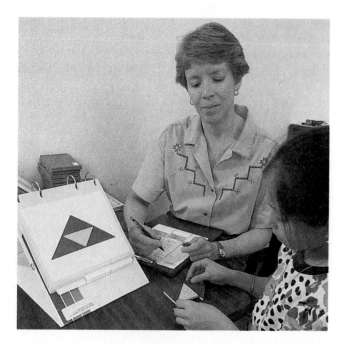

Intelligence testing often plays an important role in making a diagnosis and developing a treatment plan.

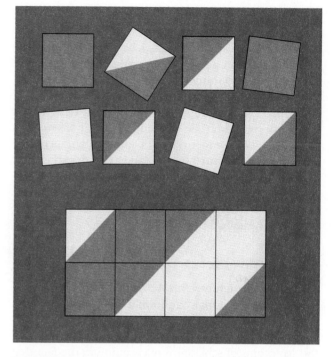

FIGURE 3.5 Block design is one subtest used to measure intelligence on the Wechsler Adult Intelligence Scale.

The most widely used test for individuals over 16 years of age is the **Wechsler Adult Intelligence Scale (Revised Edition),** generally known as the **WAIS-R.** For testing school-age children, there is the **Wechsler Intelligence Scale for Children (Third Edition),** known as the **WISC-III,** and for preschoolers, there is the **Wechsler Preschool-Primary Scale of Intelligence,** known as the **WPPSI.** The **Stanford-Binet** test can also be used with children. Because of the importance of measuring intelligence and because it is essential that the tests be unbiased with regard to culture or social class, new tests of intelligence are being developed constantly.

Individual intelligence tests are very reliable and effective for predicting school performance. Because they involve reasoning and problem solving, they can also be helpful for predicting performance in the real world. However, they are not without their problems, and I will discuss some of their limitations when I discuss mental retardation in Chapter 19.

Neuropsychological Tests. When it is suspected that an individual is suffering from some sort of organic brain damage, **neuropsychological testing** may be used to identify the location and nature of the damage. Such testing is based on the fact that different abilities are located in different areas in the brain, and therefore by measuring the pattern of an individual's abilities and disabilities, it is possible to make inferences about the location and extent of the brain damage. Some neuropsychological tests measure as many as 14 different abilities and may require a day to complete. The tests include such activities as puzzles that must be done while blindfolded, verbal tasks involving naming objects and concepts, and reaction time tasks.

Probably more important than locating the site of the damage is the fact that the testing can identify the nature of the resulting disability (e.g., loss of memory, loss of ability to form concepts, motor coordination problems). That is important in terms of designing a treatment program (i.e., deciding what abilities need to be retrained or compensated for) and making plans for the individual's future functioning (i.e., deciding how much help this individual will need in daily living). The two most frequently used neuropsychological tests are the **Halstead-Reitan Neuropsychology Battery** and the **Luria-Nebraska** battery.

Physiological Tests

Measuring Structures and Activity. Later in this book, you will learn that many abnormal behaviors are due to problems with structures in the brain or in activity levels in various areas of the brain. For example, some of the symptoms of schizophrenia are due to the fact that some parts of the brain have not developed properly or have deteriorated, and other symptoms of schizophrenia are due to the fact that some areas of the brain are overactive or underactive. For many years, it was not possible for us to see the structures of the live brain or to measure its activity, but we now have a variety of procedures for doing that, and those procedures have greatly enhanced our ability to understand and diagnose some forms of abnormal behavior.

The first technique used to assess the structures in the brain was the *X-ray*. Today, X-rays have been largely replaced by **computerized axial tomography** (to-MOG-ruh-fē), better known as the **CT scan**, and **magnetic resonance imaging**, better known as **MRI**. These techniques are similar to the X-ray in that they produce images of internal organs such as the brain. However, they differ in that rather than producing an image that shows all of the overlapping parts of the brain, with the CT and MRI techniques we get pictures of very thin "slices" of the brain, and therefore one part of the brain does not hide the parts behind it. An MRI of the human brain is presented in Figure 3.6.

The first technique that was used to measure the activity of the brain was the **electroencephalograph** (ē-LEK-trō-en-SEF-uh-lō-graf), which is usually simply called an **EEG** and is used to record the electrical activity of the brain. With this procedure, electrodes are placed at numerous locations on the skull to detect the underlying electrical activity. The procedure is analogous to putting your ear to the outside wall of a factory and listening to the sounds from inside in an attempt to determine where machines are running and how fast they are running; it works, but it is a rather primitive method.

A more recent and more sophisticated technique for measuring brain activity is **positron emission tomogra-**

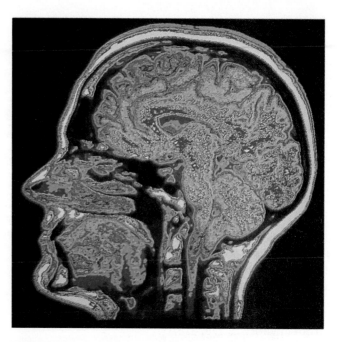

FIGURE 3.6 An MRI scan of the brain.
Source: Andreasen et al. (1986), p. 138, fig. 1.

phy, which is usually referred to as a **PET scan.** In the PET scan procedure, an *isotope* (radioactive agent) that binds to a particular chemical in the brain, such as glucose (blood sugar) or a neurotransmitter, is administered to the patient. Then, by recording where the isotope goes, we can measure the location and activity of the chemical of interest. We can record the location of the isotopes because they emit positrons, which can be recorded with equipment that is sensitive to radioactivity—hence the name *positron emission tomography*. The PET scan results in diagrams of activity in the brain taken *one slice at a time;* indeed, the word *tomography* comes from a Greek word meaning "section." PET scans reflecting glucose metabolism (energy use) in the brain of a patient during manic, normal, and depressed periods are presented in Figure 9.12 in Chapter 9. As you can see in that figure, certain areas of the brain are more active during the manic than the normal or depressed periods.

Measuring Reactions. In addition to measuring the structures and activities that cause symptoms, it is sometimes also important to measure physiological reactions such as elevations in heart rate or blood pressure during periods of anxiety. For example, we might want to know if the anxiety has resulted in chronically elevated blood pressure (hypertension). Blood pressure is measured with a **sphygmomanometer** (SFIG-mō-muh-NOM-uh-tur), and the principle is quite simple. An inflatable cuff is wrapped around the patient's arm just above the elbow and is inflated until the pressure in the cuff is high enough to pinch closed the arteries that carry blood down the arm to the hand. Then the pressure in the cuff is slowly reduced while the technician monitors the pressure and listens for a pulse in the artery just below the cuff. When the first pulse is able to get through, it means that the blood pressure is about the same as the pressure in the cuff, so the pressure in the cuff is noted and used as the measure of the **systolic** (sis-TOL-ik) **blood pressure.**

Another frequently used measure of responsiveness is the amount of moisture produced by your skin; when you are aroused, your hands become damp. That is measured by putting two electrodes on your fingers and passing a tiny electrical current (too small to be felt) from one electrode to the other. When your hands are moist, more of the current can get from one electrode to the other, and the amount of current that gets to the second electrode can be used as a measure of moisture and arousal. The bottom (smooth) line in Figure 3.7 shows the sudden change in the skin's conduction of current when a "dirty" word made the individual anxious (see point 1). With a neutral word, there was no increase (see point 2). The top line in Figure 3.7 is a measure of the blood flowing into the finger with each pulse, and as you can see, the amount of blood decreases when the individual becomes anxious. It is that decrease in blood that makes your hands cold when you are anxious. (Note that unlike skin conductance, blood flow does not return to its baseline quickly, and therefore it is a less useful measure.)

With this discussion as background, we can go on to consider some of the interesting and sometimes controversial issues associated with diagnostic testing.

ISSUES CONCERNING DIAGNOSTIC METHODS

Considerable progress has been made in the technical development and refinement of diagnostic techniques, but a number of basic issues remain troublesome and deserve comment.

Measurement of Transient Versus Enduring Traits

A paradox associated with personality testing is that even if a test is exceptionally effective for assessing the subtleties of thoughts and feelings at the time the test is given, it may not be effective for explaining past behavior or predicting future behavior. That is because some aspects of personality (and abnormality) can change, and therefore what we measure today may not have existed earlier or may not exist later. When projective

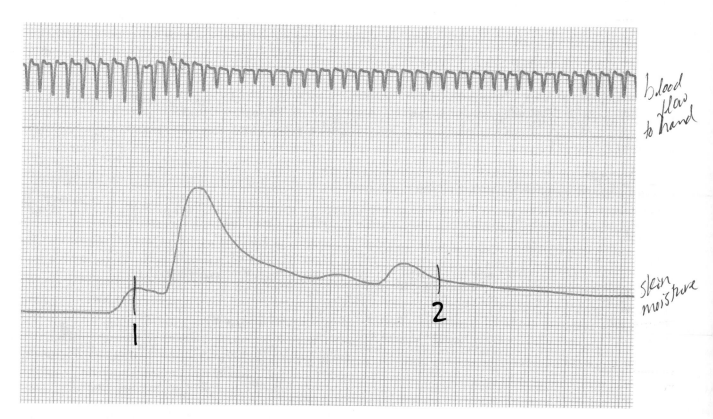

FIGURE 3.7 Increases in anxiety lead to increases in skin moisture and increases in skin conductance (see rise in bottom line). At point 1, the individual heard a "dirty" word; at point 2, the individual heard a neutral word. Increases in anxiety also reduce blood flow to the hands (see decreases in the size of pulse spikes in the top line). These effects explain why your hands feel damp and cold when you are anxious.

tests are criticized for being unreliable (yielding different results at different times), some clinicians defend the tests by suggesting that the tests are reliable but that the individual has changed and the test has picked up the change. However, even if it is true that the tests are sensitive to such changes and that is why they appear to be unreliable, the fact remains that the tests do not help us understand past behavior or predict future behavior.

Traits Versus Situations for Predicting Behavior

Our diagnostic procedures are designed to assess personality traits such as hostility, anxiety, motivation, and distractibility so that we can use those traits to explain past behavior and predict future behavior. However, it has been argued that behavior is determined by *situational factors* rather than personality traits (Mischel, 1990). For example, your professor may be reserved and constrained in class, but at a social gathering that same professor may be outgoing and uninhibited. Similarly, your friend may be relaxed and confident when alone but extremely anxious and fearful when in groups. One woman I knew felt sluggish because of low blood pressure (hypotension), but her symptoms went unexplained for years because she was very tense around physicians, and when they took her pressure, it rose to "normal." In these cases, behaviors, feelings, and physiological responses were determined by situations rather than personality traits.

There has been considerable controversy over the question of whether traits or situations are more important for determining behavior, but it now appears that both factors influence behavior. Specifically, it appears that the *level* of the trait and the *level* of the situational demands determine what will be the controlling factors. For example, an individual with a high level of hostility will probably behave in a hostile manner regardless of the situation (i.e., he or she will not be influenced by the situation), whereas an individual with a low level of hostility will behave in a hostile manner only in situations that call for hostility (i.e., he or she will be influenced by the situation). Obviously, traits and situations and the interaction between them must be considered in attempting to understand behavior. Unfortunately, most diagnostic tests do not take the situation into account. When predicting behavior, then, it may be appropriate to recall that when in Rome, individuals do what their test results suggest they will do, but they may also do what the Romans do.

Comorbidity

An individual can suffer from two or more psychological disorders at the same time (e.g., depression and schizophrenia), just as an individual may suffer from two or more physical disorders at the same time (e.g., diabetes and pneumonia). The co-occurrence of two disorders is called **comorbidity.** (The word *morbid* refers to disease, and *morbidity* refers to the *occurrence* of disease, so *comorbidity* means "the co-occurrence of two or more diseases.") Rates of comorbidity among some psychological disorders can be as high as 70%, so you should not be surprised if an individual qualifies for more than one diagnosis (Barsky, 1992; Brady & Kendall, 1992; Kendall, 1992; Rodhe et al., 1991; Sanderson et al., 1990).

There are three explanations for comorbidity, and they have different implications (Widiger et al., 1991). First, it is possible that in some cases individuals have two disorders at the same time simply by *chance* and that there is no connection between the two disorders. Second, it is possible that *one disorder leads to another.* For example, having an eating disorder may cause you to become depressed. Third, it may be that the *two disorders stem from a common cause.* For example, mood and appetite are both controlled by the same area of the brain, so a problem in that area could result in the comorbidity of depression and an eating disorder. Thus, when considering the diagnostic process, it is essential to recognize that comorbidity occurs and to examine patterns of comorbidity because they may provide clues to the causes of some disorders.

Comorbidity also has important implications for treatment. If you assume that the disorders co-occurred by chance, you would treat the disorders separately; if you assume that one led to another, you would treat the primary disorder; and if you assume that the disorders stem from a common cause, you would treat that cause. Finally, comorbidity may influence prognosis because the existence of one disorder may make the treatment of another disorder more or less difficult. For example, personality disorders may hinder the treatment of depression (Shea et al., 1992).

Subjectivity, Suggestion, and Diagnostic Fads

Despite all the attempts to make the diagnostic system objective, reliable, and valid, there is still a great deal of subjectivity in the system, and that leads to errors. The subjectivity is not in what symptoms lead to diagnoses, because the symptoms have been clearly laid out in DSM-IV or ICD-10. Rather, the subjectivity comes in the degree to which the individuals who are making the diagnoses look for particular symptoms, interpret ambiguous behaviors as symptoms, or even suggest symptoms to the individual. For example, one colleague of mine sees the symptoms of the multiple personality disorder in virtually every patient he sees, whereas most psychologists and psychiatrists never see one patient with a multiple personality disorder in their entire careers (see Chapter 7)! Do individuals with multiple personality disorders somehow seek out my colleague, are other therapists missing the diagnosis, or is my colleague biased in his probing for and interpretation of symptoms? I suspect that my colleague is biased. Similarly, in one hospital in which I worked, the staff was very interested in schizophrenia, whereas in a nearby hospital, the bipolar disorder (manic-depression) was of most interest. Each time patients were transferred between the two hospitals, their diagnoses were changed. Did the patients' symptoms and disorders change on the trip between the two hospitals? I doubt it.

It should also be noted that there are diagnostic fads during which a particular diagnosis is popular and will be widely used, only to taper off later. The obsessive-compulsive disorder provides a good case in point. In one 20-year period, there was an increase of more than 500% in the number of publications on that disorder, and in the same period the use of that diagnosis in one leading hospital increased by 400% (Stoll et al., 1992). Those findings are reflected in Figure 3.8. Clearly, diagnoses can be influenced by the specific interests of an individual who makes a diagnosis and by general fads that sweep through the profession occasionally. Unfortunately, both of those factors can reduce the validity of diagnoses.

Sociocultural Factors

It is essential to recognize at the outset that lower-class or ethnic minority group members are often less likely

to get into the mental health system (Mason & Gibbs, 1992; Paradis et al., 1994). Indeed, a number of studies have revealed that the proportion of ethnic minority individuals in the mental health system is substantially lower than their proportion in the general population. That is the case despite the fact that in some cases they suffer from a higher rate of psychiatric disorders. Some of those findings are presented in Figure 3.9.

Limited Access or Use. The fact that poor and ethnic minority individuals are less likely to be in the mental health system is due in large part to two factors related to the diagnostic process. First, poor individuals and those from minority groups are often *less likely to come in for diagnosis.* That is because they may (a) be less aware of the services that are available, (b) be less able to afford the services, (c) be more concerned about the stigma associated with seeking psychiatric help, (d) be more likely to view problems as physical rather than psychological, (e) have language barriers that keep them from seeking help, (f) have cultural backgrounds that provide nonpsychological explanations for their symptoms (e.g., possession by a spirit), or (g) have folk healers and cultural remedies such as exorcism that they use instead of psychological treatments. To overcome these obstacles, programs are being introduced to educate individuals about psychological problems and treatments, and attempts are also being made to make affordable services available in the communities in which the individuals live (see the discussion of community mental health centers in Chapter 21). Some years ago, there was a national program to make build-

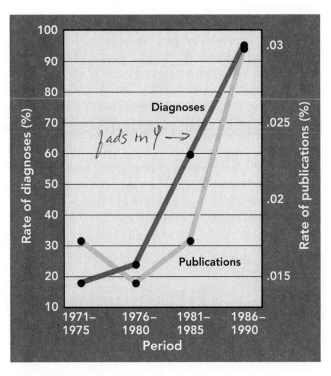

FIGURE 3.8 Publications on the obsessive-compulsive disorder and diagnoses of the disorder increased rapidly during the 1980s.
Source: Adapted from Stoll et al. (1992), p. 639, fig. 1.

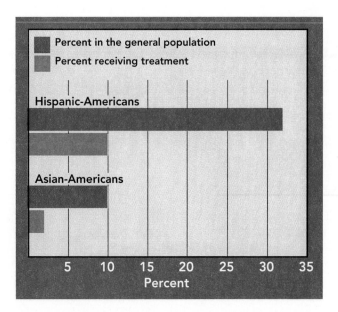

FIGURE 3.9 Members of minority groups are underrepresented in the mental health care system.
Source: Mason & Gibbs (1992), p. 449.

ings accessible to individuals with physical disabilities by eliminating physical obstacles and constructing wheelchair ramps; now we must focus our efforts on eliminating cultural obstacles and constructing "psychological ramps" to the treatment system.

Bias in Diagnostic Procedures. Unfortunately, getting poor individuals and members of ethnic minority groups "into the building" is only half the problem, because once in, they face a second problem, which is a *bias in diagnostic procedures.* That bias can come in numerous forms, but the most obvious is in *language.* Describing psychiatric symptoms is always difficult, but doing so across languages is almost impossible. (Imagine trying to explain your anxieties, depression, or hallucinations to someone in a foreign language you barely know!) For that reason, it is essential that the individuals who conduct the diagnostic evaluations be able to speak the language of the individuals whom they are evaluating. Similarly, it is necessary to have tests that are printed in the language that is spoken by the individuals being evaluated (Barbee, 1992). Fortunately, progress is being made in that area; for example, the MMPI is now available in different languages, and those new forms appear to be effective (Lucio et al., 1994; Timbrook & Graham, 1994).

A more subtle bias occurs when the individual who is conducting the evaluation does not thoroughly understand the other individual's culture, because that can lead to misunderstandings and misdiagnoses (Garretson, 1993; Good, 1992). That was illustrated in the case of a Guyanese woman who was suffering from panic attacks and agoraphobia. (Panic attacks are brief but

very intense feelings of anxiety that are associated with rapid heart rates, dizziness, and feelings that one is about to die; agoraphobia is a fear of going outside because something embarrassing might happen, such as a panic attack.) In describing her symptoms, the woman said:

> I feel like I'm going to die. . . . I worry it's not natural . . . not natural causes, evil like someone put a curse on me. . . . I'm afraid people might look at me and ridicule me because of how I look, people might talk about me." (Paradis et al., 1994, p. 611).

The woman's mention of a curse, which was consistent with her cultural beliefs, led the clinician to conclude, "The patient's bizarre delusion of an evil spirit inside her body" and "her paranoid delusions of people thinking she is ugly and laughing at her . . . all speak for the diagnosis of schizophrenia" (p. 611). In this case, then, what would ordinarily be diagnosed as a pair of simple anxiety disorders (panic and agoraphobia) was erroneously diagnosed as a very serious psychotic disorder (schizophrenia) because of the cultural insensitivity of the interviewer. Similarly, I know of an instance in which an Indian psychiatrist misdiagnosed a man as psychotic because in the interview the man referred to a woman who flew through the sky holding on to an umbrella. Of course, the woman was Mary Poppins, but the psychiatrist was not familiar with the story, so he assumed that the man was psychotic! The problem is that different cultures have different "realities," and we must be sensitive to those differences before we diagnose an individual as being "out of touch."

In other cases, the interviewer may be biased against seeing psychological problems in minority group members. For example, in one study, it was found that African-Americans who had washed their hands frequently because they suffered from the obsessive-compulsive disorder were not diagnosed as having a psychiatric disorder but instead were sent to dermatologists for treatment of skin conditions (Friedman et al., 1993). Problems such as these will be overcome when mental health professionals receive more training in cross-cultural and minority issues and when there is more ethnic diversity among mental health professionals.

Utility of Various Types of Diagnostic Information

Earlier in this chapter, I discussed a variety of sources of information about individuals that can be used in making diagnoses, including interviews, objective and projective psychological tests, and physiological tests. The question to be answered in this section is, what type of information is most helpful for making diagnoses? To answer that question, researchers have given clinicians different types of information about individuals and

Good communication is essential if diagnostic evaluation is to be complete and accurate.

then asked the clinicians to make judgments about the individuals. These investigations revealed some surprising findings (see Garb, 1985). For example, you might assume that watching an interview with an individual would yield better judgments than simply reading a transcript of the interview because the clinician could take into account the individual's gestures, vocal quality, and demeanor. However, that is not the case. Instead, clinicians were more accurate in making predictions about individuals when they only read the transcripts than when they watched videotapes of interviews. Similarly, clinicians were more accurate in making judgments when they were given only demographic information than when they were given demographic information and projective test (Rorschach, TAT) responses. Those findings suggest that the visual and auditory cues gained in interviews may distract the interviewer from the content of the interview that is most important and that interpretations of interview behavior and projective test responses may be inaccurate and lead to errors.

In sharp contrast to these negative findings are results indicating that the addition of MMPI responses to demographic data consistently led to more valid personality assessments. Furthermore, the addition of neuropsychological test results (Halstead-Reitan battery) to information from general IQ tests greatly increased the validity of judgments concerning brain damage. These results suggest that the most helpful information is information that is directly relevant and that does not require much interpretation, leaving little room for erroneous assumptions. The fact that the MMPI has consistently been found to add to the accuracy of predictions is particularly interesting because the MMPI is the least expensive and least time-consuming means of collecting information; the patient simply fills out a questionnaire and the responses can be quickly and inexpensively scored by computer.

This was clearly illustrated by an experience I had in a diagnostic case conference some years ago in which a group of psychiatrists, psychologists, nurses, and social workers were discussing the question of whether a particular patient was homosexual. (At the time, homosexuality was against the law, and it was assumed that the patient might be hiding his sexual orientation and that his orientation might have some bearing on his current problems.) While the argument went up and back and many scholarly theories and observations were offered, one psychologist became bored and fell asleep. The chief of staff became somewhat annoyed and in a loud voice said, "And Doctor Roberts, what do *you* think?" The psychologist jerked back to wakefulness and replied, "I, er, oh, he is a homosexual." The chief of staff challenged him by saying, "And what makes you think so?" to which the psychologist calmly replied, "I gave him an MMPI, and on every question that asked about homosexuality, he answered yes." Case closed! The point here is that in making diagnoses, it is best to use information that is *directly relevant* to the decision (e.g., measures of brain functioning for decisions concerning brain damage), and often direct measures such as self-report or observations are better than measures that require inferences or theories to connect them to the behaviors in question.

Clinical Versus Statistical Prediction

Up to this point, I have focused on what tests are used, how good the tests are, and which tests are most helpful. Missing in this discussion has been the diagnostician who uses the test results to make diagnoses or predictions about people. However, now I will turn to the role played by the diagnostician, usually a clinical psychologist. The question to be asked here is, are highly trained professionals more effective in making predictions from test results than relatively simple statistical formulas into which the test results are merely inserted? You might be surprised that I am even asking that question because it is widely assumed that diagnostic decisions must be made by trained professionals, but you may be even more surprised at the answer.

In the research on the effectiveness of clinical versus statistical prediction, information about individuals is collected, and then either the information is given to a group of professionals who use it to make predictions about the individuals or the information is inserted into formulas that are used to make predictions (the formulas generate scores that determine decisions, much like your test scores determine your grade in a course). The effectiveness of clinical as opposed to statistical procedures has been evaluated in the prediction of a wide variety of areas, including what diagnoses individuals will receive; how well individuals will perform in college, in medical school, or in the military; the likelihood that individuals will commit violent acts; the likelihood that individuals will commit other crimes after being paroled; and the intellectual performance of individuals following brain damage. The information that has been used to make those predictions has included things like the results of psychological tests, the results of IQ tests, school records, the history of drug use, and demographic factors such as age, gender, and social class.

Approximately 150 studies have been completed on the question of the accuracy of clinical versus statistical prediction, and the surprising finding is that in almost every study, *the statistical formulas resulted in more accurate predictions than the clinical judgments* (Dawes,

are professionals even needed?

1994; Dawes et al., 1989). In some studies the clinicians had the same information as was used in the formulas, and in other studies the clinicians had more information, but the results were the same—the formulas resulted in more accurate predictions. Furthermore, in some studies the clinicians were even given the results of the statistical predictions to use in making their own judgments, but whenever the clinicians attempted to "improve" on the statistical predictions, the accuracy of the predictions went down. It is also interesting to note that the poor performance of the clinicians was not due to the inclusion of some inept clinicians who brought the overall performance of the clinicians down. Indeed, when individual performances were examined, even the clinicians who did *best* did not do better than the statistical formulas.

It is clear that formulas outperform experts, but the question is, why? There seem to be two answers to that, the first of which is that *a formula can handle more information* at one time than a human can. Specifically, we know that humans can deal with only seven pieces of information at one time (plus or minus two), but predictions often require the consideration of many more pieces of information, and formulas do not have a limit in terms of the amount of information they can handle. Second, because some pieces of information are more important than other pieces, different pieces of information must be given different *weights* when making a prediction, and whereas humans are not particularly good at doing that, it can be done easily with formulas. *not good at priority*

Many professionals often attempt to deny or ignore the evidence concerning the effectiveness of statistical prediction because they find the evidence threatening, but that should not be the case. What is important is that we are able to build statistical formulas that can do better than we can do; not only do the formulas serve as effective tools, but they also free us up to do other things that formulas cannot do. Analogously, the fact that we built computers that can do computations faster and better than we can in our heads does not threaten or diminish us; rather we accept the computers as tools that help us work more effectively. (Do you calculate square roots in your head, or do you do them quickly on a calculator so you can get on to the more important aspects of the problem?) The statistical approach to prediction is slow in coming, but it is undoubtedly the way of the future.

From the foregoing discussions, it should be clear that diagnoses are essential for describing individuals and treating psychiatric disorders but that the process of arriving at valid diagnoses is difficult and fraught with problems. With this material as background, we can go on to consider the methods that are used for studying abnormal behavior.

RESEARCH METHODS

Finding the causes of abnormal behavior is like a complex mystery, and research methods are the tools we use to evaluate the clues and solve the mystery. An understanding of research methods will help you evaluate the current information about abnormal behavior that is contained in this book, but it will also help you evaluate the findings that you will read or hear about in the future. Unfortunately, many of the "breakthrough" findings that are touted in the media are not based on adequate research, and an understanding of research methods will make you a more sophisticated consumer of findings.

METHODS FOR STUDYING ABNORMAL BEHAVIOR

Research methods can be divided into four types: *case study, correlational, controlled experimental,* and *multiple-baseline experimental*. In the following sections, I will discuss the strengths and weaknesses of each type and illustrate how all four types are used in the attempt to answer one question: Does bad parenting lead to abnormal behavior?

Case Study Research : *aren't supportive evidence*

Through **case study research** we examine the life history of an individual in an attempt to formulate explanations for the individual's behavior. For example, when attempting to understand a disturbed patient, a clinician might learn that the patient's parents were hostile, rejecting, demanding, and only sometimes loving when the patient was a child. The clinician might then speculate that the patient's problems result from "bad parenting." Having observed this relationship in the one case, the clinician might hypothesize that bad parenting leads to abnormal behavior in general. Indeed, it was through a series of case studies that Freud developed his psychodynamic theory of abnormal behavior. Similarly, you have probably used the case history approach in attempting to understand and explain the behavior of some of your friends (e.g., "Kent is insecure on dates because when he first started going out, he got 'dumped on' a couple of times"), and you might then have gone on to use the explanations to account for the behavior of other individuals.

Case studies provide an excellent *source of hypotheses* (potential explanations) about the causes of abnormal behavior, but *they cannot be used to prove that a particular hypothesis is correct.* That is because with the case study, it is impossible to rule out other potential hypotheses. A patient may have received bad parenting, but the patient may also have seen high levels of violence on television, been frustrated in school, inhaled high levels of lead from automobile exhaust, grown up during a period of rapid cultural change, or inherited some defective genes. All of those factors have been used to account for abnormal behavior, but the case study does not allow us to determine which, if any, are responsible. Furthermore, it is also hazardous to form a general hypothesis on the basis of a case study because *we cannot determine the degree to which the relationship in one individual holds for other individuals.*

Another problem with case studies is that the observations are often *biased.* Once a clinician has a theory about the cause of a disorder, he or she may be very selective in what is reported about cases, and facts may even be distorted. For example, in one of Freud's famous case studies (that of Emma E.), he reported that a woman's nosebleeds were due to psychological causes, and he used that observation to support one of his theories. However, recently discovered letters between Freud and a colleague have revealed that Freud knew that the woman had undergone a series of operations on her nose and that during one operation a length of gauze had been accidentally left in her nasal cavity! It was the gauze rather than psychological conflicts that caused the nosebleeds, but Freud did not mention that in his case study (Masson, 1984).

Thus case studies can provide excellent descriptions of abnormal behavior, and they can suggest potential explanations for the behavior, but they cannot be used to *prove* explanations, and we must be careful about their objectivity. Numerous cases studies appear in this book, but they are included to provide descriptions of various disorders and not to suggest or support explanations.

Correlational Research

Correlational research is like case study research in that observations are made about the co-occurrence of two variables (e.g., bad parenting and abnormal behavior). However, in correlational research, observations are made of many individuals instead of just one, and then a statistical test is used to determine whether the relationship between the two variables holds for most people. For example, if we examined 100 individuals and consistently found that those who showed the most abnormal behavior had received the worst parenting

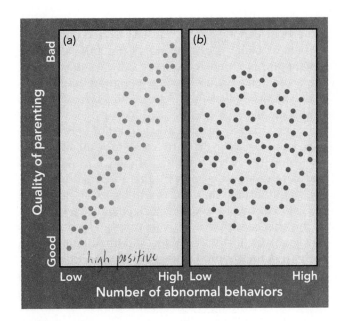

FIGURE 3.10 Scatter diagrams of correlational data: *(a)* positive correlation; *(b)* no correlation.

and that those who showed the least abnormal behavior had received the best parenting, we could conclude that there was a reliable correlation between quality of parenting and abnormal behavior. Such a relationship is presented graphically in part *(a)* of Figure 3.10. By contrast, if the relationship between quality of parenting and abnormal behavior was found in only a few of the people we studied, we could not conclude that there was a reliable correlation between parenting and behavior. Such a nonrelationship is presented graphically in part *(b)* of Figure 3.10.

The nature and strength of the relationship between two variables is expressed by means of a **correlation coefficient** (abbreviated *r*). Correlation coefficients range between + 1.00 and − 1.00. A high *positive* correlation (e.g., + .40 or + .60) indicates that individuals with *high* scores on one variable have *high* scores on the other variable (e.g., high levels of abnormal behavior are associated with high levels of bad parenting). A high *negative* correlation indicates that individuals who have *high* scores on one variable have *low* scores on the other variable (e.g., high levels of abnormal behavior are associated with low levels of bad parenting). A low correlation, regardless of its direction, indicates that there is little or no relationship between the two variables.

It is important to realize that a correlation between two variables does not necessarily mean that there is a *causal* relationship between the variables. Instead, it may be that the relationship is due to the influence of a third variable. For example, in the case of the correlation between bad parenting and abnormal behavior, it is possible that genetic factors caused both the parents and their offspring to behave in abnormal ways. Similarly, socioeconomic stress may have caused the parents to behave badly, and the same stress may also have caused the children to behave badly. In those cases, then, the relationship between parenting and abnormal behavior was actually due to the influence of a third variable.

Even if there is a causal relationship between two correlated variables, the correlation does not allow us to determine the *direction* of the causation. For example, if bad parenting was correlated with abnormal behavior, you might assume that bad parenting led to abnormal behavior, but it is possible that the abnormal behavior in the children frustrated the parents and led them to behave badly. In that case, the abnormal behavior on the part of the children caused the bad parenting.

In summary, correlational research enables us to determine whether there are reliable relationships between variables, but it does not enable us to conclude that a difference in one variable *causes* a difference in another variable. Furthermore, if there is a causal relationship, the correlation does not tell us the *direction* of the causation. To establish causal relationships, we must use the experimental approaches that will be considered next. *if there was one*

Controlled Experimental Research

In **experimental research,** we attempt to determine whether a difference in one variable *causes* a difference in another variable (Campbell & Stanley, 1963). The variable whose effects we are studying (e.g., parenting) is called the **independent variable,** and the variable that will be influenced (e.g., children's adjustment) is called the **dependent variable.** (An easy way to remember the names for the variables is to recall that the dependent variable is *dependent* on—or influenced by—the independent variable.)

The first step in **controlled experimental research** is the **random assignment** of the participants to **experimental** and **control conditions.** For example, as individuals arrive for the experiment, the first would be assigned to the experimental condition, the second to the control condition, the third to the experimental condition, and so forth. Random assignment is used in an attempt to make the participants in the two conditions comparable before the experiment begins. If the participants are randomly assigned, we assume that the participants in the two conditions are comparable, but to test that assumption, in some experiments the investigators compare the two groups with a **pretest** on the dependent variable.

The second step in controlled experimental research involves altering the independent variable in the experimental condition but not in the control condition, a procedure known as the **experimental manipulation.**

Finally, we use a **posttest** to measure the dependent variable in the two conditions. If a difference in the dependent variable is found between the individuals in the experimental and control conditions, we can assume that the manipulation of the independent variable caused the difference.

These steps can be illustrated in our hypothetical research concerning the link between parenting and abnormal behavior. To test that link, we would (a) randomly assign children to experimental and control conditions, (b) use a pretest to assess the levels of abnormal behavior in the two groups of children, (c) have the parents in the experimental condition intentionally use bad parenting techniques while the parents in the control condition use normal parenting techniques, and then (d) some years later use a posttest to assess the levels of abnormal behavior of the children in the two conditions. (Obviously, there is an ethical problem with intentionally having parents use bad parenting techniques that we think will lead to abnormality; we will discuss that later.) If children who received the bad parenting were found to have more abnormal behavior than those who received normal parenting, we could conclude that bad parenting caused abnormal behavior. Such an outcome is presented graphically in Figure 3.11.

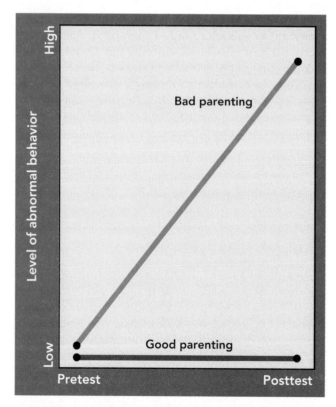

FIGURE 3.11 Results of a hypothetical experiment on good versus bad parenting.

controlled env.

In any experiment, *the participants in the experimental and control conditions must be alike and be treated alike except with respect to the independent variable.* If there are other differences between the groups, it will be impossible to determine which variable is responsible for the change that is observed in the dependent variable. For example, if we manipulated type of parenting but the participants in the bad parenting condition also happened to go to poorer schools, we could not determine whether their levels of abnormal behavior were due to bad parenting, poor schooling, or the combination of bad parenting plus poor schooling. If there is more than one difference between the conditions, the experiment is said to be **confounded.** (The word *confound* comes from a Latin word meaning "to pour together, confuse, ruin.") In the experiment just described, parenting and schooling are confounded, the results are confused, and the experiment is ruined.

Multiple-Baseline Experimental Research

Another way of experimentally testing the effects of an independent variable is to use a **multiple-baseline experimental research** procedure in which the participants are observed over a series of periods in which the independent variable is and is not manipulated. For example, in testing to determine whether hostility on the part of parents leads to social withdrawal in children, the social behavior of children would be observed for periods in which the parents (a) behaved in a normal way toward the children (first baseline period), (b) acted in a hostile manner toward the children (experimental period), and (c) again behaved in a normal way toward the children (second baseline period).

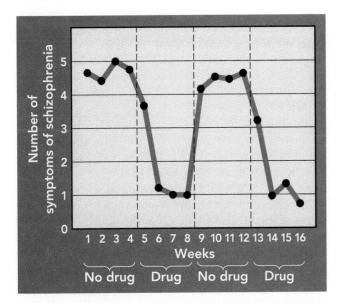

FIGURE 3.12 Results of a multiple-baseline experiment on the effects of a drug on symptoms of schizophrenia.

If the children showed more social withdrawal during the experimental period than during the baseline periods, it could be concluded that hostility on the part of parents caused social withdrawal in children. An example of results obtained with a multiple-baseline experiment is presented in Figure 3.12. In that experiment, the effects of a drug on the symptoms of schizophrenia was being tested, and the periods in which the patient was given the drug were interspersed with periods in which the patient was not given the drug. The results indicated that symptom levels were low during the drug periods and high during the no-drug (baseline) periods, therefore indicating that the drug was effective.

if drug

STRATEGIES FOR AVOIDING PRACTICAL AND ETHICAL PROBLEMS

Experiments are the best means of establishing causal relationships, but it is often impossible to conduct experiments because of practical problems. For example, when studying the effects of bad parenting, it is not feasible to get parents to behave badly toward their children for 10 years. Similarly, when studying the effects of prolonged stress, we cannot experimentally manipulate events such as wars, earthquakes, and deaths of family members.

It is also sometimes impossible to use experiments to study the causes of abnormal behavior because it is unethical to knowingly cause abnormal behavior. We could not do the experiment on the effects of bad parenting because it would be unethical to expose children intentionally to bad parenting techniques that we suspect will result in abnormal behavior. Similarly, we could not study the effects of brain damage on behavior by cutting out parts of the brains of individuals in an experimental condition. Because of these practical and ethical problems, we must sometimes rely on alternative techniques for studying the causes of abnormal behavior.

Animal Research

One strategy that is used to avoid some practical and ethical problems is to do experiments on animals. For example, when investigators were interested in determining the effects of extreme social isolation on the emotional development of infants, they raised monkeys in complete isolation (Harlow, 1959). In research on the effects of brain damage on abnormal behavior, parts of the brains of rats and monkeys were destroyed, and the effects on the animals' behavior were studied. However, research on animals does pose some problems. For example, there is always the practical

we can do cruel things to animals but not to humans

Animals are used in research when it is impractical or unethical to use humans. For example, to determine the relative importance of contact and feeding in forming attachments, this rhesus monkey was raised with a cloth "mother" and a wire "mother" that contained a feeding bottle. The study showed that the monkey preferred the cloth mother (contact) and went to the wire mother only for nourishment. Such a study could not have been conducted with a human infant.

problem of generalizing the results obtained with animals to humans. Is a monkey's emotional response comparable to a human's emotional response? Can a monkey develop schizophrenia? Furthermore, ethical standards also place limitations on what can be done with animals. Whereas once animals were treated as objects, today they are accorded many of the rights formerly reserved for humans, such as protection from undue pain.

Analogue Research

A second means of overcoming practical and ethical problems is to do **analogue** (AN-uh-log) **research.** An *analogue* is something that is *similar* to something else, and in analogue research, we study the effects of experimental manipulations that are similar to but not as

extreme as those in which we are really interested. For example, we cannot expose children to years of bad parenting, but we could bring children into a laboratory for an hour and have them interact with an individual who acted either in a mildly hostile manner (experimental condition) or in a neutral manner (control condition). We would not expect the brief experience with the mildly hostile individual to result in long-term serious abnormal behavior, but it could cause moderate and brief forms of tension, anxiety, or withdrawal. From that we might assume that if children were exposed to a more hostile individual for a longer period, real or more serious abnormal behavior would result. The problem with analogue research is that we can never be certain of the degree to which we can generalize from our analogous procedures to the real procedures in which we are interested.

Quasi-Experimental Research

A third means of avoiding some of the practical and ethical problems of experimental research is to use **quasi-experimental research** (Cook & Campbell, 1979). In quasi-experimental research, we do not actually manipulate the independent variable. Instead, we take advantage of naturally occurring situations in which there are differences in the independent variable. For example, if we were studying the effects of chronic stress on the development of depression, we might compare the people who live near a potentially dangerous nuclear power plant to those who live near a coal-fired power plant with an excellent safety record (Baum et al., 1983). If the people living near the two different types of power plants are the same on all other variables (age, sex, race, intelligence, socioeconomic status, ethnic background), but those who lived near the nuclear power plant are more depressed, we might conclude that the chronic stress of living near a dangerous power plant led to depression. The important thing to recognize about quasi-experimental research is that participants are not randomly assigned to conditions, and therefore we cannot be sure that the participants in the conditions are comparable on all variables except the independent variable. It is possible that the individuals living near the nuclear power plant were more depressed before moving to that community or that some factor in the community other than the stress of the nuclear plant led to the depression.

Delayed Treatment

When an experiment is conducted to test the effects of a particular treatment such as psychotherapy or drugs, the participants in the no-treatment control condition are not given any treatment. This raises an ethical problem because the experimenters are intentionally withholding a potentially effective treatment from individuals who need the treatment. Some researchers try to overcome this problem by arguing that when the experiment is conducted, they do not yet know for sure that the treatment is effective, and therefore they are not knowingly withholding an effective treatment from patients who need it. However, that argument is weakened by the fact that if they did not strongly believe that the treatment is effective, they would not be testing it. The ethical problem posed by withholding treatment may be avoided to some extent by providing the treatment to the participants in the control condition after the experiment is over. With such a **delayed treatment** procedure, everyone gets the treatment, but the patients in the control condition get it later. Giving the patients in the control condition delayed treatment can also add to our research findings because if the patients do not improve during the control (delay) period but then do improve when the treatment is begun, we have additional evidence from which to conclude that the treatment is effective. *quasi- multiple baseline*

Placebo and Double-Blind Procedures

Finally, there are two practical problems that can arise in research, especially in research on treatments for abnormal behavior. One problem is the so-called **placebo** (plu-SĒ-bō) **effect.** A placebo (e.g., a pill with no active ingredients) by definition has no therapeutic effect. However, some patients who are given placebos and who believe they are getting an effective treatment may show improvement in their conditions (A. Shapiro, 1980). For example, if patients are given colored water labeled "powerful pain reliever," they may actually experience some relief from their pain.

The second problem involves what are called **demand characteristics.** Individuals in experiments will sometimes intentionally do what they think the experimenter wants them to do regardless of whether the experimental manipulation was actually effective in changing their behavior (Orne, 1962). For example, patients in a treatment condition may report feeling better and act better because they think they *should* rather than because they actually *do*. Obviously, both the placebo effect and demand characteristics could influence the results of experiments on treatments and lead to conclusions that ineffective treatments were actually effective.

To avoid the problems associated with the placebo effect and demand characteristics, in research on treatments it is essential to include a placebo treatment condition in which the patients think that they are getting the treatment but in which the crucial element of the treatment is missing. In studying the effects of drugs,

we might have (a) a *treatment condition*, in which the patients receive pills containing active ingredients; (b) a *placebo condition*, in which the patients receive pills that do not contain active ingredients; and (c) a *no-treatment condition*, in which the patients do not receive any pills. The degree to which patients in the placebo condition show greater improvement than the patients in the no-treatment condition reflects the placebo effect, and the degree to which the patients in the treatment condition show greater improvement than the patients in the placebo condition reflects the actual effect of the treatment. This effect is illustrated in Figure 3.13. Note that placebo effects are not limited to drugs; they also occur with psychological interventions such as psychotherapy. Unfortunately, it is much more difficult to design a placebo control condition for an experiment on psychotherapy, but one is essential nevertheless.

The effects of suggestion influence not only the participants in experiments but also raters who are evaluating the participants. For example, if a depressed patient is given a treatment that the therapist thinks will help, the therapist may selectively notice improvements in the patient (e.g., smiles) and ignore behaviors

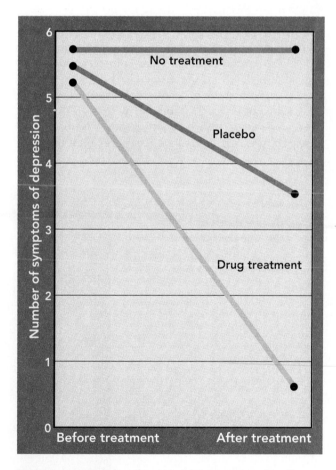

FIGURE 3.13 Results of an experiment comparing the effects of drug treatment, placebo treatment, and no treatment on the symptoms of depression.

that suggest lack of improvement (e.g., lack of activity). To avoid the effects of suggestion on both patients and raters, we can use a **double-blind procedure** in which neither the patients nor the raters know which patients are receiving the real treatment and which patients are receiving the placebo. That is, both patients and raters are *blind* to the conditions. In double-blind experiments on the effects of drugs, patients in the experimental condition are given pills containing active ingredients while those in the placebo condition are given pills with no active ingredients, but neither the patients nor the raters know which patients are receiving the medication and which are receiving the placebo. Actually, some double-blind experiments can be more difficult to pull off than you might think at first because some treatments produce side effects, and patients who experience no side effects may catch on to the fact that they are not getting the real treatment (Bystritsky & Waikar, 1994). In those cases, it is sometimes necessary to give the patients in the placebo condition a drug that causes the side effects but not the treatment effect. *ack!*

GENETIC RESEARCH

Genetic factors are playing an increasingly important role in our understanding of many physical and psychological disorders, and therefore it is essential to have an understanding of the procedures, promises, and pitfalls of this area of research (Plomin, De Fries, & McClearn, 1990; Reiss et al., 1991). Genetic research is not a *type* of research, like correlational and experimental research.

Rather, it is a *topic* of research, but because it involves some unique procedures and problems, it deserves special attention in this discussion of research methods.

Research Methods

The effects of genes are usually studied indirectly, and there are three methods by which that is done. The first is **family studies,** a method that is based on the fact that members of a biological family share more genes with one another than they share with non–family members. If abnormal behavior is due to genetic factors, it would be expected that the biological relatives of individuals with a particular disorder would be more likely to have the disorder than the biological relatives of individuals who do not have the disorder. In other words, it would be expected that abnormal behavior would "run in families." However, even if it were found that a disorder did run in families, we could not necessarily conclude that the disorder was due to genetic factors because family members usually share the same environment as well as some of the same genes.

The second method involves **twin studies. Monozygotic** (MON-ō-[zimacron]-GOT-ik; MZ) or "identical" twins have *identical* genes, and **dizygotic** (DĪ-zī-GOT-ik; DZ) or "fraternal" twins do not, so if a disorder is due to genetic factors, the disorder will be more likely to co-occur in MZ than DZ twin pairs. The rate of co-occurrence is called the **concordance** (kun-KOR-dens) **rate.** (The word *concordance* is based on *concord*, which means "agreement.")

With data obtained from monozygotic and dizygotic twins, we can estimate the degree to which a particu-

Studying monozygotic ("identical") twins who were reared apart is one way to determine genetic influences on behavior. These twins were separated at birth and reunited at age 32. Both had become firefighters and apparently share many personality traits.

$2(MZr - DZr)$

lar characteristic such as depression is due to genetic factors. The simplest way to do that is to compute correlations that reflect the concordance rates in DZ and MZ twin pairs, then subtract the correlation for DZ twin pairs from the correlation for MZ twin pairs, and finally multiply the difference by 2. For example, if depression is correlated .15 in DZ twin pairs and .40 in MZ twin pairs, we could conclude that about 50% of the variability in depression is due to genetic factors (.40 − .15 = .25 × 2 = .50; Falconer, 1960). That formula provides only a rough estimate (and sometimes an overestimate) of the effects of genes; a variety of more complicated and sophisticated methods have been developed that can provide us with more accurate and additional information.

One potential problem in the study of twins is the possibility that pairs of MZ twins share more personal experiences than pairs of DZ twins (e.g., greater overlap of friends, similar dressing), and if that were the case, part of the higher concordance rate among MZ twins could be due to their shared experiences rather than to their shared genes (Loehlin & Nichols, 1976). There is now strong evidence that the overlap in experiences is not an important factor, but we should keep that potential criticism in mind (Kendler, 1993; Plomin, De Fries, & McClearn, 1990).

The third method for studying genetic factors involves **adoptee studies.** With this method, investigators examine the rates of a disorder in children who were born to disordered or normal parents but were adopted at birth and raised by parents without the disorder. The children have the genes of either disordered or normal parents, but they are all raised in normal social environments. Therefore, if the offspring of disordered parents show a higher rate of the disorder than the offspring of normal parents, it could be concluded that genetic factors contributed to the development of the disorders. For example, in the case of schizophrenia, there is strong evidence that the biological children of parents with schizophrenia have higher rates of schizophrenia than the biological children of normal parents even when all of the children were raised by adoptive parents. This is the most convincing of the indirect methods.

A fourth approach involves studying genes themselves, a strategy that has been made possible by recent technological advances. A variety of reports have been based on this approach, but the findings have been very inconsistent, and therefore this approach has not yet yielded many firm conclusions.

Genetic Research and Environmental Factors

If we can determine how much of the variability in a disorder is due to genetic factors, by subtraction we can determine how much may be due to environmental factors. In the earlier example on depression, 50% of the variability was due to genetics, so as much as 50% of the variability could be due to environmental factors. However, two qualifications concerning that conclusion should be noted. First, when considering environmental variables, it is essential to recognize that they are not limited to the *social* variables such as economic class, interpersonal relations, and conflict, which are usually what is thought of when the concept of environment is mentioned. Environmental factors also include a host of *physiological* variables such as hormone exposure and maternal illness during prenatal development, complications during the birth process, and exposure to physical traumas and toxins such as lead later in life. We are now learning that these nonsocial environmental factors are very important in a variety of disorders.

Second, we may *overestimate* the amount of variability due to environmental factors when we subtract the variability due to genetics from the total variability (100%) and assume that the remaining variability is due to environmental factors. The problem is that other sources of variability such as errors in our measurement are also included in that remaining variability, thus artificially inflating the amount of variability that we attribute to environmental factors. Indeed, it has been estimated that errors in our measurement of personality and abnormal behavior may contribute between 15% and 30% of the variability that is not accounted for by genetic factors (Tellegen et al., 1988). That was illustrated in a study in which the investigators measured the abnormality in twins twice rather than only once as is usually done, figuring that if they missed a problem on one occasion they might pick it up on the second occasion (Kendler, Neale, et al., 1993a). The results indicated that when the more sensitive double measurement procedure was used, the amount of variability that could be attributed to genetic factors went up by about 20%. Clearly, the variability that remains after the variability that is due to genetics is removed is due to environmental factors plus other factors such as errors.

A FEW WORDS ABOUT STATISTICS

After data have been collected, it is essential that they be evaluated objectively, and to do that we use a wide variety of **statistical tests.** A thorough discussion of these tests is beyond the scope of this book, but a few general comments are necessary to put the test results into perspective so that you can evaluate them.

Most statistical tests are used to assess the *reliability* of the findings of an investigation. For example, if we collect data and then compute a correlation between

CASE STUDY 3.1

Research on Exercise and Depression: An Example of the Process

In my laboratory at the university, my students and I study stress and the physiological processes that are associated with stress. One day while we were working on a particularly difficult problem, I became frustrated and grumpy, so I took a break and went for a run. (I usually run about 6 miles a day.) When I returned from the run, I felt much better, and later my students and I talked about how running often helps me reduce stress. During that discussion, one of my students suggested that we study the effects of running on stress and possibly on depression. She joked that I provided a good *case study* but that we needed to study the effects of exercise on "real people." Everyone thought it was an interesting idea, so that day a new research program was launched.

The first thing we did was to conduct a simple *correlational study.* Specifically, we asked a group of students to fill out questionnaires concerning their levels of exercise and their levels of depression. When we computed a correlation between their exercise scores and their depression scores, we found a *statistically significant negative correlation* of −.27; that is, we found that higher levels of exercise were reliably associated with lower levels of depression. That suggested that there was a relationship between exercise and depression, but of course the correlation did not allow us to answer the question of whether exercise led to lower levels of depression or whether depressed individuals were less likely to exercise.

To answer that question, we conducted an *experiment* in which the question was, do individuals who exercise show greater reductions in depression than individuals who do not exercise? First, we administered a questionnaire that measured depression to a large number of women students, and then we invited the 45 women who were most depressed to participate in the experiment (they all agreed). Next, the women were *randomly assigned* to three conditions. The first condition was the *exercise condition;* the

women in that condition went to the gym twice a week for 10 weeks for a strenuous aerobic exercise class, and they were also asked to work out on their own at least two other times during each week. The second condition was a *placebo condition;* the women in that condition were taught relaxation exercises, and they were asked to use those exercises 4 days per week for 10 weeks. It is important to note that the women in both the exercise and the placebo conditions were told that there was evidence that the treatments they were receiving were effective for reducing depression, and therefore the women in both of those conditions expected improvements in their depressions. However, we had no reason to believe that relaxation exercises would reduce depression. The third condition was a *no-treatment condition;* the women in that condition were told that there were no longer any openings in the treatment conditions and that therefore their treatment would be temporarily postponed. All of the women completed self-report measures of depression at the beginning of the project (the *pretest*), after 5 weeks (the *midtreatment test*), and after 10 weeks (the *posttest*). The results are presented in the accompanying figure.

The statistical tests that were conducted on the data revealed that the women in the exercise condition showed significantly greater declines in depression than the women in the placebo or no-treatment conditions. More specifically, there was not a significant difference among the scores for the three conditions at the pretest, but on both the midtreatment test and the posttest, the women in the exercise condition reported significantly lower levels of depression than the women in the placebo and no-treatment conditions. On the midtreatment and posttests, the women in the placebo condition reported slightly lower levels of depression than the women in the no-treatment condition, but those differences were not statistically significant, indicating

scores measuring "bad parenting" and scores measuring "maladjustment in children," we might find that the scores are correlated +.30. Once we have the correlation, we have to determine whether it reflects a *real* relationship that would be found again if we collected a new set of data or whether it is due to *chance*—a one-time fluke. To make that determination, we use a statistical test that will indicate how

many times in 100 we could expect that particular correlation to occur by chance. If the results of the test indicate that the correlation would be expected to occur *fewer than 5 times in 100 by chance,* we can conclude that the correlation is **statistically significant.** Stated in another way, a statistically significant result is one that would be expected to occur in at least 95% of investigations (i.e., 95 times out of 100). Similarly, if

that expectancies alone were not sufficient to reduce depression. Overall, then, these findings indicated that exercise was effective for reducing depression and that the effects were not due to a placebo (expectancy) effect.

In this experiment, the results were statistically significant, but the question is, were the results also *practically* or *clinically significant?* The answer is probably yes. As I pointed out earlier, one measure of clinical significance is whether the treatment is effective for moving individuals from one category to another, and that did happen in this experiment. Specifically, the women began the experiment with depression scores of about 12, which are thought to reflect "clinical" levels of depression, but by the end of the treatment period, the women in the exercise condition had scores of about 3, which are considered to be in the "normal" range. In contrast, the women in the placebo and no-treatment conditions did not move into the normal range. It could therefore be concluded that the exercise was effective for achieving reductions in depression that were reliable (statistically significant) and practically important (clinically significant).

You might have noted that there was a potential ethical problem with this experiment in that we withheld what we thought was an effective treatment (exercise) from some seriously depressed individuals who needed treatment. To some extent, that problem was overcome by giving the exercise treatment to the women in the placebo and no-treatment conditions after the experiment was over. However, that is not a perfect solution because the women in the placebo and no-treatment conditions did have to endure their depressions for 10 weeks longer than necessary. (What would we have said if one of the women from whom we had temporarily withheld treatment had committed suicide during that 10-week period?)

This experiment answered an interesting and

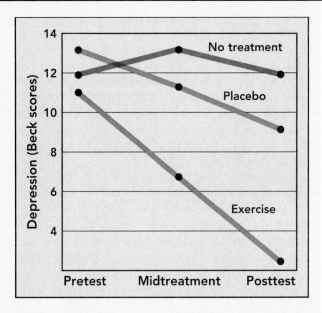

Women who exercised showed greater reductions in depression than women in a placebo or a no-treatment condition.
Source: From "Influence of Aerobic Exercise on Depression" by I. L. McCann and D. Holmes, in *Journal of Personality and Social Psychology–1984.* Vol. 46. Copyright © 1984 by the American Psychological Association. Reprinted with permission.

important question concerning the relationship between exercise and depression, but it also raised other questions: For example, what is it about exercise that reduces depression? Is exercise as effective as psychotherapy for reducing depression? Does the depression come back when the exercise is stopped? Would the same effects be found with men? Those questions led to other experiments, but as the saying goes, that's another story. . . . The process of research almost never ends.

Sources: Holmes (1993); McCann & Holmes (1984).

we conduct an experiment and find that children who were treated badly have a mean maladjustment score of 40, whereas the children who were treated well have a mean maladjustment score of 10, we have to determine whether the difference in means was due to the way children were treated or to chance. If a statistical test indicates that the difference in means would be expected to occur fewer than 5 times in 100

by chance, we can conclude that the difference in means is statistically significant.

This is fairly straightforward, but there are two conceptual problems you should keep in mind. First, the results may be statistically significant, but *if the experiment is confounded, the results are meaningless* (see the earlier discussion of confounds). In other words, the fact that the results are statistically significant does not mean that they are valid. In evaluating any finding, it is essential to determine whether it is methodologically sound.

The second problem stems from the use of the word *significant*. Most people assume that the word significant means "important," but as used by statisticians, the word *significant* means "reliable." Therefore, it is essential that you not misinterpret a "statistically significant" (reliable) effect as necessarily important because a great many statistically significant findings are in fact *trivial.* For example, we may find that a particular treatment has a statistically significant effect on patients' depression scores, but the treatment may change the scores by only 2 points on a scale that runs from 1 to 100. The 2-point change may be statistically significant (reliable) but trivial.

The problem of differentiating between statistically significant and important findings can be easily illustrated with a correlation. To determine the strength of a correlation, *square* it, and the resulting value will indicate the percentage of variability in one variable that can be accounted for by the other variable. For example, correlations of .30 are typical in the behavioral sciences and are often reliable, but with a correlation of .30 you can account for only 9% of the variability! That is, if parenting and abnormal behavior were correlated .30, knowing how bad the parenting had been would allow us to account for only 9% of the differences in behavior.

Because our statistical tests assess only statistical significance, it is essential that we also determine the **clinical significance** or practical importance of our findings. A variety of attempts has been made to develop a quantitative approach to determining clinical significance, but they have been largely unsuccessful, and in most cases clinical significance is assessed with a *subjective* judgment (Jacobson, 1988; Jacobson & Truax, 1991; Speer, 1992). One judgment that has been recommended for results concerning treatment involves determining when the change in the patients' scores on abnormality are sufficient to move the patients

from one category to another, such as from "depressed" to "normal" (Ogles et al., 1995). Statistically significant changes that moved patients to the "normal" category would also be considered as clinically significant.

Finally, it is important to recognize that there is often a bias in what findings are published; specifically, findings that are statistically significant are published, whereas those that are not significant are not published. This poses a problem because sometimes an investigator may find a statistically significant result and it will be published, but when other investigators who conduct similar investigations do not find statistically significant results, their results are not published. When that happens, an erroneous finding remains uncorrected in the literature and may mislead researchers. The bias in publication was illustrated in a comparison of the results of published and unpublished studies on the effectiveness of family therapy for treating abnormal behavior (Shadish et al., 1993). The published and unpublished studies were equally good in terms of design, but the published studies indicated stronger effects for the family therapy, and that would tend to distort the conclusions that readers would draw from the reports. Unfortunately, there is no simple solution to this problem.

In summary, then, just as all that glitters is not gold, all results that are statistically significant and published are not necessarily important or reliable, and we must be careful to separate the important from the trivial among the "significant." All of the research findings reported in this book are statistically significant (reliable), and I have attempted to select findings that were clinically or theoretically significant as well.

In the foregoing discussion, I have summarized the basic elements of research design and statistics, and with that as background, in Case Study 3.1 (pp. 82–83) I briefly describe a research program that was conducted in my laboratory. In that description, you can see how the elements of research fit together "in the real world."

SUMMARY

TOPIC I: DIAGNOSTIC TECHNIQUES

- ■ A diagnostic system helps us describe individuals who suffer from abnormalities and helps us decide how to treat them.
- ■ The diagnostic system used in the United States is contained in the *Diagnostic and Statistical Manual of Mental Disorders,* fourth edition, known as DSM-IV, and the system used elsewhere in the world is the *International Classification of Diseases,* 10th edition, known as ICD-10.

■ In DSM-IV, the symptoms for each disorder are listed, assumptions about causes are not made, and five axes are used in making a diagnosis.

■ The axes in DSM are as follows:

1. *Clinical Syndromes,* which includes the major disorders such as anxiety, depression, and schizophrenia

2. *Personality Disorders and Mental Retardation,* which includes the personality disorders, such as the obsessive-compulsive disorder and the dependent personality disorder, and the diagnoses pertaining to mental retardation

3. *General Medical Conditions,* which contains medical disorders that might be relevant for understanding and treating the individual

4. *Psychosocial and Environmental Problems,* including factors that might influence individuals' diagnoses, treatment, and prognosis

5. *Global Assessment of Functioning,* a scale on which the individuals' current and previous level of functioning can be rated

■ Any diagnostic system poses problems in that (a) unique aspects of individuals may be lost, (b) we may attribute characteristics to individuals as a function of their diagnoses, and (c) we often use a diagnosis to refer to an entire individual (a "schizophrenic") when the diagnosis only applies to one particular aspect of the individual.

■ There are four major techniques for assessing abnormal behavior:

1. Observations can be used to assess behavior and the effects of situational factors, but observations are often impractical and sometimes raise ethical questions.

2. Interviews enable individuals to tell us how they feel and react, thus sometimes substituting for observation, and we can also observe the behavior that occurs during the interview. Problems with interviews stem from the honesty or accuracy of the reports and the validity of the inferences that the interviewer draws.

3. Psychological tests can be divided into four types:

   a. Objective personality tests are like interviews in that the individuals can report how they feel and react, but the tests are often more comprehensive and time-efficient than interviews. The most widely used test is the MMPI.

   b. Projective tests are those in which individuals project their personality characteristics and feelings on to ambiguous stimuli such as inkblots and meaningless pictures. The best-known projective tests are the Rorschach and the TAT. Problems with these tests revolve around the subjective nature of the interpretation of the responses. Individuals can fake responses to the tests, and the tests measure only characteristics of which the test takers are aware.

   c. Intelligence tests are used to measure individuals' abilities in different areas (information, comprehension, arithmetic, vocabulary), and with individually administered tests, the administrator can observe the performance and make judgments about when and why problems with functioning arise. One very widely used test is the WAIS-R.

   d. Neuropsychological tests are used to identify the nature, location, and effects of brain damage. The best-known tests of this type are the Halstead-Reitan Neuropsychology Battery and the Luria-Nebraska battery.

4. Physiological tests can be used to measure the structures in the brain; for that we use X-rays, CT scans, and MRI scans. Brain activity is measured with EEGs and PET scans. Physiological reactivity is measured with tests of blood pressure and skin conductivity.

■ Seven issues or problems are associated with diagnostic methods:

1. We may be able to assess what individuals are like at the time of the assessment, but because individuals change, the results may not be helpful in understanding how the individual was in the past or will be in the future.

2. Our ability to understand and predict behavior from personality assessments may not be sufficient because to some extent behavior is determined by situational factors.

3. Comorbidity refers to the fact that an individual can suffer from two or more disorders at one time. The comorbidity of disorders may be due to (a) the chance occurrence of the two disorders at the same time, (b) the fact that one disorder leads to another disorder, or (c) the fact that both disorders stem from a common cause.

4. The diagnostic process can be influenced by the facts that diagnosticians may (a) subjectively focus on one symptom or disorder and thereby ignore others, (b) implicitly suggest symptoms to clients, and (c) be influenced by current fads.

5. Sociocultural factors can influence who receives diagnoses because individual who are poor or from ethnic minority groups are often less likely to use psychiatric services. Furthermore, when those individuals do use the services, their diagnoses may be biased because of language problems or because diagnosticians misinterpret behaviors due to unawareness of the cultural significance of the behaviors.

6. Objective information such as demographic information and self-reports that are directly related to the behaviors in question are more helpful for making predictions than inferences based on observations in interviews or projective test responses.

7. Statistical formulas that employ basic quantifiable data have been consistently found to be more effective for making predictions than the subjective judgments made by diagnosticians. That is probably because the formulas can handle more information and are more effective for applying weights to different pieces of information.

TOPIC II: RESEARCH METHODS

■ There are four basic methods for studying behavior:
1. Case studies are based on observations about an individual. Although they are a good source of hypotheses, case studies cannot be used to determine cause-and-effect relationships or whether similar relationships would hold for other individuals, and the observations are often biased.

2. Correlations are used to determine whether relationships are reliable over many individuals, but we cannot determine causal relationships on the basis of correlations.

3. Controlled experimental research involves the manipulation of an independent variable in the experimental condition but not in the control condition and then noting changes in the dependent variable.

4. Multiple-baseline research involves the repeated introduction and withdrawal of an independent variable over a series of trials while changes in the dependent variable are measured.

■ There are five strategies for dealing with practical and ethical problems:
1. Animals may be substituted for humans in some research, but care must be used not to violate the rights of the animals.

2. Analogue research involves using procedures that are similar to procedures that we would like to study, but that may not be practical or ethical. The problem with this approach is that we do not know how comparable the analogue procedures are to the procedures in which we are really interested.

3. Quasi-experimental research takes advantage of naturally occurring situations in which there are differences in the dependent variable. Confidence in the findings is limited by the fact that individuals are not randomly assigned to conditions.

4. Delayed treatment can be used to overcome the problem of withholding potentially helpful treatments from individuals in a control condition.

5. Placebos are used to test for the effects of expectancies on the part of research participants. Double-blind procedures are used to eliminate the possibility of expectancy effects for participants and assessors.

■ The effects of genes are studied indirectly by (a) studying the degree to which disorders run in families, (b) comparing the concordance rates in monozygotic versus dizygotic twin pairs, and (c) comparing siblings who were adopted and raised separately. Variability that is not accountable for by genes may be due to physiological factors in the environment, social factors in the environment, or errors in measurement.

■ Statistical results indicating that a finding is "significant" mean that the finding is reliable, usually that it will occur fewer than 5 times in 100 by chance. The clinical (or practical) significance of findings is based on subjective judgments, such as whether a treatment moves an individual from one category to another (e.g., from clinically depressed to normal).

KEY TERMS, CONCEPTS, AND NAMES

In reviewing and testing yourself on what you have learned from this chapter, you should be able to identify and discuss each of the following.

adoptee studies

analogue research - Similar

Axis I: Clinical Syndromes

Axis II: Personality Disorders

Axis III: General Medical Conditions

Axis IV: Psychosocial and Environmental Problems

Axis V: Global Assessment of Functioning

case study research

checklists of symptoms

Children's Apperception Test

clinical significance

comorbidity

computerized axial tomography (CT scan)

concordance rate - do both twins have it?

confounded

control condition

controlled experimental research

correlational research

correlation coefficient (r) - degree/relation

decision tree

delayed treatment

demand characteristics - when in Rome

dependent variable - influenced

diagnostic system - System in DSM

dizygotic

double-blind procedure

Draw-A-Person Test

DSM-IV

electroencephalograph (EEG)

experimental condition

experimental manipulation

experimental research

family studies

Halstead-Reitan Neuropsychology Battery

House-Tree-Person Test

ICD-10

Incomplete Sentences Test

independent variable - influences

intelligence tests

interview

Luria-Nebraska - neuro Y

magnetic resonance imaging (MRI)

Minnesota Multiphasic Personality Inventory (MMPI, MMPI-2, MMPI-A)

monozygotic

multiple-baseline experimental research

neuropsychological testing

objective personality tests - MMPI-2

observation

performance intelligence - puzzles, blocks

physiological testing

placebo effect

positron emission tomography (PET scan)

posttest

pretest

projection

projective personality tests

psychological tests

quasi-experimental research - using nat. occuring situations

random assignment

reliability

Rorschach test

sphygmomanometer

Stanford-Binet

statistically significant - <5 by chance

statistical tests

structured interview

systolic blood pressure

Thematic Apperception Test (TAT)

twin studies

unstructured interview

validity

verbal intelligence

Wechsler Adult Intelligence Scale (WAIS, WAIS-R) r18

Wechsler Intelligence Scale for Children, Third Edition (WISC-III)

Wechsler Preschool-Primary Scale of Intelligence (WPPSI)

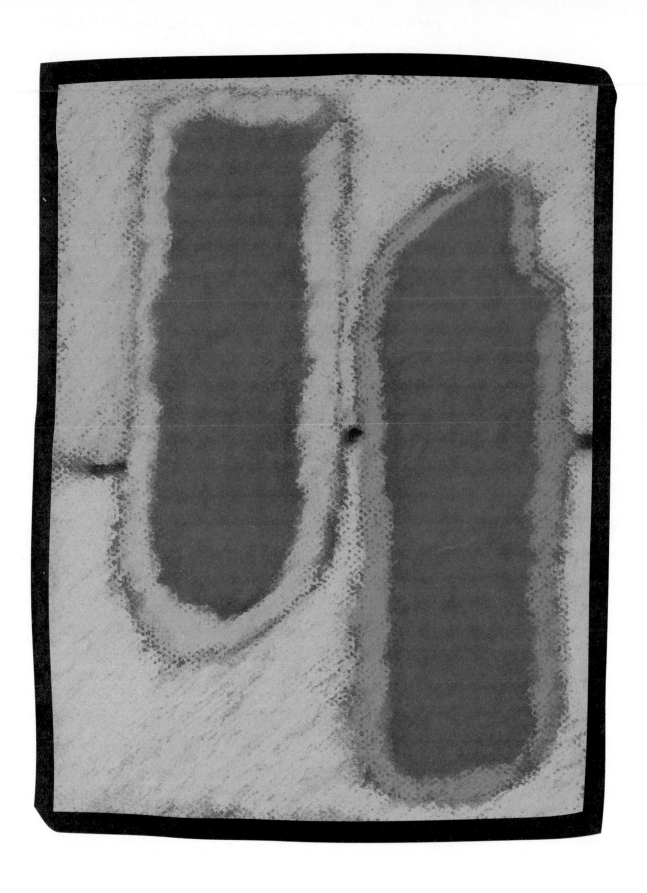

CHAPTER FOUR

ANXIETY DISORDERS: SYMPTOMS and ISSUES

OUTLINE

Symptoms of Anxiety
  Mood Symptoms
  Cognitive Symptoms
  Somatic Symptoms
  Motor Symptoms
Organization of Anxiety Disorders
Phobic Disorders
  Agoraphobia
  Social Phobia
  Specific Phobia
Anxiety States
  Generalized Anxiety Disorder
  Panic Disorder
  Obsessive-Compulsive Disorder
  Posttraumatic Stress Disorder
  Acute Stress Disorder

Issues Associated with Anxiety Disorders
  Normal Versus Abnormal Anxiety
  Prevalence of Anxiety Disorders
  Sociocultural Factors
    Gender
    Age
    Social Class
    Ethnicity
  Fear Versus Anxiety
  Trait Anxiety Versus State Anxiety
  Cognitive Anxiety Versus Somatic Anxiety
Summary
Key Terms, Concepts, and Names

hypoglycemic?

Four months ago, while Elaine was in a clothing store, she began trembling. Suddenly, she developed a sharp pain in her chest, and her heart began beating very rapidly. She was dizzy and short of breath and felt as though she were going to pass out or die. Everything was out of focus and seemed to be spinning around. She was terrified! A saleswoman called an ambulance, and Elaine was rushed to the emergency room of a nearby hospital. Tests did not reveal any evidence of a heart attack or any other abnormality. Since that first attack, she has had two others, one while at a movie and one that woke her from a very deep sleep. These attacks "just come out of the blue" and are very frightening. Elaine suffers from a *panic disorder,* a type of anxiety state.

■ ■ ■

David is afraid of snakes. Whenever he sees even a small garden snake that he knows is harmless, his palms sweat, his heart rate increases dramatically, and he feels very tense. In fact, he becomes tense when he sees snakes on television. He also shows some anxiety when he sees other reptiles such as alligators. David knows that his fear of snakes is irrational, but he cannot control his emotional response. David suffers from a *phobia.*

■ ■ ■

Over a period of a year, Mrs. Wilson began leaving her house less and less, and usually she would not go out unless someone was with her. She could not explain exactly what she was afraid of; she just felt that something terrible might happen if she left the house and that she wouldn't be able to handle the situation. Finally, she stopped going out at all; it has now been more than 4 years since she has left the house. Mrs. Wilson does not show any other unusual behavior, and she is fine as long as she is at home. Mrs. Wilson suffers from a disorder known as *agoraphobia.*

■ ■ ■

Lennie served as a rifleman in Vietnam. That was almost 30 years ago, but the experience still haunts him. He frequently has nightmares about his experiences fighting in the jungle, and occasionally during the day something will happen, such as a helicopter flying overhead, that will bring the experiences back. Lennie often catches himself scanning his surroundings looking for hidden danger. His underlying tension and fear make him emotionally distant and interfere with his personal relationships. Lennie shows the symptoms of a *posttraumatic stress disorder.*

■ ■ ■

In this chapter and the two that follow it, I will discuss the symptoms, causes, and treatment of **anxiety disorders.** In anxiety disorders, *anxiety is the major symptom* or *the cause of other symptoms.* It is important to note that anxiety is also a symptom in a variety of other disorders, such as depression and schizophrenia, but in those disorders anxiety is the *result of other problems.* For example, a woman who is suffering from depression may be anxious because she believes that she is a useless failure and doomed to a life of misery. Similarly, a man with schizophrenia may be anxious because he has a delusion that his brain is being destroyed by gamma waves from the planet Egregious. It is important to keep the distinction between primary and secondary anxiety in mind when making diagnoses and planning treatments. With that point clarified, we can go on to consider the symptoms of anxiety.

SYMPTOMS OF ANXIETY

Mood Symptoms

The mood symptoms in anxiety disorders consist primarily of anxiety, tension, panic, and apprehension. The individual suffering from anxiety has the feeling of impending doom and disaster.

Other mood symptoms associated with anxiety often include depression and irritability. The depression can stem from the fact that the individual does not see a solution for his or her problems and is ready to give up and "throw in the towel." Loss of sleep due to anxiety can lead to irritability. Both the depression and the irritability are secondary symptoms because they stem from the anxiety that is the primary symptom.

Cognitive Symptoms

The cognitive symptoms in anxiety disorders revolve around the doom and disaster that the individual anticipates. For example, an individual who has a fear of being out in public (agoraphobia) will spend a great deal of time worrying about the terrible things that might happen in public and planning how to avoid them. Furthermore, because the individual's attention is focused on potential disasters, the individual does not attend to the real problems at hand and is therefore inattentive and distractible. As a consequence, the individual often does not work or study effectively, and that can add to the anxieties.

Somatic Symptoms

The somatic (physiological) symptoms of anxiety can be divided into two groups. First are the *immediate symptoms,* which consist of sweating, dry mouth, shallow breathing, rapid pulse, increased blood pressure, throbbing sensations in the head, and feelings of muscular tension. These symptoms reflect the *high level of arousal* of the autonomic nervous system, and they are the same responses that we see in fear. Additional symptoms can occur because the individual begins breathing too rapidly, a process known as **hyperventilation.** Hyperventilation can result in light-headedness, headache, tingling of the extremities, heart palpitations, chest pain, and breathlessness. These primary somatic symptoms are what you would experience if your professor suddenly announced a pop quiz that would be worth half your grade!

Second, if the anxiety is prolonged, *delayed symptoms* such as chronically increased blood pressure, headaches, muscular weakness, and intestinal distress (poor digestion, stomach cramps) may set in. These symptoms reflect *fatigue* or *breakdown* of the physiological system that stem from the prolonged arousal. These are the symptoms you might experience if you failed the quiz referred to earlier and then worried about failing for the rest of the semester. In some cases, the prolonged arousal can cause serious tissue damage or illness, as when prolonged stomach acidity leads to ulcers (see Chapter 16).

Not everyone who suffers from anxiety experiences the same physical symptoms. That is because there are individual differences in the patterning of autonomic reactivity (Lacey, 1950, 1967). For example, when I am anxious, I tend to experience muscular tenseness, particularly in my throat (a response that, if prolonged, results in a change in or loss of my voice). Someone else may be more likely to respond with increased blood pressure (which, if prolonged, can result in hypertension).

Motor Symptoms

Anxious individuals often exhibit restlessness, fidgeting, pointless motor activity such as toe tapping, and exaggerated startle responses to sudden noise. Those motor symptoms reflect the individuals' high levels of cognitive and somatic arousal and their attempts to protect themselves from what they see as threatening. Because the activities are random or not focused on one goal, they are often unproductive and can interfere with effective functioning. For example, if you are anxious before a test, you may pace your room randomly, but the pacing does not make you feel better and will even prevent you from doing some useful last-minute studying.

ORGANIZATION OF ANXIETY DISORDERS

The anxiety disorders can be organized into two major categories, **phobic disorders** and **anxiety states.** The disorders in these two categories differ in terms of the degree to which the anxiety is *localized or diffused.* Specifically, in the case of phobic disorders, the anxiety is localized and associated with one particular object or situation. For example, an individual may become very anxious when confronted with spiders or when in a tall building. By contrast, in anxiety states, the anxiety is more likely to be diffused, not related to any one thing, and is experienced as omnipresent or free-floating. An individual suffering from an anxiety state may feel as though his or her entire life is enveloped in an electrified cloud or that every turn bodes doom and disaster from which there is no escape. In the sections that follow, I will describe the phobic disorders first because they are somewhat simpler and more clear-cut, and then I will go on to examine the anxiety states. The subtypes of the phobic disorders and anxiety states along with their major symptoms are listed in Table 4.1.

PHOBIC DISORDERS

Phobias are *persistent and irrational fears* of a specific object, activity, or situation. Phobias involve fears that have *no justification* in reality (e.g., fear of small, harmless animals) or fears that are *greater than what is justified* (e.g., extreme fear of flying).

An important aspect of the phobic fear is that *the individual is aware of the irrationality of the fear.* In other words, people with phobias know that their fear is not really justified, but at the same time they cannot stop being afraid. For example, the individual who has an elevator phobia *knows* that there are hundreds of thousands of elevators, *knows* that every day of the year those elevators each make hundreds of trips without anyone getting hurt, and *knows* that the probability of getting hurt in an elevator is very low (maybe even lower than when using the stairs). However, despite that knowledge, the individual is still afraid to ride in an elevator. This knowledge of the reality of the situation is important because it distinguishes an individual with a phobia from an individual with a **delusion,** which is an unjustified belief about the world that the individual does not recognize as wrong. Delusions usually reflect a much more serious problem (see Chapter 11). In the phobic disorders, then, we see an inappropriate separation of the cognitive and emotional aspects of psychological functioning.

There is a great deal of variability in the degree to which phobias interfere with an individual's ability to

---

TABLE 4.1 Anxiety Disorders and Their Symptoms

Phobic Disorders

Agoraphobia—fear of situations in which escape would be embarrassing if panic-like symptoms occurred

Social Phobia—fear of embarrassment over specific behaviors

Specific Phobias—fear of specific objects or situations

Anxiety States

Generalized Anxiety Disorder—persistent anxiety that is associated with a variety of situations or activities

Panic Disorder—brief periods of intense, spontaneous anxiety

Obsessive-Compulsive Disorder—recurrent obsessions and/or compulsions

Posttraumatic Stress Disorder—anxiety-related symptoms that last for a long period after a traumatic experience

Acute Stress Disorder—anxiety-related symptoms that last for between 2 days and 4 weeks after a traumatic experience

---

function. The degree to which a phobia will be disruptive is determined in part by the likelihood that the individual will encounter the feared object or situation in daily life. *Claustrophobia* (KLOS-truh-FŌ-bē-uh), a fear of small enclosed places, would not be particularly disruptive for a Kansas wheat farmer, but it could pose a serious problem for an office worker living in New York City who must frequently spend time in cramped elevators, small offices, and crowded subway cars. Many people have phobias for harmless insects, but because they do not encounter the insects on a regular basis, those fears do not have a major effect on their lives.

Phobias can lead to disruptive behavior in two ways. First, if the feared object or situation can be avoided easily, the avoidance may result in unfortunate consequences. For example, an individual with an elevator phobia who had a job on the 15th floor might have to quit the job and take a less desirable job on a lower floor in order to avoid taking the elevator. Second, if the feared object or situation cannot be avoided easily, the individual may experience uncontrollable and overwhelming fear and panic. When that occurs, the individual may show very embarrassing and inappropriate emotional outbreaks, fainting, and attempts to escape.

The case of the sportscaster John Madden illustrates the inconvenience caused by a phobia. Rather than taking a few hours to fly from New York to San Francisco to broadcast a football game, he must spend 3 or 4 days on a train or a bus to get to his destination. His symptoms are discussed in Case Study 4.1.

Phobic disorders are probably more common than you realize because people with phobias often conceal

CASE STUDY 4.1
John Madden: A 260-Pound "Fraidy Cat"?

John Madden is 6 ft 4 in. tall and weighs 260 lb. As a football player, he was an offensive and defensive tackle, and following his playing career, he was the coach of the Oakland Raiders football team for 10 years. Madden is not the sort of fellow you would expect to be afraid of much, but guess again. Madden suffers from a variety of fears, most of which seem to revolve around small spaces.

Madden's fear of being hemmed in is very general. He is afraid of planes, elevators, crowds, and even tight-fitting clothing. The anxiety that keeps him out of planes causes him considerable inconvenience because as a sportscaster, he must make frequent trips from coast to coast to broadcast football games. Rather than making the trip in a matter of a few hours by plane, it takes him 3 or 4 days to make the trip on a train.

Originally, Madden misdiagnosed his symptoms of anxiety as the effects of an inner-ear infection. Whenever he flew, he became tense, and he thought that the tension was a physiological reaction to the altitude. He soon realized, however, that the symptoms started "as soon as the stewardess closed the door"—before the plane was off the ground. "One day I had a flight from Tampa to California with a stop in Houston. I got off there, checked into a hotel, and never flew again." Madden reports that at first he was embarrassed by his phobia, but now he publicly jokes about it.

As is often the case with individuals who suffer from one phobia, Madden appears to have a variety of other anxieties. Madden's more general anxiety is reflected in the fact that he is a chronic worrier. He points out that he gave up his very successful coaching career with the Raiders because "the constant worrying made the seasons run together, and I just burned out." Undoubtedly because of his constant worrying, Madden suffers from a bleeding ulcer.

Source: Adapted from Leershen (1984).

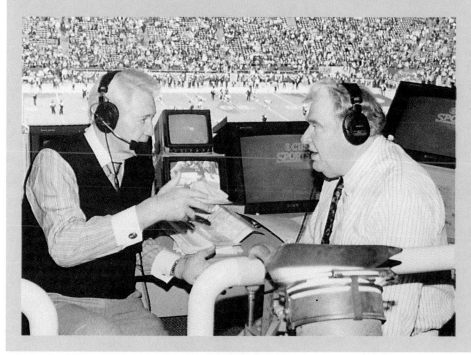

Sportscaster John Madden (right) suffers from a fear of flying that greatly interferes with his professional life. He must take a train or bus from coast to coast to broadcast football games.

their problems effectively. I was completely unaware of a colleague's rather severe elevator phobia because each time we went to our offices on the fourth floor, he would say something like, "Let's take the stairs. The exercise will be good for us." I became aware of his problem only when one day we had to move some heavy boxes to the sixth floor, and after the boxes were loaded into the elevator, he told me he would take the stairs and meet me at the top.

Phobic disorders are divided into three groups as a function of the type of situation that elicits the fear. We can now go on to consider these three types of phobias: agoraphobia, social phobia, and specific phobia.

Agoraphobia

Individuals who suffer from **agoraphobia** (AG-uh-ruh-FŌ-bē-uh) are *afraid of being in situations in which escape would be difficult or embarrassing if panic-like symptoms occurred,* and therefore the individuals *avoid those situations or insist that a companion be present to provide help if needed.* In other words, the individuals are afraid of becoming fearful (having a panic attack) and embarrassing themselves, and therefore they avoid public situations.

Because of their fear of embarrassing themselves in public, the lives of people with agoraphobia become dominated by their attempts to avoid contact with groups of people. Therefore, they may confine themselves to their homes and venture out as little as possible, and when they do go out, it might only be with someone they believe will be able to help them if they become anxious. The fact that these individuals avoid crowds does not stem from any delusions about the people or from their being depressed or wanting to be alone. Instead, being in crowds makes them fearful because "something" might happen that they cannot control. Like my friend who concealed his elevator phobia from me, individuals with agoraphobia are often successful in concealing their disorder by declining social invitations; they are always "too busy" or have "something else to do" at home. Furthermore, because they avoid social gatherings, we have less contact with them and are therefore less likely to realize that they have a problem. Agoraphobia is diagnosed in about 7% of women and in about 3.5% of men (Kessler et al., 1994). An example of agoraphobia is presented in Case Study 4.2.

CASE STUDY 4.2

The Woman Who Went to Bed Dressed: A Case of Agoraphobia

Ann is a 34-year-old college-educated woman who is married and the mother of two children. When I first met her, she impressed me as being mature, attractive, and personally outgoing. Ann had a normal childhood and adolescence, and her early adult life had gone smoothly. However, about 3 years ago, she began to feel somewhat "tense, nervous, and upset" whenever she left the house to shop, go to a party, or car-pool the children.

At first, the anxiety was relatively mild, and she described it as a "vague tension that sort of came from nowhere." As time went by, however, the level of anxiety became progressively greater. Within a year, her anxiety while out of the house was so high that she was unable to go more than a few blocks from home unless her husband or her sister were with her "for protection." Sometimes, even when she was out with her husband, she would begin to tremble, have "hot flashes," and start sweating, and she would eventually have to leave wherever she was and go home as quickly as possible. This resulted in a variety of embarrassing situations. For example, she left parties abruptly, fled from crowded stores, and once ran out of church in the middle of the service. When friends noticed her unusual behavior, she would explain it by saying that she was "tired" or "not feeling well" or had a lot of work at home that needed to be done.

It got to the point where Ann rarely ventured out of the house, and even when she did, it was only for very brief periods, and she never went far. If Ann thought about going out of the house, she would become so anxious by the time she was supposed to leave that she would not be able to leave. To get around this problem, when it was necessary for her to shop, Ann would go to bed the night before fully dressed and made up. When she awoke the next morning, she would immediately jump out of bed and run out of the house, hoping to get to the store before her anxiety got so high that she would have to stop and return home. This worked about half of the time, but sometimes she would get "trapped in the checkout line" and have to leave her basket and rush home in a panic.

Ann could not explain why she became anxious when she left the house. She could only say that there might be "an emergency," but she could not remember an emergency ever occurring, and she could not think of what emergency might occur other than getting sick. She recognized the irrationality of her fear. She also realized that her fear was disrupting her life and her family, but try as she might, she could not suppress or overcome the fear.

CASE STUDY 4.3

"Phone Phobia": A Case of a Social Phobia

The following account was written by an intelligent professional woman who describes herself as suffering from a "phone phobia." That label is something of a misnomer because she is not anxious about the telephone but rather about the social interactions that take place on the phone.

"When I'm on the phone, I am extremely tense—it's as if I'm 'on the line,' and I am almost paralyzed with fear. I feel as though I have to justify making the call, have a good reason for calling so that I don't 'bother' the other person, and have to explain what I want clearly and briefly so as not to take up too much of the other person's time. I am always sure that I am going to make an ass of myself when I call someone.

"Over the years, I have developed certain strategies for dealing with my phone phobia. For any call, I establish a day and a time for making the call—it's

on my calendar. However, I often postpone important calls if my level of tension is too high when they come up on my calendar. If I make the call and the other person is out, I am always relieved.

"I also feel threatened, tense, and anxious when I receive calls. I feel as if I'm being put on the spot, and I won't be able to think fast enough to come up with intelligent answers to the other person's questions. When the phone rings, I may start to tremble badly. To deal with my fear, I have established a firm rule for myself: I always pick up the phone after the second ring. With that rule, I give myself a little time to build up my courage, but I can't avoid the fear by not answering the phone. This phone phobia makes my professional and personal life really difficult. It's all rather crazy, but I can't get over it, so I just try to get around it."

Social Phobia

The major symptom shown by individuals with a **social phobia** is an *irrational fear that they will behave in an embarrassing way,* and as a consequence, the individuals show *high levels of anxiety in social situations* and/or they *avoid social situations.* There is a good deal of similarity between the social phobia and agoraphobia in that both involve fear of embarrassment and avoidance of situations in which the individual might be embarrassed, but the difference lies in the fact that the social phobia is limited to those situations in which *scrutiny by others is likely.* For example, an individual with a social phobia might be uncomfortable going to a crowded meeting *if he or she was going to have to make a speech,* whereas an individual with agoraphobia would be uncomfortable going to a crowded meeting because he or she might develop panic-like symptoms and escape might be difficult or embarrassing. Obviously, a social

phobia can severely constrict an individual's life. This disorder afflicts about 15% of women and about 11% of men at some point in their lives (Davidson et al., 1994; Kessler et al., 1994). An example of a relatively minor social phobia is presented in Case Study 4.3.

Specific Phobia

A **specific phobia** involves *an irrational and persistent fear about a specific object or situation* (e.g., animals, flying, heights, injections, seeing blood). Specific phobias differ from agoraphobia and social phobia in that the specific phobia involves fear of an object or a situation rather than fear of behaving in an embarrassing way. Because the category of specific phobia includes everything that is not included in agoraphobia and social phobia, the specific phobia is a *residual category.* Some specific phobias are listed in Table 4.2.

TABLE 4.2 Some Specific Phobias

Acrophobia—fear of high places	Mysophobia—fear of contamination
Algophobia—fear of pain	Nyctophobia—fear of darkness
Astraphobia—fear of storms	Ochlophobia—fear of crowds
Claustrophobia—fear of confined spaces	Pathophobia—fear of disease
Hematophobia—fear of blood	Syphilophobia—fear of syphilis
Monophobia—fear of being alone	Zoophobia—fear of animals

This playground scene made a woman with a spider phobia very anxious because it reminded her of spiders in a web.

For most people, this would be a beautiful view, but for a person with a fear of heights, it would be terrifying.

Traditionally, phobias were named with the Greek word for the feared object or situation, but this is no longer done consistently and may soon be abandoned. Specific phobias are quite common, occurring in about 16% of women and almost 7% of men (Kessler et al., 1994).

ANXIETY STATES

Anxiety states differ from phobic disorders in that in anxiety states, *the emotional response is diffused and not related to any one particular situation or stimulus.* In these disorders, the anxiety is said to be "free-floating." We can distinguish four types of anxiety states, and they will be considered in the following sections.

Generalized Anxiety Disorder

The **generalized anxiety disorder** involves *general, persistent anxiety that lasts for at least 6 months and is associated with a variety of situations or activities,* such as work, school, or relationships. The anxiety is present constantly, and there is no escape from it. At different times, the individual with a generalized anxiety disorder may focus on different factors in the environment, but the individual is always anxious about something (Brown et al., 1994).

Because the anxiety is general and not associated with a particular object, the individual does not know from where the threat will come and therefore continuously scans the surroundings for the threat. That can result in debilitating effects such as distractibility, fatigue, muscle tension, sleep disturbances, and a variety of related problems (Wittchen et al., 1994). To imagine what a generalized anxiety disorder is like, think about how you feel just before taking an exceptionally important examination, and then imagine those feelings lasting for months without your knowing why you are upset. The generalized anxiety disorder appears to afflict about 6.6% of women and about 3.6% of men (Kessler et al., 1994; Wittchen et al., 1994).

Panic Disorder

A **panic disorder** involves *brief periods of exceptionally intense spontaneous anxiety.* During a panic attack, an individual may experience physical symptoms that include shortness of breath, heart palpitations, chest pains, sensations of choking or smothering, dizziness, numbness or tingling of the extremities, hot and cold flashes, sweating, faintness, trembling, and shaking.

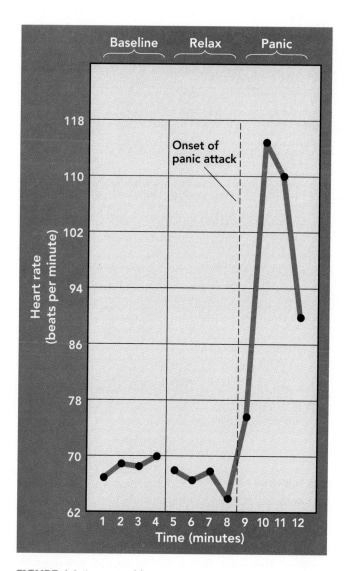

FIGURE 4.1 **Increased heart rate in a woman experiencing a panic attack.**
Source: Adapted from Cohen et al. (1985), p. 98, fig. 2.

These periods come and go suddenly, usually lasting only about 10 minutes, and their occurrence is unpredictable. They seem to come "out of the blue"; indeed, they often occur when the individual is very relaxed or in deep sleep (Craske & Barlow, 1989; Mellman & Uhde, 1989). The panic attacks that occur during sleep are called **nocturnal panic attacks,** and it is noteworthy that they are most likely to occur during the deepest level of sleep (Stage IV sleep) when the individual is not dreaming (non-REM sleep; see Chapter 16 for a discussion of sleep and dreaming).

An example of the changes in heart rate that are associated with a panic attack is presented in Figure 4.1. Those data were collected quite by chance when a woman happened to have a panic attack while she was receiving relaxation training and having her physiological responses monitored. Note that the attack occurred while she was relaxing in a nonstressful situation and that in less than 2 minutes her heart rate increased by 52 beats per minute, an increase of 81%. Because of the physical symptoms, an individual who is having a panic attack may misinterpret it as a heart attack. One patient who suffered from panic attacks said, "Most people only face dying once; I do it a couple of times a week! It's scary."

Panic attacks are very frightening. Individuals who experience panic attacks become concerned about losing control and often think that they are "going crazy," and therefore they sometimes begin avoiding public places in favor of staying home, where they feel safe. If the avoidance becomes extreme, the individual may be diagnosed as suffering from a **panic disorder with agoraphobia** rather than simply from a panic disorder. Between attacks, the individual is often anxious about possible impending attacks, causing an elevated general level of anxiety.

It is important not to confuse panic attacks with the intense periods of arousal that are associated with physical exertion or the stress of real life-threatening situations. Furthermore, it should be noted that for many years, panic attacks were misdiagnosed as cardiac or respiratory problems and treated accordingly, with no benefit to the patient. Fortunately, now that panic attacks are recognized as a psychological disorder, they are receiving widespread attention in the medical and public press, and the likelihood of misdiagnosis has been greatly reduced.

The panic disorder is thought to be rather common, occurring in 5% of women and 2% of men (Kessler et al., 1994). In one study of undergraduate students, it was found that 2.4% met the criteria for having a panic disorder (Telch et al., 1989). A description of a rather mild panic attack in an undergraduate student of mine is presented in Case Study 4.4.

Obsessive-Compulsive Disorder

The **obsessive-compulsive disorder** involves *recurrent obsessions or compulsions* (or both). An **obsession** is a *persistent idea, thought, image, or impulse* that an individual cannot get out of his or her mind and that causes the individual distress or anxiety. Common clinical obsessions are repetitive thoughts of violence (killing or harming someone), contamination (becoming infected with germs), and doubt (persistently wondering whether one has done something like hurting another individual). We all occasionally go through periods when we cannot get a thought or a tune out of our heads, but the episodes do not last too long and are not upsetting, so they are not classified as obsessions or abnormal. It is also important not to confuse obsessions with *worries* (Turner et al., 1992). Both

CASE STUDY 4.4
A Panic Attack in Class

An undergraduate student recently gave me the following account of one of her panic attacks.

"It was around 10:00 A.M. and I was taking notes in an introductory philosophy class. As I was writing, my hand started to tremble and I began having difficulty writing. My handwriting became steadily worse, and I started getting very dizzy. This had never happened to me in a class before, and I didn't know what to do. I thought about trying to leave the room, but I was afraid that I wouldn't make it to the door. I tried to get rid of the dizziness by laying my head down, but it only got worse. I was trembling so badly that I could not take notes, and in an attempt to hold on, I tried to focus all of my attention on the professor. It didn't work. I could barely see him, I couldn't hear him, and the room looked like a black-and-white photo negative. I became extremely frightened and thought that I was going to black out. The girl next to me saw that I was having trou-

ble and suggested that I leave the room, but I couldn't understand what she was saying—it was all a distant blur. Eventually I got up and stumbled out of the room—right in the middle of the lecture. I knew that if I didn't walk out, I would be carried out. I sat down outside the classroom and put my head between my knees to get rid of the dizziness and blackness. It was several minutes before the symptoms went away and I could return to the classroom.

"Since that first attack, I have had five or six similar attacks. They are always extremely frightening, but now that I understand what's happening and know that I'll get over it and won't die or something, it's not quite as bad. Having the attacks can be very embarrassing, and I worry that sometime I am really going to make a fool out of myself somewhere. Fortunately, most times people just think I am getting sick and they are very sympathetic."

involve persistent thoughts, but worries are usually related to everyday experiences (e.g., work, money, family), they occur in the form of a thought, they are seen as controllable, and they are not usually resisted by the individual. In contrast, obsessions generally revolve around a unique topic (e.g., dirt or contamination, death, aggression), they often involve impulses as well as thoughts, they are seen as uncontrollable, and they are resisted by the individual.

Obsessions can interfere with normal thoughts and thus can impair the individual's ability to function effectively. For example, it would be hard to study and perform well in school if you were constantly thinking about killing someone or worrying about the possibility that you forgot something important. Obsessions can also limit behavior. For example, an obsession with the risk of infection may lead an individual to avoid situations that involve dirt and germs.

A **compulsion** is a *behavior that an individual feels driven to perform over and over*. The individual believes that if he or she does not perform the behavior, something terrible will happen. For example, an individual may feel that it is necessary to wash his or her hands repeatedly in order to avoid contamination from germs. However, in fact the behavior is not needed or is actually unconnected to the dreaded event. For example, the individual's hands may already be clean or there may not be any germs in the area. Unfortunately, although

the individual knows that the behavior is excessive or unnecessary, the individual cannot stop performing it.

Performance of the compulsive act may temporarily relieve anxiety. For example, after washing his or her hands, an individual may feel less anxious about contamination. However, the compulsions do not lead to pleasure. In fact, because the individuals know that the compulsions are irrational, the compulsions are usually a source of distress and anxiety. Note that behaviors such as excessive eating, drinking, and gambling are sometimes referred to as "compulsive," but that is inaccurate because pleasure is derived from those activities, even if they lead to negative outcomes. True compulsions are not pleasurable.

Clinically common compulsions include hand-washing, counting, checking, and touching. As with obsessions, compulsions can seriously disrupt normal functioning. Apart from interfering with normal activities, compulsions can have other serious effects. For example, an individual with a handwashing compulsion may wash his or her hands until the skin has literally been scrubbed away.

There is some controversy over the mood that accompanies the obsessive-compulsive disorder. This disorder is classified as an anxiety disorder, and indeed individuals are often anxious about their obsessions (e.g., about thoughts of killing someone) or about the consequences of not completing a compulsive act (e.g.,

Compulsions may briefly forestall anxiety. A compulsion such as stepping over cracks may not interfere with normal activities, but some compulsions can seriously disrupt normal functioning.

dying if they step on a crack in the sidewalk). However, the mood that probably most frequently accompanies the obsessive-compulsive disorder is *depression*. Because of that, and because the obsessive-compulsive disorder can be treated more effectively with antidepressant medication than with antianxiety medication (see Chapter 6), some theorists have suggested that the obsessive-compulsive disorder should be classified as a mood disorder.

A man with a serious obsessive-compulsive disorder is described in Case Study 4.5.

Posttraumatic Stress Disorder

The **posttraumatic stress disorder** involves a variety of anxiety-related symptoms that start with a particular traumatic event and then continue for a long time after the event (Southwick et al., 1995). Four factors are necessary for a diagnosis of posttraumatic stress disorder (American Psychiatric Association, 1994): First, *the individual must have experienced or witnessed a traumatic event* in which physical injury or life was threatened. Traumatic events include natural disasters (floods, earthquakes), accidental disasters (plane crashes, fires), and deliberate disasters (wars, torture, death camps, rape, assaults). The traumatic experience provides the basis for the later disorder.

Second, *the event is persistently reexperienced*. For example, the individual frequently recalls the event, has disturbing dreams about it, experiences "flash-

backs" of reliving it, or feels the intense anxiety that was felt during the original event. The reexperiencing can persist for many years after the event (Falk et al., 1994). For example, a good friend of mine experienced savage combat as a 19-year-old GI in the Battle of the Bulge during World War II. Today, more than 50 years later, he still wakes up two or three nights a week with terrifying nightmares about the fighting.

Third, the individual *avoids stimuli associated with the trauma* and shows *a general numbing of responsiveness*. That is, the individual tries not to think or talk about the traumatic event and does not participate in activities related to it. The psychic numbing is apparent in diminished interest in usual activities, feelings of detachment from others, and blunted emotional responses when the individual is not reexperiencing the traumatic experience (Litz, 1992). In short, the individual has a limited and emotionally flattened life that is punctuated with intense emotional experiences involving the earlier trauma.

Fourth, *the individual may show a generally heightened arousal* that stems from the anxiety. That can be

A disaster can cause psychological as well as physical injury. These victims of the 1995 Oklahoma City bombing of a federal office building are at risk for the posttraumatic stress disorder.

CASE STUDY 4.5

Interview with a Man with an Obsessive-Compulsive Disorder

Here is an excerpt from an interview I had with a 35-year-old man named Bill who suffered from an obsessive-compulsive disorder for about 6 years. He was a college graduate and had been a successful middle-level manager in a relatively large company. His obsessive-compulsive behavior had interfered with his work, and at the time of the interview, he was working at a lower-level position. He was in therapy, receiving counseling, and taking both antidepressant and antianxiety medication.

Holmes: Could you begin by telling me how the problem began?

Bill: I can't tell you what the specific events were, but for a while I felt like something wasn't right in my life. I even talked to my wife about going to a marriage counselor. One of the behaviors I noticed first was that when it was time to eat, I would always reach into the cabinet and take the second dinner plate, not the top plate. The thought was that there might be germs on the top plate, but that plate would protect the second one. That's how it all started. I can't tell you what the second ritual was, but it didn't take long before I developed a lot of rituals.

There seemed to be two basic rituals. Anytime I was going anywhere, whether it was going from one part of the house to another or leaving the house, I would always walk out backward. For example, I would always back out of the house. The other thing was that I would always do things over and over. For example, I would open and close the car door twice and open and close the house door twice. If I was going through a door, I would do it twice. I would walk through and then turn around and do it again. A circular pattern developed in which I did things over and over. Numbers became very important in this whole

pattern. I had to do things a certain number of times. It wasn't always the same number. It depended on how high my anxiety was. Two was a common number, so was four, five, seven, or nine, but never would I go above eleven or twelve. Thirteen was a terribly unlucky number. The more anxious I was, the more times I had to do things.

Holmes: What was it you had to do seven times?

Bill: Any of the things. Opening and closing the car door or going through a door.

Holmes: And what did you think would happen if you didn't do this?

Bill: I think that when I first started doing rituals, I saw it more as a protection. When I took the second plate, I wouldn't get germs, and that would keep me from getting sick. Very quickly it took a negative twist, where if I didn't do one of these things, something terrible would happen. Always I had a fear of a heart attack, a fear of a stroke, and a fear of dying. Those were the three major fears. In a short time, I had a full-blown set of rituals. And the rituals covered every part of my life. For example, I'd wake up in the morning and I'd have to throw the sheets off of me, cover myself up again, and then throw the sheets off again. From that point, everything I did was controlled by the rituals. They controlled how I brushed my teeth—right down to how I picked up the toothbrush. I would pick it up, put it down, and then pick it up again. I'd put my socks on, take them off, and then put them on again. Shirt on and off and on again. Again the number two. It would take me three and a half hours to get dressed and out in the morning!

seen in problems with sleep, irritability, difficulty in concentrating, and an exaggerated startle response.

The posttraumatic stress disorder has undoubtedly existed throughout history, but it gained widespread attention when it was observed in veterans of the Vietnam conflict. An example of a posttraumatic stress disorder in a Vietnam veteran is presented in Case Study 4.6.

There is no doubt that the posttraumatic stress disorder is a real disorder that afflicts many people, but care must be taken not to apply the diagnosis indiscriminately. This is particularly the case with regard to Vietnam veterans. Those individuals were exposed to terrible stresses during their military service; undoubtedly many of them are still suffering the effects of those stresses, and they should be diagnosed and treated for

It got to the point that I couldn't go by grave-yards and couldn't go by hospitals—they reminded me of death. Then it got to where I couldn't even go by signs, like hospital signs. If I came to stop signs—"stop" meant my heart might stop—so I had to do everything to avoid these. It got to the point—let's say I came to a stop sign. I'd say, "Is it all right if I go by the stop sign?" and whoever I was with had to say, "Yes." They couldn't say "hm-mm" or "OK." I would keep badgering them until they said the word *yes*. When they said the word *yes*, it would be all right.

You can't imagine how degrading this was for me, so I'd say to myself, "By God, I'm not going to do it this time," and I'd get by the stop sign without asking permission. Maybe I'd get half a block down the street—and I'd break out in a sweat and have to make a U turn and go back through the stop sign again. I became a real U turn artist. There have been times I've made five or six U turns on a busy street in the space of ten blocks—just so I could go back through stop signs again. God, it was insane! If I didn't do one of my rituals, I'd really panic. I remember that when I left work, I would have to drive around the building twice before going home. On a bad day, I'd have to do it eleven times. Well, one day I said, "The hell with this, I'm not going to do it—bingo. I'm going to drive straight home." So I didn't drive around the building and started home, but as soon as I got about a block away, I could sense some shallow breathing, heart starting to race a little bit, all the signs. To make a long story short, about midway home I thought, "I blew it, I blew it, I've got to go back!" I just froze. Then the panic started. All the physical symptoms came, and I

thought, "I'm losing it. I've got to get back to get around the building!" Then I thought, "No, I'll never make it. I'll have to get home." So I drove seventy and eighty miles an hour down city streets—my foot just shaking on the pedal. Once I got to the top of a hill where I could see the house, I could feel the tension drop. By the time I got home, I was real shaky, but it was over.

Holmes: Your family must have become upset about this.

Bill: My youngest daughter literally hated my guts. No one understood it—I didn't understand it. Gee, anyone ought to be able to walk through a damn door without doing it twice. What do you mean you can't do that! It was very difficult.

Holmes: Earlier you said that you did your rituals to avoid possibly dying. How did you connect something like picking up a toothbrush with dying? Why did picking up a toothbrush twice protect you from possibly dying?

Bill: Well, everything is connected to living. You put the toothbrush in your mouth, but you have to breathe through your mouth. Anything that had to do with my mouth or nose was . . . Putting a shirt on over my head—put a shirt on my chest . . . What's on your chest? Your heart. All these things, ha!—There's an insane logic to it all. It all had its purpose. It's kind of like the guy sitting in a field in Kansas snapping his fingers over and over, and when another guy asks him why he is snapping his fingers, he says, "It keeps the elephants away." The other guy then says, "Hell, there aren't any elephants in Kansas." The first guy responds, "See, it works!"

the posttraumatic stress disorder. However, it is easy to attribute apathy, lack of direction, adjustment problems, and failures to a posttraumatic stress disorder resulting from a Vietnam experience when in fact those feelings are due to some other cause. Those feelings and reactions are not uncommon among males as they move through middle adulthood (the "midlife identity crisis"). Therefore, we must be careful not to "suggest" the

disorder or use it to explain current problems that may stem from other causes.

It is also important that we not limit the diagnosis of posttraumatic stress disorder to individuals who have undergone the stress of combat. Veterans have gotten the most attention with regard to such disorders, but victims of natural disasters, accidents, child abuse, rape, and other crimes also suffer from the posttraumatic

CASE STUDY 4.6

Posttraumatic Stress Disorder: A Vietnam Veteran Talks About His Life

"My marriage is falling apart. We just don't talk anymore. Hell, I guess we've never really talked about anything, ever. I spend most of my time at home alone . . . she's upstairs and I'm downstairs. Sure we'll talk about the groceries and who will get gas for the car, but that's about it. She's tried to tell me she cares for me, but I get real uncomfortable talking about things like that, and I get up and leave.

"I really don't have any friends and I'm pretty particular about who I want as a friend. The world is pretty much dog eat dog, and no one seems to care much for anyone else. As far as I'm concerned, I'm really not a part of this messed up society. What I'd really like to do is have a home in the mountains, somewhere far away from everyone. Sometimes I get so angry with the way things are being run, I think about placing a few blocks of C-4 [military explosive] under some of the sons-of-bitches.

"I usually feel depressed. I've felt this way for years. There have been times I've been so depressed that I won't even leave the basement. I'll usually start drinking pretty heavily around these times. I've also thought about committing suicide when I've been depressed. I've got an old .38 that I snuck back from Nam. A couple of times I've sat with it loaded, once I even had the barrel in my mouth and the hammer pulled back. I couldn't do it. I see Smitty back in Nam with his brains smeared all over the bunker. Hell, I fought too hard then to make it back to the World [United States]; I can't waste it now. How come I survived and he didn't? There has to be some reason.

"Sometimes, my head starts to replay some of my experiences in Nam. Regardless of what I'd like to think about, it comes creeping in. It's so hard to push back out again. It's old friends, their faces, the ambush, the screams, their faces . . . You know, every time I hear a chopper [helicopter] or see a clear unobstructed green treeline, a chill goes down my back; I remember. When I go hiking now, I avoid green areas. I usually stay above the timber line. When I walk down the street, I get real uncomfortable with people behind me that I can't see. When I sit, I always try to find a chair with something big and solid directly behind me. I feel most comfortable in the corner of a room, with walls on both sides of me. Loud noises irritate me and sudden movements or noise will make me jump.

"Night is the hardest for me. I go to sleep long after my wife has gone to bed. It seems like hours before I finally drop off. I think of so many of my Nam experiences at night. Sometimes my wife awakens me with a wild look in her eye. I'm all sweaty and tense. Sometimes I grab for her neck before I realize where I am. Sometimes I remember the dream; sometimes it's Nam, other times it's just people after me, and I can't run anymore.

"I don't know, this has been going on for so long; it seems to be getting gradually worse. My wife is talking about leaving. I guess it's no big deal. But I'm lonely. I really don't have anyone else. Why am I the only one like this? What the hell is wrong with me?"

Source: Goodwin (1980), pp. 1–2.

stress disorder, and we must be sensitive to the influence that those experiences may have on their adjustment as well.

Acute Stress Disorder

The **acute stress disorder** is similar to the posttraumatic stress disorder in that it follows a traumatic event and the individual repeatedly reexperiences the event, avoids stimuli associated with the event, shows a numbing of responsiveness, and has a generally heightened level of arousal. However, the acute stress disorder *occurs within 4 weeks of the traumatic event and lasts only between 2 days and 4 weeks.*

Now that you have an understanding of the major anxiety disorders, we can consider the questions that

are asked and steps that are taken in diagnosing them. In Figure 4.2 you will find a decision tree for diagnosing anxiety disorders.

ISSUES ASSOCIATED WITH ANXIETY DISORDERS

Normal Versus Abnormal Anxiety

It is likely that we have all experienced anxiety at some time, but that does not mean that we all suffer from anxiety disorders. In many instances, anxiety is a normal, adaptive, and positive response. For example, anxiety can serve as a drive that increases our

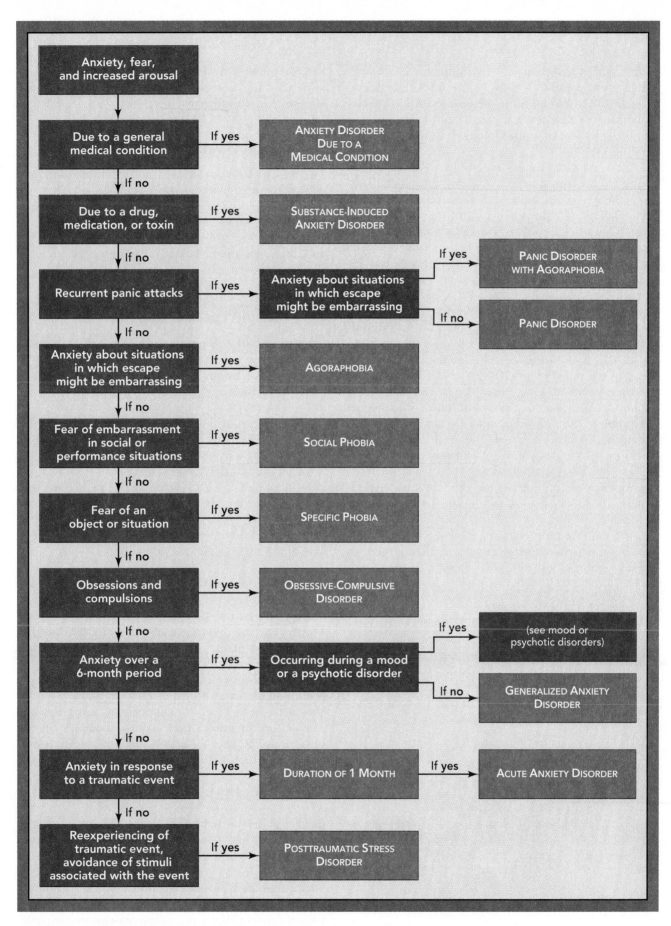

FIGURE 4.2 A decision tree for diagnosing anxiety disorders.

Source: Adapted from American Psychiatric Association (1994), pp. 698–699.

efforts and performance. Psychotherapists actually prefer their patients to have some level of anxiety because it serves to motivate patients to work on their problems. Because anxiety can be positive or negative, the question that must be asked is, when is anxiety abnormal?

There are three factors to consider when making a distinction between normal and abnormal anxiety. The first is the *level* of the anxiety. In many situations, some level of anxiety is appropriate, but if the anxiety goes beyond that level, it could be considered abnormal. For example, it is normal to be somewhat anxious about flying, but it would be abnormal if your anxiety was so high that you fainted when you got on a plane or you refused to get on a plane.

The second factor to consider is the *justification* for the anxiety. Anxiety of any level would be considered abnormal if there were no realistic justification for anxiety in the situation. The word *realistic* is important because the anxious individual may unrealistically interpret a situation as threatening and therefore become anxious, but that does not justify the anxiety. For example, an individual may be anxious around spiders, but in most cases that is not justified.

Third, anxiety is abnormal if it leads to negative *consequences*. For example, anxiety that leads to poor performance on the job, social withdrawal, or hypertension (high blood pressure) would be considered abnormal.

Although we must consider the level, justification, and consequences of anxiety in making the distinction between normal and abnormal anxiety, in the final analysis there is no simple rule or cutoff point, and eventually the decision concerning normality versus abnormality is a subjective one.

Prevalence of Anxiety Disorders

The results of a study of over 8,000 individuals indicated that about 25% reported symptoms from at least one time in their lives that would qualify as an anxiety disorder (Kessler et al., 1994). Social phobias were most common (13%), followed by specific phobias (11%), and then the other anxiety disorders (3% to 5%). Clearly, anxiety disorders are a widespread problem.

Sociocultural Factors

Gender. Anxiety disorders are more likely to be diagnosed in women than in men (Kessler et al., 1994). The prevalence of various anxiety disorders in women and men is presented in Figure 4.3.

Age. Anxiety disorders can set in at any age, but there is some evidence that the prevalence of fears appears to decrease with age. In fact, the prevalence of intense fears among women between 56 and 65 years of age is only about half of what it is among women between 18 and 25 (Costello, 1982). It appears that with time we become older, wiser, and less fearful. The relationship between age and the prevalence of various levels of fear among women is presented in Figure 4.4.

Social Class. Some data suggest that agoraphobia and specific phobia are more prevalent among individuals with less education (Robins et al., 1984). It is also noteworthy that the prevalence of some anxiety disorders may be substantially increased by where an individual lives. For example, a study of young lower-class residents in the inner city revealed a 39.1% rate of the posttraumatic stress disorder. That high rate is probably due to the fact that those individuals had a high rate of exposure to stresses such as sudden injury (9.4%), physical assault (8.3%), seeing someone seriously hurt or killed (7.1%), sudden death of a friend or a relative (5.7%), threat to one's life (2.5%), and rape (1.6%) (Breslau et al., 1991).

Ethnicity. Relatively little attention has been given to the question of whether the rates of anxiety disorders differ among ethnic groups, and the data that do exist are difficult to interpret (Neal & Turner, 1991). One notable problem revolves around biases in diagnoses, and there are two ways in which those biases occur. First, there is evidence that when patients present anxiety-related symptoms, clinicians are more likely to attribute the symptoms of African-Americans to physical disorders (e.g., handwashing as a dermatological

Most people experience anxiety when speaking in public. Here presidential candidate John Anderson wipes his brow during the presidential debates in 1992.

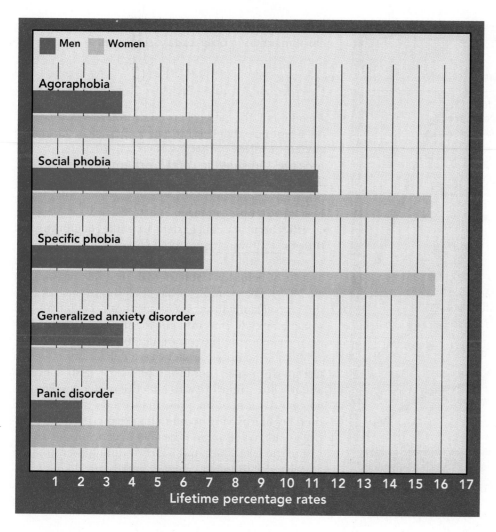

FIGURE 4.3 Anxiety disorders are diagnosed more frequently in women than in men. *Note:* Data were unavailable for the obsessive-compulsive disorder and the posttraumatic stress disorder. *Source:* Data from Kessler et al. (1994), p. 12, tab. 2.

problem) and attribute the symptoms of Caucasian-Americans to psychological problems (Paradis et al., 1994). Second, it is also likely that members of minority groups are more likely to present their symptoms as physiological than psychological.

Those biases aside, it appears that some minority group members may have higher levels of anxiety disorders than majority group members, but the differences may be due to the conditions in which the two groups live rather than ethnic differences per se. For example, high levels of anxiety are more likely to be found in minority group members who are not yet acculturated to the majority culture than those who are acculturated. That suggests that the anxiety is due to the stress of being a minority group member who is not integrated into the mainstream culture.

Fear Versus Anxiety

When reading the sections on phobias and anxiety states, you may have noticed a change in the terminology that was used to describe the emotion that is associated with the two disorders. When talking about phobias, the word *fear* was used, and when talking about anxiety states, the word *anxiety* was used. Do the words *fear* and *anxiety* reflect an important difference, or are they two words for the same thing?

Most people have an intuitive feeling that there is a difference between fear and anxiety, and they often identify *knowledge* as the crucial factor: If they know what is bothering them, they are afraid, but if they do not know, they are anxious. Using that distinction, you would be anxious if you were walking through the woods at night because you would not know what might be lurking in the shadows, but if you suddenly came face to face with a bear, you would be afraid. However, we could just as easily talk about "fear of the unknown" and "fear of the known" and thereby not use the word *anxiety*. One justification for not using the word *anxiety* is that it is a vague term to which people attach different meanings, and therefore it may not accurately communicate what is meant. If anxiety is really only a type of fear, it might be more effective to call it fear and then use a modifier to indicate what type of fear is being referred to (for example, "fear of the unknown" when walking through the woods).

FIGURE 4.4 The prevalence of women's fears decreases with age.
Source: Adapted from Costello (1982), p. 283, fig. 2.

[Graph with y-axis labeled "Rate per 1,000 population" ranging from 0 to 800, and x-axis labeled "Age" with categories 18–25, 26–35, 36–45, 46–55, 56–65. Lines labeled: "Mild fear, no avoidance of stimulus"; "Intense fear, no avoidance of stimulus"; "Mild fear, avoidance of stimulus"; "Intense fear, avoidance of stimulus"]

ious, it is important to clarify whether the arousal is a chronic trait or a brief and passing state.

Cognitive Anxiety Versus Somatic Anxiety

Anxiety can also be broken down in terms of the types of symptoms that individuals experience. **Cognitive anxiety** involves symptoms such as worry, feelings of pressure, frustration, and concerns about failure. **Somatic anxiety** involves symptoms such as feeling physically "tight" and restless and having a rapid heartbeat and an upset stomach.

Research has suggested that the cognitive and somatic symptoms constitute two separate components of anxiety and that the two may influence different aspects of behavior (Holmes & Roth, 1989; Schwartz et al., 1978). For example, it has been shown that taking a difficult examination increases both cognitive and somatic anxiety, but only the cognitive anxiety hinders performance on the examination (Holmes & Roth, 1989). The cognitive anxiety has a deleterious effect on test performance because the worry and concerns about failure interfere with effective problem solving. If you get to an item on a test that you do not know and then begin worrying about failing (experiencing cognitive anxiety), you will not be able to concentrate on the rest of the test. The rapid heart rate and upset stomach associated with somatic anxiety apparently do not influence intellectual performance. In contrast, it has been reported that somatic anxiety rather than cognitive

I did not raise the question of the similarity or difference between fear and anxiety with the expectation that the word *anxiety* will be dropped from our vocabulary, and indeed I will continue to use it throughout this book. Rather, I raised the question to draw attention to the fact that when talking about anxiety, we must understand and state explicitly what we mean by the term—usually a type of fear.

Trait Anxiety Versus State Anxiety

One widely accepted distinction regarding anxiety is the difference between *trait anxiety* and *state anxiety*. **Trait anxiety** refers to a relatively enduring characteristic of the individual that transcends the boundaries of place and time, whereas **state anxiety** is limited to a particular time or situation (Spielberger, 1971). Individuals with trait anxiety are anxious regardless of where they are or what they are doing, but individuals who suffer from state anxiety are anxious only while in particular situations (taking examinations, flying, on a date). When talking about an individual who is anx-

Somatic anxiety (e.g., rapid heart rate) does not necessarily interfere with performance on a test. However, cognitive anxiety (e.g., worry about consequences) can impede test performance.

anxiety is the best predictor of physical symptoms, sleep disturbance, and the use of a student health center (Frost et al., 1986). The distinction between cognitive and somatic anxiety is important in terms of accurately describing what individuals are experiencing and predicting what their behavior will be, and it may also be important for developing a treatment plan.

From this discussion of anxiety disorders, you should have learned the characteristics of each disorder and you should have recognized that the anxiety disorders comprise *a group of very different disorders.* They involve anxiety that can be specific to particular situations or generally free-floating, and the anxiety can stem from traumatic experiences or can come "out of the blue." Recognition of the differences among the anxiety disorders is important because although all of the disorders share the symptom of anxiety, different disorders may have distinctly different causes. In the next chapter, I will explain the causes of anxiety.

SUMMARY

- In anxiety disorders, mood symptoms include anxiety and sometimes depression and irritability; cognitive symptoms include concerns about doom and disaster; somatic symptoms include increased heart rate and blood pressure, shallow breathing, muscle tension, and intestinal problems; motor symptoms include restlessness and pointless motor behavior.
- Phobias are persistent irrational fears. There are three phobic disorders: (a) agoraphobia, which involves fear of situations from which escape would be embarrassing if panic-like symptoms occurred; (b) social phobia, which is the fear of embarrassment over behaviors; and (c) specific phobias, which are all of the other irrational fears of situations or objects.
- Anxiety states involve anxiety that is not related to any specific situation or stimulus. There are five anxiety disorders of this type: (a) The generalized anxiety disorder involves persistent anxiety that is associated with a variety of situations and activities; (b) the panic disorder involves brief periods of intense anxiety that come "out of the blue"; (c) the obsessive-compulsive disorder involves obsessive thoughts and compulsive behaviors; (d) the posttraumatic stress disorder involves anxiety that stems from a previous traumatic event; and (e) the acute stress disorder involves a brief period of anxiety following a traumatic event.
- Anxiety disorders are more likely to be diagnosed in women than in men, and anxiety tends to decrease with age. Clinicians tend to overlook anxiety disorders in minority groups, and minority group members sometimes present anxiety symptoms as physical symptoms. Higher levels of anxiety in some minority group members may be due to the stress of not fitting into the mainstream culture.
- Anxiety might be thought of as fear, and it might be helpful to distinguish between trait and state anxiety and between cognitive and somatic anxiety.

KEY TERMS, CONCEPTS, AND NAMES

In reviewing and testing yourself on what you have learned from this chapter, you should be able to identify and discuss each of the following.

acute stress disorder
agoraphobia
anxiety disorders
anxiety states
cognitive anxiety : worry
compulsion
delusion
generalized anxiety disorder

hyperventilation
nocturnal panic attacks
obsession
obsessive-compulsive disorder
panic disorder
panic disorder with agoraphobia
phobias
phobic disorders

posttraumatic stress disorder
social phobia
somatic anxiety : physical
specific phobia
state anxiety : phobia
trait anxiety : anxiety state

CHAPTER FIVE
ANXIETY DISORDERS: EXPLANATIONS

OUTLINE

David has a severe snake phobia. When his case is discussed at a clinic conference, there are strong disagreements over the cause of his phobia. A clinician who subscribes to the psychodynamic theory suggests that David has a conflict over the expression of sexual impulses and that the anxiety stems from the fact that the snake is a penis symbol. Another clinician who approaches disorders from a learning perspective believes that in the past, snakes were paired with a fear response (David saw his mother recoil in fear when she saw a snake in the garden), and because of the process of classical conditioning, the stimulus of snakes now elicits the fear response. A third clinician, who takes a cognitive approach to abnormal behavior, believes that David simply has erroneous beliefs about the degree to which snakes are dangerous and that those beliefs lead David to misinterpret or exaggerate the danger that snakes pose for him. Because David automatically thinks his erroneous thoughts when he sees a snake, he is blocked from considering more realistic views of snakes.

■ ■ ■

Lou Ann suffers from chronic free-floating anxiety, and she is diagnosed as having a generalized anxiety disorder. There is disagreement over the cause of her disorder. The psychodynamically oriented clinician believes that the anxiety stems from an underlying conflict and that the anxiety is diffused because there is no symbolic representation of the conflict. The learning theorist suggests that through the process of classical conditioning, anxiety has become associated with many stimuli and that Lou Ann is chronically anxious because at least one of those stimuli is almost always present in her environment. This clinician believes that the anxiety only appears to be free-floating because it is elicited by so many stimuli. A physiologist discounts both of those explanations. He asserts that the general anxiety is due to the fact that inhibitory neurons in Lou Ann's brain are not functioning adequately, thereby causing her to have excessive neurological activity in the areas of the brain that are responsible for arousal. That arousal is interpreted as anxiety, and it is free-floating because it is not associated with any observable external event.

■ ■ ■

Mr. Garcia also suffers from chronic anxiety, and its persistence is resulting in high blood pressure. His anxiety apparently stems from the presence of many real-life stressors around him. For example, his wife is very ill, they do not have adequate health insurance, there are rumors of layoffs in the factory in which Mr. Garcia works, and his son is being threatened by gangs at school.

■ ■ ■

Mrs. Heinz suffers from panic attacks, many of which occur during the night and begin during periods of very deep sleep when she is not dreaming. The panic attacks that occur during deep sleep are hard to explain because there are no classically conditioned stimuli to trigger the attacks and they cannot be brought on by erroneous beliefs. However, a physiologist suggests that during sleep Mrs. Heinz may not be getting enough oxygen (her respiration rate is very low), and the low level of oxygen may trigger a false alarm that she is suffocating, which leads to the sudden panic. This is more likely to occur in Mrs. Heinz than other people because the area of her brain that detects low levels of oxygen is overly sensitive.

■ ■ ■

In Chapter 4 I discussed the symptoms and issues that are associated with anxiety disorders, and with that material as background, we can now consider the explanations for anxiety disorders. Four general explanations will be discussed: psychodynamic, learning, cognitive, and physiological. In considering these explanations, you should not assume that any one explanation is necessarily the best for all anxiety disorders. Instead, it may well be that one explanation is most effective for accounting for one of the disorders and another explanation is most effective for accounting for another. It may also be that different explanations work together to account for disorders. As we work our way through the explanations, keep an open mind and wait until they have all been discussed before drawing any conclusions.

PSYCHODYNAMIC EXPLANATIONS

The basic tenet of the psychodynamic explanations is that *stress leads to anxiety disorders.* However, within the psychodynamic camp, opinions differ regarding what causes the stress and whether the causes are conscious or unconscious.

Id Impulses and Unconscious Conflicts

Freud suggested that *anxiety stems from internal conflicts over the expression of id impulses* (Freud, 1926/1959). Specifically, he theorized that anxiety is generated when the id seeks gratification of its needs but is thwarted by the superego. For example, a young man may want to have sex with a woman he is dating, but having sex is unacceptable to his superego, and that conflict results in anxiety.

Freud also suggested that anxiety can stem from the fear that the superego will not be effective in restraining the id and that unacceptable behavior will therefore break through. For example, anxiety may be generated by the possibility that sexual or hostile urges may not be adequately controlled and that if they break through, the individual will behave in an inappropriate way.

According to Freud, the experiences we have while going through the stages of psychosexual development play a crucial role in determining what conflicts will occur and how severe those conflicts will be. For example, Freud speculated that if a mother was exceptionally strict with a child about not soiling his or her diapers during the anal stage, later in life the child will have conflicts over cleanliness and control that could lead to anxiety. For the Freudians, then, early childhood experiences are the key to understanding anxiety.

It is important to recognize that according to Freud, the conflicts that result in anxiety occur on the *unconscious level,* and therefore we are not aware of why we are anxious. Anxiety is thus a signal of some underlying conflict. The unconscious nature of the conflict explains why anxiety often appears irrational and unrelated to the objective situation.

Phobias Versus Anxiety States. Why do some individuals develop phobias while others develop anxiety states such as the generalized anxiety disorder? To answer that question, Freud suggested that an individual will develop a phobia if the anxiety can be focused on a particular object that is symbolically linked to the underlying conflict. For example, if an individual has a conflict over sexual expression and snakes serve as phallic (penis) symbols, the individual's anxiety might take the form of a snake phobia. Seeing a snake would reawaken or heighten the conflict over sex and exacerbate the anxiety. Evidence that the fear stems from an unconscious conflict supposedly comes from the fact that a snake-phobic individual is afraid of snakes despite consciously knowing that snakes are not dangerous. In contrast, when the anxiety is not associated with a particular object or symbol, the anxiety will be diffused or free-floating, resulting in a general anxiety state.

Defense Mechanisms. Another factor that is important in understanding anxiety levels is the use of **defense mechanisms** (see Chapter 2). Defense mechanisms may help us avoid conflict and thereby avoid anxiety. For example, denial or suppression may be used to deal with the desires of the id that the superego finds unacceptable. Alternatively, an individual whose superego prohibits him or her from participating in sex may reduce conflict by channeling pent-up sexual energy into creative writing, a process known as *sublimation*. Obsessive-compulsive behaviors also function to control conflict because if you are obsessively counting things or humming a tune to yourself, you cannot think about or act on unacceptable drives.

The Boiler Analogy. I can summarize the relationship between conflict, anxiety, and defense mechanisms with an analogy to a boiler full of water under which there is a fire. In this analogy, (a) the boiler is a personality, (b) the heat is conflict, and (c) the pressure in the boiler is anxiety. If the level of heat (conflict) is low, the pressure in the boiler (anxiety) will be low, and it is unlikely that problems will arise. However, if the heat becomes intense, the pressure in the boiler will get very high, and a number of things could happen. One possibility is that a valve could be opened and some of the pressure could be released into another system. In human terms, pressure might be drained off through a process such as sublimation. (For example, tension over sexual conflict can be released into creative activity.) If the pressure cannot be released into another system, the sides of the boiler will be put under great tension. In human terms, the tension is an anxiety state. If there is a weakness in one part of the boiler, there will be a distortion or even a break in the weak area. In human terms, the localized distortion is a phobia. Whether or not there will be a problem depends on the level of heat (conflict) and the strength of the boiler (personality). Just as some boilers can withstand more pressure because they have better walls and stronger supporting bands, so some individuals can withstand more conflict because they have better-developed personalities and stronger defenses.

Freud's notion that anxiety stems from unconscious conflicts that were developed during childhood was originally very influential, but today more emphasis is focused on the role of current stressful life events of which we are aware. I will discuss the effects of that type of stress in the following section.

Stressful Life Events

An alternative and more contemporary psychodynamic explanation for anxiety is that *stressful life events of which we are aware can lead to anxiety*. For example, I suspect that knowing about an upcoming exam or a financial problem has caused you to become anxious, and if the anxiety is prolonged, it may result in a disorder. In an attempt to determine whether stressful life events lead to anxiety disorders, investigators identified individuals who did and did not suffer from anxiety disorders, and then they examined the levels of stress in the lives of those individuals (see Newman & Bland, 1994). For example, in one study, over 3,000 individuals were

interviewed to determine whether they suffered from an anxiety disorder and whether they had experienced any stressful life events in the preceding year. Each life event was given a stress score that could range from 1 to 20; for example, "child marries (with approval)" received a score of 3, whereas "death of a child" received a score of 19. The results indicated that individuals who suffered from the generalized anxiety disorder had a mean life stress score of 64, whereas those who did not suffer from an anxiety disorder had a mean life stress score of only 38 (Newman & Bland, 1994). That is, individuals with generalized anxiety had life experiences that were almost twice as stressful as other individuals. Clearly, stressful life events can lead to anxiety disorders.

Diathesis-Stress

Stressful life events can lead to anxiety disorders, but not everyone who is exposed to stress develops an anxiety disorder, and that leads to the question, why do some individuals develop anxiety disorders when faced with stress while others do not? One possibility is that *some individuals have a predisposition to develop the disorders*. This is known as the **diathesis-stress explanation;** *diathesis* (dī-HA-thee-sis) means "predisposition."

In one interesting test of the diathesis-stress explanation, the investigators identified individuals who either did or did not have a predisposition to develop anxiety disorders and who either were or were not under stress (Russo et al., 1995). The individuals who

Major life events can be very stressful. Even happy events, such as getting married, can lead to anxiety.

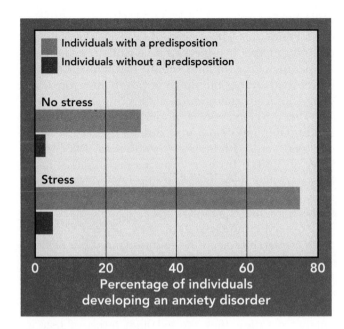

FIGURE 5.1 A predisposition and stress can combine to result in anxiety disorders.
Source: Adapted from Russo et al. (1995), p. 201, fig. 1.

were identified as having a predisposition were those who had suffered from anxiety disorders in the past, and the individuals who were identified as being under high stress were those who were responsible for the care of a spouse who was suffering from Alzheimer's disease. The results indicated that the individuals who were most likely to develop an anxiety disorder were those who had a predisposition (a history of such disorders) and who were under stress (had to take care of an ill spouse), thus offering support for the diathesis-stress explanation. Those results are illustrated in Figure 5.1.

COMMENT

There is certainly strong evidence linking stress to anxiety disorders, but three qualifications should be noted. First, although Freud's notion of unconscious conflicts (usually involving sex) was the first widely accepted explanation for anxiety disorders, today the focus is more on *conscious* conflicts and stressors as the cause of anxiety.

Second, we must be careful not to overinterpret the findings linking the reports of stressors to anxiety because there is evidence that individuals who are anxious are more likely to *remember* stressful experiences or *interpret* experiences as stressful than individuals who are not anxious. Later I will discuss research in which it was found that anxious individuals are more likely than other people to selectively attend to and recall stressors and to misinterpret ambiguous situations as stressful, and that raises questions about cause and effect.

Third, *the diathesis-stress explanation cannot account for all of the anxiety disorders.* Specifically, it cannot explain anxiety that comes "out of the blue" such as panic attacks (which can occur at night during non-dream sleep) or the generalized anxiety disorder that sometimes involves anxiety that is "free-floating." However, the fact that stress cannot be used to account for all anxiety disorders is not a reason to reject the diathesis-stress explanation; rather, it may simply be that we need more than one explanation to account for anxiety disorders and that stress is only one of them.

In sum, stress is a good explanation for anxiety, but it is not a complete explanation, and in the following sections, I will offer some alternatives.

LEARNING EXPLANATIONS

Learning theorists argue that *anxiety is a classically conditioned fear response,* and therefore they assume that *anxiety is learned.* In other words, learning theorists assume that a fear response has been paired with a previously neutral stimulus, and as a result of that pairing (conditioning), the previously neutral stimulus now elicits the fear (see Chapter 2). As a consequence, whenever you encounter the previously neutral stimulus, you become anxious. However, learning theorists also suggest that *some of the symptoms that are associated with anxiety disorders are learned through the process of operant conditioning.* Specifically, behaviors that reduce anxiety are rewarding, and therefore those behaviors will be used again in the future. In the following sections, I will explain how classical conditioning and operant conditioning can be used to account for various anxiety disorders.

Phobias: Classical Conditioning

To explain phobias, learning theorists suggest that individuals are initially frightened in the presence of a stimulus, the fear becomes associated with the stimulus through the process of **classical conditioning,** and then later the stimulus will elicit the fear. For example, an individual who was frightened while in an elevator will now become fearful whenever he or she is in or near an elevator. Not only does the originally neutral stimulus elicit the fear, but because of the process of **generalization,** other stimuli that are *similar to* the original stimulus also elicit the fear. Consequently, the individual with an elevator phobia may become fearful in other small, enclosed places.

Classically conditioned responses are not under voluntary control, and therefore an individual with a classically conditioned fear response cannot stop having a fear response when the conditioned stimulus is encountered, even if the fear response is objectively unjustified (Ohman & Soares, 1993). For example, an individual may be clearly aware that there is no justification for the fear of elevators, but if the fear has been classically conditioned, the individual has no choice but to become afraid in the presence of an elevator.

The case of Little Albert presented in Chapter 2 is probably the best-known laboratory demonstration of anxiety development through classical conditioning, but it is easy to think of other examples. A young man who goes out with a woman who is consistently critical and rejecting of him may become anxious with the woman. Furthermore, the anxiety response may generalize to other women, resulting in his having an anxiety attack whenever he is in the presence of women—or at least women who are in some way similar in appearance or style to the woman who was originally threatening.

Critics of the conditioning explanation for the development of anxiety often point to individuals with phobias who have not actually been harmed in the presence of their fear-provoking stimuli, and they ask how the fears were conditioned. Indeed, individuals with elevator phobias have probably not been in an elevator crash, and individuals with spider phobias have probably not been bitten by a dangerous spider. In reply, learning theorists point out that responses can be developed through **vicarious conditioning** (Bandura & Rosenthal, 1966). That is, the individual with a phobia may have heard about another individual's unfortunate experience, and that may have been sufficient to pair fear with the stimulus. Some spider phobias may be traced back to childhood when children learned about

Little Miss Muffett's fear response when the spider sat down beside her. The process of vicarious classical conditioning makes it unnecessary actually to experience the pairing of the stimulus and the emotional response, thereby expanding the range of possibilities for developing classically conditioned anxiety responses.

The development of phobias through vicarious conditioning was demonstrated in an interesting series of experiments with monkeys (Cook et al., 1985; Mineka et al., 1984). In these experiments, observer monkeys that had been raised in the laboratory did not show any fear when they were first exposed to a real snake, a toy snake, a model snake, or some black cord. The observer monkeys were then allowed to watch *model monkeys* interact with the snake and other objects. The model monkeys had been raised in the wild, and they showed high levels of fear in response to the snake. After watching the model monkeys, the observer monkeys were again exposed to the various stimuli, and on that occasion they showed high levels of fear in response to the snake and moderate levels of fear in response to the similar-looking toy snake, and cord. The vicariously conditioned fear persisted and was almost as strong 3 months later when the monkeys were tested again. These results are presented in Figure 5.2.

In one respect, it is fortunate that vicarious conditioning occurs, because without it we would have to experience at first hand everything of which we should be afraid. That would be an inefficient and dangerous way of learning about threats. However, vicarious conditioning can easily result in inappropriate fears. Without actually experiencing a situation to see if it really is threatening, we may unjustifiably pair a threat with the situation and develop an irrational fear. For example, a child seeing a parent's fear response to a harmless spider (or hearing about Miss Muffett's response to the spider that sat down beside her) might vicariously condition a fear of spiders.

Critics of the conditioning explanation also ask why phobic fears do not extinguish as other classically conditioned responses do. The learning theorists respond by pointing out that phobic fears can be extinguished, but they are generally not extinguished because individuals *avoid the fear-provoking stimuli.* For extinction to occur, the stimulus must be repeatedly presented without being paired with the unconditioned response, but in the case of an individual with an elevator phobia, for example, the individual stays away from elevators, and therefore the link between the elevator and the fear cannot be broken, and so the fear is maintained.

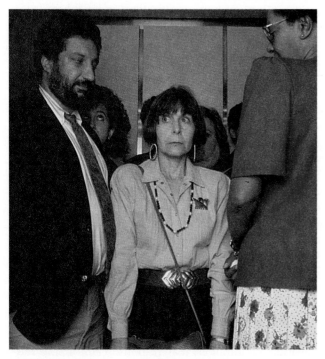

A frightening experience involving an elevator, or even hearing about an elevator accident, can lead to a classically conditioned fear of elevators.

Posttraumatic Stress Disorder: Classical Conditioning

You will recall from Chapter 4 that one of the major symptoms of the posttraumatic stress disorder is the

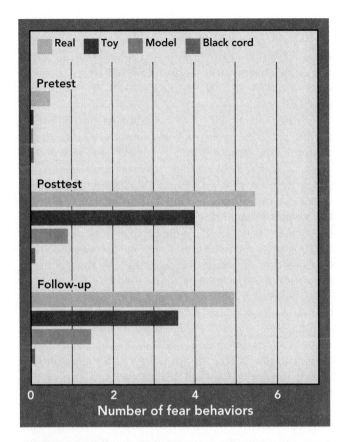

FIGURE 5.2 Monkeys showed greater fear of snakes and similar objects after observing another monkey show fear of a snake.
Source: Adapted from Cook et al. (1985), p. 603, fig. 8.

experience of anxiety that is related to a previously experienced traumatic event. For example, a woman who was raped or a GI who was exposed to terrifying combat experiences may be suddenly overwhelmed with anxiety at some later point in time. The victims of natural disasters such as floods and earthquakes may have similar experiences. Those anxiety responses can be explained in terms of *classically conditioned anxiety responses* (Charney et al., 1993; Southwick et al., 1993). That is, anxiety was paired with the stimuli in the original frightening event, and when stimuli like those in the event are encountered later, the anxiety is elicited. For example, the woman who was raped in a dark parking lot will be overwhelmed with anxiety in other dark locations, and the former GI may suddenly experience anxiety when he hears the sound of a helicopter overhead.

In addition to experiencing the anxiety, individuals with the posttraumatic stress disorder will also recall the experience; that is, they will have flashbacks to the earlier experience. Those recollections are also being elicited by the stimuli from the original situation. Thus the posttraumatic stress disorder involves the pairing of anxiety with stimuli in an initially frightening situation so that later similar stimuli will elicit the anxiety and the memories of the experience. It is interesting to

note that approached from this angle, the posttraumatic stress disorder is very similar to a phobia.

Generalized Anxiety Disorder: Generalization

The disorders I have discussed so far have involved anxiety that is associated with specific stimuli or situations (e.g., elevators or dark places). The question that now arises is, can classical conditioning also be used to explain the generalized anxiety disorder in which the anxiety appears to be free-floating and not associated with a particular stimulus? Learning theorists suggest that the generalized anxiety disorder is simply a *very broadly based phobia.* In other words, they reject the notion that the anxiety is really free-floating, and instead they suggest that the generalized anxiety disorder is actually a phobia in which the fear response has been generalized to a wide variety of stimuli, and because some of those stimuli are usually present, the individual is generally anxious. For example, if an individual develops a fear response to another person and that response is generalized to people in general, the individual would be chronically anxious and might appear to suffer from the generalized anxiety disorder because he or she is usually around other people. In other words, the *generalized anxiety* disorder is due to the *generalization of anxiety.* This explanation for the generalized anxiety disorder is theoretically possible, but it may be stretching the theory a bit, and we may find better explanations later.

Obsessive-Compulsive Disorder: Operant Conditioning

To explain the obsessive-compulsive disorder, learning theorists turned to a different type of conditioning, **operant conditioning.** You will recall that in operant conditioning, the individual receives a reward for performing a particular response, and therefore the response is used again in the future (see Chapter 2). In cases of the obsessive-compulsive disorder, it is assumed that (a) the individuals have high levels of anxiety, (b) the individuals use their obsessions and compulsions to reduce the anxiety, and (c) the anxiety reduction is rewarding, so the obsessions and compulsions continue to be used. For example, an individual who obsessively thinks a particular thought cannot think about something else that is anxiety-provoking, and an individual who compulsively washes his or her hands avoids the anxiety-provoking possibility of infection.

The Irrational Nature of Behaviors

Before concluding this discussion, I should comment briefly on the learning explanation for what appears to be the *irrationality* of many of the behaviors that are associated with anxiety. Some of these behaviors are irrational because the fear on which they are based is irrational. For example, avoiding elevators is irrational because there is no reason to be afraid of elevators. In other cases, the fear may be rational but the response is irrational because it does not really protect the individual. For example, a baseball player who is justifiably anxious about striking out may always wear a pair of "lucky socks" that he happened to wear one day when he hit a home run. In yet other cases, both the fear and the response may be irrational. For example, an individual may believe that stepping on sidewalk cracks is dangerous and thus compulsively avoid stepping on sidewalk cracks. All these behaviors may be objectively irrational, but the important point is that the individual *believes* that the behaviors provide protection from some danger, and the behaviors are therefore anxiety-reducing and rewarding.

Because these irrational responses do not really protect individuals (the baseball player sometimes strikes out while wearing his lucky socks, and the individual who avoids cracks in the sidewalk may fall and break a leg), you might ask why these behaviors do not extinguish. Actually, the fact that they seem to work *some of the time* (occasionally the baseball player gets a hit, and the individual who avoids cracks does not always fall) makes the responses more resistant to extinction because they are on an **intermittent schedule of reward,** which increases resistance to extinction (see Chapter 2).

COMMENT

Re: learning explanation

The first point to recognize when evaluating the learning explanations for anxiety disorders is that *the principles of learning and conditioning are supported by a vast body of well-controlled laboratory research* (Hilgard & Marquis, 1961; Klein, 1987). There is little doubt about the existence of classical and operant conditioning, and therefore we can have confidence in the principles on which the learning explanations for anxiety are based.

Second, however, the question that arises is, *can the principles that were developed in highly controlled laboratory situations with animals be generalized to complex abnormal behaviors that occur in humans?* The best way to test that would be to conduct experiments in which the principles of learning are used to create abnormal behavior in humans. Obviously, doing that poses serious ethical problems (see Chapter 3). For example, there is some question about whether the original experiment with Little Albert was ethically justified. Was it fair or ethical to create a phobia in the child?

However, indirect evidence that the learning explanation can be applied to complex human behaviors comes from the fact that conditioning obviously plays an important role in the development of normal human behavior. For example, inte   onally pairing

negative consequences (punishment) with misbehavior is effective for making a child anxious about using that behavior, so it is likely that inadvertently pairing negative consequences with appropriate behaviors or situations would result in similar anxieties that we would call phobias.

Third, you should note that although classical conditioning provides a good explanation for phobias and the posttraumatic stress disorder, by itself *classical conditioning does not explain why only some individuals who are exposed to fear or traumatic events develop the disorders*. The reason only some individuals develop a disorder (i.e., condition the response) may be that some individuals are more susceptible to classical conditioning, and I will discuss that possibility later when I discuss the physiological explanations. However, the point here is that by itself, the conditioning explanation may not be sufficient.

Finally, and most important, some critics suggest that *the traditional view of classical conditioning as some sort of automatic process is outdated and wrong*. The critics argue that conditioning is really a *cognitive* process; that is, if a stimulus is consistently paired with a reason to be afraid, the individual will "catch on" and expect the fearful event to follow the stimulus. The result is the same (anxiety), but the process is different, and the difference in the process can have implications for treatment. For example, if you believe that the underlying process is conditioning, you will use extinction to eliminate fears, but if you believe that the underlying process is cognitive, you simply tell the individual that the belief about the connection between the stimulus and the feared event (elevator and a crash) is wrong. In the next section, I will discuss the cognitive explanations for anxiety.

COGNITIVE EXPLANATIONS

The basic premise of the cognitive explanations for anxiety disorders is that individuals have *erroneous beliefs (cognitions) that lead to anxiety*. For example, individuals with phobias believe that specific objects or situations are more dangerous than they really are (e.g., the individual with an elevator phobia simply has an incorrect belief about how dangerous elevators are).

Erroneous Beliefs in the Anxiety Disorders

Different **erroneous beliefs** can lead to different anxiety disorders, and here are a few examples of erroneous beliefs that might go with different disorders (van Oppen & Arntz, 1994):

■ *Phobias.* "Spiders—even little ones that look harmless—are probably very dangerous." "Lots of people are killed in airplane crashes, so it is wise to avoid flying."

is anxiety based on a fear/death? [handwritten note]

■ *Posttraumatic Stress Disorder.* "This situation is a lot like the dangerous one in which I was earlier—this one could be dangerous too!"

■ *Generalized Anxiety Disorder.* "The world is really a very dangerous place, and you never know when and where trouble may arise."

■ *Panic Disorder.* "I feel slightly out of breath, and I feel a little pain in my chest. My God, I'm having a heart attack and I'll probably die!"

■ *Obsessive-Compulsive Disorder.* "There are lots of dangerous germs around, so I had better wash my hands frequently to protect myself from infection." "If I didn't turn off all of the lights in the house, a short might develop while I'm away, and the house will burn down. I'd better go back and check the lights."

Those erroneous beliefs are certainly consistent with the symptoms, but two important questions arise: first, *how were the erroneous beliefs originally developed,* and second, *how are the erroneous beliefs maintained in the face of evidence to the contrary?* In other words, how did the individual with an elevator phobia get the idea that elevators are dangerous, and how does the individual maintain that idea when there is evidence that elevators are in fact *not* dangerous?

In response to the question of how the beliefs were originally developed, cognitive theorists suggest that the erroneous beliefs are produced as a consequence of earlier experiences, possibly in very early childhood. The individual may have actually experienced a bad event, seen another individual experience a bad event, or simply heard about a bad event.

Problems with Information Processing

To explain how the erroneous beliefs are maintained, cognitive theorists suggest that once a belief is established, *the presence of that belief influences how information is processed.* For example, an individual who believes that dogs are dangerous is likely to notice and remember news reports about dogs that bite people, and the individual is likely to misinterpret a jumping dog as "attacking" rather than "playing." In other words, our erroneous beliefs guide our use of information so that our distorted views are maintained (Butler & Mathews, 1983; Ingram & Kendall, 1987; Litz & Keane, 1989; Mathews, 1990; McNally, 1990). Next I will describe four problems with information processing that help maintain erroneous beliefs and contribute to anxiety disorders.

Selective Attention. First, cognitive theorists suggest that some individuals develop anxiety disorders because they *focus excessive amounts of attention on threats and therefore they see more threats than do other individuals.* That is, **selective attention** leads them to see more threats, and the perception of all the threats makes them anxious. Selective attention apparently occurs

when information comes into the sensory memory and the individual scans it and decides what should and should not be sent to short-term memory for processing. (For a review of the cognitive processes associated with memory, see Chapter 2.)

Selective attention for threat-related information was demonstrated in experiments in which anxious and nonanxious individuals were shown a list of words in which the words were printed in different colors. The task was to *ignore the meanings* of the words and *name the color* in which each word was printed. Some of the words were threatening; others were neutral. If anxious individuals are focusing their attention on threats, it would then take them longer to name the colors in which threatening words are printed because focusing on the threat (word meaning) would interfere with attending to the color.

In one study of this type, nonanxious women and women who were suffering from a rape-related posttraumatic stress disorder were shown threat-related words (*penis, AIDS, victim*) and neutral words (*polite, moderate, typical*) (Cassiday et al., 1992). When asked to name the colors in which the words were printed, the anxious women took longer to respond to the threat-related words, thereby suggesting that they were attending to the meaning rather than the color. They also took longer in general to respond to all words, suggesting that anxiety was generally interfering with cognitive processing. These findings are presented in Figure 5.3. Other investigators have reported similar findings

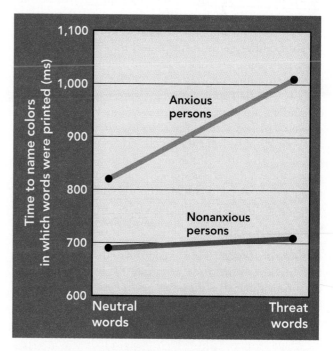

FIGURE 5.3 Anxious individuals attend more to threats than nonanxious individuals, thus slowing their ability to name the color of threat-related words.
Source: Adapted from Cassiday et al. (1992), p. 290, fig. 1.

(MacLeod & Mathews, 1988; MacLeod et al., 1986; Mathews et al., 1990; McNally et al., 1990).

Selective Recall. Second, cognitive theorists suggest that individuals who are anxious are *more likely to recall threatening experiences* than individuals who are not anxious and that recalling those experiences will contribute to their anxiety. That is, because of the **selective recall** of threatening experiences, the individuals will have more reasons to be anxious.

There are two reasons to expect that anxious individuals will be more likely to recall threatening material than nonanxious individuals. First, as just noted, anxious individuals are more likely to perceive threats and are therefore more likely to process and store them in long-term memory. Thus anxious individuals have more threatening memories on which to draw. Second, because the individuals are anxious, they are more likely to have an active associative network involving threats, so threat-related memories are more likely to be activated. (See Chapter 2 for a discussion of associative networks and activation.)

Selective recall of threat-related material was neatly demonstrated in an experiment in which individuals who did or did suffer from the panic disorder learned lists of panic-related words (e.g., *choke, fainting*), positive words (e.g., *vacation, meadow*), and negative words (e.g., *murder, brutal*), and later the individuals were unexpectedly tested for their recall of the words (Becker et al., 1994). The results indicated that the individuals who had the panic disorder recalled more of the panic-related words than the other individuals did, but there was no difference in their recall of the positive or negative words. Those findings are illustrated in Figure 5.4.

In another study, it was found that individuals also selectively recalled that stress had been paired with a phobic stimulus (de Jong et al., 1995). Specifically, individuals who had spider phobias were exposed to slides of spiders, weapons, and flowers, and the slides were *randomly* paired with a shock. Later, when the individuals were asked to indicate which slides were paired with the shock, the individuals overestimated the frequency with which slides of spiders were paired with shocks. In other words, the individuals who were afraid of spiders were more likely to recall that spiders were paired with a threat. Those findings are summarized in Figure 5.5.

Misinterpretation. Third, cognitive theorists suggest that anxious individuals are more likely than nonanxious individuals to *misinterpret neutral or ambiguous situations as threatening*, and such **misinterpretation** could contribute to anxiety. In one experiment, currently anxious individuals, recovered anxious individuals, and nonanxious individuals were read sentences that could be interpreted in either a threatening or a nonthreatening way (Eysenck et al., 1991). For example, one of the sentences was "The doctor examined little Emma's

growth." The threatening interpretation is "The doctor looked at little Emma's cancer," and the nonthreatening interpretation is "The doctor measured little Emma's height." After hearing 32 such sentences, the threatening and nonthreatening versions of the sentences were presented to the individuals, and the task was to identify which sentences they had heard earlier. The results indicated that when compared to the nonanxious individuals, the anxious individuals were more likely to choose the threatening alternative. Those results are presented in Figure 5.6. Similar results have been reported by other investigators (Butler & Mathews, 1983; MacLeod & Cohen, 1993; McNally & Foa, 1987).

The misinterpretation of ambiguous or minor physiological symptoms such as shortness of breath is central to the cognitive explanations for the panic disorder (Barlow, 1988; Carter et al., 1995; Kenardy et al., 1992; Roth et al., 1992). Specifically, it is suggested that the individual has a minor symptom but gives it a "catastrophic misinterpretation," such as, "I am having a heart attack and am going to die!" and that misinterpretation triggers the panic.

Erroneous Expectations. Finally, cognitive theorists suggest that **erroneous expectations** can also lead to anxiety. In many cases, individuals show inappropriate anxiety because they *incorrectly expect a situation to be threatening*. For example, there is now evidence that many individuals who develop agoraphobia do so

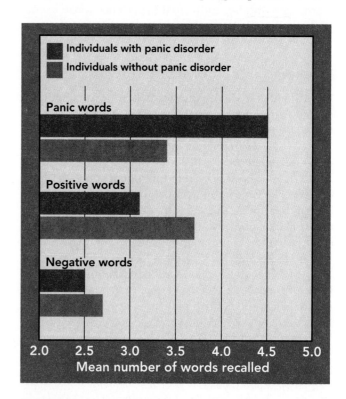

FIGURE 5.4 Individuals with the panic disorder recalled more panic-related words.
Source: Data from Becker et al. (1994), p. 397, tab. 2.

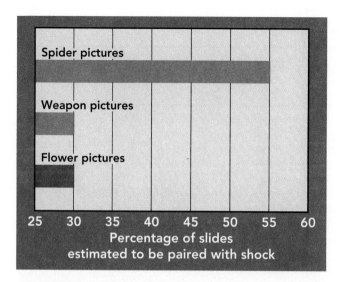

FIGURE 5.5 Individuals who had spider phobias were more likely to recall mistakenly that a threat (shock) was paired with a picture of a spider than with a picture of a weapon or a flower.
Source: Adapted from de Jong et al. (1995), p. 57, fig. 1.

A person who is sensitive to social rejection may misinterpret other people's expressions. Here this young man appears to interpret the woman's attention to someone else as a rejection of him.

because they expect to have a panic attack outside of the home (Clum & Knowles, 1991). That expectation causes them to stay home in an attempt to avoid the panic attack, and in this way the agoraphobia develops.

The effects of selective attention, selective recall, misinterpretation, and erroneous expectations in the development of an anxiety disorder are illustrated in Case Study 5.1.

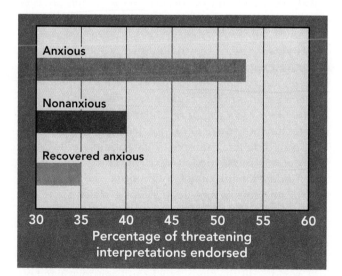

FIGURE 5.6 Anxious individuals were more likely than recovered anxious and nonanxious individuals to misinterpret ambiguous sentences as threatening.
Source: From "Bias in Interpretation of Ambiguous Sentences Related to Threat in Anxiety" by M. Eysenck et al., in *Journal of Abnormal Psychology,* Vol. 100, No. 2, 1991. Copyright © 1991 by the American Psychological Association. Reprinted with permission.

In Case Study 5.1, the skier misinterpreted physical signs and became fearful of a physical disorder. Similar misinterpretations can occur with personal or social signs, and those misinterpretations can lead to fears about personal or social problems. For example, if you are sensitive to social rejection (possibly because you were previously rejected or saw others being rejected), you may misinterpret the behavior of others as signs of rejection. Specifically, if others are preoccupied and do not greet you or do not greet you with as much enthusiasm as they usually do, you may interpret that as a sign that you have done something wrong and that you are going to be rejected. As a result of your misinterpretation, you will become anxious and begin avoiding others to avoid the embarrassment of rejection. The consequence would be a social phobia.

The effects of selective attention and misinterpretation can be seen in the behavior of students taking a course in abnormal psychology. While taking this course, you are likely to notice things about your behavior and that of your friends that you had overlooked before, and you are likely to misinterpret the behavior. The blahs become "depression," and a brief period of distractibility becomes a "schizophrenic thought disorder."

Processing Problems and Cognitive Performance

Anxiety is a problem itself, but it can also lead to another problem in that when we are anxious, our level of cognitive performance is impaired. That is, when we are anxious, we just do not think effectively. For

CASE STUDY 5.1
Erroneous Beliefs and the Development of a Panic Disorder

While skiing high in the Rocky Mountains, a 40-year-old man began to perspire heavily. In addition, he felt short of breath, weak, cold, unstable, and as though he were going to faint. He became extremely anxious, fearing that he was having a heart attack and that he was going to die. Because he was on the verge of collapse, he was taken from the slopes on a stretcher and rushed to a hospital. A thorough examination did not reveal any physical abnormalities, so it was concluded that he had suffered a panic attack—an acute *anxiety attack*.

This man had skied many times before, and because of the altitude, exertion, and weather conditions, on those occasions he had experienced the same physical symptoms of shortness of breath, chest pains, fatigue, sweating, and cold. The question then is, why did the symptoms lead to a panic attack on this occasion?

To answer that question, cognitive theorists suggested that on this occasion the man misinterpreted his normal physiological responses to exercise and altitude as the symptoms of a heart attack because several weeks earlier the man's brother, who was only a few years older, had died of a heart attack. That is, the cognitive theorists suggested that the man's thinking went something like this: "If my brother could die of a heart attack after exercising, so could I. These symptoms must mean that I am having a heart attack; *I'm about to die!*"

In other words, because of the recent death of his brother, the man had an active network associated with death. That network resulted in selective attention to the physical symptoms of altitude and fatigue because the symptoms were like those of a heart attack. Also because of the existing network, the symptoms were misinterpreted as signs of a heart attack, the man erroneously expected to have a heart attack, and this perception gave rise to anxiety.

Source: Adapted from Beck & Emery (1985).

---

example, individuals with **test anxiety** perform poorly on examinations even though they know the material well.

The cognitive problems that are associated with anxiety can be explained by what we know about information processing. In cases of test anxiety, individuals do poorly on exams because they are constantly *distracted by thoughts and feelings associated with failure* (Sarason, 1980; Sud & Sharma, 1989). For example, when individuals with test anxiety encounter a question on an exam for which they do not have a ready answer, they immediately think that they will fail; that activates a network of failure-related thoughts and feelings, and the resulting flood of failure-related thoughts and feelings interferes with thinking about the question and potential answers. The interference precludes working effectively on the question to the point that it cannot be answered, therefore confirming the beliefs about failure and starting a vicious circle. The solution for test anxiety is simply not to "spin off" into the failure-related thoughts and feelings, but that is easier said than done because the process is automatic and hence very difficult to avoid or stop (Meichenbaum, 1972).

COMMENT

The cognitive explanations for anxiety make intuitive sense, and these explanations are currently very popular among mental health professionals. Furthermore, the cognitive explanations dovetail nicely with the stress explanation for anxiety. Specifically, there is evidence that stress leads to anxiety, and the cognitive explanations suggest that erroneous beliefs can cause stress. In other words, erroneous beliefs are one of the factors that can trigger the stress that leads to anxiety.

However, there are two potential problems with the cognitive explanations that require attention. First, *the cognitive explanations cannot account for the free-floating or spontaneous anxiety that occurs in some disorders*. That is, it is difficult to use a cognitive explanation for anxiety for which the individual does not have an explanation. The most dramatic example of that occurs in the panic disorder, where the anxiety suddenly comes "out of the blue." Indeed, panic attacks often occur during sleep—specifically, during very deep sleep in which there are no dreams—so it is hard to see how cognitions play a role in those attacks. Other examples include the anxiety that occurs in the generalized anxiety disorder, in which individuals often say things like, "I just feel tense and anxious all the time, but I can't put my finger on what the problem is." However, the fact that the cognitive explanations do not seem able to account for those types of anxiety is not a reason to abandon the explanations completely. Instead, it may simply be that the cognitive explanations are helpful for some but not all anxiety disorders.

which came 1st: thought or feeling?

The second problem revolves around the question of *cause and effect*. Cognitive psychologists assume that anxiety-related thoughts lead to feelings of anxiety, but it is also possible that in at least some cases, *feelings of anxiety lead to anxiety-related thoughts*. That is, individuals who are anxious for some other reason, such as a physiological problem, may seek out cognitive explanations for their feelings, and once they find an explanation, they may misattribute the cause of their anxiety. That process was demonstrated in an experiment in which college students either were or were not made to feel anxious (Bramel et al., 1965). Then the students were asked to describe Russians, who at that time in history were considered enemies of the United States. The students who were anxious saw the Russians as hostile warmongers (which would justify the students' anxiety), whereas the students who were not anxious saw the Russians as generally nice people (because the students were not anxious, there was no reason to see others as hostile). In other words, anxiety led to cognitive explanations. *like justifications*

The findings described in the preceding paragraph indicated that at least some of the time, anxiety influences cognitions rather than vice versa. However, even in cases in which the anxiety was not originally started by cognitions, the anxiety-related cognitions triggered by the anxiety could *prolong the anxiety*. That is, if, once the anxiety has started, the individual looks for reasons to be anxious, finding reasons to be anxious could heighten or at least prolong the anxiety.

Finally, I must address the question of whether the cognitive explanations for anxiety can *replace the classical conditioning explanation*. That is, is classical conditioning simply a cognitive process? As with many things, the answer is yes and no. Yes, cognitive expectancies play a role in the conditioning process, but no, cognitive expectancies cannot account for all of it. Specifically, cognitive explanations cannot account for the apparently automatic, uncontrollable brief surge of anxiety you get when you are exposed to a once-fearful stimulus. For example, when you see a fearful object, you first have a brief surge of anxiety, and then you say to yourself, "No, that's not a reason to be afraid," and the fear subsides. In that situation, both conditioning and cognitive processes are in operation, and how that works can be understood when you recognize that there are two pathways in your brain that are involved with fear. One of those pathways goes directly to the area of your brain that is responsible for fear (the amygdala); that pathway is established through classical conditioning and is responsible for the first surge of fear. In contrast, the second pathway goes to the areas of your brain where thought processes occur (association areas) and then to the area that is responsible for fear. If you think that there is not a reason for fear, a message that suppresses the fear is sent to your fear area, and the fear response subsides. Clearly, both con-

ditioning and cognitions play a role in anxiety responses. (For a more extensive discussion, see Chapter 2.)

In short, the cognitive explanations for anxiety are helpful, but like the other explanations I have discussed, they are not the panaceas that their proponents would have us believe. Like the other explanations, they are helpful in explaining some disorders but not others. In the next section, I will discuss the physiological explanations for anxiety disorders.

PHYSIOLOGICAL EXPLANATIONS

The basic premise of the physiological explanations for anxiety disorders is that *problems with brain functioning lead to anxiety disorders*. With regard to this explanation, it is important to recognize that *different types of problems in the brain lead to different types of anxiety disorders*. Therefore, when seeking to understand the physiological basis for anxiety, we must examine the various disorders separately; that is what I will do in the following sections.

Generalized Anxiety Disorder: Insufficient Neural Inhibition

The physiological explanation for the generalized anxiety disorder is that there is *excessive neurological activity in the area of the brain that is responsible for emotional arousal* and that arousal is experienced as anxiety. The excessive neurological activity is thought to stem from the fact that the **inhibitory neurons** that ordinarily reduce neurological activity are not functioning adequately.

Inhibitory neurons serve to reduce the firing of other neurons (see Chapter 2). Specifically, at the synapse between a presynaptic and a postsynaptic neuron, there may be an inhibitory neuron that releases a neurotransmitter that inhibits the release of another neurotransmitter by the presynaptic neuron so that the impulse cannot be transmitted across the synapse. The release of the neurotransmitter by the inhibitory neuron can also make the postsynaptic neuron less sensitive, which can also reduce the transmission of the impulse. If the inhibitory neurons are not releasing enough of their neurotransmitter, the neurological activity between neurons will go unchecked. The result is a high level of neurological activity (arousal) we experience as anxiety.

The neurotransmitter that is released by the inhibitory neurons is known as **GABA** (*gamma-aminobutyric acid*), and therefore we refer to this as the *GABA explanation for general anxiety*. In short, it is believed that (a) a low level of GABA released by the inhibitory neurons results in a failure to inhibit the activity of other neurons, (b) the failure to inhibit the activity results in a high level of activity of the neurons in the areas of the brain that are responsible for arousal, and (c) that high level of activity (arousal) is experienced as anxiety. The free-floating nature of the anxiety that is seen in the generalized anxiety disorder is exactly what would be expected from low levels of GABA because GABA levels are not influenced by environmental events.

Evidence for the GABA explanation for anxiety is based on our understanding of the effects of a group of drugs called **benzodiazepines** (BEN-zō-dī-AZ-uh-pīnz) that are effective for reducing anxiety. Specifically, the benzodiazepines increase the likelihood that GABA will bind to (fit into) the receptors on the neurons that are to be inhibited, thereby reducing the activity of those neurons and reducing anxiety. The fact that increasing the effects of GABA is an effective way to reduce anxiety that otherwise appears to come "out of the blue" provides strong evidence for the GABA explanation for the generalized anxiety disorder.

Panic Disorder: Oversensitivity of the Respiratory Control Center

For many years, investigators were stymied in their search for a physiological explanation for panic attacks. A variety of clues linked panic attacks to physiological factors, but it was not clear how the clues fit together and what the underlying process was. However, recently investigators have concluded that individuals who suffer from panic attacks have *overly sensitive respiratory control centers* in the brain stem (Goetz et al., 1993; Hollander et al., 1994; Klein, 1993; Stein et al., 1995; Taylor, 1994). That may sound like a strange explanation for panic attacks, but consider the following reasoning: If an individual has an overly sensitive respiratory control center, a very minor reduction in oxygen will result in a "false alarm" that the individual is beginning to suffocate, and that false alarm about suffocation could lead to a panic. It may then be that individuals who have panic attacks are getting false alarms about suffocation when for some reason they get a little less oxygen than they normally do. In the following paragraphs, I will first give you a brief explanation of the respiratory control center, and then I will explain how this explanation fits with what we know about panic attacks.

Your brain stem is located at the base of your brain just above your spinal cord, and it monitors and controls basic physiological activities such as heart rate and respiration (see Chapter 2). Most relevant here is the **respiratory control center** that monitors the level of oxygen in your system. If you are receiving too little oxygen and building up an **oxygen debt,** the respiratory control center sends signals to higher areas in your brain indicating that you are beginning to suffocate,

The sensation of suffocation may cause a panic attack in individuals whose respiratory control centers are overly sensitive to minor increases in the level of carbon dioxide.

and so you take action to get more oxygen. Important in this explanation is that one of the factors that is used to assess the level of oxygen in the system is the level of **carbon dioxide.** Carbon dioxide is a by-product of the respiratory process, and if the level of carbon dioxide gets high relative to the level of oxygen, that indicates the presence of an oxygen debt (more by-product is being produced than oxygen is coming in). Sensing that imbalance is a normal process and necessary for survival. However, if your respiratory control center is overly sensitive, when it detects *very minor* increases in the level of carbon dioxide, it sends up false alarms that you are suffocating. Those alarms are false because you can survive on the reduced level of oxygen and there is not a crisis. With that as background, I can turn to the question of how an overly sensitive respiratory control center fits with what we know about panic attacks.

Sodium Lactate. For many years we knew that injections of **sodium lactate** (a salt) could bring on panic attacks. Importantly, that occurred only in individuals who suffered from panic attacks "normally" or who had biological relatives who suffered from panic attacks (Appleby et al., 1981; Fink et al., 1970; Gorman et al., 1988; Guttmacher et al., 1983; Kelly et al., 1971; Pitts & Allen, 1979; Pitts & McClure, 1967). In that research, individuals who did and did not suffer from panic attacks were brought into a laboratory and given sodi-

do sufferers panic attacks smoke lure?

um lactate intravenously for approximately 20 minutes. Within about 10 minutes, most of the individuals who had a history of panic attacks began experiencing severe ones. They became tense and then terrified, and they showed elevated heart rate and blood pressure. When the injections were terminated, the panic attacks subsided and the individuals returned to their normal states. It is noteworthy that the panic attacks that were induced with sodium lactate were indistinguishable from those that occur spontaneously outside of the laboratory. Furthermore, it is clear that the panic attacks were not due to the stress of the injections because when the individuals were given placebo injections they did not have panic attacks. Finally, the fact that the sodium lactate triggered panic attacks only in individuals with a personal or family history of panic attacks indicated that there was a physiological predisposition to the response that was probably due to genetic factors.

It was known that sodium lactate could trigger panic attacks, but investigators were stumped over why. However, we now know that in the body sodium lactate is converted into carbon dioxide, the carbon dioxide is then transported to the respiratory control center in the brain stem, and if the control center is overly sensitive, the increase in carbon dioxide signals suffocation and the individual panics. Clearly, the hypothesis about the respiratory control center made understandable the findings linking sodium lactate to panics.

Inhaling Carbon Dioxide and Hyperventilation. It was also known that inhaling air that contained small amounts of carbon dioxide could trigger panic attacks in individuals who have a personal or family history of panic attacks, but the reason was not initially clear (Dager et al., 1995; Gorman et al., 1994; Klein, 1994; Perna, Bertrani, et al., 1995; Perna, Cocchi, et al., 1995). For example, if, in a laboratory, individuals are given an air mixture to breathe that contains as little as 5% carbon dioxide, individuals who have a personal or family history of panic attacks will have a panic attack. Interestingly, inhaling carbon dioxide can bring on panic attacks in the biological relatives of individuals who have panic attacks (Perna, Bertani, et al., 1995; Perna, Cocchi, et al., 1995). Similarly, if individuals **hyperventilate,** individuals who have a personal or family history of panic attacks will have a panic attack. (Hyperventilation involves rapid, shallow breathing, and when individuals hyperventilate, they get less oxygen and feel "short of breath.")

Again, the links between inhaling carbon dioxide, hyperventilating, and panic attacks were not originally clear, but they were made understandable by the respiratory control center hypothesis; that is, inhaling carbon dioxide and hyperventilating triggered false suffocation alarms and panics in individuals who have overly sensitive centers.

Antidepressant Drugs. A third interesting finding that links the respiratory control center to panic attacks is that certain antidepressant drugs are effective for eliminating panic attacks. In fact, if individuals who ordinarily have panic attacks in response to sodium lactate injections are given an antidepressant drug before receiving the sodium lactate, they will not have the panic attacks (Klein, 1982; Rifkin et al., 1981). Like the other findings, the reason an antidepressant drug would stop panic attacks was not immediately understood. However, we now know that the drugs that are effective for controlling the panic attacks are those that increase the levels of the neurotransmitter **serotonin** at the synapses, and we also know that serotonin acts as an inhibitor in the respiratory control center (Eriksson & Humble, 1990). In other words, the higher levels of serotonin reduce the tendency of the respiratory control center to send up false alarms when the individual experiences a minor oxygen debt, and that controls the panic attacks. *More oxygen!*

The respiratory control center explanation also makes understandable the finding that panic attacks are more likely to occur during the premenstrual period. Specifically, about 3 days before the onset of menses, progesterone levels fall; that reduces respiration rates, thereby slightly decreasing oxygen intake, which could trigger the false alarm and panic in overly sensitive individuals. It is also interesting to note that individuals with the panic disorder cannot voluntarily hold their breath as long as individuals with the social phobia or no anxiety disorder (Asmundson & Stein, 1994). Apparently, when individuals with the panic disorder hold their breath and their oxygen levels begin to drop, their respiratory control centers send up suffocation signals sooner than is the case in other individuals, so they "let go" sooner.

Finally, a comment should be made concerning a disorder known as **Ondine's curse** in which the individual has an *insensitivity to the lack of oxygen* (Haddad et al., 1978). Individuals with this disorder do not sense the lack of oxygen, so when they are deprived of oxygen, they do not take corrective action and may even die. (*Sudden infant death syndrome* may have a similar cause; the infant may roll face down and smother before awakening.) The presence of this disorder illustrates that respiratory centers can be undersensitive as well as oversensitive, and it provides an interesting counterpoint for the panic disorder.

The panic attacks that occur spontaneously outside of the laboratory appear to occur when for some reason the individual gets less oxygen. For example, panic attacks are most likely to occur when the individual is very relaxed or deeply asleep, and in those states the rate of respiration is reduced, so oxygen intake is reduced. In sum, the overly sensitive respiratory control center explanation for panic attacks can account

So, people who have panic attacks should practice breathing techniques, avoid smoking
— what about asthma

for a wide variety of findings concerning panic attacks that cannot be accounted for by other explanations. It is an unusual and somewhat surprising explanation, but it appears to be sound.

ie why meditation is so hard for some people

Obsessive-Compulsive Disorder: Serotonin and Brain Damage

It is now widely recognized that many cases of the OCD are due to physiological problems in the brain, and I will describe three sets of evidence that lead to that conclusion.

Low Levels of Serotonin. Because the OCD is an *anxiety* disorder, for many years attempts were made to treat it with drugs that reduce anxiety. Unfortunately, those drugs were generally ineffective; the antianxiety drugs sometimes reduced the anxiety about obsessions and compulsions, but the drugs rarely reduced the obsessions and compulsions themselves. However, a few years ago it was discovered that a specific group of *antidepressant* drugs were very effective for treating many cases of the OCD (Hollander et al., 1988; Hollander et al., 1994; see also Chapter 6). I will discuss antidepressant drugs in greater detail in Chapter 10, but here it is relevant to note that the antidepressant drugs that are effective for treating the OCD *block the reuptake* of the neurotransmitter **serotonin.** (**Reuptake** is the process by which the presynaptic neuron absorbs some of the neurotransmitter that has just been released. Blocking reuptake makes more of the neurotransmitter available at the synapse, thereby increasing the activity at the synapse; see Chapter 2.) Three well-known drugs that block the reuptake of serotonin are **Anafranil (clomipramine), Prozac (fluoxetine),** and **Zoloft (sertraline),** and those drugs are effective for treating the OCD as well as for treating depression. The fact that drugs that increase the levels of serotonin at the

would exercise help this?

also inhibits RC.C. in panic attacks

do people w/ panic attacks experience OCD?

synapse can reduce the OCD suggests that *the OCD may be due to low levels of serotonin.*

Additional support for the link between low levels of serotonin and the OCD comes from an experiment in which it was found that when patients with the OCD were given a drug that *reduced serotonin activity* (it blocked the serotonin receptors at the synapse), 55% of the patients showed a substantial *increase in their OCD symptoms,* whereas none of the patients who were given a placebo showed an increase in OCD symptoms (Hollander et al., 1992). Viewed in another way, the drug that reduced serotonin activity resulted in almost a 70% increase in OCD symptoms, whereas the placebo resulted in about a 30% decrease in OCD symptoms. These findings are presented in Figure 5.7. Similarly, in a study of children with the OCD, it was found that low levels of serotonin were associated with high levels of OCD symptoms (Swedo et al., 1992).

The connection between levels of serotonin and the symptoms of the OCD was also demonstrated in an interesting study of dogs who showed severe chronic licking of their paws or flanks, behaviors that can be seen as comparable to the handwashing of humans with the OCD (Rapoport et al., 1992). These dogs were given either (a) an antidepressant drug that blocked the reuptake of serotonin (Prozac/fluoxetine), (b) an antidepressant drug that did not block the reuptake of serotonin, or (c) a placebo. The results indicated that the dogs who received the drug that blocked the reuptake of serotonin showed substantial reductions in licking, whereas the dogs who received the other drug or the placebo did not show reductions in licking. This provides an interesting animal model for understanding the OCD and support for the serotonin explanation. (As an aside, I might mention that I know of more than one family where both the humans and the dog take antidepressants for their obsessive-compulsive symptoms!)

It is clear that in many cases low levels of serotonin are related to the OCD, but they do not appear to be

dogs w/ OCD! — not cognitive?

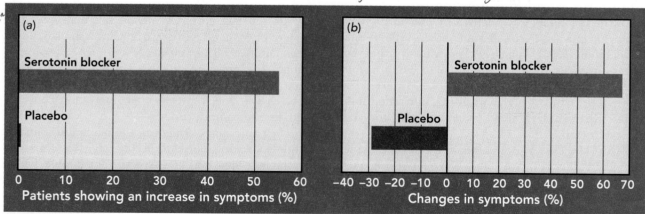

FIGURE 5.7 Reducing serotonin activity leads to increases in obsessive-compulsive disorder symptoms.
Source: Hollander et al. (1994), p. 23.

responsible for all cases of the OCD. For example, in the study in which patients were given a drug to decrease serotonin activity, the drug caused increases in the OCD in only 55% of the patients (Hollander et al., 1994). Interestingly, the drugs that block serotonin reuptake are effective for treating only about 50% of the patients with the OCD (see Clomipramine Collaborative Study Group, 1991). These findings suggest that there may be different causes of the OCD, only one of which is low levels of serotonin, which leads us to the second set of data.

Minimal Brain Damage. A second apparent cause of the OCD is some minor form of *brain damage.* Support for this notion comes from studies in which the investigators assessed the so-called **soft signs** of neurological damage in patients with the OCD (Bihari et al., 1991; Hollander et al., 1990). (Soft signs include minor problems with motor coordination such as the inability to bring together the index fingers of your two hands when your arms are stretched in front of you and your eyes are closed.) In the studies in which the soft signs were assessed, it was found that *patients with the OCD had almost four times as many soft signs of brain damage as individuals who did not have the OCD* and that among the patients with the OCD, *the patients who had more soft signs of brain damage had more severe obsessions* (r = .37). The presence of soft signs indicates the presence of damage, and research is now being conducted to identify the location of the damage (Robinson et al., 1995).

With regard to the possibility that some type of brain damage contributes to the OCD, it is relevant to note that some individuals who develop neurological disorders such as Parkinson's disease or epilepsy also show a simultaneous development of obsessive-compulsive symptoms (Insel, 1993). Indeed, in some individuals, the onset of an epileptic seizure is preceded by obsessive thoughts, suggesting that both the seizure and the thoughts are driven by some underlying brain dysfunction.

Abnormal Brain Activity. The third set of findings that link the OCD to physiological problems revolves around abnormal activity in specific areas of the brain. Specifically, it has been found that individuals with the OCD have *higher rates of metabolism* (which indicate higher rates of activity) in two connected areas of the brain (Baxter et al., 1987, 1992; Insel, 1993). One of those areas is the **caudate** (KAW-dāt) **nucleus,** which plays a role in motor functions. The higher the levels of activity in the caudate nucleus, the more severe the obsessive-compulsive symptoms, and the treatments that are effective for reducing those symptoms are associated with reductions in the levels of activity in the caudate nucleus (Baxter et al., 1987, 1992). The other area that seems to be related to the OCD is the **orbitofrontal area,** which is at the sides and rear of the frontal lobes, and it is through this area that nerves pass that link the frontal lobes to other areas of the brain (Damasio,

1994). It may be thought of as the "interface board" between the rest of the brain and the frontal lobes, where planning is done. In some extreme cases of the OCD, surgery to separate the orbitofrontal area from the rest of the brain has been effective for reducing the symptoms of the OCD (Insel, 1993). Although we know that activity in the caudate nucleus and orbitofrontal area is related to obsessive-compulsive symptoms, we do not yet understand exactly why. An interesting example of a man who developed the OCD in conjunction with a brain tumor and surgery in the orbitofrontal area is presented in Case Study 5.2.

Although it is clear that low levels of serotonin, minimal brain damage, and excessive activity in specific areas of the brain are associated with the OCD, it is not yet clear exactly how or why these factors lead to the obsessions and compulsions.

Phobias and the Posttraumatic Stress Disorder: Physiological Arousal and Classical Conditioning

When I discussed the learning explanations, I pointed out that phobias and the PTSD can probably be conceptualized best as *classically conditioned fear responses.* That is, fear was originally paired with stimuli (e.g., a spider, the darkness of the parking lot in the case of a woman who was raped there, the sound of a helicopter in the case of a Vietnam veteran), and later those stimuli are able to elicit the fear. That is a good explanation, but the question is, why do some individuals develop phobias or the PTSD and others do not? The answer seems to be that *individuals who develop phobias or the PTSD have higher levels of neurological arousal than individuals who do not develop those disorders* (Charney et al., 1993; Gerardi et al., 1994; Southwick et al., 1993).

There are three reasons why high neurological arousal would contribute to the conditioning of those disorders. First, higher levels of neurological arousal may enhance the degree to which individuals can be conditioned. (Drugs that increase arousal can enhance conditioning; see Chapter 14.) Second, highly aroused individuals may be more likely than less aroused individuals to respond with fear when confronted with a potentially fear-provoking stimulus. (Have you ever noticed that when you are tense, any little noise will cause you to jump?) If highly aroused individuals are more likely to respond with fear, they are more likely to have fear paired with stimuli in the environment. Third, high levels of neurological arousal enhance the storage of material in memory (McGaugh, 1989, 1990; Pitman, 1989; Squire, 1986). That is, you are more likely to remember material to which you are exposed when you are highly aroused. That is particularly relevant for the PTSD, which involves recurring memories of the traumatic event.

CASE STUDY 5.2

The Man Whose Brain Tumor Led to an Obsessive-Compulsive Disorder

Mr. Ervin (not his real name) was a 35-year-old accountant and the comptroller of a moderate-sized construction company. He was generally conservative in style, effective in business and personal matters, and respected as a leader. He did not have any history of obsessive-compulsive symptoms or any other psychiatric disorder. However, over a couple of months, Mr. Ervin began having problems with his vision, and he also began showing changes in his personality. In an attempt to diagnose the visual problems, Mr. Ervin was given a neurological examination. That examination revealed that Mr. Ervin had a slow-growing brain tumor that was located in an orbitofrontal area (on one side of the rear of his frontal lobes). The tumor was apparently causing the visual problems and possibly also the personality changes.

Surgery was used to eliminate the tumor, and following an uneventful 2-week stay in the hospital and a 3-month recovery period at home, Mr. Ervin returned to work. Although Mr. Ervin recovered well from the surgery, the changes in his personality persisted and got worse. Of most interest here is the development of severe obsessive-compulsive symptoms. For example, if Mr. Ervin was planning to eat out, he would spend hours considering each restaurant's seating arrangements, menu, atmosphere, and management. Having done that, he would drive to each of the restaurants to see how busy they were, but even then he would not be able to make a deci-

sion concerning where to eat. He had similar problems when he had to make any sort of minor purchase, and he had great difficulty making decisions to get rid of useless possessions. For example, at one point he had a collection of dead houseplants, old phone books, and broken fans and television sets, along with three bags of empty orange juice cans, 15 cigarette lighters, and countless stacks of old newspapers. His compulsions also extended to personal grooming; it usually took him two hours to get ready to leave the house in the morning, and sometimes he would spend the entire day shaving and washing his hair.

Despite his obsessive-compulsive symptoms, Mr. Ervin had an IQ of about 125. He did not show any other behavioral evidence of brain damage or dysfunction, but brain scans revealed that there were localized lesions in the area of the brain where the surgery had been done (orbitofrontal area). All of the other parts of his brain were normal in both structure and function.

What caused the onset of Mr. Ervin's obsessive-compulsive disorder? It is impossible to answer that question definitively, but it is relevant to note that his symptoms began to develop at the same time that his tumor began to develop and that his tumor and the subsequent surgery were in the area of the brain that we now know is linked to the OCD.

Source: Based on Eslinger & Damasio (1985).

The high level of arousal that predisposes individuals to develop phobias and the posttraumatic stress disorder helps explain why these disorders tend to run in families; that is, individuals inherit a high level of arousal, which sets the individuals up to develop the disorders (Basoglu et al., 1994).

In sum, neither learning nor physiology alone can account for the development of phobias or the posttraumatic stress disorder, but together they provide a good explanation; physiology provides the predisposition, and conditioning is the process by which the disorders develop.

Mitral Valve Prolapse: A False Lead

At this point in the discussion of the causes of anxiety disorders, I should comment on a physiological factor that is often mentioned as a cause of anxiety but

probably is not. As early as 1871, it was reported that patients who suffered from anxiety tended to have an unusual heart murmur (an odd sound that occurred when the heart beat) (Da Costa, 1871). The relationship between anxiety and that particular heart murmur has been reported by numerous investigators in the intervening 125 years (see Gorman, 1984). We now know that the heart murmur found in anxious patients is due to the fact that the *mitral valve* in the heart (the valve that normally stops blood from flowing back from the left ventricle into the left atrium) is *prolapsed* (pushed back too far), so there is some backflow of blood. In other words, with **mitral valve prolapse,** when the left ventricle contracts, some of the blood flows back into the atrium rather than into the aorta and to the rest of the body. The sound of the blood flowing back into the atrium is the heart murmur.

Mitral valve prolapse is diagnosed in 40% to 50% of anxious individuals but in only 5% to 20% of the normal population. There is a relationship between mitral valve prolapse and anxiety, but the relationship is probably *correlational* rather than *causal*. That is, although it is possible that the heart palpitations, chest pains, shortness of breath that are sometimes associated with mitral valve prolapse could contribute to anxiety, it is more likely that highly anxious individuals get more thorough physical examinations, and therefore a mitral valve prolapse is more likely to be diagnosed in them than in other people (Dager et al., 1988; Gorman et al., 1988; Margraf et al., 1988).

Genetic Factors

To this point, you have learned that anxiety disorders can be caused by physiological problems such as low levels of GABA, low levels of serotonin, minor brain damage, high levels of neurological arousal, and an overly sensitive respiratory center in the brain stem. However, the question remains, what causes those problems? One possibility is that they are due to genetic factors, and in this section I will review the evidence for the role of genetics in anxiety disorders.

Studies of Families. If anxiety disorders are due at least in part to genetic factors, it would be expected that the prevalence of anxiety disorders would be higher in the biological relatives of individuals with anxiety disorders than it is in the general population. A variety of research provides strong support for that possibility. For example, in a recent study of the parents of individuals who did or did not have the OCD, it was found that the parents of individuals with the disorder were five times more likely to have the disorder than the parents of individuals who did not have the disorder (Pauls et al., 1995). Similarly, in a study of the relatives of individuals who did or did not have the panic disorder, it was found that the relatives of those with the disorder were almost 12 times more likely to have the disorder than the relatives of individuals who did not have the disorder (14.2% versus 1.2%) (Goldstein et al., 1994). It is also interesting to note that in studies in which both first-degree relatives (parents, siblings, children) and second-degree relatives (grandparents, aunts, uncles, half siblings) were examined, the first-degree relatives of individuals with anxiety disorders were more likely also to have the disorder than second-degree relatives (e.g., Pauls et al., 1980). That would be expected if there was a genetic basis for the disorders because the first-degree relatives would share more genes with the individual with the disorder than the second-degree relatives would.

The investigations of families of individuals who have anxiety disorders provide support for a genetic basis for anxiety disorders, but firm conclusions cannot be drawn from those investigations because they do not rule out the potential role of interpersonal factors in the development of the disorders. That is, because individuals are more likely to spend more time with their first-degree relatives than with their second-degree relatives, the higher prevalence of anxiety disorders among first- than among second-degree relatives of anxiety sufferers might be due to their shared experiences and environments rather than to their shared genes. In view of that, we must turn to the study of twins.

Studies of Twins. The potential genetic contribution to the development of anxiety disorders has also been studied by comparing the concordance rates of anxiety disorders in monozygotic (MZ) and dizygotic (DZ) twin pairs. If there is a genetic basis for anxiety disorders, we would expect a higher concordance rate among MZ twins (who have identical sets of genes) than among DZ twins (who have different sets of genes). The concordance rates among twins for anxiety disorders have been examined in a variety of studies, and each revealed that the concordance rate was higher among MZ than DZ twins. For example, in four studies, the concordance rates for MZ twins were 30%, 33%, 34%, and 37%, while the concordance rates for DZ twins were only 7%, 9%, 17%, and 31% (Carey & Gottesman, 1981; Noyes et al., 1987; Torgersen, 1979, 1983). The results of other studies that focused on the generalized anxiety disorder and the PTSD revealed that the heritability of those disorders was about 30% and that the remaining variability was due to unique environmental factors rather than any shared factors such as family experiences (Kendler, Walters, et al., 1995; Kendler, Neale, et al., 1992a; True et al., 1993). (Note that "unique environmental factors" refers to *random factors in the environment* that cannot be accounted for, *not* to any specific factors associated with families.) The 30% level of heritability is similar to the level of heritability that is found for normal personality traits.

The studies of families and of twins provide strong and consistent evidence that there is a genetic basis for anxiety disorders. However, in considering these findings, you should realize that the concordance rate is not 100%, and therefore factors other than genes must contribute to the disorders.

COMMENT

The findings concerning the physiological bases for anxiety disorders are strong and often persuasive. For example, the fact that we can trigger panic attacks with physiological substances such as sodium lactate and carbon dioxide suggests a physiological basis for the disorder, and the fact that the physiological factors trigger the panic attacks only in individuals who have a personal or family history of panic attacks certainly

TABLE 5.1 Summary of Explanations for Anxiety Disorders

Disorders	Explanations			
	Psychodynamic	Learning	Cognitive	Physiological
Phobias	Unconscious conflicts or stress	Classical conditioning	Erroneous beliefs ("All snakes are dangerous")	High neurological arousal plus conditioning
Generalized anxiety disorder	Unconscious conflicts or stress	Generalized classical conditioning	Erroneous beliefs ("The world is a dangerous place")	Low levels of GABA
Obsessive-compulsive disorder	Defense against unconscious conflicts or stress	Operant conditioning to reduce anxiety	Erroneous beliefs ("I'd better wash my hands to protect myself from germs")	Low levels of serotonin or brain damage
Posttraumatic stress disorder	Unconscious conflicts	Classical conditioning	Erroneous beliefs ("This is like an earlier dangerous situation!")	High neurological arousal plus conditioning
Panic disorder	Unconscious conflicts		Erroneous beliefs ("I am going to die right now!")	Overly sensitive respiratory control center

Handwritten annotations:
- *classical maybe – cant explain why during sleep*
- *doesn't explain why some do + some dont*
- *erroneous beliefs may be result/anxiety*
- *cant explain "out/blue" anxiety*
- *cant explain specific phobias*
- *concordance rates < 100%*

suggests a genetic foundation for the disorder and tends to preclude other explanations. Similarly, the fact that we can increase and decrease the levels of obsessions and compulsions by decreasing and increasing the levels of serotonin argues strongly for a physiological basis for the OCD. In addition, the data concerning the inheritability of the OCD and other anxiety disorders is strong. Finally, a physiological factor (low levels of GABA) can be used to explain free-floating anxiety for which other approaches have not provided a good explanation.

However, at present, the physiological explanation has two limitations. First, by itself, the physiological explanation cannot account for the stimulus-specific anxieties seen in phobias. That is, by themselves, physiological factors cannot be used to explain why one individual develops a phobia for snakes whereas another individual develops a phobia for elevators. In those cases, physiological and conditioning factors must work together to produce the disorder. The second limitation is that inheritance does not account for all anxiety disorders (concordance rates are not 100%), thus suggesting that other factors are also important.

This concludes the discussion of the causes of the anxiety disorders (they are summarized in Table 5.1). In the next chapter I will explain the treatments that are used for the anxiety disorders.

SUMMARY

- The psychodynamic, learning, cognitive, and physiological explanations for the various anxiety disorders are summarized in Table 5.1
- The psychodynamic explanations for anxiety disorders suggest that anxiety stems from unconscious conflicts or from stressful life events (or both).
- The psychodynamic explanations do not explain why some individuals who are exposed to stress develop anxiety but others do not.
- The learning explanations suggest that phobias, the generalized anxiety disorder, and the posttraumatic stress disorder are due to classical conditioning of fear and that the symptoms of the obsessive-compulsive disorder are operantly conditioned responses that are used to reduce anxiety. The panic disorder might also be a classically conditioned response, but conditioning cannot be used to explain panic attacks that occur during nondreaming sleep.

■ Questions have been raised over whether the principles of conditioning can be used to explain complex human behavior, why some individuals are more likely to develop classically conditioned responses than others, and whether classical conditioning is the "automatic" process it is often represented as.

■ The cognitive explanation for anxiety disorders is that individuals have erroneous beliefs about the danger in situations, and those beliefs lead to anxiety.

■ The erroneous beliefs develop from early experiences and then are maintained by selective attention, selective recall, misinterpretations, and erroneous expectations.

■ Cognitive explanations cannot account for anxiety that comes "out of the blue" for which the individual does not have an explanation (e.g., panic attacks), and it appears that in at least some cases, erroneous beliefs may be the result rather than the cause of anxiety.

■ The physiological explanations for anxiety disorders suggest that (a) high levels of neurological arousal predispose individuals to classically conditioned phobias and the posttraumatic stress disorder; (b) the generalized anxiety disorder is due to low levels of GABA, so there is insufficient neural inhibition; (c) the obsessive-compulsive disorder is due to low levels of serotonin and minor forms of brain damage; and (c) the panic disorder is due to an overly sensitive respiratory control center in the brain stem. Some of these problems may be due to genetic factors.

■ The physiological explanations alone cannot explain why individuals develop the specific phobias they do, and therefore to explain phobias, the physiological explanations must work with the learning explanations. Because concordance rates are not 100%, factors other than genetics must contribute to anxiety disorders.

■ No one theoretical approach can account for all cases or types of anxiety disorders. That is, no one explanation prevails over all the others, but by considering the contributions of different explanations, we can develop a good understanding of the various causes of anxiety disorders.

KEY TERMS, CONCEPTS, AND NAMES

In reviewing and testing yourself on what you have learned from this chapter, you should be able to identify and discuss each of the following.

Anafranil (clomipramine): *blocks reuptake of serotonin*

benzodiazepines: *helps GABA*

carbon dioxide

caudate nucleus: *motor*

classical conditioning

defense mechanisms

diathesis-stress explanation

erroneous beliefs

erroneous expectations

GABA

generalization

hyperventilation

inhibitory neurons

intermittent schedule of reward

misinterpretation (of neutral stimuli)

mitral valve prolapse

Ondine's curse

operant conditioning

orbitofrontal area: *planning*

oxygen debt

Prozac (fluoxetine)

respiratory control center

reuptake

selective attention

selective recall

serotonin

sodium lactate

soft signs (of brain damage)

test anxiety

vicarious conditioning

Zoloft (sertraline)

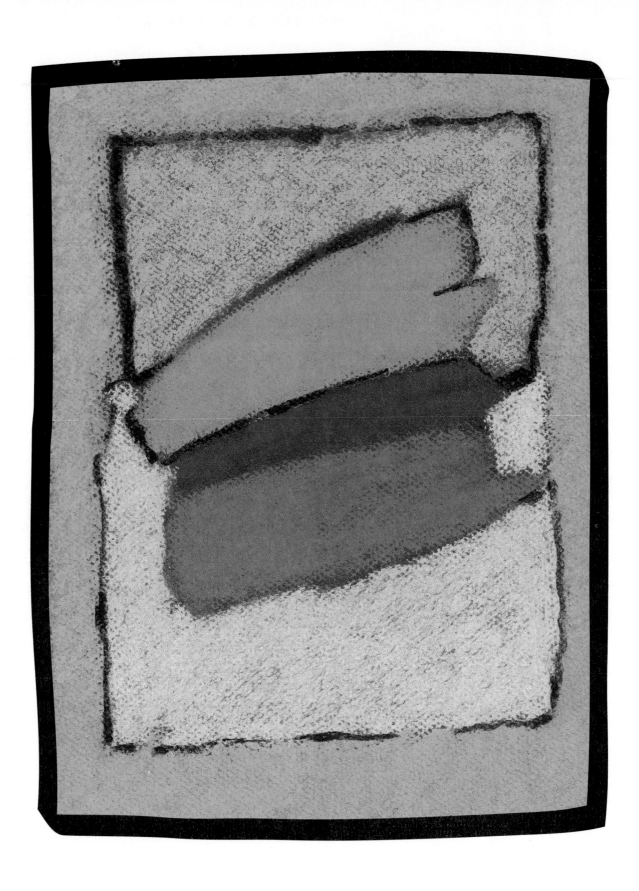

CHAPTER SIX
ANXIETY DISORDERS: TREATMENTS

OUTLINE

Julia is generally anxious, but she becomes particularly upset when she has to deal with authority figures. In the hope of overcoming that problem, she has been seeing a psychotherapist. During her weekly sessions, Julia sits facing her therapist, and they discuss her problem and the possible causes. Her therapist offers explanations and provides new ways of looking at things, but they are only suggestions. The therapist provides guidance and social support when Julia tries new ideas and behaviors. Julia and the therapist have agreed that treatment will be limited to one session a week for 6 months, so it is essential that Julia keep focused and work actively on solving her problem.

■　■　■

Elizabeth has a severe fear of heights that for years has kept her from going above the second floor of any building. She is now seeing a therapist who is using a behavioral approach for treating the phobia. The treatment involves taking Elizabeth up in tall buildings, but only one floor at a time. Each time she goes to a higher floor, she is flooded with anxiety, but she "hangs in," and eventually the anxiety subsides and she is able to go to the next floor. The therapist hopes that by exposing Elizabeth to the feared stimulus (high places) without anything terrible happening, Elizabeth's fear response to high places will extinguish. It is like Pavlov ringing the bell but not giving the dog any meat—eventually the dog will stop salivating. Elizabeth is becoming less fearful, and she is now able to go to the 10th floor before becoming anxious. The treatment seems to be working, but Elizabeth wonders whether the fear is being extinguished or whether she is just developing more realistic beliefs about high places.

■　■　■

Anthony has a phobia about dogs. His therapist is teaching Anthony how to inhibit the fear response by replacing it with a relaxation response. To do this, the therapist first taught Anthony a series of exercises he could use to achieve a state of deep muscle relaxation. Once Anthony was relaxed, the therapist had him imagine a situation that was only slightly fearful (e.g., a small dog some distance away). If the relaxation response is sufficient to inhibit the fear response in that situation, Anthony is asked to imagine a slightly more fearful situation (e.g., sitting next to a small, friendly dog). This procedure is used until Anthony is able to imagine situations that were previously very frightening to him without becoming anxious. The key to effective treatment is never to let the fear response overwhelm the relaxation response. It is hoped that the inhibition of fear that is learned by imagining situations in the office will generalize to real situations outside the office.

■　■　■

Marilyn suffers from chronic free-floating anxiety. Her therapist suspected that the problem stems from excessive neurological activity in the area of the brain responsible for anxiety. The therapist prescribed the drug Valium (diazepam), which reduces neurological activity. The Valium does reduce Marilyn's anxiety, but it has some side effects that she does not like. For example, it makes her somewhat drowsy and causes constipation. The side effects seem less severe now than when she first started taking the drug, but it may be that she is just learning to cope with them. In deciding how much of the drug she should take, Marilyn and her therapist try to find the "balance point" where the anxiety is sufficiently reduced but the side effects are not too bothersome. Marilyn knows that the drug is an effective treatment but not a cure.

■ ■ ■

George suffers from panic attacks, and because of his concern about having one in public, he developed agoraphobia. Antianxiety medication was not helpful in dealing with the panic attacks, but an antidepressant was very effective for reducing the frequency and severity of the attacks. When the fear of having a panic attack was reduced, the agoraphobia decreased. George does not understand why an antidepressant helps control panics, but he is pleased with its effects.

■ ■ ■

In this chapter we will begin our examination of the techniques that are used to treat abnormal behavior. This chapter is focused on the treatment of anxiety disorders, and in later chapters I will discuss the treatment of mood disorders (depression, mania) and schizophrenic disorders. It is essential to discuss the treatment of specific types of disorders rather than treatment in general because different disorders require different treatments, and we are more effective at treating some disorders than others. Because this is the first chapter on treatment, a number of basic issues will be introduced that will provide a background for later chapters on treatment.

The treatment of a disorder is usually directly related to its cause. For example, if we believe that a disorder stems from stress, treatment is focused on reducing the stress or at least helping the individual cope with the stress, but if we suspect that a disorder results from a physiological imbalance, treatment is designed to correct the imbalance. Because there may be psychodynamic, learning, cognitive, and physiological causes for each disorder, I will examine treatment from each of those perspectives.

PSYCHODYNAMIC APPROACHES

Psychodynamic theorists believe that anxiety is caused by *stress,* and therefore therapists who have a psychodynamic orientation treat anxiety by helping their clients *identify the sources of stress and then overcome them.* However, psychodynamically oriented therapists vary greatly in terms of what they assume causes anxiety (e.g., conflicts over sexual urges, personal problems, social problems), and there are also differences among therapists with regard to the treatment techniques they use. As a result, it is difficult to generalize about psychodynamic psychotherapy. However, a useful distinction can be drawn between the technique called **psychoanalysis,** which was developed by Freud (see Chapter 1), and the techniques that were developed later, which are generally referred to as **psychotherapy.** The term *psychotherapy* is often used to refer to all forms of psychological treatment, but in this text I will use the term *psychotherapy* to refer to psychodynamic treatments other than psychoanalysis, and I will specifically label other approaches as "learning" or "cognitive," depending on the theories from which they stem.

Psychotherapy

There are many forms of psychotherapy. In general, these approaches differ from psychoanalysis and are similar to one another in that (a) the client sits up and talks with the therapist rather than lying down and free-associating; (b) psychotherapy is usually limited to one session per week and usually does not go on for years; (c) therapists are usually more active than analysts, so the nature of the treatment is more likely to be influenced by the therapist's interpersonal style; and (d) the client may be seen individually or in a small group with four or five other clients.

In psychotherapy, therapist and patient talk about the patient's problems.

The various forms of psychotherapy share certain elements, but they also differ from one another, and in this discussion of psychotherapies, I will focus on two major dimensions along which the various psychotherapies differ. Before I discuss the differences, you should read Case Study 6.1 (pp. 136–137), which is a 26-year-old woman's report of her experience in psychotherapy.

Internal Versus External Problems. Traditional psychotherapists believe that anxiety stems from a problem *within the client,* such as an unresolved conflict, and they focus on helping the client identify and correct the problem. This approach is similar to that used in psychoanalysis, but it differs in that the problem is not necessarily assumed to be rooted in early childhood, and the psychotherapist takes more direct and active steps to identify and solve the problem.

Other psychotherapists believe that disorders arise because of *external problems,* and those problems can be of two types. First, the anxiety can stem from *stressors in the environment,* such as financial problems, interpersonal conflicts, the need to care for others, or problems associated with achieving goals. In those cases, the therapist may help the client to (a) put things into perspective and set more realistic objectives, (b) learn ways to deal with or avoid others who create stress, (c) learn ways to express anger appropriately, or (d) learn to set limits for themselves and others so that problems can be avoided. When working on problems like these,

therapists help clients resolve situations that can be resolved and cope with those that cannot be resolved. Today, this is probably the most common approach taken in psychodynamic psychotherapy (Weissman & Markowitz, 1994).

The second, less common, type of approach that some therapists take is that their clients' problems stem from the fact that *their ability to grow emotionally has been stifled by the lack of a nurturing atmosphere.* That position was developed primarily by humanistic psychotherapists (see Chapter 2), and one well-known form of this type of psychotherapy is **client-centered psychotherapy** (Rogers, 1951). The goal of the client-centered psychotherapist is to establish a nurturant interpersonal environment in which the client can grow. To establish such an environment, the therapist provides the client with *unconditional positive regard* and *sincere empathic understanding.* In other words, the therapist accepts the client uncritically as a basically good person and attempts to feel and understand what the client is experiencing. Furthermore, the therapist often shares his or her own personal reactions, feelings, and experiences, thereby becoming a more "real" person for the client. That is in sharp contrast to the private role most traditional psychotherapists take. The atmosphere of acceptance and understanding that is established by the therapist allows the client's inner strength and qualities to surface so that personal growth can occur and anxiety can be left behind. This approach is much less common today than it was in the 1970s, but the notions of uncritical acceptance and empathic understanding have been carried forward into many current approaches.

Some of the principles and techniques of client-centered psychotherapy are illustrated in Case Study 6.2 (pp. 138–139).

Past Versus Present. Traditionally, psychotherapists took the position that current problems had their foundations in the client's past experiences, and therefore most of the time in psychotherapy was spent discussing past experiences. That was an outgrowth of Freud's notion that adult problems have their roots in childhood. Some therapists still subscribe to that position, but today it is more likely that therapists will focus on the present, or at least on only the recent past. These psychotherapists do not deny that their clients' problems may be a product of their pasts, but the notion is, "The past is past; let's get on with today and tomorrow." To use an analogy, if you are lost, an individual who is helping you could take you back to the point at which you made your wrong turn and have you start over, but it might be more efficient to identify your destination and figure out how to get there from where you are now. In other words, rather than asking "where did you go wrong," the therapist might ask, "How can we get you from where you are to where you want to be?" The change in emphasis from the past to the present is in part a reflection of a change in orientation, but it is also influenced by the fact that in many cases we do not have the time or money it would take to go back to the beginning and start over.

Therapy Content and Style. An interesting finding concerning psychotherapy is that clients usually talk about whatever issues their particular therapist believes are important. For example, clients who see Freudian therapists often talk about issues related to Oedipal conflicts, whereas clients who see other types of therapists may talk about things like feelings of inferiority, lack of personal growth, or interpersonal conflict. The fact that clients talk about the issues that their psychotherapists believe are crucial is often interpreted by the psychotherapists as evidence that the issues in question are the important ones. However, the question arises, why do clients who see therapists with one orientation talk about one set of issues whereas clients who see therapists with a different orientation talk about a different set of issues?

The answer to that question is that therapists play a powerful role in guiding what clients talk about by the questions they ask and by the interest they show in the clients' answers. By asking leading questions, the therapists get the clients thinking about one topic or another. The interest that therapists show in clients' responses can be equally strong, but the process is more subtle. In that regard, it is important to recognize that the therapist is a very important person for the client, and his or her interest can be very rewarding.

The effects of interest or approval on what individuals say was examined some years ago when psychologists studied **verbal conditioning** (Holmes, 1967). In the simplest of the verbal-conditioning experiments, students were given a stack of cards, and printed on each card was a different verb and five pronouns (*I, he, she, we, they*). Each student's task was to make up a sentence for each card using the verb and any one of the pronouns. The experimenter sat quietly while the student made up sentences for the first 20 cards; after that, the experimenter showed interest (rewarded the student) by saying "good" or "uh-huh" each time the student made up a sentence using one particular pronoun that the experimenter selected at random. No response was made after sentences employing other pronouns. As indicated in Figure 6.1, the results indicated that the students rapidly increased use of the pronoun that was rewarded.

In more complex experiments that bear a greater similarity to the therapeutic situation, students were asked to talk about various early childhood experiences, and the experimenters used interest (leaning forward, taking notes, head nodding) selectively to reward the discussion of particular types of experiences, such as negative interactions with mother, sibling rivalry, or loneliness. The results indicated that

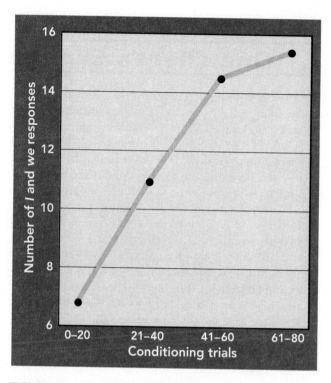

FIGURE 6.1 Students increased their use of *I* and *we* when the use of those pronouns was rewarded with interest by the experimenter.
Source: Adapted from Holmes (1967), p. 291, fig. 2.

when the students were rewarded for talking about a particular type of experience, they talked more about that type of experience. Similar processes probably go on in psychotherapy, and they can be used to explain why clients often talk about things that psychotherapists think are interesting and important.

Some psychoanalysts have argued that they do not influence their clients through verbal conditioning because they play a passive role in the treatment process. However, because they respond less, whatever responses they do make may be all the more important to the client. A colleague of mine who had been in analysis for 4 years argued that the procedure was objective because his analyst rarely said anything, but one day he told me with great excitement that his analyst had smiled at him at the end of his hour on the couch! Convinced that he had done "something right," he went over and over the material from that hour in his sessions for the next few weeks. Either the smile meant that he had said something important that pleased his analyst and his continued talking about it confirmed its importance to the analyst, or the smile meant something else (Was the analyst glad the session was over?) and my friend then misled the analyst about the importance of the material by continuing to talk about it. Clearly, psychotherapists intentionally or unintentionally do influence what their clients tell them,

---

CASE STUDY 6.1
One Client's Experience in Psychotherapy

"I've been going to a therapist for a little over a year now, and usually I go once a week. I started because I was, well, I wasn't happy. I was always tense, and that seemed to be wrecking all of my friendships, and I was a loner. I didn't know what to do about it until one day a friend of mine suggested that I might 'see someone for some professional advice.' My first reaction was, 'That's not for me. I'm not crazy!' But then I discovered that quite a few of my friends were in or had been in therapy, so I thought I'd give it a try.

"I didn't know quite what to expect at first; I thought I'd lay on a couch and talk about my mother and father a lot, but that's not what happened. My therapist is a woman about 40 years old, but I don't know for sure because she never talks about herself. (A couple of times I got up enough courage to ask her something about herself, but each time she just said something like 'We're here to talk about you, and I think it would be better if we kept focused on that.' She was very nice about it, but she drew a clear line.)

"During my sessions, I sit in a comfortable chair, and my therapist sits across from me. There is a desk in the office, but she doesn't sit behind it. The office is quiet and very comfortable.

"Originally, we spent time talking about my being tense and the problems I was having with people—we sort of had to get the issues on the table so that we'd know what we were working on. After that, we spent time talking about other things, like my family, experiences in school, and my job. It seemed like she was trying to get to know me in general, but often when we were talking about what seemed to be peripheral things, examples would come up of people or situations that upset me. In talking about it, I came to realize that what I thought was only a limited and current problem was really pretty pervasive and had been around for a long time. At first I thought, 'Gee, I've been around problem people for a long time.' We spent a lot of time talking about my interactions with other people, and then a pattern started to emerge slowly, a pattern that went way back. It seemed that I never really had any close relationships, and instead I was always fighting people. My therapist called it 'moving against or away from others rather than with or toward them.' Having realized that, I was faced with a real problem: Did I move against others for good reason—did they have a problem?—or was the problem with me? I struggled with that for a long time. Usually, I was pretty defensive and came up with long lists of problems with other people. My therapist never disagreed, but she asked gentle, prodding questions that forced me to question myself. She never pushed or argued with me; she would just pose questions or suggest alternatives. She was gentle, but some of her observations opened up some pretty painful possibilities. It isn't always fun to look at yourself from the outside and turn things upside down. The bottom line came to be, 'If I think everyone else has problems, maybe the problem is in the way I think about other people.' That was a real change in perspective for me, and to be perfectly honest, I haven't completely accepted it yet. I can buy it intellectually (it makes sense), but

---

and that must be taken into account in any evaluation of the content of psychotherapy.

Some theorists have suggested that the improvements that result from psychotherapy may be a consequence of verbal conditioning. For example, it is possible that clients are subtly rewarded for saying things such as "I don't have to be anxious because I can handle these situations," and that can lead to more adaptive behavior. Alternatively, it is possible that clients are conditioned to report improvements regardless of what is happening. Psychotherapists who want to see improvements may unwittingly reward their clients for reporting that they are doing better.

Related to therapeutic style, it is important to realize that most experienced psychotherapists do pretty much the same things in psychotherapy despite differences in their theoretical orientations and training (Lambert & Bergin, 1994). The issues on which they focus may differ and a therapist's personality may influence how he or she comes across, but most psychotherapists have genuine respect and concern for their clients, listen attentively, reflect on and clarify what is said, offer explanations for problems, and suggest potential solutions. In summary, a psychotherapist's experiences in dealing with clients and finding what works through trial and error appear to be more important than theory and training.

Group Psychotherapy. As the name implies, in **group psychotherapy,** a number of clients are seen at one time (Bednar & Kaul, 1994). The number of clients may range from three or four to eight or more. Some-

buying it emotionally is a little different. What I'm doing now is experimenting a little; when a conflict starts to emerge, I ask myself, 'Is this problem out there or in me?' I think I'm doing better, but you don't change 20 years of experience overnight.

"Even if it is true that my problems are due to me, that doesn't explain why I developed them in the first place. One day, my therapist sort of suggested that maybe I was very sensitive—insecure?—and that by finding fault and opposing or running away from other people, I avoid the risk of being rejected. That led to a long discussion about security, and the issue is still hanging there. Even if I am insecure, why am I that way? Objectively, I've got a lot going for me, but subjectively, I'm not sure. You see, one question and its answer just leads to another question, and therapy goes on and on.

"The talking has been good, but I've had ups and downs with my therapist. There were times when she really got on my nerves. For a while I almost stopped going. In fact, I skipped a number of sessions without telling her that I wasn't coming because I was convinced that she didn't like me and that the only reason she was seeing me and being nice to me was that I was paying her. I remember that there used to be a man who had an appointment before me, and my therapist would always be smiling at him when he left her office, and then she'd turn to me in a very businesslike way. When I came to the conclusion that I was just a paying customer, I really felt hurt—but I didn't say anything. The first two times I cut sessions, she made some comment about my missing, and I said that an emergency had come up, and she let it pass. The third time I did it, she told me I would have to pay for missed sessions, and she asked why I had missed. I fumbled around and came up with some dumb excuse—and she just sat there. I talked around in circles, and after letting me hang for a while, she asked whether I was upset with her and whether I was dealing with the feeling by running away—or at least by not coming in. I said, 'Of course not; why should I be upset with you? You haven't done anything to me.' I know now that I was using denial and playing word games. I didn't realize it at the time, but I was doing with her what I do—or did—with everyone.

"Earlier I said that therapy 'goes on and on,' and that poses a problem because therapy is expensive. I could never afford it myself, but fortunately my health insurance covers most of it. One glitch is that my policy only covers a certain number of visits per year, so last year, when I got beyond that number, I cut back on my visits to one a month. With the new calendar year starting, I'm back to once a week. The other day at the office, I heard that we are switching insurance companies and that the new company is going to allow only a set number of visits for a specific type of problem and after that we are on our own. I'm not sure what effect this will have on me. I hope I can get my act together before the insurance runs out. I don't have a life-and-death type of problem, but therapy sure has been great. Therapy is tough to explain, but this is what I have been going through."

times there is more than one therapist in the group. The group approach has a number of advantages. First, talking about problems in front of others may initially be threatening, but the other members of the group can be a source of support, and it can be comforting to realize that others have similar problems and are making progress in overcoming them. One woman who had been in group therapy for married couples commented, "For me, it was very instructive to see how other couples dealt with conflicts over money, sex, in-laws, whether to have children, infidelity, careers, and so on. It was valuable to see that other people could cry and that men could be intimidated." Second, the other members of the group can aid in the therapeutic process by helping the client explore problems and come up with solutions. Probably most important is the fact that the group provides a microcosm of life outside of therapy, and therefore in therapy individuals can see how they respond to others and how others respond to them, and they can practice new ways of relating.

An interesting extension of group psychotherapy is **family therapy,** in which the family group works on shared problems (Alexander et al., 1994). Having the family members come together with a therapist who can exert some control and facilitate interactions can enhance communication among family members.

Time-Limited Psychotherapy. In most psychotherapies, the client and therapist work together until the problem is solved, but in **time-limited psychotherapy,** they work together for a limited number of sessions (e.g., 10 or 15 sessions) determined in advance. The

CASE STUDY 6.2

A Client-Centered Psychotherapist and a Client

The following exchange took place between a therapist and a client in a client-centered psychotherapy session. The client has felt hopeless about herself and has spent most of this hour discussing her feelings of inadequacy and lack of personal worth.

Client: (*Long pause.*) I've never said this before to anyone—but I've thought for such a long time— This is a terrible thing to say, but if I could just— well, if I could just find some glorious cause that I could give my life for I would be happy. I cannot be the kind of a person I want to be. I guess maybe I haven't the guts—or the strength—to kill myself—and if someone else would relieve me of the responsibility—or I would be in an accident—I—I—just don't want to live.

Therapist: At the present time things look so black to you that you can't see much point in living—

Client: Yes—I wish I'd never started this therapy. I was happy when I was living in my dream world. There I could be the kind of person I want to be— But now— There is such a wide, wide gap— between my ideal—and what I am. I wish people hated me. I try to make them hate me. Because then I could turn away from them and could blame them—but no— It is all in my hands— Here is my life—and I either accept the fact that I am absolutely worthless—or I fight whatever it is that holds me in this terrible conflict. And I suppose if I accepted the fact that I am worthless,

then I could go away someplace—and get a little room someplace—get a mechanical job someplace—and retreat clear back to the security of my dream world where I could do things, have clever friends, be a pretty wonderful sort of person—

Therapist: It's really a tough struggle—digging into this like you are—and at times the shelter of your dream world looks more attractive and comfortable.

Client: My dream world or suicide.

Therapist: Your dream world or something more permanent than dreams—

Client: Yes. So I don't see why I should waste your time—coming in twice a week—I'm not worth it— What do you think?

Therapist: It's up to you. . . . It isn't wasting my time—I'd be glad to see you—whenever you come—but it's how you feel about it—if you don't want to come twice a week—or if you want to come twice a week?—once a week?— It's up to you.

Client: You're not going to suggest that I come in oftener? You're not alarmed and think I ought to come in—every day—until I get out of this?

Therapist: I believe you are able to make your own decision. I'll see you whenever you want to come.

---

number of sessions is limited in an attempt to make the client work harder and make more efficient use of the time available and thereby speed up the process. Just as students sometimes put off work on a tough term paper until just before it is due, so clients sometimes avoid the difficult issues in therapy if they think they can put them off until later sessions. The tendency to put off the work of therapy also occurs within therapy sessions, and clients often do not get to the tough issues until the end of a therapy session. That is referred to as the "end of the hour" effect. Note that time-limited psychotherapy is not a type of therapy but rather a kind of packaging for traditional forms of psychotherapy. The only difference that may emerge is that with the time-limited approach, the therapist may have to be somewhat more active to keep the client moving along.

Research has revealed that the time-limited approach is usually at least as effective as unlimited-time therapy (Koss & Shiang, 1994).

The use of the time-limited strategy was once an option, but today it is often imposed by insurance companies that have to pay for therapy. The companies have a panel of experts review the client's problem and make a judgment about how many sessions the treatment should require, and then the company will pay only for the number of recommended sessions.

Effectiveness of Psychotherapy

The question of whether psychotherapy is effective is one of the most hotly and passionately debated ques-

Client: I don't believe you are alarmed about— I see—I may be afraid of myself—but you aren't afraid of me—

Therapist: You say you may be afraid of yourself— and are wondering why I don't seem to be afraid for you?

Client: You have more confidence in me than I have. I'll see you next week—maybe.

In this exchange, the client expresses her feelings that her growth has been stifled (the gap between her ideal and what she is), and the therapist does not attempt to find or solve an underlying problem but instead accepts her uncritically (even her thoughts of suicide), expresses interest in seeing her, and indicates that he believes she can make good decisions herself.

Source: Excerpt from *Client-Centered Therapy* by Carl R. Rogers. Copyright by Houghton Mifflin Company. Reprinted with permission.

In client-centered therapy, the therapist accepts the client uncritically and works to establish a positive, nurturing environment. The therapist often shares personal reactions, feelings, and experiences.

tions in the area of abnormal psychology. For example, E. G. Boring, a leading historian of psychology, underwent psychoanalysis for a period of years and then published an article titled "Was This Analysis a Success?" (Boring, 1940). In it he wrote:

I had eagerly awaited a light from heaven, at the very least to be changed from Saul to Paul; and all that happened was that the analysis petered out in an uneventful session on June 21. . . . Now, four years after the close of the analysis, I find myself quite uncertain as to whether it has made any important change in me. . . . There is so much about this personality of mine that would be better if different, so much that analysis might have done and did not! (pp. 9–10)

[handwritten margin note: it's not up to the therapist but rather the client!]

In response, Boring's analyst wrote back saying that "without the analysis," Boring was in "danger of a breakdown" (Sacks, 1940). He went on to say that "some patients behave to the therapeutist in a manner like that of a criminal to the lawyer who has got them off: they deny that they even were seriously involved, and they want to forget all about it." This particular dispute was based on psychoanalysis, but similar differences of opinion have been documented with respect to psychotherapy. In one investigation, clients, therapists, and independent judges rated the effects of psychotherapy (Horenstein et al., 1973). Examination of the ratings revealed that the therapists rated the psychotherapy as much more effective than the clients did, and the judges agreed with the clients, thereby suggesting that therapists may overrate the value of their service.

Of more importance to the debate over the effectiveness of psychotherapy were the findings of an early

Group therapy is a popular therapeutic technique. Members of the group draw support from the fact that others are coping with similar problems. The group setting provides an opportunity for the participants to understand how they interact with one another and to practice new ways of relating.

series of investigations indicating that about 65% of "neurotic" individuals showed improvement during psychotherapy, but the same proportion of individuals who were *not* treated also showed improvement (Eysenck, 1961). From those findings it was argued that psychotherapy is no more effective than time alone or no more effective than the informal help individuals receive from friends. Those dramatic findings sparked considerable controversy and provoked a great deal of research on the effects of psychotherapy.

The recent research on the effects of psychotherapy is much more sophisticated than the earlier research, and its results consistently indicate that psychotherapy can be more effective than no therapy or placebo treatment and that in many cases the effects of psychotherapy can be long-lasting (Lambert & Bergin, 1994; Shadish et al., 1993; Weisz et al., 1995). However, it is important to recognize that psychotherapy is not equally effective for treating all types of problems. For example, it can be effective for treating depression, but it is ineffective for treating schizophrenia, and its results with anxiety disorders are mixed. It appears to be moderately effective for treating general anxiety such as that seen in the generalized anxiety disorder, but it is wholly ineffective for treating the obsessive-compulsive disorder (Svartberg & Stiles, 1991). The fact that the effectiveness of psychotherapy varies for different disorders is consistent with the notion that different disorders have different causes and therefore may require different types of interventions (see Chapter 2).

Why Does Psychotherapy Work?

Having concluded that psychotherapy can be effective, the next question that must be asked is, when it is effec-

tive, why is it effective? Three lines of research have been pursued to answer that question. First, numerous investigations were conducted to compare the *effects of different types of psychotherapy*. If one type of psychotherapy was found to be more effective than another, it could be concluded that whatever went on in that type of psychotherapy was crucial to improvement. Unfortunately, there is no consistent evidence that any one type of psychotherapy is more effective than another (Lambert & Bergin, 1994; Luborsky et al., 1975; Stiles et al., 1986).

In the second line of research, investigators attempted to determine whether the effectiveness of psychotherapy was determined by the *characteristics of the clients* (e.g., social class, age, sex, personality, expectations; Garfield, 1994), the *characteristics of the therapists* (e.g., social class, age, sex, personality; Beutler et al., 1994), or the differences in the *process of therapy* (e.g., therapy style, client involvement, type of therapeutic relationship; Orlinsky et al., 1994). Again, no consistent evidence was found linking any of these variables to the success of psychotherapy.

The third set of findings stems from comparisons of the effectiveness of *professional versus paraprofessional therapists*. **Paraprofessionals** are usually volunteers who have received some instruction in dealing with disturbed individuals, but their training is not as extensive as that of professionals. Surprisingly, the evidence indicates that paraprofessionals are usually as effective as professional therapists and in some instances may be even more effective (Dawes, 1994; Lambert & Bergin, 1994). For example, in one investigation, hospitalized patients were treated either by medical students who had no training in psychiatry or by psychiatrists (Miles et al., 1976). There was no difference in the improvement rate of those who were seen by the students and those who were seen by the psychiatrists. These find-

The immediate problem/concern

ings suggest that professional training may not contribute to the outcome of psychotherapy.

The findings reviewed here pose an awkward problem: We have evidence that psychotherapy is more effective than no treatment, but *we do not have evidence indicating what makes psychotherapy effective.* However, there are two possible explanations for the effects of psychotherapy. First, it may be that although no one of the factors we have examined accounts for the effects of therapy by itself, the combined effect of numerous variables is responsible for the improvements seen in psychotherapy. In other words, the success of psychotherapy, like the success of most interpersonal relationships, may be due to a subtle combination of factors.

The second and more probable explanation is that improvement in and out of psychotherapy is due to **social support,** and because individuals in psychotherapy are more likely to get support, they are more likely to show improvement. The argument here is that friendship or support is the crucial factor for improvement and that psychotherapy is simply the "purchase of friendship" (Schofield, 1964). The role of social support has received considerable attention lately, and we now know that social support is important for both avoiding the effects of stress and recovering from stress. That is, individuals who have close friends in whom they can confide and who can provide emotional support are less influenced by stress and recover from stress more quickly (Winefield, 1987; see also Chapter 9).

We can conclude this discussion by noting that psychodynamic psychotherapy encompasses a variety of therapeutic strategies that are widely accepted and generally effective for overcoming problems, but we do not yet know whether their effects are due to subtle interpersonal chemistry, social support, or some other, yet unidentified factor.

LEARNING APPROACHES

In Chapter 5, I pointed out that learning theorists believe that anxiety is a *classically conditioned* fear response. For example, agoraphobia occurs when fear is initially paired with the stimulus of being away from home, and after that, being away from home elicits fear. Because the anxiety is thought to result from inappropriate conditioning of a fear response, the learning approach to therapy involves correcting the inappropriate conditioning. That can be done by *extinguishing* the fear response, *inhibiting* the fear response by substituting another response, or *learning to relax* and then using the relaxation response to overcome anxiety when it occurs. In the following sections, I will discuss each of those three strategies.

However, before discussing specific therapeutic strategies, I should point out that the learning

approaches are focused on reducing the *physiological* aspects of anxiety, such as muscle tension and heart rate. That is because learning theorists assume that (a) the development of the anxiety response is based on the classical conditioning of physiological responses such as heart rate, (b) the physiological responses then provide the basis of the cognitive feelings of anxiety (i.e., increased heart rate leads you to feel anxious), and (c) the reduction of physiological responses will result in the reduction of cognitive anxiety (i.e., when your heart rate goes down, you feel less anxious). In other words, it is assumed that you are anxious because your heart is beating fast, not that your heart is beating fast because you are anxious. Actually, the relationship probably goes both ways. If you suddenly came face to face with an attacker, you would probably begin worrying about what was going to happen to you, and your heart rate would go up. In that case, your thoughts would influence your physiological responses. By contrast, if you were given a drug that increases your heart rate, you might feel anxious—that is, your physiological responses would influence your thoughts. Therapists who use a learning approach to therapy do not deny the influence of thoughts on anxiety; instead, they simply choose to focus on physiological arousal because they believe that it is a more important or more frequent cause of anxiety. With that clarified, we will now consider the three strategies for reducing anxiety that are based on the learning explanations.

The approaches to treatment that I will discuss in the following sections were developed from the principles of learning, but recently cognitive explanations have been offered to explain the effects of these treatments, and so for each treatment I will discuss both explanations. Both the learning and the cognitive explanations for these therapies are summarized in Table 6.1.

Extinction of Anxiety

One means of eliminating a classically conditioned anxiety response is through the process of **extinction** (see Chapter 2). Extinction occurs when the feared stimulus is repeatedly presented *without* the reason for being afraid. For example, if an individual who has a classically conditioned fear of dogs is repeatedly exposed to friendly dogs that do not bite, the fear associated with the dogs will eventually be extinguished. Because the initial exposure to the feared stimulus may result in the individual's being flooded with anxiety, this therapeutic technique is often referred to as **flooding** (Emmelkamp, 1994).

Individuals may be exposed to the real feared stimulus, as when an individual with a fear of heights is taken to the top of a tall building, or they may be asked simply to imagine the feared stimulus (e.g., imagine

TABLE 6.1 Learning and Cognitive Explanations for Therapies Suggested by Learning Theory

Technique	Learning Explanation	Cognitive Explanation
Flooding, implosion	Extinction of anxiety	Exposure leads to increased self-efficacy
Systematic densensitization, counterconditioning	Inhibition of anxiety	Exposure leads to increased self-efficacy
Relaxation training, biofeedback training	Blocking of anxiety	Training leads to feelings of self-control and self-efficacy

being in a tall building). Actual exposure to the feared stimulus is called **in vivo exposure,** and imagined exposure is called **in vitro exposure.** In vivo exposure is usually more effective, but in vitro is often more practical in the therapeutic setting. The use of in vivo exposure for the treatment of anxiety is illustrated in Case Study 6.3.

Numerous experiments have documented the effectiveness of exposure and extinction for reducing or eliminating fears (Emmelkamp, 1994). The results of one experiment indicated that exposure was as effective as medication (Tofranil/imipramine) for reducing agoraphobia (Mavissakalian & Michelson, 1983). In that experiment, clients with agoraphobia were assigned to one of four conditions: an *exposure* condition, in which they received in vivo exposure to open places such as large shopping malls; a *medication* condition, in which they received a drug known to be effective for reducing agoraphobic fears; an *exposure plus medication* condition, in which they received both the exposure and the drug; or (d) a *control* condition, in which the clients discussed their problems. Anxiety was measured after 1, 2, and 3 months of therapy; the results of those measures are presented in Figure 6.2. All three treatments were equally effective for reducing anxiety, and they were more effective than the control condition in which clients only discussed their problems.

It now appears that there is good evidence that exposure can be an effective strategy for reducing anxiety, but a question has been raised about why exposure works. Originally it was assumed that exposure caused the extinction of the conditioned fear response, but it now appears that the fear reduction may be due to *cognitive* factors. It may be that because nothing terrible happens when an individual is repeatedly exposed to a stimulus that was thought to be dangerous, the individual realizes that the stimulus is in fact not dangerous or that he or she can cope with the situation. Those changes in *beliefs* may result in fear reduction. For example, a man who is afraid of heights and is taken to the top of a tall building may initially be flooded with anxiety, but he soon realizes that nothing terrible happens and therefore changes

his beliefs about the situation, which in turn reduces his fears.

Support for the cognitive explanation for the effects of exposure is provided by research in which it was found that after being exposed to fearful stimuli and "getting through" the experience, individuals reported less fear and more confidence, or what is often called **self-efficacy** (Bandura, 1977). In other words, by getting through the stressful experience without ill effects, the individuals may develop more confidence in their ability to handle the situations, and that may reduce fear.

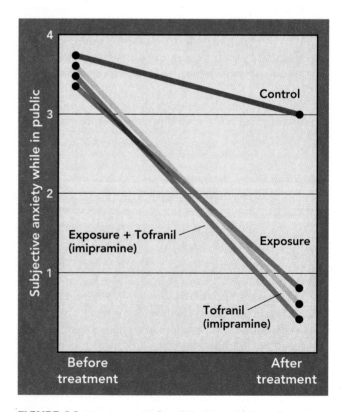

FIGURE 6.2 Exposure, Tofranil (imipramine), and exposure plus Tofranil were all equally effective for reducing anxiety.
Source: Adapted from Mavissakalian and Michelson (1983), p. 513, fig. 1.

CASE STUDY 6.3
Treatment of a Dog Phobia with In Vivo Exposure

Ned was a college senior majoring in mathematics. He was well adjusted in all respects except that he had a severe fear of dogs. So far as he could remember, he had never been hurt or bitten by a dog.

I decided to use in vivo exposure to dogs as a means of extinguishing Ned's fear. To do this, Ned and I first went to a local pet shop that had a large number of puppies for sale. The puppies were small and very friendly, and each was in a cage. At first, we simply walked around the shop looking at other things but staying away from the dogs. When Ned was relaxed and comfortable, he and I walked slowly over to a cage containing a small cocker spaniel puppy that looked somewhat sleepy. This did not bother Ned much, and I asked him to put his finger through the bars of the cage and scratch the puppy's head. He was a little tentative, thinking that the puppy might snap, but he did it, and nothing much happened. Next we went to a cage with three or four wide-awake and active puppies in it, and I asked Ned to put his hand in and play with the puppies. Again he was tentative, but he did it. After he was comfortable with that, I encouraged him to roughhouse with the puppies a little and let them chew on his finger a bit. Again he started out somewhat tentatively, but he did it, and after a few minutes he was enjoying playing with the pups. From there we went from cage to cage and back to some cages playing with the various puppies.

After about 40 minutes, Ned smiled somewhat sheepishly and said, "Once you get used to them, they're kinda fun. Their little teeth can be sharp, but if you're careful, it's all right." However, he then added, "But they're only puppies—not full-grown dogs." I told him we would take it one step at a time and that his "homework" before our next session was to go to three or four different pet stores and play with the puppies. The homework was designed to expose him to as many puppies as possible and to deal with them without me there for support.

At the beginning of our next session, Ned reported that he had gone to five different pet shops to play with puppies, that two or three times he had picked puppies up to hold them, and that he was comfortable doing that, but he hastened to add, "But those are only puppies. Dogs are a different thing." After talking for a few minutes, we went to a nearby park where a canine obedience class was being held. The dogs in the class were full-grown, on leashes, and generally well behaved because this was one of the final sessions. We watched the class for a while, noting specifically that the dogs were controllable, and after the class we talked to the owners and Ned very tentatively petted the dogs while their owners held them on a short leash. Ned then worked with the owners to put two dogs through their exercises ("sit," "stay," "come," etc.). At first, he was really nervous when the dog would come, but in time he got used to it. When the session was over, Ned was exhausted (it had been a strain), but he also felt exhilarated; he had played with dogs and enjoyed it.

At our next session, Ned and I developed a list of training exercises that would expose him to more dogs, different kinds of dogs, and dogs in different circumstances. He went to more pet stores and obedience classes as well as to dog shows and veterinarians. He also sought out friends who had dogs and spent time with them and their dogs. If the fear is to extinguish, it is important that the feared stimulus be experienced over and over in the absence of fear. Also, because the fear has generalized, it is important that all of the fear-related stimuli be experienced over and over. During the next couple of weeks, I pushed Ned really hard to increase the amount and types of exposure. With time, the fear slowly diminished, and Ned could play easily with relatively big dogs, even allowing them to lick his face. At the end of the treatment period, Ned commented, "Well, the fear is gone. There is really no reason to be afraid; dogs are like people—most of them are friendly, and the only problem is to separate the friendly ones from the others. After this treatment, I'm not afraid of dogs—I'm sick of them!"

If an individual who has a classically conditioned fear of dogs is repeatedly exposed to friendly dogs, the fear of dogs will eventually be extinguished.

It might be noted that exposure can also be used to explain why psychodynamic psychotherapy is effective. Specifically, it may be that talking and thinking about anxiety-provoking situations in psychotherapy is a form of in vitro exposure and that the exposure results in new beliefs that in turn lead to reductions in anxiety.

Inhibition of Anxiety

A second learning-based approach to therapy is founded on the idea that the anxiety response can be *inhibited* by an incompatible response, specifically, a relaxation response. In other words, if a relaxation response is paired with the feared stimulus, the relaxation response will replace and preclude the anxiety response. This therapeutic approach is known as **systematic desensitization** (Wolpe, 1958), but it is sometimes referred to as **counterconditioning.**

This procedure has three steps. First, the individual is taught how to relax. This is done with a series of exercises in which the individual tenses and then relaxes sets of muscles and in so doing learns to become completely relaxed. This procedure is known as **progressive muscle relaxation** (Jacobson, 1938). In a typi-

cal muscle relaxation training session, the individual reclines in a comfortable chair and is put through relaxation exercises by a trainer who speaks in a slow and soothing manner. The trainer gives instructions like the following:

> Settle back as comfortably as you can. Close your eyes, take a deep breath, hold it, and then let it out. Now take another deep breath, holding it deeply and then letting it out. And another. Still another. As you continue to breathe deeply, let yourself relax—more and more. Relax more and more with each breath. I am now going to make you aware of certain sensations in your body and then show you how you can reduce these sensations. First, direct your attention to your arms—to your hands in particular. Clench both fists. Clench them tightly and notice the tension in the hands and in the forearms. Notice this tension as it spreads from your fingers through your hands and through your wrists. As you continue to focus on this tension, I want you to count to yourself slowly along with me. When you reach 3, gradually relax the tension in these muscles. Gradually unclench your fists and let your hands hang loose. Ready. Now count with me: 1, 2, 3. Gradually relax. Note the difference between the tension and the relaxation. Concentrate now on the sensation of relaxation as it comes to replace the tension. Try to make this process continue. Focus on the relaxation as it spreads throughout your fingers, your hands, your wrists, and your lower arms. Once again, now, clench your hands into fists tightly, noticing the tension in your hands and forearms. Tighten. Again, count slowly with me, and when you reach 3, gradually reduce the tension in your hands and arms: 1, 2, 3. Now relax. Let your fingers spread out, relaxed, and note the difference once again between tension and relaxation.

This procedure is repeated a number of times, and then the trainer moves on to a different set of muscles (upper arms, shoulders, back, legs, neck, forehead) until the individual has learned how to relax all of the major muscle groups.

Second, a list of feared stimuli is compiled in which the stimuli are arranged in order from least feared to most feared. An individual with a phobia for dogs might list the following situations: (a) watching a small puppy in a cage 10 feet away, (b) sitting next to a small dog, and (c) petting a large German shepherd.

Third, the individual is told to begin relaxing and is then asked to imagine the least feared stimulus. The process is started with the least feared stimulus because the individual is most likely to be able to relax and inhibit the fear of that stimulus. If the individual is able to remain relaxed while thinking of the first stimulus, he or she is asked to begin thinking about the next least feared stimulus. This procedure is repeated until the individual is relaxing while thinking about the most feared stimulus. If the individual becomes anxious during the procedure, he or she is asked to go back to imagining a previous stimulus with which relaxation

CASE STUDY 6.4
Systematic Desensitization: The Case of Little Peter

A form of systematic desensitization was reported as early as 1924 in the case of Peter, a boy who had become afraid of furry objects such as rabbits and fur coats. To overcome this fear, a rabbit was presented to Peter, but it was initially presented far enough away so that Peter did not become afraid. A laboratory assistant then began feeding Peter his favorite food, and then the rabbit was slowly brought closer and closer. Feeding was used to elicit relaxation and pleasure because relaxation training would not be effective with a child as young as Peter. The hope was that the pleasure associated with eating would overwhelm and inhibit the fear. In fact, the procedure was effective in eliminating Peter's fear. Within a short period of time, Peter was sitting calmly and eating with the once-feared rabbit right next to him.

This case is often cited as an example of the effectiveness of systematic desensitization, but it should be recognized that other processes were going on as well. Most noteworthy is the fact that on most days during the treatment period, other children who were not afraid of the rabbit were brought in to play with Peter and the rabbit, and it appears that some of Peter's fear was reduced by observing the fearlessness of the other children.

Sources: Based on Jones (1924) and Kornfeld (1989).

---

was possible. The procedure is repeated a number of times until the relaxation response has been consistently paired with the feared stimulus and is effective for inhibiting the fear response.

In some cases, the procedure may be done in vivo rather than in vitro. For example, an individual who is afraid of dogs might move closer and closer to a dog while using the relaxation response to inhibit fear, or an individual who is afraid of heights might inhibit fear with a relaxation response while going up in a tall building one floor at a time. A famous example of the use of systematic desensitization is presented in Case Study 6.4.

There is evidence that systematic desensitization can be effective for reducing fears, but questions have been raised about why it is effective (Emmelkamp, 1994). Specifically, rather than inhibiting anxiety by pairing relaxation with the feared stimuli, it may be that individuals change their beliefs about the stimuli when they work through the list of feared stimuli. That is, the exposure without dire consequences may lead the individual to develop more confidence and new beliefs about the degree to which the stimulus is really dangerous.

Learning to Relax

The third learning-based approach to the treatment of anxiety involves teaching individuals how to relax and then having them apply their newly learned skill when they begin feeling anxious. Unlike the extinction and inhibition procedures, in which the client's role is passive, with this approach the client is taught a new skill (relaxation) and then actively to apply the skill whenever necessary.

There is evidence that relaxation training is effective in enabling individuals to reduce physiological arousal (Borkovec & Sides, 1979). For example, individuals who receive progressive muscle relaxation training show lower muscle tension, blood pressure, and heart rate during training sessions than individuals who do not receive the training. More important, a number of experiments have indicated that once individuals learn how to relax, they can apply what they have learned to reduce anxiety in a variety of situations. For example, after having been taught to relax, individuals show lower anxiety during interviews, while getting ready to give speeches, and while preparing for dental operations (e.g., Chang-Liang & Denney, 1976; Goldfried & Trier, 1974; Miller et al., 1978; Zeisset, 1968).

It is usually assumed that relaxation training enables an individual to use relaxation to block anxiety, but it is possible that learning to relax leads the individual to have increased beliefs about his or her ability to cope. That is, the effects of relaxation training may actually be due to cognitive factors.

Clients are usually taught to relax using progressive muscle relaxation procedures, but in some cases, attempts are made to teach clients how to relax with **biofeedback training.** In biofeedback training, electrodes that detect physiological responses such as heart rate, blood pressure, or muscle tension are attached to the individual, and then the individual watches a computer display that indicates changes in those responses. By watching the computer display, the individual tries to learn to reduce the physiological responses that are related to anxiety. For example, the individual may try to learn to lower his or her

In relaxation training, clients learn to relax and then to apply their newly learned skill in situations that cause them anxiety.

heart rate and thereby lower anxiety. I will discuss the effects of biofeedback training in greater detail in Chapter 16, but two points concerning biofeedback should be made here. First, contrary to what is usually assumed, most of the evidence indicates that biofeedback is no more effective for reducing responses such as heart rate and blood pressure than simply sitting quietly and resting (see Holmes, 1985; Roberts, 1985). In other words, biofeedback training is associated with reduced levels of arousal, but sitting quietly has the same effect, and it is likely that the effects of biofeedback training are actually due to sitting quietly rather than to the biofeedback. Second, there does not appear to be any evidence that biofeedback training has any long-term effects. That is, biofeedback training (or sitting quietly) may reduce arousal during the training session, but it does not reduce arousal in subsequent stressful situations (Bennett et al., 1978). Hence, biofeedback training does not appear to be a particularly effective means of reducing general anxiety.

COMMENT

The learning approaches to the treatment of anxiety were developed as straightforward extensions of the learning explanations for anxiety, and the treatments were found to be effective. However, there are now reasons to believe that at least some of the effects of the learning-based treatments are in fact due to cognitive factors such as reevaluation of the feared objects or increased feelings of self-efficacy that occur when the individual is exposed to the feared objects without dire consequences.

COGNITIVE APPROACHES

Cognitive theorists assume that individuals become anxious when they develop *incorrect beliefs* about potential threats; that is, anxiety disorders occur because individuals are wrong about the dangers they face. For example, an individual may have a phobia for dogs because the individual is simply wrong about the degree to which dogs are dangerous. Alternatively, an obsessive-compulsive disorder may be due to the fact that the individual believes that if he or she does not perform a ritual, something terrible will happen.

Because it is assumed that incorrect beliefs lead to anxiety, the goal of the cognitive approaches to treatment is to *change beliefs.* In the following sections, I will describe the processes that are used to change beliefs and discuss the effectiveness of cognitive therapy for treating various anxiety disorders.

Techniques for Changing Beliefs

In treating individuals with anxiety disorders, two types of anxiety-provoking beliefs can be changed. First, we can change beliefs about the *situation.* For example, a belief such as "It is dangerous to be up in a tall building" can be changed to "It is really not dangerous to be up in a tall building." Second, we can change beliefs about the *ability to cope* with the situation. For example, a belief such as "I will panic and lose control if I go up in a tall building" can be changed to "Going up in a tall building can be stressful, but I can handle it."

Cognitive Therapy. One technique that is used to change beliefs, called **cognitive therapy,** involves offering clients more accurate statements in the hope of correcting their errors and misunderstandings (Beck & Emery, 1985). The statements are initially offered as *hypotheses,* and the clients are asked to test them out and see for themselves whether the hypotheses are correct. For example, the therapist might simply suggest that tall buildings are not dangerous and suggest that the client go up in a building to see if anything unfortunate happens. After discovering that nothing bad happens, the client changes beliefs, and the anxiety is reduced.

Rational-Emotive Therapy. Some therapists believe that it is more effective if clients come up with their own new beliefs. These therapists force clients to develop more accurate beliefs by actively cross-examining the clients and challenging their beliefs. For example, when working with an individual who has a phobia for high places, the therapist might ask, "How many tall buildings have ever fallen over?" "Have you ever heard of anyone accidentally falling out of a tall building?" or "Isn't it really safer to be up in a tall building than on the ground trying to cross a busy street?" By doing this, the therapist forces the client to reexamine beliefs, recognize errors in logic, and develop more accurate beliefs. This approach is called **rational-emotive therapy** (Ellis, 1962; Ellis & Grieger, 1977, 1986).

Exposure. In some cases, individuals will simply be exposed to the stimuli or situations of which they are afraid in the hope that they will discover that nothing terrible happens and that there is really no reason for fear. That forced realization can lead to a change in beliefs.

Exposure with Response Prevention. One strategy for changing beliefs among individuals who suffer from the obsessive-compulsive disorder is to expose them to a situation in which they think they must perform a ritual to avoid some calamity but prevent them from using the ritual. For example, an individual who has a handwashing compulsion may be exposed to dirt but not allowed to wash his or her hands. If the person does not perform the ritual and nothing terrible happens, the individual may change his or her beliefs about the necessity of the ritual. This procedure is called **exposure with response prevention** (Abel, 1993).

Effectiveness of Cognitive Therapy

Phobias. Cognitive therapy has been shown to be effective for treating phobias. For example, in an experiment with individuals who had social phobias, the individuals in a cognitive-behavioral treatment condition were exposed to groups of people and were given cognitive training to change their incorrect

beliefs; for example, they were told to think, "Nothing bad will happen to me in a group of people." In contrast, the individuals in a placebo treatment condition received lectures on phobias and group support. Anxiety was measured before treatment began, immediately after treatment ended, and 3 and 6 months later. The results indicated that individuals in both conditions showed improvement but that the individuals who received the cognitive-behavioral treatment showed greater improvement (Heimberg et al., 1990). Those findings are illustrated in Figure 6.3.

From the results discussed in the preceding paragraph, it is clear that the cognitive-behavioral treatment led to improvement, but the question is, was the improvement due to the *cognitive strategies* for changing beliefs or to the fact that the individuals were *exposed* to groups of people and therefore realized that there was no reason for fear? To examine the separate effects of cognitive and behavioral components of treatments, an experiment was conducted in which some individuals with severe driving phobias received a treatment that consisted of *both* the cognitive and behavioral components and others received a treatment consisting of only the behavioral component (Williams & Rappoport, 1983). In the combined treatment condition, the cognitive component involved training in relabeling feelings (e.g., "These anxious feelings won't harm me; they're just uncomfortable"), developing positive expectations ("I will be able to manage regardless of how I feel"), focusing on task-relevant thoughts ("Keep my mind on my driving"), and using self-distraction

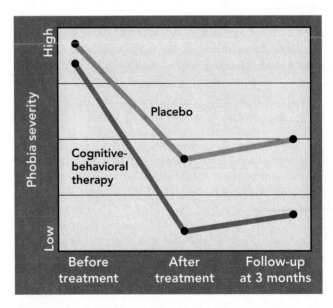

FIGURE 6.3 Cognitive-behavioral treatment resulted in greater reduction in fear than placebo treatment.
Source: Adapted from Heimberg et al. (1990), p. 11, fig. 1.

(planning recreational activities). The behavioral component of the treatment consisted of 11 hours of driving practice; that is, *exposure* to the feared situation. The behavioral-only treatment consisted only of 11 hours of driving practice. The results indicated that the individuals who received only the behavioral treatment (driving practice) showed anxiety reductions that were as great as those who received the combined treatment. From those results it was concluded that the best way to rectify the incorrect beliefs that lead to fears is to give clients firsthand demonstrations that the beliefs are incorrect and that the individuals can function effectively. In other words, demonstration via exposure is more effective for changing beliefs than cognitive retraining. These findings do not lead us to question whether changing beliefs is effective for reducing fears; they simply suggest that behavioral strategies such as exposure to the feared stimulus may be at least as effective as cognitive strategies for changing beliefs.

Panic Disorder. Cognitive theorists assume that individuals who suffer from the panic disorder misinterpret and overreact to minor physiological changes; for example, a minor chest pain or shortness of breath is interpreted as the onset of a heart attack, so they panic. To treat the panic attack, cognitive therapists attempt to (a) teach clients to interpret the physiological changes more realistically ("This chest pain is not a heart attack"), (b) convince clients that they can cope with the situation and there is no need to panic ("You can handle this situation"), and (c) teach clients how to relax instead of panicking ("Breathe deeply and slowly").

There is now a substantial amount of evidence that such cognitive treatment can reduce the frequency and severity of panic attacks (Clum et al., 1993; Klosko et al., 1990; Margraf et al., 1994; Michelson et al., 1990; Shear et al., 1991). There is even evidence that simply providing clients with written information about how to use cognitive techniques for dealing with panics can be effective, making this a very cost-effective approach (Lidren et al., 1994).

This approach is effective, but there are two questions about why it works. First, it may be that rather than changing the actual cause of the panic attacks, this approach simply helps individuals realize that they can *cope with the situation* (Mattick et al., 1990; Michelson & Marchione, 1991). For example, individuals come to realize that they are not going to die, so when an attack comes on, they simply sit down quietly, breathe deeply in an attempt to relax as much as possible, and wait for the attack to pass.

Consistent with this coping explanation is the finding that therapy that simply involved informing the clients that "panic is not dangerous" was as effective as the more traditional complete cognitive therapy (Shear et al., 1994). Similarly, it was found that simply having a "safe person" present during a par   attack greatly

reduced the symptoms of panic (Carter et al., 1995). It appears, then, that a crucial cognitive element in cognitive therapy for panic disorder may be the changed belief in the ability to cope with the situation. That change does not eliminate the disorder; it just makes it tolerable.

The second explanation for why the cognitive treatment is effective is that in most cases the treatment involves having the client try to relax by *breathing deeply,* and that may be effective because the panic is due to a brief oxygen debt that triggers a false alarm about suffocation (Klein, 1993; Stein et al., 1995; Taylor, 1994; see Chapter 5). The deep breathing overcomes the oxygen debt and terminates the panic attack. Overall, then, it is clear that the cognitive approaches to treating panic attacks are effective, but their effectiveness does not appear to be due to changed beliefs about the symptoms as originally proposed by the cognitive theorists.

Obsessive-Compulsive Disorder. The technique that has received most attention for the treatment of compulsions is *exposure with response prevention,* a technique in which the individual is placed in a situation in which he or she would ordinarily have to use some compulsion but is prevented from doing so (see earlier discussion). Estimates concerning the proportion of clients who benefit from this approach vary, but it is safe to conclude that this approach is probably effective for about 50% of the clients (Abel, 1993; Baer & Minichiello, 1990; Baer et al., 1994; Hiss et al., 1994; Stanley & Turner, 1995). Some investigators cite higher success rates, but they often do not include clients who dropped out or include clients who showed only minimal improvement.

Two things are noteworthy about the effectiveness of exposure with response prevention. First, this a behavioral strategy rather than a cognitive strategy for changing beliefs. In other words, it appears that "seeing is believing," and the seeing is more effective for changing beliefs than being told about the incorrect nature of beliefs. This is similar to the findings discussed earlier concerning the treatment of phobias by exposure.

Second, the fact that this approach is effective for about 50% of the clients is interesting because in the section on physiological treatments you will learn that drugs are also effective for treating about 50% of the clients with the obsessive-compulsive disorder. It may be that cognitive-behavioral treatments are effective for the individuals for whom the disorder has a psychological cause, whereas drugs are effective for the individuals for whom the disorder has a physiological cause.

Distraction

The last cognitive strategy I will consider for reducing anxiety is **distraction.** With distraction, the individual does not reduce anxiety by changing anxiety-provoking thoughts but instead simply avoids those thoughts. The

agoraphobia

[handwritten: hearing is better than mantra]

most popular distraction-based therapy for dealing with stress is **meditation** (D. H. Shapiro, 1980; West, 1987). The crucial factor in most forms of meditation is the use of a **mantra,** which is a nonsense word such as *abna* that the individual repeats over and over while meditating. The mantra is used to "clear the mind," and it achieves that goal by keeping the individual from thinking about anything that might be arousing. In other words, the mantra is a distractor like "counting sheep," which some people use to help them get to sleep when they are worrying about something. The act of meditating provides a distraction because you cannot think anxiety-provoking thoughts while concentrating on a mantra. Beyond that, however, it has been suggested that while meditating, you somehow refresh yourself and replenish your energy so that you can cope better afterward, but exactly how that is accomplished has never been explained scientifically.

Meditation has been practiced for centuries in the Far East, and a form called **transcendental meditation** was popularized in the West during the 1960s and 1970s (Mahesh Yogi, 1963). Another meditative technique that has gained widespread acceptance, which employs counting rather than a traditional mantra, is known as the **relaxation response** (Benson, 1975).

There are many misconceptions about the effects of meditation. Most of the attention given to meditation revolves around the possibility that it can reduce physiological arousal, and there are numerous anecdotal reports about the ability of yoga masters to reduce or stop their hearts, reduce respiration, and alter blood chemistry. Reduction of physiological arousal is relevant to the treatment of anxiety because high physiological arousal could be a cause or an effect of anxiety. There is no doubt that sitting quietly and meditating will reduce physiological arousal, but the important point that is often overlooked is that *meditation does not result in greater reductions in physiological arousal than simply sitting quietly without meditating* (see Holmes, 1984b, 1987). In more than 20 experiments, the arousal of meditating and resting individuals was compared, and the results consistently indicated that meditating and resting individuals showed comparable reductions in arousal. At present, then, it cannot be concluded that meditation is more effective than rest for reducing the physiological causes or effects of anxiety.

[handwritten: what about brain activity?]

Although meditation does not reduce physiological arousal more than rest, it is possible that it might reduce the subjective feelings of anxiety (e.g., apprehension, worry). That possibility was tested in an interesting series of experiments in which individuals were randomly assigned to conditions in which they either participated in (a) real meditation, (b) bogus meditation (sat quietly with eyes closed but did not use a mantra), or (c) antimeditation (engaged in deliberate, active cognitive activity designed to be the antithesis of meditation; Smith, 1976). The individuals in all three

[handwritten: like a mantra] *[handwritten: closing eyes reduces anxiety]*

Many people use meditation as a stress-reducing technique. However, evidence from controlled experiments indicates that meditation is no more effective than simply sitting quietly.

conditions were led to believe that the meditation they were performing would help them. The results indicated that the individuals in *all three* meditation conditions reported decreases in anxiety and that there were no differences in the degree to which the various meditation procedures reduced anxiety. Because the bogus meditation and antimeditation procedures were as effective as real meditation, it must be concluded that the anxiety reductions were due to *expectations* about the effects rather than to the meditation per se. In summary, the existing evidence indicates that meditating may reduce arousal, but it is sitting quietly and one's expectations about what will happen that are responsible for the effect. In sum, then, there is no evidence that meditation per se is effective for reducing anxiety (Hollander et al., 1994).

COMMENT

It is clear that changing incorrect beliefs can be an effective way to reduce anxiety. Incorrect beliefs can be changed with *cognitive* strategies such as teaching clients more appropriate thoughts, but it appears that in many cases *behavioral* strategies such as exposure, in which it is demonstrated that beliefs are incorrect, are more effective than the cognitive strategies. In short, seeing is believing. Furthermore, in some cases, it appears that cognitive therapy does not provide a treatment for the disorder per se but instead provides the client with new skills or beliefs for coping with the disorder. That was found to be the case with the panic disorder, and it would certainly be the case for the generalized anxiety disorder in which the anxiety comes "out of the blue" and the individual cannot give a reason for the anxiety. These new interpretations of what makes cognitive therapy work do not diminish its value; they simply help us understand why the therapy works, and with that understanding we can make better use of the "active ingredients" in the treatment.

PHYSIOLOGICAL APPROACHES

From a physiological standpoint, anxiety disorders are thought to stem from problems with brain functioning, and therefore the physiological approaches to treatment involve *using drugs to correct the problems with brain functioning.* For example, drugs can be used to adjust the levels of neurotransmitters and thereby normalize the levels of activity in the areas of the brain that are responsible for anxiety.

At the outset, it is essential to recognize that *different anxiety disorders stem from different physiological causes.* That is important because it means that *different disorders must be treated with different drugs.* In other words, no one antianxiety drug can be used for all anxiety disorders. In the sections that follow, for each anxiety disorder I will briefly review the suspected physiological cause of that disorder and then explain why a particular type of drug is effective for treating that disorder. The disorders, their suspected physiological causes, and the drugs that are used to treat them are summarized in Table 6.2.

General Anxiety and the Benzodiazepines

We now know that many cases of general anxiety are due to low levels of **GABA,** a neurotransmitter that is essential for the activity of **inhibitory neurons.** If levels of GABA are low, inhibitory neurons do not fire, the levels of neurological activity become too high, and that leads to the experience of anxiety (see Chapter 5).

To overcome that problem, a group of drugs was developed that *increase GABA activity* and thereby reduce neurological activity and anxiety (Silver et al., 1994). Those drugs are called **benzodiazepines** (BEN-zō-dī-AZ-uh-pēnz). They increase GABA activity by facilitating the entrance of GABA into the receptor sites in the neurons in the reticular activating and limbic systems, which play an important role in arousal. A widely used benzodiazepine is **Valium (diazepam),** a relatively fast-acting drug that reaches its peak concentration within 1 hour. Valium is then transported out of the brain rather quickly, but its metabolites (new substances produced during its breakdown) remain, and because the metabolites are effective for reducing anxiety, the clinical effects of Valium are prolonged. Valium is a very safe drug, and no deaths due to overdose have been recorded. The safety of Valium is due to the fact that there is an upper limit to its ability to reduce neurological activity, and that limit is below the point at which respiratory activity and other vital functions are inhibited. However, it is important to recognize that the combination of high levels of benzodiazepines and other drugs that also reduce arousal can be lethal. For example, alcohol also reduces neurological activity, and when it is taken along with a benzodiazepine, the combined effects may be enough to stop respiration and kill the individual. Frequently used benzodiazepines are listed in Table 6.3.

A substantial amount of evidence indicates that benzodiazepines are effective for reducing general anxiety (Greenblatt & Shader, 1974, 1978; Kellner et al., 1978; Silver et al., 1994). For example, benzodiazepines

TABLE 6.2 Anxiety Disorders, Suspected Physiological Causes, and Drugs Used in Their Treatment

Disorder	Physiological Cause	Drug Treatment
General anxiety disorder	Low levels of GABA, so inhibitory neurons do not inhibit arousal	Benzodiazepines increase GABA activity
Obsessive-compulsive disorder	Low levels of serotonin, but the process is not understood	Antidepressants increase serotonin levels
Panic disorder	Overly sensitive respiratory control center, probably due to low levels of serotonin	Antidepressants increase serotonin levels
Phobias	Classical conditioning or erroneous beliefs, but high levels of arousal or reactivity could contribute	Benzodiazepines reduce general anxiety, beta blockers reduce heart rate reactivity, and antidepressants have unspecified effects

TABLE 6.3 Frequently Used Benzodiazepines

Trade Name	Generic Name	Typical Daily Dose
Ativan	Lorazepam	2–6 mg
Klonopin	Clonazepam	1–4 mg
Librium	Chlordiazepoxide	15–100 mg
Valium	Diazepam	4–40 mg
Xanax	Alprazolam	1–6 mg

were found to be more effective than placebos in 22 of the 25 experiments conducted in one 5-year period. The results of one experiment in which Valium was compared to a placebo are presented in Figure 6.4. Furthermore, in double-blind experiments in which groups of clients received either benzodiazepines or placebos and then the treatments were reversed, anxiety went down when clients were taking the benzodiazepines and up when they were taking the placebos. Thus it can be concluded that benzodiazepines are effective for treating general anxiety.

Obsessive-Compulsive Disorder and Antidepressants

It now appears that for about half of the individuals who suffer from the obsessive-compulsive disorder (OCD), the cause is low levels of the neurotransmitter **serotonin** (see Chapter 5). Therefore, it follows that in treating the OCD in those individuals, the goal is to increase the levels of serotonin, but that leads to an interesting paradox: The drugs that are most effective for increasing serotonin are *antidepressant* drugs, not antianxiety drugs (DeVaugh-Geiss et al., 1992; Greist et al., 1995; Stanley & Turner, 1995; van Blakom et al., 1994). The **antidepressants** that are most effective for treating the OCD are those that *block the reuptake* of serotonin and thereby make more serotonin available at the synapse (see Chapter 2). In general, these drugs are known as **bicyclics** and **tricyclics** because their chemical structures involve two *(bi-)* or three *(tri-)* circles (see Chapter 10 for a more detailed discussion of antidepressant drugs).

The effectiveness of antidepressants for treating the OCD was clearly demonstrated in a large experiment involving over 500 patients who were given either a tricyclic (Anafranil/clomipramine) that blocked the reuptake of serotonin or a placebo, and then the patients' symptoms were assessed once each week for 10 weeks (Clomipramine Collaborative Study Group, 1991). The results indicated that by the end of the first week, the patients taking the antidepressant were already showing greater reductions in symptoms than those in the placebo group, and the difference became progressively greater over the remaining 9 weeks of the

study. These results are presented in Figure 6.5. In general, the patients taking the antidepressant drug showed a 36% decline in symptoms, whereas the patients taking the placebo showed only a 2% decline in symptoms. It is noteworthy that the drug was effective in treating the symptoms of the OCD even in patients who were not depressed, thus indicating that the drug reduced the symptoms of the OCD directly rather than reducing depression and thereby reducing the symptoms of the OCD. Similar results have been found with adolescents who suffered from the OCD (DeVeaugh-Geiss et al., 1992).

The results in Figure 6.5 are based on overall means, but a slightly different picture emerges when improvements in individual patients are considered. When that was done, it was found that by the end of the 10 weeks of treatment, only half of the patients who were taking the drug had scores in the normal range. This means that some of the patients showed large improvements, whereas others showed small or no improvements, suggesting that the drug was working for only a subgroup of patients. That result is consistent with the notion that the OCD may stem from more than one cause (see Chapter 5). Clearly, antidepressants that block the reuptake of serotonin are effective

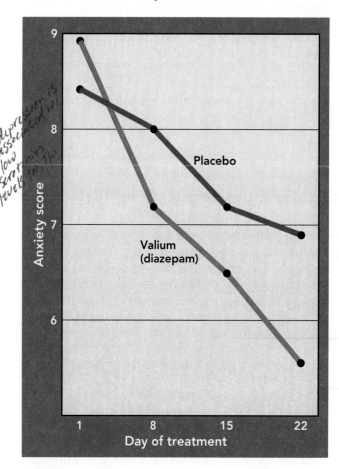

FIGURE 6.4 Valium (diazepam) was more effective for reducing anxiety than a placebo.

Source: Data from Burrows et al. (1976), p. 178, tab. 4.

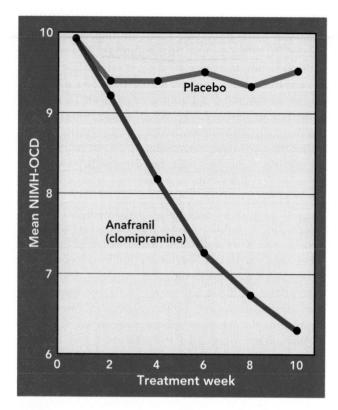

FIGURE 6.5 An antidepressant drug, Anafranil (clomipramine), was more effective than a placebo for reducing the symptoms of the obsessive-compulsive disorder.

Note: Means are for the NIMH Global OC scale. Data are collapsed over Study 1 (patients who had been ill for at least 2 years) and Study 2 (patients who had been ill for at least 1 year).

Source: Data from Clomipramine Collaborative Study Group (1991), p. 734, tab. 3.

As a footnote to this discussion of the treatment of the OCD, I should point out that in *very serious cases,* in which the individuals do not respond to any other treatments, a surgical procedure can be performed in which an area of the brain known as the **cingulate gyrus** is removed in an operation known as a **cingulotomy** (Baer et al., 1995; Hay et al., 1993; Jenike et al., 1991). It is not yet clear exactly why that should be effective, but the procedure does appear to reduce the symptoms in about 30% of the cases. However, this is a last-resort treatment for individuals with extremely serious disorders that have not responded to any of the other state-of-the-art treatments.

Panic Disorder, Agoraphobia, and Antidepressants

In Chapter 5, I explained that the panic disorder appears to be due to an *oversensitivity of the respiratory control center* in the brain stem that causes the brain stem to send up false alarms of suffocation that result in the panics (Klein, 1993; Stein et al., 1995; Taylor, 1994). Important in that regard is the fact that the activity in the respiratory center is controlled at least in part by the neurotransmitter *serotonin.* Specifically, serotonin appears to *inhibit* the activity in the respiratory center and thereby makes it less sensitive.

Because the oversensitivity of the respiratory control center appears to be due to low levels of serotonin, panic attacks could be treated with drugs that increase

for treating patients for whom low levels of serotonin is the problem underlying the OCD. It is suspected that in other patients, the symptoms may stem from minimal brain damage (see Chapter 5), but there is not yet a treatment for those patients.

It should also be noted that the widely used antidepressant drug **Prozac (fluoxetine),** which blocks the reuptake of serotonin, has been shown to be effective for treating the OCD (see Pigott et al., 1990). Indeed, strong evidence for the effectiveness of Prozac for treating the OCD comes from an experiment in which a large number of individuals with the OCD were given one of three dose levels of Prozac (20, 40, 60 mg/day) or a placebo, and then their levels of the OCD were assessed over a 13-week period (Tollefson et al., 1994). The results indicated that all of the levels of Prozac were more effective than the placebo, and the higher the level of Prozac, the better the results. Those findings are illustrated in Figure 6.6.

Case Study 6.5 provides an interesting illustration of the effects of an antidepressant on a young woman's compulsions.

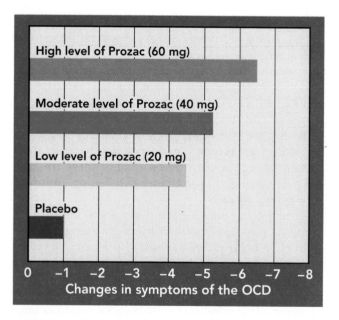

FIGURE 6.6 Higher levels of Prozac (fluoxetine) were associated with greater reductions in the obsessive-compulsive disorder.

Note: Scores are from the Yale-Brown Obsessive-Compulsive scale.
Source: Adapted from Tollefson et al. (1994), p. 564, fig. 2.

CASE STUDY 6.5

An Unexpected and Helpful Side Effect in the Treatment of Depression

A student of mine had a long history of depression, and because psychotherapy had not been effective, her psychiatrist prescribed a moderate level of an antidepressant (Prozac, 20 mg/day). (Depression and its treatment will be discussed in Chapters 8, 9, and 10.)

Initially, the depression improved, but about two months later, it got worse; the student became suicidal, and she called me. We arranged for her to stay with a friend, and in consultation with her psychiatrist, the level of the antidepressant was increased (40 mg). The dose was increased on a Friday, and when I saw the student on the following Tuesday, she surprised me with a big hug and said, "It's great—it's *great!* The rituals are gone!" I was somewhat taken aback and said, "I don't understand. What rituals?" She then smiled a bit sheepishly and explained that she had not told me or her psychiatrist, but for years she had suffered from a variety of *compulsions.* For example, she had a very specific ritual she had to go through when showering and dressing in the morning: While in the shower, she had to wash the parts of her body in a very specific order; after getting out

of the shower, she had to dry herself in the same order; and then she had to put her clothes on in a very specific order. If she did anything out of order, she would become extremely anxious, and *she would have to undress, reshower, redry, and redress following the ritual.*

She then went on to explain that what was "great" was the fact that two days after taking the higher dose of the antidepressant, she had showered, dried, dressed, and left her apartment—*and only then did she realize that she had not followed her ritual and that she was not upset about it!* She did not understand why the ritual was no longer necessary, but she thought it was great; she was really relieved and happy.

What appears to have happened with this young woman is that when the level of the antidepressant was increased, it increased the levels of serotonin enough to clear up the compulsions. The effect was surprising to the young woman because she did not know that antidepressants could influence compulsions. Clearly, this was an unexpected and distinctly positive side effect!

---

the levels of serotonin. In other words, higher levels of serotonin would decrease the sensitivity of the respiratory control center, which would decrease the false alarms and consequently the occurrence of panics. In fact, there is now a large body of evidence indicating that *antidepressant drugs that increase the levels of serotonin are effective for treating panic attacks* (Clum et al., 1993; de Beurs et al., 1995; Hollander et al., 1994). For example, in experiments in which the effects of antidepressants were compared to those of a placebo, the antidepressants were found to be more effective for reducing panic attacks than the placebo (e.g., Mattick et al., 1990; Mavissakalian & Perel, 1989, 1992a, 1992b). Furthermore, when the antidepressants were discontinued, the panic attacks returned. In another experiment, it was found that progressively higher levels of an antidepressant were progressively more effective for eliminating panic attacks, thus offering more evidence of their utility (Mavissakalian & Perel, 1995). Those results are summarized in Figure 6.7.

It should also be noted that the antidepressants are also effective for treating the agoraphobia that

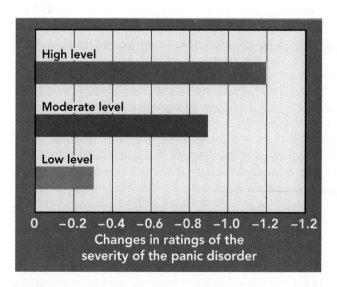

FIGURE 6.7 Higher levels of an antidepressant (imipramine) were associated with greater reductions in the panic disorder.
Note: Scores are based on clinicians' judgments on a 5-point scale.
Source: Data from Mavissakalian and Perel (1995), p. 676, tab. 2.

sometimes accompanies the panic disorder. In that regard, you should recall that agoraphobia is often linked to panic attacks because individuals become fearful of having a panic attack in public and therefore restrict their public activities. Because the drugs reduce the panic attacks, there is no longer a basis for the fear of going out in public, so the agoraphobia is diminished.

The antidepressants are effective for controlling panics, but the question arises, will individuals with the panic disorder have to stay on the drugs forever? With regard to that question, there is an interesting study in which individuals who were being gradually withdrawn from an antidepressant either were or were not given cognitive-behavior therapy in which they were taught breathing exercises (Spiegel et al., 1994). The results indicated that individuals who received the cognitive therapy showed much lower relapse rates than those who did not receive the cognitive therapy. It appears that once the drug got the individuals "over the hump," they could use the deep breathing strategy to avoid the oxygen debt and panics.

Phobias, Benzodiazepines, Beta Blockers, and Antidepressants

It is widely believed that phobias are due to classical conditioning; that is, a phobia develops when physiological arousal (fear) is paired with a specific stimulus such that later the stimulus can elicit the arousal or fear. Related to that, there is evidence that individuals who develop phobias are more physiologically aroused or more physiologically reactive than other individuals. That is, it appears that if you are very physiologically reactive, you will be likely to respond with fear, and responding with fear would make it likely that a conditioned fear response will develop. Furthermore, the symptoms of high arousal or reactivity, such as an elevated heart rate, might be misinterpreted as signs of anxiety and thereby contribute to the development of fears and phobias (Levin et al., 1989; see Chapter 5).

If high physiological arousal and reactivity contribute to phobias, phobias could be treated with drugs that reduce physiological arousal and reactivity. The drugs that are often used for that purpose are the benzodiazepines, such as Valium, that I discussed earlier. Early evidence that benzodiazepines can reduce phobias was provided by an interesting experiment on pigeons in which the birds were first taught to peck at a disk to receive food. Once that response was learned, the birds were given electrical shocks when they pecked the disk, and they ceased pecking the disk. In other words, anxiety was associated with pecking the disk, so the birds avoided that response. However, in the next phase of the experiment, the birds either were or were not given benzodiazepines, and it was found that when they were given the drug, their pecking of the disk returned almost to the normal (preshock) level, but when they were not given the drugs, they avoided pecking the disk (Houser, 1978; Sanger & Blackman, 1981). In human terms, a phobia was induced in the birds (fear of pecking the disk), which was then treated effectively with benzodiazepines. There have also been numerous experiments on humans in which benzodiazepines were effective for reducing phobias (Levin et al., 1989).

Another class of drugs that can be effective for treating phobias (and sometimes general anxiety) is known as the **beta blockers.** Beta blockers keep heart rate stable in the face of stress such as exercise or fear by blocking the stimulation of the heart. These drugs were originally developed for individuals with heart problems who had to avoid cardiac stress, but they can be used to treat individuals with phobias because if heart rate does not increase in what the individual thinks is a fearful situation such as public speaking, the individual may reevaluate the situation and reduce the fear (Levin et al., 1989; Hollander et al., 1994).

Finally, it should be noted that there is a growing body of evidence that some antidepressants are effective for treating social phobias (e.g., Gelernter et al., 1991; Levin et al., 1989; Liebowitz et al., 1992). Why this type of antidepressant is effective for reducing the social phobia is not yet clear.

Issues Associated with Drug Treatment

Before concluding this discussion of drug treatment, it is essential that I comment on some of the questions and concerns that are often raised concerning the use of drugs. These questions and concerns are relevant for the drug treatment of anxiety, but they are also relevant for the drug treatment of other disorders such as depression and schizophrenia that we will consider later.

Side Effects. The evidence clearly indicates that drugs are effective for treating anxiety disorders, but do the drugs have negative side effects? The answer is yes; the effects can include drowsiness, light-headedness, dry mouth, nausea, blurred vision, and constipation, and the side effects may be experienced by as many as 30% of the individuals who take the drugs. However, it is interesting to note that individuals who take placebos also experience many of these side effects, thus suggesting that some of the side effects are due to suggestions or expectations rather than the drugs per se. However, that does not reduce their unpleasantness (Evans, 1981).

Given that the drugs do have side effects, we must go on to ask, do the negative side effects outweigh the positive effects? The answer is generally no; in most cases, individuals would rather put up with the side effects than suffer from the symptoms the drugs relieve. Three points should be noted in this regard:

1. The side effects of the drugs are usually *not severe enough to disrupt normal living.* For example, 13% of the individuals who take Valium experience a dry mouth, but at worst that is only a minor annoyance and does not generally interfere with normal daily living.

2. Some clients report side effects of drowsiness or confusion, but there is evidence that at the proper dosages, benzodiazepines actually *enhance mental functioning* (Bond et al., 1974). This enhancement occurs because without the drug, the individual's level of anxiety is so high that it interferes with performance, whereas the drug reduces the excessive anxiety, and consequently performance improves. For most individuals, the net effect seems to be positive.

3. Over time, many of the *side effects disappear* or become relatively unimportant. That may occur because the body adjusts to the effects of the medication. Many of the side effects about which patients complain occur only at high dose levels.

In cases in which the side effects do outweigh the symptoms they replace, a good strategy is to try a different drug because different drugs often have different patterns of side effects in different individuals. It may also be possible that a lower dose of the drug will work and cause fewer side effects.

Treatment Versus Cure. Drugs are *treatments, not cures.* In other words, a drug will temporarily change the level of a neurotransmitter and thereby relieve symptoms, but *the drug will not correct the underlying problem that led to the inappropriate level of the neurotransmitter.* When the drug is withdrawn, the symptoms may return. The fact that drugs do not provide cures is certainly a limitation, but that limitation is not a reason to reject the treatment, especially because we do not have a cure at the present time. Analogously, if you have a bad headache, you may take an aspirin to relieve the pain. The aspirin will not cure the headache, but it will relieve the pain and let you get on with your activities. Should you not take the aspirin just because it is not a cure? Perhaps a better analogy is to diabetes, a disorder that stems from the fact that the individual does not produce enough insulin, a situation that is similar to not producing enough GABA. Diabetes can be treated effectively by giving the individual insulin injections on a regular basis, but the insulin does not cure the problem of underproduction of insulin by the body. Should individuals with diabetes stop taking the insulin because it does not cure the disorder? Perhaps someday we will identify cures for headaches, diabetes, and anxiety, but until then we will have to be content with symptom relief.

Long-Term Need for Drugs. Because drugs provide treatments rather than cures for anxiety, clients often ask, "Will I have to stay on the drug for the rest of my life?" The answer is probably not, because in most cases the biochemical imbalance that is being corrected by the drug is a transient aberration that will correct itself spontaneously, or the imbalance may be age-limited and will be corrected after running its course. The temporary nature of some imbalances is reflected in the fact that panic attacks, periods of generalized anxiety, and phobias tend to remit with increasing age. In those cases, the individuals can cease taking the drug as soon as the imbalance has been corrected. In other cases, the drug may be taken to help the individual cope with an otherwise overwhelming environmental stressor such as a death, and when the stressor has passed, the individual can cease taking the drug. The key to determining whether medication is still necessary is occasionally to test the lower limit of drug dosage effectiveness (can you get along with less medication?) or occasionally to take "drug holidays" (can you get along without any medication?). Of course, that should be done under careful supervision.

Drug Dependence. A potential problem with the use of benzodiazepines revolves around the development of physical **dependence** after prolonged use. (Dependence is said to occur if physical symptoms appear when an individual stops using a drug; see Chapter 17.) Some years ago, concerns were raised because physicians were prescribing benzodiazepines very widely and there were anecdotal reports suggesting that some individuals had become "addicted." Indeed, Valium was referred to as "psychiatric aspirin" and the "opium of the masses."

Research on the addictive quality of benzodiazepines is difficult to do because some of the symptoms that occur when the use of the drugs is terminated may be the symptoms for which the drugs were originally taken. For example, if the individual becomes tense and anxious, that may simply be due to the fact that the individual is no longer taking antianxiety medication, and that should not be mistaken for a symptom of dependence. However, there is some evidence that dependence can develop after *prolonged use at high levels.* For example, when patients who had been on high daily doses of benzodiazepines for at least 3 months were switched to a placebo, they showed symptoms such as muscle tremors and cognitive confusion that were not part of their original symptom pattern (Busto et al., 1986). Clearly, some dependence can develop, but there is now evidence that it can be minimized with a slow and careful withdrawal process (Rickels et al., 1991).

COMMENT

The physiological approaches to treatment have become much more sophisticated and effective since it was realized that different disorders are due to different physiological problems and therefore require different drugs. Now, rather than simply prescribing an "antianxiety" drug for all types of anxiety disorders, different types of drugs are prescribed for different anxiety disorders (e.g., benzodiazepines for general anxiety, antidepressants for the OCD and panic attacks). This has greatly increased the effectiveness of drug treatment. Furthermore, the development of new drugs that are more specific in their effects (influencing only one neurotransmitter) has improved effectiveness and reduced unwanted side effects. These changes have reduced some of the criticisms of the drug treatment of anxiety that were relevant as recently as 5 or 10 years ago.

It is also noteworthy that in many cases, the combination of drugs and cognitive therapy can be effective. For example, drugs can be used to "break the back" of the disorder, and then cognitive therapy can be used to help the individual cope with the remaining symptoms (Bruce et al., 1995).

WHAT CAN WE CONCLUDE CONCERNING THE TREATMENT OF ANXIETY DISORDERS?

The most important thing to note about the treatment of anxiety disorders is that *no one treatment is effective for all of the anxiety disorders;* rather, because the various anxiety disorders stem from different causes, different disorders require different treatments. If the anxiety stems from stressors, psychotherapy, with the guidance and social support it provides, can be effective. In the case of phobias that are due to classical conditioning, extinction procedures may be effective, although it is not clear whether the underlying process is extinction or the changing of beliefs. For anxieties that stem from incorrect beliefs, changing beliefs concerning the threats can be effective. Finally, some cases of the generalized anxiety disorder, obsessive-compulsive disorder, and panic disorder appear to be due to physiological problems, and for them the most effective treatment is drugs. Finally, it is important to note that sometimes treatments are effective even if they do not correct the basic problem. For example, changing beliefs about the ability to cope with symptoms can help even if the cause of the symptoms and the symptoms themselves are not eliminated. Furthermore, drugs that change arousal levels can be effective for reducing anxiety even if the cause of the heightened arousal is not physiological. For example, beta blockers limit arousal that may stem from stressors, classical conditioning, or incorrect beliefs. The point here is that *different treatments must be used to deal with different causes* and *different treatments can be used to intervene at different points in the chain that leads from causes to disorders.*

SUMMARY

- There are a variety of forms of psychotherapy, but in most cases, the therapist tries to help the client identify and overcome the cause of the symptoms. If the cause cannot be identified or overcome, the focus may be on helping the client learn to cope with the symptoms.
- Most clients are seen individually, but some are seen in group therapy, and because of financial pressures, more use is made of time-limited psychotherapy.
- After long debate, there is now evidence that psychotherapy can be effective, but not with all problems. With regard to anxiety disorders, for example, it is more effective with generalized anxiety than with the obsessive-compulsive disorder.
- It is not clear exactly why psychotherapy is effective, but much of its effects may be due to the social support that is provided by the therapist.
- The learning approaches to the treatment of anxiety revolve around (a) the extinction of the classically conditioned anxiety response, a procedure that is sometimes referred to as flooding; (b) the inhibition of anxiety by the substitution of a relaxation response, a procedure that is called systematic desensitization or counterconditioning; and (c) relaxation training so that the individual can relax in otherwise anxiety-provoking situations.

■ There is evidence that the various learning approaches to treatment can be effective, especially with phobias. However, it now appears that the effects may be due to changes in cognitions (thoughts about the anxiety-provoking stimuli and the ability to cope with them) rather than to the principles of conditioning on which the treatment strategies were originally founded. That is, during extinction (flooding), an individual with a dog phobia may simply learn that dogs are not dangerous.

■ Cognitive approaches to the treatment of anxiety involve changing the clients' beliefs concerning the dangerousness of situations ("Dogs are dangerous") or their ability to cope ("I can deal with dogs—even big ones"). That is done through cognitive therapy, rational-emotive therapy, exposure to the feared stimuli, and exposure with response prevention.

■ Cognitive therapy is effective for treating phobias, but exposure to the feared stimulus without dire consequences seems to be the most effective means of changing beliefs. Cognitive therapy for the panic disorder is effective, but its effects appear to revolve around enhanced coping with the symptoms or reducing the symptoms by deep breathing, which overcomes the oxygen debt. About 50% of the individuals with compulsions can be treated effectively by exposure with response prevention, a procedure in which they learn that nothing terrible will happen if they do not perform their rituals. Meditation (distraction) is not more effective for reducing anxiety than simply sitting quietly.

■ The physiological approaches to treatment of anxiety involve using drugs to correct problems with brain functioning. Benzodiazepines are used to treat the generalized anxiety disorder because they increase the activity of GABA, which is the neurotransmitter that is associated with inhibitory neurons; antidepressants that increase the levels of serotonin are effective for treating about 50% of the individuals with the obsessive-compulsive disorder; antidepressants that increase the levels of serotonin are also effective for treating the panic disorder, probably because serotonin decreases the sensitivity of the respiratory control center, so false alarms are not sent up; and benzodiazepines and beta blockers can be effective for treating phobias because they set upper limits on arousal (e.g., heart rate) so that the individual cannot experience as much fear.

■ Drugs can have unpleasant side effects. They provide a treatment but not a cure, so in some cases they will be necessary for long periods of time; and at high levels, dependence can develop.

KEY TERMS, CONCEPTS, AND NAMES

In reviewing and testing yourself on what you have learned from this chapter, you should be able to identify and discuss each of the following.

antidepressants: *blocks reuptake/serotonin*
benzodiazepines: *↑ GABA*
beta blockers: *reduces heart stress*
bicyclics: *antidepressant*
biofeedback training: *electrodes*
cingulate gyrus: *removed in serious ocd*
cingulotomy: *surgery to aid ocd*
client-centered psychotherapy: *Rogers*
cognitive therapy: *Δ beliefs*
counterconditioning: *extinction/inhibition*
dependence: *re: drugs*
distraction: *meditation*
exposure with response prevention: *OCD - block ritual*

extinction: *no*
family therapy:
flooding: *lots/anxiety, extinction*
GABA: *inhibitory neuron's neurotransmitter*
group psychotherapy *2-8 people*
inhibitory neurons: *ceases activity*
in vitro exposure: *imagined*
in vivo exposure: *real life*
mantra: *repeated word*
meditation: *not effective*
paraprofessionals: *trained, not licensed*
progressive muscle relaxation: *relax different parts/body*
Prozac (fluoxetine): *anti-dep*

psychoanalysis: *free association, lay down*
psychotherapy: *sitting + talking*
rational-emotive therapy: *therapist confronts clients beliefs*
relaxation response: *counting*
self-efficacy: *coping skills*
serotonin: *happy chemical*
social support: *friends, family who aid in therapy*
systematic desensitization: *used for inhibition*
time-limited psychotherapy: *insurance*
transcendental meditation: *a type*
tricyclics *antidepressant*
Valium (diazepam): *benzo*
verbal conditioning: *they say what therapist want to hear*

CHAPTER SEVEN
SOMATOFORM and DISSOCIATIVE DISORDERS

OUTLINE

Alice has frequently consulted physicians about a wide variety of physical symptoms, including vague pains, lumps, dizziness, blurred vision, digestive problems, and numbness. Because in many cases a cause cannot be identified, she is often sent to specialists who do additional work-ups, but even they have difficulty making a firm diagnosis. Her case becomes more complex because usually after a short period of treatment, the symptoms change, and then additional medical consultations are necessary. Alice spends a lot of time in physicians' offices, and her illnesses cause considerable disruption in her life. Recently, it was concluded that Alice is suffering from the *somatization disorder* rather than a series of actual organic disorders.

■ ■ ■

William does not frequently experience many physical symptoms, but when even a minor one occurs, he immediately thinks it is an early sign of some very serious disorder and becomes extremely tense and anxious. His fears are allayed only after a thorough physical examination. He suffers from *hypochondriasis.*

■ ■ ■

The 15 clerical staff members of a research institute had been under considerable pressure to get a large amount of data entered into the computer, and they had spent long hours working at their terminals. On Wednesday, two terminal operators went home early complaining of headaches, dizziness, and nausea. By 11 o'clock the next morning, four other operators had begun vomiting uncontrollably, three reported that their vision was so blurred that they could not see across the room, one fainted, and most of the others reported lesser forms of physiological distress. In attempting to explain this epidemic, it was first thought that the workers' computer screens were giving off excessive radiation or that chemical pollutants had gotten into the air-conditioning system. Environmental engineers were unable to confirm either of those possibilities. After two days of rest, during which the systems were checked, the staff went back to work in the same environment with no ill effects. The staff probably suffered from *mass psychogenic illness,* a modern version of the dancing manias of the 15th century.

■ ■ ■

Bob appears to be a model husband and father, but he has been going to a psychotherapist for about two years because he is "tense and dissatisfied." In the course of therapy, it has come out that Bob frequently has affairs with other women. His behavior in therapy has been somewhat inconsistent: Sometimes he does not talk about the affairs and instead focuses on his tension, but at other times he talks about his sexual escapades in a rather cavalier fashion and shows no sign of anxiety or remorse. His therapist believes that Bob may have a *multiple personality disorder,* or what is technically called the *dissociative identity disorder.*

■ ■ ■

In this chapter I will discuss two groups of interesting disorders. First, I will examine *somatoform disorders*, which involve physical symptoms for which we cannot find a physical cause. For example, an individual may appear to suffer from a wide variety of illnesses, but no organic cause for the symptoms can be found. Then I will review *dissociative disorders,* which involve a loss of contact with parts of the individual's personality. For example, the individual may suffer from amnesia, or in the case of "multiple personality," the individual may be unaware of parts of his or her personality.

TOPIC I
SOMATOFORM DISORDERS

SOMATOFORM DISORDERS

The dominant feature of most **somatoform disorders** is the presence of *physical symptoms* such as pain, paralysis, blindness, or deafness *for which there is no demonstrable physical cause.* In the absence of a physical cause, it is assumed that the symptoms stem from psychological causes.

At the outset, we must distinguish between somatoform disorders and what have traditionally been called **psychosomatic disorders** such as ulcers, tension headaches, and some cardiovascular problems. In both types of disorders, the causes are psychological and the symptoms are physical. The difference between the two is that with somatoform disorders, *there is no physical damage* (e.g., an individual may complain about stomach pain, but there is nothing physically wrong with the stomach), whereas with psychosomatic disorders, *there is physical damage* (e.g., ulcers involve lesions in the lining of the stomach). The term *somatoform* is used because there is no physical damage; the symptoms only take the *form* of a *somatic* (physical) disorder. Somatoform disorders are important because they disrupt the lives of individuals just as real physical illnesses do and also because they place a heavy and unnecessary burden on the health care system.

There are five somatoform disorders: somatization disorder, hypochondriasis, conversion disorder, pain disorder, and body dysmorphic disorder. The major symptoms of these somatoform disorders are summarized in Table 7.1.

Somatization Disorder

The diagnosis of **somatization** (sō-MAT-uh-ZĀ-shun) **disorder** is used for individuals who have *numerous, recurrent, and long-lasting somatic complaints that are apparently not due to any actual physical cause.* To be diagnosed as suffering from the somatization disorder, the individual must have reported at least two gastrointestinal symptoms (e.g., nausea, vomiting, intolerance for several foods), one sexual symptom (e.g., indifference, erectile dysfunction, irregular menses), one neurological symptom (e.g., paralysis, weakness, difficulty in swallowing), and pain in four locations (e.g., head, abdomen, joints). Individuals with this disorder reject the notion that their symptoms are caused by psychological factors, and they persist in seeking a medical solution. By middle adulthood, they have complained about almost every symptom pattern imaginable, consulted every specialist available, and stocked a medicine cabinet that

TABLE 7.1 Predominant Symptoms in the Somatoform Disorders

Disorder	Symptoms
Somatization disorder	Numerous, recurrent, and long-lasting somatic complaints that are apparently not due to any actual physical cause
Hypochondriasis	An unrealistic belief that a minor symptom reflects a serious disease
Conversion disorder	One or more major physical symptoms involving voluntary motor or sensory functions for which an organic basis cannot be found
Pain disorder	Complaint of pain in the absence of an identifiable organic cause
Body dysmorphic disorder	Preoccupation with some imagined or minor defect in one's physical appearance

Note: Symptoms must be serious enough to result in impairment in social, occupational, or other important areas of functioning.

rivals the shelves of the local pharmacy. Their medical concerns often take over and dominate their lives.

Somatization is usually a long-term, often lifelong, disorder in which the individuals seriously overuse the health care system (Bell, 1994; Smith, 1994; Williams & House, 1994). For example, during one 25-year period, a 48-year-old woman had 77 admissions to 10 different hospitals, underwent 11 operations, and spent 856 days in the hospital (the equivalent of almost 2½ years!), yet no physical disorder was ever found that could explain her symptoms. Individuals with the somatization disorder often also suffer from depression and anxiety (Noyes et al., 1994). Those complaints are not part of the disorder per se but are a consequence of the individual's belief that a serious medical problem exists. In common parlance, an individual with the somatization disorder is often referred to as a "hypochondriac," but as we will see, that diagnosis is reserved for a somewhat different set of symptoms.

Hypochondriasis

The dominant feature of **hypochondriasis** (HĪ-pō-kon-DRĪ-uh-sis) is the *unrealistic belief that a minor symptom reflects a serious disease.* That is, individuals with this disorder interpret minor physical sensations or signs as abnormalities that will inevitably lead to serious diseases, and consequently they become anxious and upset about their symptoms. For example, a headache is interpreted as a symptom of a developing brain tumor, or a slight skin irritation is seen as an early sign of skin cancer, and consequently the individual becomes distraught and seeks treatment. Medical examinations and reassurances that there is nothing wrong may temporarily allay the concern, but soon a new sign of impending physical disease will be found, and the cycle will start over again.

Hypochondriasis is similar to somatization in that both disorders involve concerns about physical symptoms. However, the disorders differ in that individuals with the somatization disorder are concerned with a wide variety of current symptoms and diseases, whereas those with hypochondriasis show excessive anxiety about one or two symptoms and the implications they could have for potential future diseases. Like somatization, hypochondriasis is a long-term disorder, more likely to be diagnosed in women, and likely to be accompanied by depression (Barsky, 1992; Noyes et al., 1994).

Conversion Disorder

In cases of **conversion disorder,** the individual has *one or more major physical symptoms involving voluntary motor or sensory functions for which an organic basis cannot be found.* Frequently cited conversion symptoms include paralysis, seizures, blindness, deafness, tunnel vision,

anesthesia (loss of feeling or sensation), and paresthesia (pricking or tingling sensations of the skin). In many cases, the symptoms are closely related to the individual's activities or occupation. For example, pilots who fly at night develop night blindness, whereas pilots who fly during the day develop day blindness (Ironside & Batchelor, 1945), and violinists develop paralysis or cramps in the hands. Because of this relationship, conversion disorders used to be referred to as **craft palsies.**

Certain features of the conversion disorder help us distinguish between it and an actual physical disorder. The most conclusive of these clues is the occurrence of a symptom pattern that could not possibly be the result of a physical cause. An example of this is the classic **glove anesthesia,** in which the individual loses feeling in the hand up to the point at which a glove would stop. Given the nerve pathways in the arm and hand, we know that such a pattern of insensitivity is impossible. The distinction between glove anesthesia and actual nerve pathways is illustrated in Figure 7.1. Unfortunately, as the level of medical sophistication in the general public increases, individuals are less likely to exhibit symptom patterns that are blatantly impossible, and hence it is becoming more difficult to separate the conversion disorder from actual physical disorders on the basis of the inappropriateness of symptom patterns.

Another clue is the absence of negative consequences that would be the inevitable result of a physical disorder. For example, individuals with the conversion disorder who suffer from epileptic-like seizures may not hurt themselves during a seizure, and psychogenically blind individuals may not bump into things.

A final clue that may be used for distinguishing between conversion and physical disorders is the consistency of the symptom pattern. In the case of an individual with the conversion disorder, the symptoms may change with changes in the stress (a paralyzed leg before a track meet and a paralyzed hand before an examination), whereas there will be greater consistency in the symptoms stemming from an actual physical disorder. Unfortunately, in many cases, all of these clues are lacking, and the differential diagnosis of these disorders can be very difficult.

A dramatic example of the conversion disorder that I observed occurred in a sophomore woman who came to the university hospital about midway through the fall semester with "intermittent blindness." This woman's vision would begin dimming on Sunday evening, and by Monday morning she would be blind. The blindness lasted until Friday evening, and by Saturday morning her vision was completely restored. This cycle persisted for 3 weeks. The student showed no surprise at the unusual nature of her disorder and evinced no concern about her condition. Indeed, she observed

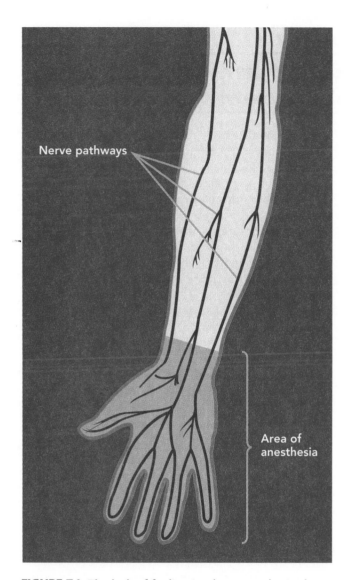

FIGURE 7.1 The lack of feeling in glove anesthesia does not follow the nerve pathways in the hand.

cheerily that she was sure we would be able to take care of the problem and, after all, it was not interfering with the important social activities associated with football weekends! After 3 weeks the symptoms remitted. It is not clear why they remitted at that point, but it may be associated with the fact that the midterm examination period was over. The student stayed in school (but did not go to many of her classes because she was "too far behind") until the last week of the semester, when she withdrew "for medical reasons."

Before concluding our description of the conversion disorder, some attention should be given to a related phenomenon that is called **mass psychogenic illness** (Colligan et al., 1982). Mass psychogenic illness involves *an epidemic of a particular manifestation of the conversion disorder.* The best known of these epidemics are the **dancing manias** that erupted in the 15th and 16th centuries. In those epidemics, large groups of

people danced, hopped, and jerked uncontrollably for hours or days until they finally fell exhausted (Martin, 1923).

Contrary to what is often assumed, mass psychogenic illnesses did not stop with the Middle Ages. In fact, numerous epidemics have been reported in recent years, but they are less extreme than the medieval dancing manias (Sirois, 1982). For example, a sudden outbreak of a peculiar illness spread quickly among Boston grade school children who were gathered at an assembly (Small & Nicholi, 1982). The children reported experiencing dizziness, hyperventilation, weakness, headache, nausea, and abdominal pain. Of the 224 children who attended the assembly, 40 to 50 required some type of treatment on the scene, and 34 had to be hospitalized. However, no physical basis could be found for any of the symptoms. Other instances of mass psychogenic illness involved 84 women in a television assembly plant in Singapore who began screaming, fainting, and going into trances (Chew et al., 1976); 85 women and 59 men working in a factory in the southeastern United States who developed dizziness, nausea, difficulty in breathing, headaches, and a bad taste in the mouth (Folland, 1975); 35 women working in an office of a midwestern university who experienced

I would too!

The dancing manias of the 15th and 16th centuries were early examples of mass psychogenic illness. In these manias, groups of people hopped and jerked uncontrollably.

CASE STUDY 7.1

Mass Psychogenic Illness in Junior High and High School Students

On April 13, 1989, approximately 600 student performers gathered at the Santa Monica Civic Auditorium for the 40th annual "Stairway to the Stars" concert. This was the major classical music performance (choral and orchestra) for students in the 6th through 12th grades. The performance started at 7:30 P.M., but shortly thereafter, it was interrupted when symptoms such as headaches, dizziness, weakness, abdominal pain, shortness of breath, chills, chest pain, and nausea began spreading through the student performers. Eleven students found themselves unable to open their eyes, and 18 fainted. The problem became so bad that the concert had to be stopped, and the students, along with the 2,000 spectators, were forced to evacuate the auditorium.

The fire department sent two paramedic squads and two engine companies, and together they set up a treatment area outside the auditorium. The students were placed on stretchers that were lined up on the lawn, and eight ambulances were used to rush the most severely ill students to local hospitals.

Physical examinations and laboratory tests performed on the students did not reveal any abnormalities. Furthermore, there was no evidence of toxic fumes or materials in the area. Because there were no confirmed physical illnesses and no evidence of

environmental threats, the school officials rescheduled the concert for the next evening, but many parents were unconvinced of the safety of the situation and therefore kept their children at home.

A follow-up study of the students who did and did not develop symptoms revealed some interesting differences. For example, when compared to students who did not show symptoms, those who did show symptoms were more likely to have had a chronic illness (25% vs. 10%), more likely to have had a recent acute illness (17% vs. 11%), more likely to have experienced the death of a relative or friend (70% vs. 55%), and, most important, more likely to have observed a friend get sick at the concert (71% vs. 41%).

The affected students truly believed that they were sick and showed signs of illness such as vomiting or fainting, but no underlying causes could be identified. The absence of underlying causes, in combination with the data concerning the influence of suggestion (e.g., previous experience with illness and seeing others become sick), clearly leads to the diagnosis of mass psychogenic illness.

Source: Small et al. (1991).

---

nausea, vomiting, dizziness, and fainting (Stahl & Lebedun, 1974); over 900 persons (mostly schoolgirls) who developed blindness, headache, stomachache, and discoloration of the skin (Hefez, 1985); and 45 schoolchildren in Bali who experienced sudden periods of fainting, visual hallucinations, and uncontrollable dancing (Suryani & Jensen, 1992). In one case of an unexplained syndrome of "allergy" among plastics workers, it was found that those who developed the illness had a higher rate of anxiety or depressive disorders (54% vs. 4%) and somatization (69% vs. 13%) than individuals who did not develop the illness, thereby suggesting a psychological predisposition or cause (Simon et al., 1990). It is interesting to note that over the past 500 years, there have been changes in the purported causes of mass psychogenic illness that parallel changes in our culture: In the 15th century, the disorders were attributed to curses; now they are attributed to factors such as radiation from computer screens. An example of mass psychogenic illness is presented in Case Study 7.1.

Pain Disorder

The **pain disorder** involves the *complaint of pain in the absence of an identifiable organic cause,* in which case the pain is thought to have a psychological origin. It is believed that some back problems may actually be manifestations of the pain disorder.

Individuals with the pain disorder are very concerned about their problem, and they may make frequent visits to physicians for treatment. The extent of the impairment caused by this disorder ranges from a slight disturbance of social or occupational functioning to total incapacity and need for hospitalization. The pain disorder could loosely be considered a subtype of the somatization disorder; the only differences between the two is that the pain disorder is limited to pain.

Body Dysmorphic Disorder

The **body dysmorphic** (dis-MOR-fik) **disorder** involves the *preoccupation with some imagined or minor defect in one's* *physical appearance*. Examples include excessive concern about a mole or the shape of one's nose. In some cases, the disorder can lead to social withdrawal, occupational dysfunction, and even suicide (Phillips, 1991). Not included in this disorder are individuals with anorexia, who are unjustifiably concerned about their weight (see Chapter 16). The dysmorphic disorder is the most recent addition to the group of somatoform disorders, added with the publication of DSM-III-R in 1987. At this point, little is known about the nature, prevalence, and implications of the body dysmorphic disorder. There is some question about whether this problem is important enough to be considered a somatoform disorder.

ISSUES ASSOCIATED WITH SOMATOFORM DISORDERS

Historical Background

Somatoform disorders (more precisely, instances of the conversion disorder) have a long history and have been associated primarily with women. From as early as 1500 B.C. we have a description of "a woman ill in seeing," and it was thought that the disorder resulted from a malpositioned uterus (Veith, 1965). Similarly, in the writings of the ancient Greeks, we find numerous descriptions of women with what appear to be conversion disorders. Those disorders were attributed to the fact that because the womb had not been sexually satisfied, it had gone wandering through the body in search of satisfaction, and in its wandering it had lodged itself in such a way as to cause the disorder. For example, if a woman had a paralyzed arm, it was assumed that the womb had become stuck in her shoulder or elbow. Because of the problem, early Greek physicians recommended sex as a treatment for these disorders. The importance of the womb in causing these problems is reflected in the fact that the problems were once labeled "hysterical"—the term *hysteria* comes from the Greek word for "womb."

Increased attention was focused on somatoform disorders in the 19th century when **Jean-Martin Charcot,** a famous French physician, dramatically demonstrated that by using suggestion, he could induce and eliminate all manner of symptoms in women patients suffering from what was then called hysteria. **Sigmund Freud** also worked with patients suffering from somatoform disorders and drew a considerable amount of attention to them. Like the Greeks before him, Freud concluded that the basis of the problem was sexual—specifically, conflicts over sexuality. Interestingly, Freud did not believe that the disorder was limited to women, and early in his career he presented a paper at a meeting of the Vienna Medical Society on "male hysteria." His suggestion that males suffer from hysteria (conversion disorder) was met with disbelief and laughter, and he was literally laughed off the stage and almost banished from the society.

In the 19th century, French physician Jean-Martin Charcot demonstrated that somatoform symptoms could be introduced and eliminated by means of suggestion. Freud was so impressed with Charcot's work that he kept a copy of this etching in his office.

Although not recognized as such at the time, the conversion disorder undoubtedly played an important role in the symptoms seen in many of the soldiers who served in World War I. It is probable that many of the symptoms that were attributed to "shell shock" were in fact instances of the conversion disorder. The presence of the conversion disorder in men was finally recognized during World War II because medical science had progressed to the point where the potential organic causes of some of the GIs' symptoms could be definitely ruled out, thereby suggesting psychological causes (Ziegler et al., 1960).

The diagnostic label "hysteria" was eliminated with the publication of DSM-III in 1980. This was done to remove the numerous connotations that had come to be associated with the term *hysteria,* such as the idea that it is necessarily caused by sexual conflict. All comments suggesting that somatoform disorders are more prevalent in women were omitted from DSM-III-R (1987).

Prevalence and Gender

It is estimated that about 2% of the population experiences the various somatoform disorders, and that rate has held steady since shortly after the turn of the 20th century (American Psychiatric Association, 1994; Stephens & Kamp, 1962). Women are more likely to be diagnosed as suffering from the conversion disorder than men. In fact, in the six investigations of the conversion disorder published in 1979 and 1980, women constituted 74% of the total number of persons diagnosed as having the disorder. In another study of 147 individuals with "multiple unexplained somatic complaints," it was found that 58% of the women and 40% of the men could be diagnosed as suffering from the somatization disorder (Golding et al., 1991). Unfortunately, we still do not know why women are more likely to receive the diagnosis. It may be that for historical reasons diagnosticians are biased in favor of diagnosing the disorder in women, that women are more likely to seek help for the types of complaints associated with the somatoform disorder, or that as with other disorders such as depression, there is something about the cause of the conversion disorder (e.g., particular stresses, physiological factors) that predisposes women to it.

Sociocultural Factors

Somatoform disorders occur throughout the world, but there can be differences across cultures in what symptoms occur and what explanations are used for the symptoms (Janca et al., 1995). For example, in Asia, there is a disorder called **koro** that involves high anxiety, the belief that the genitals are withdrawing into the body, and that death will follow. Similarly, in India, a disorder called **dhat** involves depression, numerous somatic complaints such as a decline in semen production, weakness, fatigue, and the belief that the symptoms are due to a decline in a vital fluid (*sukra*) in the body (Paris, 1992).

It now appears that the different somatoform disorders that occur across cultures are probably due to a common underlying problem, but the symptoms and explanations take different forms as a function of the cultural role models and the dominant beliefs within the culture (Chaturvedi, 1993). That is, the disorders are probably the same across cultures, but each culture molds its own form. Koro provides a good illustration of that. Specifically, we now know that koro can be successfully treated with an antidepressant drug (clomipramine) that is effective for treating disorders in Western culture that involve bodily concerns (Goetz & Price, 1994). It is also noteworthy that with immigration and the general merging of cultures, koro is now occurring in Western cultures, and it was even proposed that koro should be included in the DSM (Fishbain, 1991). With regard to dhat, it is relevant to recall that years ago in the United States, bodily complaints were often attributed to low levels of various bodily fluids, and popular traveling "medicine shows" revolved around the sale of assorted "elixirs of life" that would replenish the fluids and relieve the symptoms.

Are Somatoform Symptoms Real or Faked?

Are the symptoms seen in somatoform disorders real or faked? Can real physical symptoms exist without an underlying physical cause? Certainly there are individuals who fake somatic illnesses in deliberate attempts to gain sympathy, avoid responsibility, or obtain insurance benefits. Faking disorders to avoid responsibility is commonly called **malingering,** and in DSM-IV, disorders that are consciously faked are called **factitious** (fak-TISH-us) **disorders.** Although such cases do occur, the symptoms in somatoform disorders can be real.

The best evidence in support of the reality of somatoform symptoms comes from research on the **placebo effect** (A. Shapiro, 1980; Shapiro & Morris, 1978). The placebo effect occurs when an individual is given a treatment that has no therapeutic value (e.g., a pill does not contain any active ingredients), but the individual believes that the treatment should help and consequently shows the expected change (see Chapter 3). Many studies document the positive effects of placebos on physical symptoms such as reductions in pain, and it is generally agreed that the placebo effect is due to suggestion.

The placebo effect is relevant for understanding somatoform symptoms because placebos can be used to induce symptoms as well as reduce them. If psychological processes such as the placebo effect or suggestion can reduce real symptoms, it seems reasonable to conclude that the psychological processes are also sufficient to result in real symptoms. Some individuals undoubtedly do fake symptoms, but in other cases somatoform symptoms can be real, so we should not assume that individuals with somatoform disorders are necessarily faking.

Differential Diagnoses, Medical Costs, and Medical Progress

A serious problem stems from the difficulty of differentiating between somatoform disorders and real physical disorders. That is, in some cases, somatoform disorders are mistaken for real physical disorders, and in other cases, real physical disorders are dismissed as somatoform disorders (Gross, 1979; Slater & Glithero, 1965; Whitlock, 1967). Such misdiagnoses can be very serious because individuals do not get the psychological or medical treatment they need.

Because patients with somatoform disorders often have rather vague complaints or because a physical cause for their complaints cannot be found immediately, the patients are frequently given extensive medical tests in attempts to diagnose the problem. Those tests, along with unnecessary treatments that may be tried, can lead to extremely high medical bills.

To solve the problem of costs, programs have been put into place to identify and then screen out individuals who have somatoform disorders so that they do not proceed further in the medical system. Those programs can be very effective for cutting costs. For example, in one project, individuals who somatized were identified and their physicians either were or were not sent a letter informing them of the possible psychological nature of their patients' symptoms (Smith, Rost & Kashner, 1995). Simply informing the physicians resulted in a 33% reduction in the patients' medical costs as compared to patients whose physicians were not informed. Surprisingly, the patients whose physicians were informed also reported an improvement in physical functioning that was almost 10% greater than that reported by the other patients. It appears that when additional testing was not pursued, the patients felt comforted and assured that they were not suffering from a serious disorder.

However, a problem can arise when a patient who usually has somatoform disorders develops a real medical problem; if the new symptom is "written off" as another somatoform symptom, the individual will not get the treatment he or she needs. Therefore, psychologists and physicians who screen individuals must be careful not to dismiss a legitimate medical problem in an individual who ordinarily comes in with somatoform complaints. Of course, such caution takes us back to more testing and higher costs. Obviously, this is a thorny problem for which there is no simple solution.

Finally, you should recognize that as medical science progresses, some of what we currently think are somatoform disorders may someday be found to be actual physical disorders. Somatoform disorders consist of physical symptoms for which there is no *demonstrable* cause, but the failure to demonstrate a physical cause could be due to the fact that we have not yet identified it. For example, some years ago, women who showed the physical symptoms of pregnancy but who were not pregnant were diagnosed as having a somatoform disorder known as **pseudocyesis** (SYOO-dō-sī-Ē-sis), which means "sham pregnancy." However, with increased understanding of hormone imbalances, those individuals are now usually recognized as suffering from a physical disorder. Clearly, the problem of identifying somatoform disorders is difficult, complex, and continuing.

EXPLANATIONS OF AND TREATMENTS FOR SOMATOFORM DISORDERS

Psychodynamic Explanations

Freud's explanation for somatoform disorders was that when wishes or drives are not expressed, *the pent-up emotional energy that is associated with the wishes or drives is converted into physical symptoms* (Freud, 1920/1955). Freud speculated that pent-up emotional energy is somehow converted into physical symptoms, and that notion provided the basis for the term *conversion disorder*. Freud also suggested that the expression of emotions that were once pent up will reduce symptoms because the "charge" associated with the emotions is reduced. Today we call this **catharsis.** You may have experienced catharsis when you finally talked about a problem that you had kept "bottled up inside."

Learning and Cognitive Explanations

The basic tenet of learning theory explanations for somatoform disorders is that the symptoms are operant responses that are learned and maintained because they *result in rewards* (Ullman & Krasner, 1969). The reward can occur in three ways. First, the symptoms may enable the individual to *avoid some unpleasant or threatening situation.* For example, a form of the conversion disorder involving a paralyzed hand may enable a student to skip an examination for

This is a photo of the patient Anna O. Her treatment led Sigmund Freud and Josef Breuer to a number of their early ideas about the cause of somatoform symptoms. Her real name was Bertha Pappenheim.

which he or she is not prepared. I once worked with an athlete who always "pulled a muscle" before any track meet in which the competition was particularly good and might threaten his unbeaten record. His "pulled muscle" was rewarding because it protected his unbeaten record.

Second, somatoform symptoms can provide an *explanation of or justification for failure,* thereby relieving the individual of personal responsibility. The student who comes home at the end of the semester wearing an eye patch because of "eye trouble" is less likely to be blamed for his failing grades.

Third, somatoform symptoms can *attract concern, sympathy, and care* for the individual, and that attention can be very rewarding.

Somatoform symptoms may be maintained because they result in rewards, but how do these symptoms develop in the first place? One possibility is that individuals learn to play the role of a sick individual either by observation or through personal experience with illness. We each play many roles, and we must learn the behaviors for each role. When we first try out a new role, it requires effort and seems unreal; we are "playing" the role. However, as time goes by, the role becomes second nature, and the distinction between role and self becomes blurred. We are no longer playing the role—we have internalized the role, and the role is us.

In the case of somatoform disorders, the individual may have learned the role of a sick individual while actually being sick or by observing another individual who was sick (Schwartz et al., 1994). Later, when facing stress or in need of attention, the individual might shift to the "sick" role just as someone might change from a "partygoer" role to a "student" role as the situation required. This change to the sick role is not done with any more conscious intent than you used when you changed to your student role by picking up this book and beginning to study. The situation demanded it, you were accustomed to the role, and you used it. Furthermore, the individual with a somatoform disorder is not faking a role any more than you are now faking a student role. Just as you have internalized the role of student and are not faking it, the individual with a somatoform disorder has internalized the role of sick individual and is not faking that role.

The sick role seen in somatoform disorders is probably an extension of less extreme behaviors that most of us have used. At one time or another, most of us have developed a headache or some other minor somatic complaint that enabled us to avoid a disagreeable event. We were not necessarily lying or faking the problem, but after thinking about it for a while, we came up with a symptom that had some minimal basis in reality. If focusing on the somatic complaint was successful in getting us out of the disagreeable event or getting us some sympathy, we might do it again and again until it became a frequent and seemingly natural means of solving problems.

In one study of the effects of attention to body parts and sensations on the development of symptoms, students in one condition listened to a tape recording in which they were asked to concentrate on various bodily sites and the sensations there, whereas students in a control condition listened to music (Schmidt et al., 1994). Later, the students used a checklist to indicate what symptoms they were experiencing. The results indicated that the students who focused their attention on bodily sites and sensations reported about twice as many somatic symptoms as those who listened to the music. Similarly, when students walked on a treadmill and listened to their own breathing or to a tape recording of city sounds, those who listened to their breathing later reported more headaches, cardiovascular problems, and other symptoms of overexertion (Pennebaker, 1982). That effect is apparently exacerbated in individuals who suffer from somatoform disorders. For example, in a study in which individuals who were already suffering from hypochondriasis were asked to focus their attention on ambiguous physical sensations, those with hypochondriasis were more likely to interpret the sensations as symptoms of serious illnesses rather than as passing meaningless sensations (Hitchcock & Mathews, 1992). In other words, thinking about sensations can lead some individuals to interpret the sensations as symptoms, and individuals with somatoform disorders are very likely to do that. Therefore, if an individual's role involves paying attention to bodily sensations because the individual thinks that he or she might be getting sick, the individual is more likely to develop symptoms.

Roles and the focusing of attention on potential "symptoms" seem to provide a good explanation for somatoform disorders, but the question still remains, what leads to the roles and the focusing of attention? There is now consistent evidence that the individuals who suffer from somatoform disorders have *role models for sick behavior*. In one investigation, it was found that children with the somatization disorder were more likely to have parents with the disorder than were children with verified medical disorders (Livingston, 1993). Similarly, patients with pseudoepileptic seizures were more likely to know someone (e.g., a parent) who had seizures than were individuals who had real epileptic seizures (Eisendrath & Valan, 1994). In other words, it appears that the individuals had role models for the disorder. Approached in another way, when the children of adults with the somatization disorder were studied, it was found that they were much more likely to be taken to a hospital emergency room for unexplained illnesses and missed almost nine times more school days for "illnesses" than did the children of individuals who did not have the disorder (Livingston et al., 1995). It seems that they were being taught the disorder. Finally, information from patients revealed that three variables were strongly associated with the hypochondriacal syndrome: (a) a high level of life defeats, (b) a high level of family illness, and (c) a low pain threshold (Bianchi, 1973). It appears that when dealing with stress (defeat), individuals with a family history of illness (models) may complain of illnesses. The low pain threshold may provide at least a minimal basis for the complaints because individuals with low pain thresholds may actually experience more physical discomfort than other individuals.

To sum up, the learning and cognitive explanations for somatoform disorders runs as follows: (a) Role models or actually being sick leads the individual to learn the role of the sick person and to focus attention on bodily sensations; (b) the role and the attention to physical sensations lead to the acting or noticing of "symptoms"; and (c) the "symptoms" result in rewards (attention) or enable the individual to avoid stressful situations, so they are used repeatedly.

Children who have role models for sick behavior are more likely to develop somatoform disorders. This child is learning that being ill can result in attention, care, and sympathy.

Physiological Explanations

We generally assume that individuals who suffer from the somatization disorder or hypochondriasis complain about symptoms that are not really there. However, it may be that these individuals are actually *more sensitive to bodily sensations* or are *more physiologically aroused,* which would lead to more bodily sensations, and if that is the case, their higher levels of sensations could provide a basis for more complaints (Bell, 1994). For example, individuals who are more sensitive to pain would be more likely to notice normal aches and pains and would therefore be more likely to conclude that they were suffering from some disease than individuals who were simply not aware of the same aches and pains. I am not suggesting that these individuals have more symptoms, only that they may have more sensations that they *interpret* as symptoms.

The explanation that somatoform symptoms stem from higher levels of somatic sensations is supported by research in which it was found that individuals with hypochondriasis are better able to estimate their heart rates and thus appear to be more sensitive to internal processes than other individuals (Tyrer et al., 1980). In another investigation, it was found that individuals with hypochondriasis had unusually high levels of somatic arousal (e.g., higher heart rates and muscle tension) (Hanback & Revelle, 1978). Such increased arousal could result in more somatic sensations, which could provide the basis for symptoms. Finally, it has been found that individuals with hypochondriasis have lower pain thresholds (Bianchi, 1973). Individuals with lower pain thresholds would experience more sensations, and those sensations might then be interpreted as symptoms. Although there is evidence linking somatic sensitivity or arousal to somatoform disorders, at this point we do not know whether increased sensitivity or arousal leads to the disorders or vice versa.

It is also worth noting that anxiety results in heightened somatic arousal (see Chapter 4). The presence of anxiety could then lead to a somatic condition on which an individual could build a set of somatic complaints. In other words, the individual becomes anxious, the anxiety results in increased somatic arousal, and the sensations of somatic arousal are interpreted as symptoms of some disorder. For example, an anxious person whose heart rate is elevated might conclude that the rapid heart rate reflects an underlying cardiac problem. This sequence might be more likely to occur if the individual had a personal or family history of illness, such as heart attacks, that provided a role model and additional justification for the development of the illness explanation for the sensations.

We should also give some attention to the interesting finding that conversion symptoms are more likely to occur on the left side of the body (Galin et al., 1977; Stern, 1977). This is of interest because the left side of the body is controlled primarily by the right side of brain, and the right side of the brain is primarily responsible for emotions. On the basis of these two facts, researchers have speculated that a high level of emotional arousal on the right side of the brain disrupts other functioning on that side of the brain and produces unusual somatic symptoms on the left side of the body. This is referred to as the **hemispheric dominance** explanation for somatoform disorders. (This explanation is strikingly similar to Freud's suggestion that an emotional "charge" is converted into "unusual bodily innervations.") Alternatively, it has been suggested that symptoms are more likely to appear on the left side because they will be less incapacitating if they are on the side opposite the preferred hand. This seems unlikely, however, because frequently the symptoms do not involve the hands and thus from a functional standpoint, the side on which the symptom occurs is irrelevant.

Treatments

Change Attention and Beliefs. There are four basic approaches to treating individuals with somatoform disorders, the first of which involves *changing the patients' thoughts about their "symptoms"* (Martin & Yutzy, 1994; Visser & Bouman, 1992). Specifically, the goals are to teach the patients to stop focusing on the sensations that provide the basis for the symptoms and, when they do notice the sensations, not to interpret them as symp-

toms of some serious disorder. Unfortunately, the attempts to change attention and beliefs are often counteracted by the barrage of "medical news" to which we are constantly exposed in which new symptoms and disorders are discussed, thus increasing attention and potentially erroneous beliefs.

Reduce Depression. Second, rather than treating the somatoform disorder per se, some investigators advocate *treating the depression* that often accompanies a somatoform disorder (Fallon et al., 1993; Goetz & Price, 1994). The notion underlying this approach is that depression is the cause of somatoform disorders because depressed individuals focus their attention on bodily complaints and assume that the worst will happen (see Chapter 8), thus leading to a somatoform disorder.

Reduce Arousal. A third approach involves reducing stress and thereby *reducing the arousal that provides the basis for somatic sensations* and hence the symptoms. In that regard, it is interesting to note that "opening up" and talking about stressful experiences can reduce somatic complaints, some of which are probably somatoform (Pennebaker, 1990, 1993). Specifically, students who came to a laboratory and simply wrote for 20 minutes about previous traumatic events showed a 50% lower rate of visits to the university health center than students who wrote about trivial events. The catharsis associated with talking about the stress reduced physiological arousal, which in turn reduced the sensations that could provide the basis for somatoform complaints.

Provide Reassurance. Finally, in cases in which changing cognitions, reducing depression, or reducing arousal are ineffective, the focus may have to be on *care* rather than on *cure*, and the strategy is to *provide emotional support and reassurance* for the patients so they can cope with and endure their "symptoms" without constantly seeking medical attention (Barsky, 1993; Kellner, 1992). Whatever the strategy, the treatment of individuals with somatoform disorders is essential both for their comfort and so that their costs to the medical system can be reduced.

WHAT CAN WE CONCLUDE CONCERNING SOMATOFORM DISORDERS?

Somatoform disorders played an important role in the history of psychology because they were the disorders that originally attracted the interest of Sigmund Freud, and they remain important today because they account for a disproportionately high amount of the health care budget, especially when you consider how benign the symptoms are relative to disorders such as depression and schizophrenia. It appears that the best explanation for somatoform symptoms is that they stem from attention to and then misinterpretation of bodily sensations. The high level of attention to the sensations may occur because the individual has learned to attend to them from modeling or direct experience or because the individual is simply more sensitive to bodily sensations. The misinterpretation is probably learned. The fact that symptoms and the role of a "sick" individual can lead to rewards can serve to maintain the symptoms. Treatments are focused on changing the attention to or interpretation of bodily sensations, reducing depression that can cause the individuals to focus on bodily sensations and to assume the worst about them, reducing arousal that leads to sensations that can be misinterpreted, and when those strategies fail, reassuring the individuals that the symptoms are not serious.

With this understanding of somatoform disorders as background, we can go on to consider the dissociative disorders.

TOPIC II
DISSOCIATIVE DISORDERS

DISSOCIATIVE DISORDERS

According to DSM-IV, "The essential feature of the Dissociative Disorders is a disruption in the usually integrated functions of consciousness, memory, identity, or perception of the environment" (American Psychiatric Association, 1994, p. 477). In other words, individuals with **dissociative disorders** are *not aware of or lose contact with important aspects of their personalities or environments.* For example, individuals with the dissociative amnesia disorder cannot remember important events, and individuals with the dissociative identity (multiple personality) disorder are unaware of aspects of their personalities. The term *dissociative disorder* is used because it is assumed that the individuals with symptoms like amnesia or multiple personalities are *dissociating* themselves (escaping) from parts of their personalities that give rise to stress. In other words, the individuals are *repressing* the experiences and the parts of themselves that give rise to stress, and the repression results in gaps or holes in their awareness (e.g., amnesia).

Four dissociative disorders are identified in DSM-IV: *dissociative amnesia, dissociative fugue, dissociative identity disorder (multiple personality),* and *depersonalization disorder.* Each type involves a dissociation, but the way the dissociation is achieved differs from disorder to disorder. For example, the individual may forget some stressful material (amnesia), leave a stressful situation and develop a new identity (fugue), or develop alternative personalities (identity disorder). The major symptoms of the dissociative disorders as they are described in DSM-IV are summarized in Table 7.2. I will discuss the disorders in greater detail later, and then you will learn that there is some controversy over the existence of some of these disorders.

Dissociative Amnesia

Dissociative amnesia is characterized by a *sudden inability to remember important personal information or events,* to an extent greater than ordinary forgetfulness. This type

TABLE 7.2 Predominant Symptoms in the Dissociative Disorders

Disorder	Symptoms
Dissociative amnesia	Sudden inability to remember important personal information or events, to an extent greater than can be explained by ordinary forgetfulness
Dissociative fugue	Travel to a new locale, amnesia for previous identity, and possible assumption of a new identity
Dissociative identity disorder	Two or more distinctly different personalities, each in control of the individual at different times, and the inability to recall important personal information (e.g., the existence of other personalities)
Depersonalization disorder	Feeling detached from one's body or mental processes

Note: Symptoms must be serious enough to result in impairment in social, occupational, or other important areas of functioning.

Talented Mr. Ripley ←

According to the traditional view, dissociative amnesia may occur in response to a severe stress. The individual represses the memory of the event in order to reduce the stress associated with it. However, no reliable evidence has been found for the existence of repression, and in some cases the amnesia may even have been caused by physical trauma, such as a blow to the head.

of amnesia usually occurs immediately following some type of severe stress; the stressful event or information associated with it is forgotten. The classic examples of dissociative amnesia are soldiers who, after fighting in a terrible and traumatic battle, are unable to recall the battle but later, with the aid of psychotherapy, are able to recover the memories (Henderson & Moore, 1944). More recently, some clinicians reported that some individuals are amnesic for stressful experiences of sexual abuse during childhood but are later able to recover those memories (e.g., Terr, 1994). (We will examine these cases in greater detail later.) It has also been suggested that psychogenic amnesia can also be triggered by unacceptable impulses or acts such as an extramarital affair; the individual simply does not remember doing the unspeakable—or the unthinkable!

Obviously, there are many reasons why we are sometimes unable to recall things, and it is important not to confuse dissociative amnesia with failure to recall because of (a) the failure to process information (the individual may have been distracted by other aspects of the situation), (b) ordinary forgetting, (c) disorders such as Alzheimer's disease, (d) the use of drugs such as alcohol, or (e) the amnesia that sometimes occurs following a concussion. The factor that distinguishes between those losses and dissociative amnesia is that in dissociative amnesia, the individual is *motivated not to remember something as a way of reducing stress.*

Dissociative Fugue

An individual who is experiencing **dissociative fugue** (fyoog) suddenly and unexpectedly *travels to a new locale, is amnesic for his or her previous identity, and may assume a new identity.* This flight typically follows a severe psychosocial stress such as a marital quarrel, personal rejection, military conflict, or natural disaster. The fugue state may last only a few hours, but it generally lasts months. During the fugue, the individual behaves appropriately and does not show any signs of suffering from a psychological disorder; the person simply starts a new life and does fine. When the fugue ends, the individual returns to his or her original identity and has no memory of what took place during the fugue. The feature of fugue that distinguishes it from amnesia is that in the fugue, the individual is unaware of the lost material and substitutes new material (a new identity) in its place.

One interesting case that was diagnosed as fugue involved a man who was having serious financial and marital problems. The day following a particularly serious argument with his wife about their impending bankruptcy, the man went fishing and did not return. When his empty boat was found on the lake, it was presumed that he had fallen overboard and drowned. About a year later, the man's widow was on an automobile trip through a nearby state and stopped for lunch in a roadside restaurant. She was surprised at the quality of the food but even more surprised when on her way out, she discovered her late husband sitting in one of the booths and then learned that he was now married to the woman who owned the restaurant. When confronted, he appeared not to know her. *Tonio Kruger?*

Dissociative Identity Disorder (Multiple Personality)

The term *multiple personality disorder* has been used for many years, but in DSM-IV that term has been replaced with **dissociative identity disorder.** However, for the sake of convenience, in this chapter I will use the traditional term, *multiple personality disorder.*

An individual diagnosed as experiencing the **multiple personality disorder** appears to have *two or more dis-*

tinctly different personalities, each of which is in control of the individual at different times, and the individual is *unable to recall important personal information*. More specifically, some of the personalities will not be aware of the other personalities (Fahy, 1988; Putnam, 1989; Ross, 1989).

The multiple personality disorder has received a great deal of attention in the popular press, films, and television. Some of the best-known accounts of multiple personality are *The Three Faces of Eve* (Thigpen & Cleckley, 1957), *Sybil* (Schreiber, 1973), *The Five of Me* (Hanksworth & Schwarz, 1977), and *The Minds of Billy Milligan* (Keyes, 1981).

In a person with the multiple personality disorder, there is usually a sharp contrast between at least two of the personalities, which are ordinarily in conflict. One personality is usually "good," while the other is of more questionable character. Therapists have referred to the "saint" versus the "devil" (Prince, 1908) and the "square" versus the "lover" (Ludwig et al., 1972) in their patients. That contrast is apparent in the book and movie *The Three Faces of Eve*. Eve White was a quiet, demure, and somewhat inhibited young woman who had been in psychotherapy for the treatment of headaches and blackouts. While talking to her physician one day, Eve White put her hands to her head as if she had been seized by a sudden pain. After a moment, she seemed to shake herself loose and looked up with a reckless smile and a bright voice and said, "Hi there, Doc!" When asked her name, she immediately replied, "Oh, I'm Eve Black" (Thigpen & Cleckley, 1954, p. 137). In contrast to Eve White, Eve Black was a wild, promiscuous, devil-may-care woman. As you might have guessed, the "good" personality is usually not aware of the "bad" personality, but the "bad" personality is usually aware of (and bored with) the "good" personality.

Chris Sizemore is the woman on whom The Three Faces of Eve *is based. She claimed that she had 21 separate personalities.*

The case of Eve appears to have been more complex than it was originally portrayed. In a book published 23 years later, the woman who had been known as Eve (actually Chris Sizemore) explained that she had actually had 21 separate personalities or, as she put it, "strangers who came to inhabit my body" (Sizemore & Pittillo, 1977). Studies reveal that individuals with the multiple personality disorder report having from 2 to 60 different personalities, the average being 13 to 16 (Putnam et al., 1986; Ross et al., 1989; Ross, Miller, et al., 1990; Schultz et al., 1989). The results of those surveys also indicate that about 90% of the individuals diagnosed as having the multiple personality disorder are women.

Some comment should be made to clear up the confusion that sometimes arises over the terms *multiple personality*, *schizophrenia*, and *split personality*. Multiple personality refers to a disorder in which an individual develops a number of distinctly different and separate personalities. In contrast, the term *schizophrenia* refers to a disorder in which the individual has one personality, but that personality has split off from reality or has split itself between the functions of emotion and reasoning (Bleuler, 1950) (see Chapter 11). An individual with the multiple personality disorder does not necessarily have schizophrenia, and an individual with schizophrenia does not necessarily have multiple personalities. The term *split personality* is not a diagnostic label; it is slang, without any clinical meaning.

Depersonalization Disorder

The **depersonalization disorder** involves persistent or recurrent experiences of *feeling detached from one's body or mental processes*. Individuals feel as if they are outside of their bodies looking down on themselves or as if they are in a dream. It is important to note that during the experience, the individuals are still in touch with reality; for example, they know that they are not really out of their bodies, but it just feels as if they were. The depersonalization experience can probably be best described as an "as if" experience with regard to the self: Individuals with this disorder feel *as if* their extremities have changed in size, *as if* they were acting mechanically, *as if* they were in a dream, or *as if* they were out of their bodies and viewing themselves from a distance. In talking about depersonalization experiences, one person explained, "It was like I somehow drifted out of my body and floated way above it, and I could look down on me like I was someone else on a stage." Another said, "My body seemed to be made of rubber that could stretch.... I really didn't have any definite form. Sometimes my head would become huge, or my arms would become extremely long and I'd have big hands. It was really kind of crazy."

The "as if" nature of the disorder is important because it distinguishes the depersonalization disorder from schizophrenia, in which the individual may have the same symptoms but believes them to be true. Because the feelings are perceived as unnatural (e.g., looking down at oneself from above), individuals with the depersonalization disorder are often concerned that they might be "going crazy," and therefore the symptom pattern is often accompanied by anxiety.

The depersonalization disorder is different from the other dissociative disorders in that *it does not involve a loss of memory or identity as the others do.* That is, whereas in dissociative amnesia, dissociative fugue, or the dissociative identity disorder (multiple personality disorder) the individuals lose memory for (repress) important events and may develop a new identity, in the depersonalization disorder the individuals do not lose memory or develop a new identity; instead, they simply experience a temporary change in the way they view themselves. Depersonalization is a less extreme and less dramatic response to stress.

The occurrence of depersonalization was documented in an interesting study of journalists who witnessed the execution of a prisoner in the gas chamber of the San Quentin Prison (Freinkel et al., 1994). When questioned later, the journalists reported a high rate of symptoms of depersonalization. For example, 60% reported that they felt "estranged or detached from other people." Some years ago, I was with a woman who had just been hit by a car and whose leg was badly broken; indeed, at the knee it was bent at a 90° angle to the side! Despite the fact that the woman had not been given any medication, she was very calm, and as the medical personnel prepared to put her in the ambulance, she said rather quizzically, "You know, it's like this isn't happening to me. It's like I'm sitting up on top of the ambulance watching all of this from a distance—it's like a movie. It's really fascinating to see how the leg is bent and what everyone is doing." Clearly, in the face of stress, the woman depersonalized the situation. However, in cases like that, the depersonalization is not considered a disorder because it does not impair the individual's functioning; indeed, the depersonalization may actually aid functioning by permitting the person to perceive and act objectively.

You should note that the depersonalization disorder can appear briefly in many normal individuals. Indeed, the results of a questionnaire study indicated that in some age groups, almost 30% of the individuals sampled reported depersonalization experiences (Ross, Joshi, & Currie, 1990). The disorder is most common in early adulthood (ages 25 to 44), and then begins to drop off dramatically. The presence of the symptom pattern is considered to constitute a disorder only when it results in significant impairment of an individual's social or occupational functioning.

ISSUES ASSOCIATED WITH DISSOCIATIVE DISORDERS

In the preceding sections, I presented the dissociative disorders as they are described in DSM-IV and as they are traditionally thought to occur. However, it is important to recognize that there is now good reason to question the accuracy of those portrayals and even question the existence of some dissociative disorders. In the following sections, I will review the evidence concerning the dissociative disorders in general and the multiple personality disorder in particular.

Dissociative Disorders and the Evidence for Repression

When I introduced the dissociative disorders, I pointed out that the psychological process on which they are based is **repression.** For example, individuals with dissociative amnesia supposedly repress their memories of stressful events, and individuals with the dissociative identity disorder supposedly repress stressful aspects of their personalities. Indeed, in those cases, *dissociation* is simply a synonym for *repression.* However, the fact that most dissociative disorders are based on repression leads to a serious problem in that at the present time, *we have no objective evidence that repression occurs.* Obviously, if there is no evidence for repression, we face an awkward problem in explaining dissociative disorders. Actually, the concept of repression is widely used in psychology, and thus the question of its existence has broad implications. Because of the importance of repression, in the following paragraphs I will review the four ways in which repression has been studied, and then I will discuss the implications of the findings for dissociative disorders.

Laboratory Research. First, for over 70 years, investigators have attempted to demonstrate repression in the laboratory. In that research, individuals either were or were not exposed to stressors such as electric shocks or being told that they suffered from serious psychiatric disorders, and then their memories for related materials, such as words they had memorized, were tested. This approach did not yield any evidence for repression; at best, the individuals were temporarily *distracted* by the stress, which briefly reduced their memory performance, but they did not lose their memories for the stressor or the related materials (see Holmes, 1974, 1990). In fact, the finding that the individuals were distracted by the stressors indicated that they were *focusing on the stressors* rather than repressing them. The fact that the laboratory research did not produce evidence for repression was surprising, but it was not a source of concern because it was simply assumed that the stresses that were used in the laboratory were too "artificial" or not strong enough to result in repression. Furthermore, the absence of laboratory research was not seen as important because psychologists assumed that there was good field research (case studies) that supported the existence of repression. We will consider that evidence next.

Classic Case Studies. The classic case studies to which psychologists turned for evidence for repression involved soldiers who could not remember anything about terribly stressful battles in which they had just fought but were later able to remember the battles when they were given therapy to reduce the stress (e.g., Henderson & Moore, 1944). The notion was that the stress of the battles was so great that the entire experience had to be blocked out. For many years, those cases were accepted as evidence for repression, but a careful examination of them reveals two crucial problems. First, *in no case was the possibility of organically caused amnesia ruled out*. That is a serious omission because we know that concussions can cause amnesia (e.g., football players sometimes cannot remember plays in which they were tackled very hard and hit their heads), and in the battlefield conditions in which bombs and grenades were going off, it is very likely that the soldiers experienced concussions. In other words, if there were losses in memory, they were probably due to physiological rather than psychological factors.

The second problem is that in the cases in which the memories were later "recovered" in therapy, the recovery was accomplished with techniques such as role playing, hypnosis, or sodium amytal interviews, *all of which introduce the possibility of suggestion*. Indeed, the various professional organizations in psychology and psychiatry have explicitly warned against using those techniques for recovering information. It appears, then, that the "memories" that were supposedly "recovered" by the soldiers were actually suggested to them by their therapists. (For a more detailed discussion of the implanting of false memories, see Chapter 2; see also, Ceci et al., 1995; Hyman et al., 1995.)

Follow-Ups with Trauma Victims. Because of the problems with the early case studies, investigators next turned to the strategy of identifying individuals who were known to have undergone serious traumatic experiences and then testing the individuals some years later to determine whether they were able to remember the experiences. Examples of individuals who were studied included children who had been kidnapped and then buried alive (Terr, 1979, 1983), children who had witnessed a parent's murder (Malmquist, 1986), and individuals who had been brutalized in Nazi concentration camps (Strom et al., 1962), among many

others. Those individuals certainly underwent the types of experiences that we would expect to be repressed, but the surprising finding was that *in every case, the individual was able to recall the traumatic experience!* Indeed, rather than repressing the memories, the individuals had detailed memories of the events and in many cases could not get the memories out of their minds. In other words, rather than being repressed and leading to dissociative disorders, the traumatic experiences were vividly recalled and often led to posttraumatic stress disorders (see Chapter 4). That is exactly the opposite of what you would expect based on the theory of repression, and hence that research does not provide any evidence for repression.

However, there is one study in this group that attracted a lot of attention because it initially appeared to provide evidence for repression, and that study deserves additional comment here. In that study, the investigator identified female children who had been brought to a hospital because of sexual abuse, and then 17 years later the same individuals were interviewed concerning the traumatic experiences of their lives (Williams, 1992, 1994). The results indicated that *38% of the women did not report the abuse* that had been documented and for which they had been selected for study, and that finding was widely interpreted as evidence for repression. Unfortunately, there is a serious problem with the investigation that originally went unnoticed: Individuals who did not report the sexual abuse *were never explicitly asked about the abuse*. That is, if the individuals did not spontaneously report the experience, the investigator assumed that the experience had been repressed, but it is possible that for some reason the individuals simply *chose* not to report the experience. Strong evidence that the individuals had simply chosen not to report the abuse is provided by a similar study in which investigators followed up and interviewed individuals who had been abused as children (Femina et al., 1990). Like the earlier study, the results indicated that 38% of the individuals did not report the instances of documented childhood abuse, but when these individuals were asked directly about the possibility of the abuse, *all of them immediately acknowledged it*. When they were asked why they had not initially reported the abuse, they said things like "I try to block this out of my mind" and "My father is doing well now. If I told now, I think he would kill himself." The important point here is that although individuals may try to put stressful memories out of their minds (i.e., repress them), they are unable to do so, and the follow-up studies of trauma victims do not provide any evidence for repression.

Clinical Observations. Fourth, and finally, many therapists argue that they see evidence for repression when they are treating patients in psychotherapy; that is, the therapists see patients block out memories that they should have. The observation of repression in therapy is an interesting possibility because it was in the context of psychotherapy that Freud originally developed the notion of repression. The possibility that repression can be observed in psychotherapy was given an interesting test a few years ago when many of the "world's leading experts" on repression were brought together for a conference at Yale University. At the conference, one group of investigators showed videotapes of psychotherapy in which it was believed that repression was occurring. The experts watched the tapes, took notes about when they thought repression was occurring, and then began discussing the instances of repression. The interesting finding was that when the experts began discussing the instances of repression, there was no agreement among any of them concerning when (or whether) repression had occurred. Obviously, if a phenomenon cannot be reliably identified, the observations cannot have validity, and thus no reliance can be placed on the clinical observations of repression.

Thus, despite over 70 years of research, we still have no evidence for repression. That is a relatively new finding, and it takes many mental health professionals by surprise because repression is an important and widely accepted notion in psychology. The question that then arises is, where does the absence of repression leave us? That is, how can we account for the disorders that supposedly depend on repression? First, the fact that there is no evidence does not necessarily mean that repression does not exist because it is impossible to prove that something does not exist; new evidence may be found tomorrow. However, after 70 years of research, it would seem prudent to consider alternative explanations rather than simply to assume that evidence will be found someday. Second, it may be that the disorders that supposedly stem from repression may be due to other processes, most notably mistaken interpretations by clinicians, suggestibility, or outright faking. For example, what appear to be losses of memory that are attributed to repression may be due to organic problems, normal forgetting, or the fact that the individual never knew what the therapist assumed was known, or may be feigned to avoid responsibility. Indeed, although the role of repression is assumed in the descriptions of disorders in the DSM, some of these other possibilities are explicitly mentioned as viable alternatives. Relevant to these alternative explanations, in the following section I will discuss the evidence that the multiple personality disorder is due to repression (dissociation) or suggestibility.

Evidence for the Multiple Personality Disorder

The multiple personality disorder has long been accepted as one of the classic forms of abnormal behav-

ior, but in recent years an interesting controversy has arisen over the question of whether individuals actually do have multiple personalities as they are described in DSM-IV or whether the disorders are somehow fabricated or faked (Reisner, 1994; Spanos, 1994). That question is of theoretical interest, but it also has important legal implications because an individual might not be responsible for the acts committed by an alternative personality, especially if the individual was unaware that the other personality existed. Indeed, multiple personality is a popular disorder in the insanity defense (Keyes, 1981; Schwarz, 1981; Steinberg et al., 1993). For example, Kenneth Bianchi, known as the "Hillside Strangler" and alleged to have raped and strangled at least 12 young women, claimed he was not legally responsible for the crimes because his other personality committed the acts. A somewhat different legal complication arose in a case in which a woman apparently consented to have sex with a man and then later accused him of rape when one of her other personalities emerged and objected. In the following paragraphs, I will discuss the evidence for the multiple personality disorder, and then I will offer two alternative explanations for the behavior of individuals who appear to have the disorder.

Differences on Personality and Intelligence Tests. People who believe in the multiple personality disorder cite numerous reports indicating that personality and intelligence tests reveal large differences among the various personalities of any one patient (Brandsma & Ludwig, 1974; Congdon et al., 1961; Jeans, 1976; Keyes, 1981; Larmore et al., 1977; Luria & Osgood, 1976; Osgood & Luria, 1954; Osgood et al., 1976; Prince, 1908; Thigpen & Cleckley, 1954; Wagner & Heise, 1974). For example, tests may reveal that one personality is hostile and not particularly bright, while the other personality is loving and smart. However, those findings are not persuasive because it is easy to give false responses to tests and because the individuals who interpreted the responses to projective tests were not blind to the conditions and thus may easily have been biased in their scoring. Clearly, we must have better evidence than that.

Physiological Differences. Second, believers in the multiple personality disorder also point to research indicating that different patterns of brain wave activity (EEGs) are associated with the different personalities of any one individual (Braun, 1983b; Coons et al., 1982; Larmore et al., 1977; Ludwig et al., 1972). Indeed, in the case of one individual with four personalities, it was reported that it was "as if four different people had been tested" (Larmore et al., 1977, p. 40). These findings initially provided strong support for the validity of multiple personality, but their value has been greatly weakened by the results of a study in which EEG activity was recorded in two individuals diagnosed as having multiple personalities and one normal individual who role-played different personalities (Coons et al., 1982). In that study, it was found that the EEG differences between the personalities that were role-played by the normal individual were actually *greater* than the EEG differences between the personalities of the individuals diagnosed as having the multiple personality disorder. We now know that simple differences in concentration or mood can influence brain wave activity, and hence differences in brain wave activity cannot be used to verify the existence of multiple personalities (Coons, 1988; Coons et al., 1982; Miller & Triggiano, 1992). Differences among personalities on a wide variety of other physiological measures such as heart rate, respiration, skin conductance, and cerebral blood flow have also been examined, but as with brain waves, the differences among the multiple personalities of one individual were no greater than the differences among the roles played by normal individuals (see Miller & Triggiano, 1992). The point here is that because we all show differences in physiological responses when we are in different roles or moods, such differences cannot be used to demonstrate separate personalities.

Therapists have also reported case studies in which one personality had a toothache, was color-blind, or had an allergy but the individual's other personality did not suffer from those problems, and those cases are often cited as conclusive evidence for the existence of multiple personalities (Wilson, 1903; Braun, 1983a). However, those differences have not been independently verified or compared to differences that can be induced by suggestion. For example, a frequently cited case of an individual with diabetes who supposedly used different amounts of insulin while in different personalities can be traced back to one casual and unsubstantiated "observation" that has simply been reported over and over. Clearly, this evidence does not provide any support for the existence of the multiple personality disorder as it is described in the DSM.

Suggestion. There are two alternative explanations for the behavior of individuals who appear to have a multiple personality disorder. First, it is possible that the symptoms of multiple personalities may be *suggested to the individual by a therapist*. The possibility that therapists suggest the symptom pattern to patients gains indirect support from the fact that most therapists never see one case of multiple personality in their entire careers (Gruenewald, 1971; Rosenbaum, 1980), whereas some therapists report seeing as many as 100 or more such cases (Allison & Schwartz, 1980; Bliss, 1980, 1984; Braun, 1984; Kluft, 1982; Watkins, 1984). The implication is that therapists who are particularly interested in this disorder subtly suggest the symptom

pattern to their patients. In that regard, it is noteworthy that individuals with the multiple personality disorder are generally regarded as being highly suggestible and that the disorder is often discovered while the client is under hypnosis (a state of heightened suggestibility). Problems produced as a result of treatment (e.g., suggestions of the therapist) are called **iatrogenic** (YAT-rō-GEN-ik) **disorders.**

Evidence concerning the role that therapists' suggestions play in the development of multiple personality comes from the records of interactions between therapists and patients during therapy (Spanos et al., 1985; Sutcliffe & Jones, 1962). This is illustrated in the following quotation from an interview with Kenneth Bianchi, the Hillside Strangler, who later reported a multiple personality (see Case Study 7.2). Before Bianchi made any comments reflecting the possibility of a multiple personality, the interviewer said:

> I think that perhaps there might be another part of Ken that I haven't talked to. . . . I would like to communicate with that other part. . . . I would like that other part to come to talk to me. . . . Part, would you please come to communicate with me? . . . Would you please come, Part, so I can talk to you? (Orne et al., 1984, p. 128)

Not only did the interviewer suggest the possibility of another personality, but he actually gave the other personality a name ("Part") and repeatedly pleaded with Part to come out and talk to him!

This case led to an interesting study in which three groups of college students were asked to role-play Bianchi in an interview situation (Spanos et al., 1985). Students in one condition participated in an interview that closely followed the one used with Bianchi in that the interviewer (a) suggested that they might have another part, (b) said he would like to communicate with that part, and (c) talked directly to "Part." Students in the second condition participated in a similar interview, but the interviewer (a) suggested that we sometimes have thoughts and feelings that are "walled off" and (b) said that he would like to be in contact with "another part of you," but (c) did not address "Part" directly. In the control condition, the interviewer did not talk about a "part" or walled-off thoughts and feelings. When the students were then asked who they were and to talk about themselves, those in the first two conditions enacted another personality (used a different name, feigned amnesia for their real personality, and admitted to a crime their real personality denied). Furthermore, in a later session, when the students were asked to take personality tests as themselves and as another part of themselves, the students in the first two conditions gave very different test responses on the two administrations, whereas there was no difference in the control condition. In other words, when the interviewer suggested the possibility of a multiple personality, the students' behavior and personality test scores were consistent with multiple personalities, but when the interviewer did not suggest the possibility of a multiple personality, the students did not behave as though they had multiple personalities. These results clearly indicate that the way an interview is conducted can suggest the possibility of a multiple personality (Spanos, 1986).

Suggestions made to patients could lead them to fake the disorder deliberately or to believe that they actually had the disorder; in either case, they would act in accordance with the diagnosis. In view of the publicity the disorder gets, if an authority suggests that you have the disorder and if having the disorder explains or justifies your behavior, you may very well accede to the suggestion.

To counter the evidence implying that suggestion provides the basis for multiple personality, believers in the disorder assert first that the disorder is really more prevalent than is generally believed but that it is usually misdiagnosed as schizophrenia (Rosenbaum, 1980). They then go on to argue that the therapists who see many patients with multiple personality disorders do not suggest the disorder but are more sensitive to the subtle distinctions between multiple personality and schizophrenia and are therefore more likely to identify patients who have the multiple personality disorder.

Faking. It is also possible that in at least some cases, the individual is consciously *faking* the disorder to avoid responsibility or to get attention. The husband of a student of mine claimed to have multiple personalities when one day his wife came home unexpectedly and discovered him dressed in her clothes. He had a transvestic fetishism (see Chapter 18), but he tried to convince his wife that she was married to his "normal personality," who knew nothing about his "transvestite personality," who came out only when she was not home. During a thorough examination, he admitted the attempted deception.

The problems surrounding the diagnosis of the multiple personality disorder are highlighted in the widely publicized case of the Hillside Strangler, who is discussed in Case Study 7.2. While reading the case study, ask yourself the following questions: (a) Was Kenneth Bianchi suffering from a multiple personality disorder, or was he feigning one in an attempt to escape punishment? (b) Should he have been treated for his disorder or punished for his crimes? (c) Do people really suffer from multiple personality disorders?

Before concluding this discussion of the multiple personality disorder, three additional points should be noted. First, at present, there does not appear to be any empirical evidence for the existence of the multiple personality disorder, but *the absence of evidence does not necessarily mean that the disorder does not exist.* New evidence may come to light. Second, even if you conclude that Kenneth Bianchi was faking, this does not necessarily mean that all individuals who show evidence of multiple

personalities are faking. And finally we must distinguish between the *objective* existence and the *phenomenological* existence of the disorder. We may not be able to prove objectively that the disorder exists, but if individuals (and their therapists) believe that it does, they will behave as though it does, and therefore in some respects it does exist. However, that type of existence involves a very different type of cause and treatment than what is usually assumed. Overall, then, the question of whether or not there are individuals with the multiple personality disorder is still unanswered, and it has important psychological and legal implications.

The Faking of Dissociative Disorders

In diagnosing dissociative disorders, we must be sensitive to the possibility that the individual may be faking. For example, an individual who wanted to escape an unpleasant life situation might try to fake amnesia or a fugue. In one study of military personnel who reported being amnesic, 42% were found to be faking (Kiersch, 1962). Furthermore, in investigations of 32 individuals who were charged with crimes and who claimed to have amnesia for the acts, 66% were found to be faking, clearly indicating that individuals may attempt to use these symptom patterns to avoid difficulties. However, the fact that some individuals fake the disorders does not deny the reality of the disorders in others; it only suggests that we must be cautious in using the diagnoses.

EXPLANATIONS OF AND TREATMENTS FOR DISSOCIATIVE DISORDERS

Discussing the explanations of dissociative disorders puts us in a somewhat awkward position because in the foregoing discussion, serious questions were raised over whether these disorders really exist. However, many mental health professionals do believe that they exist and do treat them, so it is important that you know what is traditionally done. Furthermore, some individuals do show the symptoms of the disorders, so we must be able to account for that.

Psychodynamic Explanations

Psychodynamic theory suggests that dissociative disorders result from our attempts to dissociate ourselves from stressful events or to obliterate our memories of them. In other words, the dissociative disorders involve what can be considered as massive uses of repression (see Chapter 2 and earlier discussion). Although that explanation is widely held, the fact that over 70 years of research on repression has failed to produce any evidence makes the acceptance of this explanation hazardous at best.

Learning, Cognitive, and Physiological Explanations *disorder vs roles*

Learning and cognitive theorists have had very little to say about the development of dissociative disorders, probably because dissociative disorders are rare and because there is some skepticism over whether they actually exist. However, it is possible that the role explanation could be extended at least to an approximation of the multiple personality disorder. In that regard, it should be recognized that many of us have multiple personalities in that most of us play different roles in different situations (when in Rome, we do as the Romans do). Sometimes those roles are quite different, even conflicting. To avoid conflict, we may keep our conflicting roles completely separate and may not attend to the conflicts. For example, when I was an undergraduate, there was some conflict between my "jock" role and my "student" role. I behaved very differently in the two roles; usually dressed differently in the two roles; and although I did not realize it at first, when I was a senior, a friend pointed out that my different sets of friends even called me by different names (Dave vs. David).

The trouble with this explanation is that with multiple roles, we are *aware* of the "other personality" (I knew I studied and knew I was in training), but that is not the case with the multiple personality disorder. The development of different and conflicting multiple roles can be used to explain an *approximation* of the multiple personality disorder, but whether multiple roles can account for what is technically referred to as the multiple personality disorder has not yet been resolved.

Finally, it is relevant to note that dissociative amnesia, fugues, and multiple personalities could be used to avoid responsibility and thus they could be *rewarding*. For example, if an individual behaved inappropriately, he or she could simply say, "I don't remember doing that" or "Oh, it was my other personality" and thus no longer be accountable or blamed. That would not be the case for the real disorders, if they exist, but it does explain why individuals might want to have the symptom pattern. For example, whenever one individual I know faces a problem, she reverts to an infant personality: She goes to bed and demands that others take care of her.

Treatments

Traditionally, the treatment of dissociative disorders has involved, first, the resolution of the conflict that made it necessary to repress (or dissociate from) experiences or parts of the personality and, second, the integration of the previously repressed experiences or parts of the personality (Kluft, 1993; Loewenstein, 1994; Spiegel, 1994). In cases of multiple personality, the conflict must be resolved, and then each of the personalities must be reconciled and melded into the core personality. In many cases, that can take years because one personality may object or new ones may develop. In that regard, it is interesting to note that when I made the videotape that accompanies this book, I interviewed a woman who was diagnosed as having the multiple personality disorder. It took a long time to get consent to make the tape because permission had to be negotiated with each of her many personalities. In therapy, each personality must accept the solution and then agree to go away, and for that there is great resistance. Because of that, psychotherapy with individuals with the multiple personality disorder can go on for years and cost hundreds of thousands of dollars. Serious questions have been raised over whether insurance companies should pay for that therapy, especially when there is growing doubt that the disorder exists as it is described.

However, even if one takes the position that these disorders do not exist as they are traditionally described and explained, the individuals who display the symptoms probably do need some form of treatment because they obviously have a problem that led them to use the behaviors; that is, the behaviors are solving some problem (e.g., helping the individual escape responsibility) or satisfying some need (e.g., getting attention). Therefore, rather than accepting the traditional view of the symptoms, the therapist might ask why the patient has selected this set of behaviors (symptoms) and then work on that problem.

WHAT CAN WE CONCLUDE CONCERNING DISSOCIATIVE DISORDERS?

Individuals with dissociative disorders—especially those with the multiple personality disorder—have been a source of fascination for years, but now serious questions are being raised concerning the existence of the disorders as they are traditionally described and explained. There is no doubt that increasing numbers of individuals show the symptoms and that for most of those individuals, the symptom pattern is real and serves a purpose. However, the questions that must be asked are, first, are the individuals really unaware of information or other personalities because of repression, and second, did the symptoms develop spontaneously, or were they suggested to the individuals by therapists or media reports? At present, there is no objective evidence that the individuals are unaware or that the symptoms developed spontaneously. The absence of evidence poses serious problems. Of course, the fact that evidence has not been found does not mean that none exists, and consequently, no firm conclusion can be drawn. These disorders are still officially recognized in the DSM, but the diagnoses should be viewed with some caution.

CASE STUDY 7.2

The Hillside Strangler: A Case of Multiple Personality?

In the fall and winter of 1977–1978, ten young women were raped and strangled, and their nude bodies were left on various hillsides in Los Angeles County. The killer became known as the "Hillside Strangler." In January 1979, two women were raped and strangled in Bellingham, Washington. Shortly thereafter, a good-looking 27-year-old man named Kenneth Bianchi was arrested and charged with those murders and later charged with some of the murders in Los Angeles. As part of his criminal and psychiatric evaluation, Bianchi participated in a series of interviews that were videotaped. Those tapes provide a fascinating objective record of what some experts believe is a multiple personality and others believe is a scam that Bianchi used in an attempt to be declared insane so that he would not be punished for his crimes.

The presence of the second alleged personality originally came out when Bianchi participated in an interview under hypnosis conducted by a psychologist named Watkins, a specialist in multiple personalities who was working for the defense.

Watkins: I've talked a bit to Ken, but I think that perhaps there might be another part of Ken that I haven't talked to, another part that maybe feels somewhat differently from the part that I've talked to. And I would like to communicate with that other part. And I would like that other part to come to talk to me. . . . Part, would you please come to communicate with me? . . . Would you please come, Part, so I can talk to you? Another part, it is not just the same as the part of Ken I've been talking to. . . . All right, Part, I would like for you and I to talk together, we don't even have to—we don't have to talk to Ken unless you and Ken want to. . . .

Bianchi: Yes.

Watkins: Part, are you the same thing as Ken, or are you different in any way? . . .

Bianchi: I'm not him.

Watkins: You're not him. Who are you? Do you have a name?

Bianchi: I'm not Ken.

Watkins: You're not Ken. OK. Who are you? Tell me about yourself.

Bianchi: I don't know.

Watkins: Do you have a name I can call you by?

Bianchi: Steve.

Watkins: Huh?

Bianchi: You can call me Steve.

Bianchi then went on to talk about how he (Steve) had strangled and killed "all these girls," pointing out that "I fixed him [Ken] up good. He doesn't even have any idea." At the end of the interview, the psychologist asked to speak to Ken, who then promptly returned. When Ken was asked about Steve, he replied, "Who's Steve?"

In a later interview, after Ken was told about the existence of Steve, Ken talked about his "readiness for the fight" for dominance with Steve. Ken also began complaining of headaches, a symptom that Watkins attributed to the conflict and struggle over the emergence of Steve against Ken's will. When Watkins asked Ken why he was feeling bad, there was an angry snarl, and then Steve emerged complaining about the difficulty of getting out now that Ken knew about him. He said:

All these f— years I had it made. I could come and go as I pleased. He never knew about me. But now he does. I have some feeling it's partly your fault. You started this whole f— thing. . . . I try to come out. Instead I stay where I'm at, and he complains about f— headaches . . . I'd like to give him a big f— headache.

Investigations of Bianchi's past revealed that he had participated in numerous scams. In one case, he stole a psychologist's diploma, inserted a new name, and began a practice as a psychologist. He was also involved with a teenage prostitution ring. Despite clear evidence that those things occurred, Ken denied them and claimed to have had amnesic episodes during the periods in question. Watkins concluded that the illegal acts had been perpetrated by another personality of which Ken was not aware, and Watkins suggested that this was additional evidence for the multiple personality diagnosis. In contrast, the prosecution considered these to be instances of conscious misrepresentation.

The expert witnesses for the prosecution were led by a psychologist-psychiatrist named Martin Orne,

When Kenneth Bianchi was accused of being the "Hillside Strangler," he claimed that he had multiple personalities and that one of them, Steve, had committed the crimes. It was ultimately determined that Bianchi did not have the multiple personality disorder, and he was sentenced to life in prison.

who argued that rather than suffering from the multiple personality disorder, Bianchi suffered from an "antisocial personality disorder" and that he was faking the multiple personalities to avoid punishment. (Major symptoms of the antisocial personality disorder include repeated criminal behavior, lying, and a lack of anxiety; it will be discussed in Chapter 14.) A number of points were made to discredit the diagnosis of multiple personality. First, it was suggested that the disorder had not appeared spontaneously but had been suggested to Bianchi by Watkins. Some support for that is found in the transcript of the interview in which Steve originally emerged.

Second, Orne laid a small trap for Bianchi by suggesting that if he really did have a multiple personality disorder, he would have a third personality. The idea behind this was that if Bianchi was faking and if he were led to believe that having another personality would give his diagnosis more credibility, he

would begin showing one. After the suggestion was made, Bianchi was hypnotized. Steve appeared first, followed shortly by a third personality, Billy.

The prosecution also pointed to a history of crime and lying. With regard to lying, it is interesting to note that although Bianchi claimed to know nothing about the multiple personality disorder, a search of his room revealed numerous textbooks on psychology. He had also been a psychology major in college, thus making it unlikely that he was unfamiliar with the disorder. It was also discovered that Bianchi had made a number of other conscious attempts to mislead the prosecution (e.g., he had asked others to lie about where he was at various crucial times).

Facing overwhelming evidence and serious questions about the validity of his multiple personality defense, Bianchi withdrew his plea of not guilty by reason of insanity and entered into a plea bargain. (The demand for the death penalty was dropped in exchange for Bianchi's pleading guilty and testifying against another individual who had been involved in the murders.)

Despite his plea bargain, Bianchi steadfastly maintained his multiple personality. When given an opportunity to address the court before the sentence was passed, Bianchi gave an impassioned and tearful speech in which he said that he would have to devote his entire life to seeing that no one would follow in his footsteps. However, in sharp contrast to that display of emotion and regret, a detective assigned to the case reported that within three minutes of leaving the courtroom, Bianchi was sitting with his feet up on a desk, smoking a cigarette and laughing.

In his concluding comments before sentencing Kenneth Bianchi, the judge observed, "Mr. Bianchi caused confusion and delay in the proceedings. In this Mr. Bianchi was unwittingly aided and abetted by most of the psychiatrists, who naively swallowed Mr. Bianchi's story, hook, line, and sinker, almost confounding the criminal justice system."

Kenneth Bianchi was sentenced to life in prison.

Sources: Allison (1984); Orne et al. (1984); Watkins (1984); *People v. Buono* (1983).

SUMMARY

TOPIC I: SOMATOFORM DISORDERS

■ Somatoform disorders involve physical symptoms for which there is no demonstrable physical cause. They were originally called hysterical disorders and received attention from Jean-Martin Charcot and Sigmund Freud.

■ There are five somatoform disorders: (a) the somatization disorder, which involves numerous somatic complaints; (b) hypochondriasis, which involves excessive concern over a minor symptom; (c) the conversion disorder, which involves a major motor or sensory symptom; (d) the pain disorder, which involves pain without any discernible physical cause; and (e) the body dysmorphic disorder, which is a preoccupation with a minor or imagined physical defect.

■ Mass psychogenic illness is an epidemic of a particular type of conversion disorder.

■ Somatoform disorders occur in about 2% of the population and are more common among women than among men.

■ Evidence for the reality of these disorders comes from the placebo effect, in which symptoms can be induced or eliminated through suggestion.

■ Somatoform disorders can lead to high medical bills because of attempts to identify a physiological cause. Problems can arise if real medical problems are erroneously attributed to somatoform disorders. With new findings in medicine, some of what we now think are somatoform disorders may be found to be real medical disorders.

■ From a psychodynamic viewpoint, somatoform disorders are thought to stem from pent-up emotional energy that is converted into physical symptoms.

■ Learning and cognitive theorists assume that somatoform symptoms are learned and are rewarded in that they help the individual avoid stress or lead to sympathy. Furthermore, by focusing attention on bodily symptoms, the individual may misinterpret normal sensations as symptoms.

■ The physiological explanations for somatoform disorders hold that some individuals are more sensitive to bodily sensations or are more physiologically aroused and that the sensations and arousal are misinterpreted as symptoms.

■ Treatment of somatoform disorders revolves around (a) changing attention away from bodily sensations and changing beliefs about the meaning of bodily sensations, (b) reducing depression that might lead to focusing on bodily sensations and interpreting them pessimistically, (c) reducing arousal that leads to bodily sensations that might be misinterpreted, and (d) providing emotional support so that individuals can cope more effectively.

TOPIC II: DISSOCIATIVE DISORDERS

■ Individuals with dissociative disorders lose contact with important elements of their personalities or environments.

■ There are four dissociative disorders: (a) dissociative amnesia, which is an inability to remember important personal information or events that is not due to physiological causes; (b) dissociative fugue, in which the individual has amnesia for his or her previous identity and goes to a new location to assume a new identity; (c) the dissociative identity disorder (multiple personality), in which the individual has two or more personalities that take control at different times and may not be aware of one another, and (d) the depersonalization disorder, which involves the feeling of being detached from one's body.

■ Serious questions must be raised concerning the existence of most of the dissociative disorders because they are based on the concept of repression, for which we have no evidence.

■ There is no objective evidence for the existence of multiple personalities as they are traditionally described and explained; and they may be due to suggestion or faking.

■ The psychodynamic explanations for dissociative disorders hold that individuals are attempting to separate themselves from stressful events or from stressful parts of themselves.

■ Learning, cognitive, and physiological theorists have had little to say about dissociative disorders, probably because of the skepticism over their existence.

■ Treatment for individuals with these disorders is probably best focused on determining why the individual is using the symptoms (e.g., to gain attention, to avoid responsibility) and then helping the individual find better ways to achieve the goals.

KEY TERMS, CONCEPTS, AND NAMES

In reviewing and testing yourself on what you have learned from this chapter, you should be able to identify and discuss each of the following.

body dysmorphic disorder: *like anorexia — somatoform disorder*
catharsis: *talking, psychodynamic*
Charcot, Jean-Martin: *suggestion*
conversion disorder: *sensory-motor work related*
craft palsies
dancing manias: *mass pygenetic illness*
depersonalization disorder: *mind-body split — distortions / self*
dhat: *India, vital fluid*
dissociative amnesia: *forgetting stress event*
dissociative disorders: *mind-body split — personality split, env split*

dissociative fugue: *leaving on a jet plane*
dissociative identity disorder *(+ personality)*
factitious disorders: *faking disorder*
Freud, Sigmund: *repression*
glove anesthesia: *numbness in hand — conversion disorder*
hemispheric dominance: *R side causing L side problems*
hypochondriasis: *symptom → serious illness*
iatrogenic disorders: *problems as result/ treatment*
koro: *Japan, retracting genitals*
malingering: *faking to avoid responsibility*

mass psychogenic illness: *conversion*
multiple personality disorder
pain disorder: *pain w/no cause*
placebo effect: *suggest wellness or pain*
pseudocyesis: *conversion dis. — false pregnancy*
psychosomatic disorders: *damage*
repression: *#1 in dissociative disorders — no evidence*
somatization disorder: *long lasting complaints — somato. disorder w/no cause*
somatoform disorders: *no damage — aka hysterical*

CHAPTER EIGHT
MOOD DISORDERS: SYMPTOMS and ISSUES

OUTLINE

Lois is a 36-year-old woman who spends most of the day slumped in a chair staring blankly at the floor. Her face is slack and expressionless, she is rather unkempt, and she rarely moves or speaks. Occasionally, she weeps quietly to herself. Lois has difficulty getting to sleep at night, and she usually awakens at about 2:30 A.M. and cannot get back to sleep. She does not care about eating and has lost 12 lb in the past three months. When asked what was wrong, she slowly gave the following answer in a voice that was almost inaudible: "Everything is wrong; everything has gone wrong. It's just too much. *(Long pause)* I'm a complete failure. *(Long pause)* I just don't think things will get better—and I just don't care anymore. *(Begins crying)* I wish I were dead. Then I'd have it over with. . . . Everyone would be better off without me hanging around. I just can't make it anymore." Lois has been like this for about three months. She suffers from a *major depression of the retarded type.*

■　■　■

Ernst is a 68-year-old accountant for a large retail store. He has always been in good health and has always worked hard. He will retire in 2 years. Lately, he has become rather depressed. When asked what was bothering him, he replied: "What's it all for? I've kept the books balanced for 46 years, but what difference has it made to the world or to me? I came in as an assistant accountant and now I'm the senior accountant—not better, just older. The day after I leave, someone else will take over my desk and nothing will change. Old accountants don't die; they just get moved to the debit side of the ledger. I'm going to get moved over without ever having done or accomplished anything. I've been here for over 45 years, people have come and gone, and I'm just here. They don't even know who I am in the front office. If I'd been smart, I would have done something else with my life—and now it's too late." Ernst thinks of suicide sometimes, but at this point it is just a thought. Ernst suffers from *depression.*

■　■　■

Last week, Jennifer gave birth to a healthy 7-lb, 6-oz baby boy. Everyone is excited and happy—everyone, that is, except Jennifer, who became very depressed shortly after giving birth. She feels "tired and terrible." Sometimes she actually feels repulsed by the baby and does not want to see or care for him. Jennifer feels guilty about her feelings because this should be a joyous time for her, but she just cannot snap out of it. When other people are around, she sometimes tries to fake feeling good and happy about the baby, but that does not work because she often breaks into tears for no apparent reason. Nothing her friends say helps, and her husband is getting worried. She has thought about suicide. Jennifer is suffering from a *postpartum depression.*

■　■　■

Carl was a happily married 28-year-old father of two who had always been very stable. However, two years ago, he went through a period in which he became noticeably more active and extravagant. He slept less, had an unusual amount of energy, made many unrealistic plans for his small business, and spent a considerable amount of money needlessly on a new convertible and a lot of clothes. He seemed to be going off in three directions at once without giving anything much thought. After about a month, this phase passed, and Carl became his "old self" again, much to his wife's relief. Everything was normal for about a year, but then he began slipping into a mild depression. He stopped making business calls, at home he sat alone in his study, and he was convinced that he was a "rotten failure." He just wanted to be left alone. This depression lifted after a while, and once again Carl returned to his normal behavior. A week ago, however, he again started becoming very active, even agitated. He made plans for the entire family to take a vacation in the South Pacific as a celebration for a big business deal that he thought he would close but was in fact only in the idea stage. He signed a contract to have an addition put on the house but then put the house up for sale and started negotiating to buy another one that was completely out of his price range. Emotionally, he was "on top of the world" and felt as though he could achieve anything he tried. However, he never actually accomplished much because he became distracted by other ideas before he could carry through on anything. He slept very little and called people in the middle of the night to set up business appointments he never kept. After about three days of this, his wife realized that he was completely out of control, and she called the family physician, who had Carl committed to the psychiatric ward of the local hospital. He was diagnosed as suffering from the *bipolar disorder.*

■ ■ ■

Kate was a 23-year-old fashion assistant buyer for a large department store. Over the past two years, she had become somewhat depressed. She attributed her poor mood to exhaustion brought on by the constant strain of her job. She began going to a psychotherapist but stopped after only a few sessions because she didn't think she could be helped. At first she had been very successful at her job, but recently she had chosen some lines of women's clothing that had "bombed," and now her confidence was shaken. Feeling hopeless, she occasionally gave some thought to suicide; it would provide a release from the constant strain she was under— and why not? She had nothing to live for. On a number of occasions, Kate made comments to her friends like "Nothing seems to be going right; sometimes I feel like stepping in front of a truck" or "Probably the best thing for me to do tonight is to take all the pills in my medicine cabinet and just not wake up tomorrow morning." Her friends knew that Kate was depressed, but they thought she would snap out of it, and they didn't take her comments about suicide seriously. When Kate did not come in for work for two days and did not answer her phone, a friend went to her apartment. Kate was lying dead in the bathtub, her wrists slashed. She had left a short note in which she simply apologized for not being a better person.

■ ■ ■

In this chapter and the two that follow, I will examine the fascinating topic of **mood disorders.** These disorders involve disturbances in mood that range from deep **depression** to wild **mania.** It is important to understand mood disorders because their symptoms can be very serious and because many people suffer from them. Indeed, although estimates differ, it is safe to say that at least 15% of the population will suffer from a mood disorder at some time during their lives.

At the outset, it is essential to recognize that there are two major types of mood disorders. The first type is the **major depressive disorder,** in which *depression is the primary symptom.* The second type is the **bipolar disorder,** in which *depression alternates with mania.* The term *bipolar* stems from the fact that individuals with this disorder move between two extremes or "poles" of mood; depression and mania. Some years ago, the bipolar disorder was called the **manic-depressive disorder.**

In a second category of mood disorders are disorders in which the symptoms have lasted for at least 2 years and are *similar* to those of the depressive and bipolar disorders *but the symptoms are less severe.* The less severe form of the major depressive disorder is known as the **dysthymic (dis-THĪ-mik) disorder,** and the less severe form of the **bipolar** disorder is called the **cyclothymic (sī-klō-THĪ-mik) disorder.** The organization of the mood disorders along with their symptoms is illustrated in Figure 8.1. A decision tree for diagnosing mood disorders can be found in Figure 3.1 in Chapter 3.

The depressive and bipolar disorders both have depression as a major symptom, but it is important to recognize that *the depressive and bipolar disorders are different disorders.* Therefore, I will discuss the depressive disorder first and the bipolar disorder after that. Finally, I will discuss suicide, which is often closely related to the mood disorders.

TOPIC I
THE DEPRESSIVE DISORDER

Depression is the most common mood disorder, and it occurs so often that it has been called the "common cold of psychological disorders." The fact that depression is widespread is of concern, but what is also alarming is that the incidence of depressive disorders is increasing rapidly. It may be that we are moving out of the "age of anxiety" and into the "decade of depression."

SYMPTOMS OF DEPRESSION

There are two different symptom patterns in depression, retarded depression and agitated depression. **Retarded depression** is more frequent and involves a decrease in energy level such that the smallest task may seem difficult or impossible to accomplish. Individuals with retarded depression show reduced and slowed body movements. They also show reduced and monotonous speech. In contrast, individuals with **agitated depression** are unable to sit still; they pace, wring their hands, and pull or rub their hair or skin. There may also be sudden outbursts of complaining in which the individual shouts or talks rapidly. One woman who suffered from agitated depression spent her days walking in circles around her bedroom, wringing her hands and weeping, and she cried through most of the night. On the surface, agitated depression involves many of the symptoms of anxiety, and it is sometimes difficult to differentiate between agitated depression and anxiety. Agitated depression may also be confused with mania because both can involve a high level of activity. However, the individual with an agitated depression is *sad,* whereas the individual with mania is *happy.* Because retarded depression is much more common, in this chapter I will focus primarily on retarded depression.

Mood Symptoms

Obviously, the primary symptoms of the major depressive disorders revolve around mood. The individuals feel depressed, "blue," sad, hopeless, discouraged, "down." Frequently, depressed individuals also feel isolated, rejected, and unloved. Depressed individuals sometimes describe themselves as being alone in a

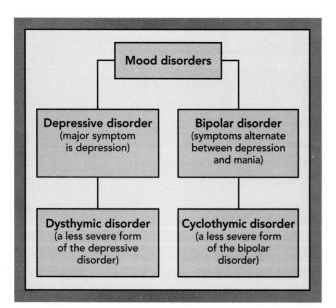

FIGURE 8.1 Mood disorders: Types and organization.

Individuals suffering from depression often feel hopeless and sad. They have a sense of being isolated, unwanted, or rejected.

deep, dark hole where they cannot be reached and out of which they cannot climb.

Cognitive Symptoms

1. **Low Self-Esteem.** Five cognitive symptoms play important roles in depression, the first of which is *low self-esteem.* Depressed individuals usually think they are inadequate, inferior, inept, incompetent, and generally worthless, and they often feel guilty about their failures.

2. **Pessimism.** A second important cognitive symptom is *pessimism.* Depressed individuals believe that they will never be able to solve their problems and that things will only get worse. That pessimism was illustrated in a study in which depressed and nondepressed students rated the degree to which they thought they *should* be able to perform a variety of tasks and also the degree to which they thought they *would* perform the tasks (Kanfer & Zeiss, 1983). There was no difference between depressed and nondepressed students in how well they thought they should perform, but the depressed students rated the degree to which they would perform much lower than the nondepressed students did. In

other words, the standards of the depressed and nondepressed students were the same, but depressed students were more pessimistic about reaching the standard. Those results are presented graphically in Figure 8.2.

3. **Low Motivation.** Third, individuals with depression exhibit *low motivation.* Because they do not believe that they will be able to solve their problems, depressed individuals see no reason to work on those problems or to seek help in overcoming them. For them, all seems lost and hopeless, so there is no point in trying. Of course, if they do not work on their problems or seek help for them, the problems will not be solved, and the accumulation of unsolved problems can provide additional reasons for depression.

Consider the case of a student who failed a midterm examination and became depressed. The failure and depression led the student to think, "I guess I'm just not smart enough to get through this course. I'll certainly flunk the final, so there is no point in going to class or working on this course anymore." Obviously, the student's low self-esteem, pessimism, and lack of motivation will result in another failure that will provide more reasons for depression and will confirm his beliefs about his inadequacy; a vicious circle will be started.

4. **Generalization of Negative Attitudes.** Unfortunately, the low self-esteem, pessimism, and lack of motivation tend to spread and encompass more than just the original cause of the depression. This *generalization of negative attitudes* is the fourth important cognitive symptom in depression. Research has shown that the degree to which individuals generalize their problems is related

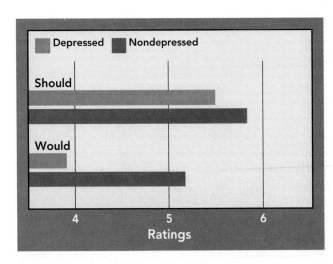

FIGURE 8.2 Depressed and nondepressed students agreed about how well they should perform on a task, but the depressed students did not think they would perform as well as the nondepressed students.
Source: Data from Kanfer and Zeiss (1983), p. 323, tab. 2.

to the severity of their depression (Carver & Ganellen, 1983). Deeply depressed individuals are more likely to agree with items such as "Noticing one fault of mine makes me think more and more about other faults" and "When even one thing goes wrong, I begin to feel bad and wonder if I can do well at *anything at all*." In the case of the depressed student who failed the midterm, he might go on to believe that in addition to being an academic failure, he is also a social failure, and that might lead him to withdraw and have fewer social contacts.

5. *Exaggeration of Seriousness.* In some cases, there is justification for feeling depressed (failing an examination can be serious and have negative long-term effects), but depressed individuals tend to exaggerate the seriousness of the problem and become excessively pessimistic. This *exaggeration of the seriousness of problems* is the fifth major cognitive symptom of depression, and it can become so extreme that the individual may develop **delusions.** That is, despite strong evidence to the contrary, the individual develops and maintains totally erroneous beliefs that are bizarre and clearly absurd. For example, a very depressed individual might believe that he or she was suffering from progressive brain deterioration. The delusions seen in depression are less bizarre than those seen in schizophrenia (i.e., the depressed individual does not think that he or she is God), and the delusions are likely to be related to the individual's mood (e.g., depression related to an imagined illness) (Junginger et al., 1992).

From the foregoing comments it is clear that depressed individuals have more negative self-perceptions than nondepressed individuals, but it is interesting to note that in at least some cases, **depressed individuals may be more accurate in their self-perceptions** than nondepressed individuals. It may be not that depressed individuals distort their perceptions downward but rather that *nondepressed individuals distort their perceptions upward.* For example, when college students were asked to estimate how well they performed on a task, depressed students gave lower estimates, but those estimates were closer to their actual performance than the higher estimates of nondepressed students. Furthermore, when college students were asked to rate their social skills, the lower estimates of depressed students were closer to the ratings made by independent judges than the higher estimates of nondepressed students (Alloy & Abramson, 1979; Lewinsohn et al., 1980). This prompted the investigators to suggest that in at least some situations, depressed individuals are "sadder but wiser."

Motor Symptoms

Psychomotor Retardation. The most prominent and most important motor symptom in depression is psy-chomotor retardation, which involves a reduction or slowing of motor behavior. Depressed persons frequently sit with a drooping posture and a blank, expressionless gaze. Some depressed individuals simply curl up in bed and attempt to sleep. If they do move, they do so very slowly and as though they were dragging a 10-ton weight. They may even report feeling like they have the weight of the world on their shoulders and just cannot move under this burden. Psychomotor retardation also affects speech patterns. Depressed individuals talk very little, and when they do talk, it is in a quiet monotone. Often they will break off talking in midsentence because they do not have the energy or the interest to finish the sentence.

Psychomotor Agitation. In contrast, some depressed persons show **psychomotor agitation** and are unable to sit still. These people are restless and constantly fidgeting or pacing. It is noteworthy that the activities of these individuals are random rather than focused on achieving any particular goal, and hence their activities do not gain them anything. Psychomotor agitation is much less prevalent than psychomotor retardation.

Somatic Symptoms

Disturbed Sleep. Depressed individuals are prone to suffer from a variety of somatic problems, one of which is a **disturbed sleep** pattern. Specifically, depressed individuals often have difficulty getting to sleep, and then they experience *early awakening;* that is, they wake up early in the morning (around 2:00 A.M., for example) and are unable to get back to sleep. Early awakening appears to be associated with more severe depressions, and as depressions begin to lift, the time of awakening becomes later and later. In some cases of depression, the individuals begin sleeping more than usual, an effect called **hypersomnia** (HĪ-pur-SOM-nē-uh).

Disturbed Eating Patterns. Disturbed eating patterns are also common in depressions. Many depressed individuals lose interest in eating, and food ceases to have any flavor for them. Consequently, they decrease their food intake. In other cases, the depressed individuals may want to eat and realize that they need to eat, but because they do not have the energy to prepare good meals, they rely on a diet of easily available "junk food" that fails to fulfill their nutritional needs. There are also some depressed individuals for whom eating becomes very important. For these people, eating becomes the only pleasant activity in their otherwise gloomy lives.

Reduced Sexual Drive. Another somatic symptom that is associated with depression is *reduced sexual interest or drive.* This is often referred to as a **loss of**

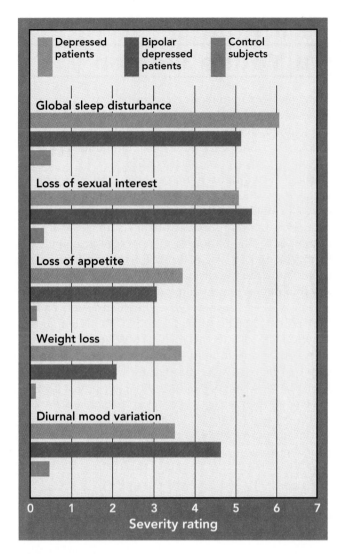

Depressed patients

Bipolar depressed patients

Control subjects

Global sleep disturbance

Loss of sexual interest

Loss of appetite

Weight loss

Diurnal mood variation

Severity rating

FIGURE 8.3 Depressed patients suffer from a variety of somatic symptoms.
Source: Adapted from Casper et al. (1985), p. 1100.

libido (li-BĒ-dō; *libido* is the psychodynamic term for "sexual drive"). The severity of somatic symptoms in depressed patients, bipolar depressed patients, and normal controls is summarized in Figure 8.3.

Physical Illnesses. Apart from the specific problems associated with sleep, appetite, and sex, depressed individuals are more susceptible to a variety of diseases. That is the result of an impairment of the functioning of their **immune systems** (Herbert & Cohen, 1993). Specifically, there is evidence that depressed individuals produce fewer of the **lymphocytes** (LIM-fō-sīts; white blood cells) that play an important role in fighting off disease (see Chapter 16). The reduction in the activity in the immune system in depressed individuals probably stems from the fact that the stress associated with the depression retards the functioning of the system, but it may also be that depression-related behav-

iors such as poor diet, less sleep, and less exercise contribute to the effect.

Less psychologically sophisticated individuals may emphasize their physical symptoms and underplay their psychological symptoms. This can result in what is called a *masked depression* in which the depressive symptoms are concealed by a mask of physical symptoms. If the individual only complains about physical symptoms, it is possible that his or her disorder will be misdiagnosed.

I will discuss the basic causes of depression in Chapter 9, but here it is important to note that the various *symptoms* of depression may serve as additional *causes* of depression or at least serve to prolong the depression. For example, cognitive symptoms such as pessimism may lead the individuals to see only negative things in life, which could lead to more reasons to be depressed. Similarly, reduced or ineffective motor activity can interfere with effective problem solving, further convincing depressed individuals of their ineptitude. Somatic symptoms such as loss of sleep and poor appetite can also sap individuals of energy, thereby reducing their effectiveness. In short, a vicious circle can develop in which the symptoms of depression lead to greater depression. An example of an individual suffering from a major depression is presented in Case Study 8.1.

Diagnostic Criteria

Now that you have seen what depression is like, I can briefly list for you the criteria for the diagnosis of major depressive disorder (recurrent type). Three things are necessary for this diagnosis; first, the individual must have experienced *two or more major depressive episodes*. A depressive episode is defined as a period of at least two weeks in which nearly every day the individual experiences five or more of the following nine symptoms: (a) depressed mood, (b) diminished interest or pleasure in activities, (c) a 5% weight loss or a dramatic change in appetite, (d) insomnia or hypersomnia, (e) psychomotor retardation or agitation, (f) fatigue or loss of energy, (g) feelings of worthlessness or guilt, (h) diminished ability to concentrate or indecisiveness, and (i) recurrent thoughts about death and suicide. Second, the symptom pattern cannot be better accounted for by some other physical or psychological disorder. Third, the individual must not have had a period of mania. (That last restriction rules out a diagnosis of the bipolar disorder, which I will discuss later.)

Dysthymic Disorder

In addition to the full-blown depressive disorder, there is a somewhat less severe disorder known as the

CASE STUDY 8.1

Major Depression in a Young Woman

Diane is a 28-year-old single woman who has suffered from severe depression since she was 16. Her first period of depression culminated in an almost fatal drug overdose. After her suicide attempt, she was hospitalized on and off for several years, and when not in the hospital, she was treated regularly in the outpatient clinic. Treatment consisted of psychotherapy and antidepressant drugs. Her adjustment during this period was only marginal, but she was able to complete high school.

Diane has remained out of the hospital now for about 7 years, but her depression has persisted. In describing her feelings, she says: "I wish someone would give me a spoon and tell me to move a mountain. Then my sense of hopeless futility would be more tangible. . . . Life is an absurd waste of time. . . . My existence is a freak accident of nature. . . . It seems that I can only handle short, sweet episodes of positive momentum."

Her overwhelming sense of worthlessness and inadequacy has prevented her from establishing any meaningful friendships that could challenge her negative self-image and provide support. Not sur-

prisingly, her ruminations concerning her "emotional hellishness" interfere with her capacity to concentrate, think clearly, or make decisions. She spends much of her time staring into space, looking but seeing only gray, negative images of life.

Diane is a bright young woman, and although plagued by almost ceaseless depression, she managed to complete college and hold several part-time jobs. However, consistent with her unrealistic self-devaluation, she minimizes these accomplishments, saying, "It took so long to finish college, my degree is useless, and the work is mindless." She seems to lack any foundation on which to build a positive self-evaluation. Despite the severity of her depression and her sense of hopelessness, Diane has not attempted suicide again. She credits therapy with providing her with at least one supportive and nurturing relationship that helps her get through the "rough spots of life." She views the possibility of long-term meaningful change skeptically: "I've been miserable all my life, and I don't know if I know how to live differently. I'm not sure I know what it is like to be happy. I probably wouldn't recognize it if I was."

dysthymic disorder (see Figure 8.1). Individuals with this disorder are depressed but just keep struggling, watching their personal relations and personal potential deteriorate, making excuses for themselves, and thinking that they are just not good people. This type of experience was beautifully described for me by a student who wrote a term paper on the topic of depression and its treatment. She opened the paper with a description of her own experience with depression before it was successfully treated; you will find her description in Case Study 8.2.

Unfortunately, because the symptoms of dysthymia are less severe, many individuals with dysthymia are not diagnosed as having a disorder and do not get treatment. As a consequence, they go through life feeling miserable and missing much that is positive, and because they do not know that they have a psychiatric disorder, they just assume that they are "bad people" or "the world is a terrible place." Even though dysthymia is less serious than depression, it can be a tragic disorder.

Some recent research revealed two interesting things about dysthymia (Kovacs et al., 1994). First, like major depressions, *dysthymia is cyclical;* it comes and goes. Second, *the presence of dysthymia in childhood is predictive of depressive disorders later in life.* Indeed, in a follow-up of children who had suffered from dysthymia,

it was found that 80% had subsequent episodes of dysthymia and 48% developed a major depressive disorder. Clearly, dysthymia is a problem in itself and may be predictive of more serious problems to come.

ISSUES ASSOCIATED WITH DEPRESSION

Normal Versus Abnormal Depression

Feelings of sadness, disappointment, grief, and depression are part of the human condition and are experienced by everyone at some time. The question that arises then is, what distinguishes normal depression from abnormal depression? The boundary is not clear, but two factors should be considered in making the distinction. The first factor is the *depth* of the depression. It is normal to feel somewhat "down," "blue," or mildly depressed occasionally, but there is reason for concern if the depression is so deep that the individual cannot function adequately. The second factor is the *duration* of the depression. Regardless of the depth of the depression, there is cause for concern if the depression is prolonged and the individual does not "snap out of it." In cases such

CASE STUDY 8.2

A Student's Struggle with Depression

"I feel as though I have spent my whole life trapped inside a glass bottle. I could look out and view the world, but it always seemed dulled and distorted by the thick, scratched glass. If anyone would shake me up the slightest bit, I felt as though I was going to crack and shatter in a million pieces. Perhaps that was precisely what I wanted so that I could cut people with the millions of jagged edges. My anger was enormous. It angered me that people were so damn happy and all I could do was watch.

"After experiencing these feelings for as much of my life as I could remember, I entered psychotherapy at the age of 17 because my parents thought I was 'depressed.' I was easily swayed by the idea because in the pit of my stomach I really did not want to go on feeling the way I did. When the time came to enter college, I quit my therapy and concluded that my feelings of entrapment and isolation must just be a major character flaw. My first year of college was filled with ups and downs. I couldn't seem to keep any relationships intact, with males or females. It seemed that everyone was always tired of being around me and accused me of being perpetually pessimistic. Sometimes I would spend days secluded by myself. When people would ask if something was

wrong, I would reply with a philosophical answer about how some people need more time to themselves than others and that I had accepted that fact about myself. I rationalized my seclusion by telling myself that people who aren't comfortable by themselves are actually more insecure than those who can be alone. As I was never happy with what I was doing in the present, I tended to move around a lot in a ploy to 'experience different things' and 'get in touch with myself.' As time went by, my depression was pushed to an all-time low, and I found myself incapacitated. I began spending more and more time in my bed huddled under my blankets with my door closed. Most of the time, I didn't feel particularly bad about not accomplishing anything because I knew that I physically couldn't get out of bed and I had lost faith that I had any academic prowess whatsoever. All of my relationships deteriorated because nobody wanted or knew how to deal with me. This only served to substantiate what I had decided about myself—that I was a worthless person who could never accomplish anything."

Note: We will return to this student's experiences later when we consider the treatment of depression in Chapter 10.

---

as the death of a loved one, it is justifiable to be depressed for a while, but if the depression is more prolonged than what is justified by the original cause, the possibility of abnormal depression must be considered.

The symptoms of depression can have longer-term effects than those of some serious physical disorders such as congestive heart failure, heart attacks, and diabetes (Hays et al., 1995). The results of a 2-year follow-up revealed that depressed individuals were doing less well in a variety of areas than their counterparts who were suffering from serious chronic physical illnesses. Those results are summarized in Figure 8.4.

Prevalence

Estimates of the prevalence of depression range from 12% to 17%, thus indicating that depression is a problem that afflicts a substantial proportion of the population (Coryell et al., 1991; Kessler et al., 1994). Actually, the problem is even greater than those numbers suggest because those estimates do not include the large number of individuals who suffer from dysthymia.

Many events can trigger feelings of depression, sadness, and grief. Unless these feelings are very severe or last a long time, the sadness these parents feel upon the departure of their daughter would not be classified as clinical depression.

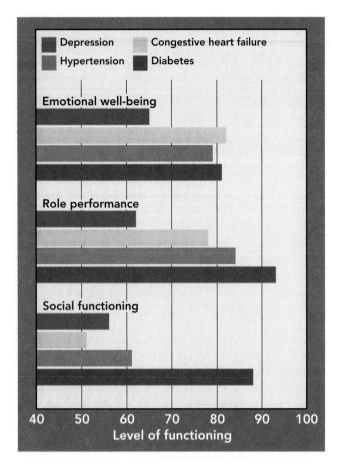

FIGURE 8.4 Depressed individuals functioned less well than individuals with serious chronic physical illnesses.
Note: Scores could range from 0 (poor) to 100 (excellent).
Source: Data from Hays et al. (1995), p. 16, tab. 3.

It is also important to recognize that *depression is very likely to recur.* In one investigation, it was found that 45% of the individuals who were studied had two episodes, and 33% had three episodes (Lewinsohn et al., 1989). The likelihood of relapse is higher for females and higher for individuals whose initial depression was more severe. In fact, for severely depressed individuals, the relapse rate may be as high as 90%. The fact that many individuals suffer from depression, in combination with the fact that it is a recurring or chronic disorder, makes depression one of the most widespread and serious disorders.

Substantial evidence indicates that *the prevalence of depression has been increasing throughout the 20th century* (e.g., Lewinsohn et al., 1993). The increase in depression is illustrated in the results of a study conducted in Sweden in which all of the individuals who lived in one particular area were examined repeatedly over a 25-year period (Hagnell et al., 1982). As indicated in Figure 8.5, the rates of "medium" and "mild" depression increased greatly over time, especially among women. The finding that severe depressions did not increase (and actu-

ally showed a decrease among women) is not completely understandable. However, that finding might be due to the fact that a variety of effective treatments for depression have been developed, and the treatments may have been more likely to be applied to severely depressed individuals, thus holding that level of depression in check. The findings concerning the increasing rate of depression have prompted some people to express concern about the coming "age of melancholy" (Klerman, 1979). This could be a serious trend.

One cautionary note should be sounded concerning the findings that the incidence of depression is on the increase. It is possible that depression is not actually increasing but that we are becoming more willing to admit to depression or more likely to diagnose it than we were. In other words, it may be that depression is becoming more acceptable or less of a stigma, and it is the change in attitude rather than a change in the actual incidence of depression that is reflected in the data. In this regard, it is noteworthy that only the mild and medium levels of depression are increasing; those are the levels that would have been easier to deny or ignore earlier.

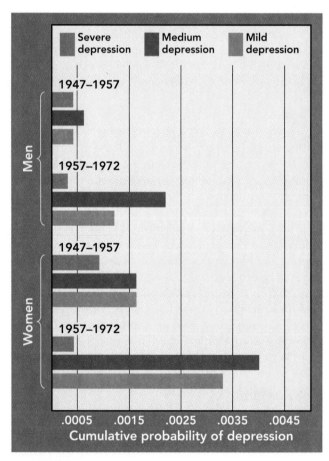

FIGURE 8.5 Rates of medium and mild depression have increased over time.
Source: Data from Hagnell et al. (1982), p. 284, tab. 3.

Sociocultural Factors

Gender. Depression is much more likely to be diagnosed in women than in men, the ratio being about 2:1 (Smith & Weissman, 1992; Kessler et al., 1994). This has been the case in 30 countries over a period of 40 years. The difference in depression rates between women and men is illustrated in Figure 8.6.

Various reasons have been advanced to account for the generally higher rate of diagnosed depression among women than men, including the following:

1. Because of their social roles, women are freer to express feelings in general and therefore freer to express the negative feelings associated with depression.
2. Women are more likely to be exposed to stresses such as oppression and lack of control that result in depression.
3. Physiological and hormonal differences between men and women predispose women to depression.

In one study that was conducted to determine the reason for the higher rate of depression among women than men, it was found that when men and women were matched in terms of level of depression, the women were not more likely to label themselves as depressed and were not more likely to seek treatment (Amenson & Lewinsohn, 1981). Those findings do not provide support for the "freer to express negative feelings" explanation. Moreover, although numerous demographic variables such as age, income, and education were related to depression, controlling for those variables did not eliminate the sex differences in depression.

It has also been found that women were more frequently exposed to more of the factors that have been shown to be related to depression, such as low education, low income, current illness, and recent illness. As before, however, when males and females were matched in terms of these stress factors, women still had higher rates of depression (Amenson & Lewinsohn, 1981; Radloff & Rae, 1979). Furthermore, a variety of psychological variables such as self-esteem, locus of control, and stressful life events were found to be related to depression, but again, controlling for those did not eliminate the sex differences. The fact that environmental and psychological variables have not been found to be related to the sex differences in depression has led some investigators to speculate that women may respond to stress differently than men or that women may have a greater physiological predisposition for depression than men. *how do estrogen & serotonin work together?*

The differences in rates of depression for men and women may be due at least in part to the effects of marriage. Some investigations have revealed that marriage increased the rate of depression in young women but decreased the rate in young men (Radloff, 1975). That effect is apparently due to the fact that marriage often

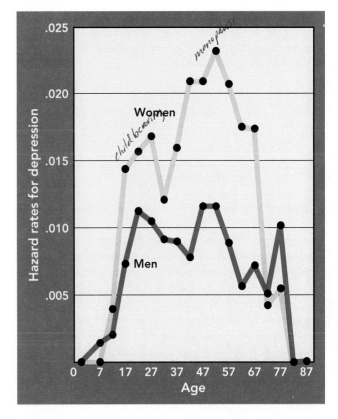

FIGURE 8.6 Women show higher rates of depression than men.
Source: From "Age at First Onset for Nonbipolar Depression" by P. M. Lewinsohn et al., in *Journal of Abnormal Psychology,* Vol. 95, No. 4, 1986. Copyright © 1986 by the American Psychological Association. Reprinted with permission.

provides an additional source of support for men whereas it entails additional demands and responsibilities for women.

The higher rate of depression in women may be due at least in part to the fact that women who become depressed do so more frequently than men (Amenson & Lewinsohn, 1981; Lewinsohn et al., 1994). In one study, the depression levels of a large number of women and men were measured at two points in time about 8 months apart. The prevalence of depression in women was found to be about twice as high as for men (11.4% vs. 5.1% at the first test, 12.8% vs. 7.1% at the second test). More important, the percentage of women who had been depressed before was higher than the percentage of men who had been depressed before (62.3% vs. 48.8%). However, that leaves unanswered the question of why the women were depressed more frequently.

It now appears that the higher rate of depression among women is due to genetic factors. In one study of adult women twin pairs, it was found that environmental factors such as stress did lead to brief transitory periods of depression, but the enduring and recurrent depressions were due to genetics (Kendler, Neale, Kessler, et al., 1993c; Kendler, Walters, et al., 1995). (I will discuss genetics and other causes of depression in greater detail in Chapter 9.)

Age. Depression occurs throughout the life span, but there are two interesting trends to note with regard to age. First, the rates of depression in females and males are the same until adolescence, but *during adolescence (ages about 11 to 15), the rate for females goes up* such that they are twice as likely to suffer from depression (Brooks-Gunn & Petersen, 1991). That change in rate is apparent in Figure 8.6. A number of psychological explanations have been offered for that dramatic change; for example, it may be that the gender differences in personality that develop during adolescence predispose girls to respond to stress with depression (Nolen-Hoeksema & Girgus, 1994). Alternatively, it may be that the biological differences that emerge during adolescence predispose women to depression.

Second, it is noteworthy that in general, the incidence of depression tends to peak sometime in the 40s, but there is also evidence of a second peak in old age (Murphy & Macdonald, 1992). Those patterns are apparent in Figure 8.6.

Social Class. Studies of large numbers of individuals suggest that those in the lower class suffer from depression more than those in higher classes, and the reason seems to be that individuals in the lower class are exposed to more stressors such as unemployment, divorce, lack of education, and poor health (Leff, 1992; Paykel & Cooper, 1992; Smith & Weissman, 1992).

The incidence of depression increases substantially after about age 65. The proportion of individuals who commit suicide also rises in this age group.

Indeed, in one community study of almost 1,000 individuals, it was found that the best predictor of depression was poor health (e.g., injuries, vision problems, hypertension) and that the next best predictor was a high level of stressful life events like moving (Brown et al., 1995). Insofar as individuals in the lower classes get poorer health care and are exposed to more stresses, class can contribute to depression. We will have to keep all these demographic factors in mind later when we examine the various explanations for depression.

Ethnicity. At the present time, there is no evidence that ethnic background per se is related to the level of depression (Weissman et al., 1991). For example, no differences were found among white Americans, African-Americans, or Hispanic-Americans. Indeed, two authors commented that what is most striking is the "similarities rather than the differences among racial groups in rates of major depression" (Smith & Weissman, 1992, p. 121). However, because members of ethnic minority groups may be overrepresented in the lower classes, where there are more stressors and more depression, there may be an indirect relationship between ethnicity and depression (Brown et al., 1995). The important point here is that the differences in depression are due to differences in stressors, not differences in ethnicity per se.

Problems with Memory

Depression is often associated with an *impairment in memory,* and deeper depressions are associated with greater impairments (Burt et al., 1995). The problems with memory can be serious because they interfere with the individual's ability to function effectively. That is a problem itself, but it can also contribute to the depression.

It is interesting to note that depressed individuals generally have more difficulty remembering positive than negative things (Burt et al., 1995). That effect probably stems from the fact that the negative things are more consistent with their moods than are positive things, and the better recall of negative things may in turn contribute to the depression, so the process becomes circular. (I will discuss the possibility that selective memory contributes to depression in Chapter 9 when I discuss the causes of depression.)

There are a number of possible explanations for the memory impairment associated with depression. First, part of the impairment may stem from the fact that the individuals are only focusing on the negative things in their lives and thus not noticing or recalling the positive things. By ignoring positive things, depressed individuals would rule out a lot of memories. Second, because of their lack of energy and motivation, depressed individuals may simply not go through the work that is involved in processing information for storage in memory. As you know, learning requires work, and depressed individuals may not have the energy to do it. Third, it may be that depressed individuals put experiences into memory, but they do not have the energy or motivation to search their memories and make responses. As with other things, they may just give up searching. Generally, then, depression is linked to problems with impairments in memory, and the impairments may be due to selective recall, limited inputting of experiences, or limited outputting of memories (Backman & Forsell, 1994).

Exogenous Versus Endogenous Depressions

We now come to the important and complex problem of determining which depressions stem from psychological causes and which stem from physiological causes. It is clear that some depressions are due primarily to *external* (psychological) factors such as stress, and those depressions are referred to as **exogenous** (eg-ZOJ-uh-nus) **depressions** (Haslam & Beck, 1994). (Exogenous depressions are also sometimes called "reactive" depressions because the individual is supposedly reacting to some environmental problem.) In contrast, it is also clear that other depressions are due primarily to *internal* (physiological) factors such as low levels of certain neurotransmitters, and those depressions are referred to as **endogenous** (en-DOJ-uh-nus) **depressions.**

The distinction between exogenous and endogenous depressions is important in terms of treatment. Specifically, individuals with exogenous (psychologically caused) depressions would probably respond best to psychotherapy, whereas individuals with endogenous (physiologically caused) depressions would probably respond better to drug therapy.

It is clear that the distinction between endogenous and exogenous depressions is important, but a problem arises in determining from which type of depression an individual is suffering. That is, how do you determine whether the cause is psychological or physiological? Initially, investigators attempted to find differences in the symptom patterns of the two types of depression, but that approach did not prove to be particularly fruitful. Indeed, the only consistent difference in symptom patterns is that endogenously depressed individuals are more likely to have a *personal or family history of depression.* (That finding suggests that endogenous depressions are likely to be due to genetic factors, and we will discuss that possibility in Chapter 9.)

Problems with Misattributions. The problem of differentiating between endogenous and exogenous depressions is complicated by the fact that we live in a psychologically oriented society, so when individuals become depressed, they usually look for psychological causes rather than physiological causes. Unfortunately, endogenously depressed individuals are often able to find what *appear* to be psychological causes of their depressions (we can always find some sort of problem in our lives), and by focusing on those, they may throw the diagnostician off the trail of the real cause. A simple example of the misattribution of the cause for an endogenous depression is presented in Case Study 8.3.

The Dexamethasone Suppression Test. Some hope for our ability to distinguish between exogenous and endogenous depression was aroused when a blood test was developed that was thought to be effective in identifying endogenously depressed individuals (Carroll, 1982). The test is called the **dexamethasone** (DEK-suh-METH-uh-sōn) **suppression test (DST),** and it is based on the following principles. First, individuals who are suffering from depressions produce high levels of **cortisol** *(hydrocortisone).* (Cortisol is a hormone that facilitates the breakdown of proteins into glycogen and sugar, thus helping the individual prepare for stress.) Second, dexamethasone suppresses the production of cortisol in exogenously depressed individuals *but not in endogenously depressed individuals.* Therefore, depressed individuals can be given dexamethasone, and then their levels of cortisol can be checked; if cortisol levels do *not* go up, it could be concluded that the depression is of the *exogenous* type. Unfortunately, a substantial amount of research has indicated that the DST test is accurate only 40% to 70% of the time, and therefore the test is not particularly effective for determining who is suffering from an exogenous depression and who is suffering from an endogenous depression. In practical terms, that means that the test is not a good device for determining who will benefit most from drugs versus psychotherapy (American Psychological Association Task Force, 1987, p. 1253).

One simple clinical test that can be used is to ask the individual (or ask yourself if you are depressed), *has there been some really important negative change in your life in the past week or so?* If nothing really dramatic has changed and you have slipped into a depression, the cause is probably biochemical.

Interaction of Exogenous and Endogenous Depressions. To this point, I have presented the question of exogenous versus endogenous depression as an *either-or* situation, but in fact it is probably a *more or less* situation. That is the case because one type of depression can lead to the other type of depression, so often a depression is a combination of both factors. On the one hand, prolonged psychological stress that leads to an exogenous depression can cause physiological changes that eventually result in an endogenous depression. For example, rats and monkeys that were

---

CASE STUDY 8.3

Misattribution of the Cause of an Endogenous Depression

I knew this student rather well, and I became very concerned one morning when he came to me very depressed and tearful, asking whether he could be excused from class that day. I asked what the problem was, and he went on at great length about his mother's serious medical problem and how upsetting it was for him. I was surprised and initially confused by his level of despair because although his mother's problem was a reason for some concern, never before had he been this distressed about it. Indeed, all of the appropriate medical steps were being taken, and until this point he had been dealing very well with the problem.

Another reason for his depression that he mentioned briefly, almost in passing, was that he had been bothered by some neck pains stemming from an automobile accident a few weeks earlier. He said the pain had been so troublesome the previous night that he had taken an additional tablet of the muscle relaxant prescribed by his physician.

We did not discuss his concerns any further, but because of the degree to which he was upset, I excused him from class but asked that he check back with me later in the day. About three hours later, he called me and with some amazement told me how, while sitting in his 11 o'clock class, the "black cloud of gloom" that had been hanging over him all morn-

ing "seemed to just lift and drift away." Everything was now "sunny and bright," and he felt great. I asked about his concern for his mother, and he said that of course he was worried, but maybe he had been a little "unrealistic" about the problem earlier in my office. He was amazed how that "black cloud" had lifted and how great he suddenly felt. My student was clearly back to his old self.

What caused this depression, and why did it suddenly lift?

After thinking about it for a while, I began to wonder whether the depression had been triggered by the pain medication. I knew that the medication he was taking had a half-life (the time it takes to be eliminated from the system and stop having its effects) of about 12 hours, and that would fit with the time that the depression lifted. To test that possibility, the next week my student again took an extra tablet of the medication, and the next morning he was depressed. Clearly, he was very sensitive to the muscle-relaxing medication he had taken, and it was the medication that had triggered the depression the preceding week. The medication caused the depression, but he then misattributed the cause of his depression to a personal or environmental factor. He is now very careful with the medication he takes.

---

exposed to prolonged stress showed changes in the levels of the neurotransmitters that are known to lead to endogenous depression (Raleigh et al., 1984; Weiss et al., 1976). On the other hand, endogenous depressions that stem from physiological factors can lead the individual to behave inappropriately, and that can lead to stress, which contributes to an exogenous depression. For example, an endogenous depression can seriously reduce an individual's ability to function (slowed thinking, lack of activity, constant crying), the inability to function leads to the loss of job or friends, and the loss provides the basis for an exogenous depression. The distinction between endogenous and exogenous depressions is important, but many depressions have both endogenous and exogenous elements, and as you will learn in the chapter on treatment (Chapter 10), treatment may have to be focused on both elements.

Primary Versus Secondary Depression

So far I have discussed individuals for whom depression is a *primary* symptom, but it is important to recognize that for individuals who are suffering from some other preexisting disorder, such as anxiety, alcoholism, schizophrenia, or a physical illness such as cancer, depression can be a *secondary* symptom (McDaniel et al., 1995). That is, depression can be the result of some other disorder rather than a disorder in and of itself. For example, an individual with schizophrenia may have a delusion that he or she is dying and may therefore be depressed, but in this case the depression is a secondary symptom of the schizophrenia. Because the causes of **primary depression** and **secondary depression** are very different, these depressions require different treatments, and the primary-secondary distinction is important when making diagnoses.

Types of Depression

Some years ago it was assumed that depressions that stemmed from different types of situations, such as getting older or giving birth, had different underlying causes and that therefore they had to be treated differently. Indeed, depressions that were related to different types of situations were given different names; for example, depressions resulting from aging were called **involutional depressions,** and depressions that followed giving birth were called **postpartum depressions.** However, later it was generally agreed that the situations in which the depression arose might be different, but the underlying factors (stress, biochemical imbalances) were the same, and therefore the situational labels were dropped. Today, we are at a midpoint between those extremes; no assumptions about differences in underlying causes are made, but in some cases qualifiers are attached to the diagnoses to indicate when the disorder developed. For example, a woman may be diagnosed as suffering from *depression,* and then the qualifier *with postpartum onset* will be added to indicate that the depression began shortly after the woman gave birth.

In the following paragraphs, I will comment on a number of commonly mentioned "types" of depression. Some of these are officially recognized in DSM-IV, others are not, and *some do not exist* (e.g., menopausal depression). Those that do not exist are included only to disabuse you of myths concerning depressions.

Involutional Depression. The term *involutional depression* was traditionally used to refer to the depression associated with the onset of *advanced age.* (*Involutional* refers to the *regressive alteration of the body as it ages.*) The incidence of depression increases substantially after the age of 65, and the predominance of female over male depressives that exists before age 65 diminishes or even reverses with increasing age. Related to the increase in depression with age are the findings that after the age of 65, the proportion of individuals who commit suicide is twice the national average. In view of the fact that life expectancies are increasing, the relationship between depression and aging is particularly important. However, onset of depression during the involutional period is not a qualifier for depression in DSM-IV.

Involutional depression was originally thought to be a consequence of the physiological factors that are associated with aging, and those factors certainly do contribute to depression in many cases. However, now attention has shifted to the role that psychological and cultural factors play. Old age and the approach of old age can be *stressful* periods because of (a) the loss of family, friends, status, and respect; (b) increased illnesses and the financial problems associated with aging; and (c) the fact that the future is limited and may appear bleak. In most Western societies in which progress is fast-paced, older individuals are seen as obsolete and are regarded as "second-class citizens" who must be moved out of the way. These individuals are often deprived of the contributing role so highly prized in our society, thus undermining their self-confidence and self-esteem. Furthermore, because their friends have died, older individuals often have less social support, and that can contribute to depression. In short, like many other depressions, depression during advanced age is due to stress; it is just that the stress is associated with aging.

A classic case of involutional depression is Willy Loman in Arthur Miller's play *Death of a Salesman* (1949). His experience is summarized in Case Study 8.4.

Depression with Seasonal Pattern. There have been numerous reports that the incidence of depression increases during the winter months, and it was generally assumed that winter depressions were simply due to the fact that winter is a dull, depressing time of year. However, some investigators have suggested that for at least some individuals, depression in winter and hypomania (a slight "high") in spring are due to the *changes in the duration and intensity of the light* that are associated with the seasons. For many years, the investigators called the light-related mood shifts the **seasonal affective disorder (SAD)** (Oren & Rosenthal, 1992; Rosenthal et al., 1984), but it is now officially called **depression with seasonal pattern** (American Psychiatric Association, 1994).

Studies of individuals who experienced the winter-related depression over a number of years have revealed a strong relationship between the number of individuals reporting depression in any one month and the average daily amount of sunlight in that month. That relationship is presented in Figure 8.7. As you might expect, the relationship between depression and months of the year is reversed in the Southern Hemisphere, where winter comes in July and August.

If the moods (depression, hypomania) are due to differences in light, then we should be able to change the moods of individuals with SAD by exposing them to more light during the winter. Some success has been reported with that approach, and we will discuss it later when we consider the treatment of mood disorders (see Chapter 10).

Depression with Postpartum Onset. Depression with **postpartum onset** refers to a *relatively severe depression that sets in within 1 month of a woman's giving birth* (American Psychiatric Association, 1994). As mentioned earlier, this was originally thought to be a separate disorder called *postpartum depression,* but now it is thought of as simply a subtype of general depression.

CASE STUDY 8.4

Willy Loman: A Case of Involutional Depression

As the play opens, Willy Loman enters slowly from the right. He is past 60 years of age, dressed modestly, and slowed by fatigue and the weight of two large sample cases he is carrying. He approaches his home, a small house that is dwarfed by the solid mass of the apartment buildings that have been built around it. Night is coming and the light is dim, but even if it were day, it is unlikely that much light could penetrate to the small plot of land on which the house sits. Willy Loman is coming back from a business trip. Actually, we can't really say coming *back,* because he never made it to his destination. He explains to his wife, "I got as far as a little above Yonkers. I stopped for a cup of coffee. Maybe it was the coffee. . . . *(pause)* I suddenly couldn't drive anymore. The car kept going off onto the shoulder, y'know?"

That is how the play opens, and that is how Willy's life is closing—a slow, grinding, uneventful but terrible close. Willy is worn out. He is through. He just can't stay on the road anymore. Like his house, Willy's life and dreams are just shells; the house is starved for light, and Willy is starved for hope.

Willy Loman has been a sales representative for a New York manufacturer for 36 years. He opened up the New England territory for the company, and ever since he has traveled the territory, carrying his heavy sample case and making calls on buyers. Willy has done a good job over the years; he had a good sales record and took pride in the fact that he could walk into any large store in his territory and people knew him. It was important to Willy that he was liked—well liked.

Unfortunately, things began to change. The line of products, the buyers, the boss all changed, and Willy was being left on the sidelines. Willy changed too; he no longer has the energy to keep up. In reflecting on how the buyers respond to him now, Willy comments, "I don't know the reason for it, but they just pass me by. I'm not noticed."

There are other disappointments to be faced—or avoided. Willy has two sons, Biff and Happy, and his dreams revolve around Biff. Biff was immensely successful in high school, athletically and socially, but somehow he never made it after that. Life beyond high school was more than a football field and giddy teenage girls, and Biff just drifted from one dead-end job to another. For years, Willy denied what was really happening to Biff—there was always that great job and success right around the corner—but the fact that Biff is not going to make it is beginning to seep into Willy's awareness like a penetrating and numbing chill. Willy's life is over, and his dreams for his son are fading. Willy, the usually optimistic and outgoing salesman, is shaken. He is slipping into depression.

Facing a bleak present and a worse future, Willy dwells on missed opportunities. Frequently, he thinks about his successful brother Ben, and at one point he says to himself, "Why didn't I go to Alaska with my brother Ben that time! Ben! That was a genius, that man was success incarnate! What a mistake! He begged me to go." But the opportunity is past, and Willy is all that he will ever be—and less than he ever hoped.

Seeking solace, Willy lapses into reminiscences in which he goes back to better times and talks aloud to persons as they were then. Often he relives times when he was a rising salesman and his sons were promising young high school athletes. His devoted

---

Disturbances of mood that are associated with childbirth are widespread and cover a wide range of severity, but not all of the disturbances are classified as disorders. At the low end of severity, some degree of depression, anxiety, irritability, loss of appetite, sleep disturbance, tearfulness, and emotional instability is normal and to be expected after giving birth. Those responses are not considered to constitute a disorder, and they probably occur because of the physical discomfort and stress associated with labor and delivery, the hormonal changes that occur with childbirth, the onset of lactation, the side effects of medication, and the hospital environment.

At an intermediate level of severity is what is often referred to as the **maternity blues.** Those "blues" involve changes in mood and crying, but because the depression is not particularly deep and usually lasts only between 2 and 4 days, the "blues" are not considered to be a disorder (O'Hara, Schlechte, Lewis, & Varner, 1991; O'Hara, Schlechte, Lewis, & Wright, 1991). Between 50% and 80% of new mothers have this reaction.

In contrast, about 0.5% of new mothers suffer from a serious and prolonged depression, and they are diagnosed as suffering from depression with postpartum onset (American Psychiatric Association, 1994; O'Hara et al., 1990; Troutman & Cutrona, 1990). By itself, that

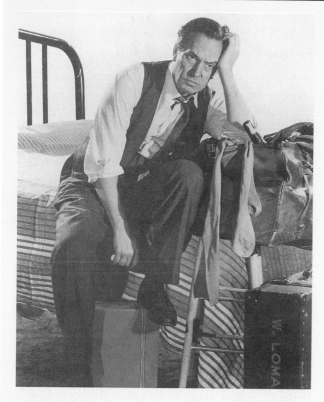

Willy Loman, the main character in Arthur Miller's Death of a Salesman, *developed a deep depression like that experienced by some people as their lives draw to an end.*

wife stands by him and gently coaxes him back to the present. When his sons come home for a visit and see their father's behavior, they are embarrassed and angry with him. His wife defends him: "A small man can be just as exhausted as a great man. He works for a company thirty-six years this March, opens up

unheard-of territories to their trademark, and now in his old age they take his salary away. . . . The man who never worked a day but for your benefit? When does he get the medal for that?"

In an emotional confrontation between the two boys and their mother, she reveals, "He's dying, Biff. . . . He's been trying to kill himself." The boys initially refuse to believe it, but she shows them an automobile insurance report and says, "They have evidence. That all those accidents in the last year— weren't—weren't—accidents." The boys are still unconvinced, so she finally tells them about a short rubber hose she has found in the basement. "There's a little attachment on the end of it. I knew right away. And sure enough, on the bottom of the water heater there's a new little nipple on the gas pipe." Clearly, Willy has attempted suicide and has planned another way.

In many respects, Willy Loman's life is over, and there is nothing left for him. He is slipping into a deep depression, and he is planning to end his life. I won't tell you about the rest of the play. You should read or see it if you can, because it is a very sensitive portrayal of the development of depression in later life. Willy Loman provides the model of what many people go through as they approach the end of their lives. They cannot keep up, so they are left behind, and it is rare that all of their dreams are fulfilled. Confronting that reality, they respond in different ways, and like Willy, many become depressed. The play is titled *Death of a Salesman*, but it could be *Death of Any of Us*.

depression can be serious, but it can also have some tragic consequences. For example, women who suffer from this disorder are often suicidal, and sometimes they have persistent thoughts of killing their babies as well. Indeed, in a growing number of documented cases, the mothers have actually killed their infants (Toufexis, 1988). Despite the fact that depression is frequently associated with giving birth, many women are not aware of the reaction, and it therefore catches them by surprise. Many women apparently try to hide their postpartum depression because they feel guilty about being depressed when tradition dictates that they should be feeling joyful.

The data concerning depression with postpartum onset suggest that it (a) is not related to age, (b) is not related to the number or order of pregnancies, (c) is more likely to recur in subsequent pregnancies following an initial episode of depression, (d) is more likely to occur in women with a history of other psychiatric disorders, and (e) is more likely to occur in women with a family history of other psychiatric disorders (Cox, 1992; Hopkins et al., 1984). Furthermore, a recent study of women who suffered from postpartum and nonpostpartum depression failed to reveal any important differences between the women or their symptoms (Whiffen & Gotlib, 1993). It appears that a

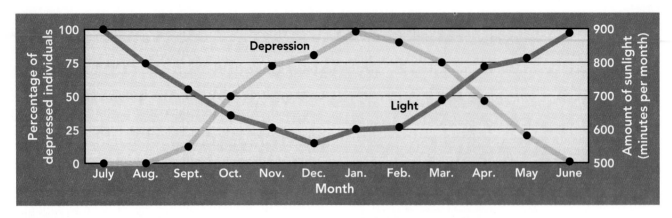

FIGURE 8.7 **For some individuals, there is a relationship between the amount of daily sunlight and their level of depression.**
Source: Adapted from Rosenthal et al. (1984), p. 74, fig. 1.

depression with postpartum onset is like any other depression except that it happens to be triggered by giving birth.

The cause of postpartum depression is complex and not yet clearly understood, but two factors merit attention. On the one hand, it is probably the case that physiological factors such as hormonal fluctuations play a role in postpartum depression because it is known that massive hormonal changes take place after delivery and during the 2-day "latency period" that usually occurs before the onset of the depression. Some indirect evidence concerning the influence of hormones is provided by research indicating that women who suffer from menstrual difficulties (dysmenorrhea and premenstrual syndrome) are more likely to experience postpartum depression (Dalton, 1971; Pitt, 1968, 1973; Yalom et al., 1968). In other words, it seems that women who have difficulty compensating physiological-

ly for normal hormonal changes will have even greater difficulty adjusting to the dramatic changes associated with birth.

On the other hand, the psychological stress associated with increased responsibilities, personal and physical limitations due to child care, changes in the family, and additional financial obligations could trigger the depression or exacerbate a depression stemming from physiological factors. In general, this is how other depressions are explained (see Chapter 9), and that is why depression with postpartum onset is viewed as being like other depressions rather than a unique type of depression (Gotlib et al., 1991; O'Hara, Schlechte, Lewis, & Varner, 1991; O'Hara, Schlechte, Lewis, & Wright, 1991; Whiffen, 1992). As with other depressions, women who experience postpartum depression are at increased risk for a subsequent depression (Philipps & O'Hara, 1991).

Many women experience a brief period of depression after giving birth, a reaction known as the "maternity blues." Depression with postpartum onset is more prolonged, can be severe, and sometimes has tragic consequences. These parents are sitting before the coffin of their 2-month-old son, whom the mother drowned because of her depression.

A mild case of postpartum depression is described in Case Study 8.5.

Menopausal Depression. For many years it was thought that women experienced emotional problems when they ceased menstruating (i.e., when they went through the "change of life"), but recent data do *not* support the existence of a unique **menopausal depression.** For example, in one longitudinal study of more than 500 healthy women, it was found that those who went through natural menopause did not show changes in depression, anxiety, anger, excitability, nervousness, problems with sleeping, Type A behavior, perceived stress, job dissatisfaction, or public self-consciousness (Matthews et al., 1990). Indeed, the only notable change was an increase in "hot flashes." Some of these results are summarized in Figure 8.8. Other investigators have reported similar findings (e.g., Schmidt & Rubinow, 1991). It should be noted that "menopausal depression" is not an official classification and does not appear to be a frequent problem.

Premenstrual Dysphoric Disorder. In recent years a heated debate has raged over whether the DSM should list the so-called **premenstrual dysphoric disorder,** which involves *depression that precedes a woman's monthly menstruation*. Critics of the diagnosis argue that the diagnosis makes "abnormal" a normal part of the female experience and that the existence of this diagnosis says, in essence, that *some women have a psychiatric disorder every month*. Obviously, that would have wide-ranging economic, professional, and political ramifications. The critics also charge that the diagnosis was introduced simply to increase the pool of patients for psychiatrists and psychologists to treat, thereby increasing their income.

In contrast, proponents of the diagnosis point out that, like it or not, there are women who suffer from serious symptoms that are associated with menstruation, and by establishing the diagnosis, we will recognize their suffering as real and give them the opportunity to obtain treatment that can be paid for by insurance. (You cannot be reimbursed for treatment for a disorder that is not listed in the DSM.) The proponents have even gone so far as to suggest that this diagnosis will enhance the women's movement because, with proper treatment, more women will be

---

CASE STUDY 8.5

A First-Person Account of a Mild Postpartum Depression

"A few days after delivering our second child, I started to feel very anxious, guilty, and depressed. Although we had a happy, healthy 4-year-old son, I now felt utterly helpless in taking care of this new infant. I felt very guilty, thinking that I should have prepared myself better by reading books or something. I couldn't remember what to do for specific problems, and I was generally anxious about everything. I felt hopelessly inadequate.

"I wasn't even slightly hungry, and when I did eat, I either vomited or had diarrhea. This made me worry that my baby wasn't getting proper nutrition because I was breast-feeding. I would awake an hour or two before the alarm went off at 6:00 A.M., and I would start worrying that I wouldn't be able to get everything done on time or that I wouldn't be a good wife and mother. It was terrible.

"I was extremely tired and exhausted all of the time, and I cried at the drop of a hat. I couldn't concentrate on anything very long, and I felt entirely overwhelmed with my predicament. I couldn't imagine how my mother had coped with six children and maintained her sanity. I remember that I did a great deal of complaining that I simply couldn't handle all of this, but somehow I kept going enough to get by.

"Meanwhile, the baby picked up on my unhappiness and anxiety and became extremely fussy, which made me feel even less capable as a mother. I recall very clearly a day when a friend stopped in, and although the baby wouldn't stop crying for me, she stopped immediately when my friend took her. My friend persuaded me to call my physician, who prescribed some antidepressants for a couple of weeks. Before long, the symptoms went away, and I was more like my normal self, even after I stopped taking the pills. Soon I was enjoying life again as I had before, and at our 6-week checkup, both the baby and I were in excellent condition and fine spirits."

Note: Although they appeared to be effective in this case, antidepressant drugs are not necessarily effective, nor are they the treatment of choice in all cases of postpartum depression. Treatment is discussed in Chapter 10.

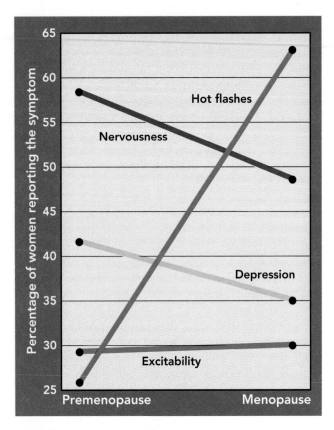

FIGURE 8.8 Natural menopause did not lead to increases in emotional problems.
Source: Data from Matthews et al. (1990), p. 350, tab. 4.

able to compete more effectively. Finally, proponents of the diagnosis point out that the fact that some women suffer from the disorder does not mean that all women do, and they draw an analogy to schizophrenia: The fact that schizophrenia exists does not mean that everyone suffers from it. Because of the controversy, in DSM-IV the premenstrual dysphoric disorder is included in an appendix of disorders that require "further study."

At present, to be diagnosed as suffering from the premenstrual dysphoric disorder, over the course of a year a woman must experience at least five of the following symptoms shortly before menstruation, the symptoms must remit within a few days after menstruation, and the symptoms must be severe enough that they interfere with the woman's normal functioning: (a) depression; (b) anxiety; (c) sudden mood swings; (d) anger or irritability; (e) decreased interest in things such as work, school, friends, and hobbies; (f) difficulty concentrating; (g) lethargy; (h) appetite changes; (i) sleep disturbances; (j) feeling overwhelmed or out of control; and (k) physical symptoms associated with the menstrual cycle (e.g., breast tenderness, headaches, weight gain). The pattern of symptoms must persist

over a number of months. Note that this diagnosis does *not* refer to what is generally called the *premenstrual syndrome (PMS)* that many women experience; the premenstrual dysphoric syndrome is a much more extreme and serious pattern of symptoms. Accurate figures are not yet available, but it is estimated that this disorder might afflict between 3% and 5% of the female population.

Depressive Personality Versus Dysthymia

For some years there has been controversy over the existence of a **depressive personality** that is separate from the depressive *disorder* (Hirschfeld & Shea, 1992; Phillips et al., 1990). Early versions of the DSM included an "affective personality" in the section on personality disorders (the term *affect* was then used to refer to depression or mood), but in later editions of the DSM, that designation was dropped and *dysthymia* was introduced to reflect mild depression (see Figure 8.1). There have been attempts to distinguish a depressive personality from the depressive disorder, but the distinction, if any, is not clear (Klein, 1990). At best, the depressive personality may represent one end of a continuum of severity running from depressive personality through dysthymia to depressive disorder. That continuum might also reflect steps in the development of a major depression, and there is now evidence that dysthymia often precedes a major depression (Lewinsohn et al., 1991).

This concludes the discussion of the symptoms and issues associated with the depressive disorder. Next I will examine the symptoms and issues associated with the bipolar disorder.

TOPIC 11
THE BIPOLAR DISORDER

The *bipolar disorder* is the second of the two major mood disorders, and it differs from the depressive disorder in that it involves *swings of mood between mania and depression* (Perris, 1992). Because of those shifts, the bipolar disorder was formerly referred to as the *manic-depressive disorder*. There are two types of the bipolar disorder (American Psychiatric Association, 1994). The **Type I bipolar disorder** involves depression and mania, whereas the **Type II** bipolar disorder involves depression and *hypomania*, which is simply a mild form of mania. In other words, in the Type II disorder, the manic component is less serious. In this chapter, I will focus primarily on the Type I disorder. (There are apparently a small number of individuals who experience mania but not depression, but because they are so rare, no separate diagnostic class has been established for them.)

SYMPTOMS OF THE BIPOLAR DISORDER

I described depression in detail in the first part of the chapter, so here I will focus only on *mania*. In many individuals with bipolar disorders, mania may have been developing for some time, and it may be quite serious before anyone realizes that there is a problem. We are often slow to recognize a manic episode because the individual is not upset, anxious, or depressed. Rather, the individual is happy, carefree, unconcerned about potential problems, self-reliant, apparently productive, and often in a playful, festive mood. During this early stage, the individual may be referred to as *hypomanic,* reflecting the low (hypo-) level of mania.

Mood Symptoms

During manic episodes, the predominant mood is *euphoria.* The patient is excited, excessively happy, emotionally expansive, and generally "flying high." DSM-IV suggests that irritability can also be present during a manic episode, but the irritability is probably only a response to the restraints imposed by people around the manic individual to limit inappropriate behavior. In other words, for the manic individual, "everything is coming up roses," but the individual may become irritated or angry if someone tries to clip those roses. For example, a 200-lb manic patient became irritated and hostile when I objected to the fact that he had torn down my office drapes. He did not like the way the office was decorated, and in his expansive mood he had decided to redo it for me!

Cognitive Symptoms

The cognitive symptoms associated with a manic episode include *inflated self-esteem* and *grandiosity.* Patients with mania have completely unrealistic beliefs about what they can accomplish. One manic person I knew had an idea for a new type of automobile engine that he thought would revolutionize the industry and make him a millionaire overnight. When major problems with his idea were pointed out to him, he brushed them aside as "minor details" that would be worked out later.

Another important cognitive symptom seen in mania is *distractibility* and *fragmentation of attention.* In their euphoric and expansive moods, manic individuals cannot keep their attention focused on any one thing for long, and they are continually shifting their attention or getting distracted by other ideas, problems, or plans. This is often referred to as a *manic flight of ideas.* In some cases, the flight of ideas is so rapid and the shifts from topic to topic are so fast that it is difficult to follow the manic person's train of thought. The inventor mentioned in the preceding paragraph was so busy recruiting investors and buying equipment to manufacture his new engine that he never took time to think the idea through carefully enough to realize that it could never work. Because of their inability to focus attention and because they keep shifting from task to task, most manic patients are ineffective and do not accomplish much. Sometimes the flight of ideas and resulting confusion can be mistaken for a schizophrenic-type thought disorder, and hence manic patients are occasionally misdiagnosed.

Some patients with the bipolar disorder also have *delusions* like those seen in schizophrenia. One manic patient talked very rapidly and jumped from topic to topic as she told me that she was married to Burt Reynolds, she was the first woman president of the United States, and her three daughters had been murdered in the hospital. Delusions such as those are not necessarily a component of the bipolar disorder but are sometimes seen in conjunction with it. When this combination of disorders occurs, the patient might be diagnosed as suffering from a **mood disorder with psychotic features.**

Motor Symptoms

The motor behavior of manic individuals parallels their excited cognitive behavior. The manic individual runs from one project to the next. During a particularly severe manic episode, one person drove through the downtown area of a large city at breakneck speed, side-swiping cars and driving wildly down sidewalks to get around cars at intersections. He had "important business deals to close" and was in a great hurry.

Their high levels of activity and exaggerated self-importance can lead some individuals with mania to very inappropriate behavior. Notable in this regard are telephoning sprees, hypersexuality, and spending money. Because they are involved in so many things and because of their exaggerated confidence in their ultimate success, manic individuals often spend very large amounts of money (usually using credit) in short periods of time. In some cases, they will quickly go through their life savings and run themselves deep into debt.

Mania does not always result in ineffective or inappropriate behavior. I once knew a very creative patient

CASE STUDY 8.6

A Bipolar Episode in a 21-Year-Old Student

"My bipolar disorder began one summer while I was living on a ranch in New Mexico. After about a month there, I began to feel increasingly self-conscious, unhappy, isolated, unmotivated, and listless. I attributed all of these symptoms to being in a new part of the country. As the depression worsened, I stopped interacting with others or participating in activities. I tried to escape in sleep, but though I spent my spare time in bed, I had great difficulty actually sleeping. I became obsessed with a desire to go away somewhere to be by myself, and I would wander aimlessly through the countryside, fantasizing about suicide. Ultimately, I spent 13 days huddled in a pile of rocks on the edge of a field, hoping to die of starvation or illness through exposure. But because I was unwilling to endure another hot day and cold night, I finally walked (or crawled) back to the ranch. My father had come to the ranch to find me when he learned that I was missing, and he brought me back home.

"After getting home, I was unable to hold a job, and I constantly thought about killing myself; I wished I were alone and unbothered, in a deep, dark hole. I was seeing a psychotherapist, and I spent the hourly sessions staring at his carpet without speaking. Toward the end of summer, though, my mood began to lift. I noticed that I wasn't as preoccupied with death and that I felt that I might have a future after all. I did not associate this improvement with psychological counseling but rather with the idea that I had somehow paid my dues and now had been given some sort of earned emotional reward. Though I am not religious, I remember feeling a spiritual significance about this; something had clicked deep inside my head, and I wasn't about to question it.

"I started to feel better and better. Within a few weeks, I was interacting well with my family, doing quite well at a job given to me by a friend of my father's, and planning to find my own apartment.

My sessions with the psychotherapist became increasingly animated, and every day I felt happier and more positive. I found an apartment and quit my job because now it seemed too boring for me. I began to learn to play the guitar and got a job in an entertainment booking agency. I soon quit to start my own agency and began leading a very active and aggressive social life. I was feeling amazingly energetic, sharp, confident, and powerful—as if I could accomplish anything I wanted to, and very quickly!

"The psychotherapist had by now become concerned about me, and he wanted me to promise to return the next week, when he would prescribe some lithium for me.* However, by this time my head was constantly spinning with new ideas and plans. My ability to concentrate was intense but changed focus rapidly. I had no concern for ethical and legal responsibilities and exercised no financial restraint. I wrote bad checks to my landlord and to Amtrak and took a train to California with my guitar and about one dollar in my pocket.

"When it became clear to me that my erratic behavior was alienating my college friends in California, particularly a woman with whom I had fallen in love, I decided to return home and commit myself to a hospital. At this time, I absolutely believed that two things were true: that I was going to father the next messiah and that this idea was crazy. After coming home, I became so agitated—feeling ready to explode—that my mother drove me to the emergency room at the medical center, where I was given an injection of 300 ml of Thorazine.† I was handcuffed by the police and taken to the psychiatric ward. The next morning, I began receiving lithium carbonate; 3 weeks later, I was released."

*Lithium is a drug that is commonly used to treat the bipolar disorder (see Chapter 10).
†Thorazine (chlorpromazine) is a drug that is often used to treat schizophrenia. It was used in this case because when injected, it has an immediate and strong sedating effect (see Chapter 13).

who was an interior decorator. Whenever she had a severe manic episode (about once a year), she would completely redecorate her home by herself. Almost without stopping to sleep, she would repaint and repaper her entire home in less than a week. She would use bright, cheery colors and do very creative things. I often envied her energy and results. Her success was probably due to the fact that her activities during the

manic phase (painting and wallpapering) did not require sustained intellectual effort.

Artists perhaps, also?

Somatic Symptoms

The only consistent somatic symptom seen in mania is a *decreased need for sleep.* Individuals suffering from mania are constantly "fired up" and "on the move," and they sleep very little. These individuals ignore fatigue, aches, pains, and other somatic problems that may actually exist.

Case Study 8.6 presents a student's description of his first experience with the bipolar disorder.

ISSUES ASSOCIATED WITH THE BIPOLAR DISORDER

Prevalence

The bipolar disorder occurs in about 1.5% of the population (Kessler et al., 1994). If the less seriously disturbed (cyclothymic) individuals are included, the percentage of individuals who have such disorders is probably twice as high, but that is still not as high as the other major disorders such as the depressive disorder and schizophrenia. We are also less likely to see individuals with the bipolar disorder than individuals with most other disorders because in most cases the bipolar disorder can be effectively treated with medication, and therefore many patients have only one or two relatively short attacks (see Chapter 10).

Sociocultural Factors

Gender. The bipolar disorder occurs about equally in men and women (Kessler et al., 1994). That is very different from the depressive disorder, in which women outnumber men 2 to 1.

Age. The risk period for onset is commonly believed to extend from about 15 to 60 years of age, with the most frequent onset occurring between ages 25 and 30 (Carlson et al., 1974; Krauthammer & Klerman, 1979; Loranger & Levine, 1978; Winokur et al., 1969). That age of onset is somewhat earlier than for the depressive disorder, which most often begins in the late 30s to mid-40s. Elderly individuals may experience their first manic episode late in life, but the symptoms in those individuals are probably due to some other diseases or medication rather than the bipolar disorder (Young & Klerman, 1992).

The manic and depressive episodes of the bipolar disorder are usually separated by normal periods, and the episodes recur, establishing a cycle of manic, normal, depressive, normal, manic, normal, and so on. If not treated, the length of the normal periods between episodes decreases and the length of each episode increases (Klerman & Barrett, 1973). Once a bipolar disorder sets in, it can last for many years.

Social Class. Whereas depression is found more frequently among lower-class individuals, class does not seem to be a factor in the bipolar disorder (Krauthammer & Klerman, 1979; Monnelly et al., 1974; Weissman & Myers, 1978; Woodruff et al., 1971).

Bipolar and Depressive Disorders as Different Disorders

Because bipolar and depressive disorders share the symptom of depression, it is tempting to assume that they are actually one disorder with the bipolar patients simply having the additional symptom of mania. However, as indicated in Table 8.1, the two disorders show a variety of differences other than symptoms, and these differences suggest that these are two separate disorders. If they were the same disorder, it would be difficult to understand why there are sex differences in one and not the other. So these appear to be separate disorders, but as with many other disorders, we will probably find that they are different but overlapping. Finally, it should be noted that some cases of depression appear to "convert" to the bipolar disorder, but what is really going on is that the individuals had a bipolar disorder all along but to that point had only shown the depressive symptoms (Akiskal et al., 1995; Coryell et al., 1995).

TABLE 8.1 **Differences Between Bipolar and Depressive Disorders**

	Bipolar Disorder	**Depressive Disorder**
Symptoms	Depression and mania	Depression
Incidence	About 1.5%	12% or more
Gender Ratio	Equal	Twice as many females
Genetics	Relatives have the bipolar disorder	Relatives have the depressive disorder

Mania as a Secondary Symptom

It is important to distinguish between mania that is part of a bipolar disorder and **secondary mania,** which is the side effect of a drug or the result of some other disease (Silverstone & Hunt, 1992). For example, secondary mania can be a side effect of some antidepressant drugs. In those cases, it appears that the drugs "overshoot the mark" and bring the patient out of depression past a normal mood state and into mania. In making diagnoses, then, care must be taken not to diagnose an individual as suffering from a bipolar disorder when in fact the individual's mania is the side effect of a drug or a symptom of another disease.

Cycle Time

A frequent question is, how long does it take individuals with a bipolar disorder to go through one cycle of mania and depression? The answer is that there is great variability in cycle time. In one study of more than 900 individuals over a 5-year period, it was found that about 35% of the individuals went through only one cycle, whereas about 1% of the individuals went through 22 cycles—about one cycle every 3 months (Coryell et al., 1992). These results are presented graphically in Figure 8.9. These figures may underestimate the natural course of the cycles because most of the patients were on medication to control their disorders.

In recent years, some interest has been shown in individuals who show **rapid cycling,** defined as four or more cycles per year (Bauer, Calabrese, et al., 1994; Coryell et al., 1992; Wehr et al., 1988; Wolpert et al., 1990). In general, rapid cycling is more likely to occur in women, and it does not show a genetic pattern (the bipolar disorder runs in families, but relatives who have the bipolar disorder do not show concordance for rapid cycling). Also, individuals who do show rapid cycling are less likely than others to recover in the first or second year of treatment but are equally likely to recover thereafter. Rather than reflecting a different type of bipolar disorder, rapid cycling probably indicates a more severe or more virulent case.

Creativity

Over the years there have been many speculations about a possible connection between mental disorders and creativity. In general, the underlying notion has been that because individuals with mental disorders often view the world differently and because creativity often involves putting things or ideas together in a different way, abnormality may lead to creativity.

There have been many anecdotal reports of artists who suffered from serious disorders, but it was not until relatively recently that objective research on the connection was reported. One problem for researchers in this area was to come up with a definition of creativity, but that problem was avoided by identifying individuals such as artists and writers who others generally agreed were creative (whatever that might mean). In other words, rather than trying to determine whether creativity was correlated with abnormality, investigators identified creative individuals and then attempted to determine whether they suffered from more disorders than other individuals. This approach has yielded two general findings. First, creative individuals appear to suffer from mood disorders

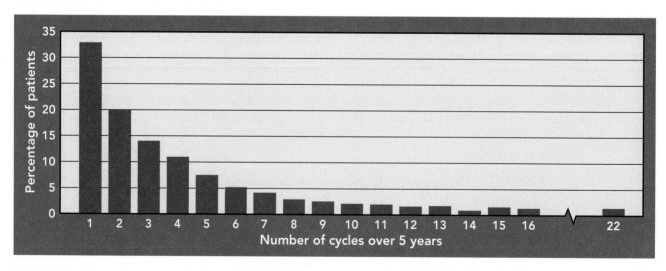

FIGURE 8.9 The number of cycles experienced by patients with the bipolar disorder shows wide variability.
Source: From "Rapidly Cycling Affective Disorder: Demographics, Diagnosis, Family History, and Course" by W. Coryell et al., in *Archives of General Psychiatry,* Vol. 49, February 1992. Reprinted by permission of the American Medical Society.

Many creative individuals have suffered from the bipolar disorder. The American writer Samuel Clemens, known as Mark Twain, described his mental condition as "periodical and sudden changes of mood . . . from deep melancholy to half-insane tempests and cyclones."

more than other individuals, and second, creative individuals seem most likely to suffer from the bipolar disorder (Andreasen, 1987; Jamison, 1993, 1994, 1995; Ludwig, 1994; Schildkraut et al., 1994). For example, in one study of creative writers, 80% had experienced at least one depressive episode, and 43% had a history of mania. In that regard, it is noteworthy that the incidence of mania in the general population is only about 1.5%, so the rate of mania in the writers was almost 30 times higher than what it is in the general population. In one study, it was even found that the more creative an individual was judged to be, the greater was his or her history of abnormal behavior. Another disorder that was often found to be linked to creativity was substance abuse (alcoholism), but as you will learn later, in many cases, substance abuse is linked to mood disorders (see Chapter 17).

Given that there seems to be a strong relationship between creativity and the bipolar disorder, the ques-

tion is, why? The answer to that question is not completely clear, but it has been argued that symptoms of the bipolar disorder such as grandiosity, expansive thoughts, high activity level, and the ability to function on a limited amount of sleep could all contribute to the production of creative works. That is, the individual ignores the restraints on what "should" be done and also produces more of everything, thus enhancing the likelihood of producing something unique (creative). The link between creativity and the bipolar disorder raises an interesting question with regard to treatment: If treatment can eliminate mania, is it appropriate to treat individuals with the bipolar disorder and eliminate their mania and possibly their creativity, thereby depriving them and us of their productions (Jamison, 1995a, 1995b)? How much great art or literature or music would we have lost if all people with the bipolar disorder had been effectively treated for their mania?

Having provided this general description of the symptoms and issues associated with the mood disorders as background, I can now go on to consider a specific problem that is often related to depression, suicide.

TOPIC III
SUICIDE

Closely linked to mood disorders is the important topic of **suicide,** so here I will discuss the basic issues that are associated with suicide. In the next chapter, after I discuss the causes of mood disorders, I will discuss the causes of suicide.

It is important to recognize at the outset that suicide is a topic of major concern. It is one of the 10 leading causes of death in the United States, and it is the second leading cause of death among young males. Some 30,000 individuals in the United States will commit suicide this year. The magnitude of the problem is actually much greater than the statistics suggest because many suicides are disguised as accidents and therefore go unrecognized. Furthermore, it is estimated that there are at least 8 to 10 attempted suicides for each one completed. The magnitude of the problem is clearly reflected in the findings of a study of college students: 26% of the students had considered suicide in the preceding 12 months, 2% had attempted suicide in the preceding 12 months, and 10% had attempted suicide at some time in the past (Meehan et al., 1992). Fortunately, many of the attempts by younger individuals fail (especially those that involve overdoses of drugs that are not lethal).

However, all too many of the attempts are successful. In view of the pervasiveness and seriousness of the problem, it is important that we give suicide thorough and careful consideration.

Issues Associated with Suicide

Sociocultural Factors

Gender. Women are three times more likely to *attempt* suicide than men, but men are three times more likely to *succeed* in committing suicide. The reason for the sex difference in attempted suicide is not clear, but it may be that women are more likely to suffer from depression than men, and depression plays a major role in suicide. The higher success rate among men reflects the fact that men use more violent techniques (guns, jumps from buildings) than women (overdoses, wrist slashing), and the more violent techniques are more likely to be successful.

Age. In almost all cultures suicide rates increase with age (Lester, 1991b). In the United States the greatest increase comes between the ages of 65 and 84; in fact, for individuals over the age of 65, the suicide rate is twice the national average (Kirsling, 1986). The generally high rate of suicide in older adults is due primarily to the very high rate of suicide among white males (McIntosh, 1992). Those findings are reflected in Figure 8.10. Older individuals are more likely to be successful in their suicide attempts than their younger counterparts, probably because they are more knowledgeable and because they are more likely to be absolutely resolute about what they are doing.

Ethnicity. There are dramatic differences among cultures in the rate of suicide, ranging from a high of about 45 suicides per 100,000 persons in countries such as Hungary and Germany to a low of less than 1 per 100,000 persons in countries such as Nicaragua and Egypt (Diekstra, 1990). There are a number of explanations for the differences. For example, suicide is a more acceptable act in some cultures than in others; indeed, in some countries like Japan, it is a normal and even an *honorable* thing to do (Domino & Takahashi, 1991). These differences across countries or cultures often appear to be due to differences in religious views concerning suicide. Specifically, in Catholicism, suicide is a mortal sin, whereas in Buddhism, it is an acceptable way to resolve serious personal problems (Iga, 1993).

Cultural differences in stress can also contribute to differences in suicide (Hawton, 1992). In countries such

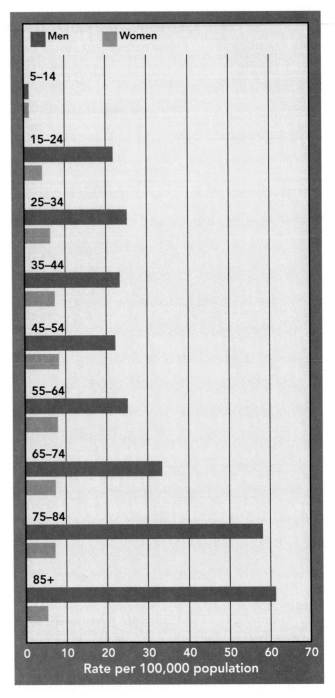

FIGURE 8.10 Men have a higher rate of suicide, which increases with age.
Source: Adapted from McIntosh (1992), p. 20, fig. 3.

as Greece and Spain where stress is apparently low, so are the suicide rates. Cultural differences in suicide also correspond to the rate of stressful cultural change that is taking place. For example, when countries go through economic depressions or dramatic social upheavals such as those we are seeing in the countries that once made up the Soviet Union, suicide rates increase.

The third contributor to differences in suicide is the difference in the degree to which depression is successfully identified and treated. Because suicide often stems from depression, the effective treatment of depression reduces the rate of suicide.

Problems in Assessing Suicide Rates

Some reports have suggested that the overall rate of suicide is increasing, and that the rate among adolescents has tripled over the past 30 years to the point that the term *epidemic* has been used to describe the problem among adolescents (Centers for Disease Control, 1986). However, the data may be somewhat misleading because at least part of the apparent increase among adolescents appears to be due to the possibility that medical examiners are becoming more willing to designate an adolescent's death as due to suicide rather than to an "accident" (Gist & Welch, 1989; Males, 1991a, 1991b). That is, it appears that today there is less of a tendency to "cover up" a suicide by calling it an accident. This conclusion is based on the fact that the overall death rate (accidents plus suicides) has remained flat in the 15–19 and 20–44 age groups. So if the suicide rate for adolescents were increasing, the accident rate for adolescents would have to be decreasing, but we have no evidence of that. It is more likely that the apparent increase in suicides is due to a change in labeling the cause of death.

The increase in reporting of suicides as suicides rather than as accidents may be due to changes in social factors. The influence of social factors was demonstrated in a study in which different medical examiners were given the same set of simulated cases and asked to decide on the causes of death (Jarvis et al., 1991). The results indicated that examiners were more likely to conclude that a death was due to suicide if the examiners lived in small towns and did not have a religious affiliation than if they lived in large cities and were Roman Catholic. Clearly, attitudes about suicide influence our willingness to report it, and as those attitudes change, we may be more willing to admit to a problem that has been with us for a long time.

Suicides, Covert Suicides, and Suicide Gestures

Many suicides are disguised and hence are not recognized as suicides. **Covert (kō-VURT) suicide** occurs when people do not want others to know what they have done either because they are ashamed or because their life insurance policies will not pay off following a suicide. Automobile accidents are one method of covert suicide (Bollen & Phillips, 1981; Phillips, 1977, 1979). Individuals who use cars when attempting suicide will intentionally drive into the paths of other cars,

trucks, or trains. For example, during two of her depressive episodes, a woman I knew drove her car at high speed into a bridge support in an attempt to kill herself, but both cases were listed as accidents rather than suicide attempts. There has also been some speculation that some individuals try to provoke the police into shooting them as a means of committing suicide.

In sharp contrast to covert suicides are **suicide gestures,** in which individuals engage in obvious suicidal behavior but do not really want to kill themselves. For example, individuals may take overdoses of pills, but not enough to kill, or may slash their wrists, but not deeply enough to bleed to death. Individuals who make suicide gestures generally make them in such a way that other people will find out. They may leave the empty pill bottle out or allow others to notice their bandaged wrists. For some individuals, suicide gestures are *cries for help* (Farberow & Shneidman, 1961). The individuals are desperate but do not know how to ask for help, are too ashamed to ask for help directly, or have asked for help and were ignored because others did not realize

For some people, suicide gestures are cries for help. In other cases, a suicide gesture is an attempt to manipulate or control others.

how upset they were. In those cases, the suicide gesture is a way of dramatizing the seriousness of the problem and asking for help indirectly.

For others, suicide gestures are attempts to *manipulate or control the people around them.* For example, an individual abandoned by a lover may make a suicide gesture in an attempt to get the lover to come back. In general, individuals who make suicidal gestures tend to be female, younger, less mature, and less depressed than individuals who actually intend to die, and suicide gestures tend to be more impulsive and less lethal than actual attempts (McHugh & Goodell, 1971; Weissman, 1974). Nevertheless, it is

often difficult to distinguish between a suicide gesture and an attempted suicide. Moreover, even when it is clear that an attempt was only a gesture, the behavior should not be taken lightly. No matter what the motive, a gesture is a sign of a serious problem, and in making the gesture, the individual might accidentally succeed.

Some suicide attempts that fail nevertheless have serious consequences. For example, taking an overdose of certain drugs can lead to long-term problems such as brain damage. A particularly distressing example of such a consequence is presented in Case Study 8.7. This case also illustrates the difficulty of determining

---

CASE STUDY 8.7
An Unsuccessful Suicide Attempt

Ann was a very bright, attractive, personable, and energetic single woman who was 52 years old. She was an avid jogger and swimmer and was in excellent physical condition. As a physical therapist at a large metropolitan hospital, Ann specialized in working with patients who were severely disabled by strokes or spinal cord injuries. She worked with patients whom others despairingly referred to as "almost vegetables."

One spring, Ann checked into a general hospital for a complete head-to-toe medical checkup. She did not complain of any particular problem; she just told the physician that it was time for a checkup. Early in the morning of Ann's second day in the hospital, a nurse walking by saw Ann standing on the narrow sill outside her 15th-floor window. As she stood there, she was lifting herself up and down on her toes "like you do just before you take a dive." The nurse walked quietly up behind Ann, grabbed her, and pulled her back into the room. Ann was subsequently sent to a psychiatric hospital for evaluation.

Ann was annoyed that she was suspected of attempting to commit suicide. She said that she had been "trying to get some fresh air" and was simply doing her "breathing exercises" on the sill. She denied any thoughts of suicide and pointed out that because of her excellent condition and balance, there was no chance of her falling. The evaluation did not reveal any signs of psychopathology, and Ann, knowing hospital routines, was helpful and compliant, a model patient.

One aspect of Ann's record that concerned the hospital staff was that both her mother and her older sister had died of heart attacks in their mid-50s, an age that Ann was quickly approaching. It was

suggested that Ann might believe that she would also experience a premature heart attack that would leave her in a condition like that of the patients with whom she worked every day. When Ann was questioned about that, she adamantly denied any such concerns and pointed out that if there was a potential problem, she had done the right thing by going into the hospital for a thorough checkup.

There was considerable debate among the hospital staff over whether or not Ann was in fact suicidal and what to do about it. Some argued that she had "too much ego strength" to commit suicide, others argued that "it takes a lot of ego strength to commit suicide," and others questioned how long this otherwise healthy patient could be kept in the hospital even if there was a consensus that she was suicidal. She was not willing to participate in therapy ("Why should I? I don't have a problem!"), and it did not seem reasonable to keep her locked up for the rest of her life.

While being evaluated, Ann had been assigned to an open ward, the door of which was watched by an attendant so that only patients with passes could leave. Three days after Ann's case conference, the attendant was briefly drawn away from the door by a scuffle between two adolescent patients, and during his brief absence, Ann walked quietly off the ward. She went directly to the center of the hospital, where there was a large circular staircase that went up four floors. She went up to the top floor, climbed up on the banister, and threw herself headfirst down the stairwell. Ann landed on her back and broke her neck. She survived but was paralyzed from the neck down. Today Ann is a complete invalid, existing in the very state she sought to avoid through her suicide attempt.

TABLE 8.2 Predictors of Suicide Risk

Variable	High-Risk Category
Age	Older
Occupation	Higher-status
Financial resources	More
Emotional disorder in family	Depression, alcoholism
Sexual orientation	Bisexual, homosexual
Previous psychiatric hospitalization	More admissions
Result of previous help	Negative or variable
Threatened financial loss	Yes
Special stress	Yes
Sleep	More sleep per night
Weight change	Gain or loss
Ideas of persecution	Yes
Suicidal impulses	Yes
Interviewer's reaction to person	Negative

Source: Adapted from Motto et al. (1985), p. 683, tab. 3.

who will and will not commit suicide and the problem of what to do with individuals who are only suspected of suicidal intentions.

Warnings and Notes

In many cases, the decision to commit suicide is not made quickly, and often the individual contemplating suicide will give some warning. Interviews with friends and relatives of individuals who committed suicide indicated that between 60% and 70% of the victims had openly said that they wanted to commit suicide (direct threats) and another 20% to 25% had talked about the topic of suicide (indirect indication of their intentions) (Farberow & Simon, 1975; Rudestam, 1971). These suicide signals can be indications of what the individuals plan to do, or they can be a means of letting others know how upset they are in an indirect attempt to get help. *Remarks about committing suicide should always be taken seriously.* Ignoring a plea for help can further convince the individual of the hopelessness of the situation. In one investigation it was found that about half of people who heard suicide threats simply denied the importance of what they were hearing and did nothing (Rudestam, 1971). In some cases, the individuals who heard the threats actually *avoided* the suicidal individuals thereafter. The other half of the individuals who heard the threats became appropriately concerned and either argued with the suicidal individuals or suggested that they seek help.

The notes left by individuals who commit suicide have attracted a lot of interest, and hundreds of such notes have been collected and analyzed (Cohen & Fiedler, 1974; Farberow & Simon, 1975; Shneidman &

Farberow, 1957; Tuckman et al., 1959). Unfortunately, these notes add little to our understanding of suicide. For the most part, they are rather matter-of-fact statements apologizing for the suicide, explaining why the suicide was necessary, saying good-bye to loved ones, and indicating the desired disposition of personal property.

Characteristics of Individuals Who Commit Suicide

Numerous attempts have been made to develop descriptions of "typical" suicidal individuals or to develop checklists to help identify individuals who are at high risk. These attempts have rarely been effective for predicting individual cases because so many idiosyncratic factors enter into each case, and we must therefore be very cautious in applying any such profiles or formulas. However, some studies have provided us with general descriptions of individuals who are at risk for suicide, and they deserve some attention.

In one investigation, almost 3,000 depressed or suicidal inpatients were interviewed with regard to a wide variety of variables. Two years after the patients were discharged, a follow-up study was conducted to determine who had committed suicide (Motto et al., 1985). Analyses were then conducted to determine which variables were the best predictors of subsequent suicide; the results are presented in Table 8.2. In reviewing these variables, it is important to realize that most individuals who commit suicide do not have all or even most of these characteristics.

In addition to the characteristics noted in the table, membership in certain groups is also related to a higher risk of suicide. For example, adolescents, the elderly, alcoholics, individuals living alone, individuals from some Native American tribes, and professionals such as physicians, dentists, lawyers, and psychologists are also at higher risk for suicide (Schaar, 1974; Wekstein, 1979). We will discuss the causes for suicide in greater detail in Chapter 9, but the increased rate of suicide in these groups appears to be due to the fact that they experience higher levels of stress and depression or lack social support.

Seasons and Day of the Week

As early as 1897, a survey of numerous European countries revealed that without exception, the six warmest months had a higher suicide rate than the six coldest months (Durkheim, 1897/1951). The rate would rise slowly from January through June and then decrease. More recent findings are consistent with the earlier ones and indicate that suicides peak in the late spring or early summer. The reason for this pattern is not clear, but it may be that the optimism many people feel in the spring contrasts sharply with the depression and hopelessness felt by suicidal individuals. The contrast may heighten their despair and may increase the likelihood of suicide—but that is only a speculation.

Twenty years ago, suicides were not more likely to occur on any particular day, but now suicides are most likely to occur on Mondays (Maldonado & Kraus, 1991). The stress of "facing the workweek" may be responsible for the effect, and the change over time may be due to the increasing number of women in the workforce. Finally, note that there is no consistent evidence for the myth that suicides are related to the phases of the moon (Campbell & Beets, 1978).

Myths About Suicide

Table 8.3 presents a number of popular myths about suicide. Recognizing that these statements are not true

"A Little Madness in the Spring Is wholesome even for the King"
—E. Dickenson
(died/suicide)

TABLE 8.3 Myths About Suicide

Myth	Reality
People who talk about suicide won't commit suicide.	Untrue. Between 60% and 80% of persons who commit suicide have communicated their intent ahead of time.
All behavior related to suicide is in the same class of behavior.	Untrue. Some people are trying to kill themselves, while others may be making suicide gestures that are calls for help or attempts to communicate the depth of their despair. There may be different motivations, but all suicide-related behavior must be taken seriously.
Only very depressed persons commit suicide.	Untrue. Many people who commit suicide are depressed, but very depressed people often do not have enough energy to commit suicide, and often they commit suicide when they are getting better. Also, reaching the decision to commit suicide can relieve stress and depression, so people may appear less depressed just before committing suicide. Finally, suicide could be the result of a delusion, or it could be a well-thought-out solution to a problem unrelated to depression.
Protestants are more likely to commit suicide than Catholics.	Untrue. The evidence concerning this is mixed, but overall there does not appear to be a difference in rates in these religious groups.
Suicide rates are higher in rainy than sunny months.	Untrue. If anything, there is some evidence that suicide rates increase as spring arrives.
Suicidal tendencies are inherited.	Untrue. The fact that suicide "runs in families" is probably due to the fact that there is a genetic basis for some depressions, and depression is often a cause for suicide, or the fact that there is a genetic basis for low levels of serotonin, and low levels of serotonin are associated with suicide.

Source: Adapted in part from Pokorny (1968).

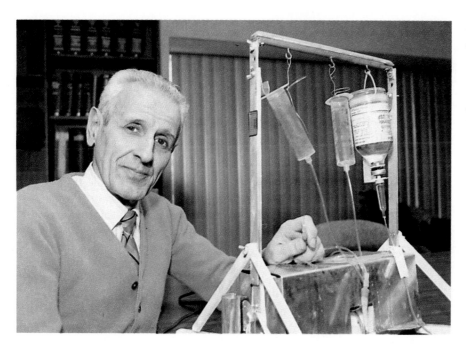

Since 1990, Michigan physician Jack Kevorkian has been lobbying to legalize doctor-assisted suicide, which he calls "patholysis," for mentally competent individuals with incurable diseases. He is shown here with one of his "suicide machines."

is important because they can lead you to misinterpret or ignore early signs of suicide attempts, possibly with tragic consequences.

Suicide as a Positive, Rational Act

Throughout this discussion, suicide has been viewed, implicitly if not explicitly, as a negative act, as abnormal behavior, as something that should be prevented. In many cases, that is certainly the case, but we should at least consider the possibility that in some cases, suicide may be a positive act that reflects a reasonable and rational judgment (Humphry, 1992; Lester, 1989; Richman, 1992). Probably the clearest examples of suicide as a positive act occur when individuals are going through excruciating pain while dying of a terminal illness. For them, there is terrible pain but no hope, and an earlier painless death might seem a reasonable alternative. Actually, in situations like that, we now legally sanction what might be called "passive suicide" in that we respect living wills (agreements that medical procedures will not be used to prolong life in a terminally ill individual). In those cases, death comes because treatment is withheld, but in some cases withholding treatment may not result in death, or at least not for a long time or after a lot of pain. In cases like that and for individuals who are not able to commit suicide without help, groups such as the Hemlock Society advocate "assisted suicide" (sometimes called *voluntary euthanasia*). Assisted suicide is illegal in most places, but it is practiced in various European countries where, contrary to the concerns of its opponents, it has not resulted in inappropriate or widespread use.

The situation becomes even less clear in cases in which the individual is not terminally ill or in great pain but for some rational reason has decided that the time for death has come. This is most likely to occur in older adults who have lived their lives and sense the beginning of a decline in their health and their ability to function. Not wanting to go through the decline,

In Final Exit, *Derek Humphry described numerous effective ways of committing suicide using readily available drugs. The book became an immediate best-seller when it was published in 1991.*

CASE STUDY 8.8

"It's Been a Great Life. Good-bye, World."

"Mother was a small, active woman of 72 who could pass for much younger. She exercised regularly, took classes at the university each semester, did volunteer work reading books onto tapes for visually impaired persons, and had a part-time job in the student union. (She took the job because she liked to be as independent as possible and because she liked the contact with the young students.) She was happy and described her current life as 'the best years of my life.'

"One day, while at the union, Mother experienced severe pains in her chest and left arm. She immediately recognized the pains as signs of a heart attack. Thinking she was going to die, she looked up and said, 'It's been a great life. Good-bye, World.' Mother was rushed to the hospital, and as she was wheeled into the emergency room, she admonished the nurse, 'I have a living will! Don't do anything extraordinary for me. I don't want some machine keeping me alive!'

"Mother recovered from the heart attack, but all was not well. An angiogram revealed that she had 90% blockages in five major coronary arteries. Her physician came to her hospital room and explained the problem to her, went on to point out that the problem could be overcome with major bypass surgery, and told her that he had already made arrangements for the surgery. Mother listened attentively, and when he was through, she said quietly but firmly, 'Thank you, but I don't think I'll have the operation.'

"'But Margaret, you don't understand. If you don't have the operation, you'll die.'

"'I understand,' she replied, 'but I am ready to die, and there are three reasons I don't want the operation. First, all I would be buying with the operation is time—time to wait to die of something else that might be more painful and difficult. I've seen too many of my friends struggle with things like cancer. . . . I've started to decline, and I am going to stop it here. I'm going to die, and a heart attack seems like the best of the alternatives. Second, I've lived my life, and it's been a good life. I've done most of the things I wanted to do, my children and grandchildren are grown, and this is a good time to go. Oh, sure, there are some things I'd like to do, but on balance, I'm ready. Third, I don't want to become a burden to anyone. The operation, the recuperation in a nursing home, and the limitations on my activities after that will put a strain on everyone, and I don't want that. Also, this whole thing will wind up costing a lot of money. I know that insurance will pay for most of it, but why spend that kind of money on me at this point in time? It just doesn't make sense; others need those resources more than I do.'

"The physician argued with her, and finally Mother took his hand as if to console him and said, 'No, Doctor, you don't understand because you're not where I am. You're 50 years old; you're healthy; you have many important things to do—

dependence, and degradation that often come with old age and deteriorating health, they elect to end their lives. In those cases, the decision to die is based on a risk-benefit analysis: The individual weighs the risk of losing some remaining good years against the benefit of ensuring not having to go through some of the terrors and suffering of old age. Is suicide a rational act in those cases?

Case Study 8.8 was written by the son of a woman who elected to die despite the fact that her life could have been saved and she might have had some productive years ahead of her. This case falls in the large gray area in the definition of what behavior is appropriate and what behavior constitutes suicide. Did this woman commit suicide? Did she make a rational and reasonable decision? Should the woman in Case Study 8.8 have been diagnosed as a danger to herself, committed to a hospital as a psychiatric patient, and treated against her will (part of which treatment would have been the coronary surgery)? Or was she a strong woman with strong beliefs about her own personal control of her destiny who simply took control of the situation—*her* situation? Is signing a living will an act of suicide? Are there situations in which suicide is a reasonable, rational, positive act? These questions have far-reaching philosophical, theological, and legal implications that are beyond resolution here, but they are questions of which you should be aware. These questions have implications for how we view suicide, and they are questions that you may have to face someday—professionally, for yourself, or for someone you love.

you have lots of living left. I'm 72; life is good and I am happy, but my health is obviously failing, I'm going to begin to decline, and this is a good time to wind it up. I really don't have much in front of me, and I'd rather go now while I'm ahead. No, Doctor, I'm going to check out of the hospital and go home. For years I've been very careful about my diet and I've denied myself what I've wanted, but tonight if I want butter on my potato, I'll put *real butter* on it, and if I want chocolate cake for desert, I'll have *two* pieces.'

"Mother checked out of the hospital that evening, went home, and continued doing 'her thing.' She wasn't happy about this turn of events, and in letters to friends she mused over things that she would have to leave undone, but she concluded that on balance she was making the right decision.

"About five days after Mother left the hospital, she had another attack. She sat and waited to die, but the pain became unbearable, so she finally had to call the hospital and go to the emergency room. The physician and I met her there, and he explained that if we acted quickly, the bypass surgery could still be done. Mother declined and asked how much time 'the process' would take and whether the pain could be controlled. Shaking his head with dismay, the physician told her that without the operation she would probably live only another day or so and that, yes, the pain could be controlled with morphine.

Mother quipped with a grin, 'Morphine—gee, I get to be a junkie before I go—another new experience!'

"Mother was taken to the intensive care unit, where she was hooked to a morphine pump and a vital signs monitor. We spent that evening and the next day talking and reminiscing. As the time went by, the level of morphine had to be increased, and consequently Mother would occasionally drift off to sleep. When a nurse would come in to check on her, she would wake up, we would talk some more, and then she would drift off again. Late that night, I sat by Mother's bed holding her hand and watching the heart rate monitor. Finally, her heart began to slow, gave a few erratic beats, and then stopped. Mother had died. As I looked at her and wept, I thought of how much I loved her, how much I would miss her, and how *proud* I was of her. Mother had been a positive woman who had remained in control. She had died with as little pain and as much dignity as possible. She arranged her death so that she was not a burden to others, and by saving resources, she contributed to others who she thought needed them more.

"As I said earlier, I was very proud of Mother, and it did not occur to me until sometime later that in a technical sense, *Mother had committed suicide.* Suicide—we usually think of that as a desperate act of a hopeless person. Maybe we need to rethink our conception of suicide and death with dignity."

SUMMARY

TOPIC I: THE DEPRESSIVE DISORDER

■ In the major depressive disorder, mood symptoms involve depression, cognitive symptoms include low self-esteem, pessimism, low motivation, a generalization of negative attitudes, and an exaggeration of the seriousness of problems; motor symptoms involve psychomotor retardation or agitation; and somatic symptoms include disturbed sleep, disturbed eating patterns, reduced sexual drive, and sometimes additional physical illnesses.

■ A somewhat less serious depressive disorder is the dysthymic disorder, which involves a lower level of depression and related symptoms.

■ Estimates of the prevalence of depression range from about 12% to 17%, and the rate seems to be increasing. Depression is twice as likely to occur in women than in men, and it seems to peak at midlife and in old age. Depression is more likely to occur in the lower class, probably because of the additional stress there, and there is no evidence that ethnic background per se is related to depression.

■ Exogenous depressions are due to external (psychological) causes, whereas endogenous depressions are due to internal physiological causes, a distinction that can be important for treatment. Individuals often misattribute the causes of endogenous depressions to psychological factors. The dexamethasone suppression test is used to distinguish between these types of depression, but it is not reliable.

■ Secondary depressions can stem from other factors such as anxiety, alcoholism, or physical illness.

■ Distinctions are sometimes made between involutional depression, depression with seasonal onset, depression with postpartum onset, and the premenstrual dysphoric disorder, but most of those subtypes are not officially recognized in DSM-IV.

TOPIC II: THE BIPOLAR DISORDER

■ The bipolar disorder involves shifts in mood between depression and mania. The Type I disorder involves depression and mania, whereas the Type II disorder involves depression and hypomania.

■ The mild form of the bipolar disorder is called the cyclothymic disorder.

■ In mania, the mood is characterized by euphoria; the cognitive symptoms include inflated self-esteem, grandiosity, problems with attention, and in some cases, delusions; motor symptoms involve excessive activity; and the primary somatic symptom is a decreased need for sleep.

■ The bipolar disorder occurs in about 1.5% of the population, occurs with equal frequency in women and men, and has an onset between the ages of 15 and 60. There do not appear to be class differences.

■ The depressive and bipolar disorders share the symptom of depression, but they appear to be different disorders.

■ Secondary mania can be a side effect of drugs or the result of other disorders.

■ There are individual differences in cycle time, with rapid cycling more frequent in women and probably indicating a more virulent disorder.

■ There seems to be a link between creativity and the bipolar disorder, and it may be that the grandiosity and high activity levels lead to creative productions.

TOPIC III: SUICIDE

■ Women are more likely to attempt suicide, but men are more likely to succeed, so the rate of suicide is higher in men than women. Individuals over 65 have the highest suicide rate.

■ Reports of a rapidly increasing suicide rate among adolescents are probably due to an increasing willingness to record a death as a suicide rather than hide it as an "accident."

■ Covert suicides are suicides that are disguised as accidents. Suicide gestures are behaviors that are designed to look like suicide attempts but in fact are not and are probably used to communicate a level of despair, attract attention, or manipulate others.

■ Warnings about interest in committing suicide should always be taken seriously. Notes left by individuals who commit suicide are usually only apologies, explanations, or good-byes and usually tell us little about the act.

■ Suicide rates rise as winter turns to spring and then decrease, and suicides tend to occur on Mondays.

■ There are numerous myths about suicide, such as "People who talk about suicide won't commit suicide" and "Only depressed individuals commit suicide."

■ It can be argued that in some circumstances (e.g., when facing a terribly painful death), suicide might be a rational and positive act rather than an abnormal behavior.

KEY TERMS, CONCEPTS, AND NAMES

In reviewing and testing yourself on what you have learned from this chapter, you should be able to identify and discuss each of the following.

agitated depression
bipolar disorder
cortisol
covert suicide
cyclothymic disorder
delusion
depression
depression with postpartum onset
depression with seasonal pattern
depressive personality
dexamethasone suppression test (DST)
disturbed sleep
dysthymic disorder
endogenous depression

exogenous depression
hypersomnia
immune system
involutional depression
loss of libido
lymphocytes
major depressive disorder
mania
manic-depressive disorder
maternity blues
menopausal depression
mood disorders
mood disorder with psychotic features
postpartum depression

premenstrual dysphoric disorder
primary depression
psychomotor agitation
psychomotor retardation
rapid cycling
retarded depression
seasonal affective disorder (SAD)
secondary depression
secondary mania
suicide
suicide gesture
Type I bipolar disorder
Type II bipolar disorder

CHAPTER NINE
MOOD DISORDERS: EXPLANATIONS

OUTLINE

Charles is a 26-year-old salesman who was admitted to a psychiatric hospital because he was very depressed and was talking about "ending it all." In his admission interview, he reported that he had been under a lot of stress for the past year. For example, his sales quotas were being set higher and higher, and he could not keep up. It seems that stress played a role in the development of his depression, but how? One possibility is that because he had to work so hard and business had not been good, he did not have time for pleasure and did not receive many rewards. The low levels of pleasure and rewards could have led to the depression. It is also possible that because the stressful factors in his life such as sales quotas were not under his control, he developed a sense of hopelessness that in turn led to the depression. A third explanation is that the prolonged stress led to a reduction of a neurotransmitter in his brain that was responsible for pleasure, and the low level of the neurotransmitter caused the depression.

■　■　■

Marilyn is a 36-year-old woman who has been very depressed for three months. This is her fifth bout of depression in the past four years. There are a number of potential explanations for her depression. First, it might be that the depression stems from the fact that Marilyn's husband left her five years ago and she is turning some of the anger she feels toward her husband in on herself; in other words, the anger turned on herself might be causing the depression. Second, it might also be that Marilyn is not really as depressed as she seems, but she is reporting symptoms as a means of getting attention and sympathy from the people around her. Third, it is noteworthy that when she was a child, Marilyn developed a tendency to see the worst in herself, her situation, and her future. As a consequence, when she comes up against even a small problem, she is likely to say something like "This is too hard for me" or "I will always be a failure." Those negative feelings about herself and her world may have led to her depression. Finally, it is possible that Marilyn's depression stems from a genetically determined low level of a neurotransmitter in her brain. In that regard, it is interesting to note that Marilyn's mother suffered from depression, and it may be that Marilyn inherited the problem from her. Before beginning treatment, Marilyn's psychologist will have to determine the cause of the depression.

■　■　■

Russ is depressed and considering suicide. A relationship that he had been in for three years just fell apart, and he doesn't know what to do. He can't think of any way to get the relationship back together, and now that he is out of college, he isn't sure where to go to get another relationship started. So in addition to being depressed, he feels hopeless. Suicide seems like the only way out—it seems like a nice peaceful escape. Because he doesn't have any family responsibilities or any strong religious beliefs, there is nothing holding him back. The only question now is, how? That question may have been answered by a news report he saw about a man who committed suicide by simply running his car in the garage with the door closed.

■ ■ ■

In Chapter 8 I reviewed the symptoms of mood disorders and discussed suicide. In this chapter I will discuss the factors that are thought to lead to mood disorders and suicide. As you read this chapter, you will see that there are some sharp differences among theorists about the causes of mood disorders and suicide. However, rather than competing with each other, in many cases the various explanations complement each other and work together to give us a more complete understanding of the mood disorders and suicide.

TOPIC I
THE DEPRESSIVE DISORDER

PSYCHODYNAMIC EXPLANATIONS

Loss with Anger Turned Inward

Freud's most widely accepted theory of depression revolves around the consequences of **loss** (Freud, 1911/1955; Mendelson, 1992). First, Freud noted some similarities between depression and *mourning* (the feelings of sorrow and grief that occur when a loved one dies). Specifically, he observed that both mourning and depression occur after the *loss of a loved individual*. Second, Freud recognized that we often have *ambivalent feelings* about the loved individual who was lost. That is, we may love the lost individual, but at the same time we are angry with or even hate the individual for leaving or rejecting us. Such ambivalent feelings are frequently seen in a mourning individual who, though sad and tearful about the death of a loved one, will suddenly say, "Why did you have to leave me! How could you do this to me?" Third, Freud pointed out that depressed individuals are often unjustifiably *self-critical and angry with themselves* and blame themselves for things that are not their fault. Freud suggested that these individuals are self-critical because they are attempting to deal with the loss by symbolically *taking the lost object in as part of themselves,* but when the lost object becomes part of the self, the negative feelings associated with the lost object

get turned in on the self, and therefore the individuals become self-critical and angry with themselves. For Freud, then, the crucial factor in depression is **anger turned inward,** and the event that triggers the process is loss. Freud thought that losses that occur during childhood (e.g., the loss of a parent) are particularly hard to bear and are important for determining the individual's response to later losses; specifically, later losses will reactivate the overwhelming feelings of grief that were associated with the earlier loss.

Numerous early investigations linked losses of many types to depression. For example, people who have recently experienced the death of a relative show higher levels of depression than other people, and those who have lost a spouse are at significantly greater risk for suicide (Bornstein et al., 1973; Bunch, 1972; Clayton et al., 1968; MacMahon & Pugh, 1965).

Freud believed depression to be the result of the negative feelings associated with loss. However, the fact that not all depressed individuals have experienced a loss suggests that depression may be due to stress and that loss is only one type of stress.

The findings linking loss and depression are often taken as support for Freud's theory, but two qualifications should be noted. First, the fact that depression is often preceded by loss does not necessarily mean that the depression stems from the process of taking the lost object in as part of the self and then turning anger inward. Depression may be associated with loss, but these data do not offer any evidence concerning how the two are related. Second, it is important to realize that although losses often precede depressions, many depressed individuals have not experienced a loss, and therefore using the concept of loss to explain depression may be too limited. The fact that some but not all depressions are associated with loss might be explained by suggesting that depression is due to stress and that loss constitutes only one type of stress. In view of this possibility, we must examine the research concerning stress and depression.

Stress

One of the most popular explanations for depression is that it stems from **stress,** and there is a substantial amount of evidence that links stress to depression. For example, we now know that stressors such as physical illnesses and geographic moves are the best predictors of depression (Brown et al., 1995). In one study, it was found that stressful life events such as the loss of a job, illness, and the breakup of a relationship were linked to depression and that the greater the number of stressful events experienced, the greater the likelihood that the individuals would become depressed (Brown & Harris, 1978). Those results are summarized in Figure 9.1. In another study, the investigators examined the lives of women who either did or did not relapse following

treatment for depression (Paykel & Tanner, 1976). The results indicated that the women who relapsed had experienced more undesirable events, especially in the month before the relapse, than the other women. That led the investigators to conclude that even treatment may not protect people from the effects of stress. In another study, it was found that the best predictor of who would relapse was the response to the question, How critical is your spouse of you? (Hooley & Teasdale, 1989). Apparently, critical spouses create stress and precipitate relapses.

Results like these appear to provide evidence for the influence of stress on depression, but one interpretive problem should be noted. Rather than stress causing depression, it is possible that at least in some cases, the *early effects of the depression may cause the stress.* For example, an individual who is becoming depressed does not function well and might therefore lose a job before being diagnosed as suffering from depression. In such a case, the depression might be attributed to the stress of losing the job when in fact the depression caused both the loss of the job and the stress.

Does stress cause depression, or does depression cause stress? The fact is that the relationship goes both ways. Evidence that stress causes depression comes from research in which investigators compared the levels of depression in groups of individuals who either were or were not exposed to some clearly definable stressor such as surgery, heart attack, financial loss, or the need to provide long-term care for an elderly spouse. For example, in one investigation, it was found that 29% of the individuals who experienced a catastrophic financial loss when a bank failed developed severe depression, whereas only 2% of individuals who did not experience that loss developed depression (Ganzini et al., 1990). Overall, the research consistently reveals more depression in individuals exposed to stress, thus providing strong evidence linking stress to the onset of depression.

There is also evidence that depression can contribute to stress. One investigator conducted a longitudinal study in which she assessed the types and levels of stress faced by depressed women (Hammen, 1991). She found that when compared to medically ill and normal women, depressed women were more likely to generate stresses such as interpersonal conflict and that the stresses they generated were more serious than the other stresses they faced. Similarly, in a study of disadvantaged mothers over the course of a year, it was found that stresses such as relationship problems, child care problems, and financial problems led to depression but also that depression led to increases in those problems (Pianta & Egeland, 1994). From these results it is clear that stress does lead to depression but the depression can then also cause stress, so the process can be circular, and the problem can become progressively worse.

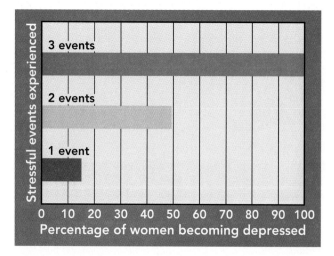

FIGURE 9.1 Women who experienced more stressful life events were more likely to become depressed.
Source: Brown and Harris (1978), p. 108.

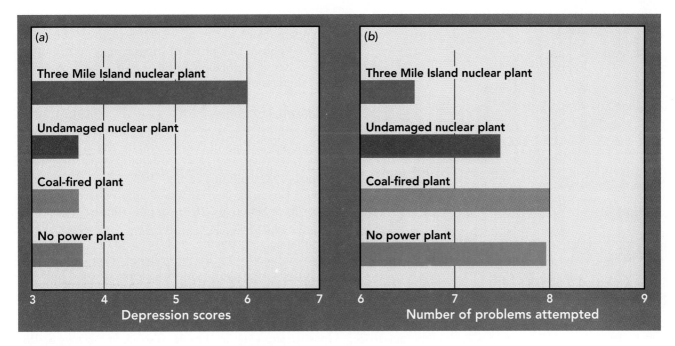

FIGURE 9.2 Individuals living near the damaged Three Mile Island nuclear power plant showed higher levels of depression than individuals living elsewhere *(a)*, and they made fewer attempts to solve problems than individuals living elsewhere *(b)*.
Source: Data from Baum et al. (1983), pp. 568–569, tabs. 2 and 3.

So far, I have focused attention primarily on the effects of *acute* stress, but *chronic* stress that results from factors like long-term interpersonal conflict, job dissatisfaction, poverty, or prolonged illness also appears to contribute to depression. The effects of chronic stress on depression were documented in a series of studies of individuals who lived near the Three Mile Island (TMI) nuclear power plant at the time of a serious accident in which deadly nuclear radiation was almost released. After the accident, living near the power plant was a source of chronic stress because the residents were never sure if and when they would be exposed to radiation. In one study, people living near the TMI plant were compared to people who lived near an undamaged nuclear plant, people who lived near an undamaged coal-fired plant, and people who did not live anywhere near an energy plant (Baum et al., 1983). Tests conducted a year and a half after the accident at the TMI plant revealed two interesting findings: First, the people living near the TMI plant reported higher levels of depression, anxiety, and somatic distress than the other people. Second, when the people from the four locations were given a series of problems on which to work, those who lived near the TMI plant made fewer attempts to solve the problems and did not perform as well. These findings clearly demonstrate the effects of stress on depression and depression-related behaviors. The results are presented in Figure 9.2.

Some attention has also been given to the role of persistent "daily hassles" as a potential cause of depression (Fry, 1989; Holahan et al., 1984; Kanner et al.,

1981; Wolf et al., 1989). Investigators found that the frequency with which individuals reported being annoyed by things like "misplacing or losing things," "social obligations," "too many responsibilities," and "home maintenance" was related to depression, sometimes more strongly than the presence of more serious forms of stress. It is probably true that a lot of little nagging problems can get an individual "down," but it is unlikely that hassles will lead to clinical levels of depression. Furthermore, getting upset by those little things may be more a *result* of an existing depression than a *cause* of depression (Johnson & Bornstein, 1991). That is, you may be more likely to notice and respond to hassles if you are depressed than if you are not depressed.

Moderating Factors in the Stress-Depression Relationship

It is clear that stress is often related to depression, but it is also clear that not everyone who is exposed to stress becomes depressed. Therefore, we must consider what factors moderate the stress-depression relationship (i.e., protect individuals from the effects of stress).

Social Support. One important factor in the stress-depression relationship is the amount of **social support** the individual has available when facing the stress. There is now evidence that individuals who have a close friend are less likely to become depressed when under stress (e.g., Andrews et al., 1978; Billings et al., 1983;

Chronic stress, such as stress resulting from poverty, can lead to depression.

Brown & Harris, 1978; Miller & Ingham, 1976; Monroe et al., 1983; Roy, 1978; Tennant & Babbington, 1978; Warren & McEachren, 1983). For example, in one study, college students reported on the number of "close friends" they had, and later their levels of depression were assessed after the stress of final examinations (Monroe et al., 1983). The results revealed that students who had the most close friends were the least likely to become depressed. Apparently, the presence of friends helped the students through the stress of finals.

Note that it is not simply the *number* of friends but also the *quality of the relationships* that is important (Billings et al., 1983). One friend with whom you can be really close is more important than several superficial relationships. However, having a close friend does not necessarily mean that you will get social support from that individual. In one study, it was found that friends sometimes simply echoed what the other individual was saying and therefore actually reinforced the depression (Belsher & Costello, 1991). The key seems to be understanding and support in working through the problem.

We know that individuals who have social support are less likely to be depressed, but we do not yet understand the process by which social support protects us from depression (Brehm & Smith, 1986). One possibility is that stressful events are less stressful when the burden can be shared with others. In that regard, it is interesting to note that in laboratory experiments, it was found that when awaiting a stressful situation (a painful electric shock), most individuals preferred to wait with others (Schachter, 1964). In other words, misery likes company—or more likely, company makes trouble less upsetting.

Social support tends to reduce depression, but unfortunately, depressed individuals are less likely to get social support because they are unpleasant to be around. That is, because depressed individuals are frequently crying, complaining, pacing, and being irrita-

ble, sluggish, or unresponsive, they are simply not good company (McLeod et al., 1992; Segrin & Abramson, 1994). Thus a lack of social support may contribute to the onset of depression and may also serve to maintain the depression.

Individual Differences. A variety of individual difference factors serves to moderate the stress-depression relationship. One of those factors is the **coping strategies** individuals use when exposed to stress (Billings & Moos, 1981; Billings et al., 1983; Coyne & Whiffen, 1995; Coyne et al., 1981; Folkman & Lazarus, 1980; Pearlin & Schooler, 1978). In general, depressed individuals are more likely to use *passive* strategies such as avoidance, acceptance, wishful thinking, eating, and smoking, and they are more likely to seek advice and emotional support. In contrast, nondepressed individuals are more likely to use *active* strategies that are focused on solving and overcoming the problem. Unfortunately, from this research it is not clear that passive strategies lead to depression, and it may be that passive strategies are a result of depression. However, regardless of what caused what, passive strategies could certainly serve to maintain depression because in many cases they would be ineffective for solving problems and reducing stress.

Another individual difference factor that has received a lot of attention is **aerobic** (ā-RŌ-bik) **fitness.** Aerobic fitness refers to the effectiveness with which an individual can process oxygen, and it is improved by exercises such as jogging, swimming, and cycling in which the heart rate is elevated for prolonged periods of time. There is a substantial amount of evidence that individuals who are in better aerobic condition show smaller responses to stress, and the lessened response to stress may serve to reduce the possibility of depression (Holmes & McGilley, 1987; Holmes & Roth, 1985; McGilley & Holmes, 1988; Sinyor et al., 1983). In one study, the investigators identified a group of students who were experiencing a high degree of life stress (e.g., divorce of parents, geographic moves, broken relationships) that might be expected to lead to depression (Roth & Holmes, 1987). The students were then given either 10 weeks of aerobic training, 10 weeks of relaxation training, or no treatment. The students who received the aerobic training showed higher levels of aerobic fitness and lower levels of depression than the students in the other conditions (see also Roth & Holmes, 1985). Apparently, improvements in aerobic fitness protected students from the effects of stress and from depression.

COMMENT

Stress is clearly a cause of depression, but three important qualifications concerning the stress-depression

Individuals who are in better aerobic condition show smaller physiological responses to stress.

relationship should be noted. First, *stress does not always lead to depression.* Some individuals who are exposed to high levels of stress do not show any abnormal behaviors. That can be explained in part by the effects of moderating variables such as coping strategies and individual differences that may protect some individuals from the effects of stress. However, it may also be that for stress to lead to depression, an individual must be somehow *predisposed to respond with depression.* We will examine that possibility later.

Second, *stress can lead to disorders other than depression.* In other words, in some cases, stress leads to disorders such as anxiety rather than to depression. Probably the best explanation for why an individual develops depression rather than some other disorder lies in the notion of predisposition; some individuals are predisposed to develop depression rather than some other disorder.

The third qualification to be noted is that *depression can occur in the absence of stress.* That is, in many cases individuals who have not been exposed to stress become depressed. That clearly indicates that *stress is not the only cause of depression,* and in the following sections of this chapter I will discuss other potential causes of depression. In sum, stress is an excellent explanation for many depressions, but it is not a complete explanation because it appears that a predisposition may be necessary and it does not account for all depressions.

LEARNING EXPLANATIONS

Learning theorists have offered two explanations for depression. One is that depression stems from *low levels*

of rewards or high levels of punishments (or both). The other explanation is that depressive behaviors are learned and maintained because they lead to rewards such as sympathy and support. In the following sections, I will discuss each of these explanations.

Insufficient Rewards and Excessive Punishments

The most prominent learning-related explanation for depression is that receiving a low level of **rewards** or a high level of **punishments** will lead to depression (Ferster, 1973; Lazarus, 1968; Lewinsohn, 1974; Rehm, 1977). Low levels of rewards and high levels of punishments are thought to contribute to depression in any or all of three ways:

1. An individual who receives fewer rewards or more punishments will have a generally less pleasant life, and that could contribute to depression.

2. If an individual's behavior does not result in rewards or results in punishments, the individual might have a reduced sense of self-worth and develop a low self-concept, which can contribute to depression.

3. If a behavior is not rewarded or is punished, the likelihood of using the behavior again will be reduced, thus resulting in the reduced activity commonly seen in depression. The reduced activity could further decrease the probability of getting rewards, and thus a vicious circle could develop that would contribute to greater and greater depression.

With these possibilities in mind, we must go on to determine whether depressed individuals actually do get fewer rewards or more punishments.

Levels of Environmental Rewards and Punishments. Rewards and punishments can come from two sources, our environment (people and events around us) and ourselves. A variety of evidence indicates that *depressed individuals receive fewer rewards and more punishments from others.* For example, in one study, students who were not depressed each spent time talking to other students who either were or were not depressed (Gotlib & Robinson, 1982). The interactions between the pairs of students were videotaped and analyzed. The results revealed that the students who interacted with depressed students smiled less often, showed less pleasant facial expressions, talked about fewer positive things and more negative things, and made fewer supportive statements to the other student than those who talked to nondepressed students. Clearly, the depressed students got fewer rewards and more punishments from their peers than the nondepressed students did. Other investigations have also revealed that we are more rejecting and less pleasant to depressed than nondepressed individuals (see Marcus & Nardone, 1992).

Environmental factors can reduce the level of rewards one receives and can bring on depression. For example, moving to a new location might cause an individual to lose contact with previous sources of rewards.

There is also evidence that depressed individuals gravitate toward persons who view them unfavorably and solicit unfavorable feedback from other people (Swann et al., 1992). Specifically, when college students were given the opportunity to interact with other students and obtain feedback about themselves, depressed students were more likely than nondepressed students to ask to interact with individuals who had evaluated them negatively and to seek negative information about themselves. That behavior reduces their rewards and adds to their punishments.

The situation with regard to rewards and punishments is made even worse by the fact that when depressed individuals receive the *same* amount of rewards or punishments as nondepressed individuals, the depressed individuals *think* that they receive *fewer rewards* and *more punishments*. For example, in one experiment, depressed and nondepressed individuals worked on a task, and regardless of how they actually performed, they received standard levels of rewards and punishments (Nelson & Craighead, 1977). The individuals were then asked to estimate the number of rewards and punishments they had received. The results indicated that the depressed individuals underestimated their levels of rewards and overestimated their levels of punishments. In other words, the depressed individuals always recalled the situation as less pleasant (fewer rewards, more punishments) than it actually was. Those results are presented in Figure 9.3.

Another factor that reduces rewards and increases punishments is that depressed individuals are *less effective at solving social problems* than nondepressed individuals (Marx et al., 1992). Their social inepti-

tude undoubtedly makes life less pleasant. Overall, then, depressed individuals (a) get low levels of rewards and high levels of punishments from the people around them, (b) seek out individuals who will not reward them, (c) underestimate their rewards and overestimate their punishments, and (d) are poor social problem solvers. All of those factors would lead to a serious reward-punishment imbalance that could result in an unpleasant life and contribute to the depression.

Environmental factors can also influence rewards and punishments and may bring on depression. For example, moving from one location to another may cause an individual to lose contact with previous sources of rewards, and changes in what behaviors are rewarded make once rewarding activities useless. Also, sometimes standards are increased, making higher levels of performance necessary for rewards to be achieved. Consider the college jock who after graduation moves away from the university and is no longer the darling of all the cheerleaders. Now his rewards are no longer based on his ability to throw a ball, and depression might set in if he does not find alternative sources of rewards.

Levels of Self-Reward and Self-Punishment. Some theorists have emphasized the role of self-reward and self-punishment in depression, and there is evidence that *depressed individuals give themselves fewer rewards and more punishments* for their behaviors. In one experiment, depressed and nondepressed individuals were asked to work on a simple laboratory task and to give themselves rewards (small amounts of money) and punishments (withdrawal of money) for their performance (Rozensky et al., 1977). The results indicated that the depressed individuals gave themselves fewer rewards and more punishments than the nondepressed

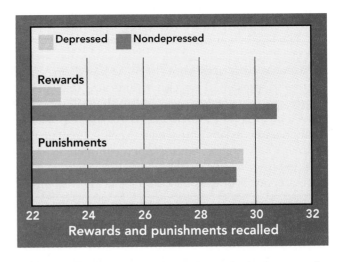

FIGURE 9.3 Depressed individuals recalled more punishments and fewer rewards than nondepressed individuals.

Source: Data from Nelson and Craighead (1977), p. 383, tab. 2.

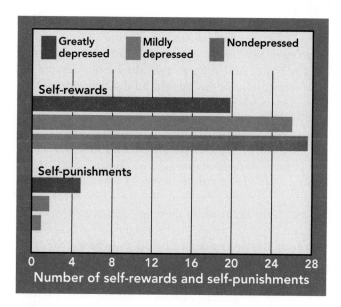

FIGURE 9.4 Depressed individuals gave themselves fewer rewards and more punishments than nondepressed individuals.
Source: Data from Rozensky et al. (1977), p. 36, tab. 1.

individuals. These results are presented in Figure 9.4. Similar results have been found with hospitalized depressed patients and depressed university students (Lobitz & Post, 1979; Nelson & Craighead, 1977, 1981).

From the evidence, it is clear that depressed individuals get fewer rewards from other people and give themselves fewer rewards than individuals who are not depressed. It is usually assumed that the low levels of rewards cause the depression, but it may be that in at least some cases, the low levels of rewards are the result of depression. For example, we may be less pleasant to depressed individuals, and they may give themselves fewer rewards because they do not think they are any good. However, even if low levels of rewards do not cause depression, they may help maintain depression once it gets started.

Depression as an Operant Behavior

In sharp contrast to the theory just discussed is the possibility that some *depressive behaviors may be the result of rewards*. We may be more attentive, caring, and supportive of individuals who are "down in the dumps" or depressed. We may also do nice things for them to cheer them up, and all of those things could serve to reward the depressive behavior. Furthermore, by doing everything for depressed individuals in the hope of making them feel better, we may actually be convincing them that they are not good people or not well enough to do things for themselves, and that could also lead to more depression.

However, there are two potential problems with this explanation. First, research presented earlier indicated that we usually punish rather than reward depressed individuals; in view of that, the number of individuals for whom depression would be caused by rewards would seem to be very limited. Even if we are initially rewarding and supportive of depressed individuals, that quickly changes as our tolerance and patience diminish. Second, we have to ask whether the behavior that is rewarded is actually depression or whether it is a facade covering normal or near-normal feelings. In other words, the individual might simply *act* depressed in order to get the attention but not really *be* depressed. Such an effect is sometimes seen in hospitalized patients who are about to be discharged and who do not want to leave the protected atmosphere of the hospital (Braginsky et al., 1969). In those cases, the patients sometimes put on a brief show of abnormal behavior so that they can stay in the hospital. Generally, this explanation seems to have very limited applicability and is probably related to "depressive-like" behavior rather than true depression.

COMMENT

The best learning-based explanation for depression seems to be that few rewards and many punishments can lead to depression, at least to mild depression. However, this explanation does not really add much to what we already know because few rewards and many punishments can be thought of simply as *stress*, and we already know that stress can lead to depression. In other words, the evidence linking few rewards and many punishments to depression simply provides more evidence for the stress-depression relationship.

COGNITIVE EXPLANATIONS

There are two cognitive explanations for depression. In one, it is hypothesized that individuals become depressed because they *focus on the negative aspects of life*, whereas in the other it is assumed that individuals become depressed because they *feel helpless about controlling* the negative outcomes of life. I will discuss each of these in the following sections.

Negative Cognitive Sets and Information Processing

The first cognitive explanation revolves around the notion that depressed individuals have **negative cognitive sets** that lead them to focus their attention on personal shortcomings and other reasons to be depressed, and *thinking negative thoughts leads to the depression* (e.g., Beck, 1967, 1976). For example, an individual who is

neg. thoughts positively [directly] related to depression

generally successful might ignore successes or misinterpret them as flukes and instead dwell on failures. As a result of those negative perceptions, the individual will have a self-image as a failure, will assume that the future will be filled with failures, and consequently will fall victim to depression.

To understand how these negative cognitive sets develop and operate, psychologists have applied what we know about human **information processing.** In general, the information processing approach has three components. First, depressed individuals are thought to have strong and active **associative networks** that link together memories that involve depression. The depression networks were probably originally established when the individuals had some depression-related experiences. That is, early experiences with depression laid down ("burned in") the depression networks. (For a review of associative networks, see Chapter 2.)

Second, because of their active depression networks, depressed individuals are more likely to attend to depressing things around them. That is, depressed individuals use **selective attention** and focus on the depressing information. Furthermore, because the individuals are thinking about the depressing information, they are likely to process it and send it on to storage in their long-term memory. Of course, seeing and thinking about reasons for depression contribute to depression, and the storage of that information adds to the depression network.

Third, because extensive depression networks keep developing, depressed individuals are more likely to recall depressing information. That is, if you have more depressing memories, and if those memories have numerous associative links to other memories, it is very likely that one of those depressing memories will be activated. Activating that memory will activate the entire depression-related network, with the result that you will be flooded with depressing memories. In other words, the depressed individual is constantly recalling old reasons for depression.

The picture that develops from this information-processing model is consistent with the picture of clinical depression: Depressed individuals are always seeing reasons for depression and remembering other reasons for depression, and the process is cyclical and builds on itself. Depressed individuals cannot help themselves because the process is automatic; just as your computer operating system "boots up" when you turn the computer on, so the depressed individual's negative network is activated when he or she begins thinking. In the following sections, I will review the evidence for this explanation.

Presence of Negative Thoughts. The first question we must ask is, do depressed individuals actually have more negative thoughts than nondepressed individuals? The answer is yes, and furthermore it appears that negative thoughts may increase and decrease as depressions increase and decrease. In one investigation, depressed psychiatric patients, nondepressed psychiatric patients, and normal individuals completed a 40-item questionnaire that measured the degree to which they had negative thoughts (Hamilton & Abramson, 1983). Using items like "If I fail at my work, then I am a failure as a person," the questionnaire measured negative expectancies about outcomes, excessive self-blame for failures, beliefs about lack of control, and beliefs about negative evaluations by others. The patients filled out the questionnaire when they were admitted to the hospital and again when they were discharged (on the average, 17 days later). The normal control individuals also took the test twice, with 17 days between the tests.

The results revealed three interesting findings. First, at the time of admission, the depressed patients as a group had more negative thoughts than the nondepressed patients or the normal individuals, thus indicating that negative thoughts were associated with depression. Second, the high level of negative thoughts among depressed patients was due to the extreme scores of a *subset* of patients, thus indicating that negative thoughts are not characteristic of *all* depressed individuals. Third, over the course of their treatment, the depressed patients who had negative thoughts showed a decline in those thoughts such that at the time of their discharge, their thoughts were no different from those of the nondepressed patients or the normal individuals. In other words, as the depression declined, so did the negative thoughts. The results of this investigation are presented in Figure 9.5.

Selective Attention. The second question we must ask is, do depressed individuals selectively attend to negative information? Again, the answer is yes. In one interesting demonstration of selective attention, mildly depressed and nondepressed individuals were shown "happy" and "sad" faces while their eye fixations were recorded (Matthews & Antes, 1992). The results indicated that the depressed individuals looked more often at sad parts of faces than the nondepressed individuals, thus suggesting that they sought out negative aspects of life.

Selective Recall. Next we must ask, are depressed individuals more likely to recall negative events than nondepressed individuals? Yes; depressed individuals are more likely than nondepressed individuals to recall things such as failures, being left out of peer groups, or being criticized by teachers or employers (Isen et al., 1978; Laird et al., 1982; Madigan & Bollenbach, 1982; Natale & Hantas, 1982; Snyder & White, 1982; Teasdale & Fogarty, 1979; see reviews by Blaney, 1986; Bower, 1981, 1987; Johnson & Magaro, 1987).

The effect of mood on recall was neatly demonstrated in an experiment in which students who were in

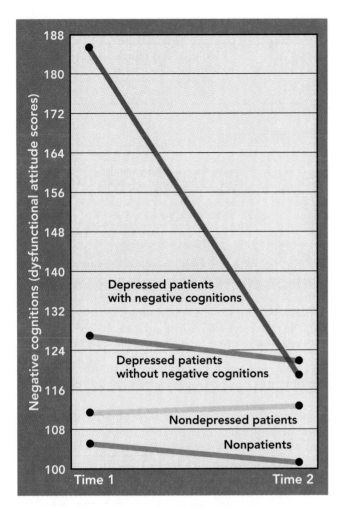

FIGURE 9.5 Depressed patients used fewer negative cognitions as psychotherapy progressed.
Source: Adapted from Hamilton and Abramson (1983), p. 181, fig. 1.

a neutral mood learned a group of pleasant and unpleasant personality-related words (*considerate, helpful, thoughtful, pleasant, kind, friendly, rude, cruel, hostile, ungrateful, impolite, mean;* Clark & Teasdale, 1985). Following that, the students were made to feel happy or depressed, and then they were asked to recall the words. The results indicated that female students recalled more pleasant than unpleasant words when they were happy and recalled more unpleasant than pleasant words when they were depressed. Mood did not influence the recall performance of men. The fact that mood was more likely to influence the recall of women than men may help account for the finding that women are more likely to become depressed than men (see Chapter 8).

The fact that depressed individuals are likely to recall negative events can be explained in terms of **priming.** That is, the depression activates the depression-related network and makes it more sensitive to later activation, so the memories of negative events that are stored in that network are more likely to be activated and recalled. Furthermore, recalling the negative events again primes the network, so the process becomes circular.

Negative Thoughts as a Cause of Depression. Now that you know that depressed individuals have more negative thoughts than nondepressed individuals, we must go on to ask whether the negative thoughts *cause* depression or are the *result* of depression. To answer that question, some theorists have pointed to a series of experiments in which it was found that reading negative or sad statements led to increases in mild depression (Coleman, 1975; Frost et al., 1979; Frost et al., 1982; Hale & Strickland, 1976; Natale, 1977; Strickland et al., 1975; Teasdale & Bancroft, 1977; see reviews by Blaney, 1986; Bower, 1981; Goodwin & Williams, 1982). The statements the individuals read were like the following: "I'm discouraged and unhappy about myself," "I feel worn out," "My health might not be as good as it's supposed to be." When compared to individuals who read positive or neutral material, individuals who read negative material (a) reported higher levels of depression, anxiety, and hostility; (b) were more likely to prefer solitary or sedentary activities; (c) performed worse on an intelligence test; (d) wrote more slowly; (e) paused more often in their speech; (f) made more constricted doodles; and (g) altered their eating behavior.

Clearly, reading negative statements led to depressions, but it is important to recognize that the depressions were not particularly deep, did not last more than a few minutes, and could be completely eliminated by a simple distraction such as working briefly on another task (Frost & Green, 1982; Isen & Gorgoglione, 1983). In other words, thinking the negative thoughts resulted in feelings that were more like the sadness we feel while watching a "depressing" movie than they were to the clinical depression we see in patients. Because of that, the findings concerning cognitively induced changes in mood do not provide evidence that negative thoughts result in clinical depression. However, the induction procedures used in these experiments were very brief, and it might be that more intense or prolonged procedures that more closely approximate what some individuals experience in daily living could result in greater depression.

In another approach to the question of causation, investigators measured negative thoughts in almost 1,000 individuals, and then 1 year later they assessed the individuals to determine which ones became depressed (Lewinsohn et al., 1981). The results indicated that those who became depressed did not have more negative thoughts before becoming depressed than individuals who did not become depressed. The fact that negative thoughts did not precede depression raises serious questions about whether negative thoughts cause depression or whether depression causes negative thoughts.

Questions about the causal role of negative thoughts were also raised in an investigation in which depressed patients were given either cognitive therapy that was designed to treat the depression by changing thoughts or were given antidepressant drug therapy (Simons et al., 1984). Both treatments were effective for reducing depression, but the relevant finding here was that *both treatments reduced negative thoughts.* The fact that lifting the depression with medication reduced negative thoughts suggests that depression may cause negative thoughts rather than vice versa. Numerous other investigations have also failed to reveal a causal link between thoughts and depression, so we must conclude that there is at present no reliable evidence that negative thoughts cause clinical levels of depression (see Haaga et al., 1991).

Negative Thoughts as a Predisposing Factor in Depression. The lack of consistent evidence that negative thoughts cause depression poses a serious problem for the theory. However, it may be that rather than causing depression, negative thoughts *predispose* individuals to become depressed when under stress. This can be referred to as the **cognitive diathesis-stress hypothesis.** The word *cognitive* is noteworthy here because usually when we use the term *diathesis* (which means "predisposition"), we are referring to *physiological* factors such as genes, but in this case the predisposition is based on a cognitive factor.

To test the cognitive diathesis-stress hypothesis, a number of investigators have collected data on negative thoughts, life stress, and symptoms of depression (Kwon & Oel, 1992; Olinger et al., 1987; Robins & Block, 1989; Segal et al., 1992). In general, it was found that *some* of the depressed individuals had experienced stressful life events, but *most* depressed individuals reported *both* negative thoughts *and* stressful life events. It appears that the perception of the world as difficult may heighten the impact of stress and thereby result in depression. This model is illustrated in Figure 9.6.

The predisposing effect of negative thoughts was clearly illustrated in a study of college students who failed an examination (Metalsky et al., 1993). First, the students were tested to determine the degree to which they felt hopeless and had low self-esteem, then they were given their grades on an important examination, and finally their levels of depression were assessed on each day for 5 days after they received their grades. The results indicated that there was a general increase in depression immediately after the students received their failing grades, but only the students who had earlier reported feeling hopeless and having low self-esteem were still depressed 5 days later; those who had more positive attitudes "popped back" from the initial depression. Those findings are illustrated in Figure 9.7. Similarly, in a prospective study of high school students, it was found that those who were originally more pessimistic were most likely to develop depression later (Lewinsohn et al., 1994). Taken together, those find-

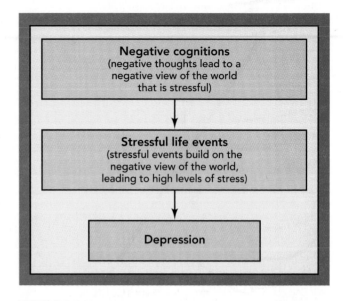

FIGURE 9.6 Cognitive diathesis-stress model of depression: Negative conditions may predispose individuals to depression when they face stressful life events.

ings provide strong support for the notion that negative thoughts can predispose individuals to depression.

Negative Thoughts and the Maintenance of Depression. In addition to predisposing individuals to depression, negative thoughts may also provide explanations for depression once they set in (e.g., "It's understandable that I'm depressed because . . ."). In that case, negative thoughts could serve to *maintain* depression. This is supported by the results of a study in which it was found that depressed individuals who had more negative thoughts were less likely to *improve* than those who had fewer negative thoughts (Lewinsohn et al., 1981). There is also evidence that the negativity may feed on itself, spiraling and increasing as the depression wears on (Davis & Unruh, 1981; Nolen-Hoeksema, 1991; Teasdale, 1988). In short, having a negative cognitive set may lead to greater and greater negativity, and the negativity may preclude seeing the positive aspects of life, thereby prolonging the depression.

To sum up, it is clear that (a) depressed individuals have more negative thoughts than nondepressed individuals, (b) the negative thoughts apparently stem from selective attention and enhanced recall of negative factors, (c) the negative thoughts may not cause depression but do predispose individuals to depression when they are exposed to stress, and (d) the negative thoughts do serve to maintain depression.

Learned Helplessness

The second cognitive explanation for depression asserts that individuals learn (correctly or incorrectly) that they cannot control future negative outcomes; consequently, the individuals feel helpless, and the feel-

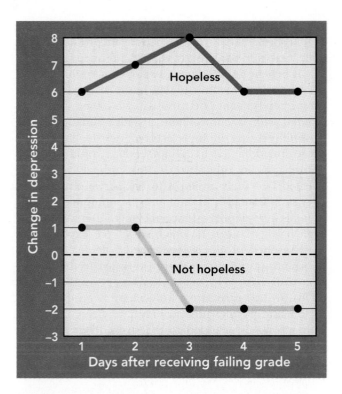

FIGURE 9.7 After failing an examination, students who generally felt hopeless remained depressed, whereas others "popped back."

Note: Scores reflect change in depression from a baseline period before the grades were received. Depression was measured with the Beck Depression Inventory.

Source: Adapted from Metalsky et al. (1993), p. 107, fig 1.

ings of helplessness lead to depression. This is referred to as the **learned helplessness** explanation (Abramson et al., 1978; Miller & Norman, 1979; Peterson & Seligman, 1984; Roth, 1979; Seligman, 1975).

The major difference between the negative-thoughts explanation and the learned-helplessness explanation is that individuals with negative thoughts believe that they are *responsible* for the negative things that happen in their lives, whereas individuals who have learned helplessness believe that they are *helpless* in controlling the negative things (Abramson & Sackeim, 1977; Blaney, 1977). The difference, then, is one of self-blame (negative thoughts) versus lack of control (learned helplessness).

Early Laboratory Research on Helplessness and Depression. The learned-helplessness explanation was discovered quite accidentally in a series of experiments on conditioning with animals (see Maier & Seligman, 1976). In one of those experiments, dogs were exposed to one of three conditions. The dogs in one condition were placed in a cage and given a series of *inescapable* (uncontrollable) shocks. When the shocks first came on, the dogs jumped, barked, scratched, and generally thrashed around, but their responses were ineffective, and they simply had to endure the shocks. The dogs in a second condition were placed in the cage and given a

series of *escapable* (controllable) shocks. Specifically, the dogs could escape the shocks by jumping over a small barrier and going to the other side of the cage. These dogs quickly learned to escape the shocks. The dogs in the third condition were placed in the cage but were never shocked, so they had no reason to learn an escape response. Twenty-four hours later, all of the dogs were returned to the cage and given shocks that they could escape if they jumped over the barrier.

The results indicated that on the first trial, the dogs who had learned the escape response the day before jumped the barrier very quickly to avoid the shock. That was not unexpected. The dogs who had not been shocked before required a little more time to jump over the barrier because they had not had any experience with it before, but by the third or fourth trial they were also quickly avoiding the shocks. That also was not unexpected. However, the surprising finding was that the dogs who had received the inescapable shock on the previous day made little attempt to avoid the shock (did not jump the barrier) and eventually simply lay down and endured it. Apparently on the basis of their previous experience in which they had been unable to do anything about the shock, these dogs simply gave up in this new situation. After three or four trials, some of the dogs did happen to cross the barrier and thereby escape the shock, but they did not catch on to the effectiveness of their response and did not use it again in later trials. In view of the similarity between the responses of the dogs and the responses of depressed individuals, the investigators inferred that the experience with inescapable stress had caused depression in the dogs. The responses of the three groups of dogs are presented in Figure 9.8.

After observing learned helplessness in animals, similar experiments were conducted with humans, and those experiments yielded comparable results. For example, in one experiment, students were exposed either to a loud aversive noise that they could not terminate or to a loud aversive noise that they could terminate by pushing a button; other students were not exposed to a noise (Hiroto, 1974). When the students were later put in a test situation in which they could terminate an aversive noise by moving a lever from one side of a panel to another (a situation analogous to the dogs moving from one side of the cage to the other), the students who had been exposed to the uncontrollable noise did not perform as well as the students in the other conditions. Because lack of control over negative outcomes led to depressive-like behavior, researchers concluded that lack of control and learned helplessness caused depression in humans (Hiroto & Seligman, 1975).

Beliefs About Control as a Cause of Depression. On the basis of the research just described, it was widely assumed that learned helplessness caused depression. However, before accepting that conclusion, we must

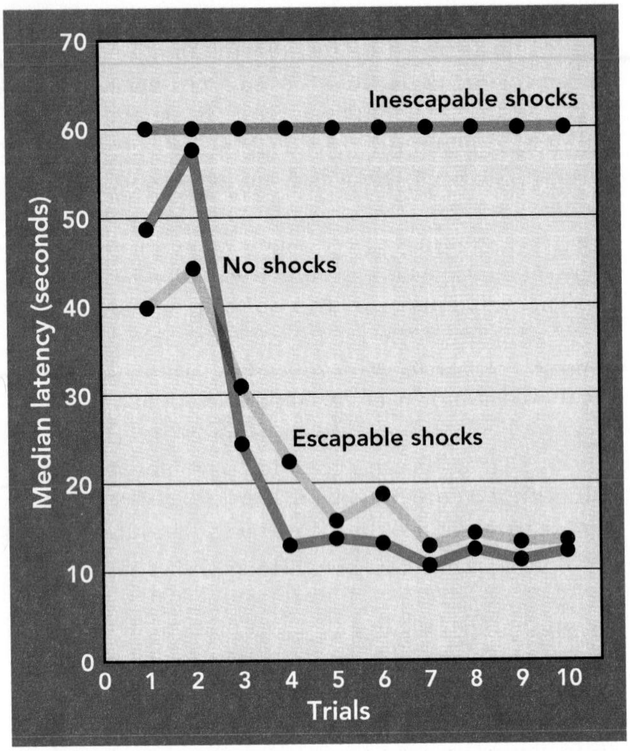

FIGURE 9.8 Dogs that had been exposed to inescapable shocks did not jump the barrier to avoid shocks in a new situation.
Source: Adapted from Maier et al. (1969), p. 328, fig. 10-13.

examine the question of whether thoughts about helplessness actually preceded the onset of depression. To answer that question, it is necessary to conduct research in which individuals' beliefs about control are measured, and later the individuals are followed up to determine whether those who originally felt that they were not in control were more likely to become depressed. Contrary to what might be expected on the basis of the original laboratory research, most of the research does not provide evidence that learned helplessness precedes and causes depression (Cutrona, 1983; Danker-Brown & Baucom, 1982; Lewinsohn et al., 1981; Manley et al., 1982; Peterson et al., 1981; see also reviews by Brewin, 1985; Coyne & Gotlib, 1983). In other words, feelings of helplessness appear to be a consequence rather than a cause of depression.

Further doubts about the value of learned helplessness for explaining depression were raised by a series of experiments in which it was found that individuals who showed the learned-helplessness effect (i.e., performed poorly on a task after not being in control on an earlier task) were *not aware* that they had not been in control on the first task and were not depressed (Oakes & Curtis, 1982; Tennen, Drum, et al., 1982; Tennen, Gillen, & Drum, 1982). In other words, the lack of control influenced behavior, but the effect was not due to beliefs about control, and the behavior did not reflect depression. Those findings have sparked considerable contro-

versy and raised serious questions about whether learned helplessness plays a role in causing depression (Alloy, 1982; Oakes, 1982; Silver et al., 1982; Tennen, 1982).

If beliefs about control do not cause depression, it must be asked why the animals in the original laboratory studies became "depressed" when they were confronted with uncontrollable negative situations. One possibility is that the high levels of inescapable stress in those situations led to *learned inactivity* rather than to depression. In other words, the animals may have learned that their attempts to escape were useless, so they simply stopped trying, and the inference that the animals were depressed was incorrect. Alternatively, the high levels of stress to which they were exposed may have resulted in *physiological changes* (decreases in certain neurotransmitters) that in turn led to the depression (Anisman, 1978; Glazer & Weiss, 1976; Weiss et al., 1976). In that case, stress would have been the crucial factor, and helplessness would have been important only insofar as it added to the stress. That possibility will be discussed shortly, when I examine the physiological explanations for depression.

COMMENT

At present, the cognitive explanations are among the most popular psychological explanations for depression, and that popularity is understandable because what people think and say certainly fits with their moods and behaviors. That is, depressed individuals say things like "I'm no good," "Life is terrible and probably won't get better," and "Things are just out of control." Unfortunately, not all of the enthusiasm for the cognitive explanations is justified because there is still no consistent evidence that negative thoughts or learned helplessness *cause* depression. That does not mean, however, that we should abandon the cognitive explanations for depression. On the contrary, although negative thoughts by themselves may not cause depression, there is good evidence that negative thoughts can establish a *predisposition* such that when the individual is exposed to stress, depression will result. That is, the negative thoughts make the individual more vulnerable. Furthermore, negative thoughts and learned helplessness can serve to *maintain* the depression (Eaves & Rehm, 1984). That occurs because when feeling negative and helpless, individuals do not make attempts to overcome their problems, thus precluding the possibility of finding solutions for the problems that initially caused the depression.

Finally, it might be noted that negative thoughts and beliefs about helplessness may be thought of as sources of *stress*. That is, insofar as those factors may be linked to depression, there is nothing unique about those factors beyond the fact that they create stress, and stress can contribute to depression.

Overall, then, cognitive factors add to our understanding of depression, but by themselves they are not a sufficient explanation.

PHYSIOLOGICAL EXPLANATIONS

From a physiological standpoint, depression results from *low levels of neurological activity in the areas of the brain that are responsible for pleasure* (George et al., 1995). The question then is, what causes the low levels of neurological activity? One explanation is that there are *low levels of neurotransmitters in the areas of the brain that are responsible for pleasure* (Delgado et al., 1992). In other words, if there are insufficient amounts of neurotransmitters at the synapses, the transmission of the nerve impulse from neuron to neuron will be limited, thus limiting neurological activity and pleasure. The two neurotransmitters that have been implicated in depression are **serotonin** (SEH-ruh-TŌ-nin) and **norepinephrine** (NOR-ep-i-NEF-rin). Collectively, these neurotransmitters are known as **catecholamines** (KAT-uh-KŌ-luh-mēnz), and consequently this physiological explanation for depression is often called the **catecholamine hypothesis.** (For the sake of simplicity, in this discussion I will use the term *neurotransmitters* rather than *catecholamines*.)

At first, low levels of neurotransmitters appears to be an excellent explanation for depression, and the drug treatment of depression is based on this explanation. That is, drugs are used because they increase the levels of the neurotransmitters and reduce the depression. However, the results of the drug treatment pose a problem because although the drugs increase the levels of the neurotransmitters to their normal levels almost immediately, the depression is not reduced until 2 to 3 weeks after drug therapy has begun. The fact that there is a lag between the increase in neurotransmitter levels and the decrease in depression suggests that *something in addition to low levels of neurotransmitters is involved in the depression.* Unfortunately, we have not yet identified exactly what that something is. One possibility is that the low levels of the neurotransmitters somehow caused the *postsynaptic neurons to become less sensitive to stimulation* so they are less likely to fire and it requires a few weeks of normal levels of neurotransmitters for the sensitivity to return to normal. Another possibility is that depressed individuals may have fewer receptor sites for the neurotransmitters, and it may take time for additional sites to develop (Nemeroff et al., 1994). Because we do not yet know what the other factor is, in this section I will focus on what we do know about the low levels of neurotransmitters.

In this part of the chapter, I am focusing on depression rather than mania, but it is relevant to note that whereas an excessively low level of a neurotransmitter can result in depression, *an excessively high level can result in mania.* In other words, too little or too much of a neurotransmitter can cause problems with mood. With this overview as background, we can now go on to examine the evidence for the catecholamine hypothesis.

Neurotransmission and Depression

Evidence Based on the Effects of Drugs. Neurotransmitters cannot be studied directly in the live brain, so we must rely on two types of indirect evidence concerning the relationship between neurotransmitter levels and depression. The first type of evidence stems from studies of the effects of drugs that increase or decrease the levels of the relevant neurotransmitters. The results of this large body of evidence are clear: First, drugs that increase neurotransmitter levels and decrease depression in depressed individuals can lead to mania in normal individuals. Apparently, increasing neurotransmitter levels in depressed individuals brings those levels up to normal and thereby reduces the depression, whereas increases in nondepressed individuals who already have normal levels of the neurotransmitters result in excessively high levels and bring on mania. Second, drugs that decrease the level of the neurotransmitters cause depression in normal individuals and reduce mania in individuals who are manic. In general, then, *drugs that increase neurotransmitter levels elevate mood, and drugs that decrease neurotransmitter levels depress mood.* Those results are summarized in Table 9.1 (see also Altshuler et al., 1995).

TABLE 9.1 Effects of Drugs That Alter Neurotransmitter Levels

Types of Individuals	Change in Neurotransmitter Level	
	Increase	**Decrease**
Depressed	Reduces depression	—
Normal	Causes mania	Causes depression
Manic	—	Reduces mania

Source: Adapted from Zis and Goodwin (1982), p. 176, tab. 12.2. See also Altshuler et al., 1995.

There is one notable exception to this pattern of findings. A drug called *lithium* reduces both depression and mania in individuals who suffer from the bipolar disorder. This double-barreled effect is probably due to the fact that lithium moderates the level of norepinephrine and does not allow it to get too high or too low. We will discuss lithium in greater detail later when we consider the treatment of the bipolar disorder.

Finally, it should be noted that mood changes based on changes in neurotransmitter levels can be caused by a variety of drugs other than those that are usually used to treat mood disorders. For example, amphetamines and cocaine cause "highs" (mania) because they result in higher levels of the neurotransmitters.

Evidence Based on the Study of Metabolites. The second body of evidence concerning the influence of neurotransmitters on depression is based on studies of **metabolites.** Metabolites are the substances that are produced when neurotransmitters change their chemical structure as a result of interactions with other chemical agents, and so by studying metabolites of neurotransmitters, we can study neurotransmitters indirectly. It is easier to study the metabolites of neurotransmitters than the neurotransmitters themselves because the metabolites are transported out of the brain and into the urine and the cerebrospinal fluid, where they can be measured. The assumption in this research is that finding low levels of the metabolites means that there are low levels of the neurotransmitters at the synapses in the brain. The metabolites that are of most interest are **MHPG,** which is the metabolite of norepinephrine, and **5-HIAA,** which is the metabolite of serotonin.

The relationship between MHPG and mood is illustrated in Figure 9.9, where the daily levels of MHPG excretion are plotted for a patient along with an indication of whether the patient was in a depressed or manic state. Inspection of the figure indicates that MHPG levels are low during depression and high during mania. Furthermore, it is important to note that MHPG levels rise a few days *before* the mood shifts from depression to mania and fall before the mood shifts from mania to depression. The fact that MHPG levels change before the mood change occurs is important because it suggests that the change in neurotransmitter level causes the mood change rather than vice versa. This effect has been documented in numerous investigations (Agren, 1982; Beckman & Goodwin, 1980; Bond et al., 1972; De Leon–Jones et al., 1975; Jones et al., 1973; Maas, 1975; Maas et al., 1972; Muscettola et al., 1984; Schildkraut et al., 1973; Schildkraut et al., 1978). Furthermore, there is evidence that increases in MHPG secretion are associated with recovery from depression (Greenspan et al., 1970; Pickar et al., 1978). Taken together, these findings provide strong support for the hypothesis that depression is related to levels of norepinephrine.

Diet and Depression. If depression is due to physiological factors, a question that arises is, can diet influence depression? There does not appear to be any consistent evidence that normal variations in diet influence depression (at least not clinical levels of depression), but extreme changes in the intake of **tryptophan** (TRIP-tuh-fan) can influence mood in some individuals. Tryptophan is an amino acid that is found in protein, and there are particularly high levels of it in dairy products and turkey. Tryptophan is relevant for depres-

proteins

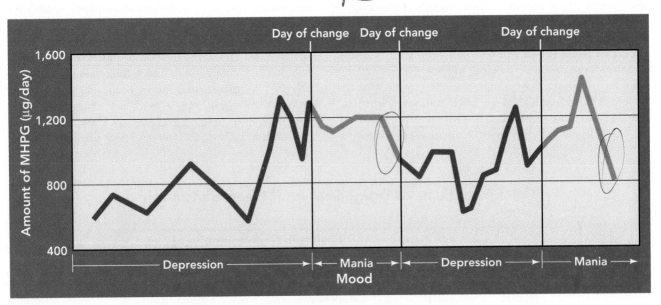

FIGURE 9.9 A patient showed lower levels of MHPG just before and during depression and higher levels just before and during mania.
Source: Adapted from Maas (1975), p. 122, fig. 2.

Changes in the intake of tryptophan, an amino acid, can influence mood in some individuals. Turkey and dairy products have particularly high levels of tryptophan.

why do we get sleepy then?

sion because once in the body, *tryptophan is converted into serotonin*, which is crucial for depression.

In one experiment, individuals who did or did not have a family history of depression were put on a 1-day diet that had either low or normal levels of tryptophan, and their moods were monitored (Benkelfat et al., 1994). The results indicated that within the first 5 hours, 30% of the individuals who had a family history of depression and who were on the low-tryptophan diet entered a mild depression (i.e., they reported more depression and less confidence in themselves), whereas none of the other individuals became depressed. From these findings, it appears that a low-tryptophan diet (which leads to low levels of serotonin) can push individuals with predispositions to depression over the line into depression.

In another test of the tryptophan-depression link, it was found that some individuals who were already depressed became more depressed when they were given a low-tryptophan diet (Delgado et al., 1994). Interestingly, the individuals who became more depressed on the low-tryptophan diet were also the ones whose depression improved when they were given drugs to increase serotonin levels. In other words, low levels of tryptophan lowered serotonin levels and increased depression, and drugs that then increased the serotonin levels reduced the depression.

Depression in the Absence of Stress. Earlier in this chapter, I pointed out that some depressions were due to stress but that others appeared to be independent of stress and that those might be due to physiological factors. If that is the case, it would be expected that individuals who become depressed in the absence of stress would show physiological causes for their depressions. To test that possibility, in one investigation the levels of

neurotransmitters were compared in depressed individuals whose depression had or had not been preceded by a stressful life event (Roy et al., 1986). The results indicated that individuals whose depressions were not associated with stress had lower levels of serotonin and norepinephrine. In a related study, the investigators first identified individuals whose previous depressions were thought to be due to stress or physiological factors, and then they examined the presence or absence of stress in later depressions (Frank et al., 1994). The results indicated that among individuals with a history of stress-related depressions, over 70% of subsequent depressions were stress-related, whereas among individuals who did not have a history of stress-related depressions, only 46% of their subsequent depressions were preceded by stress. In other words, some individuals clearly show a pattern of developing depression in the absence of stress, and in those individuals, the crucial factor appears to be a physiological problem. Clearly, then, physiological factors are effective for accounting for depressions that cannot be accounted for with other explanations.

Neurotransmitters and the Symptoms Associated with Depression. In the earlier description of depression, I pointed out that depression is often associated with reductions in sleep, appetite, and sex (see Chapter 8). Related to that, it is important to note here that in addition to accounting for the depression, low levels of serotonin and norepinephrine can also be used to account for the symptoms that are associated with the depression. Specifically, serotonin and norepinephrine play a crucial role in the functioning of the **hypothalamus,** and *the hypothalamus controls sleep, appetite, and sex.* It appears, then, that low levels of the neurotransmitters can account for both the depression and the other symptoms that are associated with the depression. That fact increases the power and usefulness of the physiological explanations.

The Role of GABA. Many depressed individuals also suffer from anxiety, but the anxiety is not linked to serotonin or norepinephrine. Therefore, we must ask, what gives rise to the anxiety seen in depressed individuals? Some of the anxiety is undoubtedly a response to the unpleasant state of being depressed, but there is also evidence that some of the anxiety may have a physiological basis. Specifically, it has been found that many depressed patients have lower levels of the neurotransmitter known as **GABA** than nondepressed individuals (Gerner & Hare, 1981; Gold et al., 1980; Kasa et al., 1982; Petty & Sherman, 1984). That is relevant because as you will recall from Chapter 5, GABA plays a role in anxiety; specifically, GABA is essential for the activity of the inhibitory neurons that reduce the activity of the neurons responsible for anxiety. Finding low levels of GABA in depressed individuals is important because it enables us to explain their anxiety physiologically.

GABA: cuts activity that leads to anxiety

From the results that were reviewed in this section, it is clear that some depressions are related to low levels of the neurotransmitters serotonin and norepinephrine. However, it is not enough to know that low levels of the neurotransmitters result in depression; we must also determine why those levels are low. One possibility is that the neurotransmitter levels and depression are determined by genetic factors, and I will examine the evidence for that in the following section.

Genetic Factors : *Why levels are low*

Studies of Families. Some evidence that depression is inherited is provided by the fact that depressed individuals are more likely than nondepressed individuals to have first-degree relatives (brothers, sisters, parents, or children) who are also depressed. For example, in a summary of nine studies, it was found that 8.6% of the relatives of depressed individuals suffered from depression, whereas only 4% of the relatives of nondepressed individuals suffered from depression (Nurnberger & Gershon, 1992). Unfortunately, in these studies, it is possible that it was the social contact with the relatives rather than the overlap of genes that resulted in the depression, so we must consider other evidence.

maybe social

Studies of Twins. The results of numerous studies have revealed that the concordance rate for depression is higher in monozygotic (MZ) twins (those who are genetically identical) than it is in dizygotic (DZ) twins (those who are genetically different) (Nurnberger & Gershon, 1992). For example, in one recent study the concordance rate for MZ twins was almost 70%, whereas the rate for DZ twins was only about 30% (Kendler, McGuire, et al., 1993b). Looked at in another way, the results of one study of twins indicated that the heritability of depression was between 33% and 45% and that the remaining variability was related to the unique experiences of the individuals rather than to specific family characteristics (Kendler, Neale, et al., 1992b). That range of heritability is similar to what has been found for anxiety (see Chapter 5) and for many ordinary personality traits.

Additional evidence for the role of genetics in depression comes from a study in which it was found that the level of depression in one twin was linked to the likelihood of depression in the other twin (Bertelsen, 1979; Bertelsen et al., 1977). Specifically, the concordance rate for depression in twin pairs in which one twin had fewer than three depressive episodes was only 33%, whereas the concordance rate for depression in twin pairs in which one twin had three or more depressive episodes was 59%. Furthermore, it has also been found that the levels of depression in twins are similar and that those levels are similar to the levels of depression in their parents (Kendler, Walters, et al., 1994). The findings based on the study of twins provide strong evidence for a genetic basis for depression.

Studies of Adoptees. The most convincing evidence of a genetic basis for depression comes from the study of individuals who either did or did not have depressed biological parents and were adopted and raised by nondepressed adoptive parents. In one study of this type, almost 40% of the adopted biological offspring of depressed parents were later found to be depressed, whereas only .07% of the adopted biological offspring of nondepressed parents were found to be depressed (Cadoret, 1978a).

An interesting experiment with rhesus monkeys provides evidence concerning the process by which genetics can lead to depression in offspring. In that experiment, the investigators examined the levels of serotonin and norepinephrine in (a) monkey biological parents, (b) monkey "adoptive" parents, and (c) the offspring that were raised by the biological or adoptive parents (Higley et al., 1993). The results revealed that the levels of serotonin and norepinephrine in the biological parents were related to the levels of those neurotransmitters in their offspring regardless of whether the offspring were raised by the biological or adoptive parents. In other words, genetic factors influenced levels of serotonin and norepinephrine, and as you learned earlier, levels of serotonin and norepinephrine influence depression.

In view of all of these results, it seems safe to conclude that genetic factors do play a role in depression. However, it is also essential to realize that (a) not all relatives of depressives become depressed, (b) the concordance rate for depression in monozygotic twins is not 100%, and (c) many people who become depressed do not appear to have a family history of depression. Therefore, from these findings we must conclude that genetic factors play an important role in depression but that genetic factors alone do not account for all depressions (Faraone et al., 1990).

Genetics and Stress. From the findings just presented, it is clear that genes contribute to depression, and the pathway appears to be as follows: Genes result in lower levels of neurotransmitters, and then the lower levels of neurotransmitters result in depression. However, there is another pathway by which genes can contribute to depression: *Genes can lead to stressful life events that can in turn lead to depression.* It may surprise you that genes are linked to stressful life events, but I will describe how the relationship works.

In most discussions, it is assumed that stressful life events are random and due to chance; that is, having a lot of stressful life events is "bad luck." However, stressors may not be completely random. Have you ever noticed how some people have more bad

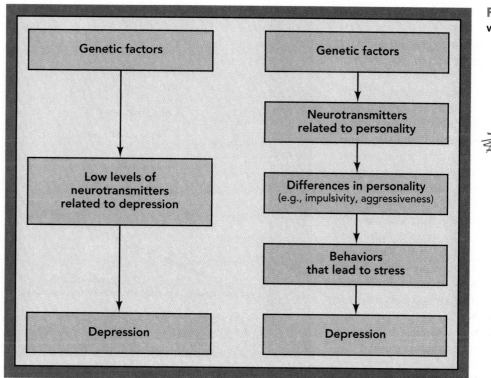

FIGURE 9.10 Genetic pathways to depression.

things happen to them or are involved in more personal crises than others? Indeed, there is now objective evidence that some individuals are more likely than other individuals to have automobile accidents, suffer industrial injuries, endure financial crises, and be the victims of criminals (Kendler, Neale, et al., 1993c). The fact that stressful events are not random suggests that there is an underlying explanation for their occurrence, and part of that explanation is genes. No, you do not inherit stressful life events per se; rather you inherit levels of various neurotransmitters that influence your personality, and then your personality influences the stress in your life. For example, a low level of serotonin, determined in part by genetics, is related to impulsivity (discussed later in this chapter and in Chapter 14), and impulsivity can easily lead an individual to make foolish decisions that will lead to stress.

Evidence for the role of genetic factors in stressful life events comes from the study of twins. For example, in one study of almost 400 twins who were reared together or apart, it was found that there was a higher concordance rate for stressful life events among MZ twin pairs than among DZ twin pairs (Plomin, Lichtenstein, et al., 1990). The effect was the same regardless of whether the twins were raised together or apart, thus indicating that a common family environment could not account for the effect.

In another study, it was also found that the concordance rate for stressful life events was higher among MZ than DZ twins, but when the investigators examined different *types* of stressful events, they found that genetics played a much stronger role in events in which the individual was *directly involved* than those that happened to others but caused stress for the individual (Kendler et al., 1993). Specifically, the concordance rate was higher for events such as personal illnesses, injuries, criminal assaults, and interpersonal conflicts than was the case for deaths, illnesses, or injuries of someone else close to the individual. Clearly, many of the stressful events in which individuals are directly involved are not random events or bad luck; they are due to behaviors that are influenced by genetic factors.

The link between genes and stressful life events increases the role that genetic factors play in the development of depression. That is, not only do individuals inherit a physiological problem that can predispose the individuals to develop depression or can actually cause the depression, but individuals can also inherit traits that will lead to stress that can trigger depression. The two pathways by which genes can lead to depression are illustrated in Figure 9.10.

The Link Between Stress and the Physiological Factors

Throughout this chapter, it has become clear that stress can cause depression, but the question arises, how does stress cause depression? That is, what is the underlying process? Fortunately, an understanding of the physiological basis for depression enables us to answer that question. Specifically, there is now strong evidence that *stress results in lower levels of serotonin and norepinephrine,* and the lower levels of those neurotransmitters lead to depression.

Evidence for the link between stress and lowered levels of neurotransmitters comes from research in which animals were or were not exposed to stressors, and then the levels of serotonin and norepinephrine in their brains were assessed (see E. A. Stone, 1975). The stressors have included such things as electric shocks, heat, noise, conflict, social separation, fighting, and observing other animals fighting. In almost every case, the stress led to reduced levels of serotonin and norepinephrine. Furthermore, when the experiments involved more than one level of stress, higher levels of stress led to lower levels of serotonin and norepinephrine. In some cases, the levels of the neurotransmitters were reduced by as much as 40% or 50%. The exact process by which stress reduces neurotransmitter levels is not yet understood, but it may be that the high levels of neurological activity associated with stress somehow use up the available neurotransmitters.

In a particularly interesting study that is relevant for depression in humans, the investigators studied the changes in serotonin in monkeys that were moved from one social group to another (Raleigh et al., 1984). In the first social group, the monkeys were leaders and enjoyed high social status, but in the group to which the monkeys were moved, they were isolated at the bottom of the social network. When the monkeys' status dropped and they were isolated, their levels of serotonin dropped, and the monkeys appeared to be depressed. There is a striking parallel between those findings and the effects of changes in our lives such as going away to school, moves, job demotions, or forced retirement. The next time you are under stress and you become depressed, you will know that your levels of serotonin and norepinephrine have probably been lowered by the stress. Understanding this process can have implications for treatment. For example, if an individual is depressed because of a stress that cannot be relieved, drugs might be used to bolster the levels of the neurotransmitters lowered by the stress.

Diathesis-Stress

Why do some individuals become depressed in the face of stress while others do not? The findings that low levels of neurotransmitters lead to depression and that stress lowers the levels of neurotransmitters enable us to answer that question. Individuals who become depressed in the face of stress are probably those who already have low or variable levels of the neurotransmitters, and the stress forces their levels down below some threshold level. In contrast, individuals who are less likely to become depressed when confronted with stress are probably those who have high or stable levels of the neurotransmitters, so a stress-related reduction of those levels is less likely to force their levels below the crucial

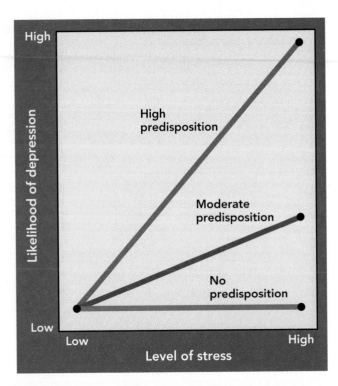

FIGURE 9.11 **The likelihood of depression increases as the level of stress or level of predisposition (diathesis) increases.**
Source: Adapted from Monroe and Simons (1991), p. 415, fig. 4.

threshold for depression. In other words, some individuals are *predisposed* to depression because of initially lower or unstable levels of the neurotransmitters, and then stress triggers the depression. This is referred to as the **diathesis-stress explanation** for why only some individuals become depressed (Monroe & Simons, 1991). (Recall that *diathesis* means "predisposition.")

Note that diathesis is not an either-or phenomenon; instead, there are gradations in the degree to which an individual may be predisposed to depression, so individuals are at greater or lesser risk. The diathesis model is portrayed in Figure 9.11. In that figure, different lines are used to indicate individuals with different degrees of predisposition, and as you can see, as stress or disposition increases, so does the likelihood of becoming depressed. That explains why in some individuals a slight stress will trigger a depression, whereas in others depressions are brought on only by major stresses.

COMMENT

There is very strong evidence that low levels of neurotransmitters, specifically serotonin and norepinephrine, can lead to depression. In addition, the low levels of neurotransmitters can also be used to explain the symptoms such as problems with sleep, appetite, and sex that often accompany depression, thereby providing a more complete account than other explanations.

However, the important question that must be asked is, what causes the low levels of neurotransmitters? Clearly, in many cases, they are due to genetic factors, and in those cases, the depression can be independent of psychological and environmental factors. In other cases, the low levels of neurotransmitters may be the "final common pathway" by which stress leads to depression. That is, stress leads to low levels of the neurotransmitters, which then lead to depression. That may be most likely to happen in individuals who already have low levels of the neurotransmitters and who are then "pushed over the edge" by the stress.

WHAT CAN WE CONCLUDE CONCERNING THE CAUSES OF DEPRESSION?

Probably the most important thing to recognize is that depression can be caused by a number of different factors. However, those factors can be organized into two groups: *stress* and *physiology*. With regard to stress, there is strong evidence that *psychological stressors* such as interpersonal conflict, financial problems, and overwhelming demands can result in depression. Furthermore, it appears that low levels of rewards, high levels of punishments, negative cognitive sets (thinking you are no good or that the world is a hostile place), and feelings of hopelessness can also be stressful and lead to depression.

Two qualifications should be noted with regard to the stress-depression relationship. First, the co-occurrence of stress and depression does not always mean that the stress caused the depression. Instead, in some cases, depression may lead an individual to behave in such a way as to cause stress. Second, there is not a direct link between stress and depression. Instead, stress (whatever its cause) leads to low levels of neurotransmitters, which in turn lead to depression. That is, a lowered level of neurotransmitters is the final common pathway to depression.

With regard to physiology, there is strong evidence that low levels of serotonin or norepinephrine can cause depression and the related symptoms of problems with sleep, diet, and sex. The low levels of the neurotransmitters may be caused by stress, or they may be due to genetic factors. In the latter case, the depression can occur in the absence of stress.

In many cases, depression results from the interaction of a number of factors. For example, for genetic reasons individuals may have somewhat low levels of serotonin or norepinephrine (not low enough to cause depression), but then the presence of a stressor forces the levels of those neurotransmitters lower and causes depression. In other cases, individuals may have negative cognitive sets that lead them to overinterpret minor problems as serious,

thus creating stress that can lower neurotransmitters and cause depression. In other words, physiological factors and cognitive factors can *predispose* individuals to depression, for example.

Finally, it should be noted that once an individual is depressed, a number of factors may serve to prolong the depression, sometimes for long periods of time after the original cause of the depression has dissipated. For example, an individual may become depressed because of a loss, but the depression will activate negative expectations and the recall of negative experiences, and those factors may maintain the depression after the problems related to the loss have been overcome.

TOPIC II
THE BIPOLAR DISORDER

PSYCHODYNAMIC, LEARNING, AND COGNITIVE EXPLANATIONS

For most major disorders, there are widely held psychodynamic, learning, cognitive, and physiological explanations. However, that is not the case for the bipolar disorder because the psychodynamic, learning, and cognitive explanations have been largely abandoned in favor of physiological ones. The demise of interest in psychological explanations for the bipolar disorder probably stemmed from the fact that the drug **lithium carbonate** was found to be highly effective for treating the disorder (see Chapter 10). Furthermore, treatments based on the psychological explanations were ineffective. In other words, because the physiologically based treatment was very effective and the psychologically based treatment was ineffective, we have come to believe that the psychological theory was wrong. However, to provide a historical perspective, I will examine the once popular psychological explanation for the bipolar disorder and then go on to discuss the physiological explanations.

The basic tenet of the psychological explanation was that individuals with the bipolar disorder are basically very depressed (which they show during their depressive phase), but when the depression becomes too great, they attempt to *escape the depression with manic behavior* (Freeman, 1971; Lewin, 1951). During the manic phase, the patients were said to be in a "manic flight from depression." In other words, the manic behavior was seen as a defense against overwhelming depression. The flight-from-depression explanation for mania had a good deal of intuitive appeal because a commonly suggested remedy for depression is to "go out and do something wild" or to "put on a happy face." There were also numerous case studies that could be interpreted as supporting the flight-from-depression explanation. For example, I knew one patient with a bipolar disorder who had a husband who was having affairs with other women, and that upset and depressed her. In her manic phase, she would sometimes dance around the ward singing, "I'm going to wash that man right out of my hair"—and on a number of occasions, she dumped washbasins of water over her head. The interpretation was that she used the singing and dancing to distract herself from the "underlying depression" about her husband, but even then her "real concern" about her husband came through in the content of what she sang (she wanted the unfaithful husband "out of her hair").

Anecdotal reports such as those are interesting, but there is no reliable evidence that psychological factors such as a flight from depression cause the bipolar disorder. However, psychological factors can contribute to it. Specifically, there is now evidence that sometimes stress can bring on or prolong the symptoms or cause a relapse in individuals who are physiologically predisposed to the bipolar disorder (Johnson & Roberts, 1995). For example, it was found that among individuals with the bipolar disorder, those who had a high number of life stresses were 4½ times more likely to relapse than individuals who had a low number of life stresses (Ellicott et al., 1990). In considering the influence of stress on the bipolar disorder, it is important to keep separate the stresses that bring on the disorder from the stresses caused by the disorder because sometimes the onset of the manic phase can bring on stress. However, overall it does appear that stress can contribute to some cases of the bipolar disorder, probably because it exacerbates an underlying physiological problem.

PHYSIOLOGICAL EXPLANATIONS

Physiological Imbalances

The fact that the symptoms in the bipolar disorder involve shifts between depression and mania suggests that the underlying problem involves some form of *physiological instability* (Schou et al., 1981; Siever & Davis, 1985). So far, no specific instability has been definitely identified, but there are two likely possibilities: *changing levels of neurotransmitters* and *changing levels of postsynaptic sensitivity* (Bunney & Murphy, 1976).

Changing Levels of Neurotransmitters. The presynaptic membrane that regulates the release of the neurotransmitter may vary the amount of the neurotransmitter it allows into the synapse. When it allows an excessive amount of the neurotransmitter into the synapse, there will be a high level of neurological activi-

ty, and the individual will become manic. In contrast, when the membrane allows an insufficient amount of the neurotransmitter into the synapse, there will be a low level of neurological activity, and the individual will become depressed.

Changing Levels of Postsynaptic Sensitivity. It is also possible that changes in the sensitivity of the postsynaptic receptor sites may be the crucial factor in the bipolar disorder. At some times, the receptor sites may be very sensitive to stimulation, leading to more neurological activity and manic behavior. At other times, the receptor sites may be insensitive to stimulation, resulting in decreased neurological activity and depression.

We do not know exactly what aspect of the system is unstable or why. However, we do know that administering lithium carbonate is effective in eliminating symptoms in most patients with the bipolar disorder, and we assume that the drug serves to stabilize the erratic system. How that is achieved is still a topic of debate and research.

The changes in brain activity in mania and depression can be seen by measuring changes in glucose metabolism. Energy is required for all the activities that occur in the body, and that energy is provided by a type of sugar called **glucose.** The process of using glucose to produce energy is known as **glucose metabolism.** Just as your leg muscles require glucose when you run, your brain requires glucose when neurological activity occurs, and therefore we can measure brain activity by measuring glucose metabolism with PET scans (see Chapter 3). Figure 9.12 shows PET scans from a patient with a bipolar disorder. The three scans in the top row were taken during a depressed phase, and the three scans in the bottom row were taken during a manic phase. You are looking down on the brain from the top,

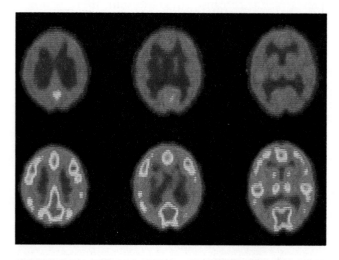

FIGURE 9.12 PET scans indicate higher levels of cerebral glucose metabolism and higher levels of brain activity during manic than during depressive phases.
Source: From "Cerebral Metabolic Rates for Glucose in Mood Disorders" by L. R. Baxter et al., in *Archives of General Psychiatry,* Vol. 42, May 1985. Reprinted by permission of the American Medical Society.

and the three scans in each row represent three levels (planes) of the brain. The colors indicate different amounts of glucose metabolism; red and yellow indicate higher metabolism, and blue and purple indicate lower metabolism. On the manic day, the patient had a much higher rate of cerebral glucose metabolism than on the depressed day; in fact, the rate of glucose metabolism on the manic day was 36% higher than on the depressed day (Baxter et al., 1985). Although these findings clearly indicate differences in brain functioning between manic and depressed days, we should not conclude that differences in glucose metabolism are the cause of the bipolar disorder. Instead, they reflect the effects of the problems with neurotransmission that were discussed earlier.

Is glucose metabolism related to weight? Are overweight people more sad, depressed?

Genetic Factors

If the bipolar disorder stems from problems with neurological activity, we must go on to ask, what causes those underlying problems? One possibility is that individuals may inherit a neurological instability that results in a bipolar disorder.

Studies of Families. If there is a genetic basis for the bipolar disorder, we would expect that first-degree relatives (children, parents, siblings) of individuals with the disorder would have a higher rate of bipolar illness than individuals in the general population. A review of 15 studies that together involved thousands of individuals revealed that 7.6% of the relatives of individuals with the bipolar disorder also suffered from the disorder, whereas only .8% of the relatives of individuals who did not have the disorder suffered from it (Nurnberger & Gershon, 1992). In other words, individuals who have a first-degree relative with the bipolar disorder have a risk of developing the disorder that is 9½ times higher than individuals who do not have a relative with the disorder. *8% vs 1% Is this significant?*

Studies of Twins. Studies of monozygotic and dizygotic twins also provide evidence for the role of heredity in the bipolar disorder. For example, in one study, it was found that among MZ twin pairs, the concordance rate for the bipolar disorder was 58%, whereas among DZ twin pairs, the concordance rate was only 17% (Bertelsen et al., 1977). In these studies, the concordance rate among MZ twins was more than three times higher than the concordance rate among DZ twins.

Studies of Adoptees. The role of genetic factors in the development of bipolar disorder was also established in a study of the biological and adoptive parents of individuals who developed the bipolar disorder (Mendlewicz & Rainer, 1977). In that study, it was found that 31% of the biological parents of the patients had a bipolar disorder, but only 2% of the adoptive parents had one.

Direct Examination of Genes. In a number of studies, the investigators actually examined the genes of a large number of individuals who did and did not have a bipolar disorder (Detera-Wadleigh et al., 1987; Egeland et al., 1987; Hodgkinson et al., 1987). In one study, it was reported that individuals with a bipolar disorder had an additional gene on the short arm of chromosome 11, but other investigators were unable to replicate the finding, and therefore we are not yet able to draw a conclusion concerning specific genes or sets of genes.

Taken together, the evidence from studies of families, twins, and adoptees provides strong and consistent support for the speculation that heredity plays a role in the development of the bipolar disorder.

WHAT CAN WE CONCLUDE CONCERNING THE CAUSES OF THE BIPOLAR DISORDER?

It is now clear that the bipolar disorder is due to *physiological factors*. Specifically, it appears that it is due to *changing levels of neurotransmitters* or *changing levels of postsynaptic sensitivity* (or possibly both). The exact mechanisms are not yet understood. It is also clear that genetic factors play an important role in the bipolar disorder. Although physiological factors provide the foundation for the bipolar disorder, psychological stress can play a role in that it can trigger relapses.

This completes the discussion of the causes of mood disorders. However, before concluding this chapter, we must consider the causes of suicide. Suicides and mood disorders are often related, and there is some overlap in some of their causes. Therefore, your understanding of the causes of mood disorders will provide you with some of the foundation that is necessary to understand suicide.

TOPIC III
SUICIDE

PSYCHODYNAMIC EXPLANATIONS

Freud's View of Suicide

Freud once wrote that suicides could be regarded as disguised murders. In this view, the suicidal individual's goal is not so much self-destruction as the destruction of another person, a lost person with whom the individual has identified. According to Freud, individuals who lose a loved person take the person in as part of themselves as a means of symbolically avoiding the loss (recall our discussion of the causes of depression). However, while loving the lost person, these individuals also hate the person for deserting them. (That anger turned inward is thought to be the cause of depression.) A suicide attempt may in that case be an expression of *aggression against the internalized other* rather than aggression against the self. Freud considered suicide the ultimate act of anger turned inward (Menninger, 1938).

Freud also hypothesized that there was a **death instinct,** the goal of which was returning the conflicted individual to a state of calm and nonexistence from which he or she came. When the death instinct became stronger than the life instinct that usually held it in check, the result was suicide (Freud, 1920/1955).

Stress and Suicide

A widely held psychodynamic explanation for suicide is that *people commit suicide to escape stress.* Consistent with that explanation, a variety of investigations indicated that just prior to their attempts, people who attempt suicide experience up to four times as many negative life events (e.g., separations, major financial reversals, diagnoses of serious illnesses) as nonattempters over a comparable period of time (Cochrane & Robertson, 1975; Paykel et al., 1975; Slater & Depue, 1981).

Other evidence for the influence of stress on suicide is that during the Great Depression of the early 1930s, the suicide rate jumped from under 10 per 100,000 to 17.4 per 100,000. Similarly, the rate of suicide increased during the economic recession of the 1970s (National Institute of Mental Health, 1976; Wekstein, 1979).

When considering the effects of stress on suicide, we should also consider the role played by social support in moderating the effects of stress. Individuals who attempt suicide often have less social support than nonattempters, suggesting that the absence of support intensifies the effects of stress (Braucht, 1979; Slater & Depue, 1981). Suicide attempters are often demographically dissimilar from their neighbors, so it appears that being a misfit could serve to isolate these individuals from needed sources of support. Finally, it is noteworthy that the stress experienced by individuals who commit suicide often involves losses such as deaths of relatives or friends that reduce social support.

There is absolutely no doubt that stress plays an important role in many suicides. However, two problems remain. First, not everyone who is exposed to stress commits suicide, so we must go on to consider the processes that might link stress to suicide for some individuals. Second, some individuals who commit suicide are not under stress, so we must also consider explanations for suicide other than stress.

Depression and Suicide

Depression plays a very important role in many suicides. It has been estimated that at least 80% of suicidal patients are depressed, and the rate of suicide among depressed individuals is 22 to 36 times higher than among nondepressed individuals (Kraft & Babigian, 1976; Lesage et al., 1994; Robins & Guze, 1972; Slater & Depue, 1981). Depressed individuals commit suicide because from their perspective, life is not worth living. A frequent comment made by depressed individuals is "I wish I were dead."

The rate of suicide among depressed individuals would probably be even higher were it not for the fact that many severely depressed patients simply do not have the energy to commit suicide. Because of this, many suicides occur after the individuals begin to get better (Shneidman, 1979). The individuals are still depressed, but as they start to improve, their energy begins to return, and they are better able to carry out the suicidal act. For example, during the worst of her depression, one depressed woman sat motionless and simply stared into space (she was experiencing psychomotor retardation). When her depression began to lift and she started to move around, one of her first actions was to go to the bathroom and take an overdose of medication, which killed her.

Fantasies and Suicide

From the psychodynamic standpoint, an important factor in determining whether someone will commit suicide is **fantasies** about what suicide will accomplish (Furst & Ostow, 1979). Four fantasies have been singled out as most important.

Identification with the Lost Person. In the discussion of the causes of depression, I pointed out that psychodynamic theorists believe that depression is triggered by a stressful loss. Some theorists suggest that depressed individuals attempt to regain the lost person by identifying with him or her. If the person has been lost through death, the ultimate act of identification is one's own death, and thus it may be that attempts to identify with lost (dead) persons result in suicide. In support of that explanation, theorists have pointed to what are called "anniversary suicides," whereby an individual commits suicide on the anniversary of the other individual's death. An alternative explanation for anniversary suicides is that the anniversary brings back the individual's stress and despair, and the heightening of those factors leads to the suicide. Clearly, anniversaries of severe stresses are a time when increased social support is needed.

Rebirth. Another fantasy that has been suggested as relevant for understanding suicide is the fantasy that after death, the individual will be reborn free of his or her current problems. This fantasy gains support from religious beliefs concerning an afterlife or heaven. Indeed, in many religious funerals, the deceased individuals are described as having been relieved of their worldly burdens and having gone to a new life in a better place. (However, it is interesting to note that in many religions, suicide is viewed as a sin, and the individual may be refused entry to heaven.) Consistent with this rebirth fantasy, one therapist reported that patients in a psychiatric hospital located next to a large river had the fantasy that they would "escape from this place, run out on the bridge, jump off and drown, and later come out alive and new on the other side" (Furst & Ostow, 1979).

rivers are symbolic / life change

Self-Punishment. When we do things of which we do not approve, we often punish ourselves in a variety of little ways, such as depriving ourselves of some pleasure or treat. Psychodynamic theories suggest that in extreme cases, this self-punishment can result in suicide. They suggest that the "bad me" (associated with the ego) and the "good me" (associated with the superego) get separated, and to punish the "bad me," the "good me" may kill the "bad me."

Revenge. Revenge may play a role in suicide in that it appears that some individuals commit suicide to make the people around them feel sorry or guilty. This motivation is often reflected in suicide notes that say, in effect, "This would not have happened if you had not done thus and so." This is common in children who commit suicide. They are powerless to attack the adults who control them and commit suicide in an attempt to get back at the adults. It is not unusual for a child to think or say, "When I'm dead, you'll be sorry you weren't nicer to me!" *lots/ego*

LEARNING EXPLANATIONS

Rather than examining the underlying factors that cause an individual to want to commit suicide, learning theorists have focused their attention on the processes that facilitate committing suicide once the individual is motivated to do so. In that regard, learning theorists have pointed to the role played by *imitation* and *behavioral contagion*. We will consider those processes, and we will also consider the possibility that suicidal gestures may be carried out because they are a means of getting rewards (attention).

Imitation

The basic premise of the learning explanations is that suicide occurs in large part because of **imitation.** When encountering a problem, an individual may hear of another individual's suicide, and that may suggest suicide as a solution. The other individual's suicide may also suggest an effective way of committing suicide.

Evidence for the effects of imitation on suicidal behavior is provided by the fact that suicide rates increase dramatically following reports of suicides on television or in newspapers (Bollen & Phillips, 1982; Phillips, 1974; see review by Stack, 1990). Examples of this are provided in Table 9.2, where you will find the dates of seven suicides that were reported on nationally televised evening news programs. With each date is the number of individuals who committed suicide in the United States during the following week and during a comparable control week that was not preceded by the report of a suicide. Those data indicate that the number of suicides increased by 7% after a nationally publicized suicide, resulting in 244 additional suicides. Other research has shown that levels of publicity given

was this when suicide coverage was few + far b/t?

TABLE 9.2 Increases in Suicides Following Stories About Suicides on Television Evening News Programs

Date of Story	Suicides After Story	Suicides During Control Period	Difference
April 25, 1972	554	444	110
June 4, 1973	528	435	93
September 11, 1973	487	514	−27
July 15, 1974	482	462	20
April 11, 1975	593	572	21
September 3, 1975	553	501	52
May 13, 1976	550	575	−25
Totals	3,747	3,503	244

Source: Adapted from Bollen and Phillips (1982), p. 804, tab. 1.

to suicides were related to the levels of subsequent suicides (more publicity, more suicides) and that the effect was limited to the geographic area receiving the publicity (Phillips, 1974).

The effect of imitation on suicide is probably stronger than the data in Table 9.2 suggest because those data reflect only overt cases of suicide. Data from other investigations indicate that motor vehicle fatalities increase following well-publicized suicides (Bollen & Phillips, 1981; Phillips, 1977, 1979), and it is likely that the accidents in which the individuals were killed were actually disguised or covert suicides.

It is interesting to note that suicides following publicized suicides come in two waves. There is a surge of suicides on the day of the report and the following day, then there is a lull, and finally there is another surge on the sixth and seventh days after the report. That has been the case for both overt and covert suicides (Bollen & Phillips, 1982; Phillips, 1977). These findings suggest that there may be two types of suicide responders. Those who respond immediately may be more impulsive or have already contemplated suicide, and the publicized suicide may have only hastened an act that would have occurred anyway. In contrast, those who respond after six days may be making a more considered response or may not have seriously contemplated suicide as a solution prior to the example provided by the publicized suicide.

An interesting but unfortunate example of the effects of imitation on suicide is seen in the "epidemics" or clusters of suicide that occur among adolescents (Gould et al., 1989). In numerous instances, one adolescent has committed suicide, followed by a number of his or her peers, often using the same or a similar procedure. For example, in 1983, Bill Ramsey was killed in a drag-racing accident. Two days later, Bruce Corwin, Ramsey's best friend, said he would see Bill again "some sunny day" and then committed suicide by running his car engine in a closed garage. Six days later, Glen Curry, a friend of Bill and Bruce, committed suicide in the same way. That was followed by the suicide of Henri Droit, who did not know the others but had newspaper articles about their suicides on his bulletin board at home. In addition to these four successful suicides, there were 12 unsuccessful suicide attempts in the following 8 weeks. Another example of imitation occurred in a small town in Connecticut in which during one 5-day period, eight young girls were brought to the hospital because of suicide attempts (Rosenberg & Leland, 1995). Consistent with those findings are the results of a study of adolescents in which it was found that the best predictors of suicide were (a) a history of attempts, (b) depression and thoughts about suicide, and (c) a recent attempt by a friend (Lewinsohn et al., 1994). In other words, depressed individuals can be led to suicide by the example of others.

Finally, the effects of imitation on the strategies that individuals use to commit suicide is illustrated by the number of people who kill themselves by jumping off of the Golden Gate Bridge in San Francisco. More than 1,000 people have committed suicide by jumping off that bridge, but fewer than 200 have committed suicide by jumping off the San Francisco–Oakland Bay Bridge, a short distance away. Indeed, some individuals drive over the Bay Bridge to get to the Golden Gate Bridge so they can jump from it. Given its history, apparently the Golden Gate Bridge is "the place to do it."

Occasional attempts have been made to prevent suicidal imitation. For example, to end a rash of sensational suicides in subways (individuals throwing themselves in the way of trains), news reporters agreed to stop publicizing the suicides. The reduction of publicity was associated with a reduction in those specific suicides (Etzersdorfer et al., 1992).

Behavioral Contagion

Simply getting the idea to commit suicide is rarely enough to result in the act. Even if an individual wants very much to do it, there are usually cultural restraints against committing suicide ("It is wrong to commit suicide," "Nice people don't commit suicide"). However, those restraints can be overcome through the process of **behavioral contagion** (Wheeler, 1966). Behavioral contagion occurs when (a) an individual wants to do something, (b) is restrained from doing it because society says that the behavior is wrong, (c) sees someone else do it and "get away with it," and then (d) thinks that he or she can get away with it also. Examples of behavioral contagion include crossing the street against the traffic light and smoking in no-smoking areas when others do so first. (Contagion differs from imitation in that *contagion reduces restraints against performing a known behavior,* whereas *imitation introduces a new behavior.*)

The concept of behavioral contagion is useful in understanding suicide, especially epidemics of suicide, because it explains why it is suddenly "all right" to take one's own life. Fortunately, behavioral contagion does not reduce all restraints, and thus its effect is limited. Observing others commit prohibited acts can reduce *external* restraints that stem from social rules, but it is relatively ineffective for reducing *internal* restraints that stem from one's own beliefs (Ritter & Holmes, 1968). This means that contagion would occur if the individual was originally restrained by the fact that society says that suicide is wrong, but contagion would not occur if the individual was restrained by the personal belief that suicide was wrong.

Clearly, hearing about suicides plays an important role in increasing their incidence, but hearing about suicides is not itself a sufficient explanation for suicide. Like other explanations, the learning explanations provide part, but not all, of the answer to the question of why people commit suicide.

Rewards

Suicide threats and gestures are often calls for help, but they may also be operant behaviors used to manipulate others and get *rewards* (Bostock & Williams, 1975). In one case, a man began threatening to kill himself when a woman he had been dating broke off the relationship and refused to see him. He wrote to her, saying, "Without you, there is nothing in life for me. Unless there is a chance that you will see me, I will end it all." At first, the woman gave in because the threats frightened her, but they were not a basis for a relationship, so she eventually told the police of his threats and stopped seeing him. Individuals who use suicide threats to manipulate others pose difficult problems because if we attempt to extinguish the behavior by ignoring it, we run the risk that the individual will succeed at suicide, accidentally or intentionally.

COGNITIVE EXPLANATIONS

The cognitive explanations for suicide suggest that some people lack adequate problem-solving skills, so when they face stress-provoking problems, they develop an attitude of hopelessness and eventually commit suicide because they see no other alternative. In this explanation, *poor problem-solving skills* and *hopelessness* provide the link between stress and suicide.

Poor Problem Solving

Research has demonstrated that suicidal individuals have poor problem-solving skills when compared to nonsuicidal individuals (Orbach et al., 1990; Patsiokas et al., 1979; Schotte & Clum, 1987). Specifically, suicidal individuals suffer from **cognitive rigidity,** which means that they lack the flexibility to see alternative solutions for their problems. In one study, suicidal and nonsuicidal psychiatric patients were asked to list alternative uses for a number of common items such as pencils and paper clips. The suicidal patients came up with only 40% as many uses as the nonsuicidal patients. Furthermore, when each patient was reminded of an interpersonal problem from real life and was asked to generate solutions for it, the suicidal patients generated fewer than half as many solutions as nonsuicidal patients and rated them as less likely to be effective.

The inability to solve problems because of cognitive rigidity can have a number of serious implications. First, people who are unable to solve problems will experience more failures, and that increases the stress on them. Second, the inability to solve problems leads to feelings of hopelessness, which, as we will see, is closely related to suicide. Third, once cognitively rigid individuals decide on suicide as a solution for their problems, they will pursue only that solution and not consider or develop other, better solutions. For example, a poor problem solver who faces financial difficulties may not be able to come up with an effective solution and may simply repeat the actions that led to the difficult situation in the first place. That may cause increased stress and feelings of hopelessness and, with no solution in sight, encourage suicide.

The poor problem-solving ability may stem from two sources. First, the individual may never have learned how to solve problems, and second, the individual's problem-solving ability might be impaired by depression (see Chapter 8). In the latter case, poor problem-solving ability provides the link between depression and the hopelessness that leads to depression. Indeed, there is now evidence that short-term changes in depression lead to short-term changes in problem-solving ability (Schotte, Cools, & Payvar, 1990). For at least some individuals, poor problem solving may be dependent on their state of depression rather than an enduring trait.

Hopelessness

The other important factor in the cognitive explanation for suicide is **hopelessness** (Beck et al., 1990; Ivanoff & Jang, 1991). Hopelessness is the belief that "things won't get better," and it is a component of depression, but depressed individuals can feel more or less hopeless, and the degree to which an individual feels hopeless is closely related to suicidal behavior. In fact, hopelessness is a better predictor of suicidal intent than depression in general. It has also been found that as hopelessness increases, so do thoughts about suicide, intentions to commit suicide, and suicide attempts (Beck et al., 1974; Beck et al., 1985; Minkoff et al., 1973; Motto, 1977; Rifai et al., 1994; Wetzel, 1977). Table 9.3 contains some of the items from the questionnaire that is usually used to measure hopelessness. Those items will give you some understanding of what is meant by hopelessness and why individuals who answer yes are more likely to commit suicide.

The important role that hopelessness plays in suicide was demonstrated in a study in which more than 200 inpatients who had taken the Hopelessness Scale were followed up 5 to 10 years later to determine which ones had committed suicide (Beck et al., 1985). Of the 14 patients who had committed suicide, 13 had scores of 10 or greater on the Hopelessness Scale. These results clearly reflect the role of hopelessness in suicide.

In one test of the cognitive model of suicide, investigators examined the levels of hopelessness and

TABLE 9.3 Sample Items from the Hopelessness Scale (High Scores Are Related to Suicide)

I might as well give up because I can't make things better for myself.

My future seems dark to me.

I just don't get the breaks, and there's no reason to believe I will in the future.

All I can see ahead of me is unpleasantness rather than pleasantness.

Things just won't work out the way I want them to.

It is very unlikely that I will get any real satisfaction in the future.

There's no use in really trying to get something I want because I probably won't get it.

Source: Beck et al. (1974), p. 862, tab. 1.

thoughts about suicide in individuals who experienced high or low life stress and who had good or bad problem-solving skills (Schotte & Clum, 1982). The results indicated, first, that individuals under high stress felt more hopeless and thought more about suicide than individuals under low stress. Second and more important, it was the individuals who were under high stress *and* who had poor problem-solving skills who felt most hopeless and thought most about suicide. The results concerning suicidal thoughts are presented in Figure 9.13. Overall, then, there is consistent and strong evidence that stress and poor problem solving are related to feelings of hopelessness and that hopelessness is in turn related to suicidal thoughts and behavior.

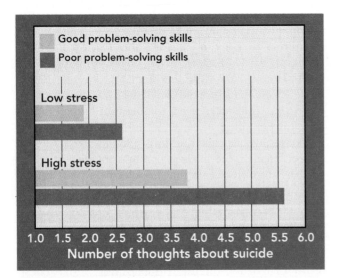

FIGURE 9.13 Individuals who are under stress and have poor problem-solving skills think more about suicide.
Source: Some data from Schotte and Clum (1982), p. 693, tab. 2.

Delusions and Hallucinations

It is noteworthy that the rate of suicide among individuals who suffer from schizophrenia is relatively high (Roy, 1983). In one study of 264 individuals who had been hospitalized with schizophrenia, it was found that the suicide rate was 10.6% among men and 4.7% among women (Westermeyer et al., 1991). The elevated rate of suicide in individuals with schizophrenia may be due to at least three factors. First, those individuals may have **delusions** that lead them to kill themselves. For example, individuals with schizophrenia may believe that they are the Devil and do not deserve to live, that they are cornered by foreign agents and must escape by poisoning themselves, or that they must kill themselves so that they can rejoin God. Second, individuals with schizophrenia may have auditory **hallucinations** (voices) telling them to kill themselves. Finally, **despair** over their condition may lead to suicide.

Delusions and hallucinations are cognitive explanations for suicide, but those explanations are qualitatively different from the cognitive explanations based on problem-solving abilities and hopelessness. It thus appears that suicide can stem from two different classes of cognitions: normal cognitions involving problem-solving skills and hopelessness and abnormal cognitions involving delusions and hallucinations. It is interesting to note that stressful life events and hopelessness are related to suicide in persons who do not have schizophrenia but not among persons with schizophrenia (Breier & Astrachan, 1984; Minkoff et al., 1973).

Reasons for Not Committing Suicide

You have seen that a variety of cognitive factors contribute to suicide (poor problem-solving skills, hopelessness, hallucinations, delusions), but there are also a number of cognitive factors that make suicide less likely in people who are otherwise at risk for suicide (Dyck, 1991; Linehan et al., 1983). Here is a list of six factors that have been shown to reduce suicidal intent, each followed by sample questions that are used to measure that factor.

1. *Survival and coping beliefs.* "I still have many things left to do." "No matter how badly I feel, I know that it will not last."

2. *Responsibility to family.* "It would hurt my family too much, and I would not want them to suffer." "My family depends on me and needs me."

3. *Child-related concerns.* "The effect on my children would be harmful." "It would not be fair to leave the children for others to take care of."

4. *Fear of suicide.* "I am a coward and do not have the guts to do it." "I am afraid that my method of killing myself would fail."

5. *Fear of social disapproval.* "I would not want other people to think I did not have control over my life." "I am concerned about what others would think of me."
6. *Moral objections.* "My religious beliefs forbid it." "I am afraid of going to hell."

Note that the positive cognitions about survival and coping are the flip side of the hopelessness that was discussed earlier (if you have positive beliefs about survival and coping, you cannot be hopeless), but the other cognitions are relatively independent of hopelessness.

Finally, it should be noted that one other important reason why some individuals do not commit suicide is that they *lack an effective means by which to do it.* For example, accessibility of guns is related to the suicide rate; if guns are not available, suicide rates are lower (Carrington & Moyer, 1994; Clarke & Lester, 1989; Kellermann et al., 1992). Other factors that have been linked to reductions in suicide include the introduction of exhaust emission controls that reduced the poisonous carbon monoxide that comes from automobiles (Clarke & Lester, 1989), the detoxification of home

---

CASE STUDY 9.1
Suicide of a 27-Year-Old Male Graduate Student

Chuck was a mature, upper-middle-class 27-year-old graduate student in chemistry. After graduating from college, he married a woman he had dated for 2 years and took a job with a large chemical company. Although he did very well at his job, he became dissatisfied. He attributed his unhappiness to the fact that without more education, he could not move up in the company. With his wife's support, he quit his job and returned to graduate school to get a master's degree.

Graduate school was demanding and often stressful. Although his grades were excellent and his professors cited him as one of the most promising students, Chuck began to wonder whether he had what it took to "make it." More important, he began to wonder whether he wanted to make it. He frequently asked himself, "Was it all worth it?" He continued to do well in his coursework, but he seemed to lose his sense of direction and found it increasingly difficult to enjoy himself. His worry about keeping up in school, in combination with his self-doubts about his future, led him to become anxious, moody, and depressed, and he became increasingly difficult to live with. After about a year, he and his wife separated. She was opposed to the separation and wanted to stay together to work on the problem and help him. However, as his depression deepened, Chuck easily became angry and wanted to be left alone. Figuratively, he pushed her away. His wife moved back to her parents' home in a distant city, and Chuck moved into a small apartment, where he lived alone.

When Chuck started missing many of his classes and stopped going to the laboratory, his professors insisted that he "see someone for help." Chuck saw no point in it ("I'm not crazy. I just don't know what

I want to do. I'm behind and unhappy, not crazy!"), but under pressure from his professors, he finally went to a psychiatrist.

During the first few sessions with the psychiatrist, Chuck admitted that he sometimes got quite depressed and that he was having difficulty sleeping through the night. He also acknowledged that sometimes he would spontaneously say to himself, "I wish I were dead" or "Life is terrible." Chuck occasionally talked about suicide in the abstract, but he denied that he was seriously considering suicide. When discussing suicide, it came out that his mother had once attempted suicide when he was about 12. He knew that she had subsequently received some psychiatric help, but he was too young at the time to know what had been done for her, and she had been killed about 4 years later when a car she was driving ran off the road.

The psychiatrist prescribed a tricyclic antidepressant for Chuck, but after two weeks of taking it, his depression had not improved. Chuck stopped taking the drug against the advice of the psychiatrist, who felt that not enough time had elapsed to give the drug a chance to have an effect. With the depression getting worse, the psychiatrist became concerned and recommended that Chuck voluntarily check into a psychiatric hospital where other treatments could be tried and where he could be more closely supervised. Chuck objected but agreed that he would think about hospitalization over the next couple of days and that they would discuss it again at their meeting the following Thursday.

Sitting on his bed that night, Chuck placed the end of a shotgun in his mouth and pulled the trigger.

heating gas (Lester, 1990), and lower heights of buildings (Marzuk et al., 1992). An elderly and very ill man in a hospital commented to me, "I want to die and I would commit suicide, but locked up in here, *I can't find a way to do it.*"

Overall, it appears that some individuals feel hopeless and consider suicide but do not attempt it because of the offsetting effects of cognitions about responsibility to family and children, fear of suicide, fear of social disapproval, moral objections, or the lack of effective means. The presence of these cognitions and options helps us understand why not everyone who feels hopeless commits suicide.

Many of the psychological factors that have been shown to contribute to suicide are reflected in the background and experiences of the young man who is discussed in Case Study 9.1 (p. 249).

PHYSIOLOGICAL EXPLANATIONS

Low Levels of Serotonin ∿ Suicide

Some of the most interesting new findings concerning suicide revolve around the neurotransmitter serotonin. Specifically, *low levels of serotonin are associated with suicide* (Lester, 1995; Mann et al., 1992; see reviews by Korn et al., 1990; Rifai et al., 1992; Roy, 1990; Stanley & Stanley, 1989). In one of the classic studies on this topic that was done with depressed patients, it was found that only some of the patients had low levels of serotonin, but it was the patients with low levels of serotonin who were more likely to have attempted suicide (40% vs. 15%; Asberg et al., 1976). Furthermore, it was the patients with low levels of serotonin who were most likely to use violent means for attempting suicide.

You know that low levels of serotonin can cause depression, and therefore you might assume that the serotonin-suicide relationship is simply mediated by depression—low levels of serotonin lead to depression, and the depression leads to suicide. That may be the case with some individuals, but serotonin must do something more because low levels of *both* serotonin and norepinephrine lead to depression, whereas suicide is higher only among individuals with low levels of serotonin. Furthermore, it has been found that when patients were given drugs that increased levels of serotonin or norepinephrine, the drugs that increased serotonin levels were more effective for reducing suicide than those that increased norepinephrine (Sacchetti et al., 1991). Clearly, low levels of serotonin are linked to suicide.

The effect of serotonin that is important here is that low levels lead to *aggression* as well as depression (Higley et al., 1992; Kruesi et al., 1992; Mehlum et al., 1994; see reviews by Brown & Goodwin, 1986; Van Praag, 1986). For example, in one study of men in the military, it was found that 80% of the differences in their levels of aggression could be accounted for by differences in their levels of serotonin; lower serotonin was associated with more aggression (Brown et al., 1979). Actually, low levels of serotonin do not lead to an increase in aggressive drive. Instead, normal levels of serotonin serve to *inhibit* aggressive responses or responses that had been punished in the past, so when the levels of serotonin drop, the inhibition lifts, and the aggressive or punished responses are used (Sanger & Blackman, 1976; Tye et al., 1979). For example, rats that were given electrical shocks when they ran into a goal box to get food stopped going into the box, but when they were given a drug that lowered their levels of serotonin, they ignored the possibility of shock and ran into the goal box. So the process that apparently links serotonin to suicide is as follows: A low level of serotonin causes an increase in depression and a decrease in the inhibition of inappropriate responses, so when the depression leads to thoughts of self-destruction, there is not enough inhibition of self-destructive behavior, and the individual attempts suicide.

Having established that low levels of serotonin are linked to suicide, the question arises, what causes the low levels of serotonin? There are two explanations. First, *stress* can cause a reduction in the levels of serotonin, and as you learned earlier, suicidal individuals experience as many as four times as many stressful life events as nonsuicidal individuals. Thus the stress-depression-suicide relationship can be mediated by lowered levels of serotonin. In that case, the relationship would actually be *stress-serotonin-depression-suicide.* Second, low levels of serotonin can be *inherited*, and that inheritance can be used to account for the serotonin-depression-suicide relationship in individuals who are not exposed to stress. In that case, the relationship would be *genes-serotonin-depression-suicide.* In view of the role that genetic factors might play in suicide, it will be instructive to consider the evidence linking genetics and suicide.

Low Levels of Cholesterol

It may surprise you, but another factor that can lead to suicide is a low level of **cholesterol.** Indeed, in one study, it was found that men with cholesterol levels that were below the 25th percentile were twice as likely to make a serious suicide attempt than their counterparts with higher levels of cholesterol (Muldoon et al., 1992). Why should low cholesterol lead to suicide? The first clue to the answer to that question came from studies of the health benefits of reducing cholesterol. In those studies, it was found that the lowered levels of cholesterol resulted in lower levels of heart disease, but the overall death rate did not go down because there was an increase in non-illness-related deaths. That is, deaths due to heart disease went down, but deaths due to suicide, violence, and accidents went up. The fact that there was an increase in violent types of death that are known to be associated with low levels of serotonin led investigators to speculate that the low levels of cholesterol led to low levels of serotonin. To test that possibility, investigators fed monkeys a diet that was low in fat and cholesterol and found that the monkeys' levels of serotonin activity went down and their level of aggression went up (Kaplan et al., 1991; Muldoon et al., 1992). We now know that *any* factor that can lower serotonin levels (stress, genetics, diet) can increase suicide rates.

Genetic Factors

Studies of Families. In seeking to determine whether inheritance plays a role in suicide, some investigators have examined the family histories of suicidal individuals. Their results consistently indicate that the incidence of suicide among the relatives of suicidal individuals is substantially higher than the rate among the relatives of nonsuicidal individuals (Farberow & Simon, 1969; Roy, 1982; Stengel, 1964). One investigator found that 49% of the patients who attempted suicide had a family history of suicide (Roy, 1983). These results suggest a genetic influence, but of course it is also possible that the effects were due to social modeling, so we must go on to consider other evidence.

Studies of Twins. The occurrence of suicide in monozygotic and dizygotic twins has been examined in two investigations that involved hundreds of sets of twins (Roy et al., 1991). Among the MZ twins in the two studies, the concordance rate for suicide was 14%, whereas among the DZ twins, the concordance rate for suicide was less than 1%. In other words, when the twins had identical genes, the concordance rate was about 15 times higher than when they had different genes, thus providing evidence for a genetic influence on suicide. These results are summarized in Figure 9.14.

Studies of Adoptees. In a study based on the adoptee method, the investigators found that among the relatives of children who were adopted and later committed suicide, the suicide rate among the adoptees' *biological* relatives was 4.5%, whereas the suicide rate among the adoptees' *adoptive* relatives was 0% (Schulsinger et al., 1979).

Studies of Genes. Recently, investigators have identified a specific gene that is linked to lower levels of serotonin (it is called the *TPH gene*), and in one study it was found that individuals who had a history of suicide were more likely to have the gene than nonsuicidal individu-

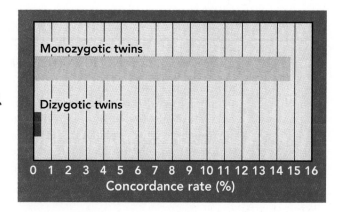

FIGURE 9.14 The concordance rate for suicide is almost 15 times higher in monozygotic twins than in dizygotic twins.
Source: Adapted from Haberlandt (1967) and Roy et al. (1991).

als (Nielsen et al., 1994). As you might expect, the suicidal individuals also had lower levels of serotonin.

Evidence for a genetic influence on suicide is clear. In considering these findings, however, it should not be concluded that there is a gene for suicide. Instead, it is probable that genetic factors lead to low levels of serotonin, which lead to depression and reduced inhibition for self-destructive acts.

WHAT CAN WE CONCLUDE CONCERNING THE CAUSES OF SUICIDE?

There is much more to suicide than an individual's simply wanting to "end it all" because he or she is under stress or depressed. Indeed, many factors contribute to suicide—and to the inhibition of suicide. For example, once the individual is depressed, role models for suicide and the fact that other people do it can reduce the restraints against suicide. Furthermore, feelings of hopelessness and poor problem-solving skills can move individuals closer to suicide because they do not see any other solution for their problems. Finally, low levels of serotonin can be important both because they contribute to depression and because they make the individual more impulsive and therefore more likely to suddenly carry out a violent act of self-destruction. The low levels of serotonin can stem from genetic factors and even from cholesterol-lowering diets.

Although suicide gestures are not designed to kill the individual, they must be taken very seriously because they reflect a serious problem and because they may accidentally succeed in killing the individual. The problem is that in some cases, individuals use suicide gestures to manipulate others and get attention.

SUMMARY

TOPIC I: THE DEPRESSIVE DISORDER

■ Freud suggested that depression was caused by a loss and, more specifically, by anger toward the lost individual that is turned inward. A more contemporary psychodynamic explanation is that depression is due to stress, and there is good support for that explanation. Loss may simply be a type of stress.

■ The effects of stress may be moderated by social support, individual differences in coping strategies, and aerobic fitness.

■ Learning theorists suggest that depression is due to (a) insufficient rewards, (b) excessive punishments, or (c) rewards for depressive behavior. The roles of insufficient rewards and excessive punishments are probably best understood in terms of the stress they cause, and there is little evidence that true depressive behaviors are learned.

■ Cognitive theorists suggest that depression is due to negative cognitive sets that lead individuals to focus on and recall the negative aspects of life. There is strong evidence that depressed individuals use selective attention and recall for depressing thoughts, but it may be that those are the result rather than an initial cause of depression. However, negative thoughts may predispose individuals to depression when they are exposed to stressors, and the negative thoughts may help maintain depression.

■ Cognitive theorists also suggest that depression is caused by feelings of helplessness in controlling the negative outcomes of life (learned helplessness). However, the evidence suggests that feelings of helplessness lead to depression because helplessness is a stressor.

■ From a physiological standpoint, depression is thought to stem from low levels of neurological activity in the areas of the brain that are responsible for pleasure. The low levels of activity may be due to low levels of neurotransmitters (serotonin, norepinephrine) or because the postsynaptic neurons are relatively insensitive to stimulation.

■ Evidence for the role of neurotransmitters comes from findings that drugs that increase their levels reduce depression, metabolites of the neurotransmitters are low in depressed individuals, and diets that are low in substances the body uses to make the neurotransmitters can lead to depression.

■ Low levels of neurotransmitters due to genetic factors can explain depressions that develop in the absence of stressors, and the low levels of neurotransmitters can also explain the associated problems with sleep, appetite, and sex.

■ There is strong evidence that genetic factors lead to depression, probably because they lower neurotransmitter levels, but genetic factors can also lead to stress, which can in turn reduce neurotransmitter levels and lead to depression.

■ Stress leads to depression because it lowers neurotransmitter levels. Some individuals may be predisposed to depression because they have genetically low levels of neurotransmitters, which are then forced below a critical point by stress. That is the diathesis-stress explanation.

TOPIC II: THE BIPOLAR DISORDER

■ Psychodynamic, learning, and cognitive explanations for the bipolar disorder have been largely abandoned because they did not prove helpful and because the drug lithium carbonate was found to be effective for treating the disorder. However, there is some evidence that stress can trigger the disorder, prolong the symptoms, and cause relapses.

■ The physiological explanations are that the vacillations in depression and mania are due to changing levels of neurotransmitters or changing levels of postsynaptic sensitivity. There is strong evidence for a genetic basis for this disorder.

How does St. Johns Wort work?

God Loves You

So it says:

- low levels / serotonin are related w/ impulsivity + aggression
- impulsivity is a characteristic / mania in bi-polar
- mania is associated w/ high levels / serotonin
  — so which is correct?

Also,

- tryptophan (in turkey) is converted into serotonin
- tryptophan is commonly related w/ sleepiness
- low-tryptophan diets lead to mild depression — so how does that work? sweet dreams?

TOPIC III: SUICIDE

■ Freud suggested that suicide was due to aggression turned inward or to a death instinct. A more contemporary psychodynamic explanation is that suicide is used to escape stress. Depressed individuals may commit suicide because the depression leads them to conclude that life is not worth living.

■ Learning theorists point to the evidence for the roles of imitation, behavioral contagion (restraint reduction), and rewards in suicide and suicide gestures.

■ Cognitive theorists suggest that suicide is due to poor problem solving (individuals do not see another solution), hopelessness (they don't think things will get better), hallucinations, and delusions. Cognitions involving responsibility to families, effects on children, and fear of social disapproval can deter suicides.

■ From a physiological standpoint, suicide, especially suicide through violent means, is thought to be due to low levels of serotonin, which can lead to depression and to increased impulsivity and aggression. There is evidence for a genetic basis for suicide in that genetics can determine levels of serotonin. Finally, low levels of cholesterol can lead to suicide because they contribute to low levels of serotonin.

KEY TERMS, CONCEPTS, AND NAMES

In reviewing and testing yourself on what you have learned from this chapter, you should be able to identify and discuss each of the following.

aerobic fitness ↑serotonin

anger turned inward: Freud

associative networks: cognitive

behavioral contagion: reduces social restraints

catecholamine hypothesis: neurot. affect dep.

catecholamines: serotonin + norepinephrine

cholesterol↓ serotonin ↓

cognitive diathesis-stress hypothesis neg. thoughts/hopeless

cognitive rigidity: no problem solving skills

coping strategies: reduces suicide

death instinct: Freud, ID

delusions: ↑ suicide in schizo

despair: ↑ depression↑ suicide↑

diathesis: physiological disposition

diathesis-stress explanation: predisposition + stress = disorder below critical pt.

fantasies: suicide

5-HIAA: serotonin metabolite

GABA: inhibitor

glucose: sugar - for energy in brain funct.

glucose metabolism: ↑ in mania

hallucinations: ↑ suicide in schizo

hopelessness: ↑ depression/suic. (cog)

hypothalamus: in charge / sleep eat sex

imitation: suicide factor

information processing:

learned helplessness: can't control life

lithium carbonate: bipolar drug - effective

loss: often connected w/ suicide + depression

metabolites: can measure for neurot.

MHPG: norephinephrine metabolite

negative cognitive sets: relations in memory

neurotransmitters:

norepinephrine: neurotransmitter

priming: setting up network/recall

punishments↑ depression↑

rewards: learned depression/suicide gest.

selective attention: depression

selective recall: depression

serotonin: neuro

social support helps depression

stress: psychodynamic; leads to disorders

tryptophan: converts to serotonin

determined life

CHAPTER TEN
MOOD DISORDERS: TREATMENTS

OUTLINE

Carla has been very depressed since her father died last year. She now sees a therapist once a week. During her sessions, she talks about what her father meant to her and how lost and vulnerable she feels without him. Often she will reflect on childhood experiences, good and bad, in which her relationship with her father was molded. Her therapist says relatively little during the sessions but will occasionally ask a question to help Carla explore an issue that she overlooked or avoided. The therapist will also help her clarify her feelings by pointing out similarities or conflicts between things she says or feels. In general, however, her therapist is nondirective, and the actual work of psychotherapy is Carla's responsibility. Through this psychodynamic therapy, Carla is gaining a better understanding of the relationship she had with her father, learning why losing him was so traumatic, and developing mature methods of coping with the loss and stress. It may be a long process, but Carla feels that she is making progress and that she is getting better at dealing with her problems.

■ ■ ■

The therapist speculated that Mike's depression stemmed from the fact that there were too few rewards and too many punishments in Mike's life. As a first step in correcting that, Mike was asked to make lists of the things he found rewarding and punishing. Next, Mike and the therapist set up a program of goals that could be reasonably achieved, and each goal was paired with a reward. For example, now when Mike completes a report, he rewards himself with a movie. (Before he would have just gone on to work on the next report.) Mike and his therapist also developed ways of reducing some of the unpleasant parts of Mike's life. One thing that bothered him was saying no to people who asked him to do things. He just did not have the courage to say no, and consequently he was overwhelmed with responsibilities, which really got him down. To help with that, the therapist gave Mike assertiveness training so that he would be able to say no and social skills training so that he could say no without offending. Mike's life is a lot more pleasant now, and he feels much better about himself and his future.

■ ■ ■

Joan had a low self-concept and was depressed. Every time she faced a task, her first thought was, "I can't do that. I'll probably fail and make a fool of myself. I'm never going to be successful or happy!" She just never gave herself a chance. To overcome these automatic self-defeating thoughts, she and her therapist first conducted several experiments to see whether she really was incompetent and ineffective. When they revealed that she was not, she and her therapist began a program of replacing the automatic negative thoughts with more accurate thoughts. The program also involved activities in which she would act effectively in accordance with her new positive thoughts. The activities provided her with new behavior patterns and evidence that the positive thoughts were accurate. Joan feels better about herself and is less depressed. Now whenever she thinks a negative thought, she stops and asks herself whether the thought is realistic.

■ ■ ■

When Ann became depressed, her physician prescribed medication, a *tricyclic antidepressant*. Ann was warned that it would probably be two or three weeks before the medication would begin reducing the depression. When she first started taking the medication, she had some annoying side effects such as dizziness, slightly blurred vision, and fatigue, so the dosage level had to be reduced somewhat. Four weeks after beginning the medication, her depression is gone, and she and her physician are working to reduce the dosage to the point at which she can take as little as possible and still keep the depression under control. They also plan "medication holidays" during which she will not take any medication to see if she can get along without it.

■ ■ ■

Although nothing particularly important had changed in his life, a little over a year ago, Fred became very depressed and could not snap out of it. Neither talking about his feelings nor antidepressant drugs seemed to help much. Three weeks ago, he began a course of *electroconvulsive therapy* in which twice a week he received a 140-V shock for half a second along the right side of his brain. The shock causes a brief convulsion. After six shocks, his depression lifted. Before treatment, he was told that the treatment caused a loss of some memories for some patients, but that has not occurred with Fred. He admits that the first time he went in for treatment, he was frightened, but he points out that he is not conscious during the procedure and that now "it's not a big deal."

■ ■ ■

Paul suffers from a bipolar disorder that takes him from wild periods of mania to desperate periods of depression. When he was brought to the hospital by police after one of his manic periods, he was given *lithium carbonate*. Within three days, his mood had stabilized, and he was released from the hospital. Paul now takes time-release lithium pills every day, and his mood remains on an even keel. Because he was doing so well, he once thought that he did not need the medication anymore and stopped taking it, but shortly thereafter he went into a terrible depression and wound up in the hospital.

■ ■ ■

In Chapters 8 and 9 I explained the symptoms and causes of the depressive disorder, the bipolar disorder, and suicide. In this chapter I will discuss the various treatments that have been developed for those problems. In presenting each treatment, I will briefly review the suspected cause of the disorder, and then I will discuss how the treatment is designed to overcome that cause. Finally, I will examine the treatment's effectiveness and any potential problems with its use. This chapter is divided into three parts; one on the treatment of the depressive disorder, one on the treatment of the bipolar disorder, and one on suicide prevention.

TOPIC I
TREATMENT OF DEPRESSION

PSYCHODYNAMIC APPROACHES

As you learned in Chapter 9, psychodynamic theorists believe that depression stems from stress, and therefore the psychodynamic approaches to treating depression are aimed at helping the individual *overcome or reduce the stresses* and *develop better ways of responding* so that in the future stresses can be avoided or dealt with more effectively. The traditional technique for treating individuals who are depressed because of stress is *psychotherapy,* and in this section I will examine the effectiveness of that approach.

Effectiveness of Psychotherapy

Psychotherapy is now generally recognized as effective for treating depression (Frank & Spanier, 1995; Weissman & Klerman, 1992). Studies carried out in the 1920s and 1930s (before therapeutic drugs were available) indicated that 40% of the individuals who were hospitalized for depression recovered within the first year and that 60% recovered within 2 years (Alexander, 1953). However, the problem with these and many other studies was that they did not include a no-treatment control condition in which patients did not

receive therapy. The absence of that control condition is crucial because a high proportion of depressed individuals will improve even without treatment, an effect known as **spontaneous remission** of symptoms. Without a no-treatment control condition, we cannot determine how much of the improvement actually stemmed from the therapy. Fortunately, there are now a variety of controlled experiments from which we can draw firm conclusions.

In one experiment, acutely depressed patients were randomly assigned to a condition in which they received psychotherapy at least once a week or to a control condition in which they received "nonscheduled treatment"—no active treatment was scheduled, but if necessary, the patient could arrange one 50-minute session per month (Weissman et al., 1979). A clinician who was unaware of the type of treatment the patients were receiving assessed each patient's depression at various times during treatment. An analysis of those ratings indicated that the patients who received psychotherapy showed fewer relapses in depression than the patients in the control condition. Those results are presented in Figure 10.1. Other investigators have reported similar results (e.g., Klerman et al., 1974).

In an attempt to refine our understanding of what contributes to successful therapy, a considerable amount of research has been focused on the problem of identifying the personal characteristics of patients that are associated with successful therapy outcome. Unfortunately, most of the findings have been inconclusive or inconsistent (Beutler et al., 1994; Garfield, 1994; Orlinsky et al., 1994). Only one generalization

Psychotherapy is frequently used to treat individuals suffering from depression. It is effective both in reducing the relapse rate for depression and in helping individuals improve their social adjustments and interpersonal relationships.

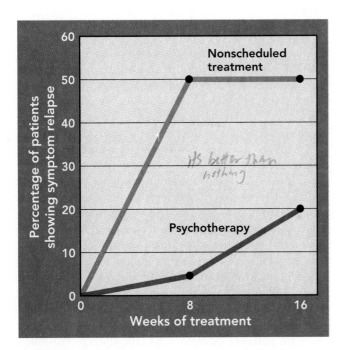

FIGURE 10.1 Psychotherapy was more effective than "nonscheduled treatment" for reducing relapses in depression.
Source: Adapted from Weissman et al. (1979), p. 557, fig. 1.

can be made: More severely depressed individuals will be less likely to benefit from psychotherapy or will require more time to benefit. Beyond that, no personal patient characteristics are consistently related to improvement.

COMMENT

Two points should be made concerning the effectiveness of psychotherapy for depression. First, although in many cases psychotherapy is effective for treating depression, it is not always effective (Mohr, 1995). Indeed, one study revealed a 20% failure rate (Weissman et al., 1979), and we would expect more failures among more severely depressed patients. However, psychotherapy is not alone in failing to reduce all depressions, and later you will learn that other therapeutic techniques also have only limited success. (I will discuss the relative effectiveness of different therapeutic approaches later in this chapter after I have presented some of the other approaches.)

Second, we do not yet understand what it is about psychotherapy that makes it effective for treating depression (Lambert & Bergin, 1994; Weinberger, 1995). It is encouraging that a wide variety of psychotherapies are effective, but if people get better almost regardless of what is done for them, it is difficult to determine what the crucial factor is that makes psy-

chotherapy effective. If all of the techniques are effective (long-term psychoanalysis, group therapy, attention from a social worker, etc.), we are in the awkward position of concluding that the differences among the techniques may in fact be irrelevant. The only element that is common to all of the approaches is **social support,** and that support may be the crucial element in the psychotherapeutic treatment of depression. That speculation is consistent with the wide variety of evidence indicating that social support is important for minimizing the effects of stress.

LEARNING APPROACHES

Learning theorists hypothesize that low levels of rewards or high levels of punishment result in a less pleasant life, low self-esteem, and a decreased level of activity. Those factors then lead to depression. The learning approaches to the treatment of depression are aimed at helping patients increase the rewards and decrease the punishments in their lives.

Increasing Rewards and Decreasing Punishments

There are three steps for changing the levels of rewards and punishments. The first is to *identify* the aspects of the environment (people, activities, situations) that are the sources of rewards and punishments for the depressed individual. To do that, the individual draws up a list of the most frequently occurring pleasant and unpleasant events and then monitors them to determine which are the most important in promoting good or bad feelings.

The second step is to teach the individual new skills or strategies to overcome, avoid, or *minimize the punishing experiences*. That step might include assertiveness training for patients who become upset when intimidated by others, time management training for those who are concerned about not getting things done, social skills training for those who have difficulty with interpersonal relationships, financial counseling for those beset with money problems, and relaxation training for those who find themselves under stress.

The third step involves teaching the individual to *increase the rewards* in his or her life. That is accomplished initially through a program of self-reinforcement. A "reward menu" is established using the list of rewards that was prepared earlier, and each reward is paired with a "price"—a task that must be accomplished to get the reward. Prices must be set high enough (tasks made difficult enough) so that the

Changing response patterns can be one way to overcome depression. Here people in an assertiveness training class are learning to express themselves more forcefully.

individual accomplishes something meaningful but not so high that he or she never gets a reward. Getting the rewards can result in reduced levels of depression, and this approach can also help the individual become more active and accomplish more. In the case of one depressed man who loved going to the movies, a plan was established whereby he could not go to a movie until he had completed a specific task such as writing a report at work or painting a room at home. Within a short time, he was seeing more movies than he had before, which made him happy, and he was accomplishing more, which made him feel better about himself, and that also helped with his depression.

Three points should be noted: (a) The techniques used with any one individual are highly individualized and specific to the rewarding and punishing aspects of that particular individual's life; (b) a wide variety of techniques that would not be part of traditional psychotherapy are used to change behaviors in order to maximize rewards and minimize punishments; and (c) the therapist plays a very active role in teaching the individual the skills that are necessary to maximize rewards and minimize punishments.

Effectiveness of Learning Therapy *(self-control)*

In one interesting experiment, 28 moderately depressed women between the ages of 18 and 48 participated in one of three conditions: *self-control* therapy, *nonspecific* therapy, or a *waiting-list* control condition (Fuchs & Rehm, 1977). The self-control therapy was based on the learning approach to depression. It was called self-control therapy because with the learning approach, patients strive to gain more control over the rewards and punishments in their environments. Over the course of six weekly sessions, the patients in self-control therapy (a) were taught to identify the events that made them feel good and bad, (b) selected specific and realistically attainable goals that would make them feel better (e.g., "making better friends with women in my neighborhood"), (c) worked on achieving one or more of those goals, and (d) set up and used a self-reward system in which they gave themselves rewards for completing activities that were not inherently rewarding.

The patients in the nonspecific therapy condition also participated in six sessions, but their activities revolved around nondirective group therapy in which they discussed problems and feelings in an empathic manner. The patients in the waiting-list control condition were informed that they had been accepted for treatment but that all of the groups were filled and that they would have to wait 8 weeks before they would begin treatment.

The results indicated that the patients in self-control therapy reported greater declines in depression than the patients in the other conditions. Those results are summarized in Figure 10.2. Furthermore, the patients who received self-control therapy also showed greater increases in social behavior. Apparently, the therapy influenced not only how patients felt but also how they subsequently behaved. Because increased social interaction could lead to increased rewards, it might be expected that the effects of self-control therapy would be maintained over time. Indeed, in a longitudinal study of the effects of a learning-based approach for the treatment of depression, it was found that the learning-based approach was superior to a control treatment (relaxation) and that the effect lasted at least 27 months (McLean & Hakstian, 1979, 1990).

COMMENT

The findings just discussed are encouraging, but you should note that the idea of increasing rewards (pleasant experiences) and decreasing punishments (unpleasant experiences) is not unique to the learning approaches to treating depression. Indeed, it is basic to most psychotherapeutic approaches. What is different about the learning approaches is the very direct, systematic, active, and varied ways in which the therapist

patients can manipulate situations to their disadvantage

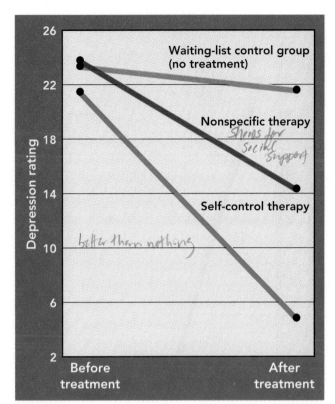

FIGURE 10.2 **Self-control therapy resulted in greater decreases in depression than nonspecific therapy or no treatment.**
Source: Data from Fuchs and Rehm (1977), p. 210, tab. 1.

[handwritten on graph: Sharves for social support]
[handwritten on graph: better than nothing]

works with the patient to overcome the punishments and increase the rewards. The tactic of increasing rewards and decreasing punishment is probably effective because it reduces stress.

COGNITIVE APPROACHES

From a cognitive perspective, depression stems from inaccurate negative beliefs that lead people to view themselves, their world, and their future in inappropriately negative ways ("I'm no good, my situation is terrible, and the future is bleak"). The goal of cognitive therapy is to *replace the inaccurate negative beliefs with accurate positive beliefs* (Beck et al., 1979; Wright & Beck, 1994).

Replacing Negative Beliefs : *3 steps*

In cognitive therapy, the therapist tries to replace negative beliefs through a three-step process. The first step is to *identify the negative beliefs* that are influencing the patient's mood and behavior ("I am depressed and withdrawn because others do not like me, and I will always be rejected by others in the future"). Rather than letting the patient accept the negative beliefs as

true, the therapist tells the patient to consider them *hypotheses* to be tested. In other words, the therapist does not agree or disagree with the patient's views but takes a "let's see if you are correct" approach.

The second step involves *testing to determine whether the hypotheses are valid*. For example, if a patient is depressed because of the belief that he or she is disliked, the therapist and patient might conduct a little experiment in which the patient asks someone for a date to see if others actually do dislike and reject the patient.

Once the patient has done some carefully directed testing and finds that many of the negative beliefs are false (or at least not as serious as they were thought to be), the third step in the therapeutic process can begin. That step involves the *replacement of the erroneous negative beliefs* with more accurate beliefs. For example, a patient will be instructed to replace negative thoughts with thoughts like "I may not be perfect, but I am not a bad person, and others do like me." That is not a simple step, and it takes some practice to get those positive thoughts to be as automatic as the previous negative thoughts. An important part of this phase of therapy involves activity planning. Rather than just thinking more accurate thoughts, the therapist and patient work together to plan activities that are consistent with the new accurate thoughts. In the case of a patient who feels rejected, they may plan a variety of social activities such as dates and parties. This is important because the patient needs consistent confirmation of the new beliefs concerning social acceptability. Without direction and planning, the individual may slip back into old ways. It is essential that the scheduled activities be carefully graded in terms of difficulty. A young man who felt depressed and rejected and who isolated himself socially for two years before therapy should probably start with a casual coffee date rather than attempt a weekend with the homecoming queen!

Because improvements in cognitive therapy occur when the patient collects data that actually disprove his or her negative beliefs, the individual will not be dependent on the therapist in the future. If negative beliefs crop up again, the patient will have learned to check and eliminate them. Indeed, the long-term success of cognitive therapy depends on the patient's careful monitoring of thoughts so as to avoid slipping back into the habit of using negative thoughts. Whenever they begin, the patient is taught to ask three questions (Hollon & Beck, 1979):

1. What is my evidence for this belief?
2. Is there another way of looking at this situation?
3. Even if it is true, is it as bad as it seems?

In cognitive therapy, the patient and therapist actively work together to develop more accurate beliefs that will lead to more positive feelings and behaviors.

Effectiveness of Cognitive Therapy

Initially, excitement about cognitive therapy was high because the results of an early experiment indicated that cognitive therapy was more effective than drug therapy for treating depression (Rush et al., 1977). In that experiment, 41 depressed patients were treated for 12 weeks with either cognitive therapy or an antidepressant drug (Tofranil/imipramine), and the patients who received cognitive therapy showed greater decreases in depression than the patients who received the drug treatment. Unfortunately, the results of numerous subsequent experiments have failed to confirm the superiority of cognitive therapy, and now even its advocates have concluded that "cognitive therapy is neither more nor less effective than antidepressant medication in the treatment of nonpsychotic, nonbipolar depressed outpatients" (Hollon et al., 1991, p. 97). The results of an experiment comparing cognitive therapy, drug therapy, cognitive therapy plus drug therapy, and cognitive therapy plus placebo therapy are presented in Figure 10.3. The sharp declines in depression reflect the strong and comparable effects of the various treatments.

It is generally assumed that cognitive therapy works because the patients learn to change their negative beliefs, but some doubts have been raised about that explanation. In one experiment on the effects of cognitive therapy and drug therapy, the experimenters collected data on changes in depression and also on changes in negative beliefs (Simons et al., 1984). What they found was that cognitive therapy and drug therapy were equally effective for reducing depression but also that cognitive therapy and drug therapy were *equally effective for reducing negative beliefs.* The reduction in negative beliefs would be expected in the cognitive therapy condition, but it would not be expected in the drug therapy condition unless negative beliefs were an *effect* rather than a *cause* of depression. The investigators suggest that "cognitive change may be more accurately seen as a part of improvement rather than the primary cause of improvement" (p. 45) and that we must rethink the explanation of cognitive therapy. Since then, even advocates of cognitive therapy for depression have concluded that the evidence does not support the notion that cognitive changes are "sufficient mediators" in the reduction of depression (De Rubeis et al., 1990). Cognitive therapy can be effective, but it is not clear exactly why (Whisman, 1993).

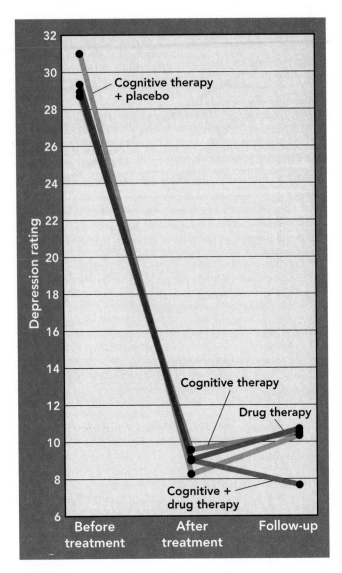

FIGURE 10.3 Cognitive therapy, drug therapy, cognitive plus drug therapy, and cognitive therapy plus placebo were all equally effective for reducing depression.
Source: Data from Murphy et al. (1984), p. 37, tab. 4.

| COMMENT |

Although cognitive therapy is not more effective than drug therapy, the fact that it can be *as effective* as drug therapy is very important because cognitive therapy does not have the unpleasant side effects that are sometimes associated with drug therapy. Furthermore, cognitive therapy does not require maintenance treatment, which is usually necessary with drug therapy. However, it should be recognized that the effectiveness of cognitive therapy is limited to *mild to moderately depressed outpatients;* it is *not* appropriate to use it with severely depressed individuals or those with the bipolar disorder. Nevertheless, for many people, cognitive therapy is an effective treatment that can be a viable alternative to drug treatment. Future research will have to be focused more on why it works than on whether it works, and with a better understanding of the underlying process, psychologists may be able to enhance its effects.

PHYSIOLOGICAL APPROACHES

The physiological approaches to the treatment of depression can be divided into two types: *drug treatment* and *convulsive treatment* (the use of electrical shocks to induce convulsions). Both approaches have been effective, but the nature of their effects and the situations in which they are most effective are very different. We must give careful attention to physiological treatments because they are playing an increasingly important role in the treatment of depression today, but they are often misunderstood.

Drug Treatments

You learned in Chapter 9 that depression stems in part from low levels of the neurotransmitters serotonin and norepinephrine at the synapses in the areas of the brain that are responsible for emotion. Those low levels are related to any or all of three processes: *reuptake* (reabsorption) of the neurotransmitter by the presynaptic neuron, *catabolism* (chemical destruction) of the neurotransmitter, and *insufficient production* of the neurotransmitter by the presynaptic neuron. Drug treatments are designed to reverse these processes and thereby restore an appropriate level of the neurotransmitter.

Tricyclics and Bicyclics: Drugs to Reduce Reuptake.
The drugs that are most widely used for the treatment of depression are the **tricyclics** and the newer **bicyclics** (Goodwin, 1992). These drugs work by *reducing the reuptake* (reabsorption) of serotonin or norepinephrine by the presynaptic neuron. Specifically, these drugs fit into the channels in the presynaptic neuron through which the neurotransmitters would be reabsorbed, thus blocking their reuptake. Blocking the reuptake makes more of the neurotransmitters available at the synapse, thus increasing neurological activity. The terms *tricyclic* and *bicyclic* are derived from the chemical structures of these drugs, which involve three or two circles as illustrated in Figure 10.4. The bicyclics that have attracted most attention lately are Prozac, Zoloft, and Paxil. In Table 10.1, you will find a list of the most widely used antidepressant drugs.

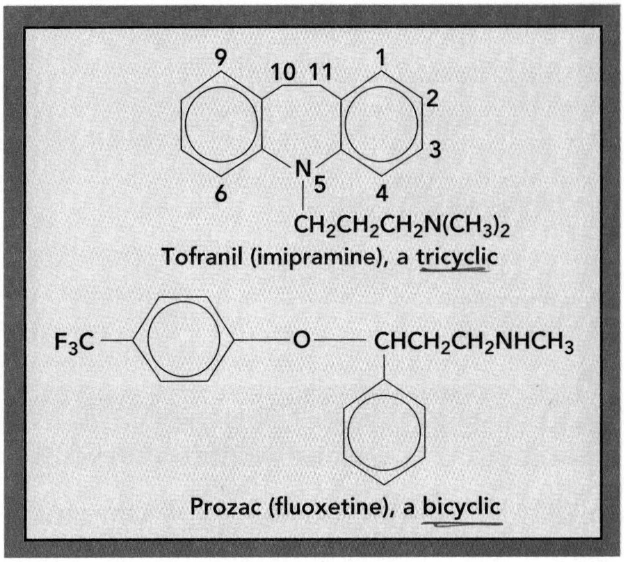

FIGURE 10.4 The chemical structure of a tricyclic antidepressant and a bicyclic antidepressant.

TABLE 10.1 Frequently Used Antidepressant Drugs

Type	Trade Name	Generic Name	Usual Maximum Daily Dose (mg)
Tricyclic	Anafranil	Comipramine	250
	Elavil	Amitriptyline	300
	Pamelor	Nortriptyline	150
	Sinequan	Doxepin	300
	Tofranil	Imipramine	300
Bicyclic	Paxil	Paroxetine	60
	Prozac	Fluoxetine	80
	Wellbutrin	Bupropion	450
	Zoloft	Sertraline	150
Monoamine oxidase inhibitor (MAOI)	Marplan	Isocarboxazid	50
	Nardil	Phenelzine	90
	Parnate	Tranylcypromine	50

Note: Some drugs are sold under more than one trade name (e.g., amitriptyline is sold as Elavil and Endep).

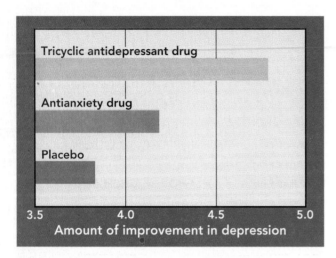

FIGURE 10.5 A tricyclic drug was more effective for reducing depression than an antianxiety drug or a placebo.
Source: Data from Covi et al. (1974), p. 196, tab. 4.

Do the tricyclic and bicyclic drugs relieve depression, and must the treatment be continued even after the depression has lifted? There is now strong and consistent evidence that these drugs are more effective than no drugs or placebos for reducing depression. Figure 10.5 presents the results of one experiment in which acutely depressed patients were treated with (a) a tricyclic (Tofranil/imipramine), (b) a drug that is usually used to treat anxiety (Valium/diazepam), or (c) a placebo (Covi et al., 1974). The patients who took the tricyclic showed greater improvement in depression than the patients who took either the antianxiety medication or the placebo.

With regard to the effects of drugs, it is interesting to note that although in some experiments cognitive therapy was found to be as effective as drug treatment in the long run, the patients who took drugs showed improvement much faster than those who received cognitive therapy (Watkins et al., 1993).

Tricyclics and bicyclics are effective for reducing depression, but in many cases the treatment must be continued because the chance of relapse increases greatly if the drugs are withdrawn. That was clearly demonstrated in three experiments in which depressed patients were first successfully treated with tricyclics and were then assigned to conditions in which they either continued to take the drug or began taking a placebo (Klerman et al., 1974; Mindham, 1973; Prien et al., 1974). The results of each experiment revealed that the patients who continued to take the drug had lower relapse rates than the patients who were switched to the placebo. In general, the drugs reduced the relapse rate by about 50%. Those results

are summarized in Figure 10.6. (Note that the overall differences in relapse rates across the different experiments are associated with differences in the severity of the depression; experiments in which the patients were more severely depressed had higher overall relapse rates.)

One important practical point to note about the antidepressant drugs is that there is a delay of 2 weeks or more (sometimes as long as 6 weeks) before they begin reducing depression (Quitkin et al., 1984). We do not yet understand the reason for this delay, but patients should be warned about it so that they do not become disappointed with the lack of immediate effects and cease taking the medication. The delayed effect of antidepressant medication is illustrated in Figure 10.7.

The delayed effect of the antidepressant drugs has implications for patient management, especially for patients who are suicidal and for whom immediate relief is necessary. For those patients, hospitalization might be necessary until they are no longer a danger to themselves, or it might initially be necessary to use some other, faster-acting treatment, such as electroconvulsive therapy (to be discussed shortly), to break the depression.

The bicyclic antidepressants were developed after the tricyclics, and they differ from the tricyclics in two important ways. First, whereas tricycles block the reuptake of serotonin or norepinephrine, *most bicyclics block*

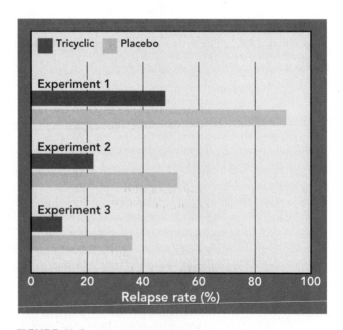

FIGURE 10.6 In three experiments, tricyclic drugs reduced relapse rates for depression by about 50%.
Sources: Data from Prien et al. (1974); Mindham (1973); Klerman et al. (1974).

did patients know it was a placebo?

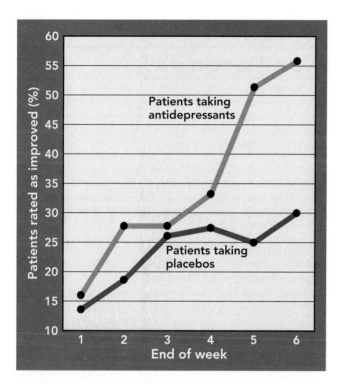

FIGURE 10.7 The effects of antidepressant drugs are usually delayed.
Source: Adapted from Quitkin et al. (1984), p. 240, fig. 1.

only the reuptake of serotonin. Indeed, bicyclics are often referred to as **selective serotonin reuptake inhibitors (SSRIs)**. Second, *most bicyclics have fewer or less serious side effects than tricyclics.* For example, whereas tricyclics can cause a considerable weight gain, bicyclics do not result in a weight gain and may even result in a small loss in weight. (We will discuss side effects in greater detail later.)

The introduction of bicyclic antidepressants such as Prozac attracted a lot of attention, and in many respects the bicyclics are an advance over the older tricyclics. For example, there is evidence that even if Prozac is not more effective than other drugs, it does have fewer side effects (Greenberg et al., 1994). That is important because individuals who could not take the tricyclics may be able to take Prozac, and severely depressed individuals may be able to take higher doses of Prozac. Furthermore, there is evidence that Prozac is effective for treating the depression that often accompanies PMS (premenstrual syndrome), something for which the other drugs were not particularly effective (Steiner et al., 1995).

Despite the facts that Prozac and other bicyclics are effective for reducing depression and have relatively few side effects, Prozac was involved in a controversy over the possibility that it might lead to suicide. That controversy is discussed in Case Study 10.1.

Lithium: A Drug to Stabilize Neurotransmission. **Lithium carbonate** is often used to treat the bipolar disorder, but it is sometimes also used to treat depression that is separate from the bipolar disorder (Joffe et al., 1993; Price & Heninger, 1994). Specifically, lithium is used alone or in combination with tricyclics or bicyclics when those other drugs are not completely effective. In other words, lithium is a "second line of defense." For example, in one experiment, depressed patients who had not shown improvement with a bicyclic (Prozac) were put on a combination of the bicyclic and lithium, and the results indicated that the combination was more effective than the bicyclic alone (Fava et al., 1994). It is not clear exactly why lithium works, but it probably stabilizes the release of neurotransmitters or stabilizes the sensitivity of the receptors on the postsynaptic neuron. (We will return to a discussion of lithium when we review treatment of the bipolar disorder.)

MAO Inhibitors: Drugs to Reduce Catabolism. Neurotransmitters are catabolized (destroyed) at the synapse by an enzyme called **monoamine oxidase** (MON-ō-uh-mēn OK-si-dās; **MAO**). That is a normal process that is necessary for keeping the synapse "clean." However, if too much of a neurotransmitter is catabolized, there will not be enough to facilitate synaptic transmission, and depression will set in. Drugs that are used to treat depression by *inhibiting* the effects of monoamine oxidase are known as **MAO inhibitors (MAOIs)** (Davidson, 1992). That is, by inhibiting the monoamine oxidase, catabolism of the neurotransmitter is reduced so that more of the neurotransmitter will be available, and therefore the basis for the depression will be reduced or eliminated.

The effectiveness of MAOIs for protecting against low levels of norepinephrine during stress was demonstrated in an interesting experiment with rats. As you learned in Chapter 9, when laboratory animals are exposed to stress, their levels of norepinephrine decline, suggesting that stress brings on depression by reducing norepinephrine. However, in one experiment, the animals were given an MAOI before being exposed to the stress, and those animals did not show the decrease in norepinephrine (Maynert & Levi, 1964). This suggests that by slowing down the catabolism of norepinephrine, MAOIs allow normal levels of norepinephrine to be maintained during stress, thus protecting the individual from the depressing effects of stress. Consistent with that process, there is a large body of evidence that indicates that MAOIs are effective for treating depression (Silver et al., 1994).

CASE STUDY 10.1
Prozac: Panacea or Paradox?

Prozac (fluoxetine) has been heralded as a wonder drug for the treatment of depression, but it has also been cited as a drug that leads people to suicide and even murder.

Prozac was introduced in 1987 and immediately became one of the most widely used drugs in the United States. *Newsweek* magazine even featured a capsule of Prozac on its cover. Prozac's widespread acceptance was based on two facts. First, the drug was very effective for reducing depression as well as other disorders such as the obsessive-compulsive disorder, anorexia, and bulimia. Second, it did not have many of the side effects that were associated with other antidepressants. For example, Prozac did not cause the weight gain that is associated with the use of some antidepressants, and that made it very popular. Sales of Prozac skyrocketed; more than a million prescriptions for Prozac were being filled every month! Prozac was seen as a panacea for a wide variety of disorders, and it quickly became the dandy of the drug market.

However, the view of Prozac changed suddenly when an article appeared in which it was reported that six patients who had been taking Prozac for major depression had experienced the emergence or intensification of thoughts about suicide (Teicher et al., 1990). After being put on Prozac, one man reported "nearly constant suicidal preoccupation" and "violent self-destructive fantasies," and when a woman who planned to commit suicide was given an increased dose of Prozac, she became violent and mutilated herself. That article was followed by reports of four other adults and six children who also experienced increases in thoughts about suicide after they began taking Prozac (Dasgupta & Hoover, 1990; King et al., 1991; Masand et al., 1991). Those reports opened the floodgates, and people telling sensational horror stories about the alleged effects of Prozac were on all of the TV talk shows. Furthermore, Prozac "survivor" groups were formed around the country to provide support for those who had

gone through the "perils of Prozac." Possibly the most dramatic aspect of the Prozac story involved the allegation that Prozac led people to commit murder. For example, it was alleged that Joseph Wesbecker was under the influence of Prozac when he stormed into a building with an AK-47 assault rifle and shot 20 people (8 fatally) before killing himself. Many defendants in murder cases began using what came to be known as the "Prozac defense"—using Prozac to explain their violent acts, thereby relieving themselves of responsibility and opening up the manufacturer to huge lawsuits.

The alleged increase in violent behavior (toward self and others) associated with taking Prozac was particularly surprising in view of the drug's biochemical effects. We know that *low* levels of serotonin are associated with aggressive behavior and suicide (see Chapter 9), but Prozac blocks the reuptake of serotonin and therefore Prozac results in *higher* levels of serotonin. In other words, from a biochemical standpoint, if Prozac has any effect on aggression, it should *reduce* it. However, it is always possible that Prozac has some paradoxical effect on behavior, as some other drugs do. For example, we know that *stimulants* have the effect of *calming* hyperactive children (see Chapter 15). Might Prozac also have a paradoxical effect? Is Prozac a dangerous drug? Should it be withdrawn from the market?

Case studies can provide a signal that a problem may exist, but we cannot draw conclusions from case studies because the reported effects might be due to other factors. For example, in some of the cases that were reported, the individuals were also on other medications and were suffering from other psychiatric disorders, and it may have been those factors rather than the Prozac that led to the disturbed behavior. So case studies aside, what results have been generated by controlled research?

First, there is some evidence that when compared to a placebo, antidepressant drugs in general may lead to a *slight* increase in suicide of about 1%

Although the MAOIs can be effective for treating depression, care must be used with them because if they are taken in combination with certain foods or drugs, they can cause a dangerous increase in blood pressure called a *hypertensive crisis*. Indeed, the increase in pressure may be so great that the individ-

ual will suffer a stroke and die. Such a crisis can occur when a patient who is taking an MAOI eats foods that contain **tyramine** (TĪ-ruh-mēn) in large amounts (unpasteurized cheese, aged meats or sausages, yeast extract, wines, some beers, avocado) or takes other drugs (stimulants, decongestants, antihypertensives,

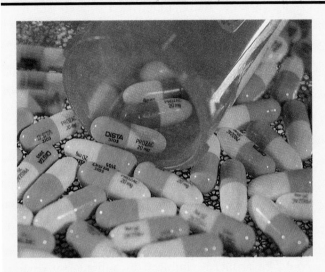

Prozac is the best known of the bicyclic antidepressants.

(Gardner & Cowdry, 1985; Rouillon et al., 1989; Soloff et al., 1987; see review by Mann & Kapur, 1991). If such an effect occurs, it is probably due to the fact that as the depression begins to lift, the individuals have more energy and are more active and are thus more likely to act on their lingering suicidal thoughts. In any event, if this effect occurs, it does not appear to be anything like the effect attributed to Prozac.

Second, the results of at least three large-scale double-blind controlled experiments did *not* reveal *any* evidence that Prozac resulted in an increase in suicidal thoughts or behavior (Altamura et al., 1989; Muijen et al., 1988; Sacchetti et al., 1991; see review by Mann & Kapur, 1991). Instead, Prozac was found to be generally *more* effective than the other drugs and placebos in reducing suicidal urges and depression (Beasley et al., 1991; Fava & Rosenbaum, 1991).

If the controlled research does not support the initial claims that Prozac leads to increased rates of suicidal thoughts, how do we account for the case studies? First, it is possible that the behaviors were the result of the other medications the patients were

taking or the other disorders from which they suffered. Second, it is also possible that in some instances the behavior was indeed an abnormal reaction to the Prozac. In the case of virtually every drug, there are individuals who have abnormal reactions (e.g., some people cannot take aspirin), so there are undoubtedly people who cannot tolerate Prozac. However, the number of those individuals appears to be very small. If some patients do show abnormal reactions, the solution is not to abandon the use of Prozac but rather to alert patients to the potential side effects and monitor the patients carefully, a strategy that is essential with any drug.

And what about the "Prozac defense"? In one case, a woman who murdered her husband while allegedly under the influence of Prozac was convicted of manslaughter rather than murder, but the lesser conviction was probably due to the jury's concern about the woman's advanced age of 74 rather than to her use of Prozac. Other cases involving the Prozac defense have been unsuccessful, and there now appears to be less interest in the Prozac defense.

Finally, you may recall my student in Case Study 8.2 who described her depression, her feelings of living inside a glass bottle, and how she huddled under the covers in her bed. She wrote that description as the introduction to her term paper on depression and its treatment with Prozac. She concluded her paper with the following:

As I sit at my computer successfully completing the first major term paper I've been able to tackle this semester, I am thankful for the development of Prozac, and I am willing to risk the possible side effects. I am now able to experience everyday joys like others who I once could only envy. I still have good days and days when I feel "blue," but that is perfectly normal, and Prozac is no panacea. It has not been determined how long I will remain on Prozac, but as for now, I am just enjoying life. I like people, I'm proud of what I'm accomplishing, and I love myself.

tricyclic antidepressants). Because so many common foods and drugs can cause negative reactions to MAOIs, some authorities believe that MAOIs should only be taken by patients who are in a hospital where their diet can be carefully supervised and where help is available in the event of complications. At present,

MAOIs are usually used only after other antidepressant medications have been tried and found to be ineffective.

Psychomotor Stimulants: Drugs to Increase Neurotransmitter Production. A group of drugs known as

psychomotor stimulants (e.g., amphetamines) can decrease depression by increasing the production of the neurotransmitters by the presynaptic neurons. Unfortunately, most psychomotor stimulants are addicting and have relatively short-term effects. Furthermore, after their effects wear off, the depression often worsens, an effect known as **postamphetamine depression.** That occurs because after the effects of the drug wear off, the presynaptic neuron produces even less of the neurotransmitter than it did before the drug was taken. Because of those problems, the psychomotor stimulants are not used widely and not used for long periods.

Side Effects. I have already mentioned the sometimes lethal side effects that can occur with the use of MAOIs and the addictive nature of psychomotor stimulants, but the widely used tricyclics and bicyclics also have side effects (Post, 1994; Silver et al., 1994). These can include dryness of the mouth, blurring of vision, difficulty in urination, constipation, palpitations of the heart, hypotension (low blood pressure), weight gain, drowsiness or excitation, and problems with sexual functioning (e.g., delayed orgasm). However, these unwanted side effects are generally correlated with the dosage level of the drug and thus can sometimes be minimized by using the lowest effective dosage level (Mindham, 1982). Furthermore, in many cases, the side effects diminish over time (the body seems to adjust to the medication) or patients learn ways to avoid or cope with the side effects. It is crucial to inform patients about possible side effects so that they can deal with them and not misinterpret them as additional symptoms of their disorder. Indeed, the presence of unexpected side effects can sometimes convince patients that they are "going crazy." Unfortunately, individuals who treat depression (and other disorders) are often insensitive to the problems side effects can pose.

The serious nature of some side effects was made very clear to me when I participated in a study of the effects of Prozac. I describe that experience in Case Study 10.2.

It is important to consider the trade-off between side effects and symptom relief. Regrettably, some side effects may be intolerable, and the use of the drug will have to be terminated (though another drug might then be tried). In other cases, there may be side effects, but the negative aspects of the side effects may be an acceptable price to pay for the relief from the misery and depression the patient might have to endure without the drug. As with most things, then, drug treatment for depression is a matter of balances, compromises, risks, and benefits, and the important thing is for both therapist and patient to be informed about the options and the consequences.

Electroconvulsive Therapy

The other physiological treatment for depression is **electroconvulsive therapy (ECT),** commonly called "shock therapy" (Fink, 1992). ECT is used widely for the treatment of depression, and it has been estimated that more than 10,000 patients in the United States receive ECT each day. Because ECT is widely used, frequently misunderstood, and often the focus of public and professional outcries (Breggin, 1979; Frieberg, 1975; Palmer, 1981; Weiner, 1982), it is essential that we give careful consideration to the procedures, effects, and side effects of ECT.

Background. ECT was originally developed as a treatment for schizophrenia when it was observed that patients who suffered from both schizophrenia and epilepsy appeared to remit their schizophrenic symptoms immediately following an epileptic convulsion. Clinicians speculated that if epileptic-like convulsions could be artificially induced in patients with schizophrenia, the convulsions might be effective for reducing the schizophrenia. Originally, the convulsions were induced with drugs such as insulin (Meduna, 1935), but it was quickly learned that greater control over the convulsions could be achieved if they were induced with an electrical shock to the brain, and electroconvulsive therapy was born (Cerletti & Bini, 1938). Since then, we have learned that ECT is not effective for treating schizophrenia, but evidence has accumulated that it can be effective for treating some types of depression.

Procedures. In the typical portrayal of shock therapy in grade B horror movies, a screaming patient is held down on an operating table by brutish attendants, a physician holds large electrodes to the patient's temples, a flash of lightning-like electrical current arcs between the electrodes, and the patient shudders in pain and falls comatose, brain-damaged and changed for life. The early use of ECT may have involved some elements of that scenario, but it bears no resemblance to the procedures in use today! Regrettably, those portrayals and certain horror stories (some true) based on the early misuse of ECT have colored the general perception of the treatment.

Today, the patient is first given a strong sedative and a muscle relaxant. The sedative induces sleep, so the patient is not conscious when the convulsion is induced. The relaxant reduces muscular contractions during the convulsion. (Before muscle relaxants were used, patients often broke bones during the convulsions.) Once the patient is unconscious and relaxed, electrodes are placed on the skull and an electrical current of between 70 and 150 V is passed between the electrodes for 1/10 second to 1 second to induce the

CASE STUDY 10.2
"I Can't Sit Still!" A Potential Side Effect of Prozac

Akathisia →

There is substantial evidence that Prozac can relieve depression, but some individuals claim that it does more than that—it makes them "better than well." Specifically, after relieving their depression, it makes them more outgoing, more assertive, and generally more effective personally and professionally. That notion was popularized in the best-selling book *Listening to Prozac* (Kramer, 1993). To test that possibility, I participated in a project in which I first monitored my mood for a period of a month and then began taking Prozac to see if my mood improved. The project was planned as a multiple-baseline study (see Chapter 3) in which I would or would not take Prozac at different times to see if my mood went up and down between "normal" and "better than normal." Unfortunately, I never got beyond the first "on drug" period because within a day of beginning the drug, I developed a serious side effect. Specifically, *I felt as though there was a huge motor in my chest that was running at top speed, and I simply could not sit still!* At the time, I was writing a chapter for this book, and prior to taking the drug, I was able to sit and work at my computer for hours at a time. However, after taking the drug, I would sit and work for about five minutes, and then I would have to get up and walk around. I would then go to another room, where I would try to read, but that would only last for about five minutes, when I would

again have to get up. Then I would take my portable computer and try to work in another room, but I was able to work for only a few minutes. I kept moving from room to room, trying one thing and then another, never getting much done. By the end of the day, I had tried to work in every chair in every room and probably walked miles, but I had not gotten anything done.

It is important to note that I did not go into a manic state; that is, I did not feel elated or motivated, and I did not have any grandiose ideas. Furthermore, I did not feel anxious, except about the fact that I was not getting any work done—*I just could not sit still!*

For two days, I kept telling myself, "David, these side effects will go away; just hang in there." (How many times in the past had I heard myself say that to other people!) After three days, there was no improvement and I wasn't getting any work done, so I stopped taking the drug, and in less than 12 hours I was back to normal.

The side effect from which I suffered is called **akathisia** (ak-uh-THIZH-yuh), which means "restlessness," and it is a relatively common side effect of Prozac (Lipinski et al., 1989; Silver et al., 1994). I am one of the people who cannot take Prozac, and my experience made me much more sensitive to the problems people have with side effects.

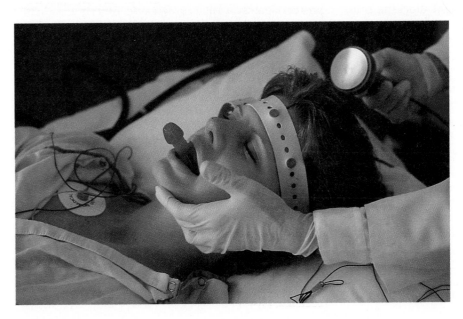

Modern procedures used to administer electroconvulsive therapy (ECT) bear little resemblance to those of the past. Today, the patient is unconscious during treatment and is given a muscle relaxant to reduce muscle contractions during the seizure.

convulsion. While the convulsion runs its course (usually 45 to 60 seconds), the patient shows some minor muscle contractions. These can range from an arching of the back and movement of the arms to only a slight movement of the toes. The degree to which muscle contractions occur depends on the amount of the muscle relaxant that is administered. During the convulsion, it is necessary to put something in the patient's mouth to prevent swallowing of the tongue. The patient does not breathe during the convulsion and some carbon dioxide builds up, and so the patient is usually given oxygen for 10 to 15 seconds immediately following the convulsion. A few minutes later, the patient regains consciousness. The entire procedure can take less than 15 minutes, and after having been through it once, most patients do not report any greater concern than would be expected for any other minor medical procedure. Indeed, many patients I know say that they would rather undergo ECT than go to the dentist to have a cavity filled!

ECT is generally given three times per week. Treatment only twice a week results in fewer side effects and is just as effective, but the rate of improvement is slower, and that is a problem with severely depressed (possibly suicidal) individuals (Lerer et al., 1995). The number of treatments necessary to obtain results differs widely from patient to patient. Many respond after 5 to 8 treatments. Today, if 8 or 10 treatments have not resulted in improvement, it is usually concluded that the treatment will not be effective, and it is stopped. The old adage "an ounce of prevention is worth a pound of cure" probably provided the basis for an early belief that a few additional treatments should be given after the depression had lifted, but there is no evidence that the extra treatments help (Barton et al., 1973). ECT can be given on either an outpatient or an inpatient basis, but it is usually used for inpatients because they are more severely depressed. Giving four to eight shocks in one session has been tried in an attempt to speed up the effects of the treatment, but that was not found to be as effective as separating the shocks by 1 or 2 days.

Effectiveness of ECT. The first question we must ask is, is ECT more effective than a placebo treatment? Two types of placebos have been used, a drug placebo and an ECT placebo. With the ECT placebo, the patient receives the sedative and muscle relaxant but is not given the shock. However, upon regaining consciousness, the patient is told that the shock was given. The results of at least 19 experiments have consistently indicated that ECT is more effective than either type of placebo for relieving depression (see Fink, 1979; Janicak et al., 1985; Scovern & Kilmann, 1980). The only qualification is that effectiveness of ECT is limited to patients suffering from severe endogenous (physiologically caused) depressions (Greenblatt et al., 1964).

Understandably, ECT is not more effective than placebos for treating individuals with mild exogenous (environmentally caused) depressions; there is no reason to expect that an electrical shock to the brain would help individuals overcome depression that was due to an environmental event such as the loss of a loved one.

Next we must ask, is ECT more effective than antidepressant drugs? The evidence indicates that when treating individuals with severe endogenous depressions, ECT is generally more beneficial than the drugs (Scovern & Kilmann, 1980). For example, in one study with severely depressed patients, ECT had an 83% success rate, whereas tricyclics had only a 35% success rate (Avery & Lubrano, 1979).

In addition to being more effective than drugs, ECT has the advantage of producing its effects faster than drugs. The antidepressant drugs take at least 10 to 14 days to produce an effect and may take much longer, but ECT can begin showing its benefits within 3 or 4 days. The speed with which ECT works makes it very helpful in treating suicidal patients who may be a danger to themselves as long as they are depressed, and it may decrease the length of time that endogenously depressed patients must be hospitalized. Indeed, in one study, it was found that patients who received ECT spent 13 fewer days in the hospital than patients who received tricyclics (Markowitz et al., 1987). That not only saved the patients time, but it would have saved each patient over $13,000.

Is ECT a long-lasting treatment, or are patients treated with ECT more likely to relapse than patients treated with drugs? That is a very important question, but before answering it, we must consider how the two treatments are usually used. ECT is administered until the depression lifts, and then it is discontinued. In contrast, drugs are administered until the depression lifts, and then the patient is kept on a maintenance dose to protect against a relapse. Because ECT is terminated but the drug therapy is not, it is not fair to compare ECT to extended drug therapy. From a practical standpoint, however, there is probably a somewhat higher relapse rate with ECT.

The findings that ECT can eliminate depression quickly and that drugs can serve to reduce relapse rates after the depression has lifted would suggest that the two treatments might be combined for best effects: Use ECT to lift the depression quickly, and then use drugs to protect against relapse. The empirical evidence concerning the efficacy of combining ECT and drug therapy is limited, but it does suggest that the combination of treatments is more effective than ECT alone for relieving depression and reducing relapses (American Psychiatric Association, 1990).

Despite the substantial evidence that ECT is effective for treating endogenous depressions, we still do not know why it works. More than 50 theories have been advanced to account for its effects, but we have not reached any firm conclusions on the mechanism responsible (Lerer et al., 1984; Silver et al., 1994). Some dramatic effects of ECT were revealed in a recent study in which the changes in cerebral blood flow were measured in individuals who were undergoing ECT (Nobler et al., 1994). Increases in blood flow are relevant because they reflect increases in the use of blood sugar (glucose) by the neurons, and that is in turn a reflection of increased activity of the neurons; that is, more blood flow indicates more neurological activity. The results of the study revealed that individuals for whom the ECT was effective showed great increases in cerebral blood flow. Those differences are illustrated in Figure 10.8, where darker colors indicate greater increases in blood flow. Clearly, in successful cases, ECT resulted in greater increases in neurological activity, but the process that led to that effect is not yet understood.

Side Effects. It is clear that ECT can be effective for treating depression, but is it safe? The answer is yes; when used appropriately, ECT is a very safe treatment.

With regard to its overall safety, it is noteworthy that in a study of almost 19,000 patients who received an average of more than five shocks, it was found that not one fracture or death occurred (Kramer, 1985). Even elderly individuals who are at risk because they have preexisting cardiovascular disease do not develop more major complications than individuals not at risk (Rice et al., 1994).

One occasional side effect of ECT that some patients find upsetting is **retrograde amnesia.** Patients receiving ECT may lose their memories for some events that occurred prior to the treatment, and as the number of treatments increases, the memory loss extends farther back in time. This memory loss is called *retrograde* amnesia because it starts with recent events and works back from those. In most cases, the loss is minimal and little more than a minor annoyance. Although an event or a name may be forgotten, it can be relearned, and there is no permanent impairment. Furthermore, there is now evidence that as time goes by, the memories that were lost as a consequence of the shock may be regained (Calev et al., 1991). In that investigation, the memory performance of depressed

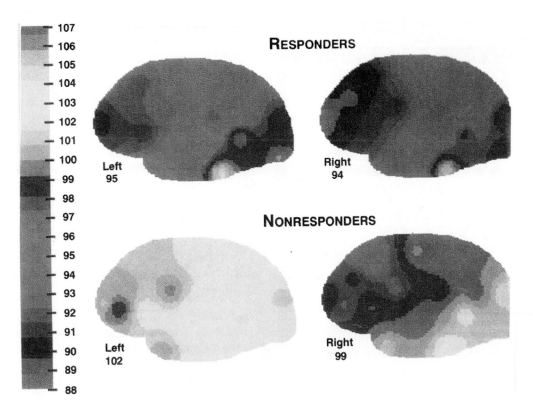

FIGURE 10.8 Patients who responded to ECT showed increases in blood flow in the brain that suggested higher levels of neurological activity.
Source: From "Regional Cerebral Blood Flow in Mood Disorders: 3. Treatment and Clinical Response" by M. S. Nobler et al., in *Archives of General Psychiatry*, Vol. 51, November 1994. Reprinted by permission of the American Medical Society.

patients was measured before and immediately after receiving ECT and then again 1 month and 6 months later. The patients received an average of nine treatments. The results indicated that there was a considerable loss in memory immediately after the treatment, but memory was back to the pretreatment level 1 month later and even a little higher 6 months later (probably due to the fact that the patients were generally functioning better after the depression had lifted). Those results are presented in Figure 10.9. Note that in some cases, memory loss may be exaggerated by patients who blame the treatment for the normal forgetting that we all experience.

The degree to which memory is disturbed may be influenced by where the electrodes are placed. Originally, they were placed *bilaterally* (one on either side; see Figure 10.10), but the results of a number of experiments have suggested that *unilateral* placement on the *nondominant* side (e.g., both on the right side for right-handed individuals; see Figure 10.10) may result in less retrograde amnesia (d'Elia & Raotma, 1975). The unilateral placement probably results in less memory disturbance because with that placement the current does not traverse the dominant side of the brain, which is responsible for most language functions.

One question that is often asked with regard to ECT is, does it cause brain damage? Obviously, the

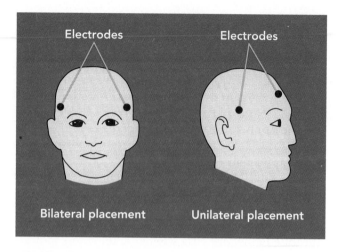

FIGURE 10.10 Electrode placement for electroconvulsive therapy.

no more than drug use probably

application of 150 V of electrical current to brain cells will result in some damage. However, with modern techniques such as using low-level shocks and providing the patient with oxygen during the convulsion to prevent anoxia, it is impossible to detect any brain damage even with highly sensitive CT and MRI scans (Devanand et al., 1994).

A more important question is, does ECT result in impaired cognitive functioning? The data on this are limited, but they indicate that ECT may actually *improve* cognitive functioning (Sackeim, 1985). The improvement stems from the fact that the depression reduced cognitive functioning, so when the depression was eliminated by the shock, functioning improved. There are even data indicating that patients who received more than 100 ECT treatments over their lifetimes did not differ from nonshocked patients on measures of cognitive functioning (Devanand et al., 1991, 1994). Because of the effectiveness of ECT and the fact that it can be given in such a way that side effects are minimized, the use of ECT is increasing dramatically (Thompson et al., 1994).

Light Therapy for Depression with Seasonal Pattern

In Chapter 8, you learned that a subset of depression is likely to occur during seasons of the year when there is less light, a disorder known as *depression with seasonal pattern*. (That disorder is also commonly referred to as the *seasonal affective disorder*, or *SAD*.) If reduced light leads to depression in some individuals, exposing those individuals to more light should relieve their depression. That prescription was offered initially more than 2,000 years ago when Aretaeus said, "Lethargics are to

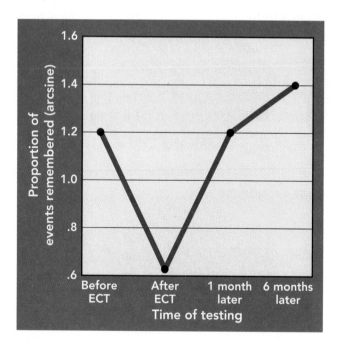

FIGURE 10.9 Memory for important events was not impaired 1 month after electroconvulsive therapy (ECT).
Source: From "Early and Long-Term Effects of Electroconvulsive Therapy and Depression on Memory and Other Cognitive Functions" by A. Calev et al., in *The Journal of Nervous and Mental Disease*, Vol. 179, No. 9. Copyright © 1991 by Williams and Wilkins.

be laid in the light and exposed to the rays of the sun." Despite the amount of time that has elapsed since light therapy was suggested, there is still controversy over this treatment, and it is still being refined (Bauer, Kurtz, et. al., 1994; Lam, 1994; Murphy et al., 1993; Oren et al., 1994; Teicher et al., 1995; Termal et al., 1989; Wirz-Justice et al., 1993). However, it does appear that the treatment is effective for at least some individuals and that *bright light (2,500 lux) is more effective than dim light* (Wehr & Rosenthal, 1989). Indeed, dim light is often used as a control condition in experiments on light therapy. Second, some investigators have found that light in the *morning* is more effective than light in the evening, but the data are not consistent (e.g., Avery et al., 1993; Wirz-Justice et al., 1993). Regardless of when the light is used, the crucial factor seems to be to extend the time during the day that the individual gets light—that is, to create an earlier morning or a later night.

The process underlying SAD and light therapy is not clear. One hypothesis revolves around the production of **melatonin** (mel-uh-TŌ-nin), a hormone that regulates sleep activity cycles and at high levels may depress mood. Melatonin production is increased when periods of light are shorter, as they are in the winter. By exposing the individual to light in the morning

This could keep me awake!

Exposure to bright light has been shown to be effective for some individuals who suffer from depression with seasonal pattern. Why light therapy works, however, is still unclear.

or at night, the total period of light is increased, and that may suppress the production of melatonin. This explanation is still under investigation, and it is too early to draw a conclusion (Checkley et al., 1993). Other explanations revolve around the effects of light on metabolic rate and circadian rhythms (Gaist et al., 1990; Wehr & Rosenthal, 1989). Finally, it should be noted that drugs such as Prozac are also effective for treating depression with seasonal pattern (Lam et al., 1995).

↑ melatonin ↓ mood

COMMENT

The evidence for the effectiveness of the physiological treatments for depression is strong and growing stronger. With regard to drugs, it is probably not an understatement to say that we are in the midst of a revolution with regard to the treatment of depression, and as new drugs are introduced, the level of treatment effectiveness goes up and the level of side effects goes down. However, it is important to recognize that drug therapy is still not effective in all cases. For example, as many as 30% of patients do not improve or experience intolerable side effects. One explanation for the failures is that some patients have not been given the right drug. For example, if an individual is depressed because of low levels of serotonin but is given a drug that influences levels of norepinephrine, it is unlikely that the drug therapy would be effective. Finally, drugs may not be effective because the dosage was not high enough or the drug was not used for a long enough period of time. Because there are many reasons why drugs may not be effective, it is often necessary to experiment with a number of drugs and dosage levels before abandoning drug therapy.

With regard to ECT, it is clear that after half a century of use (and abuse), we can conclude that ECT can be effective for treating severe endogenous depression. Furthermore, ECT produces results faster than drug therapy, making it especially helpful for treating suicidal patients for whom a rapid intervention in the disorder is essential. Unfortunately, because ECT is not a cure and because patients cannot be put on a maintenance dose of ECT, the most effective treatment is probably to use ECT to break the depression and then to follow it up with drug treatment to protect against relapse. It is important to note that although ECT is often effective for treating depressions, despite five decades of use, we still do not understand why it works, and it continues to be a controversial treatment.

Light therapy is still in its infancy; it does appear to help some individuals, but it is not yet clear who it helps and what mode of treatment is most effective.

Finally, it is important to note that the physiological treatments are treatments rather than cures, and therefore individuals may have to continue with these treatments for long periods of time. That is certainly a limitation, but it is not a limitation that is unique to psychiatric treatment and not a sufficient reason to reject physiological treatments. For example, insulin is an effective treatment for diabetes, not a cure, but that has not been a reason to reject it.

The physiological treatments are effective, but are they more effective than other treatments? I will examine the data related to that question in the next section.

COMPARISONS AND COMBINATIONS OF TREATMENTS FOR DEPRESSION

From the preceding sections, it is clear that a variety of very different approaches can all be effective for treating depression. In view of those findings, two questions that are often asked are, *which treatment is most effective, and is a combination of treatments more effective than any one treatment alone?* The answers to those questions have important implications for the effective and efficient treatment of depression.

Comparisons of Psychotherapy, Cognitive Therapy, and Drug Therapy

For many years, there has been a hot debate over the question of which type of therapy is most effective for treating depression. After reviewing the research, one group of authors concluded that "initial analysis suggested some differences in the efficacy of various types of treatment; however, once the influence of investigator allegiance was removed, there remained no evidence for the relative superiority of any one approach" (Robinson et al., 1990, p. 30). In other words, investigators with different orientations found evidence to support their own positions. In an attempt to overcome this problem of bias, the National Institute of Mental Health (NIMH) called together investigators who represented a number of different orientations and conducted an experiment in which about 250 depressed individuals were randomly assigned to four treatments: (a) *interpersonal psychotherapy,* (b) *cognitive behavioral therapy,* (c) tricyclic *drug therapy,* and (4) *placebo pill therapy* (Elkin et al., 1985, 1989). The therapy was conducted by experts in each area over the course of about 16 weeks, and a number of different measures of effectiveness were used.

The initial report of this investigation revealed two notable findings (Elkin et al., 1989). First, when indi-

viduals who were initially *less* depressed were considered, *there were no reliable differences among the treatments in terms of effectiveness.* In other words, for mildly depressed individuals, neither psychotherapy nor cognitive therapy nor drug therapy was more effective than the placebo. The lack of effectiveness of the treatments was surprising and needs more exploration. Second, when individuals who were initially *more* depressed were considered, *there were differences among the effects of the treatments, but the differences were not particularly large.* For example, with one measure of effectiveness, it was found that (a) the drug therapy was reliably more effective than the placebo therapy, (b) the interpersonal psychotherapy and cognitive behavioral therapy showed levels of effectiveness that were between those of the drug and placebo therapies, and (c) the levels of effectiveness of the interpersonal psychotherapy and cognitive behavioral therapy were not reliably different from those of the drug and placebo therapies. Those findings are presented in Figure 10.11. (Note that if a difference is said to be *not reliable,* it means that the difference is relatively small and could be due to chance.) It is also noteworthy that in a reanalysis of the data, it was found that individuals who received any one of the treatments were not more likely to move from "dysfunctional" to "functional" categories than the individuals in any other treatment (Ogles et al., 1995). In other words, there do not appear to be practical or clinically significant differences among the treatments.

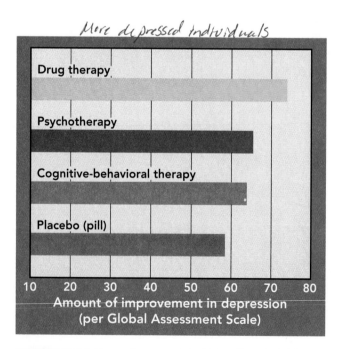

FIGURE 10.11 **Drug therapy was more effective than placebo therapy, but other differences were unreliable.**
Source: Adapted from Elkin et al. (1989), p. 976, fig. 1.

These relatively weak findings were met with mixed emotions by therapists representing different points of view; they were disappointed that their therapy didn't "win" but relieved that it didn't "lose." The question that arises is, why weren't greater differences found in the effects of therapies that involved such different procedures?

There are at least two answers to that question. First, it could be argued that although there were major differences among the various therapies, there were also some factors that were common to all of the therapies (a caring therapist, a rationale for symptoms, a treatment plan, expectations for improvement), and it may have been that those *common factors were responsible for the effects* (Frank, 1982; Imber et al., 1990; Weinberger, 1993, 1995). This is referred to as the **nonspecific (common) factor explanation.** The nonspecific factor explanation could even be applied to the placebo condition because the sessions in which patients were given their pills lasted 20 to 30 minutes, so there was more going on than just the giving of pills.

The second explanation is that *each therapy was effective, for a different type of patient or a different type of symptom,* and when different types of patients and symptoms were "lumped together," the different effects of the therapies were canceled out and all of the therapies appeared to have similar and only moderate effects. This can be called the **specific patient-symptom explanation,** and I will discuss it in the following sections.

Types of Patients and Types of Therapy

There are numerous differences among patients, such as intelligence and verbal ability, that could influence the type of therapy that would be most effective for a given patient (Beutler, 1991; Shoham-Salomon & Hannah, 1991; Smith & Sechrest, 1991; Snow, 1991; Sotsky et al., 1991). Probably one of the most important variables to consider is the type of depression with which the patient is suffering. We know that depressions can stem from a number of different factors, and therefore it is overly simplistic to assume that any one therapy would be effective for patients with different types of depression. For example, psychotherapy may be more effective for individuals with environmentally caused depressions, and drug therapy may be more effective for individuals with physiologically caused depressions.

In one study relevant to this possibility, it was found that depressed patients who did not respond well to tricyclic drugs reported almost three times as many undesirable events in their lives during therapy than patients for whom the tricyclic drugs were effective (Lloyd et al.,

1981). The events tended to be health-related and were perceived as being beyond the patients' control. These results suggest that the patients who did not respond to the drugs were suffering from exogenous (stress-related) depressions for which we would not expect the drugs to be effective.

Types of Symptoms and Types of Therapy

It is also possible that different types of therapies influence different types of symptoms. A series of comprehensive experiments concerning this possibility has revealed two interesting findings (Covi et al., 1974; Friedman, 1975; Klerman et al., 1974). First, psychotherapy was found to be more effective than drug therapy for helping patients deal with problems of living, social functioning, and interpersonal relations. However, drug therapy was found to be more effective than psychotherapy for reducing the feelings of depression and preventing relapse (see reviews by Klerman & Schechter, 1982; Weissman, 1979). In other words, psychotherapy influenced *behaviors,* and drugs influenced *moods.* This does not mean that psychotherapy did not influence depression and that drugs did not influence the problems of daily living. It means only that the different approaches were relatively more effective with the different sets of symptoms.

Psychotherapy plus Drug Therapy

Because psychotherapy and drug therapy may influence different aspects of the depressive disorder, we might expect that the combination of the two therapies would result in the greatest effect. However, it has been argued that drug therapy may actually interfere with psychotherapy when the two are used in combination. For example, patients may rely on their pills for help and not devote sufficient effort to psychotherapy.

Controlled research on the separate and combined effects of psychotherapy and drug therapy permits two conclusions. First, there is no evidence that drug therapy interferes with psychotherapy or vice versa (Covi et al., 1974; Friedman, 1975; Klerman et al., 1974). In other words, patients who are in psychotherapy but also taking drugs do not work less or do less well in psychotherapy. Second, there is good evidence that the combination may be more effective than either treatment alone (Di Mascio et al., 1979; Frank et al., 1989; Frank et al., 1990; Klerman, 1990; Klerman et al., 1974; Weissman et al., 1979). For example, in one experiment, acutely depressed patients were given *psychotherapy alone, drug therapy* (Elavil/amitriptyline) *alone, psychotherapy plus drug therapy,* or *nonscheduled treatment,* in which active treatment was not scheduled but the patient could call for one 50-minute session per month (Weissman et al., 1979). The results indicated that (a) the patients who received psychotherapy plus drug therapy were least likely to relapse, (b) the patients who received the nonscheduled treatment were most likely to relapse, and (c) the patients who received either psychotherapy alone or drug therapy alone showed intermediate relapse rates. Those results are summarized in Figure 10.12. The additive effect of psychotherapy and drug therapy occurs because when the symptoms of depression are reduced or eliminated with the drug, the patient can benefit more from the support and guidance provided in the psychotherapy (Klerman & Schechter, 1982).

In other research, it was found that among individuals who were at high risk for relapse after treatment for depression (they had a history of recurrent depression), relapse following drug treatment could be reduced if the individuals received psychotherapy (Frank, 1991; Frank et al., 1990). Furthermore, it was found that among the individuals who received psychotherapy, those whose therapy was more interpersonal (i.e.,

focused on social relations, support, and feelings rather than symptoms or intellectual issues) showed the lowest relapse rates (Frank et al., 1991). These findings offer additional support for the notion that the combination of drugs and psychotherapy is most effective, and they highlight the findings noted earlier that it is the personal rather than the technique-specific aspects of psychotherapy that are most important.

WHAT CAN WE CONCLUDE CONCERNING THE TREATMENT OF DEPRESSION?

Most important to conclude is that today most depressions can be effectively treated and that a number of different strategies are useful. Specifically, for treating mild or moderate levels of depression, psychotherapy, cognitive therapy, and drug therapy have all been shown to be effective. The psychotherapy and cognitive therapy appear to be effective because they reduce stress (i.e., provide social support, solutions to problems, a more positive outlook). The stress reduction may then lead to a normalization of neurotransmitter levels, which constitute the final common pathway to depression. In contrast, drugs appear to work because they have a direct effect on neurotransmitter levels. For severe depression, electroconvulsive therapy followed by drugs may be necessary. Light therapy appears to be effective for individuals who are suffering from depression with seasonal pattern.

Although psychodynamic, cognitive, and drug therapy are often found to be equally effective for treating depression, it is probably the case that the different therapies are effective for different individuals or different symptoms. For example, drugs would be more effective for depressions that stem from strictly biochemical causes. In other cases, the most effective outcomes are achieved when different therapies are combined. For example, a severe depression might be treated with drugs, and then relapse can be prevented with psychotherapy or cognitive therapy.

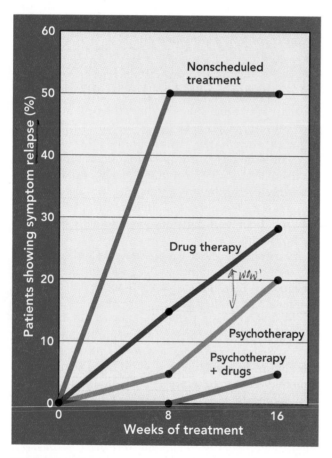

FIGURE 10.12 The combination of psychotherapy and drug therapy was most effective for reducing relapses in depression.
Source: Adapted from Weissman et al. (1979), p. 557, fig. 1.

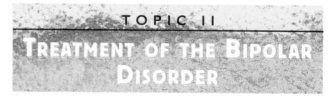

TOPIC 11

TREATMENT OF THE BIPOLAR DISORDER

Effective treatment of the bipolar disorder is important because during manic phases, individuals with the bipolar disorder can pose difficult management problems. As recently as 1970, our treatments for this disorder were ineffective, and we were limited to controlling the patients with straitjackets, heavy doses of sedatives, and confinement in seclusion rooms. That picture has changed dramatically, and today most cases of the bipolar disorder can be treated effectively.

THE USE OF LITHIUM

In 1949, it was discovered that *lithium carbonate* was effective for controlling both the mania and the depression seen in the bipolar disorder (Cade, 1949). Although lithium was used extensively in Europe to treat the disorder, it was not approved for use in the United States until 1970 because of its potentially serious side effects. Since its approval for use, it has been the treatment of choice for the bipolar disorder, and it is sometimes used to treat depression (the unipolar disorder) when other approaches fail.

Effectiveness of Lithium

There is strong and consistent evidence that lithium is effective for treating between 60% and 70% of the adults and children who suffer from the bipolar disorder (Abou-Saleh, 1992; Alessi et al., 1994; Goodwin & Jamison, 1990; Price & Heninger, 1994; Thau et al., 1993; Tohen et al., 1990). In one series of studies in which patients with the bipolar disorder were given either lithium or a placebo, 62% of the patients who were given lithium remitted their symptoms, whereas only 5% of the patients who were given the placebo did so. In another series of studies, patients whose symptoms had been eliminated with lithium were either maintained on the lithium or were switched to a placebo without being informed (Baastrup et al., 1970; Hullin et al., 1972; Melia, 1970). The patients who remained on the lithium had a relapse rate of only 11%, but the patients who had been switched to the placebo had a relapse rate of 51%.

Lithium is clearly effective for treating the bipolar disorder, and once the proper level of medication is stabilized, the individual may live a "normal" life. However, the picture is not always completely rosy. A number of follow-up studies have indicated that some individuals are likely to be rehospitalized briefly and may show continuing problems in social or occupational functioning even if they are not rehospitalized (e.g., Gitlin et al., 1995; Goldberg et al., 1995). One predictor of poor response is whether the individuals are also taking antipsychotic drugs. The fact that the individuals are taking an antipsychotic drug may reflect the fact that they are also suffering from some other disorder that is interfering with their adjustment. Another factor in relapse is high stress, and that is consistent with the fact that stress can trigger the bipolar disorder in individuals who are predisposed (see Chapter 9).

Lithium has been found to be an effective treatment for the bipolar disorder, but the reason for its effectiveness is not yet clear (Manji et al., 1991; Risby et al., 1991). As you learned in Chapter 9, the bipolar disorder appears to stem from fluctuations in the amount of the neurotransmitter that is released by the presynaptic neurons or from fluctuations in the sensitivity of the postsynaptic neurons. Lithium probably reduces symptoms by stabilizing the processes responsible for transmitter release and neuron sensitivity, but exactly how it works has not yet been definitely established.

Monitoring Lithium Levels and Side Effects

Low levels of lithium are not effective for treatment, and high levels are poisonous, so it is essential to monitor the levels of lithium in the bloodstream (Bassuk & Schoonover, 1977; Blom & Moore, 1978). During the first week, while levels are being established, it is necessary to take blood samples every day. Following that, weekly samples are necessary, and eventually checkups can be reduced to about one a month.

The most common side effects of lithium are thirst and frequent urination (to eliminate the fluids taken in to quench the thirst). At somewhat higher dosage levels, lithium can cause difficulty with concentration, memory, and motor coordination (Shaw et al., 1987). When the dosage level is too high, muscle tremors, gastric distress, and dizziness may set in (Herrington & Lader, 1981). Some years ago, patients would go through cycles in which side effects would set in shortly after the medication was taken and then dissipate as the effects of the drug wore off, only to appear again when the next dose was taken. The initial side effects occurred because patients had to be given a high enough dose to carry them through to the next administration. Fortunately, timed-release lithium tablets are now available, and thus the drug can be maintained at a uniform level throughout the day without the side effect cycles.

Problems with Patient Compliance

Lithium is an effective drug for treating the bipolar disorder, and its side effects are minimal when compared to the symptoms they replace. So you may be surprised to learn that it is frequently difficult to get patients to continue taking their lithium. Patients often stop taking it soon after their moods have stabilized. This usually occurs for one of three reasons: (a) Once the symptoms are gone, the patient does not think that he or she needs the drug anymore, (b) the patient becomes annoyed with the side effects or the inconvenience of taking the medication, or (c) the patient misses the fun of the manic highs and goes off the medication in the hope of experiencing those highs again (Jamison &

other 30%

Akiskal, 1983; Van Putten, 1975). Going off the lithium in an attempt to "get high" is mostly likely to occur when the patient is facing a stress or crisis. It is interesting to note that bipolar patients are more likely to discontinue their drugs than unipolar patients, who experience only depression (Kocsis & Stokes, 1979).

An individual who goes off lithium is 28 times more likely to have a manic episode than an individual who stays on the medication (Suppes et al., 1991). However, in some cases, the patient is foiled in the attempt to bring on mania because depression sets in instead. The experience of one patient who voluntarily discontinued his medication is presented in Case Study 10.3. (This is a follow-up report by the student who described his original experience with a bipolar disorder in Case Study 8.6 in Chapter 8.)

Alternatives to Lithium

Lithium is effective for treating only about 70% of the individuals who suffer from mania, and some individu-als develop unacceptable side effects. For those individuals, anticonvulsive drugs may be used effectively (Silver et al., 1994). The **anticonvulsive drugs** that are used most widely to treat mania are Tegretol (carbamazepine), Klonopin (clonazepam), and Depakene (valproic acid). As is the case with lithium, it is not clear why these drugs work, but it is suspected that they inhibit the random and erratic firing of neurons that may lead to mania. That explanation is based on the fact that erratic firing of neurons is responsible for convulsions (e.g., epileptic seizures), and the drugs are effective for controlling that firing and the seizures.

ELECTROCONVULSIVE THERAPY

Clearly, lithium and the anticonvulsive drugs are effective for treating mania, but there are some individuals for whom the drugs are not effective, and in those cases

---

CASE STUDY 10.3

A 21-Year-Old Student with a Bipolar Disorder Who Discontinued Lithium Carbonate

"After being 'normalized' on lithium carbonate, I began to wonder whether I could exercise any conscious control over my moods. Having been through both extremes of bipolar illness, I believed that I would be able to detect the warning signals that would tell me when a mood swing was coming on. An inability to sleep and lack of appetite signaled a high coming on, and unwarranted depression and listlessness signaled a low. I rationalized that during my level period, I was medicating myself needlessly. Also, various aspects of taking lithium carbonate bothered me. The side effects of stomach discomfort, dry mouth, and the need to urinate frequently were very annoying, as was the simple hindrance of having to carry and take pills three times a day.

"I also missed the wonderful feeling involved in the manic high. I believed that if I were to stay off lithium long enough to notice the first signs of mania coming on, I could then medicate myself to the point of holding my mood at a mild 'hypomanic' state. This would let me feel happier and more energetic than usual, and I thought that with 'a little medication,' I could keep from climbing too high.

The problem, as I found out, is that it is very difficult to detect those first signals—especially those of depression. When I went off my medication, I found myself so depressed that I didn't even care enough to start the lithium again. Lithium does not have a fast-acting antidepression effect, and it took a long time for me to benefit when I did resume taking the medication.

"My attempt to keep track of my high and control it was also unsuccessful. When I was feeling better (higher), I thought, 'I can handle this—I'm sure I can handle a little more.' Unfortunately, during the manic state, it is very hard to be objective, and I lost control. In the end, the expression 'letting it get away from you' seems a very apt way to describe what generally happened when I went off my medication.

"After a couple of disastrous experiences (I had to drop out of school and go back into the hospital until I was again normalized on lithium), I am now back on the medication for good, or at least until we have established that I am no longer at risk for bipolar mood swings. I now take my lithium in timed-release capsules, and the side effects are no longer noticeable."

electroconvulsive therapy (ECT) can be effective. Indeed, research over the past 50 years has revealed that ECT can be effective for bringing about a quick recovery for about 60% of individuals with mania for whom drugs did not work (Mukherjee et al., 1994). (ECT appears to be effective for about 80% of manic patients in general.) Interestingly, individuals with mania appear to have lower thresholds for seizures than depressed individuals have; therefore, lower levels of shock can be used in the treatment, which can reduce the cognitive side effects. As in the treatment of depression, the most effective strategy for severe cases may involve the use of ECT in combination with drugs such as lithium (Mukherjee, 1993).

What Can We Conclude Concerning the Treatment of the Bipolar Disorder?

One of my colleagues once commented to me that if he had to have one psychiatric disorder, he would want it to be the bipolar disorder, for two reasons. His first reason was that if he had to have symptoms, they might as well be ones that made him feel good; his second reason was that he wanted a disorder that could be treated relatively quickly and effectively. He was at least half right. Half of the symptoms of the bipolar disorder (the mania) do make individuals feel good, and in most cases the symptoms of the bipolar disorder can be brought under control quickly and relatively inexpensively with drugs such as lithium or anticonvulsant drugs that have very few side effects. Although we still do not understand the basis of the bipolar disorder or why the drugs are effective, in most cases today it is a manageable disorder, and one of the biggest problems associated with its management is getting the individuals to continue taking their medication.

TOPIC III
SUICIDE PREVENTION

In Chapter 8 you learned that suicide is a leading cause of death, and the question to be addressed here is, can suicide be prevented? The answer to that question is definitely yes, but what we do and how effective we are depend on when in the process we attempt to intervene. In general, there are two types of suicide prevention programs; one is focused on the *education* of individuals about suicide so that they will not get to the point of actually attempting suicide, and the second is *crisis management,* in which we intervene with individuals who are about to commit a suicidal act.

EDUCATION

Suicide Prevention Programs

Educational programs are used to teach individuals about suicide and the sources of help that are available for individuals who are contemplating suicide. Specifically, in these programs individuals are taught (a) how to recognize the signs of suicidal behavior in themselves and others, (b) why it is important to get help, and (c) where to get that help. These educational programs are run for individuals of all ages, but they are often focused on schoolchildren or young adults who are just entering or going through a high-risk period for suicide.

Effectiveness of Educational Programs

The evidence concerning the effectiveness of the educational programs is mixed. On the one hand, there is evidence that participants in programs of this type do become more knowledgeable about the signs of suicides and how to respond to them. It also appears that if individuals are taught effective strategies for coping with the problems that are leading to suicide, their reported levels of suicidal feelings can be decreased (Abbey et al., 1989; Orbach & Bar-Joseph, 1993). That is, teaching them that there are solutions other than suicide can reduce hopelessness and hence suicide. On the other hand, there is some evidence that at least in some cases, participation in a school-based program can be associated with an increase in suicide (Garland & Zigler, 1993; Lester, 1992). The explanation for the latter finding may be that the programs stigmatized suicidal individuals and therefore discouraged them from seeking help. In that regard, it is interesting to note that prevention programs appear to be more effective for females than for males, possibly because seeking help may be more consistent with the traditional female role (Overholser et al., 1990). Clearly, education about suicide is important, but it must be presented in a positive, constructive, and noncritical fashion.

CRISIS MANAGEMENT

Suicide Prevention Centers

If early identification and intervention are not effective, we may face an individual who is about to kill himself or herself, and that calls for crisis management. At that point, we must do something to stop or at least slow down the process so as to have an opportunity to find an alternative solution for the individual. This is often done by the staff in a **suicide prevention center.** The first of these centers were established in the mid-1950s in Los Angeles, California, and London, England. They were walk-in type clinics to which individuals could go for help during a crisis. The idea quickly caught on, and now there are hundreds of such centers. Furthermore, the programs that were originally designed specifically for suicide prevention centers have been adapted for use in a variety of other settings, including hospital emergency rooms, general crisis centers, and community mental health centers. In addition, there are now telephone hot lines that individuals who are contemplating suicide can call for help. Those hot lines are particularly helpful because it is easier to pick up a phone than to travel to a clinic and the individual may feel more comfortable talking over the phone than face to face with a counselor. A key feature of all of these programs is *easy accessibility.* If an individual is contemplating suicide, we want to make it as easy as possible for that person to get help as soon as possible. Unlike other services in which the motto often is something like "Take an aspirin and see me next week," with suicide prevention it is "What's the problem and let's see what we can do about it *now.*" (For a fascinating description of one student's experience working in a crisis center, see Case Study 21.5 in Chapter 21.)

In most cases, crisis management programs are staffed by **paraprofessionals,** individuals who have received some training in counseling but who are not professional mental health workers such as psychologists, psychiatrists, social workers, or nurses. For example, many of my undergraduate students spend some time volunteering in crisis centers. Of course, the paraprofessionals have professionals on whom they can rely for advice and backup when necessary.

The specifics of the strategies for intervention differ from program to program, but in most programs, the counselor has five general goals:

1. *Establish a Relationship.* First, the counselor must establish a positive relationship with the individual who has come in or called for help. A trusting relationship is important so that the individual will be honest about his or her seriousness about suicide and so that later the individual will have confidence in what the counselor says and suggests. One of the crucial features in developing that relationship is not being judgmental. The counselor should not agree with the decision to commit suicide but must accept the individual's concerns and positions so that together they can begin seeking an alternative solution.

2. *Assess the Risk of Suicide.* Early in the discussion the counselor must determine whether a suicidal act has already been started (e.g., have pills already been taken?), if the individual is on the brink of a suicidal act, or if the individual is just thinking about it. This assessment has serious implications for what is done; do we send the police and an ambulance, or do we try to talk the person out of going further?

3. *Clarify the Problem.* If it is determined that the individual is not in imminent danger of dying, the counselor must identify what the problem is—what led to this crisis? That is essential if a solution other than suicide is going to be found.

Suicide prevention counseling is often done by paraprofessionals. Here a young volunteer tries to help a young man who is contemplating suicide.

4. *Activate the Individual's Strengths.* Next it is essential to give the individual support, encouragement, and reasons for going on rather than giving up. In doing this, one can point to the strengths and contributions of the individual as well as the important role he or she has in the lives of others. In essence, positive factors have to be introduced.

5. *Develop a Plan.* Once the problem has been identified and the individual has been stabilized, a plan for solving the problem that led to the interest in suicide must be developed, and in most cases the counselor has to play a major role in developing the plan. Obviously, if the individual could do it, there would not be a crisis. However, it is important to keep the individual involved; it has to be "our" plan so that the individual gets a sense of control and support. As I have pointed out numerous times in this book, social support plays an important role in dealing with stress and diminishing symptoms. Often the plan involves a "contract" between the counselor and the suicidal individual in which the person agrees not to attempt suicide before contacting the counselor. This serves as a protection, but it also reinforces the sense of the counselor's concern for and commitment to the individual.

Effectiveness of Crisis Management

Suicide prevention programs are used widely, but it is not clear how effective they are. One factor that limits their effectiveness is that only a very small proportion of suicidal individuals come for help. That is not surprising because individuals who recognized that there was help for their problems probably wouldn't be planning suicide. Indeed, it has been estimated that as few as 2% of suicidal individuals contact the programs for help, and those who do contact the programs do not belong to the demographic groups that are at greatest risk for suicide (Lester, 1989). People who use the programs are most likely to be young African-American women, whereas the individuals who are most likely to commit suicide are older white males (see Chapter 9). Obviously, if the programs are not used much and not used by individuals who are at high risk, their effectiveness will be limited.

It is clear that the underuse of the programs limits their effectiveness, but do the programs reduce suicide rates in the individuals they serve? The evidence *suggests* that the programs are effective, but because of methodological problems in studying the issue, there is no hard evidence from which we can draw firm conclusions (Neimeyer & Pfeiffer, 1994). For example, in one approach to the problem, an investigator compared the change in suicide rates in communities that did or did not introduce prevention programs and found that the rate of increase was less in the communities in which the programs were introduced (Lester, 1991a, 1991b, 1993). That certainly suggests that the programs were effective, but because programs were not randomly assigned to communities, it is possible that the communities that elected to have the centers were somehow different from those that did not and that the difference influenced suicide rates. For example, might it be the communities that elected to have the program were more affluent or more "psychologically minded"? In another approach to the problem, investigators followed up high-risk individuals who had called a suicide prevention center for help and found that only 2% of those individuals subsequently committed suicide (Farberow & Litman, 1970). That figure was in contrast to the 6% rate of suicide that is usually found for similar individuals. Again the findings suggest that the program was effective, but it is also possible (even likely) that individuals who call for help are somehow different from those who do not call for help. For example, might those who call be less firmly committed to suicide and thus at somewhat lower risk?

These findings suggest that suicide prevention programs can be effective, and in view of the seriousness of the problems, it seems clear that the programs should be continued and that additional research is necessary to evaluate and increase their effectiveness.

SUMMARY

TOPIC I: TREATMENT OF DEPRESSION

■ Psychotherapy has been found to be effective for the treatment of depression, but it is not clear exactly what makes it effective. The one common element across forms of psychotherapy is social support, and that support may help reduce stress.

■ The learning approaches to treatment involve increasing rewards and decreasing punishments. Those approaches have been found to be effective, probably because they reduce stress.

■ The cognitive approaches to treatment involve replacing inaccurate negative beliefs with accurate positive beliefs. Cognitive therapy has been found to be effective for treating individuals with mild or moderate levels of depression, and in some cases it is as effective as drug treatment.

■ One physiological approach to treatment involves drugs; tricyclics and bicyclics block the reuptake of serotonin and norepinephrine, lithium stabilizes the levels of the neurotransmitters, and MAOIs reduce the catabolism of the neurotransmitters. Drugs are effective for treating depression, but there is usually a delay of at least 2 weeks before their effects become apparent, and in some cases they can have side effects. Stimulants can also reduce depression, but they are not used because when they are withdrawn, the depression may become worse than it was originally.

■ A second physiological treatment is electroconvulsive therapy (ECT). ECT can be effective for treating severe depressions, and its effects are relatively fast. The most effective approach involves ECT followed by drugs to maintain the effects. ECT can cause retrograde amnesia, but with proper administration, those effects can be minimized or eliminated. We do not yet understand why ECT is effective.

■ Light therapy can be effective for treating individuals with depression with seasonal pattern, but we do not yet understand why it works.

■ Comparisons indicate that the differences in the effectiveness of interpersonal psychotherapy, cognitive therapy, and drugs were minimal, and interpersonal psychotherapy and cognitive therapy were found to be not reliably more effective than a placebo treatment. The lack of differences in effectiveness may be due to the presence of nonspecific factors (e.g., expectations for improvement) that were present in all treatments and which were responsible for the improvements. It is also possible that different treatments were effective for different types of patients or symptoms, and when they were lumped together, effects were canceled out. A combination of psychotherapy or cognitive therapy and drugs may be most effective.

TOPIC II: TREATMENT OF THE BIPOLAR DISORDER

■ Lithium carbonate is effective for treating between 60% and 70% of patients with the bipolar disorder. For patients who do not improve with lithium, anticonvulsive drugs may be effective for controlling the mania. For patients who do not respond positively to drugs, ECT can be effective.

■ A major problem with drug treatment is patient compliance; once the mood is stabilized, the patients may think they no longer need the drug, be annoyed by the side effects, or miss the "highs."

TOPIC III: SUICIDE PREVENTION

■ Some suicide prevention programs are focused on educating people about the signs of suicidal behavior and the sources of help, whereas others are focused on crisis management for individuals who are actively contemplating suicide.

■ Data concerning the effectiveness of suicide prevention programs are sparse and problematic from a methodological standpoint, but in general they suggest that the programs can be effective. The effectiveness of the programs is limited in that they are not used widely or by the individuals in most need of them.

KEY TERMS, CONCEPTS, AND NAMES

In reviewing and testing yourself on what you have learned from this chapter, you should be able to identify and discuss each of the following.

akathisia: *cant sit still!*

anticonvulsive drugs: *bi-polar, other 30%*

bicyclics: *depression*

electroconvulsive therapy (ECT): *dep + bi-pl.*

lithium carbonate: *bipolar + dep*

MAO inhibitors (MAOIs): *reduces destruction neurot.*

melatonin↑ *mood↓ SAD*

monoamine oxidase (MAO): *enzyme to keep synapse clean*

nonspecific (common) factor

explanation: *most therapies effective, all share a common factor* — *why therapies differ*

paraprofessional: *non-professional*

postamphetamine depression: *down after upper*

psychomotor stimulants: *amphetamine*

retrograde amnesia: *ECT recent + earlier*

selective serotonin reuptake inhibitors
(SSRIs): *bicyclics — blocks reuptake/serotonin*

social support: *important for dep. relief*

specific patient-symptom explanation:

spontaneous remission: *w/o treatment*

suicide prevention center: *crisis ctr*

tricyclics: *depression*

tyramine: *interferes w MAOIs cause blood pressure↑ found in wine, aged sausage beer avacado unpast. cheese*

CHAPTER ELEVEN
SCHIZOPHRENIA and OTHER PSYCHOTIC DISORDERS: SYMPTOMS and ISSUES

OUTLINE

All of Lauren's friends thought that she was a typical, normal 24-year-old woman, but over a period of a few weeks, she began behaving more and more strangely. She did not recognize it, but she had a hard time concentrating, and when talking, she would jump from topic to topic with no apparent connection. She became very concerned about pollution and "cosmic radiation," and she attributed many personal as well as world problems to these factors. Sometimes she would laugh uncontrollably for no apparent reason. Lauren was admitted to a psychiatric hospital on an emergency basis when, according to her friends, "she just wasn't making sense anymore" and they became worried about her. After about three weeks in the hospital, many of her symptoms diminished, and she was transferred to the outpatient clinic, where she saw a social worker once a week. Within a month, she was judged to be "symptom-free," and her treatment was terminated. Four years have gone by since that episode, and during that time, she has not had any problems. She still does not understand what caused what she refers to as her "out-of-it period." The diagnosis in her records is "schizophreniform disorder."

◼ ◼ ◼

Allan had always been a loner, and somehow he had just never "gotten his act together." He drifted through high school without ever really getting involved; he had no friends and joined in no outside activities. After high school, he tried working in a couple of fast-food places, but he could not seem to "keep things straight," and he lost those jobs. Allan was brought to a psychiatric hospital when the police found him on the street only half dressed. During his admission interview, he could give his name but did not know the day of the week, the month of the year, or where he was. It was impossible to learn much more about him because he was completely incoherent; his sentences were gibberish, and what could be understood was not related to the questions he had been asked. He kept talking about "them," but it was not clear who "they" were. Allan was admitted to the hospital with a diagnosis of "schizophrenia, disorganized type."

◼ ◼ ◼

Ben has been hospitalized for over 30 years. During that time, he has received psychotherapy, numerous types of drugs, and electroconvulsive therapy. Every day for the past eight years, he has sat in the same chair staring straight ahead but attending to nothing. The sides of his mouth twitch constantly, and his head jerks occasionally. He is able to take care of himself, go to meals, and feed himself. When asked questions, he only mumbles and then seems to "drift away." The ward staff cannot remember when he had his last visitor, and they refer to him as a "burned-out schizophrenic." It is unlikely that he will ever be able to leave the hospital.

◼ ◼ ◼

The term **schizophrenia** (SKIT-zō-FRĒ-nē-uh) refers to a set of disorders that encompasses what are undoubtedly the most complex and frightening symptoms we will encounter. For example, individuals suffering from schizophrenia may hear voices, think that they are controlled by other persons, feel bugs crawling through passages in their bodies, believe that other people are plotting against them, and speak in language that may not make any sense at all. These symptoms are particularly frightening because they are totally beyond the realm of experience of most people. Many of us can understand disorders involving anxiety and depression because we have experienced those symptoms, but few of us have had hallucinations and delusions, so we have great difficulty understanding them, and we often react to them with fear. Furthermore, until recently, our fear of schizophrenia was intensified by the fact that schizophrenia was considered untreatable, and therefore the diagnosis of schizophrenia meant a life of misery and hopelessness on a back ward of a mental hospital. However, as we progress through this chapter and the two that follow, you will learn that our understanding of schizophrenia is changing rapidly and that many of our earlier conceptions and fears of the disorder may no longer be appropriate.

I should also point out that schizophrenia occurs in between 1% and 2% of the population and that the annual financial cost of schizophrenia is well over $100 billion per year (Black & Andreasen, 1994; Robins et al., 1984). Overall, then, schizophrenia is an important disorder in terms of the seriousness of the symptoms, the number of people who suffer from it, and its financial implications.

Clearly, schizophrenia is a serious problem, but it is important to recognize that a number of other psychotic disorders share some of the symptoms of schizophrenia and can cause grave problems. For example, the *schizoaffective disorder* is a combination of schizophrenia and a mood disorder.

Before discussing the symptoms of schizophrenia, I want to make a brief comment about the labels that are used when talking about individuals who suffer from schizophrenia. We usually talk about these individuals as "schizophrenics," but that is not appropriate. Just as we do not talk about people with cancer as "cancers," we should not talk about people with schizophrenia as "schizophrenics." In doing so, we may imply more than is true. That is, having schizophrenia can be very serious, but it does not necessarily influence the individual's entire being, and therefore it is not appropriate to write the whole individual off as "schizophrenic." Many people have mild cases and have learned to cope with the symptoms (e.g., they may hear voices, but they may also ignore them), or their symptoms may not interfere with their lives. Indeed, many individuals with schizophrenia function effectively in society, and other peo-ple may not even be aware that people they know well have the disorder.

Instead of talking about "schizophrenics," in this book I will talk about "individuals with schizophrenia" or "individuals who suffer from schizophrenia." In some cases, that may seem awkward and wordy, but the way we label people is important because those labels influence our perceptions and conceptions. For example, the use of nonsexist language has reduced some of the stereotypes associated with gender. When I originally wrote these chapters on schizophrenia, I used the traditional approach and talked about "schizophrenics," but when I revised the chapters using the phrase "individuals with schizophrenia," a subtle but important change emerged: The people I talked about become *people with a problem* rather than *problem people*. With this clarified, let's go on to discuss the symptoms of schizophrenia.

SYMPTOMS OF SCHIZOPHRENIA

Cognitive Symptoms

The cognitive symptoms of schizophrenia include *hallucinations, delusions, disturbed thought processes,* and *cognitive flooding,* and these may be the most obvious and serious symptoms of the disorder.

Hallucinations. **Hallucinations** are *perceptual experiences that do not have a basis in reality*. An individual who hears, feels, smells, or sees things that are not really there is said to be hallucinating. *Auditory* hallucinations are the most common. They frequently involve hearing voices that comment on the individual's behavior, criticize the behavior, or give commands. For example, a woman named Betty whom we will discuss later hears monks chanting, "Cut yourself and die. Cut yourself and die" (see Case Study 11.2). Less frequently, hallucinations involve hearing other sounds, such as motors. It is also common for individuals with schizophrenia to have *tactile* and *somatic* hallucinations in which the individual imagines tingling or burning sensations of the skin or internal bodily sensations. Finally, *visual* and *olfactory* hallucinations (seeing or smelling things that are not there) also occur in schizophrenia. For example, Betty sees monks who parade through her apartment or gather around her desk to criticize her while she is trying to work. Visual and olfactory hallucinations are somewhat less common than the other types of hallucinations.

It is important to realize that to the individuals having them, *hallucinations appear to be real perceptions,* and the individuals are *unable to distinguish hallucinations from real perceptions*. For example, Betty is very bright, and on one level she knows that monks are not really chanting at her, but the experience is so real that she sometimes has to call me for what she calls a "reality check" to get reassurance that in fact there are no monks chanting at her. *Can she destroy them w/o the hallucination?*

Delusions. Delusions are *erroneous beliefs that are held despite strong evidence to the contrary.* Some delusions are bizarre and patently absurd, whereas others are possible but unlikely. For example, the belief that there is a machine in the state capitol building that sends out waves that make you think constantly about sex is a bizarre delusion, whereas the belief that there are FBI agents hiding behind the trees in your backyard to spy on your sexual behavior is a nonbizarre delusion. The more bizarre the delusion, the more likely it is that the individual is suffering from schizophrenia.

The most common delusions are **delusions of persecution** in which individuals think that others are spying on them or planning to harm them in some way. Also common are **delusions of reference** in which objects, events, or other people are seen as having some particular significance to the person. For example, one male patient believed that if a woman across the room folded a newspaper in a certain way, that was a sign that he was being followed by spies. Similarly, another patient interpreted a television advertisement touting Coca-Cola as "the real thing" as a message that

usually regarding being controlled in some way.

controlled

"codes"—determined by outside worlds

Shattered and distorted thought patterns are characteristic of patients suffering from schizophrenia.

the people she was with at that time could be trusted. Individuals who suffer from schizophrenia may also experience **delusions of identity** in which they believe that they are someone else. Common examples of this include delusions that they are Jesus, Joan of Arc, the president of the United States, Michael Jackson, or some other famous person. In many cases, individuals with schizophrenia develop very elaborate delusional systems involving many interrelated delusions, and the hallucinations they experience are often related to their delusions. One woman who thought she was the Virgin Mary (delusion of identity) heard voices (auditory hallucinations) that she thought were the voices of sinners crying out to her for mercy. Similarly, the stomach pains (somatic hallucinations) felt by another individual with schizophrenia were taken as evidence that he had been poisoned (delusion of persecution).

Most normal individuals also maintain some beliefs that are inconsistent with reality. For example, we are sometimes incorrect in our assumptions about the motives of others, we see ourselves or others as better or worse than is actually the case, or we attach more importance to some things or behaviors than may be appropriate. However, the delusional beliefs in schizophrenia are more bizarre, more pervasive, and more resistant to change in the face of contrary evidence than the distortions most of us live with from day to day (Oltmanns & Maher, 1988).

Disturbed Thought Processes. In addition to the problems with *what* individuals with schizophrenia think (e.g., delusions), there are also problems in the *way* they think. Specifically, the *thought processes* of these individuals are characterized by a "loosening" of the associative links between thoughts so that the individuals frequently spin off into irrelevancies (Bleuler, 1936). For example, a patient may be talking about his coat and then with no apparent transition will begin talking about medieval castles in Spain.

Disturbances in thought processes are illustrated by the following response to the question "Who is the president of the United States?":

> I am the president, I am the ex-president of the United States, I have been a recent president. Just at present I was present, president of many towns in China, Japan and Europe and Pennsylvania. When you are president you are the head of all, you are the head of every one of those, you have a big head, you are the smartest man in the world. I do testory and all scientist of the whole world. The highest court of doctoring, of practicing, I am a titled lady by birth of royal blood, (pointing to another patient) he has black blood, yellow blood, he is no man, a woman, a woe-man.... (Bleuler, 1936, pp. 72–73) *sounds like beat poetry!*

The phrases used by individuals with schizophrenia are generally grammatically correct, but the thoughts

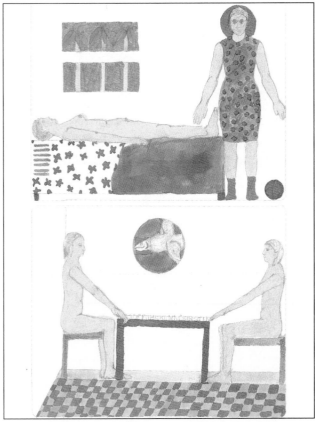

This artwork was done by Betty, a woman who suffers from schizophrenia and who is profiled in Case Studies 11.2 and 13.4

would ritalin work?

expressed are disjointed and do not make sense when put together. Because of the apparent random nature of their thoughts, the language of individuals with schizophrenia has been described as a **word salad.** Each ingredient or phrase is separately identifiable, but they have been mixed or tossed so that there is no order to them.

If individuals who suffer from schizophrenia have disturbed thought processes, their intellectual functioning is going to be impaired, and therefore in many cases we find that these individuals perform at *reduced intellectual levels* (Heaton et al., 1994). For example, it would be difficult to perform well in an interview or on a test if you were giving responses that consisted of random thoughts strung together. Interestingly, the original term for schizophrenia was **dementia praecox** (di-MEN-shuh PRE-koks), which means "premature deterioration." When that term was introduced, it was thought that the patients suffered from the type of intellectual deterioration that underlies senility but that it had set in prematurely. However, it was later realized that the deterioration in schizophrenia is very different from that in senility, and consequently the impaired intellectual functioning seen in schizophrenia is now referred to as the **schizophrenic deficit** in order to distinguish it from other forms of intellectual impairment.

are genius often mis-diagnosed?

Cognitive Flooding (Stimulus Overload). An important element in the cognitive experience of individuals with schizophrenia is the *inability to screen out irrelevant internal and external stimuli.* It is as though the "filter" that most of us have for eliminating extraneous stimuli is missing or broken. As a consequence, individuals with schizophrenia are forced to attend to everything around and within them, and they feel as if they are being flooded to the point of overload with perceptions, thoughts, and feelings. This is called **cognitive flooding** or **stimulus overload.** The inability to screen out stimulation, flooding, and overloading of the cognitive system is reflected in the following quotations from patients:

> Things are coming in too fast. I lose my grip of it and get lost. I am attending to everything at once and as a result I do not really attend to anything.

> Noises seem to be louder to me than they were before. . . . I notice it most with background noises.

> Colors seem to be brighter now almost as if they are luminous. (McGhie & Chapman, 1961, p. 105)

One author provided the following description of the cognitive experience of schizophrenia:

> The problem is that schizophrenia makes you so goddamned fragile. I was reacting appropriately, but to so many different things, so strongly, and in such a personal way that I didn't look that way to anyone else. More importantly, my being that fragile and reactive meant I

couldn't do many things I wanted to do. I was so distractible that even very simple tasks were impossible to complete. (Vonnegut, 1975, p. 209)

This flooding can be seen in terms of brain activity. If you present a series of sounds, such as clicks, to individuals who are not suffering from schizophrenia, the brain will show a considerable response (increased electrical activity) to the first sound but a greatly reduced response to subsequent sounds. In other words, the individual adapts to the stimulation, "closing the gate" on it, so to speak. However, individuals who suffer from schizophrenia do not show the adaptation or gating. Instead, they show as great a response to subsequent stimuli as they did to the first stimulus (Braff et al., 1992; Judd et al., 1992). This effect is illustrated in Figure 11.1, in which the brain activity responses to two clicks in individuals who were or were not suffering from schizophrenia are plotted. The decline in responsivity shown by the individuals who were not suffering from schizophrenia was more than six times greater than the decline shown by individuals who were suffering from schizophrenia (−1.24 vs. −7.50). Obviously, the inability to close the gate on incoming stimulation could be very disruptive.

Note that cognitive flooding is not listed as a symptom of schizophrenia in DSM-IV. It is included here because it is an effective way of conceptualizing the nature of cognitive problems experienced by some individuals with schizophrenia.

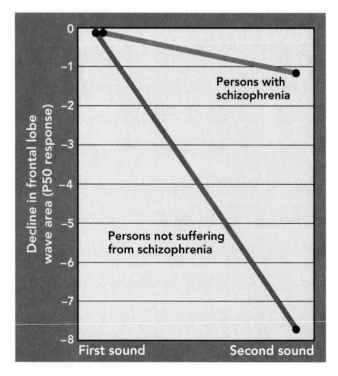

FIGURE 11.1 Individuals with schizophrenia show less adaptation to repeated stimulation than individuals who do not suffer from schizophrenia.
Source: Data from Judd et al. (1992), p. 491, tab. 1.

is there a lapse/time — get lost in the moments — need control — split b/t in+out
is God fetish a social thing or a control thing

Mood Symptoms

There are two important things to note about the mood symptoms, the first of which is that *as many as 60% of individuals with schizophrenia also suffer from serious depression* (Black & Andreasen, 1994). Their moods are often described as "blunted" or "flat." Some of the depression may be a side effect of the drugs that are used to treat schizophrenia, or it may stem from the depressing effects of struggling with the disorder. However, the effects of drugs and the struggles with the symptoms are not sufficient to account for all of the depression, and it may simply be that depression is a symptom that co-occurs with schizophrenia. Obviously, depression can contribute to the symptom pattern by decreasing motivation, increasing withdrawal, and making individuals less responsive.

The second thing to note concerning mood is that individuals with schizophrenia often show emotional responses that are *inappropriate or situationally inconsistent.* For example, when hearing of a death in the family or watching a very funny film, an individual who has schizophrenia may remain impassive and show little or no emotional response. Alternatively, at another time when discussing an injury or some other serious topic, the same individual may break into laughter.

One explanation for the situationally inappropriate emotional responses is that individuals with schizophrenia are responding to their hallucinations and delusions rather than to the elements in the situation that you and I perceive. For example, one day I was having lunch with a friend of mine who suffers from schizophrenia, and although we were talking about a very pleasant topic, she began to appear upset, depressed, and even distraught. I became concerned, and when I asked if something was wrong, she replied, "Oh, I'm sorry; it's just that everyone in the restaurant has blood running down their faces. It's just one of my hallucinations." (My friend describes her symptoms in greater detail in Case Study 11.2.) This situation is analogous to one in which four persons are listening to recordings on headphones. Three of the people are listening to quiet mood music, while unknown to the others, the fourth person is listening to a very funny comedy album. To those listening to mood music, the laughing of the fourth person would appear inappropriate. Viewed in this way, in some cases schizophrenia does not involve a disturbance of mood per se but rather a mood disturbed because of underlying cognitive problems.

To sum up, individuals with schizophrenia suffer from depression or otherwise inappropriate emotions, and those problems with mood may occur because depression is part of the disorder or because the individuals are responding to the hallucinations or delusions rather than the reality of the situation. In some cases, if we knew what the individuals were responding to, their responses might be perfectly appropriate. For example, my friend's response to the bleeding faces was appropriate; I just did not know to what she was responding.

Somatic Symptoms

DSM-IV does not list any somatic symptoms for schizophrenia, but over the years a considerable amount of attention has been focused on differences in physiological arousal (heart rate, blood pressure, sweating palms). At present, the evidence is contradictory; in some studies, individuals with schizophrenia are found to be more physiologically aroused than normal individuals, but in other studies, they are found to be less aroused. The conflicting findings may be due to the possibility that different levels of arousal are associated with different types of schizophrenia or different phases of the disorder. For example, it may be that individuals with acute cases are overaroused but those with chronic cases are underaroused. It is also possible that level of arousal is a function of the types of delusions experienced. Individuals who believed that others were plotting to kill them would probably be more aroused than individuals who thought that they were already dead.

Hallucinations and delusions often involve somatic complaints (the individual may feel pains for which there is no organic basis or may believe that parts of his or her body are rotting away), but we must be careful not to confuse those cognitive symptoms with actual somatic symptoms. Also, because many of the drugs that are used to treat schizophrenia have somatic side effects such as dryness of the mouth and increased sensitivity to the sun, we must be careful not to confuse the effects of the treatment with the effects of the disorder.

Motor Symptoms

The range of motor symptoms in schizophrenia is wide. Some individuals with the disorder remain immobile for long periods of time, whereas others are very agitated and exhibit a high level of activity. In some cases, individuals with schizophrenia have difficulty sitting still, and they repeatedly get up and sit down. Other motor symptoms include unusual facial grimacing and repetitive finger and hand movements. Many of the movements of patients appear random and purposeless, but in a few cases they are related to the patients' delusions. For example, individuals with delusions of persecution may direct large amounts of activity toward hiding or defending themselves from their persecutors.

As with some of the other symptom patterns, it is important to distinguish between the motor symptoms of schizophrenia and the side effects of the medications that are used to treat it. As we will learn later, many of the drugs that are given to individuals with

— moments/clarity

idea
— dance/hallucinations: dance troup enacting typical sch. hallucinations

CASE STUDY 11.1

The Three Christs of Ypsilanti: A Confrontation of Delusions

Some years ago in a hospital in Ypsilanti, Michigan, a psychologist brought together three patients, each of whom believed that he was Christ. The goal was to see how—or if—these three men could resolve their conflict over who was Christ. Although each believed that he was Christ, they went by the names of Joseph, Clyde, and Leon. What follows is a summary of some of their interactions with one another and the psychologist. The first day, each man was asked to introduce himself:

Joseph: My name is Joseph Cassel.

Psychologist: Joseph, is there anything else you want to tell us?

Joseph: Yes, I'm God.

Clyde: My name is Clyde Benson. That's my name straight.

Psychologist: Do you have any other names?

Clyde: Well, I have other names, but that's my vital side and I made God five and Jesus six.

Psychologist: Does that mean you're God?

Clyde: I made God, yes. I made it seventy years old a year ago. Hell! I passed seventy years old.

Leon: Sir, it so happens that my birth certificate says that I am Dr. Domino Dominorum et Rex Rexarum, Simplis Christanus Pueris Mentalis Doktor. [In Latin, this means "Lord of Lords and King of Kings, Simple Christian Boy Psychiatrist."] It also states on my birth certificate that I am the reincarnation of Jesus Christ of Nazareth,

and I also salute, and I want to add this. I do salute the manliness in Jesus Christ also, because the vine is Jesus and the rock is Christ, pertaining to the penis and testicles, and it so happens that I was railroaded into this place because of prejudice and jealousy and duping that started before I was born, and that is the main issue why I am here. I want to be myself. I do not consent to their misuse of the frequency of my life.

Psychologist: Who are "they" that you are talking about?

Leon: Those unsound individuals who practice the electronic imposition and duping. . . . I want to be myself; I don't want this electronic imposition and duping to abuse me and misuse me, make a robot out of me. I don't care for it.

Joseph: He says he is the reincarnation of Jesus Christ. I can't get it. I know who I am. I'm God, Christ, the Holy Ghost, and if I wasn't, by gosh, I wouldn't lay claim to anything of the sort. I'm Christ. . . . I know this is an insane house and you have to be very careful.

And so it went, each patient asserting that he was God and often rambling off into other associations and delusions. One day when Leon was holding his head as if in pain, the psychologist asked, "Do you have a headache?"

Leon: No, I don't sir, I was "shaking it off," sir, Cosmic energy, refreshing my brain. When I grab cosmic energy from the bottom of my feet to my

---

schizophrenia influence the areas of the brain that are responsible for motor behavior, and thus some (but not all) of the tremors, muscular contortions, and stiff gait these individuals exhibit are due to the treatment and not the disorder (Fenton et al., 1994).

Before concluding this discussion of the symptoms of schizophrenia, I should point out that in a high proportion of the cases, individuals with schizophrenia *are not aware of their symptoms* (Xavier et al., 1994). For example, in one sample of over 400 patients, 33% were unaware that they had any mental disorder, 40% were unaware that they had hallucinations, 58% were unaware that they had delusions, and 53% were unaware that they had a thought disorder. The fact that individuals

may not know that they have these serious symptoms is important because if they do not know about the symptoms, they cannot compensate for them.

Some of the delusions and problems with thought processes seen in schizophrenia are illustrated in Case Study 11.1.

Diagnostic Criteria

From the foregoing discussion, it should be clear that the clinical picture of schizophrenia encompasses a wide variety of symptoms. However, it is important to recognize that *an individual does not have to have all or*

brain, it refreshes my brain. The doctor told me that's the way I'm feeling, and that it is the proper attitude. Oh! Pertaining to the question that you asked these two gentlemen [a question about why they were here], each one is a little institution and a house—a little world in which some stand in a clockwise direction and some in a counterclockwise, and I believe in a clockwise rotation.

Sometimes the men developed other delusions to explain the conflicts brought on by their original delusions. For example, when Clyde was asked to explain the fact that Joseph and Leon both also claimed to be God, he explained: "They are really not alive. The machines in them are talking. Take the machines out of them and they won't talk anything. You can't kill the ones with machines in them. They're dead already."

When asked where the machines were located, Clyde pointed to the right side of Joseph's stomach. The psychologist then asked Joseph to unbutton his shirt, and with his permission, Clyde tried to feel around for the machine. When he couldn't find it, he said: "That's funny. It isn't there. It must have slipped down where you can't feel it."

The bizarre nature of the symptoms of these men and their interactions is reflected in the following descriptions of some of their typical ward behavior.

Coming to a table at which Clyde and Joseph are sitting, Leon says, "Ah, good morning, ye instrumental gods," and sits down with a self-satisfied smile.

"These men are victims of electronic imposition," he continues.

Clyde leaps up, yelling: "Joseph, I made the place!"

Later Joseph stands up, banging his fist on the table, and talks to Leon about "good old England." Leon, who is sitting down, stands up, and Joseph sits down. "My salute to you, sir," says Leon. Joseph gets to his feet again, and they salute each other. Then they shake hands, after which Leon shakes hands with Clyde, who is sitting close by, telling him he's an instrumental God, hollowed out four or six times. "Hallowed," Clyde insists, "not hollowed."

Queen Elizabeth is on TV. Joseph says he's not interested in watching the queen because she is taking his place, although he saved her years ago by preventing two men from throwing her off London Bridge.

After living together constantly for over two years and after meeting every day in an attempt to resolve their conflict, each of the three Christs of Ypsilanti still thought that he was Christ. Furthermore, none showed improvement in his schizophrenia.

go figure!

Source: Adapted from Rokeach (1964).

---

even most of those symptoms to be diagnosed as suffering from schizophrenia, and different individuals with the same disorder may have very different sets of symptoms. For example, one individual might have hallucinations and delusions, another might have hallucinations and disorganized behavior, a third might have disorganized speech and flat affect, and a fourth might have bizarre delusions, but they would all receive the diagnosis of schizophrenia. Indeed, to be diagnosed as suffering from schizophrenia, an individual need only show *a decline in social or occupational functioning* (e.g., poor work, interpersonal relationships) and *any two of the following:* (a) delusions, (b) hallucinations, (c) disorganized speech, (d) grossly disorganized behavior, or (e) flat affect or apathy. Actually, only one of those symptoms is necessary if the delusions are bizarre delusions or the hallucinations involve a voice that talks constantly. Because of that, there are 12 different possible combinations of symptoms that could lead to the diagnosis of schizophrenia, and aside from a decline in functioning, no single symptom is common to all individuals with the diagnosis. The diagnostic criteria for schizophrenia are summarized in Table 11.1.

It is also important to note that the diagnosis of schizophrenia is arrived at by *exclusion*. That is, individuals who suffer from certain medical conditions or are taking particular drugs sometimes show the same symptoms, and therefore an individual is diagnosed as

TABLE 11.1 Diagnostic Criteria for Schizophrenia

1. Two or more of the following:
   a. Delusions
   b. Hallucinations
   c. Disorganized speech
   d. Grossly disorganized behavior
   e. Flat affect, apathy (negative symptoms)

   or one of the following:

   a. Bizarre delusions
   b. A constant hallucination in which a voice talks constantly or two voices converse

2. A decline in social or occupational functioning
3. Symptoms that persist for at least 6 months
4. Other psychotic disorders and other medical conditions have been ruled out *(exclusion)*

Source: Adapted from American Psychiatric Association (1994).

having schizophrenia only after those other possible causes have been ruled out.

Finally, it is crucial to note that despite all of these strange symptoms, *schizophrenia does not necessarily imply an inability to operate effectively outside of a hospital.* The diagnosis requires that there be a deterioration from a previous level of functioning, but if the demands on the individual are low or do not involve areas in which the symptoms will be disruptive, the individual may be able to function effectively and undetected in society. Whether or not individuals with schizophrenia are able to function in society depends on factors such as (a) the nature of the symptoms (delusions may be less disruptive for daily functioning than stimulus overload), (b) the context in which the individual must function (hallucinations will be less disruptive for a farmer plowing a field than for a secretary in a busy office), (c) the degree to which others will tolerate deviance (eccentricities are better tolerated in a university than in a law firm), and (d) the severity of the symptoms. A colleague of mine is widely known as a brilliant scientist, but what most people do not know is that this individual suffers from schizophrenia. Similarly, I know of a student who graduated from a prestigious medical school and then announced that he had been hallucinating and delusional for the previous five years. Indeed, as part of his medical school training, he had done an intensive psychiatric rotation on the ward to which he was later admitted, but during his rotation no one detected his problem!

Many of the symptoms and problems of individuals with schizophrenia are illustrated in Case Study 11.2.

PHASES OF SCHIZOPHRENIA

Individuals who suffer from schizophrenia are thought to go through three phases. First, some patients go through a **prodromal phase,** which precedes the onset of the full-blown disorder. (*Prodromal* is from the Greek for "running before.") In this phase, intellectual and interpersonal functioning begins to deteriorate, some peculiar behaviors appear, emotions start to become inappropriate, and unusual perceptual experiences begin to occur. This phase can last anywhere from a few days to many years. In cases in which the prodromal phase is prolonged and the individual shows an insidious downhill course, the long-term prognosis is usually poor.

Second is the **active phase,** in which the symptom patterns are clear-cut and prominent. Hallucinations, delusions, and disorders of thought and language become identifiable, and behavior may become more grossly disorganized.

Third, some patients go through a **residual phase** that is similar to the prodromal phase in that the symptom picture again becomes less clear. Symptoms such as

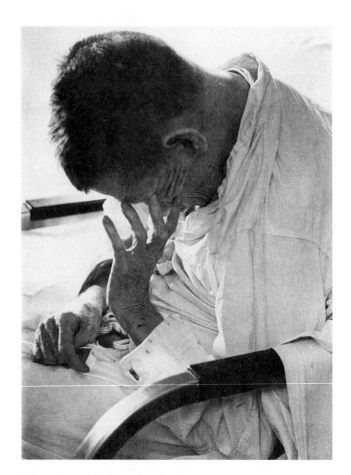

The prognosis for burned-out patients is very poor.

CASE STUDY 11.2
A Talk with Betty About Her Symptoms

Betty is a good friend of mine who suffers from a severe case of schizophrenia. Betty is a very bright, articulate, and friendly woman who graduated from college with a degree in fine arts and later earned a master's degree in library science. Her father was president of a large state university, her mother is a teacher and nurse, and she has three sisters who are successful professionals.

Betty's schizophrenia first appeared when she was in college, and she has struggled with the symptoms ever since. She has been hospitalized many times and has had just about every treatment imaginable. She is currently on a variety of drugs that we will discuss in Chapter 13. It has been about three years since her last hospitalization, and she now lives by herself in an apartment. Betty calls me three or four times a week for brief chats and what she calls "reality checks." Each semester, she comes to my class to talk about schizophrenia. Below is an excerpt from an interview with Betty in which she and I talked about some of her symptoms. Later in the book we will consider Betty's treatment.

Betty

David: Betty, let's talk a little about your symptoms. Could you begin by telling me about your hallucinations?

Betty: Hallucinations have been a major part of my illness. Probably the first hallucination I had was the sound of glass breaking when people walked. You know, that real fine crystal, and it would be kind of crunchy when people walked. It seemed strange and I couldn't understand it, but I heard it all the time.

The next hallucination that developed was that when certain people were around, I would hallucinate electricity coming out of their bodies, in colors. I could see it, and I didn't want to get radiation. *aura reader*

David: What did it look like?

Betty: Like neon, just coming out of their bodies in different colors. People looked like they had bands of color coming out of their bodies, and it was too hot for me to be close to them, physically, because I could feel the waves, the heat. I don't see the radiation much anymore, but now I see auras around people. Different people have different colors.

David: Do I have an aura now?

Betty: Oh, yes, blue. Blue is good. People with blue auras are good.

David: Have you had other visual hallucinations?

Betty: I think the most awful hallucination I had—and still have—is the blood, blood pouring down people's faces. Sometimes everybody has blood pouring down their foreheads and down their front. When I look at people, they are all bloody. It's really horrible. The first time it happened, I was so scared, and nobody believed me. They didn't understand what I was seeing, and they kind of ignored me and sneered. It still happens, usually at night, but sometimes in the afternoon. It's like living in a slaughterhouse, and I don't want to look at anybody, so I just kind of keep to myself.

David: How do you deal with this? What do you do when it happens when you are talking to someone and the person starts bleeding?

Betty: I try and just finish the conversation and get away, but sometimes I can't. I just try to act normal. I have this thing about acting normal, which has nothing to do with reality whatsoever. I

continued

CASE STUDY 11.2 (continued)

just say, "Hi, how are you," and then I get out of there. I see it, I can't stop seeing it, so I have to get away from the bloody people.

David: Could you tell me about the demons?

Betty: They started up a long time ago. They used to come and go, but now they are constantly with me—around me all the time. One set is in my head—I see them; they wear cloaks, and they chant.

David: Are they in your head or in the room?

Betty: These are my in-head ones; I have two sets. These are in my head, and they chant, "Cut yourself and die. Cut yourself and die." And sometimes they come out of my head; that really frightens me, and I want to get armed.

David: Armed?

Betty: Yes, get a knife or something to protect myself.

David: What about the out-of-head demons?

Betty: Well, they look like the demons, but their cloaks are bigger and black. They are men; I can't see their features, but they are human. They wear those leather pointy shoes, like the ones they wore in the Middle Ages. They don't chant; they talk to me. They tell me I'm stupid and worthless.

David: Where do you see them?

Betty: They are in my apartment all of the time, but I don't think I've ever seen them on the street. When I sit at my desk, they line up behind me, and when I go to bed, they stand at the foot at the bed. They say all kinds of horrible things, like I should have been a dead fetus and that I'm useless and I hurt so many people in my life that I could never repay them all. I'm unsure anyway, and with the demons telling me those things, it's terrible.

David: How real do the demons appear?

how does she know what it smells like?

What if she befriended them?

Betty: How real? *Absolutely real.* I mean, intellectually, I know they are hallucinations, *but they are real to me.* I know they are hallucinations, but sometimes I have my doubts. That's when I have to call you for a "reality check"—to have you assure me that they are hallucinations.

Hallucinations are very real, and they can lead you to do some strange things. One night, I had this hallucination that I was covered in blood and dead, and I went into the kitchen and got a knife and cut my arm up. I thought, if I can bleed, I'm not dead, I'm alive.

David: Do you ever have other kinds of hallucinations, say, smell things?

Betty: Rotting flesh. I smell that off and on, not often. I often taste things. Things taste like metal—very unpleasant.

David: Let's shift to delusions. Can you tell me about your delusions?

Betty: Well, there's what I call the "ticker tape" delusion that everyone can read my forehead.

David: I don't understand.

Betty: You know, like in Times Square, where the words go around the front of the building in light bulbs. That's what I thought was here on my head, and as I had thoughts, they were flashed across my forehead, and I thought that everyone could read my thoughts. I was convinced that people could read my thoughts that way, and I couldn't figure out how to make it stop, so sometimes I would walk around with my hands over my forehead to keep people from reading my thoughts.

Talking about mind reading, I should tell you about the "shower" delusions. I had a male friend, and every morning when I got in the shower, I thought he was able to read my mind. I thought he could read my mind while I was in the shower, so whenever I was in there, I tried to keep thinking good thoughts about him. You know, "Andy is so nice," "Oh, gee, I really like Andy." I wanted him to think that I only thought good things about him.

David: This happened only in the shower?

Betty: Yep, but I thought that my mother could read my mind anywhere. That's what I made the code for.

David: The code?

Betty: Yes, if Mother said a certain sentence, that meant she was reading my mind but wasn't telling me. And the sentence would be something inane, like "How are you?"

David: So if your mother said, "How are you?" that was a signal that she was reading your mind?

Betty: Yes, and I was furious that she was doing it. I confronted her and she denied it, but I didn't believe her.

David: Have you had any other delusions?

Betty: Oh, yes, lots. Probably my major delusion has been that the police are after me. Whenever I see a patrol car, I am sure they are following me, and they can really frighten me. I am convinced that they can read my mind with their equipment, on their radios, and they are after me. They do it real cleverly; they don't just come out and get me. They watch; they're waiting for a chance. It's really scary.

David: Do you think that now?

Betty: (Pauses with a somewhat sheepish smile) Well . . . I know it's a delusion, but . . . well, yes, I still think they are after me. Now I think, well, I'm not going to be paranoid about the police, and then a patrol car goes by and . . . I don't know . . . The funny thing is, I don't know what they would do to me or what I've done. You know, I have this feeling, a profound feeling of guilt. . . . When I see a patrol car, it is a sign of oncoming psychosis.

David: A symbol of oncoming psychosis? I don't understand.

Betty: Well, they zap me with their radar, and eventually it will destroy my brain.

David: Let's talk a little about disturbances of thought processes. What's that like?

Betty: Well, it's like you have roads through your brain. When you think, you travel on them. Mine have detours and barricades. My thoughts get blocked or get detoured, and it gets all mixed up. I don't know quite when it started, but when I get a thought, I can't always follow it to completion. Sometimes it happens when I am talking. I get confused, or all of a sudden I'll think, "The demons are here," and then I'll start to worry about them or listen to them, so I get distracted.

David: Betty, can you tell me what it's like to function, to get through the day, with all of these symptoms?

Betty: It's like hell. You know, you see people doing things, just doing things, and it's so hard for me. People get up and eat and read and clean the house, and I have such a hard time just getting into the shower—and then I might have to worry about someone reading my mind. Everyone seems so competent, and I can't do it. . . . I think it's a dirty trick from the demons. . . .

I can't always think right, and then there is the paranoia. It makes everything so hard to do. When I am around people, I think they can read my mind, that they know about my illness, that they are making fun of me, so I leave. I remember one day when I was working at the library and I had to alphabetize some cards, and I just couldn't do it. Sometimes when I am really sick, it is like everyone is speaking in Greek to me, and I can't understand it. It is like being in Italy and not speaking Italian, and no one can speak English to you. You just can't understand what is happening. It is just like being out of it. It's *hell.*

CASE STUDY 11.3

"Old Alex": A Case of Burned-Out Schizophrenia

The ward staff usually calls the patient "Old Alex." When he was hospitalized 36 years ago, he was diagnosed as "schizophrenic." He was described as intelligent and articulate but agitated and suffering from delusions of omnipotence. Then Alex thought he was "the brother of God, sent to free those who were damned by the Devil." Today, Alex sits slumped in a metal chair in a lonely corner of Ward G. His mouth twitches frequently, and his head occasionally jerks involuntarily to the left. He is dressed in wrinkled blue pants and a plaid shirt, the laces of his shoes are not tied, and he does not wear socks. There is a large urine stain on his pants just below the belt.

Much of the time, Alex seems to be dozing, but when he is awake, he stares blankly at the wall a few feet in front of him. *Wheel of Fortune* is on the television and Vanna White is smiling and turning letters, but he doesn't seem to notice her—or anything else. Old Alex has been sitting there and staring at the wall for as long as any of the ward staff can remember.

At 11:30, when it is time for lunch, a young attendant comes over, shakes Alex's shoulder gently, and says, "Come on, Alex, it's time for lunch. Come on, Alex, lunch." Alex turns his head and looks up. He looks at the young attendant for a few moments with great effort, as if he were straining to see through a dense fog. Then he gets up and shuffles with a stiff-legged gait toward the door where the other patients are waiting to be taken to the dining room. Once in the dining room, he eats his food with his fingers rather than with a fork, but when scolded by the attendant, he wipes his fingers on his shirt and begins using his fork.

Alex never makes any trouble on the ward, and he is liked by the staff. He has to be prodded to dress in the morning, and four or five times a day he has to be reminded about going to the bathroom, but he is compliant and does whatever he is told, in a mechanical way. His bad table manners do not reflect symptoms; it is more as if he has simply forgotten to use his fork.

Other people are often around Alex on Ward G, but he seems isolated and not really with them. Alex has an older sister in New Jersey who sent him a small box of cookies at Christmas two years ago, but that is the only contact he has had with his family for many years. Once every couple of years, the students from an abnormal psychology class visit the hospital, and Alex is one of the patients they interview. The interview is usually rather disjointed because Alex tends to lose the thread and drift off. When asked whether he still thinks he is the brother of God, he concentrates for a while as if trying to remember the plot of a long-forgotten movie and then responds somewhat distractedly, "Er . . . I don't think so. . . . Maybe . . ."

Every 6 months, Alex is brought up for a routine evaluation at a ward staff meeting. This is strictly routine; his behavior has not changed in years, and there are no new treatments to be tried with him. The entries in his hospital file are repetitive: "No change. Recommend that care on domiciliary ward be continued." Alex will live out his life slumped in the chair, staring at the wall, unaware that the woman on TV has just turned over a winning set of letters. There is a small graveyard behind the hospital, and someday Old Alex will be quietly moved there.

---

hallucinations and delusions may still exist, but they are less active and less important to the individual. Associated with the muting of symptoms is a general blunting or flattening of mood and often a general decline in intellectual performance (Davidson et al., 1995). This combination of symptoms often makes it impossible for the individual to return to the level of functioning he or she enjoyed before the onset of the illness.

Although it is not officially recognized as such, there is another phase, often referred to as the **burned-out phase.** This is a more extreme form of the residual phase, and it is most likely to be seen in patients who

have been hospitalized for many years. The symptom picture is probably due in large part to the effects of long-term institutionalization. Burned-out individuals do not show many of their original symptoms of schizophrenia, but they show a very serious deterioration of social skills. They may eat with their hands, urinate in their clothing, and be completely insensitive to people around them. It is unlikely that burned-out patients will ever be able to function outside the hospital. These patients are sometimes referred to as "back ward" patients because they are generally "warehoused" out of sight of other patients and the public. Fortunately, the number of such patients seems to be declining. That is probably because we now have more effective treatments than we did when these patients were originally hospitalized, and so fewer patients deteriorate to this point. Also, with the new emphasis on community-based treatment, even disturbed patients are less likely to be kept in a hospital for long periods of time, and therefore they avoid the effects of institutionalization (see Chapter 21). An example of a burned-out patient is presented in Case Study 11.3.

TYPES OF SCHIZOPHRENIA

So far I have discussed schizophrenia as though it were one disorder, but it is generally agreed that schizophrenia probably involves a group of disorders, and it is now common to talk about the "schizophrenias" or the "schizophrenic disorders." In DSM-IV, distinctions are made among five types of schizophrenia. Each type has as a core the symptom pattern discussed earlier, but each type is differentiated from the others by the relative predominance or absence of a particular symptom or set of symptoms.

Disorganized Type

As the name indicates, individuals with **disorganized schizophrenia** show the greatest degree of *psychological disorganization*. They are frequently incoherent and have disorganized speech, they show odd or disorganized behavior, and they have blunted, inappropriate, or "silly" moods. In most of these cases, the disorder showed a slow and progressive development until finally the individuals crossed the line into schizophrenia.

Catatonic Type

Catatonic (KAT-uh-TON-ik) **schizophrenia** is characterized by a *psychomotor disturbance*. In the classic form, the catatonic patient is stuporous and shows what is called **waxy flexibility.** Patients with this symptom pattern are like wax statues in that they are generally mute, and when placed in a particular position, they will remain in that position for long periods of time. One patient was so immobile that he did not blink his eyes, and they had to be taped shut so that the surface would not dry out and be damaged. In contrast, some patients show a high level of motor activity involving frenzied and excited behaviors, and yet other patients may vacillate between stupor and excitement.

Although catatonic schizophrenia was apparently quite common several decades ago, individuals with this disorder are now very rare. The reason for the decline in catatonia is not clear, but it may be that these

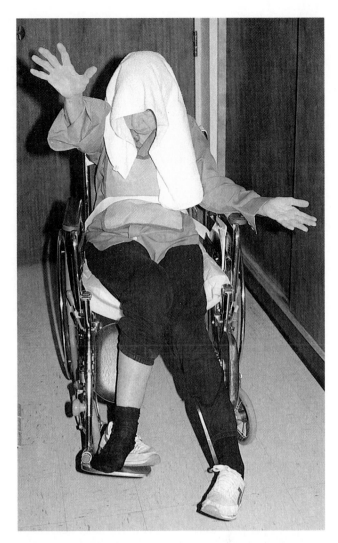

Persons who suffer from catatonic schizophrenia may remain immobile, sometimes in strange positions, for long periods of time. This disorder is now relatively rare.

types of symptoms are particularly amenable to the medications that are available today.

Paranoid Type

The dominant symptoms in **paranoid** (PAR-uh-noyd) **schizophrenia** are *delusions of persecution and grandiosity*. For example, patients may think that family members are plotting against them in order to steal a long-lost inheritance (persecution) that would place them among the wealthiest people in the world (grandiosity). Patients with paranoid schizophrenia also frequently have hallucinations with a persecutory or grandiose content (e.g., voices criticize them or tell them they have special talents). It is noteworthy that patients with paranoid schizophrenia do not show disorganization of thoughts or behavior. Indeed, apart from their delusions, they often behave in very normal

CASE STUDY 11.4

A Psychologist Talks About His Own Struggle with Schizophrenia

Frederick J. Frese III was a 26-year-old college graduate when the symptoms of schizophrenia began to develop. At the time, he was a lieutenant in the U.S. Marine Corps, where he was responsible for guarding atomic weapons and providing security for the Fleet Intelligence Center for Europe. Fred wrote the following about his symptoms and his means of dealing with them.

"Work became very difficult for me, and I could not understand why everything seemed so hard to do in a proper manner. After several months of struggling to understand why things were so difficult, I suddenly figured it all out. It became quite obvious to me that during the Korean War, the Chinese had taken prisoners and given them posthypnotic suggestions. By the use of certain 'key words,' the Chinese were controlling those who had been their prisoners. It was very easy for me now. All I had to do was to find out which Marines and others had served in Korea, and avoid them, because if they found out that I knew about them, surely they would take steps to neutralize me. My immediate superior, a certain major, often talked about his experiences in the Korean War. He needed to be helped, and our country needed protection from him and the others under Chinese control. In order to help him, I decided to call the base hospital, where I talked to a psychiatrist about how we might best go about 'deprogramming' the persons who had been hypnotized. The psychiatrist asked me to come to the hospital to talk with him. I did so, but after a brief chat, I was escorted to a small single room in the hospital, where I was told that I was now a psychiatric patient

and could not leave. Soon thereafter, I learned that I had been given the diagnosis of paranoid schizophrenia. Clearly, in my mind, I had made a serious mistake. Obviously, the psychiatrist had been in Korea, too.

"Those whom the Chinese controlled now knew that I had discovered them, and I knew that it was only a matter of time before one of them would be 'activated' to kill me. I started demanding that a priest administer the last rites before they got to me. After about three days, a kindly priest visited me and administered the sacrament, and I was prepared to die.

"But I was lucky. Before long, a plane arrived that took me to Washington, where I became a patient in the Naval Hospital in Bethesda, Maryland. I was promptly escorted to the psychiatric ward. There I would remain for five months while I very carefully probed everyone I came in contact with to find out if they had ever been to Korea. I totally resisted the idea that I had a psychiatric problem. I just knew something very important that others did not know, and I did not seem to be able to convince anyone of the great threat that our country was facing. There was nothing wrong with me other than the fact that 'I knew too much.' After five months, I was released from the hospital and from the Marine Corps.

"Because I had learned to speak some Japanese when I was in the service, I enrolled in a graduate school to study international business. Those who were controlled by the Chinese did not seem to be around the school. Maybe I was safe. Maybe they had forgotten me, and I could quietly live a regular life.

ways. Probably because of their concerns about persecution and their need to defend their high self-concepts, these individuals tend to be anxious, argumentative, and sometimes violent if confronted. In Case Study 11.4, a colleague of mine describes his experience with paranoid schizophrenia.

Undifferentiated Type

Undifferentiated schizophrenia is essentially a catchall or "wastebasket" category consisting of individuals who

cannot be placed in any of the preceding categories or who meet the criteria for more than one of them.

Residual Type

Individuals who are diagnosed with **residual schizophrenia** have had at least one schizophrenic episode in the past and currently show some signs of schizophrenia such as blunted emotions, social withdrawal, and eccentric behavior, but do not have any prominent delusions, hallucinations, disorganized speech, or behavioral dis-

After a year, I graduated from business school and secured employment with a *Fortune* 500 company. The company needed my skills in Japanese to deal with Japanese manufacturing firms. It was very exciting to be receiving so much attention. But then, in all the excitement, I started behaving very strangely. I suddenly started being controlled by numbers and lights. Red lights stopped me and green lights started me, and all tasks were translated through numbers. I began stopping everything whenever I saw a red light no matter where the red light might be, and not starting again until I saw a green light. Finally, after a lot of desperate acts, one Sunday I went to a cathedral in the downtown area, where, without invitation, I started assisting the priest celebrating the High Mass. Shortly thereafter, I began feeling and behaving more strangely. I started grunting, then barking. I began turning into a monkey, then into a doglike animal, then into a reptile, a dragon, then into a wormlike creature. Later I was to 'realize' that what I was experiencing was like going backward through an evolutionary process. Finally, I degenerated totally. I had become only one atom, and it was the atom in the center of an atomic bomb. I was being loaded onto a bomber airplane. The world was going to end in nuclear holocaust, and I had been turned into the mechanism for its destruction. Everything was over. It was only a matter of time. . . .

"The next thing that I remember, I was in a bed with my legs and arms strapped down, inside a small room. It was another psychiatric ward. I was to remain there for several weeks.

"Unusual experiences like these happened to me numerous times during the past 23 years. But after the first 10 years, during which I was in nine different hospitals for a total of about 300 days, I have not had to be rehospitalized. I still have breakdowns, but I have learned to sense when they are coming on and to 'cut short' the mechanism of the breakdown. I usually handle these circumstances or attacks by taking time off from work and staying around home singing, dancing, synthesizing the religions of the world, eating raw acorns, or behaving in some other strange manner as I work out my problems. *funny!*

"During the time between breakdowns, I have earned a PhD in psychology and worked as a psychologist and administrator in a large state hospital, helping other people with schizophrenia who have not learned to cope as well as I have. I very much like being around the patients because I can see a lot of myself in each of them. We have a common experience. Whether the patients might be a 'mystic Abyssinian warrior' or hiding from 'the Green Gang,' whether they are hearing voices or cannot button their shirts properly, I remember 'being there' myself, and I know it is possible to return from that 'parallel reality' that one enters through the mechanism of psychosis."

Today, Dr. Frese works as a psychologist and mental health administrator in Ohio. His case clearly illustrates the symptoms of schizophrenia and demonstrates that it is possible for some individuals to lead very productive lives while suffering from the disorder.

We are all here to some extent!

turbances. Actually, rather than having a particular *type* of schizophrenia, it appears more likely that they are simply in the residual *phase* of the disorder.

Problems with the Typology

symptoms ↑ no cause cant treat

The five types of schizophrenia that I have described here are officially recognized in DSM-IV, but there are three serious problems with that classification system. First, many individuals who suffer from schizophrenia *do not fit neatly into any one type,* or *their symptoms change*

over time such that their classification must be changed. Second, the classification of individuals into these types has *not led to an understanding of what causes schizophrenia.* 2 Third, the classification of individuals into these types has *not led to an understanding of how to treat individuals who are suffering from schizophrenia.* Indeed, individuals who suffer from the different types do not show differences in their responses to therapy (Hawk et al., 1975; Strauss & Carpenter, 1972; Strauss et al., 1974). Consequently, the five DSM-IV-recognized types of schizophrenia appear to have little theoretical or practical value and tend to be ignored. For diagnostic (descriptive) purposes, in the future it might be better to abandon the official types and instead simply describe an individual as "suffering from schizophrenia with . . ." and then list the individual's specific symptoms (e.g., "schizophrenia with delusions" or "schizophrenia with thought process problems").

POSITIVE VERSUS NEGATIVE SYMPTOMS OF SCHIZOPHRENIA

Because the traditional typology of schizophrenia did not prove to be helpful in understanding or treating schizophrenia, investigators began searching for an alternative means of classifying symptoms and individuals. The alternative that is most promising involves grouping symptoms into two types, **positive symptoms** and **negative symptoms,** and in this section I will discuss that classification of symptoms (Andreasen, 1982; Andreasen & Olsen, 1982; Easton et al., 1995; McGlashan & Fenton, 1992).

Nature of Positive and Negative Symptoms

Positive symptoms include *hallucinations, delusions, thought disorders,* and *bizarre behaviors.* These are called *positive* symptoms because they are *additions* to normal behavior; that is, normal individuals do not have hallucinations and delusions. In contrast, negative symptoms include *flat mood, poverty of speech, inability to experience positive feelings, apathy,* and *inattentiveness.* These are called *negative* symptoms because they reflect the *absence* of normal behaviors; that is, normal individuals have fluent speech and can experience positive feelings.

Recent analyses have revealed that there are probably two types of positive symptoms (Andreasen et al., 1995). One type, called **psychoticism,** consists of hallucinations and delusions. In other words, psychoticism is characterized by the *production of false stimulation (hallucinations) or ideas (delusions).* The second type, called **disorganization,** consists of thought disorders (confusion), bizarre behaviors, and inappropriate affect. It is characterized by *disorganization of thinking and behavior.* This organization of positive and negative symptoms is illustrated in Figure 11.2.

The symptoms of schizophrenia clearly fall into the types described in Figure 11.2, but it is important to recognize that those types do not necessarily reflect distinct types of schizophrenia. Instead, it is better to think of positive and negative symptoms as ends of a dimension of schizophrenic symptoms (Andreasen et al., 1995). In other words, individuals do not have positive *or* negative symptoms, but rather they may have more symptoms of one type than another.

Characteristics Associated with Positive and Negative Symptoms

It seems clear that there is a difference between positive and negative symptoms, but the question is, is it a difference that makes a difference? That is, are positive and negative symptoms related to factors that help us understand and treat schizophrenia? The answer appears to be yes, and in this section I will discuss the characteristics that are associated with the positive and negative symptoms.

Premorbid Adjustment. It is consistently found that negative symptoms are more likely than positive symptoms to be associated with a *poor premorbid adjustment.* For example, before being diagnosed as suffering from schizophrenia, individuals with primarily negative symptoms (a) showed poorer social and sexual functioning, (b) progressed less far in school, and (c) performed worse in work settings. There also appears to be

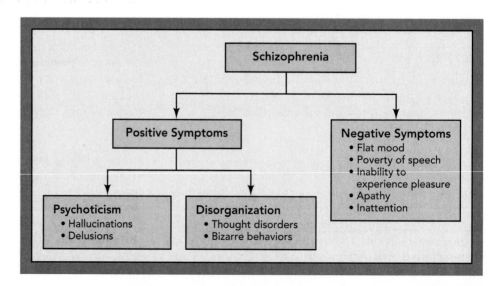

FIGURE 11.2 Organization of positive and negative symptoms of schizophrenia. Positive symptoms are behaviors that are not usually found in normal individuals. Negative symptoms are the absence of behaviors that are usually found in normal individuals.

TABLE 11.2 Characteristics Associated with Positive and Negative Symptoms

Characteristic	Positive Symptoms	Negative Symptoms
	– chemical △	*– brain damage*
Onset	Later	Earlier
Stability over time	Symptoms fluctuate	Symptoms consistent over time
Frequency of occurrence	More frequent in women	More frequent in men
Response to treatment	Good	Poor

Adjustment Before onset | *Bleuler OK* | *Kraepelin poor*

a tendency for negative symptoms to be associated with lower scores on intelligence tests.

Consistency over Time. It is also noteworthy that *negative symptoms are consistent over time*, whereas positive symptoms tend to wax and wane (Arndt et al., 1995; Davidson et al., 1995; McGlashan & Fenton, 1992). Insofar as negative symptoms change over time, they tend to get worse.

Gender. *Men are more likely than women to suffer from negative symptoms.* The reason for the gender differences is not clear, but it reflects the less optimistic prognosis for males suffering from schizophrenia.

Response to Treatment. Finally, it is important to note that in general, *positive symptoms respond better to drug treatment* than negative symptoms do. Indeed, until very recently, no treatments were known to be effective for negative symptoms, and even the newly developed treatments are only moderately effective for negative symptoms (see Chapter 13).

The findings that positive symptoms are associated with better premorbid adjustment, show a more rapid onset, are less consistent over time, and respond better to drug treatment than negative symptoms have been used to suggest that positive and negative symptoms have different causes. Specifically, it may be that positive symptoms are due to fluctuations in brain chemistry, whereas negative symptoms are due to progressive brain damage and deterioration. (I will discuss those possibilities in Chapter 12.) In any event, the distinction between positive and negative symptoms is promising and is clearly more valuable than the traditional typology of schizophrenia. The characteristics that are associated with the positive and negative symptoms are summarized in Table 11.2.

ISSUES ASSOCIATED WITH SCHIZOPHRENIA

History and Current Views

Now that you understand the symptoms of schizophrenia, it will be helpful to consider briefly how our views

of schizophrenia developed historically. The history of modern attempts to describe and explain schizophrenia goes back to the beginning of the 20th century when **Emil Kraepelin** (ā-MĒL KRĀ-puh-lin) (1856–1926) in Germany and **Eugen Bleuler** (OY-gen BLOY-lur) (1857–1939) in Switzerland focused their attention on the problem. *influenced by Freud* These two men offered very different views of the disorder, and the views they introduced a century ago still influence our thinking today.

Kraepelin's Views. Kraepelin argued that schizophrenia began *early in life* and that the symptoms reflected a *progressive and irreversible intellectual deterioration* that was like that of senility. Indeed, he is the one who labeled the disorder *dementia praecox.* Consistent with his notion that the disorder was like senility and progressive, Kraepelin believed that the disorder had a *physiological cause* and that the *prognosis was very poor.* Kraepelin had a basically pessimistic view of the disorder.

Bleuler's Views. In sharp contrast to Kraepelin, Bleuler argued that schizophrenia could develop at *any point in life* and that rather than being a senility-like deterioration, the disorder was due to a *disorganization or breakdown of the associative threads that connect words, thoughts, and feelings.* He suggested that the disordered language patterns of patients stem from their use of misconnected words, problems in thought processes stem from the use of misconnected thoughts, and inappropriate moods stem from the fact that emotions are disconnected from thoughts. To reflect that disorganization and breakdown of associations, Bleuler coined the term *schizophrenia,* which literally means "splitting of the mind." With regard to cause, Bleuler agreed with Kraepelin that the underlying cause of the disorder was *physiological,* but he argued that the *symptoms could be brought on by psychological factors* such as stress. Finally, Bleuler offered a more optimistic view concerning the prognosis, suggesting that some individuals did get better. The views of Kraepelin and Bleuler are summarized in Table 11.3.

Kraepelin and Bleuler offered two strikingly different views of schizophrenia, and the questions that arise are, how did they come up with such different views, who was correct, and what view is held today? It appears that Kraepelin and Bleuler came up with their different

TABLE 11.3 Views of Kraepelin and Bleuler Concerning Schizophrenia

	Kraepelin	Bleuler
Onset	Early	Early or late
Process	Progressive deterioration (like senility)	Disorganization (breaking of associations)
Cause	Physiology	Physiology, but can be triggered by stress
Prognosis	Poor	Poor or good
Term	*Dementia praecox* (premature deterioration)	*Schizophrenia* (splitting of the mind)

Note: Kraepelin seems to have been describing *negative symptoms*, whereas Bleuler seems to have been describing *primarily positive symptoms*.

views because they were working with different types of patients; Kraepelin must have been working with patients who suffered primarily with negative symptoms (e.g., early onset, deterioration, poor prognosis), whereas Bleuler seems to have been working with patients who suffered from primarily positive symptoms (e.g., later onset, disorganization, good prognosis). Who was correct? Obviously, they were both correct, but for different subsets of patients. However, Kraepelin's views prevailed while Bleuler's were largely ignored, and that is unfortunate because Kraepelin's views precluded our recognition of what might be considered "the other side of schizophrenia" (the positive symptoms) and retarded our understanding of the disorder. Today, we recognize that the disorder involves both positive and negative symptoms, and therefore our view of schizophrenia is an amalgamation of the views of Kraepelin and Bleuler, but the more pessimistic views of Kraepelin still seem to be dominant.

Prevalence

In a community study in which almost 10,000 individuals were interviewed, it was found that *1.5% of the population suffered from schizophrenia at some time during their lives* (Robins et al., 1984). The seriousness of the problem is magnified by the fact that schizophrenia is often a long-term disorder. That is, not only do a lot of people suffer from schizophrenia, but they suffer from it for a long period of time.

Sociocultural Factors

Age. Schizophrenia is most frequently diagnosed during *early adulthood*. In the community study that was described in the preceding paragraph, it was found that schizophrenia was most likely to be diagnosed between

the ages of 25 and 44 (Robins et al., 1984). In fact, in early editions of the DSM, it was specified that the onset of schizophrenia must be before the age of 45, but DSM-IV does not set an upper age limit for onset. In many cases, especially those involving negative symptoms, the disorder undoubtedly started much earlier, but the full symptom picture does not develop and the individual is not diagnosed until young adulthood.

Gender. The evidence concerning a possible link between gender and schizophrenia is inconsistent; some studies reveal a higher rate for women, others reveal a higher rate for men, and still others show no difference (e.g., Hambrecht et al., 1994; Iacono & Beiser, 1992; Robins et al., 1984). However, there is consistent evidence that *men are usually first diagnosed as having the disorder at a younger age than women* (Gorwood et al., 1995; Loranger, 1984; Szymanski et al., 1995). That difference has been found in more than a dozen studies in numerous countries. The relationship between gender and age at the time of diagnosis is illustrated in Figure 11.3.

more stress is a male

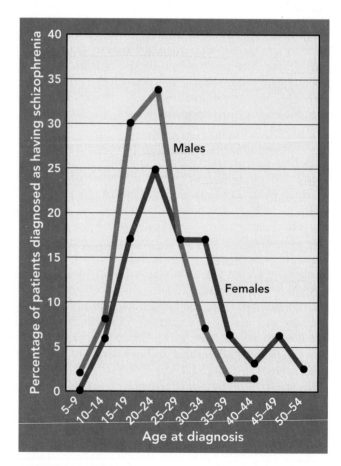

FIGURE 11.3 Schizophrenia is diagnosed earlier in males than in females.
Source: From "Sex Difference in Age at Onset of Schizophrenia" by A. W. Loranger, from *Archives of General Psychiatry*, Vol. 41, February 1984. Reprinted by permission of the American Medical Society.

We do not know exactly why the onset is earlier in men than in women, but there are three possibilities. First, it is possible that women are more likely to be at home than men, so their pathology is more likely to remain hidden for longer than would be the case for men. Another possibility is that the biochemical or hormonal differences between men and women play a role by either triggering the disorder earlier or suppressing it until later in one of the sexes. For example, it is thought that estrogen plays a role in suppressing the activity of the neurotransmitter that leads to the symptoms of schizophrenia (see Chapter 12) (Seeman & Lang, 1990). A third explanation is that women are more likely to suffer from positive than negative symptoms, and as I mentioned earlier, positive symptoms have a later onset than negative symptoms. All of these factors may contribute to the gender difference in the age of onset of schizophrenia.

Ethnicity. It is noteworthy that the rate of schizophrenia is about the same across virtually all of the countries and cultures in which it has been studied, and insofar as differences are sometimes found, they appear to be due to differences in how the disorder is defined or diagnosed (Edgerton & Cohen, 1994; Mete et al., 1993). Although the rate of schizophrenia is the same across cultures, the content of the delusions may differ as a function of the culture (El-Islam, 1991). For example, in highly industrialized societies, delusions may involve thought control by radar or computer microchips, whereas in less developed societies, delusions may revolve around the effects of spirits or demons. There is evidence that in countries such as Sweden, Japan, England, Germany, and the United States, the rate of schizophrenia is higher in cities than it is in rural areas. However, that is probably due to the effects of social class, infectious diseases, and migration to the cities by disturbed individuals rather than to anything unique to cities per se (Freeman, 1994). I will discuss some of the variables in the following sections.

Social Class. One very consistent finding is that individuals in the lower class are more likely to be diagnosed as suffering from schizophrenia than individuals from the middle or upper classes. In fact, the rate of schizophrenia has been reported to be as much as *eight times higher* in the lower class (Dohrenwend & Dohrenwend, 1974; Kohn, 1973; Strauss et al., 1978). It may be that the link between class and schizophrenia is due to the high level of stress that is associated with life in the lower class and that the stress triggers the disorder. I will discuss the role of stress in schizophrenia in Chapter 12; here I will consider five alternative explanations for the relationship between social class and schizophrenia.

Downward Social Drift. One explanation is that suffering from schizophrenia leads individuals to drift downward into the lower social classes (Myerson, 1940). Such a drift might be expected because schizophrenia frequently results in greatly reduced levels of social and intellectual functioning, thus making it more difficult for the individual to maintain a position in society. Consider the case of Betty from Case Study 11.2. Betty's father was a university president, her mother is a nurse, and Betty has a master's degree, but her symptoms are so severe that she is unable to work and is supported by disability insurance. If the social drift hypothesis is true, the lower-class status of individuals with schizophrenia would be a result rather than a cause of the disorder.

In one study of the social drift hypothesis, the investigators compared the social class of a group of

It has been suggested that because schizophrenia involves impaired functioning, it results in a downward drift into the lower classes. In extreme cases, a person with schizophrenia may become homeless.

male patients who had schizophrenia to the social class of the patients' fathers (occupational level was the measure of social class; Turner & Wagonfeld, 1967). The results indicated that about 43% of the patients had drifted downward from the levels of their fathers, whereas national census data suggested that only 26% of males in general showed such a drift.

Clearly, schizophrenia can result in a downward social drift, but by itself that drift does not appear sufficient to account for the strong relationship between class and schizophrenia, so we must consider additional possibilities.

Bias in Diagnosis. Because it is widely believed that schizophrenia is more likely to occur among lower-class individuals, it is possible that social class is used as a factor in making diagnoses. A class bias in the diagnostic process would enhance this relationship and perpetuate a potentially erroneous belief.

In an attempt to determine whether social class influenced diagnosis, I once gave two groups of psychiatrists sets of written descriptions of patients, and I asked the psychiatrists to make diagnoses based on the descriptions. The descriptions given to the two groups were identical except that in one set the patients were described as having an upper-class background, whereas in the other set the patients were described as having a lower-class background. When a comparison was made of the patients who had the *same symptoms,* it was found that the lower-class patients were more likely to be diagnosed as suffering from schizophrenia, whereas the upper-class patients were more likely to be diagnosed as suffering from the bipolar disorder. It does seem then that social class influences diagnosis, but by itself the bias effect does not appear strong enough to account for the strong relationship between social class and schizophrenia.

Bias in Treatment. If lower-class patients get lower-quality treatment than upper-class patients (and they probably do because they cannot afford the better treatment), then the lower-class individuals with schizophrenia will be in treatment for longer periods of time and their numbers will increase over time. Therefore, when counts are made, more lower- than upper-class individuals would be found with schizophrenia, but the difference would be a reflection of the differences in treatment rather than in the incidence of the disorder among upper- and lower-class patients (Kramer, 1957).

Bias in Self-Presentation. It is also possible that differences in the ways that upper- and lower-class individuals present themselves and interact with the hospital staff will influence whether or not they are diagnosed as suffering from schizophrenia. For example, given the same set of symptoms, a poorly educated lower-class individ-

ual with inadequate social skills may be seen as having schizophrenia, whereas an upper-class individual will be seen as "eccentric" (Hollingshead & Redlich, 1958).

Prenatal and Perinatal Complications. In Chapter 12, you will learn that some cases of schizophrenia can be linked to prenatal complications, such as poor diet or diseases of the mother during pregnancy, and to perinatal complications, such as problems during labor or illness immediately after birth. Because those problems might be more likely to occur among poorer individuals, they might account for the higher proportion of schizophrenia in lower classes (Goodman & Emory, 1992).

From the foregoing discussion, it should be clear that lower-class individuals are more likely to be diagnosed as having schizophrenia than upper-class individuals and that there is evidence supporting a number of explanations for that relationship. However, the nature of the relationship is not completely clear, and it is probably determined by a combination of several factors.

This concludes the discussion of schizophrenia. In the next section, I will describe some other psychotic disorders that appear to be related to schizophrenia.

OTHER PSYCHOTIC DISORDERS

Now that you understand the symptoms of schizophrenia, we can go on to consider what are referred to as the "other psychotic disorders" (American Psychiatric Association, 1994). There are five disorders in this group, and their symptoms and relationship to schizophrenia are described in Table 11.4. It is important to be aware of the similarities and differences between each of these disorders and schizophrenia so that you will not confuse them with schizophrenia.

Brief Psychotic Disorder / *Brief Reactive Psychosis*

The **brief psychotic disorder** is similar to schizophrenia in that the symptoms involve delusions, hallucinations, disorganized speech, and disorganized behavior, but only *one* of those symptoms is necessary for a diagnosis, so the disorder can be somewhat less serious than schizophrenia. More important, the brief psychotic disorder differs from schizophrenia because it only lasts between 1 day and 1 month; that is, it is a *brief* disorder. Furthermore, in some cases, the brief psychotic disorder is thought to stem from an *overwhelming stress.* Indeed, prior to the publication of DSM-IV, this disorder was called the *AKA brief reactive psychosis;* the term *reactive* was used to reflect the fact that the symptoms were a reaction to stresses. We see instances of the brief psychotic

TABLE 11.4 Symptoms of the Other Psychotic Disorders

Brief psychotic disorder
- One or more of the following: delusions, hallucinations, disorganized speech, grossly disorganized behavior, negative symptoms.
- Symptoms last 1 day to 1 month.
- *stems fr: stress (ie war)*

Schizophreniform disorder
- Two or more of the following: delusions, hallucinations, disorganized speech, grossly disorganized behavior, negative symptoms.
- Symptoms last 1 to 6 months.

Schizoaffective disorder
- Major mood symptoms (depression, mania, or both).
- Two or more of the following that occur with mood symptoms: delusions, hallucinations, disorganized speech, grossly disorganized behavior, negative symptoms.
- Delusions or hallucinations sometimes occur in the absence of mood symptoms.

Shared psychotic disorder
- A delusion develops in the context of a relationship with another person who has an existing related delusion.

Delusional disorder
- Nonbizarre delusions.
- No hallucinations, disorganized speech, grossly disorganized behavior, or negative symptoms.
- Apart from the effects of the delusions, functioning is not impaired.

disorder after disasters such as earthquakes and wars (Susser et al., 1995).

Schizophreniform Disorder

The **schizophreniform** (SKIT-zō-FREN-i-form) **disorder** is very much like schizophrenia in that the core symptoms that are required for a diagnosis are the same (two from the group that includes delusions, hallucinations, disorganized speech, disorganized behavior, and flat affect). However, the schizophreniform disorder differs from schizophrenia in two ways: First, it does not involve a decline in social or occupational functioning, and second, it lasts only between *1 month and 6 months*. In other words, this disorder has the *form* (core symptoms) of schizophrenia, but because it has a shorter duration and the individual does not deteriorate, it is not considered to *be* schizophrenia. If an individual is diagnosed as suffering from the schizophreniform disorder but the symptoms last longer than 6 months, the individual will be rediagnosed as suffering from schizophrenia.

A comparison of the disorders beginning with the brief psychotic disorder and going on to the schizo-

phreniform disorder and then schizophrenia reveals two important differences. First, as we move toward schizophrenia, there are *more symptoms.* The brief psychotic disorder involves *one* of the core symptoms (delusions, hallucinations, disorganized speech, disorganized behavior, flat affect), the schizophreniform disorder involves *two* of the core symptoms, and schizophrenia involves *two* of the core symptoms *plus* a decline in social or occupational functioning. Second, as we move toward schizophrenia, the *symptoms last longer.* Specifically, in the brief psychotic disorder, the symptoms go away within *1 month,* in the schizophreniform disorder the symptoms go away within *6 months,* and in schizophrenia the symptoms may persist at one level or another *indefinitely,* even throughout the individual's life. It is assumed that individuals with the brief psychotic disorder and the schizophreniform disorder will soon be symptom-free regardless of what is or is not done for them, so the prognoses with these disorders is very good.

Historically, the diagnoses of brief psychotic disorder and schizophreniform disorder were introduced to provide diagnoses for individuals who had the symptoms of schizophrenia *but who got better.* In other words, the new disorders were necessary because it was widely assumed that schizophrenia is a progressive disorder that does not remit, so when it was found that some individuals got better, new diagnoses were needed. However, it may be that the brief psychotic disorder, the schizophreniform disorder, and schizophrenia are not three separate disorders but just different levels of severity of one underlying disorder, schizophrenia. For example, the schizophreniform disorder might simply be a "mild" form of schizophrenia.

Schizoaffective Disorder : *schizop + mood dis.*

As the name implies, the **schizoaffective** (SKIT-zō-uh-FEC-tiv) **disorder** involves a *combination of schizophrenia and a major mood disorder* (depression or mania). To be diagnosed as having the schizoaffective disorder, the individual must at one time have shown the core symptoms of schizophrenia *and* a mood disorder and at another time shown *only* symptoms of schizophrenia (delusions and hallucinations). This is a somewhat controversial disorder because it can be asked why the individual is not simply diagnosed as suffering from schizophrenia *and* a mood disorder, just as an individual might have a cold and a broken arm.

And what about depression—as most people w/ schizophrenia have?

Shared Psychotic Disorder

The diagnosis of **shared psychotic disorder** is used when an individual develops a *delusion as a consequence* *of a close relationship with another individual who has a delusion.* For example, a woman who has a delusion that she is a movie star might have a friend who thinks she is an important producer. *like Tom thinking a meteor will kill us b/c Will claims there is.*

Delusional Disorder

In the **delusional disorder,** the major symptom, as the name implies, is the *presence of one or more delusions.* However, unlike many of the delusions seen in schizophrenia, the delusions that are present in the delusional disorder are *nonbizarre.* In other words, they involve situations that could occur in real life, such as being followed, poisoned, infected, loved from a distance, or deceived by others. It is important to note that individuals with the delusional disorder do not show the general decline in social or occupational functioning that is seen in schizophrenia. Indeed, the presence of an unshakable delusion in an individual who otherwise appears normal and functions well is one of the striking things about the delusional disorder. Case Study 11.5 involves a man with a very limited delusional disorder, whereas Case Study 11.6 was written by a young woman who had a very pervasive delusional disorder. It is interesting to note that to some extent the young

woman may also have a suffered from a shared psychotic disorder because her mother had "taught" her most of the delusions. *are superstitions part/this?*

Relationship to Schizophrenia

Earlier I pointed out that as we move from the brief psychotic disorder to the schizophreniform disorder and then to the schizophrenia, the number of symptoms and the duration of the symptoms increases. That has led to the speculation that rather than there being a group of distinctly separate disorders, there may be a **spectrum of schizophrenic disorders.** The schizoaffective, delusional, and shared psychotic disorders might also be part of that spectrum in that they consist of some of the symptoms that make up schizophrenia. An analogy can be drawn to the common cold. In its most severe and complete form, the cold involves a runny nose, congested head, cough, and that "ache all over" feeling. However, different individuals may have more or fewer of those symptoms, different sets of those symptoms, and more or less severe symptoms, but they all have a cold. Similarly, individuals with the other psychotic disorders may have different forms or less severe cases of schizophrenia.

mild

CASE STUDY 11.5

A Successful Executive with a Delusional Disorder

George Arronson was a very successful executive in a large corporation. He was intelligent, hardworking, and quietly competitive. Those were the traits he thought were necessary to "keep one step ahead of the competition." Arronson was happily married, the father of two children, and well liked by his friends and colleagues. He had done well, his future was bright, and there was no sign of any problems.

One day, Arronson got to the office before his secretary had arrived. At about 9 o'clock, a telephone repairman arrived to install a new phone in Arronson's office. The secretary did not know that Arronson was already in his office, so she sent the repairman in without announcing him. When the door to his office opened and Arronson saw an unknown man carrying a heavy metal case and wearing a jacket with a phone company emblem on it, he reached into his desk drawer, took out a .38 caliber revolver, and shot the repairman at point-blank range. He then ran from the office but was soon caught.

A psychological examination revealed that for years, Arronson had suffered from a delusion that "others" were plotting against him, were trying to steal his ideas, and would eventually try to "eliminate" him. Arronson could not explain who the "others" were, but he believed that "they" got access to his mail and tapped his phone to "track" his ideas. Arronson was in a competitive business in which there was some "corporate espionage," but his beliefs were clearly delusional. The extremity of his delusions was reflected in the fact that he kept vans stocked with cans of food in four parts of the city (north, south, east, and west). The vans and food were to be used to help with his "getaway if they ever closed in." When the repairman entered the office unannounced carrying a black metal case, Arronson thought "they" were coming for him, and he shot in self-defense.

CASE STUDY 11.6

A Serious Delusional Disorder in an Undergraduate Woman

"I was raised in a very chaotic family. Both my parents were alcoholics, and I experienced the usual madness that is always present within an alcoholic family. When I was a very young child, my mother taught me a complex fantasy life designed to 'escape all of the people who would like to take advantage of us.' By the age of 5 or 6, I was already having a difficult time distinguishing between fantasy and reality. I usually played by myself for a number of reasons. Many of the parents of classmates thought I was odd, and their children were not allowed to play with me unless the play was supervised. I often tried to pull them into my fantasies.

"My mother was very concerned about established organizations such as school and government that might learn too much about our family. 'They' might try to lock us up. I was never allowed to fill out any of the typical enrollment forms in grade school, but instead I had to take them home so that Mom could pick and choose what was pertinent for the school records. Often this rigorous screening would end in parent-teacher conferences, after which Mom would tell me, 'They will definitely be watching you now.'

"By age 10, I totally believed my mother. The teacher would send home notes about the fact that I was talking to myself or some other aberrant behavior. Mom would tell me that I shouldn't do these things in public but that I could be 'normal' at home. And so I often stayed in the closet for hours talking to myself and enjoying the praise from Mom for being such a 'good girl.'

"The punishments my mother gave me for misbehavior were often bizarre. They typically involved cleansing rituals in which I would be placed in a bathtub full of water and told to pray for purification and forgiveness.

"In an attempt to flee this disturbed atmosphere, my brother entered the Marine Corps at 17. He was away for 3 years, and I felt as if my only link with sanity had been transferred from home. I was not allowed to write to him for fear that 'they would read the mail.' Once I wrapped a letter in a box and disguised it as a birthday present and mailed it to him. It was the only letter he received from me.

"1At 15, I entered high school, and this was the beginning of the serious downhill slide. There were too many people, and they were constantly staring at me, or so I thought. I adopted many strategies for avoiding them. I wouldn't look into their eyes. I wouldn't participate in any school activities. I was an honor student, but I wouldn't attend any of the functions associated with that status. I did attend one academic award ceremony at my mother's insistence. She didn't believe that I was a scholar, but she wanted us to go to 'find out why they are persecuting the family.'

"I always attempted to avoid social contact. I would dress in unusual clothing (often my brother's or my mother's) and use a lot of makeup in an attempt to keep people from recognizing me. For relaxation, I sat in front of a strobe light and thought cosmic and mystic thoughts.

"By my sophomore and junior years, my paranoia was fairly intense. The girls I knew had begun to date and establish their femininity, but I was being taught at home that sex was the work of the Devil and that all men are suspect. I began to question the motives of my girlfriends and their relationships with boys. As a consequence, they discontinued their friendships with me. Now I was sure it wasn't just the men who were suspect but that these girls were actually boys who were sent to trick me. I began to keep files on everyone I knew.

"After graduation from high school, I got a job and moved out of the house. Things seemed relatively calm, but they were anything but calm within my mind. My fears about governmental agencies became so intense that I started checking my apartment for bugs and telephone taps whenever I returned home. Whenever I got a wrong-number call, I was certain that this marked the beginning of some complex eavesdropping scam whereby 'they' could now hear everything going on inside my home. I changed my telephone number so often that finally the phone company refused to change it anymore without a fee. Now, I concluded, the phone company was in on the plot.

"It was at this stage that I began to hear voices. At first they were friendly, and I thought I had been chosen by God for some special mission. I sat in the backyard or in the bedroom closet for hours and waited for messages that never came. After several weeks, the theme of the voices changed, and I felt damned and doomed. The voices would tell me of

continued

CASE STUDY 11.6 (continued)

elaborate traps that were designed to get me, and they often involved the people with whom I worked. Whenever I spent any time with other people, I was sure they could hear my thoughts.

"I took the following summer off to get my act together. I worked on some projects around my apartment and visited with friends. My concentration and motivation were quickly deteriorating, and I did not complete any of the projects. In an effort to elude my persecutors, I packed my car one fall evening and escaped in the night to wander around the southeastern United States. The money ran out in about three weeks, and 'they' were still following me anyway, so I returned home.

"When I returned, everything was the same. I still checked the apartment, I still sat in the closet, and often I stayed up the entire night roving from room to room so that 'they couldn't get a fix on me.' Finally, I could no longer cope with it all by myself, so I got in my car and drove to my parents' house. I drove in a roundabout fashion to elude my followers. When I arrived at their home, I had my 'breakdown.' I felt as if my limbs were not attached to my body and that my brain and mind were separate entities. I was waving my arms about madly in an attempt to get my mind to return to my brain and the two of them to reestablish themselves in my body. My mother held and rocked me in a darkened bedroom. I wanted to get to a mental hospital, but she wouldn't allow it. She called our family doctor of 30 years and described my state. The doctor called it a 'psychotic break' and told Mom that if I had what he thought I had, it would pass regardless of the type of intervention used, so Mom decided to keep me at home. When I spoke (which was not frequent because I felt that everyone could hear my thoughts anyway), I was usually incoherent and began to cry. I knew that God was punishing me for all of my sins and that I

would surely go crazy and die. Only one of these two things occurred.

"I spent the next two or three months at my parents' home. After a couple of months, I began to feel better, although I was still extremely paranoid. The voices had dissipated, and I slowly reoriented myself to the outside world. I told my family that I still needed psychiatric help, but they refused to listen because 'nobody in our family gets sick.' Finally, I got a job delivering packages. I could work alone, and it didn't tax me mentally. I found any mental activity difficult, and occasionally I thought that my mind was going to blow up and my employer would find me dead in the streets from insanity. At that point, I sought the aid of a psychologist.

"I immediately didn't like her, but I thought this was due to the paranoia. She gave me an MMPI and I lied on all of the questions to appear normal because I was sure she would send this information to the government. I wouldn't allow her to take notes, and after two sessions, I stopped going.

"Next I went to the local mental health center. I was the only person in the waiting room, and I sat quietly until I noticed one of those big round mirrors that are mounted near the ceiling at corners. I could see them and they could see me. I began to pace and hide myself behind pillars. When the receptionist saw my behavior, she quickly assigned me to a social worker, who seemed concerned and sympathetic. I didn't tell her my 'real' symptoms, but I am sure she was aware of them after my behavior in the waiting room. We could not get a schedule of meeting times worked out, so I left. Two weeks later, I had another breakdown. The dismembered feeling was back, so I called the social worker. She referred me to another social worker who had more flexible hours. I saw that social worker for a year, but I never

WHAT CAN WE CONCLUDE CONCERNING SCHIZOPHRENIA?

First of all, it is important to recognize that many different combinations of symptoms can lead to the diagnosis of schizophrenia. Therefore, different individuals with the same diagnosis may have very different symptoms and prognoses. It is also important to note that

there are five other psychotic disorders that involve one or more of the symptoms of schizophrenia, and it may be that rather than there being a number of different disorders, there may be a spectrum of schizophrenic disorders. For example, the brief psychotic disorder and schizophreniform disorder may simply be mild forms of schizophrenia.

The major symptoms of schizophrenia are cognitive and include hallucinations, delusions, and dis-

told her any of my symptoms. One night, I finally told her about the voices, and she immediately sent me to a psychiatrist. After asking me how to spell my name properly, the psychiatrist prescribed Triavil. By the end of the week, the drug had offered no relief, so he prescribed Elavil as a supplement. My symptoms only got worse. While driving around at work, I was convinced that no one could see me. Some rational part kept saying that wasn't so, but the irrational part was winning. I became so delusional that I stopped at a self-serve gas station and asked the attendant in the little glass booth, 'Can you see me?' He promptly closed his little window and picked up his phone. Poor man! I jumped back in my car and drove off, debating about whether I should admit myself to a local hospital, but my mother's words about no one in our family getting sick were still with me, so I didn't. Somehow I completed my work that day and returned to the psychiatrist and told him what he could do with his pills, and then I went to the social worker and told her what she could do with her practice.

"About two years ago, I started seeing a psychologist. She has been teaching me social skills and coping techniques. During the first four months of therapy, I would not discuss the nature of the problem with her, although my symptoms were very pronounced. If she looked at me for too long, I thought that she was judging me, and I would hide behind the chairs in the office. She could not take notes. She could not record the sessions, and occasionally I would hide from her in her outer office. She worked very slowly with me, beginning with the issue of trust. After the first year, I did trust her somewhat. Sometimes she would 'goof up' in my mind, and we would have to start all over with the trust thing. She told me to call her anytime I thought I was losing control, and I did. Sometimes I wouldn't talk while on the phone, but she would know it was me and would talk as if I were responding.

"I started college as a part-time student and soon ran into many of the same problems I had faced in high school. However, my therapist helped me with everything from maintaining eye contact to processing information. I am continually scanning my environment for clues as to how I am doing (instead of who is trying to do what to me). I liken the techniques that I am learning in therapy to what a color-blind person learns; after many years, the color-blind person learns how other people process colors, and he identifies colors in those terms so that other people will understand him. There are still many stumbling blocks, but I am slowly learning to overcome them. I always sit in the front of the class, not because I am one of the smart folks, but because if I need to ask a question, I won't notice that everyone is looking at me. I prefer to perform all of my social activities in groups. When I speak alone with anyone for more than two or three minutes, I become quite frightened and think that they will know that I'm ill. I have two friends who know of my illness, and I often seek refuge with them when I feel about to collapse and I am unable to see my therapist. The collapses are still frequent (two to five a year) and usually consist of reducing me to a jelly-like state both mentally and physically, but they are getting less and less frequent and less overwhelming."

Note: This account was written when the woman was a senior in college. I have kept in contact with her over the years and can report that she is now for the most part symptom-free and is doing very well in a professional career. When I recently asked how she was getting along, she commented about how busy and behind schedule she was at work but said that it was a lot easier working now that she did not have to spend time checking every room for bugs. One clear sign of her improvement is her willingness to allow me to print her story.

turbed cognitive processes. Disturbances of mood are also prevalent, and as many as 60% of the individuals with schizophrenia also qualify for a diagnosis of a major mood disorder. Indeed, the schizoaffective disorder is a combination of schizophrenia and a mood disorder.

In an attempt to bring some organization to the symptom patterns in schizophrenia, five types were identified (e.g., disorganized, catatonic, paranoid), but they have not proved helpful in understanding or treating the disorder. Currently, attention is focused on the distinction between positive symptoms (hallucinations, delusions) and negative symptoms (lack of emotion, poverty of language). That distinction is related to the course and prognosis of the disorder (e.g., negative symptoms set in earlier, last longer, are more resistant to treatment, and are more likely to occur in men). In the following chapters, you will learn that positive and negative symptoms appear to have different causes and require different treatments.

Historically, schizophrenia was viewed as an incurable and untreatable disorder. That view is now changing because new explanations are leading to effective treatments. I will discuss those explanations and treatments in the next two chapters, but before going on to those, consider the following whimsical description of schizophrenia by Lynne Morris:

I
am
the
rear tire
of a bicycle,
not trusted enough
to be a
front tire,
expected to go
round and round
in one narrow rut,
never going very far,
ignored
except

when I
break down.
Then
I get lots of
frightening,
angry
attention
and
I am put into
a
garage,
sometimes for months,
where
I forget my function
and
I become afraid
to function
and all functions seem useless.
Next time out
I think I will be
an off-ramp
from a
freeway.

SUMMARY

- The cognitive symptoms of schizophrenia include hallucinations, which are perceptual experiences that do not have a basis in reality; delusions, which are erroneous beliefs that are held despite strong evidence to the contrary; disturbed thought processes, which can be seen in loose associations and intruding thoughts; and cognitive flooding (stimulus overload), which is the inability to screen out irrelevant stimuli.

- Mood symptoms include depression in as many as 60% of individuals with schizophrenia. Mood is often inappropriate.

- Motor symptoms range from immobility to agitation. With all symptoms, it is important to distinguish between those that are due to the disorder and those that are side effects of drugs.

- To be diagnosed as suffering from schizophrenia, a person must show a decline in social or occupational functioning and present any two of the following symptoms: delusions, hallucinations, disorganized speech, disorganized behavior, and flat affect. Hence there are wide differences among individuals with the diagnosis of schizophrenia. Some individuals with the disorder can function effectively.

- The phases of schizophrenia include the prodromal phase, when the symptoms develop; the active phase, when symptoms are full-blown; and the residual phase, when symptoms are less active. Unofficially, there also appears to be a burned-out phase in which patients have very few symptoms but show a serious deterioration of social and personal functioning.

- DSM-IV lists five types of schizophrenia: disorganized, catatonic, paranoid, undifferentiated, and residual. However, this is not a useful way to classify patients.

- An unofficial but effective way to classify types of schizophrenia involves positive and negative symptoms. Positive symptoms are additions to normal behavior and include hallucinations, delusions, thought disorders, and bizarre behaviors.

(Negative symptoms) reflect the absence of normal behaviors and include flat mood, poverty of speech, inability to experience positive feelings, apathy, and inattentiveness.

■ Relative to positive symptoms, negative symptoms are more likely to be associated with poor premorbid adjustment, be consistent over time, occur in men, and show poorer response to drug treatment.

■ Our conceptions of schizophrenia are influenced by the early work of Kraepelin and Bleuler. Kraepelin believed that the disorder had an early onset and was a progressive deterioration like that in senility; he called it *dementia praecox* ("premature deterioration"). Bleuler believed that the disorder could have an early or late onset and was a breaking of associations; he called it *schizophrenia* ("splitting of the mind").

■ About 1.5% of the population suffer from schizophrenia.

■ Schizophrenia is most frequently diagnosed in early adulthood, but negative symptoms probably begin developing much earlier. Men are usually diagnosed as suffering from schizophrenia earlier than women, and the rate of the disorder is consistent across cultures.

■ Schizophrenia is diagnosed more frequently in individuals from the lower than the middle or upper classes. Class differences may be due to downward social drift, bias in diagnosis, bias in treatment, bias in self-presentation, or prenatal and perinatal complications more common in the lower class that can lead to schizophrenia.

■ Five other psychotic disorders are currently recognized:
1. The brief psychotic disorder involves only one or more of the symptoms of schizophrenia (delusions, hallucinations, disorganized speech, disorganized behavior, negative symptoms) and lasts no longer than 1 month.
2. The schizophreniform disorder involves two or more of the symptoms of schizophrenia and lasts only between 1 and 6 months.
3. The schizoaffective disorder involves major mood symptoms (depression or mania) and two of the symptoms of schizophrenia.
4. The shared psychotic disorder involves a delusion that develops in the context of a relationship with another person who has a related delusion.
5. The delusional disorder involves nonbizarre delusions but no other symptoms of schizophrenia, and apart from the effects of the delusion, the individual's functioning is not impaired.

■ Schizophrenia and the other psychotic disorders may represent different sets of symptoms or levels of severity in a spectrum of schizophrenia disorders.

KEY TERMS, CONCEPTS, AND NAMES

In reviewing and testing yourself on what you have learned from this chapter, you should be able to identify and discuss each of the following.

active phase: *clear cut symptoms #2 symph. phase*

Bleuler, Eugen : *studied "positive sympt."*

brief psychotic disorder *= 1 symp., 1 mo max*

burned-out phase: *#4 phase: serious deterior.*

catatonic schizophrenia: *h2 symp waxy flexibility*

cognitive flooding: *symptom*

delusional disorder : *#1 nonbizarre delusions*

delusions : *belief*

delusions of identity: *belief that someone else*

delusions of persecution: *belief others against you*

delusions of reference: *codes*

original term premature deterioration

dementia praecox: *progressive dimensia*

disorganization: *thoughts / behaviors*

disorganized schizophrenia: *hallucinations, but lots/disorganiz.*

hallucinations: *perceptions of ...*

Kraepelin, Emil *negative symptoms*

negative symptoms:

paranoid schizophrenia: *persecution + grandiosity*

positive symptoms

prodromal phase: *#1, some indication*

psychoticism: *hallucinations + delusions*

residual phase: *symptoms less clear*

like in residual phase

residual schizophrenia: *some signs*

schizoaffective disorder: *schiz + mood*

schizophrenia:

schizophrenic deficit: *lack/intellectual functioning*

schizophreniform disorder: *<6 mos*

shared psychotic disorder: *shared delusions*

spectrum of schizophrenic disorders: *rather than #6*

stimulus overload: *flooding*

undifferentiated schizophrenia: *wastebasket*

waxy flexibility : *catatonic*

word salad: *how they talk*

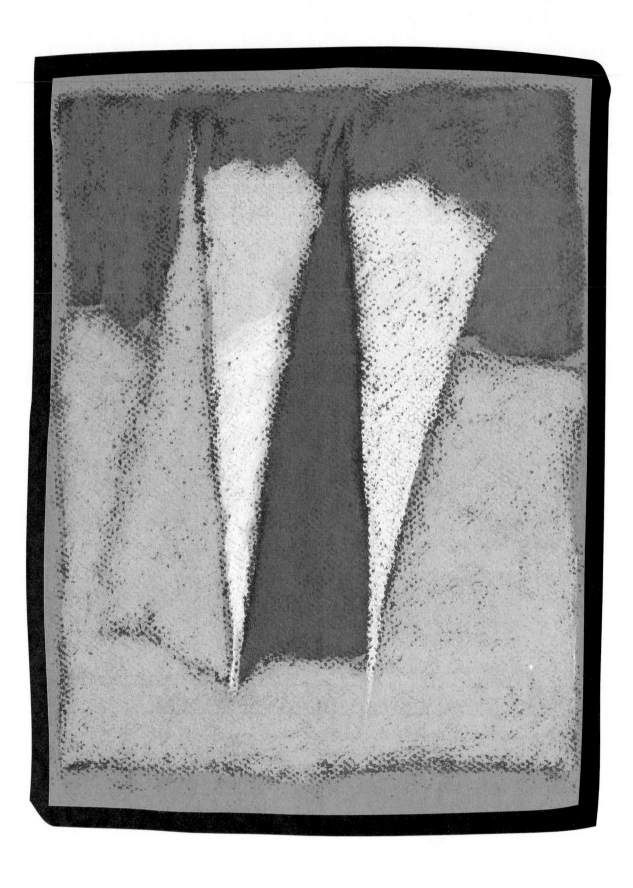

CHAPTER TWELVE
SCHIZOPHRENIA and OTHER PSYCHOTIC DISORDERS: EXPLANATIONS

Marion's therapist believes that many of Marion's symptoms are due to her social isolation and her preference for "her own little world." As a young child, Marion was a little different from her peers in that she preferred to play by herself with her dolls and with imaginary friends she invented. Even when she was with other children, she seemed to play "around" them rather than with them. In time, her peers began avoiding her because they did not share any interests with her and she seemed very distant. When one of Marion's high school classmates was asked about her, she replied, "Marion? Oh, she's out of it, a little weird. She marches to the tune of a distant drummer, and no one else hears that drummer." As Marion got older, she became more withdrawn, and she did not seem to realize how strangely she was behaving. She lost her reference points for what was appropriate and inappropriate, what was real and what was in her head.

■ ■ ■

Brian suffers from schizophrenia, and because of the disturbance in his thought processes, it is difficult for him to carry on a normal conversation. For example, recently, when the ward attendant said, "Come on, let's go to lunch," Brian responded, "Oh yes, in the church. That's where he was, you know the one, Notre Dame. Boy, she was beautiful. I wish we had some like her in here." Brian's "crazy" response stemmed from the fact that hearing the word *lunch* made him think of the word *hunch* and the book title *The Hunchback of Notre Dame*. That explains his talking about the church. He then seems to have picked up on the slang meaning of the word *dame*, which explains his comment about a beautiful woman. Brian's disturbance can be accounted for by problems with rapid and uncontrolled word associations.

■ ■ ■

Edwin is hospitalized with schizophrenia. Because of his diagnosis, it is expected that he will behave strangely, so when he becomes upset and begins throwing things or screaming to "blow off stream," no one does anything to restrain or stop him; after all, he's "crazy," so bizarre behavior is what you would expect of him. If he behaves really strangely, the nurses will try to calm him down, which is just about the only time they give him any attention. As time goes by, Edwin's behavior is getting more and more unusual, and the nurses are spending more and more time with him.

■ ■ ■

Ruth suffers from Parkinson's disease, which causes problems with her physical movements. Those problems are due to a low level of the neurotransmitter dopamine, so she is treated with a drug called L-dopa that increases the level of dopamine. However, when she takes high levels of L-dopa, she develops the symptoms of schizophrenia. In contrast, Jane suffers from schizophrenia, which is thought to stem from high levels of dopamine. The drug she takes reduces the level of dopamine and reduces her schizophrenia, but in high doses it causes problems with her physical movements like those in Parkinson's disease.

■ ■ ■

Mark began showing the early symptoms of schizophrenia at about the age of 15 and was diagnosed as having the disorder when he was 22. He suffers primarily from negative symptoms such as the inability to experience pleasure, poverty of speech, and inattentiveness. There is no family history of schizophrenia or any related disorders, and psychological and medical history does not contain anything unusual other than the fact that his mother had a very serious case of the flu when she was pregnant with Mark and there were some complications during the birth.

■ ■ ■

In Chapter 11 I discussed the symptoms and issues associated with schizophrenia, and in this chapter I will explain the causes of schizophrenia. Finding those causes is exceptionally important because schizophrenia afflicts hundreds of thousands of people, sometimes for life, and it can be a terrifying and debilitating disorder. However, at the outset I should point out that finding the causes of schizophrenia has been a difficult and frustrating task because there have been many suspected causes and numerous dead ends. In this chapter I will explain even the dead ends because knowing what does *not* cause the disorder will help us dispel widely held erroneous beliefs. For example, for many years it was thought that mothers were responsible for the development of schizophrenia because of the way they raised their children, but now we know that is not the case and we need to get mothers "off the hook." Furthermore, as I describe the various explanations, you will see that often the investigators were on the right track but their explanations were inadequate or incomplete. However, over time we were able to put the pieces together to form a more accurate and fuller understanding of this serious disorder.

Two other points should be made before beginning. First, because schizophrenia is a complex disorder with a variety of symptoms, the general explanations are made up of a number of subexplanations. Therefore, at the beginning of each section, I will review the specific subexplanations and then go on to elaborate and examine the evidence. Second, in this chapter I will focus on schizophrenia, but the explanations also apply to the other psychotic disorders insofar as those disorders share symptoms with schizophrenia. With this as background, we can begin the search for the causes of schizophrenia and other psychotic disorders.

PSYCHODYNAMIC EXPLANATIONS

The psychodynamic theorists offered the following four basic explanations for schizophrenia:

1. In the face of stress, individuals *regress* to an earlier stage of development, and the symptoms of schizophrenia reflect the "childlike" behavior of the earlier stage.

2. When faced with interpersonal stress, individuals *withdraw* from interpersonal contact. That withdrawal reduces feedback about what behaviors are appropriate and normal, and the absence of that feedback leads to the symptoms of schizophrenia.

3. High levels of stress disrupt cognitive functioning, which leads to the symptoms of schizophrenia.

4. Problems in child rearing make it difficult for the individual to distinguish between reality and unreality, and the loss of contact with reality results in the symptoms of schizophrenia.

I will discuss and evaluate each of these explanations in the following sections.

Regression

Freud suggested that when facing overwhelming conflict or stress, some individuals deal with the problem by *returning to an earlier stage of psychosexual development at which they felt more secure.* He called that strategy **regression** (Arieti, 1974; Fenichel, 1945). To use a military analogy, the individual can be thought of as an advancing army that suddenly encounters fierce resistance and must retreat to an earlier but more secure and defensible position. Just as some armies are not prepared for battle and are more likely to retreat in the face of resistance, some individuals are not prepared for life (have poorer defenses) and are more likely to regress in the face of conflict and stress. In the case of schizophrenia, psychodynamic theorists suggest that the individual has regressed all the way back to an infantile or oral stage of psychosexual development. The behavior of an individual with schizophrenia is thought to be infantile or childlike.

At the very early stages of psychosexual development, the ego and superego are not well developed, and consequently the id is dominant. Hallucinations and delusions then supposedly represent the unchecked activities of the id; that is, the individual who wants something only needs to fantasize about it for it to exist. Many children have "imaginary friends" who become almost real; for the person who has regressed and developed schizophrenia, those imaginary people are real. Freud suggested that even well-adjusted individuals appear to have occasional lapses in ego control that permit glimpses of psychotic-like thinking. That is most likely to occur during sleep when the ego is less vigilant and our wishes and desires break through in the form of dreams.

Regression provides an interesting description of schizophrenia, but there is no empirical evidence to support the regression explanation for schizophrenia. For example, although the verbal and intellectual performance of individuals with schizophrenia may appear to be childlike, careful analysis of those behaviors reveals that the kinds of errors that are made by individuals with schizophrenia are different from the kinds of errors made by young children (Buss & Lang, 1965). In other words, individuals with schizophrenia may perform intellectual tasks at the same level as children, but

the individuals with schizophrenia perform at those levels because of different types of responses and errors. So even though it is common to think of individuals with schizophrenia as regressed and childlike, we must dismiss the regression explanation for schizophrenia.

Withdrawal

Another psychodynamic theory suggests that individuals with schizophrenia find contact with other individuals to be stressful, so they *withdraw* (Faris, 1934). This interpersonal **withdrawal** cuts the individuals off from feedback about what behaviors or thoughts are inappropriate, *and in the absence of corrective feedback, the individuals begin behaving strangely.* Think how you might behave if for the past five years you had not noticed people's responses to you or you had not been given feedback about what behaviors, emotions, or clothes were appropriate. *your giving appropriateness for much value.*

A variety of research has revealed that, indeed, individuals who developed schizophrenia were more socially isolated as adolescents than individuals who did not develop schizophrenia (Barthell & Holmes, 1968; Bower et al., 1960; Kohn & Clausen, 1955; Schofield & Balian, 1959; Watt, 1978; Watt et al., 1970). For example, an analysis of the activities reported in high school yearbooks indicated that the students who later developed schizophrenia participated in fewer social activities than other students (Barthell & Holmes, 1968).

The major problem with these findings lies in the question of cause and effect. Individuals who developed schizophrenia were more socially isolated, but did

Social isolation at a young age is more likely to be an early symptom of schizophrenia than a cause.

the isolation cause the schizophrenia, or was the isolation an early symptom of schizophrenia? Evidence for the conclusion that isolation is an early effect rather than cause comes from the fact that many individuals who choose to lead very isolated lives (hunters or scientists who must live alone in isolated areas for long periods of time) do not develop schizophrenia, and others who have social isolation forced on them (prisoners of war who are held in solitary confinement for long periods of time) do not develop schizophrenia. Furthermore, the results of two studies indicated that when the biological children of individuals with schizophrenia were adopted and raised by normal parents, they showed greater social isolation than biological offspring of normal parents who were adopted and raised by normal parents (Kendler et al., 1982; MacCrimmon et al., 1980). Because the children of individuals with schizophrenia are at greater risk for the development of schizophrenia, it appears that their social isolation was an early symptom of the disorder. Thus social isolation is often associated with the development of schizophrenia, but it appears to be an early symptom rather than a cause.

Family Influences

The family provides the context in which individuals spend their important formative years, and so for many years theorists speculated that problems in the family were at the root of schizophrenia. Most attention was focused on the personality characteristics of the parents and communication patterns within the family.

Personality Characteristics of Parents. Psychodynamic theorists consider the mother-child relationship to be one of the crucial factors in the development of schizophrenia. They suggest that mothers of children who develop schizophrenia are *overprotective* and *controlling* but at the same time are *rejecting* and *distant.* The mother's overprotection supposedly stifles the child's emotional development, and her emotional distance deprives the child of personal security. The limited emotional development, in combination with the lack of security, leaves the individual vulnerable, and when dealing with stress, the individual breaks down. The term **schizophrenogenic** (SKIT-zō-fren-uh-JEN-ik) **mother** was coined to describe such overprotecting but distant mothers.

Research on the personality and child-rearing practices of the parents of individuals with schizophrenia yields two general conclusions. First, *there is no evidence that the mothers of individuals with schizophrenia are more likely than other mothers to fit the description of the schizophrenogenic mother* (Goldstein & Rodnick, 1975; Hirsch & Leff, 1975; Jacob, 1975; Mishler & Waxler, 1968a;

Wynne et al., 1979). Second, *there is evidence that in many cases the mothers and fathers of individuals with schizophrenia are generally less well adjusted than the parents of normal individuals* (Hirsch & Leff, 1975). In fact, the parents of individuals with schizophrenia often suffer from schizophrenia.

The co-occurrence of poor adjustment in parents and children is clear, but we cannot necessarily conclude that the poor adjustment is transmitted to the children through the process of child rearing. Instead, there is evidence that having a severely disturbed child poses problems for the parents, and those problems can have a negative effect on the parents' adjustment (Liem, 1980; Mishler & Waxler, 1968a). In other words, rather than parents causing problems in children, children cause at least some of the problems in the parents.

Alternatively, it may be that the co-occurrence of schizophrenia in parents and children is due to their shared genes rather than the process of child rearing. Support for this possibility is provided by evidence that children of normal parents who are adopted and raised by disturbed foster parents are not more likely to develop schizophrenia than children of normal parents who are adopted and raised by normal foster parents (Wender et al., 1974). In other words, the "worse-case scenario" in which a child is raised by a parent with schizophrenia does not necessarily lead to schizophrenia in the child if the child had normal biological parents.

Communication Patterns. For many years, a popular explanation for schizophrenia was the **double-bind hypothesis** (Bateson et al., 1956). This hypothesis suggests that the messages given to children who later developed schizophrenia actually contained two conflicting messages, and the child would be punished for disobeying either of the messages. The conflict posed by the two messages and the fear of punishment for disobeying supposedly led the child to respond in deviant ways (ignore messages, see hidden meanings in them, give an irrelevant response) to avoid the conflict and punishment. The strategy seemed to be, when unsure about the message you are getting, to avoid trouble, confuse the situation. Those deviant responses are thought to lead to schizophrenia.

Consider the situation in which a father and son disagree on something. The father spends 15 minutes trying his best to get the son to agree with his position and then concludes by saying, "But of course, I want you to make up your own mind." What is the child to do? If he finally agrees with his father, he has given in and has not made up his own mind as his father instructed him to do. But if he stands his ground and makes up his own mind, he disobeys his father's advice on the issue. In that situation, the child cannot win and must do something to extricate himself from the situation. The classic (though somewhat contrived) example of a double-bind statement is "I order you to disobey me." Try to respond appropriately to that one! If you disobey, you are obeying the command, and if you obey, you are disobeying the command.

Communication explanations for schizophrenia have considerable intuitive appeal, but despite a large amount of research on the topic, there is no evidence linking any particular communication problem or style to schizophrenia. For example, the parents of individuals with schizophrenia are not more likely to give double-bind communications than the parents of normal children (Mishler & Waxler, 1968a). Communication difficulties with people who are important to us do not help our adjustment, but they do not lead to schizophrenia.

Stress

A more contemporary psychodynamic explanation for schizophrenia is focused on the role of stress, regardless of its source. Specifically, it is suggested that high levels of stress disrupt cognitive functioning and that *the disruptive effects of stress lead to the symptoms of schizophrenia.* Support for a link between stress and schizophrenia comes from a variety of sources. For example, in one study, individuals who did or did not suffer from schizophrenia were interviewed about their experiences during a 13-week period (Brown & Birley, 1968). For the individuals with schizophrenia, the period in question was the 13 weeks immediately prior to the onset of their symptoms, whereas for the normal individuals it was a period that was not followed by any symptoms of schizophrenia. The results revealed that the individuals with schizophrenia were more likely to have experienced stressful life events (e.g., job loss, geographic move, divorce) than the normal individuals. Furthermore, the individuals with schizophrenia were more likely to experience their stressful events in the 3-week period just prior to the onset of their symptoms. Those results are summarized in Figure 12.1. It has also been found that stressful life events are likely to precede relapses and readmissions to hospitals (see Dohrenwend & Egri, 1981).

The role of stress in schizophrenia has also been studied by examining the incidence of the disorder in extremely stressful situations such as combat. Diagnoses made under battlefield conditions may not be comparable to those made under civilian conditions, but it does appear that the rate of schizophrenia is higher in combat than in civilian conditions. However, it should be recognized that many of the cases that were diagnosed in the battlefield may actually have been instances of the *brief psychotic disorder* rather than schizophrenia. Indeed, the battlefield patients were found to have very good prognoses and were sometimes described as having "3-day" psychoses or "5-day schizophrenia" (Kolb, 1973; Kormos, 1978). That symptom pattern, in combination with the fact that there was an obvious precipitating stressful event, would certainly suggest the diagnosis of brief psychotic disorder rather than schizophrenia.

In summary, stress does appear to play a role in the development of schizophrenia, but three qualifications should be noted. First, in some cases, *the stress may have been the result rather than the cause of the onset of the disorder.* That is, because the symptoms of schizophrenia cause problems in daily functioning, the individual's life may become more stressful as symptoms develop. Second, stress does not result in schizophrenia in everyone, and therefore it appears *that stress by itself is not sufficient to produce schizophrenia.* Instead, it is probable that stress leads to schizophrenia in individuals who have a biological predisposition to the disorder. (I will discuss that later when I discuss the physiological and diathesis-stress explanations for schizophrenia.) Third, because

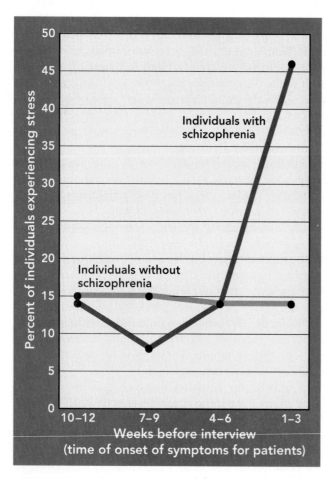

FIGURE 12.1 Stress was related to the onset of schizophrenia.
Source: Adapted from Brown and Birley (1968).

The intense stress of combat may lead to a brief psychotic disorder.

many individuals develop schizophrenia in the absence of stress, it is clear *that stress is not necessary for the disorder to develop*. That is, factors other than stress may cause schizophrenia. Overall, then, stress can trigger schizophrenia, but it is neither a sufficient cause (stress must occur with a predisposition) nor a necessary cause (the disorder can occur without stress).

COMMENT

Originally, there was widespread acceptance of the ideas that schizophrenia was due to regression, withdrawal, child-rearing practices, and communication problems. However, years of research have failed to provide any evidence for those explanations. The explanations initially appeared valid because we misinterpreted behavior (schizophrenia is not really regression), we confused cause and effect (withdrawal appears to be an early symptom rather than a cause of schizophrenia), and we did not realize that family and communication difficulties are not unique to persons with schizophrenia. We made those mistakes largely because the explanations fit what we saw, but we did not go on to test our hypotheses about cause and effect.

In contrast, there is strong evidence that stress can contribute to schizophrenia. By itself, stress does not appear to cause schizophrenia, but it appears to trigger it in some people. Furthermore, some family influences may be important because they increase stress. Because psychodynamic explanations are not sufficient to explain schizophrenia, we must go on to consider other explanations.

LEARNING EXPLANATIONS

Learning theorists offered four simple explanations for schizophrenia:

1. Individuals with schizophrenia have a *high level of drive* (arousal), and the symptoms of schizophrenia stem from the disruptive effects of the drive on thinking and from the attempts to reduce the high level of drive.

2. Some individuals are *not rewarded for appropriate social behaviors,* so they ignore the usual social cues and begin behaving inappropriately.

3. *Bizarre behaviors lead to rewards* (attention), so those behaviors are used over and over and become the symptoms of schizophrenia.

4. Being labeled as a "schizophrenic" leads to a *social role* in which bizarre behaviors (symptoms) are permitted and expected.

I will discuss and evaluate each of these explanations in the following sections.

High Drive, Response Disruption, and Drive-Reducing Behaviors

The first explanation for schizophrenia offered by learning theorists was that *schizophrenia is the result of high drive* (Mednick, 1958). Learning theorists assume that thoughts (and other responses) are influenced by underlying drives, and *if drive levels are too high, extraneous thoughts will be triggered that can distract the individual and disrupt cognitive functioning.* That disruption results

are genius people schizophrenic? (perhaps pretty close)

in the cognitive symptoms (Mednick & Schulsinger, 1968; Neale, 1971). You may have had a similar but less severe experience when you became anxious on an exam and were unable to concentrate and make correct responses. Indeed, some of your responses may have been a little "crazy."

The learning theorists also suggest that because high drive is unpleasant, individuals attempt to reduce the unpleasantness by focusing on thoughts that are irrelevant to the drive. *The attempts at self-distraction lead to the irrelevant thoughts and disruptions of thought processes that we diagnose as schizophrenia.* You may have seen this process operating in yourself in unpleasant situations like preparing for or taking an examination. The anxiety (drive) associated with the examination was unpleasant, so to reduce the anxiety, you thought about something else. However, thinking about irrelevant things interfered with your cognitive functioning. The presence of the irrelevant thoughts could also be used to explain the inappropriate mood seen in schizophrenia; that is, individuals who are thinking irrelevant thoughts would be expected to show inappropriate moods.

Initially, these hypotheses concerning the effects of drive generated a lot of interest, but because the theory could not explain why some individuals had high drive, the drive explanation for schizophrenia was largely abandoned. However, later when I discuss the physiological explanations for schizophrenia, you will learn that the drive explanation has been revived in a more sophisticated form. Specifically, it has been suggested that some of the symptoms of schizophrenia are due to excessively high levels of neurological activity in the brain (what the learning theorists called drive), which disrupts cognitive functioning. In other words, the learning theorists were on the right track, but their explanation needed refinement.

Extinction of Attention to Relevant Cues

Second, learning theorists suggested that schizophrenia might stem from the *extinction of attention to relevant cues in the environment and consequent attention to irrelevant cues* (Ullman & Krasner, 1969). In other words, they suggested that some individuals who find their social situations unrewarding or punishing start to ignore the relevant aspects of their environment and focus instead on irrelevant things that are rewarding or at least neutral. The attention to irrelevant cues results in behaviors that are irrelevant and inappropriate to the situation—that is, the symptoms of schizophrenia.

This process can be illustrated with a simple, less extreme example. A student who finds a lecture boring (unrewarding) may stop paying attention and begin daydreaming. If the student is then suddenly called on to answer a question, the response will probably completely miss the point and may seem childish, illogical, or inappropriate. That is the same sort of characterization applied to the responses of individuals with schizophrenia. In the case of an individual with schizophrenia, the diversion of attention is more pervasive and of greater duration than with the bored student, and consequently the individual's responses will be even more disjointed, tangential, or irrelevant.

Delusions are accounted for by suggesting that if a particular set of beliefs is not effective for obtaining rewards or is punishing, the individual may alter his or her beliefs so that they will be rewarding. Because the individual is no longer attending to the relevant cues in the environment, the new beliefs will not be accurate or corrected. The development of a delusion through this process can also be illustrated with a simple example. If a young man finds the social environment punishing because he cannot make friends, he may cease attending to the painful social cues in the environment and develop a belief (delusion) that he has not been able to make friends because he is exceptionally bright and therefore threatening to others. Inattention to the relevant social cues in the environment will preclude correction of the erroneous belief. Furthermore, the individual's inappropriate behavior (stemming from attention to irrelevant cues and erroneous belief) could lead the individual's peers to actually reject him, which could in turn cause him to develop delusions of persecution. With regard to this explanation, a substantial amount of research indicates that if we are comfortable with a particular set of beliefs, we will not seek out or will actually avoid evidence that is inconsistent with our beliefs, thereby reducing the possibility that erroneous beliefs will be corrected (Lord et al., 1979; O'Sullivan & Durso, 1984; Sweeney & Gruber, 1984).

Hallucinations can also be explained by selective attention. There is a fine line between "thinking thoughts" and "hearing voices when no one else is there" (auditory hallucinations). We often recall or mentally rehearse conversations that involve numerous "voices." Because the world is threatening, the individual with schizophrenia may cease attending to external cues and focus attention inward. (The unhappy individual is said to turn inward for solace.) Then, because he or she is not attending to the relevant social cues in the environment, the individual will not realize that attending to the internal cues is inappropriate. From there it is only a short jump to dealing with those internal stimuli as if they were real.

Unfortunately, it is overly simplistic to assume that schizophrenia is due to a voluntary lack of attention to relevant cues in the environment. If that were the case, we could cure schizophrenia by simply rewarding the individual for paying attention to the relevant cues, but that does not work (see Chapter 13).

Symptoms and Rewards

Third, learning theorists suggested that individuals with schizophrenia *use their abnormal behavior to get rewards* such as attention. On an overcrowded and understaffed hospital ward, a quiet, symptom-free patient will not get much attention, and therefore it behooves the patient who wants attention to act a little "crazy." Just as the squeaky wheel gets the oil, so the "weird schizophrenic" gets the attention. Attention can be a particularly powerful reward in hospitals where patients are rarely visited and are usually ignored by an overworked staff. Nurses have reported to me that some patients start acting "crazier" when they learn that I am bringing a group of students to the hospital for a tour because the patients want to be picked to visit with the students.

The results of a variety of experiments demonstrate that patients can and will manipulate their symptoms to gain rewards (Braginsky & Braginsky, 1967). In one of those experiments, randomly selected groups of hospitalized patients were told that they were going to be interviewed (a) to determine whether they should be discharged, (b) to determine whether they should be placed on a very desirable open ward where they could come and go as they wished, or (c) simply to determine their mental status. The interviews were recorded, and later the responses of the patients were scored by three psychiatrists in terms of how disturbed the patients were. It was found that the patients who thought they were being interviewed for the open ward presented themselves as having the lowest level of abnormal behavior. These patients were able to fake relative health so that they could get on the desirable open ward. In contrast, the patients who thought that they

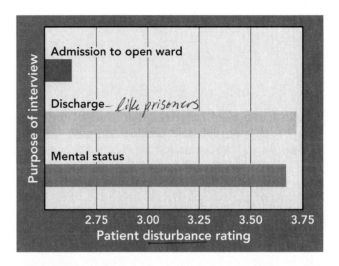

FIGURE 12.2 **Patients reduced their symptoms to qualify for admission to an open ward.**
Source: Data from Braginsky and Braginsky (1967), p. 545, tab. 1.

were being interviewed for discharge or to determine their mental status showed higher levels of pathology. That is, the patients in the discharge condition did not fake health because they liked the hospital and did not want to risk being released. Those results are presented in Figure 12.2.

Other evidence that symptoms may be used to get desired rewards comes from the finding that the amount of time patients stay in the hospital versus the community is related to the degree to which they like the hospital versus the community (Drake & Wallach, 1979). Among patients who were capable of living in the community, those who preferred the hospital stayed in the community an average of 9.5 days, whereas those who preferred the community stayed in the community an average of 233.9 days. Clearly, the patients manipulated their symptoms to achieve their desired result, hospitalization or life in the community.

To sum up, there is evidence that the symptoms shown by individuals with schizophrenia can be influenced by rewards, but there are two serious problems with the notion that schizophrenia is learned. First, many of the symptoms of schizophrenia are simply *not under voluntary control*, and therefore *patients cannot manipulate them to get rewards*. For example, individuals are simply not able to stop hallucinations or stop the disruptions in thought processes that plague them. The second problem is that in most cases, *the symptoms of schizophrenia are not rewarding*. Indeed, in many cases, the symptoms are troublesome or terrifying, and individuals will do almost anything to get rid of them. For example, recall that my friend Betty reported the terrible hallucinations of blood pouring down people's faces and monks telling her that she is a terrible person who should have been killed as a fetus (see Case Study 11.2). Rewards may be able to account for some

In some cases, patients may use bizarre behavior to attract attention, which can be rewarding. Also, being labeled mentally ill permits a wide range of "acceptable" behaviors.

superficial behaviors, but not for the real symptoms of schizophrenia.

Labels, Roles, and Expectations

Finally, it has been suggested that some of the symptoms of schizophrenia may develop because *individuals are labeled as "schizophrenic."* Giving individuals such labels could result in abnormal behavior in two ways. First, because we expect individuals who are labeled as suffering from schizophrenia to behave in "crazy" ways, we may subtly suggest abnormal behaviors to them. Consider the case of a woman who was admitted to a psychiatric hospital with the diagnosis of schizophrenia. Because individuals with schizophrenia often hallucinate, the woman's therapist assumed that she hallucinated, and he therefore frequently asked her whether she heard voices when no one else was around. The woman did not have hallucinations, but after being asked about it by an individual of authority, the woman began to wonder whether she did indeed hallucinate. Given the suggestion that she might (or should?) and some time to think about it, the distinction between listening to one's thoughts and hearing voices became blurred ("Maybe those thoughts in my head are hallucinations"). The next time she was asked, she acknowledged hallucinating, thus fulfilling the therapist's expectations, and thereafter talked about her thoughts as if they were hallucinations.

Being labeled as suffering from schizophrenia can also lead to symptoms because *the role of being "schizophrenic" permits a wider variety of behaviors than the role of being "normal,"* and therefore an individual who is labeled as suffering from schizophrenia might use behaviors that ordinarily would be suppressed. For example, an individual who is defined as suffering from schizophrenia may not be expected to be responsible for his or her behaviors and is therefore allowed to act more deviantly. One day, a patient became very frustrated, and to vent his anger he picked up a chair and began breaking it up by hitting it against the wall. When a ward attendant grabbed him and told him to stop, the patient yelled, "I'm going crazy!" The attendant then yelled back, "You may be crazy, but you can't break up furniture when *I'm* on duty!" Hearing that, the patient stopped, looked thoughtfully at the attendant for a moment, and then said he was sorry and walked away. In the future, that patient showed his "obvious deterioration of ego strength" only when a more tolerant attendant was on duty.

The effects of roles and expectations on abnormal behavior were demonstrated in research on **sensory deprivation.** In the early experiments, the investigators did not know what would happen to people who were deprived of stimulation, and therefore the participants in the experiments were asked to sign elaborate release

forms before they were sent into the isolation chamber. The participants were also told that if they wanted to end the session for any reason, they could hit the large red "panic button" on the wall of the chamber. The results of those investigations revealed that if individuals were placed in a soundproofed chamber for a few hours, they experienced a variety of potentially serious symptoms such as changes in perceptual experiences, inability to concentrate, and spatial and temporal disorientation (Bexton et al., 1954; Scott et al., 1959). Indeed, these findings led some theorists to hypothesize that schizophrenia was caused by sensory deprivation. However, that speculation was in error. Later investigators speculated that the "symptoms" were being suggested by the procedures ("panic buttons," etc.) rather than caused by the isolation (Orne & Scheibe, 1964). To test that possibility, an experiment was conducted in which one group of individuals was treated in the usual way while another group was exposed to the same isolation but were told that they were in a "control" condition, and nothing was said about release forms, symptoms, or panic buttons. The results indicated that individuals who were warned about symptoms developed symptoms much like those seen in schizophrenia ("There are multicolored spots on the wall," "Objects on the desk are becoming animated and moving about," "The buzzing of the fluorescent light is growing alternately louder and softer, so that at times it sounds like a jackhammer"), whereas individuals in the control condition were simply bored. In other words, taking away the panic button and the implicit suggestion about symptoms eliminated the schizophrenic-like symptoms. Clearly, roles, expectations, and suggestions can influence symptoms.

Labels and roles can influence what people do, but *another individual's label or role can also influence our interpretation of what the individual does and why the individual does it.* For example, if you observe an individual who is labeled as "schizophrenic" staring off into space, you would probably assume that the individual is hallucinating rather than just thinking or daydreaming. If the individual misunderstands something you say, you might attribute it to an "underlying thought disorder" rather than to a simple misunderstanding. Those interpretations will then influence how you respond to the individual, which might in turn influence how the individual responds to you. The influence of labels on the interpretation of behavior is illustrated in Case Study 12.1, which involves the labeling of normal individuals as "schizophrenics."

I had an experience similar to that of the people described in Case Study 12.1 when I was beginning my clinical internship at a large psychiatric hospital. The first day, I was instructed to dress informally and "hang out" on one of the wards so that I could "get the feel of the place." Most patients quickly recognized me as "another one of the new trainees," and they spent time

---

CASE STUDY 12.1

Normal Individuals in a Mental Hospital: The Effects of Being Labeled as a "Schizophrenic"

This case study does not involve a disturbed individual. It focuses on the experiences of eight *normal* individuals, some of them students, who were admitted to various psychiatric hospitals under the guise of being abnormal. It illustrates what can happen to people when they are simply *labeled* as abnormal.

The people in this study did not have any signs or history of abnormal behavior, but when they presented themselves at the hospitals, they complained of hearing voices. When asked about the voices, they said that they were "unclear" but seemed to say words like *empty, hollow,* and *thud.* All of the other information given by the individuals (personal background, frustrations, joys) was true and did not reflect any serious problems. All of the individuals were diagnosed as suffering from schizophrenia and admitted to the hospitals as patients. Once admitted, the pseudopatients *ceased simulating any symptoms and behaved as they ordinarily did.* They talked to other patients, cooperated with all requests from the staff, and when asked how they were feeling, they said that they were fine and were no longer having any symptoms.

The pseudopatients were kept in the hospital and treated for between 7 and 52 days. Despite the extended periods of hospitalization, *none of the hospital staff recognized that the patients were in fact normal.* That was the case despite the fact that once admitted, they did not show any symptoms. They were in the hospital and were labeled as "schizophrenic," so they must be disturbed. In contrast, however, the real patients in the hospital (i.e., individuals who are supposedly out of touch with reality) were very likely to recognize the pseudopatients as fakes. They made comments like "You're not crazy. You're a journalist or a professor [referring to the continual note taking]. You're checking up on the hospital."

Not only did the hospital staff not recognize that the pseudopatients were normal, but because the pseudopatients were labeled as "schizophrenic," the staff interpreted their normal behaviors as abnormal. For example, when the pseudopatients were seen sitting outside the cafeteria half an hour before lunch, a psychiatrist interpreted the behavior as reflecting the "oral-acquisitive nature of the syndrome." Apparently, the fact that there was little to do in the hospital other than go to meals was not considered an explanation for their behavior.

In the case of one pseudopatient who experienced the normal ebb and flow in personal relationships, his file contained the following summary:

> This white 39-year-old male . . . manifests a long history of considerable ambivalence in close relationships, which begins in early childhood. . . . Affective stability is absent. . . . And while he says that he has several good friends, one senses considerable ambivalence embedded in those relationships.

In other cases, when patients became upset, it was always assumed that their behavior was due to their disorders rather than to some factor in the environment, such as intentional or unintentional mistreatment by a ward attendant.

Clearly, everything normal about these normal persons was turned around and interpreted as evidence that they were disturbed. There was no way out for these normal persons. Even when they were finally discharged, they were discharged as "schizophrenic 'in remission.'" The fact that they were discharged implied that they were behaving normally, but the label implied that the disorder still lurked beneath the surface.

How would your daily behavior be interpreted if you were suddenly labeled as a "schizophrenic"?

Source: Adapted from Rosenhan (1973).

---

talking to me and "showing me the ropes." I spent quite a bit of time talking with one middle-aged man who frequently made religious or biblical references, often called me "son," and once offered to pray for me in my "current time of need." Because I had been instructed not to probe, I did not attempt to identify this man's disorder, but I assumed that he had some delusion revolving around himself as God. Two days later, at a staff meeting, the man and I were both a bit red-faced when I discovered that he was the new ward chaplain and he realized that I was the new intern!

It is clear that labels, roles, and expectations are responsible for some of the symptoms seen in schizophrenia. However, those factors cannot be used to account for all of the symptoms because the labels, roles, and expectations can only have their effects *after the individual has been diagnosed (labeled) and has assumed the role of patient.* To reach that point, some symptoms must have already existed. Furthermore, the notion that the symptoms of schizophrenia are due to labels, roles, and expectations suggests that to a large extent the symptoms can be changed easily by simply changing labels and roles, but clearly that is not the case. We can conclude, then, that labels and roles can influence the behaviors of individuals with schizophrenia and our expectations can influence how we interpret their behaviors, but labels, roles, and expectations are not sufficient to explain schizophrenia.

COMMENT

The explanations for schizophrenia that were offered by learning theorists may help account for some symptoms, but the explanations have some serious limitations. First, the high-drive explanation can account for disturbances in cognitive functioning, but it does not account for why some individuals have a high level of drive. Second, inattention to relevant cues can account for inappropriate social behavior and some cognitive symptoms, but it is questionable whether simple inattention is sufficient to explain the serious and uncontrollable symptoms of schizophrenia. Furthermore, it is not clear whether inattention to relevant cues is a cause or an effect of schizophrenia. Third, some symptoms may be influenced by rewards such as attention, but rewards cannot be used to explain the uncontrollable problems with thought processes. Finally, labels, roles, and expectations also seem to explain some of the symptoms associated with schizophrenia, but these could influence patients only after they were initially diagnosed, and thus they do not seem sufficient to explain all of the symptoms of schizophrenia. In sum, the learning explanations, like the psychodynamic explanations, offer some clues but no firm conclusions concerning the causes of schizophrenia, and again we will have to consider other explanations.

COGNITIVE EXPLANATIONS

The cognitive explanations for schizophrenia involve the following three points:

1. Individuals with schizophrenia actually have *sensory experiences that are different from those of normal individuals* (e.g., they hear or feel things that other people do not).

2. Many of the symptoms of schizophrenia (e.g., hallucinations, delusions) stem from the attempts of individuals to *explain their different sensory experiences* (e.g., sounds will be interpreted as voices, and if others do not hear the voices, the individuals who hear them will think that they are somehow special).

3. The disrupted intellectual and verbal performance evident in schizophrenia is due to the fact that *the sensory experiences interfere with the individuals' otherwise normal cognitive functioning.*

The cognitive explanations differ from the psychodynamic and learning explanations in two important ways. First, rather than suggesting that the unusual sensory experiences in schizophrenia are not real and are caused by the disorder, the cognitive explanation suggests that the sensory experiences *are real* and *are the cause of the disorder.* In other words, the individuals do not hallucinate because they have schizophrenia; rather, they have different sensory experiences, and symptoms arise when an individual tries to *explain* the sensory experiences. Second, rather than suggesting that the thought processes in schizophrenia are deranged and different from those of other people, cognitive theorists suggest that the thought processes in schizophrenia are *like those of normal individuals but seem deranged* because the individuals are dealing with different sensory experiences that interfere with the normal thought processes. In the following sections, I will elaborate on these points.

Sensory Experiences, Hallucinations, and Delusions

It is important to recall that many individuals who suffer from schizophrenia experience **cognitive flooding** or **stimulus overload** (see Chapter 11). That is, individuals with schizophrenia cannot screen out sounds, sights, and sensations that normal individuals screen out, so they are flooded or overloaded with stimulation. The question then arises, how do these sensory experiences lead to the symptoms of schizophrenia?

The nature of the overloading and its relationship to the development of symptomatology are illustrated in Case Study 12.2 (p. 328). Was the man in the case study suffering from schizophrenia when he called me? Was he in the process of developing schizophrenia? In the following sections, I will explain how changes in sensory sensitivity like those experienced by this man could result in the development of hallucinations and delusions.

Hallucinations. Traditionally, hallucinations have been interpreted as sensory experiences that do not have a basis in reality (Bentall, 1990). However, the extraordinary sensitivity to stimulation experienced by some people may provide the basis for what we call hallucinations. For example, individuals who report tactile hallucinations (e.g., tingling of the skin, gnawing sensations inside the body) may be more sensitive to somatic sensations and may therefore experience sensations that other individuals do not experience. Similarly, individuals who hear voices that others do not hear may be more sensitive to sounds than other individuals.

feeling itchy → bugs crawling all over you
overactive brain → voices

Persons with schizophrenia may experience stimulus overload; many are aware of sights, sounds, and sensations that normal individuals screen out.

This does not mean that the highly sensitive individuals are actually feeling and hearing exactly what they think they are feeling and hearing. Instead, it may be that these individuals are experiencing some vague or irrelevant stimulation, and in an attempt to make sense of it, they "fill in the blanks" and come up with a complete and meaningful perception. This filling-in process is not unusual or abnormal, and there is abundant evidence that we all use it. From this perspective, then, hallucinations may be interpreted as an expected consequence of the normal process of dealing with sensory experiences.

Delusions. Delusions can also be accounted for by the presence of extra stimulation (Maher, 1988a, 1988b). It is generally assumed that we all have the same sensory experiences and therefore have access to the same information. Consequently, if an individual holds a belief that is contrary to the commonly held evidence, it is assumed that the individual is suffering from a delusion. However, it may be that some individuals have different sensory experiences (e.g., they hear or feel things that others do not), and those different experiences lead the individuals to reach different conclusions about the world, conclusions that we might refer to as delusions. Furthermore, if an individual has sensory experiences that other individuals clearly do not have, the individual having the different experiences would have to come up with explanations for why only he or she has those experiences, and those explanations could result in additional delusions such as "I am special."

With regard to this explanation, consider the old parable about the five blind men who each felt a different part of an elephant and therefore had different sensory experiences concerning the shape of the elephant. If four of the blind men each felt a leg and the fifth felt the tail, the four who felt a leg might conclude that the fifth man who thought that the elephant was small and thin suffered from a delusion about the shape of elephants. Given some creativity, the four "normal" men who felt a leg might be able to come up with an explanation for the fifth man's "delusion." They might suggest, for example, that the fifth man was threatened by the obvious size of the elephant and that he resolved the threat by developing the delusion that the elephant was small and thin.

Some other examples may illustrate how attempts to explain differences in sensory experiences can result in the development of delusions. Consider the case of a young student who, because of a problem with heightened sensitivity, became aware of the buzzing noise made by the fluorescent lights and to the muffled voices of the students talking in the next room. Those sounds seemed very prominent to her, but when she mentioned them to her roommates, they denied hearing them. The sounds were real to the young woman and had to be explained. The denial of those sounds by her roommates also had to be explained. Could it be that the students in the next room were talking about her, that they were causing the light to make noise to annoy her, and that her roommates were now lying to her?

Consider also the example of the man in Case Study 12.2 who became sensitive to sights and sounds while driving his car. He would have to account for the fact that he was now seeing and hearing things that he had not seen or heard before and that others were not seeing or hearing. He might assume that he now had some special powers or that the things he was seeing were special signs for him.

Finally, consider the case of an elderly woman who was losing her hearing. Because of that loss, it appeared to the woman as though everyone around her was whispering, and she was faced with the problem of explaining that behavior. She might recall earlier times when she had disagreements with other people, and she might conclude that the people around her were now planning to get back at her, perhaps to take her money. Why else would they be whispering? This woman's delusion was rooted in her different sensory experiences,

CASE STUDY 12.2
Stimulus Overload and Potential Schizophrenic Symptoms

One morning I received a telephone call from a friend, a very bright, psychologically sophisticated 34-year-old executive. He was in a state of near panic as he told me that he was afraid that he was "losing his mind" and "going crazy." When I asked what had happened, he told me that while driving to his office that morning, he began having strange experiences. First, he explained that everything he saw was very "intense" and that he could not ignore anything. For example, while driving by billboards, he saw things that he had never noticed before, such as the very small print at the bottom of the billboard that gives the name of the company that owns it. Second, he was having great difficulty with sounds. He explained that while he was driving on the expressway, he was constantly afraid that he was going to be run over by a huge truck because it sounded to him as though a truck were almost on top of him. However, when he looked in the rearview mirror, it was obvious that the truck was a long distance away and of no danger to him. Moments later, however, it again sounded like the truck was about to run him down.

One of the most psychologically frightening experiences associated with sound occurred when he pulled up at a stoplight. There were two men in the car in front of him, and as one man turned his head

to talk to the other man, my friend suddenly thought that because of his unusual sensitivity to sound, he would be able to hear the man talk despite the fact that he was in another car and the windows were up in both vehicles. Terrified by the possibility of something he knew to be impossible, he looked away, hoping that if he did not see the man speak, he might not hear him.

In his panic over these strange experiences and his loss of control, he called me for help. This was the first such "attack" that he had experienced, but as I listened to him talk, I recalled a number of related experiences of which I was aware. For example, he had become extremely uncomfortable and disoriented when he had to drive through a long tunnel in which lights flashed by as he drove along, he had always disliked loud rock music, and he had complained about movies in which there were sudden and rapid flashes of scenes. Clearly, he was generally sensitive to sensory stimulation, but never before had it been so severe, and in the past he had always been able to cope with it by avoiding it. For some reason, his sensitivity had suddenly been heightened, he was being overwhelmed by stimulation, and he did not know what was happening to him or how to deal with it.

if we focus on it, it becomes worse.

and the delusion was simply given form by the nature of her prior experiences. No amount of psychotherapy concerning her earlier experiences with others would relieve the basis for her delusion—but a hearing aid would do it immediately!

There is also laboratory evidence to support the notion that differences in sensory experiences can result in delusions. In one experiment during the Cold War, college students were shown pictures of Russians, and while they were looking at the pictures, the students were given false physiological feedback concerning their anxiety levels (Bramel et al., 1965). The members of one group received feedback indicating that they were very anxious while looking at the pictures, whereas the members of another group received feedback indicating that they were not anxious while looking at the pictures. After getting the feedback, the students were asked to rate the degree to which they thought the Russians were hostile. The results indicat-

ed that the students who were led to believe that they were anxious rated the Russians as more hostile than the students who were not led to believe that they were anxious. These results suggest that the students who thought they were anxious had to explain or justify their apparent sensory experiences, so they attributed the threat to the Russians ("I am anxious because of the threat posed by the Russians"). It might be said that those students developed "delusions of persecution" concerning the Russians. *what if a neutral picture was used?*

In considering this explanation, it is relevant to note that there is a strong correspondence between the occurrence of cognitive flooding and delusions. Both are more likely to occur in acute cases of schizophrenia (Payne, 1962; Payne & Friedlander, 1962). The fact that cognitive flooding is *correlated* with delusions does not prove that flooding *causes* delusions, but the implication is very strong and is supported by the laboratory research discussed earlier.

A crucial point in this explanation is that the cognitive process by which disturbed individuals develop delusions is *identical* to the cognitive process by which normal individuals develop explanations. The problem for individuals with schizophrenia is not in the nature of their thought processes but rather in the fact that they have more and different stimuli to incorporate into their views of the world than normal individuals do. It is the incorporation of the additional material that leads to delusions.

Cognitive Intrusions, Distraction, and the Schizophrenic Deficit

A notable feature of schizophrenia is a decline in intellectual functioning that we call the **schizophrenic deficit.** It is now widely assumed that the deficit is due to the *intrusion of irrelevant thoughts that distract the individuals and disrupt their thought processes* (Maher, 1968, 1972, 1983; McGhie & Chapman, 1961; Shakow, 1963; Venables, 1964). In other words, it is as if there is a breakdown in the **filter mechanism** that is responsible for screening out stimuli that are not related to the current thought, and in the absence of that filtering, the individual is flooded with distracting stimuli.

Clinical support for the influence of **distraction** on cognitive performance is readily available in the subjective reports of patients. Newly admitted patients consistently report problems in controlling the flow of incoming information (McGhie & Chapman, 1961), and the personal reports written by patients reflect their attentional problems (Freedman, 1974). One patient reported that with books he had

> a hard time concentrating, getting into the actual reading of them [because] probably an external stimulus would take my attention off the book . . . a sound or something like a piece of sunlight is going on over here and that would probably start me thinking. (Freedman & Chapman, 1973, p. 50)

Another patient reported:

> My mind was so confused I couldn't focus on one thing. I had an idea and I was wondering whether I should press charges and then all of a sudden my mind went to something pleasant, and then it went back to my work, and I couldn't keep it orderly. (p. 50) *like manic epis.*

In addition to this clinical evidence, the results of many laboratory experiments attest to the influence of distraction on the performance of people with schizophrenia (see Lang & Buss, 1965; Neale & Oltmanns, 1980). For example, in one experiment conducted with individuals who did and did not have schizophrenia, a series of numbers was read by a female experimenter, and the individuals' task was to recall the numbers after they had been read (Lawson et al., 1967). On half of

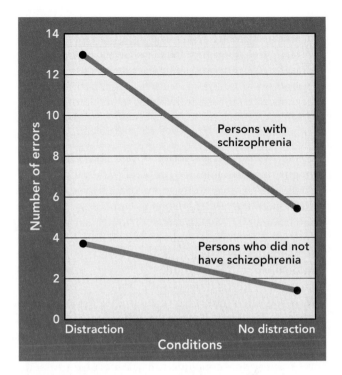

FIGURE 12.3 Distraction resulted in more errors by persons with schizophrenia than by persons who did not have the disorder.
Source: Data from Lawson et al. (1967), p. 529, tab. 2.

the trials, a male experimenter read irrelevant (distracting) numbers while the female read the test numbers. On the other trials, irrelevant numbers were not read. The most important aspect of the findings is that the reading of irrelevant numbers had a more deleterious effect on the performance of individuals with schizophrenia, an effect that is probably attributable to the fact that they could not screen out the distracting irrelevant numbers. Although we cannot be sure, the fact that the individuals with schizophrenia did less well than normal individuals even when they were not intentionally being distracted is probably due to the fact that they were distracted by other stimuli in the situation. The performance of the individuals who did and did not have schizophrenia is presented graphically in Figure 12.3.

In summary, both clinical and experimental evidence indicates that the poor intellectual performance associated with schizophrenia is due to the fact that individuals with the disorder are unable to filter out irrelevant stimuli, and those stimuli disrupt thought processes.

Cognitive Intrusions, Distraction, and Language Problems

Another symptom of schizophrenia is that language is often garbled and distorted. To explain that, cognitive theorists suggest that individuals with schizophrenia are constantly being *distracted by interfering and irrelevant thoughts,* and therefore the individuals jump from thought to thought. Those transitions between thoughts are not obvious to the listener, and hence the sentences of disturbed individuals seem chaotic. In the following sections, I will explain how those distractions might occur.

Unusual Word Associations. Originally, researchers thought that the language problems exhibited by individuals with schizophrenia occurred because the individuals had *different meanings or associations for words* than normal individuals did. Obviously, serious communication problems would arise if people had different meanings for the words they were using. To test that possibility, lists of stimulus words were read to individuals who did or did not suffer from schizophrenia, and it was their task to give their first association to each stimulus word. The results indicated that the associations of individuals with schizophrenia were *less common* than the associations of other persons, and therefore it was widely concluded that associative problems lay at the base of schizophrenia (Kent & Rosanoff, 1910; Moran, 1953; Moran et al., 1964; Murphy, 1923; Shakow & Jellinek, 1965).

 too bright?

Unfortunately, the early investigations did not contain controls to ensure that the stimulus words were correctly heard or understood. That was a serious omission because in later research it was found that individuals with schizophrenia were more likely to *misunderstand* the stimulus words than normal individuals. (Perhaps stimulus overload was causing interference.) When procedures were introduced to ensure that everyone was responding to the same stimulus, there were no differences between the associations of individuals who did or did not have schizophrenia (Lang & Luoto, 1962; Moran et al., 1964; Pavy, 1968). In light of those findings, it does not appear that the language problems associated with schizophrenia can be attributed to unusual word associations.

Associative Intrusions. A better explanation for the language problems is that they stem from an *inability to maintain attention and from the consequent intrusion of irrelevant thoughts* (Chapman et al., 1964, 1984; Maher, 1983). That is, when constructing sentences, an individual may have lapses in attention during which other thoughts intrude, causing the individual to "spin off" and begin dealing with the new thoughts. These intrusions are due to the individual's *associations* with the words being used, and therefore the problems are said to be due to **associative intrusions.** In the following paragraphs, I will describe four types of associative intrusions.

1. *Semantic Intrusions.* The first is a **semantic intrusion** in which *an alternative meaning for a particular word*

introduces a new thought. All of us have more than one association for many of the words we use. Examples of common words with multiple meanings are *rare, diamond, corn, bat, tip, yard,* and *pit.* Each of these words has a strong association (the first or most common association) and at least one weak association (the second or third most common association). For example, a strong association for *date* is "an appointment to go out with someone," whereas a weak association is "a fruit from a palm tree." In explaining disordered language, it has been suggested that individuals with schizophrenia are likely to use the *strong association for a word regardless of whether that is the appropriate association.* Consider the following sentence: "When the farmer bought some cattle, he needed a new pen." The word *pen* has two meanings; the strong association is "a writing instrument," and the weak association is "a fenced-in enclosure." *usually for pigs, cows stay in a corral* If you pay attention to the context in which the word *pen* was used in the sentence, you will realize that in this case the weak association, "fenced-in enclosure," is the correct association. However, individuals with schizophrenia are likely to ignore the context and use the strong association for the word *pen,* "writing instrument" (Chapman et al., 1964). *So am I!*

It is easy to see how problems in communication can arise when one individual uses the word *pen* to indicate a fenced-in enclosure and another individual responds and talks about a writing instrument. The individual who responded with the situationally wrong association would probably be judged to have a thought disorder.

Problems can also arise in constructing sentences because an individual with schizophrenia might start out using one meaning for a word but then get distracted and complete the sentence using another meaning. In the case of the word *pen,* the sentence might be "The cattle were in the pen, which I put in my shirt pocket."

2. *Thought Content Intrusion.* A second type of associative intrusion involves a **thought content intrusion.** That occurs when *a word reminds the individual of a different topic, which then intrudes.* For example, an individual may be telling a story about a particular cat, but in mentioning the topic of cats, the individual thinks of another story about another cat and in midsentence launches off into that story without making the transition clear.

3. *Clang Intrusions.* A third type of associational intrusion is based on the *sound* of the word, and these are called **clang associations.** Examples of clang associations include *bang* and *fang, dog* and *bog,* and *heed* and *deed.* In the process of constructing the sentence "When I saw the clown, I began to laugh," the individual with schizophrenia might get to the word *clown* and think of the word *down* and then complete the sentence with a phrase involving the word *down,* such as "Jack fell down and broke his crown and Jill came tumbling after." The resulting sentence might be "When I saw the clown, Jack fell down and broke his crown," which does not make sense.

The disrupting effects of clang associations are obvious in the following statement by a patient suffering from schizophrenia:

> Oh you can have all the keys you want, they broke into the store and found peas, what's the use of keys, policeman, watchman, dogs, dog shows, the spaniel was the best dog this year, he is Spanish you know, Morrow castle what a big key they have Sampson, Schley, he drowned them all in the bay, gay, New York bay, Broadway, the White Way, etc. (Bleuler, 1936)

4. *Habit Strength Intrusions.* Fourth, there are **habit strength intrusions.** Certain words or phrases are frequently used together, and if one word or phrase is used, an individual is likely to think of and then use the word or phrase that is habitually associated with it. For example, in answering the question "Who was living at home?" an individual with schizophrenia who had a strong Christian background might say, "The father, the son, and the Holy Ghost." The phrase "the Holy Ghost" intruded because in Christian religious services, "the Holy Ghost" often follows "The Father, the Son." Other examples might be drawn from phrases in commercials that we hear over and over or from familiar clichés. For example, when you hear the following phrases, what are you likely to think of? *A penny for . . .* [your thoughts]. *You can't have your cake . . .* [and eat it too]. *When it rains, . . .* [it pours]. If a sentence contained one of these phrases and you were not attending carefully, you might complete the sentence with the words that are frequently associated with the phrase rather than with words that are appropriate.

Because there are different types of associational intrusions and a large number of potential associations of each type, a great many intrusions can appear in any given sentence. Thus in any one sentence, it is very difficult to understand where an individual with schizophrenia has gone wrong in terms of associations.

If it is true that the language problems seen in schizophrenia are due to associative intrusions, it must be asked why those intrusions occur. Cognitive theorists suggest that the intrusions stem from the interaction of two factors: *momentary lapses in attention* and *cognitive flooding*, which provides the individual with numerous competing stimuli, each of which may be accompanied by associations.

Two lines of evidence support the idea that lapses in attention lead to the intrusions that disrupt the language of individuals with schizophrenia. First, *intrusions are most likely to occur at transition points in sentences* (at commas, the ends of sentences, or other pauses) where attention would be most likely to lapse. It is probably because intrusions occur at the ends of phrases that any

one phrase in a sentence makes sense but the phrases do not fit together. Second, in the thought processes and speech patterns of normal individuals, *intrusions are most likely to occur when attentiveness is lessened.* For example, normal individuals are more likely to come up with disjointed and irrelevant thoughts "out of the blue" when they are tired, especially relaxed, just waking up, or bored.

Two final points should be made concerning language problems associated with schizophrenia. First, it is important to recognize that the content of the intrusion may be related to something in the individual's background, but *that background factor is not the cause of the intrusion or the schizophrenia.* For example, the associative intrusion of "the Holy Ghost" following the phrase "the father, the son" may indicate that the individual comes from a Christian background, but it does not indicate that issues or conflicts associated with religion are the basis of the schizophrenia. Therefore, understanding the content of the intrusion will not lead to an understanding of the schizophrenia. This position is very different from that of the traditional psychodynamic theorists, who see symbolic significance in the content of the language of individuals with schizophrenia.

The second point to be noted is that *the processes that result in language problems in individuals with schizophrenia are no different from those that lead to errors or mistakes in the language of normal individuals.* In other words, the errors made by disturbed individuals are not unique; they are simply more extreme or more frequent errors of the types made by normal individuals (Cohen & Servan-Schreiber, 1992; Hoffman, 1992).

COMMENT

The cognitive explanations seem to deal effectively with a wide variety of the symptoms that are exhibited in schizophrenia. Furthermore, the principles on which the explanations are based are rooted in broadly accepted scientific research. However, cognitive explanations have two major limitations. First, *they do not explain why individuals with schizophrenia have different sensory experiences and are more distractible than normal individuals,* and therefore they do not provide an explanation for the factors that are thought to underlie the disorder. In other words, the cognitive theory explains the process that leads to the symptoms, but it does not explain what started the process.

The second limitation is that although the cognitive theory can account for positive symptoms such as hallucinations and delusions, it does not account for negative symptoms such as flat mood, poverty of speech, and apathy. As it stands, then, cognitive explanations are incomplete. They provide parts of the puzzle of schizophrenia, but we will have to look elsewhere for other pieces. Next I will examine the physiological explanations.

PHYSIOLOGICAL EXPLANATIONS

There are four major physiological explanations for schizophrenia:

1. Excessively *high levels of neurological activity* in some areas of the brain serve to disrupt cognitive activity and thereby result in the positive symptoms of schizophrenia such as disturbed thought processes and hallucinations.

2. Excessively *low levels of neurological activity* in some areas of the brain serve to retard cognitive activity and thereby result in the negative symptoms of schizophrenia such as poverty of speech and apathy.

3. *Structural abnormalities in the brain* (malformations, damage, deterioration) serve to retard cognitive activity and thereby result in the negative symptoms of schizophrenia.

4. The problems with neurological activity and brain structure are due to *genetic factors and biological traumas* (problems during prenatal development and birth).

The links between the various physiological explanations and between those explanations and various symptoms are illustrated in Figure 12.4. I will examine the evidence for each of these explanations in the following sections.

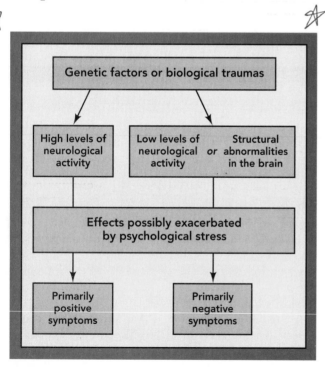

FIGURE 12.4 Sequence of physiological causes in the development of schizophrenia.

Positive Symptoms:
High Neurological Activity in the Brain

It is widely agreed that *high levels of neurological activity in the brain cause many of the symptoms of schizophrenia* and that the crucial neurological activity occurs primarily in the areas of the brain where the major neurotransmitter is **dopamine** (Davis et al., 1991). In other words, high dopamine activity leads to high neurological arousal in certain areas of the brain, and those high levels of neurological activity disrupt cognitive functioning and cause some of the symptoms of schizophrenia.

Effects of Decreasing Dopamine Activity. The first evidence that links high levels of dopamine activity to schizophrenia comes from the finding that a group of drugs called **neuroleptics** (NOO-rō-LEP-tiks) that *reduce dopamine activity* also *reduce the symptoms of schizophrenia* (see Chapter 13). In other words, because neuroleptics reduce dopamine activity and reduce the symptoms of schizophrenia, researchers believe that high levels of dopamine activity result in the symptoms of schizophrenia. Further support for the relationship between dopamine and schizophrenia is provided by the finding that in most cases, the neuroleptics that are most effective for blocking dopamine activity are also those that are most effective for reducing schizophrenic symptoms (Carlsson, 1978; Horn & Snyder, 1971; Snyder, 1976).

Effects of Increasing Dopamine Activity. The second evidence for the dopamine explanation comes from the finding that drugs that *increase dopamine levels increase schizophrenic symptoms.* For example, it is known that amphetamines and cocaine increase dopamine levels and have the effect of causing schizophrenic symptoms in normal individuals and exacerbating symptoms in individuals who are already suffering from schizophrenia (Angrist et al., 1974; Baker, 1991; Griffith et al., 1972; Janowsky et al., 1973; Satel & Edell, 1991; Satel et al., 1991; Snyder, 1976).

In that regard, it is interesting to note that the drug **L-dopa** (dihydroxyphenylalanine), which is used to treat **Parkinson's disease,** can also result in the symptoms of schizophrenia. The reasons for the relationships between Parkinson's disease, L-dopa, dopamine, and schizophrenia are as follows. Parkinson's disease involves muscle tremors that stem from low levels of dopamine in the area of the brain (the *basal ganglia*) that is responsible for motor movements. L-dopa is used to treat Parkinson's disease because in the body L-dopa is converted into dopamine, thus increasing the level of dopamine and reducing the muscle tremors. Unfortunately, however, the increase in dopamine is not limited to the area of the brain that is responsible for motor movements, and the increase of dopamine in the other areas of the brain results in

low dop (Parkinsons) → use L-dopa to ↑dop. → schizo symp.

Parkinsons: Schizophrenia on a continuum

schizophrenic symptoms. Conversely, the use of drugs that reduce schizophrenia by reducing dopamine can have the effect of causing Parkinsonian symptoms (see Chapter 13).

Effects of the Number of Dopamine Receptors.

Third, there is also evidence that some individuals who suffer from schizophrenia have *more dopamine receptors than other people* (Hietala et al., 1994; Wong et al., 1986). The higher level of dopamine receptors would be expected to result in more dopamine activity because with more receptors, it is more likely that one of the receptors will get stimulated. Related to this, it is interesting to note that in men the number of dopamine receptors declines sharply between the ages of 30 and 50, whereas in women the decline is somewhat less dramatic (Wong et al., 1984). The more rapid decline of dopamine receptors in men than women may account for the fact that men are more likely to remit their symptoms earlier than women. In other words, not only do individuals with schizophrenia have more dopamine receptors, but decreases in the numbers of receptors also appear to be consistent with decreases in symptomology. The relationship between age and dopamine receptors is illustrated in Figure 12.5.

Effects of Increasing Serotonin Activity.

There is now evidence that the neurotransmitter **serotonin** can also play a role in increasing the neurological arousal that leads to schizophrenia (Meltzer, Bastani, Kwon, et al., 1989; Pickar et al., 1991; Spoont, 1992). In areas of the brain where dopamine is a major neurotransmitter,

serotonin serves to *inhibit neurological activity*, so if serotonin levels are too low, there will not be enough inhibition of dopamine activity, and neurological activity will become too high (Jenner et al., 1983; see discussion of inhibitory neurons in Chapter 2). By itself, a low level of serotonin is probably not sufficient to lead to schizophrenia, but in some cases, a low level of serotonin may combine with a high level of dopamine to cause or exacerbate schizophrenia.

Evidence for the role of serotonin in schizophrenia comes from the fact that a group of drugs called **atypical neuroleptics** that reduce dopamine activity and increase serotonin activity can be more effective for treating schizophrenia than regular neuroleptics that only reduce dopamine activity (see Chapter 13). That is, increasing serotonin levels adds to the treatment effect, indicating that serotonin plays a role. There is also evidence that taking neuroleptics in combination with antidepressant drugs such as Prozac that increase serotonin activity can be more effective for reducing the symptoms of schizophrenia than taking neuroleptics alone (Brancato et al., 1994).

It is essential to recognize that the presence of schizophrenic symptoms is related to neurological activity in the areas of the brain in which dopamine is the neurotransmitter *but not to activity in general.* This is attested to by the fact that drugs that increase and decrease dopamine-related activity are associated with increases and decreases in symptoms, but drugs that increase and decrease general activity are not associated with changes in symptomology. For example, using caffeine to increase general arousal in mildly disturbed patients does not exacerbate their symptoms, and using barbiturates to decrease their general arousal does not decrease their symptoms (Angrist & Gershon, 1970; Angrist et al., 1973).

How High Neurological Activity Leads to Symptoms.

The question that now arises is, how does the high level of dopamine activity lead to the symptoms of schizophrenia? To answer that question, it is essential to understand that there is an area of the brain that produces neurological activity and that dopamine is the major neurotransmitter in the nerve tracts that link that area to three other areas in the brain where behaviors related to the symptoms of schizophrenia can be produced. In other words, the nerve tracts in which dopamine is the neurotransmitter provide the crucial links between a source of neurological activity and the areas of the brain where high levels of neurological activity can cause symptoms. Therefore, if those nerve tracts are very easily activated because of the high levels of dopamine, the activity from the activity-producing area is very likely to be transmitted to the symptom-related areas, possibly overstimulating those areas and causing the symptoms of schizophrenia. The part of the

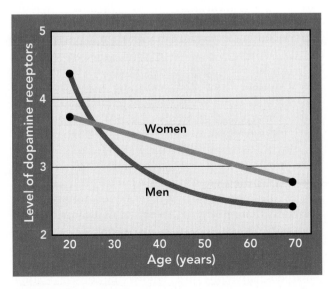

FIGURE 12.5 Dopamine receptors decline more rapidly with age in men than in women.
Source: Adapted from Wong et al. (1984), p. 1394, fig. 3.

how is external stimulation (memory) "saved" in matter???

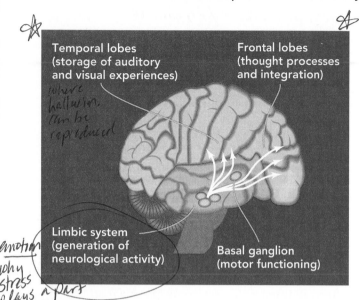

where hallucin. can be reproduced

Temporal lobes (storage of auditory and visual experiences)

Frontal lobes (thought processes and integration)

Limbic system (generation of neurological activity)

emotion
why stress plays a part

Basal ganglion (motor functioning)

FIGURE 12.6 Dopamine is a neurotransmitter in nerve tracts that lead from the limbic system to the frontal lobes, temporal lobes, and basal ganglia of the brain.

brain that generates the neurological activity is the *limbic system,* and the activity is conducted to the *frontal lobes,* the *temporal lobes,* and the *basal ganglia.* Those parts and the dopamine-related nerve tracts are illustrated in Figure 12.6. In the following paragraphs, I will discuss the parts of the brain in this system and explain how they are related to the production of the symptoms of schizophrenia.

The Limbic System. The **limbic system** is a set of structures in the midbrain that are *involved in emotions* and that can *generate neurological activity.* The activity that is generated by the limbic system is crucial because the dopamine-related nerve tracts originate there and then carry activity up to other areas of the brain. The fact that the limbic system is involved with emotion is relevant because that may explain why stress can exacerbate the symptoms of schizophrenia; that is, during stress, even more activity is generated that can be conducted to the other areas of the brain.

The Frontal Lobes. The **frontal lobes** are *where thought processes occur and are integrated.* That is important because if the frontal lobes are overstimulated by arousal from the limbic system, *thought processes will be disrupted,* and that could lead to the disturbed cognitive processes evident in schizophrenia. Specifically, the problems with associations and interference that contribute to the positive symptoms of schizophrenia may be due to overactivity of the frontal lobes.

The Temporal Lobes. The **temporal lobes** are *where memories for auditory and visual experiences are stored.* (These memories can be of *real* experiences or of *thoughts* that involve sights and sounds.) The storage of perceptual memories in the temporal lobes is

important because if the temporal lobes are overstimulated, *random perceptual memories could be activated,* and that could result in hallucinations. To understand how that could occur, a little background might be helpful.

It is generally assumed that each perceptual memory is stored in a group of cells in the temporal lobes and that when the group of cells is stimulated, the perception will be reproduced (Hebb, 1949). The storage and reproduction of perceptual memories was demonstrated in a series of studies in which investigators opened up the skulls of humans and then electrically stimulated specific areas of the temporal lobe (Penfield, 1955; Penfield & Perot, 1963). The stimulation resulted in immediate, clear, and specific perceptual experiences. For example, when one point in the temporal lobe of a young man was stimulated, he said, "Oh, gee, gosh, robbers are coming at me with guns" (Penfield & Perot, 1963, p. 616). When the stimulation was applied to another point, the young man reported hearing his mother talking. For this young man, both visual and auditory hallucinations could be produced with simple electrical stimulation. In the case of a young woman, when stimulation was applied at one point, she said, "I hear singing. . . . Yes, it is 'White Christmas,'" and when stimulation was applied at another point, she reported, "That is different, a voice—talking—a man . . . a man's voice—talking" (p. 618). In both cases, when the stimulation was applied at the same points some time later, the same perceptions were reproduced. *how is external stimulation "saved" in matter?*

From the foregoing discussion it is clear that by electrically stimulating areas of the temporal lobe, it is possible to produce hallucinations—perceptual experiences that do not have a basis in reality. Analogously, then, it may be that the excessive and erratic stimulation of the temporal lobes by the dopamine-related nerves coming from the limbic system are responsible for the hallucinations that occur in schizophrenia.

Two other findings are relevant here. First, from investigations using PET scans, we know that when patients who suffer from schizophrenia have hallucinations, they show high levels of neurological activity in the temporal lobes (McCarley et al., 1994; Silbersweig et al., 1995). Furthermore, reducing those levels of activity with drugs reduces the hallucinations. Clearly, high activity in the temporal lobes is related to hallucinations. *r/. hallucinathr*

Second, we know that a variety of nonpsychiatric disorders that involve high levels of neurological activity in the temporal lobes can also involve hallucinations (Anderson & Rizzo, 1994). For example, individuals who suffer from **temporal lobe epilepsy** often experience hallucinations just before the onset of their seizures; that is, they have hallucinations at a time when we know that they are experiencing excessive and erratic neurological activity in the temporal lobes. Similarly, individuals who suffer from a disorder known as

Charles Bonnet syndrome, which is due to problems in the visual pathway in the brain, have very vivid hallucinations but do not have any other psychiatric symptoms (Teunisse et al., 1994). It is noteworthy that individuals with these disorders do not attribute any personal meaning to their hallucinations and do not let their hallucinations affect their lives; the individuals simply recognize that because of a neurological disorder, they sometimes have visual experiences that do not have a basis in reality, and they try to ignore the hallucinations. (Unfortunately, most individuals with schizophrenia do not realize that their hallucinations are neurological artifacts and often attach importance to them.)

Basal Ganglia. The **basal ganglia** are structures in the midbrain that play a crucial role in the *control of motor movements.* Problems with motor movements are not an official symptom of schizophrenia, but many individuals who suffer from schizophrenia show unusual motor movements such as facial grimacing, repetitive hand movements, and sometimes an inability to sit still. Those problems can be explained by the fact that the dopamine-related nerve tracts carry stimulation to the basal ganglia, where the motor movements originate.

In summary, high levels of neurological activity in specific areas of the brain may account for the disturbed thought processes and hallucinations of schizophrenia—the positive symptoms. However, to understand the negative symptoms of schizophrenia, we must examine the roles played by low levels of neurological activity and structural abnormalities in the brain.

Negative Symptoms: Low Neurological Activity in the Brain

For some years it has been suspected that the cognitive deficit that is characteristic of schizophrenia (e.g., poverty of thought and language, apathy) might be due to *excessively low levels of neurological activity in the frontal lobes of the brain,* where thought processes are developed. This explanation is referred to as the **hypofrontality hypothesis,** and a variety of investigations have provided support for it (e.g., Berman et al., 1992; Buchsbaum et al., 1992; Wolkin et al., 1992; see review by Andreasen et al., 1992). For example, in one study, the investigators used PET scans to measure brain activity (metabolism) in individuals who were or were not suffering from schizophrenia (Buchsbaum et al., 1992). Measurements were made while the individuals worked on a challenging cognitive task in which they had to watch numbers that appeared briefly every 2 seconds and then push a button every time a zero appeared. The results revealed that the individuals with schizophrenia had lower levels of activity in the frontal lobes. Those effects are illustrated in Figure 12.7, where you will notice that in the brains of the individuals with schizophrenia (bottom row), the frontal lobes are less "lit up" (activity is indicated by lighter colors)

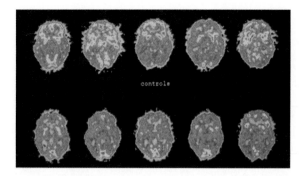

FIGURE 12.7 Some individuals with schizophrenia *(bottom row)* show low levels of neurological activity in their frontal lobes. (Activity is highest in the yellow and red areas.)
Source: From "Frontostriatal Disorder of Cerebral Metabolism in Never-Medicated Schizophrenics" by M. S. Buchsbaum et al., in *Archives of General Psychiatry,* Vol. 49, December 1992. Reprinted by permission of the American Medical Society.

than those of normal individuals (top row). Similar effects have been reported by other investigators using different techniques, and in some studies it was found that the reduced frontal lobe activity was found primarily in individuals with negative symptoms (e.g., Andreasen et al., 1992; Wolkin et al., 1992).

One particularly interesting investigation was done using twins who were concordant (both twins had the disorder) or discordant (only one twin had the disorder) for schizophrenia (Berman et al., 1992). The results indicated that only the member of the twin pair who suffered from schizophrenia showed lower levels of neurological activity. Finally, some indirect evidence for the hypofrontality explanation comes from the fact that neuroleptics (drugs that *reduce* activity) are *not* effective for reducing negative symptoms. Indeed, those drugs often cause side effects that are like the negative symptoms (flat affect, lack of motivation). Thus there is consistent evidence that low levels of neurological activity in the frontal lobes are linked to the negative symptoms of schizophrenia.

Structural Abnormalities in the Brain

Another explanation for the symptoms of schizophrenia involves **structural abnormalities of the brain.** Malformation, damage, or deterioration could result in abnormalities that could interfere with brain activity, and as early as 1919, Kraepelin (1919/1971) cited cerebral lesions as a cause of dementia praecox. Since then, numerous investigators have pointed to the similarities between some of the negative symptoms of schizophrenia and the symptoms of other disorders such as general paresis and encephalitis that are known to stem from structural abnormalities. In the following sections, I will discuss five structural problems in the brain that are linked to schizophrenia.

Enlarged Ventricles. Going through the brain from front to back are canals through which cerebrospinal fluid flows and wastes are drained away. Those canals are called **ventricles,** and there is now strong evidence that between 20% and 50% of the individuals who suffer from schizophrenia have **enlarged ventricles;** that is, their ventricles have become wider (Andreasen et al., 1982; Degreef et al., 1992; Flaum et al., 1995). Enlarged and normal lateral ventricles are depicted in the MRI scans presented in Figure 12.8. There are three ventricles: one *lateral ventricle* on each side of the brain and a *third ventricle* that goes through the center of the brain. The greatest widening is usually found in the third (center) ventricle (Raz & Raz, 1990). That is of interest because it is believed that when schizophrenia is due to structural abnormalities in the brain, the problems appear first in the center and then extend to the lateral areas only in the more severe cases (Weinberger, 1987).

The significance of the enlarged ventricles probably lies in the fact that as the ventricles get larger, *brain mass is reduced,* and the reduced brain mass then influences brain functioning. In other words, enlarged ventricles are not important themselves, but they reflect a loss of neurons that may be important.

Enlarged ventricles are more closely associated with negative symptoms (poverty of speech, flat mood, inability to experience pleasure, apathy) than with pos-

itive symptoms (Andreasen et al., 1982; Johnstone et al., 1976; Pearlson et al., 1989; Seidman, 1983). They are also more prominent in males, which is consistent with the finding that males are more likely to have negative symptoms than females.

Unfortunately, we do not yet understand what causes the enlargement of the ventricles. However, it is probably due to a general process of **atrophy** (AT-ruh-fē), which is a general *loss or deterioration of the nerve cells.* (The word *atrophy* means "wasting away, progressive decline, degeneration.") That is, as the brain cells are lost, the ventricles become larger. The progressive nature of the atrophy is reflected in the fact that individuals with greater ventricle widening have suffered from schizophrenia longer and been hospitalized longer than individuals with less widening.

Cortical Atrophy. Atrophy is not limited to the ventricles; it also affects the cortex of the brain. **Cortical atrophy** can be seen in the widening of the grooves (*sulci*) covering the cerebral cortex, in the enlargement of the clefts (*fissures*) between parts of the brain, and in the general deterioration of the surface of the brain. Obviously, a loss of cells in the cortex could have serious implications for functioning because the cortex is where higher mental processes are carried out. Cortical atrophy appears to characterize the brains of 20% to 35% of the individuals with schizophrenia, and it is also most likely to be found in chronic patients with negative symptoms.

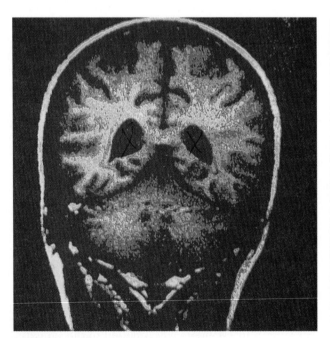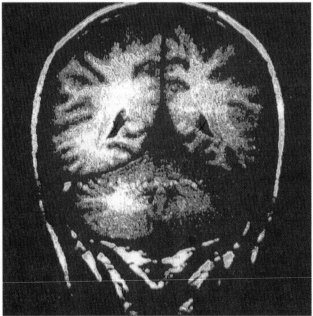

FIGURE 12.8 Some individuals with schizophrenia have enlarged ventricles *(left)* relative to normal individuals *(right).*

Source: From "Brain Imaging: Applications in Psychiatry" by N. C. Andreasen, in *Science Magazine,* March 1988. Reprinted by permission from *Science Magazine.* Copyright © 1988 by American Association for the Advancement of Science.

Subcortical Atrophy. Originally, most attention was focused on atrophy in the ventricles and cortex of the brain, but there is now evidence that individuals with schizophrenia also show atrophy in various structures inside the brain beneath the cortex (Arnold et al., 1995; Bloom, 1993; Breier et al., 1992; Flaum et al., 1995; Zipursky et al., 1992). This **subcortical atrophy** has been found in three crucial subcortical areas, the first of which is the **hippocampus.** The hippocampus is responsible for *information processing* (storing information in long-term memory), and hence damage there could contribute to the intellectual deficit and negative symptoms of schizophrenia. Second, there is evidence of atrophy in the **thalamus,** which is *where incoming information is screened.* Problems there could interfere with incoming information. Third, atrophy has been found in the **amygdala,** which is an area that in normal individuals plays a role in *emotional arousal* and *assertiveness,* both of which are lacking in patients with negative symptoms. Thus subcortical atrophy can lead to problems with screening and processing of information and with emotional arousal, and those problems can lead to the negative symptoms of schizophrenia.

Before concluding this discussion of brain atrophy, I should point out that the brain damage in individuals with schizophrenia is often very subtle and not detectable by direct examination. That was demonstrated in an investigation in which individuals who did and did not suffer from schizophrenia were given tests that involved the "soft signs" of neurological damage. (Soft signs of damage involve, for example, tests of coordination such as trying to bring your index fingers together at arms' length while keeping your eyes closed.) The results indicated that 23% of the individuals who had schizophrenia showed soft signs of neurological damage, whereas none of the individuals who did not have schizophrenia showed signs of such damage (Gupta et al., 1995; see also Sanders et al., 1994). Those differences were found with individuals who had never been on medication for schizophrenia, so the differences cannot be blamed on the effects of drugs. Clearly, brain deterioration and damage are associated with schizophrenia, primarily the negative symptoms.

Failure of Neural Migration. As your brain develops, *neurons move from one area to another,* and *neurons grow so that connections can be made with other neurons in other parts of your brain.* In general, neurons appear to move and reach from lower to higher areas of the brain. This process is called **neural migration.** The failure of neural migration would have serious consequences because there would not be enough of the right neurons in the right places, and connections among areas would not be made.

There is now evidence that in many individuals who suffer from schizophrenia, *neural migration was retarded* (Akbarian, Bunney, et al., 1993; Akbarian, Vinuela, et al., 1993; Cannon et al., 1995; Selemon et al., 1995). When compared to normal individuals, individuals with schizophrenia have fewer neurons in the gray matter of the cortex than in the white matter that lies beneath the cortex. That is particularly true in the frontal and temporal lobes. It appears that in schizophrenia, the cells have not migrated up.

Related to the migration of neurons from the white matter up to the gray matter, it has been found that in the brains of individuals with schizophrenia, a type of neuron that is responsible for producing an enzyme that aids in neurotransmission tends to be located in the white matter rather than in the gray matter of the cortex, whereas the reverse is true in the brains of individuals who do not have schizophrenia (Akbarian, Bunney, et al., 1993; Akbarian, Vinuela, et al., 1993). Apparently, those neurons did not migrate up, and the relative absence of that type of neuron would reduce the activity level (neurotransmission) in the cortex, which in turn would lead to the negative symptoms of schizophrenia.

Finally, with regard to neural migration, in a recent comparison of the brains of individuals who had either schizophrenia, the bipolar disorder, or no disorder, it was found that the individuals with schizophrenia had *smaller amounts of gray matter (cortex) in an area of the frontal lobes* (the *heteromodal association area*) where input from different areas (e.g., sensory, motor) are integrated (Schlaepfer et al., 1994). The reduced amount of gray matter may have been due to a lack of neural migration; such a reduction in that particular area of the brain would impair an individual's ability to "put things together" and could therefore greatly diminish the individual's ability to function. So it now appears that problems with neural migration may play a role in the development of schizophrenia, especially the negative symptoms (Bloom, 1993).

Reversed Cerebral Asymmetry. In normal individuals, the left side of the brain tends to be larger than the right side, but in some individuals with schizophrenia, *the right side of the brain tends to be larger than the left side.* That is called **reversed cerebral asymmetry.** Furthermore, the enlarged ventricles that were discussed earlier are more likely to be on the left side (Suddath et al., 1990). The finding that many individuals with schizophrenia have problems on the left side of the brain is relevant for understanding their symptoms because different cognitive functions tend to be located on one side of the brain or the other. For example, *language function is on the left side of the brain,* so damage on that side could lead to the poverty of language often exhibited in schizophrenia. Indeed, the reversed cerebral asymmmetry is particularly apparent in the areas of the brain that are responsible for language, and the degree to which the asymmetry was reversed was related to the severity of the language problems (Petty et al., 1995; Yokoyama et al., 1993).

From the foregoing discussions, it should be clear that the symptoms of schizophrenia are due to high and low levels of neurological activity and to structural problems in the brain (enlarged ventricles, atrophy, neural migration, reversed cerebral asymmetry). The question that then arises is, what causes the problems with the activity and structures in the brain? Those problems are apparently due to *genetic factors* and to *biological traumas* such as problems during fetal development and problems during the birth process (Cannon et al., 1993, 1995). In the following sections, I will discuss the roles of genetics and biological traumas in schizophrenia.

Genetic Factors

Studies of Families. Numerous studies have been conducted to determine whether schizophrenia tends to run in families. The results of some of those studies are summarized in Table 12.1, from which it can be concluded that the prevalence of schizophrenia in the rela-

TABLE 12.1 Schizophrenia Risk: Higher for Individuals with Relatives Who Suffer from the Disorder

	Risk (%)
Children of two parents suffering from schizophrenia	40–68
Children with one parent suffering from schizophrenia	9–16
Parent of a person suffering from schizophrenia	5–10
Nontwin siblings of a person suffering from schizophrenia	8–14
Grandchildren of a person suffering from schizophrenia	2–8
Stepsiblings of a person suffering from schizophrenia	1–8
Half siblings of a person suffering from schizophrenia	1–7
Cousins of a person suffering from schizophrenia	2–6
Nieces and nephews of a person suffering from schizophrenia	1–4

Source: Zerbin-Rudin (1972).

tives of individuals with schizophrenia is higher than in the general population. Furthermore, it can also be concluded that the closer the biological relationship to the afflicted individual, the higher the prevalence of schizophrenia. For example, the concordance rate among siblings is between 8% and 14%, whereas the concordance rate among cousins is only 2% to 6%. It is also noteworthy that the prevalence of schizophrenia among individuals who had two parents with the disorder (40% to 68%) is substantially higher than among individuals who had only one parent with the disorder (9% to 16%). Clearly, the greater the degree to which an individual shares genes with a person who suffers from schizophrenia, the higher the likelihood that the individual will develop the disorder.

In addition to the data linking schizophrenia in parents to schizophrenia in their offspring, there are also data linking schizophrenia in parents to the physiological processes that lead to some of the symptoms of schizophrenia in the offspring. For example, in Chapter 11, I pointed out that individuals with schizophrenia suffer from *cognitive flooding* because they cannot physiologically "close the gate" on incoming stimuli, and there is now evidence that the adolescent offspring of individuals with schizophrenia lack that same ability despite the fact that they do not yet suffer from schizophrenia (Hollister et al., 1994). Specifically, adolescents were identified who either had (a) two parents who suffered from schizophrenia, (b) one parent who suffered from schizophrenia, or (c) no parent who suffered from schizophrenia. All of the adolescents were presented with a series of tones that were followed by rest periods, during which the number of bursts of *electrodermal activity* were measured. (Electrodermal activity reflects the amount of moisture on the hands, and brief increases in moisture reflect responses to internal and external stimulation.) The results indicated that adolescents whose parents suffered from schizophrenia showed more electrodermal responses during the rest periods than the adolescents whose parents did not suffer from schizophrenia. In other words, the biological children of individuals with schizophrenia showed problems in screening out stimulation despite the fact that they did not yet suffer from schizophrenia. Those findings are presented in Figure 12.9. As an aside, it is interesting to note that in a follow-up of these adolescents, it was found that those who showed the most responsiveness (least ability to screen out stimulation) were most likely to develop schizophrenia later in life.

It is also noteworthy that individuals who are closely related to individuals with schizophrenia often show cognitive problems, although the problems might not be serious enough to qualify as schizophrenia (Docherty, 1994; Park et al., 1995).

These results certainly suggest that there is a genetic basis for schizophrenia. However, because individu-

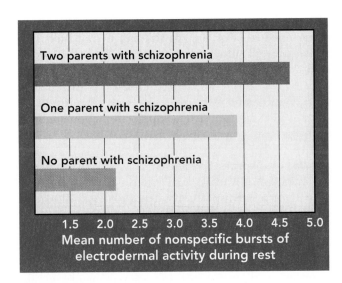

FIGURE 12.9 Children of individuals with schizophrenia showed problems in screening out stimuli.
Source: Adapted from Hollister et al. (1994), p. 556, fig. 1.

als who are more closely related are also more likely to share the same environment, we cannot definitely conclude from these results that there is a genetic basis for schizophrenia. Therefore, we must turn to other types of studies for more definitive data.

Studies of Twins. In the studies of twins, the concordance rate for schizophrenia among dizygotic (DZ) twins is compared to the concordance rate for schizophrenia among monozygotic (MZ) twins. At least 13 studies of this type have been completed, involving more than 600 sets of MZ twins and more than 1,300 sets of DZ twins (see Gottesman, 1991). In every one of

these studies, there was a higher concordance rate among MZ twins than among DZ twins. A typical concordance rate for MZ twins was about 50%, whereas the rate for DZ twins was about 15%. These findings consistently indicate that genetics does play an important role in schizophrenia.

The studies of twins have yielded two other relevant findings. First, the concordance rate for schizophrenia among MZ twins was found to be much higher if one of the twins was severely disturbed rather than only moderately disturbed (Gottesman & Shields, 1972; Kringlen, 1967, 1968; Rosenthal, 1961). Second, when MZ twins are concordant for schizophrenia, both twins tend to show the same types of symptoms. Specifically, in 31 of 34 sets of twins studied, both twins received the same subtype diagnosis (Fischer, 1971, 1973; Gottesman & Shields, 1972; Kringlen, 1967). This suggests not only that schizophrenia is inherited but also that a propensity for a specific set of symptoms may be inherited.

Studies of Adoptees. Evidence for the role of genetic factors has also been provided by studies of adoptees. Four different approaches have been used to study adoptees.

1. *Schizophrenia in adopted children whose biological parents suffered from schizophrenia.* In the first approach to this problem, the investigators compared the rates of schizophrenia in children whose biological parents did or did not have schizophrenia but who had been adopted and raised by normal adoptive parents (Heston, 1966; Rosenthal et al., 1968; Rosenthal et al., 1971). In one study of this type, it was found that among individuals whose biological mothers had schizophrenia, 11%

typical – see chart –

Studies of families and twins have yielded compelling evidence for a genetic basis for schizophrenia. Shown here are the Genain quadruplets; each of the four developed a schizophrenic disorder.

developed schizophrenia, but among those whose biological mothers were normal, none developed schizophrenia (Heston, 1966). (Actually, the rate of schizophrenia among the offspring of mothers with schizophrenia jumps to 16.6% when the data are age-corrected. Age corrections are sometimes used when working with younger subjects who still have time to develop schizophrenia.)

2. *Schizophrenia in the biological and adoptive parents of children with schizophrenia.* In the second approach to studying adoptees, the investigators started with a group of individuals who had been adopted and who were or were not suffering from schizophrenia, and then the investigators determined the rates of schizophrenia among the biological and the adoptive *parents* (Kendler et al., 1982; Kety et al., 1975; Kety et al., 1994). That is, rather than going from parents to children, in this study the analysis went from children to parents. The results indicated that among the persons with long-term schizophrenia, 5% had biological parents who had the disorder, whereas none of their adoptive parents had the disorder. In contrast, among the normal individuals, none of their biological parents had schizophrenia, whereas 1% of their adoptive parents had the disorder. Again the disorder was linked to the biological parents.

3. *Schizophrenia in the Biological and Adoptive Siblings of Children with Schizophrenia.* The third approach to studying adoptees focused on the siblings of six persons with schizophrenia who had been raised in foster homes (Karlsson, 1966). The disturbed individuals had 29 biological siblings who were raised in other foster homes and 28 foster siblings who were raised in the same homes as the children with schizophrenia. When the prevalence of schizophrenia in the biological and foster siblings was determined, it was found that 21% of the biological siblings had the disorder but none of the foster siblings, despite the fact that they had been raised in the same homes as the children with schizophrenia. Clearly, schizophrenia was linked to shared genes and not to shared environments.

4. *Children raised by foster parents who suffered from schizophrenia.* In the last approach, the investigators compared the rates of schizophrenia in individuals who had normal biological parents but had been raised by foster parents who were either normal or were suffering from schizophrenia (Wender et al., 1974). The results revealed essentially the same rates of schizophrenia among individuals who were and were not raised by foster parents with schizophrenia. That is, being raised by a foster parent with schizophrenia did *not* increase the likelihood of developing the disorder, indicating that the disorder is not passed on through a social process.

The results of the studies in which the adoption method was used clearly and consistently indicate that whether or not individuals develop schizophrenia is determined in large part by whether or not their biological parents suffered from schizophrenia and not by environmental factors such as who raised them. Because the adoption method enables us to separate the genetic and environmental effects, the results of these studies provide strong support for a genetic basis for some cases of schizophrenia.

Studies of Disorder Specificity. Now we must consider the question of whether one inherits schizophrenia in specific or a predisposition to psychological disorders in general. To answer that question, investigators examined the disorders developed by children of parents who had schizophrenia or mood disorders. The results indicated that the children tend to develop the same disorder as their parents (Kendler, McGuire et al., 1993a; Ödegärd, 1972; Winokur et al., 1972). For example, in one study, it was found that among disturbed children whose parents suffered from severe cases of schizophrenia, 78% developed schizophrenia and only 14.7% developed a bipolar disorder. In contrast, among the disturbed children of parents with a bipolar disorder, only 19.1% developed schizophrenia and 70.2% developed a bipolar disorder. Those results are summarized in Figure 12.10. Not only do the data indicate a genetic basis for schizophrenia, but they also indicate a high degree of specificity in the relationship. These findings are consistent with those mentioned earlier that indicated that MZ twins who were concordant for schizophrenia were almost always found to suffer from the same type of schizophrenia.

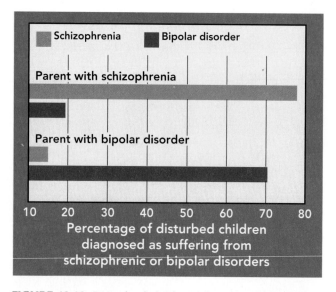

FIGURE 12.10 Disturbed children of parents with schizophrenia developed schizophrenia, and disturbed children of parents with a bipolar disorder developed a bipolar disorder.
Source: Adapted from Ödegärd (1972).

When considering the pattern of heritability, it is clear that the offspring of parents with schizophrenia are more likely to develop schizophrenia than a mood disorder, but it is also clear that they are also more likely to develop one of the "other psychotic disorders" that are related to schizophrenia (e.g., the delusional disorder or the schizophreniform disorder) (Kendler, Walters, et al., 1995; Kendler, Neale, et al., 1995; Parnas et al., 1993). For example, in one study, it was found that 16% of the children of parents with schizophrenia developed schizophrenia, but an additional 19% developed the schizotypal personality disorder that appears to be a mild form of schizophrenia. It appears then that the genes lead not only to schizophrenia but also to the other disorders in the schizophrenia spectrum.

Studies of Specific Genes.

In all of the studies discussed so far, the genetic effect has been determined indirectly by studying relatives who shared genes rather than by studying the genes themselves. However, recent technological advances have made it possible to examine genes directly. Some investigators who used the new technology reported finding a link between a specific gene on chromosome 5 and schizophrenia (Sherrington et al., 1988). That finding was especially intriguing because the gene in question is one of the genes that influence dopamine and dopamine receptors. Unfortunately, other investigators were not able to replicate the finding (Kennedy et al., 1988; Sherrington et al., 1988). Examining specific genes holds out great promise, but the task is exceptionally difficult because not all cases of schizophrenia stem from genetic factors, and in cases in which there is a genetic basis, it is likely that the disorder stems from the complex interaction of a number of genes.

Overall, there is strong evidence that genetic factors play a role in schizophrenia. However, it is important to recognize that *genetic factors do not account for all cases of schizophrenia*. For example, not all of the biological offspring of parents with schizophrenia develop schizophrenia, and there is not a 100% concordance rate for schizophrenia among monozygotic twins. Indeed, genetic factors probably account for less than 10% of the cases of schizophrenia. Does this mean that the genetic explanation is wrong? No, it simply means that genetic factors are only one of the primary causes of schizophrenia. In the next section, we will consider the other major group of primary causes, biological traumas.

Biological Traumas

Another primary cause of schizophrenia appears to be **biological traumas** such as illness or physiological problems during the prenatal or perinatal periods. It may be that those traumas can account for the cases of schizophrenia that cannot be explained by genetic factors.

Prenatal Complications.

The term *prenatal* refers to the time between conception and birth. Recent interest in the link between **prenatal complications** and schizophrenia came from the initially puzzling finding that in the Northern Hemisphere, individuals who later develop schizophrenia are most likely to be born during the month of January, February, or March (see Bradbury & Miller, 1985). This is known as the **season-of-birth effect.** This effect appears to be due to the fact that the mothers had become ill earlier in the winter when the rate of influenza was high, and the illness came during the *second trimester of pregnancy*, a period that is important for fetal brain development. The mothers' illnesses apparently retarded brain development or caused brain damage in the fetuses, and that led to the later development of schizophrenia. In view of that explanation, it is not the season of birth that is important but rather the *time of mothers' illnesses* that is crucial, so the effect might better be called the **second-trimester-illness effect.**

The possibility that schizophrenia is related to exposure to illness during the second trimester of fetal development has been supported by a variety of investigations (Barr et al., 1990; Wright et al., 1995). For example, in a retrospective study that covered 39 years, the investigators identified periods of high, medium, and low rates of influenza in the general population, and then they assessed the rates of schizophrenia in individuals who were born 3 months after each of those periods. The results indicated that schizophrenia was higher for individuals born after periods of high influenza, and the effect was specific to individuals who were in the second trimester of development during the peak influenza period. In this research, it was not possible to determine whether the pregnant women actually had influenza, so an inference about their infections was made based on the elevated rate of infection in the general population at that time. If mothers who actually had an infection could be identified, the correlations would probably be much stronger.

It is clear that the mother's illness influences the brain of the fetus, but we do not understand the underlying process. It is unlikely that the fetus itself becomes infected because the virus probably cannot cross the blood-brain barrier between mother and fetus. However, brain damage might result from *elevations in temperature* because fever accompanies influenza, and it has been shown that increases of only 2.5°C can cause brain damage in mammalian fetuses. The second trimester is particularly important because it is a time when the brain is going through a period of rapid growth and crucial connections between parts of the brain are being established (Jakob & Beckmann, 1986).

Why does damage that occurs in the second trimester of fetal development not result in schizophrenia until 20 or 25 years later? The answer is that the areas of the brain that are affected are normally slow to develop, so the effects of the damage (or nondevelopment) do not become apparent for some time (Weinberger, 1987). The symptoms that do eventually become evident are those that we usually characterize as negative symptoms (Opler et al., 1984).

Before concluding this discussion, it should be noted that (a) the seasonal effect is reversed in the Southern Hemisphere, where winter comes during July, August, and September; (b) the effect will occur during other months if a major influenza epidemic occurs sometime other than during the early winter; and (c) the effect does not hold for other psychiatric disorders such as anxiety and depression (Barr et al., 1990; Bradbury & Miller, 1985; Mednick et al., 1988; Mednick et al., 1990; Torrey et al., 1988; Watson et al., 1984).

Finally, it should be noted that the season-of-birth effect probably accounts for only 5% or 10% of the individuals who suffer from schizophrenia (Takei et al., 1994; Waddington et al., 1992). However, the important point that is illustrated by the season-of-birth effect is that prenatal complications can lead to schizophrenia, and mothers' influenza is undoubtedly only one of many potential complications. For example, it has been reported that extreme food deprivation during the first trimester is linked to schizophrenia later in life (Susser & Lin, 1992). Indeed, there was a substantial increase in schizophrenia among individuals who were in prenatal development during the terrible Dutch hunger during the winter of 1944–1945 (Susser & Lin, 1992). The prob-lem we face is to identify the other prenatal complications, but that is a difficult task because relevant events such as illnesses occurred many years before the onset of the disorder, and usually there is no record of them.

Perinatal Complications. The term *perinatal* refers to the time immediately around birth. **Perinatal complications** include such problems as prolonged or difficult labor, deprivation of oxygen during birth *(anoxia),* and the use of forceps in delivery. The notion here is that perinatal complications may result in brain damage that could later contribute to the development of schizophrenia.

A substantial amount of evidence now links perinatal complications to schizophrenia (Cannon et al., 1989; Kanofsky et al., 1990; Lyons et al., 1989; Machon et al., 1987; Wilcox, 1986; Wilcox & Nasrallah, 1987a, 1987b). In one longitudinal study of individuals who were at high risk for developing schizophrenia (their parents suffered from schizophrenia), it was found that those who developed the disorder were almost twice as likely to have experienced perinatal complications as those who did not develop the disorder (Mednick et al., 1987). In a more recent investigation of individuals with schizophrenia, it was found that those who had experienced perinatal complications such as bleeding, seizures, and hypertension were more likely to have structural abnormalities in the brain and that the relationship was stronger among individuals who did not have a family history of schizophrenia (Kanofsky et al., 1990). In other words, it appears that perinatal complications led to brain damage, which in turn led to schizophrenia, and that perinatal complications may account for schizo-

Complications of a difficult birth may result in brain damage that could later contribute to schizophrenia.

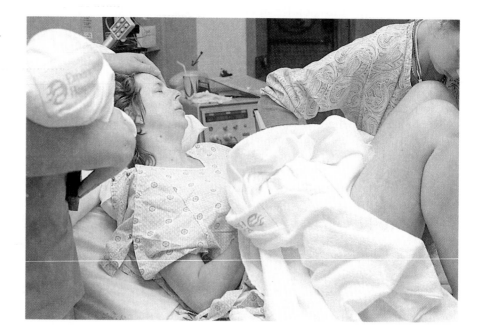

phrenia in cases in which genetics is not a factor (individuals who do not have a family history of the disorder).

In another study that was part of a 40-year follow-up of over 500 individuals with schizophrenia, it was found that those who had not recovered were more likely to have had perinatal complications than those who improved (Wilcox & Nasrallah, 1987a, 1987b). This finding is consistent with the notion that perinatal complications lead to brain damage, which in turn leads to negative symptoms that are more difficult to treat. Clearly, research on prenatal and perinatal complications is providing more of the pieces of the puzzle of schizophrenia.

Diathesis-Stress Hypothesis

A very popular explanation for schizophrenia is that *physiological factors establish a predisposition for schizophrenia, and then environmental stress triggers the symptoms.* In other words, genetic factors place the individual at risk, and then stress factors push the individual over the edge. This is known as the **diathesis-stress hypothesis.** (As explained in Chapter 2, the word *diathesis* means "a constitutional predisposition to a particular state.") The diathesis-stress hypothesis can be illustrated with the following quip: "Humpty Dumpty had a fragile shell, but he didn't break until he fell."

Indirect support for the diathesis-stress explanation comes from the findings that stress can lead to schizophrenia in some but not all individuals. The notion is that the stress triggered the schizophrenia only in individuals who were predisposed to the disorder. Other indirect evidence can be found in the fact that individuals with schizophrenia are more likely to suffer relapses after leaving the hospital if they return to a stressful home environment than if they are released to a nonstressful home environment (see Chapter 13).

However, we must be careful in applying the diathesis-stress explanation because what in some cases appears to be stress leading to a worsening of symptoms may actually be a worsening of symptoms leading to stress. For example, if because of a fluctuation in dopamine levels an individual's symptoms became worse, the individual's ability to function might decline, and he or she might then lose a job. In that case, the stress of the job loss would be associated with the increase in symptoms, but the stress did not increase the symptoms.

The results of one well-known study of children are often cited as evidence for the diathesis-stress hypothesis, but those results are subject to an alternative interpretation, and they deserve comment here (Mednick, Cudeck, et al., 1984). In that study it was found that among the children of parents who suffered from schizophrenia (i.e., children who had a biological predisposition to the disorder), the children who developed schizophrenia were those who experienced more personal stresses. That might be evidence for the diathesis-stress hypothesis, but examination of the stresses indicated that *the stresses were associated with higher levels of abnormality in the parents,* such as the mother's having a psychotic episode. It may be that the children who developed schizophrenia did so because of a greater genetic contribution (their parents were more severely disturbed) rather than because of stress per se. In that regard, recall that the concordance rate for schizophrenia among twins was higher if one of the twins was severely disturbed rather than only moderately disturbed (Gottesman & Shields, 1972; Kringlen, 1967, 1968; Rosenthal, 1961).

Thus a genetic predisposition and stress do appear to interact to result in schizophrenia, but it should not be concluded that stress is necessary. Just as stress levels can fluctuate and affect symptom levels, so physiological factors can fluctuate and affect symptom levels.

COMMENT

In Chapter 11 you learned that schizophrenia is a heterogeneous disorder and that different individuals can suffer from different symptoms. The physiological approach to schizophrenia offers three different explanations (high neurological activity, low neurological activity, structural abnormalities) that can be used to account for the different symptoms. This approach is more comprehensive than the other approaches.

The physiological approach does not conflict with other approaches but rather complements them. Specifically, (a) the role of stress that is emphasized by the psychodynamic approach is incorporated into the diathesis-stress explanation, (b) the high drive that is central to the learning explanations can be understood in terms of excessively high neurological arousal, and (c) the disruptions in cognitive processing (stimulus overload, problems with attention) on which the cognitive approach is focused can be explained by excessively high neurological arousal. Furthermore, the physiological approach provides explanations for negative symptoms, whereas those symptoms are largely ignored by other approaches. Because the physiological approach to schizophrenia is more comprehensive and because the other approaches can be encompassed within it, the physiological approach is becoming the dominant theory for understanding schizophrenia. As we will see later, it also provides the best model for treatment.

WHAT CAN WE CONCLUDE CONCERNING THE CAUSES OF SCHIZOPHRENIA?

After many years of research and after following many blind alleys, it is now clear that schizophrenia is a biological disorder or, more accurately, a group of biological disorders. The symptoms stem from high or low neurological activity in the brain or structural abnormalities in the brain. Those problems appear to be due to genetics or biological traumas such as prenatal and perinatal complications. Although the basis for schizophrenia is biological, that does not mean that psychological factors play no role. Indeed, psychological stress may trigger or exacerbate the disorder in individuals who have a biological predisposition toward it. Also, once an individual has developed the disorder, the symptoms may be strengthened if they lead to rewards such as attention from other people.

SUMMARY

- Psychodynamic explanations for schizophrenia revolve around (a) regression, (b) withdrawal, (c) the disruptive effects of stress, and (d) family influences. Stress can trigger schizophrenia, but it is not a necessary condition, and there is no evidence that the other factors cause schizophrenia. Instead, withdrawal may be an effect of schizophrenia, and disturbed family factors may be a correlate of the disorder.

- Learning theorists posit that schizophrenia is due to (a) high levels of drive that disrupt thought processes, (b) a lack of rewards for normal behavior, (c) rewards for abnormal behavior, and (d) the social role of being "crazy" that comes with being labeled "schizophrenic." Problems with these explanations revolve around the facts that (a) it is not clear why some individuals have high drive, (b) rewards and punishments cannot be used to explain the uncontrollable nature of the symptoms, and (c) the effects of social roles would appear only after the individuals developed some symptoms.

- Cognitive theorists suggest that (a) individuals with schizophrenia have different sensory experiences, (b) delusions stem from attempts to explain the different experiences, and (c) problems with thought processes are due to interfering sensory experiences and distractions. There is evidence to support the effects of those processes, but the cognitive approach does not explain why individuals with schizophrenia have different sensory experiences or why they are more prone to distraction.

- Physiological explanations include (a) high levels of neurological activity that lead to positive symptoms such as disturbed thought processes and (b) low levels of neurological activity that lead to negative symptoms such as apathy. The problems with neurological activity are thought to stem from (a) structural abnormalities in the brain, (b) genetic factors, and (c) biological traumas during prenatal and perinatal development.

- The neurotransmitter on which most attention is focused is dopamine, which is important for carrying arousal to higher areas of the brain. Evidence indicates that increases in dopamine activity lead to increases in positive symptoms of schizophrenia and decreases lead to decreases in symptoms.

- Structural abnormalities in the brain include enlarged ventricles, cortical atrophy, subcortical atrophy, failure of neural migration, and reversed cerebral asymmetry, all of which appear to be related primarily to negative symptoms.

- Evidence for the role of genetic factors comes from studies of families, twins, adoptees, and disorder specificity (similar disorders in related individuals), but genetic factors appear to play a role in only about 10% of cases of schizophrenia.

- There is evidence linking prenatal and perinatal complications to the later development of schizophrenia, probably because the complications disrupt brain development. Prenatal complications can be used to account for the sea-son-of-birth effect.

■ The diathesis-stress hypothesis suggests that physiological factors predispose the individual to the disorder and that the symptoms are triggered by stress. There is some support for that (stress can trigger symptoms or relapses), but stress is not a necessary precursor of schizophrenia.

KEY TERMS, CONCEPTS, AND NAMES

In reviewing and testing yourself on what you have learned from this chapter, you should be able to identify and discuss each of the following.

amygdala
associative intrusions
atrophy
atypical neuroleptics: ↓dop ↑serotonin
basal ganglia
biological traumas
Charles Bonnet syndrome: hallucinations
clang associations
cognitive flooding
cortical atrophy
diathesis-stress hypothesis
distraction
dopamine
double-bind hypothesis
enlarged ventricles
filter mechanism

frontal lobes
habit strength intrusions
hippocampus
hypofrontality hypothesis
L-dopa
limbic system
neural migration
neuroleptics
Parkinson's disease
perinatal complications
prenatal complications
regression
reversed cerebral asymmetry
rewards
schizophrenic deficit
schizophrenogenic mother

season-of-birth effect
second-trimester-illness effect
semantic intrusions
sensory deprivation
serotonin: dop inhibitor
stimulus overload
structural abnormalities of the brain
subcortical atrophy
temporal lobe epilepsy
temporal lobes
thalamus
thought content intrusions
ventricles
withdrawal

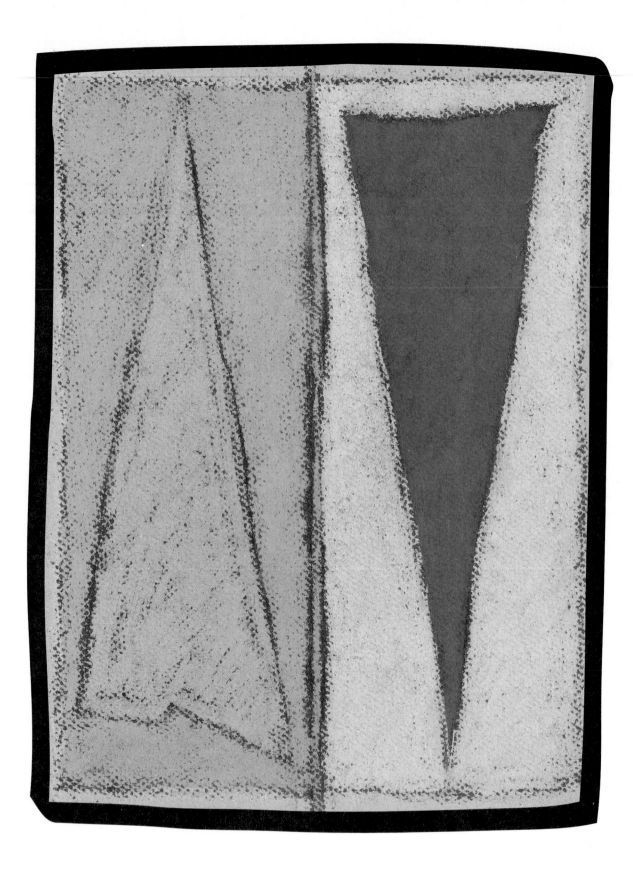

CHAPTER THIRTEEN
SCHIZOPHRENIA and OTHER PSYCHOTIC DISORDERS: TREATMENTS

OUTLINE

Bill was hospitalized with a diagnosis of schizophrenia. Neuroleptic drugs were effective for reducing his symptoms, and he was released from the hospital after three months. Then he and his family participated in family therapy once a week for eight weeks. The therapy involved teaching Bill's family more effective communication and problem-solving skills. The goal of therapy was not to develop any new "insights" about Bill's psychological problems. Instead, it was designed to help his family accept Bill's illness and to foster a less stressful and more supportive environment for him. The therapy seems to have been effective; Bill has been able to remain out of the hospital on a reduced level of medication.

■ ■ ■

Over a period of a few months, Ann became very confused and developed a delusion that all of her coworkers were against her. She thought that they were sabotaging her work at night and putting "contaminants" in her drinking water that made her skin itch so that she would not be able to concentrate. One afternoon, she locked herself in a closet "for protection." She was admitted to a psychiatric hospital and immediately given a neuroleptic drug. During the three weeks that she was in the hospital, her medication was changed twice in an attempt to find the drug that would be most helpful and cause the fewest side effects. Ann is now out of the hospital and back at work, but she is on a maintenance dose of the medication, which is generally effective for holding her symptoms in check. However, sometimes she gets a little suspicious of her colleagues. Although the drug keeps her free of schizophrenic symptoms, its side effects sometimes make her head swim a bit. Because the side effects are somewhat annoying, Ann and her physician try to keep the drug dosage level as low as possible.

■ ■ ■

Ed has been hospitalized for 12 years with a diagnosis of schizophrenia. During that time, he has been on 8 or 10 different drugs and combinations of drugs. Nothing seems to help much. For the past couple of years, Ed has been having difficulty with involuntary muscle movements that make his tongue twist in his mouth and his head twist suddenly to the side, and he is unable to sit still for more than a minute or two. He gets up, paces briefly, sits down, and then gets up again. These motor symptoms are not part of his schizophrenia but are the symptoms of a disorder known as *tardive dyskinesia*, which can result from the use of some antipsychotic drugs. There is no effective treatment for this disorder. Ed appears to be one of those patients for whom we do not yet have an effective treatment. Ed will probably have to live out his days in a hospital.

■ ■ ■

Sid had been hospitalized with a diagnosis of schizophrenia for almost nine years. Eighteen months ago, he was transferred to a ward that was organized as a "token economy." Whenever Sid shows appropriate behaviors (making his bed, initiating social interactions), he is given a plastic poker chip, and he can use his chips to buy privileges (TV time, grounds passes, better food). Through this procedure, Sid is learning to behave more "normally." He appears much better and may be released to a sheltered living environment, but he still suffers disturbances in his thought processes that he cannot control.

■ ■ ■

In Chapter 12 you learned about the various causes of schizophrenia, and in this chapter we will use that information as a foundation on which to build an understanding of the treatment of schizophrenia. The effective treatment of schizophrenia is crucial because the disorder afflicts hundreds of thousands of individuals, and without an effective treatment, many of those individuals would be doomed to a life of progressive deterioration on the back ward of a mental hospital or as a homeless individual on the streets. There are also practical reasons for developing effective treatments. For example, the direct cost of caring for an individual with schizophrenia can be well over $80,000 per year in a public hospital and much more in a private hospital. In addition, there are indirect costs, such as lost productivity. These costs pose an overwhelming public and personal burden, but they can be reduced with effective treatments. The treatment of schizophrenia is not a simple problem; it stymied researchers for many years, but as you will learn in this chapter, we may have "turned the corner" with regard to our ability to treat this disorder (Hegarty et al., 1994).

In the following sections, I will discuss the psychodynamic, learning, cognitive, and physiological approaches to treatment. Because each treatment approach is based on a different suspected cause, before discussing a particular treatment I will briefly review the suspected cause it is designed to overcome. As you will learn, no one approach is completely effective, but together there are some impressive synergistic effects.

PSYCHODYNAMIC APPROACHES

The original psychodynamic explanation for schizophrenia was that early childhood experiences led to conflicts that the individual dealt with by regressing to an earlier stage of development or by withdrawing from interpersonal contacts. To overcome those problems, some therapists tried using *psychotherapy* with their patients. In contrast, the more contemporary psychody-

namic explanation for schizophrenia is that stress in general leads to the disorder. To help reduce stress, some therapists use an *educational* approach in which they teach patients and their families how to avoid or cope with stress. In the following sections, I will explain the use of psychotherapy and education for treating schizophrenia. I will also discuss *milieu therapy*, which is a strategy for improving the lives of patients while they are in the hospital.

Psychotherapy

The use of **psychotherapy** to treat individuals with schizophrenia was begun in the 1950s, but the results of the early research on its effectiveness were very discouraging. For example, in one classic experiment, it was found that the addition of psychotherapy to the usual hospital care did not improve the release rate, length of hospital stay, nurses' assessment of outcome, therapists' assessment of outcome, or patients' intellectual functioning (May, 1968). Furthermore, it was found that the combination of psychotherapy and drug therapy was not more effective than drug therapy alone. The findings indicated flatly that psychotherapy did not add to what could be achieved by routine hospital care or drug therapy. Those results are summarized in Figure 13.1.

However, advocates of the use of psychotherapy argued that the results of the early research were not more positive because the patients were not treated long enough, the therapists were not sufficiently trained, or the treatment programs were not intense or sophisticated enough. Therefore, an investigation was conducted in which a group of 20 patients with chronic schizophrenia was given essentially the best of everything for 2 years (Grinspoon et al., 1968, 1972). The patients lived in a special ward that was designed to provide them with a therapeutically ideal environment. For example, in addition to excellent physical facilities, there was a nursing staff of 25, an occupational therapist, and a social worker. Psychotherapy was provided by senior psychiatrists chosen from among the best in the Boston area. In addition, the patients were involved

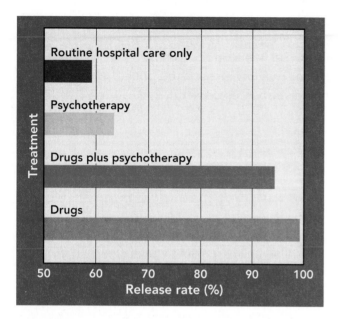

FIGURE 13.1 Patients who received drugs had higher release rates than patients who received just routine hospital care or routine hospital care plus psychotherapy.
Source: Adapted from May (1968), p. 138, fig. 5-1.

in an intensive program that included ward meetings, occupational therapy, and frequent outings to the beach, museums, and sports events. If it were available today, such treatment would easily cost in excess of $150,000 per year per patient. Unfortunately, despite the herculean effort at intervention, there was no evidence that the patients showed any improvement over the 2 years of treatment. However, as you will learn later, the patients did improve when they were given

drugs, thus indicating that the patients were capable of improvement but that psychotherapy was not effective in achieving it.

To date, the well-controlled research has not supplied any evidence that traditional psychotherapy is effective for treating schizophrenia regardless of the outcome measure used. The fall from favor of psychotherapy for the treatment of schizophrenia is dramatically illustrated by the fact that when research on the treatment of schizophrenia was initiated in the early 1960s, it was considered unethical to have a control condition in which the patients did not receive psychotherapy. However, less than a decade later, it was considered unethical to have a control condition in which the patients received *only* psychotherapy (Mosher & Keith, 1980)!

Family Therapy, Psychoeducation, and Social Skills Training

The findings concerning the effects of traditional psychotherapy are discouraging, but you should not conclude that psychotherapeutic interventions are not effective, for they are. However, in seeking effective psychotherapeutic interventions, we must use a somewhat different model from what has been used in the past. The model that is emerging is often referred to as **family therapy** because it involves the family members as well as the patient. This approach is also referred to as **psychoeducation** or **social skills training** because it is focused primarily on *education* and *training* rather than on complex "underlying" or "dynamic" problems (McFarlane et al., 1995).

Teaching problem-solving skills to patients and their families is more effective for maintaining recovery than teaching such skills to patients alone.

In general, this approach to treatment consists of three elements (Halford & Hayes, 1991). The first element involves *educating the patient and the family* so that they can *understand the disorder.* For example, the patient and family are taught that schizophrenia, like other disorders such as diabetes and epilepsy, is due to biochemical imbalances. To some extent, this "normalizes" the disorder and makes it less frightening so that everyone can deal with it more realistically.

The second element involves teaching the patient and family how to *reduce the stress that exacerbates the symptoms.* Regardless of whether or not stress causes schizophrenia, we know that an intense emotional climate can make the symptoms worse and contribute to relapse (Doane et al., 1985; Leff, 1976; Vaughn & Leff, 1976; Vaughn et al., 1984). This is not unique to schizophrenia; indeed, many of us do not function well when we are under high stress. Therefore, patients and families are taught strategies for "cooling" the emotional climate in which the patient lives. This may involve placing fewer demands on the patient or being less critical when he or she does not measure up to expectations. After all, because of his or her symptoms, the patient may be working under a distinct handicap. (Understanding that goes back to the educational element already mentioned.)

The third goal in this approach is to teach the patient strategies for *coping with the symptoms.* In many cases, it is not possible to eliminate all of the symptoms with whatever treatment is being used (e.g., drugs), and therefore it is essential for the patient to learn to cope with the remaining symptoms. Like the educational component, this is not unique to schizophrenia because patients with disorders such as diabetes and epilepsy must also learn ways of coping with their symptoms. Coping can take many forms and often requires help from others. For example, Betty (Case Study 11.2) calls me for a "reality check" when she begins to lose confidence in her ability to distinguish between reality and her hallucinations. In other cases, the patient may learn to avoid overly stimulating environments. For example, it would be disastrous for a patient suffering from stimulus overload to attend a rock concert; in some cases, even a noisy party could be difficult.

The goal of this approach is not to treat the schizophrenia per se but rather to prevent a relapse after the disorder has been brought under control with some other means (usually drugs). With this approach, we attempt to take the stress component out of the diathesis-stress mixture and thereby reduce the likelihood of igniting or exacerbating symptoms.

This approach to helping individuals with schizophrenia has been shown to be quite successful. In one of the best tests of this approach, the investigators assigned patients to one of four conditions: (a) drugs

By teaching families to accept disturbed family members and by helping the families deal with their problems, stress for the disturbed person can be reduced, and that aids adjustment and reduces relapse.

only, (b) drugs plus patient social skills training, (c) drugs plus family psychoeducation, or (d) drugs plus patient social skills training and family psychoeducation (Hogarty et al., 1986, 1991). All of the patients were returning to family environments that could be characterized as highly emotional, and therefore these patients were at high risk for relapse. The results indicated that 1 year after discharge from the hospital the relapse rates in the conditions were as follows: (a) drugs only, 38%; (b) drugs plus patient social skills training, 20%; (c) drugs plus family psychoeducation, 19%; and (d) drugs plus patient social skills training and family psychoeducation, 0%. After 2 years, the relapse rates were generally higher, and it appeared that the psychoeducation for family members had a more lasting effect than the social skills training for the patients (29% vs. 50% relapse rates, respectively), but they were still both more effective than drugs alone (62%). These results are summarized in Figure 13.2.

It is noteworthy that the decline in the effectiveness of patient social skills training between the 1- and 2-year evaluation points corresponds with the time at which contact with patients was being terminated because the study was ending. That is important

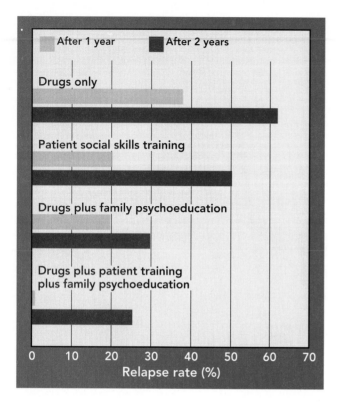

FIGURE 13.2 Family psychoeducation and patient social skills training are effective for reducing relapse rates.
Source: Data from Hogarty et al. (1991), p. 342, tab. 1.

because it indicates that individuals with schizophrenia cannot be treated and then dismissed; they need *continued maintenance therapy* to keep them "on track."

Another experiment was conducted to determine whether patients who received family therapy would have lower relapse rates and would be able to get along with *less medication* (Goldstein, 1980). In that experiment, when patients were discharged from the hospital, they were put on either a high or a low dose of an antipsychotic drug and either were or were not given family therapy. The major goals of the family therapy were to identify future stresses to which the patients would be exposed and to make plans so that the stresses could be minimized or avoided. Therapy occurred only once a week for a 6-week period. The results concerning relapse after 6 months are presented in Figure 13.3.

Two important findings should be noted. First, the patients in the high-drug-plus-family-therapy group showed the lowest relapse rate (0%), whereas the patients in the low-drug-and-no-family-therapy group showed the highest relapse rate (almost 50%). Second, relapse rates in the high-drug-and-no-family-therapy and low-drug-plus-family-therapy groups were nearly the same. That suggests that family therapy reduced the level of drugs that was necessary to keep the patients out of the hospital.

In a more extensive experiment, one group of patients was given family therapy in which the patient and the patient's family learned problem-solving skills designed to reduce the stress in the patient's life, while another group of patients was given the same type of therapy (teaching of problem-solving skills), but it was given only to the individual patient (Falloon et al., 1985). The investigation produced encouraging findings in three areas. First, patients in the family therapy condition showed lower levels of schizophrenia symptoms. Those results are presented in Figure 13.4.

The second finding was that after 9 months, the relapse rates were lower among patients receiving family therapy than among those receiving individual therapy. For example, only 11% of the patients receiving family therapy had to be rehospitalized, compared to 50% of the patients receiving individual therapy. Similarly, the rates of going to jail or being placed in other residential care facilities were also lower for patients receiving family versus individual therapy (6% vs. 17%, respectively, for each measure). Overall, the patients who received family therapy spent an average of only 1 day out of the home, whereas patients in individual therapy spent an average of 12.22 days out of the home.

The third finding of interest is that the patients in the family therapy group were able to take somewhat lower levels of drugs during the treatment period than the patients in the individual therapy group. That finding is particularly noteworthy when considered with the fact that those patients also did better on other measures of adjustment (level of symptoms, relapse rates).

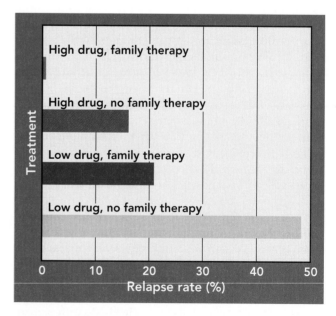

FIGURE 13.3 The combination of drugs and family therapy was most effective for reducing relapse rates of patients after they left the hospital.
Source: Adapted from Goldstein (1980), p. 81, fig. 1.

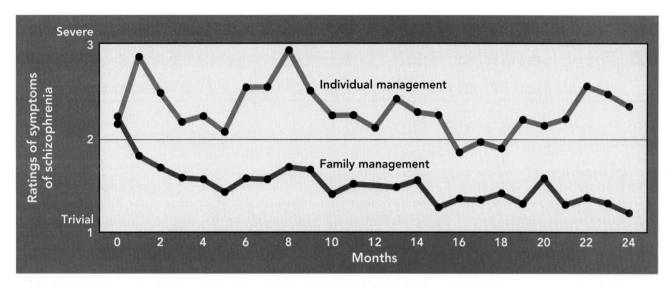

FIGURE 13.4 Family management was more effective than individual management for reducing symptoms of patients who had been released from the hospital.

Source: From "Family Management in the Prevention of Morbidity of Schizophrenia" by I. R. Falloon et al., in *Archives of General Psychiatry*, Vol. 42, September 1985. Reprinted by permission of the American Medical Society.

In other words, the patients receiving family therapy took less medication and showed better adjustment. In summary, the results of this experiment are particularly noteworthy because they indicate that teaching problem-solving skills to patients and their families is more effective for maintaining recovery than teaching problem-solving skills only to patients. It is also noteworthy that this effective approach is based on straightforward training procedures rather than on the in-depth analyses and insights that were traditionally thought to be necessary for effective therapy.

It is clear from the research discussed here that teaching basic coping skills to disturbed persons and their families may not cure schizophrenia, but it can be an effective means of helping them deal with the day-to-day problems that are posed by the disorder. Case Study 13.1 focuses on a psychologist who has struggled successfully with his own schizophrenia for over 20 years.

Milieu Therapy

Patients who are hospitalized for schizophrenia might be in therapy for only two or three hours a week, so they spend a great deal of time on the ward. However, long ago it was recognized that letting patients simply sit passively all day would have negative effects, so in most hospitals attempts are made to enrich the patients' daily lives by providing activities such as occupational therapy, music therapy, art therapy, recreational therapy, ward meetings in which patients and staff work on problems, and perhaps field trips outside the

hospital. All of these experiences are thought to contribute to the patients' recovery and are collectively referred to as **milieu** (mil-YOO) **therapy.**

The potential value of milieu therapy for many patients is obvious, and no one would propose that we return to the time when patients were simply allowed to vegetate. However, there is evidence that the stimulating environment provided by milieu therapy may not be good for all patients and may even hinder the recovery of some. For example, in one investigation, patients with chronic schizophrenia were assigned to either an experimental ward that had an intensive and stimulating milieu therapy program (meetings, trips, much staff contact, brightly decorated rooms designed in part by the patients, etc.) or to a regular ward that provided care but little more (Schooler & Spohn, 1982). The patients' social behavior and their levels of abnormal behavior were assessed before, during, and after the 2-year treatment period. The results indicated that the patients who received the intensive milieu therapy showed a tendency to initiate more social interactions with other individuals, but they also showed a substantial increase in their levels of abnormal behavior relative to the patients on the regular ward. Furthermore, the patients who received intensive milieu therapy were not discharged from the hospital sooner, and after discharge, they did not remain in the community longer than patients who received the regular treatment. Similar results have been reported by numerous other investigators (see Van Putten & May, 1976; Wing, 1975).

It is interesting to note that intensive milieu therapy had its most negative effects on the most disturbed

CASE STUDY 13.1

A Psychologist with Schizophrenia Talks About What Helps Him Function Effectively

Fredrick J. Frese III is a psychologist who has struggled with schizophrenia for over 20 years. In Case Study 11.4, he described the onset of his symptoms and talked about his occasional "breakdowns." Dr. Frese believes it is important that the individual with schizophrenia be aware of the nature of the problem in order to develop effective coping strategies. Despite his illness, most of the time he functions effectively. Here he describes some of the things that help.

"Persons with schizophrenia need to study carefully how they function. Until they can identify their deficits, it is very difficult to start building compensatory mechanisms that will enable them to function better.... Persons recovering from schizophrenia should be able to identify, and be on the lookout for, the sorts of persons, places, and things that can cause the type of stress that may precipitate their breakdowns. They should know how to get to environments that are helpful.

"Just as a diabetic must take action to control his or her blood sugar level, persons recovering from schizophrenia must learn to monitor and take measures to counteract an imbalance in subcortical neurochemical activity. But unlike diabetes, schizophrenia seriously interferes with rational processes, and once the irrationality begins, the person may have great difficulty acting in a rational or responsible manner.

"Because of our disability, it is very difficult for us to know what we do that normals do not understand. Therefore, it is very helpful to have a trustworthy normal person around to let us know what it is about our thoughts that perhaps it would be better not to share with everyone else. In my case, my wife constantly gives me feedback whenever I am saying or doing things that normal people may consider bizarre or offensive. Some things are rather obvious. If you are hearing voices, it is generally best not to talk back to them while normals are around. If your thoughts are dominated by the importance of the colors or similar sounds in the environment, you probably do not want to reveal too much about this to others.

"With help, other disabled persons learn to compensate for their disabilities and frequently lead dignified, productive lives. The blind learn to use canes and Seeing Eye dogs; people with limited use of their legs learn to use crutches and wheelchairs. For the mentally ill, however, the parameters of our disability are often not easily defined. We need help and feedback so that we can understand exactly the nature of our disability.

"Unfortunately, feedback is not always enough. Sometimes the symptoms overwhelm the person, who then loses the ability to function. When that occurs, some flexibility on the part of other people in the environment is necessary.

"Schizophrenia tends to be an episodic disorder. We are going to have periodic breakdowns. This makes holding employment very difficult because the usual practice is to terminate employees who require frequent periods of leave. Work for us should be structured so that our disabilities are taken into account. Many of us are well educated or have useful skills when we are not having episodes. Why can't jobs be structured for us so that our episodic breakdowns do not automatically result in our loss of employment? Like the general population, we like and need to work, but the world of the chronically well needs to be a little more flexible in understanding that we are going to behave strangely from time to time and there are going to be times when we do not function well at all."

---

patients. The negative effects of milieu therapy seem to be due to the fact that the stimulation provided by the therapy contributed to stimulus overload, which is one of the components of schizophrenia (see Chapters 11 and 12). Specifically, milieu therapy increased hallucinations and reduced intellectual performance, both of which are related to stimulus overload.

In summary, it appears that either extreme in the environmental milieu can have deleterious effects on patients: A socially impoverished environment can result in social withdrawal and lack of motivation, whereas a very stimulating environment can exacerbate symptoms such as hallucinations, delusions, and problems of speech and language. Contrary to what is generally thought, then, milieu therapy is not universally effective, and like almost any other therapy, it must be tailored to the needs and capacities of the patient because in some cases "overdoses" can have negative effects.

COMMENT

Psychological interventions for schizophrenia got off to a poor start with traditional psychotherapy. In retrospect, it appears that the ineffectiveness of psychotherapy is due to the fact that it is not focused on what really causes schizophrenia. However, with the development of the education or training model and with the involvement of the family, considerable strides have been made in the treatment of individuals with schizophrenia. It is noteworthy that therapy based on the education or training model can be conducted by a variety of professionals other than psychologists and psychiatrists and even by paraprofessionals. That reduces costs. However, it is important to recognize that the education and training approach is not a cure but only a strategy for avoiding some of the stress that can contribute to schizophrenia. Because it is an aid, not a solution, we must go on to consider other treatment possibilities.

LEARNING AND COGNITIVE APPROACHES

In Chapter 12 I pointed out that one of the learning explanations for schizophrenia is that individuals *learn their symptoms;* that is, individuals with schizophrenia behave strangely because their behaviors are effective in obtaining rewards. Based on that assumption, the learning theory approach to treatment involves the *manipulation of rewards or punishments so that abnormal behaviors (symptoms) are no longer rewarded and may be punished,* whereas *normal behaviors are rewarded.* Because the focus of the treatment is on *behaviors,* this is usually referred to as **behavior therapy.** Case Study 13.2 illustrates this procedure.

Behavior Therapy and Token Economies

Since the 1960s, numerous controlled experiments have demonstrated that many of the symptoms of schizophrenia can be brought under control by manipulating the reward and punishment contingencies that are associated with the symptoms. In many of the experi-

ments, patients were given tokens when they behaved appropriately, and those tokens could later be used to buy desired rewards (hospital passes, better living conditions, better food, TV time, etc.). In other words, the tokens were used like money (earned, saved, and spent), and therefore this approach is often referred to as the **token economy** approach to treatment.

In one of the most impressive tests of the effectiveness of the token economy approach to treatment, 56 chronic mental patients were assigned either to a ward on which a token economy approach was used or to a ward on which an active milieu therapy approach was used (Paul & Lentz, 1977). On both wards, the patients were kept very busy with a variety of activities (classes, group meetings, gym time, housekeeping, meals, individual assignments), and it was made clear to the patients that they were expected to act appropriately and to take responsibility for their behavior. When patients on either ward behaved appropriately, they were rewarded with positive statements and encouragement.

However, the important difference between the two wards was that patients on the token economy ward were systematically rewarded with tokens for good behavior, whereas those on the other ward were not. For example, if a patient did a good job of cleaning his room, an attendant would say something like, "You did a really good job smoothing the sheets and putting things away this morning, George; here is a token for keeping your room in order." When the patients did not behave well, that was pointed out, and they were told that a token was being withheld; for example, "You don't earn your appearance token this morning, Herman, because your hair is all tangled." The tokens were then used like money to buy meals, rent better sleeping quarters (a four-bed dormitory room cost 10 tokens per week; a furnished one-bed room cost 22 tokens), obtain passes to leave the hospital, purchase recreational time (TV, piano, games, radio, phonograph, etc.), buy privileges like staying up later, and get other miscellaneous things such as use of the phone, laundry service, a haircut, or extra baths.

The investigation generated two positive findings and two negative findings with regard to behavior. On the positive side, the token economy approach was effective for improving *general behavior* such as cooperation, social activity, housekeeping, grooming, care of belongings, and appropriate mealtime behaviors. The improvement in interpersonal skills is illustrated in Figure 13.5. Also on the positive side, the token economy approach was effective for reducing *disorganized and bizarre motor behaviors* such as constant rocking, repetitive movements, and blank staring.

On the negative side, the token economy approach was ineffective for reducing *disorganized and bizarre cogni-*

CASE STUDY 13.2
Treatment of Bizarre Symptoms with Techniques Based on Learning Theory

The patient was a 47-year-old woman who had been hospitalized for 9 years and was diagnosed as suffering from chronic schizophrenia. She had a wide variety of symptoms, but three of them were particularly troublesome. The first was her continual stealing of food and overeating. She always ate everything on her tray and then stole food from the counter and from other patients. Because of her excessive eating, she weighed over 250 lb, and that was posing a risk to her physical health. Her second annoying symptom was hoarding hospital towels in her room. Despite the fact that the nurses kept retrieving them, the patient often had as many as 30 towels. The third and most extreme symptom was excessive dressing. At any one time, she might wear six dresses, several pairs of underwear, two dozen pairs of stockings, two or three sweaters, and a shawl or two. In addition, she often draped herself in sheets and wrapped a couple of towels around her head in a turban-like headdress. These behaviors had persisted for a number of years, and various attempts to change them (therapy, pleading) had been ineffective. Finally, it was decided to try a learning theory approach to treating the symptoms.

The patient's food stealing was treated by punishment (withdrawal of food). Nurses simply removed her from the dining room as soon as she picked up unauthorized food, so she missed a meal whenever she stole food. Within two weeks, the patient's food stealing was eliminated, and she ate only the diet prescribed for her. Her weight dropped to 180 lb in 14 months, a 28% loss.

The hoarding of hospital towels was treated with satiation. Rather than restricting the number of towels the patient had, the staff began giving her more towels. The notion was that if she had more towels than she wanted, the value of the towels would be reduced, and consequently the hoarding would be reduced. (This is like letting workers in a candy factory eat all they want; soon they do not want any more, and they stop eating the product.) At first, when a nurse came into her room with a towel, the patient said, "Oh, you found it for me, thank you."

As the number of towels increased rapidly in the second week, the patient responded by saying, "Don't give me no more towels. I've got enough." By the third week of the treatment period, she was being given as many as 60 towels a day, and she said, "Take them towels away. . . . I can't sit here all night and fold towels." Soon her room was overflowing with towels, and in the sixth week, she complained to a nurse, "I can't drag any more of these towels, I just can't do it." When the number of towels in the patient's room reached 625, she started taking towels out of the room, so the staff stopped giving them to her. The patient had apparently had it with towels, and for the next 12 months, the average number of towels found in her room was 1.5 per week.

The patient's excessive dressing was treated by punishing overdressing and rewarding reduced dressing. Before each meal, the patient was required to get on a scale, and if she exceeded a predetermined weight (her body weight plus a specified number of pounds for clothing), she was simply told, "Sorry, you weigh too much; you'll have to weigh less," and she was not allowed in the dining room for that meal (punishment). The patient quickly learned that if she took some of her clothes off, she could meet the weight requirement and thereby get to eat (reward). Originally she was allowed 23 lb for clothes, but that was gradually reduced. Within a short period of time, the weight of her clothing dropped from 25 to 3 lb, and she was dressing normally.

It should be noted that the patient responded with some anger when she was first denied food as part of the treatment of her food stealing and overdressing. When that behavior was not rewarded (it was ignored), it disappeared, and no other inappropriate behaviors were introduced. Finally, it is interesting to note that as the patient's behaviors became less bizarre, patients and staff began interacting with her more, and she began to participate somewhat more actively in social functions.

Source: Adapted from Ayllon (1963).

---

tive behaviors such as incoherent speech, hallucinations, and delusions. Nor was it effective for reducing *emotional behaviors* such as aggression, screaming, and cursing.

This pattern of findings indicates that the use of rewards was effective for improving *overt behaviors* but that it was not effective for *improving cognitive processes or emotional responses.* Whether or not the behaviors can be influenced by rewards is apparently due to whether or not they are under the voluntary control of the individual; for example, overt motor behaviors

The token economy approach is effective for improving a patient's general behavior.

are under voluntary control, whereas cognitive processes are not.

The fact that the use of rewards is not effective for controlling cognitive processes places a limitation on the use of this approach. However, despite that limitation, it is important to note that the results of the investigation revealed that more patients from the token economy ward than the milieu ward were *released from the hospital* (96.4% vs. 67.9%) and that more patients from the token economy ward than the milieu ward achieved release to *independent functioning and self-support* as opposed to some form of continuing community care (10.7% vs. 7.1%). In other words, the token economy approach led to improved behaviors, and the improvements in behaviors were crucial for getting the patients out of the hospital and functioning effectively. To sum up, the token economy was not effective for

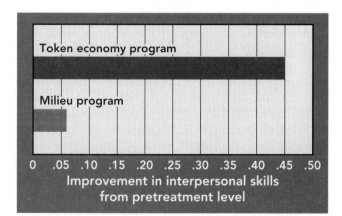

FIGURE 13.5 Token economy treatment was effective for improving the behavior of patients hospitalized for schizophrenia.
Source: Adapted from Paul and Lentz (1977), p. 317, fig. 29.4.

reducing all of the symptoms, but it did reduce some that were important in terms of daily functioning.

Cognitive Therapy

In view of the fact that many of the symptoms of schizophrenia involve cognitive problems such as hallucinations and delusions, it would seem that cognitive therapy, which is designed to correct erroneous beliefs, could be helpful (Alford & Correia, 1994; Bentall et al., 1994; Chadwick et al., 1994; McNally, 1994). Indeed, while behavior therapy might be used to treat the overt behaviors as just described, cognitive therapy might be used to treat the cognitive problems for which the behavior therapy is ineffective. The goal of cognitive therapy would be to replace erroneous beliefs such as "I hear demons talking to me" (hallucinations) or "I am God" (delusions) with more accurate beliefs. That is similar to cognitive therapy for depression in which the goal is to replace beliefs such as "I am a failure and will never succeed."

Formal cognitive therapy is rarely used with individuals who suffer from schizophrenia, but the general strategy is often used informally. For example, when Betty (see Case Study 11.2) calls to talk with me about her belief that the police are monitoring her thoughts, I simply assure her that, no, the police are not monitoring her thoughts and that her belief is a delusion. Similarly, when she talks about demons talking to her, I tell her that the experience is a hallucination. In other words, my "cognitive therapy" with her involves helping her correct and relabel her experiences so as to bring them into line with reality. That can work, but the problem is that *correcting and labeling the experience as a hallucination does not eliminate the hallucination.* The individual may not act on the hallucination (e.g., Betty will not kill herself when the "demons" tell her to do so), but she still has the hallucination. Therefore, the cognitive therapy may be an aid, but it is not a treatment for the schizophrenia.

COMMENT

There is no doubt that in many cases the alteration of reward and punishment contingencies is effective for modifying the behavior of individuals with schizophrenia. However, critics have questioned whether with this approach we are actually treating schizophrenia or whether we are simply altering superficial behaviors and ignoring or glossing over the real underlying problem. Consider the simple and probably not infrequent situation in which a therapist says something like this to a patient:

Look, as long as you keep wearing a cowboy hat and telling everyone that you are John Wayne, we are going to have to keep you locked up in this hospital, and life here is not pleasant. However, if you want to get out, just stop wearing the cowboy hat and telling everyone you are John Wayne. Now I don't care who you think you are; it's really irrelevant. The point is, if you want out, you just can't tell everyone who you think you are. Be John Wayne at home but not in public if you want to stay out of this hospital.

If the patient wants to leave the hospital and takes the advice, the patient will be judged as being "in remission" and will be discharged. This straightforward exercise of behavior modification (the patient was rewarded for not acting crazy) has resulted in an individual who no longer appears to suffer from schizophrenia, but has the schizophrenia really been treated or changed? Obviously not, but many learning theorists would respond by saying, "So what? The patient's happy, and so is everyone else." Similar criticisms can be applied to cognitive therapy for schizophrenia; it can be helpful for the individual's functioning, but it does not change the underlying problem.

PHYSIOLOGICAL APPROACHES

The findings reviewed in Chapter 12 led to the conclusion that the primary causes of schizophrenia are physiological—specifically, high or low levels of neurological activity or structural problems in the brain. The physiological approaches to treatment are designed to reverse those processes as far as possible. I will divide this discussion of physiological treatments into two sections. The first section is devoted to the early therapies, which involved electroconvulsive shocks or surgery. Those treatments were not based on any particular theory of schizophrenia; rather, they were used simply because they might work. In the second section, I will discuss drug therapy, in which medication is used to adjust the levels of neurological activity that underlie some of the symptoms of schizophrenia.

Early Therapies

Convulsive Therapy. In the 1930s, a physician noticed that patients who suffered from both schizophrenia and epilepsy showed reductions in their schizophrenic symptoms immediately after having an epileptic seizure. He therefore speculated that schizophrenia might be treated by inducing seizures (Meduna, 1938). Initially, drugs such as insulin were used to cause the seizures, but the drugs were soon replaced by **electroconvulsive therapy (ECT),** in which the convulsions are induced with an electrical shock (see Chapter 10). Convulsive therapy was widely used to treat schizophrenia for many years, but research now clearly indicates

that ECT is not helpful for treating schizophrenia and is far less effective than drug therapy (Greenblatt et al., 1964; Heath et al., 1964; Miller et al., 1953).

Today, ECT is rarely used to treat schizophrenia per se. However, because depression often accompanies schizophrenia (see Chapter 11), ECT may be used to treat individuals with schizophrenia, *but the target symptom is their depression.* Unfortunately, the use of ECT with individuals who suffer from schizophrenia can result in serious side effects, including extensive retrograde amnesia and cognitive confusion. That is in sharp contrast to the case with individuals who are only depressed; for them, amnesia and confusion may not occur or are minimal. The difference stems from the fact that the degree of amnesia and confusion following ECT is determined by the amount of confusion that exists before the ECT (Sobin et al., 1995). In other words, ECT temporarily exacerbates existing cognitive problems. That was illustrated with Betty (see Case Study 11.2) who was hospitalized last year and given ECT because her depression had become very severe. One afternoon when I stopped by to see her and asked how she was doing, she said, "Oh, I'm fine. We went ice skating on the pond today!" With some surprise I responded, "Ice skating on the pond? I don't think so, Betty—it's August and 90 degrees outside." She thought for a while and then said, "I guess I'm confused." With regard to retrograde amnesia, I should point out that Betty was in the hospital for three weeks, but she does not remember any of it. The ECT did help with her depression, her confusion has cleared up, and now she laughs when she is told about it.

Generally, then, ECT can be effective for treating depression in individuals who suffer from schizophrenia, but it is not a treatment for schizophrenia, and it can have some temporary side effects. In cases in which ECT is used to treat schizophrenia, the often heard justification is, "Well, it probably won't hurt, and it might help."

Psychosurgery. **Psychosurgery** is another physiological treatment that was once popular but has now been generally abandoned (Swayze, 1995; Valenstein, 1980). Psychosurgery involves severing the connections between the frontal lobes and the rest of the brain. Psychosurgery was performed as early as the 19th century (Burckhardt, 1891), but the procedure as we know it today originated in 1935 when an operation known as a **prefrontal lobotomy** (luh-BOT-uh-mē) was introduced. The idea for the operation stemmed from a report that an excitable and sometimes violent chimpanzee had become docile and friendly after the destruction of her prefrontal cortex (Jacobsen et al., 1935). The notion was that the disorder stemmed from problems in the frontal lobes, so to treat the disorder, the frontal lobes should be destroyed or at least separated from the rest of the brain.

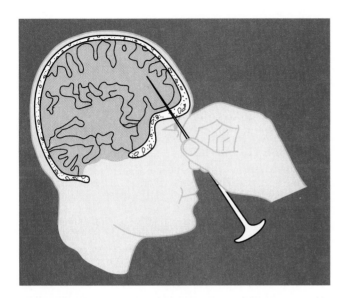

FIGURE 13.6 A transorbital lobotomy could be performed in the physician's office.

To perform a prefrontal lobotomy, holes were drilled in the top of the skull, and then a knife was inserted and pivoted up and back so that a cut was made separating a portion of the frontal lobes from the rest of the brain. If the operation was not successful in reducing symptoms, it was performed again, but the second time the holes were drilled farther back on the skull so that more of the frontal area would be separated from the rest of the brain.

In 1948, the **transorbital lobotomy** was introduced. This procedure involved inserting an icepick-like knife through the top of the eye socket and up into the brain. The knife was then swung up and back to destroy brain tissue. The procedure is illustrated in Figure 13.6. Transorbital lobotomies could be performed as an office procedure and were widely used. (In some cases, electroconvulsive shocks were used to induce unconsciousness before the transorbital was performed!)

In the years between 1935 and about 1955, thousands of patients received lobotomies. Unfortunately, it is difficult to determine how effective the operations were because the nature of the operation differed greatly from hospital to hospital, and objective records were not kept on patients' pre- and postoperation symptoms. However, there is some agreement that the operations did result in a reduction in the intensity of the patients' emotional responses (it reduced anxiety or alleviated depression). However, it is not clear whether the operations were effective for reducing specific symptoms or simply made the patients calmer and more docile. In any event, the patients were easier to manage and more likely to be discharged. Needless to say, psychosurgery can have a wide variety of serious side effects, such as loss of cognitive abilities and some-

times a loss of emotional control. Psychosurgery was also misused. For example, I knew of a physician who performed transorbital lobotomies on adolescents who had behavior problems in school.

The use of psychosurgery diminished sharply in the mid-1950s in large part because of the introduction of drugs that were more effective and resulted in fewer negative side effects. As a footnote to this discussion of psychosurgery, it might be mentioned that the physician who introduced the use of psychosurgery received the Nobel Prize for his work but was paralyzed later in life when he was shot in the spine by an angry lobotomized patient.

Drug Therapy

The introduction of antipsychotic drugs in the mid-1950s revolutionized the care and condition of mental patients. Almost overnight, psychiatric wards were transformed from "snake pits" where patients lived in straitjackets and were largely out of control to places of relative calm and order. Of course, some antipsychotic drugs can have serious side effects, and critics argue that the benefits achieved by these drugs are superficial and are outweighed by the side effects they cause.

In this section, I will discuss the general nature and effects of the drugs that are used to treat schizophrenia and the controversies over their use. A thorough and balanced understanding of this often misunderstood and sometimes controversial area is important for at

Before the introduction of neuroleptic drugs, scenes like this were common in psychiatric hospitals.

least three reasons: The drugs are widely discussed in the mass media, they play an important role in today's treatment, and someday you may have to make a decision concerning the use of one of these drugs for yourself or someone close to you.

Overview of Neuroleptic Drugs. One of the physiological causes of schizophrenia is excessively high neurological activity in the areas of the brain where **dopamine** is the major neurotransmitter. The high level of dopamine-related activity leads to symptoms because it disrupts cognitive activity (see Chapter 12). Therefore, the primary goal of modern drug therapy is to *reduce the high level of neurological activity.* That is done with a group of drugs known as **neuroleptics.** The term *neuroleptic* is derived from the Greek *neuro,* which refers to the brain, and *leptic,* from a word that means "to seize or arrest." In short, then, neuroleptics relieve the symptoms of schizophrenia by *arresting brain activity.*

Neuroleptic drugs reduce brain activity in three ways. First, they *block the receptors on the postsynaptic neuron* so that the neurotransmitter (dopamine) cannot enter the receptor and cause the neuron to fire. It is like putting the wrong key in a lock; you cannot open the lock with the wrong key (the neuroleptic), but if that key is in the lock, you cannot get the right key (the dopamine) in either. The degree to which a drug enters receptors is often a good predictor of how effective the drug will be in reducing symptoms; that is, more blocking is usually associated with greater symptom reduction.

The second way in which neuroleptics may reduce brain activity is by *reducing the sensitivity of the postsynaptic receptors.* If the receptors are less sensitive, they will be less likely to fire even when stimulated. The belief that neuroleptics reduce receptor sensitivity stems from the fact that although neuroleptics block receptors immediately, some symptoms do not diminish for days or even weeks after drug treatment is started. It appears that over time, the presence of the drug changes the sensitivity of the receptors, and this delayed change in sensitivity is responsible for the delay in symptomatic relief. This process has not yet been documented, and it is still a matter of speculation.

Third, some new neuroleptics (called *atypical neuroleptics*) also increase the levels of the neurotransmitter **serotonin.** That can be effective for reducing symptoms because serotonin serves to *inhibit dopamine activity.*

Neuroleptic drugs are sometimes incorrectly referred to as "major tranquilizers" to distinguish them from the "minor tranquilizers" that are used to treat anxiety (see Chapter 6). However, calling neuroleptic drugs "major tranquilizers" is misleading because although these drugs do calm disturbed and agitated patients, they are not simply stronger versions of the "minor tranquilizers," and they are not particularly effective for treating anxiety. The notion of an

TABLE 13.1 Widely Used Neuroleptic Drugs

Trade Name	Generic Name	Typical Daily Dose
Low-potency neuroleptics		
Thorazine	Chlorpromazine	200–600 mg
Mellaril	Thioridazine	200–600 mg
High-potency neuroleptics		
Haldol	Haloperidol	2–12 mg
Navane	Thiothixene	6–30 mg
Atypical neuroleptics		
Clozaril	Clozapine	200–900 mg
Risperdal	Risperidone	2–6 mg

antipsychotic drug as a "major tranquilizer" is probably a holdover from the days before we had true antipsychotic drugs and patients were treated (or at least controlled) with large doses of muscle relaxants (e.g., Miltown).

Neuroleptic drugs can have a number of side effects that I will discuss later. One particularly troublesome side effect involves a *disturbance in muscle activity.* The disturbance can include involuntary tremors, twitches, shaking, and jerking. Those occur because dopamine is also a neurotransmitter in the area of the brain that is responsible for motor activity (the basal ganglia), and when the general level of dopamine is altered with a neuroleptic drug, the activity level in the motor area of the brain is changed, resulting in the muscle movements. These motor side effects are referred to as **extrapyramidal** (EK-struh-puh-RAM-i-dul) **symptoms** because the neurons that are responsible for motor movements extend from a group of cells that look like a series of pyramids.

Numerous neuroleptic drugs are available today, and in this discussion I will organize them in terms of their biochemical and behavioral effects. I will refer to them as *low-potency, high-potency,* or *atypical neuroleptics.* In this discussion, *potency* refers to the degree to which the drug blocks the dopamine receptors. Some of the most widely used neuroleptics are listed in Table 13.1.

Low-Potency Neuroleptics. **Low-potency neuroleptics** were the first neuroleptics to be developed, and as the label implies, they are less effective for blocking dopamine receptors than the high-potency drugs that were developed later. However, they are effective for treating schizophrenia and are still used widely.

The best-known low-potency neuroleptic is **Thorazine (chlorpromazine).** Thorazine was first introduced in the mid-1950s, and it immediately became a very popular drug for treating schizophrenia. Indeed, in the 1960s and 1970s, the question was not whether patients were on Thorazine but how much were they taking. Thorazine is still widely used today.

The widespread use of Thorazine and other low-potency neuroleptics was justified by their clinical effectiveness. In what is probably the classic experiment on the effects of these drugs, patients with schizophrenia at nine different public and private hospitals were randomly assigned to one of four conditions (Cole et al., 1964; Cole et al., 1966). The patients in three conditions received one of three different neuroleptics (Thorazine, Mellaril, Prolixin), while the patients in the fourth condition received a placebo. The patients' psychological functioning was assessed before treatment began and after 6 weeks of treatment.

The results of this experiment clearly indicated that the three neuroleptics were much more effective for reducing the symptoms of schizophrenia than the placebo was. In fact, as indicated in Figure 13.7, fully 75% of the patients who received neuroleptics were "much improved," compared to only 25% of the patients who received the placebo. Only 2% of the patients who received neuroleptics got worse, whereas almost 50% of the patients who received the placebo got worse.

It is important to recognize that the improvements in the patients who received the neuroleptics were not simply due to the fact that the patients were sedated and therefore easier to manage. It is true that the patients were less hostile, less irritable, and less agitated, which may be interpreted as a tranquilizing effect.

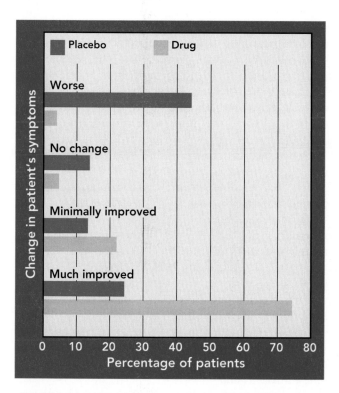

FIGURE 13.7 Patients with schizophrenia who took neuroleptic drugs were more likely to improve and less likely to get worse than patients who took placebos.
Source: Davis et al. (1980), p. 71, fig. 1.

However, the patients who received the neuroleptics were also more socially active, less indifferent to their environment, more coherent in their speech, less disoriented, better able to take care of themselves, and subject to fewer hallucinations and delusions. Obviously, the neuroleptics had effects well beyond the sedating of the patients, and in some ways the drugs actually served to activate the patients—they became more socially active and more involved and took better care of themselves.

The positive effects of a neuroleptic (Mellaril) were also demonstrated in an interesting long-term experiment with patients who suffered from chronic schizophrenia (Grinspoon et al., 1968, 1972). In this investigation, 20 male patients who averaged only 27 years of age but had already spent an average of 6.5 years in mental hospitals were first moved to a special-treatment ward where they were given a placebo for 3 months. Following that period, half of the patients were given the neuroleptic for 15 months, while the other half continued to receive the placebo. After that period, all of the patients were again given a placebo for a 3-month period. Finally, half of the patients were again given the neuroleptic for a 3-month period, while the other half continued to receive the placebo. Thus the phases of the experiment involved placebo versus placebo, neuroleptic versus placebo, placebo versus placebo, and neuroleptic versus placebo.

If the neuroleptic was effective, it would be expected that the patients would show improvements in their symptomatology while taking the drug but not while taking the placebo. That is exactly what was found; the results are summarized in Figure 13.8. Note that the patients did not immediately get worse when they were switched from the neuroleptic to the placebo. The delay in the deterioration of the patients stems from the fact that the medication remains active in the patients' systems for some time after it has been taken.

Clearly, low-potency neuroleptics are effective for treating schizophrenia, but they are not effective with all patients, and they can have a number of side effects such as involuntary motor movements (the extrapyramidal symptoms). I will discuss the side effects in greater detail later.

High-Potency Neuroleptics. In view of the effectiveness of the low-potency drugs, chemists began working to develop drugs that would block more of the dopamine receptors, and in the 1970s a number of **high-potency neuroleptics** were developed. The best known of these is **Haldol (haloperidol).** Thorazine blocks 80% of the receptors, whereas Haldol blocks about 85% (Farde et al., 1988).

In experiments comparing the effects of Thorazine and Haldol, Haldol was often found to be more effective for reducing the symptoms of schizophrenia, and therefore Haldol became widely used. However, it was

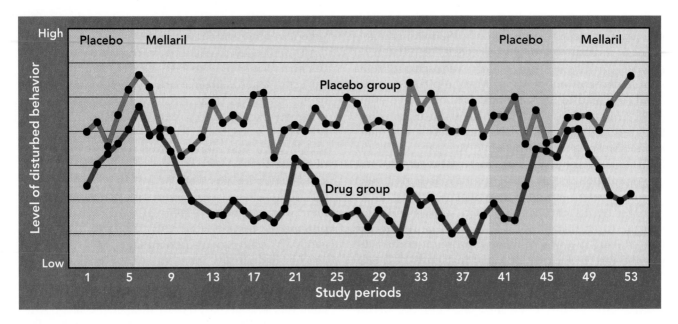

FIGURE 13.8 Patients showed fewer disturbed behaviors when given antipsychotic medication but got worse when they were switched to a placebo. During placebo periods, patients in both groups received the placebo, but during the Mellaril periods, one group received the drug and the other received the placebo.

Source: From *Schizophrenia: Pharmacotherapy and Psychotherapy* by L. Grinspoon et al. Reprinted by permission of Williams and Wilkins Publishers.

quickly discovered that the increased effectiveness of Haldol had a price—an increase in the troublesome extrapyramidal side effects. That is understandable because Haldol blocks more dopamine receptors, and the blocking of certain dopamine receptors leads to the motor problems. Today Haldol continues to be used with many patients, but to reduce the side effects, the dose levels are kept as low as possible and other drugs are often prescribed to help reduce the extrapyramidal side effects.

Atypical Neuroleptics. The latest development in drug treatment revolves around a new type of neuroleptic called **atypical neuroleptics.** These drugs are called *atypical* neuroleptics because they differ from regular neuroleptics in three ways. First, atypical neuroleptic drugs *block fewer dopamine receptors* than the regular neuroleptics. Indeed, whereas Haldol blocks 85% of the receptors, an atypical neuroleptic blocks only 65% (Farde et al., 1988). At first you might think that the lower blocking rate would make atypical neuroleptics less effective for treating schizophrenia, but before drawing that conclusion, note the second difference.

The second difference is that atypical neuroleptics are *more selective in the sets of dopamine receptors that they block.* Specifically, unlike regular neuroleptics, which block dopamine receptors in general, atypical neuroleptics block dopamine receptors in the nerve tracts that lead to the frontal and temporal lobes, but they do not block dopamine receptors in the nerve tracts associ-

ated with motor movements (Coward et al., 1989; Creese, 1985). This selectivity in blocking leads to reductions in cognitive symptoms (disorganized thinking in the frontal lobes and hallucinations in the temporal lobes) without causing the side effects involving motor functioning (extrapyramidal activity) that often occur with the normal neuroleptics. The receptors in the nerve tracts that lead to the frontal and temporal lobes and are blocked by atypical neuroleptics are called **D-2 receptors,** whereas the receptors in the nerve tracts that lead to the motor area and are not blocked by atypical neuroleptics are called **D-1 receptors.**

The third difference is that atypical neuroleptics also appear to *influence serotonin activity.* However, the effects of atypical neuroleptics on serotonin is complex in that they *increase the levels of serotonin* while at the same time they *block certain serotonin receptors* (the 5-HT$_2$ receptors), and the influence of these effects on symptoms is still unclear (Borison, 1995; Breier, 1995; Carpenter, 1995; Huttunen, 1995; Meltzer, 1995b). The increase in serotonin may serve to inhibit dopamine activity (recall that serotonin often serves as an inhibitory neurotransmitter), and the blocking of some serotonin receptors may serve to reduce some symptoms. These possibilities are under investigation now, and the findings will help us understand both the drugs and schizophrenia.

The first and best known of the atypical neuroleptics is **Clozaril (clozapine),** which produced some surprising effects. The landmark experiment on the effects of Clozaril was based on over 300 patients who had not responded to previous treatments (Kane et al., 1988, 1989). The typical patient was 35 years old, was diagnosed as suffering from chronic schizophrenia, was first hospitalized at about age 20, and had been hospitalized about eight times since then. In short, these were severely and chronically ill individuals who were ultimately bound for long-term custodial care in a state hospital.

The experiment involved two phases that each lasted 6 weeks. In the first phase, all of the patients were given Haldol (a high-potency neuroleptic) plus medication to relieve extrapyramidal side effects. This phase was used to be sure that the patients did not respond to other medication. Any patients who showed improvement during this phase were dropped from the experiment. In the second phase, the remaining patients were randomly assigned to a condition in which they received Thorazine (a low-potency neuroleptic) plus medication to relieve extrapyramidal side effects or to a condition in which they received Clozaril. The patients' symptoms were evaluated each week by raters who did not know which patients were taking which drug.

The results revealed three interesting findings. First, the patients who took Clozaril showed *greater reductions in positive symptoms* (e.g., hallucinations, delusions, thought disorder) than the patients who took Thorazine. Second, somewhat surprisingly, the patients who took Clozaril also showed *greater reductions in negative symptoms* (e.g., flat mood, poverty of speech, disori-

entation). Third, the patients who took Clozaril showed *fewer extrapyramidal side effects* (i.e., involuntary muscle movements) than the patients who took Thorazine. That was the case despite the fact that the patients who were taking Thorazine were also taking medication to offset such side effects. The results concerning the reductions in positive and negative symptoms are summarized in Figure 13.9. Looked at in another way, 30% of the patients who took Clozaril showed significant clinical improvement (i.e., a 20% improvement or posttreatment scores in the "mild" range of pathology), whereas only 4% of the patients who took Thorazine showed such improvement.

Since that initial experiment, a number of other investigators have reported similar results (e.g., Breier et al., 1994; Honigfeld & Patin, 1989; Leppig et al., 1989; Lieberman et al., 1994; Lindstrom, 1989; Meltzer, Bastani, Ramirez, & Matsubara, 1989; Miller et al., 1994; Pickar et al., 1992). In one study, patients with chronic schizophrenia who were given Clozaril showed improvements of more than 30% in both positive and negative symptoms (Miller et al., 1994). In that study, it was also found that the improvements in negative symptoms were not correlated with the improvements in the positive symptoms, thus suggesting that Clozaril was having a direct influence on the negative symptoms rather than influencing them indirectly by influencing positive symptoms. In Clozaril we apparently have a treatment for both positive and negative symptoms that is effective for otherwise hard-to-treat patients and does not lead to extrapyramidal side effects.

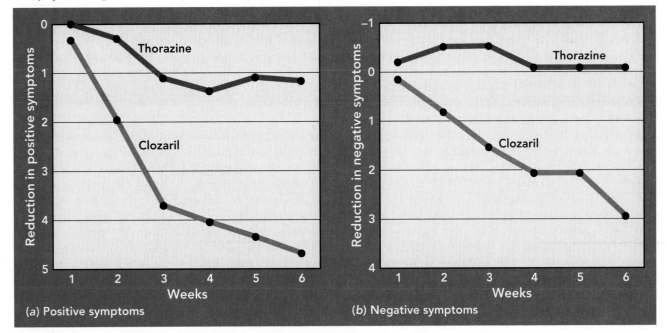

FIGURE 13.9 Clozaril is more effective for treating both positive and negative symptoms than a typical neuroleptic.
Source: From "Clozapine for the Treatment-Resistant Schizophrenic" by J. M. Kane et al., in *Archives of General Psychiatry*, Vol. 45, September 1988. Reprinted by permission of the American Medical Society.

A recent investigation revealed yet another benefit of Clozaril: It can greatly reduce the rate of suicide attempts among patients who are difficult to treat (Meltzer & Okayli, 1995). Specifically, when patients were switched to Clozaril, their rate of serious suicide attempts dropped from 6% to zero. The reduction in suicide attempts was attributed to the fact that the Clozaril reduced feelings of depression and hopelessness (negative symptoms). However, it may also be that because Clozaril increases serotonin activity, it led to a decrease in impulsivity, which decreased suicide attempts (recall from Chapter 10 that low levels of serotonin can increase impulsivity, which can lead to suicide attempts).

Clozaril was an important breakthrough, but there is a potentially serious problem associated with its use in that 1% to 2% of the individuals who take it develop a disorder in which there is a *sudden drop in white blood cells* (leukocytes). That can be very serious because white blood cells are essential for fighting infection, and if the level of white cells gets too low, an individual may die from infection. That disorder is called **agranulocytosis** (uh-GRAN-yuh-lō-sī-TŌ-sis). Fortunately, agranulocytosis can be eliminated within about two weeks by simply taking the patient off the Clozaril.

The possibility of developing agranulocytosis posed a dilemma because on the one hand, Clozaril was effective for treating previously untreatable individuals, but on the other hand, it could result in fatal side effects. This dilemma was resolved in the mid-1980s when the company that produces Clozaril developed a procedure for monitoring leukocyte levels. Specifically, each week, a sample of the patient's blood is taken and analyzed for leukocyte levels, and if the levels are within normal limits, the patient is given a week's worth of medication. However, if the leukocyte levels are low, the patient is not given the Clozaril until the leukocytes return to their normal levels. This procedure is known as **bundling** because the blood test is "bundled" with the distribution of the medication. The bundling procedure resolved the dilemma posed by the possibility of triggering agranulocytosis, but it posed another problem—very high costs. The cost of the combination of Clozaril and the company's blood tests came to about $9,000 per year. That amount was well beyond what most patients were able to pay, and it was also beyond what Medicaid was willing to pay. In the Clozaril bundle, then, we had a rich person's drug for a poor person's disorder. (It is interesting to note that in Europe, where the blood monitoring is not required, the drug costs only between $1,000 and $1,500 per year.)

As it turned out, the $9,000 cost was much higher than necessary because the company was placing a very high price on its blood test. Physicians and pharmacists claimed that the blood test could actually be done for much less, but the company would not release the drug unless its own blood test was used. Company officials argued that the blood test was essential because of the potential side effects and that the high cost of the test was necessary to offset the expense of developing the drug.

Eventually two things happened to make the drug more accessible and cheaper. First, a number of patients sued Medicaid to force that program to pay for Clozaril. The patients argued that it was cheaper to pay $9,000 for the drug than to pay $40,000 for hospitalization. They also argued that it was discriminatory to pay $50,000 a year for kidney dialysis for individuals with kidney disease but not to pay $9,000 a year for Clozaril for individuals with schizophrenia. (Betty, whose experiences are described in Case Study 11.2, is one of the individuals who successfully sued Medicaid.) Second, powerful public and governmental pressure was brought to bear on the company that produces Clozaril, so the firm finally relented and agreed that the blood test could be done by less expensive companies. Now the average cost per year for Clozaril and the blood tests is approximately $8,000 (500 mg/day)—still expensive, but a real help to many individuals, and Medicaid will pick up some of the expense.

Recently, a new atypical neuroleptic drug called **Risperidal (risperidone)** was introduced that has generated considerable excitement and hope (Land & Salzman, 1994). Like Clozaril, Risperidal is more effective than other neuroleptics for treating positive and negative symptoms, and it does not cause the side effects of involuntary muscle movements (Borison et al., 1992; Kerwin, 1994; Marder & Meibach, 1994). In addition, however, Risperidal is an improvement over Clozaril in that *it does not trigger agranulocytosis* and *it is less expensive.* With Risperidal, then, we may have taken another step on the path to the effective and economical treatment of schizophrenia.

Side Effects of Drug Therapy. We now come to the complex and sometimes serious problem of the side effects of drug therapy for schizophrenia. Just as there is no denying that neuroleptic drugs can reduce the symptoms of schizophrenia, so there is no denying that these drugs can induce a variety of **side effects.** In considering drug therapy, then, we must determine what the side effects are, whether they are serious and treatable, and whether they outweigh the benefits of the drugs.

There are two levels of side effects. At the relatively superficial level, patients who are taking neuroleptics often experience symptoms such as dryness of the mouth or excessive salivation, blurred vision, grogginess, constipation, sensitivity to light, reduced sexual arousal, weight gain, and awkward or slowed motor activity. These effects can be annoying and sometimes embarrassing or disruptive, but they may be acceptable trade-offs for the dramatic reductions in serious symptoms. For example, Betty, about whom you read earlier, has gained a considerable amount of weight and often drools because of excessive salivation, but she says she would rather be "fat and relatively free of symptoms than thin and crazy as a loon."

On the more serious level, there can be side effects that are very dangerous and that can have important long-term implications. Three of those need attention here. First, the most common of the serious side effects involves *involuntary motor movements*. The movements are most often associated with the mouth, lips, and tongue, and patients experience involuntary sucking, chewing, lateral jaw movements, smacking and pursing of the lips, thrusting and twisting of the tongue, and ticlike motions of the lips, eyes, and eyebrows. In some cases, there are also involuntary movements of the arms and trunk, such as twisting of the body and shrugging of the shoulders. In other cases, there can be an involuntary contraction of the diaphragm, which causes the patient to make a noise like a bark. These behaviors are not under voluntary control and go on continually while the patient is awake. This side effect is known as **tardive dyskinesia** (TAR-div dis-ki-NĒ-zhuh). With low-potency neuroleptics, it may be some years before tardive dyskinesia sets in, but with high-potency neuroleptics, minor symptoms may begin appearing within days or weeks (Sweet et al., 1995). Tardive dyskinesia is thought to stem from the fact that the drugs cause the dopamine receptor sites to become *supersensitive* to dopamine. (They seem to be naturally compensating for the fact that the drugs limit the effect of dopamine.) Note that *tardive* means "late-developing" and reflects the fact that there is a delay between when the individual begins taking the drug and when the side effect begins. *Dys-* means "abnormal," and *kinesia* refers to body movements, so the term literally means "late-developing abnormal body movements."

Paradoxically, for some patients, the neuroleptic drugs may be effective in treating the schizophrenia yet leave the patients acting even "crazier" than when they suffered from the schizophrenia. For example, when Betty was taking a high-potency neuroleptic, occasionally her head would snap back and her tongue would stick out. Furthermore, because tardive dyskinesia can interfere with speech, dexterity, eating, and respiration, it can result in serious disabilities and even death.

There are drugs that can diminish the tardive dyskinesia. However, in some cases, the symptoms of tardive dyskinesia are irreversible, suggesting that some permanent structural alterations of the brain have occurred. Because of that, in most cases, the drug is withdrawn or the dosage is reduced as soon as symptoms appear.

Although neuroleptics can bring on tardive dyskinesia, there is now evidence that other factors such as organic brain damage can cause the disorder in the absence of neuroleptics (Khot & Wyatt, 1991; Wegner et al., 1985). We now know that tardive dyskinesia can be part of a general disease process, so not all cases should be blamed on the use of neuroleptics.

A second serious side effect of neuroleptics is the *inability to sit still* (Sachdev & Kruk, 1994). This occurs in about 35% of the individuals who take neuroleptics, and it differs from tardive dyskinesia in that rather than involving random involuntary jerking behaviors, it involves continual and coordinated movements; the individual is constantly moving from place to place. This side effect is called **akathisia** (ak-uh-THIZH-uh), from the Greek for "not to sit." Akathisia can be very disruptive because the patient is constantly moving or using all of his or her attention to stop the moving, thus interfering with other activities. (Note that akathisia can be a side effect of other psychiatric drugs; see Chapter 10 and Case Study 10.2.)

Finally, a relatively rare but very serious side effect is the **malignant neuroleptic syndrome,** the symptoms of which include muscular rigidity, very high temperature that can lead to brain damage, fluctuating blood pressure and heart rate, confusion, agitation, and stupor or coma (Addonizio, 1991; Caroff et al., 1991; Keck et al., 1991; Pope et al., 1991). This side effect is more likely to occur with the high-potency neuroleptics, is more common in women, and appears to be due to a sudden drop in dopamine activity that causes a general dysregulation of the hypothalamus and other control centers in the brain. (This syndrome can also occur when patients stop taking medication for Parkinson's disease, that is, medication that keeps dopamine levels up.) Obviously, this is a very serious syndrome, but it occurs in fewer than 1% of the patients taking neuroleptics, it can be treated effectively if it is diagnosed early, and there is no evidence that it is more likely to return after treatment (Pope et al., 1991).

It is important that patients be warned about the side effects because if the symptoms are not recognized as side effects, they can be very frightening and contribute to the disorder. For example, changes in vision or sensitivity to light could provide the bases for additional delusions, and an unexplained impairment in sexual performance could be very upsetting. However, if these symptoms are initially explained as normal and expected side effects that can be compensated for or treated, their impact will be minimal, especially when compared to the benefits obtained by reduction of the schizophrenic symptoms.

In summary, some patients are troubled by relatively minor side effects, whereas others suffer considerably from serious side effects of their medication, and we must be careful not to ignore or grow insensitive to those problems. However, we must also be cautious in responding to the demands of people who believe that drug therapy should be abandoned because of the side effects. It would be inappropriate to "throw the treatment out with the side effects." At present, the alternative to the side effects is a return to the straitjackets, padded cells, and the "snake pit" wards of earlier days. That is certainly not an attractive option.

Length of Drug Therapy. A question that always arises is, how long do individuals with schizophrenia have to take the medication? Unfortunately, in many cases, schizophrenia is a lifelong disorder, and therefore *many individuals will have to take medication for the rest of their lives.* The fact that many individuals must stay on the drugs for the long term was illustrated by the results of an investigation in which more than 4,000 patients were followed up after their neuroleptic medication was either withdrawn or maintained (Gilbert et al., 1995). The results indicated that within an average of 10 months, 53% of the patients from whom the drugs were withdrawn had a relapse, whereas only 16% of the patients for whom the drugs were maintained had a relapse. In other words, withdrawal of the drugs resulted in an almost 40% increase in relapse rates. The relapse rates over a 2-year period are presented in Figure 13.10.

Actually, there is both bad news and good news in the findings linking drug withdrawal to relapse. The bad news is that many patients relapse when the drugs are withdrawn, and that means that many individuals will have to stay on the medication permanently. The good news is that *not everyone relapses* when the drugs are withdrawn (almost 50% did not), and that means that after an initial period of treatment, some individuals can go off the drugs without dire consequences.

There are two other encouraging findings concerning drug withdrawal. First, there is evidence that the rate of relapse can be reduced by about one-third if the withdrawal is *gradual* rather than abrupt (Baldessarini & Viguera, 1995). Second, the estimates of the relapse rates that were derived from the research may be too high because in the research the patients were selected for drug withdrawal on a *random* basis, but if we carefully select patients for withdrawal who we suspect can survive without the drugs, it is likely that the relapse rate will be reduced (Carpenter & Tamminga, 1995; Greden & Tandon, 1995; Jeste, Gilbert, et al., 1995; Meltzer, 1995a).

Level of Drug Therapy. Even if it is not possible to withdraw the drug, it may be possible to reduce the level of the drug once the symptoms have been stabilized. In one study of patients who had been hospitalized for more than a year and who were taking high levels of Haldol, it was found that on the average it was possible to reduce the drug level by over 60% before the patients' symptoms began to get noticeably worse (Liberman et al., 1994). In fact, some patients even showed *improvements* when the drug levels were reduced, an effect that was probably due to the fact that at the high levels, the drug was causing side effects such as flat affect and slowed thought processes that were misinterpreted as symptoms of the disorder.

Of course, if the drug level is reduced and the symptoms get worse, the drug level can be increased to head off a complete relapse. In one experiment, patients were given small "supplements" in drug dose levels when their relatives reported the onset of minor symptoms such as trouble concentrating, withdrawal, and depression, and those supplements were effective for reducing relapse rates (Marder et al., 1994).

With regard to drug levels, it should be recognized that whereas moderately high levels of neuroleptics are often more effective than low levels, the evidence suggests that *very high levels are not more effective than moderately high levels* (Cole, 1982; Volavka et al., 1992). Insofar as very high doses sometimes seem effective, the benefit is probably due more to the sedation effects (patients are so "knocked out" that they don't show symptoms) than to the antipsychotic effects (Lerner et al., 1979).

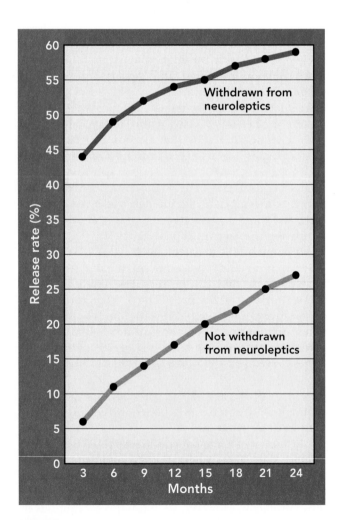

FIGURE 13.10 Relapse rate was higher among patients who were withdrawn from neuroleptics.
Source: Data from Jeste, Gilbert, et al. (1995), p. 210.

It is interesting to note that *women often require lower levels of neuroleptics than men* (Baldessarini et al., 1995; Szymanski et al., 1995; Yonker et al., 1992). When women and men of comparable body size are given comparable doses, women show higher levels of the drugs in their bloodstreams. In terms of symptom relief, it appears that women require only about half as much medication as men. It also appears that women are more responsive to the drugs. For example, in one study, it was found that women had a remission rate of 91%, whereas the figure for men was only 66%, a difference of 25% (Szymanski et al., 1995).

In general, the best overall strategy seems to be first to use whatever level of the drug is necessary to get the symptoms under control and then to slowly reduce the level. If the symptoms do not get worse, further reductions can be tried, and it may even be possible to withdraw the drug completely. However, if the symptoms get worse, a slight increase in the drug can be tried, but if that is not sufficient, the drug can be returned to its originally effective level, and a reduction can be tried again later. The point is that we must always be testing the lower limit of drug level where we can find an acceptable balance in drug level, level of symptoms, and level of side effects. Of course, the frequent testing of the lower limit requires more attention to the patient than the set-it-and-leave-it approach, but symptom monitoring can be done by case managers such as social workers or by family members.

Finally, before concluding this discussion, I should mention two other points. First, at present we do not have any way to determine which drug will be most effective for which patients, and so in many cases we must resort to trial and error (Pickar et al., 1991). The fact that one drug does not work with a particular patient does not necessarily mean that other drugs will not work, and therefore other drugs and combinations of drugs must be tried. Second, the treatment of schizophrenia often involves the use of drugs other than neuroleptics. Use of antidepressants is common because, as you learned earlier, 60% of individuals with schizophrenia also suffer from serious depression. Antidepressants can be very effective for the depression, though they usually have little effect on the schizophrenia (Siris et al., 1994).

COMMENT

There is no doubt that for many patients neuroleptic drugs can be effective for reducing the symptoms of schizophrenia, and the new drugs that are being developed are increasing our effectiveness for treating the disorder. However, three qualifications should be noted. First, the drugs are a treatment, not a cure, and therefore many individuals will have to take the drugs for an extended period of time—possibly for the rest of their lives.

Second, for some individuals the drugs have disruptive and potentially serious side effects. To avoid those side effects, it is essential that we use as low a drug level as possible and try alternative drugs that may not produce the side effects. In most cases, some side effects must be expected, but they may be acceptable trade-offs for the symptom relief that is made possible by the drugs.

Third, neuroleptic drugs can be effective for reducing the symptoms that stem from problems with high levels of neurological activity in the brain, but the drugs cannot do much or anything for the symptoms that stem from structural problems in the brain. For example, in one study, it was found that drugs were effective for treating 83% of the individuals and that *the best predictor of who would not recover was the presence of structural problems in the brain* such as enlarged ventricles (Lieberman et al., 1993). In other words, drugs can be used to treat problems with brain functioning, but they can do little to overcome structural problems in the brain. That places a limitation on their effectiveness.

WHAT CAN WE CONCLUDE CONCERNING THE TREATMENT OF SCHIZOPHRENIA?

The crucial question that is asked by individuals with schizophrenia and their families is, can this terrible disorder be treated? The answer to that question is a guarded yes; *in most cases, schizophrenia is a treatable disorder.* That conclusion is in sharp contrast to what was true only a few years ago. Having drawn that conclusion, let me comment on what treatments are effective and what their limitations are.

First, it must be recognized that *the basic treatment for schizophrenia is physiological;* in most cases, the symptoms are due to problems with neurological activity in the brain, and *neuroleptic drugs are used to adjust those levels of activity.*

Second, because stress can exacerbate the problems with neurological activity, it can be helpful in some cases to reduce the stress in the individuals' lives. That stress reduction or management can be achieved through programs that are loosely called *family therapy, psychoeducation,* or *social skills training.* It is important to note that stress reduction is an adjunct to drug treatment, *not an alternative.*

Third, in some cases it may be helpful to use a program of rewards and punishments to teach the individual to use appropriate behaviors and suppress inappropriate behaviors. That strategy is probably most effective for chronic patients who have not been helped by drugs and whose behavior has deteriorated. Note that although rewards and punishments can be effective for overt behaviors such as grooming and

---

CASE STUDY 13.3

"Can We Talk?" A Personal Account of Therapy Written by a Recovering Patient

"A year and a half ago my therapist asked me if psychotherapy had helped me. I was a bit stunned but answered almost automatically, 'Yes, of course it's helped me.' . . . My therapist's question was prompted by the controversy about whether schizophrenic patients could truly benefit from talk therapy or were best helped by drug therapy. I was somewhat angered by the thought that some schizophrenic patients were being treated only with pills and a monthly rendezvous to pick up a prescription. Perhaps the most dramatic symptoms such as delusions and hallucinations may respond to such treatment, but there is so much more involved in the life of a schizophrenic patient than just these manifestations.

"Even if one adheres to the belief that psychotherapy lends itself more to emotionally oriented problems than to something which appears to be more biochemical, one must take into consideration the emotional aspects of schizophrenia. Besides the day-to-day stress of contending with what often seems to be a monster raging inside one's mind, there are emotional problems that have evolved and accumulated over the course of the patient's life.

"If this is true, the confusion I felt about myself was compounded by what seemed irrational or conflicting actions directed toward me. A child destined to become schizophrenic must deal not only with the seeds of illness within himself but also with the attitudes of others toward his 'idiosyncrasies,' whether these feelings are voiced openly or subtly

manifested in everyday life. Even if medication can free the schizophrenic patient from some of his torment, the scars of emotional confusion remain, felt perhaps more deeply by a greater sensitivity and vulnerability.

"Like so many schizophrenic patients I have my own history of hospitalizations, medication trials—good and bad—setbacks, milestones, turns in the road, light appearing and disappearing at the end of the tunnel. I have seen lights in the sky, heard choruses of people inside me—taunting, tormenting me, pinning me against the wall, driving me into insanity. The drama is endless, and the agony and terror are even more so.

"I have had bright spots in my life, but they all seem to have been achieved in the shadow of illness, and the effort was so exhausting as to dim the exhilaration of the moment. I fought my way through Harvard in the midst of psychosis and 'spaciness,' which I now believe to have been a reaction to neuroleptics and which usually proved worse than psychosis. More than half my college life was spent in a private psychiatric hospital. Between hospitalizations, I attended a day program and spent 3, 4, or 5 nights a week there. In fact, I trudged up the hill leading to the hospital 6 days a week, sometimes twice a day, while I tried to juggle my education with my illness.

"There is no doubt in my mind that therapy helped me get through school. My freshman year and the first half of my sophomore year (until my

---

social interactions that are under voluntary control, the strategy is not effective for altering the problems with cognitive functioning (disorganized thoughts, hallucinations) that form the core of schizophrenia.

Today's neuroleptic drugs can be effective for treating schizophrenia, but they do have some limitations. First, neuroleptics provide a *treatment* for schizophrenia but *not a cure.* You will recall that the same was true in the drug treatment of anxiety and mood disorders (see Chapters 6 and 10), and a similar situation exists for disorders such as diabetes. This means that in many cases, individuals may have to stay on the drugs for prolonged periods of time.

Second, in many cases, the drugs are effective for treating only *some of the symptoms* (primarily positive symptoms), or they *reduce but do not eliminate symptoms*

(hallucinations may be less frequent or less intense). That partial reduction in symptoms may be enough to enable the individual to function effectively in society but not enough to eliminate the burden of coping with the remaining symptoms.

Third, *not all patients are helped by drugs.* Neuroleptics such as Thorazine and Haldol can help about 80% of patients, and atypical neuroleptics such as Clozaril can help about another 10%, but that still leaves about 10% without help. We have come a long way in the drug treatment of schizophrenia, but if you or someone you love is in that remaining percentage, you realize that we have a way to go.

Drugs do not relieve all symptoms and are not effective with all patients because for the most part the drugs only work to reduce high levels of neurological

first hospitalization) I was involved in supportive therapies with two different therapists who seemed to offer day-to-day support that was well-intentioned but was not enough. It was the combination of support and learning to understand why I thought the way I did, why I felt so bad, that gave me the strength to finish school.

"For so long I wondered why my therapist insisted on talking about my relationship with him. He was not my problem; the problem was my life—my past, my fears, what I was going to do tomorrow, how I would handle things, sometimes just how to survive. . . . I took a long time, but finally I saw why it was important to explore my relationship with my therapist—it was the first real relationship I had ever had: that is, the first I felt safe enough to invest myself in. I rationalized that it was all right because I would learn from this relationship how to relate to other people and maybe one day leave behind the isolation of my own world. . . . I often felt at odds with my therapist until I could see that he was a real person and he related to me and I to him, not only as patient and therapist, but as human beings. Eventually I began to feel that I too was a person, not just an outsider looking in on the world.

"With the struggles back and forth it almost seems questionable at times whether all this is really worth it. There are days when I wonder if it might not be more humane to leave the schizophrenic patient to his own world of unreality, not to make him go through the pain it takes to become a part of humanity. Those are the days when the pain is so great, I think I might prefer craziness until I remember the immobilizing terror and the distance and isolation that keep the world so far away and out of focus. It is not an easily resolved dilemma. Either way the schizophrenic patient must withstand intolerable suffering, but it seems that only through psychotherapy can the world of unreality truly be dispelled. There are those bad days, but I must admit that there are other days when I am glad that they did not give up on me and there is someone standing beside me guiding me to the knowledge of another existence.

"Medication or superficial support alone is not a substitute for the feeling that one is understood by another human being. For me, the greatest gift came the day I realized that my therapist really had stood by me for years and that he would continue to stand by me and to help me achieve what I wanted to achieve. With that realization my viability as a person began to grow. I do not profess to be cured—I still feel the pain, fear, and frustration of my illness. I know I have a long road ahead of me, but I can honestly say that I am no longer without hope."

Source: "A Recovering Patient" (1986).

arousal, and some of the symptoms of schizophrenia are due to low levels of neurological arousal or structural abnormalities in the brain. Unfortunately, we do not yet have effective treatments for those latter causes. There is no doubt that drugs can be very helpful in the treatment of schizophrenia, but they are not a panacea.

At the beginning of this chapter, I pointed out that we had made great progress in developing effective treatments for schizophrenia and that we had "turned the corner" in our search for effective treatments. That is true, but unfortunately, not all individuals who suffer from schizophrenia have been able to come around that corner. Some, like Betty, about whom I have talked frequently in this chapter, are still on the dark side, and we can only hope that our progress in the next few years will be as fast as it has been in the past few years.

Through three chapters, we have examined schizophrenia and its treatment from an objective and dispassionate point of view. Before concluding, however, it might be interesting to consider the disorder and its treatment from the patient's perspective. Case Studies 13.3 and 13.4 are patients' personal accounts of their treatment experiences. These cases are not presented as evidence for or against any particular approach, and the experiences of these patients are not necessarily representative of the experiences of all patients. What is most noteworthy about these reports is the importance of medication and also the importance of having another person to whom the patient can turn for help and support during the confusing and sometimes terrifying experience of schizophrenia.

CASE STUDY 13.4
Betty's Therapy: Drugs and More

Case Study 11.2 focused on my friend Betty, who suffers from a severe case of schizophrenia. Betty has numerous symptoms, including hallucinations that monks are chanting, "Cut yourself and die" and that people dissolve into blobs of blood. In this case study, we will review the various therapies Betty has received over the past 20 years. Betty has been hospitalized numerous times, but here we will focus on types of treatment rather than on the experience of hospitalization. (We will discuss hospitalization in Chapter 21.)

David: Would you tell me what type of therapy you tried first?

Betty: Well, I was living in New York City when I had my first break, and not knowing anything about mental illness at the time, I went to see a psychoanalyst. That was a big and costly mistake. We spent hours talking about things that had nothing to do with any of my symptoms. He just didn't understand. He would ask me about my toilet training, and I would try to talk about that while I was hallucinating his plants marching around the room. It was crazy. I saw him for several years, but we got nowhere. I should have been hospitalized.

David: After analysis where did you go?

Betty: Next was megavitamins; that was hot then. I took 40 different vitamins a day. I carried them around with me in a box along with little cups for water and small bits of food to take with the vitamins. At first I felt better, but it didn't last. I don't really think the vitamins helped; I think I just happened to be going through a period in which the symptoms were less intense. When I started becoming ill again, the vitamins did nothing. Finally I just crashed.

David: OK, the vitamins didn't work. What was next?

Betty: When I crashed the doctor gave me CO_2 therapy. I'd never heard of it before, but he seemed to think it would help. First they give you some anticonvulsion medication, and you lay on a table with a mask over your face. You're breathing, but there's no oxygen. You breathe harder and harder, but you can't get your breath, and then all of a sudden, bang, and you're out—unconscious. Oh God, it's terrible; it's like drowning. And while you're out you are supposed to have these good dreams, but my dreams were hideous. God, they were terrible. I don't know how all of this was supposed to help me, but it didn't. I had the treatment once a week for about a year, and it did nothing. In fact, I got worse.

David: All right, CO_2 therapy didn't work. What did you try next?

Betty: Well, for a while I was on and off a lot of different drugs, mostly antidepressants, but they weren't working, so I went into the hospital for shock therapy, ECT.

David: Did it help?

Betty: When I first woke up—for a few hours after a treatment—I guess I felt a little better, but not much. I wasn't as depressed, but the shocks didn't stop my hallucinations or delusions. My doctors didn't want to give up on shocks, though, so they kept giving me more. They were desperate to find something that would work. After I left the hospital, I kept getting the shocks on an outpatient basis. Three times a week, Mom and I would drive to the hospital in the morning so I could get my shocks. But there really wasn't much improvement—even after about 30 shocks.

David: Well, what was next?

Betty: Then I changed doctors, to a specialist in drugs. He tried a lot of drugs; I was always changing drugs trying to find the right one or the right combination.

David: Thorazine? Any help from Thorazine?

Betty: Made me drowsy, but didn't stop the symptoms—I was just drugged.

David: Haldol?

Betty: I had the best response to that, although even that wasn't much. Actually, on Haldol I felt so drugged that I didn't care if I was hallucinating.

David: Side effects? Tardive dyskinesia?

Betty: Off and on. I had a lot of facial twitches—my mouth jerked—and I rocked up and back all the time. That drove my mother nuts! For a while I had really bad side effects. I remember that my head would suddenly jerk back, my eyes would roll up, and my tongue would stick out. That was frightening. When that happened, we reduced the dose level and I started taking more drugs to counteract the side effects.

I don't know if this is a typical reaction to taking a lot of drugs, but I just felt like my world was coming apart inside me—coming and going—all very strange. I took Haldol, Stelazine, all of the tricyclics, and all of the MAO inhibitors. I took everything in every combination. Then we tried Clozaril.

David: Tell me about the Clozaril.

Betty: When it first became available, my doctor thought I would be a good candidate. It was very expensive, but I was getting worse and they were getting ready to admit me to the state hospital. I couldn't afford Clozaril, so we went to court to sue Medicaid to pay for it. It was a class-action suit so other patients could get it too. The argument was, it's expensive, but less expensive than going in the hospital—which was the direction I was headed. We won, so I could get the drug.

David: Did the Clozaril help?

Betty: Well, first they had to put me in the hospital while I changed drugs. Every two weeks they would reduce my other medication and up the level of the Clozaril a little. And when I finally got off the Haldol and onto the Clozaril, I felt really good—almost back to normal. I was feeling like normal people do, and I was thrilled. I was doing so well that when I came back home, the public television station did a special report on me and the effects of the Clozaril. Being on Clozaril was like the patients in the movie *Awakenings:* I was back, I was normal, and it was wonderful! I was really doing great for a few months—*(long pause)*—and then bam, they were back.

David: "They?"

Betty: The demons, the voices, the monks chanting, the fears about the police—everything. All the symptoms came back. It was terrible, so depressing. But I would never put Clozaril down because it helped a lot for a while, and things are better now than they could be. I'm on the highest dose possible, 900 milligrams a day! I'm just very drug-resistant.

David: You think the Clozaril is helping. Are you having any side effects?

Betty: The weight gain is the worst; I gained more than 20 pounds. I'm becoming a blimp, but I'd rather be fat than mentally ill. Oh, and sometimes the Clozaril makes me drool, but that's not a big deal.

David: Are you on any other drugs?

Betty: A lot. Zoloft for depression—two 100-milligram tablets twice a day. Klonopin, an antianxiety medication—four 2-milligram tablets at bedtime. That helps me sleep. Next is chloral hydrate. That's a classic old sleeping medication, and I take one before going to bed. Oxybutynin—that is for my bladder problem. The medication makes me incontinent, and this takes care of that. Oh, yes, I also take Ativan for anxiety.

David: That's a lot of medication, but you still have the serious symptoms. How do you handle what can't be controlled with the drugs?

Betty: What people have to understand is that schizophrenia is a physical disease—a problem with the brain—so it has to be treated with drugs. Unfortunately, in most cases, the drugs are not enough. People with schizophrenia have to cope with a lot of problems—symptoms that can't be completely controlled with the drugs and problems in daily living that are caused by the symptoms. For those other problems we need social support.

David: Where do you get that social support?

Betty: Well, my case manager is important. She checks with me regularly and helps with all kinds of problems, like taking care of all of the Medicaid forms and things like that. Then I have some very good friends who are also patients. We can support each other because we know what the other person is going through. We can be frank with each other. We know what the symptoms are, so we understand. It makes you feel less alone. Other patients are important, but it is also very important to have friends who are not sick. The problem is, it is hard to make those connections; we get stuck in a psychiatric clique, a psychiatric ghetto. You have to make contacts in the real world, but that's hard. It's like trying to make integration work. One of the most important

continued

CASE STUDY 13.4 *(continued)*

---

things for me is to have someone to call when I get really sick—someone to call when I am depressed or bothered by a delusion and need reassurance. That's when I call you, like last week when I was hallucinating voices from the drain and outside my window that were so real—I called you for reassurance that it was a hallucination. Those "reality checks" and support are important because the drugs can't do it all.

In a recent note to me, Betty summed up the importance of contact with others, and she gave me permission to print part of that note here.

Thank you for talking with me yesterday. I don't understand quite what was wrong, but things weren't adding up. You were most helpful in making things more cohesive for me. Thank you. I usually handle things better when I can identify the source. Most of the time my logic is random. Some things get processed, and others are like black holes. I guess I should be grateful for what I have. I am so much better than when I was on the Haldol. I am slowly coming to accept myself as something more than a broken doll. You have been wonderful to me. You gave me stature and took me seriously. *You saw me as something besides illness.* You have no idea what a gift you gave to me.

SUMMARY

- Traditional psychotherapy is not effective for treating schizophrenia.
- Family therapy, psychoeducation, and social skills training are focused on teaching the patient and family (a) about the disorder, (b) how to reduce the stress that exacerbates the symptoms, and (c) how to cope with the symptoms. These approaches can be very effective for reducing symptoms, reducing the need for drugs, and reducing relapses.
- Milieu therapy is designed to enrich the lives of hospitalized patients. It can be helpful, but caution must be used not to overstimulate patients who are suffering from stimulus overload.
- Behavior therapy and token economies are effective for changing general behaviors (cooperation, grooming) but are not effective for changing disorganized cognitive behaviors or emotional behaviors.
- Cognitive therapy is focused on changing erroneous beliefs, but merely recognizing that a "voice" is a "hallucination" does not eliminate the hallucination.
- ECT is not effective for treating schizophrenia, but it can be helpful for treating the depression that often accompanies schizophrenia. ECT can increase amnesia and confusion in individuals with schizophrenia.
- Psychosurgery (prefrontal and transorbital lobotomies) were not effective for treating schizophrenia.
- Neuroleptic drugs are used to reduce high levels of dopamine-related neurological activity by blocking dopamine receptor sites and possibly by making postsynaptic neurons less sensitive to stimulation. Certain (high-potency) neuroleptics influence symptoms by altering serotonin activity.
- Low-potency neuroleptics (e.g., Thorazine) and high-potency neuroleptics (e.g., Haldol) are effective for treating positive symptoms, whereas atypical neuroleptics (e.g., Clozaril, Risperidal) are effective for treating both positive and negative symptoms.
- Low- and high-potency neuroleptics have a variety of side effects, the most serious of which is tardive dyskinesia (involuntary muscle movements). Atypical neuroleptics do not lead to tardive dyskinesia because they block only the D-2

receptors, but one atypical neuroleptic (Clozaril) can cause agranulocytosis, which is a serious decline in immune system functioning.

■ Patients may have to take neuroleptics for the rest of their lives because without them, the chance of relapse is increased. However, in some cases, it may be possible to reduce the level of medication gradually. Very high levels of medication are not more effective than moderate levels (the higher levels simply sedate more), and men often require higher doses than women. It may be necessary to experiment to determine which drug at which dose level is most effective for a particular patient.

KEY TERMS, CONCEPTS, AND NAMES

In reviewing and testing yourself on what you have learned from this chapter, you should be able to identify and discuss each of the following.

agranulocytosis	extrapyramidal symptoms	psychosurgery
akathisia	family therapy	psychotherapy
atypical neuroleptics	Haldol (haloperidol)	Risperdal (risperidone)
behavior theory	high-potency neuroleptics	serotonin
bundling	low-potency neuroleptics	side effects
Clozaril (clozapine)	malignant neuroleptic syndrome	social skills training
D-1 receptors	milieu therapy	tardive dyskinesia
D-2 receptors	neuroleptics	Thorazine (chlorpromazine)
dopamine	prefrontal lobotomy	token economy
electroconvulsive therapy (ECT)	psychoeducation	transorbital lobotomy

CHAPTER FOURTEEN
PERSONALITY DISORDERS

OUTLINE

For Louise, everything must be "just right." She can spend hours laying out and preparing her clothes for the next day, and then she is still not satisfied. When it comes to studying, she uses three colors of felt-tipped pens for underlining: red for very important ideas, blue for less important ideas, and yellow for ideas that are merely interesting. She has her pens and 10 perfectly sharpened pencils carefully arranged on her desk, which is always extraordinarily neat (books are put away, the top is dusted every day, and the drawers are meticulously arranged). Louise is never happy because she never feels "on top of things." She has few friends because her organizational activities take up so much time. Also, other people become annoyed with her need for control and lack of spontaneity, so they avoid her. Louise suffers from the *obsessive-compulsive personality disorder*.

■ ■ ■

Darryl is very distrustful of everyone. He does not have any obvious delusions that others are plotting against him, but he is constantly and unjustifiably suspicious of everyone. Because of this, he is anxious and distant, and he works best alone. Darryl appears to have a *paranoid personality disorder*.

■ ■ ■

Stan can be a lot of fun to be around because he is charming, bright, articulate, outgoing, and always ready to do something wild. Although Stan is very gregarious, he is actually self-centered and insensitive to the needs of others, and he will often take advantage of others. For example, while living with one woman, he was "sleeping around" and not making much of an attempt to cover his tracks. When confronted, he talked his way out of it, effectively blaming the other women. A careful review of his background reveals that he has been in and out of a lot of scrapes, usually because he acted impulsively to satisfy some spur-of-the-moment want. For example, as an adolescent, he frequently cut school, was drunk, used other people's money without repaying it, and a couple of times stole a car to go joyriding. In most cases, he was able to con his way out of the trouble, only to repeat the behavior a short time later. Although he has frequently hurt those around him, he has never shown anxiety or remorse about his behavior. He just does not seem to have a conscience. Stan would be diagnosed as suffering from the *antisocial personality disorder*, but it is actually the people around him who suffer.

■ ■ ■

In this chapter I will discuss a variety of problems that are known as **personality disorders.** These disorders differ from the others we have discussed in that in most cases individuals with personality disorders behave in *less deviant ways* and are usually *less distressed*. In fact, some critics have suggested that many of the behaviors seen in personality disorders are not really abnormal but simply reflect differences in adjustment within the normal range. The issue that underlies the controversy over whether these behaviors are disorders revolves around the question of where we should draw the line between normal and abnormal behavior. At present, the trend seems to be to set the cutoff point low and include more people in the abnormal category. However, because the personality disorders are recognized as less severe, they are organized on Axis II of the DSM. (Note that all of the disorders that have been discussed so far were on Axis I in the DSM; see Chapter 3 for a discussion of the DSM.)

It is important to recognize that at one time or another most of us have shown some of the symptoms seen in the personality disorders. For example, we may have been dependent, passive, self-centered, emotionally detached, or guilt-free after doing something wrong. However, that does not mean that we have one of the disorders. Three factors separate people who have the disorders from those who do not. First, an individual with a disorder will *consistently* use the behaviors in question, whereas nondisturbed individuals will use them only occasionally. Second, an individual with a disorder will show a *more extreme* level of the behavior. For example, there is a difference between being orderly and being compulsive. Third, in disturbed individuals the behavior results in *serious and prolonged problems with functioning or happiness.* It is important to keep these distinctions in mind so that you do not erroneously attribute a personality disorder to an individual who only sometimes shows a low level of the behavior in question and whose life is not disrupted by those instances.

This chapter has two major sections. In the first section, I will discuss the *antisocial personality disorder* in some detail, and in the second section, I will review a variety of other personality disorders.

Antisocial personality disorder is the official diagnostic label for the problem we will discuss in this section, but individuals with this disorder are commonly referred to as **psychopaths** or **sociopaths.** For the sake of convenience, in this chapter we will use the abbreviation **APD** for *antisocial personality disorder.*

A thorough understanding of the APD is important because individuals with the disorder are among the most interpersonally destructive and emotionally harmful individuals in our society. Interestingly, with most other disorders, most of the problems are suffered by the individual *with* the disorder, but in the case of the APD, most of the problems are suffered by the *people around the disordered individual.* One of the difficulties with individuals who have the APD is that they do not

show any of the traditional signs of abnormal behavior such as anxiety or hallucinations, and in fact they often appear to be very well adjusted. This makes them exceptionally difficult to recognize and diagnose, and as long as they go unrecognized, they continue causing problems for the people around them.

SYMPTOMS OF THE ANTISOCIAL PERSONALITY DISORDER

Diagnostic Criteria

Individuals with the APD do not have any of the traditional symptoms of abnormal behavior such as depression, anxiety, hallucinations, or delusions. Instead, the diagnosis of this disorder is based on a *history of antisocial behavior.* The specific symptoms that are necessary for a diagnosis of APD are listed in Table 14.1.

Discussion of Symptoms

Here I will discuss the symptoms necessary for a diagnosis of APD as indicated in Table 14.1 and describe some of the other symptoms that are often associated with the disorder so that you will be better able to recognize and understand the disorder. It now appears that there

TABLE 14.1 Diagnostic Criteria for the Antisocial Personality Disorder

1. The individual shows a *pervasive disregard for the rights of others* since age 15 as indicated by at least three of the following:
   a. Repeated illegal behavior
   b. Repeated lying or conning of others for profit or pleasure
   c. Impulsivity
   d. Aggressiveness as indicated by repeated fights or assaults
   e. Disregard for the safety of self or others
   f. Irresponsibility as indicated by poor work performance or failure to honor financial obligations
   g. A lack of remorse as indicated by being indifferent to hurting, mistreating, or stealing from others
2. The individual is *at least 18 years old.* (This requirement is included to ensure that the individual has had time to learn the appropriate behavior.)
3. There is *evidence of a conduct disorder* before the age of 15. (A conduct disorder involves essentially the same type of behaviors as the APD but occurs in children; see Chapter 15.)

Source: Adapted from American Psychiatric Association (1994).

are two major dimensions to the APD; the first involves *antisocial behaviors,* and the second involves a *lack of anxiety* (Frick et al., 1994; Hare et al., 1991; Harpur et al., 1994). The lack of anxiety apparently leads to the antisocial behavior because without anxiety, there is nothing to inhibit the individual, and lower levels of anxiety are related to more severe and chronic levels of antisocial behavior.

Lack of Anxiety. As just indicated, the most important of the symptoms associated with the APD is a *lack of anxiety or guilt.* Individuals with the APD are often said to be "conscienceless" individuals. For example, after doing something wrong, inappropriate, or illegal (not returning borrowed money or killing someone), an individual with the APD will show no anxiety, guilt, or remorse. Because they do not have the restraints that are typically provided by anxiety, individuals with the APD tend to be "loose," and impulsive, and have a devil-may-care attitude.

In one interesting demonstration of the lack of anxiety in individuals with the APD, individuals who did or did not have the disorder heard sentences that were neutral (e.g., "I am relaxing on my living room couch looking out the window on a sunny autumn day") or threatening (e.g., "Taking a shower, alone in the house, I hear the sound of someone forcing the door, and I panic") while their heart rates were monitored (Patrick et al., 1994). The results indicated that when exposed to the neutral sentences, individuals who did and did not have the APD showed similar small changes in heart rate, but when exposed to the threatening sentences, individuals who did not have the disorder showed large increases in heart rate whereas individuals who did have the disorder showed only small increases in heart rate. In other words, when

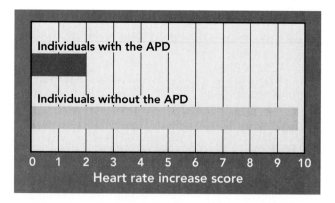

FIGURE 14.1 Individuals with the antisocial personality disorder (APD) showed less heart rate response (anxiety) to threat than individuals without the APD. Score reflects the heart rate response to threatening sentences minus the response to neutral sentences.
Source: Adapted from Patrick et al. (1994), p. 532, fig. 3.

exposed to a threat, the individuals with the APD did not show the physiological responses that reflect anxiety. Those findings are summarized in Figure 14.1.

Another interesting demonstration of the lack of anxiety in individuals with the APD was based on the finding that we are more likely to tense our facial muscles and to blink our eyes when we see something stressful (Patrick et al., 1993). In the experiment, individuals who did and did not have the APD were shown slides of pleasant subjects (e.g., food, sports scenes, children) and slides of unpleasant subjects (e.g., mutilated bodies, aimed guns, snakes) while their facial muscle activity and eye blinks were recorded. A comparison of the responses to the pleasant and unpleasant scenes indicated that the individuals with the APD showed smaller increases in facial muscle tension and fewer eye blinks than the individuals who did not suffer from the APD.

Narcissism and Hedonism. Individuals with the APD are *narcissistic* (self-centered) and *hedonistic* (pleasure seeking). They seem to be guided by the dictum "I want what I want when I want it"—and they take what they want regardless of the cost to others. In many cases, individuals with the APD appear to be unable or unwilling to delay gratification of their needs, and consequently they act impulsively, with only their own wants in mind. In doing so, they frequently harm people around them.

Shallow Feelings and Lack of Attachment to Others. A third symptom is a *shallowness of feelings* and *lack of emotional attachment to others.* Individuals with the APD often verbalize strong feelings and commitments (e.g., they quickly profess love), but their behavior indicates otherwise. For example, an individual with the APD may be involved in numerous sexual relationships, but those relationships come and go without having any real impact on the individual.

Social Skills and the Ability to Rationalize Behaviors. It is especially noteworthy that people with the APD typically appear to be *very intelligent,* have well-developed *verbal and social skills,* and have the ability to *rationalize* their inappropriate behavior so that it appears reasonable and justifiable. Because of these abilities, when they get themselves in trouble, they are often able to talk their way out of it.

Consider the example of a charming 26-year-old male who, three days before he was to be married, was discovered by his fiancée to be having a very active affair with another woman. When confronted with irrefutable evidence of his inappropriate behavior, the young man first professed his unfaltering love for his fiancée and then went on to explain in the most sincere manner imaginable that he had no real feelings for the other woman (which in a sense was probably true) and that he was having the affair only as a means of testing his love for his fiancée. Indeed, he explained that he participated in the affair for the good of his fiancée so that once his love had been tested and found to be true, no one else would ever pose a threat to their relationship. He expressed some surprise at her lack of understanding of his affair, but he promised that nothing like that would ever happen again. They were married as planned, but the young man proceeded to engage in a long series of indiscretions, each of which was "explainable" and was followed by professions of remorse and more promises to reform.

Impulsivity and Sensation Seeking. Lack of anxiety leads individuals with the APD to behave *impulsively*. An interesting aspect of their behavior that has been receiving attention lately is what is referred to as high *sensation-seeking behavior*. These people often engage in wild and dangerous activities (e.g., fast driving, skydiving) "for kicks" rather than to achieve some goal. If they take drugs, the drugs are more likely to be stimulants than sedatives. In a less dramatic vein, individuals with the APD tell lies from which they cannot possibly reap any benefit other than the intrigue and "danger" associated with perpetrating the deception.

Inability to Benefit from Punishment. Most individuals with the APD also appear *unable to benefit from punishment*. In many situations, these people can avoid punishment by talking their way out of it, but when they are punished, the punishment does not appear to have any effect, regardless of its severity. One individual I know of was jailed for car theft, and when he was released on bail, he stole a car to get home! Because individuals with the APD do not seem to learn or benefit from their experiences, they are not deterred and tend to engage in the same inappropriate behavior again and again, even when they are repeatedly punished for the behavior.

Physical Aggression. Individuals with the APD frequently cause emotional and financial harm to those around them, but as a general rule, they do not engage in overt physical aggression. However, there is a subset of individuals with the disorder who may act very aggressively in some situations. The attention given by the media to aggressive behavior of these individuals is disproportionate to the frequency with which that symptom occurs. The acts of aggression get attention because they are so extreme and senseless. Examples of widely publicized cases include Richard Speck, who killed eight nurses one evening in an apartment in Chicago; the two killers who were made famous in Tru-

Serial killer Ted Bundy could probably be diagnosed as having suffered from the antisocial personality disorder. He used his good looks, intelligence, and charm to get close to his victims—all young women—whom he sexually abused and then murdered. Bundy was executed in Florida.

man Capote's book *In Cold Blood;* Ted Bundy, who was suspected of killing more than 20 women in five states (including two women in a sorority house whom he battered to death); and Kenneth Bianchi, the Hillside Strangler (see Case Study 7.2).

An example of an individual with an APD is presented in Case Study 14.1.

ISSUES ASSOCIATED WITH THE ANTISOCIAL PERSONALITY DISORDER

Prevalence and Duration

Community studies have indicated that about 5% of men but only about 1% of women suffer from the APD (Kessler et al., 1994; Golomb et al., 1995; Robins et al., 1984;). The disorder seems to be most apparent during late adolescence and early adulthood, and then, for reasons that are not yet understood, it seems to "burn out" at around age 40 (Craft, 1969; Gibbens et al., 1955; Maddocks, 1970; Weiss, 1973). It is fortunate that

CASE STUDY 14.1

An Individual with the Antisocial Personality Disorder

As a child, Doug was well liked because of his good looks and charming manner. His parents thought he could do no wrong. In fact, however, Doug often disobeyed his parents and teachers, but he usually had a convincing explanation for his actions, or he blamed his friends. Therefore, he was seldom punished for this misbehavior. Once, when he was 7, he told all of his friends that he was having a birthday but that he was not going to have a party or get any presents because his father was not working. Hearing that, the neighbors gave him a big party and lots of presents—only to learn that he had lied. His father was working, and it was not even his birthday! His parents thought it was "cute," and he was not punished.

In high school, Doug had a series of girlfriends (indeed, he was much sought after) and many casual male buddies, but he never formed close attachments with anyone. His peers looked up to him because he was extroverted and daring, always ready to try something new. The first clear sign of antisocial behavior occurred when Doug was 15. He stole a car that belonged to an older friend and took three buddies on a joyride that lasted several hours. When they were finally caught, Doug lied about his part in the theft, blaming the friends who had accompanied him. His parents believed him, and they convinced the local police that Doug was innocent, so he again went unpunished for his actions.

Doug went to college but never graduated. He had the intelligence to do well, but he just stopped going to class. When he was about to be thrown out of school, he conned a woman in the admissions office into ignoring that last semester's grades (all Fs) by telling her that he had missed class because he had been going home to take care of his parents, who had been in a serious accident. Impressed with his devotion to his parents and his sincere hope to do better, she gave him an exemption.

One summer, when his parents thought that he was in school taking "extra courses," he was in fact in Aspen tending bar. He got his roommate to forward his checks from home to Colorado.

After college, Doug did not hold any job for long. Although he could be hardworking, he usually lost his jobs because he did something foolish. For example, a number of times he simply did not show up for

a few days because on the spur of the moment he had decided to go backpacking. Once while working as an automobile salesman, he drove off one night in a very expensive demonstrator model and did not return. He made no attempt to conceal the car and was caught within a week. When taken to court, he claimed that he had intended to return to work the next day and that it was all a "misunderstanding." In exchange for his promise to pay for the use of the car, he was given a suspended sentence. Two days later, he left town.

At age 26, Doug married a girl of 18 who worked in one of the bars he frequented. They married almost "as a lark," and neither knew much about the other. He was unemployed, but she believed one of his "lines" in the bar and thought he was a stockbroker. Without her knowing it, they lived for the first couple of months off her savings, which he took from the bank. He also forged checks to pay for a car he leased and the numerous items of clothing he bought for himself. Also unknown to his wife, within two weeks of the marriage, he was having affairs with two other women (his wife thought he was seeing clients). He was eventually caught and convicted for check forgery and served six months in jail. A month after he was jailed, his wife discovered that she was pregnant. When his wife went to pick him up on the day he was scheduled to be released from jail, she discovered that he had been released early "for good behavior" and had left town.

In another state, Doug assumed another name, soon met the daughter of a wealthy family, and began to court the woman. She was completely taken in by Doug's good looks, charm, attentive manner, and intelligence. He portrayed himself as a sensitive and lonely man who was rejected by his parents. He told her that he had plans to develop a retirement home, and the woman began giving him substantial amounts of money to lay the groundwork for the project. Doug took the money, opened a lavish office, and started an affair with his secretary.

The problems described here probably constitute only the tip of the iceberg of Doug's inappropriate behavior; because he was so effective at conning people, much of his misbehavior went undetected or unreported.

the burnout occurs because, as we will learn later, this disorder is exceptionally resistant to treatment.

Primary Versus Secondary Disorders

There appear to be two types of the APD, the **primary** and the **secondary.** Low levels of anxiety are characteristic of both types, but the types differ in the *processes that are responsible for the low levels of anxiety.* In the primary APD, the individual is thought to be largely *incapable of developing anxiety.* In contrast, in the secondary APD, the individual is thought to be capable of developing anxiety but has *learned to avoid it.* The difference in the processes that lead to low anxiety is important for understanding the development of the disorder and planning treatment strategies. For example, there could be little done to treat individuals who are incapable of developing anxiety, but those who avoid it might be treatable. (I will consider the development and treatment of the types later.)

Historical Background

The concept of the antisocial personality disorder has gone through four steps in its development, and an understanding of those steps is helpful for understanding current thinking about the disorder. The concept initially developed from the recognition that there was a disorder in which individuals behaved inappropriately but did not have other symptoms. This form of "madness" was referred to as "insanity without delirium" (Pinel, 1806). The disorder was also sometimes referred to as **moral insanity** because the inappropriate behaviors involved things such as lying, cheating, and stealing (Prichard, 1835).

The second step in the development of the concept occurred when it became generally accepted that the disorder had a *physiological basis.* That is, individuals with the disorder were thought to be suffering from a "moral depravity" because of a problem in the area of the brain that is responsible for "moral faculties" (Rush, 1812). Similarly, it was common to talk about the "born delinquent" and the "constitutional inferiority" of these individuals (Lombroso, 1911). The label that was then used for individuals with this disorder was *psychopath,* a term that reflected the suspected underlying physiological problem, a "pathology of the psyche" (Koch, 1891).

Next, in the 1930s and 1940s, attention was shifted to the potential *interpersonal and social causes* of the disorder (Cleckley, 1941). That shift was consistent with the growing awareness of psychological causes for disorders, and it resulted in the adoption of the

label *sociopath* for individuals with the disorder, an obvious reference to potential *societal* contributions to the disorder.

The current approach to the labeling of disorders in general avoids any explicit or implicit inferences concerning the causes of disorders. Therefore, in DSM-IV the terms *psychopath* and *sociopath* are not used, and the disorder has been given the neutral descriptive label of *antisocial personality disorder.*

With this information as background, I can go on to describe the current explanations for the disorder. Most attention has been focused on explaining the lack of anxiety that is seen in this disorder because it is the lack of anxiety that appears to underlie the other symptoms; that is, without anxiety, there is nothing to inhibit the individuals' inappropriate behaviors. A variety of explanations have been offered, and although they originally competed with one another, they now seem to be coming together as different pieces of the puzzle.

PSYCHODYNAMIC EXPLANATIONS

Early Family Influences

Traditionally, the APD was thought to stem from *bad parenting*—rejection, neglect, lack of love, abuse, and inconsistencies in parents' responses to the child (e.g., Bowlby, 1952; Cleckley, 1976; Lindner, 1944; McCord & McCord, 1964). Consistent with that, there is evidence that many individuals with the APD are raised in homes in which the parenting can be described as bad on almost every relevant dimension. For example, in one early study, the investigators identified 30-year-old men who either had the APD, had an anxiety disorder, or were normal, and then the investigators used information that had been gathered 20 years earlier to compare the backgrounds of the men (Roff, 1974). The results indicated that when compared to the anxious and normal men, those with the APD had mothers who were more likely to have (a) neglected them, (b) not exerted control over them, (c) wished to be rid of them, (d) abandoned them, and (e) been physically cruel to them. Similarly, their fathers wished to be rid of them and were more likely to abandon them. The fact that the men with the anxiety disorders did not have backgrounds of abuse and neglect suggests that those factors were linked specifically to the development of the APD rather than to abnormality in general. Some of those findings are illustrated in Figure 14.2. In a more recent study, it was found that the amount of abuse to which individuals were exposed as children was related to the severity of their APD as adults (Luntz & Widom, 1994).

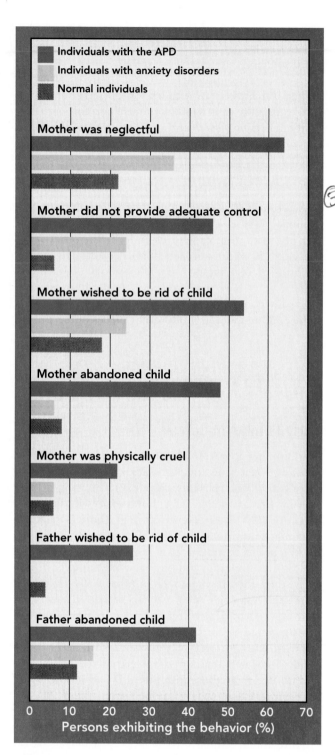

Mother was neglectful

Mother did not provide adequate control

Mother wished to be rid of child

Mother abandoned child

Mother was physically cruel

Father wished to be rid of child

Father abandoned child

Legend:
- Individuals with the APD
- Individuals with anxiety disorders
- Normal individuals

0 10 20 30 40 50 60 70
Persons exhibiting the behavior (%)

FIGURE 14.2 Individuals with the antisocial personality disorder were exposed to neglect and abuse as children. *Source:* Data from Roff (1974).

It is clear that there is a link between bad parenting and the APD, but the question is, why? There are three possibilities. First, it is usually assumed that *bad parenting causes the APD.* That could occur in a variety of ways, one of which would be modeling. That is, children who see their parents as cruel and neglecting may adopt those traits themselves.

Second, it is also possible that the *antisocial behavior of the child caused the parents to behave inappropriately* and to become bad parents (Bell, 1968). That is, when faced with incorrigible antisocial behavior on the part of a child, in desperation the parents might try different approaches to child rearing (become inconsistent), attempt more severe measures for gaining control (use excessive punishment), or withdraw in frustration (appear to reject the child).

Third, it is possible that the bad parenting and the antisocial behavior of the child both stemmed from a third factor, a *common gene pool*. In that regard, it is noteworthy that the descriptions of the parents of antisocial children suggest that the parents were themselves antisocial. If that is the case, and if it is assumed that personality is at least partly inherited, we could conclude that the similarity in the behavior of the parents and the children was determined by their shared genes rather than their social interactions.

Which explanation is correct? Before attempting to answer that question, let's consider some other explanations.

LEARNING EXPLANATIONS

Deficit in Classical Conditioning

Learning theorists have offered two explanations for why individuals with the APD do not develop anxiety. The first explanation begins with the idea that *anxiety is a classically conditioned response* and goes on to suggest that individuals with the primary type of the APD *do not classically condition well* and therefore do not develop anxiety. In other words, individuals with the APD are not anxious because they have a deficit in the ability to develop classically conditioned anxiety responses.

It is important to recognize that the **deficit in classical conditioning** explanation is limited to *classical* conditioning. It does not suggest that individuals with the APD have an impairment in the ability to develop *operantly* conditioned responses. (Those two types of conditioning apparently occur in different parts of the brain.) Therefore, the ability of these individuals to learn nonemotional responses is not impaired. Indeed, the clinical picture presented by individuals with the APD suggests that they are of average or superior intelligence and that they know what is right and wrong but do not conform their behavior to the rules. Having made that distinction, we can now consider the research that is relevant to the deficit-in-classical-conditioning explanation.

Classical Conditioning. The first set of experiments to be considered was conducted to determine whether individuals with the APD do in fact classically condition anxiety responses less well than other individuals. In these experiments, individuals who either did or did not have the APD participated in a series of conditioning trials in which they were presented with a tone, followed by a brief pause, and then a painful electric shock. The question was, would individuals with the APD be less likely to develop a conditioned anxiety response to the tone than other individuals? In these experiments, anxiety was measured during the pause following the tone, and the measure of anxiety was their electrodermal responses. (Electrodermal responses involve increases and decreases in moisture on the hand, which are influenced by anxiety. You may have noticed that when you are anxious, your palms sweat.)

The results of a variety of experiments indicate that individuals who had the APD required more trials to learn (condition) the anxiety response and that they gave fewer anxiety responses than individuals who did not have the disorder (Hare, 1965a; Hare & Craigen, 1974; Hare & Quinn, 1971; Lykken, 1957; Schachter & Latané, 1964). The results of one of these experiments are presented graphically in Figure 14.3.

In another investigation, the classical conditioning of 104 adolescents was measured, and the individuals were followed up 10 years later to determine which of them engaged in some form of antisocial behavior (Loeb & Mednick, 1976). If we assume that the antisocial behavior was due to the APD, and if it is true that the APD is due to poor classical conditioning, then it would be expected that the individuals who engaged in antisocial behavior would have demonstrated poorer classical conditioning than individuals who did not engage in antisocial behavior. That is exactly what the investigators found; individuals who engaged in antisocial behavior had shown poor classical conditioning 10 years earlier. Hence there is substantial and consistent evidence that people with the APD do not develop classically conditioned anxiety as well as other people. With that established, we must examine the question of whether a deficit in classical conditioning influences the *behavior* of individuals with the APD, and for that we must turn to the research on avoidance conditioning.

Avoidance Conditioning. Before discussing the results of the research on **avoidance conditioning,** it will be helpful if I briefly describe the procedures and their relevance here. In experiments on avoidance conditioning, individuals work on problems that involve making a series of responses, and the individuals are punished (usually with electrical shocks) each time they respond incorrectly. For example, an individual working on a "mental maze" (throwing a series of switches in a specific order) is given an electrical shock each time a mistake is made. Performance in avoidance conditioning situations improves when, through the

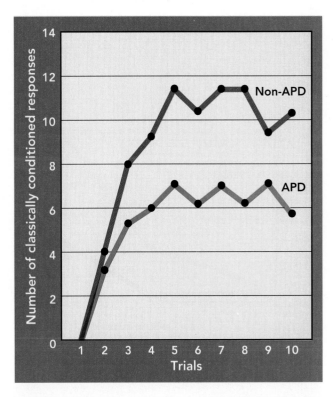

FIGURE 14.3 Persons with the antisocial personality disorder classically condition more slowly than other people.
Source: Hare (1965a), p. 369, fig. 1-A.

process of classical conditioning, anxiety is associated with the incorrect response and then that response is avoided in order to avoid anxiety.

Avoidance conditioning experiments are relevant for studying the APD because if individuals with the disorder are less likely to develop classically conditioned anxiety, they should also be less anxious about making incorrect responses, and therefore they should perform less well than individuals who do not have the disorder. Avoidance conditioning experiments provide a good analogue for numerous real-life situations in which you are punished for making an inappropriate response and hence in the future you avoid that response and use a more appropriate response instead. For example, if an individual cheats on an examination and gets punished, the next time he or she thinks about cheating, anxiety will increase, and to avoid that, the individual will not cheat.

The results of numerous experiments indicate that individuals with the APD evidence poorer avoidance conditioning than other individuals (Hare, 1965b; Hare & Craigen, 1974; Lykken, 1957; Rosen & Schalling, 1971; Schachter & Latané, 1964; Schmauk, 1970). The results of one of these experiments are presented in Figure 14.4. In that experiment, the participants sat in front of a box containing four switches. The box was programmed so as to constitute a compli-

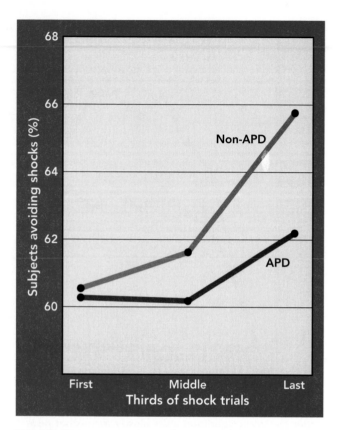

FIGURE 14.4 Individuals with the antisocial personality disorder did not learn to avoid shock responses as well as other individuals.
Source: Adapted from Schachter and Latané (1964), p. 248, fig. 2A.

cated mental maze with 20 decision points. For each decision point, the participant had to press one of the four switches. One of the switches was designated as "correct" and advanced the participant to the next choice point, but the other switches were designated as "incorrect." Pressing an incorrect switch did not advance the participant and instead caused delivery of an electrical shock. The results in Figure 14.4 indicate that the individuals with the APD showed less avoidance of the shocked switches than the other individuals. It can be inferred from these results that the individuals with the APD did not develop the classically conditioned anxiety that underlies performance in avoidance conditioning.

The results of this experiment indicate that individuals who have the APD do not learn to avoid incorrect responses that are punished. These results are consistent with the clinical picture of individuals with the APD; they do not inhibit inappropriate responses. Thus a considerable amount of evidence supports the deficit-in-classical-conditioning explanation for the lack of anxiety and consequent lack of inhibitions in individuals with the APD.

Operantly Conditioned Avoidance of Anxiety

The second learning explanation begins with the premise that during a normal childhood, children are punished for misbehaviors and that in an attempt to avoid the punishment and the anxiety associated with it, children stop misbehaving and instead behave appropriately. However, the **operantly conditioned avoidance** explanation suggests that during childhood, individuals *learn* with the APD learn operant responses that they can use *to be* to *avoid the punishment* that should follow the inappropri-*cunning* ate behavior, and thus they avoid the anxiety and eliminate the restraints against misbehavior (Maher, 1966).

Consider the following simple example: 4-year-old Billy is caught eating cookies before dinner, an act that his mother has expressly forbidden. When caught, but before his mother begins to punish him, Billy contritely admits that he knew that he was not supposed to eat the cookies, and he professes sorrow over the fact that he did not obey. Furthermore, he goes on to point out that the problem was that his mother is "such a *wonderful* cook" and "the cookies were *so good*," he just could not help himself! Billy also adds in the most endearing manner that in the future, he will try hard to avoid falling prey to temptation.

An interaction like this can have a number of effects that may be relevant to the development of the APD. If Billy can con his mother and thereby avoid the punishment, he will learn that "fast talking" is an effective way of avoiding punishment after misbehaving. In other words, the misbehavior is not punished and the fast talking is rewarded. Even if the punishment is only postponed by the fast talking, the effectiveness of the punishment will be reduced because punishment is effective only if it closely follows the misbehavior. Furthermore, even if the talking is not always effective, the intermittent nature of its effectiveness will actually contribute to the ultimate strength of the strategy because responses that are rewarded *intermittently* are more resistant to extinction than responses that are rewarded 100% of the time (see Chapter 2).

Individuals can learn through trial and error how to avoid punishment and anxiety by fast talking, but they could also learn it through observation (Bandura, 1969). The opportunity for observing inappropriate behaviors would certainly exist because, as you learned earlier, people with the APD are often raised by parents with the APD. Seeing parents misbehave and then talk themselves out of punishment would certainly provide a basis for the development of this pattern of behavior in children.

The operant conditioning explanation is based on well-established laws of learning, but no research has been conducted to test directly whether this type of learning history in fact leads to the APD. That is because it would be unethical to attempt to condition an individual to use antisocial behavior.

Before concluding our discussion of the learning explanations for the APD, it might be helpful to compare the two explanations that have been put forward. The fundamental difference lies in the fact that the deficit-in-classical-conditioning explanation suggests that the individual is *impaired in the ability to develop anxiety*, whereas the operant conditioning explanation suggests that the individual has the normal ability to develop anxiety but has *learned techniques to avoid the anxiety*. In both cases, the individual has a relative lack of anxiety, but the lack stems from very different processes. One problem for the deficit-in-classical-conditioning explanation is that it does not explain why the individual has a deficit, but that might be accounted for by the physiological explanation we will consider later.

COGNITIVE EXPLANATIONS

Inaccurate Evaluation of Situations

Recently, cognitive theorists have suggested that individuals with the APD do not respond with anxiety because *they do not accurately evaluate situations as threatening* (Gorenstein, 1991; Lang, 1995). In other words, whereas individuals with anxiety disorders misperceive everything as threatening and anxiety-provoking (see Chapter 5), individuals with the APD do not see anything as threatening or anxiety-provoking. At first, that seems like a reasonable explanation, but the problem is that even when the individuals are clearly aware that the situation is threatening (e.g., they consistently receive electrical shocks or are punished in other ways), they still do not respond with anxiety. It appears, then, that it is probably not a case of inaccurately interpreting the situation but rather that the anxiety response has not been paired with the cues in the situation (i.e., failure of classical conditioning) or that for some reason the individuals cannot experience the physiological arousal that is the basis for anxiety. I will examine the latter possibility in the next section.

PHYSIOLOGICAL EXPLANATIONS

Low Neurological Arousal

One physiological explanation for the APD is that individuals who suffer from the primary type of the disorder have *low levels of neurological arousal* in the areas of the brain that are responsible for emotional arousal. If those areas are underactive, the individuals would not be able to experience anxiety, and the absence of anxiety could lead to antisocial behavior and the APD.

Low Arousal and Later Behavior. Strong evidence linking low arousal to antisocial behavior comes from studies in which arousal levels were measured in adolescents, and then some years later the individuals' behaviors were assessed to determine which individuals showed evidence of the APD (Kruesi et al., 1992; Raine et al., 1990, 1995). For example, in one study, electrodermal (sweating) and heart rate responses to stimulation were measured in 15-year-olds, and then their records of criminal behavior were examined 14 years later (Raine et al., 1995). The results indicated that those who engaged in criminal behavior were those who earlier had showed lower levels of arousal. It is particularly noteworthy that it is the responses that are usually associated with anxiety (hand sweating and heart rate) that were low in individuals who later became criminals.

EEG Abnormalities and Symptoms. Neurological arousal in the brain is often measured with electroencephalograms (EEGs), recordings that reflect electrical impulses (see Chapter 3). The EEGs of individuals with the APD have been examined in at least 20 investigations that together have encompassed the records of almost 2,000 individuals, so we have a large database from which to draw conclusions (see Holmes, 1991). In every one of those studies, it was found that there was a higher incidence of **EEG abnormalities** among individuals with the APD than among normal individuals. Importantly, the abnormality that was identified most frequently was the presence of unusually high amounts of **slow-wave activity**, electrical impulses in the range of 8 to 12 cycles per second rather than the normal 16 to 20 cycles per second. Slow waves reflect a low level of activity or arousal, and these findings provide the basis for the inference that individuals with the APD suffer from neurological underarousal.

What is particularly interesting is that the slow-wave activity is found primarily at the temporal and posttemporal areas of the skull. That is important because activity at those areas reflects activity in the **limbic system,** which is directly in from those areas of the skull, and the limbic system plays a crucial role in emotional arousal (see Chapter 2). In other words, there is a substantial amount of evidence that individuals with the APD have underactive limbic systems, and that could account for the low level of anxiety in those individuals.

Those findings are interesting, but the question that arises is, is the low level of neurological activity a cause or an effect of the APD? That is, does the low level of activity cause the low anxiety, or does the low anxiety cause the low level of activity? A number

pr. mary: low levels / anxiety
Secondary: learned to avoid it

which is why they are sensation-seeking

Numerous studies have shown that people with the antisocial personality disorder have a high incidence of electroencephalogram abnormalities. The abnormal EEGs seem to indicate a connection between reduced cortical arousal and the APD.

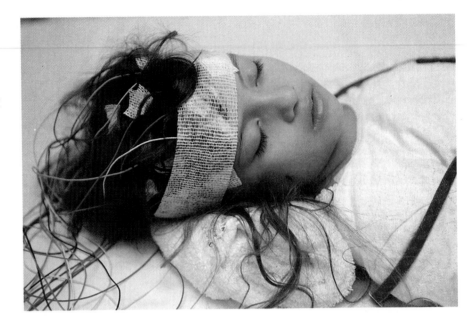

of experiments have shed light on that question. In one experiment, individuals who did or did not have the APD were injected with either a placebo or a stimulant, epinephrine (adrenaline), that would increase their levels of neurological arousal, and then they participated in an avoidance conditioning experiment (Schachter & Latané, 1964). The results indicated that after being injected with the placebo, the individuals with the APD performed less well than the individuals who did not have the APD. In contrast, after being injected with the stimulant, the individuals with the APD performed as well as or better than the individuals who did not have the APD, thus suggesting that the stimulant and the consequent increase in arousal caused the individuals with the APD to perform "normally." Similar results have been reported in another experiment in which arousal was manipulated with noise rather than drugs (Chesno & Kilmann, 1975). These results provide strong support for the contention that differences in arousal cause the behavior seen in the APD.

If increases in arousal decrease the symptoms of the APD, then the question arises, would decreases in arousal increase the symptoms of the APD? That possibility was tested in an experiment in which university students took an important examination and then were administered either a placebo or a drug (chlorpromazine) that decreased their arousal (Schachter & Latané, 1964). Following that, each student was allowed to score the examination that he or she had taken earlier. The results indicated that students who had taken the arousal-decreasing drug cheated more frequently when scoring their examinations than the students who had taken the placebo. Indeed, the difference in cheating in the two conditions was almost 20%. If cheating is taken as an indication of the APD, the

results of this experiment provide strong evidence that decreasing neurological arousal leads to the symptoms of the APD. Thus there is strong and consistent evidence linking low levels of neurological arousal to the low level of anxiety that characterizes individuals with the APD.

A second type of EEG abnormality that is found in some individuals with the APD involves what is called **positive spiking.** At intermittent points during the slow waves, some individuals show sudden bursts of electrical activity. A number of investigators have suggested that positive spiking is more likely to occur in individuals with the APD who are prone to act aggressively, and the investigators have implied that the bursts of electrical activity lead to sudden acts of aggression. That causal link has not been confirmed yet.

It is interesting to note that the slow-wave activity and the positive spiking that are found in the EEGs of individuals with the APD are also found in the EEGs of young children, for whom those characteristics are normal. That similarity has led to the suggestion that individuals with APD suffer from **delayed neurological development.** That is, in an individual with the APD, it may be that for some reason the area of the brain that is responsible for emotional arousal (anxiety) has not developed sufficiently. Consistent with the delayed-development notion, it has been reported that EEG abnormalities among individuals with the APD tend to decrease with age (Hill, 1952; Hill & Watterson, 1942) and that individuals with the APD have typically been described as "burning out" when they get older (Robins, 1966). In other words, with time, the EEG abnormalities seem to clear up, and so does the APD. However, no direct test of the relationship between declines in EEG abnormalities and declines in the APD has yet been reported.

Serotonin and Testosterone

Recently, some biochemical abnormalities were identified that can explain the lack of restraint and impulsivity seen in individuals with the APD. Specifically, it was found that individuals who suffered from the APD had *low levels of serotonin,* and so did criminal offenders who repeated a criminal act after being released from prison (Virkkunen et al., 1989; Virkkunen et al., 1994). These findings are consistent with numerous other findings indicating that low levels of serotonin are related to impulsivity; serotonin serves to inhibit behaviors that are punished, so when serotonin levels drop, the individual ignores the possibility of punishment and acts impulsively. Related to this, you will recall from the discussion of suicide that individuals with low levels of serotonin are more likely to commit suicide with impulsive violent acts. In those cases, the individuals are depressed, and the violence is expressed against themselves. In the case of the individuals with the APD, the impulsivity and violence are expressed against others.

It was also found that individuals with the APD had *high levels of testosterone* (the "male" hormone) and that those levels were associated with higher activity levels and more aggression (Virkkunen et al., 1994). The combination of low serotonin and high testosterone would lead to high activity, high aggression, and high impulsivity—characteristics of the individual with the APD.

Genetics

In most of the studies that have focused on the heritability of the APD, criminal behavior was used as a measure of the disorder. However, criminal behavior is not the only measure of the disorder, and insofar as it is not a good measure, the results of the research will be distorted.

Studies of Twins. There are numerous studies in which it was found that the concordance rate for criminal behavior in monozygotic (MZ) twin pairs was higher than it was in dizygotic (DZ) twin pairs (Merikangas & Weissman, 1986; for a review of earlier studies, see Dalgaard & Kringlen, 1976). Indeed, the concordance rate for MZ twin pairs is often more than three times higher than for DZ twin pairs.

Additional analyses conducted in one of the studies of twins revealed that the difference in concordance rates between MZ and DZ twins was greater in rural areas than in urban areas (Christiansen, 1968). That finding suggests that in rural areas, where there may be fewer social reasons for crime (e.g., fewer adolescent gangs, more close-knit communities), genetic factors play a greater role in determining who will commit a crime than they do in urban areas, where there may be more social reasons for crime. In other words, both social and genetic factors may contribute to crime, and where the social factors are minimized, the genetic factors may be more apparent.

Studies of Adoptees. Stronger evidence for the role of genetics in the APD comes from studies in which it was found that individuals who had *biological parents* who suffered from the APD were at high risk for developing the APD even if they were adopted at birth and raised by parents who did not suffer from the disorder (Bohman et al., 1982; Cadoret, 1978b; Crowe, 1974; Hutchings & Mednick, 1974; Mednick, Gabrielli, & Hutchings, 1984; Schulsinger, 1972). In one such study, 17% of a sample of adopted children whose biological parents had the APD developed the disorder themselves, whereas none of the adopted children in the control group did (Cadoret, 1978b).

Taken together, the results of the studies of twins and the studies of adoptees provide strong and consistent evidence that genetic factors play a role in the development of antisocial behavior. However, it is essential to recognize that these results do not demonstrate that heredity accounts for all or even the majority of cases of antisocial behavior. For example, the concordance rate among MZ twins was not 100%.

TREATMENT

Because individuals with the APD do not have any of the traditional symptoms of abnormal behavior (e.g., anxiety, depression, delusions, hallucinations), they are often not diagnosed as having a psychological problem and are therefore not brought in for treatment. Furthermore, because their behavior is often illegal, they are more likely to be sent for punishment rather than treatment. Unfortunately, however, even when treatment is tried, it is usually ineffective, so now many psychotherapists are reluctant to accept individuals with the APD for treatment. Indeed, it is interesting to note that in one recent comprehensive handbook on psychotherapy, treatment of the antisocial personality disorder is not even mentioned (Bergin & Garfield, 1994).

A variety of factors contribute to the ineffectiveness of the treatment of individuals with the APD. For example, there is nothing to motivate these individuals to change their behaviors, anxiety cannot be classically conditioned in these individuals, and giving rewards for good behavior is ineffective because these individuals are already getting the rewards they want. However, insofar as the APD is due to low levels of neurological arousal, it is possible that stimulants that increase arousal might be effective for treating the disorder, and there is evidence to support that possibility (Satterfield & Cantwell, 1975; Schachter & Latané, 1964; Suedfeld

& Landon, 1978). For example, you will recall that earlier I discussed an experiment in which individuals with the APD who were given a stimulant learned to avoid punishment like normal individuals. Unfortunately, the effects of stimulants are short-lived, and at present, it is not feasible to keep individuals on stimulants for long periods of time.

Prognosis

We are not yet able to control or treat the APD. That conclusion, in combination with the fact that individuals with the disorder do a great deal of harm, has led some frustrated and exasperated observers to suggest, only partly in jest, that all individuals with the APD

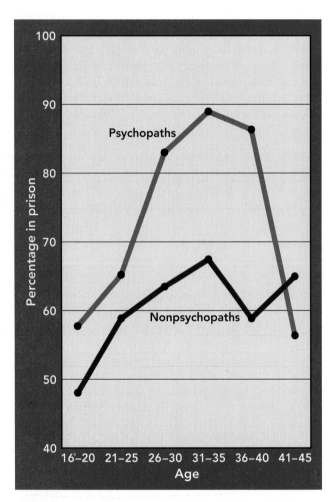

FIGURE 14.5 Men classed as psychopaths are most likely to spend time in prison during their 30s; apparently because the disorder "burns out," during their 40s their rate becomes comparable to that of men who do not have the disorder.

Source: From "Male Psychopaths and Their Criminal Careers" by R. Hare et al., in *The Journal of Consulting and Clinical Psychology,* Vol. 56, No. 5, 1988. Copyright © 1988 by the American Psychology Association. Reprinted with permission.

should be banished to a desert island. However, despite our apparent inability to treat the disorder, the prognostic picture is not completely gloomy, and individuals with the disorder may not require so drastic a response as banishment.

The ray of hope in the otherwise gloomy prognosis is provided by the evidence indicating that many individuals with the disorder burn out or settle down as they enter their late 30s or early 40s (Harpur & Hare, 1994). For example, one investigator found that 34% of the individuals who were studied remitted their symptoms by the age of 40 (Robins, 1966).

In one interesting study related to burnout, 521 prisoners who were or were not classified as psychopaths were studied over a period of years to determine changes in their criminal behavior (Hare et al., 1988). Figure 14.5 presents the data concerning the percentage of men who were in prison during various 5-year age segments between the ages of 16 and 45. The men classified as psychopaths are most likely to be in prison during their 30s, but their rate of imprisonment drops to the level of the nonpsychopaths by age 45. Although these findings are encouraging, it is important to note that the remission of symptoms does not occur with all individuals and that even those who do remit their symptoms can cause considerable personal and legal havoc before burning out.

What Can We Conclude Concerning the Antisocial Personality Disorder?

The symptoms of the primary form of the antisocial personality disorder revolve around a lack of anxiety that leads to illegal behavior, impulsivity, aggressiveness, disregard for others, and a lack of guilt. It now appears that in many cases, the primary form of the antisocial personality disorder is due to low levels of neurological arousal in the area of the brain that is responsible for anxiety. Support for that comes from studies in which it was found that (a) individuals with low levels of arousal as children are likely to engage in criminal behavior as adults, (b) individuals with the disorder show low levels of neurological arousal (EEG activity) in the limbic system, and (c) drugs that increase and decrease arousal can cause corresponding decreases and increases in the symptoms of the APD. The low levels of arousal also explain why these individuals do not classically condition and hence do not learn avoidance responses. The low levels of arousal appear to be due in large part to genetic factors. The genetic factors account for the frequent finding that parents of individuals with the disorder often behave inappropriately, a pattern that was once used to suggest that the disorder was due to bad parenting. That is, it now appears that problems with parents are a correlate rather than a cause of the disorder. At present, there is no effective treatment, and so we must wait until the disorder burns out.

TOPIC II
OTHER PERSONALITY DISORDERS

The remaining personality disorders can be organized into two groups. The first group contains less serious disorders that involve the *exaggeration of normal personality traits* such as dependence, passivity, and narcissism. I will refer to the disorders in this group as **trait disorders.** The second group contains disorders that are *more serious and involve symptoms like some of those found in paranoia and schizophrenia.* Because these disorders fall into the gray area bordering on other serious disorders, I will refer to them as **marginal disorders.**

Although nine different personality disorders are identified in DSM-IV, the rate of comorbidity with these disorders is high (Ekselius et al., 1994; Starcevic, 1992). In other words, nine separate disorders have been identified, but it is likely that an individual with any one of them will suffer from more than one and may also suffer from depression. The reason for this is not clear. It may be that there is an overlap in symptoms that makes multiple diagnoses likely, or it may be that these disorders reflect different manifestations of some general underlying problem.

Note that in addition to discussing trait and marginal disorders, at the end of this chapter I will also briefly discuss *impulse control disorders,* a group that includes disorders such as *kleptomania, pyromania,* and *gambling.*

TRAIT DISORDERS

Traits are generally thought of as enduring ways in which individuals respond to other individuals and situations. For example, an individual with the trait of hostility will generally respond to others in antagonistic, belligerent, or contrary ways, and an individual with the trait of compulsivity will be orderly, methodical, and lacking in spontaneity. Traits lead to personality disorders when they interfere with personal functioning or cause distress. For example, an individual with a lot of hostility may drive others away and therefore become lonely and depressed. An individual who is very compulsive may spend so much time planning that he or she never gets anything done. It is interesting to note that in many cases, the individual does not object to having the trait but does object to the *effects* of the trait. A friend of mine with the obsessive-compulsive personality disorder states adamantly that "there is nothing wrong with being highly organized" but later says, "I get anxious and depressed because I am always planning but never get anything done!" He does not seem to mind the trait, but he does not like its effects on his life.

The symptoms of the obsessive-compulsive, avoidant, dependent, histrionic, and narcissistic personality disorders are summarized in Table 14.2. In the following sections, I will describe each of those personality disorders, and then I will comment on their explanation and treatment.

Avoidant Personality Disorder

Individuals with the **avoidant personality disorder** are exceptionally sensitive to potential social rejection and the humiliation that goes with it. Because of their concerns about rejection, these individuals avoid relationships unless they are guaranteed uncritical acceptance. They want affection, closeness, and acceptance, but they avoid relationships that might satisfy those needs because of their stronger need to defend against rejection. In other words, avoidance is a defense; if they do not attempt to make friends, they cannot be rejected.

One young man with the avoidant personality disorder wanted desperately to have close friends with whom he could share experiences, but he was so afraid of rejection (it would prove him inadequate) that he never attempted to establish friendships. Instead, he focused his efforts on "achieving," with the hope that others would accept him because of his competence, but acceptance based on his achievements and competence did not satisfy his need for friendship. This very competent young man lived an isolated and unfulfilled existence.

Because individuals with the avoidant disorder cannot satisfy their need for closeness and constantly feel as though they will be rejected, they tend to have a low self-concept and to suffer from anxiety and depression. In addition to causing personal unhappiness, their avoidance of relationships can interfere with their occupational functioning.

It might be noted that the avoidant personality disorder is similar to the social phobia disorder (see Chapter 4) in that the symptoms revolve around concern with criticism (Hofmann et al., 1995; Jansen et al., 1994; Widiger, 1992). However, the avoidant disorder seems to be a central element in the individual's personality rather than an isolated problem, it sets in earlier, and it is more likely than the social phobia to be associated with depression (Holt et al., 1992). The behavior of the individual with the avoidant personality

TABLE 14.2 Symptoms of the Trait Personality Disorders

Disorder	Symptoms	Behavioral Examples
Avoidant	A pervasive pattern of social inhibition, feelings of inadequacy, and sensitivity to negative evaluation	Person avoids interpersonal contact, does not get involved with others unless certain of being liked, views self as socially inept or inferior
Dependent	A pervasive and excessive need to be taken care of that leads to submissive and clinging behavior and fear of separation	Person has difficulty making decisions without help, needs others to assume responsibility, has difficulty expressing disagreement, has difficulty initiating projects because of lack of self-confidence, seeks nurturance, is uncomfortable when alone, is preoccupied with concerns about having to take care of self
Histrionic	A pervasive pattern of excessive emotionality and attention seeking	Person must be the center of attention, acts seductive, exhibits rapid shifts of emotion, uses physical appearance to draw attention, employs dramatic expression of emotion, is suggestible, overestimates the intimacy of relationships
Narcissistic	A pervasive pattern of grandiosity, need for admiration, and lack of empathy	Person has an exaggerated sense of importance; harbors fantasies of great success, power, brilliance, or ideal love; believes he or she is special; requires admiration; expects favorable treatment; exploits others; lacks empathy; behaves arrogantly
Obsessive-compulsive	A pervasive pattern of preoccupation with orderliness, perfectionism, and control, at the expense of flexibility, openness, and efficiency	Person is preoccupied with details, rules, lists, order, and organization; perfectionism interferes with task completion; devotion to work precludes leisure activities and friendships; person is overconscientious, scrupulous, and inflexible; is unable to discard useless or worn-out items; hoards money in case of future catastrophe; is rigid and stubborn

Source: Adapted from American Psychiatric Association (1994).

disorder is intended primarily to reduce anxiety about rejection. The individual simply concludes, "If I don't get close, I can't be rejected or hurt."

Dependent Personality Disorder

Individuals with the **dependent personality disorder** passively allow others to make major decisions for them. They are often easy to get along with because they will not do anything to jeopardize their relationships with the persons on whom they rely for major decisions. The inability of these individuals to make decisions can result in anxiety and depression and can interfere with their ability to get anything done if they are placed in roles involving responsibility or leadership. They may feel uncomfortable or helpless when alone, and they will go to great lengths to keep others around them.

One middle-level business manager with the dependent personality disorder got along well in the company because he always went along with the group. When votes were taken in meetings, he always looked both ways to see which direction the vote was going before casting his vote. He went along but did not advance in the company because he never contributed leadership or unique ideas. He was frustrated and depressed about his position but too afraid to do anything about it. His disorder probably stemmed from a time when as a newcomer in the company, he offered a new idea and, from his perspective, got "stepped on."

This disorder is more frequently seen in women, but that may be due to the fact that the stereotype of women traditionally involves dependence. The cause of this disorder is not clear, but it probably stems from a lack of self-confidence. Overly dependent individuals seem to be saying to themselves, "I am probably going to be wrong, so if I do not initiate anything, I cannot be blamed or criticized."

Histrionic Personality Disorder

There are three notable characteristics of individuals with the **histrionic** (HIS-tre-ON-ik) **personality disorder.**

First, such people are usually attractive, charming, appealing, and sexually seductive. However, although they try to charm and seduce everyone, if things start to get serious, they back off quickly. Freud speculated that the immature and inconsistent behavior of histrionic individuals resulted from their interest in but fear of sex. Like the moth and the flame, these individuals flutter around sex, but when things get hot, they back off.

Second, histrionic individuals like to be the center of attention and often act in overly dramatic and emotional ways to attract attention (crying, weeping, threatening to commit suicide). In the excitement and tragedies they generate, they always play the starring role, and others are relegated to supporting roles.

Third, despite their great shows of feelings, histrionic individuals are emotionally very shallow, and their emotions may shift quickly from person to person or from positive to negative. Because of their emotional shallowness and lack of sincere consideration for others, their relationships tend to be stormy and short-lived.

In general, these individuals are outgoing (especially with potential sexual partners), but their behavior is designed to gain them attention and assurance, and they can become extremely demanding, egocentric, dependent, vain, inconsiderate, and manipulative when things do not go their way. An individual with the histrionic personality disorder can be a lot of fun (especially to flirt with) at a party, but the relationship is best ended when the party's over. We have no firm theory on the cause and treatment of the histrionic personality disorder; fortunately, it is not a particularly debilitating disorder.

Narcissistic Personality Disorder

The archetype for the **narcissistic** (NAR-suh-SIS-tik) **personality disorder** is Narcissus, the character in Greek mythology who fell in love with his own reflection in a pond. Individuals with the narcissistic personality disorder have a grandiose sense of their own importance, and they are preoccupied with fantasies about their ultimate success, power, brilliance, or beauty. Because they think they are "special," they demand constant attention and admiration from everyone around them. These individuals see themselves as entitled to favors from others because of their importance, and consequently they take advantage of the people around them. If criticized rather than praised, they may respond with cool indifference, or their overblown egos may collapse like a punctured balloon. Also, because they are so self-centered, they have difficulty maintaining relationships. Legend has it that because Narcissus was so absorbed in himself, he spurned the love of Echo, who then went off to die alone in a cave. There may be a moral in that story for people who deal with individuals who have the narcissistic personality

According to Greek mythology, Narcissus fell in love with his own reflection in a pond. Persons with the narcissistic personality disorder have a grandiose sense of their own importance and are preoccupied with fantasies about their success, power, brilliance, or beauty.

disorder. The disorder is more prevalent in men than women (Golomb et al., 1995).

Obsessive-Compulsive Personality Disorder

Individuals with the **obsessive-compulsive personality disorder** have high needs for perfection, order, and control, and their lives become dominated by getting organized and prepared. Problems arise because they get so bogged down with organization and details that they do not get started on the projects they plan. Also, their overattention to details prevents them from seeing the "big picture," so they may spend too much time on meaningless or trivial aspects of problems they must solve. A student with the obsessive-compulsive personality disorder who has to write a paper may spend endless hours collecting material, organizing it into neat piles, and worrying about tiny details for footnotes but may never clearly define the goal of the paper or never actually get around to writing it. The student spends all the available time preparing and never actually produces anything.

Individuals with the obsessive-compulsive personality disorder do not have meaningful interpersonal relations because they are so tied up getting organized that they do not take time for friendships. Furthermore, because of their need for control, they often insist that others do things *their* way rather than allowing for the give-and-take that is necessary in a friendship. Also, their need for control makes these individuals personally stilted, stiff, and unable to feel or to express emotions that are necessary for warm, close relationships. In short, rather than "going with the flow" and being spontaneous in their interpersonal relations, these individuals live behind a dam where everything is controlled and emotionally flat.

Finally, individuals with the obsessive-compulsive personality disorder are not particularly happy; they do not take time for pleasure or relaxation, and they are constantly worrying about missing some detail and failing.

The obsessive-compulsive personality disorder differs from the obsessive-compulsive anxiety disorder in that the major symptom in the personality disorder is a need for perfection and order, whereas the major symptom in the anxiety disorder is recurrent thoughts or actions. There is some overlap in the disorders in that the individual with the personality disorder may persistently think or worry about being organized, but the persistent thoughts are focused on organization (rather than on violence, for example), and the personality disorder is less disruptive of normal living.

Explanations and Treatments

We know very little about the cause and treatment of the trait personality disorders (Phillips & Gunderson, 1994). Indeed, in a recent comprehensive handbook of psychiatric disorders, the chapter on personality disorders was the shortest and was limited primarily to descriptions (Hales et al., 1994). At present, the only treatment that may be effective is social skills training (Stravynski et al., 1994). That approach does not solve the problems, but at least it provides the individuals with some skills for working around their problems.

MARGINAL DISORDERS

The symptoms of the four personality disorders in this group overlap somewhat with those of the psychotic disorders such as schizophrenia, but the symptoms are milder, at the less severe end of the schizophrenia spectrum (see Chapter 11). It is tempting to assume that these personality disorders are the early stages of the more serious disorders, but at present they are considered distinct and separate disorders. In examining these personality disorders, we must note how they are similar to the other disorders but also how they are different. I will describe the disorders in the following sections, and then I will comment on their explanation and treatment. The major symptoms of the paranoid, schizoid, schizotypal, and borderline personality disorders are summarized in Table 14.3.

Paranoid Personality Disorder

The dominant feature of the **paranoid personality disorder** is *an unwarranted suspicion and mistrust of people* that persists even in the face of strong evidence that there is no justification for such concern. Because these individuals perceive threats as coming from everyone around them, they tend to be anxious, distant, humorless, and argumentative, and they often "make mountains out of molehills" when dealing with problems. Their lack of trust in others and their "protective" behaviors undermine their interpersonal relationships and may interfere with their job performance. However, these individuals often work very hard (they think they must do so to "keep ahead" of others), and if they are in a situation in which they can work independently, they may do very well. This disorder is diagnosed more commonly in men, and it is not yet clear what causes it. The paranoid personality disorder differs from the delusional (previously called paranoid) disorder in that individuals with the delusional disorder have clearly formed delusions (see Chapter 12), whereas those with the paranoid personality disorder have only vague suspicions and mistrust.

Schizoid Personality Disorder

The primary symptom of individuals with the **schizoid** (SKIT-zoyd) **personality disorder** is a *lack of interest in other people or social relationships*. Not only do they not reach out to others, but they also rarely respond to others. For example, they are indifferent to the praise or criticism of others, and they rarely make reciprocal gestures such as smiling or nodding. Individuals with the schizoid disorder are loners—physically, intellectually, and emotionally.

Individuals with the schizoid disorder also show very little emotion and hence appear aloof, humorless, cold, and emotionally flat. Although they show the social isolation and flat affect that are characteristic of schizophrenia, they do not show any evidence of a thought disorder (no hallucinations, delusions, or lan-

TABLE 14.3 Major Symptoms of the Marginal Personality Disorders

Disorder	Symptoms	Behavioral Examples
Paranoid	A pervasive distrust and suspicion of others such that their motives are interpreted as malevolent	Individual suspects that others are being deceptive, doubts the loyalty of others, does not confide in others, reads hidden meanings into benign events, holds grudges
Schizoid	Detachment from social relationships and a restricted range of emotional expression	Person does not enjoy relationships, chooses solitary activities, lacks friends, is emotionally cold and has flat affect, is indifferent to praise and criticism, takes little pleasure in life.
Schizotypal	A pervasive pattern of interpersonal deficits plus cognitive and perceptual distortions and eccentricities	Person adopts odd beliefs or magical thinking such as clairvoyance or telepathy, experiences bodily illusions, acts suspicious, limits emotional expression, exhibits behavior that is odd or peculiar
Borderline	A pervasive pattern of instability in interpersonal relationships, self-image, and mood, plus marked impulsivity	Person has feelings of abandonment and emptiness; forms intense but unstable interpersonal relationships; shows impulsivity in spending, sex, eating, substance abuse, and other behaviors; engages in recurrent suicidal or self-mutilating behaviors; is emotionally unstable

Source: Adapted from American Psychiatric Association (1994). ..

guage problems), and therefore they cannot be considered to be suffering from schizophrenia.

Schizotypal Personality Disorder

The individual with the **schizotypal** (SKIT-zō-TĪ-pul) **personality disorder** has many more of the characteristics of schizophrenia than the individual with the schizoid disorder, but the symptoms are not severe enough to justify the diagnosis of schizophrenia. These individuals may have bizarre beliefs (e.g., they may think that they are clairvoyant or have mental telepathy), be socially inept and isolated, or engage in eccentric or peculiar behaviors (e.g., they may talk to themselves or have strange rituals and motor behaviors), and they may not pay any attention to their appearance. However, despite their symptoms, they stay just barely on the normal side of the fine line that separates normality from schizophrenia. For example, they may say, "I feel *as if* my dead mother were in the room with me," which is subtly different from saying, "My dead mother *is* in the room with me." In other words, the individual with the schizotypal disorder has *illusions*, whereas the individual with schizophrenia has *delusions*. Similarly, schizotypally disordered individuals also have odd speech patterns in that they are digressive and vague, but they do not suffer from the serious distortions ("word salads") exhibited in schizophrenia. The schizotypal personality disorder may be a mild form of schizophrenia.

Borderline Personality Disorder

The last major personality disorder we will discuss is the **borderline personality disorder.** Interest in this disorder is high, but the disorder is complex and not yet well understood. Originally, the term *borderline* was used to refer to individuals whose adjustment was on the borderline between normal and psychotic. For example, we would refer to individuals as having "borderline schizophrenia" if they were disturbed but not enough to be classified as suffering from schizophrenia. However, now the term *borderline* is used to refer to a specific personality disorder that is characterized primarily by *instability.* Unlike an individual with a mood disorder or schizophrenia who has one set of relatively stable symptoms, the individual with the borderline personality disorder shows *different symptoms at different times.* For the most part, the symptoms revolve around problems of mood, mild disturbances in thought processes, and impulsive self-injurious behavior. Together, those symptoms disrupt the individuals' interpersonal relationships. Although individuals with the borderline disorder show some of the symptoms seen in mood or schizophrenic disorders, their symptoms are usually not as severe as those shown by individuals with full-blown mood or schizophrenic disorders. In short, individuals with the borderline disorder seem to stand on the borderline of various disorders and move in and out of them.

Individuals with the borderline personality disorder usually show symptoms in four areas, as shown in

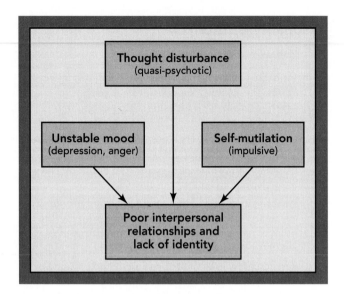

FIGURE 14.6 There are four major symptom areas in the borderline personality disorder.

Figure 14.6 (Zanarini, Gunderson, Frankenburg, & Chauncey, 1990). First, they show unstable *mood*. For example, they will plummet into depression, only to come out of it after a while. They usually do not go through manic phases as in the bipolar disorder, but instead they vacillate between normal or flat mood to moderate or severe depression. These individuals also go through periods of intense anger that can interfere with effective social functioning.

Second, individuals with the borderline personality disorder have intermittent periods during which they experience *thought disturbances,* but the disturbances are not as extreme as those seen in schizophrenia (Zanarini, Gunderson, & Frankenburg, 1990). That is, rather than suffering from full-blown hallucinations, individuals with the borderline personality disorder show "unusual perceptions" that include illusions and depersonalization. For example, one woman told me that sometimes she felt as though she could see through people and that other times she felt as though she were dead. Similarly, rather than having clear-cut delusions, individuals with the borderline disorder reflect "odd" thinking that includes suspiciousness and magical beliefs. For example, a student reported that sometimes he felt like he could control events by thinking about them. Important phrases here are "as though" and "like"; the individuals did not completely believe that they were really dead or could control events, but they were approaching those conclusions. These thought disturbances are more like those seen in the schizotypal personality disorder than those in schizophrenia. Because these disturbances are not as extreme as those seen in schizophrenia, they are sometimes called **quasi-psychotic thought disturbances.**

The third notable symptom in the borderline disorder is intermittent *self-mutilating and suicidal behavior* (Dulit et al., 1994; Mehlum et al., 1994; Shearer, 1994; Soloff et al., 1994; Winchel & Stanley, 1991). The suicidal behavior appears to stem from the combination of depression and impulsiveness. The self-mutilation often involves acts like burning oneself with cigarettes, carving up one's body with a razor blade, making deep scratches with the fingernails, sandpapering the skin, or pouring acid on oneself. This behavior is not intended to result in death; rather, the self-mutilation is often done in an emotionally detached way, and the patients report that they self-mutilate in an attempt to feel or experience themselves as "real." Concerning her self-mutilation, one patient reported to me, "If I bleed, I know I'm alive. If I cut myself up, I may feel *something.*" In another case, a woman carved the word *slut* into her stomach after having sex with a man. She said she did it to make herself feel bad about what she had done. Self-mutilation is a serious symptom, one that it is not yet well understood.

The fourth symptom is associated with *interpersonal relationships.* Individuals with the borderline personality disorder tend to have intense relationships that are very unstable, so they vacillate between love and hate. Individuals with the disorder do not simply drift in and out of friendships, but instead show abrupt, frequent, and dramatic changes between intense love and equally intense hate in any one relationship. The disruption of their interpersonal relationships may be a by-product of the other symptoms. That is, the fluctuations in their mood (especially their anger), their thought disturbances (especially paranoid thoughts about betrayal and abandonment by others), and their impulsiveness make it difficult to maintain relationships with others.

Some of the symptoms of the borderline disorder are seen in other personality disorders, but the symptoms are seen more frequently and are more likely to occur in combination with one another in the borderline disorder. The frequency of these behaviors in the borderline personality disorder and other personality disorders is illustrated in Figure 14.7.

The instability in mood, thoughts, behavior, and interpersonal relationships that is characteristic of the borderline personality disorder has led theorists to suggest that individuals with this disorder have a problem with *identity.* That is, the instability reflects the lack of any real sense of self or self-direction, and indeed, these individuals often report a sense of being "empty." One woman reported that she felt as though there was a big hole inside of her. The word *unstable* is usually used to describe individuals with the borderline personality disorder, but that word does not do justice to their lives. Indeed, their personal and interpersonal lives are better described as *intermittently chaotic.*

likely in adolescents/teens?

A major question concerning the borderline disorder is whether this is *one* disorder or a *combination* of disorders, as the schizoaffective disorder is a combination of schizophrenia and a mood disorder. One widely held explanation is that the borderline disorder may be a "low-grade" combination of schizophrenia (or the schizotypal disorder) and a mood disorder (primarily depression) that is further complicated by problems of impulse control. Unfortunately, we have a long way to go for an adequate description, understanding, and treatment of this important disorder. In Case Study 14.2, one of my students talks about her struggle with the borderline personality disorder.

Explanations and Treatments

Probably the most consistent and most important finding concerning the paranoid, schizoid, schizotypal, and borderline disorders is that they are most likely to be found in the *biological relatives of individuals who suffer from schizophrenia and the other psychotic disorders* (Gladis et al., 1994; Kendler, McGuire, et al., 1993a; Maier et al., 1994; Siever et al., 1990; Webb & Levinson, 1993). That finding suggests that there is a strong *genetic basis* for these personality disorders. Specifically, when schizophrenia is due to genetic factors, there are probably a number of genes involved, and it appears that when individuals inherit only some of those genes, they develop the personality disorders that resemble mild forms of schizophrenia. Additional evidence for a genetic basis for these personality disorders is provided by research in which it was found that the parents and siblings of individuals with these disorders are more likely to suffer from these disorders than unrelated individuals are (Nigg & Goldsmith, 1994; Thapar & McGuffin, 1993).

However, it should be noted that not all cases of the marginal personality disorders are due to genetics. Just as some cases of schizophrenia are due to prenatal and perinatal problems (see Chapter 12), so some cases of these personality disorders may be due to prenatal and perinatal problems.

In many cases, individuals with these personality disorders do not receive treatment; instead, they just drift along on the brink of psychosis and on the fringes of society. When they are treated, treatment often involves the same drugs that are used to treat schizophrenia and other psychotic disorders, but at lower levels. Neuroleptic drugs such as Thorazine or Haldol are used to treat the schizophrenic-like symptoms, antidepressants or lithium may be used to treat the unstable moods, and drugs that enhance serotonin activity may be used to diminish impulsive behavior (Coccaro & Kavoussi, 1991; Mehlum et al., 1994; Soloff, 1994; Soloff et al., 1994; Teicher & Gold, 1989). (The link between

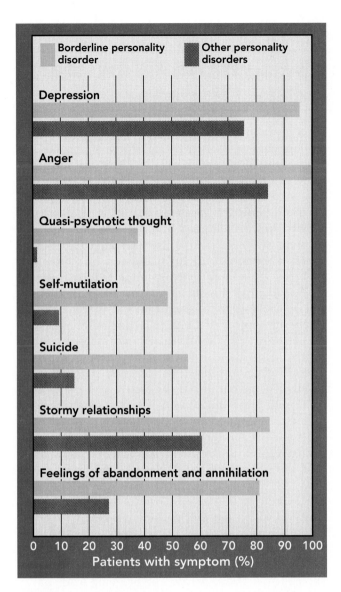

FIGURE 14.7 Problems with mood, cognitions, self-mutilation, and interpersonal relationships are higher in individuals with the borderline personality disorder than in individuals with other personality disorders.
Source: Data from Zanarini, Gunderson, Frankenburg, and Chauncey (1990), p. 164, tab. 2.

The borderline personality disorder is diagnosed more frequently in women than in men, but it is not yet clear whether that is due to an actual difference in the incidence of the disorder or to a bias in the use of the diagnosis (Castaneda & Franco, 1985). There is evidence that homosexual activity occurs more in individuals with the borderline disorder than in other individuals (Zubenko et al., 1987). The homosexuality may be a reflection of the individuals' lack of identity. That is, they may be trying other roles or orientations in an attempt to find an identity or interpersonal closeness. In that case, the homosexuality may be more a case of transient behavior than a firmly established orientation.

CASE STUDY 14.2

A Student Writes About the Symptoms of Her Borderline Personality Disorder

Linda is a tall, attractive, and bright young woman. When she was a senior in high school, she received a scholarship to a six-year combined college–dental school program that would begin immediately after graduation. However, Linda did not graduate with her classmates. As they marched across the stage, she was confined to a mental hospital with a serious borderline personality disorder. For the next three years, Linda was in and out of a number of hospitals. She was finally able to enter college, and with support and treatment she was able to graduate. Her symptoms are better but not gone. Here she writes about some of her symptoms.

Concerning Her Feelings and Self-Mutilation

"It is very hard for me to explain how I feel and how I felt. Feelings really overwhelm me. There are times when I felt like I would explode or burst because of the feelings. It was like my skin would crawl and I felt trapped. I felt like screaming or doing something to release the feelings. I usually chose to burn or cut myself. That was a release for me. When I saw the blood coming out, it was like seeing the hurt drip away. Other times when I would hurt myself it was because of the hatred I felt for myself.

"From the very first time I hurt myself I loved the feeling. I don't think there are words to explain how it feels. There is so much involved. I felt very 'out of control' with everything in my life, and the cutting and burning gave me a sense of control. The act of mutilating yourself is a very powerful thing. More than control, it gives you a sense of *being*. You *see* the blood or the burnt flesh and you know *you are real*.

"I remember burning myself one time when I was feeling rejected and very alone. I felt a very intense and overwhelming pain inside, in my gut. The pain was emotional, not physical. I got in my car and just drove. I had tears in my eyes because I hurt so badly. I felt very spaced. That was always how I felt when I hurt myself. I was numb to the point of feeling outside of my body. It is like when you are dreaming. You can see yourself from the outside and all that is going on from that view. I felt very light, as if I were weight-

less. I drove to a parking lot. I did not go there with the intention of hurting myself, it just happened. I had a cigarette lighter in my car. I lit it and let the flame touch my flesh. I burned a section of my arm that was about 2 inches by 3 inches. The skin blistered and burned. It gave me a warm feeling all over. It didn't hurt, it felt good. I'm not sure what made me stop, but tears came to my eyes after it was all over. Not because it hurt, but because of the release. I felt better when I was done. All of the pain was gone. Maybe the physical mutilation let me focus my attention on the outside, instead of on the internal pain. Whenever I hurt myself I had a feeling of renewal. It was like starting fresh without all of the emotions.

"The cutting was a lot like the burning, but it seems like I cut myself when I was angry, especially at myself. When I cut myself deeply, I wasn't trying to kill myself, I just wanted to bleed. One time when I cut myself, I dripped the blood all over two pieces of paper and saved it. The blood did something for me. It was a high to see the blood. Maybe it made me feel 'real' or maybe it was just a release—a release of the pain.

"The release I experienced with the cutting was similar to what I felt with my bulimia. I consider my eating behavior a part of my self-destructive behavior. There was a period of time that I was bingeing and purging five to six times a day. It engulfed my whole life—it *became my life*. The bingeing made me feel kind of high and I felt like I could start fresh. I never did start fresh. I just kept eating to fill the emptiness and purging to release the emotions. I couldn't stop."

About Mood

"I felt depressed most of the time. Sometimes I felt like I couldn't go on in life. It's not that there was something so *wrong* with my life, but there was something *missing*. I still feel like that. It is like there is a huge hole inside of me. Sometimes when I am alone I can feel it—the emptiness inside of me. There's nothing there. I have tried many things to fill that void—food, alcohol, drugs, sex, relationships—but none of those things make it go away. *I want so badly to feel whole but I just don't*. I have wanted to kill myself because I don't think I will ever feel whole. More than really wanting to die, I just wanted to be in a coma-like state for a while and then wake up and have everything be better, like I was only having a bad nightmare. I really struggle with finding a meaning in my life—and finding me!"

Concerning Her Paranoia and Interpersonal Relationships

"I felt like the whole world was against me. I thought people wanted to hurt me. I knew that everyone talked about me and hated me. I knew if 'they' would just leave me alone I would be OK. I felt like people were hurting me on purpose. I thought if they only knew how much I already hurt inside, they would be sorry for pushing me to hurt more. I grew to hate everyone because of this. It was like a double-edged sword. I felt like no one loved or cared about me, but when they would try to get close, I would push them far away. It was a never-ending circle.

"I have not been able to have any really stable relationships. Most of the men I have gotten involved with are 'safe' in some way. They are really unavailable before I even get involved. I always have an out with these kinds of people. My last relationship was with a drug addict. As long as he had problems, I always had a good excuse to get out. When he was clean for eight months, I got out of the relationship. My biggest fear is rejection, so I do it first.

"One time I jumped into a relationship with a man from out of state. I thought that we would just date for the summer and then he would go home. Well, he did go home but I went to visit him one weekend. The very next Friday I dropped out of college and moved into an apartment with him. I had always thought, 'If I could only get to another place my life will be better.' It was another desperate attempt to fill the emptiness. Well, it was a disaster and two months later I moved back but he came with me. Driving back in the U-Haul, I was so desperate that I drove straight through a dangerous ice-storm. I hated him so much at that point that I wanted to have a bad wreck and have him die. I had my seatbelt on so I felt relatively safe. I just wanted so badly

for him to die. For two and a half years after that I went through loving him and wanting to marry him one day to hoping he would just overdose and die the next day. I loved him and I hated him.

"I don't understand why I am like this; I wish I did. I think a part of it is that I don't have a grasp of who I am and what I want in life, so I am always changing my mind. One day a man is the love of my life and I want to marry him, and the next day I hate him. It is a lot like how I feel about *myself*."

Her Summary

"The best way to describe how I feel is to share something I wrote a few years ago when I was struggling the most:

The way that I feel inside is so strange. I can't believe after all the tears I've cried I still feel the same. I want pain on the outside, I want to hurt myself, but I don't want pain on the inside. What will I gain? I don't know.

Emptiness. That's what I feel. Yet there's so much inside. There's so much hurt. The hurt is what I want gone. I cut myself and let it out, I burn myself.

I always run from the pain. I run and run. I never know what it is, I just run. Right now I want to run, far away where no one will find me, to a place where I will be safe.

I don't like this feeling. I want it to end. I want to cut myself. It's like all of a sudden someone invaded my body. I'm different now than I was.

I don't want to tell anyone because when I change back they will still watch me and I can't take that. I can't tell anyone how I feel. I am trapped here. There's no way to win, not even suicide. I'm stuck here to hurt and to feel all of this pain and all of this agony.

Her Treatment

Linda has taken Prozac (a bicyclic) for her depression, Haldol (a high-potency neuroleptic) for her psychotic-like symptoms, Tegretal (an anticonvulsant), which can be helpful for controlling her mood swings, and Ativan (a benzodiazepine) for her anxiety. With the medication and intensive psychotherapy and counseling, Linda was able to do well in college and graduate. She has come a long way, but as her comments indicate, she still has a way to go.

low levels of serotonin and impulsivity was discussed earlier in the discussion of the antisocial personality disorder.) In addition, supportive counseling may be used to help the individuals cope and get from one day to the next (Linehan et al., 1994; S. G. Miller, 1994).

To sum up, the paranoid, schizoid, schizotypal, and borderline personality disorders appear to be mild forms of schizophrenia or combinations of mild forms of schizophrenia and the other psychotic disorders. As such, these personality disorders constitute the less severe disorders in the schizophrenic spectrum of disorders. As is the case with schizophrenia, these personality disorders appear to be comparable across cultures. For example, a comparison of Japanese and American individuals with the borderline disorder revealed basically identical sets of symptoms (Ikuta et al., 1994). Finally, the treatment of individuals with these personality disorders is similar to that used with the more serious disorders.

IMPULSE CONTROL DISORDERS

Before concluding this chapter, a comment should be made concerning a number of other disorders that are not technically personality disorders but are listed under the related heading of **impulse control disorders.** Under that heading, DSM-IV contains five disorders: the **intermittent explosive disorder, kleptomania** (KLEP-tuh-MĀ-nē-uh), **pyromania** (PĪ-ruh-MĀ-nē-uh), **pathological gambling,** and **trichotillomania** (TRIK-uh-TIL-uh-MĀ-nē-uh). Those disorders, along with their major symptoms, are listed in Table 14.4.

In general, impulse control disorders are characterized by three features: (1) They involve the inability to resist an impulse to perform behaviors that are dangerous to the individual or others; (2) the individual

experiences an increase in tension before committing the act, and (3) the individual experiences a sense of guilt or regret after committing the act.

Although behaviors such as shoplifting, fire setting, gambling, and hair pulling are common in the general population, it is rare that those behaviors are due to *irresistible impulses,* and therefore *disorders* associated with those behaviors are relatively rare (McElroy et al., 1992). In other words, not all cases of shoplifting, fire setting, gambling, and hair pulling are disorders. The impulse disorder that may not be particularly rare is pathological gambling, which may occur in as much as 3% of the general population. Indeed, it has been suggested that the "addiction" to playing video games that is prevalent today may be a form of pathological gambling (S. Fisher, 1994).

In general, relatively little is known about most of the impulse control disorders, but a number of findings are emerging. First, these disorders usually begin in childhood or adolescence and become chronic or episodic after that. Second, the impulse control disorders are often linked to depression and sometimes to eating disorders (Goldman, 1992; McElroy et al., 1991, 1992). Interestingly, some patients report that the "rush" that is associated with their stealing or gambling is a pleasurable alternative to their depressive symptoms. The "rush" may provide a brief antidote for the depression, but it is not believed that the disorders stem from attempts to avoid depression; rather, mood disorders and impulse control disorders may simply share a common underlying cause.

With regard to cause, it was originally speculated that impulse control disorders were substitutes for sex (note the pattern of building tension, the rush or excitement, and then release), but there is no evidence to support that link (e.g., Rice & Harris, 1991). Today, most attention is focused on the frequent finding that individuals with these disorders have *low levels of sero-tonin* (Carrasco et al., 1994; McElroy et al., 1992; Stein

TABLE 14.4 Impulse Control Disorders and Their Symptoms	
Disorder	**Symptoms**
Intermittent explosive disorder	Discrete episodes of failure to resist aggressive impulses that result in assaults or destruction of property
Kleptomania	Recurrent failure to resist impulses to steal objects that are not needed
Pyromania	A pattern of fire setting for pleasure or relief of tension
Pathological gambling	Recurrent and persistent maladaptive gambling
Trichotillomania	Recurrent pulling out of one's hair for pleasure or relief of tension

et al., 1993). That finding is understandable because serotonin serves to inhibit behavior, and low levels lead to impulsivity (see the earlier discussion of the antisocial personality disorder and the discussion of suicide in Chapter 9). The low levels of serotonin can also explain the finding that individuals with impulse disorders are often depressed because low levels of serotonin are a cause of depression (see Chapter 9). At present, the best guess concerning the cause of the low levels of serotonin is genetics, but because the disorders are so rare, there are no good studies of twins on which we can rely. All we can say is that serotonin seems to be the link that brings the symptoms of these disorders together. However, although serotonin levels can explain the impulsivity and the depression, what remains unexplained is why some individuals impulsively set fires whereas others impulsively steal, pull their hair out, or act aggressively.

Evidence concerning the effectiveness of various treatments is sparse, but two tentative conclusions may be drawn. First, there is some evidence that behavioral

Many fires are deliberately set in order to collect insurance or cover up another crime. However, individuals suffering from pyromania set fires for pleasure or to relieve stress.

For some individuals, the impulse to gamble is difficult to control. They are convinced that the next spin of the wheel or roll of the dice will bring wealth and happiness.

approaches can be effective, but their effects seem to be due to the *restraints* that are imposed by the therapists rather than to any change in the underlying cause of the disorder (McElroy et al., 1989; Murray, 1992). For example, one treatment for kleptomania is to not allow the individual to go shopping (Goldman, 1992). Second, evidence is now accumulating that the new antidepressant drugs such as Prozac that increase the levels of serotonin can be effective for treating these disorders (Goldman, 1992; McElroy et al., 1989). Apparently, increasing the levels of serotonin reduces the underlying impulsivity. In summary, then, our understanding of the causes and treatments of impulse disorders is limited but growing.

WHAT CAN WE CONCLUDE CONCERNING PERSONALITY DISORDERS?

In general, the personality disorders appear to fall along a continuum between normal behaviors and serious disorders such as anxiety, depression, and schizophrenia. For example, the avoidant, dependent, and obsessive-compulsive personality disorders seem to be extreme forms of normal behaviors, whereas the schizoid, schizotypal, and borderline personality disorders appear to be less serious forms of disorders such as schizophrenia. At present, we know less about the causes of the personality disorders than we know about the causes of the more severe disorders. Indeed, what we know about disorders such as the schizoid disorder stems in large part from what we know about schizophrenia and depression. Similarly, in most cases, the treatments for the personality disorders such as the schizotypal disorder are derived from the treatments for the more severe disorders; that is, we treat them in the same way that we treat the more severe disorders but less aggressively.

SUMMARY

TOPIC I: THE ANTISOCIAL PERSONALITY DISORDER

- The personality disorders involve more extreme forms of what can be normal behaviors and less severe forms of the other disorders discussed in this book. Personality disorders are diagnosed on Axis II in DSM-IV.

- The major symptom of the antisocial personality disorder is a pervasive disregard for the rights of others (e.g., illegal behavior, lying, aggressiveness). Also noteworthy are (a) a lack of anxiety, (b) impulsiveness, (c) an ability to rationalize inappropriate behavior, and (d) an inability to benefit from punishment.

- The APD occurs in about 5% of men but only 1% of women, and it "burns out" at about age 40.

- Originally, the APD was referred to as *moral insanity,* and more recently individuals with the disorder were called *psychopaths* or *sociopaths.*

- The main psychodynamic explanation is that the APD stems from bad parenting. There is evidence that the parents do behave inappropriately, but it is also possible that the disruptive behavior of the children causes inappropriate behavior in the parents or, more likely, that the problem behavior in parents and children is due to shared genes.

- The main learning explanation is that the individuals do not develop classically conditioned responses and therefore do not develop anxiety (avoidance conditioning). There is evidence for that, but this explanation does not make clear why the individuals do not classically condition. It is also suggested that the individuals learn how to avoid anxiety, thus leading to the secondary form of the disorder.

- The main cognitive explanation is that the individuals do not accurately perceive the possibility of threat or punishment in situations and therefore act inappropriately. There is little evidence for this, and it is contrary to the finding that the individuals behave inappropriately even when the possibility of threat or punishment is clear.

- The main physiological explanation is that these individuals have low levels of neurological arousal in the areas of the brain that are responsible for emotion, and that precludes the development of anxiety. Evidence for that comes from (a) follow-up studies of individuals with high and low levels of arousal, (b) EEG studies, and (c) the effects of drugs. There is also evidence that some of the symptoms stem from low levels of serotonin, which lead to impulsivity, and high levels of testosterone, which lead to activity and aggression. Finally, there is evidence for a genetic basis for the disorder.

- There is no effective treatment for the APD, and apart from burnout, the prognosis is poor.

TOPIC II: OTHER PERSONALITY DISORDERS

■ The five personality disorders in what can be called the trait category are (a) the avoidant disorder, which involves social inhibition and the avoidance of others; (b) the dependent disorder, which involves the need to be cared for; (c) the histrionic disorder, which involves excessive emotionality and attention seeking; (d) the narcissistic disorder, which involves grandiosity and a need for admiration; and (e) the obsessive-compulsive personality disorder, which is a preoccupation with orderliness, perfectionism, and control. We do not have particularly good explanations or treatments for these disorders.

■ The four personality disorders in what can be called the marginal category are (a) the paranoid disorder, which involves a pervasive distrust and suspicion of others; (b) the schizoid disorder, which involves detachment from others and a lack of emotion; (c) the schizotypal disorder, which involves cognitive and perceptual distortions; and (d) the borderline disorder, which includes instability in interpersonal relationships, impulsivity, and emotional instability.

■ These disorders appear to be minor forms and combinations of the psychotic disorders (e.g., schizophrenia, delusional disorder), and treatment is similar to the treatment of the more serious disorders.

■ There are five impulse control disorders: (a) the intermittent explosive disorder, which involves aggressive assaults and destruction of property; (b) kleptomania, which is repeated stealing of objects that are not needed; (c) pyromania, which is fire setting for pleasure or tension reduction; (d) pathological gambling, which is recurrent and persistent maladaptive gambling; and (e) trichotillomania, which is the pulling out of one's hair for pleasure or tension reduction.

■ These disorders may be due to low levels of serotonin, which lead to a lack of impulse control. Treatment involves social restraints and drugs that increase levels of serotonin.

KEY TERMS, CONCEPTS, AND NAMES

In reviewing and testing yourself on what you have learned from this chapter, you should be able to identify and discuss each of the following.

antisocial personality disorder (APD)
avoidance conditioning
avoidant personality disorder
borderline personality disorder
deficit in classical conditioning
delayed neurological development
dependent personality disorder
EEG abnormalities
histrionic personality disorder
impulse control disorders
intermittent explosive disorder
kleptomania

limbic system
marginal disorders
moral insanity
narcissistic personality disorder
obsessive-compulsive personality
  disorder
operantly conditioned avoidance of
  anxiety
paranoid personality disorder
pathological gambling
personality disorders
positive spiking

primary type of the APD
psychopath
pyromania
quasi-psychotic thought disturbance
schizoid personality disorder
schizotypal personality disorder
secondary type of the APD
slow-wave activity
sociopath
trait disorders
trichotillomania

CHAPTER FIFTEEN
DISORDERS of INFANCY, CHILDHOOD, and ADOLESCENCE

OUTLINE

Charlie is 6 years old and is absolutely out of control. He cannot keep his attention on anything for more than a few seconds, and he is constantly squirming, fidgeting, running around, or interrupting people. He does not listen to instructions or ignores them. Because of his wild activity, he sometimes hurts children around him. When he was younger, his parents thought he was just an "active child," but they now know that he suffers from the *attention-deficit/hyperactivity disorder*. It has been recommended that Charlie be given a drug called Ritalin that is effective for treating the disorder, but his parents are not sure they want to start a 6-year-old on drugs.

■ ■ ■

Evan is 5. He spends his days sitting cross-legged on the floor, rocking back and forth and staring into space. He is oblivious to what is going on around him. When he is touched or picked up, he is unresponsive and limp. This lack of response to others has been apparent since he was born; he just never cuddled like other infants. Evan has not developed any verbal behavior, but in a very mechanical way he will sometimes repeat words that are said to him. He is diagnosed as suffering from *autism,* and his prognosis is poor.

■ ■ ■

Carolyn is 7 years old and is still wetting her bed at night, and therefore she is diagnosed as suffering from *enuresis*. Recently, her parents bought a pad that goes on her bed. When Carolyn urinates, the pad becomes damp and causes a bell to ring. That wakes Carolyn up, and she stops urinating. This treatment seems to be working, but the therapist cautioned that Carolyn might have relapses.

■ ■ ■

Tim is 14 and shows a variety of twitches and tics. His head sometimes jerks, and he often blinks and grimaces. Most surprising is that occasionally he blurts out words, usually vulgarities. He does not mean to do it, and he is embarrassed by it, but he cannot control it. Because of his strange behavior, most other children avoid him. His isolation and embarrassment are interfering with his social development. Tim suffers from a rare disorder known as *Tourette's disorder.*

■ ■ ■

In this chapter we will consider a variety of disorders that are grouped together because they usually appear first during infancy, childhood, or adolescence. Disorders in this group range from relatively minor ones like tics to very serious ones like autism. Some of these disorders disappear as the child grows older, but others persist into adulthood if they are not treated. Indeed, in a recent study it was found that almost 30% of children with psychological problems still had serious problems as young adults (Ferdinand & Verhulst, 1995). Clearly, it is important that these problems be detected and treated early.

Interest in these disorders has increased greatly during the past 30 years. DSM-I listed only six disorders of infancy, childhood, and adolescence, but in DSM-IV, more than 30 such disorders are identified. It will not be possible to discuss each disorder thoroughly, so I will focus on those that are of greatest concern.

This chapter is divided into three parts, and in each I will discuss a number of specific disorders. The first part is focused on **disruptive behavior disorders.** Children with these disorders have problems with attention, hyperactivity, and antisocial behavior, and their behavior is disruptive for the people around them. In the second part, I will review the **developmental disorders.** Children with these disorders have problems with emotional and academic development. The effects of these disorders may be pervasive, as in the case of autism, in which the individual's entire life is affected, or they may be very specific and influence only one skill, such as reading or arithmetic. In the third part, I will discuss a group of unrelated disorders that includes problems with elimination (urination, defecation) and tics. Mental retardation is also a disorder of infancy, childhood, and adolescence, but I will consider that problem in Chapter 19.

TOPIC I
DISRUPTIVE BEHAVIOR DISORDERS

The two most important disruptive behavior disorders are the *attention-deficit/hyperactivity disorder,* which involves overactivity, and the *conduct disorder,* which involves aggression and delinquency.

ATTENTION-DEFICIT/HYPERACTIVITY DISORDER

Children with the **attention-deficit/hyperactivity disorder** are unable to focus their attention for any reasonable length of time and are physically very active and impulsive. These children are almost constantly running, climbing, speaking out without regard to what is appropriate, and behaving in other disruptive and impulsive ways. In the long run, their inattention and inappropriate behaviors can result in serious personal, social, and academic problems. The attention-deficit/hyperactivity disorder appears in children before the age of 7, it is between 5 and 10 times more common among boys than girls, and it may occur in as many as 5% of elementary school children.

Symptoms

There are two major symptoms in the attention-deficit/hyperactivity disorder, the first of which is the *inability to maintain attention.* Children with this disorder do not seem to listen to directions, are easily distracted, lose things, are careless in their schoolwork, cannot do or dislike tasks that require sustained effort, and often fail to finish tasks they begin. Those problems seriously hamper their performance, especially in school.

The second major symptom is *hyperactivity or impulsivity.* The children fidget, squirm, run about, or climb on things, and are "on the go" as if they were driven by a high-speed motor. To use another analogy, a child with this disorder is often a human cyclone! The impulsivity leads the children to blurt out comments inappropriately, have difficulty waiting their turn, or interrupt others. Children with this disorder are likely to hurt themselves or others because they have a high activity level and because they do not think through the consequences of their actions (Farmer & Peterson, 1995). Note that in one study of adolescents who suffered from the bipolar disorder (see Chapter 8), almost 60%

Children with the attention-deficit/hyperactivity disorder are unable to focus their attention. They do not listen to directions, are easily distracted, and often fail to complete tasks. As a result, these children often have great difficulty succeeding in school.

of them met the diagnostic criteria for the attention-deficit/hyperactivity disorder when they were in the manic phase of their disorder (West et al., 1995). However, although the attention-deficit/hyperactivity disorder and mania share symptoms, these are different disorders, and you should not confuse them.

Secondary symptoms include serious academic difficulties that stem from the inability to study. The disorder also retards social development because even though children with the disorder are often liked as "class clowns," they do not develop close personal relationships (J. Wheeler & Carlson, 1994).

Issues

Disorder Versus Misbehavior. Some critics argue that rather than considering problems with attention and hyperactivity as a *disorder* and treating the child with psychotherapy or medication, the behaviors should simply be thought of as *misbehavior,* and treatment should be focused on environmental factors such as poor parenting or poor school environments that permit or even foster the misbehavior (Prior & Sanson, 1986). However, the data that we will consider in the following sections generally lead to the conclusion that hyperactivity is a serious disorder with a biological basis and not simply misbehavior.

Long-Term Effects. For some years, there was a controversy over how long the attention-deficit/hyperactivity disorder lasted. Some theorists assumed that the disorder is due to "delayed development" and is therefore only a temporary problem during childhood. Others assumed that the disorder involves a serious underlying problem that can persist into adulthood. To resolve this controversy, investigators conducted more than 30 studies in which they followed up children with the disorder to see what they were like as adults (Fischer et al., 1990; Lilienfeld & Waldman, 1990; Mannuzza et al., 1991; Mannuzza et al., 1993). The results of those studies clearly indicate that between 30% and 80% of children with the attention-deficit/hyperactivity disorder continue to show symptoms of the disorder in adolescence and adulthood. Indeed, one of the most important things to happen with regard to this disorder in the past few years is that professionals and the public recognized that many adults suffer from the disorder. Now, rather than thinking that they are bad, stupid, or maladjusted, these individuals recognize that they have a disorder and that it can be treated. In that regard, a few months ago I met a charming couple who were in their 60s, and while the husband hugged his wife affectionately, he told me that he had always loved her but until recently she had always been "the far side of scat-

ter-brained." His wife grinned and explained that six months earlier, she had been diagnosed as suffering from the attention-deficit/hyperactivity disorder and given medication. She said, "It took almost 60 years, but I finally got my act together—or had it put together for me by that medication. It's great!" Unfortunately, many cases of the disorder go undiagnosed and can lead to serious problems later, including the conduct disorder (to be discussed shortly) or substance abuse (Shaffer, 1994).

Case Study 15.1 is focused on a student of mine who suffers from the attention-deficit/hyperactivity disorder. She does not have a particularly severe case, but as you will see, it does interfere with her life, and there is no doubt that her life would have been easier and more productive if she had been diagnosed earlier. The fact that attention-deficit/hyperactivity can be a long-term disorder contributes to the importance we must attach to it.

Diagnostic Procedures. Not all problems with attention, activity level, and performance are due to the attention-deficit/hyperactivity disorder, so it is essential that care be used in making a diagnosis. (Many of my students who are not doing well immediately assume either that they have a "learning disability" or the adult form of the attention-deficit/hyperactivity disorder, but in most cases, those self-diagnoses are not correct.) Unfortunately, there is no simple test for the presence of the disorder, so the diagnosis is based on a clinical judgment. In making that judgment with children, the clinician can rate the child on the 12 items in Table 15.1. There is no specific cutoff score for a diagnosis, and the child can be judged as suffering from a more or less severe form of the disorder.

TABLE 15.1 Items for Rating the Attention-Deficit/Hyperactivity Disorder in Schoolchildren

1. Fails to finish things he or she starts
2. Can't concentrate, can't pay attention for long
3. Can't sit still, is restless or hyperactive
4. Fidgets
5. Daydreams or gets lost in his or her thoughts
6. Acts impulsively, without thinking
7. Has difficulty following directions
8. Talks out of turn
9. Does messy work
10. Is inattentive, easily distracted
11. Talks too much
12. Fails to carry out assigned tasks

Source: Adapted from *The Child Attention/Activity Profile* by. C. Edelbrock, Pennsylvania State University.

CASE STUDY 15.1

A College Student Writes About Her Attention-Deficit/Hyperactivity Disorder

"I'm not your typical case of attention-deficit/hyperactivity disorder because I wasn't diagnosed until my sophomore year in college and because I'm a female, but I've got it and it causes problems. Knowing that I have the disorder helps because now I know what is going on, but knowing does not help the symptoms.

"The best way I can illustrate what it is like to have an attention-deficit disorder is to tell you that focusing on writing this case study is very difficult and frustrating! I've been trying for hours to come up with the next logical thought or sentence. It is taking me forever, and it is still disorganized. I keep drifting off the track. It is no wonder that I was called the 'Space Queen' by one of my high school teachers.

"It's difficult for me to stay on task, whether it's writing a paper, listening to a lecture, or reading a book. Because of this, I'm at an immediate disadvantage academically. It often takes me hours to get through one short textbook chapter, and writing a paper can take forever. My mind just keeps wandering—regardless of how interesting the topic may be.

"Restlessness also contributes to the long length of time it takes me to complete a task. I have to take 'study breaks' very frequently because I simply cannot sit still for long. When I am forced to remain in one place for a period of time, such as in a lecture, I'll generally be swinging my leg or tapping my foot.

"Time is my biggest enemy: The fact that it takes me so long to do anything completely disrupts my life. The amount of time I use to perform anything is the largest disruption in my life. Because my distractions and restlessness make me slower at doing things, I always feel incompetent and rather stupid, which is why I struggle with a bad self-image.

"Low self-esteem is a major component of my disorder. It takes me a long time to do anything, so I feel abnormal and like I'm not intelligent enough to finish assignments as quickly and easily as others. However, some of my problem with self-image is due to my social relationships that get fouled up because of my disorder. I'm typically labeled an 'airhead' because my mind wanders. Frequently I only hear a portion of a conversation and, embarrassingly, I have to ask people to repeat it. That annoys people.

"I've been taking Ritalin for about a year now. It helps, but it's only a treatment, not a cure. It helps me focus and concentrate much better while I study, but it does not completely prevent me from daydreaming. Because Ritalin helps me focus my attention, I'm able to accomplish more in less time than I did before, so I feel a little better about myself. And because it is a stimulant, I feel more motivated to study.

"While on the drug, I am also calmer and not so uptight or agitated in social situations. I don't take sarcastic comments or constructive criticism as personally as I did in the past. I feel that the drug has resulted in some very positive changes. My sister noticed a definite difference and improvement in my personality just days after I began using it. I haven't experienced any negative side effects except for an occasional dry mouth, feeling of thirst, and slight weight loss. But the positive effects far outweigh the negative side effects, and I'm thankful for the difference it has made in my disorder and in my life.

Explanations

Physiological Factors. Learning and cognitive theorists initially speculated that children with the attention-deficit/hyperactivity disorder have simply *not learned effective strategies for controlling and focusing attention*. However, interest in that explanation has waned, and it is now widely believed that most cases of the disorder are due to *organic brain dysfunction*. Specifically, there is now evidence that the disorder involves *underactivity* in the areas of the brain that are responsible for the control of

attention and motor activity (Zametkin et al., 1990). For example, recent findings indicate that individuals with the attention-deficit/hyperactivity disorder show lower levels of metabolism in the brain than individuals who do not have the disorder and that the greatest differences are in the superior prefrontal cortex and premotor cortex, which control attention and motor activity. The differences in metabolism as measured with a PET scan are presented in Figure 15.1. The reduced metabolism probably reflects lower levels of activity in the areas of the brain responsible for *inhibition,* and

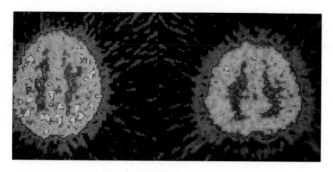

FIGURE 15.1 Individuals with the attention-deficit/ hyperactivity disorder show lower levels of brain activity than other individuals. The image on the right is from a person with the disorder, and the image on the left is from a person who does not have the disorder. Brighter yellow indicates more activity (glucose metabolism).
Source: From "Cerebral Glucose Metabolism in Adults with Hyperactivity of Childhood Onset" by A. J. Zametkin et al., in *The New England Journal of Medicine,* November 15, 1990. Copyright © 1990 Massachusetts Medical Society. Reprinted by permission of The New England Journal of Medicine.

when inhibition is reduced, attention and motor behavior run wild. A parallel situation occurs when you drink alcohol: Alcohol is a depressant, and at low levels, it depresses the inhibitory areas of the brain, thereby resulting in a loosening up of behavior (see Chapter 17). As we will see later, drugs that stimulate activity in the inhibitory areas of the brain are effective for reducing the attention-deficit/hyperactivity disorder.

Environmental Factors. Having identified brain dysfunction as a cause of the attention-deficit/hyperactivity disorder, we must go on to identify the causes of the brain dysfunction. There are now data indicating that some cases of the disorder appear to be due to *infections* during the first 12 weeks of pregnancy or to **anoxia** (uh-NOK-sē-uh) (lack of oxygen) during the birth process (Gualtieri et al., 1982; Towbin, 1978). Probably most important among the environmental factors is the *ingestion of lead.* Lead ingestion occurs when children eat chips of paint containing lead or when they inhale air that is polluted with the emissions from automobiles run on gasoline containing lead (David et al., 1979; Marlowe et al., 1985; Needleman et al., 1979). The influence of lead ingestion in children is illustrated in Figure 15.2, which indicates that children who had higher levels of lead deposits in their teeth were more distractible, hyperactive, and impulsive.

Another environmental factor that was identified but overemphasized is *food additives* (coloring, preservatives, flavorings). It was originally suggested that hyperactivity was an allergic reaction and that as many as 50% of hyperactive children could be returned to normal levels of functioning when placed on an additive-free diet (Feingold, 1975, 1976). However, in better-controlled studies in which hyperactive children were given diets containing additives or placebos, it was found that additives accounted for only about 5% of the cases of increased hyperactivity (Conners, 1980; Marshall, 1989). The effects of food additives are not as powerful or as pervasive as they were once thought to be, but we must not ignore any factor that accounts for even 5% of a disorder as serious as the attention-deficit/hyperactivity disorder.

Genetic Factors. Genetic factors have also been implicated in the attention-deficit/hyperactivity disorder, and three sets of findings deserve attention. First, it was found that biological relatives, especially male relatives, of hyperactive children were more likely to have been hyperactive as children than the adoptive relatives of hyperactive children (Cantwell, 1972; Lombroso et al., 1994; Morrison & Stewart, 1971). Indeed, in one study it was found that 57% of the children of parents with the disorder also had the disorder (Biederman et al., 1995). Second, the activity levels of members of monozygotic twin pairs were more similar (correlation, .96) than the activity levels of members of dizygotic twin pairs (correlation, .59) (Willerman, 1973). Third, parents of children with the attention-deficit/hyperactivity disorder tended to have problems with cognitive

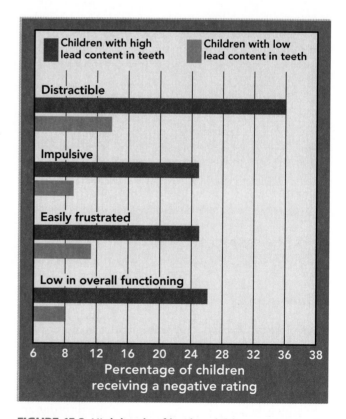

FIGURE 15.2 High levels of lead in children were associated with high levels of distractibility, hyperactivity, and impulsivity.
Source: Data from Needleman et al. (1979), p. 692, tab. 3.

functioning even if they could not be diagnosed as suffering from an attentional deficit per se (August & Stewart, 1982). This combination of findings clearly suggests that genetic factors play a role in at least some cases of the attention-deficit/hyperactivity disorder.

Treatments

Psychological Treatments. Both psychological and physiological approaches have been used to treat the attention-deficit/hyperactivity disorder. Psychological approaches have revolved around teaching children **self-instruction** procedures that are designed to help them focus their attention and improve self-control (Kendall, 1984; Meichenbaum & Goodman, 1971). The underlying notion is that if children think through what they are going to do before doing it, they will slow down and act more appropriately. For example, while working on a problem, the children are given a "reminder card" with questions on it: "What's the problem?" "How can I do it?" "Am I using my plan?" "How did I do?" Children are also given "say it before you do it" exercises in which they are given a task but must verbalize what they are going to do before doing it. These training procedures are accompanied by rewards for thinking through and for appropriate subsequent behaviors. Unfortunately, this strategy has met with only limited success. The children seem to be able to gain some control in the clinic while supervised closely, but the effects do not generalize beyond the clinic.

Physiological Treatments. The physiological approach to treatment usually involves the administration of a drug marketed under the trade name **Ritalin (methylphenidate).** A less widely used drug is **Dexedrine (dextroamphetamine).** Contrary to what you might expect, the drugs that are used to *calm* hyperactive children and adults are actually *stimulants.* Apparently, these drugs work because they stimulate activity in the *inhibitory* areas of the brain, and that activity then reduces distractibility and motor behavior.

Students sometimes ask how it was discovered that a stimulant was effective for treating the attention-deficit/hyperactivity disorder. As was the case with many other findings concerning drugs, the effects of stimulants were discovered accidentally (Gross, 1995). A physician was using stimulants to treat headaches in children, and when he happened to treat children who had both headaches and the attention-deficit/hyperactivity disorder, he discovered that the stimulants reduced both sets of symptoms. That discovery occurred in 1937, but not until relatively recently was the treatment generally accepted.

There is now abundant evidence that stimulants are effective for treating the disorder. For example, in one experiment, the investigators compared the effects of a placebo and three dosage levels of Ritalin on academic performance (arithmetic and reading scores), negative classroom behaviors (destruction of property, being out of seat, disturbing others, inappropriate talking, name calling, swearing, teasing), and task behaviors (appropriate actions directed toward completing the assignment) (Pelham et al., 1985). The results indicate that Ritalin was more effective than the placebo for improving academic performance, increasing task behaviors, and reducing negative behaviors. Furthermore, moderate or higher levels of the drug were more effective than very low levels of the drug. These results are presented in Figures 15.3 and 15.4. The fact that higher levels were more effective can be used to explain the ineffectiveness of some drug treatment programs in which lower levels of the drugs were used.

Similar results have been reported in a variety of other investigations, and it appears that the drugs are effective for treating almost 90% of the children with the attention-deficit/hyperactivity disorder (Klorman et al., 1994; Mayes et al., 1994). Furthermore, the drugs are also effective for reducing the aggressive and antisocial behavior that often accompanies the disorder (Frederick & Olmi, 1994; Hinshaw, 1991; Hinshaw et al., 1992). In some experiments, the drugs resulted in improved *social* behavior but did not immediately influence the performance on standardized *achievement*

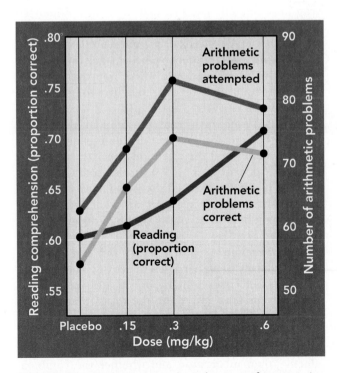

FIGURE 15.3 Ritalin improved academic performance in children with the attention-deficit/hyperactivity disorder.
Source: Pelham et al. (1985), p. 950, fig. 1.

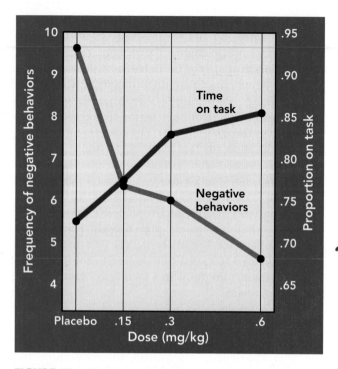

FIGURE 15.4 Ritalin increased on-task behaviors and decreased negative behaviors in children with the attention-deficit/hyperactivity disorder.
Source: From "Methylphenidate and Children with Attention Deficit Disorder" by W. Pelham et al., in *Archives of General Psychiatry*, Vol. 42, October 1985. Reprinted with permission of the American Medical Society.

tests, and it was therefore argued that the effects of the drug were limited. The fact that the drugs influenced social behavior but not academic achievement is due to the fact that a 6- or 8-week drug treatment period would not be expected to influence performance on tests that measure years of academic work; improvements on those tests could only be expected after long-term use of the drug.

It is also noteworthy that the stimulant drugs have the same beneficial effects on the attention and activity levels of adults with the attention-deficit/hyperactivity disorder (Spencer et al., 1995). In one study, a moderate dose of Ritalin reduced the hyperactivity of adults by more than one-half in a brief period of time. However, when adults who do not have the disorder take the drug, they get "high" (Volkow et al., 1995). That is because the stimulant pushes adults with normal levels of brain activity to higher levels of activity. The fact that the drugs can create a high poses a problem because some parents take and abuse the drugs that are prescribed for their children.

Numerous experiments have been conducted to determine whether cognitive training is more or less effective than medication and whether the combination of cognitive training plus medication is more effective than either treatment alone (Abikoff & Gittelman, 1985; Brown et al., 1985; Cohen et al., 1981; Gittleman-Klein et al., 1976; Hinshaw et al., 1984a, 1984b; Horn et

al., 1983; Pelham et al., 1980; Pelham et al., 1985; Pelham et al., 1986; Schroeder et al., 1983; Wolraich et al., 1978). The results of those experiments have generally indicated that medication is more effective than cognitive training and that the combination of medication and cognitive training is not superior to medication alone (Pelham et al., 1993). Although it is now widely recognized that drugs are effective for overcoming the attention-deficit/hyperactivity disorder, it is important to recognize that they are a *treatment* and not a *cure*. Therefore, it is sometimes necessary to keep individuals on a maintenance dose of the drug.

Before concluding, four comments must be made concerning the use of the drugs. First, we must be careful not to use the drugs unless they are really necessary. Surveys of teachers and parents indicate that they consider as many as 50% of all children as restless, distractible, or hyperactive (Schultz, 1974; Werry & Quay, 1971), but it is unlikely that all of those children suffer from the attention-deficit/hyperactivity disorder, and it would be inappropriate to medicate them all. Nor should medication be used as a substitute for appropriate parenting and classroom discipline.

Second, we must be careful that children who do require medication are not given excessively high dosages. The drugs seem to be effective for treating the disorder because they limit the range of stimuli to which the individual will respond, but if the dosage level is extremely high, the individual will respond to only a very limited range of stimuli, and that may result in social withdrawal and repetitive or "mechanical" behaviors (Solanto & Conners, 1982; Wender, 1971). For example, after receiving a high dose of medication, one originally hyperactive child persisted in writing one homework assignment for five hours. In another case, a previously talkative and sociable child withdrew to a corner, where he read the same story over and over and refused to interact with others. In other words, excessively high levels of the drugs will result in abnormal behavior that is the opposite of the attention-deficit/hyperactivity disorder, a symptom pattern called **response stereotypy** (STER-ē-ō-TĪ-pē). The problems of drug overuse and excessively high dosages are not unique to the drug treatment of the attention-deficit/hyperactivity disorder, and the potential problems associated with medication misuse should not be invoked as reasons for limiting the appropriate use of medication.

Third, with regard to treatment, there is some evidence that the use of Ritalin might slow growth in children who are taking the drug (Klein et al., 1988). Evidence concerning this effect is inconsistent, and in some cases in which the drug did initially retard growth, the deficit was made up when the children were taken off the drug. At present, the potential side effect of methylphenidate on growth does not appear to have serious long-term consequences, but it is a controversial issue that requires additional attention.

Finally, it is important to note that despite the effectiveness of stimulants for treating the attention-deficit/hyperactivity disorder, there is a problem with keeping children consistently on the drug (Stine, 1994). Indeed, rates of noncompliance range between 20% and 70%, and symptoms return within hours of the time at which a dose was skipped. Fortunately, since it is immediately apparent when a child has skipped a dose, the medication can be given, and within minutes its effects are apparent.

CONDUCT DISORDER ½ boys

The second major disruptive behavior disorder is the **conduct disorder.** The symptoms of this disorder revolve around a persistent pattern of misbehavior in which the individual breaks rules and violates the rights of others.

The conduct disorder is important not only because it causes problems when the individuals are children but also because it is related to disruptive and criminal behavior later in life. For example, aggression in childhood is the best predictor of aggression in later life, and many children with the conduct disorder go on to become serious juvenile delinquents or criminals as adults (Quay, 1986; White et al., 1994). However, not all criminals displayed the conduct disorder as children, thereby indicating that criminal behavior stems from a number of causes of which the conduct disorder is only one.

Symptoms

To be diagnosed as suffering from the conduct disorder, an individual must have shown behaviors in three or more of the following four categories within the preceding year:

1. *Aggression toward people and animals:* the individual bullies, threatens, picks fights, and is cruel to people and animals or forces others into sexual activities.
2. *Destruction of property:* The individual deliberately destroys the property of others, as by setting fires.
3. *Deceitfulness or theft:* the individual breaks into buildings or cars, lies ("cons" others) to get what he or she wants, steals, or commits forgery.
4. *Serious violations of rules:* the individual stays out all night before the age of 13 despite rules to the contrary, runs away from home, or is often truant from school.

The conduct disorder usually begins in childhood or adolescence. It occurs in 6% to 16% of males under the age of 18 and 2% to 9% of females in the same age range (American Psychiatric Association, 1994). In some individuals, the disorder will diminish as the individuals approach adulthood, but in other individuals, it may persist and develop into the antisocial personality disorder (see Chapter 14).

Note that there is a somewhat similar disorder called the **oppositional defiant disorder** that involves some of the hostility and disobedience seen in the conduct disorder, but also prominent are *negativistic* and *defiant* behaviors such as arguing with adults, refusing to comply with requests, being easily annoyed, and being spiteful or vindictive. In some respects, the oppositional defiant disorder can be seen as a less severe form of the conduct disorder; that is, the hostility toward others takes a passive, negativistic form and has not yet crossed the line to overt aggression. Often we see negativistic behavior in individuals who are suffering from mood disorders, but in those cases, the negativity is a secondary symptom of the depression and not a disorder itself.

Aggression against people, animals, or objects is a symptom of the conduct disorder. Many children with the conduct disorder establish a pattern of criminal activity early in life.

lower b/t serotonin + mortality rates

Explanations

Psychodynamic theorists believe that the conduct disorder has its origin in the child's relationship with his or her parents. If parents are *overindulgent,* children grow up believing that they can do anything without the fear of punishment, whereas if parents are overly *restrictive* and *withholding,* children grow up believing that to meet their needs, they must take what they want regardless of the consequences. The crucial element is *frustration,* and in many cases, frustration leads to aggression (Berkowitz, 1989; Dollard et al., 1939; Geen, 1990). However, it is also true that when they encounter frustration, many individuals withdraw, so frustration is not a comprehensive explanation.

Learning theorists suggest that the inappropriate behaviors seen in the conduct disorder are *learned through imitation and reward* (Bandura, 1983). Consistent with that explanation are numerous findings indicating that individuals who observe aggression in others subsequently perform more acts of aggression. Indeed, the evidence indicates that not only do observers of aggression perform more acts like the ones that they saw, but they also perform more aggressive acts in general. In one classic study, it was found that mothers who used more aggressive child-rearing behaviors had children who were more aggressive in general than mothers who used less aggressive methods (Sears et al., 1957). That is, punishment seemed to foster aggression rather than suppress it. However, it is also possible that the link between aggression in the mothers and children was due to genetic factors or that aggressive and unmanageable behavior in children brought out aggression in the parents (Bell, 1968; Frick et al., 1992).

Cognitive theorists believe that individuals with the conduct disorder behave aggressively because *they perceive others as hostile and threatening;* that is, their behavior is a defensive response to what they see as a hostile world. There is now substantial evidence that chronically aggressive individuals do perceive others as hostile (Crick & Dodge, 1994; Dodge & Coie, 1987; Dodge & Tomlin, 1987). For example, in one study, aggressive and nonaggressive boys were shown a videotape in which one boy "accidentally" spilled paint on another boy's project (Dodge & Somberg, 1987). When asked about the accident, the aggressive boys were more likely than nonaggressive boys to perceive the accident as maliciously intentional and to report that they would respond with anger. It has also been found that after viewing a videotape in which an individual acts in a confrontational but not openly hostile manner, adolescents who have a history of violence are more likely to see the other person as hostile, expect aggression from the person, and see fewer solutions for the problem than adolescents who do not have a history of violence (Lochman & Dodge, 1994). In other words, it appears that individuals with the conduct disorder view the world as a hostile place and are prepared to respond in kind.

The physiological explanation for the conduct disorder is focused on two factors, the first of which is *low levels of serotonin* (Lahey et al., 1993; Rogeness et al., 1992; Zubieta & Alessi, 1993). Serotonin is important because it plays a role in the inhibition of punished responses (Soubie, 1986). That is, if an animal has learned not to make a response because it will be punished, but then the animal's level of serotonin is lowered with a drug, the animal will disregard the possibility of punishment and make the response. This disregard for punishment is similar to what we see in the behavior of individuals with the conduct disorder. Furthermore, there is now substantial evidence linking low levels of serotonin to aggression in humans. For example, in a study of young men in the military, it was found that 80% of the variability in their levels of aggression could be accounted for by their levels of serotonin; lower levels of serotonin were associated with higher levels of aggression (Brown et al., 1979). Similarly, in a prospective study of children and adolescents with the conduct disorder, it was found that levels of serotonin measured at one time were correlated −.72 with levels of aggression two years later (Kruesi et al., 1992). That is, low levels of serotonin were linked to high levels of subsequent aggression.

The second physiological factor of interest is *high levels of the male hormone testosterone.* The link between aggression and testosterone was illustrated in a study of young prison inmates who differed in their levels of aggression and social dominance (Ehrenkranz et al., 1974). Those who were most aggressive (those who were probably suffering from the conduct disorder) had the highest levels of testosterone, those with intermediate levels of aggression had intermediate levels of testosterone, and those with low levels of aggression had the lowest levels of testosterone. Those findings are presented in Figure 15.5.

Given that low levels of serotonin and high levels of testosterone are related to the aggression seen in the conduct disorder, the question arises, what leads to those deviant biochemical levels? Prolonged stress can influence levels of serotonin and testosterone (see Chapters 9 and 18), but most of the chronic differences in those levels are probably due to genetic factors. Consistent with that are the findings indicating that genetic factors play an important role in conduct disorders (e.g., Cadoret & Cain, 1980; Jarey & Stewart, 1985; Lahey et al., 1995; Mednick, Gabrielli, & Hutchings, 1984). Specifically, biological children of parents with the conduct disorder or the antisocial personality disorder (an adult form of the conduct disorder) show high rates of the conduct disorder even when they are adopted at birth and raised by parents who do not have the disorder.

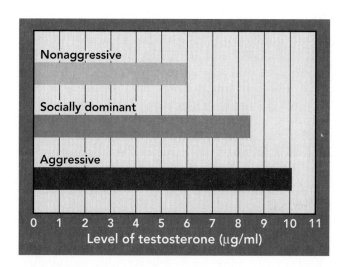

FIGURE 15.5 Higher levels of aggression were associated with higher levels of testosterone.
Source: Data from Ehrenkranz et al. (1974), p. 471, tab. 1.

Each of the explanations just described probably accounts for some cases of the conduct disorder, but many cases probably result from the interaction of causes. That is, physiological factors provide a predisposition to aggressive behavior, and then frustration, the observation of models, or the perception of a threat may trigger or give form to aggressive acts.

Sociocultural Factors

Social and cultural factors can play an important role in some cases of the conduct disorder. One of the best predictors of who will develop the disorder is lower social economic status (Lahey et al., 1995). Statistically, African-Americans are more likely to develop the conduct disorder than other groups, but analyses have revealed that *ethnicity per se had nothing to do with the development of the disorder.* Instead, the African-Americans were overrepresented only because they were overrepresented in the lower class. Lower-class membership could contribute to the development of the conduct disorder in a variety of ways, but one of the strongest is learning. That is, the rewards and role models for antisocial behavior that are available in the lower class can contribute to the development of the disorder.

Concerns have been raised over the possibility that in some cases a diagnosis of conduct disorder may be misapplied to individuals in high-crime areas who are using behaviors such as fighting to *protect themselves.* Therefore, in DSM-IV it is pointed out that "the Conduct Disorder diagnosis should be applied only when the behavior in question is symptomatic of an underlying dysfunction within the individual and not simply a reaction to the immediate social context" (American

Psychiatric Association, 1994, p. 88). That is, the conduct disorder involves behaviors that are generated by the individual, not elicited by a situation.

Treatment

As with other disorders that can stem from different causes, different approaches must be taken, depending on the suspected cause. If it is suspected that the conduct disorder was learned, the strategy may be to punish the behavior. It might also be effective to reward alternative behaviors that are more appropriate, but unfortunately that is rarely done. Some evidence for the effectiveness of punishment is provided by a study of the arrest records of almost 30,000 males in Denmark (Brennan & Mednick, 1994). The results indicated that among those who were arrested for personal-property offenses such as breaking and entering or car theft, 52% of those who were not punished after their first arrest were arrested in the future, versus only 20% of those who were punished after their first arrest. In other words, punishment resulted in a 32% reduction in future illegal behavior. Furthermore, among individuals who were arrested multiple times, those who were consistently punished were less likely to be arrested in the future than individuals who were punished inconsistently. However, it is important to note that even among individuals who were consistently punished following three or four arrests, there was still a recidivism rate of 67%. In other words, punishment can be effective, but there are individuals for whom punishment does not appear to be effective.

Punishment by itself is often ineffective because it serves to *suppress* the inappropriate behavior temporarily, when what is needed is to learn and be rewarded for alternative appropriate behavior. That is, it is not enough to say, "Don't do that" and punish the behavior; it is also essential to say, "Do this instead" and then reward the better behavior. In fact, there is now considerable evidence that if started early, education in combination with social support can be effective for reducing delinquency in children who are at high risk (Yoshikawa, 1994).

For individuals for whom punishment and education are not effective, the problem may be low levels of serotonin that lead to impulsivity, and for those individuals it may be effective to use a drug that increases the levels of serotonin (Ghaziuddin & Alessi, 1992). I recently saw an interesting example of this in a college student who was suffering from serious depression and the conduct disorder. An antidepressant drug was prescribed for the depression, and to our surprise, the drug cleared up the depression *and* the conduct disorder. Why? You will recall from Chapter 10 that most antidepressants increase the level of serotonin, and in this case, that helped with both problems.

TOPIC II
DEVELOPMENTAL DISORDERS

Developmental disorders involve problems that interfere with emotional and academic development in infants and children. We will give careful attention to the very serious disorder known as autism and to the somewhat less serious learning disorders that are associated with language, academic, and motor abilities.

AUTISTIC DISORDER

The word *autism* means "self-centered and withdrawn from reality," and the **autistic disorder** involves extreme social impairment and lack of communication. Children with this disorder are "in their own little world" and usually cannot be reached.

Symptoms

DSM-IV lists three major symptoms for the autistic disorder.

Impairments in Social Interactions. Children with autism appear to be off in their own world; they do not respond to others around them and seem even to be unaware of the presence of others. As infants, they do not cry when left alone, do not smile at others, and do not vocalize in response to others. When picked up, they are stiff or limp and do not cuddle against their parents' bodies as normal infants do. Later in life these individuals do not relate to others, but neither do they get into conflicts with others. They are simply "on their own wavelength" and are unable to respond to other people in the way humans usually do.

The lack of interpersonal interest shown by children with autism was demonstrated in a study in which disturbed and normal children were allowed to look at human and nonhuman environmental stimuli (Hutt & Ounsted, 1966). When compared to the nonautistic children, those with autism spent more time gazing at environmental stimuli and less time gazing at human stimuli.

Impairments in Communication. Even by the age of 5 or 6, many children with autism cannot use language at all. They are mute or will make only meaningless sounds that are not used to communicate with others. The absence of language is a very important factor in determining the child's prognosis. Specifically, if the child does not have language skills by the age of 5, there is a 75% chance that he or she will never make an adequate personal or social adjustment (Eisenberg & Kanner, 1956; Gillberg, 1991).

Children with autism who do talk will often show a variety of peculiar speech patterns. For example, they may simply repeat what is said to them; if you say, "Hello, Jimmy," the child may say, "Hello, Jimmy." This response pattern is referred to as **echolalia** (EK-ō-LĀ-lē-uh) because the child repeats what is said without a sense of meaning, much as an echo comes back from a mountainside. In some cases the echolalia is delayed, and the child will repeat the phrase hours later, completely out of context and with no apparent stimulus. Another unusual speech pattern is **pronoun reversal,** whereby the child will use *he, she,* or *you* for *I* or *me.* For example, a boy with autism who wants a cookie may say, "You want a cookie" or "He want a cookie."

Children with the autistic disorder show little response to other people, a reduced ability to communicate, and a restricted repertory of activities and interests. Many require special education.

Restricted, Repetitive, and Stereotyped Behaviors.
Children with autism may sit alone for hours with a fixed stare, or they may rock back and forth endlessly. In other cases, they may repeat certain behaviors such as spinning a toy for hours, or they may repeatedly make ritualistic gestures with their fingers and hands. For example, for hours at a time they may move their fingers as if playing a piano. Often these children engage in self-mutilation behaviors such as scratching or hitting themselves. In one case, a child who was not restrained banged his head 1,800 times in 8 days (Lovaas & Simmons, 1969).

Children with autism also seem to prefer sameness with regard to environmental stimuli. They will rigidly keep things such as toys or clothing in careful order and become upset if there is any change in their daily routine.

The symptoms of autism appear *very early.* Indeed, if a child is to be diagnosed as suffering from autism, the symptoms must be apparent before the child is 3 years old. Parents who have some experience with infants and who know what to expect notice a problem with the child almost from the time of birth. The early onset of this disorder is reflected in its original name, *infantile autism.*

Autism is not an either-or disorder; there are degrees of severity. Individuals with less severe cases are generally referred to as **high-functioning individuals** (Yirmiya & Sigman, 1991). High-functioning individuals show less disruption in social and cognitive functioning and may show normal levels of intelligence. With regard to performance on IQ tests, high-functioning individuals do less well on subtests that measure social intelligence (e.g., arranging pictures to make a story) than they do on nonsocial subtests (e.g., arranging blocks to make a design).

In Case Study 15.2, you will find portions of an interview I had with the mother of a child with autism. In the interview, she describes the child's behavior and her reactions.

Issues

Sociocultural Factors. Autism is a relatively rare disorder and may occur in only about 1 in 2,000 births, but it is four times more likely to occur in males than in females.

The results of early studies suggested that autism was more likely to occur in the upper socioeconomic classes and that the parents of children with the autistic disorder were more likely to be professionals (Eisenberg & Kanner, 1956). However, more recent and better studies have consistently indicated that autism is not related to social class (Gillberg & Schaumann, 1982; Tsai et al., 1982). The initial findings relating autism to upper-class status were probably due to the fact that the studies were conducted in prestigious and expensive

hospitals where the children of wealthy parents were more likely to be brought for treatment.

Autism Versus Schizophrenia in Childhood. For many years there was a controversy over whether autism was a separate disorder or a type of schizophrenia in childhood. However, it is now generally agreed that autism and schizophrenia in childhood are separate disorders. A variety of factors separate infantile autism from schizophrenia in childhood:

1. Individuals with autism rarely have a family history of schizophrenia, but individuals with schizophrenia often have a family history of schizophrenia.
2. Individuals with autism often show a lack of intellectual development, but that is not the case with individuals who suffer from schizophrenia.
3. Individuals with autism have limited speech, whereas individuals with schizophrenia have normal speech ability but communicate bizarre ideas.
4. Autism is apparent almost at birth, whereas schizophrenia develops later.
5. Neuroleptic drugs are generally effective for treating individuals with schizophrenia but have relatively little effect on individuals with the autistic disorder.

With regard to the differences between autism and schizophrenia, it can be said that children with autism appear *unoriented* and *detached,* whereas children with schizophrenia appear *disoriented* and *confused.* For these reasons, autism and schizophrenia are considered separate disorders, and you should not assume that the causes and treatments for one can be applied to the other.

Autism and Asperger's Disorder. Although autism is clearly a different disorder from schizophrenia, there is a strong relationship between autism and a disorder known as **Asperger's** (uh-SPUR-gurz) **disorder,** which like autism involves impairments in social interactions, is characterized by repetitive or stereotyped patterns of motor behavior, and is four times more likely to occur in males than females (American Psychiatric Association, 1994). However, the difference between autism and Asperger's disorder is that *Asperger's does not involve problems with communication or delays in development* (i.e., language development follows a normal course) and the problems with motor behavior are often characterized as a general *clumsiness* (Gillberg, 1993). Because the symptoms of Asperger's disorder are similar to but less serious than those of autism, individuals with Asperger's disorder are often likened to high-functioning individuals with autism (Manjiviona & Prior 1995). The existence of Asperger's disorder suggests that there is a *spectrum or continuum of autism;* that is, rather than autism's being one disorder, the symptoms may appear in different combinations and at different levels of severity (Eaves et al., 1994; Szatmari, 1992). In that

CASE STUDY 15.2

A Mother Talks About Her 15-Year-Old Son, Who Was Diagnosed as Suffering from Autism

Holmes: Can you tell me when you first noticed that something was wrong with Tom?

Mother: In retrospect, I think I always felt there was something wrong, even as early as the pregnancy. The pregnancy was technically normal—tests didn't show any problems—but it just wasn't like my other two pregnancies. He was always moving and kicking, and I just thought he was unhappy in the womb. Then right after he was born, I noticed a couple of things that were different from my other children. Tom had difficulty sucking at the breast, and he never seemed to be comforted when he was picked up or cuddled. In fact, picking him up seemed to upset him more; his muscles would become rigid, and he would scream at the top of his lungs. This worried my husband and me; we thought we were doing something wrong in the bonding process.

Holmes: Can you tell me about his reactions to other people?

Mother: Well, at first he would scream and twist if touched by anyone, but as he got older, he stopped showing that extreme reaction, but he didn't react positively either. He was just neutral and limp. However, when he was picked up by an unfamiliar person, he would have a severe negative reaction, a real tantrum.

Apart from that, he seemed to be in his own little world. When he was an infant, it was difficult to get his attention, and then it was impossible to hold it for more than a few seconds. He never played with other children or adults. Instead, he would do activities like looking in mirrors or at shiny objects for hours at a time. He also liked to spin the lids from jars over and over. One of his favorite things was to sit in front of the washing machine and watch the clothes go round

and round. Sometimes he would sit in a corner and rock back and forth, or he would flap his arms and sing "da da de la da" over and over. For a while, we tried to force social interactions on him, hoping we could "break through." That never worked, and he would resist by banging his head on the floor and screaming. At around 8 or 9, he started interacting with others a little, and now he will sometimes initiate a conversation or an activity. I'm not sure whether we had an influence or he finally matured a little.

Holmes: How about developmental tasks, things like smiling, walking, and talking? Did he start doing those things on schedule?

Mother: Tom did everything much later than other children. He didn't roll over until 8 months, and he didn't walk until 26 months. When he finally did walk, he walked only on his toes until he was 5. He started talking at around 4, but even then he didn't talk, he just repeated what others were saying. We had a terrible time getting him toilet-trained. It wasn't until he was 5 that he could stay dry during the day, and he wet himself at night until he was 12.

Holmes: Did Tom show any unusual behaviors other than his lack of social interest and delayed development?

Mother: One thing that has been a real problem is that he just cannot deal with change. To keep peace in the house, everything in his room—which is where he stayed most of the time—had to be kept exactly the same all the time. One time, I threw away an old beat-up wastebasket that had been in his room, and for two weeks he cried, demanding that it be returned. When he was moved from the fifth to the sixth grade, he refused to go to school for three weeks and

regard, it is interesting to note that Asperger's disorder is more common in the relatives of individuals with autism than in the relatives of other individuals (Ehlers & Gillberg, 1993; Gillberg et al., 1992).

Explanations

Autism poses one of the major unsolved mysteries of abnormal psychology. However, since the disorder was

first identified (Kanner, 1943), we have ruled out a number of erroneous explanations, and we are now developing some viable hypotheses about what might cause the disorder.

Psychodynamic Explanations. Early psychodynamic explanations for autism focused on the role of parents' personalities and their styles of child rearing. For example, it was suggested that the parents of chil-

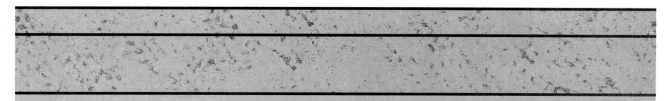

became violent when we tried to drag him out of the house. As long as things were perfectly constant and no one tried to get into his little world, he would be all right. Well, I don't mean "all right," but he wouldn't become agitated or violent.

Holmes: You mentioned school. How's he been doing in school?

Mother: School has always been a struggle for us all. Just getting him to go has been tough, but on the whole, Tom has done pretty well. Most of the time, he has been in a special class for children with behavior disorders, so he gets more structure and more individualized instruction. Once he was "mainstreamed" into a regular typing class, but the change and additional stimulation were too much for him. He is now doing tenth-grade-level work, which is just about where he should be. For the past year, he has been in a special occupational program where he earns school credit for working 3 hours a day. First he worked in a veterinary clinic, where he did odd jobs. He loved being around the animals, but he couldn't handle the lack of structure—different chores all the time—so he started withdrawing and finally stopped going. Then he was switched to a fast-food restaurant where he had a consistent assignment, but for some reason that didn't work out either. I think there was too much activity and pressure to keep up.

Holmes: When was Tom first diagnosed as suffering from autism?

Mother: (long pause; rubs her temples and slumps in her chair a little) All along, we'd been very worried about Tom's development, and we'd taken him to a variety of specialists, but it was the language problem at age 4—the delay and the echolalia—

that convinced everyone that Tom was autistic. *(pause)* I will never forget the day the diagnosis was finally made. The possibility that he was autistic had been mentioned earlier, but we had always avoided confronting it. We kept looking somewhere else for a "better" explanation— something that could be cured. When the social worker told us the diagnosis, it was like we had been hit by a truck. We had seen the truck coming, but we had intentionally looked the other way. We had a son who was autistic—what were we going to do? First we got books and started reading about autism, but that made things worse because they said it was the parents' fault for being cold and distant. We felt terrible, but then the psychologist explained that those were old theories and that now it is believed that autism is due to some genetic problem or a problem during pregnancy. That didn't make the problem less serious, but it helped relieve some of our guilt. *(pause)*

We've come to accept the fact that Tom is different from other children. There are limits to what he can do and limits to what we can do for him. Autism isn't an either-or thing—there are degrees of it, and Tom's case isn't as severe as many others. He can live at home and function to some extent in the community. Someday, when we aren't around to take care of him, he will probably have to be moved to some sort of sheltered-living situation. I've grown to recognize that we have to accept people the way they are. We need to keep helping Tom, but we also need to accept him and his limitations. We think or hope he is happy, but a lot of the time it is hard to know what is going on in his world.

dren with autism were cold, formal, humorless, detached, highly rational, and objective (Bettelheim, 1967; Kanner, 1943). Supposedly, parents of that type did not provide their children with interpersonal warmth and nurturance, and it was assumed that the children then turned away from these "mechanical" parents and turned inward for comfort and stimulation. The psychodynamic explanations have lost most of their credibility and supporters because numerous

investigations have revealed that the parents of children with autism do not differ from the parents of normal children or from parents of other types of disturbed children.

Learning Explanations. Learning theorists attempted to explain autism by suggesting that the abnormal behaviors such as headbanging, uncooperativeness, tantrums, and mutism are often followed by rewards such as attention, food, and toys that are designed to distract the child and reduce the abnormal behavior (Ferster, 1961; Lovaas & Smith, 1989). However, rather than reducing the abnormal behavior, it was suggested that the rewards reinforced and increased the abnormal behaviors. In other words, these theorists suggest that autistic behavior is taught by parents who reward the wrong behavior.

The learning explanations for autism were tested indirectly with experiments in which attempts were made to eliminate autistic behavior by changing what behaviors were rewarded. The notion was that if autistic behavior was caused by rewarding the abnormal behavior, ceasing those rewards and rewarding normal behavior would eliminate the autism. Those experiments will be discussed in the section on therapy, but for now we should note that ignoring or punishing autistic behaviors and rewarding normal behaviors has been only slightly effective in making children with autism more manageable, and it has not resulted in a reversal of the autism (Lovaas et al., 1973). In view of that, much of the interest in learning as the cause of autism has waned.

Physiological Explanations. Comparisons of children who do and do not have autism have revealed numerous differences in brain structure and neurochemistry, and those differences strongly suggest that autism is due to some form of brain dysfunction (e.g., Piven et al., 1995; Zilbovicius et al., 1995). Unfortunately, we do not yet understand the nature of the dysfunction or how it results in autistic behavior, and it would be premature to speculate on any one causal factor. Indeed, as was found to be the case with schizophrenia, it is likely that the different symptoms of autism will be found to be due to a number of different factors.

Some support for the physiological explanations comes from the findings that biological hazards during pregnancy and birth are related to autism. For example, there is substantial evidence that the mothers of children with autism experience more problems during pregnancy than mothers of normal children (Finegan & Quarrington, 1979; Kagan, 1981; Nelson, 1991; Torrey et al., 1975). These problems include bleeding, infections, poisoning, and physical trauma. These hazards are most likely to result in autism when they occur during the first trimester of pregnancy, when the fetus is going through crucial stages of development and is particularly vulnerable.

There is also substantial evidence that children with autism experience more problems during the birth process than normal children. In one study, the birth records of 23 children with autism were compared to the birth records of their 15 normal siblings, and it was found that the children with autism had

more difficulties in the birth process than their siblings did (Finegan & Quarrington, 1979).

Apart from problems with pregnancy and birth, there is also evidence that as many as 11% of individuals with autism suffer from rare diseases that could influence brain development and functioning (Ritvo et al., 1990). The 11% figure is much higher than what would be expected in a normal population because the diseases are generally very rare, and thus the high co-occurrence rate suggests a causative role. There is also evidence that individuals with autism are more likely to have problems with their immune systems, and the reduced effectiveness of the immune systems would make the individuals more vulnerable to infectious diseases that could affect the brain (Zimmerman et al., 1993).

The evidence for the influence of biological hazards is impressive, but biological hazards alone cannot account for all cases of autism. Therefore, we must go on to consider the role that genetic factors play in the disorder. We cannot test for a genetic basis for autism by studying the offspring of individuals with autism because individuals with the disorder rarely marry or have children. However, we can examine the rates for autism among siblings, and investigations of that type indicate that between 2% and 5% of the siblings of individuals with autism also suffer from the disorder (August et al., 1981; Folstein, 1991; Hanson & Gottesman, 1976; Minton et al., 1982; Ritvo et al., 1982; Rutter, 1967). Concordance rates of 2% and 5% are not high, but they are much higher than the rate of autism in the general population, so they provide evidence that there is a genetic basis for at least some cases of autism.

Investigators have also found that the "normal" siblings of individuals with autism are more likely to suffer from cognitive impairments such as delayed speech development or reduced verbal abilities (Bartak et al., 1975; Folstein & Rutter, 1977; Minton et al., 1982; Rutter et al., 1971; Vaillant, 1963). For example, delayed language development was found in 25% of the siblings of individuals with autism. In other words, although they are not autistic, many of the siblings of autistic children exhibit what might be thought of as mild symptoms of autism.

The genetic basis for autism has also been examined in studies of the concordance rates for autism in monozygotic and dizygotic twin pairs (see Fish & Ritvo, 1979; Folstein, 1991; Hanson & Gottesman, 1976; Smalley et al., 1988). In the best study of this type, it was found that the concordance rate among MZ twin pairs was 36%, while the concordance rate among DZ twins was 0% (Folstein & Rutter, 1977). Those results clearly indicate that at least some cases of autism have a genetic basis.

In the study just mentioned, the investigators also checked to see if the nonautistic members of twin pairs suffered from any cognitive impairments such as delayed speech development that might reflect a mild form of autism. The results indicated that among MZ twin pairs, the concordance rate for autism in one twin and cognitive impairment in the other was 46%, while among DZ twin pairs, the rate was only 10%. When the autism-impairment concordance rate was combined with the autism-autism concordance rate, the overall concordance rate for cognitive disturbance among MZ twin pairs was 82%, versus only 10% among DZ twin pairs. These results suggest that there is a genetic basis for a range of impairment and that only for some individuals is the impairment severe enough to justify the diagnosis of autism.

As the evidence concerning the causes of autism mounts, it is becoming clear that both biological hazards and genetic factors must be considered. The fact that multiple factors must be considered was neatly demonstrated in an investigation in which both genetic and biological hazards were examined in 21 twin pairs (Folstein & Rutter, 1977). First, it was determined that 32% of the cases of autism could be accounted for by genetic factors (i.e., there were four sets of MZ twins who were concordant for autism). Next, an examination of pregnancy and birth records revealed that 40% of the children with the autistic disorder had been exposed to biological hazards during pregnancy or birth (e.g., delay in breathing, neonatal convulsions, congenital anomalies, low birth weight, narrow umbilical cord, neonatal apnea). It is particularly interesting that none of the MZ twins who were concordant for autism had experienced such hazards, a finding that strengthens the interpretation that those cases were due to genetic rather than biological factors. Taken together, the genetic and hazard factors accounted for 72% of the cases of autism. The task facing investigators now is to determine the cause of the remaining 28% of the cases.

Treatment

Numerous approaches have been used in attempts to treat childhood autism, but none has been shown to be consistently effective. In the 1950s and early 1960s, a great deal of attention was devoted to intensive, long-term psychodynamic treatment, but there is virtually no evidence that it was effective, and that approach has now been generally abandoned.

An exciting development was introduced in the mid-1960s when behavior modification strategies were introduced. In those treatment programs, children with autism were rewarded for appropriate behaviors and punished for inappropriate or self-destructive behaviors (Lovaas & Simmons, 1969; Lovaas et al.,

1966; Wolf et al., 1967). This can be an extremely difficult and prolonged task. For example, it may require thousands of trials in which a child is given bits of food for correct responses in order to teach the child simply to say one word, and then it is unlikely that the child will know what the word means or be able to use it in a sentence. Indeed, the child may be imitating rather than talking. These programs required a great deal of time, effort, and money, but the initial results were very encouraging, and a film of the progress made by autistic children in this program is still shown widely in college classes on psychology (Lovaas, 1969). At the end of that film, children who were once mute, echolalic, self-destructive, and unable to interact with others are shown to be behaving much more normally. The implication was that behavior modification procedures are effective for treating autistic children.

Regrettably, the original film and the related research reports may imply or promise more than what was actually accomplished. The results that were reported suffer from two serious problems that generally go unrecognized. The first is that the treatment effects did not last (Lovaas et al., 1973). Despite 6 hours of one-on-one treatment per day for a period of 14 months, the newly developed appropriate behaviors dropped out when the treatment was stopped, and the old, inappropriate behaviors returned. This is illustrated for two children, Pam and Rick, in Figure 15.6. During the year of treatment (1964–1965), appropriate play increased and self-stimulation decreased, but when Pam and Rick

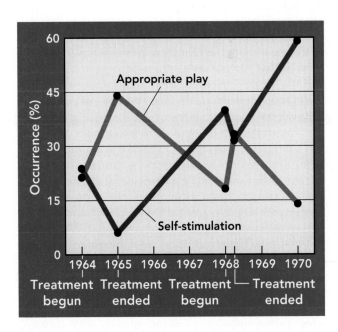

FIGURE 15.6 Appropriate behaviors declined and inappropriate behaviors returned after a behavior modification program for autistic children was ended.
Source: Adapted from Lovaas et al. (1973), p. 149, fig. 8.

were assessed 3 years later, these activities had returned to their original levels. At that time (1968), treatment was reinstituted, and for a brief time appropriate play increased and self-stimulation decreased. However, when the children were assessed again after another 2 years in which they were not treated (1970), the gains made in treatment had disappeared. Indeed, as indicated in the figure, 5 years after the end of training, Pam and Rick were showing less appropriate play and more self-stimulation than they had before treatment was begun.

The second problem is that the treatment did not actually result in the hoped-for behavior even during the treatment period. The behavior therapists suggest that the treatment increased social and affectionate behavior, and as an example they point out that after treatment, the previously withdrawn autistic children would run across the room with outstretched arms to their therapist in the hope of being picked up and hugged (Lovaas, 1969). However, what is not made clear in the film is that the children were barefooted and the behavior occurred in a room that had a shock-grid on the floor that would be used to administer punishment to the children (Lovaas et al., 1965). The children ran across the room to be picked up by the therapist to avoid getting shocks to their feet and not in an attempt to get or express affection! It is also noteworthy that the purportedly affectionate behavior did not generalize to another room that did not have a shock grid on the floor. Unfortunately, then, the responses achieved with the behavior modification program were not always what they appeared to be, and the improved behavior did not last or generalize to other situations. A sad footnote to this attempt at treatment is that the children who were treated in the film and for whom there were such high hopes were subsequently readmitted as full-time residents of psychiatric institutions.

The story does not end there because the investigators tried again with a more extensive program (Lovaas, 1987, 1993). In this second investigation, treatment was started earlier (at about 3 years of age), was more intensive (more than 40 hours per week of one-on-one treatment), and lasted longer (at least 2 years), and the parents were actively involved in the treatment. The notion was that the children needed more treatment and that other people in the children's lives should be involved so as to enhance the generalization and maintenance of the newly learned behaviors. Treatment involved ignoring or punishing inappropriate behaviors (aggression, self-stimulation, noncompliance with instructions) and rewarding appropriate behaviors (attempts to talk, prosocial activities, compliance with instructions). When the children started kindergarten, treatment was reduced to 10 hours per week, and when they started first grade, the treatment was usually limited to

consultation with parents. The second investigation also included a minimal treatment control condition (10 hours or less per week of one-on-one treatment).

The results indicated that 47% of the children in the treatment condition successfully passed through normal first grade in a public school and demonstrated a normal IQ, whereas none of the children in the control condition got through first grade or demonstrated a normal IQ (Lovaas, 1987). Symptoms of autism such as self-stimulation and abnormal speech were assessed before treatment began but not at the end of treatment, so we do not know the degree to which those behaviors were influenced. However, the investigator implied that if they had not been improved, the children would not have been able to complete first grade.

These results are certainly positive, but the investigation has come under severe criticism, and the results are surrounded in controversy (Lovaas et al., 1989; McEachin et al., 1993; Schopler et al., 1989; Smith et al., 1993). For example, the critics pointed out that (a) the children were not randomly assigned to the treatment and control conditions, (b) no data on behavior were reported, (c) changes in IQ scores may reflect changes in compliance rather than changes in cognitive functioning, and (d) the children in the treatment condition may have been pushed through school by staff pressure. At present, it is hazardous to draw firm conclusions concerning this approach to treatment; the children in the treatment condition were more likely to complete first grade, but it is not clear how or why. In the absence of good data, we must be careful neither to hold out false hopes nor to abandon hope.

Before concluding our discussion of the behavioral approach to treatment, we should give some attention to the controversy over the use of punishment for suppressing inappropriate and potentially dangerous behaviors (Etzel et al., 1987; Guess et al., 1987; Kiernan, 1988; Lavigna & Donnellan, 1986; Wedell et al., 1987). Children with autism frequently engage in very serious self-injurious behaviors such as head banging, which they might do hundreds of times a day, and there is no doubt that the use of **aversive procedures** such as slapping them, giving them painful electrical shocks, or spraying noxious substances in their faces can quickly bring those behaviors to a stop. However, the question is, is it ethical to use aversive procedures on children who are not in a position to object? Does the end justify the means?

Some people have argued that aversive procedures are not justified, and they have taken steps to outlaw them. For example, a bill was introduced in Congress in 1987 to withhold funding from any agency that used aversive procedures in the treatment of "any individual with a severe disability." The bill died in committee and

The prognosis for children suffering from the autistic disorder is poor; fewer than 25 percent make a satisfactory adjustment by adolescence or adulthood. Dustin Hoffman (left) portrayed an autistic adult in the movie Rain Man.

has not been reintroduced. In another case, the state of Massachusetts attempted to suspend the operation of a treatment center where aversive procedures were used in the treatment of children with autism (Fuller, 1986). Opponents of aversive procedures argued that the procedures constituted "officially sanctioned child abuse." In response, the parents of a boy named Brendon filed a class-action suit in which they argued that by denying the use of aversive procedures, the state was denying Brendon and other children the *right to an effective treatment in the absence of an effective alternative.* They pointed out that over a period of 15 years, Brendon had been discharged as "untreatable" from a number of prestigious institutions for autistic children but that while being treated with the aversive procedures at the Behavioral Research Institute, he had shown remarkable improvement. The judge found in favor of the parents and thereby permitted the use of the aversive procedures. Since that decision, there have been a number of other challenges to the use of aversive procedures, but all have failed. Aversive procedures work, and although they seem harsh, they are more humane than letting people do serious harm to themselves. The key

to their effective and ethical use is to apply only the amount that is necessary to suppress the inappropriate behaviors and to institute a system of checks to ensure that the procedures are not misused.

Numerous drugs have been used in attempts to treat autism, but the results have been mixed at best. For example, the neuroleptic Haldol (see Chapter 13) may help reduce the hyperactivity, outbursts of rage, and sleeplessness that are sometimes present in autism (Anderson et al., 1984; see review by Gittelman & Kanner, 1986). However, although the drug may have made the children somewhat easier to manage, it did not reduce the core symptoms of the autism. It has also been found that the antidepressant drug that is effective for treating the obsessive-compulsive disorder (clomipramine) was more effective than a placebo for eliminating the repetitive ritualized behaviors, such as object spinning and hand movements, that are often seen in autism (Gordon et al., 1993).

In view of the ineffectiveness of our treatments and the fact that in most cases the disorder does not diminish as the individual gets older, the prognosis for autistic children is poor. Fewer than 25% make a satisfactory adjustment by adolescence or adulthood (De Myer et al., 1981; Eisenberg & Kanner, 1956; Rutter & Lockyer, 1967), and between 40% and 70% continue to live in institutions (Lotter, 1978). The number of autistic individuals who live in institutions increases as they become older, a finding that is probably attributable to the fact that as the children get older, the parents are less able to cope with them (De Myer et al., 1981). Overall, autism represents one of the most conspicuous and most serious failures of psychology and psychiatry, and we can only hope for a breakthrough in the future. At present, however, the picture is bleak.

LEARNING, COMMUNICATION, AND MOTOR SKILLS DISORDERS

Before concluding the discussion of developmental disorders, some comment should be made concerning a relatively new set of disorders called **learning, communication, and motor skills disorders.** These disorders are summarized in Table 15.2. Serious questions have been raised about whether these problems should be considered psychological disorders or whether they might be more appropriately considered educational problems. Some critics have suggested that labeling these problems as psychological reflects a psychological or psychiatric "imperialism" whereby psychologists and psychiatrists are trying to gain control over problems that are beyond their traditional and appropriate

TABLE 15.2 Learning, Communication, and Motor Skills Disorders

Disorder	Symptoms
Reading disorder	Reading ability is markedly below what would be expected on the basis of the child's intellectual ability.
Mathematics disorder	Mathematic ability is markedly below what would be expected on the basis of the child's intellectual ability.
Expressive language disorder	Use of language is markedly below what would be expected on the basis of the child's intellectual ability (e.g., poor vocabulary, overly simple sentences, limitation to the present tense).
Written expression disorder	Composition of written text is markedly below what would be expected on the basis of the child's intellectual ability (e.g., poor spelling and grammar).
Phonological disorder	Child fails consistently to use speech sounds as expected for age and dialect.
Stuttering	Child fails consistently to speak without involuntary disruption or blocking.
Developmental coordination disorder	Performance in motor skills activities is markedly below what would be expected on the basis of the child's chronological age and intellectual ability.

Note: In all disorders, low ability must interfere with achievement and activities.

scope. The decision about whether they are psychological or educational problems will ultimately rest on the determination of the cause or causes of the problems. For the most part, we currently know very little about their causes and treatment.

TOPIC III
OTHER DISORDERS

ELIMINATION DISORDERS

Symptoms

Enuresis (en-yoo-RĒ-sis) is the voluntary or involuntary voiding of urine into the child's clothing or bed after the age at which the child should be able to control the flow of urine. Specifically, an individual is diagnosed as suffering from enuresis if he or she voids inappropriately at least twice a week for 3 months after the age of 5. The disorder is thought to occur in about 7% of males and 3% of females.

Encopresis (en-kuh-PRĒ-sis) is the voluntary or involuntary passage of feces in inappropriate places, such as in clothing or onto the floor. To be diagnosed as suffering from encopresis, the child must be at least 4 years old because toilet training should be completed by that age, and inappropriate bowel movements must occur at least once a month for a period of 3 months so as to ensure that the symptoms are not just accidents.

Explanations

In this discussion, I will focus on enuresis because it is a more widespread problem than encopresis and because more is known about it.

Psychodynamic Explanations. The psychodynamic explanations assume that enuresis stems from intrapsychic conflict. For example, Freud (1905/1953) suggested that it was a substitute for masturbation, which was forbidden. Other theorists posited that enuresis is a form of passive aggression or that it results from a regression to an earlier stage of development in the face of conflict (Fenichel, 1945; Mowrer, 1950). These explanations do not have any empirical support.

More general psychodynamic theories suggest that stress inhibits the learning of bladder control or disrupts learning that may have already occurred (Couchells et al., 1981; Douglas, 1973; Morgan & Young, 1972; Shaffer, 1973). As evidence for the role of stress, theorists point out that in many cases, children with enuresis show other adjustment problems (Stehbens, 1970). In other words, stress leads to enuresis as well as other problems. Alternatively, it is possible that the other adjustment problems seen in children with enuresis are not a reflection of stress in general but rather a result of the enuresis. Consistent with that possibility, there is evidence that when the symptoms of enuresis are treated and reduced, the other problems also diminish (Baker, 1969; Baller, 1975; Starfield, 1972). Stress undoubtedly plays a role in many cases of enuresis, but whether it is a cause, an effect, or both has not yet been determined.

Learning Explanations. A widely held explanation for enuresis is that the individual has simply not yet learned the urine retention response (Lovibond & Coote, 1969). Evidence for this explanation comes from research indicating that the use of training procedures in which bladder control is taught are very effective for overcoming enuresis in many individuals. Those procedures and results will be considered in greater detail in our discussion of treatment.

Physiological Explanations. There are a number of physiological explanations for enuresis, the first of which is that the disorder stems from a maturational lag or delay in the normal development of the neurological system that governs bladder control (Troup & Hodgson, 1971). In other words, the neurological development necessary for bladder control may be delayed in some individuals, thereby preventing them from learning bladder control. Consistent with the developmental-lag hypothesis is the finding that almost all individuals do outgrow the disorder eventually.

A second physiological explanation is that the level of bladder pressure that is necessary to stimulate urination is lower in some children than in others. The lower pressure that is required for urination in children with enuresis may not be sufficient to wake them up if they are sleeping or alert them if they are awake, thus resulting in uncontrolled or unexpected urination (Yates, 1975).

A third physiological explanation is that children with enuresis sleep more deeply than other children, and their bladder tension is not sufficient to awaken them so that they can go to the toilet. The evidence for differences in sleep patterns between children who do and do not have enuresis is contradictory at best. Moreover, the deep-sleep hypothesis has difficulty explaining problems with bladder control experienced by some children during waking hours (Gillin et al.,

1982). For these reasons, this explanation has largely been rejected.

The exact physiological mechanism underlying enuresis is not clear, but we do have evidence linking genetic factors to enuresis. Indeed, approximately 75% of the children with enuresis have a first-degree relative with the disorder (American Psychiatric Association, 1994). Furthermore, in one study of twins, there was a concordance rate of 70% for enuresis among monozygotic boys, but the rate was only 30% among dizygotic boys (Bakwin, 1971).

Treatment

Traditional psychotherapy is not effective for treating enuresis, and at present the most popular approach involves what is known as the **bell-and-pad procedure.** An electrically wired pad is placed beneath the sheet of the child's bed. When the child urinates in the bed, the fluid serves to close a circuit in the pad, which immediately sounds a bell that awakens the child, who then stops urinating in bed and goes to the toilet (Friman & Vollmer, 1995; Lovibond & Coote, 1969).

A review of the research on the bell-and-pad technique suggests that it is effective with about 75% of the treated cases and that it is more effective than drugs (Doleys, 1977; Houts et al., 1994). The problem is that among the individuals who are originally helped with this technique, about 40% relapse. However, if the treatment procedure is reinstituted, about 30% of the individuals regain bladder control.

There are two theories to explain the effectiveness of the bell-and-pad procedure. The *classical conditioning* explanation suggests that bladder tension becomes associated with the bell, awakening, and cessation of urination so that eventually the child wakes up and withholds urine when the bladder tension develops (Mowrer & Mowrer, 1938). The *operant avoidance conditioning* explanation suggests that being suddenly awakened by the bell is unpleasant, and the child learns to avoid that by withholding urination (Lovibond, 1963). At present, we do not understand why the bell-and-pad technique works, but from a practical standpoint, the important thing is that it does work.

TIC DISORDERS

In general, **tics** involve *recurrent involuntary motor movements*. The movements range from small twitches to large movements of major portions of the body. Some tics involve the muscles of the diaphragm and result in grunts, barks, and even words, but those are rare.

Almost a third of individuals with Tourette's disorder may yell out obscenities when there is no reason to do so. The fear of behaving in such a manner in public often makes suppressing the symptoms more difficult.

Individuals with tics can consciously suppress the tics for short periods of time, but as soon as attention is turned away, the tics return. Tic disorders occur more frequently in males than in females, but generally they are rare. There are two types of tic disorders; simple tic disorders involve small to moderate muscle movements, whereas Tourette's disorder involves larger muscle movements and vocal utterances.

Tic Disorders

Children with **tic disorders** experience recurrent and involuntary contractions of skeletal muscles that result in jerking or twitching movements of the body or face. Eye blinks and facial twitches are most common. By themselves, tics are usually not particularly serious or disruptive, but they can lead to unfortunate secondary effects if the child with a tic becomes the target of ridicule from peers, which may lead the child to feel ashamed and to withdraw socially. Tics can occur during a brief transient period or may be a chronic problem.

Tourette's Disorder

Tourette's disorder involves tics like those in a simple tic disorder, but they often involve more and larger muscle groups, so the motor movements are more pronounced. More important, Tourette's disorder includes **vocal tics** that result in grunts, yelps, barks, and words. As many as 30% of individuals with Tourette's disorder have a verbal tic that involves the involuntary uttering

of obscenities (Comings, 1990). For example, in the absence of any reason for doing so, the individual might yell out words that most other people find shocking. This syndrome, known as **coprolalia** (kop-ruh-LĀ-lē-uh), can obviously be very disruptive of normal psychosocial functioning. The tics seen in Tourette's disorder can be voluntarily suppressed for short periods of time, but as soon as attention is diverted, they return.

In one interesting case, a radio disc jockey suffered from a severe form of Tourette's disorder, but he was able to suppress his vocal outbursts during the 15- or 20-second periods he was on the air between records. However, as soon as the mike was off, he would begin yelling things uncontrollably. He reported that he often yelled things he was thinking about but would not ordinarily say out loud. For example, at the beginning of the interview he yelled, "Get me a hamburger!" At that time, he was hungry and thinking about lunch. He described the verbal outbursts as being like a cough that can be suppressed temporarily but eventually wells up and bursts through uncontrollably.

The symptoms of Tourette's disorder are made worse by stress, and a vicious circle can develop in which the symptoms result in social stress, which in turn increases the likelihood of the symptoms. The disorder usually appears around age 7, it is three times more likely to occur in males than females, and it lasts throughout adulthood (Comings, 1990). Individuals with Tourette's disorder often also show symptoms of the attention-deficit/hyperactivity disorder and the obsessive-compulsive disorder (Comings & Comings, 1990).

Explanations

Psychodynamic theorists have speculated that tics reflect the breaking through of pent-up energy associated with unconscious conflicts and that tics that involve blinking of the eyes or turning away represent attempts by the individual to avoid conflicts (Fenichel, 1945).

A more widely accepted explanation is that tics are due to an organic brain dysfunction (Hyde & Weinberger, 1995, Kerbeshian & Burd, 1994; McDougle et al., 1994, Rogeness et al., 1993). More specifically, tics are probably due to excessively high levels of dopamine activity. In that regard, recall that dopamine is the neurotransmitter in the area of the brain responsible for motor activity and that it is involved in the involuntary twitching movements seen in tardive dyskinesia and Parkinson's disease (see Chapters 13 and 19).

Evidence linking Tourette's disorder to dopamine activity includes findings that drugs that increase dopamine activity exacerbate tics and drugs that reduce dopamine activity (neuroleptics such as Haldol) can be effective for treating tic disorders (Gittelman & Kanner, 1986; Kurlan, 1989; Zamula, 1988). It has been suggested that coprolalia can be explained by the fact that dopamine is also an important transmitter in the limbic system, which is responsible for emotion; the elevated emotion in combination with the elevated tic behavior might result in the spontaneous utterance of obscenities (Messiha & Carlson, 1983). A number of factors could contribute to the excessive dopamine activity, but primary among them is genetics (see Devor, 1990). For example, there is evidence that the incidence of the disorder is higher in family members with the disorder than it is in the general population (7.4% vs. .05%) and that the concordance rate is higher among monozygotic than dizygotic twins (Messiha & Carlson, 1983; Pauls et al., 1984; Shapiro & Shapiro, 1982).

Treatment

Tourette's is treated most effectively with neuroleptic drugs such as Haldol that reduce dopamine activity (Hyde & Weinberger, 1995; Rapoport, 1994). Those effects were illustrated in an interesting case of a professional baseball player who suffered from Tourette's. After playing successfully for some years, his performance began to decline, and he was eventually dropped from the team. At that point, he sought treatment for his disorder and was prescribed a neuroleptic drug that blocked dopamine activity. Taking the drug had two interesting effects: First, it reduced his Tourette's disorder, and second, it improved his general physical coordination such that he was able to make a successful comeback in the major leagues. In this case, it appears that the excessive dopamine activity resulted in muscle problems that led to both Tourette's and to a reduced ability to play baseball; when the dopamine problem was corrected, both symptoms went away.

SUMMARY

TOPIC I: DISRUPTIVE BEHAVIOR DISORDERS

- The attention-deficit/hyperactivity disorder involves the inability to maintain attention and hyperactivity or impulsivity. Although once thought to be misbehavior, it is now recognized as a disorder that can persist into adulthood.
- The attention-deficit/hyperactivity disorder is due to low levels of activity in the areas of the brain responsible for the control of attention and motor behavior. That physiological problem can stem from infections during pregnancy, anoxia during birth, ingestion of toxins such as lead, and genetic factors.
- The disorder in children and adults can be treated effectively with stimulants such as Ritalin and Dexedrine.
- The conduct disorder involves persistent misbehavior such as aggression, deceitfulness, and other forms of delinquency.
- Psychodynamic theorists suggest that the conduct disorder stems from overly indulgent or restrictive parenting; learning theorists attribute it to learning and rewards for inappropriate behavior; cognitive theorist believe that the disorder is

due to the perception of others as hostile, which elicits defensive behaviors; and the physiological explanations revolve around low levels of serotonin that reduce inhibitions and perhaps high levels of testosterone that enhance aggression.

■ Depending on the cause, effective treatment may involve punishment, teaching and rewarding more appropriate responses, and the use of antidepressant drugs that increase levels of serotonin.

TOPIC II: DEVELOPMENTAL DISORDERS

■ The autistic disorder involves (a) impairments in social interactions, (b) impairments in communication, and (c) unusual and stereotyped behaviors, such as head banging, finger movements, or gazing at objects. The symptoms appear shortly after birth and are more common in males than females.

■ The autistic disorder is different from schizophrenia but is related to Asperger's disorder; the latter is different only in that it does not involve impairments in communication.

■ It was once thought that autism was caused by cold and detached parents, but that explanation has been abandoned. Interest in the idea that the symptoms are learned has waned because treatment based on this approach was not very effective. Numerous physiological explanations have been offered, but no one explanation has been consistently supported. It is clear that the disorder is linked to genetic factors and problems with pregnancy and birth. At present, the autistic disorder is unexplained, and it may be due to a combination of factors.

■ Conditioning and aversive procedures may be useful for controlling some symptoms, but at the present time there is no generally effective treatment for the autistic disorder.

■ Learning, communication, and motor skills disorders involve delays or problems with reading, mathematics, spoken language, written language, speech, stuttering, or coordination. Questions have been raised over whether these are psychiatric disorders or educational problems.

TOPIC III: OTHER DISORDERS

■ Elimination disorders include enuresis, which is inappropriate urination after the age of 5, and encopresis, which is inappropriate bowel movements after the age of 4.

■ Explanations for enuresis include stress that disrupts previously learned responses, the failure to learn bladder control, and a maturational lag in the neurological system that governs bladder control. Evidence that such a lag stems from genetic factors comes from the high concordance rate for enuresis in relatives.

■ The bell-and-pad procedure, in which a bell is rung when a child urinates in bed, is very effective for treating enuresis.

■ Tic disorders involve involuntary muscle contractions that result in jerking or twitching movements.

■ Tourette's disorder involves muscle tics but also vocal tics that result in grunts, yelps, or the involuntary blurting out of words that are sometimes inappropriate and embarrassing.

■ Tic disorders appear to be due to high levels of dopamine, which is the neurotransmitter in areas of the brain that are responsible for motor activity. In some cases, tic disorders and Tourette's disorder can be treated with neuroleptic drugs that block dopamine receptors.

KEY TERMS, CONCEPTS, AND NAMES

In reviewing and testing yourself on what you have learned from this chapter, you should be able to identify and discuss each of the following.

anoxia
Asperger's disorder
attention-deficit/hyperactivity disorder
autistic disorder
aversive procedure
bell-and-pad procedure
conduct disorder
coprolalia
developmental disorders

Dexedrine (dextroamphetamine)
disruptive behavior disorders
echolalia
encopresis
enuresis
high-functioning individuals
learning, communication, and motor
  skills disorders
oppositional defiant disorder

pronoun reversal
response stereotypy
Ritalin (methylphenidate)
self-instruction
tic disorders
tics
Tourette's disorder
vocal tics

CHAPTER SIXTEEN
EATING, SLEEP, and PSYCHOPHYSIOLOGICAL DISORDERS

OUTLINE

nn is an attractive college freshman. She is bright, slim, and athletic, and she appears normal to her friends. In fact, many of her friends envy her slimness. What nobody knows is that Ann suffers from *bulimia.* Five or six times a week, Ann goes on uncontrollable eating binges during which she stuffs herself with tremendous amounts of food in a short period of time. She does this by going to three or four different drive-through fast-food restaurants. To relieve the abdominal pain caused by the binge and to avoid gaining weight, Ann forces herself to vomit all that she ate during the binge. This behavior pattern is upsetting to Ann, and she is often depressed, but somehow she cannot stop it. Because the vomiting brings gastric acid into her mouth, she is developing sore spots in her throat, and the enamel on her teeth is beginning to deteriorate.

■ ■ ■

osé has a great deal of difficulty getting to sleep at night, and even when he does get to sleep, he does not sleep soundly and often wakes up. As a result, José is constantly tired and drags through the day. José's problem is known as *primary insomnia,* and it stems from the fact that too much stimulation is getting to the upper levels of his brain. To overcome the problem, he is receiving relaxation training and taking a drug called a hypnotic. His friend Katia has a very different problem; she has uncontrollable attacks in which she suddenly falls sound asleep. Sometimes when that occurs, she collapses because all of her muscles go limp. She suffers from *narcolepsy,* which is due to sudden decreases in the stimulation of the upper areas of the brain. Katia takes a stimulant to overcome the problem.

■ ■ ■

ill was an enthusiastic, aggressive, effective midlevel executive who was rapidly climbing the corporate ladder at a computer company. Bill always set high goals for himself, and while others complained about pressure, he sought it out. Because of the demands he placed on himself, Bill was always "on the run." He became impatient in meetings when others talked slowly or took time to state the obvious. When that happened, he would jump in and finish their sentences for them so they could "get on with it." Even while driving, he conducted business over his car phone. Bill was making progress, but it was brought to an immediate halt when, at the age of 43, he had a serious heart attack. The combined effects of stress and a poor diet had resulted in an almost total blockage of the arteries that provide blood for the muscles of the heart. Bill survived the attack, and now, with his usual enthusiasm and commitment, he is involved in a rehabilitation program. He has changed his diet, is on a rigorous program of aerobic exercise, and tries to "stop to smell the flowers" now and then.

■ ■ ■

elen has been under a lot of stress during the past six months. Her mother was seriously ill and then died three months ago; just weeks after that, she and her husband moved from Chicago to Los Angeles; and now she is struggling with the problems of establishing herself in her new job as well as looking after their 3-year-old son. Lately she has been sick a lot: colds, sore throats, the flu. The prolonged stress may well have reduced the functioning of her immune system, making her less able to fight off infections.

◼ ◼ ◼

Chris has been having severe pains in his stomach, and the other day, he coughed up some blood. He knew before he went to his physician what the problem was: ulcers. His father had them, so he knew the symptoms. His physician prescribed some medication that reduced the production of stomach acid but also warned him that the medication was just a stopgap measure; he would have to reduce the stress in his life.

◼ ◼ ◼

In this chapter I will discuss a variety of physical disorders that are caused at least in part by psychological factors. These disorders include problems with weight, problems with sleep, heart attacks, high blood pressure, strokes, headaches, joint pains, and cancer.

At the outset I should distinguish between the disorders to be discussed here and the **somatoform disorders** that were discussed in Chapter 7. In somatoform disorders, *psychological factors cause symptoms of physical disorders, but there is no actual physical disorder.* For example, an individual with a conversion disorder may have a paralyzed arm, but there is no actual damage to the nerves, muscles, or bones of the arm. In contrast, in the disorders discussed in this chapter, *psychological factors cause real physical disorders.* For example, prolonged psychological stress can cause the production of excess acid in the stomach, and the acid in turn causes ulcers.

The fact that psychological factors such as stress can influence physiological functioning provides an interesting balance for the findings reviewed earlier that physiological factors such as neurotransmitters can influence psychological functioning. Clearly, the more we learn, the more we realize that there is a considerable degree of overlap and interaction between the psychological and physiological causes of psychological and physiological disorders.

This chapter is divided into three parts. In the first I will deal with *eating disorders* such as anorexia and bulimia; the second is focused on *sleep disorders,* which range from insomnia to narcolepsy; and the third includes a variety of *psychophysiological disorders,* including heart attacks, strokes, headaches, ulcers, and arthritis.

TOPIC 1
EATING DISORDERS

ANOREXIA AND BULIMIA

Anorexia nervosa and *bulimia nervosa* are eating disorders that together may afflict as many as 4% of young women and in some cases can be serious enough to cause death. Because these disorders are so widespread and serious, they deserve careful consideration.

Symptoms

Anorexia Nervosa. The major symptom of **anorexia nervosa** (an-uh-REK-sē-uh nur-VŌ-suh) is an individual's *refusal to maintain body weight* above the minimal normal weight for the individual's age and height (American Psychiatric Association, 1994). The maintenance of a weight *15% below the expected minimum* is the cutoff point for a diagnosis of anorexia. (*Anorexia* comes from the Greek for "lack of appetite.")

Other symptoms include an intense *fear of gaining weight* or becoming fat and a *distortion of body image.* Regardless of how thin and emaciated the individuals become, they are still afraid of becoming fat, they "feel fat," and therefore they continue their attempts to lose weight. Because of their distorted self-perception, individuals with anorexia do not see themselves as too thin or as suffering from a serious disorder, and hence they do not seek help. One student of mine had become

Regardless of how emaciated individuals with anorexia may be, they still feel fat and may continue to lose weight.

The course of anorexia is quite variable. Some individuals experience a single episode followed by complete recovery with no residual problems. Others have a number of serious episodes that are interspersed with relatively normal periods in which they are simply careful about what they eat. Unfortunately, in some individuals anorexia is a chronic condition that ultimately leads to death.

It is interesting to note that individuals with anorexia do not lose their interest in food and in fact will sometimes go to great lengths to prepare elaborate meals for others but will not eat the meals themselves. One student of mine who suffered from anorexia frequently brought me rich and wonderful chocolate desserts but never ate any of them herself. She made the desserts for me after jogging a few miles, going to her aerobics class, and limiting her food intake for the day to a bowl of cereal and a few carrots.

Bulimia Nervosa. The first major symptom of **bulimia nervosa** (byoo-LIM-mē-uh nur-VŌ-suh) is *eating binges*. During an eating binge, the individual consumes very large amounts of food in a short period of time. Binges are usually carefully planned and carried out in secret. The eating binge is often accompanied by a feeling of lack of control over the eating behavior. The binge ends when the individual cannot eat any more and develops abdominal pains. (*Bulimia* comes from a Greek word meaning "great hunger.")

The second major symptom is inappropriate *compensatory behavior designed to prevent weight gain*. That is, to relieve the pain that comes from eating too much and to avoid gaining weight, the individuals use self-

seriously anorexic, weighed only 85 lb, thought she looked great, and could not understand why her boyfriend from back home was repelled by her appearance when he came for a visit.

The last major symptom of anorexia in females is the *absence of at least three consecutive menstrual cycles*. This is known as **amenorrhea** (uh-MEN-uh-RĒ-uh). In some cases, amenorrhea sets in before there is significant weight loss, but the reason for that is not yet clear.

Secondary symptoms that stem from inappropriate diets and weight loss include slow heart rate (bradycardia), low blood pressure (hypotension), low body temperature (hypothermia), and other problems associated with disturbances in metabolism. One woman with anorexia had a heart rate of only 28 beats per minute and had blood pressure so low it could not be measured (Brotman & Stern, 1983). Finally, most of the individuals who suffer from anorexia also suffer from serious depressions, obsessions, and compulsions (Thiel et al., 1995; Vitousek & Manke, 1994).

After her separation from Prince Charles, Princess Diana admitted in a television interview that she had suffered from bulimia for several years. Without that admission, her disorder would probably have remained secret, despite constant media attention.

induced vomiting, laxatives, enemas, fasting, or excessive exercise to get rid of the food. The use of vomiting, laxatives or enemas is often referred to as a **purge.** Because the purging is effective for helping the individual maintain a normal weight, it helps hide the disorder. In that regard, it is interesting to note that Diana, Princess of Wales, suffered from bulimia for years, yet despite constant public scrutiny, she was able to conceal it with careful purging.

The fact that individuals with bulimia often vomit to purge themselves leads to numerous secondary symptoms such as sore throats, ulcers of the mouth and throat, swollen salivary glands, and destruction of tooth enamel. Those symptoms occur because the vomit contains high levels of stomach acid, which destroys tissues and tooth enamel. Individuals with bulimia can also suffer from nutritional problems and dehydration because they are not getting any benefit from the food they consume. Finally, as is the case with anorexia, depression and obsessive-compulsive symptoms are often associated with bulimia. One woman's struggle with bulimia is presented in Case Study 16.1.

Issues

Historical Trends. Because anorexia and bulimia have attracted so much attention in recent years, it is widely thought that these are relatively new disorders, but that is not so. Cases of these eating disorders can be found in the records of the ancient Greeks, and the modern history of "fasting girls" began with publications in 1873 (Vandereycken & Lowenkopf, 1990). Even then the disorders were described as common, but they were subsumed under other diagnoses such as *sitophobia* ("fear of eating"), so they did not attract separate attention. In fact, a study of the incidence of anorexia over a 50-year period in Rochester, Minnesota, revealed a steady rate of the disorder over time with perhaps a slight increase in the 1980s (Lucas et al., 1991). That increase may simply have reflected a greater willingness to admit to the disorder because of the attention and acceptance it began receiving then. Indeed, in some cases, mothers whose daughters are being treated for eating disorders admit somewhat sheepishly that they had similar problems when they were younger but that they never admitted the problems to anyone. Interestingly, new data indicate that the rate of eating disorders may actually be decreasing from the high observed a few years ago, and it may be that the disorder is "going back into the closet" (Heatherton et al., 1995).

Gender and Age. Women are 10 times more likely than men to suffer from anorexia and bulimia, and the disorders have an earlier onset in women than men, a difference that may be due to the fact that women

mature earlier than men (Carlat & Camargo, 1991; Lucas et al., 1991).

Anorexia and bulimia are disorders primarily of late adolescence and early adulthood, with the most frequent age of onset being between 15 and 19 (Lucas et al., 1991; see Figure 16.1). Fortunately, in most cases, the disorder burns out within a few years, although the individuals may experience some lingering concerns about weight. That is, the more serious symptoms of eating disorders appear to be time-limited.

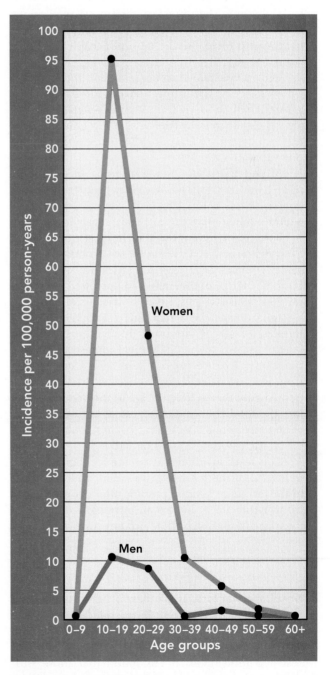

FIGURE 16.1 **Anorexia occurs most frequently in adolescence and early adulthood.**
Source: Data from Lucas et al. (1991), p. 919, tab. 2.

CASE STUDY 16.1
A Student Talks About Her Bulimia and Her Desperation

The following account was written by an honors student of mine who had suffered from anorexia while in high school and had suffered from bulimia for approximately two years before writing this.

"If I were to use one word to describe how it feels to be bulimic, I would use *desperate*. I experience many feelings while bingeing, purging, and waiting for the next cycle, but the most noticeable is desperation.

"Once I've decided to binge, I can't think of anything else. The first thing I have to do is get off by myself. I will lie to my friends and skip classes to get away. I usually tell my friends that I'm going to class or to study. I even leave for class early or late so no one will walk with me.

"After I figure out how I'm going to get off by myself, I think about money. What I eat when I binge depends on how much money I have. If I have quite a bit, I'll binge on whatever I crave regardless of cost. If I have only a little, I buy the cheapest things I can. Even if I'm broke, I will find a way to binge. At the sorority house, I will pack a big sack lunch. I've sold books for binge money, and I've borrowed from others. When all else fails, I'll even write a bad check.

"Next comes the actual binge. I usually eat at a number of places because I don't want anyone to know how much I actually eat. I almost always buy something I can carry out, and then I eat as I go from place to place. I do that because I have an irrational belief that as long as I am in the process of eating, the food is not being digested, but when I stop eating, my stomach will start working double-time to get all the calories out of the food.

"This irrational belief leaves me feeling desperate to get rid of the food I've just eaten, and that leads to the purge. As soon as possible after eating, I travel from bathroom to bathroom purging. I don't want to spend too much time in any one bathroom because I'm afraid someone might walk in. I'm also afraid of leaving a noticeable odor. I think that I know every public bathroom in town, and I know when most of them are likely to be empty.

"My bingeing will take on different tones depending on why I am doing it. Sometimes it's just habit and I can't think of an alternative. In that case, I'm fairly calm and my actions have a determined, inevitable quality. It's almost like I'm in a trance. I purposefully move from place to place, and I don't get anxious about little inconveniences.

"More often, however, a specific event or emotion triggers a binge. It can be just about anything—fear, anger, depression. Whatever the reason for bingeing, the procedure takes on a frantic quality. I need to binge, and I need to do it immediately! I still take precautions so nobody knows what I'm doing, but I'm more likely to take some risks. The binge takes precedence over everything else. I eat faster, and I'm more likely to take laxatives if I don't think I've gotten rid of enough.

"Sometimes I feel relieved afterward, especially if it was an overwhelming or upsetting emotion that triggered the binge. If I'm bingeing out of habit, I usually feel depressed and might cry afterward wondering why I'm doing this to myself. Often I go right into another binge.

"It's not only when I'm bingeing that I feel desperate. In between binges, I am desperately searching for a strategy to stop the behavior. I've spent endless hours in the library and bookstores looking for an answer. I've read many diet books and tried their diets hoping that the structure of a diet will help me stop bingeing. I've read antidiet books, books on nutrition, and books on anorexia and bulimia. Ironically, I often read these books as I pig out. For me, bingeing, purging, and the desperate struggle have become a way of life."

Sociocultural Factors. It is widely believed that eating disorders are more prevalent in the middle and upper classes, but there is no evidence for that, and in fact the opposite appears to be the case. Indeed, in a study of almost 400 individuals, it was found that those with lower incomes were more likely to report eating disorders (Pope et al., 1987). The original impression that middle- or upper-class individuals are more likely to have eating disorders was probably based on the observation that middle- or upper-class individuals were more likely to come for treatment. However, who gets treated is not a good index of who has the disorder because we know that lower-class individuals are less likely to come in for treatment even when they need it, and when they do come in, they are more likely to present their problems as physical rather than as psychological and so do not get into the psychiatric system (see Chapter 2). The higher rate of eating disorders in the lower classes is interesting because there is a strong link between eating disorders and depression, and the rate of depression is higher in the lower class (see Chapter 8).

Strategic Eating Disorders. Before discussing the causes of anorexia and bulimia, it is helpful to make a distinction between what appear to be two types of anorexia and bulimia. On the one hand, there are individuals like the student in Case Study 16.1 in whom the behavior appears to be *out of control* and *involuntary.* Just as the individual with schizophrenia cannot voluntarily stop hallucinating, so these individuals cannot control their inappropriate eating behaviors. On the other hand, there are also individuals who show many of the symptoms of anorexia or bulimia but for whom the behavior is *under voluntary control.* Many people diet excessively, numerous others abuse stimulants to curb appetite, and I know numerous women students who keep bottles of ipecac syrup hidden in their dresser drawers to use occasionally for purging when they have eaten too much and have to get into that special dress. (Ipecac is a nonprescription medication designed to induce vomiting in children who have swallowed poison.) In these cases, however, the behavior is *voluntary, controllable, and designed to achieve a specific goal.* These behaviors might be called **strategic eating disorders** to distinguish them from the other eating disorders in which the behavior is out of control. The distinction between strategic and other eating disorders might be helpful when considering causes and treatments, but it should be noted that the distinction is not made in DSM-IV.

Case Study 16.2 focuses on the eating behavior of actress Jane Fonda, who seems to have suffered from strategic anorexia and bulimia. Her experiences and behaviors are in sharp contrast to those of the young woman in Case Study 16.1, who described her behavior as uncontrolled and desperate.

Explanations

Psychodynamic Explanations. When eating disorders began attracting more attention, psychodynamic theorists offered a variety of explanations that revolved around various conflicts. For example, it was suggested that eating was a substitute for sex and that a young girl's refusal to eat represented *a symbolic denial of her emerging sexual urges* (Ross, 1977). Of course, anorexia can limit the development of secondary sexual characteristics, can reduce sexual drives, and can lead to amenorrhea. It was also suggested that women with anorexia were using their refusal to eat as a means of

As a young woman, Jane Fonda suffered from what might be called strategic bulimia.

passively rebelling against their mothers or as a means of controlling the one element in their lives over which they had control, their bodies (Bruch, 1982). Although these explanations were once very popular, they are not supported by the research, did not lead to effective treatments, and are now generally dismissed.

Other psychodynamic theorists suggested that anorexia and bulimia were somehow related to *childhood sexual abuse.* In support of that hypothesis, many therapists reported that their clients with eating disorders reported memories of childhood sexual abuse. However, we still have no evidence that reports of childhood sexual abuse are higher in women with eating disorders than they are in the general population or other patient populations, leaving that explanation without controlled support (Kinzl et al., 1994; Pope & Hudson, 1992; Pope et al., 1994; Rorty et al., 1994; Welch & Fairburn, 1994).

A more general psychodynamic explanation is that *stress leads to eating* and that extreme stress could lead to the binge eating seen in bulimia (Greeno & Wing, 1994). This hypothesis was originally based on research with rats in which it was found that when rats were stressed with a tail pinch or an electric shock, they showed dramatic increases in eating. To test the effects

CASE STUDY 16.2
Jane Fonda: A Case of Strategic Anorexia and Bulimia

In the introduction to her first book on exercise, Jane Fonda (1981) talked about how for many years she binged, purged, and misused medication to control her weight. The bingeing apparently began at the age of 14, when she went away to boarding school. She and her classmates developed "a preoccupation with food," and she recalls bingeing on coffee ice cream by the gallon, pound cake by the pound, and brownies by the bagful. For the young Fonda, "eating binges were *de rigueur*" [required by fashion, etiquette, or custom]. The routine of eating binges became firmly established and was broken only by an occasional crash diet to slim down for a dance or a weekend away from school. In other words, bingeing was an activity, not a compulsion, and it could be stopped when necessary, as when she needed to fit into a certain dress.

Fonda and her classmates discovered purging in a class on Roman civilization in which they learned that during large feasts the Romans would go to a room called a *vomitorium,* vomit up what they had eaten, and then return to the feast and start all over again. This was a great discovery for Fonda and her friends because, as she put it, they thought, "Ah-ha, here's a way to *not* have our cake and eat it too!" (p. 14).

When she went to college, Fonda discovered another way to avoid gaining weight: taking stimulants to curb appetite. She used Dexedrine and reports becoming addicted to the drug. She then experienced "a terrible sense of fatigue and depression" when she stopped taking it. (That effect was probably a poststimulant depression; see Chapter 10.)

After college, Fonda worked as a model to support her acting lessons. She was thin but still concerned about gaining weight. She wanted to lose more weight because at the time, the extremely thin

and angular look was the "ideal." The answer was more pills. She writes, "In boarding school I had discovered vomiting, in college Dexedrine, and as a model I learned about diuretics" (p. 15). Diuretics have the effect of reducing fluids in the body and thereby reducing weight. With diuretics, inches seemed to evaporate overnight, and Fonda took them for the next 20 years. Because her body adjusted to them (a process called tolerance; see Chapter 17), she had to keep increasing the dosage. The prescribed level was one pill every 3 days, but soon she was taking two or three pills a day. It wasn't until many years later that she learned that prolonged use of high levels of diuretics can be very dangerous unless the diuretics are accompanied by dietary supplements to replace the vitamins and minerals flushed out of the body with the fluids.

Clearly, for a long time, Fonda engaged in serious and potentially dangerous eating, dieting, and vomiting patterns that might qualify as an eating disorder. These patterns started in her early teens, lasted well into adulthood, and involved bingeing, purging, and the inappropriate use of medication to reduce appetite and weight. As Fonda describes it, however, her behavior seems to have been *goal-directed* and *voluntary*. She wanted to achieve a culturally valued look (lean and lovely) that was essential for social acceptance and her profession. She used inappropriate eating behaviors to achieve her goal until she realized the dangers and found alternatives. Her actions had been "strategic," that is, effective for gaining acceptance and a professional goal, and over a long period of time had become part of a style of life. Although the pattern of her behavior was serious, it was quite different from the irrational and uncontrolled starvation, bingeing, and purging seen in many individuals with eating disorders.

in humans, stress was induced with electric shocks, frightening films, or difficult tests, and then the amount of food the individuals ate was measured. The results indicated that women were more likely to eat during stress than men, and the women who were most likely to eat during stress were those who are trying to control their weight through procedures like dieting (e.g., Cools et al., 1992; Heatherton et al., 1991; Schotte, Cools, & McNally, 1990). It appears, then, that

stress might contribute to bulimia in those individuals who are already struggling with problems of weight, but the process and the factors that predispose some individuals to eat when stressed are not yet clear.

Learning Explanations. Learning theorists suggest that anorexia may be brought on by *rewards* from the environment. Specifically, because "slim is in," individuals who are losing weight may get rewarded for being "lean and lovely," and that reinforces inappropriate diet behavior. In women's dorms and sorority houses, it is not unusual for there to be weight-loss programs and even contests between groups, with the women losing the most weight getting attention, praise, and even prizes. The anorexic student who used to bring me desserts was particularly successful in this regard and was envied and consistently rewarded by her peers. Unfortunately, they did not realize that they were rewarding her for the symptoms of a potentially fatal disorder.

It is also possible that some cases of anorexia are due to a *classically conditioned phobia for fatness or eating* (Crisp, 1967). The thought of gaining weight may be anxiety-provoking, and because eating leads to weight gain, anxiety may become associated with eating. The individual then reduces that anxiety by avoiding eating. One woman told me that when she went through a cafeteria line, she would feel fine while in the salad section (nonfattening food) but would become increasingly anxious as she came closer and closer to the main course and dessert sections. She would therefore rush by those sections very quickly; her anxiety would subside when she got to the beverages, where she would take only water. The woman had developed a phobia for fattening foods, and she reduced her classically conditioned anxiety by avoiding them.

Learning theorists also suggest that the binge eating seen in bulimia is a brief but intensely pleasurable experience and that the bingeing is used to distract the individuals and help them briefly *avoid anxiety* (Heatherton & Baumeister, 1991). Many students "pig out" on foods like ice cream or french fries when under stress, and they find it pleasurable (rewarding). In one group of women with bulimia, tension was the most frequently mentioned factor that preceded a binge, and almost 70% of the subjects reported relief from the ten-sion as a consequence of the binge (Abraham & Beumont, 1982).

Finally, learning theorists also suggest that anorexia may stem from attempts to *imitate* the ultraslim women identified as beautiful in Western culture. The Duchess of Windsor was said to have commented that one "can never be too rich or too thin," and the women in centerfold pictures and Miss America pageant winners have become progressively thinner over the decades (Garner et al., 1980). Furthermore, we are also constantly reminded of the importance of slimness by the numerous advertisements and articles pertaining to weight loss and dieting that appear in national magazines. Consistent with this emphasis on slimness, one study indicated that even though only 4% of girls between 12 and 18 years of age were medically overweight, 40% of them considered themselves overweight (Davies & Furham, 1986).

In one study of the possible link between media exposure to thinness and eating disorders, college women completed a questionnaire in which they indicated how many magazines related to health, fitness, beauty, and fashion they had looked at during the preceding month, and they also reported on their symptoms of eating disorders (Stice et al., 1994). The results indicated that more media exposure was associated with more symptoms of eating disorders. Of course, those findings could be interpreted either as indicating that media exposure led to eating disorders or that eating disorders and the related concerns about health and beauty led to more media exposure.

Cognitive Explanations. Cognitive theorists hypothesize that individuals with anorexia have *incorrect beliefs* about their "weight problem" and that they exaggerate the consequences of gaining weight. The individual starts out thinking, "I'm a little overweight," is

The idealization of slim female beauty promoted by advertisers sets a standard that many women cannot achieve without extreme measures.

concerned that the weight might become a problem, and so embarks on a reasonable diet. However, as time goes by, the individual begins exaggerating the seriousness of the "weight problem," focusing on any information suggesting that there is a problem and ignoring information to the contrary. This selective attention leads to increasingly erroneous beliefs, severe dieting, and ultimately anorexia.

In one investigation, women who suffered from bulimia, women who dieted frequently, and women who neither suffered from bulimia nor dieted (controls) recorded what they were thinking about every 30 minutes for 2 days (Zotter & Crowther, 1991). The results indicated that the women with bulimia and the women who were dieting thought more about eating and weight than the control women, and more important, the women with bulimia had *more distorted* thoughts about eating and weight than the dieting or control women; for example, they had more incorrect beliefs about how overweight they were. These findings demonstrate a link between incorrect beliefs and eating disorders, but they do not necessarily indicate that the incorrect beliefs *caused* the eating disorders. That is, it is possible that the eating disorders caused the incorrect beliefs about eating and weight just as increases in depression have been shown to increase incorrect beliefs about one's abilities and worth (see Chapters 9 and 10).

Physiological Explanations. The physiological explanations for anorexia and bulimia revolve around a suspected malfunction of the **hypothalamus,** which is the area of the brain that is responsible for appetite. As mentioned in earlier chapters, it appears that low levels of **serotonin** and **norepinephrine** cause problems with the functioning of the hypothalamus, and that can disrupt eating patterns. This explanation has its origins in early experiments with rats and monkeys in which it was found that if lesions were made in the lateral (side) portions of the hypothalamus, the animals greatly reduced or ceased eating (Anand & Brobeck, 1951a, 1951b; Anand et al., 1955). It was also found that if the animals could be kept alive by forced feeding, many of them eventually recovered and began eating normally again, a pattern like that seen in humans with anorexia (Teitelbaum & Steller, 1954). In contrast, lesions made in the ventromedial (front center) portion of the hypothalamus resulted in excessive eating like that seen in bulimia (Duggan & Booth, 1986). The parallel between animal and human behavior is provocative, but it does not necessarily prove that anorexia in humans is due to problems in the hypothalamus.

However, convincing evidence for the roles of serotonin and norepinephrine in humans came from studies in which the investigators measured the levels of the neurotransmitters in individuals who were or were not

suffering from eating disorders. For example, in one study the investigators measured the levels of neurotransmitters in patients who had a high frequency of binges (mean of 23 binges per week), patients who had a low frequency of binges (mean of 10 binges per week), and individuals who did not have eating disorders. Levels were measured at the time the patients were admitted for treatment and again 4 weeks later after eating patterns were stabilized (Jimerson et al., 1992). The results indicated that high-frequency bingers had lower levels of serotonin than low-frequency bingers both at the time of admission and later when eating patterns were stabilized. These results are presented in Figure 16.2.

Other interesting evidence concerning the role of serotonin comes from a study in which women who were and were not suffering from bulimia were put on a diet that was low in **tryptophan,** and then changes in their eating were determined (Weltzin et al., 1995). Tryptophan is relevant here because once in the body, it is converted into serotonin, so a diet that is low in tryptophan would lead to low levels of serotonin (see Chapter 9). The results indicated that among the women with bulimia, a low-tryptophan diet led to an increase in food intake, that is, to an exacerbation of the symptoms of their eating disorder. These findings provide more evidence for the role of serotonin, and they also indicate how the dietary problems that are associated with eating disorders can in turn contribute to the disorders. That is, avoiding or purging foods

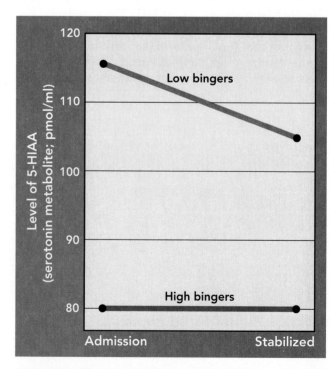

FIGURE 16.2 High-frequency bingers had lower levels of serotonin than low-frequency bingers.
Source: Adapted from Jimerson et al. (1992), p. 134, fig. 1.

such as dairy products that contain tryptophan would further lower serotonin levels and make the disorder even worse.

If low levels of serotonin and norepinephrine cause eating disorders, it would be expected that correcting those levels with drugs would correct the eating disorders. In fact, as you will learn later when I discuss treatment, drugs that increase the levels of serotonin and norepinephrine are indeed effective for treating eating disorders. Furthermore, it is noteworthy that anti-obesity drugs reduce appetite by decreasing serotonin activity. In other words, drugs that increase serotonin activity increase eating behavior, and drugs that decrease serotonin activity decrease eating behavior. Those findings clearly establish a causal link between serotonin and eating disorders.

Two other points should be made concerning the link between serotonin and eating disorders. First, it is important to note that the low levels of serotonin can also explain the depressions and obsessive-compulsive symptoms that often accompany eating disorders (Thiel et al., 1995; Vitousek & Manke, 1994). Specifically, you will recall that many depressions and obsessive-compulsive disorders are due to low levels of serotonin (see Chapters 5 and 9). The fact that serotonin levels can account for the eating disorders and the other disorders that co-occur with them adds considerable credibility to the serotonin explanation. Second, because low levels of serotonin are linked to impulsivity and decreases in inhibition (see Chapter 9), they can explain the impulsive eating and purging in bulimia that would ordinarily be inhibited.

Low levels of serotonin and norepinephrine provide a good explanation for eating disorders, but they provide only half of the explanation because we must also know what causes the low levels of those neurotransmitters. There are two possibilities, the first of which is *genetic factors*. Supporting this possibility are the results of investigations of anorexia in monozygotic and dizygotic twins. In two studies, the concordance rate for the disorder was high in MZ twin pairs (75% and 45%, respectively), whereas the concordance rate in DZ twin pairs was zero (Nowlin, 1983; Schepank, 1981). In a more recent study, it was found that if one twin had an eating disorder, the other twin was 2.6 times more likely to have a disorder than if the first twin did not have an eating disorder (Walters & Kendler, 1995). This provides strong evidence that some cases of eating disorders have a genetic basis.

The second possibility is that *prolonged stress* lowers the levels of the neurotransmitters. The results of numerous experiments have indicated that stress leads to reduced levels of serotonin and norepinephrine (see Chapter 9), so prolonged psychological stress could trigger the physiological process that leads to the eating disorder.

At present, we have some good explanations for eating disorders, but no one explanation accounts for all cases. As with other disorders we have discussed, it is probable that more than one explanation is correct and that different types of eating disorders have different causes. For example, strategic eating disorders may be accounted for by learning or incorrect beliefs, whereas involuntary eating disorders may be due to physiological factors. Different causes would require different approaches to treatment, which I will consider next.

Treatments

Alarm over the prevalence and seriousness of anorexia and bulimia led to the development of *eating disorder clinics.* These are inpatient facilities that are usually part of a general hospital. Clinics may differ in their therapeutic orientation (e.g., psychodynamic, learning, eclectic), but most place a heavy reliance on external control of eating behavior. Diets are carefully prepared, food intake is closely monitored, and opportunities for purging are eliminated by controlling access to bathrooms and other areas where an individual might vomit. Such clinics are usually rather expensive ($800/day), and clients usually stay for 60 or 90 days (the amount of time covered by health insurance). Of course, not all individuals with anorexia and bulimia require or can afford this form of treatment, so many are treated in more typical outpatient clinics.

Psychodynamic Approaches. Psychodynamic treatments usually involve attempts to relieve depression and improve self-concept because those factors are believed to be the causes of anorexia and bulimia. There have been numerous claims for the effectiveness of psychodynamic treatment, but in most cases, the investigations did not have adequate control conditions. The absence of control conditions is particularly important because eating disorders tend to burn out in time even if left untreated, and thus without a no-treatment condition, the improvements that are due to time alone may be erroneously attributed to the therapy. Similarly, when different treatments are compared and yield similar results, it may not be that they are all working but that a placebo effect is responsible for the improvements (Fairburn et al., 1993; Jones et al., 1993). Finally, however, insofar as the disorders may be brought on by stress, which lowers the levels of neurotransmitters, psychotherapy may be effective because it can reduce stress (see Chapter 6), but so far the evidence for that effectiveness is limited at best.

Learning Approaches. Therapists have also used the principles of learning and have provided rewards such as visitors, television, and tokens for appropriate eating and weight gains (Azerrad & Stafford, 1969; Geller et al., 1978; Halmi et al., 1975; Mizes & Lohr, 1983). Unfortunately, the absence of controlled research makes it impossible to conclude that these techniques are effective.

Cognitive Approaches. A substantial amount of controlled research has been conducted to assess the effects of cognitive therapy on eating disorders, and a variety of positive results have been reported (see Wilson & Fairburn, 1993). For example, in one experiment, 40 women who were suffering from bulimia were randomly assigned to either an immediate cognitive-behavioral treatment condition or to a delayed cognitive-behavioral treatment condition (Telch et al., 1990). Women in the immediate treatment condition participated in one 90-minute group therapy session per week for a 10-week period and then were followed up after another 10-week period. In contrast, women in the delayed treatment condition did not receive any treatment for the first 10-week period but then participated in the treatment program during the next 10-week period. In the treatment sessions, the women were taught first how to identify the patterns of eating, thinking, and mood that triggered binge-eating episodes. Then they were taught how to gradually develop alternative patterns that would lead to healthy, binge-free eating. Self-reports of binge eating were collected at the beginning of the project, after the first 10-week period (treatment or delay), and after the second 10-week period (treatment or follow-up). The results indicated that the women who were treated in the first 10-week period showed reductions in binges relative to the women whose treatment was delayed. Those results are presented in Figure 16.3. It was also found that the women who were treated in the second 10-week period showed reductions in binges like those shown earlier by the other women. Other research has indicated that about two-thirds of the individuals who benefit from cognitive therapy maintain their improvements for at least 6 months (Thackwray et al., 1993). Clearly, for some individuals, cognitive therapy seems to be an effective treatment.

Physiological Approaches. The physiological approaches are founded on the notion that the disorders stem from low levels of serotonin or norepinephrine, and therefore treatment involves the use of antidepressant drugs that increase the levels of those neurotransmitters (see Chapter 10 for a discussion of those drugs).

Substantial evidence has accumulated indicating that antidepressant drugs are effective for treating many cases of anorexia and bulimia (Fairburn et al., 1992; Fluoxetine Bulimia Nervosa Collaborative Study Group, 1992; Hughes et al., 1986; Marcus et al., 1990;

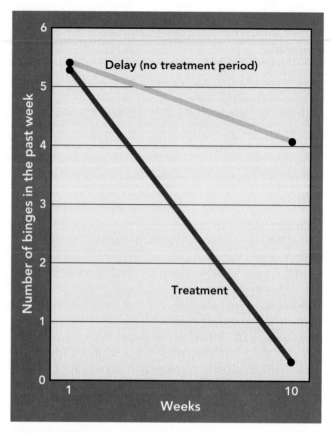

FIGURE 16.3 Cognitive-behavioral therapy was effective for reducing binge eating.
Source: Data from Telch et al. (1990), p. 632, tab. 1.

Mitchell & Groat, 1984; Pope & Hudson, 1982, 1984; Pope et al., 1983, 1985; Walsh et al., 1982; Walsh et al., 1984; Walsh et al., 1991). For example, in one experiment, almost 400 patients with bulimia were either put on a relatively low level of Prozac (20 mg/day), a relatively high level of Prozac (60 mg/day), or a placebo (Fluoxetine Group, 1992). Prozac was used because it blocks the reuptake of serotonin, thereby increasing the level of serotonin at the synapse. When reductions in vomiting were assessed, the high dose of Prozac was most effective, followed by the low dose and then the placebo. Those results are presented in Figure 16.4. Similar results were found when reductions in binge eating were considered.

In another experiment, patients suffering from bulimia were given either an antidepressant (Norpramin/desipramine) or a placebo for 6 weeks (Hughes et al., 1986). The patients taking the drug experienced a 91% decrease in binge eating and a 30% decrease in depression. In contrast, the patients taking the placebo showed only a 19% decrease in binge eating and only a 5% decrease in depression. Later, when the patients who originally took the placebo were given

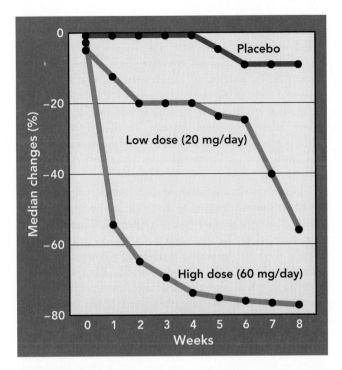

FIGURE 16.4 Prozac was effective for reducing vomiting in women with bulimia.
Source: Adapted from Fluoxetine Bulimia Nervosa Collaborative Study Group (1992), p. 142, fig. 1.

the drug, they showed an 84% decrease in binge eating, thus offering additional support for the effects of the drug.

Other evidence concerning the effects of drugs comes from analyses of the levels of the drug found in the patients' blood. In 10 patients, the drug level in the blood was below the level that is thought to be necessary to be effective. Four of those patients had recovered, but the other six still had symptoms. When the dosage level was increased for the six patients who still had symptoms, four of them recovered completely, thus suggesting that when the drug did not work, in most cases it was probably due to an insufficient dose.

The research on drugs consistently indicates that they are fast-acting and effective for treating eating disorders, but note that no drug was effective for treating all patients. Therefore, it may be that there are subgroups of patients who are responsive to different types of drugs (just as different types of depressive patients respond to different types of drugs) or that eating disorders stem from different causes, only one of which is physiological. It is also noteworthy that the drugs appear to be more effective for treating bulimia than anorexia, but it may simply be that the cessation of bingeing and purging can occur faster than eating can be returned to normal.

In summary, cognitive therapy and drugs can be used effectively to treat eating disorders, and thus the outlook for individuals with those disorders is much more positive than it was a few years ago.

OTHER EATING DISORDERS

Two other eating disorders that deserve mention are relatively rare and usually limited to infants or very young children. Although the symptom patterns have been described, little is known about the etiology of these disorders.

Pica

The major symptom of **pica** (PĪ-kuh) is the persistent eating of nonnutritive substances such as paint, plaster, hair, cloth, sand, bugs, leaves, pebbles, and animal droppings. For reasons that are not understood, the child prefers to eat nonnutritive substances over food. This symptom pattern can result in serious weight loss, malnutrition, poisoning, and intestinal problems.

Rumination Disorder

The word *rumination* comes from a Latin word meaning "to chew the cud," and the major symptom of the **rumination disorder** is the repeated regurgitation of food. The regurgitation does not involve typical vomiting activity (retching, nausea, disgust). Instead, the young child brings partially digested food up into the mouth and either spits it out or rechews it and reswallows it much as a cow chews its cud. The activity seems to result in considerable pleasure and satisfaction. The disorder can be serious because if the food is continually spit out, the child will suffer from malnutrition and may die. Fortunately, spontaneous remissions are thought to be common (see Franco et al., 1993; Fullerton et al., 1992).

TOPIC II
SLEEP DISORDERS

Sleep is crucial for our ability to perform effectively; for example, too little sleep leaves us tired and can impair our performance, and sleeping too much can interfere with our performance. In this section, I will discuss sleep disorders, but to understand those disorders thoroughly, it is essential to understand sleep and dreams, so I will begin with a brief introduction to the causes of sleep and dreams.

THE NATURE OF SLEEP AND DREAMS

Circadian Rhythms

We all go through a normal daily pattern of wakefulness and sleep called the **circadian** (sur-KĀ-dē-in) **rhythm.** (*Circadian* is based on the Latin *circa*, which means "about," and *die*, which mean "day," so the word means "about a day.") There are two important things to note concerning circadian rhythms: First, *they are controlled primarily by an internal "biological clock"* rather than by external factors such as light. You can "reset" your clock with light or by going to bed early, but the clock always runs at the same speed. Second, there are *wide differences among individuals in the length of the circadian rhythm.* The average length is about 25 hours, which is why most people tend to go to bed later and later until it gets very difficult to get up on time, so they reset their clocks. However, for some individuals, the rhythms are much longer or much shorter, and that can cause the individuals to become seriously "out of synch" with other people and the day-night cycle.

Stages and Cycles of Sleep

After you fall asleep, you go through four **stages of sleep** that become progressively deeper. For example, Stage 1 sleep is the light sleep you enter just after falling asleep and from which it is easy to awaken, whereas Stage 4 sleep is the very deep sleep that occurs later and from which it is difficult to awaken. After reaching Stage 4 sleep, you reverse the process and work your way back up to Stage 1 sleep. That **cycle of sleep** is repeated three or four times each night.

REM (Rapid Eye Movement) Sleep and Dreams

During the Stage 1 sleep that occurs in the *second and later* cycles of sleep (i.e., not during the Stage 1 sleep that occurs when you are first going to sleep), your eyes begin moving from side to side very rapidly. That is called **rapid eye movement sleep,** or **REM sleep** for short. The eye movements are not important by themselves, but they are of interest because *they co-occur with dreams;* that is, they usually signal the presence of dreams. You should note that the rapid eye movements are not *due* to the dreams; that is, they do not occur because you are watching the action in the dream. Rather, rapid eye movements and dreams stem from the same underlying process, but they are separate effects. (I will discuss the underlying process shortly.)

Causes of Sleep

Sleep occurs when the *level of electrical activity in the cortex of the brain is lowered.* We measure electrical activity in the cortex by placing electrodes on the surface of the skull and then using the electrodes to detect the electrical impulses that are occurring inside the skull. This is called an **electroencephalogram,** or **EEG** (see Chapter 3). In general, sleep is associated with slower and more regular waves of electrical activity than are seen in wakefulness.

The electrical activity in the cortex originates in the **brain stem,** which is at the base of the brain where it joins the spinal cord (see Chapter 2). The activity is then carried up to the cortex via a network of nerve tracts called the **reticular activating system.** In other words, the brain stem can be thought of as an electrical generating plant and the reticular activating system as the power lines to the neighborhood. Sleep sets in (the "lights" in the cortex dim) when the reticular activating system carries less stimulation to the cortex.

Sleep occurs when the reticular activating system supplies less stimulation to the cortex, but why does that happen? Most people assume that you simply run out of energy or electrical stimulation, but that is not the case. Instead, sleep is an *active* process, a process that "kicks in" to *stop stimulation from going up the reticular activating system to the cortex,* and it is that active inhibition of stimulation that brings on sleep. Specifically, at the base of the reticular activating system, where it leaves the brain stem, there is a group of inhibitory neurons called the *raphe* (RĀ-fē] *nuclei,* and when those neurons fire, they block impulses from traveling up the reticular activating system to the cortex, and thus sleep begins. Exactly what causes the inhibitory neurons to fire is not completely understood, but they probably receive stimulation from the hypothalamus, which is involved in the circadian rhythms. To sum up, then, sleep occurs when stimulation that is generated in the brain stem is blocked so that it cannot travel up through the reticular activating system to the cortex of the brain.

Causes of REM and Dreams

REM. Now that you have a basic understanding of sleep, I can turn to the questions of what causes REM sleep and dreams. I have pointed out that sleep is caused by a *general decrease* in the electrical activity in the cortex, but the onset of eye movements is caused by a specific increase in electrical activity in the area of the cortex that is responsible for eye movements. That is, there is a second set of nerves, known as the *PGO* (pons, geniculate, occipital) system, that during Stage 1 sleep carries stimulation up to the part of the cortex where eye movements are controlled, and that stimulation is responsible for the REM. That stimulation explains REM, but what about dreams, and why do they co-occur with REM?

Dreams. Originally, Freud suggested that dreams occur when material that had been repressed and stored in the unconscious breaks through into consciousness. That breakthrough supposedly occurs because during sleep the ego is less vigilant. The strange nature of dreams was explained by suggesting that the content was being distorted as a means of protecting the individual from its real meaning (see Chapter 2).

Freud's explanation for dreams was widely accepted, but there is now an intriguing alternative explanation that is based on what we know about brain physiology. Before explaining this theory, I should remind you that memories and thoughts are stored in sets of neurons (called *cell assemblies*) in the brain and that the memories and thoughts can be activated by stimulating those neurons (Penfield & Perot, 1963; see Chapter 12). In view of that, it was suggested that dreams occur when electrical impulses come up from the brain stem and stimulate the areas of the cortex in which various memories and thoughts are stored, and then the brain puts those memories and thoughts together to form a dream (Hobson, 1988). For the most part, the stimulation of memories and thoughts is *random,* and that explains why the story line of most dreams is so "weird": we have to put together generally random memories and thoughts to make a story. Analogously, if I gave you 10 random pictures, you could make up a story to fit the pictures, but the story might be a little strange—and remember, with dreams, you have to do it while you are asleep. The fact that dreams often involve parts of recent or important experiences is explained by the fact that recently or frequently used thoughts and memories are more easily activated; that is, those images and thoughts are "primed."

This explanation for dreams is consistent with the notion that hallucinations are the result of the excessive and erratic firing of neurons in the brain, which stimulates images and thoughts (see Chapter 12). In view of that, dreams might simply be considered *nocturnal hallucinations.* This explanation of dreams is more consistent with what we know about brain physiology than Freud's explanation, and its acceptance is growing.

In summary, inhibitory neurons reduce the transmission of electrical activity up through the reticular activating system so the activity cannot get from the brain stem to the cortex, and the lowered level of electrical activity in the cortex results in sleep. However, during Stage 1 sleep that occurs after the first sleep cycle has ended, a second system carries stimulation up to the cortex, and that stimulation results in rapid eye movements and dreams. With this material as background, we can go on to consider sleep disorders.

PRIMARY SLEEP DISORDERS

Primary sleep disorders are due to *physiological problems associated with the process that leads to sleep.* These disorders are divided into two types, *dyssomnias* and *parasomnias.* A **dyssomnia** (DIS-SOM-nē-uh) is a disorder that involves *problems with the amount, quality, or timing of sleep.* For example, individuals with dyssomnias sleep too much or too little, do not get good sleep, or cannot control when they fall asleep. (*Dys* means "abnormal," and *somnia* means "sleep," so *dyssomnia* means "abnormality of sleep.") In contrast, a **parasomnia** (PAR-uh-SOM-nē-uh) involves *abnormal behaviors that are associated with sleep.* For example, individuals with parasomnias may have nightmares or may walk in their sleep. (*Para* is Latin for "alongside," so *parasomnia* refers to things that happen *along with sleep.*) The dyssomnias and parasomnias are summarized in Table 16.1. In the following sections I will describe the symptoms, explain the causes, and examine the treatments. for each disorder.

Dyssomnias

Primary Insomnia. The major symptoms of the **primary insomnia** *disorder are difficulty getting to sleep, difficulty staying asleep long enough,* or *difficulty getting sleep that is restful.* The problems with sleep can lead to tension, frustration, or anxiety. Those are secondary symptoms and not the cause of the sleep problem, but of course tension and anxiety can lead to additional sleep problems. Primary insomnia is a relatively widespread disorder; it may occur in as many as 30% to 40% of the population. Older individuals, especially older women, are most likely to suffer from primary insomnia.

This disorder is due to *excessive levels of internally generated neurological arousal;* in other words, the reticular activating system is carrying too much activity up from the brain stem to the cortex, therefore precluding sleep. At present, we do not understand exactly why or how the excessive arousal is generated, but we take two general approaches to reducing the arousal, physiological and psychological.

The physiological approach to reducing arousal involves the use of drugs known as **hypnotics** (hip-NOT-iks). (The word *hypnotic* comes from a Greek word that means "to put to sleep.") Most hypnotics are in a class of drugs called **benzodiazepines,** the same class of drugs that is used to treat anxiety (see Chapter 6). In

TABLE 16.1 Primary Sleep Disorders and Their Symptoms

Disorder	Symptoms
Dyssomnias (problems of quantity or timing of sleep)	
Primary insomnia	Problems getting to sleep or staying asleep
Primary hypersomnia	Excessive sleepiness, prolonged sleep, daytime sleep
Narcolepsy	Irresistible attacks of sleep, loss of muscle tone, intrusions of REM
Breathing-related sleep disorder	Sleep disruption due to apnea or hypoventilation
Circadian rhythm sleep disorder	Sleep problems due to a mismatch between internal rhythms and external demands
Parasomnias (abnormal behavioral or physiological events occurring during sleep)	
Nightmare disorder	Repeated frightening dreams that disrupt sleep
Sleep terror disorder	Awakening with a panicky scream or cry
Sleepwalking disorder	Walking during sleep

Note: Secondary sleep disorders include those due to *another mental disorder* (e.g., anxiety or depression), a *general medical condition*, or the *ingestion of substances* (e.g., drugs). Those should not be confused with the *primary* sleep disorders.
Source: Based on American Psychiatric Association (1994).

general, these drugs *increase the activity of inhibitory neurons,* and the increased activity of the inhibitory neurons serves to reduce general arousal, thus facilitating sleep. This is the same process by which these drugs reduce anxiety (see Chapter 6.) Commonly used hypnotics include Halcion (trizolam), Restoril (temazepam), and Dalamine (flurazepam). In some cases, *antidepressants* such as Elavil (amitriptyline) or *antipsychotics* such as Haldol (haloperidol) are used.

The benzodiazepines that are used as hypnotics are those that have a relatively short **half-life.** *Half-life* refers to the amount of time it takes for half of the drug to be eliminated from the body, and a short half-life is necessary so that the level of the drug will be reduced below its effective level before morning. That is, a short half-life is necessary to reduce "hangover" effects that include drowsiness, cognitive confusion, and problems with muscle coordination the next day (Neylan et al., 1994). Elderly individuals often suffer from primary insomnia and are often treated with hypnotics (Wooten, 1992), but that poses a problem because elderly individuals eliminate the drugs from their bodies more slowly than younger people, thus increasing the likelihood of hangover effects (Greenblatt et al., 1991). It should also be noted that if the drug's half-life is too short, the drug will be out of the individual's system before the night is over, and the individual will awaken early. Like so many other things, treating insomnia is a matter of timing.

Even if hangover effects are minimized by using a drug with an appropriate half-life, problems can devel-op because the individual may develop a *tolerance* for the drug and consequently require higher and higher levels to achieve the desired effect (see Chapter 17). Finally, concern has been expressed about the possible **rebound effect** when the individual stops taking the drug; that is, it is possible that the symptoms will be worse than they were before the drug was taken. To some extent, the rebound effect is simply the sudden return of the symptoms that had been controlled with the drug. However, there is some evidence that the symptoms can be worse than they were originally if the individual was on a high level of the drug and if the drug was terminated quickly (recall the discussion of drug dependence in Chapter 6).

Because of the possible side effects of drugs, in some cases psychological strategies are used to reduce arousal and aid in sleep (Murtagh & Greenwood, 1995). Those strategies include (a) *cognitive therapy,* in which the individual's beliefs about sleep are changed (e.g., "I can get along with less than 8 hours of sleep") so that tension over the lack of sleep is reduced; (b) *relaxation training,* in which the individual is taught how to relax muscles and thereby reduce tension and arousal; (c) *stimulus control,* in which the individual goes to bed only when tired and does not use the bedroom for anything other than sleeping (no reading or sex) so that the stimuli of the bedroom become paired with sleep; and (d) *paradoxical intention,* in which the individual is instructed to try to stay awake, and that "permission" actually reduces the tension that is associated with staying awake and allows the individual to fall asleep. The research indicates that compared to various placebo treatments, all of these strategies are generally effective for decreasing the length of time required to get to sleep, increasing the total amount of sleep, reducing the number of awakenings, and enhancing the quality of sleep (Morin et al., 1994; Murtagh & Greenwood, 1995).

Primary Hypersomnia. The major symptom of **primary hypersomnia** is *excessive sleepiness,* which can lead to long periods of sleep at night and the necessity of taking naps during the day. Unfortunately, the sleep and naps do not relieve the sleepiness, so the individual drags through the day and can become grouchy and ineffective. In some cases, the sleepiness and need for naps poses a danger, as when the individual is driving. It is important to note that many of us often become tired and need a good night's sleep or a nap; what distinguishes that from primary hypersomnia is that the sleep or nap refreshes us and we "snap back." That does not happen in cases of primary hypersomnia. (*Hyper* means "excessive," so *hypersomnia* literally means "excessive sleep.")

Primary hypersomnia is caused by *insufficient neurological arousal* being generated in the brain stem, a condition that can result from a wide variety of factors including lesions in the hypothalamus. In other words, the cause of primary hypersomnia is the opposite of the cause of insomnia. The problem is usually treated with *stimulants,* just as you might take caffeine to increase alertness and stay awake. Frequently used stimulants include Ritalin (methylphenidate) and various amphetamines.

Narcolepsy. Individuals who suffer from **narcolepsy** (NAR-kuh-lep-sē) have daily *irresistible attacks of sleep.* (The term comes from *narco,* meaning "sleep," and *lepsy,* meaning "seizure;" individuals with the disorder are literally "seized by sleep.")

Four characteristics of narcolepsy should be noted. First, the sleep is *irresistible;* the individual cannot simply fight the sleep off and stay awake. Second, the sleep is often associated with a sudden and complete *loss of muscle tone,* such that the individual collapses. Third, there is usually evidence of *REM sleep* at the beginning or end of the sleep period, and the individual has *vivid dreams* that are sometimes described as hallucinations. In some cases, the dreams or hallucinations are so vivid that they are confused with reality and the individuals believe the event really happened. Indeed, there is some reason to believe that reports of being visited by space aliens may stem from narcoleptic dreams (Spanos et al., 1993). And fourth, the sleep is *temporarily refreshing;* the individual wakes up feeling good, but a few hours later, he or she may have another sleep attack. The sleep attacks

can be embarrassing, and more important, they can be very dangerous because they result in falls and accidents (Richardson et al., 1990).

Like hypersomnia, narcolepsy is due to *insufficient neurological arousal,* but for reasons that are not yet understood, the arousal drops very quickly, resulting in the sleep attack. Unfortunately, we have no completely satisfactory treatment for narcolepsy, but stimulants can be effective (Mitler & Hajdukovic, 1991). In some cases, frequent naps during the day may help, probably because they forestall the need for sleep (Neylan et al., 1994).

Breathing-Related Sleep Disorder. Individuals with the **breathing-related sleep disorder** have their *sleep frequently disrupted because of problems with breathing.* For example, an individual may suffer from **apnea** (AP-nē-uh), which is a *brief cessation of breathing* (*a* means "no," and *pnea* means "breath," so *apnea* means "no breath"), and the reduction of oxygen intake wakes the individual up. That occurs frequently during the night, and so by morning the individual has not had a good night's sleep.

Sleep apneas fall into two general types, depending on their cause. The first type is **obstructive apnea,** which involves *obstruction of the airway to the lungs such that the individual is briefly deprived of oxygen.* The upper airway path at the top of the throat is flexible and can collapse, thus cutting off the air supply to the lungs. Normally, muscles hold the airway open when the individual inhales, but three factors can interfere with that process. First, in some cases, *the muscles that keep the airway open may not receive enough stimulation,* and therefore they relax and allow the airway to collapse. This is most likely to occur during REM sleep because during that time, stimulation to the muscles is generally decreased. It is also possible that insufficient stimulation of muscles can stem from the use of sedatives that cause low levels of general arousal. Second, *obesity can lead to a narrowing of the airway,* thus making it more likely that the airway will become closed. Third, the *position in which an individual sleeps* can increase the likelihood that the airway will collapse.

Behavioral treatments for obstructive apnea include the avoidance of sedatives so that the muscles will get more stimulation, weight loss that increases the size of the airway, and sleeping on the side or face down so that the airway does not fall closed (Cartwright et al., 1991). Drug treatment involves the use of antidepressants. Those drugs work because they suppress REM sleep, which is when the brain provides the least amount of stimulation to the muscles that hold the airway open. Mechanical approaches to treatment include using a device that fits in the individual's mouth and holds the tongue down or repositions the jaw so that air can pass through the lower airway when the upper airway is blocked. In other cases, a tube is placed in the individual's nose through which a current of air is passed, and the air forces the pathway to remain open (Nakazawa et al., 1992). Finally, surgery can be used to increase the size of the airway.

The second general type of sleep apnea is **central apnea,** and it stems from a problem in the brain that causes a brief interruption in breathing. That problem occurs most often in older individuals.

Circadian Rhythm Sleep Disorder. The **circadian rhythm sleep disorder** involves a *mismatch between the timing of an individual's natural sleep-wake cycle and the demands made on the individual by the circumstances in which he or she lives.* For example, the individual's circadian rhythm may follow a 28-hour sleep-wakefulness cycle, while the rest of the world is running on a 24-hour cycle. In that case, the individual would be "out of synch" with others, and that could lead to conflict and stress. You may have seen minor forms of this in individuals who are "morning people" who are up and going long before anyone else (they have short cycles) or "night people" who are still going long after everyone else has gone to bed (they have long cycles).

Circadian rhythms are controlled by the "biological clock," and because that clock can be reset by bright light, the circadian rhythm sleep disorder can be treated by exposing the individual to a bright light (Rosen-

thal et al., 1990). Specifically, light early in the morning will start a new phase when the problem is that the phase is too long, and light in the evening will prolong an existing phase when the problem is that the phase is too short (Neylan et al., 1994).

This concludes the discussion of dyssomnias. Next I will discuss the parasomnias, which involve abnormal events that occur with sleep.

Parasomnias

Nightmare Disorder. Individuals who suffer from the **nightmare disorder** repeatedly experience *frightening dreams (nightmares) that awaken them* (American Psychiatric Association, 1994; Bearden, 1994). After awakening, the individuals can remember the nightmare, but they are immediately oriented and alert, and they realize that the nightmare was "only a dream." However, the individuals may find the experience frightening, and they have a lingering sense of fear or anxiety that may cause problems in getting back to sleep. Of course, the disruptions in sleep and problems getting back to sleep can lead to sleepiness and problems with normal functioning.

Nightmares occur frequently in children, especially after some frightening event, but the children should not be diagnosed as having the nightmare disorder unless the nightmares are causing considerable distress and impairment. Fortunately, nightmares become less

The circadian rhythm sleep disorder is an occupational hazard for many shift workers, for airline pilots and flight crews, and for others who must cope with irregular schedules or time zone changes.

frequent after childhood, and most children outgrow the disorder. The effects of nightmares can be greater in individuals who believe that dreams have spiritual or supernatural implications because for those people, the nightmares are not "just dreams"; instead, the nightmares may be interpreted as important messages from gods or others.

Sleep Terror Disorder. The major symptom of the **sleep terror disorder** is the *abrupt awakening from sleep with a panicky scream.* The panicky scream is accompanied by feelings of intense fear and a very high heart rate. While in the state of panic or terror, the individual is disoriented and cannot be comforted by others. Indeed, the individual may resist being touched or held by others, probably because the individual is confused and being self-protective. After calming down, the individual does not remember a nightmare that might have triggered the terror. In that regard, it is noteworthy that the terrors *usually occur during non-REM sleep,* when it would not be expected that the individual would be dreaming. That leads to the speculation that the terrors stem not from dreams but rather from a physiological process that is analogous to what happens in a panic attack (see Chapters 4 and 5). Unfortunately, we do not yet understand the process that leads to the terror, nor do we have an effective treatment (Taylor, 1993). On the positive side, this is a relatively rare disorder, and it is suspected to occur in fewer than 6% of children and fewer than 1% of adults.

Sleepwalking Disorder. The **sleepwalking disorder** involves *rising from bed and walking while asleep.* During the walking, the individual is deeply asleep and consequently has a blank expression and is usually unresponsive to others. However, in some cases the individual may respond to simple commands, such as an order to go back to bed. If awakened while walking, the individual will be confused initially about where he or she is and will not have any memory of the sleepwalking. It is noteworthy that sleepwalking occurs during periods of *non-REM sleep,* so it seems unlikely that the individual's walking is in response to a dream. Sleepwalking is more frequent in children (between 10% and 30% have at least one episode) than adults, in whom it is rather rare. Contrary to a widely held myth, an individual who is awakened during an episode of sleepwalking will not die.

It is interesting to note that some individuals will engage in relatively complex activities, such as eating, while asleep. In fact, there are cases of individuals who have committed murder while apparently sleepwalking (Broughton et al., 1994; Gilmore, 1991). Those cases raise difficult legal questions.

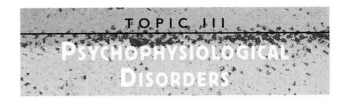

TOPIC III
PSYCHOPHYSIOLOGICAL DISORDERS

In this section we will consider how psychological stress can cause or exacerbate physical disorders such as heart attacks, high blood pressure, strokes, headaches, ulcers, muscle and joint pain, colds, and even cancer. The realization that psychological factors contribute to many physical disorders has led to the development of the new area of **health psychology,** in which psychologists work to identify, prevent, and treat the psychological factors that lead to physical illnesses.

STRESS AND PHYSIOLOGICAL RESPONSES

Stress provides the basis for the disorders that will be considered in this section, and therefore I will begin with a brief review of the concept of stress.

A *stressor* is a problem or situation that overtaxes us and leads to high levels of *psychological arousal* (anxiety) and *physiological arousal* (increased heart rate or blood pressure); *those increases in arousal are what we call stress.* The increase in physiological arousal is most important in this discussion because if physiological arousal is prolonged, it can result in a variety of physical disorders. For example, the prolonged elevation of responses such as heart rate, blood pressure, and muscle tension and the production of excessive gastric acid can lead to physical disorders such as heart attacks, hypertension, headaches, and ulcers.

To understand the physiological aspects of stress, it is essential to understand the organization of the nervous system. As indicated in Figure 16.5, the system is divided into two major parts, the **central nervous system** and the **peripheral nervous system.** The central nervous system consists of the *brain* and the *spinal cord,* and its major function is to *interpret information* and *initiate responses.* In contrast, the peripheral nervous system involves all of the nerve connections that are *not* in the brain and spinal cord, and its major function is to *carry information* to and from the central nervous system.

The peripheral nervous system is in turn broken into two divisions. The **somatic division** connects the central nervous system to the *muscles* and *skin,* and the **autonomic division** connects the central nervous system to various *glands* and *organs.* The autonomic division is of most interest in our study of stress because it controls organs such as the heart that play a crucial role in the physiological stress response.

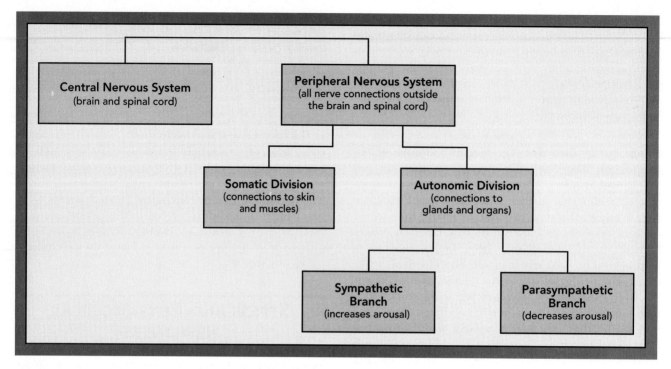

FIGURE 16.5 Organization of the nervous system.

Finally, the autonomic system is divided into the **sympathetic branch,** which is responsible for *increasing arousal,* and the **parasympathetic branch,** which is responsible for *decreasing arousal.* However, the two branches are connected, so activity in one branch eventually leads to activity in the other branch, and therefore a balance is usually achieved. For example, when confronted with a stressor, the sympathetic branch is activated so that there is an increase in arousal (e.g., higher heart rate). However, activation of the sympathetic branch also leads to the activation of the parasympathetic branch, which then decreases arousal (e.g., lowers heart rate). If the systems were not interconnected and one or the other system were allowed to run unchecked, our arousal would soar out of control or we would lapse into a comatose state.

There are three important points to recognize concerning the organization and function of the nervous system. First, *stressors cause intense and prolonged stimulation of the sympathetic branch of the autonomic system,* thereby overwhelming the calming effect of the parasympathetic branch. As long as new and stressful stimulation is coming in, the sympathetic branch will be continually activated, and you will remain in a high state of arousal.

Second, *the sympathetic branch responds as a unit,* so when it is stimulated there is *general arousal.* Unfortunately, some components of that general arousal may be irrelevant for a particular stressor. For example, when confronted by an attacker, it is helpful to have an increased heart rate that supplies more blood to the muscles so you can fight or run, but an increased heart rate is irrelevant when what you are confronting is a difficult examination. The general physiological response to stressors may have been adaptive for our ancestors, whose survival depended on running away from wild animals, but it is maladaptive today when most stressors are of the cognitive or intellectual type.

Third, *the autonomic division is not under voluntary control* (the autonomic division is *automatic*), so you cannot voluntarily control the arousal generated by the sympathetic branch. For example, when under stress, your heart will beat fast and your blood pressure will go up, but under most circumstances you cannot do much to control those responses. Overall, then, stressors lead to prolonged general arousal that is not under voluntary control.

With this understanding of stress as a background, we can now begin our examination of some of the disorders that are linked to stress. I will discuss cardiovascular diseases, headaches, ulcers, and illnesses related to the immune system because those disorders are widespread, have clinical repercussions, and reflect different processes. Although these disorders are relatively common, many people do not really understand them. For example, the exact mechanisms of heart attacks and strokes are not widely understood, and few people understand what causes the pain in a migraine headache. Therefore, I will review the nature of each disorder before discussing the role that psychological factors play in its development. This will provide you with a better understanding of the disorders and will enable you to see how physiological and psychological factors work together to cause and maintain the disorders.

CARDIOVASCULAR DISORDERS

Here I will discuss two related disorders, *coronary artery disease* and *hypertension*. These disorders are leading causes of death because they contribute to heart attacks, strokes, kidney failure, and a wide variety of other serious problems.

Coronary Artery Disease

Coronary artery disease involves the buildup of fats (*cholesterol* and *triglycerides*) inside the arteries. That buildup results in a narrowing of the passage through which the blood must flow, and the narrowing reduces blood flow. A reduction of blood flow can be serious because blood delivers oxygen and nutrients to the tissues throughout the body. If an artery becomes *occluded* (clogged and closed) because of the buildup of fats, blood flow to the tissues served by that artery is progressively reduced, and the tissues may die. The buildup of fats in blood vessels is called **atherosclerosis** (ATH-uh-rō-skluh-RŌ-sis). Figure 16.6 shows a cross section of a coronary artery that is almost completely occluded due to atherosclerosis.

Atherosclerosis often results in what is commonly called a *heart attack*. A heart attack occurs when the arteries that supply blood to the muscles of the heart become occluded; that deprives the muscles of blood, and they die. When the muscles die, the heart stops pumping or does not pump enough. The heart muscle is known as *myocardium*, and an area of tissue that has

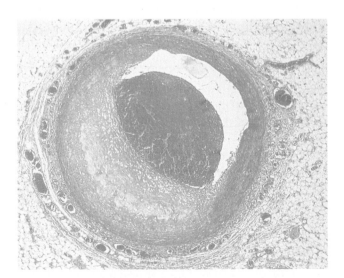

FIGURE 16.6 This coronary artery is almost completely occluded by the buildup of fats (cholesterol and triglycerides).

died is called an *infarct,* and therefore the technical term for a heart attack is a **myocardial** (Mī-ō-KAR-dē-ul) **infarction (MI).** A heart attack is most likely to occur during periods of exercise or stress because then the heart must beat faster and its muscles require more blood.

An early sign of insufficient blood to the myocardium is a sharp pain around the heart. This pain is called **angina** (AN-Jī-nuh), and it usually occurs with exercise. When individuals experience angina, they usually take a tablet containing **nitroglycerin** (Nī-trō-GLIS-uh-rin) that causes the artery to dilate temporarily and allow more blood through. Unfortunately, that is only a short-term solution for the problem.

Atherosclerosis can lead to problems with blood supply in four ways. First, it can lead to a general narrowing of arteries. Second, when blood comes into contact with a rough cholesterol deposit on the wall of an artery, the blood tends to form a clot. Such a blood clot is called a **thrombus** (THROM-bus), and a thrombus can add to the blockage of the artery. Third, a thrombus may break off and be carried downstream to a smaller artery or capillary, where it will block the blood flow entirely. When that occurs, the individual is said to have an **embolism** (EM-buh-liz-um), and the tissues farther downstream will be deprived of blood and will die. Fourth, when fat deposits build up, the arteries become thick and brittle, and that makes them more likely to rupture. Such ruptures are called **vascular accidents,** and if an artery ruptures, the tissues it serves will be deprived of blood and will die.

In this chapter, I will focus on problems associated with reduced blood flow to the heart, but it is important to recognize that all tissues need blood to live, and therefore the development of atherosclerosis has implications far beyond heart failure. For example, a general occlusion, a thrombus, an embolism, or a vascular accident in the brain can lead to a **cerebral infarction** (death of a part of the brain), or what is more commonly called a **stroke.** Cerebral infarctions are serious because a loss of tissue in the brain can result in the loss of the functions for which the tissue was responsible. That could involve a minor loss of memory, the loss of muscle control over activities like walking or talking, or the loss of some function that is essential to life itself. (Cerebral infarctions are discussed in greater detail in Chapter 19.)

With the description of coronary artery disease as background, I can now explain how psychological and physiological factors interact to result in the disease.

Influence of Type A Behavior and Hostility

Numerous factors contribute to coronary artery disease, including genetics, diet (high intake of fats, cholesterol, triglycerides, and salt), carbon monoxide from cigarette smoking, and stress. Many of these factors are related to lifestyle and thus are psychological in nature.

The psychological factor that has received most attention is the **Type A behavior pattern,** and it is on that behavior pattern that I will focus attention. The notion of the Type A behavior pattern gained prominence in the late 1950s when two cardiologists noted that their patients who had heart attacks tended to be intense, competitive, concerned with achievement, aggressive, hostile, overcommitted, and driven by a sense of time urgency (Friedman & Rosenman, 1959, 1974). They termed this the *Type A* behavior pattern and contrasted it with the *Type B* pattern, which involves a more relaxed, leisurely, mellow approach to life that is not associated with the development of coronary artery disease. Actually, this was not a new idea, because as early as 1892 it was observed that the individual who is most likely to develop coronary artery disease is "vigorous in mind and body," is "keen and ambitious," and behaves as though his or her "engine is always at full speed ahead" (Osler, 1892).

An understanding of the Type A behavior pattern can be gained by examining how it is measured. One method is known as the **structured interview** (Rosen-

Individuals with the Type A behavior pattern are overcommitted, competitive, hurried, and often hostile. It now appears that the hostility component of the pattern is associated with an increased risk of heart attack.

man, 1978). During the interview, the interviewer asks about a variety of behaviors that are related to the Type A behavior pattern—for example, "Do you often do two things at the same time?" "Do you eat and walk rapidly?" "Do you always feel in a hurry to get going and finish what you have to do?" The answers to those questions help in diagnosing an individual with Type A behavior, but of most importance is the *way* the individual responds during the interview. Compared to individuals with Type B behavior, individuals with Type A behavior speak more vigorously, more rapidly, and louder; they also answer faster and give shorter answers that are more to the point. In addition, Type A individuals are more alert, tense, and hostile and are more likely to try to hurry the interviewer and jump in and finish a sentence if the interviewer pauses (Chesney et al., 1981).

The Type A behavior pattern can also be measured with a number of paper-and-pencil questionnaires (Glass, 1977; Haynes et al., 1978). The questionnaires include items like this:

> When waiting for an elevator, I
> (a) wait calmly until it arrives.
> (b) push the button again even if it has already been pushed.

These questionnaires are widely used because they are fast and easy, but they are not as effective for making the diagnosis as the structured interview.

Type A Behavior and Cardiovascular Disease. A connection between the Type A behavior pattern and coronary artery disease has been demonstrated in a number of major investigations. In the classic study on this topic, a wide variety of risk factors such as smoking, blood pressure, cholesterol in the blood, lack of exercise, education, and personality were originally measured in more than 3,000 men between the ages of 39 and 59 (Rosenman et al., 1975; Rosenman et al., 1976). An examination of the men 8½ years later revealed that when compared to men who originally showed the Type B behavior pattern, those who originally showed the Type A behavior pattern were more than twice as likely to have developed coronary artery disease (have occluded arteries) and have a heart attack. It is important to note that the relationship between the Type A behavior pattern and coronary artery disease existed even after the effects of other risk factors such as smoking, blood pressure, and diet were controlled, thus clearly indicating that something about the Type A behavior itself led to the coronary problems. Other large-scale studies have yielded similar findings (see Matthews, 1988).

The Role of Hostility. Once investigators established the link between Type A behavior and cardiovascular disease, they began to speculate about whether one aspect of the overall Type A behavior pattern was more

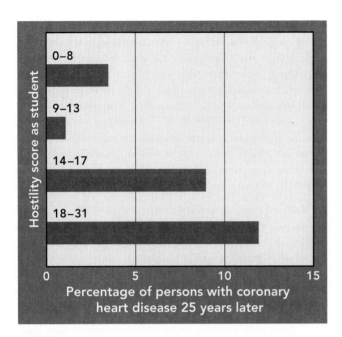

FIGURE 16.7 High hostility among students was found to be related to coronary heart disease 25 years later. *Source:* Adapted from Barefoot et al. (1983), p. 60, fig. 1.

important than other aspects. As it turns out, the overall Type A behavior pattern is made up of three components—*competitiveness, time urgency,* and *hostility*—and *the* **hostility** *component is the best predictor of coronary artery disease* (Barefoot et al., 1983; Chesney & Rosenman, 1985; Deary et al., 1994; Houston et al., 1992; MacDougal et al., 1985; Matthews et al., 1977; Meesters & Smulders, 1994; T. Q. Miller et al., 1996; Patel, 1994; Smith, 1992; Williams et al., 1980). For example, in one study of more than 400 individuals for whom Type A and hostility scores were available, it was found that among those with low hostility scores, only 48% had an occlusion, whereas among individuals with high hostility scores, 70% had an occlusion (Williams et al., 1980).

In another study, the investigators followed up 255 physicians who had taken a test of hostility 25 years earlier when they were in medical school (Barefoot et al., 1983). The results indicated that physicians with hostility scores above the median were almost five times more likely to have a heart attack than those with scores below the median. The relationship between hostility and cardiovascular problems held up even when other risk factors such as smoking were controlled. These results are presented in Figure 16.7. (Note that high hostility scores were also related to higher rates of death due to other factors such as cancer, accident, suicide, and gastrointestinal problems, thus suggesting that hostility may play a very broad role in human health.) From these and other results, we know that the Type A behavior pattern is related to coronary artery disease and that it is the hostility component that is responsible for the effect.

A classic example of the relationship between Type A behavior or hostility and coronary artery disease is the case of Mike Ditka. Ditka was known as a particularly driven and hostile player on the Chicago Bears football team, and those characteristics were also apparent when he later coached the team. He was an effective coach, but the media made much of his hostility. At age 49 he had a serious heart attack (three days after the Bears suffered a shattering 30–7 loss to the New England Patriots). In typical Type A manner, two weeks later Ditka was back on the sidelines. His assistant was coaching, but Ditka was pacing up and back (probably muttering under his breath), with his cardiologist right behind him.

Processes Linking Type A Behavior or Hostility to Disease. The next question that must be addressed is, what is it about the Type A pattern or hostility that leads to coronary artery disease? That is, why do individuals with the Type A behavior pattern develop the disease? To answer that question, we must turn first to laboratory research on how Type A individuals respond to stress, and there are two findings of particular interest. First, *Type A individuals show higher heart rates and higher blood pressure in stressful or challenging situations than Type B individuals do* (see Glass, 1977; Holmes,

Mike Ditka, former coach of the Chicago Bears, showed the Type A behavior pattern and experienced a heart attack.

1983; Houston, 1983; Lyness, 1993; Matthews, 1982). For example, in one experiment, college students who were either Type A or Type B worked on an intelligence test that was either easy or difficult while their blood pressure was monitored (Holmes et al., 1984). The results indicated that while working on the difficult test the Type A students showed higher systolic blood pressure than the Type B students. Those results are presented in Figure 16.8.

The second notable finding is that *Type A individuals set higher goals for themselves than Type B individuals,* and therefore they *force themselves into more stressful or challenging situations.* For example, in the preceding experiment, when students were asked to indicate whether they would like to work on harder or easier tasks in a second part of the experiment, Type A students chose more difficult tasks than Type B students (Holmes et al., 1984). In another experiment, in which Type A and Type B individuals ran on a treadmill, Type A individuals ran until they were closer to their actual limits of physical exhaustion before giving up than Type B individuals (Carver et al., 1976).

The combination of increased arousal during challenge and increased challenge seeking would lead the Type A individuals to be more highly aroused more frequently than Type B individuals. The next question then is, how does the arousal lead to the disease? Actually, there are four ways in which increased arousal can lead to cardiovascular disease:

1. *Arousal leads to the increased production of cholesterol.* In one study, the cholesterol levels of corporate accountants and tax accountants were assessed periodically between January and June (Friedman et al., 1958). The results indicated that the corporate accountants who

were under chronic stress showed consistently high levels of cholesterol, whereas the tax accountants showed high levels of cholesterol only around April 15 when they were under the stress of getting tax returns filed. That relationship is presented in Figure 16.9. Increased cholesterol has also been found in students during the stress of final examinations (Dreyfuss & Czaczkes, 1959). (Cholesterol production is increased during stress because cholesterol is a basic building block in the body, so its production is a defense against the deterioration that comes with stress.)

2. *Arousal leads to greater clotting of cholesterol.* During stress, catecholamines (e.g., epinephrine and norepinephrine) are secreted into the bloodstream, and they cause the particles of cholesterol that are floating through the blood to become sticky and form clots in the blood or on the artery walls (Ardlie et al., 1966). Those clots could then lead to occlusion of the arteries.

3. *Arousal leads to higher heart rates and hence to more rapid accumulation of cholesterol on the artery walls.* Stress leads to a higher heart rate, and there is evidence that the higher heart rate enhances the buildup of cholesterol on the artery walls. The link between heart rate and cholesterol buildup was neatly demonstrated in an experiment in which the heart rates of six monkeys in an experimental group were artificially lowered by destroying part of the nerve node that controls heart rate (Beere et al., 1984). Eight other monkeys in a control condition underwent the same operation, but the node was not destroyed, so the heart rates of those monkeys were not lowered. After the operation, the monkeys in both conditions were fed a high-cholesterol diet for 6 months. Examination of the coronary arteries of the monkeys at the end of the 6-month period revealed that the monkeys whose heart rates had been lowered showed occlusions of about 20%, whereas the monkeys whose heart rates had not been lowered showed occlusions of 55%. In other words, the monkeys with slower heart rates had occlusions that were about 35% less extensive than the monkeys with higher heart rates. It appears that higher heart rates lead to greater occlusions because the brief pause of blood flow that occurs between heartbeats provides an opportunity for cholesterol to become attached to the walls of the arteries. More heartbeats lead to more pauses in blood flow, which in turn lead to more buildup on the artery walls.

4. *Arousal leads to high blood pressure, and the consequent stretching of the arteries causes their walls to become rough, making it easier for cholesterol to adhere.* That process enhances the buildup of cholesterol on the artery walls and leads to occlusions.

In summary, Type A and hostile individuals have higher and more frequently elevated levels of arousal,

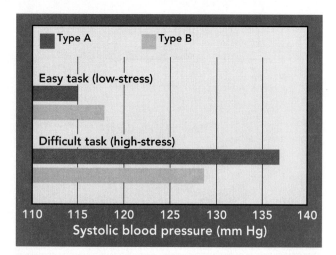

FIGURE 16.8 Students with the Type A behavior pattern showed higher blood pressure when working on a difficult (stressful) task than students with the Type B behavior pattern.
Source: Adapted from Holmes et al. (1984), p. 1326, fig. 1.

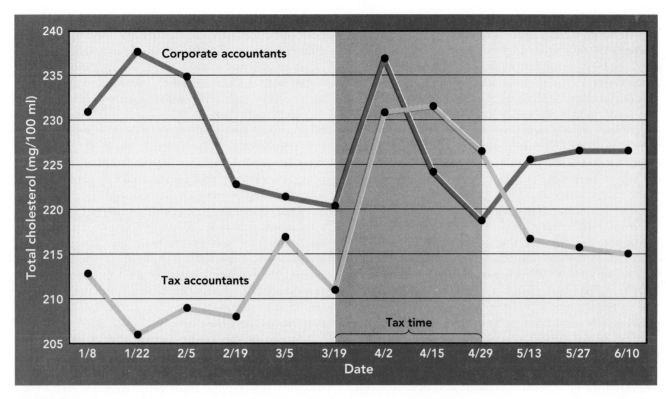

FIGURE 16.9 **Cholesterol levels increase during periods of stress, as in accountants at tax-filing time.**
Source: Adapted from Friedman et al. (1958), p. 856, fig. 2.

and those elevated levels of arousal lead to the development of coronary artery disease because they increase (a) the production of cholesterol, (b) the clumping of cholesterol particles, (c) the likelihood that cholesterol will stick to the artery walls, and (d) the ease with which cholesterol can adhere to the artery walls. Taken together, these findings provide strong evidence linking behavior to the development of coronary artery disease.

Hypertension

The other major cardiovascular disease is **hypertension** (HĪ-pur-TEN-shun), which involves *high blood pressure*. There are two types of hypertension, *essential* and *secondary*. **Essential hypertension** is high blood pressure *for which a physical cause has not been found,* and so it is assumed that the elevated pressure is due to psychological factors. (Essential hypertension is sometimes referred to as *primary hypertension*.) In contrast, **secondary hypertension** is high blood pressure that stems from *known physiological causes* such as excessive salt in the diet, kidney malfunction, or atherosclerosis. It is called *secondary* because the elevated blood pressure is a side effect of some other physical disorder. In this chapter, I will focus on essential hypertension.

Hypertension is a widespread and potentially serious disorder. It has been estimated that 1 out of every 6 adults has hypertension and that 90% of those individuals suffer from essential hypertension. Many individuals are not aware that they have hypertension because it does not have any noticeable symptoms. With regard to its seriousness, hypertension has been shown to increase the risk of coronary artery disease, heart attacks, vascular accidents, and kidney failure.

There are two important measures of blood pressure, the *systolic* and the *diastolic*. The **systolic** (sis-TOL-ik) **blood pressure** is the high level of pressure that occurs immediately after each heartbeat when blood is suddenly forced through the system. In contrast, the **diastolic** (DĪ-uh-STOL-ik) **blood pressure** is the low level of pressure that occurs just before each heartbeat. Blood pressure is measured in terms of the height of a column of mercury that could be supported by the pressure. Normal systolic pressure is about 120 mm Hg (millimeters of mercury), and normal diastolic pressure is generally considered to be 80 mm Hg. When talking about blood pressure, we give the systolic pressure first and then the diastolic pressure, and thus we might say that an individual's pressure is "120 over 80" (written 120/80). Although 120/80 is considered "normal," pressure varies widely. Women generally have lower pressure, older individuals have higher pressure, and any one individual's pressure may go up and down during the day due to a variety of factors.

Individuals are usually diagnosed as suffering from hypertension if they have sustained blood pressure readings of 140/90 or higher. However, both figures need not be high for a problem to exist, and there is no agreement over whether elevation of the systolic or the diastolic pressure is more important. It might be noted that some individuals suffer from **hypotension** (HĪ-po-TEN-shun), or *low blood pressure*. Hypotension is not a serious problem, but when getting up quickly from a chair or a bed, it can result in sudden dizziness because for a brief period there is not enough pressure to get blood to the brain.

The development of essential hypertension involves two steps. First, stress results in a temporary increase in blood pressure. Second, the increased blood pressure causes the arteries to stretch, and the stretch is detected by a set of sensors called **baroreceptors** (BAR-ō-rē-SEP-turz) that then send signals to the central nervous system to reduce blood pressure. Specifically, peripheral blood vessels are dilated, heart rate is reduced, and the strength of the heart's contraction is reduced, all of which serve to reduce pressure. However, if pressure is high for a prolonged period of time, the baroreceptors adjust to the higher level of pressure and signal the central nervous system only when the pressure goes even higher. In other words, after an extended increase in pressure, the baroreceptors reset themselves, and high pressure becomes the norm.

Psychological factors, specifically the Type A behavior pattern and hostility, play an important role in the development of essential hypertension because those factors contribute to more frequent and more prolonged elevations in blood pressure, and those elevations increase the likelihood that the baroreceptors will be reset at higher levels.

The long-term effect of individual differences in blood pressure responses to stress was illustrated in a study in which the investigators followed up men who 15 years earlier had shown either high or low blood pressure responses to a threat of electrical shock (Light et al., 1992). The results indicated that the men who had shown high blood pressure reactivity 15 years earlier had developed higher chronic blood pressure than the men who earlier had shown low blood pressure reactivity. Clearly, individual differences in the response to stress have long-term implications.

Treatment

An individual whose coronary arteries are approaching the point of occlusion might undergo **coronary bypass surgery,** which involves grafting in an unclogged piece of artery so that the blood can bypass the occluded area and hence get to the heart. Another operation that is frequently performed involves taking a tiny flexible tube with an inflatable balloon on the end and insert-

ing it into the occluded artery. At the point of the occlusion, the balloon is inflated, forcing the fatty material against the side of the artery and making a larger passageway in the artery. This operation is called **angioplasty** (AN-jē-ō-PLAST-ē). A related procedure involves inserting a tube with a rotating knife blade on the end, and when the blade spins, it chops up the obstructing material so that it can be carried away in the bloodstream. More recently, drugs referred to as **"clot busters"** have been developed that if administered immediately after a heart attack or stroke can dissolve clots and prevent further damage.

One type of drug that is widely used to treat hypertension is the **diuretic** (DĪ-yuh-RET-ik). Diuretics reduce the amount of fluid in the body, and when the fluid level is lower, there is less pressure in the cardiovascular system. Hypertension is also treated with drugs called **vasodilators** (VĀ-zō-dī-LĀ-turz) that cause the blood vessels to dilate, making more room in the system and thereby reducing the pressure.

Stress on the cardiovascular system can also be reduced with drugs known as **beta** (BĀ-tuh) **blockers** (such as propranolol, sold under the trade name Inderol) that reduce heart rate (Kristal-Boneh et al., 1995). If heart rate is reduced, the heart's need for oxygen is reduced, and therefore the likelihood of heart attack is reduced. These drugs are called beta blockers because they block synaptic transmission at what are called *beta receptors* at the synapses of the sympathetic nervous system.

Prevention

Surgery and medication can be effective for treating existing problems, but unless appropriate preventive steps are taken, the problems will return. Indeed, it is not unusual to see patients coming in for second or third angioplasties or bypass operations. Therefore, the key is *prevention,* and most prevention programs are nonmedical. Prevention is usually focused on two factors, *diet* and *stress reduction* (Dubbert, 1995; Reid et al., 1994; Smith & Leon, 1993). First, attempts are made to change the individual's diet so that the ingestion of fats is reduced, thereby reducing the basic building blocks of cholesterol and atherosclerosis. Second, attempts are made to teach the individual how to control or reduce the stress. In the following sections, I will discuss three widely used approaches for controlling stress.

Stress Management. Originally, **stress management training** programs were designed to make Type A individuals more like Type B individuals. For example, in one investigation, individuals who had experienced heart attacks were randomly assigned either to a condition in which they participated in a standard cardiac rehabilitation program (in which they received instructions concerning diet and exercise), or they were assigned to a condition in which they participated in the same rehabilitation program but also participated in group counseling sessions designed to reduce their Type A behavior patterns (Friedman et al., 1984; Friedman & Ulmer, 1984). The results indicated that the individuals who received counseling to reduce the Type A behavior showed reductions in Type A behavior, and they were less than half as likely to have another heart attack as the individuals who participated in only the traditional rehabilitation program.

These results suggest that it is possible to change the Type A behavior pattern, but achieving such a change is difficult. One impediment to change is that many individuals do not want to give up their Type A behaviors because those behaviors are very effective for achieving success. Indeed, in Western society the Type A behavior pattern is generally admired and rewarded, and unless individuals face imminent death from another heart attack, they are resistant to change their behavior patterns.

Another strategy for managing stress revolves around enhancing **social support** because there is consistent evidence that social support is associated with lower heart rate and blood pressure (Bland et al., 1991; Dressler, 1991; Gerin et al., 1992; Unden et al., 1991). For example, individuals who participate in more club activities and individuals who report more social support at home or at work show lower cardiovascular arousal when they come for physicals, and they also show lower arousal when cardiovascular measures are taken in social and work settings. Of course, it is possible that social support does not reduce arousal but that individuals who are less aroused attract more support (e.g., they may be less hostile). To determine whether social support actually leads to lower cardiovascular arousal, an experiment was conducted in which an accomplice of the experimenter argued with an individual while the individual's blood pressure was taken (Gerin et al., 1992). In a social-support condition, a third person defended the individual, whereas in a no-social-support condition, the third person did not come to the individual's defense. The results indicated that when individuals were given social support, they showed smaller increases in blood pressure and heart rate, thus confirming the link between social support and reduced cardiovascular arousal.

In addition to helping prevent the onset of cardiovascular disease, social support can also help prevent relapse after the disease has set in and has been treated with bypass surgery (Fontana et al., 1989; King et al., 1993; Kulik & Mahler, 1989). For example, patients who have high levels of social support experience less angina, thus indicating that they have a better blood supply to the heart than patients who have low levels of social support.

Aerobic Exercise. Until around 1970, rest was prescribed for individuals who had experienced a heart attack. The notion was that the heart was weakened and should not be strained. However, now it is generally agreed that **aerobic exercise** can aid in the treatment and prevention of cardiac disorders in a number of ways. (Aerobic exercises include jogging, swimming, cycling, and others that elevate heart rate to 70% of its maximum for at least 20 minutes. Your maximum heart rate is determined by subtracting your age from 220.) For example, aerobic exercise can reduce the buildup of cholesterol in arteries. That is the case because there are two types of cholesterol, one "bad" and one "good." The bad type, known as **LDL** (low-density lipoproteins), comes from fat in the diet and builds up in the arteries. The good type, known as **HDL** (high-density lipoproteins), is produced when we exercise and carries away the LDL before it can build up. In other words, by exercising, we increase the production of HDL, which reduces the buildup of LDL.

Aerobic exercise also serves to enlarge and strengthen the heart so that it can pump more blood more efficiently (i.e., the volume of blood pumped with each beat is increased). The increased efficiency of the heart means that it will have to work less hard (beat slower and require less oxygen) both under normal conditions and under stress.

Aerobic exercise can help reduce the buildup of cholesterol in the arteries and can reduce cardiovascular responses to stress. The relationship between aerobic fitness and improved cardiovascular responses during stress has been demonstrated in a number of studies.

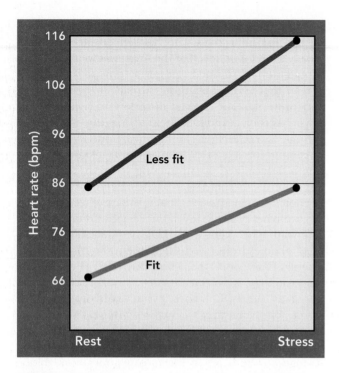

FIGURE 16.10 When exposed to stress, aerobically fit students showed smaller increases in heart rate than less aerobically fit students.
Source: Adapted from McGilley and Holmes (1988), p. 129, fig. 3.

The relationship between aerobic fitness and improved cardiovascular responses during stress has been demonstrated in a number of investigations (Holmes, 1993). For example, in one study, the heart rates and blood pressure of students were measured while they rested and while they worked on a stressful intellectual task (subtracting by 7 as fast as possible from the number 3,584; McGilley & Holmes, 1988). The results indicated that during stress, the students who were in better aerobic condition had heart rates that were almost 30 beats per minute lower than the less fit students. Those results are presented in Figure 16.10. During stress, the more fit students also had systolic blood pressure readings that averaged almost 14 mm Hg lower than those of the less fit students.

Exercise programs have also been demonstrated to be effective for physiological and psychological rehabilitation of individuals after a heart attack or bypass surgery. One experiment revealed that compared to patients who received routine medical care, patients who participated in an exercise program showed (a) lower heart rate, (b) lower blood pressure, (c) better performance on a treadmill, (d) better self-concept, (e) less employment-related stress, (f) more enjoyment of leisure time, and (g) greater sexual activity (Roviaro et al., 1984). Unfortunately, when the patients were examined again 7 years later, the patients who had been in the routine-care condition were doing better than the patients who had been in the exercise condi-

tion (McGilley et al., 1993). The problem was that the patients in the exercise condition thought they were "cured" when the program was over, so they stopped exercising, but the patients who received routine care were still concerned about themselves, so they slowly began to increase the amount they exercised, and that exercise led to improvements in their physical and psychological health. Clearly, *exercise must be part of a change in lifestyle,* not just a temporary treatment.

Biofeedback Training. Responses of the autonomic branch of the peripheral nervous system are generally not under voluntary control, and that makes it difficult to control the physiological responses to stress. For example, ordinarily you cannot voluntarily reduce your heart rate or blood pressure during periods of stress. However, some years ago it was suggested that our inability to control autonomic responses was due to the fact that we had not had sufficient opportunities to learn such control. Feedback about performance is essential to learning (e.g., you cannot learn to decrease your blood pressure unless you know when it is going up and down), and thus it could be that we do not learn to control autonomic responses because ordinarily we do not get enough feedback about them. That speculation led to the development of **biofeedback training** procedures in which sophisticated electronic equipment is used to provide individuals with instant feedback about changes in their autonomic responses and then, ideally, the individuals can learn to control those responses.

Blood pressure biofeedback has been widely publicized as an effective treatment for hypertension, and a number of investigators have reported that hypertensive patients who received biofeedback showed decreases in blood pressure of as much as 26 mm Hg. They also reported that after biofeedback training individuals could maintain normal blood pressure without the aid of medication. However, in most of those studies, the changes in blood pressure in patients receiving biofeedback were not compared to changes in patients who did not receive biofeedback (no-treatment controls), so from those studies we cannot determine whether biofeedback was actually effective. To correct that problem, a series of experiments was conducted in which some patients received blood pressure biofeedback training while others simply sat quietly for a comparable length of time. Surprisingly, the results of those experiments indicated that the biofeedback training was no more effective than sitting quietly (see Holmes, 1981). Thus despite widespread publicity and extensive clinical use of biofeedback training, there is no reliable controlled evidence that biofeedback is effective for treating hypertension.

To sum up, cardiovascular disorders pose a variety of serious medical problems, and there is now substantial evidence that psychological factors are related to cardiovascular problems. The most important of those factors seems to be hostility. Hostility is correlated with and perhaps causes cardiovascular disorders because it is associated with increased levels of arousal, which lead to the cardiovascular disorders. The arousal levels that lead to cardiovascular disorders can be reduced with medication (beta blockers), aerobic exercise, and some stress management programs.

HEADACHES

Headaches are among the most common causes of pain. It is estimated that between 10% and 30% of Americans suffer from chronic headaches. Here attention will be focused on *migraine* and *muscle tension* headaches because they pose the most serious and frequent problems.

Migraine Headaches

A **migraine headache** produces pain so severe that it can completely incapacitate an individual. Some patients describe the pain as if a burning rod were being driven through the brain. There are two types of migraine headaches. The *classic* type afflicts about 2% of headache sufferers and consists of two phases. The first phase begins about 30 minutes before the actual headache starts, and the symptoms involve visual problems such as flashing lights and blind spots, dizziness, and sometimes abdominal pain. These are called **prodromal symptoms,** and they serve as a warning that a headache is about to begin. The headache begins in the second phase, and at first it involves a unilateral (one-sided) throbbing pain that usually occurs in the temporal or occipital areas (side or back of the head). In addition to the pain, the individual usually becomes nauseated and very sensitive to light and is most comfortable in a dark, cool place. As time goes on, the pain changes from throbbing to constant. The headache lasts for a few hours, usually less than 24.

The second type of migraine is the *common* type, and it afflicts about 12% of headache sufferers. The common migraine is not preceded by prodromal symptoms, and the pain is usually generalized rather than limited to one area of the head. However, the common migraine does involve the other symptoms such as nausea and sensitivity to light and is just as painful as the classic type. The severity of the pain associated with migraine headaches cannot be understated.

The prodromal symptoms of the classic migraine are due to an extreme *constriction of the cranial arteries* (the arteries that supply blood to the head). The constriction limits the blood supply, and that causes the

symptoms. As the process progresses, the cranial arteries change from a state of constriction to a state of *extreme dilatation*. When the arteries dilate and increase in size, they put pressure on the surrounding pain-sensitive nerves, and it is that pressure that results in the pain. The initial throbbing nature of the pain is due to the hydraulic pulsations of blood through the dilated arteries. As the attack continues, the arteries become inflamed and rigid in their dilated state, and therefore the pain changes from throbbing to steady.

We know that migraine pain is due to extreme dilatation of the cranial arteries, but we do not yet clearly understand the factors that cause the arteries to dilate. However, it does appear that genetic factors play a role in predisposing individuals to migraine headaches and that the genetic link is stronger for women than men. It also appears that estrogen is somehow connected to migraine headaches because the incidence of migraines in women drops sharply after menopause and because the incidence of migraines in women who are taking estrogen supplements drops sharply when those supplements are reduced. Finally, over the years, there have been numerous speculations concerning the role of stress in precipitating migraine headaches, but as yet the effects of stress have not been demonstrated to be particularly important (see Robbins, 1994; Solomon, 1994). Individuals often report that stress precedes the onset of migraines, but they ignore the fact that more frequently stress does not lead to migraines.

Tension Headaches

Tension headaches, sometimes called **muscle contraction headaches,** are very common (Silberstein, 1994). The pain is constant (nonpulsating), usually occurs on both sides of the head, and most frequently occurs primarily in the frontal area (forehead) or the suboccipital area (back of the head just above the neck). The pain of tension headaches stems from the fact that the muscles in the afflicted area have been contracted for prolonged periods of time. Exactly how the pain is generated is not clear, but it is probably related to reduced blood flow and reduced energy stores that are associated with prolonged static contractions of the muscles. The prolonged muscle contractions are generally believed to stem from psychological stressors. For example, individuals who are attempting to deal with stressors may frown persistently, contracting the frontalis muscles, or they may hold their heads rigidly for long periods of time, causing prolonged contraction of the muscles at the base of the skull.

Treatment

Migraine. The medical approach to the treatment of migraines involves the administration of stimulants such as *ergotamine tartrate* and *caffeine.* Stimulants are effective for reducing the pain because they result in constriction of the dilated arteries and therefore reduce the pressure on the surrounding pain-sensitive nerves. However, to be effective the stimulants must be taken during the very early stage of the headache, before the dilated arteries become rigid. If the attempt to constrict the arteries is made after they become rigid, the treatment will not be effective and the individual will have to endure the pain until the headache runs its course.

The most widely publicized psychological treatment of migraine headaches involves *finger temperature biofeedback training* in which the individual attempts to increase his or her finger temperature with the aid of biofeedback. Finger temperature increases when more blood flows to the area, and the assumption is that if more blood is flowing to the hands, less blood will be flowing to the head, thus decreasing pressure and pain there. A variety of early case studies seemed to provide support for this treatment, and it quickly became very popular. Unfortunately, subsequent controlled research has not provided any support for the efficacy of biofeedback for the treatment of migraine headaches (see Holmes, 1981; Holmes & Burish, 1984). For example, in one experiment, the individuals were given either true biofeedback or false biofeedback that did not accurately reflect skin temperatures (Mullinix et al., 1978). The results indicated that the individuals in the true biofeedback condition were better able to increase their finger temperatures, but they did not show greater reductions in headaches or medication usage than the individuals who received the false biofeedback. It was also found that the degree to which headaches did or did not improve was not correlated with the degree to which patients did or did not increase their finger temperature. In other words, the control of finger temperature (blood flow) was not related to the headache activity. Even more devastating were the findings of another investigation in which it was demonstrated that individuals who were given biofeedback training could learn to relax and control blood flow but that the changes in blood flow to the hands were not related to changes in blood flow to the cranial arteries (Largen et al., 1978). Furthermore, it now appears that the dilatation of the cranial arteries is not due to changes in blood flow. Thus finger temperature biofeedback has not been found to be effective for treating migraine headaches and, for physiological reasons, probably cannot be effective. However, because of the publicity given to the results of the early case studies and the intuitive appeal of the approach, biofeedback is still widely advertised and used as a treatment for migraine headaches.

Tension. The goal of treatment of tension headaches is to reduce muscle tension. In some cases, that is achieved with muscle-relaxing drugs, but a more frequent approach involves teaching individuals how to relax in general and how to relax the muscles of the face, neck, and shoulders specifically. Two approaches have been used to teach relaxation, **progressive muscle relaxation training** and **electromyographic** (ē-LEK-trō-Mī-uh-GRAF-ik) **(EMG) biofeedback training.** Progressive muscle relaxation training is a procedure in which individuals tense and then relax sets of muscles. This is done so that they can become familiar with the sensations and techniques that are associated with muscle relaxation, and with this increased awareness they become more effective at achieving relaxation at will (see Chapter 6). By focusing the training on the muscles that are associated with tension headaches (forehead and neck), progressive muscle relaxation training can be an effective way to reduce the headaches (Holmes & Burish, 1984; Holroyd & Penzien, 1994).

In EMG biofeedback training, electrodes are used to detect muscle activity, and the individual is given immediate feedback about whether muscles are tensing or relaxing. A tone is usually used to provide the feedback; the tone goes higher when the muscles become tense and lower when they relax. By listening to the tone and trying to get it to go lower, the individual can learn to relax specific sets of muscles. There is substantial evidence that EMG biofeedback training is more effective than no treatment for reducing muscle tension headaches (see Holmes & Burish, 1984). Those findings are encouraging, but it is important to note that in experiments in which the effects of EMG biofeedback training were compared to the effects of progressive muscle relaxation training, both techniques were *equally effective.* In other words, EMG biofeedback training is effective for reducing tension headaches but not more effective than the cheaper and easier progressive muscle relaxation training, so muscle relaxation training is probably the treatment of choice.

In summary, at present, there is no strong evidence linking psychological factors to migraine headaches and no evidence that psychological approaches such as biofeedback are helpful for treating those headaches. However, stress that leads to prolonged muscle contractions does appear to provoke muscle tension headaches, and those headaches can be treated effectively with either EMG biofeedback or progressive muscle relaxation training.

PEPTIC ULCERS

The word *ulcer* refers to any abnormal break in the skin or a mucous membrane. The ulcers from which most people suffer are **peptic ulcers,** which occur in the digestive system, and about 10% of Americans suffer

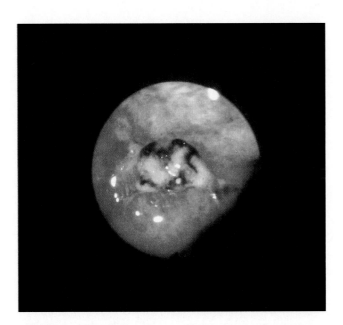

FIGURE 16.11 Peptic ulcers are holes in the wall of the duodenum or the stomach.

from them. (*Peptic* is derived from *pepsin,* the gastric acid that breaks down proteins in the digestive tract.) In addition to causing considerable pain, ulcers can be dangerous because they lead to internal bleeding and can result in death. Figure 16.11 is a photo of an ulcer.

Before going on to discuss the psychological factors that contribute to ulcers, I should note that many ulcers are due to bacteria (Blaser, 1996). How many are due to bacteria and how many are due to psychological factors is not clear, but as you will learn, psychological factors can play an important role in many ulcers.

Types and Causes

Peptic ulcers result from an imbalance between the level of *gastric acid* (primarily hydrochloric acid and pepsin) that is produced to break down foodstuffs and the level of *mucus* that is produced to neutralize the acid and thereby protect the walls of the intestinal tract. If the acid level gets too high because too much acid is being produced or because not enough mucus is being produced, the acid will eat holes (ulcers) in the walls of the intestinal tract. The ulcers result in pain and sometimes the vomiting of blood (Weiner, 1991).

Peptic ulcers are divided into two types, depending on where in the digestive system they occur. **Duodenal** (DOO-uh-DĒ-nul) **ulcers** occur in the *duodenum,* which is the first part of the small intestine, where food enters the intestine from the stomach. About 85% of duodenal ulcers are caused by *overproduction of gastric acid* rather than by underproduction of mucus.

In contrast, **gastric ulcers** occur in the stomach, and in contrast to duodenal ulcers, they are usually the result of *too little protective mucus* rather than too much

gastric acid. (The exception is when food from the small intestine backs up into the stomach and brings additional acid with it.) In many cases, individuals develop gastric ulcers because they have ingested high levels of substances like aspirin or alcohol that reduce mucus, thus causing an acid-mucus imbalance.

Stress. A major reason for the overproduction of gastric acid is stress (Magni et al., 1994; Wilhelmsen et al., 1994). Evidence for the influence of stress on the development of ulcers is provided by an early study of air traffic controllers who worked in towers in what were characterized as high- or low-stress situations (Cobb & Rose, 1973). The results indicated that (a) the air traffic controllers were more likely to have ulcers than a control group of men, (b) the air traffic controllers developed their ulcers earlier than the controls, and (c) the air traffic controllers who worked in the high-stress towers were more likely to have ulcers than those who worked in the low-stress towers.

In early research with rats that were given stressful electrical shocks, it was found that the rats were more likely to develop ulcers if they did not know when the shocks were coming or if they could not control the shocks (turn them off) by pushing a lever (Seligman, 1968; Weiss, 1968, 1970). From those findings it was widely concluded that unpredictable and uncontrollable stresses were most likely to lead to ulcers, but that conclusion requires a qualification. Specifically, it may not be the *nature* of the stress (i.e., unpredictable or uncontrollable) that is crucial but rather the *level* of stress that is important. If you (or a rat) do not know when stress will come (i.e., unpredictable stress), you will be constantly under stress and thus under more stress than an individual who knows when the stress will come. Similarly, if you cannot control stress, you will not know when the stress will end, and thus you will be under more stress than an individual who can control the stress. In other words, predictability and control may simply be factors that influence the *level of stress,* and the level of stress may be the crucial factor in the development of ulcers.

Physiological Predisposition. Stress can lead to ulcers, but it is clear that by itself stress is not sufficient to cause ulcers. That is, many people who undergo stress do not develop ulcers. It now appears that in addition to being exposed to stress, the individuals who develop ulcers also have a *physiological predisposition* to produce high levels of gastric acid (Weiner, 1991).

Individual differences in the gastric response to stress and their relationship to ulcers was illustrated in an early study in which individuals who did or did not have ulcers were exposed to the same level of stress, after which the levels of acid in their stomachs were measured (Mittelmann et al., 1942). The results indicated that when exposed to the stress, the individuals who had ulcers showed higher levels of the acid and more stomach churning than the individuals who did not have ulcers.

More convincing evidence concerning the interaction of acid production and the development of ulcers comes from a prospective study in which the investigators identified newly inducted army draftees who had either high or low levels of pepsinogen (a chemical that becomes gastric acid) but who did not have ulcers (Weiner et al., 1957). When the men were followed up after 16 weeks of stressful basic training, it was found that 15% of the men with high levels of pepsinogen had developed ulcers, whereas none of the men with low levels of pepsinogen had done so.

In summary, the research consistently indicates that a predisposition to produce high levels of gastric acid in combination with stress leads to the development of ulcers. This is another example of the diathesis-stress model used in earlier chapters to account for other disorders. So rather than talking about the *stress-ulcer* relationship, we should talk about the *predisposition-stress-ulcer* relationship.

Finally, one important qualification should be noted: A predisposition to produce acid in combination with stress can lead to ulcers, but it is now known that ulcers can also stem from infections, so it should not necessarily be assumed that all ulcers are stress-related.

Treatment and Prevention

Medical treatment for ulcers sometimes involves surgically removing the portion of the stomach or intestine that is ulcerated. That obviously removes the ulcer, but because it does not remove the underlying problems (acid production and stress), the ulcers are likely to return. Another medical procedure involves partially cutting the vagus nerve, which stimulates acid production in the stomach, but this extreme treatment is rarely used. Other treatments include the use of antacid drugs to neutralize the excess gastric acid and the use of a drug (cimetidine) that blocks nerve transmission to the stomach and reduces the production of gastric acid by 70% to 80%. These are effective maintenance treatments and can be used for prolonged periods of time by individuals who normally produce excess gastric acid or are constantly under stress. However, because in many cases the excess acid is due to stress, the treatment of choice often involves various types of stress management training programs in which individuals are taught to avoid or control stress.

IMMUNOLOGICAL DISORDERS

We are constantly exposed to infectious and toxic agents such as bacteria, viruses, fungi, and parasites. If allowed to go unchecked, these agents can result in a wide variety of disorders, ranging from colds to cancer. Fortunately, the body has an **immune system** that fights these disease-causing agents. In recent years, we have learned that psychological factors play an important role in the functioning of the immune system (Maier, Watkins, & Fleshner, et al., 1994). Here I will review how the immune system works, examine the role that psychological factors play in its functioning, and then consider the role that psychological factors play in rheumatoid arthritis, a disorder that is influenced by the immune system.

Immune System Functioning

The disease-causing agents that enter the body are known as **antigens** (AN-ti-junz). The function of the immune system is to destroy antigens and thereby prevent disease. The major combatants in the war against antigens are the **white blood cells** that circulate throughout the body via the bloodstream. White blood cells are technically called **leukocytes** (LOO-kuh-sīts), from the Greek for "light-colored cells." Leukocytes are produced in the lymph nodes, bone marrow, spleen, and parts of the gastrointestinal tract.

There are a number of kinds of leukocytes, but most attention has been focused on the **lymphocytes** (LIM-fuh-sīts), which are produced in the lymph nodes and are particularly effective for destroying antigens. Some lymphocytes are called **killer cells** because they destroy antigens, others are called **helper cells** because they identify antigens and signal the lymph nodes when it is necessary to produce more killer cells, and some are called **suppressor cells** because they cause a reduction in the production of killer cells when the killer cells are not needed.

The degree to which the immune system is active and effective is referred to as the individual's level of **immunocompetence.** High immunocompetence is characterized by high levels of killer and helper cells and a low level of suppressor cells. It is because the number of leukocytes increases to fight infection that your white blood cell count is checked to determine whether you have an infection. It is important to recognize that there are wide individual differences in immunocompetence; the less responsive the immune system, the more an individual will suffer from infections and diseases. Let us now take a look at the factors that influence immunocompetence.

Psychological Factors and Immune System Functioning

Decreases in Immunocompetence. Immunocompetence can be influenced by both physiological and psychological factors (Maier, Watkins, & Fleshner, 1994).

A physiological factor that has attracted widespread attention is the **HIV** (human immunodeficiency virus) virus, which kills lymphocytes instead of being killed by them. Specifically, the HIV virus kills the helper cells, and therefore the system is not stimulated to produce more killer cells when the body is invaded by antigens. In the absence of sufficient killer cells, the individual develops AIDS and usually dies of various infections, often pneumonia.

Of most importance for our discussion here is the fact that *psychological stress often causes a decrease in the functioning of the immune system,* which in turn leads to physical illnesses (see Andersen et al., 1994; Cohen et al., 1993; Herbert & Cohen, 1993; Jemmott & Locke, 1984; Weisse, 1992). For example, in one of the early studies in this area, the investigators measured the levels of life stress (e.g., family or financial problems) in a group of seamen before they left for an extended cruise and then tracked the number of illnesses the men experienced during the cruise (Rahe et al., 1970). The results indicated that the men who had experienced higher levels of life stress experienced more illnesses than those who had experienced lower levels of life stress. Those results are presented in Figure 16.12.

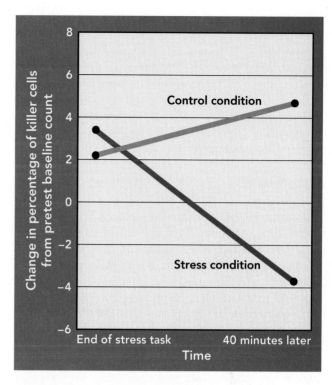

FIGURE 16.13 Students showed a drop in killer cells in their immune systems after a brief stress.
Source: Data from Cohen et al. (1993), p. 127, tab. 2.

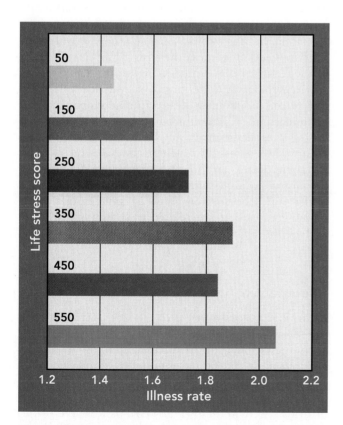

FIGURE 16.12 Men who experienced high life stress were more likely to get sick than men who did not experience high life stress.
Source: Adapted from Rahe et al. (1970), p. 404, fig. 1.

There is now a wide variety of evidence linking stress to lower immune system functioning. For example, in one experiment, individuals in a stress condition worked on a challenging intellectual task for 30 minutes while individuals in a control condition read magazines (Cohen et al., 1993). Measures of the levels of killer cells indicated that the levels were comparable before and during the tasks, but the individuals in the stress condition showed substantially lower levels 40 minutes later. Those findings are summarized in Figure 16.13. In other research it was found that stressful final examinations led to lower immunocompetence among students, and the effect was greater among lonely students who lacked social support (Kiecolt-Glaser et al., 1984). Another study revealed that students had lower immunocompetence following a stressful period in school than following a vacation (Jemmott et al., 1983). Those findings explain why you are likely to become sick after finals. It has also been demonstrated that individuals who are undergoing the prolonged stress of bereavement (death of a family member or loved one) show lower levels of immunocompetence than individuals who are not experiencing such stress (Bartrop et al., 1977; Linn et al., 1982; Schleifer et al., 1984).

Immunocompetence has also been found to be related to depression: It is lower in depressed than nondepressed individuals (Denney et al., 1988; Kronfol et al., 1983; Schleifer et al., 1984), and the level of depression is related to the level of immunocompetence, with more depressed individuals showing lower immunocompetence (Denney et al., 1988; Kronfol et al., 1983; Linn et al., 1982). Depression is probably associated with lowered immunocompetence because depression reflects the presence of stress or because depression itself is a stressor (see Chapter 8). Thus it can be concluded that psychological stress has the effect of reducing immunocompetence, which can in turn influence physical health.

Increases in Immunocompetence. The finding that increases in psychological stress can lead to decreases in immunocompetence leads to the question of whether psychological treatments that reduce stress could increase immunocompetence in people who are exposed to stress. That possibility gained support from an experiment in which students participated in a series of stress reduction training sessions before taking an important examination (Kiecolt-Glaser et al., 1984). Levels of immunocompetence were assessed a month before the examination and again after the examination. The results indicated that the students showed generally lower immunocompetence after the exams than they had a month earlier (i.e., stress reduced immunocompetence), but the students who attended more stress reduction training sessions showed higher immunocompetence. In another experiment, elderly individuals had their immune systems assessed before and after receiving relaxation training, social contact, or no treatment over a period of 1 month (Kiecolt-Glaser et al., 1985). Comparisons of the groups revealed that the individuals who received relaxation training showed increases in immunocompetence, whereas the individuals in the other conditions did not. Thus there is now some evidence that stress management techniques are effective for reducing the effects of stress on the immune system.

Another behavior strategy that is effective for increasing immunocompetence is aerobic exercise training. Ample evidence now indicates that an acute bout of strenuous aerobic exercise will increase the levels of various lymphocytes (e.g., Edwards et al., 1984; Hedfors et al., 1983; Landmann et al., 1984; Robertson et al., 1981).

The results of one study suggest that aerobic exercise and fitness may serve to facilitate immune system functioning and reduce illness (Roth & Holmes, 1985). In that study, the investigators identified students who either were or were not experiencing high levels of life stress and then determined which students were high or low in aerobic fitness. When the health records of the students were examined for the following 8-week period, it was found that among the students who were

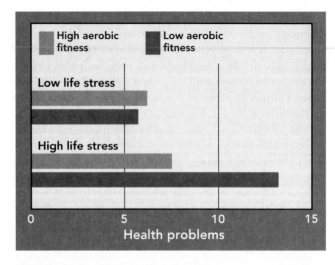

FIGURE 16.14 When exposed to life stress, aerobically fit individuals were less likely to get sick than less aerobically fit individuals.
Source: Adapted from Roth and Holmes (1985), p. 169, fig. 1.

under high stress, those who were low in aerobic fitness showed high levels of illness, whereas those who were high in fitness showed low levels of illness. In fact, the fit students who were under high stress showed illness levels that were comparable to those of students under low stress. In other words, aerobic fitness served to offset the effects of stress in the stress-illness relationship. These results are presented in Figure 16.14.

In summary, a wide variety of evidence links stress to reduced functioning of the immune system, and it is generally agreed that reduced immunocompetence following stress is the mediating factor in the stress-illness relationship. Stress management and aerobic exercise programs have been shown to be effective strategies for increasing immunocompetence. With this material as background, we can now go on to consider one of the many diseases that are related to the immune system and are influenced by psychological factors.

Rheumatoid Arthritis

Arthritis is a disease that involves *pain in the joints.* It is the second most prevalent disease in the United States, following coronary heart disease. Although arthritis is rarely fatal, it can be exceptionally painful and often results in severe crippling. There are three types of arthritis, but in this section I will focus on **rheumatoid arthritis** (ROOM-uh-toyd ar-THRĪ-tis), which occurs when the membrane that covers the joints is damaged. When the protective membrane is damaged, friction develops that leads to pain.

Rheumatoid arthritis afflicts about 1% of the population, and the ratio of female to male sufferers is 3:1. Most cases occur between the ages of 20 and 50, but a rare juvenile form occurs in young children. Rheumatoid arthritis usually affects the small joints in the hands, wrists, knees, and ankles.

Psychological Factors Contributing to Rheumatoid Arthritis. In studying the psychological factors in arthritis, investigators first attempted to determine whether a specific personality type was associated with arthritis, that is, if an "arthritic personality" existed (see Anderson et al., 1985). A wide variety of personality characteristics were proposed (e.g., depression, hostility, inhibition), but after more than 40 years of research there is still very little reliable evidence connecting specific personality characteristics to the disease. Furthermore, insofar as there are consistencies in the findings, most can be attributed to the fact that personality was measured after the onset of the disorder, and therefore the characteristics observed in the patients may be effects rather than causes of the disease. At present, then, there does not appear to be any reliable evidence that specific personality characteristics are related to the development of rheumatoid arthritis.

In contrast to the findings concerning personality, there is a growing body of evidence that *psychological stress* (such as financial problems, loss, and marital conflict) is related to the development of rheumatoid arthritis (Anderson et al., 1985; Stewart et al., 1994; Zautra et al., 1994). In one study, extensive interviews dealing with life events were conducted with a group of patients who were believed to be developing rheumatoid arthritis and with an age-matched group of patients suffering from other medical problems (Baker, 1982). (Using patients who were just developing the disorder helped reduce the possibility that the presence of the disease influenced the patients' reports.) A year later,

the patients who had a confirmed diagnosis of rheumatoid arthritis were compared to the general medical patients. The results indicated that 68% of the arthritic patients reported an important life stress in the year before the onset of their symptoms, whereas only 36% of the general medical patients reported such a stress.

Stress and Subtypes of Rheumatoid Arthritis. Although numerous studies have indicated a relationship between stress and the development of rheumatoid arthritis, in a variety of cases stress was not found to be a factor. One possible explanation for the inconsistency in the findings is that stress may be only one of a number of factors that can lead to the disease, and therefore only a subset of cases is related to stress. Support for that possibility comes from a number of studies in which the investigators identified what appear to be two forms of the disease, one stress-related and one not stress-related (Rimon & Laakso, 1985; Stewart et al., 1994). The characteristics of the two forms are listed in Table 16.2. What is most noteworthy is the fact that in one form, the symptoms are associated with stress and there is *not* a family history of the disease, whereas in the other form, the symptoms are not related to stress but there *is* a family history of the disorder. In other words, rheumatoid arthritis may be related to stress *or* to a genetic factor.

A 15-year follow-up of the patients who were used to make the original distinction between stress-related and non-stress-related rheumatoid arthritis revealed two interesting findings (Rimon & Laakso, 1985). First, the patients in the stress-related group showed symptoms that were sometimes better and sometimes worse, whereas the course of the disease for the other patients was constant and progressive. Second, the increases in symptomatology that were observed in the stress-related group were most likely to occur during times of major life stress, thus suggesting that for these patients, stress was the crucial factor in their disease.

TABLE 16.2 Characteristics of Stress-Related and Non-Stress-Related Forms of Rheumatoid Arthritis

Stress-Related Form	**Non-Stress-Related Form**
Rapid onset of symptoms	Slow, insidious onset of symptoms
Varying severity of symptoms	Fairly constant symptoms
Little or no family history of rheumatoid arthritis	High proportion of family members with rheumatoid arthritis
Onset of symptoms associated with stress	Onset of symptoms not associated with stress

Source: Adapted from Rimon and Laakso (1985).

CASE STUDY 16.3

Stress and Rheumatoid Arthritis in a Physically Active 34-Year-Old Woman: A Personal Account

I have always been healthy, physically active, and interested in sports. I ride my horse a couple of times a week, play golf and tennis frequently, and play on a softball team. Because of my interest in sports, four years ago I took all of my savings, borrowed some money, and opened a sporting goods store. More about that later; first let me tell you about the physical problems that developed.

One day about three years ago, I started having a pain and some swelling in my right wrist. It bothered me, but I didn't worry about it at first because I assumed that it stemmed from some tendinitis I had from a skiing accident a few years earlier. However, a few days later, I also began to have pain in my other wrist, and my fingers began swelling. Then I noticed that my feet and ankles were swollen, and I started having trouble putting on my shoes. The problem got worse very fast, and soon I couldn't open a bottle or a car door, couldn't shift my car, and couldn't bend my knees, which made fitting people for athletic shoes really tough. Things came to a head when I had to make a long drive and developed severe aches in all of my joints. My feet and knees hurt so badly that I had to stop every half hour to stretch and rest them. The next day, I went to my physician, who took some blood tests and told me that I had rheumatoid arthritis. Arthritis? Me? How could that be? Arthritis is for old people—how did I get it?

I went to a rheumatologist for a second opinion, but she came to the same diagnosis. In talking with me, the rheumatologist asked whether anyone in my family suffered from arthritis and whether I was under stress. No, no one else in the family suffered from arthritis, but yes, I was definitely under a tremendous amount of stress. The stress was associated with my new business. The problem was that I had paid a contractor $75,000 to remodel my store

in a mall, but the contractor left town without paying the subcontractors who had done the work. I was left responsible for paying the $75,000 again. The store was making money, but not enough to pay off the start-up costs twice. I was trying to run the store, I was deep in debt, and I was being constantly harassed by creditors, lawyers, and vendors. I was struggling to keep my head above water, but I was slowly slipping under—and now I was rapidly developing a crippling case of rheumatoid arthritis.

I was put on some expensive medication to reduce the inflammation in my joints, and my physical activities were restricted so that I would not hurt my inflamed joints and cause permanent damage. I also did simple exercises with a physical therapist so that my joints wouldn't freeze up.

The medication held the symptoms in check, but I had to stay on it. And though the arthritis was under control, my business problems weren't, and finally I had to sell out and give up. It had been a terrible time; I was personally and financially devastated, but it was over and behind me. I decided to take a year off, come back to school, and try to figure out what to do next. I really enjoyed being back in school, and after a couple of months, I noticed that my joint pain was becoming less and less and I was getting more movement and flexibility. In consultation with my physician, I began slowly to reduce the amount of medication I was taking until I was completely off it. I have now been off the medication *and symptom-free* for a little over a year. I can't prove that the stress of the business failure caused the arthritis, but the arthritis came and went with the stress. I've got my fingers crossed that neither will come back—and the fact that I can cross my fingers tells you how well I'm doing!

Overall, these findings refine our understanding of rheumatoid arthritis and suggest that stress plays an important role in the development of at least one form of the disease. The possible relationship between stress and rheumatoid arthritis is illustrated in the experience of the 34-year-old woman who describes her experience in Case Study 16.3.

To sum up, there is now a substantial amount of evidence linking psychological stress to the development of rheumatoid arthritis, but we still do not under-

stand the process involved. Most theorists assume that the effect is mediated by the immune system. It is possible that in these patients, stress results in an excessive response of the immune system that leads to the joint damage, but this is still very speculative. In most individuals, stress leads to a diminished response of the immune system, but there is now some evidence that the reverse can also be true, and it may be that persons who develop rheumatoid arthritis are somehow predisposed to that type of response.

SUMMARY

TOPIC I: EATING DISORDERS

■ The major symptom of anorexia nervosa is the refusal to maintain weight over a minimal normal weight. Other symptoms include a fear of gaining weight, distortion of body image, and in women, amenorrhea.

■ The major symptom of bulimia nervosa is eating binges. The other important symptom is inappropriate behaviors such as purges that are designed to prevent weight gain.

■ Depression and obsessive-compulsive symptoms often accompany these eating disorders.

■ These disorders are not new, are not limited to middle- or upper-class individuals, and are more prevalent among women in adolescence and early adulthood.

■ Initially it was thought that these disorders stemmed from conflicts of sexuality, passive rebellion, attempts at control, or childhood sexual abuse, but there is no reliable evidence for those explanations. There is evidence that in some individuals, stress can lead to excessive eating.

■ Learning theorists suggest that the disorders are due to rewards for being slim, a classically conditioned fear of fatness, attempts to gain pleasure through eating, or modeling the cultural standard of slimness.

■ Cognitive theorists suggest that anorexia is due to incorrect beliefs about "weight problems," beliefs that are supported by selective attention.

■ From a physiological perspective, the disorders are thought to stem from low levels of serotonin or norepinephrine, which disrupt the functioning of the hypothalamus, the brain center responsible for eating behavior. The low levels of serotonin also explain the accompanying symptoms of depression, obsessions, and compulsions. Neurotransmitters could be low due to stress or genetic factors.

■ Cognitive therapy focused on changing beliefs and the use of antidepressants to increase levels of serotonin (and norepinephrine) can be effective in overcoming eating disorders.

■ Other eating disorders include pica, which is the persistent eating of nonnutritive substances, and the rumination disorder, which involves the repeated regurgitation of food, sometimes accompanied by rechewing and swallowing of the food.

TOPIC II: SLEEP DISORDERS

■ The circadian rhythm is the daily pattern of sleep and wakefulness. It is driven by a "biological clock," and there are wide individual differences in the timing of sleep.

■ There are four stages of sleep, and we cycle up and down through the stages three or four times each night.

■ Stage 1 sleep in the second and later cycles involves rapid eye movements, and it is during this REM sleep that dreams occur.

■ Sleep occurs when stimulation that is generated by the medulla in the brain stem is stopped from going to higher areas of the brain. The raphe nuclei inhibit impulses going up the reticular activating system.

■ Rapid eye movements are due to stimulation that travels up via the PGO (pons, geniculate, occipital) system.

■ Freud originally suggested that dreams were due to material breaking out of the unconscious, but it now seems clear that they occur when activation from the PGO system stimulates groups of neurons in which memories and thoughts are stored.

■ Primary sleep disorders are divided into the dyssomnias, which are problems with too little, too much, or the timing of sleep, and the parasomnias, which are abnormal behaviors or events that occur with sleep.

- There are five dyssomnias:
  1. Primary insomnia involves problems getting to sleep or staying asleep. It stems from excessive neurological arousal reaching the higher areas of the brain. It is treated with hypnotics such as benzodiazepines that reduce arousal and with behavioral strategies such as relaxation training, which are also designed to reduce arousal.
  2. Primary hypersomnia is excessive sleepiness. It is due to insufficient arousal and is treated with stimulants.
  3. Narcolepsy involves irresistible attacks of sleep due to sudden drops in arousal, and it is treated with stimulants.
  4. The breathing-related sleep disorder involves disruptions in sleep because of problems with breathing. In obstructive apnea, the airway to the lungs closes briefly, depriving the individual of oxygen. Treatment involves strategies to keep the airway open, such as stimulating muscles or mechanical devices. Central apnea is due to problems in the control of respiration in the brain.
  5. The circadian rhythm sleep disorder involves a mismatch between the individual's sleep pattern and the demands of the environment. The rhythm can be reset with bright light.
- There are three parasomnias:
  1. The nightmare disorder involves frightening dreams that awaken the individual and disrupt sleep. They are most common in childhood.
  2. The sleep terror disorder involves awakening with intense fear and disorientation, but it is not triggered by a nightmare (it occurs during non-REM sleep).
  3. The sleepwalking disorder involves walking while asleep.

TOPIC III: PSYCHOPHYSIOLOGICAL DISORDERS

- Certain physical disorders are caused at least in part by stress. Stressors stimulate activity in the sympathetic branch of the autonomic nervous system, thereby increasing general arousal, which is not under voluntary control. Prolonged physiological arousal leads to the disorders.
- Coronary artery disease involves the narrowing of arteries because of the buildup of fats (atherosclerosis), and the narrowing reduces blood flow that is necessary to sustain life in tissues. Occlusions (general narrowing, thrombus, embolism) and vascular accidents (ruptures) can result in a myocardial infarction (heart attack) or a cerebral infarction (stroke).
- Individuals with the Type A behavior pattern, and particularly those who are hostile, are at greater risk for coronary artery disease. That occurs because the Type A pattern and hostility lead to higher arousal, and arousal leads to increased production, clumping, and accumulation of cholesterol on artery walls.
- Essential hypertension is high blood pressure for which a physiological cause has not been found. Stress increases pressure, the baroreceptors that control pressure become adapted, and thus high pressure becomes "normal."
- Treatments such as bypass surgery, angioplasty, "clot busters," diuretics, vasodilators, and beta blockers may not have long-term effects, so attention is focused on prevention through stress management, social support, and aerobic exercise.
- Migraine headaches are due to the dilation of cranial arteries, which puts pressure on pain-sensitive nerves. The effects of stress on that process have not been reliably confirmed. Treatment usually revolves around stimulants that cause the arteries to constrict.
- Tension headaches are due to prolonged muscle contractions due to stress. Treatment involves muscle relaxation training, sometimes with EMG biofeedback.
- Peptic ulcers result when acid eats a hole in the wall of the digestive tract (stomach or duodenum). Stress can lead to ulcers, but only in individuals with a biological predisposition.

■ Certain white blood cells (called lymphocytes) destroy foreign substances (antigens) that could cause disease. Stress can cause a decrease in immunocompetence, which can lead to increased rates of illness. Stress reduction (as from social support) and aerobic exercise can increase immunocompetence and decrease illness.

■ In rheumatoid arthritis, the immune system attacks the protective membrane in the joints. Some cases are caused by stress.

KEY TERMS, CONCEPTS, AND NAMES

In reviewing and testing yourself on what you have learned from this chapter, you should be able to identify and discuss each of the following.

aerobic exercise
amenorrhea
angina
angioplasty
anorexia nervosa
antigens
apnea
arthritis
atherosclerosis
autonomic division
baroreceptors
benzodiazepines
beta blockers
biofeedback training (EMG and finger temperature)
brain stem
breathing-related sleep disorder
bulimia nervosa
central apnea
central nervous system
cerebral infarction
circadian rhythm
circadian rhythm sleep disorder
"clot busters"
coronary artery disease
coronary bypass surgery
cycle of sleep
diastolic blood pressure
diuretic
duodenal ulcers
dyssomnias
electroencephalogram (EEG)
electromyographic (EMG) biofeedback training

embolism
essential hypertension
gastric ulcers
half-life
HDL
health psychology
helper cells
HIV
hostility
hypertension
hypnotics
hypotension
hypothalamus
immune system
immunocompetence
killer cells
LDL
leukocytes
lymphocytes
migraine headache
muscle contraction headaches
myocardial infarction (MI)
narcolepsy
nightmare disorder
nitroglycerin
norepinephrine
obstructive apnea
parasomnias
parasympathetic branch
peptic ulcers
peripheral nervous system
pica
primary hypersomnia
primary insomnia

primary sleep disorders
prodromal symptoms
progressive muscle relaxation training
purge
rapid eye movement (REM) sleep
rebound effect
reticular activating system
rheumatoid arthritis
rumination disorder
secondary hypertension
serotonin
sleep terror disorder
sleepwalking disorder
social support
somatic division
somatoform disorders
stages of sleep
strategic eating disorders
stress
stress management training
stroke
structured interview
suppressor cells
sympathetic branch
systolic blood pressure
tension headaches
thrombus
tryptophan
Type A behavior pattern
vascular accidents
vasodilators
white blood cells

CHAPTER SEVENTEEN
SUBSTANCE-RELATED DISORDERS

OUTLINE

Len Bias was a talented college basketball player who had just signed a multimillion-dollar contract to play for the world-champion Boston Celtics. His future was bright when he shot some cocaine and died of cardiac arrest. Thousands of cases of heart attacks from unknown causes are undoubtedly due to cocaine use.

■ ■ ■

Ruth is a bright, anxious, tense, sensitive, and somewhat inhibited 34-year-old woman who rarely drinks alcohol. However, every few months, she goes on a binge. She buys a bottle of vodka, takes it home, and drinks until she passes out. After 8 or 10 hours, she comes to with a terrible hangover and is sick for a day or so. She is always ashamed of what she has done, and most people do not know about her problem. Ruth suffers from the binge type of alcoholism. The very high level of alcohol may serve briefly to reduce her high level of arousal.

■ ■ ■

John is an uninhibited, impulsive guy who often takes risks just for kicks, and consequently he has frequent scrapes with the law. John always seems to be drinking—always having a drink or having just finished one. He does not drink a lot at any one time, so he is rarely really drunk, but he is usually just a little high. John appears to have the persistent type of alcoholism. The low level of alcohol may have the effect of depressing the inhibitory areas of the brain, thereby resulting in a higher level of arousal for him.

■ ■ ■

After smoking marijuana, an engineer ran his train through a red signal light and hit another train. Seventeen people died. . . . A man with twice the legal limit of alcohol in his blood drove his pickup truck down the wrong side of the road and hit a school bus head on. He survived, but 27 schoolchildren were killed. . . . An autopsy revealed cocaine in the body of a pilot whose plane crashed, killing all passengers.

■ ■ ■

Cynthia used LSD occasionally with some of her friends, and the "trips" were usually pleasant and fun. However, twice she had really bad trips that were terrifying, and during one, she tried to kill herself. Because of the bad trips, she has stopped using LSD, but now she is having "flashbacks" (trips that occur when she does not take the drug). She never knows when a flashback will occur, and she feels out of control. She is now afraid to be alone because she does not know when she will need help.

■ ■ ■

We are constantly bombarded with stories documenting the fact that the misuse of drugs is one of the most serious problems facing Western civilization today. At this point, the "war on drugs" is not being won. If anything, we seem to be losing, and the topic of drugs is one to which we must give very careful attention.

In this chapter I will not take a moral stand concerning whether or not it is appropriate to use drugs. Instead, I will focus on understanding the effects of drugs and the reasons some individuals become dependent on them. Armed with that background, you will be able to make your own informed judgments concerning what is and what is not appropriate.

ISSUES ASSOCIATED WITH DRUG USE AND ABUSE

Definition and Nature of Psychoactive Drugs

The substances that I will discuss in this chapter are generally referred to as psychoactive drugs. Stated simply, a **psychoactive drug** is any substance that *alters your mood* (e.g., makes you happy, sad, angry, depressed), *alters your awareness of the external environment* (e.g., changes your perception of time, location, conditions), or *alters your awareness of the internal environment* (e.g., induces dreams, images). For example, after taking a psychoactive drug, an individual may feel elated, be unaware of the passage of time, and focus on fantasies rather than what is going on in the immediate environment.

Over the years the term *psychoactive* has taken on numerous negative connotations. It often conjures up images of the "junkie," the individual who is "spaced out on dope," the rock star sniffing coke, or the disheveled heroin addict slumped in a doorway. However, the term *psychoactive* does not imply good or bad, legal or illegal. Marijuana, cocaine, heroin, and LSD are all psychoactive substances, but so are sugar, caffeine, nicotine, alcohol, and codeine. Furthermore, although psychoactive drugs are often abused and can lead to serious problems, they also have many important and valuable uses, such as the reduction of anxiety and the control of pain.

Factors That Influence the Effects of Drugs

A number of factors other than the chemical makeup of a drug can influence its effects, and those factors deserve some attention before we go on.

Dose-Dependent Effects. One of the first things to recognize is that the effects of drugs can vary with the *amount that is taken*. In other words, most drugs have **dose-dependent effects.** First, dose level can influence *how much* of an effect will occur. This is obvious in the case of alcohol: A few beers can result in a slight slurring of speech; a few more, in a greater slurring of speech. Second, dose level can influence the *type* of effects that will occur. For example, small doses of nicotine produce physiological stimulation, but larger doses result in physiological sedation that can be great enough to cause death.

Individual Differences. The effects of many drugs are also influenced by the personality of the individuals taking them. For example, a small dose of caffeine (the equivalent of two cups of coffee) can improve the intellectual performance of extroverted individuals (e.g., enable them to study better), but the same dose can impair the performance of introverted individuals (Revelle et al., 1976). That effect stems from the fact that extroverts are often neurologically underaroused, so the stimulating effect of the caffeine brings them up to an optimal level of arousal, but introverts are already at an optimal level of arousal, so the additional stimulation provided by the caffeine pushes them beyond the optimal level, and consequently their performance declines.

Individual differences in previous experiences with drugs can also influence the effects of drugs. For example, individuals who are inexperienced in the use of marijuana do not report any effects of the drug even when physiological measures indicate that effects are occurring. In contrast, experienced users notice the effects right away. The reasons for that are not yet completely understood.

The influence of genetic factors can be seen in the fact that there is a higher concordance rate for alcoholism among monozygotic than dizygotic twins (Goodwin, 1985a, 1985b; Hopper, 1994; Kendler, Heath, et al., 1993; Kendler, Walters, et al., 1994, 1995; McGue et al., 1992). In other words, genetic factors seem to predispose some individuals to become dependent on alcohol and other drugs.

Interaction Effects. The effects of a drug can be drastically altered if it is taken in combination with another drug. That is, when taken together, drugs often interact and produce an effect that is greater than the sum of the two drugs taken separately. For example, the combination of Valium and alcohol results in much greater levels of physiological sedation than would be the case if the effects of each drug were simply added together. Some individuals will intentionally take combinations of drugs to get stronger effects, but that can be very dangerous because the degree of the effect is hard to predict and the overall effect can prove fatal.

Tolerance and Cross-Tolerance. **Tolerance** refers to the fact that after repeated administrations of the same dosage of a drug, *that dosage level begins having less and less effect.* As tolerance for the drug develops, the individual must take greater amounts of the drug to achieve the same effect. In ancient Greece, tolerance was used as a defensive strategy by individuals who thought that someone might attempt to poison them. The individuals would take increasing amounts of the poison an enemy might use so that they would eventually be immune to a dose given by the enemy. Today, many individuals who take drugs over prolonged periods develop very high levels of tolerance, and therefore they must take very large amounts of the drugs to achieve the desired effects. That can have serious consequences because at high doses, the drugs may have dangerous side effects.

Cross-tolerance refers to the fact that when a drug of one type is taken, *tolerance can develop for other drugs of that type.* For example, taking an opiate such as morphine will reduce the effects of other opiates such as heroin.

Because of the factors discussed in this section, any one drug can have different effects at different times for the same individual, and any one drug can have different effects in different individuals. Therefore, when attempting to explain the effects of a drug, it is important to understand the individual, the situation, and the history of that individual's use of drugs as well as the drug itself.

Problems Related to Drug Use

Most people use a psychoactive drug occasionally, such as a cup of coffee with caffeine to provide a lift or an alcoholic drink to help with relaxation. The question is, when does normal use cross the line and constitute a substance-related disorder? According to DSM-IV, the presence of any one of four factors can lead to a diagnosis of substance-related disorder (American Psychiatric Association, 1994). The four factors are as follows:

1. *Abuse.* Drug **abuse** is said to occur when *the use of a drug leads to clinically significant impairment or distress.* Examples include the failure to meet responsibilities at school, work, or home; engaging in physically hazardous behaviors such as driving while intoxicated; recurrent legal problems such as arrests for disorderly conduct; and social or interpersonal problems such as arguments or physical fights that result from taking drugs. In essence, when an individual begins wrecking his or her life or the lives of others because of the effects of drugs, that individual is abusing drugs.

2. *Intoxication.* **Intoxication** is defined as *reversible symptoms,* such as belligerence, changes in mood, impaired judgment and impaired functioning, *that stem from the recent ingestion of a drug that influences the central nervous system.* A key term here is *reversible;* that is, the symptoms will go away when the drug wears off. A common example of intoxication is drunkenness from alcohol.

3. *Withdrawal.* **Withdrawal** refers to the *physiological symptoms that occur when an individual stops taking a drug or takes less of the drug than was taken before.* An individual can be defined as suffering from withdrawal when the withdrawal symptoms cause *clinically significant impairments in functioning or in personal distress.* In some cases, withdrawal symptoms are relatively mild, such as the feelings of tension that occur when an individual stops smoking. In other cases, withdrawal symptoms are terrifying and can be fatal. For instance, withdrawal from alcohol or heroin can involve uncontrollable movements of the body (kicking, jerking), nausea, and hallucinations. Because the physiological symptoms of withdrawal can be so severe, the anticipation of those symptoms often produces psychological symptoms such as fear and anxiety.

It is important to note that the symptoms of withdrawal can be quickly reduced or eliminated by taking another dose of the drug or by taking a dose of a different drug from the same class of drugs. For example, the frightening symptoms of withdrawal from barbiturates can be quickly eliminated with another dose of barbiturates or a dose of another depressant such as alcohol. Withdrawal symptoms play a crucial role in the development of drug dependence (discussed next) because the individual must continue taking the drug (get a "fix") to avoid the withdrawal symptoms.

4. *Dependence.* Essentially, **dependence** is said to occur when *tolerance develops,* so the individual must take higher doses to achieve the desired effect; *withdrawal symptoms occur,* so the drug must be taken to avoid those symptoms; and much of the individual's life is devoted to obtaining or taking drugs. For example, an individual who must take alcohol to avoid the "shakes" is drug-dependent. A common word for dependence is *addiction;* the individual who must have the drug or high doses of the drug is said to be addicted.

In summary, abuse, intoxication, withdrawal, or dependence can lead to the diagnoses of substance-related disorders.

Substance-Related Disorders

In DSM-IV, substance-related disorders are organized in terms of *the drug that is causing the problem,* as follows (American Psychiatric Association, 1994):

Alcohol-related disorders

Amphetamine-related disorders

Caffeine-related disorders

TABLE 17.1 Psychoactive Drugs, Their Modes of Action, Their Effects, and Examples

Category	Action	Effects	Examples
Depressants	Depress arousal centers	Sedation	Alcohol, barbiturates, benzodiazepines
Narcotics (opiates)	Decrease neural transmission	Dulling of senses	Opium, morphine, heroin, methadone
Stimulants	Increase neural transmission (but may also block transmission)	Arousal	Amphetamines, caffeine, cocaine, nicotine
Hallucinogens	Vary, depending on drug	Distortion	Cannabis (marijuana, hashish), LSD, mescaline, psilocybin

Cannabis-related disorders (e.g., marijuana)

Cocaine-related disorders

Hallucinogen-related disorders (e.g., LSD)

Inhalant-related disorders (glue, paint thinner, spray propellants)

Nicotine-related disorders

Opioid-related disorders (morphine, heroin)

Phencyclidine-related disorders (e.g., PCP, "angel dust")

Sedative-, hypnotic-, or anxiolytic-related disorders (e.g., tranquilizers such as barbiturates, sleeping pills, and antianxiety medication)

Polysubstance-related disorder (multiple drugs)

However, within each drug-type diagnosis there can be subdiagnoses of abuse, intoxication, withdrawal, or dependence. For example, within the alcohol-related disorders, there are subdiagnoses of *alcohol abuse, alcohol intoxication, alcohol withdrawal,* and *alcohol dependence,* and one or more can be applied to a given individual. The use of the subdiagnoses makes it possible to specify the exact nature of the problem stemming from the drug use for each patient so that treatment can be more focused and, it is hoped, more effective.

Types of Drugs

It should be clear from the list of diagnoses that numerous drugs are involved in substance-related disorders. However, most of the drugs can be organized into four types on the basis of the *effects* they produce:

1. Depressants, which have a general *sedating* effect
2. Narcotics, which have a *dulling* effect on sensory experiences
3. Stimulants, which have a general *arousing* effect
4. Hallucinogens (huh-LOO-sin-uh-jinz), which have a *distorting* effect on sensory experiences

The types of drugs, their mode of action, their effects, and the names of specific drugs are summarized in Table 17.1. Because the drugs of any one type

share characteristics and effects, in this chapter the discussions of drugs will be organized around types of drugs rather than specific drugs. For each type of drug, I will consider the background and effects of the drug, the physiological process that is responsible for the drug's effects, and the problems that are associated with misuse of the drug. This organization will enable you to make comparisons among drugs and will prepare you to understand the causes and treatments of substance-related disorders.

DEPRESSANTS

Depressants *reduce physiological arousal, reduce psychological tension, and help individuals relax.* They are most frequently used to counteract the stress of daily living. Examples include a drink at the end of the day, a sleeping pill, and Valium taken when anxiety or muscle tension gets too high. Although depressants usually reduce arousal, large quantities consumed at one time can cause a brief high or "rush." There are three types of depressants: *alcohol, barbiturates,* and *benzodiazepines.*

Alcohol

You may be surprised that **alcohol** is a depressant because after a few drinks, many people become upbeat rather than subdued; they are more outgoing, more expansive, and less inhibited. The uplifting effect of alcohol is due to the fact that at first alcohol depresses *inhibitory* centers in the brain, causing the individual to become less inhibited and more expansive. However, as the level of intoxication increases, the depression effect becomes more widespread and reduces activity in the areas of the brain that are responsible for *arousal,* and then sedation and sleep set in.

It should be noted that at least some of the disinhibiting effects of alcohol are due to *expectancies* about its effects. Many people believe that they will be a little "loose" after drinking, so some of their uninhibited behavior is due to how they expect they should behave.

Evidence for this is provided by research indicating that individuals who drink nonalcoholic beverages that they think contain alcohol will act more aggressively, become more sexually aroused, and be less anxious (Hittner, 1995; Kidorf et al., 1995; Lang et al., 1975; Wilson & Abrams, 1977; Wilson & Lawson, 1976). Because of expectancies, some individuals may actually get "drunk" on nonalcoholic beer or wine.

Apart from its elating and depressing effects, alcohol affects vision and balance and reduces muscle control, so speech becomes slurred and coordination decreases. It also impairs concentration and judgment, so individuals make poor decisions. The combination of impaired vision, lessened muscle control, and impaired cognitive functioning can lead to disastrous consequences, especially in the case of driving.

The alcohol we drink (technically called *ethyl alcohol* or *ethanol*) is produced by a process called *fermentation*. Fermentation occurs when sugar is dissolved in water and then microorganisms called yeasts convert the sugar into alcohol and carbon dioxide. The carbon dioxide bubbles off and leaves the alcohol and water. Fermentation of sugar from different sources leads to different types of beverages; fermentation of grapes leads to wine, and fermentation of grains leads to beer. Alcohol makes up between 3% and 12% of the volume of these beverages.

Because the yeasts that convert sugar into alcohol die in solutions that contain more than 10% or 15% alcohol, the fermentation process stops when the alcohol content is still relatively low. To produce beverages

with alcohol content higher than 10% or 15%, the process of *distillation* is used. In distillation, the liquid containing alcohol is heated until the alcohol vaporizes, leaving the water behind. The vapor is then cooled and condensed to yield a liquid with a higher alcohol content. The familiar still in pictures of "moonshiners" was used for distillation. Distilling the alcohol from different sources leads to different drinks: Grapes produce brandy; grains, whiskey; molasses, rum; and potatoes, schnapps. (Gin and vodka are mixtures of pure alcohol, water, and flavoring.) Alcohol makes up between 40% and 50% of the volume of these drinks.

Physiological Processes. Alcohol is usually drunk and then absorbed from the digestive tract. Drinking alcohol just before or during a meal reduces the rate of absorption because most of the absorption occurs in the small intestine, and the alcohol will be diluted and delayed in getting there if it is mixed with food that is being digested in the stomach. Once the alcohol is absorbed, it is widely distributed to tissues throughout the body, including the brain, where it depresses inhibitory centers and later depresses arousal centers. Some of the alcohol also goes to the tissues of the lungs, where it is vaporized into the air. It is possible to use the alcohol content of expired air as an index of the amount of alcohol in other areas of the body, and that provides the basis for the *Breathalyzer test*, which is used for determining intoxication levels of individuals who are suspected of driving while under the influence of alcohol.

Many automobile accidents occur as a result of the impaired vision, loss of muscle control, and poor judgment associated with alcohol consumption. Because alcohol is released from the blood in the lungs and exhaled as vapor, a Breathalyzer test can determine how much alcohol is in the body.

Alcohol can also be consumed by inhalation. When inhaled, the alcohol vapors are absorbed by the lungs, dissolved in the blood, and then distributed throughout the body. The traditional brandy snifter is designed to facilitate the inhalation of alcohol vapors. The large base of the glass can be cupped in the hand so that heat from the hand aids vaporization, and the small opening at the top of the glass concentrates the vapors so that they can be effectively inhaled. Brandy produces a substantial amount of vapor because it has a very high alcohol content.

Problems of Misuse. Tolerance for alcohol develops rapidly, and within a few weeks, dose levels must be increased by 30% to 50% to achieve the desired effect. The tolerance develops because drinking alcohol stimulates the body's production of substances that destroy alcohol, so the more alcohol that is consumed, the more is destroyed.

After a period of chronic consumption, cessation of alcohol intake leads to withdrawal symptoms that can be severe and even lethal. The first withdrawal symptoms include agitation and involuntary contraction of the muscles (the "shakes"). Next the individual experiences muscle cramps, nausea, vomiting, and profuse sweating. In extreme cases, the withdrawal involves delirium (hallucinations) and seizures. This is referred to as *delirium tremens,* or *the d.t.'s.* These symptoms can be very serious, but withdrawal can be eased by giving the individual small amounts of other short-acting depressants such as Valium, thereby permitting withdrawal with fewer symptoms.

Barbiturates and Benzodiazepines

Barbiturates were the first type of tranquilizer, and they are very effective for reducing arousal. At low levels, barbiturates result in relaxation, light-headedness, and a loss of motor coordination. Higher doses bring on slurred speech, greater reductions in motor control, mild euphoria, and sleep. At very high doses, they cause a brief rush that is followed by relaxation or sleep. In some cases, barbiturates lead to aggression, an effect that probably occurs because they reduce inhibitions.

Benzodiazepines are the latest generation of tranquilizers. Well-known drugs of this type include Ativan (lorazepam), Librium (cholodiazepoxide), Valium (diazepam), and Xanax (alprazolam) (see Chapter 6). These drugs are misused by two different groups of individuals. One group consists of individuals who use them simply to reduce daily tensions and aid in sleep, but they use the drugs too frequently or in excessively high dosages. This is a normal extension of the appropriate use of the drugs, and these users have unwitting-

ly slipped across the fine line that separates appropriate use from abuse.

The other group of misusers consists of the "street" drug users. They use barbiturates and benzodiazepines to produce a brief rush, to achieve a state of relaxed euphoria, or to aid in "coming down" from a high caused by taking a stimulant. Barbiturates and benzodiazepines are very similar in many respects, but barbiturates are more powerful, more likely to be misused, and more likely to result in dependence, so I will focus attention on them.

Physiological Processes. Barbiturates are quickly absorbed into the bloodstream from the digestive system and then pass rapidly into the brain, where they have their effects. However, after a very short period, they are redistributed to fatty areas of the body and then are slowly released. Because of this pattern of absorption, storage, and release, barbiturates quickly achieve their major effects, but then the effects drop off and persist at a low level for some time. Barbiturates differ in the speed with which effects occur, and those differences determine the clinical use of the drugs. Barbiturates that act fast but have relatively brief effects are used as anesthetics (painkillers), those with a less rapid onset but moderately long-lasting effects are used as sleeping pills, and the long-lasting ones were once used to treat anxiety and epilepsy. In most cases, barbiturates are taken orally, but injecting them directly into the bloodstream will quicken their effects and result in a brief period of very intense euphoria.

Barbiturates reduce arousal by *reducing neural transmission.* They do that in two ways. First, they enhance the effects of inhibitory neurotransmitters such as GABA, which serve to inhibit neural transmission (see Chapters 5 and 6). Second, barbiturates block the effects of excitatory neurotransmitters. Paradoxically, at very high levels, barbiturates *facilitate neural transmission,* and that effect is responsible for the rush. As the drug level drops, the rush turns to relaxation.

Problems of Misuse. Prolonged use of barbiturates results in serious withdrawal symptoms. The symptoms begin between 12 and 36 hours after the drug is taken, depending on whether it was the fast- or slow-acting type, and the symptoms include tension, tremors, loss of motor control, nausea, and often delirium that can include visual and auditory hallucinations. If the individual has been taking high doses, withdrawal can be very dangerous and actually lethal if it is done too quickly. In those cases, it may be necessary to begin giving the individual a less potent depressant (e.g., phenobarbital or even alcohol) for which the dose level can be controlled and slowly reduced. In less severe cases in which substitution is not necessary, the symptoms of withdrawal fade slowly over a 2-week period, but they can last for months in minor forms.

A serious problem associated with barbiturate use is death due to accidental overdose. Death stems from the fact that barbiturates cause a reduction in respiration, and at high doses, they may cause an individual to stop breathing completely. The possibility of accidental death increases with prolonged use because individuals develop a tolerance for barbiturates and therefore must take increasingly higher doses to achieve the desired effects. The amount that is necessary to kill also increases over time, but not as fast as the amount necessary to obtain the desired effects, so as time goes by, the amount necessary to get the effect approaches the lethal dose, thus reducing the room for error. This is illustrated in Figure 17.1. The possibility of overdose and death is greatly enhanced when barbiturates are taken in combination with other depressants such as alcohol because the two depressants work together to suppress respiration.

In summary, depressants such as alcohol, barbiturates, and benzodiazepines reduce physiological arousal and thereby reduce tension. At high levels, the barbiturates and benzodiazepines can cause a brief rush. The use of depressants can lead to serious withdrawal symptoms, and at high levels, they can cause death because they cause respiration to cease.

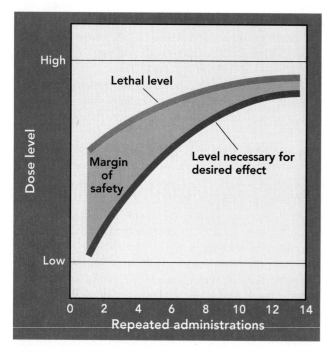

FIGURE 17.1 The dose level for intoxication rises faster over usage than the lethal dose level, so death due to overdose becomes ever more likely.
Source: Adapted from Wesson and Smith (1977), p. 35.

NARCOTICS

The term *narcotics* is often used to refer to illegal drugs, but technically it refers to a specific class of drugs derived from *opium*. These drugs are usually referred to as **opiates** (Ō-pē-its). Narcotics have the effect of dulling or numbing the senses and produce a sleeplike state. However, when high doses are rapidly delivered to the brain, opiates can cause a sudden high or rush. Opiates include *opium, morphine,* and *heroin.* There are also a number of synthetic (artificially produced) opiates such as Dolopine (methadone), which is used as a substitute for heroin in addiction treatment programs, and Demerol (meperidine) and Darvon (propoxyphine), which are used to control pain.

Opium

Opium (Ō-pē-um) is the sap of the poppy plant, and the name *opium* comes from a Greek word that means "sap." In the form of sap, opium can be chewed, and it will produce a prolonged state of mellow relaxation. The use of opium in this way dates at least as far back as 4000 B.C., and it is still chewed by the natives of Southeast Asian countries (Myanmar, Laos, and Thailand) where the poppies are grown. Opium can also be inhaled (smoked). Smoking it is an effective way of getting greater quantities to the brain faster, and it results in a deep, stuporous state that can be maintained for many hours. It has been described as a state of "divine enjoyment."

One of the most notorious early uses of opium occurred in Chinese opium dens, where it was smoked in pipes and the smokers would languish for days in a stuporous state. Ironically, the Chinese developed the technique of smoking opium in 1644 when the emperor forbade the practice of smoking tobacco. Opium was also used in Britain during the 19th century when it was incorporated into pills, candies, vinegars, and wines. One notable use was in preparations such as Mrs. Winslow's Soothing Syrup, which was used to "dope" the children of working mothers while the mothers were away. Because of opium's widespread use, many individuals became addicted to it, including such literary notables as Lord Byron, Percy Shelley, John Keats, Sir Walter Scott, Elizabeth Barrett Browning, and Samuel Coleridge. In an attempt to break his addiction, Coleridge once hired a man to follow him and physically block his entry to any store in which he might buy opium. The use of opium reached epidemic proportions in Britain, and finally its nonprescription use was banned in 1868 with the Pharmacy Act. Opium

Smoking opium results in a stupor that can be maintained for hours. The Chinese developed the technique of smoking opium in 1644 when the emperor forbade smoking tobacco.

was also used widely in the United States until 1914, when its nonmedical use was outlawed.

Morphine and Codeine

Morphine (MOR-fēn) is one of the active ingredients in opium, and it is extracted from opium and used as a drug itself. It is dissolved in liquid and then injected into the bloodstream. After a brief high, it results in a mellow state of relaxation. The name *morphine* comes from Morpheus, the Greek god of sleep. Morphine and other narcotics cause sleepy sensations, but unlike the depressants, they do not actually increase sleep and may decrease it. The most widespread use of morphine is as an analgesic (painkiller) in hospitals.

Codeine (CŌ-dēn) is another but less powerful ingredient of opium that is isolated and used by itself. It is widely used as an analgesic and is found in various prescription painkillers and cough medicines.

Heroin

Heroin (HĀR-uh-win) is also derived from opium, but it is a semisynthetic drug that is produced by adding chemical structures to the morphine molecule. The difference in chemical structure enables heroin to get to the brain faster, and once in the brain, it is changed back into morphine. The faster delivery makes heroin about 3 times more potent than morphine and 10 times more potent than opium. Heroin was invented in

1898 by the chemist who had invented aspirin, and it was initially advertised by the Bayer company as a safe, superior aspirin.

Heroin is usually used in powdered form. It is mixed with tobacco and smoked, inhaled directly into the nostrils (an act known as "snorting"), dissolved and injected under the skin ("skin popping"), or dissolved and injected directly into the veins ("mainlining"). Heroin can cause a rush that users say is similar to orgasm. The rush lasts about 60 seconds and is followed by a 4- to 6-hour stuporous period during which bodily needs for food and sex are greatly diminished. This has been described as a pleasant time of relaxation, reverie, and mild euphoria. After the period of relaxation, the symptoms of withdrawal begin setting in. With increased use, tolerance for the drug develops, and larger and larger quantities are needed to achieve the effects.

Physiological Processes. Opiates achieve their dulling or numbing effects by *reducing neural transmission*. The reduced transmission occurs because the opiates stimulate receptor sites on presynaptic neurons, and that stimulation inhibits the release of neurotransmitters.

Many of the positive medical effects of opiates can be traced to the fact that they reduce neurological activity in various parts of the central nervous system. For example, their analgesic effect is due to the fact that in the spinal cord they inhibit the incoming nerve

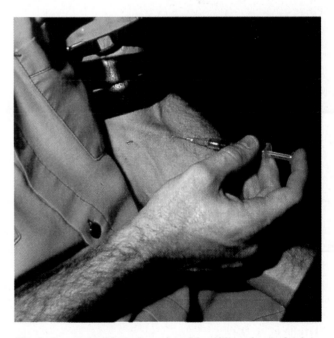

Heroin is a semisynthetic drug created by adding chemical substances to the morphine molecule. The resulting chemical structure enables heroin to get quickly to the brain, where it is changed back into morphine.

impulses that signal pain. Opiates also reduce the emotional aspects of pain by reducing neural transmission in the limbic system of the brain, where emotions originate. Opiates are effective cough suppressants because they reduce activity in the cough center of the brain. (Codeine has been used in cough medicines for many years but is now being replaced with *dextromethorphan,* which is less addicting.) Opiates are also effective for reducing diarrhea because they disrupt and reduce activity in the intestines, and that slows the movement of digested materials. (A side effect of analgesics containing opiates is constipation.)

Problems of Misuse. The prolonged use of opiates leads to dependence and serious problems of withdrawal that begin about 8 hours after the last use of the drug. The individual has chills, hot flashes, and difficulty breathing. Some individuals then fall into a deep sleep, but others have prolonged insomnia. Next the individual experiences a loss of motor control resulting in twitches, shaking, and kicking. These may be accompanied by painful muscle cramps, diarrhea, vomiting, and extreme sweating. During withdrawal, it is as though all of the systems that had been suppressed by the opiates are now turned on full blast and going wild; tranquility has turned to terror, and heaven has turned to hell. The process of withdrawal usually takes about 3 days, but it can be stopped immediately by another dose of opium, and so when the early symptoms of withdrawal begin, users will do almost anything to get more opiates.

The use of high doses of opiates can lead to death because they cause respiration to stop. In that regard, it is noteworthy that many terminally ill individuals who are given high doses of morphine for their pain do not die because of their illnesses but because eventually the morphine causes them to stop breathing. Heroin overdose deaths "on the street" usually occur because individuals take *too much* heroin; take heroin that is *of higher quality* than what they are used to, so more gets to the brain than it can handle; or take heroin *in combination with depressants* such as alcohol or barbiturates that also reduce respiration. The singer Janis Joplin died because she took heroin after drinking heavily. The likelihood of an overdose increases with time because the individual builds up a tolerance for opiates and therefore must take greater amounts to achieve the desired effects. Finally, it should be noted that sharing syringes when injecting heroin leads to a substantial increase in the risk of contracting AIDS (Grella et al., 1995).

In summary, narcotics such as opium, morphine, and heroin are derived from the poppy plant. At low levels, they dull the senses and lead to a sleeplike state, but at high levels, they can cause a rush. Their use can lead to serious withdrawal symptoms, and at high levels, they can cause death because they stop respiration.

STIMULANTS

Stimulants *increase arousal* and *cause states of euphoria* that are generally referred to as "highs." They have those effects because they increase the levels of certain neurotransmitters and thereby increase the level of neurological activity in the limbic system, which is responsible for pleasure. The two most powerful stimulants that are abused are the *amphetamines* and *cocaine,* but attention should also be given to *caffeine* and *nicotine.*

Amphetamines

When **amphetamines** (am-FET-uh-mēnz) are taken orally, they result in feelings of well-being, high spirits, high energy, vigor, elation, and reduced fatigue. Because amphetamines are absorbed slowly from the digestive system, when they are taken orally the effects come on slowly but last between 3 and 6 hours. In contrast, when amphetamines are inhaled or injected into the bloodstream, they are delivered to the brain faster and in greater quantity, so they produce a sudden rush. Regardless of whether amphetamines are swallowed or injected, the high or rush is followed by a low or a depression.

When used appropriately, the arousing effects of amphetamines have a number of beneficial effects such as reducing fatigue (pep pills), reducing appetite (diet pills), dilating air passages in the lungs to relieve asthma attacks, and treating the attention-deficit hyperactivity disorder (see Chapter 15). During World War II, amphetamines were given to the GIs so that they could fight longer and harder. The inappropriate use of amphetamines involves using them to "get high." Street users of amphetamines refer to them as "speed."

Physiological Processes. The arousing effects of amphetamines are due to the fact that they increase the level of neurotransmitters (norepinephrine, serotonin, and dopamine) in the limbic system of the brain, which is responsible for pleasure.

Problems of Misuse. Prolonged use of amphetamines leads to withdrawal symptoms of depression, listlessness, and fatigue. Apart from the problems of withdrawal, the use of amphetamines has three serious consequences. First, high doses cause dramatic increases in blood pressure that can result in cerebral infarctions (breaking of blood vessels in the brain; see Chapter 19), which in turn lead to brain damage and death.

Second, high doses of amphetamines can result in **amphetamine psychoses** that involve delusions like those seen in paranoid schizophrenia. The psychotic behavior stems from the fact that amphetamines stimulate the production of the neurotransmitter dopamine, and high levels of dopamine are related to schizophrenia (see Chapter 12). Although amphetamine psychoses can be serious, they dissipate as the drug wears off and therefore do not usually have long-term consequences. The third serious effect of high levels of amphetamines is that the individuals sometimes become dangerous. While under the influence of amphetamines, some individuals become very aggressive or do foolish things that endanger their own lives or the lives of others. Some of these erratic behaviors may be due to delusions associated with the amphetamine psychoses.

Cocaine

Cocaine is the other major stimulant that is often abused. The effects of cocaine on mood are similar to those of amphetamines, but much more intense. The drug causes an intense high or rush that is characterized by feelings of exhilaration, energy, well-being, self-confidence, and being "on top of the world." The high lasts about 30 minutes and is followed by a period of mild depression. Contrary to the widely held belief, cocaine results in a high but it does not stimulate the sex drive in women (Henderson et al., 1995).

Cocaine comes from the leaves of the coca plant, which is grown in South America, and its use has a long history. The Indians of Peru chewed coca leaves as early as 2500 B.C., and stone idols found in Colombia dating back to 500 B.C. have puffed-out cheeks suggesting that they were chewing coca leaves (an image not dissimilar from that of the modern baseball player with his wad of chewing tobacco). The Spanish who conquered the Incas did not chew the coca leaves but used them as rewards for the enslaved Indians. Giving the Indians coca leaves also reduced the cost of their upkeep because the coca reduced their appetites.

When cocaine was shipped to Europe, its pleasant effects were quickly recognized by the young Sigmund Freud, who found the stimulating effects of cocaine to be helpful in dealing with his depression. In fact, Freud was so impressed with its effects that he sent some to his fiancée and encouraged her to use it. (In doing this, Freud may have been one of the first "pushers.") The value of cocaine was also proclaimed by writers of the period, such as Robert Louis Stevenson, who believed that it stimulated their creativity and enabled them to write better.

Probably the most widespread use of cocaine occurred between 1886 and 1906 when coca leaves were used in the recipe for Coca-Cola. The "classic" Coke was indeed "the real thing." Coca leaves are still used in Coca-Cola, but the cocaine has been removed, and the stimulant effect of Coca-Cola now comes from caffeine. In its original version with the cocaine base, Coca-Cola was thought to have health benefits, and therefore it was sold in drugstores. It is probably for that reason that soda fountains originally developed in drugstores.

Cocaine can be processed and used in a number of ways. The simplest way is to chew the coca leaves, as the Indians of South America still do. Like the amphetamines, cocaine is absorbed slowly from the digestive system, and therefore taking it orally results in a prolonged mild euphoria.

Most of the cocaine used in the United States is in the form of a powdered white salt called *cocaine hydrochloride* that has been diluted ("cut") with various substances. By inhaling ("sniffing" or "snorting") the salt or dissolving it and injecting it into the bloodstream, high doses of cocaine can be gotten to the brain quickly, producing the rush. The strength of a rush is determined by the degree to which the cocaine has been diluted with other substances, and consequently a number of processes have been developed to purify cocaine so as to enhance the rush. One common procedure is to heat the cocaine hydrochloride until it forms a vapor that is free of the impurities with which it was diluted, and then the vapor can be inhaled. An even more refined and powerful form can be obtained by chemically separating the cocaine molecule from the hydrochloride. Freed from its hydrochloride base, the cocaine can then be burned, and the vapors of the pure cocaine can be inhaled. This is known as "freebasing." "Crack" is a highly concentrated form of cocaine.

Physiological Processes. The cocaine rush results from the fact that cocaine increases the levels of various neurotransmitters, and those higher levels result in more neurological activity in the limbic system of the brain, which is responsible for pleasure. In contrast, high levels of cocaine can block the conduction of nerve impulses along the axon and thereby reduce neurological activity. Because of that blocking, injections of cocaine can be used as a local anesthetic. In fact, Novocain, which is often used as an anesthetic in dental procedures, is a synthetic form of cocaine that lacks the stimulant properties. With regard to its anesthetic properties, it is interesting to note that inhaling cocaine hydrochloride is sometimes called a "freeze" because the cocaine anesthetizes the nose.

Problems of Misuse. Cocaine use is not generally thought to lead to physiological dependence, but there is some controversy over that. However, there is no

When cocaine is separated from its hydrochloride base, it can be burned and inhaled. This process is known as freebasing.

question that because of the extreme pleasure cocaine can provide, individuals can develop an extremely strong psychological dependence on it. Once dependent, individuals will do almost anything to get cocaine, and it is estimated that as much as half of the violent crime in the United States may be cocaine-related. As is the case with amphetamines, when cocaine wears off, the individual experiences depression. The depression can be eliminated with another dose of cocaine, but when that dose wears off, the depression will be deeper and more prolonged.

In addition to dependence and depression, there is now evidence that in some individuals, cocaine can induce a psychosis that usually involves paranoid delusions (Satel & Edell, 1991; Satel et al., 1991). In individuals who already have disorders, the psychosis may last for months; in others, it will dissipate as the drug wears off. We do not know exactly why cocaine precipitates a psychosis, but the symptoms can be controlled with neuroleptic drugs (Gawin, 1991; see Chapter 13).

The use of cocaine also poses serious medical risks because it can block conduction of nerve impulses.

That can be lethal when it blocks the impulses that stimulate the actions of the heart, and it is now suspected that many emergency room cases of heart failure for "unknown reasons" may actually be cocaine-related.

An unfortunate combination of the psychological and medical effects of cocaine occurred in a case in which police were summoned to a house in which they found an irrational man who was brandishing a knife and threatening to kill the people around him. The police attempted to subdue the man, but while doing so, he suddenly fell dead. An autopsy revealed high levels of cocaine in the man's system. Apparently, the strange behavior that caused the police to be called was a cocaine psychosis, and his sudden death was the result of cardiac arrest due to the cocaine.

Another medical problem associated with the sniffing of cocaine is severe damage to the mucous membranes of the nose, sometimes resulting in the destruction of the inside of the nose. Because of the anesthetic

Basketball player Len Bias (in the Maryland uniform) died of cardiac arrest after injecting cocaine.

TABLE 17.2 Levels of Methylxanthines in Frequently Used Products

Product	Caffeine (mg)	Other Methylxanthines (mg)
One cup of coffee		
Decaffeinated	1–2	
Instant	29–117	
Perked	39–168	
Drip	56–176	
One cup of tea	30–75	
One cup of cocoa		75–150 total
Coca-Cola (12 oz)	45	
Pepsi-Cola (12 oz)	30	
Chocolate bar		150–300 total
Analgesics (1 tablet)		
Anacin	22.7	
Dristan	16.2	
Excedrin	65.0	
Stimulants (1 tablet)		
No-Doz	100	
Vivarin	200	

effect of cocaine, the pain associated with the damage can be reduced with additional cocaine (the freeze), but that, of course, leads to even more damage.

Caffeine

Caffeine is the most prominent and strongest stimulant in a group of drugs called **methylxanthines** (METH-ul-ZAN-thēnz). Caffeine occurs naturally in coffee and tea, and it is also added to many cola drinks and over-the-counter drugs. The levels of methylxanthines found in various preparations are listed in Table 17.2.

The discovery of caffeine in coffee is often attributed to a herd of goats that belonged to an Islamic monastery (Jacob, 1935). As the story goes, one day the goats wandered off and ate some berries from a *Coffea arabica* bush, and for the next five days they frolicked continuously without showing any signs of fatigue. Having observed this, the abbot of the monastery sampled the berries late one evening, with the result that he was still wide awake and invigorated when it came time for midnight prayers. As the saying goes, "The rest is history."

It is interesting to note that at about the same time that opium dens were popular in China, the tradition of the coffeehouse was getting started in England. In contrast to the opium dens, in which the customers were "doped" and lay semiconscious, in coffeehouses the patrons were stimulated and participated in animated discussions late into the night. These discussions fre-

quently revolved around politics, and because there was concern that the coffeehouses were hotbeds of sedition and revolution, an attempt was made to outlaw them in 1675. The attempt failed, and the tradition of the coffeehouse continues to this day. Indeed, today there is a great resurgence of interest in coffee and coffeehouses.

The arousing effect of caffeine is usually used for maintaining wakefulness (Muehlbach & Walsh, 1995). For example, a 300-mg dose of caffeine (the equivalent of two or three cups of coffee) more than doubles the amount of time before an individual falls asleep and cuts the time in sleep by about a quarter (Brenesova et al., 1975). Apart from increasing wakefulness, the stimulating effects of caffeine can enhance performance on a wide variety of tasks (Muehlbach & Walsh, 1995; Weiss & Laties, 1962). However, it is important to recognize that caffeine does not improve the performance of rested individuals. Instead, it only serves to offset the effects of fatigue and enable tired individuals to perform at normal levels (Lorist et al., 1994). These effects seem to be stronger for simple tasks (e.g., driving) than for complex intellectual tasks (e.g., solving mathematical equations) or tasks requiring fine motor coordination (e.g., Bovim et al., 1995).

Physiological Processes. Caffeine in coffee and tea is absorbed from the digestive system and reaches peak blood levels in 30 to 60 minutes. Caffeine then remains active in the system for about 3½ hours. It is interesting to note that smoking cigarettes speeds the elimination of caffeine from the system, and therefore the frequent pattern of smoking and drinking coffee actually reduces the effect of the coffee. The process by which caffeine has its stimulating effect is not well understood, but it appears to revolve around the heightened release of norepinephrine, which increases arousal.

Problems of Misuse. Ingestion of large amounts of caffeine (500 to 800 mg/day, or 8 to 10 cups of coffee) results in agitation, tension, irritability, insomnia, loss of appetite, increased heart rate, and headaches. In short, it results in the symptoms of an anxiety disorder. At extremely high levels (1,800 mg, or more than 20 cups of coffee), it can result in a toxic psychosis with symptoms revolving around mania that can lead to violence. High levels of caffeine can also exacerbate existing psychological problems because it increases arousal and blocks the effects of antianxiety and antipsychotic medications (benzodiazepines and neuroleptics) (Greden et al., 1978; Kulhanek et al., 1979; Paul et al., 1980).

Withdrawal symptoms occur even in individuals who drink as few as five cups of coffee a day. The symptoms usually include tension, agitation, and muscle tremors. As with other drugs, the symptoms of caffeine withdrawal can be terminated with a dose of caffeine. A common and mild form of withdrawal can be seen in

The consumption of caffeine is woven into the social fabric of our society. Coffeehouses provide a place to socialize as well as drink coffee.

individuals who are grouchy in the morning until they have their first cup of coffee. Their withdrawal symptoms (e.g., tension, headache, agitation) set in because the individuals did not get any caffeine while sleeping during the night. In most cases, abuse of caffeine does not result in the dire consequences that stem from abuse of many of the other substances discussed in this chapter, but the fact that caffeine use is so widespread makes it worthy of serious attention.

Nicotine

Nicotine is derived from tobacco, and most people get nicotine from smoking. People use nicotine for two reasons; they use it when they are sluggish and want to increase arousal (e.g., after a meal or during a break), and they use it when they are tense and want to decrease arousal (e.g., during periods of stress). In other words, nicotine is classed as a stimulant, but it can serve as *both a stimulant and a depressant.* I will explain nicotine's sometimes contradictory effects after reviewing its background.

Nicotine is naturally produced by the tobacco plant, which was originally cultivated and used by the Indians of North America. In 1492, when Columbus arrived in what is now the Bahamas, the natives presented him with some "dry leaves" and showed him and his crew how to smoke them (McKim, 1986). At first, the explorers did not understand the smoking behavior (they called it "drinking smoke") and found it repulsive. However, when one of the crew realized that smoking could be pleasurable and took up the habit, he was tried and imprisoned for his "devilish habit." This con-

flict between smokers and nonsmokers still goes on today, and although smokers are not imprisoned, numerous laws are being passed that limit where and when they may smoke.

Physiological Processes. Most people get nicotine from smoking cigarettes or cigars that consist of the dried (cured) leaves of the tobacco plant. When the tobacco is burned, nicotine vapors are absorbed by the lungs, and then the nicotine is passed into the bloodstream, where it is carried first to the heart and then to the brain. Because this is a very direct route, absorbing nicotine from the lungs results in a relatively strong and fast effect.

Increasing numbers of people are now also getting nicotine from the chewing of tobacco. Tobacco designed for chewing consists of the leaves of the tobacco plant that have been soaked in a solution of sugar and licorice and then dried. When the tobacco is chewed, nicotine is absorbed through the membranes of the mouth and passed to the bloodstream, and the tobacco is spit out. Absorption from the mouth results in less effect than absorption from the lungs.

Once in the brain, nicotine has an influence on both the central and the peripheral nervous systems. In the central nervous system, nicotine stimulates numerous nerve centers and causes higher levels of neurological arousal. For example, nicotine stimulates the area of the brain that is responsible for respiration and thereby increases breathing rate. It also stimulates the area of the brain stem that is responsible for vomiting, and that is why new smokers who have not yet developed a tolerance for nicotine get sick to their stomachs when they first try smoking. That is also why nonsmokers become nauseated when they are around smokers and must inhale tobacco smoke. With regard to the peripheral nervous system, nicotine stimulates the release of adrenaline into the bloodstream, which increases arousal in terms of responses such as heart rate and blood pressure.

However, at high levels the effects of nicotine are *reversed,* and it blocks the stimulation of various nerves, thus serving as a depressant. The blocking of nerve transmission can be very serious because some of the nerves that are blocked are responsible for respiration, and when those nerves are blocked, the individual can die of respiratory arrest. Unfortunately, each year a number of children die because they eat tobacco and get too much nicotine into their systems.

Problems of Misuse. The stimulation produced by nicotine results in muscle tremors, increases in heart rate, increases in blood pressure, and constriction of the blood vessels in the skin. The limitation of blood flow to the skin is what is responsible for the cold hands of smokers (skin temperature is determined by the amount of blood in the area), and it is also responsible for the fact that the skin of smokers wrinkles and ages faster than that of nonsmokers.

Probably the most notable problems associated with nicotine revolve around withdrawal, the symptoms of which include tension, irritability, inability to concentrate, dizziness, drowsiness, nausea, constipation, muscle tremors, headaches, insomnia, and an increase in appetite that results in weight gain. The withdrawal symptoms usually last less than 6 months but can persist for years.

The physical symptoms of nicotine withdrawal are certainly not as severe as those of heroin withdrawal, but some individuals who have gone through both nicotine and heroin withdrawal report that psychologically it is as difficult to give up smoking as it is to give up heroin (McKim, 1986). Indeed, there is a growing body of evidence that nicotine withdrawal can lead to a wide variety of psychiatric symptoms such as depression and anxiety disorders (Breslau et al., 1992, 1993; Leibenluft et al., 1993). These symptoms occur in many individuals but are seen most often in those with a history of depression or anxiety. I am aware of one individual who began having hallucinations when she stopped smoking, but she could quickly stop the hallucinations by having a cigarette. Because another cigarette will reduce the unpleasant withdrawal symptoms immediately and because cigarettes are readily available, it is often very difficult to give up smoking. Indeed, there is now strong evidence that *nicotine obtained from either smoking or chewing tobacco can be highly "addicting"* (Boyle et al., 1995; Fowler et al., 1996; Stolerman & Jarvis, 1995). The addictive effects of smoke

(probably the nicotine in the smoke) stem from the fact that it reduces an enzyme that ordinarily breaks down dopamine; when there is less of that enzyme there is more dopamine, and the higher levels of dopamine lead to pleasure because dopamine is a neurotransmitter in an area of the brain that is responsible for pleasure.

With regard to the development of nicotine dependence (addiction), evidence is growing that there are individual differences in the ease with which the dependence develops and that some of those differences are linked to genetic factors (Gilbert & Gilbert, 1995; Heath et al., 1995). For example, an individual might inherit a low or high level of physiological arousal, and those levels of arousal could then be "normalized" by taking in either low or high amounts of nicotine.

Many of the relatively mild short-term effects of nicotine, such as increased heart rate and blood pressure, can result in serious long-term problems such as coronary artery disease (see Chapter 16). Also, the process of getting nicotine through smoking can result in other serious problems such as cancer because the smoke introduces carcinogens into the body.

Before concluding this discussion of nicotine, we should return to the paradox mentioned earlier concerning the fact that nicotine can serve as both a stimulant and a depressant. This paradox is interesting in and of itself, but understanding it is also important in helping us understand why and in what situations individuals use nicotine. There are three reasons nicotine can be both a stimulant and a depressant. The first is the *amount of nicotine* that is taken. As noted earlier, the effects of nicotine are dose-dependent; at low levels, nicotine stimulates nerve activity, and at high levels, it blocks that activity. However, dose level cannot account for all of the contradictory effects because the same dose (e.g., one cigarette) will serve to arouse at one time and relax at another time.

The second explanation revolves around the *reduction of withdrawal symptoms.* The symptoms of nicotine withdrawal involve unpleasant increases in tension, but those symptoms can be quickly reduced by another dose of nicotine. Therefore, a habitual smoker who has not had a cigarette for a while and who is aroused because of withdrawal symptoms can reduce this arousal by taking another cigarette.

A third explanation for the arousal-reducing effect of nicotine is strictly psychological. If an individual is tense, smoking a cigarette may be calming because it gives the individual something to do; that is, it serves as a temporary *distraction.* The very tense individual who is constantly lighting a cigarette, taking a puff or two, putting it aside, and then lighting another is not getting more nicotine than the individual who smokes the cigarette all the way through, but the repeat lighter is certainly getting more breaks and distraction, and that may temporarily reduce arousal.

In summary, stimulants include amphetamines, cocaine, caffeine, and nicotine, and they increase arousal, sometimes leading to states of euphoria. At high doses, nicotine can also serve as a depressant. The use of stimulants can lead to serious symptoms of withdrawal and in some cases to periods of psychosis.

HALLUCINOGENS

The effect of the hallucinogens is to *distort* sensory experiences. In other words, while under the influence of hallucinogens, the things people see or hear are altered, changed, or deformed so that they seem different. These distortions can be termed *hallucinations* (perceptual experiences that do not have a basis in reality), hence the term *hallucinogen*. However, it is important to note that a high dose of almost any drug can result in hallucinations, and therefore the term *hallucinogen* should be reserved for drugs that produce hallucinations even at low levels. The commonly used hallucinogens that will be discussed in this section include cannabis (marijuana), LSD, psilocybin, and mescaline.

Cannabis

Marijuana, hashish, and *hash oil* all come from the hemp plant, *Cannabis sativa;* the name for the drug they all contain is **cannabis** (KAN-uh-bis). **Marijuana** (ma-ri-HWA-nuh) is simply the dried leaves of the cannabis plant, and it is the most common form in which cannabis is used. Marijuana is usually inhaled by smoking the leaves in the form of a cigarette (the "joint" or "reefer"), but it can also be taken orally by grinding the leaves and baking them in cookies and candy ("Alice B. Toklas brownies"). **Hashish** (ha-SHESH) is the dried resin from the top of the female plant, and it is usually in powder form. Like marijuana, hashish can be mixed with tobacco and smoked or baked in cookies and eaten, but because it is more concentrated, it has stronger effects than marijuana. An even more concentrated form of cannabis is **hash oil,** which is obtained by first mixing the hashish with alcohol, which extracts the active ingredients from the hashish. The alcohol is then boiled away, and what remains is a red oil that contains a high concentration of the active ingredients. Hash oil is used by putting a drop on a normal cigarette and then smoking it or by putting a drop on hot metal and inhaling the vapors.

Cannabis can affect mood, sensory experiences, and cognitive functioning, but its effects vary greatly from individual to individual and time to time. Probably the most common effect is to cause mood swings that range from a placid dreaminess or a floating sensation called "getting off" to euphoric gaiety referred to as a "high." The high brought on by cannabis is very different from the high achieved with the stimulants like amphetamines or cocaine. Rather than a "rush" of excitement and arousal, the cannabis high involves mild euphoria and feelings of gaiety. During the high, everything may seem funny or even hilarious. Cannabis usually results in a positive mood shift, but sometimes it results in depression or negative experiences. The negative mood shifts are relatively rare and mild, and they should not be confused with the "bad trips" that will be discussed later in connection with drugs like LSD.

Cannabis also affects sensory perceptions in that experiences seem richer, fuller, brighter, and more intense. Users describe the cannabis experience as like going from black-and-white to color TV, from mono to stereo sound, and from bland to spicy food. The sense of time is also distorted; time seems stretched out, and a 5-minute period seems to last at least twice as long.

Finally, cannabis has a number of cognitive effects. The simplest things may seem very important, interesting, and profound. While under the influence of cannabis, individuals have what they think are great insights, and they believe themselves to be more creative. However, research has consistently shown that while on cannabis, individuals are *not* more insightful or creative and in fact are probably *less* so (Braden et al., 1974; Grinspoon, 1977). Other cognitive effects of cannabis include an increase in distractibility and a decline in short-term memory such that sometimes individuals start sentences but cannot finish them because they forget what they started to say.

It is interesting that cannabis may not have much effect the first times it is used. That is probably due in part to the fact that the novice user does not know how to take the drug effectively (e.g., the smoke is not held in the lungs long enough, so not enough is absorbed), but it may also be that it takes some experience to recognize and respond to the effects of the drug. Like exotic food, cannabis may be an acquired taste that takes time to develop. It is also relevant that the effects of the drug seem to be influenced to some degree by the mood of the other individuals with whom the drug is taken.

Physiological Processes. The active ingredients in cannabis are substances called **cannabinoids** (KAN-uh-bin-oydz). When cannabis is inhaled, the cannabinoids are quickly absorbed through the lungs, and the effects are noticed within a few minutes, with the peak effect occurring in 30 to 60 minutes. The effects of smoking cannabis can be enhanced by taking a deep draw on the cannabis cigarette and then holding the smoke in the lungs for 15 or 20 seconds before exhaling, thus allowing more time for absorption. Absorption of cannabinoids from the digestive system is much slower, so the effects of eating cannabis do not peak for 3 hours, but once started, the effects may last 5 hours or even longer.

The chemical basis for the effects of cannabis is very complex and not well understood. That is the case in part because cannabis contains more than 80 different cannabinoids that may contribute to the effects in different ways. Furthermore, burning cannabis (as is done when it is smoked) changes some of the cannabinoids and creates other ones, and when cannabis is eaten (as in brownies), new cannabinoids are formed during digestion and metabolism.

Problems of Misuse. There are numerous controversies over the alleged benefits and dangers of cannabis use. Proponents argue that when it is used in moderation, cannabis is an effective and safe relaxant and that its use is less troublesome than the use of alcohol or tranquilizers. Furthermore, they point out that cannabis has a number of medical applications, such as the reduction of the nausea and vomiting that often accompany chemotherapy for cancer. It may also be effective as an anticonvulsant and useful for treating glaucoma (a disorder involving increased pressure in the eyeball that can lead to blindness). The fact that cannabis has medical uses but is an illegal drug has resulted in a number of court cases in which patients sought to have the drug made available on a prescription basis.

Critics have argued that the use of cannabis leads to increased violence, higher rates of abnormal behavior, the use of more dangerous drugs, and overall reductions in motivation. Those accusations were widespread in the 1930s and were in large part responsible for the passage of laws such as the Marijuana Tax Act that restricted the use of cannabis. However, it was more recently concluded that "there is absolutely no systematic data to support the myth" that cannabis use leads to violence (McKim, 1986, p. 228). Indeed, long-term studies in controlled hospital settings have never provided evidence that cannabis use leads to violence. Instead, mood ratings indicated decreased feelings of hostility and increased feelings of friendliness when cannabis was used.

In sharp contrast to the preceding findings, there is evidence that using cannabis can exacerbate the symptoms of schizophrenia. Specifically, although the occasional smoking of small or moderate amounts of cannabis will not lead to schizophrenia in most individuals, it can trigger a relapse among individuals who

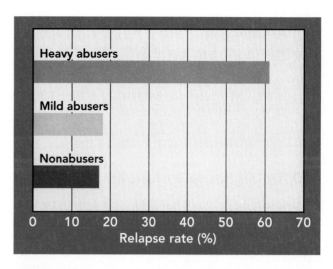

FIGURE 17.2 Cannabis use is associated with relapse of schizophrenia.
Source: Data from Linszen et al. (1994), p. 276.

have recovered from the disorder (Linszen et al., 1994; Martinez-Arevalo et al., 1994). For example, in a follow-up study of individuals who had recovered from schizophrenia, it was found that the relapse rates were 61% for heavy users, 18% for mild users, and 17% for nonusers. Those results are summarized in Figure 17.2. There were no other differences among the groups that could account for the differences in relapse rates, and the connection between the use of cannabis and relapse is strengthened by the fact that in most cases, the psychotic symptoms increased immediately after the cannabis was taken.

Why does cannabis increase the symptoms of schizophrenia? The answer lies in the fact that one of the active ingredients in cannabis serves to *enhance the activity of dopamine* in the nerve tracts that lead to the frontal lobes of the cortex (Gardner & Lowinson, 1991), and you will recall from the discussion of schizophrenia that high levels of dopamine activity in those tracts are one of the causes of schizophrenia (see Chapter 12). In that regard, it is interesting to note that the primary effect of cannabis was to increase the *positive symptoms* of schizophrenia such as hallucinations, delusions, disturbances of thought processes, which are the symptoms that are most influenced by dopamine activity. The connection between cannabis use and the exacerbation of symptoms is clearly reflected in the comments of an individual with a history of a serious delusional disorder (this is the individual who was featured in Case Study 11.6). The person is now functioning normally but made the following comments concerning the consequences of smoking cannabis:

I do not smoke marijuana because when I do, all of my paranoid symptoms come back. I have never experienced a "nice high" like many of my friends have. In an attempt to understand what happens, I have smoked alone with a tape recorder so I could record what happens. However, it all happens so fast that I freak out and go into a paranoid panic. I check the house for bugs and of course I turn the tape recorder off! All of the behaviors are present that I experienced during my rough moments without the drug—and that's no fun. I simply don't smoke marijuana anymore.

LSD, Psilocybin, and Mescaline

The remaining group of hallucinogens contains a wide variety of drugs, but probably the best known and most widely used are **LSD (lysergic acid)**, which is a synthetically produced drug; **psilocybin** (sī-luh-SĪ-bin), which is found in the *Psilocybe mexicana* mushrooms of Mexico; and **mescaline,** which comes from small button-like growths on the peyote cactus of Mexico and the southwestern desert of the United States (Strassman, 1995).

These drugs come from very different sources and have very different modes of action, and the effects of any one drug may be quite variable from individual to individual and from time to time for any one individual. However, they generally result in periods of dramatically changed sensory experiences. Colors are brighter, sounds are more intense, and shapes are often distorted. Because everything is so different, it is like taking a trip to a different world, and for that reason the period of the drug effect is called a "trip." Trips usually last between 4 and 8 hours.

The changes in perception and feelings of being transported lead to a variety of emotional experiences such as depersonalization and detachment. If the changed perceptions are pleasant, the trip can be enjoyable and exciting, but if the changed perceptions are unpleasant, the trip can be terrifying and traumatic. "Bad trips" get most of the public attention because they can lead to dangerous acts or hospitalization. However, even "good trips" can lead to serious consequences, as in the case of a young woman who thought she had supernatural powers and jumped out of a 12-story window in an attempt to fly. We do not understand what makes some trips enjoyable and others terrifying, but the individual's mood or expectations when beginning the trip appear to play some role.

In the 1960s, it was thought that hallucinogens caused brief periods of schizophrenia and that the hallucinogens and hallucinogenic experiences might be helpful for understanding schizophrenia. However, we now know that the causes and nature of the hallucinogenic experience are very different from schizophrenia, and consequently the use of hallucinogens to study schizophrenia has been abandoned. However, there is one very important exception to that; the drug phencyclidine, which is better known as PCP or "angel dust,"

can lead to schizophrenia and as such *is very dangerous* (Olney & Farber, 1995).

It was also once thought that hallucinogens might help people discover important personal insights about themselves, and therefore hallucinogens were sometimes used as an adjunct to psychotherapy. That also turned out to be erroneous. What seemed important to the drug user while taking the drug turned out to be silly, meaningless, or wrong when the drug wore off.

Physiological Processes. Hallucinogens are taken orally, absorbed through the digestive tract, and then carried to the brain via the bloodstream. Most hallucinogens are structurally similar to certain neurotransmitters in the brain (e.g., LSD and psilocybin are similar to serotonin, and mescaline is similar to norepinephrine), and it is assumed that once in the brain, they stimulate the postsynaptic receptor sites that are normally stimulated by the neurotransmitters they resemble (Jacobs, 1987; McKim, 1986). The fact that the hallucinogens generate such a wide variety of effects can probably be attributed to the fact that the nerves they stimulate are very basic and interconnect and stimulate many other nerve networks, thereby setting in motion a cascade of complex neurological activity.

Problems of Misuse. The use of LSD, psilocybin, and mescaline has a number of negative consequences. First, during the trip, individuals may do things that are dangerous to themselves or others. An example of this is the woman who jumped out a window because she thought she could fly. Second, at least 5% of the individuals who use LSD experience **flashbacks,** which are sudden and uncontrollable recurrences of perceptual distortions like those experienced during the trip (Abraham & Aldridge, 1993; Smith & Seymour, 1994). These are particularly frightening because the individual does not understand what is happening or why. After experiencing a flashback, the individual may become chronically anxious, worry about having another one, and worry about losing control in a potentially dangerous situation. We do not yet know why flashbacks occur. Third, there is some evidence that LSD can result in chromosomal damage, and thus its use poses serious problems for children born to hallucinogen users. Finally, hallucinogens are generally not physiologically addictive, but some individuals become psychologically dependent on the drugs as a means of escaping from the tedium of their everyday lives.

In summary, the major effect of hallucinogens such as cannabis (marijuana), LSD, psilocybin, and mescaline is to distort sensory experiences by interfering with neural transmission in the brain. These drugs are probably not physiologically addicting, but individuals can become psychologically dependent on them for pleasure and escape. The problems posed by the use of hallucinogens include foolish and dangerous behaviors, flashbacks, and the exacerbation of symptoms of schizophrenia.

This concludes our discussion of the various substances on which individuals become dependent. In the next section, I will examine the important question of why some individuals abuse and become dependent on drugs.

EXPLANATIONS FOR DRUG USE AND ABUSE

Accounting for substance abuse or dependence has always been a thorny problem, and explanations have ranged from the moral (those who abuse drugs are "bad" people) to the medical (those who abuse drugs are trying to overcome an underlying physiological problem) (Petraitis et al., 1995). The major conflict is over the question of whether drug abuse is *voluntary misbehavior* or an *illness*. The misbehavior explanation received some legal support in a Supreme Court decision concerning alcoholism. That case revolved around the fact that veterans must use their educational benefits within 10 years of completing their military service. However, two veterans who had not used their benefits asked for an extension based on the fact that they had been suffering from alcoholism and therefore had not been able to use the benefits. The Veterans Administration denied their request on the grounds that alcoholism was "willful misconduct" and not an illness. When the men appealed the case to the Supreme Court, the justices concluded that they were not in a position to decide whether or not alcoholism was an illness, but they voted 4 to 3 to affirm the right of the Veterans Administration to label alcoholism "willful misconduct." Even the justices who considered alcoholism an illness agreed that "the consumption of alcohol is not regarded as wholly involuntary." This ruling lent credence to the misbehavior explanation for alcoholism, but it should be noted that the ruling was a *court opinion* and not a *scientific fact*. The justices admitted that they were not in a position to come up with a better conclusion, so they simply let stand the prevailing "misbehavior" opinion. Our task in this section will be to determine whether substance abuse and dependence are due to willful misconduct or whether there is a better explanation.

There are a number of explanations for substance dependence, and I will discuss each of them. Initially, it may appear that the explanations are independent and compete with one another, but as we have found in our attempts to explain other disorders, it may be that there is a common element that is simply being viewed from different perspectives.

Exposure

Early theorists assumed that exposure to drugs and initial light usage would necessarily lead to substance-related disorders. It was that orientation that led early antidrug crusaders to predict that one puff on a marijuana cigarette would ultimately lead to opium dens and heroin addiction.

Of course, exposure is *necessary* for a problem to develop but is not *sufficient* to explain drug problems. Convincing evidence for that comes from the fact that among the soldiers who became dependent on heroin while in Vietnam, only 12% relapsed within 3 years of their return to the United States (Robins et al., 1974; Robins et al., 1975). The drugs were still available at home, but the life situations of the veterans had changed, so their patterns of drug usage changed. (For a review of other evidence contradicting the exposure explanation, see Alexander & Hadaway, 1982, and Craig, 1995.)

Situational Factors

It is possible that situational factors such as stress or boredom might lead to drug abuse. For example, an individual in a stressful job may drink too much or take excessive numbers of sleeping pills to escape the stress, and an individual who has nothing to do and is bored may look for "kicks" with stimulants or take "trips" with hallucinogens. Also, an individual who is trapped in the slums may abuse drugs in an attempt to temporarily escape an intolerable situation.

The effects of situational factors on drug abuse were clearly demonstrated in experiments in which laboratory animals were given free access to drugs in their cages. The interesting finding was that animals that were housed alone in standard laboratory cages consumed 16 times more morphine than animals who were housed in a large colony of other animals (Alexander et al., 1978; Alexander et al., 1981; Hadaway et al., 1979). It appears that the restricted, isolated conditions of the standard cages may have been stressful for mobile and social animals like rats and monkeys, and their drug use may have been a response to the stressful situation. The very high rate of substance abuse and dependence among soldiers serving in Vietnam may have been due to the high stress of that situation, and the lessening of stress on returning to the United States may account for the substantial drop-off in drug use among the veterans. Those who continued to abuse drugs may have been those for whom the conditions in the United States were also stressful (e.g., lack of jobs, broken homes).

From these results, it appears that situational factors do contribute to substance abuse and dependence, but situational factors do not account for all of the problems because there are many individuals who exist in stressful, boring, or otherwise unpleasant situations who do not turn to drugs. Why are only some individuals affected? Let us consider family and personality factors that might predispose individuals to substance abuse.

Family Characteristics

Theorists have long suspected that family characteristics during childhood predispose individuals to later drug abuse. Often-cited factors are poor role models, lack of discipline, and stress in the form of family disorganization (divorce, separation, inappropriate punishment) from which the child might want to escape through the use of drugs. To determine whether family characteristics are related to alcoholism, numerous prospective investigations have been conducted in which families were studied and then the children were followed up as adults and examined for alcoholism. A review of the results of those investigations revealed that children who went on to develop alcoholism (a) were raised in homes with more marital conflict, (b) received inadequate parenting, and (c) had parents who were more likely to be alcoholic, sexually deviant, or antisocial (see Zucker & Gomberg, 1986).

Many of the parental behaviors that were related to drug use by their children could be labeled as *antisocial,* so the role of the antisocial personality disorder in parents deserves attention. On the one hand, it is possible that antisocial parents could serve as bad role models for their children and that one of the inappropriate behaviors that the children learn is substance abuse. In that way, parental behavior could cause substance abuse. On the other hand, it is also possible that the antisocial behavior of the parents and the antisocial behavior (drug abuse) of the children is due to a third factor, *shared genes.* In our discussion of the antisocial personality disorder in Chapter 14, it was pointed out that the disorder is due in large part to genetic factors, and therefore antisocial parents may contribute to antisocial behavior and drug abuse through gene transmission instead of or in addition to role modeling and parenting.

Personality

Antisocial Behavior and Impulsivity.
In seeking an explanation for drug abuse, a considerable amount of early research was devoted to identifying an *addictive personality* (see Nathan, 1988; Sutker & Allain, 1988). A unique addictive personality was not found, but the research did reveal two consistent findings that are important. The first is that *antisocial behavior and impulsivity* in childhood and adolescence are related to substance abuse in adulthood (Nathan, 1988; Sher & Trull,

1994). Specifically, children and adolescents who are frequently in trouble, show poor impulse control, do not value conventional institutions, and are independent, aggressive, and pleasure-seeking are more likely to abuse drugs as adults than children who do not have those characteristics.

The question then arises, what causes the antisocial behavior pattern of which substance abuse is a part? One possibility that was mentioned earlier is that the behavior is learned from antisocial parents or other role models. A second possibility is that individuals who are antisocial and abuse drugs suffer from the antisocial personality disorder. You will recall from Chapter 14 that in most cases, that disorder appears to be due to a low level of neurological arousal that results in a low level of anxiety, which in turn reduces inhibitions and permits antisocial behavior. The low level of neurological arousal may play a role in reducing restraints against drug abuse, and it may also contribute to drug abuse because underaroused individuals may use drugs to raise their arousal levels (perhaps simply to the normal levels experienced by other people). Indeed, when individuals with the antisocial personality disorder abuse drugs, they are most likely to use stimulants. Thus we can conclude that the antisocial personality disorder may lead to a lack of restraints against using drugs and a physiological need for drugs to increase arousal.

Depression.
The second personality factor that has been consistently related to substance abuse is *depression.* However, there is some question about whether the depression is a cause or an effect of substance abuse. In some cases, depressed individuals use stimulants as an antidote for their depression, as Freud took cocaine, or they may take depressants to deaden their senses and thereby avoid their problems. However, in other cases, individuals become depressed because of the problems caused by their substance abuse (loss of jobs and friends).

Differences in Personality and Patterns of Abuse.
The findings linking both antisocial behavior and depression to substance abuse may seem inconsistent at first because antisocial behavior is not usually associated with depression. The explanation for the inconsistency lies in the possibility that substance abuse may be associated with antisocial behavior *or* depression rather than the two in combination. In other words, there may be two different personality types related to substance abuse, antisocial and depressive.

Support for the notion that two different personality patterns may be linked independently to substance abuse was supported by research in which it was found that there are *two types of alcoholism* and that the different types are associated with *different personality charac-*

TABLE 17.3 Characteristics of Individuals Who Suffer from the Persistent and Binge Types of Alcoholism

Persistent Type	Binge Type
Early onset (before age 25)	Late onset (after age 25)
Persistent	Periods of abstinence
Moderate to heavy	Severe binges
Cannot abstain	Cannot stop binges
Lack of anxiety	Anxious
Impulsive	Inhibited
Risk-taking	Cautious
Novelty-seeking	Shy
Independent	Dependent
Distractible	Depressed
Antisocial	Socially sensitive
Equally prevalent in men and women	More prevalent in women
Persons are physiologically under-aroused; frequent low doses of alcohol serve as stimulants that increase arousal.	Persons are physiologically overaroused; high doses of alcohol during binges serve as depressants that decrease arousal.

teristics (Cloninger, 1987; Gallant, 1990; Penick et al., 1990; Sullivan et al., 1990). One type of alcoholism is characterized by *persistent drinking* at moderate to heavy levels. In those cases, it appears that the individual does not have the ability to abstain from using alcohol regularly. We will refer to this as the **persistent type of alcoholism.**

The persistent type of alcoholism is associated with impulsivity, lack of anxiety, risk taking, novelty seeking, independence, distractibility, and antisocial behavior. In other words, individuals with the persistent type of alcoholism are uninhibited and seem to suffer from at least a mild form of the antisocial personality disorder. These personality characteristics are generally associated with *neurological underarousal* (see Chapter 14), and it is assumed that the individuals use alcohol persistently but at low levels to increase their arousal to optimal or normal levels. Recall that at low levels, alcohol is a stimulant.

In contrast, the other type of alcoholism is characterized by *long periods of abstinence* during which the individual is able to control the drinking, but once drinking begins, the individual *cannot stop,* and the drinking takes the form of a *binge.* We will call this the **binge type of alcoholism.**

Individuals with the binge type of alcoholism are characterized as anxious, inhibited, cautious, shy, dependent, depressed, and emotionally sensitive. It is assumed that these individuals are neurologically overaroused and that the high levels of alcohol they con-

sume during a binge serve to reduce arousal. Recall that at high levels, alcohol is a depressant. The characteristics associated with the persistent and binge types of alcoholism are summarized in Table 17.3. The persistent and binge types are usually discussed as though they were distinct types, but they are probably the endpoints of a continuum.

In summary, there is now consistent evidence linking the antisocial personality pattern and depression to substance abuse, and there is reason to believe that the link between personality and substance abuse may be due to underlying differences in arousal. Low levels of arousal lead to low levels of anxiety, uninhibited behavior, and the use of substances to increase arousal. In contrast, high levels of arousal lead to high levels of anxiety, inhibitions, and the use of substances to reduce arousal.

Anxiety Reduction

It has long been argued that the consumption of alcohol *reduces anxiety* and therefore leads to more consumption. The anxiety reduction explanation was originally based on research with laboratory animals in which it was found that stressors such as electrical shocks increased alcohol consumption and that the animals would come closer to a feared stimulus if they had been given alcohol (Conger, 1951; Freed, 1971; Wright et al., 1971). Similar results have been reported with humans (Sher & Levenson, 1982). It appears that

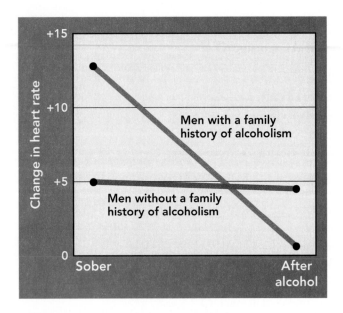

FIGURE 17.3 Alcohol reduced stress-induced arousal in males with a family history of alcoholism.
Source: Adapted from Finn et al. (1990), p. 83, fig. 2.

alcohol can reduce anxiety, and the question we must answer here is why.

The first explanation is that alcohol reduces anxiety because it is a *physiological depressant*, and as such it can reduce the arousal we label as anxiety. In one study, males who either did or did not have a family history of alcoholism were exposed to stressful electrical shocks while sober or after drinking alcohol (Finn et al., 1990). For the men who had a family history of alcoholism, drinking alcohol greatly reduced their responsiveness to the stressful stimuli. In contrast, the alcohol did not affect the responsiveness of the men who did not have a family history of alcoholism. The results for heart rate are presented in Figure 17.3. These results clearly indicate that at least among individuals with a family history of alcoholism, alcohol can reduce arousal or anxiety.

The second explanation is that alcohol reduces anxiety because it *impairs cognitive functioning* (information processing) that is essential for recognizing the existence of a problem (Steele & Josephs, 1988; Steele et al., 1986). For example, individuals who are drunk cannot focus their attention clearly and therefore may not be aware of problems. You may have noticed that individuals who have been drinking tend to focus on one or two ideas and ignore other ideas that may be more relevant or more important. If they do not attend to all of the relevant factors in their environment, they may not see or remember a problem that is anxiety-provoking.

Third, alcohol may reduce anxiety because it *enhances positive feelings.* There is evidence that the stimulating effects of small doses of alcohol reduce anxiety

because they lead to more feelings of energy, power, well-being, and confidence (Yankofsky et al., 1986). In summary, alcohol can reduce anxiety through physiological sedation, cognitive interference or distraction, and energization of positive feelings. All three types of anxiety reduction would be rewarding and could encourage drinking.

Expectations

It has also been suggested that drug use is influenced by *what the individuals expect* the drug will do for them (Aas et al., 1995; Downey & Kilbey, 1995; Evans & Dunn, 1995; Grube et al., 1995; P. B. Johnson, 1994; Jones & McMahon, 1994; Kushner et al., 1994). For example, if individuals expect that the use of a drug will help them get a lift, relax, or perform better, they are more likely to become dependent on the drug than if they do not have those expectancies. Indeed, among college freshmen, expectancies about the positive and negative effects of alcohol were good predictors of the students' levels of drinking at the end of the year; positive expectancies were linked to more drinking (Werner et al., 1995). The recent resurgence in the popularity of LSD may be due to the fact that LSD is now perceived as "safer" than other drugs, and individuals do not expect negative outcomes from its use (Gold, 1994).

In some cases, expectations about the effects of drugs can lead to *self-fulfilling prophesies* (Darkes & Goldman, 1993; Smith, Goldman, et al., 1995) For example, in a variety of experiments it was found that individuals who expected that drinking alcohol would reduce inhibitions and who then drank a nonalcoholic placebo that they thought contained alcohol showed reductions in inhibitions that were as great as individuals who drank alcohol (Cooper et al., 1992; Leigh, 1989; Wilson, 1987). In other research, individuals who thought that drinking alcohol would lead to poorer motor coordination showed poorer motor performance even when they drank a placebo that they thought was alcohol (Fillmore & Vogel-Sprott, 1995). Similarly, expectations about unpleasant nicotine withdrawal symptoms are linked to reports of higher levels of withdrawal symptoms (Tate et al., 1994). It is clear that expectations can influence the effects of drugs, so positive expectations could contribute to drug use.

Expectations can also be used to account for *uncontrolled drinking*—the possibility that one drink will necessarily lead to another and eventually to a state of drunkenness. Support for the role of expectancies in uncontrolled drinking comes from studies in which individuals were allowed to drink either alcoholic or placebo (nonalcoholic) beverages and their drinking was monitored (Berg et al., 1981). The results indicated that the best predictor of how much was drunk was not whether the beverages contained alcohol but whether the participants thought they could control their drinking; those who did not think they could control their drinking drank more, regardless of whether the drink contained alcohol. The belief that drinking cannot be controlled may account for relapses after periods of abstinence (Marlatt, 1978; Rollnick & Heather, 1982). In other words, relapse may be a self-fulfilling prophecy.

Physiological Factors

The most widely held physiological explanation for substance abuse and dependence is that some individuals are predisposed to the problem because they have *different physiological needs* or because they *process drugs differently.*

There are a variety of physiological differences between individuals who do and do not suffer from alcoholism, but the question is, are those differences a cause of the alcoholism or an effect of the long-term use of alcohol? To answer that question, many investigators now focus on the differences between the children of individuals who do or do not suffer from alcoholism (e.g., Pihl et al., 1990; Volavka et al., 1996). The logic behind this approach is as follows: (a) Alcoholism is in large part an inherited disorder, (b) parents who suffer from alcoholism pass on to their children the physiological factors that lead to alcoholism, and (c) comparing the children of parents who do and do not suffer from alcoholism *before the children begin drinking* will make it possible to identify differences that exist before the effects of drinking set in.

This type of research has revealed that the sons of parents who suffer from alcoholism have *higher levels of neurological arousal* and show *greater reductions in neurological arousal after drinking alcohol* than the sons of parents who do not suffer from alcoholism. Specifically, it has been found that *before* drinking alcohol, sons of parents who suffered from alcoholism showed brain wave activity that indicated *higher arousal,* and that *after* drinking alcohol, they showed *greater decreases* in that brain wave activity. These findings suggest that some individuals are genetically predisposed to abuse alcohol because they have unpleasantly high levels of arousal that will be reduced (perhaps to a "normal" level) by the alcohol. A similar effect was illustrated earlier with heart rate in Figure 17.3: When compared to men who did not have a family history of alcoholism, men who had a family history of alcoholism showed a greater heart rate response to stress when sober but a smaller response to stress after drinking alcohol (Finn et al., 1990).

Other evidence for genetic effects on alcoholism come from studies in which the investigators examined the rates of alcoholism in adopted children

whose biological parents either did or did not suffer from alcoholism (Searles, 1988). In one adoption study, the investigators examined two large groups of adoptees (Cadoret et al., 1986). The first group had biological relatives who had histories of either alcoholism or antisocial behavior, whereas the second group did not have biological relatives with either of those problems. When the adoptees were examined as adults, three interesting findings emerged: First, it was found that a biological family history of antisocial behavior was related to antisocial behavior in the adoptees and that the antisocial behavior in the adoptees was in turn related to the abuse of all types of drugs (stimulants, depressants, narcotics, and hallucinogens). That finding suggests that one route to drug abuse involves the inheritance of the antisocial personality disorder, which in turn leads to drug abuse. Some theorists have referred to this type of alcoholism as *secondary* or *psychopathic alcoholism* because it is mediated by the antisocial behavior (Cadoret et al., 1984).

The second finding of interest is that a biological family history of alcoholism was also related to the abuse of all types of drugs but not to any particular personality characteristic. This suggests that some individuals may have a biological predisposition to drug abuse that is independent of antisocial behavior or personality. This type of alcoholism is referred to as *primary alcoholism* because it is not mediated by personality factors.

The third noteworthy finding is that some of the adoptees who did *not* have a biological family history of antisocial behavior or alcoholism did develop drug abuse problems. Those adoptees were more likely than others to be raised in adoptive families in which there was parental discord (separation or divorce) or a disturbed parent. In other words, *situational stress* contributed to drug abuse independent of a biological family history of antisocial behavior or alcoholism. The results of this study therefore suggest that there are three routes to substance abuse: (a) a genetic predisposition that is mediated by antisocial behavior, (b) a genetic predisposition that is independent of antisocial behavior, and (c) environmental stress.

Strong evidence for the role of genetic factors in alcoholism was recently provided by a study of 1,030 monozygotic and dizygotic female twin pairs (Kendler, Heath, et al., 1992). The results indicated that the concordance rate for MZ twin pairs was 46.9%, whereas the concordance rate for DZ twin pairs was 31.5%. Using these data, the authors estimated the heritability of alcoholism to be about 60%. These findings are particularly interesting because they are based on women, whereas most other findings are based on men. In a second study of female twins and their parents, it was concluded that vulnerability to alcoholism was transmitted equally by fathers and mothers and that the transmission was due to genetic and not environmental factors (Kendler, Neale, et al., 1994).

In this discussion of physiological and genetic factors, I have focused primarily on alcoholism, but it is important to recognize that physiological and genetic factors also play important roles in the abuse of other substances. For example, studies of families and of twins have revealed that genetic factors play an important role in nicotine dependence (Breslau et al., 1993; Kendler, Neale, MacLean, et al., 1993). In the case of nicotine, it may be that genetic factors lead to a low level of arousal and that the individuals become dependent on the nicotine because it is a stimulant that brings their level of arousal up to a more normal level.

From the research reviewed in this section, it is clear that physiological factors play an important role in drug use and abuse. That is, genetic factors appear to establish different levels of arousal and different responses to drugs. The physiological factors are clearly important, but their role must be considered in context. For example, there is no evidence that physiological factors somehow take over or "commandeer" the individual and trigger uncontrollable drinking bouts (Goldman et al., 1991). Instead, it is undoubtedly the case that physiological factors establish needs for drugs and responses to drugs, and then personality and environmental factors determine whether the drugs will be used. A popular phrase associated with the treatment of substance abuse is "Just say no!" Saying no is certainly a solution, but it is important to recognize that for physiological reasons, *saying no is much harder for some individuals than it is for others,* and we must be sensitive to those differences.

Sociocultural Factors

Finally, it is essential to comment on the role of sociocultural factors in drug use. I left these factors for last not because they are unimportant but because their effects are mediated by factors such as exposure, situational variables, expectancies, and physiological differences that required comment first.

The role of sociocultural factors is clearly apparent in cultural differences in drug use. For example, consider the high consumption of wine by adults and even children in France, the high consumption of vodka in Russia, the high consumption of beer in Germany, and the generally low consumption of alcohol in areas where there are many Muslims or Mormons. Those differences in use are due to differences in the *exposure* of individuals to alcohol and to differences in *religious prohibitions* concerning the use of alcohol. The role of cultural differences in exposure is particularly clear in these examples because the differences influence both how much alcohol is consumed and the type that is consumed (e.g., wine versus vodka versus beer).

Differences in drug use across cultures and within any one culture may also be due to differences in levels of *stress.* For example, the greater level of stress and depression in lower classes may offer a partial explanation for why substance abuse is often higher in lower classes. Recognition of the class-stress-use relationship is important because it helps account for some of the ethnic differences in drug use. That is, the high level of drug use by some minority groups such as African-Americans and Native Americans may not be linked to their ethnicity per se but rather to the fact that they are more likely to be members of a lower class (Collins, 1993; D. Johnson, 1994).

It is interesting to note that there are some preliminary data indicating that dietary differences that may be related to social class may also contribute to alcohol consumption (Adams et al., 1995). In studies of rats, it was found that a low-tryptophan diet greatly increases alcohol consumption. Tryptophan is a protein found in dairy products, and a poor diet on the part of lower-class individuals might contribute to their alcohol consumption.

Finally, it should be recognized that some ethnic differences in drug use may be due to *genetic* factors. There is growing evidence that a set of genes (e.g., $ALDH_2$) is related to an individual's response to alcohol and the amount of alcohol that is consumed; that is, individuals with a specific gene have a more pleasant response to alcohol and are more likely to drink more. This is relevant to our consideration here because Asians are more likely to have this gene than members of other groups, and that might explain their expectancies concerning the effects of alcohol and their high level of alcohol consumption (O'Hare, 1995; Roberts et al., 1995; Thomasson & Li, 1993; Tu & Israel, 1995; Wall et al., 1992).

COMMENT

It is clear that a wide variety of factors can contribute to substance abuse. For example, individuals must be exposed to the drugs before the drugs can be a problem, situational factors such as stress or boredom can influence the attractiveness of drugs, an antisocial personality may lead the individual to disregard rules against taking drugs, high levels of anxiety can lead to the use of drugs to reduce the anxiety, expectations about the effects of the drugs can motivate drug taking, and physiological factors such as high or low arousal and the drugs' effects on that arousal can lead to drug use. It is interesting to note that many of the explanations for taking drugs revolve around *attempts to adjust or normalize arousal levels*—either to bring down arousal levels in stressful situations or to bring up or down genetically determined levels of arousal that are too low or too high. The notion that drugs are used to adjust arousal levels is referred to as the **self-medication hypothesis,** and it is simply an extension of what we "normally" do with drugs, as for example when we give individuals with anxiety or schizophrenia medication to reduce neurological arousal (Geekie & Brown, 1995; also see Corrigan et al., 1994; Khantzian, 1985; Meisch, 1991; Schinka et al., 1994). The difference here is that the individual writes his or her own prescription and in some cases may use drugs that are illegal. The self-medication hypothesis certainly does not account for all substance abuse, but when seeking to understand why an individual is taking a drug, it is often helpful to begin by asking what the physiological effect of the drug is and what need it might be fulfilling for the individual.

PREVENTION AND TREATMENT

Reduced Availability, Penalties, and Legalization

Four strategies are employed for solving the substance abuse problem. The first involves *eliminating the availability* of drugs so that individuals cannot begin misusing them. That can be done effectively in closed or highly controlled societies, but it is very difficult to achieve in more open societies. For example, when the Communists took over China in 1949, they simply eliminated the availability of opium and eliminated the drug problem posed by the opium dens. However, now that the government in China is reducing some of its restrictions, drug use is on the increase.

The second strategy is to use *severe penalties* for drug abuse. Proposed penalties include stiff fines, long prison sentences, and mandatory execution of individuals involved in drug-related murders. An interesting instance of a stiff fine is the confiscation of personal property associated with illegal drug use. This approach allows police officials to seize and then sell any property such as cars, boats, and planes in which even the smallest amount of drugs is found. In one case, a 133-ft, $2.5 million yacht was seized when .1 oz of marijuana was found on board. The penalty strategy breaks down because of problems with enforcement: insufficient numbers of police, long and expensive delays in prosecution, and lack of space in facilities to incarcerate all of the convicted offenders.

The third strategy is the *legalization of drug use.* This strategy essentially says, "If you can't beat 'em, join 'em," and making drug use legal at least eliminates the criminal element. Most drugs are easy and cheap to produce, and they are expensive only because they are illegal. If they were made legal, the profit and crime associated with them would be eliminated, and people

who abused drugs could be identified, helped, or at least provided with safer drugs and procedures. This approach is used in England, where heroin addicts are registered and provided with heroin or a heroin substitute. Although this strategy may eliminate the crime associated with drug abuse, it does not reduce the drug abuse, and if drug abuse is tolerated, it is possible that increasing numbers of individuals will begin using drugs, which could have a negative overall effect on society. Some critics have charged that legalization of heroin use in England has resulted in increased numbers of heroin users.

Treatment

The fourth strategy for dealing with drug abuse problems involves treatment, and there are four different approaches to treatment: *self-control, maintenance, blocking,* and *correction.*

Self-Control. The **self-control approach to treatment** is based on the assumption that substance abuse is due to a "weakness of character," and the treatment involves using moral suasion and social support to help the individual avoid the use of drugs. The self-control approach is used by Alcoholics Anonymous and by Synanon, the latter of which is a program designed for individuals who are addicted to opiates (McCrady, 1994). Unfortunately, gaining and maintaining self-control is very difficult for substance abusers. In fact, Synanon claims that only 10% of the treated individuals maintain abstinence. Even that may be an overly optimistic figure because Synanon accepts only highly motivated clients who are most likely to improve. As noted earlier, physiological factors may make self-control very difficult for some individuals, so it is not surprising that this approach is often ineffective.

In one interesting experiment, the investigators tested to determine whether rewards might be effective for keeping individuals off cocaine (Higgins et al., 1994). The individuals who participated in the experiment were cocaine-dependent adults in a treatment program for cocaine abuse, and they had urine specimens tested for cocaine three times per week. The individuals were randomly assigned to two groups, reward and no reward. For each individual in the reward group, the first urine specimen that tested negative for cocaine was worth $2.50, and each additional consecutive negative specimen was worth an additional $1.25, so, for example, the sixth consecutive negative specimen was worth $8.75. Furthermore, a bonus of $10.00 was paid for every three consecutive negative specimens, so six consecutive negative specimens were worth a total of $28.75. The presence of a positive urine specimen caused the reward level to be reset at $2.50. The individuals in the no-reward group did not receive

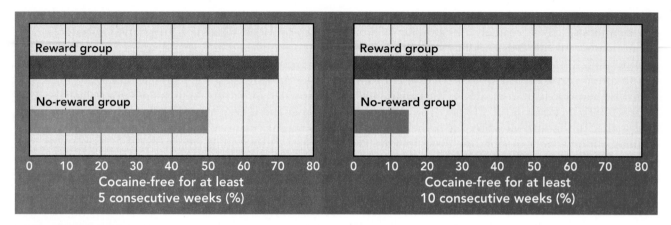

FIGURE 17.4 **Rewards were effective for reducing cocaine use.**
Source: Data from Higgins et al. (1994), p. 572.

rewards for negative specimens. The results indicated that 70% of the individuals in the reward group were continuously cocaine-free for at least 5 weeks, whereas only 50% of the individuals in the no-reward group showed that level of improvement. The results of this experiment are summarized in Figure 17.4. Those results clearly indicate that the use of rewards can be an effective strategy for reducing drug abuse, but the procedures raise an interesting question: Should individuals be given substantial rewards for doing what they should be doing anyway? If you are not on cocaine now, should we start paying you? That is an interesting philosophical question, but the bottom line here is that

Persons who are dependent on heroin may be given methadone to help forestall withdrawal symptoms and begin the weaning process. However, the results of research on this method of treating heroin addiction are discouraging.

behavior that is illegal and dangerous can be brought under control with a system of rewards.

Maintenance. The **maintenance approach to treatment** involves giving individuals a relatively harmless substitute for the substance on which they are dependent. In the case of heroin addiction, a substitute called **methadone** (Dolopine) is used (Rosenbaum, 1995). Methadone prevents the painful effects of withdrawal, and therefore the individuals do not need to resort to illegal behavior to get drugs to avoid the feared withdrawal. Important too is the fact that methadone partially blocks the opiate receptors, so taking heroin produces weaker positive effects (Jaffe, 1995). Heroin could in fact be used in maintenance therapy (as is sometimes done in Britain), but there are three advantages in using methadone: (a) The methadone can be taken orally and therefore avoids the problems associated with needles; (b) it puts off withdrawal symptoms for 24 hours rather than 8 hours with heroin, so it needs be taken only once a day; and (c) it partially blocks the effects of heroin, so if heroin is taken to obtain a rush, its effects are somewhat diminished. Although addicted individuals can be kept on methadone indefinitely, the goal is to wean them slowly from the drug. This is difficult, however, because eventually withdrawal symptoms set in.

The maintenance approach to treatment is based on two assumptions. The first is that the addiction probably cannot be cured and that its most serious effect is to force many individuals into illegal behavior to support their habits. Providing addicted individuals with methadone eliminates their need to get opiates to avoid withdrawal and therefore indirectly protects society. The second assumption is that continued opiate use is due primarily to the fear of withdrawal rather than the pleasure derived from the drugs. Methadone does eliminate the withdrawal symptoms, but it does not provide the pleasurable sensations of heroin.

The results of research concerning the effects of methadone maintenance are mixed. One explanation for the sometimes weak effects of the maintenance approach is that although methadone reduces the fear of withdrawal, it does not provide the pleasure that the heroin does. If continued opiate use is due even in part to the pleasure derived from the drug, methadone is doing only part of the job. A second explanation for treatment failures is that the patients may not have been given high enough doses of methadone (Hartel et al., 1995; Ward et al., 1994). Indeed, there is now consistent evidence that higher levels of methadone are related to higher levels of treatment success, probably because at low levels the methadone does not adequately block the effects of heroin, so individuals on low levels can still occasionally use heroin to get high.

The use of nicotine patches, gum, or inhalants for treating nicotine dependence is a type of maintenance treatment. The patches and gum deliver a constant low level of nicotine into the bloodstream, thereby eliminating the need to smoke. Inhalants can be used to get nicotine on an as-needed basis. This approach can be quite effective for reducing nicotine withdrawal symptoms when smoking is stopped and thus is helpful in smoking treatment programs (Cepeda-Benito, 1993; Fiore et al., 1992; Fortmann & Killen, 1995; Hatsukami et al., 1995; Hughes et al., 1991; Killen et al., 1990; Kornitzer et al., 1995). Indeed, in a long-term follow-up, the combination of patch use and traditional psychological treatments such as group support for smoking was found to be more than 50% more effective than the psychological treatments alone. However, eventually the individual must be weaned off of the patch or the gum, and that can result in withdrawal symptoms and relapse (Hatsukami et al., 1995; Hurt et al., 1995). In other words, substituting the patch or gum for the cigarettes eliminates the use of cigarettes, but it does not overcome the problem of nicotine dependence.

Blocking. The **blocking approach to treatment** was developed because continued substance abuse may be due to the pleasure derived from taking the drugs. With the blocking approach, individuals are given drugs that block the positive effects of the substances that are being abused or cause the individual to become nauseated (Kosten & Kosten, 1991). For example, in the case of heroin addiction, the person is given an **opiate antagonist** (naloxone), which completely blocks the effects of heroin, thereby eliminating the pleasure it usually provides. Opiate antagonists work by fitting into the opiate receptors, thus shutting out the opiates so that they cannot have any effect. Opiate antagonists are also effective for treating alcoholism because some of the pleasure derived from alcohol is due to the stimulation of the opiate system, so blocking that system can help reduce alcohol consumption

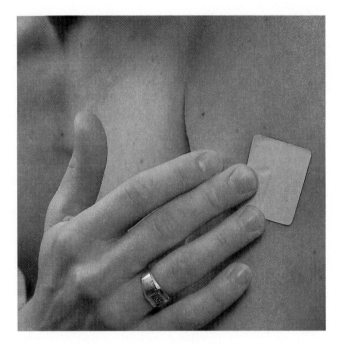

The use of patches for nicotine dependence is a form of treatment through maintenance. The patches deliver a low level of nicotine into the bloodstream, thereby eliminating the craving to smoke.

(O'Malley et al., 1992, 1996; Swift et al., 1994; Volpicelli et al., 1992).

In a somewhat different approach to blocking, an individual suffering from alcoholism may be given Antabuse (disulfiram), a drug that will cause severe nausea and vomiting if alcohol is drunk, thus not only eliminating alcohol's positive effects but also producing distinctly negative effects. The results of this type of treatment are mixed (Elkins, 1991). Individuals do stop taking the forbidden drugs while they are taking the antagonist, but once out of the clinic, they often stop taking the antagonist so that they can again derive pleasure from the drugs and then go back to using the forbidden drugs. However, a more powerful version of disulfiram was patented recently that might be used in patches or inserts that would slowly release the medication into an individual's system. Those delivery systems might make it more difficult to stop taking the medication and increase the effectiveness of the approach.

Correction. The fourth strategy is the **correction approach to treatment,** which involves correcting the problem that initially led to the abuse (Acierno et al., 1994). That may involve changing an entire lifestyle or removing an individual from a social environment that is contributing to the drug use. In many cases, that may be very difficult or not realistically possible, and hence many attempts to overcome substance-related disorders with correction have been rather ineffective.

SUMMARY

- Psychoactive drugs alter mood, awareness of the external environment, or awareness of the internal environment.
- A number of factors other than the drug per se influence the effects of a drug:
  1. Dose-dependent effects refer to the fact that drugs can have different effects at different dose levels.
  2. Factors such as personality, previous experience, and genetics can influence a drug's effects on an individual.
  3. Drugs taken in combination can have a greater effect than the simple sum of their separate effects.
  4. Tolerance refers to the fact that increasing amounts of a drug may have to be taken to achieve a given effect.
  5. Cross-tolerance refers to the fact that taking a drug of one type will lead to tolerance for other drugs of that type.
- Four factors can lead to a diagnosis of substance-related disorder:
  1. *Abuse* occurs when taking a drug leads to impairment or distress.
  2. *Intoxication* involves reversible symptoms such as impaired judgment that result from taking a drug.
  3. *Withdrawal*—the onset of unpleasant physical symptoms—occurs when the level of the drug is reduced.
  4. *Dependence* occurs when the individual must take a drug to avoid withdrawal symptoms.
- Substance-related disorders are organized first in terms of the drug that is involved and then in terms of the problems its use causes (abuse, intoxication, withdrawal, dependence).
- Depressants include alcohol, barbiturates, and benzodiazepines. At low levels, they reduce arousal, but at high levels, they can produce a rush. Misuse can cause withdrawal symptoms and even death because respiration is stopped.
- Narcotics include opium, morphine, and heroin, which are all derived from the seeds of the poppy. At low levels, they dull or numb the senses and bring on a sleeplike state, but at high levels, they can produce a rush. Misuse can cause withdrawal symptoms and even death because respiration is stopped.
- Stimulants include amphetamines, cocaine, caffeine, and nicotine. At low levels, they increase arousal, and at high levels, they produce a high. Misuse leads to withdrawal symptoms (e.g., depression, amphetamine psychoses), dangerous behavior, and possibly death. Nicotine can act as both a stimulant and a depressant.
- Hallucinogens include cannabis, LSD, psilocybin, and mescaline. They distort sensory experiences. Their use is not linked to withdrawal symptoms, but it can lead to dangerous behavior, flashbacks, and exacerbation or relapse of schizophrenia.
- Exposure to drugs is necessary but not sufficient to lead to substance-related disorders.
- Situational factors such as stress or boredom can lead to drug usage but cannot account for all cases.
- Family characteristics, particularly antisocial parents, are linked to drug use, and the underlying mechanism may be modeling or shared genes.
- Personality, particularly antisocial behavior and depression, are linked to drug use. The lack of anxiety in the antisocial personality disorder may permit drug taking. Antisocial behavior and depression may be linked to different patterns of drug use (e.g., persistent versus binge drinking, respectively) that are used to adjust ("normalize") underlying levels of arousal.
- Anxiety reduction may play a role in drug use because some drugs reduce arousal, distract the individual, or induce positive feelings.

- Expectations influence drug use because they influence individuals' beliefs about the positive and negative effects of drugs. In some cases, expectations can lead to self-fulfilling prophecies.
- Physiological factors such as genetically determined high or low levels of arousal and genetically determined differences in the effects that drugs have on individuals (e.g., greater arousal reduction in some individuals) can influence drug use.
- Sociocultural factors are linked to drug use, but the links appear to be due to differences in factors such as exposure, tolerance, stress levels, expectancies, and possibly genetic factors.
- Strategies for reducing drug use have included reducing the availability of drugs, imposing severe penalties for possessing drugs, and advocating the legalization of drugs.
- Four approaches have been used for treating drug abuse:
  1. Self-control involves moral suasion and social support. This is the basis for Alcoholics Anonymous.
  2. Maintenance involves giving the individual a harmless substitute for the dangerous drug that is being abused. Examples include methadone and the nicotine patch.
  3. Blocking involves giving the individual a drug that will block the effects of the drug that is being abused, thus rendering it ineffective and useless.
  4. Therapy is sometimes used to correct the personal problem that led to the drug use.

KEY TERMS, CONCEPTS, AND NAMES

In reviewing and testing yourself on what you have learned from this chapter, you should be able to identify and discuss each of the following.

abuse
alcohol
amphetamine psychoses
amphetamines
barbiturates
benzodiazepines
binge type of alcoholism
blocking approach to treatment
caffeine
cannabinoids
cannabis
cocaine
codeine
correction approach to treatment
cross-tolerance

dependence
depressants
dose-dependent effects
flashbacks
hallucinogens
hashish
hash oil
heroin
intoxication
LSD (lysergic acid)
maintenance approach to treatment
marijuana
mescaline
methadone
methylxanthines

morphine
narcotics
nicotine
opiate antagonist
opiates
opium
persistent type of alcoholism
psilocybin
psychoactive drugs
self-control approach to treatment
self-medication hypothesis
stimulants
tolerance
withdrawal

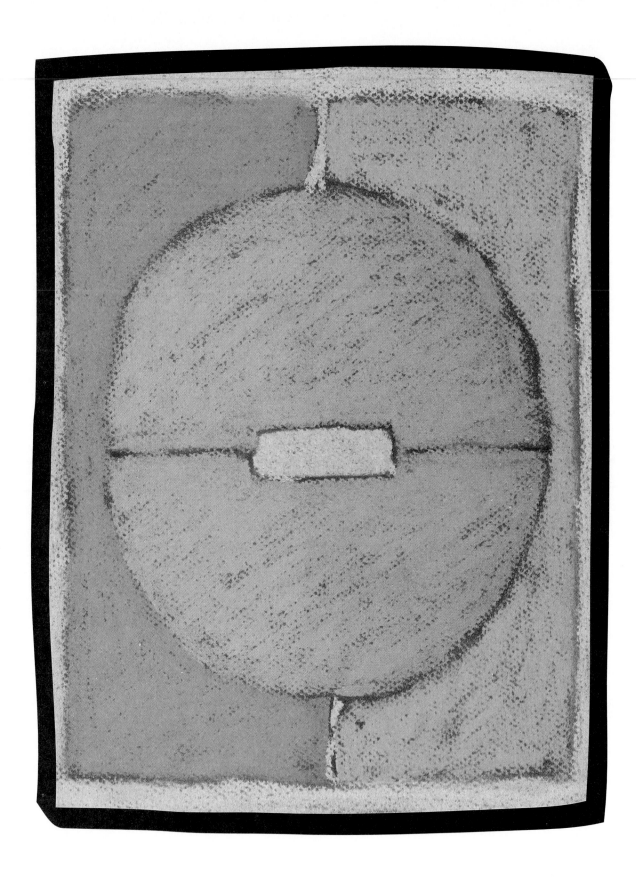

CHAPTER EIGHTEEN
SEXUAL and GENDER IDENTITY DISORDERS

OUTLINE

Ken is worried about his sex life—or more accurately, his lack of sex life. There are a lot of good-looking women around, and a few have "put a move on him," but he just isn't interested in sex. Good friendships with women are fine, but unlike most of the other guys his age, he has little or no sexual desire. He knows he is not gay, but he worries about his lack of interest in women. Ken suffers from a *sexual dysfunction* known as a *desire disorder.*

■　■　■

Alice is a 33-year-old woman who has always enjoyed sex. The problem is that during intercourse, she cannot reach orgasm, regardless of how long the sexual activity is maintained. She is confused because she can achieve orgasm easily through masturbation. Alice does not blame her sexual partners and instead assumes that she has some "unconscious problem" about men. This is beginning to interfere with her relationships. Alice suffers from a very common and easily treated sexual dysfunction known as an *orgasmic disorder.*

■　■　■

Margaret and her husband love each other very much and would not think of hurting each other. However, for Margaret to become sexually aroused, it is necessary for her husband to slap her face and twist her arm behind her back until it hurts. He does not like doing it, but Margaret wants him to do it, and it is the only way she can become aroused, so they have gone through this ritual every time they have had sex for the past 8 years. Margaret suffers from *sexual masochism.*

■　■　■

Carl has had sexual relationships with a couple of women, but his favorite way of achieving sexual gratification is to dress in women's clothing and then masturbate. Wearing the women's clothing is very exciting for him, and he has three different outfits hidden in the bottom drawer of his dresser. This is an example of *transvestic fetishism.*

■　■　■

As long as Daniel can remember, he has wanted to be a girl. As a child, he preferred to play with girls, and when they played house, he wanted to be the mother. When the other boys in the neighborhood called him a sissy, he didn't care; he thought boys were disgusting. In adolescence, Daniel tried to "become a man," but it just didn't "feel right." Later he drifted back and forth across the sex-role line. He would try to play the traditional male role in public, but in private or with close friends, he took the role of a woman and was more comfortable. Now age 30, he says he is tired of "fighting the battle of who I am" and is being considered for sex reassignment surgery. He says, "On the outside I may have a penis, but inside I am a woman, and that is who I like being, so let's change the outside." Daniel has the *gender identity disorder.*

■　■　■

In this chapter I will consider three types of disorders that are associated with sex. The first type is known as *sexual dysfunctions,* which involve insufficient sexual *desire,* insufficient sexual *arousal,* and problems with *orgasm.* Second, I will discuss *paraphilias,* which are disorders in which individuals achieve sexual arousal through *inappropriate means.* For example, individuals may gain sexual pleasure from exposing their genitals to others, dressing in the clothes of the opposite sex, or hurting their sexual partners. The third type is called the *gender identity disorder,* and individuals with this disorder have a *strong cross-gender identification that is accompanied by discomfort with their own physiologically determined sex.* For example, a male may believe that he would be more comfortable if he were a woman, or he may believe that he actually is a woman. The types of sexual and gender identity disorders are summarized in Table 18.1.

When discussing sexual disorders, it is important to distinguish between *illegal* behaviors and *abnormal* behaviors. Illegal behaviors are not necessarily abnormal, and vice versa. For example, oral sex is illegal in many states, but it is not defined as abnormal in DSM-IV. In contrast, wearing clothes of the opposite sex to gain sexual pleasure is not illegal, but it is defined as abnormal. In this chapter, the focus will be on abnormal behaviors.

It is also important to note that sociocultural factors play an important role in determining what is defined as abnormal. That was clearly illustrated with the case of homosexuality. Specifically, up until 1980, homosexuality was identified as a disorder in the DSM, but then, as attitudes toward homosexuality changed, it was considered a disorder only if it made the individual anxious or uncomfortable. That is, the focus was changed from the homosexual behavior itself to the feelings it generated. Finally, as attitudes became even more liberal, in 1987 *homosexuality was dropped as a disorder in DSM.* Similarly, in China, the very existence of lesbianism was denied until very recently, but it is now being recognized and may someday be regarded as more acceptable (Ruan & Bullough, 1992). It is also interesting to note that in some Native American societies, a clear distinction is not always made between "man" and "woman," and therefore in those societies behaviors such as homosexuality and transvestism (dressing in the clothes of the "opposite sex") would not be problematic (Schnarch, 1992). Clearly, when considering the normality or abnormality of sexual behavior, we must take the time and the culture into account.

Sexual disorders are usually not as debilitating as other disorders such as anxiety, depression, and schizophrenia, and therefore they are often seen as less serious. However, sexual disorders can be very serious because of the impact they can have on other people.

TABLE 18.1 Sexual and Gender Identity Disorders

(Sexual Response Cycle)

Sexual Dysfunctions
- Desire disorders *(Appetitive Phase)*
  —Hypoactive sexual desire disorder
  —Sexual aversion disorder
- Arousal disorders *(Excitement Phase)*
  —Female sexual arousal disorder
  —Male erectile disorder
- Orgasmic disorders *(Orgasm Phase)*
  —Female orgasmic disorder
  —Male Orgasmic Disorder
  —Premature ejaculation

Paraphilias
- Exhibitionism
- Fetishism
- Transvestic fetishism
- Frotteurism
- Pedophilia
- Sexual masochism
- Sexual sadism
- Voyeurism

Gender Identity Disorder
- Gender identity disorder

Note: DSM-IV also contains a category of "Sexual Pain Disorders" that includes *dyspareunia* (pain associated with intercourse) and *vaginismus* (involuntary contraction of muscles of the vagina that interferes with sexual intercourse).

This is particularly true when the disorders involve behaviors such as rape, sadism, or the sexual abuse of children. Because sexual disorders are very prevalent in our society and because some of them can pose a danger, it is important that we give them careful consideration.

TOPIC I
SEXUAL DYSFUNCTIONS

Sexual dysfunctions involve the *absence or failure of the sexual response at some point during the sexual response cycle.* Three types of dysfunction disorders have been identified, and each is associated with a different phase of the sexual response cycle.

1. The *desire disorders* are associated with the *appetitive phase,* in which the individual has fantasies about sexual activities and develops a desire for sex. Desire disorders involve a lack of sexual desire.

2. The *arousal disorders* are associated with the *excitement phase,* which consists of subjective sexual pleasure and physiological changes such as erections in males and vaginal lubrication in females. Arousal disorders involve insufficient physiological arousal despite the presence of desire.

3. The *orgasmic disorders* are associated with the *orgasm phase,* which involves a peaking of subjective sexual pleasure with heightened physiological changes such as ejaculation in males and the contraction of the walls of the vagina in women. Orgasmic disorders involve either failure to achieve an orgasm despite the presence of desire and arousal or premature orgasm.

DESIRE DISORDERS

Desire disorders involve a *deficiency or lack of desire for sexual activity.* Individuals with desire disorders lack the sexual urge, have few sexual fantasies, and therefore may not seek sexual stimulation. However, if the individuals are sexually stimulated, they can become sexually aroused. Technically, there are two desire disorders, and they generally reflect different levels in the lack of desire. The **hypoactive sexual desire disorder** involves a *lack of sexual desire,* and the **sexual aversion disorder** involves an extreme *aversion to sexual activities.* Desire disorders occur in up to 15% of males and in up to 35% of females (Nathan, 1986).

Individuals differ greatly in terms of the degree to which they are upset by desire disorders. Al and Peg Bundy from television's Married . . . with Children *make their lack of desire for each other a source of frequent jokes.*

Individuals differ greatly in the degree to which they are upset by desire disorders. Some individuals are not concerned about their lack of desire, and they simply do not miss the sexual activities in which they are not interested. However, others are very upset because they want the sexual pleasure they once experienced or they see portrayed in the media or read about in literature. Furthermore, for some individuals, the lack of desire is inconsistent with their cultural role (e.g., the "macho" male or the female "sex symbol"), and they become concerned about how they are perceived by others. In those cases, desire disorders can lead to depression because the individuals think they are missing out on something, or the disorders can lead to anxiety because the individuals think they are not measuring up. Finally, lack of sexual desire can cause depression and anxiety for the individual's partner, who may assume that the lack of desire is a reflection on his or her sexual attractiveness.

Psychological Explanations and Treatments

Psychological explanations for desire disorders generally fall into one of three categories. The first of these involves the *defensive suppression* of desire. The notion is that the individuals were raised to believe that sex is "bad" or "dirty," so they avoid the forbidden attraction by suppressing their desire.

Second, it has been suggested that lack of desire is due to *stress.* Individuals who are under stress must focus their attention and energy on the problem of coping with the stress, and that leaves little attention or energy available for sex. For example, in a study of almost 200 men and women, it was found that men who were under stress because of unemployment experienced more sexual difficulty than men who were not under stress (Morokoff & Gilliland, 1993). Stress did not influence desire in women.

The third explanation is *interpersonal,* and it revolves around the possibility that desire disorders may reflect a way of manipulating, punishing, or instilling feelings of inadequacy in one's partner. For example, an individual who wants to make the partner feel bad as punishment for something may develop a desire disorder and then blame the lack of desire on the partner, thereby undermining the partner's feelings of worth and attractiveness.

Psychotherapy is a popular technique for treating desire disorders, but there is no consistent evidence that this approach is particularly helpful (Becker & Kavoussi, 1994; Bergin & Garfield, 1994; O'Carroll, 1991).

Physiological Explanations and Treatments

The physiological explanation for desire disorders is based on *hormone imbalances,* and treatment revolves

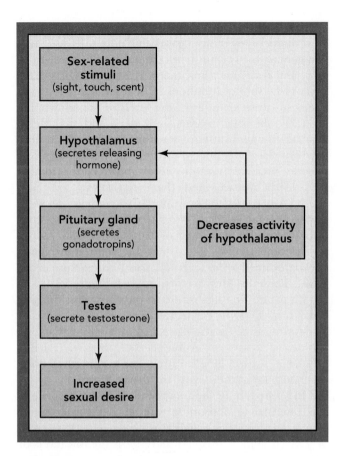

FIGURE 18.1 Hormones influence sexual desire in males.

around restoring the balances. Before discussing this explanation and treatment, it will be helpful if I describe the physiological process that is responsible for normal desire.

The process begins in the **hypothalamus,** the area of the brain that is responsible for arousal in general. In the male, when the hypothalamus is stimulated by some sex-related stimulus such as a visual image, a touch, or a scent, the hypothalamus secretes a **releasing hormone** that stimulates the **pituitary gland,** which in turn secretes hormones known as **gonadotropins** (guh-NAD-uh-TRŌ-pinz). (*Gonad* refers to any reproductive gland, such as the testes or ovaries, and *tropin* means "alter or influence.") As the name implies, the gonadotropins stimulate the male's testes, which then produce **testosterone** (TES-TOS-tuh-rŏn), the hormone responsible for the arousal of desire. Testosterone results in desire, but it also causes the hypothalamus to *reduce* production of the releasing hormone that started the process. In other words, there is a negative-feedback loop in the system so that the level of testosterone is maintained within a narrow range. If that were not the case, once stimulated, the system would run unchecked. The chemical process responsible for arousal in men is illustrated in Figure 18.1.

The chain of events is similar in women, but it is considerably more complex because the production of

hormones varies greatly during a woman's monthly cycle and because additional hormones are involved. In general, however, in women, the gonadotropic hormones stimulate the ovaries to produce **progesterone** (PRŌ-JES-tuh-rŏn). That hormone contributes to desire, and like testosterone in the male, it is involved in a negative-feedback loop that reduces hypothalamic production of the releasing hormone that started the process.

When considering this system, it is important to recognize that it involves a number of different parts (hypothalamus, pituitary gland, sex organs), as well as a variety of hormones (releasing hormone, gonadotropin, testosterone or progesterone), and that all of the components must operate within narrow tolerances if the system is to work effectively. If any of the components of the system are thrown off by spontaneous fluctuations, damage, disease, or external factors, the individual will experience an altered level of sexual desire.

Support for the notion that hormone imbalances can result in desire disorders comes from two sets of research results. First, there is ample evidence that *low levels of the sex hormones are associated with low sexual desire* (e.g., Bancroft, 1984a, 1984b; Lo Piccolo, 1983). For example, in one investigation the sexual responses (erections) of men with normal or low levels of testosterone were compared when the men engaged in erotic fantasy and when they were exposed to an erotic film (Bancroft, 1984a). The results indicated that men with low levels of testosterone showed much lower sexual arousal in response to fantasy but only slightly lower sexual arousal when stimulated by the erotic film. In other words, the males with low hormone levels showed *less sexual desire* but *unimpaired physical response to stimulation.* These results are presented in Figure 18.2.

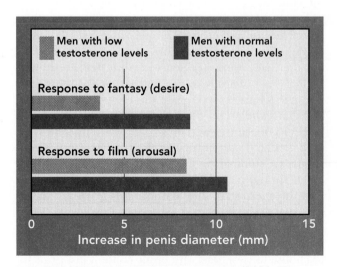

FIGURE 18.2 Men with low levels of testosterone showed low desire responses to fantasy but normal arousal responses to stimulation by films.
Source: Adapted from Bancroft (1984a), p. 6, fig. 2.

Are high testosterone men always in arousal then?

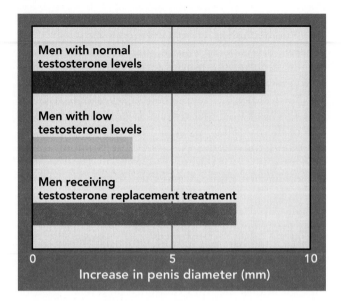

FIGURE 18.3 Testosterone replacement therapy increased men's desire responses (erections) to fantasy.
Source: Adapted from Bancroft (1984a), p. 6, fig. 2.

Related to the finding that low hormone levels are associated with low desire is the finding that as men grow older, their levels of testosterone decline, and so they experience diminishing sexual desire and arousal (Schiavi et al., 1990; Schiavi et al., 1991). However, once the men become stimulated and aroused, they report normal levels of desire, enjoyment, and satisfaction.

The second set of research findings supporting the hormone explanation for desire disorders comes from data indicating that *increasing the levels of the sex hormones increases sexual desire* (e.g., Bancroft, 1984a; Bancroft & Wu, 1983; Davidson, 1984; Davidson et al., 1979; Kwan et al., 1983). For example, in one investigation men with low levels of testosterone either were or were not injected with testosterone, and then their responses to sexual fantasy and erotic films were assessed (Bancroft, 1984a). The results of this investigation indicated that the men who were injected with testosterone showed higher levels of arousal while fantasizing about sex than the men who were not given the testosterone. In fact, the men who were given the testosterone showed a level of arousal during fantasy that was almost as high as that of men with normal levels of testosterone. Those results are summarized in Figure 18.3.

It should be noted that there is some controversy over the question of whether hormone levels are linked to sexual desire in women (Schreiner-Engel et al., 1989; Zillmann et al., 1994). In one study that supported the relationship, it was found that women were most likely to choose to view films with erotic content just prior to, during, and just after menses.

Now that we have established that low levels of sex hormones are related to low levels of sexual desire, at least in men, we must go on to examine possible causes

for the low levels of the hormones. Hormone levels can be influenced by many factors, including disease, age, and genetic background, but external influences are of most interest here. For many years, zoologists have known that subtle alterations in weather and amount of light can cause changes in the levels of gonadotropins produced in sheep, goats, and deer and that those changes in turn influence the animals' desire and mating behavior. In humans, turning the lights down low may not increase hormone levels, but recent evidence has clearly documented that *psychological stress can decrease hormone levels.* For example, when men who were under normal levels of stress were compared to men who were under high levels of stress, as in military training or combat, it was found that the men under higher stress produced lower levels of testosterone (Rose et al., 1969). These findings are presented in Figure 18.4.

From the findings reported in this discussion, it is clear that physiological factors play an important role in determining sexual desire in humans but that psychological factors can influence the physiological factors. That is, psychological stress can lead to physiological changes that then cause the desire disorder.

In approaching the treatment of arousal disorders, it is essential to determine whether a disorder stems from a physiological problem (disease, genetic factors) or a psychological problem (stress). If the low levels of testosterone are due to low levels of production because of a physiological problem, treatment for male patients may simply involve administering testosterone to bring the level up to normal, a procedure called **testosterone replacement therapy** (Bagatell & Bremner, 1996). This procedure can be very effective. For example, the results reported in Figure 18.3 indicated that when the men with low levels of testosterone were administered testosterone, their levels of sexual arousal were almost as high as those of normal men.

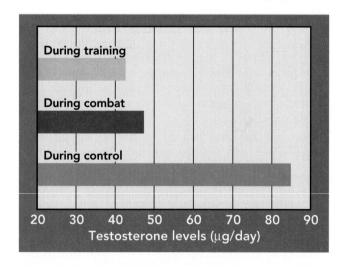

FIGURE 18.4 Men under stress showed lower levels of testosterone than men not under stress.
Source: Adapted from Rose et al. (1969), p. 425, fig. 3.

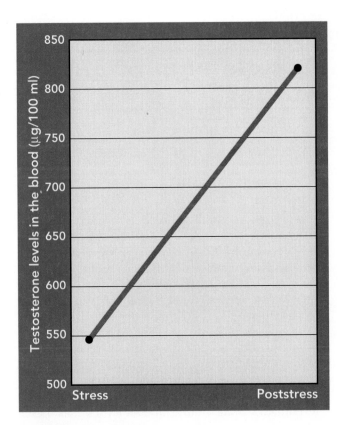

FIGURE 18.5 Decreases in stress were associated with increases in testosterone.
Source: Data from Kreuz et al. (1972), p. 480, tab. 1.

In contrast, if the low levels of testosterone are due to the effects of stress, treatment can be directed at reducing stress. An interesting illustration of the effects of stress reduction on testosterone levels is provided by a study of men in officer candidate school (Kreuz et al., 1972). The testosterone levels of these men were measured during the first phase of the training, when stress was very high, and then again during the second phase of the training, when the men were "over the hump" and stress levels were greatly reduced. The levels of testosterone during the first and second phases of training for the men are presented in Figure 18.5. Inspection of those data indicate that testosterone levels went up when stress went down.

AROUSAL DISORDERS

Individuals with **arousal disorders** desire and participate in sexual activity, but once the activity is initiated, they *cannot achieve an adequate level of physiological arousal or cannot maintain an adequate level of arousal*. In males, the major symptom is the failure to achieve or maintain a complete erection. The prevalence of arousal disorders is estimated to be 10% to 20% in males, but we do not have sufficient data to estimate the prevalence in women (Nathan, 1986). Case Study 18.1 is an excerpt

from an interview with a young man who came to a clinic because of an arousal disorder.

Diagnostic Procedures and Problems

Arousal disorders can stem from either psychological or physiological causes. One approach to determining what is causing a disorder is to determine whether or not the individual is physiologically capable of arousal (Conte, 1986). One technique for determining whether a male is capable of sexual arousal involves the measurement of **nocturnal penile tumescence** (tyoo-MES-ins). *Tumescence* refers to the state of erection, and in physiologically normal males erection occurs occasionally during periods of rapid eye movement (REM) sleep. If the individual has erections during sleep, it can be assumed that he is physiologically capable of sexual arousal and that his problems in achieving or maintaining arousal while awake must be due to psychological factors. (Note that erections occur during REM sleep, which is associated with dreams, but the erections are not necessarily related to the nature of the dreams; rather, both the dreams and the erections are due to an increase in neurological arousal.)

Nocturnal penile tumescence is measured by placing a cuff on the penis. If erection occurs, the cuff expands, breaking a series of small seals. In the morning, the seals can be checked to determine whether erection occurred.

Psychological Explanations and Treatments

There is widespread agreement that *anxiety* is the major psychological cause of arousal disorders. Often, it is anxiety about problems with arousal that prevents arousal or causes a premature drop in arousal (Barlow, 1986; Kaplan, 1981; Masters & Johnson, 1970; Wolpe, 1958). The question is, what process links anxiety to reduced arousal? In answering that question, it is important to recognize that anxiety has a cognitive component: thoughts about failure. Those anxiety-related thoughts are important for understanding arousal disorders because they lead to *distraction,* and distraction can in turn lead to a reduction of sexual arousal.

The role of distraction in reducing sexual arousal has been demonstrated in a variety of ways (Cerny, 1978; Geer & Fuhr, 1976; Henson & Rubin, 1971; Laws & Rubin, 1969). For example, it has been shown that individuals can voluntarily suppress sexual arousal while watching erotic films if they shift their attention to something else (watch the film but think about something else). Also, involuntary reductions in sexual arousal occur when subjects hear erotic material in one ear but distracting material (e.g., math problems) in the other ear.

CASE STUDY 18.1

Interview with a Man Complaining of an Arousal Disorder

The client was a handsome 34-year-old man. The early part of the interview did not offer any evidence of adjustment problems, and it was apparent that the client had an active and mature social life. The following discussion ensued when the interviewer turned the conversation to the problem that had brought the client to the clinic.

Client: Well, the problem is that—Well, I just have a hard time getting an erection when I get physically involved with a woman. It's not that I don't want sex—I really do. But somehow when we get right down to it . . . when the time comes to begin making love, I can't get an erection. I'm just limp.

Interviewer: Hmmm. Can you tell me a little more about it? Can you describe a typical situation in which you have a problem?

Client: (pause) Well, let's say I've gone out with a woman for a while and it comes to the point where one night things are getting physical. Everything goes great—I mean, I'm aroused and excited—and she is too, but then I just can't seem to go further. It's not that I don't stay excited; I'm really excited and enjoying what we're doing, but when it gets to the point at which I should have a good erection, it doesn't come.

Interviewer: Have you ever had an erection? For example, do you ever wake up in the morning with an erection, or can you get an erection with masturbation?

Client: Oh, yeah, I frequently wake up with an erection—that's normal—and I can masturbate. Sometimes it takes me a little while to get started, but I always get there.

Interviewer: How about with a woman? Do you ever get an erection with a woman?

Client: Yes. Sometimes when we just get started and we're just necking I'll get an erection for a while and then I think, "Great, this time we're going to make it," but then I lose it and can't get it back. It's really annoying.

Interviewer: Have you ever completed intercourse with a woman?

Client: Oh, sure. It didn't used to be a problem, but lately it just hasn't been working. It's a relatively recent problem. (pause) It gets kind of embarrassing. I get to a high point, and then I just can't go further. I usually hide what's happening—or not happening—and make up some excuse to, well, to bring things to an end. (pause) Not long ago, I dated a woman who caught on to what was going on, but she was pretty relaxed about the whole thing. She just laughed and said, "Don't worry. We'll get around it," and we just kept making out. She kept playing with me and eventually I came around, at least for a while. She seemed to know what she was doing.

Interviewer: Has anything changed for you that might be associated with the problem? Have you had any physical or psychological problems?

Client: (sighs) No, nothing that I can think of. When the problem started, I did a little reading about it. The articles I read said that anxiety was the problem and that the trick was not to let yourself get distracted by upsetting thoughts, so I worked real hard to concentrate on what I was doing, how much I enjoyed the woman's body, and I tried not to think about the problem. (sighs) Great idea but tough to pull off. The problem is always there. Forcing yourself to concentrate on what you are doing is . . . well, by working to avoid the problem, you admit that there is a problem, and it doesn't seem to work for me. The work of concentrating is almost enough to wreck my arousal. (sighs) It's a mess—and it's frustrating as hell.

The distracting thoughts that are most common among individuals with arousal disorders involve concerns about sexual performance and failure. In other words, it is assumed that problems with arousal are due to the fact that individuals worry about their sexual performance, those thoughts distract them, and then the distraction reduces arousal.

It is also worth noting that individuals with arousal disorders underestimate their levels of sexual arousal. That was demonstrated in an investigation in which males estimated their levels of sexual arousal while their actual levels of arousal were measured in terms of penile erection (Sakheim et al., 1984). The results indicated that males with psychologically based arousal disorders underestimated their arousal more than normal males or even males with physiologically based arousal disorders. Comparable results have been reported for females (Morokoff & Heinman, 1980). The tendency for individuals with arousal disorders to underestimate their arousal levels is important because their erroneous assumptions about their underarousal could contribute to their concerns and lead to additional distraction.

Treatment for psychologically based arousal disorders revolves around attempts to reduce anxiety by instilling more confidence in the client and thereby reducing the cognitions that interfere with sexual arousal (Lo Piccolo & Stock, 1986). Cognitive therapists might also teach the client to focus on the positive aspects of sex and in so doing reduce distraction. Therapists and clients usually report success with these techniques, but so far we have little adequately controlled research to document the long-term effectiveness of these approaches (Bergin & Garfield, 1994).

Physiological Explanations and Treatments

It was once assumed that over 90% of erectile failures were due to psychological problems, but more recent research indicates that as many as 50% or 60% of the problems may actually be due to various organic conditions (Fisher et al., 1979; Kaya et al., 1979).

Before discussing the physiological explanations for arousal disorders, a brief comment should be made concerning the physiology of sexual arousal. Sexual arousal can be initiated either in the brain by sexual thoughts and desires or in the genital area by stimulation of the sex organs and the area around them. In both cases, nerve impulses are sent to the lower portion (sacral section) of the spinal cord. From there, parasympathetic nerve impulses are sent to the male's penis or to the female's clitoris. (The clitoris is the major site of arousal for the female, and it will be described and discussed in greater detail later when we consider orgasmic disorders.) The parasympathetic impulses cause a dilation of the **erectile tissues** in those organs. Erectile tissues consist of blood channels that are normally empty, but when stimulated they dilate tremendously and fill with blood. Considerable pressure builds up in erectile tissues because blood flow out is restricted. Dilation and filling of the erectile tissues in the penis cause it to become enlarged and erect. In the female, the dilation and filling of erectile tissues results in a swelling and firming of the clitoris. For the female, the parasympathetic impulses also cause the secretion of mucus just inside the vaginal opening.

A number of physiological problems can reduce sexual arousal. For example, *neurological damage* to the hypothalamus, spinal cord, or connecting nerve pathways could result in the reduction or absence of the nerve stimulation that causes changes in blood flow. Unfortunately, because damage to the central nervous system is irreversible, arousal disorders due to nerve damage are usually permanent.

Reduced arousal can also stem from *blockage of the arteries* that supply blood to the penis or clitoris. If those arteries are blocked, the filling of the erectile tissues will be limited, and therefore arousal will be limited. This problem is more pronounced in men, probably because during midlife men are more prone to the development of atherosclerosis (see Chapter 16). When the disorder is due to artery blockage, treatment is focused on enhancing blood supply, but in some cases a prosthetic device may be implanted in the penis (Metz & Mathiesen, 1979; Michal et al., 1977). The prosthetic device consists of an inflatable balloon that is implanted in the penis and connected to a pump. When an erection is desired, the pump is turned on, the balloon is inflated, and the penis becomes erect.

Finally, *anxiety* can lead to physiological effects that can reduce sexual arousal. Specifically, anxiety is associated with increased physiological arousal (e.g., heart rate, blood pressure) that is due to increased activity of the *sympathetic* branch of the autonomic nervous system. That is important because sexual arousal is associated with *parasympathetic* activity, and the sympathetic and parasympathetic are *antagonistic* (competing) reactions that lead to different types of activity. Most important, the parasympathetic activity leads to the *dilation* and filling of the peripheral and erectile tissues that is crucial to sexual arousal, but the sympathetic activity leads to *constriction* of these tissues and consequently to a drop in sexual arousal. Because sympathetic activity initially dominates parasympathetic activity, the sympathetic activity associated with anxiety can overwhelm the parasympathetic activity and reduce or eliminate sexual arousal. In this case, a psychological factor (anxiety) causes a change in a physiological factor (reduced parasympathetic activity), which produces the arousal disorder. (Recall from the earlier discussion that anxiety also has a cognitive component that involves thoughts that can distract the individual and reduce arousal.)

The effects of chronic and acute stress (anxiety) on sexual arousal in males was demonstrated in a study of employed and unemployed men (Morokoff et al., 1987). In this study it was assumed that unemployed men were under chronic stress and that employed men were not under stress. To manipulate acute stress, half of the men in each group were told that at the end of the laboratory session they would be asked to give a short talk about their sexual behavior to a group of students. The other half of the men were not led to believe that they would have to talk about their sexual behavior. During the laboratory session, the men watched an erotic film of a heterosexual couple making love, and while they watched the film their sexual arousal was measured by assessing changes in penis diameter (erection). The results indicated that among men who were under chronic stress, the addition of the acute stress (expecting to talk about their sex lives with students) resulted in a lower level of arousal in response to erotic stimulation than in the other men. In other words, the combination of chronic and acute stress resulted in a reduction in arousal that might be interpreted as an arousal disorder.

ORGASMIC DISORDERS

Individuals with **orgasmic disorders** desire and participate in sexual activity, become aroused, and maintain the arousal, but *they do not experience an orgasm or, in the case of males, they experience orgasm too soon.* Orgasmic disorders pose problems because they deprive individuals of the pleasure they seek, and the disorders may lead to feelings of inadequacy. Indeed, we used to refer to individuals who did not experience orgasm as sexually "inadequate" or "frigid." Those pejorative labels have been abandoned, but it is still common to talk about the "failure to achieve orgasm," and that phrase reflects an underlying negative evaluation. Orgasmic disorders occur in both men and women, but they are more common in women.

Explanations and Treatments of Orgasmic Disorders in Women

In women, a distinction is sometimes made between the **primary orgasmic disorder,** in which the woman has never experienced an orgasm through any means, and the **secondary orgasmic disorder,** in which the woman can experience orgasm during masturbation but not during sexual intercourse. Together, these problems affect between 5% and 10% of women (Spector & Carey, 1990).

Traditionally, orgasmic disorders in women have been explained in terms of anxieties and unconscious conflicts associated with sex. For example, it was assumed that women who did not experience orgasm were unable to "let go" sexually. The resistance was thought to be rooted in childhood experiences that led the women to believe that sex was dirty or harmful. If women with orgasmic disorders were not aware of such thoughts, it was assumed that they had *unconscious conflicts* about sexuality, probably revolving around unresolved attractions for their fathers or mothers.

For many years, the concepts of anxiety and conflict were widely used to explain orgasmic disorders, but the popularity of those explanations has declined

since the late 1960s. That decline occurred because there was no evidence to support the effects of anxiety and conflict and because a more contemporary and simpler explanation was developed that led to a very effective treatment. Specifically, it is now widely believed that many orgasmic disorders are due to the fact that women or their sexual partners *simply do not know what should be done to achieve maximal stimulation* or fail to do what they know should be done. In other words, the fact that a woman does not reach orgasm is probably due to a lack of knowledge or inadequate sexual technique rather than underlying conflicts. Support for this explanation comes from the finding that teaching women more about their bodies and educating sexual partners about what type of stimulation is most arousing are very effective methods for overcoming orgasmic disorders. To understand the problems that women may encounter in achieving orgasm, it will be helpful if I briefly discuss how stimulation does and does not occur during intercourse.

As the penis moves in the vagina during intercourse, the friction created by the penis rubbing against the walls of the vagina stimulates the sensitive penis, thereby maintaining the male's arousal and leading to his orgasm. In contrast, the movement of the penis in the vagina does not result in much direct sexual stimulation for the woman because the first two-thirds of the vagina has relatively few nerve endings and hence is not particularly sensitive to stimulation. Stated simply, intercourse is maximally effective for the attainment of the male's orgasm but is not particularly effective for achieving that goal for women. (In that regard, it is interesting to note that men and women require about the same amount of time to achieve orgasm through masturbation, but during intercourse, men experience orgasm much faster than women; Offir, 1982.)

Some investigators believe that some women have a short sexually sensitive area just inside the vagina known as the **G spot** and that stimulation of that area may lead to arousal and orgasm (Addiego et al., 1981; Alzate & Hoch, 1986; Goldberg et al., 1983; Ladas et al., 1982; Perry & Whipple, 1981). However, the existence of the G spot is not well documented, and its importance is a matter of some controversy.

The fact that the vagina is not particularly sensitive does not mean that intercourse is not pleasurable and cannot result in orgasm for the woman. Instead, the pleasure, arousal, and orgasm experienced by women during intercourse appear to be due primarily to the stimulation of the **clitoris** (KLIT-uh-ris), which is a pea-sized body located a small distance above the vaginal opening (see Figure 18.6). The clitoris is normally covered by a hood (a small flap of skin). Gently pulling the hood back reveals its tip, called the **glans.** In contrast to the vagina, the clitoris contains many nerve endings

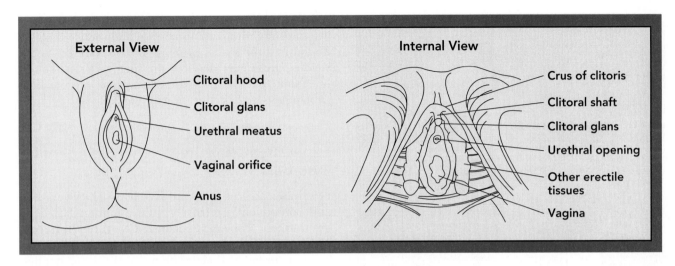

FIGURE 18.6 The clitoris is made up of erectile tissue and is the primary area of sexual stimulation for most women.

(probably more than the larger penis), and it is exceptionally sensitive to stimulation. In fact, it is so sensitive that some women do not want it touched directly and prefer that it be stimulated indirectly by caressing the area around it, which serves to move the hood and thereby stimulate the glans.

Because the clitoris is easily manipulated and its manipulation results in sexual arousal, the clitoris plays an important role in achieving orgasm through masturbation. The clitoris also plays an important role in sexual arousal and orgasm during intercourse because as the penis moves in and out of the vagina, it causes the tissues around the vaginal opening to move, and that movement causes the hood over the clitoral glans to move, stimulating the glans and thereby providing pleasurable sensations and orgasm.

The clitoris is actually the end of the **clitoral shaft,** which extends back into the body and then divides into two leglike structures (see Figure 18.6). The clitoral shaft contains erectile tissue like that in the penis, and during sexual excitement, the erectile tissue of the clitoris fills with blood, causing a swelling such that the shaft doubles or triples in size. The pressure caused by the increase in size results in greater sensitivity, which contributes to increased arousal. Because of the size and importance of the underlying structures, the tiny clitoris and glans have been referred to as the "tip of an erogenous iceberg."

Treatment for the primary orgasmic disorder using the education approach entails a number of steps. First, it may be necessary for the woman to learn more about her body and what gives her pleasure. This may involve sitting down with a mirror and visually exploring her body. That is followed by gentle touching, fondling, or massaging in the genital area to discover where and what type of stimulation is most effective for achieving sexual arousal. Such exploration and self-stimulation may have been avoided or forbidden by traditional attitudes toward sexuality. In most cases, manual stimulation is sufficient to achieve arousal and orgasm, but sometimes a manual device or vibrator will be used as an adjunct. Essentially, the woman learns to achieve orgasm through masturbation. (This would not be necessary in the case of the secondary orgasmic disorder, in which the woman can already achieve orgasm through masturbation.)

The next phase involves having the woman communicate to her partner what arouses her. Because it is sometimes difficult to talk about those things, some therapists suggest that the woman take her partner's hand and gently guide him and show him the kind of stimulation she wants. Once the couple is comfortable with this form of genital stimulation, it is suggested that they attempt intercourse. Many therapists suggest that the first intercourse should be done with the woman on top because that way she has the major responsibility for movement and can better control the nature of the stimulation. Once orgasm has been achieved in this position, the couple is encouraged to experiment with other positions.

Education, self-exploration, self-stimulation, communication with the partner, and practice are all important steps in this therapy. However, couples must also develop attitudes of self-acceptance and responsibility for their own sexual pleasure. The woman must realize that *sex is not something that just happens or is done to her* but rather something in which she *actively participates and shares control* with her partner. Sometimes this type of therapy will be combined with counseling designed to reduce interpersonal

Education is an important part of therapy for sexual dysfunctions.

anxiety or tension, thereby facilitating communication and mutual acceptance.

This approach to the treatment of orgasmic disorders is very effective, with success rates usually reported to be greater than 75% (see reviews by Marks, 1981; Masters & Johnson, 1970; Offir, 1982). The proportion of women with the primary orgasmic disorder who are subsequently able to experience an orgasm with masturbation may be as high as 95%.

It should not be concluded that overcoming an orgasmic disorder is always a strictly mechanical or educational process. There is no doubt that anxiety about sex or interpersonal tensions with her partner can interfere with the woman's arousal and enjoyment of sex and can reduce the likelihood of an orgasm. However, it is now clear that anxiety is less important than it was once thought to be, and in many cases, anxiety and interpersonal tension may be the *result* of problems with sex rather than their cause. For example, a woman who feels that her partner does not understand or is not sensitive to her needs may become tense or resentful in her sexual relationship, and that may disrupt her

personal relationship with her partner. That disruption will interfere with communication and reduce the likelihood that the sexual problem will be resolved, and a vicious circle may develop. In such cases, attention must sometimes be given to personal and interpersonal problems as well as education and technique.

Explanations and Treatments of Orgasmic Disorders in Men

Fewer than 10% of males are unable to achieve orgasm, and consequently relatively little attention has been given to this problem (Spector & Carey, 1990). In contrast, an orgasmic disorder that occurs in almost 40% of males is **premature ejaculation.** As the term implies, this disorder involves reaching orgasm *too soon.* Specifically, ejaculation occurs after only minimal stimulation, and therefore the orgasm occurs before the male wishes it and before his partner has been sufficiently stimulated and satisfied.

Numerous explanations have been offered to account for premature ejaculation. For example, it has been attributed to (a) hostility on the part of the male who is depriving the female of the pleasure of sex by terminating the act early; (b) high levels of anxiety that contribute to heightened arousal; (c) the inability to perceive arousal accurately, which makes it impossible to exercise control; (d) abstinence from sexual activity, which results in higher arousal; (e) hypersensitivity of the penis, which leads to excessively high stimulation, and (f) experiences in situations that encouraged short ejaculatory times (e.g., places where the return of parents or others was imminent, pay-by-the-hour motels, backseats of cars, "quickies" with prostitutes). Unfortunately, there is no good evidence for any of these explanations, and we do not yet have a confirmed explanation for the disorder (see Lo Piccolo & Stock, 1986; Ruff, 1985).

However, despite the fact that we do not yet understand the cause of premature ejaculation, there are three effective treatments for the problem. The first is known as the **start-stop technique.** It involves stimulation of the penis, as would be done in masturbation, until a high level of arousal is achieved (the start phase). Then the stimulation is stopped before the level of arousal gets to the point of ejaculation. During that stop phase, the arousal subsides, and then the procedure is repeated. This is done three or four times on any one day and is usually practiced two or three times per week. Over time, the length of time between the start of stimulation and the point of ejaculation becomes longer. The prolongation of arousal before ejaculation in the practice sessions appears to generalize well to sexual activity with a partner.

The second treatment is known as the **start-squeeze technique** (Masters & Johnson, 1970). The start-squeeze technique is very similar to the start-stop technique except that when arousal becomes high, instead of simply stopping the stimulation, the individual firmly squeezes the end of the penis. Doing so does not hurt, but it immediately reduces arousal and eliminates the urge to ejaculate. The squeeze seems to be a fast way to reduce arousal between periods of stimulation. Both the start-stop and start-squeeze techniques are very effective for treating premature ejaculation, and success rates as high as 90% to 98% have been reported (Kilmann & Auerbach, 1979). It is encouraging that these treatments are effective, but we still do not understand the cause of premature ejaculation or why these treatments are effective for overcoming the disorder (Lo Piccolo & Stock, 1986).

The third effective treatment involves the use of *antidepression drugs that block the reuptake of serotonin.* (Drugs in that group include Prozac and Zoloft.) When I discussed these drugs in Chapter 10, I pointed out that one negative side effect was that they eliminated or greatly prolonged the time to orgasm or ejaculation. Prolonging time to ejaculation may pose a problem for individuals without ejaculatory difficulties, but it is exactly what individuals with premature orgasm want. Indeed, in one study, the use of an antidepressant increased the time to ejaculation from 30 seconds to 10 minutes (Waldinger et al., 1994). Although the drugs work, in view of their expense and side effects, it seems wiser to use the start-stop or the start-squeeze techniques first.

Having discussed problems with sexual functioning, we can now turn our attention to the paraphilias, in which individuals achieve arousal and pleasure through abnormal means.

TOPIC II
PARAPHILIAS

Paraphilias (PAR-uh-FIL-ē-uz) revolve around *abnormal means of achieving sexual arousal.* The major symptoms of paraphilias are recurrent sexual urges, fantasies, and arousal that are associated with (a) nonhuman objects such as articles of clothing, (b) suffering or humiliation, or (c) nonconsenting individuals such as children. (The term *paraphilia* is derived from *para,* meaning "abnormal," and *philia,* meaning "attraction," so paraphilias are abnormal attractions.)

We do not know how widespread paraphilias are because the behaviors are usually private and often occur without a partner or with a partner who consents and who therefore does not report the behavior. Furthermore, in some cases, the partner may not even be aware that the other individual's arousal stems from a paraphilia. For example, a woman having sex with a man may not realize that his arousal stems from her clothes or from fantasies about harming her rather than from her and her body.

Despite the fact that reports of paraphilias are relatively rare, it is believed that the prevalence of these disorders is high. That assumption is based in part on the fact that there are hundreds of catalogs for paraphiliac paraphernalia such as whips, chains, handcuffs, and leather sex suits, and there are numerous magazines devoted to things such as child pornography and transvestism (dressing in the clothes of the opposite sex). It is generally assumed that with the exception of sexual masochism, paraphilias are found primarily in men.

Because many or most individuals with paraphilias go undetected, our understanding of these disorders is based on a very limited and probably unrepresentative subset of individuals, and we must therefore be very cautious in drawing conclusions from the existing data. For example, individuals with paraphilias are sometimes described as less intelligent and more likely to have other adjustment or legal problems, but it is likely that only the more inept individuals have been caught and studied.

Before beginning our discussion of paraphilias, three qualifications should be noted. First, abnormal means of gaining sexual arousal are not diagnosed as paraphilias unless "the fantasies, urges, or sexual arousal cause clinically significant distress or impairment in social, occupational, or other important areas of functioning" (American Psychiatric Association, 1994, p. 523). For example, a man may find women's underwear arousing, but that is not considered abnormal unless the man is distressed by the arousal or it interferes with his functioning. Second, for a diagnosis of paraphilia to be made, the behavior must have resulted in "recurrent, intense sexual urges or behaviors" for a period of at least 6 months (American Psychiatric Association, 1994). In other words, occasional arousal or brief experimentation does not constitute a disorder and should not be a source of alarm. Third, in many cases paraphilias such as fetishes (using objects of clothing as a part of the sex act) are relatively harmless when acted out with a consenting partner. In that case, the major problem is that the partner may not share the paraphilia and will therefore not find the behavior pleasurable. However, paraphilias can be *very serious when they involve nonconsenting individuals or children.*

Eight paraphilias are identified in DSM-IV. I will briefly describe each and then go on to consider their

TABLE 18.2 Paraphilias and Their Symptoms

Paraphilia	Symptoms
Exhibitionism	Sexually arousing fantasies, sexual urges, or behaviors involving exposure of the genitals to an unsuspecting stranger
Fetishism	Sexually arousing fantasies, sexual urges, or behaviors involving the use of nonliving objects
Transvestic fetishism	Sexually arousing fantasies, sexual urges, or behaviors involving cross-dressing by a heterosexual male
Frotteurism	Sexually arousing fantasies, sexual urges, or behaviors involving touching and rubbing against a nonconsenting person
Pedophilia	Sexually arousing fantasies, sexual urges, or behaviors with a prepubescent child
Sexual masochism	Sexually arousing fantasies, sexual urges, or behaviors of being humiliated or made to suffer
Sexual sadism	Sexually arousing fantasies, sexual urges, or behaviors in which the psychological or physical suffering of the victim is sexually exciting to the person
Voyeurism	Sexually arousing fantasies, sexual urges, or behaviors involving the act of observing an unsuspecting person who is naked, in the process of disrobing, or engaging in sexual activity

Note: To be considered a disorder, the fantasies, urges, or behaviors must have lasted for at least 6 months and cause distress and impairment in functioning.
Source: Adapted from American Psychiatric Association (1994).

suspected causes and treatments. The symptoms of the paraphilias are summarized in Table 18.2.

TYPES OF PARAPHILIAS

Exhibitionism : streaking/flasher

Exhibitionism involves fantasies about or actually *exposing the genitals to an unsuspecting stranger* in order to achieve sexual arousal. Exhibitionism does not involve further sexual activity with the stranger, and therefore exhibitionists do not pose a physical danger to others. The classic example of the exhibitionist is the "flasher" who suddenly opens his coat to expose himself to an unsuspecting woman. Some years ago, "streaking" (running nude in public places) was a frequent prank on college campuses, but it did not result in arousal (at least not for the streaker) and therefore would not be considered exhibitionism.

A variety of surveys suggest that about 60% of exhibitionists are married and that they do not differ from the general population in intelligence, educational level, or vocation. There is also evidence that they do not suffer from other forms of abnormal behavior at a rate greater than the general population (see by Blair & Lanyon, 1981). An example of an exhibitionist is presented in Case Study 18.2.

Fetishism

The major symptom of **fetishism** is the use of *nonliving objects (fetishes)* to obtain sexual arousal. The most common fetish objects are articles of women's clothing such as bras, underpants, stockings, shoes, and boots. The individual will often masturbate while fondling, kissing, or smelling the fetish object. In other cases, the individual's sexual partner will wear the object during sexual encounters, thereby providing an arousing stimulus that enables the fetishist to participate in otherwise normal sexual behavior. The diagnosis of fetishism is not used when an individual gains sexual pleasure from the use of nonhuman objects such as vibrators that were designed to provoke sexual arousal.

Transvestic Fetishism

Heterosexual men who suffer from **transvestic fetishism** gain sexual pleasure from *dressing in women's* *clothing,* a behavior that is often referred to as **cross-dressing.** Cross-dressing can range from wearing only one article of women's clothing while alone to dressing completely in women's clothing and appearing that way in public. In some cases, the cross-dressing is so effective that it is difficult to distinguish a cross-dressed transvestite from a woman. However, the individual's goal is not to "pass" but to achieve arousal. It is interesting to note that DSM-IV limits this disorder to *heterosexual men;* a homosexual male or a woman who cross-dresses would not be diagnosed as suffering from transvestic fetishism.

A man with a transvestic fetish will often masturbate while dressed in women's clothes and will fantasize about other men being attracted to him while he is dressed in those clothes. In a very limited number of cases, homosexual males may cross-dress to attract other men, but the homosexual males are not diagnosed as having transvestic fetishism because the cross-dressing is not used to gain arousal. Similarly, female impersonators may cross-dress as part of an act, but unless they gain sexual pleasure from the cross-dressing itself, they are not diagnosed as having transvestic fetishism. Finally, it is important to recognize that the presence of transvestic fetishism does not necessarily preclude participation in normal sexual relationships. Such a possibility is illustrated in Case Study 18.3.

Frotteurism

The diagnostic label **frotteurism** (FRŌ-TUR-iz-um) is derived from the French word *frotter,* which means "to rub," and the disorder involves *rubbing against or touching a nonconsenting individual.* The rubbing is usually done in crowded public places such as stores or on public transportation where minor instances of rubbing can be attributed to simply bumping into the other person. In those situations, a male might rub his genitals against the thighs or buttocks of a woman. In more overt cases, the male may actually fondle the woman's genitalia or breasts and then flee when she realizes what is happening.

Pedophilia

Pedophilia (PED-uh-FIL-ē-uh) refers to a *sexual attraction to children.* (*Ped* comes from a Greek word meaning

---

CASE STUDY 18.2
Exhibitionism in a 43-Year-Old Man

The client was a married, 43-year-old college-educated man of average appearance who was the manager of a small printing business. He was referred to the clinic by the court after his second arrest for exposing himself in public. On each occasion, he had exposed himself to an attractive woman. In his initial interview, he admitted that he had probably exposed himself as often as once a month for the past 20 years.

His acts of exhibitionism always occurred in public places such as busy streets, entrances to department stores, or subway platforms as the train pulled out. After exposing himself, he would run and quickly lose himself in the crowd.

The exposures were not spontaneous events but were carefully planned over a couple of days, and the planning was associated with increasing anticipation, excitement, and tension. Just before the exposure, he would have an erection, and by slipping his hand through an opening in the bottom of his coat pocket, he would unzip his pants and pull his penis and testicles forward and out of his pants. Then when he was directly in front of the woman, he would open his coat and stand with his genitals exposed. After 2 or 3 seconds, he would pull his coat closed and run away. He would usually run two or three blocks, often dodging through stores and across streets. He described "the chase" as a "very exciting part of the whole thing." After the chase, he felt "exhausted but relaxed—you know, like you feel after good sex."

A psychological examination did not reveal anything particularly striking about the client. The only other unusual sexual behavior he reported involved going to a "male peep show" in the back of a porno bookstore a few times. His wife reported that he always seemed "completely normal." She commented that their sex life was "limited but OK." She repeatedly mused, "I can't figure this out. It just doesn't make sense." The patient's reaction was mixed. He seemed thoroughly ashamed and chagrined about being caught, but there was a tone of futility and hollowness in his promise that he would not do it again, an attitude shared by the clinic staff. To avoid prosecution, the client agreed to treatment.

Men suffering from transvestic fetishism gain sexual pleasure from dressing in women's clothing. These men are shown at the Miss Florida beauty pageant in Miami.

"child.") In most cases of pedophilia, the child is younger than 13 years old (prepuberty) and the molesting individual is a male aged 16 or older (postpuberty). Attraction to girls is reported to be twice as common as attraction to boys, but many individuals with pedophilia are attracted to both girls and boys.

The activities undertaken by the child molester include undressing the child and looking, exposing himself to the child, masturbating in the presence of the child, fondling the child, engaging in oral sex with the child, and penetrating the child's vagina, mouth, or anus with fingers or penis. In many cases it is not necessary for the offending individual to use physical force because the child is not aware of the inappropriate nature of the activities and the offender presents them as "games." However, force is used in some cases, and sometimes elaborate ruses or threats of punishment are used to prevent the child from informing others about the activities.

Individuals who sexually molest children are often thought of as "marginal characters" or "dirty old men," but that is usually not the case. Child molestation is a very serious act reflecting a serious problem, but the typical child molester is an otherwise respectable, law-abiding individual who began the behavior while a teenager (Groth et al., 1982). Furthermore, most child molesters are not strangers to their victims, and in many cases, they are brothers, fathers, or uncles of the victims (Conte & Berliner, 1981). It is probably because child molesters do not fit the stereotype that many of them go undetected; no one suspects these otherwise normal individuals of

engaging in such behavior, and reports by the children may be disregarded.

An important distinction has been made between molesters who *have a preference for children* and molesters who *use children as substitutes for adult sexual partners* (Groth & Birnbaum, 1978; Groth et al., 1982; Howells, 1981). Those who prefer children to adults are usually unmarried, their victims are often males rather than females, and their offenses are generally planned and form a consistent part of their lives. In contrast, individuals who use children as substitutes are primarily attracted to adults as sexual partners, they have more or less normal heterosexual histories, and their use of children seems to be impulsive and associated with periods of life stress or rejection. As with most distinctions in psychology, the distinction between preference and substitute probably represents the two ends of a continuum rather than a dichotomy. However, the distinction highlights the fact that it is difficult or impossible to generalize about individuals who suffer from pedophilia (Lanyon, 1986).

Sexual Masochism

The diagnosis of **sexual masochism** (MAS-uh-KIZ-um) is used when an individual derives sexual pleasure from *being abused* or from *suffering*. The abuse may be verbal and involve humiliation, but it is more likely that the abuse is physical and involves being beaten, bound, or tortured. Masochistic activities may be used indepen-

CASE STUDY 18.3

Transvestic Fetishism in a Happily Married Man: His Wife's Report

"Allan and I were married during the summer before our senior year in college. Married life was great. We had a cozy apartment close to campus, our classes and grades went well, and we really loved being married. It was wonderful—until one terrible afternoon in December. I had classes in the afternoon, but that day I didn't feel very well, so I cut my 2 o'clock chem lab and went home to the apartment. When I walked in, I got the shock of my life. *Allan was sitting on the bed dressed in my clothes—hose, skirt, blouse, and jewelry—the works!* He even had one of my bras under the blouse, but he couldn't snap it because it was too small. I couldn't believe it, and at first I just stood stock-still and stared.

"As soon as Allan saw me, he jumped up and started to 'explain.' I became so upset, I don't remember everything he said, but I know he tried to tell me that he had a multiple personality. He said that I married the 'straight' half and this was his 'other half.' He said that the half that married me didn't know about this and that everything was all right with that half. I didn't believe a word he was saying. I thought that he was making it up as an excuse. I didn't know what to think; I was in shock. There sat my husband dressed in my clothes—and he'd been doing it for months! I finally just broke down and cried; my neat little world was coming apart. Allan changed clothes and tried to comfort me, but I didn't want him to touch me. Finally, he went out for a walk so that I could be alone for a while.

"By the time he came back I had settled down emotionally, but I still didn't know what to do. He sat down and explained that he was ashamed of what he had done and that the story about having a multiple personality was just an excuse. He admitted that he had been secretly dressing in women's clothing since he was 12 or 14 but that he didn't know how it all started. It just did, and it had been going on for a

long time. He told me that sometimes he just sat in the clothes and other times he masturbated. He seemed really ashamed of that. He said he never went out of the house dressed that way and that he never did it with anyone else. He told me he wasn't a homosexual. After a while, he told me that he loved me, that our sex had always been really good for him, that dressing in women's clothes was something that was just 'separate from everything else,' and that he was sorry. My feelings were confused. I loved Allan, but I felt weird with him. That night, he slept on the couch. The next day we went to a counselor at the university clinic. I didn't know what would happen. I thought that maybe there was some form of drug therapy or that we should consider divorce. The counselor was pretty calm about the whole thing, but he really didn't have much to say, either. We saw him once a week for a couple of months. One thing that came from the sessions is that I learned that Allan's cross-dressing problem is a 'stand-alone' problem, and it does not mean that there is anything else wrong with Allan. I was relieved about that. The other thing that happened in our sessions was that we came to view Allan's cross-dressing as a 'mistake' or as an 'alternative sexual behavior.' The analogy was to an affair—it was an inappropriate indiscretion that could be stopped. You couldn't erase the past, but you could try to forget (forgive?) it and go on. That may be stretching the point a bit, but it is a way of thinking about it that helps us. It's been two years since that December afternoon. The topic of the cross-dressing is still a bit touchy, but usually I don't think about it, and Allan and I are very happy. Sometimes you just have to 'go with the flow' and take things one step at a time. Allan had kind of an unusual affair, but it's over and behind us now."

dently of other sexual acts, as when an individual gains sexual pleasure from simply being hurt by another person, or the masochistic activities may be combined with sexual acts, as when an individual wants to be beaten during intercourse.

One woman client reported that she could become aroused only if her partner "treated me like a whore and pretended to rape me," and a male client could

maintain arousal during intercourse only if his partner scratched or dug into his back with a sharp fork. For these individuals, being humiliated or experiencing pain was the only way they could achieve or maintain sexual arousal. In some cases the masochism is played out only in fantasies. The fantasies may involve being raped or being held or bound by others so that there is no possibility of escape. The case of an otherwise well-adjusted individual with a sexual masochism disorder is presented in Case Study 18.4.

Sexual Sadism

Sexual sadism (SĀ-diz-um) is the flip side of sexual masochism in that an individual with this disorder derives sexual pleasure from *causing others to suffer.* Sadists may physically abuse their partners during sexual activity as a means of achieving arousal and satisfaction. An "ideal couple" might involve a sadist and a masochist. Case Study 18.5 involves a case of sexual sadism; we will return to this case later when we discuss treatment. In some cases sexual sadism becomes extremely brutal and bizarre, and individuals such as Jeffrey Dahmer attract widespread publicity. Unfortunately, at present, we know relatively little about these individuals, and their "profiles" do not distinguish them from many other individuals (Dietz et al., 1990).

Voyeurism

The disorder known as **voyeurism** (VWA-YUR-iz-um) involves gaining sexual pleasure from *observing an unsuspecting individual who is naked, disrobing, or engaging in sexual activity.* The "peeping Tom" who looks into a woman's window at night is the classic example of the voyeur. It is important to note that the voyeur does not seek contact or actual sexual activity with the individual he or she is watching. Instead, the simple act of looking and fantasizing about being with the individual is sufficient to achieve sexual pleasure; in some cases, the voyeur may masturbate while watching or later while recalling what was seen.

A huge industry is built on the needs of voyeurs. It includes pornographic magazines, movies, videotapes, strip shows, and "peep shows" where a man can sit alone in a small room and "peep" through a small window at a woman stripping. It should not be concluded that all viewing for sexual pleasure necessarily reflects a disorder. On the contrary, viewing is often an important component of normal sexual behavior, and the viewing is considered a disorder only if it results in distress for the viewer.

Other Problems

Before concluding this section I should point out that we now know that some individuals gain sexual arousal by *depriving themselves of oxygen* for brief periods of time,

---

CASE STUDY 18.4
Sexual Masochism in an Otherwise Normal Man

One 26-year-old middle-class college-educated man routinely visited a prostitute who would remain dressed but undress him and then beat him with a rolled-up newspaper. The beating was only somewhat painful, but the slapping of the paper against his skin made a considerable amount of noise. Taking a beating like this resulted in intense sexual arousal, and as the beating became harder and faster, he would ejaculate.

The man's ability to attain sexual arousal in normal foreplay with a woman was very limited, and usually he became aroused only if he fantasized that after becoming aroused, he was going to be severely beaten by the woman. He never told his partners that his arousal was due to his fantasies. Because his normal sexual activities with women were relatively unsuccessful and because he did not want to tell his partners what they would have to do to really "turn him on," he limited most of his sexual activities to the prostitute whom he paid to "do what I needed."

The young man came to the clinic for a "check-up" to make sure that he did not have any other problem. He said that some years ago, he had come to terms with the fact that he "did things a little differently," but he wanted assurance that his "eccentricity" was not a sign of some other problem of which he was not aware. Despite a very thorough examination, no signs of any psychological disturbance could be found other than the masochism. The only relevant childhood experience he was able to recall was that he once became very upset when his older brother was severely spanked with a rolled-up newspaper. He was informed that no other problems were apparent, and he was offered treatment for the masochism. He declined treatment, pointing out, "It's not causing me any other problems, I'm not hurting anyone, I'm not doing anything illegal, and I'm enjoying myself. What I do is a little different, but so what?" He mused that it might be easier if he enjoyed normal sex but indicated that he did not want "to fix what is working pretty well for me." A follow-up call made a year later by a member of the clinic staff did not reveal any evidence of change in the young man's sexual behavior, attitude, or general adjustment.

CASE STUDY 18.5
Sexual Sadism in a 47-Year-Old Married Man

The patient was a 47-year-old man who was unable to obtain sexual satisfaction unless he hurt his wife. Throughout the 25 years of their marriage, the patient had frequently handcuffed his wife, shaved her head, stuck pins in her back, and hit her as a means of achieving ejaculation. Although his behaviors were often extreme, he never hurt his wife seriously enough for her to require medical attention, and because she never took legal action, the problem went undetected. In addition to the actual behavior, the patient was preoccupied with sadistic fantasies, which made it difficult for him to concentrate and work.

The patient was clearly aware of the inappropriate nature of his behavior, and after each occurrence, he was disgusted with himself and remorseful. To avoid the problem, when he felt the tension mounting, he would stay at the office late. Alternative means of obtaining sexual gratification were largely ineffective. Masturbation led to an erection, but he could achieve ejaculation only if he hurt his wife.

Source: Adapted from Berlin and Meinecke (1981), p. 605.

Serial killer Jeffrey L. Dahmer, who suffered from sexual sadism, was convicted of murder after parts of 11 human bodies were found in his apartment.

nition of paraphilias, but it is not yet defined as a disorder. A related strategy for increasing sexual arousal involves inhaling substances (e.g., amyl nitrate) that reduce oxygen to the brain. The arousal induced by the oxygen debt apparently spreads to sex and increases the intensity of the experience. This *inhalation masturbation* is less dangerous than hanging, but it can be dangerous; for example, it can lead to a heart attack.

A huge industry is built on the needs of voyeurs as well as normal individuals who like to look.

as, for example, by hanging themselves. Apparently, when they are deprived of oxygen and fighting for their lives, the individuals become very aroused and that arousal leads to sexual arousal. Unfortunately, in some cases the process goes too far, and the individuals die (Hucker & Blanchard, 1992; O'Halloran & Dietz, 1993; Tough et al., 1994). That is known as **autoerotic asphyxiation.** This behavior pattern fits within the defi-

EXPLANATIONS AND TREATMENTS

Psychodynamic Approaches

The psychodynamic explanation for sexual sadism is based on Freud's idea that sex and aggression are basic instincts and that *the arousal from those instincts is interchangeable*. In other words, the arousal that is associated with aggression could be transferred to (spill over to) sex, and in that way aggressive acts such as whipping or beating could lead to sexual arousal (Bieber, 1974; Freud, 1920/1955). In contrast, the transfer of arousal from sex to aggression can be used to explain instances in which sadism occurs after the individual is sexually aroused and sex is in progress; in that case, the sexual arousal increases aggressive arousal. It is noteworthy that minor aggressive acts such as biting often occur at the height of normal sexual behavior, and that has been used as evidence for the sex-to-aggression transfer.

The explanation of masochism posed a problem for most psychodynamic theorists because Freud asserted that humans were driven by the *pleasure principle* (see Chapter 2), but masochism involves the seeking of *pain* (Bieber, 1974; Freud, 1915/1955, 1919/1955, 1925/1955). However, Freud (1920/1955) suggested that there was another instinct, the *death instinct*, and masochism is a reflection of our unconscious wish to be hurt and die.

The traditional psychodynamic explanation for exhibitionism and transvestism is that they are attempts to deny the possibility of castration (Bak & Stewart, 1974). The notion is that the male is concerned about castration (see Chapter 2), and paraphilias reflect the male's attempts to deny the possibility that he could be castrated. For example, with exhibitionism, the male can convince himself and others that he has not been castrated, and with transvestic fetishism (cross-dressing), he can deny that women have been castrated because beneath the women's clothing he will find a penis. These psychodynamic explanations were once widely accepted, but there is no evidence for them; today they are largely ignored and of only historical interest.

Learning Approaches

Learning theorists attribute paraphilias to *classical conditioning*. Specifically, they suggest that paraphilias develop when sexual arousal is paired with an object or activity so that later the object or activity can elicit the sexual arousal. For example, a young boy may happen to experience sexual arousal while being punished, and the pairing leads to an association between punishment and sexual arousal. Therefore, in the future, when the young man is punished, he will experience sexual arousal. As a consequence, he will seek punishment to achieve sexual arousal, and thus develop a sexual masochism disorder.

Support for the classical conditioning explanation comes from laboratory research in which paraphilias were developed by pairing sexual arousal with previously neutral stimuli (Rackman, 1966; Rackman & Hodgson, 1968). For example, in one investigation, 10 men were first shown a slide of a pair of women's boots (a neutral stimulus) while their sexual arousal was assessed. (Sexual arousal was assessed with a device that measured changes in penis size.) Next, on a series of trials the men were shown the slide of the boots again, but immediately after each time the boots were shown, the men were shown a slide of a scantily dressed woman (a source of sexual arousal). In other words, the boots were paired with sexual arousal. Finally, the men were shown the slide of the boots alone, and when that was done, every one of the men responded with sexual arousal! That is, after the boots were paired with the sexual arousal, simply seeing the boots resulted in an erection. Furthermore, for some of the men the effects of the conditioning generalized to related objects, and the men showed sexual arousal when they were shown slides of a pair of high-heeled black shoes or a pair of gold sandals. In these experiments, then, paraphilias were developed in the laboratory through classical conditioning. Finally, it is interesting to note that in a recent study of individuals with foot fetishism, many reported that the feet (shoes, socks, etc.) reminded them of a pleasurable (arousing) experience (Weinberg et al., 1994).

When considering this explanation, the question arises, how does sexual arousal originally get paired with nonsexual stimuli? In answering that question, it should first be noted that emotions such as anger, anxiety, and sex *all result in similar patterns of physiological arousal*. Indeed, unless changes in the genital area are taken into account, it is usually impossible to determine what emotion an individual is experiencing by measuring only physiological arousal. One implication of the similarity of arousal across emotions is that *arousal generated by one emotion can be transferred and therefore can provide the basis for another emotion* (Schachter, 1964; Zillmann, 1983). The transfer is usually due to *relabeling* of the arousal. For example, an individual who is fearful will experience arousal, but the arousal may be labeled as sex rather than fear, and therefore the arousal will be *experienced* as sex rather than fear. The transfer of arousal across emotions is referred to as **arousal transference.**

Evidence that arousal from other emotions can be transferred and lead to sexual arousal has been provided by a number of interesting experiments (e.g., Berscheid & Walster, 1974; Dutton & Aron, 1974; Redmond et al., 1982; Roviaro & Holmes, 1980). For example, it has been shown that males who had just been frightened by walking across a swaying suspension bridge showed more interest in a female experimenter and used more sexual themes in the stories they told in response to Thematic Apperception Test cards than males who had just walked across a stable bridge (Dutton & Aron, 1974). In another experiment, college students who rode a bicycle vigorously before meeting a woman rated the woman as more attractive than men who did not ride the bicycle before meeting her (White et al., 1981). Indeed, men even felt more romantically attracted to a woman after listening to a gruesome description of a man being mutilated by a mob than after listening to a description of the circulatory system of a frog. That is, the arousal generated by the exercise or gruesome story got transferred to sex.

Arousal transference involving sex is apparently frequent among adolescents, for whom sex is relatively new and not yet well defined. For example, studies of adolescent boys indicate that approximately 50% experience an erection from some type of nonsexual but exciting stimulus such as an accident, a fire, being chased, or being punished (Bancroft, 1970).

This learning explanation for paraphilias has led to a treatment strategy known as **aversion therapy** that involves pairing anxiety with the paraphiliac object or activity so that in the future the object or activity will elicit anxiety in addition to or instead of sexual arousal (Barker, 1965; Cooper, 1964; Kushner, 1965; Marks & Gelder, 1967; Marks et al., 1970; Raymond & O'Keefe, 1965). In one study of aversion therapy, individuals with transvestic fetishes participated in training sessions in which they wore electrodes through which they could be given painful shocks by remote control (Marks & Gelder, 1967). Shocks were administered whenever the individuals began putting on any article of women's clothing or when they indicated that they were fantasizing about women's clothing. The results indicated that as training progressed, the clients became less and less likely to have erections while handling or thinking about women's clothing. It is noteworthy that the training procedures did not reduce the clients' sexual responsiveness to appropriate sexual stimuli (e.g., slides of nude women). In other words, aversion therapy reduced the response to women's clothing but not to women. The results of a follow-up study conducted 2 years later indicated that for most individuals, the effects of the training were still apparent (Marks et al., 1970).

One individual in the study initially became sexually aroused when he fantasized about "being tied up" (a mild sexual masochism disorder). Treatment involved administering a mild electrical shock whenever he indicated that he was having one of his masochistic fantasies. The degree to which the individual experienced

an erection while thinking about being tied up declined sharply with training and by the end of the third session was virtually eliminated. That finding is illustrated in Figure 18.7.

Aversion therapy can be effective for two reasons. First, if the paraphiliac object or activity can be made to elicit anxiety, it will be avoided. In other words, the therapist attempts to develop a classically conditioned *phobia* for the paraphiliac object, and it is hoped that the client will then avoid the paraphiliac object and return to normal sexual relationships. Second, if the paraphiliac object can be made to elicit anxiety, the anxiety may interfere with and inhibit the sexual arousal.

A potential problem with aversion therapy is that clients may become anxious about paraphiliac objects while in the therapist's office where they know the objects will be paired with negative consequences (e.g., shock), but the clients may realize that the negative consequences will *not* occur when the objects are used in the privacy of home. In other words, clients may distinguish between situations, and the conditioned anxiety will not generalize.

A second learning explanation for paraphilias is also based on the concept of classical conditioning, but in this explanation it is assumed that for some reason the appropriate sexual partner is *not available*, and therefore the individual achieves sexual arousal or

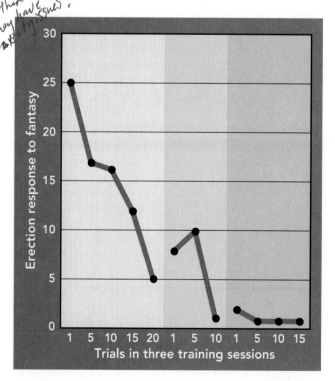

FIGURE 18.7 Aversion therapy was effective for reducing the arousal (erection) response in sexual masochists to the fantasy of being tied up. *Source:* Adapted from Marks and Gelder (1967), p. 715, fig. 2.

pleasure from some object that is associated with the desired but absent partner. In this explanation, the paraphilia is a *substitute*. For example, men find women arousing, and because articles of women's clothing are associated with the women, those objects could give rise to arousal and pleasure through the process of *generalization*. Therefore, when the woman is not available, the male might use a woman-associated substitute object to achieve arousal and pleasure. Support for this explanation comes from the fact that most paraphiliac objects are associated with women; that is, men with paraphilias usually collect women's clothing, not garbage can covers, and when men with paraphilias dress inappropriately to gain sexual pleasure, they do so in women's clothing, not in animal costumes.

A crucial question concerning this explanation and the related approach to treatment is, why is the sexual partner not available? In many cases, a partner is not available because women and sexual relationships are perceived as threatening and hence are avoided. Indeed, some individuals with paraphilias are characterized as timid and lacking in social skills. In those cases, social ineptitude may have resulted in failed social or sexual relationships, and that might have led the individuals to seek alternative sources of sexual gratification.

Treatment based on this explanation revolves around making members of the opposite sex more psychologically accessible. That is usually accomplished with some form of social skills training that will increase the likelihood of social success. Relaxation training (systematic desensitization) is also used to reduce the anxiety associated with interacting with members of the opposite sex (Bond & Hutchinson, 1960; Wolpe, 1958). However, treatment based on social skills training and relaxation training may not be completely effective because although it may make members of the opposite sex seem more approachable, the paraphiliac behavior has a long history of reward (sexual gratification), and the individual may not wish to give it up. Consequently, the most effective approach to treatment may involve social training and systematic desensitization to increase the accessibility of a normal sexual relationship, followed by aversion therapy to decrease the attraction of the paraphiliac behavior. In other words, first make the appropriate sex object accessible, and then develop an avoidance of the inappropriate sex object.

Physiological Approaches

One popular explanation for paraphilias is that they result from *excessively high sex drive*. It is assumed that males with paraphilias have higher than normal levels of the male hormone testosterone. The underlying notion seems to be that the high level of drive somehow "spills over" into inappropriate sexual behavior or drives the individual to abnormal behavior. This explanation and the image of the "oversexed pervert" are widely held by the general public. However, the data supporting this explanation are very limited and inconsistent. For example, when men who did and did not have transvestic fetishes were compared on a variety of sex-related hormones, no differences were found (Buhrich et al., 1979).

The notion that paraphilias are due to excessively high sex drive has led to the use of surgery (castration) or medication to reduce the sex drive of individuals with paraphilias. In some cases, those treatments have been effective, but that does not necessarily mean that the paraphilias are due to excessively high sex drive. Instead, it is possible that paraphilias are due to *misdirected* sex drive, and reducing the drive might reduce paraphilias because it *reduces sexual behavior in general,* not necessarily because the drive was too high.

Independent of whether or not paraphilias are due to excessively high sex drive, we must carefully examine the treatments designed to reduce sex drive because they may be effective and because they have generated considerable controversy. The most drastic approach is *castration* (surgical removal of the testicles), which removes the source of testosterone. The use of this approach is limited to individuals such as rapists whose sexual behavior poses a serious danger to others. Castration does reduce sexual desire, but contrary to what many people believe, it does not necessarily eliminate sexual arousal and behavior. For example, rapists who had been castrated and released from jail reported that after castration, they had greatly reduced frequencies of sexual thoughts, masturbation, and sexual intercourse, but 50% of the men reported that they were still able to have sexual intercourse (Heim, 1981). Overall, then, the main effect of castration may be to reduce the sexual desires that lead to the inappropriate sexual behavior.

While discussing the use of surgery to reduce sexual drive, it might be noted briefly that brain surgery has also been used to reduce the drive (Rieber & Sigusch, 1979; Schmidt & Schorsch, 1981). Specifically, portions of the hypothalamus were destroyed because that is the area of the brain responsible for sexual arousal. However, because the basis of the operation was questionable and the results equivocal, this procedure has been abandoned.

The second approach to lowering sex drive involves the use of *medication*. The drugs that are used to reduce sex drive in males are known as **antiandrogens** (AN-tī-AN-druh-jenz) because the male hormones they reduce belong to a class of hormones known as **androgens** (AN-druh-jenz). The most frequently used antiandrogen is **MPA** (medroxyprogesterone acetate), which is widely known by its trade name, **Depo-Provera** (DEP-ō prō-VĀR-uh). Depo-Provera is injected into a muscle, from which it is slowly released into the bloodstream. Because it is released slowly, patients undergo-

CASE STUDY 18.6
Use of Depo-Provera for Treating a Case of Sexual Sadism

The patient was a 47-year-old man who was obsessed with thoughts of sexual masochism and who had handcuffed, beaten, and stuck pins in his wife to achieve sexual satisfaction throughout their 25-year marriage. (This man's symptoms were described in greater detail in Case Study 18.5.) The patient voluntarily sought treatment when he became frightened that he might seriously harm or even kill his wife.

For 4 years, the patient was given Depo-Provera, which maintained the testosterone in his blood at below-normal levels. During the treatment period,

the patient did not report a single instance of sexual sadism, did not have any extramarital sexual relationships, and reported that conventional sexual activities became a regular part of his marriage. In addition, the patient reported that his sexual sadistic urges and obsessions were greatly reduced. In this case, then, the medication was effective for reducing the inappropriate sexual obsessions, urges, and behaviors.

Source: Adapted from Berlin and Meinecke (1981), p. 605.

---

ing treatment need to be given a shot only once or twice a week. Once in the bloodstream, Depo-Provera inhibits the release of sex-related hormones from the pituitary gland. That inhibition is important because ordinarily the hormones from the pituitary gland stimulate the testes and cause the release of testosterone, which is responsible for sexual arousal (see Figure 18.1). Depo-Provera thus reduces the male sex drive by reducing the release of the sex-related hormones.

The major side effects of Depo-Provera include drowsiness, weight gain, and increased blood pressure (Berlin & Krout, 1986). With regard to side effects, it should be noted that the drug is not a "feminizing" medication, and men who take it do not develop female sex characteristics such as breasts. All of the effects of Depo-Provera are eliminated within about 10 days after its discontinuance, and therefore its use does not have long-term effects.

Depo-Provera has often been found to be effective for controlling inappropriate sex behavior (e.g., Berlin & Meinecke, 1981; Gange, 1981; Kiersch, 1990; Wincze et al., 1986). For example, in one study in which patients were followed for 5 to 15 years, it was found that only 15% of those who received Depo-Provera relapsed (Berlin & Meinecke, 1981). However, two points should be noted in considering these findings. First, many of the findings were based on the patients' self-reports, and those reports may not be accurate because patients may be hesitant to report inappropriate (even illegal) sex behavior. Second, insofar as the drug does reduce inappropriate sexual behavior, its effects seem to be due primarily to the fact that it reduces subjective sexual *desire* rather than reducing physiological sexual *arousal* (Langevin et al., 1979; Wincze et al., 1986). In other words, like castration, Depo-Provera appears to reduce the thoughts or

desires that lead to sexual behavior, but if the individual is properly stimulated, he can become sexually aroused and active. This pattern of results is less than what was expected of the drug, but if the drug does reduce sexual desire, it may forestall inappropriate behaviors. Case Study 18.6 describes the use of Depo-Provera for treating a case of sexual sadism. (As an aside, it might be noted that in women, Depo-Provera can be an effective drug for birth control.)

The use of antiandrogens to treat paraphilias is controversial, and some writers have questioned whether the procedures are ethical (e.g., Berlin, 1989; Halleck, 1981; Melella et al., 1989). Some individuals, such as sadists, rapists, and child molesters, pose serious threats, and in the absence of other effective treatments for those individuals, medication may be appropriate. However, concerns are raised about the possibility of forcing medication on nondangerous individuals. Some abnormal sexual practices may be matters of preference or eccentricity and do not endanger others, and in those cases, medication may not be appropriate.

Before concluding this section, I should mention that there are some findings that sexual sadism may be related to a problem in brain structure (Hucker et al., 1988; Langevin et al., 1988). Brain scans have revealed that sadists are more likely to have abnormalities in the right temporal lobe than individuals with other sexual disorders or individuals who do not have sexual disorders. Abnormalities in the temporal lobes are particularly relevant because aggressive or attack behavior is controlled there. (Individuals who have temporal lobe epilepsy sometimes show spontaneous aggression.) The arousal associated with sex might set off aggression, and the combination of sex and aggression would lead to sadism.

Recidivism and New Laws

One of the most distressing findings concerning the treatment of paraphilias is that the rate of **recidivism** (repeat offenses) among sexual criminals is very high (Furby et al., 1989; Hanson et al., 1993; Marshall et al., 1991; M. E. Rice et al., 1991; Rubinstein et al., 1993). For example, in one sample of individuals who had been convicted of sexual offenses such as child molestation and rape, it was found that 31% were later convicted of a second sexual offense and that individuals who received treatment for their disorder were just as likely to be convicted of another offense as those who did not receive treatment (M. E. Rice et al., 1991). In another sample, it was found that the recidivism rate was over 40% (Hanson et al., 1993). Even those high rates are probably underestimates of the actual rate because sex crimes often go unreported and because the individuals had to be actually convicted of the second offense, and such convictions are often difficult to obtain. The high rate of recidivism reflects the persistent nature of the disorder and the fact that thus far we have not developed effective psychological interventions.

The rate of repeat offenses is very high among individuals who commit sexual offenses such as child molestation and rape. One study showed that individuals who were treated for their disorders were just as likely to be convicted for another offense as those who did not receive treatment.

Because of the general ineffectiveness of traditional treatments for sexual offenders and because of the fear that these individuals engender in the public, **sexual predator laws** have been passed that are designed to confine these individuals in prison for periods beyond their usual criminal sentences. Specifically, if a jury finds that an individual is *likely* to commit another sexual offense *in the future,* the individual can be confined for an indeterminate length of time. This procedure is a drastic departure from our usual legal procedures, in which an individual is confined *after* having committed an illegal act, not because it is suspected that he or she *might* commit an illegal act in the future. Other laws have been passed that require that residents of a neighborhood be notified, often with newspaper announcements, when a convicted sex offender who has served a criminal sentence is being returned to the community. (These are often called *Megan's laws* because they were passed in response to the case of a little girl named Megan who was raped and murdered by a previously convicted sex offender.) Concerns about the presence of a previous offender in the community may be justified, but these laws raise serious constitutional questions. That is, other criminals such as murderers who have served their time are not subject to additional confinement, and their return to the community does not require public announcement. I will discuss this issue in greater detail in Chapter 20 when I discuss legal issues in general.

T O P I C I I I

GENDER IDENTITY DISORDER

It will be helpful if I begin this discussion by making a distinction between **physiological sex identification,** which is the objective knowledge of whether you are a male or female based on the genitalia you have, and **psychological gender identity,** which is the subjective feeling of being a male or a female. Most individuals have a gender identity that is consistent with their physiological sex identification, but there are exceptions. For example, an individual may possess a penis, have all of the normal male secondary sex characteristics (e.g., deep voice, facial hair), and play a traditional male role in public but may feel that he is in fact a woman. When there is an inconsistency between an individual's physiological sex identification and his or her gender identity, the individual is diagnosed as suffering from the **gender identity disorder.** *Why a disorder?*

There are two major symptoms in the gender identity disorder, the first of which is a *persistent cross-sex identification.* That is, the individual wants to be or claims to be a member of the opposite sex. Second, the individual is *uncomfortable about his or her actual sex.* For example, a young girl may reject typical feminine behavior and dress, believe that she will grow a penis and not grow breasts or menstruate, and refuse to urinate in a sitting position. A young boy may reject masculine behavior and dress, believe that he will grow up to be a woman, and feel that his genitals are disgusting and that it would be better not to have a penis or testes. During adolescence and adulthood, individuals with the disorder are more realistic and realize that their physiological sex identification will not change, but they are still very uncomfortable with it. Some individuals with the gender identity disorder dress as members of the opposite sex, but they do so because they are more comfortable in those clothes, not because doing so gives them sexual gratification, as in the case of transvestic fetishism.

Individuals differ in the degree to which they experience an incongruence between their sex and gender identities. For some individuals, the incongruence is relatively mild and the individuals experience only "discomfort" with their physiological sex. In more severe cases, the individuals have the sense of actually belonging to the opposite sex (e.g., "a woman trapped in a man's body"). These individuals are often preoccupied with actually changing their primary and secondary sexual characteristics to those of the opposite sex.

A phrase that is often used when discussing sexual practices or disorders is "sexual preference," and the phrase is usually taken to imply that the individual has voluntarily or consciously *chosen* one type of sexual partner or identity over another. For example, it is implied that an individual with the gender identity disorder has *chosen* to identify with an opposite-sex role. However, when one works with individuals who have the disorder, it becomes clear that *they do not feel that they have a choice about their sexual identity.* Individuals with the gender identity disorder often fight the cross-sex identity, but they usually fail in that fight and eventually give up and accept the cross-sex identity as their "fate." For these individuals, the expression "sexual imperative" seems more appropriate than "sexual preference."

The consequences of fighting the cross-sex identification are reflected in the results of a survey that was conducted on male transvestites whose behavior appeared to be part of the gender identity disorder. About 70% of the individuals surveyed reported that at one time or another they had gone through a "purge" in which they had destroyed or given away all of their feminine clothing. However, the pressure to cross-dress had become too great, and at the time of the survey, 99% had given up trying to stop cross-dressing and over 70% had decided to expand their activities and develop their feminine selves more fully (Prince & Bentler, 1972). It seems that just as individuals with anxiety cannot voluntarily reduce their arousal and individuals

with schizophrenia cannot suppress their delusions, so persons with the gender identity disorder may not be able to avoid or deny their cross-sex identification.

EXPLANATIONS AND TREATMENTS

Psychological Approaches

One clear and consistent finding is that individuals with gender identity problems showed cross-sex behavior patterns even as young children. Numerous studies have documented that as children, the males were described as "sissies" who preferred feminine activities and the females were described as "tomboys" who preferred masculine activities (e.g., Green, 1974, 1976, 1985).

In considering the early onset of these disorders, it is important to recognize that although virtually all adults with gender identity disorder were sissies or tomboys during childhood, *not all children who are sissies or tomboys have the gender identity disorder as adults.* In fact, the gender identity disorder is relatively rare, and even among childhood sissies or tomboys, the probability of being diagnosed with the disorder later in life is low. For these reasons, *you should not assume that a child who has interests and behaviors characteristic of the opposite sex is necessarily showing the early signs of the gender identity disorder.*

The finding that the symptoms of the gender identity disorder appear first in childhood has led some theorists to assume that the disorder stems from training in *inappropriate gender roles during early childhood.* Specifically, it has been suggested that parents or other adults somehow foster the development of cross-sex behaviors, possibly because they wanted a child of the other sex. The father who wanted a son may treat his daughter like a son, taking her to football games or the office, thereby teaching her to be "one of the boys." It has also been suggested that the disorder stems from the possibility that the child has *identified with the opposite-sex parent* because the same-sex parent was not available for identification due to factors such as a broken home or hostility on the part of the same-sex parent. If a father is away much of the time or is so threatening that he cannot be approached, a young boy may spend most of his time with his mother and learn her gender role.

Explaining the gender identity disorder in terms of inappropriate sex-role socialization is initially appealing, but three problems should be recognized. First, it is possible that parents respond to children in a cross-sex fashion because the children behave in a cross-sex manner. Fathers may get out and throw the football with their tomboy daughters because the daughters are good at it and enjoy it. In other words, the responses of the parents may be an *effect* rather than a *cause* of the children's behavior.

Second, for every case in which parents may have encouraged cross-sex behavior, there are many cases in which frustrated parents did everything possible to *discourage* the cross-sex behavior. Fathers sometimes literally drag their feminine sons to sporting events to teach them to be men, and failing that, they bring them to the clinic for help.

Third and most important, there is no evidence to support the inappropriate-socialization explanation, but there is some evidence that seems to contradict it. For example, when an investigator compared feminine boys who showed "extensive cross-gender behavior" (early gender identity disorder) to boys who showed normal masculine behaviors, no differences were found on any social or family variable that might be related to child rearing and gender role development (Green, 1976). Overall, then, at present we remain without an empirically verified psychological explanation for this group of disorders, and therefore we must turn to possible physiological explanations.

Physiological Approaches

A very different explanation for the gender identity disorder is based on the possibility that during *fetal development* these individuals were exposed to higher than average levels of *hormones related to the opposite sex* (Collaer & Hines, 1995). There is a good deal of evidence that the physical sex characteristics and sexual behavior of many animals can be greatly influenced and even reversed by exposing the fetus to opposite-sex hormones. However, the question that arises is whether the hormones could also influence more subtle social behavior that is generally thought to be learned.

To test that possibility, investigators exposed one group of female monkeys to androgens (male hormones) while they were in the womb but did not do that to another group of monkeys, and then the social behavior of the monkeys was monitored as they grew up (Young et al., 1964). The results indicated that the monkeys who were exposed to the androgens behaved more like male monkeys than those who were not exposed to the androgens. For example, like male monkeys, the androgen-exposed females were more likely to threaten other monkeys, initiate play, and engage in more rough-and-tumble play patterns. Especially noteworthy was the fact that these masculine behaviors were strictly social and were not related to sexual behavior per se, thereby providing an interesting parallel for the behavior seen in humans with the gender identity disorder.

The results with animals are interesting, but it must be asked whether the same effects would be found in humans for whom it is believed that social factors play an important role in psychosexual development. A number of studies are relevant when considering this

Christine Jorgensen was the first person to undergo sex reassignment surgery. In this 1979 photo, she holds up the account of her transformation that appeared in the December 1, 1952, New York Daily News.

question; three of them will be considered here. Two of the studies focused on girls whose mothers had been given high levels of androgens while pregnant in attempts to avoid complications during pregnancy (Ehrhardt et al., 1968; Ehrhardt & Money, 1967). The results of both studies indicated that when compared to other girls, those who had been exposed in utero to the androgens were more likely to be described as "tomboys," participate in rough-and-tumble play, prefer boyish clothes, and aspire to culturally masculine ideals. The third study was conducted on two groups of boys whose mothers had been given high levels of estrogens (female hormones) during pregnancy (Yalom et al., 1973). One group was 16 years old at the time of the study, and the other group was 6 years old. These groups were compared to age-matched boys whose mothers had not been exposed to the estrogens. Comparisons of the 16-year-olds indicated that those exposed to the estrogens were rated as less "masculine"; more feminine when throwing and catching a ball, swinging a bat, and running; less aggressive; and having fewer masculine interests. Ratings of the 6-year-olds revealed only that those who had been exposed to the estrogens were less assertive and less athletic. The finding that differences were less pronounced in the 6-year-olds can be attributed to the fact that because they were younger, normal sex-role development had not progressed as far, so possibilities for differences were more limited.

Taken together, the results of these and other investigations are consistent and provocative but not conclusive. Therefore, the hormone explanation for the gender identity disorder will have to await additional research.

Sex Reassignment Surgery

In an attempt to cope with their problem, some individuals with the gender identity disorder take on the gender role with which they feel comfortable. In other words, they behave socially like opposite-sex individuals, and for some this provides an acceptable, albeit imperfect, solution for their problem. Others seek a more drastic solution, **sex reassignment surgery,** or what is commonly called a *sex-change operation.* The first of the modern sex reassignment surgeries was the celebrated case of Christine Jorgensen in 1952 (Hamburger et al., 1953); since then, many such operations have been performed, but there is controversey over the procedure (Petersen & Dickey, 1991; Olsson et al., 1995; Collyer, 1994; Pfafflin, 1992).

Surgery can be effective in making the individuals look like individuals of the opposite sex, but the operations are more than just cosmetic. In the case of the male-to-female change, it is possible to create an artificial vagina-like opening so that the individual can have intercourse and even experience orgasm (Lief & Hubscham, 1993). The female-to-male change is more difficult and less successful because although it is now possible to construct a penis, it has not been possible to reroute blood flow to enable the individual to have an erection. In addition to the surgery, in many cases the individuals take the hormones of their adopted sex (testosterone, estrogen). The hormones contribute to the physical characteristics (e.g., development of breasts) and behaviors of the new sex (Asscheman & Gooren, 1992; Cohen-Kettenis & Gooren, 1992). Case Study 18.7 concerns a woman who applied for sex reassignment surgery.

Apart from appearance and sexual performance, the important question is, does sex reassignment surgery result in improved gender identity adjustment? Since 1975 there have been at least 14 studies in which data have been collected from individuals who underwent sex reassignment surgery, and they have generated three noteworthy findings (see Abramowitz, 1986). First, about two-thirds of the individuals who undergo sex reassignment surgery report improved adjustment after surgery. Second, although about three times as many males as females apply for the surgery and the male-to-female operation is cosmetically more effective, it appears that the female-to-male surgery is psychologically more effective. The reasons for that are not clear.

CASE STUDY 18.7

Marilyn: An Applicant for Sex Reassignment Surgery

Marilyn presented herself as a tall, rugged-looking male with masculine voice quality, gait, and mannerisms. She is the fifth of six children. Her father died in an automobile accident 10 years ago at age 60. There is no family history of psychiatric contacts, alcoholism, or suicide. The family is described as deeply religious and supportive apart from one sister, who refers to the patient as a "queer."

As early as Marilyn can remember, she wanted to be like "other guys." In fact, as a young child she prayed for a penis. When she entered grade school, she became very upset when she wore dresses. Her family and school finally consented to her wearing overalls. Marilyn preferred boys' games to girls' activities, which led her peers to dub her "half boy, half girl." Marilyn has lived as a male since she left school and currently manages a section of a large drugstore.

Marilyn reports a long-standing sexual attraction to females but disgust with her own genitals and breasts. At age 17, she attempted heterosexual intercourse, which she describes as a dismal failure. She had a brief romance some 20 years ago with another female who left her to marry a male; that woman divorced her husband recently and is now living with Marilyn. Marilyn sought out sex reassignment surgery approximately 15 years ago, but she did not follow through on it due to the state of the surgical technology at that time.

Marilyn does not allow women to touch her breasts or vagina during sex play. She is adamant about not being a lesbian or interested in lesbian women. She feels that sex reassignment surgery will enhance her relationships with desired partners and enable her to live more comfortably as a male.

Source: Adapted from Roback and Lothstein (1986), pp. 407–408.

Third, about 7% of the operations result in bad or tragic outcomes such as serious adjustment problems or suicide. Sometimes individuals request another operation to restore the original sex. One of the best predictors of success is whether the individual tried living the life of the other sex for a period of time before the operation (Pfafflin, 1992). That is, a real-life pretest may reveal to the individual that the change in sex roles does not solve all of his or her problems, so the surgery is not undertaken and therefore disappointment is avoided.

Most positive conclusions about the effects of sex reassignment surgery must be accepted somewhat tentatively because most of the studies did not involve comparisons with control individuals who did not have the surgery (Snaith et al., 1993). Indeed, the results of a controlled study done at the Gender Identity Clinic of Johns Hopkins University raises serious questions about the success of the operations (Meyer & Reter, 1979). Its results indicate that control individuals who were not operated on showed improvements in adjustment over the follow-up period that were comparable to improvements in individuals who underwent the operation (i.e., both groups improved). The controversy over the effects of sex reassignment surgery is similar to the early controversy over the effects of psychotherapy, and we will have to wait until more and better experiments are reported before drawing firm conclusions about the psychological consequences of the surgery.

wouldn't it be their choice, tho?

SUMMARY

TOPIC I: SEXUAL DYSFUNCTIONS

- There are three types of sexual dysfunctions: (a) desire disorders, (b) arousal disorders, and (c) orgasmic disorders. All involve the absence or failure of sexual arousal at some time during the sexual response cycle.
- Desire disorders involve a deficiency or lack of desire for sexual activity. This can involve a simple lack of interest (hypoactive sexual desire disorder) or an active dislike and avoidance of sex (sexual aversion disorder).
- Psychological explanations for desire disorders revolve around defensive suppression, stress, and interpersonal factors (e.g., punishing the partner). The physiological explanation involves hormone imbalances (e.g., low levels of testosterone).
- There is little evidence for the effectiveness of psychotherapy, but hormone replacement therapy can be effective.
- Arousal disorders involve the inability to achieve or maintain an adequate level of sexual arousal, although desire is present.
- Psychological explanations for arousal disorders are focused on anxiety and distraction, whereas physiological explanations involve neurological damage, blockage of the arteries that supply blood to the penis or clitoris, and stimulation of the sympathetic nervous system by anxiety.
- Psychological treatment is focused on anxiety reduction, whereas physiological treatment involves enhancing blood supply or the implanting of a prosthetic device.
- Orgasmic disorders involve the inability to experience orgasm or, in the case of males, premature orgasm.
- Orgasmic disorders in women appear to be due to the fact that the women or their partners do not know what to do to achieve maximal sexual stimulation, and treatment involves education. The cause for premature ejaculation is not yet understood, but it can be treated with the start-stop and the start-squeeze techniques as well as with antidepressant drugs that block the reuptake of serotonin.

TOPIC II: PARAPHILIAS

- Paraphilias involve abnormal means of achieving sexual arousal, and they include exhibitionism, fetishism, transvestic fetishism, frotteurism, pedophilia,

— peeping Tom

sexual masochism, sexual sadism, and voyeurism. Autoerotic asphyxiation is another abnormal means of gaining arousal.

■ Psychodynamic explanations revolve around the interchangeable nature of drives such as sex and aggression. The learning explanation is based on classical conditioning. It has also been suggested that paraphilias are due to excessively high sex drive, but there is little evidence for that, and it is probably that the drive is misdirected rather than excessive.

■ Treatment based on learning often involves aversion therapy in which anxiety is paired with the arousing stimuli so they are avoided or the anxiety blocks the sexual arousal. Physiological treatments involve antiandrogens and castration, and they are effective because they reduce desire, so the individual is less inclined to act.

■ There is a very high rate of recidivism among sexual offenders, and that has led to the passage of sexual offender laws.

TOPIC III: GENDER IDENTITY DISORDER

■ The gender identity disorder involves a persistent cross-sex identification and discomfort with one's actual sex.

■ The psychological explanation for the gender identity disorder is that the individual was given inappropriate gender role training as a child, but there is little support for that. The physiological explanation is that during fetal development, the individual was exposed to high levels of opposite-sex hormones. In extreme cases, treatment can involve sex reassignment surgery.

KEY TERMS, CONCEPTS, AND NAMES

In reviewing and testing yourself on what you have learned from this chapter, you should be able to identify and discuss each of the following.

androgens *— male hormones*
antiandrogens
arousal disorders
arousal transference
autoerotic asphyxiation
aversion therapy
clitoral shaft
clitoris
cross-dressing
Depo-Provera
desire disorders
erectile tissues
exhibitionism
fetishism
frotteurism
gender identity disorder

glans
gonadotropins
G spot
hypoactive sexual desire disorder
hypothalamus
MPA
nocturnal penile tumescence
orgasmic disorders
paraphilias
pedophilia
physiological sex identification
pituitary gland
premature ejaculation
primary orgasmic disorder
progesterone
psychological gender identity

recidivism
releasing hormone
secondary orgasmic disorder
sex reassignment surgery
sexual aversion disorder
sexual dysfunctions
sexual masochism
sexual predator laws
sexual sadism
start-squeeze technique
start-stop technique
testosterone
testosterone replacement therapy
transvestic fetishism
voyeurism

CHAPTER NINETEEN
COGNITIVE DISORDERS and MENTAL RETARDATION

OUTLINE

Emma is 68 years old, and her daughter describes her as "slipping a lot lately." Most notable has been her loss of memory for recent events. For example, Emma will carry on a normal conversation, but 15 minutes later she will begin discussing the same topic again as though it had not already been discussed. At other times, she will go to get something in another room, but halfway there she will forget why she is going. Emma realizes that she is losing control, and that makes her very nervous. Recently she has also experienced a lack of coordination in her left arm. Sometimes she will go for weeks or months without showing any decline, and then she will show a sudden drop in functioning. Emma is suffering from *senile dementia,* probably due to a *multi-infarct disorder.* In other words, the decline in her mental status is probably due to a series of small strokes.

■ ■ ■

A few years ago, Harlan's hands began shaking a little. Not long after that, he began having trouble doing things like writing. It seemed like he was losing control of some of his small muscles. As time went by, the effects became more widespread, and he began walking with a stiff, shuffling gait. Harlan was diagnosed as suffering from *Parkinson's disease.* He is now being treated with a drug call L-dopa. The drug is effective for controlling his symptoms, but sometimes it interferes with his cognitive performance, and he begins hallucinating.

■ ■ ■

Michael suffers from a moderate level of mental retardation due to *Down syndrome.* His abilities are very limited, but he is a lovable, good-natured, and playful child. There is no treatment for Down syndrome. When he is older, Michael will probably spend his days working in a sheltered workshop, but he will always require a great deal of care and supervision. His parents worry about who will take care of him after they are gone.

■ ■ ■

In this chapter I will discuss a variety of disorders that involve *problems with cognitive functioning that occur independently of traditional psychiatric disorders such as depression or schizophrenia.* First I will review the cognitive disorders that stem from physiological problems such as Alzheimer's disease and strokes, and then I will examine the problem of mental retardation. Although many of the traditional psychiatric disorders, including depression and schizophrenia, can involve problems with cognitive functioning such as slowed thinking or confusion, in those disorders the cognitive problems are among *numerous symptoms* that make up the disorder. In contrast, in the disorders I will discuss in this chapter, cognitive problems are the *main symptom* of the disorder, and if there are other symptoms such as depression, they are secondary and occur because of the cognitive symptoms. For example, individuals who have had strokes and have lost some cognitive abilities such as language may be depressed, but the depression stems from the loss of the ability, not from the stroke per se.

Here I will discuss disorders that involve *declines in cognitive functioning that are due to underlying physiological problems,* primarily the disruption, deterioration, or death of the neurons that make up the brain. Some years ago, these were called *organic mental disorders,* but because we now know that many other disorders such as depression and schizophrenia can also have physiological (organic) causes, the term *organic mental disorders* is no longer useful for distinguishing between types of disorders. Therefore, that term was replaced by **cognitive disorders** to reflect the type of symptoms that predominate in these disorders.

The cognitive disorders can be divided into three types as a function of the nature of the cognitive symptoms (dementia, delirium, and amnesia). I will describe and explain each of those types.

DEMENTIA DISORDERS

The symptoms of **dementia** (di-MEN-shuh) **disorders** revolve primarily around problems with *memory.* (The word *dementia* is derived from the Latin *de,* which means "away," and *ment* or *mens,* which means "mind," so the word literally refers to losing—moving away from—the mind.) An individual who is suffering from dementia may not be able to recall previous experiences or previously learned material or may not be able to put new experiences into memory. Initially, individuals who are suffering from dementia may be unable to remember small things such as names, phone numbers, directions, or minor events. However, as the disorder progresses, the individuals may not remember people whom they have known for many years (parents can even "forget" their children), and they may not remember a conversation they had only minutes earlier, so they repeat conversations over and over. Furthermore, in some cases the problems with memory can impair language functioning because the individuals will not be able to recall names or words; that is known as **aphasia** (uh-FĀ-zhuh). (The word *aphasia* is based on *a,* which means "not," and *phasia,* which means "speech," so *aphasia* literally means "no speech.") In extreme cases, the problems with memory can lead to problems with simple motor activities such as dressing and cooking, and the individuals may even become lost in their own homes. Some individuals may be unable to recognize simple objects such as a chair, or they may even be unable to recognize their own reflections in a mirror.

In the early stages of the disorder, individuals who suffer from dementia often develop coping strategies that allow them to compensate somewhat for their loss of memory. Probably the most common coping strategy is note writing. Individuals who are losing their memories write notes to remind themselves of the things they cannot effectively store in memory. One 76-year-old woman who had lost much of her memory due to Alzheimer's disease took extensive notes while watching various television programs because during the commercial breaks she would forget what had happened and become very confused about the story line. She also left notes to herself all around the house reminding herself to do things: "Turn off the stove," "Lock the front door," "Put toothpaste on your brush," "Don't turn the knobs that control the color on the television." Strategies like that can be very helpful in the early and middle stages of dementia, but in the final stages, not even they can make up for the intellectual loss.

In some cases dementia can cause changes in the individual's personality or temperament. The extent

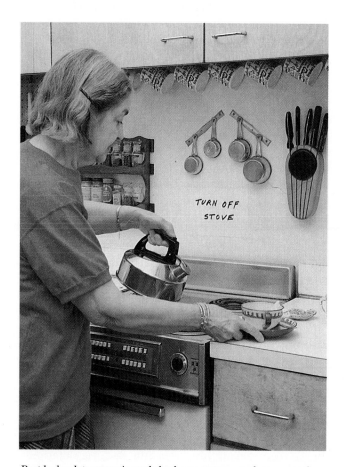

People develop strategies to help them compensate for memory loss. Reminder notes, at least during the early stages of dementia, can help individuals function more competently.

and nature of the changes differ greatly from one individual to another. As they begin to lose control, some people become irritable and difficult to manage; others essentially give up and become very compliant. Some individuals develop paranoid delusions. The delusions probably stem from the fact that these individuals are losing control and do not understand what is happening around them, so they make up explanations. For example, an elderly man who cannot find his money may assume that someone is stealing it. The changes in personality are a *secondary effect* of the dementia rather than part of the dementia per se.

The rate of decline in functioning due to dementia is usually relatively slow and smoothly progressive because the underlying deterioration of the brain is slow and smoothly progressive. However, with some disorders such as strokes, declines may be sudden and steplike because when each stroke occurs, it suddenly destroys a section of brain tissue. Furthermore, in those cases, there may be differences from time to time in what functions are lost because the strokes are destroying neurons in different parts of the brain. For example, an individual may show a steady level of functioning and then a sudden drop in memory performance, followed by a plateau and then a sudden loss of some motor ability. The nature of the decline (smooth vs. steplike) is sometimes an important factor in determining the cause of the dementia.

If the decline begins before the age of 65, it is referred to as **presenile dementia;** if it begins after age 65, it is referred to as **senile dementia.** The age of onset of dementia is of course important for the individual suffering from the disorder, but it is also important for family members because in the case of disorders for which there is a genetic basis, early onset is associated with a greater likelihood that biological relatives will also suffer from the disorder.

Finally, it is important to distinguish between primary and secondary dementia. **Primary dementia** refers to a decline in intellectual functioning that is due to a *physiological problem in the brain,* whereas **secondary dementia** refers to a decline in intellectual function that is the result of *some other disorder.* For example, declines in abilities due to Alzheimer's disease are primary dementia, whereas the declines in functioning that are associated with depression are instances of secondary dementia. In one case it was thought that a woman with Alzheimer's disease had gone through a period of particularly rapid deterioration or had had a stroke because she became listless, disoriented, and almost mute. However, a month later she showed striking improvement. Because deterioration from organic causes cannot be reversed, it was concluded that her temporary decline in functioning had been due to a period of depression. Recent research indicates that it is difficult or impossible to distinguish between dementia that stems from mild Alzheimer's disease and the symptoms of depression (Rubin et al., 1991). That poses a serious problem because almost 20% of the individuals admitted to nursing homes may suffer from severe undiagnosed depression (Rovner et al., 1991). Obviously, if the basis for the dementia were misdiagnosed, treatment would be focused on the wrong problem. In this chapter, we will focus on primary dementia.

Different diagnoses are made depending on the nature of the underlying physiological cause. Specifically, there are diagnoses of dementia due to (a) Alzheimer's disease, (b) vascular disorders (e.g., strokes), and (c) other general medical conditions. In the sections that follow, I will describe and explain three specific dementia disorders.

Alzheimer's Type: General Brain Deterioration

Alzheimer's (OLTS-hī-murz) **disease** is probably the most common cause of dementia among elderly people, and it is three times more prevalent among women than men. In the early phases, the individual is generally forgetful, and the major problem is with *short-term memory.* In the middle phase, problems with short-term memory increase and may become so severe that the individual is unable to hold a memory long enough to transform it into purposeful action. That problem is known as **cognitive abulia** (uh-BYOO-lē-uh). (The word *abulia* refers to an abnormal lack of ability to act or make a decision.) For example, an individual may go into a room to do something but once in the room may completely forget why he or she is there. (That happens to all of us at times, but in Alzheimer's disease it is a persistent problem.)

In the final stage of the disorder, both short-term and long-term memory functions are lost. The individual is not only unable to recall what happened a few minutes earlier but also unable to recognize family members such as his or her own children. In this stage, people suffering from Alzheimer's disease are disoriented and may not be able to take care of themselves. Problems with other systems may also develop; for example, there may be a loss of motor control, meaning that the individual can no longer control elimination processes.

In the early phases of the disorder, some individuals with Alzheimer's disease do not show obvious problems with memory, but they may develop paranoid delusions. For example, they may think that members of the family are plotting against them. We do not know why that pattern develops. It may be that the individual is beginning to experience some cognitive confusion and attributes the loss of control to external sources. In

In the final stages of Alzheimer's disease, the memory loss suffered may be so severe that a patient may be unable to carry out basic self-care.

years, the deterioration had reached the point at which she had difficulty talking because she could no longer remember words. If an individual survives to the age of 80, it is unlikely that he or she will then develop the disorder (Silverman et al., 1994).

The age of onset of Alzheimer's disease is related to the probability that biological relatives will also suffer from the disorder. The earlier the onset, the greater the likelihood that the patient's offspring will also develop the disorder (Li et al., 1995; Silverman et al., 1994).

Autopsies of individuals who suffered from Alzheimer's disease have revealed three types of brain deterioration. First, the neurons in the cortex appear to be tangled and in disarray. This is referred to as **neurofibrillary** (NYOO-rō-FIB-ruh-ler-ē) **tangling,** and it is illustrated in Figure 19.1. It is suspected that the tangled neurons result in disruptions in neurological functioning, which in turn cause the cognitive confusion that is associated with Alzheimer's disease. It is as though "all the wires got crossed." Second, the nerve endings in the brains of individuals with Alzheimer's disease show high levels of deterioration. The patches of deterioration are called **plaques** (plaks). The fact that the nerve ends are deteriorated probably serves to inhibit effective transmission of nerve impulses, which would interfere with cognitive functioning. Third, there may be small holes in the body of the nerve that reflect general deterioration. This is called **granulovacuolar** (GRAN-yuh-lō-VAK-yoo-ō-lur) **degeneration.** This type of deterioration seems to be limited to the area of

other words, instead of saying, "I can't find things because I am getting old and losing my memory," the individual might say, "I can't find things because other people are taking them or hiding them." If that is the case, the personality changes would be a secondary rather than a primary symptom of the neurological deterioration.

In all cases of Alzheimer's disease, the decline in cognitive functioning eventually becomes apparent and is the dominant symptom. However, because the disorder sets in gradually, its onset is hard to identify. It is commonly thought that death will occur 5 to 10 years after the start of the disorder, but it has not been demonstrated that the disorder is necessarily the cause of death. Given the late onset of Alzheimer's, it is quite possible that the patients would die within 5 to 10 years even if they did not have the disorder.

Alzheimer's disease is most likely to occur late in life (after age 65), but presenile cases do occur. One woman was afflicted in her early 50s, and within three

After President Ronald Reagan left office, it was announced that he was suffering from Alzheimer's disease. As the disease has progressed, he has made fewer public appearances.

FIGURE 19.1 Brain cells of persons with Alzheimer's disease are characterized by neurofibrillary tangling, plaques, and granulovacuolar degeneration.

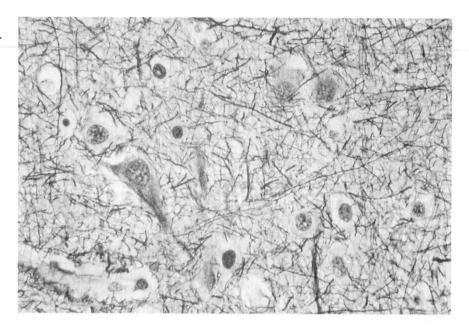

the brain known as the *hippocampus,* which plays a major role in memory. In addition to causing problems with cognitive functioning, in some cases these types of neurological problems can cause other symptoms such as involuntary motor movements (twitches or facial grimaces) or slurring of speech. Whether or not motor behavior is influenced is determined by where in the brain the deterioration occurs.

Researchers have identified the structural problems associated with Alzheimer's disease (tangles, plaques, granulovacuolar degeneration), but they have not yet identified exactly what causes those problems. Numerous promising explanations are under investigation, but because most of them are still highly speculative, it would not be appropriate to focus on any one theory here. However, it has been discovered that patients with Alzheimer's disease who have a family history of the disorder have a defect on *genes 14 and 21* (Cohen, 1995; Saint George–Hyslop et al., 1987). It was also found that the area of gene 21 where the defect occurs is responsible for the production of amyloid proteins that are associated with abnormal tissue development (plaques, granulovacuolar degeneration) in the brain (Goldgaber et al., 1987; Selkoe et al., 1987; Tanzi et al., 1987). The location of the defect on gene 21 is also interesting because an extra gene 21 is associated with the form of mental retardation known as Down syndrome, and individuals with that syndrome have a high prevalence of Alzheimer's disease in later life. It should not be concluded that the genetic defect that has been isolated is responsible for all cases of Alzheimer's disease. It is possible that there may be more than one cause, and environmental factors may play a role. For example, there are long-lived monozygotic twin pairs in which one twin suffers from the disorder but the other twin does not (Rapoport et al., 1991). In fact, it is possible that

Alzheimer's symptoms may reflect a group of degenerative disorders rather than a single disease.

In general, a diagnosis of Alzheimer's disease can only be confirmed with an autopsy, and therefore in living patients a diagnosis of Alzheimer's disease is made by exclusion. In other words, when all other possible explanations for the dementia have been ruled out, it is assumed that the individual has Alzheimer's disease. The chromosomal problem that is responsible for cases of Alzheimer's disease that are due to heredity can be detected with a blood test, but the complicated nature of the test makes it impractical for general screening (Murrell et al., 1991).

Finally, a comment should be made concerning the so-called **nootropic** (NŌ-uh-TRŌ-pik; "mind-acting") **drugs** (e.g., Piracetam, Oxiracetam) that have been proposed as a treatment for Alzheimer's disease. Early research on animals suggested that these drugs might reverse neurological problems associated with memory loss and learning disabilities. These findings sparked hope in relatives of individuals with Alzheimer's disease and received widespread attention. However, the effects in animals are questionable, and there is no reliable evidence that the drugs have any effects in humans (Bartus, 1990).

Case Study 19.1 reflects the early and middle phases of Alzheimer's disease in a woman as seen by her daughter, who, because of the genetic basis of the disease, may also be at risk.

Vascular Type: Death of Brain Tissue Due to Lack of Blood

Blood provides the nourishment that cells must have to survive, and if the supply of blood is cut off, the cells

CASE STUDY 19.1

A Daughter Talks About Her Mother's Experience with Alzheimer's Disease and Her Concerns About Her Own Future

"My mother was once an active, healthy, charming, independent, and very intelligent woman. When my father died, Mother took a position with a small importing company, and in a short time she became the company's executive manager. After she retired, she had a very active social life. She had lots of friends, traveled a lot, did volunteer work, gardened, and gave splendid parties. In short, she really 'had it together,' and she was fun to be around.

"Around age 68 or 69, however, Mother began to slow down. She stopped going out and ceased seeing friends. She spent most of her time at home reading or watching television. I really wasn't too concerned; after all, she was almost 70. After a while, however, her behavior seemed to deteriorate somewhat. She became very forgetful and sometimes seemed a little confused, although she covered it up well. I attributed most of these changes to the fact that she wasn't getting much social stimulation, and undoubtedly that did play a role. As time went on, however, her forgetfulness became very pervasive, and she had to leave notes for herself everywhere reminding her what to do (e.g., 'Be sure to lock the door,' 'Remember to turn the oven off,' 'Feed the cat'). Most noticeable was the fact that when she read books or watched television, she would take extensive notes. I soon realized that without the notes, she would not be able to remember what had happened at that point in the story. As this got worse I became concerned about her living alone, so I arranged for a woman who lived across the hall to look in on her a few times a day. Over the next year, Mother got by on her own, but she was doing less and less well. Because of my increasing concern, I made arrangements for her to have a complete checkup at the medical center.

"Four days after her examination, I was called in for a conference with the physician, neurologist, psychologist, and social worker who had seen her. The physician came right to the point and said that there were three things I needed to know. First, he said that Mother was in excellent physical condition (90th percentile for her age group on most measures) and that she would probably live another 15 years. Second, he said that it was their judgment that Mother was suffering from a serious and rapidly pro-

gressing case of Alzheimer's disease. He said—these are his words—that at the rate her disease was advancing, '*she will be a vegetable in five years.*' I had been prepared for bad news, but that really stunned me. He went on to point out that given Mother's life expectancy and the speed with which the Alzheimer's was progressing, she would need *total* care for an *extended* period of time, and therefore I was going to have to face a very substantial financial responsibility. I had barely taken that in when he made his third point. 'Finally, I have to tell you that Alzheimer's is inherited, and it is highly probable that you will develop the disease. You should take that into account in making financial plans for your own future.' Clearly, *I was facing serious problems.*

"The first thing I had to do was find a place for Mother to live. Because she could still take care of herself, she didn't need to live in a nursing home, and I was fortunate to find a 'minimal care' facility that was operated by the Catholic church. Originally, the building had been a college dormitory, but it had been converted to a home for elderly persons when the college no longer needed it. Residents have individual rooms, which they furnish with their own furniture. The homelike rooms are good-sized and have washbasins, but like in many old dorms, the residents share bathroom facilities on each floor. Meals are provided in a dining room just as in a college dorm. Residents must be relatively healthy because there is no nursing care. However, the staff will remind residents to take medication as needed. All of the staff members are caring and wonderful, and the facility has been a godsend.

"Of course, Mother did not want to move out of her own home, and as she left, she said to her neighbor, 'I'll never have another happy day in my life. It's over.' I almost broke down and cried, but the move had to be made.

"Over the next two years, Mother began showing a slow and progressive deterioration. After the first year, she had almost no short-term memory. While talking with her on the phone one evening, for example, I asked her to check to make sure she had clean socks in her dresser drawer. She put down the phone to go to the dresser, but before she got there

(continued)

CASE STUDY 19.1 *(continued)*

she forgot what she was supposed to do, and then she forgot that she was on the phone, so she just went and sat in her chair, leaving the phone off the hook. I had to hang up, call to the front desk, and have them send someone up to hang the phone up so I could call back.

"She also started having trouble with aphasia [loss of the ability to use certain words]. One evening on the phone, she said, 'It's broken.' I asked, 'What's broken, Mother?' but she couldn't tell me. She just couldn't find the word. Finally, in frustration she said, 'You know, the thing on the wall.' 'Where on the wall, Mother?' 'Next to the window.' 'Do you mean the clock, Mother?' 'Yes, the clock's broken and not working.' Sometimes talking with mother is like playing twenty questions because she just can't find the words she needs. She gets very frustrated and sometimes just gives up.

"As time went by, Mother became less and less aware of what was happening around her. On a number of occasions I noticed that Mother would become very confused for a couple of days, and when the confusion cleared up, she would not be functioning as well as she had before. I think she may be having little strokes. The Alzheimer's is causing the slow deterioration, and the strokes are probably responsible for the sudden drops in ability.

"As her level of functioning has declined, Mother has withdrawn and interacts less and less with other residents. She goes to meals and 'goes through the motions' of social interaction, but I don't think she really understands what is going on around her. Most of the time now she simply sits in her room, hunched forward, looking at the floor. Sometimes the television is on, but it doesn't make much difference because she really can't follow it anymore. The *TV Guide* that used to be heavily marked with reminders about what to watch now lies unopened on the floor.

"One of the saddest things is that at times Mother is aware of the fact that she has lost control. One day I told her that I thought she was looking good, and after a moment's pause, she frowned and said in a weak little voice, 'Oh, maybe I look good, but I'm not really good. I get all mixed up about everything. I don't know what to do. I don't know what's happening.' Sometimes she seems absolutely terrified. It tears me apart to see her like that. Sometimes I think it might be better if she lost that one last vestige of insight.

"I've heard that some people become hostile or paranoid as they go through this deterioration, but I'm very fortunate in that so far Mother has remained very sweet, affectionate, and considerate. She always says she is 'fine,' but I know that she is worried and very unhappy. The other day, she told one of the other residents that she wishes she were dead and would like to jump out of her window but can't open it.

---

will die. For example, when the blood supply to a part of the brain is cut off, that part of the brain dies, and the individual is said to have had a **cerebral infarction.** The common term for a cerebral infarction is **stroke.**

If the infarction affects a part of the brain that is essential to life, the individual will die. However, if the infarction affects a part of the brain that is responsible for motor or cognitive functioning, the individual will live but will lose the ability that was associated with that part of the brain. For example, an infarction in the motor area will result in paralysis; an infarction in an area that is responsible for language will result in the inability to use words. The case of a professor in a large midwestern university provides a particularly poignant example of the language difficulties that sometimes follow a cerebral infarction. After his first infarction, he developed aphasia, which posed problems when he lectured. He was a nationally recognized expert on Shakespeare and had not forgotten anything he knew about Shakespeare, but he could not remember Shakespeare's name. His lectures would go something like this: "Yesterday, I began lecturing about the sonnets of . . . of . . . oh, you know, the chap who wrote *Hamlet*." Over time he developed a list of important words that he could not bring to mind, and when he drew a blank during a lecture, he would quickly go down his "cheat sheet" to find the word or name he needed. Unfortunately, he suffered several more cerebral infarctions and has completely lost his ability to communicate.

Because neurons in the central nervous system (brain and spinal cord) cannot replace themselves, once the neurons are dead, they are gone forever. For-

"We've had a couple of crises recently. About three months ago, I was called at my office and told that Mother had put all of her clothes in a pile outside her door, stating that she was leaving. When I got there 20 minutes later, I found Mother sitting on her bed weeping with her head in her hands. She knew that she had done something wrong, but she could not remember what it was, and she was frightened. I put the clothes away, and the incident passed. Two weeks ago, I was called early in the morning and told that I had to come over right away. Mother had not come down for breakfast, and when the staff had gone to her room to check on her, they found her disoriented, mute, and incontinent. She had soiled herself and was wandering around half dressed. After cleaning her up, I took her to the medical center. A checkup did not reveal any physical problem; indeed, she was pronounced 'physically very healthy.' When the tests were done that afternoon, some of the confusion had cleared up, so I took her back to her room. The crisis passed, but Mother's level of functioning did not return to what it had been. She is much more confused and less verbal, and for some reason she can't seem to change clothes by herself anymore. Now every evening I have to stop by and help her get ready for bed and put out her clothes for the next day. With this help she can get by, but the woman who administers the home says that she doesn't think they will be able to keep Mother much longer. I have begun looking for a facility that can provide more care.

"I'm struggling with three rough problems. First, it's a terrible experience to watch Mother go through this. I love her, she has done so much for me, and now there's so little I can do for her as she slowly loses control. It's tearing me apart emotionally.

"Second, I'm not sure how I'm going to handle all of this financially. It's clear that soon Mother will have to be moved to a nursing home, but nursing home care is terribly expensive, it isn't covered by insurance, and Mother might need it for years and years. This could wipe me out financially. I'm not sure how I'm going to handle it, and if I can't, what will happen? What will happen to Mother when we can't afford the care she needs?

"Last, I worry about what is ultimately going to happen to me. Sometimes when I see Mother confused and slumped in her chair staring at the floor, I see myself 20 years from now. It's like looking into a horrible crystal ball. Is this going to happen to me? Is this my future I'm looking at, slumped alone in the chair? If it is, who is going to look after me when I lose control, become incontinent, and can't dress myself? Will I waste away like that—and be alone with no one to help? It's frightening. . . ."

tunately, however, sometimes other areas of the brain may take over the functions of the dead areas. Therefore, with time and retraining, approximately 20% of stroke victims regain their abilities (20% die, and 60% have some residual impairment; Lishman, 1978).

Many individuals have one massive cerebral infarction that kills them or leaves them with large and sudden disabilities (e.g., major paralyses, lack of language), but other individuals have a series of small infarctions, each of which destroys a small area of the brain. Over time, these small infarctions can result in the loss of a large part of the brain and in considerable dementia. This is known as **multi-infarct dementia** (dementia that results from multiple small infarcts). Other parts of the brain may take over some of the lost functions, but the speed with which functions are lost exceeds the rate at which they can be taken over, and thus there is a net loss over time.

Two things about the symptom pattern in multi-infarct dementia distinguish it from other dementias. First, the decline in abilities is *uneven* rather than smoothly progressive. This is because a sudden loss in function following an infarction is followed by a plateau until the next infarction. The sudden loss of function may be large or small, and it may influence any of a number of abilities. Overall, this results in an uneven and erratic rate of decline in abilities. The second distinguishing feature of multi-infarct dementia is that it usually results in the loss of *specific abilities* (loss of language, loss of memory, paralysis of parts of the body) rather than a general deterioration of function. In other words, the loss of abilities is "patchy" rather

With time and retraining, approximately 20% of stroke victims regain abilities lost due to their strokes.

than general. The patchy nature of the loss is due to the fact that specific areas of the brain are destroyed by the infarcts. However, over time, many infarcts will result in a widespread loss of functions, and therefore the deterioration will appear to be more general. In some individuals, the loss of abilities can be very frightening and result in high levels of anxiety.

Cerebral infarctions stem from four factors. The first is a progressive narrowing and eventual blockage of the blood vessels because of the buildup of fatty material on the walls of the blood vessels. You will recall from Chapter 16 that this is known as **atherosclerosis,** and it results in reduced blood flow to parts of the brain, which in turn leads to the death of those parts of the brain. Second, infarcts occur because blood vessels lose their elasticity and rupture when blood pressure increases. When a rupture occurs, the blood flow to the area of the brain served by that artery is interrupted. The process by which the vessels lose their elasticity is known as **arteriosclerosis** (ar-TĒ-rē-ō-skluh-RŌ-sis). This is the "hardening of the arteries" that is often referred to when discussing cerebral problems in older individuals. The third cause of infarcts also involves a rupture, but in this case the rupture occurs when the wall of a blood vessel develops a weak spot, swells, and finally breaks. Such a weak spot is called an **aneurysm** (AN-yur-iz-um). Fourth, a clump of atherosclerotic plaque may develop and suddenly clog an artery, thereby reducing blood flow. That is known as an **embolism.**

Once the syndrome of multi-infarcts begins, there is little that can be done to arrest it, but numerous things can be done to prevent or reduce the likelihood of its beginning. Among those things are diets that lower low-density cholesterol to reduce atherosclerosis and controlling blood pressure with medication or aerobic exercise (see Chapter 16) to reduce the likelihood of rupturing blood vessels.

Due to a General Medical Condition

Dementia disorders can also stem from a variety of general medical conditions such as an HIV infection, a trauma (blow) to the head, Parkinson's disease, Huntington's disease, Pick's disease, and Creutzfeldt-Jakob disease.

Dementia due to a medical condition can be illustrated with Parkinson's disease, which is due to low levels of the neurotransmitter dopamine. The physical symptoms of Parkinson's disease involve problems with muscle movements—tremors; impairment of fine motor movements, such as a stiff or shuffling gait; and rigidity of the face and other parts of the body. Some individuals with Parkinson's disease become depressed and withdrawn. Those psychological symptoms may be part of the disorder, but it is more likely that they are secondary symptoms that stem from anxiety over the physical symptoms and the attempt to cope with them. The disorder is relatively common, affecting at least 500,000 people in the United States at any given time (Duvoisin, 1984). It is usually diagnosed in individuals over the age of 50.

Parkinson's disease is due in part to the destruction of the **substantia nigra** (sub-STAN-she-uh NĪ-gruh; "dark matter"), a dark gray area of the midbrain that is responsible for motor movements. A secondary effect of the loss of the substantia nigra is a drop in the production of dopamine, and the resulting imbalance in neurotransmitters is thought to be responsible for some of the other motor symptoms. It is not clear what causes the destruction of the substantia nigra, but it could result from infections, infarctions, tumors, or drugs. The drug **L-dopa** is effective for reducing, if not eliminating, the symptoms in approximately 80% of the individuals who suffer from Parkinson's disease (Bauer et al., 1982). L-dopa interacts with an enzyme and is converted into dopamine. The increased levels of dopamine that result are nearer to normal levels and thereby reduce the symptoms. Thus L-dopa is effective for *treating* but not for *curing* Parkinson's disease.

You may recall from Chapters 12 and 13 that schizophrenia stems from high levels of dopamine activity and that the neuroleptic drugs that are used to treat schizophrenia reduce dopamine activity. At high levels, those drugs may decrease schizophrenia, but they can also bring on the symptoms of Parkinson's disease because of an excessive reduction of dopamine activity. Not surprisingly, the high levels of L-dopa used to treat Parkinson's disease can result in excessively high levels of dopamine activity and bring on the symptoms of schizophrenia. In treating these disorders, then, it is necessary to achieve the delicate balance of a dopamine level that is neither too low nor too high.

DELIRIUM DISORDERS

Delirium (di-LIR-ē-um) **disorders** are characterized by *disturbances in consciousness,* such as a *reduced awareness of the environment* so that the individual may not know where he or she is, and *problems in focusing attention,* so that the individual is easily distracted and cannot stay "on track." In addition, delirium disorders involve *problems with memory and language,* probably because the individuals are not concentrating effectively, and may also involve *perceptual distortions* (hallucinations). In short, the symptoms of delirium involve problems with awareness, attention, memory or language, and perception. (The word *delirium* comes from a Latin word meaning "to leave the track" or, used figuratively, "to be crazy," and individuals who are delirious behave more strangely and hence appear more "off track" and "crazy" than individuals who are suffering from dementia.)

Due to a General Medical Condition

Delirium disorders can be caused by a variety of medical conditions, such as encephalitis and meningitis, which involve inflammation of the tissues that surround the brain. Malaria can also cause delirium. In most cases the factor that causes the delirium is the *high fever* that accompanies the diseases; the increased

temperature causes a disruption in brain functioning. For example, brief periods of delirium will be seen in children who are running very high fevers and in individuals who are suffering from "heat stroke" (hyperthermia). An important point here is that when the medical condition goes away, so will the delirium, and there will not be any long-term effects.

Due to Substance Intoxication or Withdrawal

Delirium disorders can be brought on by a variety of drugs, including narcotics (opiates) such as morphine, hallucinogens such as LSD, and depressants such as barbiturates and alcohol. Delirium can also be triggered by many poisons and allergic reactions. One of the most frequent causes of delirium disorders is a high level of alcohol; indeed, individuals who are very drunk might be considered to be suffering from a minor form of delirium in that they are not completely aware of what is going on around them, they have difficulty with attention, they have problems with memory and language, and they may even hallucinate. Furthermore, individuals who have been on high levels of alcohol for long periods of time and whose bodies have adjusted to those levels may experience a delirium disorder when the alcohol is withdrawn. That is referred to as **delirium tremens** because in addition to the cognitive symptoms of delirium, the individuals experience uncontrollable muscle tremors. (*Tremens* means "tremor," so *delirium tremens* is literally "delirium with tremors.") The substances that cause delirium do so because they disrupt neurological activity in the brain and that disrupts cognitive functioning. Treatment usually involves using a drug that will offset the effects of the original drug and restore normal brain functioning. Because delirium disorders are usually triggered by an acute infection, sudden change in temperature, or drug administration, they usually show a rapid onset.

AMNESIA DISORDERS

In **amnesia** (am-NĒ-zhuh) **disorders,** the symptom is a problem with memory. Specifically, either the individual cannot recall previously known things or cannot put new information into memory. (The word *amnesia* comes from a Greek word that means "forgetfulness.") Problems with memory are also central to the dementia disorders that were discussed earlier, but the difference between those disorders and amnesia disorders is that in the amnesia disorders, the symptoms are limited to problems with memory and the problems are usually less profound.

It should be noted that there are two types of amnesia: **retrograde amnesia,** in which the problem is with the retrieval of information that was effectively stored earlier, and **anterograde amnesia,** in which the problem is with the storage of new information. A classic example of anterograde amnesia is H. M., who at the age of 27 had to have portions of his brain removed to treat a life-threatening case of epilepsy. In the operation, part of H. M.'s hippocampus was removed, and thereafter he was unable to put new memories into storage (Milner, 1970; Scoville & Milner, 1957). H. M. could remember things that happened to him *before* the operation, and he had an effective short-term memory, so he could carry on a normal conversation (as long as he was talking about something, it was held in his short-term memory), but a few minutes later, H. M. had no memory of what had happened. For example, if you met and talked with H. M. and then left the room for a few minutes, when you returned, H. M. would have no memory of ever having met or talked with you. It is interesting to note that H. M. and his family moved shortly after his operation, but he was never able to remember that they moved or recall the new address. In essence, H. M. is trapped in time at the point at which he had his operation. Indeed, when asked what date it is, he gives a date a few days before his operation, which occurred many years ago.

Due to a General Medical Condition

Amnesia disorders can stem from a variety of factors such as Korsakoff's disease, malnutrition, convulsions, and concussions. In the case of retrograde amnesia, those factors either disrupt the functioning or destroy the neurons that form the networks in which memories are stored, and therefore the memories are lost. Greater damage results in greater loss. For example, an individual who experiences a concussion from a blow to the head may lose only the memory for the events that immediately preceded the blow, but an individual who has a disease that has widespread effects in the brain may lose the ability to recall events extending back many years. In the case of anterograde amnesia, the primary problem is in the part of the brain called the hippocampus through which memories must go on their way to storage, so if the hippocampus is disrupted or destroyed, new experiences cannot be stored in memory. The problems with memory may be temporary if the functioning of the neurons is merely disrupted, but the problems may be permanent if the neurons are destroyed.

Due to a Substance

Amnesia can also be caused by various drugs that destroy or disrupt brain functioning. Transient amnesia

TABLE 19.1 Symptoms and Course of Cognitive Disorders

Dementia Disorders
- Problems with memory (recall and learning)
- Problems with language, recognition, and the ability to carry out actions (e.g., dressing)
- Usually develop slowly

Delirium Disorders
- Reduced awareness
- Problems with attention
- Problems with memory and language
- Perceptual distortions (hallucinations)
- Usually develop quickly

Amnesia Disorders
- Problems with memory (recall and learning)
- May be transient (less than 1 month) or chronic

occurs when drugs such as anesthetics or alcohol reduce neurological activity and thereby reduce the ability to retrieve information or store new information. In some cases, drugs can cause permanent damage that results in chronic amnesia. For example, excessive use of alcohol leads to the destruction of the hippocampus and therefore to anterograde amnesia, a disorder known as Korsakoff's disease.

The symptoms and the course of the three types of cognitive disorders are summarized in Table 19.1.

TOPIC II
MENTAL RETARDATION

It is estimated that there are well over 6 million people in the United States who have IQs in the retarded range (under 70). *That is as many people as live in Los Angeles and Chicago combined,* and it makes mental retardation one of our most widespread health problems. If individuals with borderline IQs (between 70 and 85) are included, the number of afflicted individuals rises to well over 40 million—*more than twice the combined populations of the 10 largest cities in the United States!* Stated in another way, 1 out of every 6 Americans suffers from mental retardation to some extent. The personal, social, and economic impact of mental retardation is especially great because it is usually a chronic and irreversible condition. Clearly, this is a problem to which we must give careful consideration.

DSM-IV sets out three criteria that must be met to reach a diagnosis of **mental retardation:**

1. The individual must have an IQ of 70 or below.

2. The individual must have problems in daily functioning that are due to low intelligence. For example, individuals may have problems taking care of themselves, supporting themselves, or getting along with others.

3. The disorder must set in before the age of 18. If an individual functions normally until the age of 18 and only thereafter shows a decline, the individual is diagnosed as suffering from some form of dementia rather than retardation.

The line between normal ability and retardation is not always clear or consistent because it is often difficult to measure IQ exactly. Also, what is demanded of an individual in terms of functioning varies widely from one situation to another. For example, the intellectual demands on a secretary in an urban office may be much higher than those on a farm laborer. Therefore, an individual may move back and forth across the line between normality and retardation depending on the circumstances of testing and demands of life situations.

There are three major causes of mental retardation: *genetic factors; physical factors* in the environment,

such as problems during pregnancy and diet; and *psychosocial factors,* such as impoverished living conditions. In the following section, I will discuss some of the difficult and controversial issues that are associated with mental retardation, and then I will examine the types of retardation that stem from genetic, physical, and psychosocial factors.

ISSUES ASSOCIATED WITH MENTAL RETARDATION

Levels of Retardation

There are four **levels of retardation.** Just as the line between normality and retardation is not clear, the lines between the various levels of retardation are not clear, but for general descriptive purposes, it is helpful to identify ranges of retardation. The four generally accepted ranges of retardation are described in Table 19.2.

TABLE 19.2 The Four Levels of Mental Retardation

Mild Mental Retardation (IQ = 50–70)
This is roughly equivalent to what was once called "educable." This group constitutes the largest segment of persons with retardation—about 85%.
- *Education and Training Potential.* People with this level of retardation typically develop social and communication skills during preschool years and are often indistinguishable from normal children until a later age. They can acquire academic skills up to about the sixth-grade level.
- *Long-Term Outlook.* During their adult years, they usually achieve minimal self-support. Virtually all people with mild retardation can live successfully in the community, independently or in supervised apartments or group homes.

Moderate Mental Retardation (IQ = 35–50)
This is roughly equivalent to what used to be referred to as the "trainable" level of retardation. This group constitutes about 10% of individuals with retardation.
- *Education and Training Potential.* These individuals can learn to communicate during the preschool years. They may profit from vocational training and, with moderate supervision, can take care of themselves. They can profit from social and occupational training but are unlikely to progress beyond the second-grade level in academic subjects.
- *Long-Term Outlook.* During adolescence, their retardation may interfere with peer relationships. In adulthood, they may be able to contribute to their own support by performing unskilled or semiskilled work under supervision in sheltered workshops or in the competi-

tive job market. They adapt well to life in the community, usually in supervised group homes.

Severe Mental Retardation (IQ = 20–35)
This group constitutes 3% to 4% of individuals with retardation.
- *Education and Training Potential.* During preschool, they display poor motor development and acquire little or no communicative speech. During school age, they may learn to talk and can be trained in elementary hygiene skills. They profit to only a limited extent from training in such things as the alphabet and simple counting. They can be taught to sight-read words such as *men, women,* and *stop.*
- *Long-Term Outlook.* In their adult years, they may be able to perform simple tasks under close supervision. Most adapt well to life in the community, in group homes, or with their families.

Profound Mental Retardation (IQ = below 20)
This group constitutes 1% to 2% of individuals with retardation.
- *Education and Training Potential.* As children, these people display minimal capacity for sensorimotor functioning. A highly structured environment with constant aid and supervision by a caregiver is required for optimal development. Motor development and self-care and communication skills may improve if appropriate training is provided.
- *Long-Term Outlook.* These individuals can perform simple tasks under close supervision.

Source: Adapted from American Psychiatric Association (1994).

Problems with Measuring Intelligence

IQ scores are usually the major factor in determining whether an individual is suffering from mental retardation. However, there are three potentially serious problems with using traditional IQ tests for measuring retardation.

Sociocultural Factors. First is the possibility that traditional IQ tests are not always effective for measuring the abilities of children who come from poor or minority group backgrounds because those children may have had cultural experiences that are different from those of white middle-class children, on whose cultural tradition IQ tests are based. Evidence for that is provided by a study in which it was found that African-American and white children showed comparable levels of functioning in their daily lives but the African-American children scored lower than the white students on traditional IQ tests (Adams et al., 1973). In that case, it appears that the traditional IQ tests did not adequately measure the intelligence of the African-American students. Insofar as that is true, traditional measures of IQ may be irrelevant or invalid for diagnosing retardation in members of groups with different cultural backgrounds.

Measurement of Relevant Abilities. A second problem is that the traditional IQ tests may not measure abilities that are relevant for the "real world," and therefore the retardation they measure may be limited to the schoolroom (Ginsberg, 1972). In this regard, it is interesting to note that when **Alfred Binet** (bĕ-NĀ) (1857–1911) developed the first widely used IQ test in 1905, the test was explicitly designed to predict how well students would do *in school.* Thus an IQ test may indicate that an individual is retarded in terms of the types of tasks performed in school, but that does not necessarily mean that he or she is retarded with regard to tasks that may be important outside of school.

Physical and Emotional Factors. A third problem stems from the fact that in some cases individuals with retardation also suffer from a variety of physical and emotional problems in addition to their retardation, and those other problems may interfere with their performance on the test and distort the results. For example, a retarded child who also suffers from depression or dyslexia may receive a particularly low score on an IQ test. The level of performance that results from the combination of the retardation and other problems may reflect the individual's current *functional* level of ability (what he or she is able to do given all the problems), but it does not reflect what the individual would be able to do if his or her other problems were treated. In that sense, then, the IQ test

About 85% of persons with mental retardation are only mildly retarded and are able to achieve minimal self-support.

may provide an unrealistically low estimate of the abilities of some individuals.

In summary, cultural bias, the measurement of irrelevant abilities, and physical and emotional problems can all serve to invalidate the measurement of intelligence and lead to an erroneous diagnosis of retardation. However, note that in DSM-IV it is explicitly required that the assessment of IQ be based on one or more of the *individually administered* general intelligence tests (see Chapter 3) rather than on paper-and-pencil tests. Individually administered tests usually involve up to two hours of interactions between the client and a highly trained test administrator, and the test administrator should be able to recognize when a problem is interfering with a client's performance so that allowances can be made or the test can be disregarded. Note also that the diagnosis of mental retardation requires that the individual perform poorly on an intelligence test and *also demonstrate an inability to function adequately.* Therefore, even if the IQ test provides a low but invalid measure of the individual's capacity, by itself that will not result in the diagnosis of retardation. Clearly, safeguards are built into the system, but the system is not perfect, and we must constantly be on guard against misdiagnosis.

Mental Defect or Delayed Development?

There is no doubt that *severe* retardation is due to **mental defects** such as damaged chromosomes or brain damage. That is, individuals who suffer from severe retardation have problems with the structure or functioning of their brains. However, there is some controversy over the cause of *mild* retardation. On the one hand, some theorists believe that even mild retardation is due to mental defects and that we have not yet found the defects because they are very small and subtle (Milgram, 1969). On the other hand, other theorists believe that mild retardation is due to **delayed development** (Zigler, 1969; Zigler & Balla, 1982). These theorists suggest that individuals go through stages of cognitive development and that for some reason the intellectual development of some individuals is retarded at an early stage. (Note that the term *retarded* implies that there is a *delay* in development rather than a *defect*.) The delay could stem from (a) growing up in a culturally impoverished environment, (b) attitudes about achievement ("I can't do it, so I won't try"), (c) lack of motivation ("I don't care about doing it, so I won't try"), or (d) lack of parental encouragement ("You're dumb, so don't bother to try").

The answer to the question of whether mild retardation is due to a defect or a delay in development has important implications in terms of what we do for individuals who suffer from retardation. If retardation is due to a defect, treatment should be focused on teaching individuals ways of *compensating* for the problem because it cannot be corrected. For example, individuals might be given vocational training designed to provide them with income-producing skills that do not require great intelligence. In contrast, if retardation is due to a delay in development, treatment should be focused on *correcting* the problem. For example, individuals might be placed in a program in which they are exposed to experiences that will enable them to grow intellectually and change their attitudes about themselves and their abilities.

The answer to the defect-or-delay controversy also has implications for the prevention of mild retardation. If it is assumed that retardation is due to defects, attention must be focused on things such as good prenatal care and the elimination of lead in the environment so that there will be no impediments to brain development. In contrast, if mild retardation is due to delayed development, it is important that we expose children to cultural opportunities and positive attitudes. Indeed, the Head Start program was founded on the assumption that retardation was due to delays in development, and the program was designed to prevent or offset those delays. Delayed development is certainly a more optimistic explanation because it suggests that with proper experiences, mild retardation can be prevented or effectively treated.

A variety of attempts have been made to resolve the defect-versus-delayed-development controversy. The results have been mixed, and it is probably safest to conclude that mild retardation can be due to a defect or a delay in development and that attention should be given to both possibilities when considering prevention and treatment. The problem may not be to determine which explanation is correct in general but rather to determine which explanation is correct for a particular individual.

With an understanding of these issues as background, we can now go on to consider the causes and types of mental retardation. In the following sections, I will describe types of retardation that result from genetic, physical, and psychosocial factors.

RETARDATION DUE TO GENETIC FACTORS

Retardation due to genetic factors accounts for only about 25% of the cases of mental retardation, but this type of retardation is particularly important because it is often the most severe.

Down Syndrome: The Effect of an Extra Chromosome

Down syndrome results in a moderate to severe level of general retardation (IQs range from 35 to 49). Individuals suffering from Down syndrome are easily recognizable because they have almond-shaped eyes that slant upward, a small nose with a low bridge, and a furrowed tongue that protrudes because the mouth is small and has a low roof. Their hands are usually small with short stubby fingers, and as adults these individuals are often short and stocky. Because the eyes of individuals with Down syndrome give them a somewhat Asiatic appearance, the disorder was originally referred to as "Mongolism." This syndrome occurs in about 1 of every 1,000 live births and is therefore one of the most common causes of retardation.

In most cases, Down syndrome is due to the fact that the individual has an *extra chromosome 21*, a problem known as **trisomy** (TRĪ-sō-mē) **21** (Pueschel & Thuline, 1983). (That term stems from the fact that the individuals have three rather than two of the chromosomes in question.) We know that the extra chromosome 21 is responsible for Down syndrome, but we do not yet know how it has its effect.

One important finding concerning Down syndrome is that older women are more likely to give birth to infants with the disorder. In fact, the number of Down syndrome births per 1,000 live births increases from .58 in mothers who are 20 years old to 87.93 in

Down syndrome results in a moderate to severe level of retardation. The facial features of persons with this disorder include almond-shaped eyes that slant upward, a small nose with a narrow bridge, and a tongue that protrudes because the mouth is small and has a low roof. The syndrome is the result of the individual having an extra chromosome 21.

mothers who are 49. Figure 19.2 dramatizes this increase in the rate of Down syndrome births. We do not yet understand why the mother's age is associated with the syndrome. It is possible that because older women's eggs have been held in "suspended animation" longer, they have been exposed to more environmental agents or stresses that disrupt them. It is also possible that the hormonal changes that occur in midlife influence the process (Crowley et al., 1982; Mikkelsen & Stene, 1970; Smith & Wilson, 1973).

There is also evidence that the father's age can be related to the disorder (Erickson & Bjerkedal, 1981; Regal et al., 1980). However, whereas the risk greatly increases after the mother passes her mid-30s, the risk on the father's side does not increase until he passes his mid-50s.

Fortunately, there are now a variety of tests that can be used to determine early in pregnancy whether the fetus has an extra chromosome 21. Because of the serious long-term problems associated with Down syndrome, those tests are generally recommended, especially for older pregnant women who are at highest risk for giving birth to a child with the syndrome.

Although individuals with Down syndrome are seriously retarded, they are usually good-natured, happy, affectionate, socially well adjusted, and playful in a "clownish" way. Unfortunately, as they age, they are more likely to suffer from Alzheimer's disease and

other disorders that add appreciably to the problems of their care (Miniszek, 1983).

It is important to recognize that some individuals with Down syndrome are only moderately retarded and that with careful guidance they can make a somewhat normal adjustment. In Case Study 19.2, a mother talks about her moderately retarded daughter who has Down syndrome.

Phenylketonuria (PKU): A Genetic Problem with Metabolism

Phenylketonuria (FĒ-nul-KĒ-tun-YOO-rē-uh), usually abbreviated **PKU,** results in a severe level of retardation with IQ rarely higher than 40 or 50. Many individuals with this disorder are so retarded that they cannot walk or talk. They are also likely to be irritable, unpredictable, and hyperactive, and they are generally unresponsive to other persons (Robinson & Robinson, 1976). Furthermore, they often show aimless motor behavior such as arm waving, rocking, and unusual finger movements. This combination of emotional and motor symptoms is similar to the symptom pattern seen in children with autism (see Chapter 15), and therefore some children with PKU are misdiagnosed as suffering from autism. Individuals who suffer from PKU are likely to have blond hair, blue eyes, and very fair skin. PKU occurs in approximately 1 of every 15,000 live births (Carter, 1975).

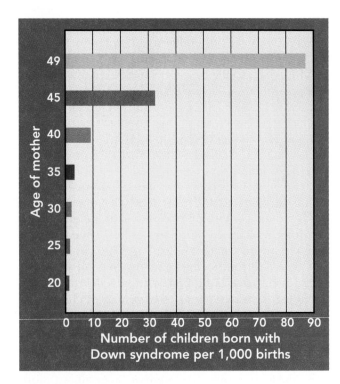

FIGURE 19.2 Older mothers are more likely to give birth to children with Down syndrome.
Sources: Hook (1982); Hook and Chambers (1977); Hook and Fabia (1978); Hook and Lindsjo (1978).

PKU results from a low level of an enzyme that is necessary to break down the amino acid **phenylalanine** (FĒ-nul-AL-uh-nīn). If the phenylalanine is not broken down, it forms **phenylpyruvic** (FĒ-nul-pī-ROO-vik) **acid,** which destroys the brain (Jervis, 1939, 1947). In other words, when the enzyme level is low, the acid level builds up and destroys the brain. The destruction of the brain results in mental retardation and inappropriate behavior. The low level of the critical enzyme that ultimately leads to brain damage is due to a recessive gene that is carried by as many as 1 individual in 50 (Rosenthal, 1970). If two individuals with the gene give birth to a child, there is a 25% chance that the child will have PKU.

Although an infant with PKU is born with an inability to break down phenylalanine, at birth the acid levels have not had time to build up and begin destroying the brain. Therefore, if the disorder is diagnosed early and steps are taken to treat the problem, the effects of the disorder can be reduced or eliminated. Screening for PKU is done with a simple urine or blood test when the infant is only a few days old. Infants found to have PKU are put on a diet that is low in phenylalanine, thereby preventing the buildup of the phenylpyruvic acid and preventing the destruction of the brain. The sooner the low-phenylalanine diet is begun, the less severe the retardation will be. Indeed, if the diet is begun early in infancy and is maintained for at least 6 years, the retardation will be minimal (Berry et al., 1967; Tredgold & Soddy, 1970). There is one difficulty with a low-phenylalanine diet, however: Phenylalanine is found in almost all foods that contain protein. This means that there is very little that the child can eat without being deprived of protein, which is essential for growth. To get around the problem, the child must eat synthetically developed foods that contain protein but not phenylalanine (Lofenalac, PKU-Aid, Phenylfree). Unfortunately, those foods are expensive, they usually do not taste good, and it is often difficult to get the child to eat them. In sum, PKU can and must be treated, but the process can be difficult. Because the disorder can be corrected if the diet is begun early, it is especially tragic when it is misdiagnosed (usually as autism) and treatment is delayed. If the treatment is delayed more than a couple of years, severe and irreversible damage occurs.

One more important fact concerning PKU should be mentioned: Women who had PKU as children but were effectively treated are likely to give birth to brain-damaged children. That is because the mothers still have high levels of phenylalanine, which can damage the fetus while it is developing in the womb. This was not a problem before we knew how to treat PKU because females with PKU became so retarded as children that they were institutionalized and did not reproduce. In view of the problem posed for the children of women with PKU both in terms of passing the recessive gene on and in terms of the dangerous fetal environment they provide their children, these women should give serious consideration to not having children (Carter, 1975; Pueschel & Goldstein, 1983).

Other Types of Retardation Due to Genetic Factors

Many other types of retardation stem from genetic problems, but most of them are rare. However, some brief attention should be given to three of the more notable types.

Turner's Syndrome. **Turner's syndrome** (or **gonadal dysgenesis**) is limited to women and only sometimes results in general retardation. When retardation does occur, it is usually associated primarily with deficits in *space-form perception* rather than in verbal abilities (Bock & Kolakowski, 1973). The problem with space-form perception affects the ability to see relationships between objects and how things fit together. The disorder is due to the fact that the woman is missing one of the two female chromosomes (X instead of XX). As you might expect from the cause, physical symptoms consist primarily of a lack of secondary sex characteristics after puberty. That can be treated with female hormones, but the treatment does not help the deficits in cognitive abilities.

Klinefelter's Syndrome. In contrast to Turner's syndrome, **Klinefelter's syndrome** is limited to men and results from the presence of extra female chromosomes. Instead of having an XY chromosome configuration (one female and one male chromosome), which is normal for males, the individual will have an XXY or XXXY configuration. In some cases, the man may have as many as five female chromosomes. This genetic problem causes retardation in only about half the cases, but the severity of the problem increases as the number of extra X chromosomes increases (Forssman, 1970).

Cretinism (Hypothyroidism). The most notable physical characteristic of **cretinism** (or **hypothyroidism**) in adults is very short stature (dwarfism), which is sometimes associated with obesity, a protruding abdomen, stubby fingers, dry skin, and sparse and brittle hair. Cretinism is frequently but not always associated with retardation, which can range from moderate to severe. In infants, cretinism can be detected by a low heart rate, low respiratory rate, and low body temperature. Cretinism is usually due to a recessive gene that interferes with the production of **thyroxin** (thī-ROK-sin) by the thyroid gland. Thyroxin is responsible for maintaining a proper metabolic rate, and if there is too little thyroxin, metabolism and development are slowed. This low metabolism is responsible for the low heart rate,

CASE STUDY 19.2

A Mother Talks About Her 15-Year-Old Daughter, Who Has Down Syndrome

"I am the mother of a 15-year-old daughter with Down syndrome. Kimberly is currently attending junior high school and is in the ninth grade, enjoying all the ordinary things that teenage girls enjoy. Her passions are rock music and movie stars. She is looking forward to being able to work next summer and earn some money (probably to buy more music tapes) and to eventually move into her own apartment, just like her brother did when he graduated from high school.

"When Kimberly was born, the city had numerous support programs for developmentally disabled children and their families, but the problem was finding the programs. The medical community and social service offices were not coordinated, and therefore new parents in the hospital with a disabled child could not get all the information they needed to help them adjust to this dramatic change in their lives. Trying to deal with the shock of having a child that was not 'normal' and not being able to find support services was traumatic for both my husband and me. All our pediatrician told me was that I did not have to take her home if I didn't want to, that there were institutions available. I remember thinking that she is only a baby, and a baby only needs love and care and a family. There was no way that I was going to put her in an institution. Fortunately, my mother lived across the street from a family that had a son with Down syndrome, and she immediately brought as much information as she could to the hospital.

"Adequate support is critical at this time because the parents in this situation go through a grieving process—grieving for the normal child that they did not have. The hopes and dreams that you have for your children must be adjusted to encompass your special child, and this takes time. I believe that it is important to recognize this process, for it helps us finally to accept the situation and move positively toward the future.

"We found that at first we were able to plan ahead for only a short period of time, and we did not look too far down the road. When Kim was a baby, for instance, my hopes were only that she be able to go to a preschool. When she was 3 years old, we started thinking about what would be available for her when she was 5. We also learned not to let our own thoughts and objectives create limits for Kim. When she was 3, it never occurred to me that she would ever be reading at the third- or fourth-grade level and that she would be interested in the things that she is interested in today.

"We were fortunate to be in a school district in which she had the opportunity to be mainstreamed into some regular classrooms, and for many classes that was successful. In one case, however, I think Kim realized that she was not comfortable in a regular classroom, and she seemed much happier when we returned her to her special-education classroom. She is currently attending special-education classes but is mainstreamed into regular physical education, art, and music classes and enjoys participating in all

---

low respiratory rate, and low body temperature. Although the low level of the thyroxin is usually due to a genetic problem, it can also result from radiation (X-rays) during pregnancy that interferes with the normal development of the thyroid gland. It can also be caused by an iodine deficiency in the mother during pregnancy, but that cause has been largely eliminated in countries where iodine is added to table salt.

If detected early and treated with thyroid medication (thyroxin obtained from animals), the problem can often be cured or reduced. The treatment reverses the progression of the disease following birth but cannot repair any damage that might have occurred before birth.

RETARDATION DUE TO PHYSICAL FACTORS IN THE ENVIRONMENT

A variety of physical factors such as infections, drugs, temperature, pressure, nutrition, injuries, and abuse can damage the brain. These factors can have their influence while the fetus is in the womb, during the birth process, and during the first few years following birth. The retardation that results from these factors is usually less severe than that caused by genetic factors, but it is still very serious. Attention to such retardation is important because in most cases it can be avoided.

of them. She is learning, in a somewhat structured environment, to participate in the real world.

"Kim's wants and desires are not that different from those of normal teenagers, but trying to meet those wants and desires is. As parents of a child with Down syndrome—or any disability, for that matter—we usually have to go to bat for our child in order for her to have some experiences that ordinary children take for granted. It is normal for seventh and eighth graders to gather with their friends on Friday or Saturday night, and Kim wants to do the same thing, but she doesn't always have the capacity to handle the situation. We also have to be careful that other people do not take advantage of her. Fortunately, we have been able to work with the city's Parks and Recreation Department to develop some structured weekend activities in which Kim and her friends can participate successfully and safely.

"Kim wants to drive a car when she is 16, which is not too far away, and we haven't quite figured out how to deal with that. Our stock answer is that if she can pass the written driving test like everyone else, she can get her learner's permit. That's the same answer that we give to her younger sister. In essence, we are trying, and have always tried, to treat Kimberly as normally as possible and to expect the same responsibilities from her that we do from the other children. The hard part is to give her enough leeway to try so that she (and we) can learn her limits but to do so without being too lax and assuming that she can handle everything. When Kim was only 2 months old, a good friend told me that I shouldn't put limits on what I thought Kim was capable of becoming. I have never forgotten her advice, and I know that Kim has far exceeded anything that I could have imagined when she was only a few months old.

"As a parent of a disabled child who is soon to be an adult, I am learning that it is important for Kim to learn to cope with the real world. I want her to be able to go to movies, go to the store, go on a date if she wants, and do ordinary things independently, without having people stare at her and think she is weird. I want her to learn to dress nicely, to keep her hair combed and her face washed. I want her to care that her clothes match and that she looks presentable. I want her to move out of the house when it is appropriate, just as I want my other children to do the same thing. Our hopes and dreams for Kim are the same as our hopes and dreams for our other children: that she will build a life for herself beyond the family; that she will have her own job, her own home, and some independence; that she can cope with the world around her and be happy. I want people around her to accept that she has the same rights to these goals and happiness that anyone else does. Our fears are that she will be rejected because of her disability, that there will not be anyone to watch out for her when we are gone, and that necessary services for people with developmental disabilities will disappear."

Fetal Alcohol Syndrome: Effects of Maternal Drinking During Pregnancy

We now know that the consumption of alcohol by pregnant women can result in a variety of problems in their offspring, and this has come to be known as **fetal alcohol syndrome,** sometimes abbreviated **FAS.** One of the symptoms is mental retardation, which can range from mild to severe. Other cognitive symptoms can include attentional difficulties and hyperactivity (see Chapter 15). Physical abnormalities include microcephaly (small brain), distortions of the face, and cardiac abnormalities. Not all of these symptoms are always present, and they appear in different combinations.

Fetal alcohol syndrome may affect as many as 1 in 750 live births, and between 25% and 75% of the children born to alcoholic women suffer from fetal alcohol syndrome, making alcohol one of the most common causes of physically based mental retardation (Streissguth et al., 1978). Furthermore, many victims of fetal alcohol syndrome grow up to abuse alcohol as adults, thereby producing another generation of sufferers. This serious and widespread form of mental retardation is all the more tragic because it can be prevented so easily.

Alcohol has a number of serious effects on fetal brain structure and functioning. Specifically, it can kill cells in the brain, it can disrupt neural migration such

Symptoms of children with fetal alcohol syndrome can include mental retardation, attentional difficulties, hyperactivity, small brain, facial distortions, and cardiac abnormalities.

that neurons in one part of the brain do not grow to make connections with other parts of the brain, it can result in the disorganization of the connections when they are made, and it may cause problems with the production of neurotransmitters. We do not yet completely understand when the critical period is, but it may be that exposure to alcohol at different times may have different effects. For example, exposure early in pregnancy may result in malformation throughout the body, whereas exposure somewhat later may influence brain development (Able, 1990; Niccols, 1994). In view of the exceptionally serious effects, the best rule of thumb is *to avoid all alcohol consumption during pregnancy.*

Alcohol is not the only drug that can have detrimental effects on fetal development. Many other drugs (e.g., tranquilizers) taken by pregnant women can also result in deformities and retardation in their offspring, and pregnant women must be cautious about taking almost any medication.

Rubella (German Measles): Effects of Infection During Pregnancy

The symptoms of a pregnant woman suffering from a case of **rubella** (roo-BEL-uh) (**German measles**) consist only of a low-grade fever and a slight skin rash. However, her infection can cause an inflammation of her fetus's brain, which in turn leads to a degeneration of the brain tissue. Different parts of the brain are

destroyed, depending on its stage of development when the inflammation occurs, and thus the effects of rubella may differ from one child to another. Retardation may be mild or very severe, and there may also be defects involving sight, hearing, and heart function. The likelihood of mental retardation is 50% if the infection occurs in the first month of pregnancy but declines thereafter. As with most other forms of retardation, there is no treatment for the disorder once it occurs, but it can be effectively prevented by vaccination before pregnancy.

Lead Poisoning: Effects of Exposure During Pregnancy and Early Childhood

Exposure to lead early in life can disrupt neurological development and cause mental retardation. The retardation may be of only moderate severity, but this form of retardation is very widespread and therefore a serious problem. Children develop lead poisoning when they eat chips of paint that contain lead, play in dirt in contaminated areas, or inhale lead in the air (automobile or industrial pollutants). The poisoning can also occur during fetal development when pregnant women are exposed to lead.

The effects of exposure to lead on IQ were demonstrated in a study in which lead concentrations were assessed in pregnant women and later in their offspring (Baghurst et al., 1992). The lead exposure stemmed from the fact that the individuals were living in a city with a large lead-smelting plant and where there were high levels of lead in the air. IQ was measured when the children were 7 years old. The results indicated that high and low levels of maternal lead were linked to differences in IQ of almost 10 points (99.8 vs. 108.5, respectively) and that high and low levels of lead in the children at age 7 were linked to differences in IQ of more than 10 points (98.7 vs. 109.6).

RETARDATION DUE TO PSYCHOSOCIAL FACTORS

Severe forms of mental retardation constitute only a small proportion of the cases of mental retardation; they are found in equal proportions in all levels of society, and they stem from physiological problems. In contrast, moderate forms of mental retardation are much more prevalent; they are more likely to be found in the lower social classes, and in most cases they are presumed to be due to psychological or social factors. The severe forms of retardation can be linked to specific causes and broken into distinctly different types (e.g., Down syndrome, PKU), but moderate retardation is usually not linked to specific causes and is not broken into different types. We will consider some of the psychosocial factors that may contribute to moderate levels of mental retardation. In most cases, the psychosocial factors that are thought to be related to retardation are associated with differences in social class.

The influence of socioeconomic status and cultural background on intellectual ability was illustrated in an early study in which various abilities were assessed in Chinese, Jewish, Puerto Rican, and African-American children who came from middle- and lower-class backgrounds (Stodolsky & Lesser, 1967). Some of the results are presented in Figure 19.3, and they reveal two findings. First, children from the lower class generally performed less well than children from the middle class, and second, children from different ethnic backgrounds showed different patterns of ability. Those findings provide strong evidence for the effects of class and culture on intellectual abilities.

The effects of psychosocial factors were also dramatically illustrated in the case of a child who was locked in an attic until she was 6 years old (Davis, 1947). When she was found, her IQ was estimated to be

only 25, but within 3 years she was functioning at the appropriate level for her age. This child's retardation was more extreme than what is usually thought to stem from psychosocial factors, but of course the psychosocial factors to which she was exposed were more extreme than what most children experience. Case Study 19.3 focuses on an individual whose retardation stems from psychosocial factors.

The findings in Figure 19.3 and the case of the confined child provide strong support for the relationship between psychosocial factors and intellectual abilities. The question is, what specific psychosocial factors influence intellectual development? Despite years of research, the answer to that question remains controversial, but I will mention some of the factors that are generally thought to be important. In most cases these factors are associated with social class, which is probably why members of the lower class are more likely to suffer from moderate retardation.

1. *Limited Psychosocial Environments.* Enriched social environments are thought to contribute to enhanced brain development and superior cognitive skills. Unfortunately, lower-class children have fewer toys to play with, their homes contain fewer objects of any kind, and they are less likely to be taken on trips to places like museums or zoos (Deutsch, 1967).

2. *Language Habits.* Verbal behavior plays an important role both in the assessment of intelligence and in daily functioning, and therefore language habits are a crucial factor in mental retardation. A problem that arises for some minority group members who speak English is that they use a nonstandard form of English. The nonstandard English enables the individuals to communicate with other members of their group, but it does not enable them to communicate with or learn from individuals in the larger society or to perform well on tests of intelligence. In many respects, the nonstandard English is like a foreign language, and its use to the exclusion of standard English can contribute to retardation. Also, lower-class children often learn very restricted language patterns because the adults around them do not talk with them or use very restricted language patterns themselves, and the limited language skills limit the children's thinking processes and hamper the development of problem-solving abilities.

3. *Child-Rearing Style.* A variety of studies have demonstrated that relative to middle-class mothers, lower-class mothers are more authoritarian and allow their children fewer opportunities for self-exploration. They are also less likely to explain things, are more critical, talk less with their children, and use shorter and less complex sentences with fewer abstract words. These interactions do not foster critical thinking or academic challenges.

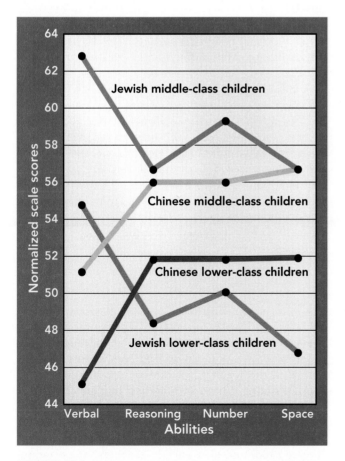

FIGURE 19.3 Chinese and Jewish children showed different patterns of abilities, and children from the lower class performed less well than children from the middle class.
Source: Data from Stodolsky and Lesser (1967), p. 568, figs. 2 and 3.

CASE STUDY 19.3

The Contribution of Psychosocial Factors to a Boy's Mild Retardation

Lester was raised in a tough, severely blighted urban ghetto. His father deserted the family soon after Lester was born, so he, his mother, and his two older sisters lived on welfare. Occasionally his mother worked as a cleaning woman and was paid "under the table," but for the most part they had to subsist on public assistance. In the first eight years of Lester's life, the family moved six times because the buildings in which they were living were condemned, set on fire, or unheated in winter or because the family was evicted for not paying rent. Lester's diet during his early childhood consisted largely of soft drinks, donuts, and junk food. His major activities consisted of watching television and roaming the streets at all hours of the day and night.

Elementary school started badly. He was not prepared for the limitations it placed on him (despite his young age, he was used to doing what he wanted when he wanted), and he could not see any value in what he was supposed to learn. Even at age 6, in his world, "street-wise" was better than "book-wise." He told his teacher, "Letters 'n them don't git ya nothin'." Because of his lack of interest and the frequent disruptions he caused, he alienated his teacher. Within three months, he and his teacher had implicitly arrived at a standoff: He came to school (or usually did) because he had to, but once there, he did nothing, and as long as he did not cause trouble, the teacher ignored him. He wasted away the days doodling, napping, or goofing off. Because he was not an overt troublemaker, he was not disliked, and he was passed along from grade to grade without having learned anything.

His entrance into high school changed little except that when he did not feel like going to school, he simply "cut." Letters to his mother were useless, and threats of suspension were empty because he did not want to be in school anyway. Lester was not alone in coming to and going from school as he wished; on a typical day, almost half the students would be absent from any one of his classes. The only class in which he showed any consistent interest and ability was auto shop, where he became adept at fine-tuning automobiles. Lester did not graduate, but it is not clear from the records whether he ever formally dropped out. Apparently, he just drifted out of school and no one bothered to try to bring him back.

When he was 17, Lester was picked up by the police on suspicion of auto theft, and as part of the pretrial assessment, he was sent to a juvenile detention center, where he was given an individual intelligence test. The results revealed that his IQ was only 62. Follow-up was never done because he was released when the case was dropped.

Today Lester is functionally illiterate. He cannot effectively read or write, and his math skills are limited to simple addition and subtraction. Socially, he is pleasant and gets along well with just about anyone. He works as a "gofer" in a local automobile repair shop. When he is not running errands, he acts as a helper for one of the mechanics, who is teaching him the business. In this hands-on situation, Lester is learning quickly, but ultimately his progress will be limited by the fact that he cannot read the repair manuals.

4. *Motivation.* Motivation is crucial for effective intellectual performance, but lower-class children are often not encouraged to do well in school and do not see school performance as relevant or important. In some cases, lower-class individuals see themselves as locked into their situation and develop feelings of helplessness. In other words, they do not see themselves as in control but rather as controlled by external factors, so they give up and do not try (Battle & Rotter, 1963). This view of control has been documented in children as young as 3 years old (Stephens & Delys, 1973).

5. *Schooling.* There are often important differences between the facilities that are available to students from different classes or racial groups. Also important is the nature of the teaching or interaction that goes on in the classroom. There is evidence that in classrooms consisting solely of African-Americans, 50% to 80% of the classroom time is devoted to disciplining children, versus 30% in all-white classrooms (Deutsch, 1967).

As I pointed out earlier, teachers' expectations about how well students will do and the attention they give them may also play a role. In the classic study in this area, teachers were told that some of their students would probably bloom by the end of the year but others would not (Rosenthal & Jacobson, 1968). At the end of the year, all of the students were given an IQ test, and it was found that the students who the teachers were led to believe would bloom in fact had higher scores even though the children had been randomly assigned to the bloomer and nonbloomer groups. A related study revealed that children who were not expected to do well were generally ignored by the teacher, and the reduced attention could certainly result in lowered performance (Rist, 1970). These detrimental effects of expectations can be serious, and therefore it may be fortunate that not all investigators found the effects (Elashoff & Snow, 1971).

6. *Poor Physical or Medical Care.* Individuals in the lower class often receive poorer prenatal and postnatal care than individuals in the middle class, and those differences in care can lead to retardation. Strictly speaking, infection, trauma, premature birth, and nutrition are not psychosocial factors, but they are associated with psychosocial factors (economic class) and therefore deserve mention in this context.

Overall, then, social class is related to a variety of psychological as well as physical factors that contribute to mental retardation.

It is important to recognize that in most cases, the evidence linking the psychosocial factors to mental retardation is correlational, and therefore we cannot definitely say that psychosocial factors cause retardation. However, because it seems highly likely that they do cause retardation and because their effects are reversible, it is important that we continue to focus

attention and efforts on psychosocial factors as causes of retardation.

INDIVIDUALS WITH RETARDATION IN THE COMMUNITY

Until the late 1960s, most individuals who suffered from mental retardation were kept in large institutions where they were essentially "warehoused." In 1967, there were almost 200,000 retarded individuals in public institutions, many more were in private facilities, and others were kept behind closed doors at home. The notion was that individuals who suffered from retardation could not care for themselves and needed protection. It also seems likely that many parents were ashamed of their retarded children and attempted to hide them. Since then, however, great strides have been taken to modify, if not reverse, that position and to bring the retarded out into the mainstream of society. Indeed, since 1967 the number of retarded individuals in public institutions has decreased by over 50%.

This change in the treatment of retarded individuals was motivated by two factors. First, it was suggested that if retarded individuals were exposed to normal living conditions, they were more likely to develop more normal behavior patterns than if they were left to languish in institutions. This is known as the principle of **normalization** (Landesman & Butterfield, 1987). The principle of normalization does not deny that intellectual limitations influence the behavior of retarded indi-

The move toward deinstitutionalization of individuals with mental retardation has led to efforts to integrate them into mainstream society. Community-based programs that involve group homes and supervised work situations have been effective in many cases.

CASE STUDY 19.4

Cottonwood: A Community Program That Is "Good Business" and a Whole Lot More

Cottonwood, Inc., is a community-based program for individuals who suffer from mental retardation in Lawrence, Kansas, a university town of about 80,000 people. Cottonwood serves two major functions. First, it provides supervised home living for its clients. It does this through 10 group homes that are scattered throughout the city. Rather than being "institutional," these homes are indistinguishable from other homes in the area. Most people are not even aware that the houses are group home facilities. Between four and six residents and a home supervisor live in each home. During the times when the residents are not working, the supervisor provides training in nutrition, grocery shopping, cooking, grooming, hygiene, clothing care, housekeeping, home maintenance, money management, leisure skills, and social skills. Residents pay a monthly fee to cover rent, utilities, and food, and they are responsible for the care and maintenance of the homes. As residents develop the necessary skills, they progress to a semi-independent living arrangement in which they have their own apartments, but they are still given up to 5 hours a week of training and guidance that is tailored to their particular needs.

Cottonwood's second major function is to provide occupational training and opportunities for its clients. There are three levels of training. First, approximately 30 clients work in the "sheltered workshop" program. In this program, clients are brought to the Cottonwood building, where, with close supervision and training, they work on projects involving light manufacturing, packaging, collating, and the preparation of bulk mailings. These are not meaningless or "make-work" projects. Instead, Cottonwood has contracted for real work on a competitive basis with local businesses, and the clients are paid for their work. Because the projects are let on a competitive basis and because the Cottonwood clients may work somewhat more slowly than other people, the wages paid to the clients may be somewhat lower than those paid to others. The important point is that the Cottonwood clients become produc-

tive, contributing members of society and are paid on a fair basis. Everyone wins.

The second level of job training and experience involves supervised group work in the community. For example, companies such as Quaker Oats often need a workforce to complete a particular project, and a group from Cottonwood will take on the job. In those cases, Cottonwood transports its clients to and from the work site and provides on-site supervisors for them. This real-world work is an important experience for Cottonwood's clients because they can use their nonretarded coworkers as role models. In one case, a client stopped carrying his Snoopy lunch box when he saw that everyone else was carrying a plain black lunch box. The clients want to fit in, and with normal models available, they quickly learn how. Having the clients on the production line is also an important experience for the other workers, who learn to overcome their stereotypes about persons with retardation and come to accept them.

Some clients go on to normal independent and competitive community employment. Typical employment involves work in fast-food restaurants, janitorial services, housecleaning jobs (especially in hotels and motels), and some light industry.

Employing retarded persons is not charity. As one executive after another says, *"It's just good business."* Indeed, the experiences of employers across the country consistently indicate that retarded workers are often more reliable, happier, and more likely to remain in the job than their nonretarded coworkers. The Cottonwood clients find their jobs challenging and interesting, and that makes them good employees. With this approach, everyone wins: Retarded persons get meaningful jobs and a chance to grow, employers get an excellent workforce, and the economy is helped because people who were once consumers of tax dollars become producers of tax dollars. Cottonwood's logo is a "thumbs up" sign, and that is appropriate because the program is making things work for everyone. It's good business *and a whole lot more.*

viduals, but it suggests that the intellectual limitations are only *part* of the problem. In an attempt to overcome the problems caused by experiential limitations, it was proposed that efforts be made to integrate retarded individuals into the mainstream of society.

The second factor in the deinstitutionalization of retarded individuals was economics. The average yearly cost per institutionalized individual is well over $40,000, and costs are rising sharply. The cost to the federal and state governments is over $4 billion per year. In addition, there are the enormous costs of private hospitalization and many hidden costs associated with keeping retarded individuals at home (e.g., a potential wage earner has to stay home to care for the individual).

Both normalization and economic pressures led to deinstitutionalization, but the deinstitutionalization had mixed effects. In some cases, retarded individuals were taken out of institutions only to be ignored and left alone in deplorable circumstances. In other cases, specialized programs were developed and the deinstitutionalization was very effective. Case Study 19.4 describes one effective program for helping retarded individuals in the community. In this case, not only did the community help the retarded individuals, but the retarded individuals also made a meaningful contribution to the community.

SUMMARY

TOPIC I: COGNITIVE DISORDERS

■ Cognitive disorders are defined as problems with cognition (thinking) or memory that are due to a medical problem such as Alzheimer's disease or vascular accidents (strokes). In other words, they are not secondary problems that stem from a psychiatric disorder such as depression or schizophrenia.

■ There are three types of cognitive disorders: (a) dementia, (b) delirium, and (c) amnesia.

■ Dementia disorders revolve around problems with memory, and there are three types: (a) Alzheimer's type, (b) vascular type, and (c) the type that is due to a general medical condition.

■ The Alzheimer's type is due to a general and progressive deterioration of the brain that is caused by Alzheimer's disease (neurofibrillary tangling, plaques, granulovacuolar degeneration). There is a genetic basis for this disorder, and it is stronger in cases with earlier onset.

■ The vascular type is due to cerebral infarctions (strokes) that result in the death of various areas of the brain. The infarctions occur when the blood supply to the area is cut off because of atherosclerosis (narrowing of the blood vessels), an embolism (a clot in a vessel), rupturing of vessels because of arteriosclerosis ("hardening of the arteries"), or an aneurysm (weak spot in the vessel wall).

■ The type due to a general medical condition stems from disorders such as HIV infections, a physical trauma, Parkinson's disease, or Huntington's disease.

■ Delirium disorders involve problems with awareness, attention, memory or language, and perception. In other words, delirious individuals may not know who or where they are, cannot concentrate, have trouble thinking and speaking, and may have hallucinations.

■ Delirium disorders often occur in connection with disorders in which the individual has a high fever or temperature (e.g., meningitis, hyperthermia). The temperature appears to interfere with brain functioning, and when the temperature is reduced, the delirium is eliminated.

■ Delirium disorders can also be caused by drugs such as narcotics (morphine), hallucinogens (LSD), and depressants (alcohol) and by poisons and allergic reactions. In those cases, the delirium occurs because the drugs and poisons disrupt brain functioning.

■ Amnesia disorders involve problems with memory. (Amnesia disorders differ from dementia disorders in that with amnesia the symptoms are limited to memory and are less profound.) There are two types of amnesia. Retrograde amnesia is the loss of memories that were once established and recallable, and anterograde amnesia is the inability to put new memories into storage.

■ Amnesia disorders can be caused by general medical conditions such as Korsakoff's disease, malnutrition, convulsions, and concussions. In retrograde amnesia, the medical conditions disrupt or destroy the neurons that form the networks in which memories are stored, whereas in anterograde amnesia the medical conditions disrupt or destroy the neurons in the hippocampus, through which memories must pass on their way to storage.

■ Amnesia disorders can also be caused by substances (drugs) that disrupt or destroy brain functioning (e.g., alcohol can destroy the hippocampus and lead to anterograde amnesia, a disorder known as Korsakoff's disease).

TOPIC II: MENTAL RETARDATION

■ To be diagnosed as suffering from mental retardation, an individual must meet three criteria: (a) have an IQ of 70 or below, (b) experience problems in daily functioning (e.g., be unable to take care of himself or herself), and show signs of the disorder before the age of 18.

■ There are four levels of retardation: mild (IQ 50–70), moderate (IQ 34–50), severe (IQ 20–35), and profound (IQ below 20).

■ Problems with the measurement of intelligence revolve around sociocultural factors (e.g., poor individuals or those from ethnic minorities may have had different experiences), the measurement of abilities that are relevant for functioning in the "real world," and the presence of physical or emotional problems that interfere with intellectual performance. However, many of these problems can be overcome with individually administered tests.

■ There is a controversy over whether mild retardation is due to mental defects or delayed development that stems from culturally improvised environments, attitudes about achievement, lack of motivation, or lack of encouragement. This issue is relevant for what is done for individuals who suffer from retardation (compensation or correction). It now appears that severe retardation is due to defects, whereas mild retardation can be due to defects or delayed development.

■ Retardation due to genetic factors is usually the most serious form of retardation. Major examples include Down syndrome, which is due to an extra chromosome 21 (trisomy 21) and is seen more often in the children of older women and sometimes older men, and phenylketonuria (PKU), which is caused by the inability to break down phenylalanine, which then forms phenylpyruvic acid which destroys the brain.

■ Retardation due to physical factors in the environment (e.g., infections, drugs, temperature, nutrition, injuries) can also be serious. Major examples include (a) fetal alcohol syndrome (FAS), which is caused by exposure to alcohol during fetal development that kills neurons, disrupts or disorganizes neural migration, or influences neurotransmitters; (b) rubella (German measles), which, contracted during fetal development, destroys neurons in different parts of the developing brain; and (c) lead poisoning during infancy and early childhood, which disrupts brain development.

■ Mental retardation due to psychosocial factors is less severe than retardation due to genetic or physical factors in the environment but is more widespread. In most cases, it is caused by socioeconomic and cultural factors that limit the child's exposure and development (e.g., impoverished environments, limited language exposure, lack of encouragement and motivation, poor schooling).

■ Many individuals who suffer from retardation can function effectively in the community if they are provided with sufficient support and structure. This helps overcome problems that stem from isolation in institutions and can also reduce the costs of caring for individuals who are retarded.

KEY TERMS, CONCEPTS, AND NAMES

In reviewing and testing yourself on what you have learned from this chapter, you should be able to identify and discuss each of the following.

Alzheimer's disease	dementia disorders	phenylalanine
amnesia disorders	Down syndrome	phenylketonuria (PKU)
aneurysm	embolism	phenylpyruvic acid
anterograde amnesia	fetal alcohol syndrome (FAS)	plaques
aphasia	German measles	presenile dementia
arteriosclerosis	granulovacuolar degeneration	primary dementia
atherosclerosis	Klinefelter's syndrome	retrograde amnesia
Binet, Alfred	L-dopa	rubella
cerebral infarction	levels of retardation	secondary dementia
cognitive abulia	mental defects	senile dementia
cognitive disorders	mental retardation	stroke
cretinism (hypothyroidism)	multi-infarct dementia	substantia nigra
delayed development	neurofibrillary tangling	thyroxin
delirium disorders	nootropic drugs	trisomy 21
delirium tremens	normalization	Turner's syndrome (gonadal dysgenesis)

CHAPTER TWENTY
LEGAL ISSUES

OUTLINE

Andrew was arrested for stealing a car. Before his trial, his attorney discovered that Andrew had a serious thought disorder that made it difficult or impossible for Andrew to understand the legal proceedings or to testify accurately. (Andrew was probably suffering from schizophrenia.) When this was confirmed by a psychologist, the judge ruled that Andrew was *incompetent to stand trial.* That ruling postponed the trial, and Andrew was committed to a hospital for treatment until he was judged competent. The incompetence ruling protected Andrew from an unfair trial, but there was still a problem because his confinement for treatment might be longer than his confinement would be if he stood trial and was convicted.

■ ■ ■

Leslie believed that the man next door was building a nuclear device in his basement and that he was going to use it to blow up the Capitol. One night, while listening to a commercial on TV, she received a "secret message from the president" instructing her to kill the man next door and thereby save civilization. The next morning, she shot the man with a .38 as he left for work. She knew that killing was wrong, but this was "self-defense for the world—I had no choice." At her trial, her attorney argued that Leslie's behavior had been a result of a "mental disease or defect," and therefore under the laws of the state, she should be found *not guilty by reason of insanity.* The jury agreed, and Leslie was committed to a hospital for treatment rather than to a prison for punishment. It is interesting to note that if Leslie had been tried in a nearby state where the laws were different, she would have been found guilty regardless of her mental state because she knew that killing another person was wrong. After a year and a half in the hospital, Leslie was released.

■ ■ ■

In a fit of passion, Donald bludgeoned to death a man who had made a pass at his wife. At his trial a year later, Donald testified that he had been so upset at the time of the killing that he would have hit the man even if a police officer had been standing there and he knew that he would be caught. The defense argued that at the time of the killing, Donald was *temporarily insane,* but he was normal now. The defense suggested that Donald should be found not guilty by reason of insanity and released. After all, they argued, if he is normal now, there is no point in confining him for treatment. The prosecution argued that it is difficult enough to determine an individual's mental state at the present, much less a year ago, and that a convincing case had not been made for insanity. Apart from that, one might wonder whether without treatment, Donald might become insane again the next time he became upset.

■ ■ ■

Martha has been a patient in a huge state hospital for six years. She was committed to the hospital against her will after a neighbor reported to the police that Martha was talking about killing herself, and a panel of psychiatrists agreed that she was a "danger to herself." Martha has petitioned the court for release on the grounds that "talk therapy" once a week is not doing her any good. The court is in a difficult position because the law requires that patients be treated or released, but there is no rule for determining what is appropriate treatment.

■ ■ ■

Lois is suffering from severe depression and is suicidal. Psychotherapy and drugs have had little or no effect, and it appears that she will have to be hospitalized for a long time. In the face of this, it has been decided to try electroconvulsive (shock) therapy. Lois has refused the treatment. However, Lois can be given the electroconvulsive therapy against her will because she was *involuntarily committed* to the hospital and because not using the treatment would result in greatly increased costs to the hospital.

■ ■ ■

Craig signed himself into the hospital voluntarily when he thought he was "losing control" of his thoughts. After being in the hospital a week, he feels somewhat better, but he does not like the drugs he is being given, and he generally dislikes the hospital. Two days ago he told the ward nurse that he wanted to sign out of the hospital and go home. She gave him the appropriate forms to fill out and told him that there would be a 48-hour waiting period before he could be discharged. During the waiting period, the hospital staff decided that Craig needed to be hospitalized, so they changed his status from voluntary to involuntary commitment. Now he cannot leave the hospital. He is furious and argues that if he had not come in voluntarily, he would not be there and that if he were a medical patient with cancer, they would let him leave. He claims his right of equal protection is being violated, and he wants out.

■ ■ ■

In this chapter I will discuss a variety of important legal issues that are related to abnormal behavior. Specifically, I will consider (a) the rules that are used to determine whether individuals are competent to stand trial, (b) the rules that are used to determine whether individuals are insane and not responsible for their crimes, (c) the procedures that are used to commit individuals to mental hospitals voluntarily and involuntarily, (d) the rights of hospitalized mental patients, and (e) the right of the public to be protected from potentially dangerous mental patients.

These are important topics because they reflect the protection that is given to disturbed individuals and to other members of society who may be threatened by disturbed individuals. For example, in 1980 John W. Hinckley Jr. attempted to assassinate the president of the United States. In his defense, he claimed that he had a mental disorder and therefore was not responsible for his act. Should he have been treated for his disorder and then released, or should he have been punished for the crime as another citizen would be punished? Joyce Brown lived next to a heat vent on a New York City street and sometimes burned money that was given to her by passersby. Should she have been committed to a hospital against her will, or should she have been allowed to continue living on the street as she wished? These are some of the questions we will try to answer in this chapter. The issues linking abnormal behavior and the law are complex because of the delicate balance that must be achieved in protecting the rights of disturbed individuals while also protecting the rights and safety of other members of society.

COMPETENCE TO STAND TRIAL

It is important that individuals who are accused of crimes be given the best opportunity to defend themselves in court. However, individuals who cannot adequately defend themselves because they suffer from mental disorders can be declared **incompetent to stand trial,** and their trials will be postponed (Appelbaum, 1993; Grisso, 1992; Philipsborn, 1990). To be declared incompetent to stand trial, it must be determined that the individual *cannot understand the proceedings* or *cannot contribute to his or her defense.* For example, an individual with schizophrenia whose thought processes are so disturbed that he or she cannot understand what is being said or cannot respond appropriately would be declared incompetent to stand trial. The incompetence defense is an extension of the notion that an individual should not be tried in absentia. In other words, defendants must be physically and mentally present at their trials.

The decision concerning whether an individual is competent to stand trial is made by a judge, who usually obtains recommendations from experts such as psychiatrists and psychologists (*Dusky* v. *United States,* 1960; *Pate* v. *Robinson,* 1966). In a review of a large number of defendants whose competence had been evaluated, it was found that individuals were most likely to be judged incompetent if they showed psychotic behavior such as hallucinations, delusions, disturbed behavior, or disturbed mood that would interfere with their ability to participate in their defense (Nicholson & Kugler, 1991; Slovenko, 1995).

It is important to note that *incompetence does not relieve the individual of responsibility for an illegal act.*

Instead, it simply allows the trial to be postponed until he or she can participate appropriately. During the postponement, the defendant is confined in a hospital or a prison for the criminally insane. This confinement is for the purpose of treating the individual so that eventually he or she will be competent to stand trial.

There are three potential problems with the use of the incompetence defense. First, some individuals attempt to *fake* incompetence as a means of stalling the legal proceedings against them. Fortunately, experts are usually able to detect attempts to fake incompetence, and even if the attempts are successful, they only postpone the trial and do not get the individual off.

The second problem is that it is possible for individuals to be *confined longer for the treatment of the incompetence than they would be confined if they stood trial for their crimes and were convicted.* That does not seem fair. The results of one investigation revealed that the average length of incarceration for incompetence was almost 6 years, which is much longer than the time most criminals spend in jail for serious crimes (McGarry & Bendt, 1969). In one institution, three individuals were found who had been incarcerated for incompetence but then overlooked for 17, 39, and 42 years, respectively.

Obviously, confinement for that long is inappropriate, and the U.S. Supreme Court has ruled that the confinement must not be longer than what is necessary to treat the individual and render him or her competent to stand trial. If it is unlikely that the individual will ever become competent, the individual must either be committed to a hospital or released (*Jackson* v. *Indiana,* 1972). Apart from the problem posed by the fact that confinement because of incompetence may be longer than imprisonment for the crime, there is always the

The embezzlement trial of television evangelist Jim Bakker was stalled when his attorney claimed that Bakker was incompetent to stand trial. After three days of evaluation, Bakker was ruled competent.

possibility that after a prolonged confinement for incompetence, the individual will be found not guilty of the crime.

The third problem occurs when the system is *misused* by law enforcement officials. When dealing with individuals who are a nuisance but who do not commit serious crimes, law enforcement officials may arrest the individuals and then have them declared incompetent as a means of getting them off the streets for longer periods than are justified by their illegal acts (Appelbaum et al., 1993). In those cases, what was originally developed as a defense becomes a tool for prosecution. This type of confinement is particularly onerous because unlike other pretrial confinements, incarceration for incompetence does not permit release on bail.

In summary, the concept of incompetence to stand trial is used to protect disturbed individuals from unfair trials. However, the question arises whether disturbed individuals should be tried at all; that is, if their illegal acts were caused by their disorders, maybe they should not be held responsible for their illegal acts. We will consider that possibility in the next section.

THE INSANITY DEFENSE

In our society, it is generally agreed that individuals are in control of their behavior, and therefore they are responsible for their behavior and should be punished if they do something that is illegal. However, if for some reason individuals cannot control their behavior, then it is not appropriate to hold them responsible or punish them for their behavior. That line of reasoning led to the **insanity defense.** Stated most broadly, the insanity defense asserts that *individuals who cannot behave appropriately because of mental disorders should not be held responsible for their behavior and should not be punished for their illegal behavior.*

If an individual is judged to be "not guilty by reason of insanity," he or she is committed to a hospital for treatment rather than to a prison for punishment. When the authorities agree that the individual no longer suffers from the disorder that led to the criminal behavior, the individual is released and does not have to go to prison. The insanity plea is very controversial, and we must give it careful consideration because it has a variety of important implications.

General Issues

Before discussing the rules that are used to determine whether or not an individual is insane, we should briefly mention three related issues. First, note that the term *insanity* is a *legal* term and not a psychological or medical one. This is relevant because it means that whether or not an individual is judged insane is determined by the laws of a given state rather than by what is defined as abnormal in DSM-IV. For example, under some laws an individual could be hallucinating, delusional, and diagnosed as suffering from schizophrenia, but if he or she knew the difference between right and wrong, the individual would be judged to be sane.

Second, different states employ different rules for determining whether an individual is insane. Because of these differences, in one state an individual might be declared not guilty by reason of insanity and be treated rather than punished, but in another state the same individual would be judged guilty and punished rather than treated.

Third, there are wide differences of opinion concerning how strict or lenient the rule for determining insanity should be. On the one hand, some critics argue that insanity should be defined very narrowly so that individuals who willfully commit crimes will be punished. The most conservative position is that all humans are always responsible for their behavior, and the insanity defense should be abolished. Indeed, it has been abolished in Utah, Montana, and Idaho. On the other hand, some people contend that insanity should be defined broadly so as to avoid the possibility of punishing disturbed individuals who need treatment. The most liberal position is that anyone who commits an illegal act is suffering from some sort of problem and should be rehabilitated rather than punished. As will become apparent in the subsequent discussion, the rules that are used for defining insanity differ widely, and as you read about each, you should consider which rule you think is most appropriate. Because insanity is determined by laws, someday you may be asked to vote to determine how insanity will be defined in your state.

Rules for Defining Insanity

At present, there are two basic rules for defining insanity, and I will consider each rule, along with its strengths and weaknesses. The rules will be considered in chronological order so that you can see how the concept is evolving. An understanding of these rules is important because they determine whether individuals who commit serious crimes such as murder will be punished, treated, or simply set free (Wettstein et al., 1991).

The M'Naghten Rule: Knowledge of Right Versus Wrong. This rule is named for Daniel M'Naghten, who in 1843 murdered the secretary of the British prime minister. M'Naghten actually meant to kill the prime minister but mistook the male secretary for his intended victim. During the trial, it was discovered that M'Naghten thought that the prime minister was plotting against him and that "the voice of God" had instructed him to kill the prime minister. Because M'Naghten's behavior had resulted from delusions of

In 1843, Daniel M'Naghten murdered a public official, but the British court ruled that he was not guilty by reason of insanity. Outrage over this verdict resulted in a new standard for determining insanity, the M'Naghten rule. That rule holds that an individual can be declared insane if at the time of the crime the individual did not know what he or she was doing or did not know that the act was wrong.

persecution and hallucinations rather than evil intent, he was found not guilty by reason of insanity, and therefore instead of being punished, he was committed to a mental hospital, where he remained for the rest of his life.

There was widespread public outrage over the fact that an individual who had willfully committed murder was not punished. Most important, Queen Victoria was infuriated by the insanity verdict because numerous attempts had been made on the lives of members of the royal family, and she thought that the failure to punish M'Naghten would encourage more such attempts. Therefore, the queen demanded that a tougher rule be developed for determining who is insane. The rule that was then developed in the House of Lords holds that an individual can be declared insane if at the time of the crime he or she *did not know what he or she was doing* or *did not know that it was wrong.* This rule came to be known as the **M'Naghten** (mik-NOT-un) **rule.**

The M'Naghten rule has been severely criticized because it is based entirely on the individual's knowledge of *right versus wrong,* and therefore it ignores all of the other mental abnormalities that can contribute to behavior. For example, it does not take into consideration the possibility that the individual knew that the act was wrong but could not exercise control because of overpowering emotions ("crimes of passion" or "irresistible impulses"). Furthermore, it does not take into consideration the possibility that the individual knew that the act was wrong but had to commit it because of hallucinations or delusions. An individual who suffers from schizophrenia might know that killing is wrong but believe that it must be done in self-defense because

the other person is sending brain-killing X-ray waves. The critics of the M'Naghten rule argue that overwhelming emotions and mental aberrations such as hallucinations and delusions are at least as important as the simple knowledge of right versus wrong, and hence they believe that the M'Naghten rule is too narrow.

In some states that employ the M'Naghten rule, an additional rule has been introduced that takes into account the influence of an **irresistible impulse** (sudden overwhelming emotion) that can lead to illegal behavior (*Smith* v. *United States,* 1929). The irresistible impulse rule is sometimes known as the **elbow rule** because it essentially asks, *would this individual have committed the crime if a police officer had been standing at his or her elbow, thereby ensuring that he or she would be caught?* The notion is that if the police were standing next to you so that you certainly would be caught and you still committed the illegal act, you must be out of control and should be judged to be insane.

Problematic as the M'Naghten rule may be, it stood unchallenged for over 100 years, and it is still used in some states today.

The American Law Institute Rule: Mental Disease or Defect.

Because of the dissatisfaction with the M'Naghten rule, a number of alternatives were suggested, and in 1972 the court adopted a new rule that had been developed by the American Law Institute, called the **American Law Institute rule** (*United States* v. *Brawner,* 1972). The first part of the rule reads as follows:

> A person is not responsible for criminal conduct if at the time of such conduct as a result of mental disease or defect he lacks substantial capacity either to appreciate

the criminality (wrongfulness) of his conduct or to conform his conduct to the requirements of law.

This rule greatly expanded the basis for insanity because in addition to using knowledge of right versus wrong (i.e., appreciate the wrongfulness of the conduct), the rule indicates that illegal behavior that results from a *mental disease or defect* could also be considered to be the product of insanity. For example, an individual who commits a murder because he or she has hallucinations or delusions could also be found to be insane. (Interestingly, that was the basis on which M'Naghten was originally ruled insane.) It should also be noted that in the American Law Institute rule, *mental disease or defect* was defined very broadly so as to include "any abnormal condition of the mind which substantially *affects mental or emotional processes* and substantially *impairs behavior controls*" (emphasis added). That is, mental diseases could lead to disturbed thoughts or disturbed emotions. That would allow for "crimes of passion" in which the individuals lost emotional control. Clearly, the American Law Institute rule was much more liberal than the M'Naghten rule.

A second part of the American Law Institute rule reads:

The terms "mental disease or defect" do not include an abnormality manifested only by repeated criminal or otherwise antisocial conduct.

This provision is important because it explicitly precludes habitual criminals from using repeated criminal activities as evidence of a mental disease or defect. That is, they cannot argue, "The fact that I repeatedly break the law is evidence that I have a mental disease and therefore I should be judged to be insane and not responsible for my acts." This provision also precludes an individual with the antisocial personality disorder (a psychopath) from pleading insanity because, as you learned earlier, one of the major signs of that disorder is repeated criminal behavior (see Chapter 14).

To recap, under the M'Naghten rule, insanity is defined very narrowly in terms of knowledge of right versus wrong, whereas under the American Law Institute rule, insanity is defined rather broadly and includes knowledge of right versus wrong and also mental disease or defect.

Practical Problems with the Insanity Defense

Independent of the philosophical questions of whether there should be an insanity defense and how broadly or narrowly it should be defined, a number of practical problems are associated with implementing the insanity defense. One problem revolves around the fact that the decision concerning whether an individual is insane or not is determined by the vote of a jury. This is problematic because jurors may not have the technical knowledge or training that is necessary to make informed judgments concerning insanity. Leaving the decision concerning sanity to jurors might be like asking 12 individuals with no training in medicine to decide whether an individual with a pain on the right side of the abdomen has strained a muscle, has appendicitis, or is faking. After reading this book, you will probably be more knowledgeable about abnormal behavior than most jurors, but would you be comfortable judging whether an individual has a mental disease or defect, or would you rather leave that decision to an expert? In that regard, it is interesting to note that the decision concerning *competence to stand trial* is put in the hands of experts (psychologists and psychiatrists), whereas the more complex decision concerning sanity is left to untrained jurors. Should the decision concerning insanity be left to a panel of independent experts?

Related to the fact that juries make the decision is the fact that in many cases, the jury must rely on opinions of expert witnesses, and often those witnesses disagree. What are juries to do when expert witnesses disagree?

The decision concerning competence to stand trial is put in the hands of experts, but the more complex decision concerning insanity is left to untrained jurors.

Another problem revolves around the fact that in making a decision about insanity, we must determine the nature of the individual's state of mind *at the time the act was committed.* It is difficult enough to determine an individual's present mental condition; it is almost impossible to determine what it was days, weeks, or even years earlier.

There is also the related problem of treating the individual who was insane at the time of the act but is sane now. How do you treat an individual for a disorder he or she no longer has? Is the individual simply to be turned loose? Will the public stand for that? What is to prevent the "temporary insanity" from coming back and leading the individual to commit another crime?

Still another problem is that individuals who are found not guilty by reason of insanity are incarcerated until they are "cured," but in many cases, the resulting period of incarceration is longer than what would have occurred if they had been found to be sane and simply sent to prison. Is that appropriate?

Finally, in most cases, the individual is presumed sane until proven insane. However, in our system of justice, the burden of proof is on the prosecution, and therefore we may ask whether the individual should be presumed to be insane until proven sane.

Some of the problems associated with judging insanity are illustrated in Case Study 20.1, of John W. Hinckley Jr., who attempted to assassinate President Ronald Reagan and then pleaded insanity. Hinckley's symptoms were somewhat vague and can lead to different diagnoses (e.g., was he suffering from schizophrenia or only the schizoid personality disorder? was he depressed or only dysthymic?). Because his symptoms can be interpreted in various ways, there is room for disagreement about whether or not he was insane (e.g., did his symptoms impair his behavioral control?). It is important to understand the facts and issues of this case because it will serve as a legal benchmark and point of controversy for many years to come. In some respects, the Hinckley case has had an effect in America like the M'Naghten case had in England. As you read this case, you might try to arrive at your own diagnosis for John Hinckley and determine for yourself whether or not he was insane. (Read Case Study 20.1 now, before continuing in the text.)

RULE CHANGES IN RESPONSE TO THE HINCKLEY VERDICT

Return to M'Naghten. When Hinckley was found not guilty by reason of insanity, there was a considerable backlash against the use of the insanity defense. In some states, the insanity defense was simply abolished; in others, the rules for determining insanity were changed. Indeed, the American Psychiatric Association recommended that the basis for insanity should no longer include mental disease or defect as an acceptable reason for not conforming behavior to the requirements of the law (Insanity Defense Work Group, 1983). In essence, that change returned the basis for insanity to the M'Naghten rule (knowledge of right versus wrong), and the change was accepted by the U.S. Congress, so it now applies in all U.S. federal courts. It was also adopted by about half of the state courts. Knowledge of right versus wrong is certainly a more restrictive definition of insanity, but it is noteworthy that returning to that rule has not resulted in a dramatic decline in the use or success (acquittal rate) of the insanity defense (McGreevy et al., 1991).

"Guilty but Mentally Ill" Rule. One alternative rule that was proposed is the **"guilty but mentally ill" rule.** Under that rule there would be two trials. The first would be used to determine whether the defendant was guilty or innocent, and the second would be used to determine whether the defendant was sane or insane. If found to be both guilty and insane, the individual would first be sent to a mental hospital for treatment until he or she was found to be sane, and then the individual would be sent to prison to be punished for the crime (Bumby, 1993). This procedure was developed to satisfy both supporters and opponents of the insanity defense, but you cannot satisfy both without some logical contradiction. Specifically, how can you agree that an individual was insane and therefore not responsible for his or her behavior and then punish the individual for the behavior for which you had agreed he or she was not responsible?

Other proposed changes involve making the defense prove insanity rather than making the prosecution prove sanity (that is already the case in some states) and barring psychiatrists and psychologists from testifying so that the judgment would be left entirely to the jury.

In recent years the insanity defense has been invoked in trials that received widespread publicity in the media. Most cases still hinge on the effects of psychotic symptoms such as hallucinations and delusions, but increasing numbers of defendants are using the multiple personality disorder as a defense (Serban, 1992). Those defendants allege either that they are incompetent to stand trial because they do not know what their other personality did, so they cannot defend themselves, or that they are insane because they are not responsible for the actions of their other personality. A second currently popular defense involves the posttraumatic stress disorder. Defendants who use that defense allege that their crimes (usually shooting sprees) are defensive reactions that occur during a "flashback." These are usually linked to

CASE STUDY 20.1

John W. Hinckley Jr.: An Insanity Defense After Attempting to Assassinate the President

Hinckley's Background

John W. Hinckley Jr. was the youngest of three children in a wealthy family. In elementary school he quarterbacked the football team, starred in basketball, became an avid Beatles fan, and appeared to be a well-adjusted child. When John was in the sixth grade, the family moved to an affluent and prestigious suburb (the home had its own swimming pool and even a soft-drink machine), and it was then that things seemed to change for John. As his mother put it, he was no longer the "kingpin"—he was the manager of the football team rather than the quarterback, he took up solitary activities such as playing the guitar, and he developed "his own little withdrawn personality."

After John graduated from high school, he enrolled at Texas Tech. During the following summer and fall he lived in Dallas, a period he described this way: "I stayed by myself in my apartment and dreamed of future glory in some undefined field, perhaps music or politics." He returned to Texas Tech for the spring and fall semesters, but after that his life became chaotic and disjointed. For example, he lived in at least 17 different places between his junior year in college and the time four years later when he attempted to assassinate the president. Because of space limitations, I cannot describe those years in detail, but some facts are particularly noteworthy.

Midway through the spring semester of his junior year, John dropped out of school and sold his car to finance a trip to California, where he planned to sell songs he had been writing. Six weeks later, a letter he wrote to his parents was filled with optimism, but the tide soon turned, and when he wrote a month later, he said: "Through a series of sorry circumstances, I am in trouble. For the past 2 and a half weeks I have literally been without food, shelter and clothing." He asked for money, which his parents sent. On the positive side, he wrote about an encouraging contact with United Artists and a girlfriend named Lynn Collins. In fact, however, no contact had been made with United Artists, and Lynn Collins did not exist.

One fact about the period in California that later took on great significance was that John saw the movie *Taxi Driver* 15 times. The major character in

In 1980, John W. Hinckley Jr. attempted to assassinate President Ronald Reagan in an effort to impress actress Jodie Foster. He was judged not guilty by reason of insanity and sent to a hospital for treatment.

the film is Travis Bickle, a lonely New York taxi driver. Travis meets a girl named Betsy, who works for a presidential candidate, but after their first date, she walks out on him, leaving him heartbroken. Travis goes to kill the candidate for whom Betsy works but is scared off by the Secret Service men. Later Travis encounters a 12-year-old prostitute named Iris (played by Jodie Foster), whom he decides to rescue. When Travis attacks Iris's pimp, he is shot and wounded, and the newspapers portray him as a hero. Some time later, by chance, Travis picks up Betsy in his cab, and because of his notoriety, she shows renewed interest in him.

John Hinckley apparently identified with the lonely Travis and subsequently took on many of his characteristics: John dressed as Travis did, drank peach brandy, bought and played with guns, and began taking pills of various sorts. The film and his identification with Travis also led him to an intense interest in Jodie Foster, whom he saw as needing to be loved and rescued.

After returning from California, John worked for a while as a busboy and later returned to Texas Tech.

continued

CASE STUDY 20.1 *(continued)*

While in school, he complained of a variety of physical ailments such as a sore eye, sore throat, earache, and light-headedness. He also became interested in the National Socialist (American Nazi) party and later wrote, "At the age of 23, I was an all-out anti-semite and white racist." In September 1979, he started publishing a newsletter for the American Front, an organization that he described as "an alternative to the minority-kissing Republican and Democrat parties." John called himself the "national director" and listed members in 37 states, but in fact there was no organization and he had made the whole thing up. The next year, he founded a mail-order company called Listalot from which people could buy lists of different types, but the lists were fictitious.

Off and on during this time, John sought help for more physical symptoms and was given a prescription for an antihistamine. Later he complained of hearing problems, dizzy spells, heart palpitations, and an "anxiety attack." The physician who saw him for those symptoms wrote in the record: "Patient showed a flat affect throughout examination and depressive reaction." An antidepressant (Surmontil) was prescribed. In a letter to his sister, John wrote: "My nervous system is about shot. I take heavy medication for it which doesn't seem to do much good except make me very drowsy. By the end of the summer, I should be a bone fide basket case." After more visits to the physician, a tranquilizer (Valium) was prescribed.

John returned to Colorado to house-sit while his parents were away, and at that time he began seeing a psychologist, Darrell Benjamin, who was a consultant on personnel matters for John's father. The psychologist regarded John as very immature and suggested that he formulate a plan for his life. Following that suggestion, John worked out an agreement with his parents whereby he could sell some stock to finance a course in writing at Yale. He left for New Haven but did not register for class. Instead, he called Jodie Foster on the phone twice (she was then a student at Yale) and then, after only five days, flew back to Colorado. Of that time he wrote: "My mind was on the breaking point. A relationship I had dreamed about went absolutely nowhere. My disillusionment with EVERYTHING was

complete." After four days in Colorado, he flew to Lubbock and then to Washington, D.C., where he wrote to his sister, "Yale is such a disappointment. These past weeks have been strange times. I keep getting hit over the head by reality. It doesn't feel good."

This was followed by a series of trips to Columbus, Dayton, New Haven, Lincoln, Nashville, Chicago, New York, and Dallas. Some of these trips involved the stalking of President Jimmy Carter, whom John planned to shoot, but he decided against that. Before one flight between Nashville and New York, airport security guards found three pistols in John's suitcase. He was fined $62.50, held five hours, and then released.

At the end of this frenzy of traveling, John took an overdose of the antidepressant that had been prescribed for him, but he survived, and at his parents' insistence, he began seeing a psychiatrist named John Hopper. Between weekly sessions with Dr. Hopper in Colorado, John started making trips to Washington, New York, and New Haven. Sometimes he traveled under the assumed name of John Hudson. On trips to New Haven, he left notes, poems, and presents for Jodie Foster at her dormitory at Yale. One note read: "Just wait. I'll rescue you very soon. Please cooperate." Another said: "I love you six trillion times. Don't you maybe like me just a little bit? (You must admit I am different.) It would make all of this worthwhile."

On March 6, 1980, John ran out of money and called home for help. His father arranged for him to fly to Colorado and met John at the airport. Dr. Hopper, John's psychiatrist, advised the elder Hinckley, "Give John a hundred dollars and tell him good-bye," so Hinckley gave his son $210 and sent him off on his own. John spent the next couple of weeks living in motels. On March 25, his mother drove him to the airport. Of the trip to the airport she recalled:

> It was so hard to see John go, because I felt in my mind that once again John might be leaving and maybe he might try to take his own life. . . . He looked so bad, and so sad, and so absolutely in total despair and I was frightened, and I didn't know what he was going to do. . . . [At the airport,] John got out of the car and I couldn't even look at him. And he said, "Well, Mom, I

want to thank you for everything. I want to thank you for everything you have ever done for me."

John flew to Hollywood, but the next day he took a bus to Washington, D.C., where he arrived on the afternoon of March 29 and registered at the Park Central Hotel.

The Shooting

On the morning of March 30, 1980, John took a Valium and went to McDonald's for breakfast. On the way back, he bought a copy of the *Washington Star,* in which he noticed President Ronald Reagan's schedule. Back in his room, John took a shower and took some Valium to help him calm down. He then loaded his .22 caliber pistol, specifically using exploding-head Devastator bullets. Next he wrote a letter to Jodie Foster. In that letter, he wrote of his plan to kill the president. He also wrote of his love for her and the reason for attempting to kill the president:

> As you well know by now I love you very much. Over the past seven months I've left you dozens of poems, letters and love messages in the faint hope that you could develop an interest in me. . . . I honestly did not wish to bother you with my constant presence. I know the many messages left at your door and in your mailbox were a nuisance, but I felt that it was the most painless way for me to express my love for you. . . . I will admit to you that the reason I'm going ahead with this attempt now is because I just cannot wait any longer to impress you. I've got to do something now to make you understand, in no uncertain terms, that I am doing all of this for your sake! By sacrificing my freedom and possibly my life, I hope to change your mind about me. This letter is being written only an hour before I leave for the Hilton Hotel. Jodie, I'm asking you to please look into your heart and at least give me the chance, with this historical deed, to gain your respect and love. I love you forever.

John then went to the Washington Hilton, where the president was scheduled to speak at 1:45. He waved as the president went in and then waited for him to come out. The president came out at 2:25, surrounded by aides and protectors. In response to a call from the crowd, the president turned, and as he did, John crouched like a marksman and fired six shots in rapid succession. The first bullet hit the

president's press secretary in the face and entered his brain. The second hit a policeman in the back. The third went over the president's head. The fourth hit a Secret Service agent in the chest. The fifth bullet hit the glass of the president's limousine, and the sixth ricocheted off the limousine and entered the president's chest, where it glanced off a rib and came to rest in a lung only inches from his heart. John was wrestled to the ground by a Secret Service agent, who reported that John "was still clicking the weapon," now empty, as they went down.

The Trial

The trial opened in May 1982 and lasted until mid-June. The facts of the attempted assassination were clear and indisputable. Indeed, they were recorded by a television news cameraman, and the trial was begun with a showing of the videotape. John W. Hinckley Jr. had attempted to assassinate the president; the question was, *was he sane or insane at the time of the attempt?* Because the assassination was attempted in the District of Columbia, where the American Law Institute rule is used to determine sanity or insanity, the crucial question was, did John lack substantial capacity to appreciate the wrongfulness of his act or conform his conduct to the requirements of the law? The prosecution and defense waged a legal tug-of-war using teams of experts in an attempt to pull the jury in one direction or another.

The Defense

The defense attorneys first called John Hopper, the psychiatrist who had treated John after the attempted suicide and who had suggested that the family turn the young man out on his own. Hopper testified that John's problems during late adolescence and early adulthood were "typical" of an unsuccessful son in a successful family. In other words, Hopper did not see John as particularly disturbed. That testimony would have played into the hands of the prosecution, which was to argue that John was not insane, but the defense attorneys cleverly turned the testimony around. First, they suggested that Hopper was mistaken in his judgment. As support for that, they pointed out that despite the fact that John had

continued

CASE STUDY 20.1 *(continued)*

had 22 therapy sessions with Hopper, Hopper knew nothing of John's extensive trips around the country, intense interest in the movie *Taxi Driver*, arrest in Nashville, or numerous other relevant facts about the young man's life. Then the defense attorneys used the fact that Hopper had been misled to suggest that John was so clever at disguising his problems that he was able to fool even a trained psychiatrist. The conclusion to be drawn by the members of the jury was that they should not also be misled by John's superficial appearance of normality. The defense also called William Carpenter, another psychiatrist, who testified that it was his judgment that John was suffering from major depression and from schizophrenia. It was Carpenter's opinion that because schizophrenia is a serious disorder that results in breaks from reality and delusions of reference, John was not responsible for his acts.

Another important and controversial defense witness was David Bear, a psychiatrist who had special expertise in brain structure. Bear brought two things to the defense. First, he pointed out the role the movie *Taxi Driver* had played in John's symptoms. He pointed out that it was normal for a young man to fall in love with an actress, but he said that after being rejected by Jodie Foster, it was not normal for Hinckley to continue pursuing her and to believe that she was a "prisoner at Yale" and that he had to "rescue" her. Bear asserted that Betsy's renewed interest in Travis after he shot the pimp suggested to John that violence is rewarded by the attention of a woman and that John's fantasies about Travis and Iris had taken over his mind. According to Bear, John was essentially acting out the movie script. He had to rescue Jodie/Iris, and he could get her attention and love through violence. That, Bear concluded, "was psychosis."

Second, Bear testified about the results of a CT scan that was done on John's brain (for a discussion

of CT scans, see Chapter 3). Bear testified that the brains of many persons with schizophrenia are characterized by widened sulci (folds on the surface of the brain; see Chapter 12) and that John Hinckley's CT scan indicated that his brain had widened sulci. The implication was that the CT scan provided evidence that John was suffering from schizophrenia. On cross-examination, the prosecutor tried to make the point that widened sulci are not a perfect sign of schizophrenia (i.e., some normal individuals have widened sulci) and that the CT scan could not be used to "confirm" a diagnosis of schizophrenia because the diagnosis had not been made in the first place. There was considerable controversy over whether the CT scan should be allowed as evidence, but eventually the judge ruled that it would be allowed. That ruling set an important precedent because never before had evidence of that type been allowed at a trial.

The defense also called Ernst Prelinger, a psychologist from Yale, as a witness. Prelinger testified that on the Wechsler Adult Intelligence Scale, John had an overall IQ of 113. More important, Prelinger reported that on the MMPI, John had abnormally high scores on all but one of the scales that measured abnormal behavior (e.g., measures indicative of schizophrenia, depression, anxiety) and that there was no evidence that he was faking his responses.

In summary, the defense argued that there was both psychological and physiological evidence that John Hinckley was suffering from schizophrenia and that his schizophrenia had rendered him unable to appreciate the wrongfulness of his act.

The Prosecution

The major expert witness for the prosecution was a psychiatrist named Park Dietz. Dietz had led the

---

military experiences in Vietnam, but some defendants have claimed that growing up in dangerous slums caused posttraumatic stress disorder, leading to flashbacks and hence to the crimes. These defenses have been referred to as "trendy alibis," and although they

receive a lot of attention, there is no evidence that they are more effective than other insanity defenses (Appelbaum et al., 1993).

In conclusion, many people believe that it is better to treat than punish individuals whose illegal behavior

team of government psychiatrists that produced a 628-page report concerning Hinckley's mental status, and Dietz was on the stand for five days testifying about the conclusions. It was Dietz's conclusion that John was suffering from a dysthymic disorder (a mild form of depression that falls between normal depression and the more serious major depressive disorder; see Chapter 8) and that he had three types of personality disorders: schizoid, narcissistic, and a combination of the borderline and passive-aggressive types.

In essence, the prosecution witnesses agreed with those of the defense with regard to the general *nature* of John's problems, but they saw the problems as *less serious*. They saw John as suffering from *dysthymia* rather than depression and as having the *schizoid* or *borderline* personality disorder rather than schizophrenia. In their report, the team of psychiatrists for the prosecution concluded that "Hinckley's history is clearly indicative of a person who did not function in a usual, reasonable manner. However, there is no evidence that he was so impaired that he could not appreciate the wrongfulness of his conduct or conform his conduct to the requirements of the law." Dietz argued that rather than suffering from schizophrenia, John was a lazy, fame-seeking, spoiled loner who lied and cheated to get what he wanted from his parents. As evidence of John's need for attention, Dietz pointed out that following the shooting, John had asked if reports of his assassination attempt would preempt the Academy Awards telecast scheduled for that night.

The other witness for the prosecution was Sally Johnson, a psychiatrist who had spent more time interviewing John than anyone else. Johnson testified that John suffered from numerous personality disorders, but she did not consider them psychotic, nor did she think that they prevented John from being responsible for his acts.

In summary, the prosecution argued that John Hinckley was an immature and disturbed individual but that he was not suffering from schizophrenia and his level of disturbance was not enough to interfere with his ability to appreciate the wrongfulness of his act or conform his behavior to the law.

The Verdict

After months of testimony, Judge Barrington Parker gave the jury its instructions. As part of those instructions, he told the jury that mental illness was defined as "any abnormal condition of the mind" that "substantially affects mental or emotional processes and substantially impairs [a person's] behavior controls." The judge then made two important points: First, he told the jury that the burden was on the prosecution to prove that John was *not* insane at the time of the assassination attempt. In other words, Hinckley was *insane until proven sane*, and if there was any reasonable doubt about his sanity, the jury had to bring in a verdict of not guilty by reason of insanity. Second, the judge addressed the effect of finding John not guilty by reason of insanity. The judge pointed out that if found to be insane, John would be committed to Saint Elizabeth's Hospital and that within 50 days, a hearing would have to be held to determine whether he could be released. In essence, he warned the jury that if they found John insane, he would not be punished and might soon be eligible for release.

After 4½ days of deliberation, the jury returned its verdict: on all counts, not guilty by reason of insanity. John W. Hinckley Jr. was remanded to Saint Elizabeth's Hospital, where he remains to this day.

Source: Based on Caplan (1984).

is due to a mental disorder. However, it is exceptionally difficult to formulate a generally acceptable rule for determining who is insane. Furthermore, because the attitudes about insanity change with the political climate and events, the debate over the insanity defense

will continue. It is important that you understand the issues and appreciate the implications of the various options so that you can make an informed decision if you must confront the question of insanity. What rule would you use for determining insanity, and whose responsibility should it be to determine whether an individual is sane or insane?

VOLUNTARY AND INVOLUNTARY HOSPITALIZATION

It is generally believed that many psychological disorders can be treated most effectively in a hospital and that many disturbed individuals must be confined in hospitals for their own safety and for the safety of others. Because of these beliefs, disturbed individuals are often hospitalized, many of them against their will. In the following sections, I will consider the difficult question of who can be hospitalized voluntarily and involuntarily.

Voluntary Hospitalization

Anyone who feels in need of help can apply for **voluntary admission** to a mental hospital. The individual will be examined by an admitting psychiatrist or a psychologist, and if the symptoms are judged to be serious, the individual will be admitted for at least a period of evaluation. However, now that hospitals are facing serious economic cutbacks, individuals will not be admitted unless it is really necessary, and the individuals may not be held as long as was once the case.

When considering voluntary hospitalization, it is important to realize that *voluntary admission does not guarantee voluntary release.* For example, an individual may voluntarily sign into a hospital and then later decide to sign out, but if the hospital staff decides that the individual requires hospitalization, the staff may change the admission from voluntary to involuntary. That can occur because to be discharged, the patient must sign a form requesting discharge and then wait a period of time (often 72 hours). During that waiting period, the nature of the discharge can be changed, and the patient is then surprised to learn that he or she cannot leave. Perhaps we should give warnings to individuals who are about to sign into a mental hospital voluntarily, to the effect that "anything you say or do can and will be used against you, and you may be involuntarily committed." We protect suspected criminals in that way; why not potential mental patients?

It is interesting that the conversion of a voluntary admission to an involuntary commitment is not done with medical patients who want to terminate treatment. A medical patient who wishes to leave must sign a form indicating that he or she is doing so "against medical advice" but is nevertheless permitted to go. Clearly, we treat medical and mental patients differently.

Recently, the Supreme Court raised concerns about the validity of some voluntary admissions when it ruled that *some individuals may not be legally competent to make the decision concerning admission.* That is, some individuals may be too disturbed to be able to consent to hospitalization (Cournos et al., 1993; Hoge, 1994). One case revolved around a man who was found walking along a highway, bruised, bloodied, disoriented, and thinking he was "in heaven." He was taken to a mental hospital, where he was given voluntary commitment papers to sign, which he did. He was then held for 5 months, during which time he was not given a hearing concerning his willingness to stay in the hospital because he had admitted himself voluntarily. When he was finally released, he filed a suit alleging that he had been deprived of his liberty without due process; his argument was that he had been admitted as a voluntary patient but was at the time incompetent to give his informed consent to such an admission (*Zinermon* v. *Burch,* 1990; R. D. Miller, 1994; Winick, 1991). Interpreted narrowly, this decision could mean that patients who want to admit themselves voluntarily would first have to be examined for competence; if they were found to be competent, then they could sign in voluntarily, but if they were found to be incompetent, they would have to be committed involuntarily. This could add an expensive and time-consuming step to the admission procedure.

Involuntary Hospitalization

Many individuals in mental hospitals have been hospitalized against their will by means of **involuntary commitment.** The act of committing individuals to mental hospitals against their will must be done carefully because in doing so, we are depriving the individuals of their civil liberties; indeed, we are depriving them of their freedom. There are two justifications for committing an individual to a mental hospital: the *protection of the individual* and the *protection of society.*

Protection of the Individual (Parens Patriae). It is generally agreed that the state has the right and responsibility to protect and provide for the well-being of people within its jurisdiction. That right and that responsibility are referred to as the doctrine of *parens patriae* (PAR-enz PĀ-trē-ī; the term is Latin for "parent of the country"), which under English law held that the king was "the general guardian of all his infants, idiots, and lunatics." There are three situations under the doctrine of *parens patriae* in which the state has the right to commit an individual to a mental hospital:

1. If the individual *needs treatment*
2. If the individual is *dangerous to himself or herself*
3. If the individual *cannot take care of himself or herself*

Most people agree that individuals meeting one or more of these requirements need hospitalization. For example, suicidal individuals are dangerous to themselves, need treatment, and in many cases should be hospitalized at least until the crisis has passed. However, problems arise when the disturbed individuals do not think they need treatment but the authorities think they do. For example, suicidal individuals usually think they know what is best for themselves and do not want to be hospitalized.

In court decisions it has been stressed that *individuals should not be committed to hospitals involuntarily if they are capable of making their own decisions on the matter.* For example, in one case the court ruled that unless it could be proved that a mentally ill individual is unable to make an appropriate decision about hospitalization because of the mental illness, the individual should be allowed to decide about hospitalization (*Lessard* v. *Schmidt,* 1972). The problem with this ruling is that if the authorities want to hospitalize an individual but the individual decides that he or she does not want to be hospitalized, the authorities can simply conclude that the individual is not able to make an appropriate decision, and then they can hospitalize the individual involuntarily. In essence, the ability to make an appropriate decision about hospitalization is operationally defined as agreeing with the authorities on the decision. This places the potential patient in a catch-22 situation: *The patient has the right to make the decision about hospitalization only as long as that decision is the same as that of the authorities.*

There is also a potential legal problem with committing individuals to mental hospitals under the doctrine of *parens patriae.* We do not involuntarily hospitalize individuals with medical disorders such as cancer, so if we involuntarily hospitalize individuals with mental disorders, we may be violating their **right to equal protection,** a right guaranteed by the 14th Amendment to the U.S. Constitution. In other words, individuals who suffer from mental disorders must not be treated differently from individuals who suffer from medical disorders. Because of these problems, the states of Pennsylvania, Michigan, Washington, Alabama, West Virginia, and Kentucky no longer permit involuntary hospitalization on the basis of *parens patriae.*

Protection of Society (Police Power of the State).

Involuntary commitment may also be justified under the **police power of the state** if the individual is considered dangerous to others (*Humphrey* v. *Cady,* 1972; *Jackson* v. *Indiana,* 1972). Most persons would probably agree that individuals who are dangerous to others should be confined. However, a problem arises because the results of numerous studies indicate that psychologists and psychiatrists are not particularly accurate at predicting who is dangerous (Diamond, 1974; Ennis &

Litwack, 1974; Kozol et al., 1972; Monahan, 1973, 1976, 1978, 1984; Rofman et al., 1980; Steadman, 1973; Steadman & Keveles, 1972, 1978; A. A. Stone, 1975). If we cannot predict who is dangerous, we may commit individuals who do not need to be committed and thereby unjustifiably deprive them of their freedom.

In one study, almost 1,000 criminally insane patients who were assumed to be dangerous were released from prison hospitals, and investigators followed them up to determine their rate of dangerous acts (Steadman & Keveles, 1972). The patients were released because of a change in the law rather than because they were judged to be "cured," but after 4 years only 2.7% of them had behaved dangerously and were back in a hospital or in prison. In other words, 97.3% of the individuals who had been incarcerated because they were supposedly dangerous did not commit dangerous acts when they were released! That finding is particularly noteworthy because these individuals were originally hospitalized because they had committed a dangerous act, and therefore we might expect them to be more likely to commit another dangerous act.

There has been recent movement toward requiring that the danger posed by the individual be "imminent" rather than at some unspecified time in the future. Because we are probably better able to assess an individual's current mental and emotional state of mind than predict what he or she will be like sometime in the future, we may be better able to predict imminent danger than danger in general.

A potential legal problem is also associated with hospitalizing individuals who are only suspected of being dangerous because doing so may violate their right to equal protection. Mentally ill individuals who are suspected of being dangerous are confined, but individuals who are not mentally ill and are suspected of being dangerous (e.g., a suspected "hit man" for the Mafia) are not confined. Furthermore, mentally ill individuals who might be dangerous *in the future* are confined, but others who are not mentally ill cannot be locked up until it has been proved that they have *already* committed a dangerous act. Thus it appears that in many cases, mentally ill individuals are not treated equally under the law, and it must be asked whether it is fair to treat them more harshly than we treat suspected criminals.

In recent years questions about the appropriate use of involuntary commitment have arisen with regard to the treatment of homeless people in cities such as New York and Washington (Cohen & Thompson, 1992). In those cities, sweeps were occasionally conducted in which individuals who were living on the streets were picked up and taken to mental hospitals against their will. City officials justified the sweeps by saying that the commitments were for the good of the individuals involved, but civil libertarians argued that the homeless people were not a danger to anyone and were able to take care of themselves, albeit in a somewhat different manner than most other people. In short, the critics argued that the street people were being taken off the street and committed to hospitals because *they disturbed other people* rather than because *they were disturbed.* This problem is illustrated in Case Study 20.2. Read this case study before continuing in the text.

The case of Joyce Brown illustrates a number of the problems and issues we have discussed in this book. First, how do we define "abnormal"? From a personal perspective, Brown was neither distressed nor disabled, but from a cultural perspective, she was deviant. The case also illustrates the point that behavior must be considered in a context. Burning or throwing money away certainly sounds "crazy," but doing so in an attempt to convince people who are forcing it on you that you have all you need and do not want more may

Disturbed individuals are sometimes hospitalized against their will. The justifications for this include protection of the individual and protection of society. Committing individuals against their will must be done carefully because it deprives them of their civil liberties. Many observers have argued that involuntary commitment of homeless people has occurred because the homeless disturb other people and not because the homeless are disturbed.

not be crazy. More germane to the concerns of this chapter is the question of the protection of the rights of individuals. Brown's right to live as she wished must be protected, but at the same time, we must be sensitive to the concerns of people visiting businesses and restaurants in the area who might be offended by her.

There is also the question of how we determine whether a person presents a danger to self or others. Joyce Brown was forcibly taken off of the street, purportedly for her own good, but in fact she was physically healthy, and life on the street was the life she preferred. She was also picked up because of concern that others would attack her, but in our society we usually incarcerate the *attackers,* not the *individuals they attack.* The case of Joyce Brown illustrates all of these problems and questions, but it does not solve or answer any of them. What decision would you have made about Joyce Brown?

Finally, as with all case studies, it is important that we not generalize from Brown to all homeless people. Many are not on the street by choice, many have been literally thrown out of hospitals in which they would rather be living and getting treatment, and many are not able to function effectively, so they desperately cling to—and sometimes fall from—a thin ledge of existence.

Before concluding this discussion of involuntary commitment, a comment should be made concerning the possibility of **involuntary outpatient commitment** (Lefkovitch et al., 1993; McCafferty & Dooley, 1990; Mulvey et al., 1987). With this procedure, the individual would not be confined to a hospital but would be required to attend outpatient therapy. This is a middle-ground approach that does not deprive individuals of their basic freedom and saves the state the cost of hospitalization, but at the same time it ensures that individuals receive the treatment and supervision they need. Involuntary outpatient commitment could not be used with all patients (e.g., clearly dangerous individuals would not be eligible), but it might be an appropriate and advantageous approach for many.

It should be clear from the foregoing discussion that our attempts to help disturbed individuals and to protect society through involuntary hospitalization are fraught with legal, logical, and practical problems. At best, the system is an imperfect series of compromises designed to protect the rights of all. As with other such compromises, sometimes the protection of one individual's rights infringes on the rights of another, and we must constantly be sensitive to the needs of all and work to maintain the delicate balance between protection and infringement.

Procedures for Involuntary Hospitalization

Earlier you learned that the grounds for involuntary hospitalization are need for treatment, danger to self,

CASE STUDY 20.2
The Woman Who Burned Money

The case of the woman who burned money began on Thursday, October 29, 1987, when the *New York Times* carried a front-page story under the headline "Mentally Ill Homeless Taken off New York Streets." The article explained how vans carrying a psychiatrist, a nurse, and a social worker had been dispatched to begin a "vigorous campaign to remove severely mentally ill homeless people from Manhattan streets, parks and byways" so that the city could "forcibly provide them with medical and psychiatric care."

The first person to be picked up and taken to the Bellevue Hospital Center was described as "a disheveled woman in her 40's who lived for nearly a year against the wall of a restaurant . . . and often defecated in her clothes." The mayor had visited the woman once six months earlier, and in a speech to the American Psychological Association he said, "She lies there all year around, and she defecates in her clothing when she is not lucid, and when she is lucid she defecates on the sidewalk."

The woman, who was thought to be named Ann Smith (but was sometimes called Joyce), had been living on the sidewalk on Second Avenue near 65th Street, where she kept warm by sitting in front of a 1-by-3-ft heat vent from a restaurant. Local merchants and residents had shown sympathy for her and had often left her food or given her money. A florist had given her flowers. "She liked them," he said, "but was troubled that they die." The article went on to point out that one of the most confusing aspects of this "troubled person" was her vacillation between begging and belligerence, belligerence that often involved throwing away or burning money that she had been given. A woman from the restaurant reported, "She asks for a quarter and then when you give her three quarters, she is going to throw the other two away. . . . I don't know why. It's very strange. A lot of people were worried about her. . . . They stop and give her money, but sometimes she won't take it. 'I don't need your money,' she yelled." The florist reported that "around Christmas time, that's the only woman I know who rips up $100 and $50 bills. . . . She rips them up in teeny little pieces." His coworker added, "She likes to burn them."

At a news conference the next day, the mayor called the roundup program a "breakthrough" that "should have been started five years earlier." However, resistance was developing among civil libertarians, who believed that the rights of the people being

Joyce Brown lived on the streets until she was hospitalized against her will. In a court hearing, she effectively argued that she was not disturbed but had an eccentric lifestyle. She was hospitalized for 84 days. She later spoke about her case at the Harvard Law School.

picked up were being violated. A staff attorney with the New York Civil Liberties Union said he had received a call from the first person picked up (Ann Smith), who wanted help getting out of Bellevue. (In New York, involuntarily committed patients must be given a hearing within 5 days.) Smith, he said, was "lucid and extremely articulate and extremely angry. . . . She was aware of her rights and felt strongly that they had been violated." When concerns were raised about people being forced to come in against their will, in one case in handcuffs, the director of the project commented, "People say, 'We don't want to come.' With the police with us, we say, 'You must come, we want to help you.' I don't think voluntarily is the word, but cooperatively."

The next development in the case was on Monday, November 2, when it was reported that in a telephone interview from a psychiatric ward at Bellevue,

(continued)

CASE STUDY 20.2 *(continued)*

Smith had said, "I like the streets, and I am entitled to live the way I want to live. . . . I know that there are people and places I can go to if I don't choose to be on the streets. . . . In this day and age, in the 80s in the United States of America, where everyone comes to be free, my rights are being violated." With regard to her burning of money, she said that she did it because she was sometimes insulted that people threw money at her. She was angry about a press release distributed by city hall describing her as "dirty, disheveled and malodorous, . . . delusional, withdrawn and unpredictable." In fact, her comments did not sound like those of the derelict described in the press release. Smith asked the reporter to visit her at Bellevue, but despite the fact that legally Smith was entitled to visitors and had been visited by a neighborhood resident, hospital officials barred the reporter, assigned a security guard to follow him through the public areas of the hospital, and then barred Smith from making additional phone calls. These restrictions were justified by suggesting that "the kind of media attention that is being requested by members of the press would be detrimental to her condition."

On Monday, November 2, a 5-hour hearing was conducted in a courtroom at Bellevue to determine whether New York City had the right to take Smith off the street and treat her in a psychiatric ward against her will. Psychiatrists for the city testified that she was suffering from chronic schizophrenia, ran in front of cars, lived in her own feces, was so sick that she was completely unaware of her illness, and had to be hospitalized for her own good because she was a danger to herself and might be assaulted by others.

The defense attorneys challenged those allegations and argued that Smith (who was now giving her name as Billy Boggs) was only an "eccentric" who wanted to live on the streets and be left alone. They also pointed out that on five occasions during the past year, Smith (Boggs) had been taken to other psychiatric hospitals, but on each occasion, she had not been admitted because there was no evidence that she was a danger to herself. On cross-examination, the city officials admitted that they had no evidence that Smith (Boggs) had ever harmed herself. Furthermore, during the cross-examination the defense attorney read hospital records in which it was stated that Smith (Boggs) "had a delusion that she was unfairly incarcerated." The attorney then asked whether he would also be judged to have a delusion if he felt that Smith had been incarcerated unfairly. The psychiatrist on the stand said no.

A particularly noteworthy fact about the hearing was that throughout the proceedings, Smith (Boggs) was well groomed and attentive, and "much like any defendant, she penciled notes to her lawyer during testimony." In addition, as in her earlier comments, she was consistently articulate, lucid, and knowledgeable. She certainly did not fit the stereotype of the disoriented homeless person or appear to be "so sick that she was completely unaware of her illness," as alleged earlier.

The next surprising turn of events occurred on the second day of the hearing, when three women identified Ann Smith as Joyce Brown and reported that for 10 years she had been a secretary for the Human Rights Commission in Elizabeth, New Jersey. The women who identified her were her sisters, and they had recognized her from an artist's sketch that had been used on a television news broadcast. The women had been searching hospitals, morgues, and

---

inability to care for self, and danger to others. The question we must consider now is, what procedures are used to commit an individual to a hospital? Stated more personally, what would someone have to do to get you hospitalized against your will?

There are big differences from state to state, but in most states, the procedure is very simple. The process starts when a police officer, a mental health professional, or simply another citizen alleges to the police or a judge that a person is dangerous to self or others. Note that no real evidence is necessary other than the opin-

ion of the individual filing the complaint, and often that individual has no training, knowledge, or expertise concerning abnormal behavior.

Once the allegation is made, the police pick the individual up and take him or her to a mental hospital, where a brief examination is conducted by at least one physician. Often this examination lasts only a few minutes, and it may be conducted by a physician who is not necessarily a psychiatrist. That examination usually leads to **emergency (involuntary) hospitalization** so that additional observations and examinations can be

police stations for their sister since she had disappeared a year earlier after a family fight.

The sisters explained that Brown had been raised in a middle-class family in Livingston, New Jersey, had graduated from high school and business college, and then had worked as a secretary for 19 years. Over several years, she had used cocaine and heroin and eventually lost her job. She then moved in with her family, but she became abusive and was asked to leave. Next she lived in shelters in Newark, but according to her sisters she was asked to leave those when she became abusive. Brown was then briefly hospitalized, and her sisters lost contact with her when she was released. At the hearing, Brown's sisters asked that she be confined for treatment.

On the third day of the hearing, Brown defended her life on the street and her right to continue living there. She argued that she was a "professional" homeless person who was able to care for herself on the streets and was longing to get "back to the streets." She explained that she could live effectively on a budget of $7 a day and that she could easily panhandle between $8 and $10 per day. Local businesses allowed her to use their rest rooms, and the air from the heating vent kept her warm, so all of her needs were taken care of. She described how she talked with passersby such as executives, lawyers, and doctors about movies, restaurants, current events, and their families. When asked if she could care for herself, she replied, "That's what I have been doing all along, and I have done a good job. . . . My mental health is good, and my physical health is good." She explained that she used false names to help her evade her sisters, who were looking for her and wanted to put her in a hospital.

When asked about tearing up money, she replied that she only did it when people insisted on throwing money at her when she already had enough for the day. "If money is given to me and I don't want it, of course, I am going to destroy it. . . . I've heard people say: 'Take it, it will make you feel good.' But I say: 'I don't want it, I don't need it.' It is not my job to make them feel good by taking their money."

Brown said that the only time she became abusive was when the city workers from Project Help kept offering her help she did not need and then "swooped down" and took her to the hospital. "Every time I was taken before, I was treated like a criminal. . . . I didn't need their food, I didn't need their conversation, I didn't need them around."

In his closing argument, Brown's defense attorney said that the city had not provided any evidence that Brown had hurt herself or was dangerous to others, and he added that she was skilled in living on the streets. The attorney for the city rebutted, "Decency and the law and common sense do not require us to wait until something happens to her. It is our duty to act before it is too late."

If you had been the judge, what would you have decided in this case? Was Brown disturbed, unable to care for herself, and a danger to others, or had she chosen an unconventional lifestyle in which she functioned effectively and posed no threat to others? Was she disturbed, or was she simply disturbing to others?

The judge ruled against Brown. She was involuntarily committed in the psychiatric ward at Bellevue Hospital Center for 84 days. Upon her release, Harvard University invited her to speak. After her lecture at Harvard, she returned to the streets.

Source: Based on *New York Times* reports, October 29–November 7, 1987.

---

conducted. The probability of an emergency hospitalization is very high because physicians do not want to take chances and let individuals go who might hurt themselves or others. Depending on the state, the emergency hospitalization can be as short as 24 hours (Texas) or as long as 20 days (New Jersey). Some states require that a judge approve an emergency commitment, but that approval is usually only a formality because it is unlikely that a judge who is not trained in psychology or psychiatry will reverse the recommendation of the physician. In some states, a preliminary hearing must be conducted within 48 hours to determine whether there is probable cause for continued detention of the individual. At the end of the emergency hospitalization period, the individual must (a) agree to voluntary hospitalization, (b) be committed for an indeterminate length of time, or (c) be released.

Clearly, it is quite easy to have an individual committed and detained for a considerable length of time. Indeed, in many cases an individual who is suspected of having committed a crime will be released from jail sooner than an individual who is suspected of suffering from a mental disorder will be released from a hospital.

RIGHTS OF HOSPITALIZED MENTAL PATIENTS

Now that you understand the principles and procedures that determine why and how individuals are hospitalized, we can go on to consider the rights that individuals have once they are hospitalized.

Right of the "Least Restrictive Alternative"

At one time treatment meant total hospitalization, but it is now recognized that there is a continuum of treatment options that differ in the degree to which the patient is confined. Those options include (a) total hospitalization in a closed ward; (b) hospitalization in an open ward where patients have the right to leave and go to other parts of the hospital; (c) day hospitalization, in which patients spend the day in the hospital but spend the night at home; (d) night hospitalization, in which patients spend the evening and night in the hospital but spend the day at work or at home; and (e) outpatient care, in which patients live at home and come to a clinic only for treatment sessions. Recognition of these options is important because the courts have consistently ruled that if individuals are committed for treatment, they have the right to be treated in the **least restrictive alternative** that will serve the purpose of the treatment (*Lake* v. *Cameron*, 1966; *Lessard* v. *Schmidt*, 1974; *Shelton* v. *Tucker*, 1960; *Welsch* v. *Litkins*, 1974; *Wyatt* v. *Stickney*, 1971, 1972). Not only does this mean that they should be treated outside of the hospital if that is feasible, but if they must be hospitalized, they must be treated in the least restrictive ward possible (*Covington* v. *Harris*, 1969).

Because it was traditionally assumed that individuals needed to be in a hospital, in the past we probably overhospitalized disturbed individuals. One study conducted in Texas revealed that 60% of the hospitalized patients could be treated effectively at home and therefore did not need to be in the highly restrictive hospitals (Kittrie, 1960). Appropriate use of the least restrictive alternative for treatment should have eliminated that problem.

Right to Receive Treatment

You may have assumed that individuals who were hospitalized against their will would at least be treated so that

they could improve and someday be released. Unfortunately, that has not necessarily been the case, and many patients languished in mental hospitals for years without being treated. Four important legal decisions have concerned patients' rights to treatment, and I will consider those decisions in chronological order so that you can see how the laws concerning the right to treatment are evolving.

The Right to Treatment. Charles C. Rouse was charged with carrying a dangerous weapon, but when tried, he was found not guilty by reason of insanity and was therefore involuntarily committed to a mental hospital. After 4 years of confinement during which he was not treated, Rouse applied for a discharge, arguing that the crime for which he had been charged carried a maximum prison sentence of only 1 year and that he was therefore being held too long without treatment (*Rouse* v. *Cameron*, 1966). When the case was taken to the court of appeals, the judge ruled that "the purpose of involuntary hospitalization is treatment, not punishment" and that if patients are not treated, a hospital would be turned "into a penitentiary where one could be held indefinitely for no convicted offense." The judge also ruled that the hospital does not necessarily have to prove that the treatment will be effective, only that a serious attempt at treatment is being made. This case provided an important step in establishing patients' rights to treatment in that the ruling required that at least some effort has to be made to treat hospitalized patients.

Standards for Treatment Staff. The next step in the evolution of the right to treatment occurred when a suit was filed against the Alabama Commissioner of Mental Health on behalf of more than 8,000 involuntarily committed mental patients in Alabama (*Wyatt* v. *Stickney*, 1971, 1972). The suit charged that the patients were not receiving adequate treatment, and it asked that the court take over the supervision of the treatment programs. There was good evidence to support the charge of inadequate treatment; for example, the Alabama state mental hospitals averaged *one physician for every 2,000 patients!* Assuming that the physicians did nothing but see patients 8 hours a day, 52 weeks a year, that would mean that each patient would receive approximately 1 minute of therapy a week!

In ruling on this case, the judge first reaffirmed that the patients had a right to treatment and then went on to specify the numbers and types of staff members who must be available to provide treatment. He ruled that for every 250 patients, there had to be at least 2 psychiatrists, 4 psychologists, 3 general physicians, 7 social workers, 12 registered nurses, and 90 attendants. This standard was much higher than the one that was then in use in Alabama, but it was still substantially lower than what was recommended by the American Psychiatric Association as the minimum standard.

Determination of Appropriate Treatment. Once it was ruled that patients had a right to treatment and the minimum number of staff members was specified, the question arose, what is appropriate treatment? This question was raised in the case of Nicholas Romeo, a profoundly retarded 33-year-old man with an IQ between 8 and 10. His mother brought suit against the superintendent of the hospital in which Nicholas was a patient because Nicholas had injured himself on at least 63 occasions in one 29-month period (one of his symptoms was self-mutilation). She argued that if Nicholas was injuring himself that frequently, he must not be receiving adequate treatment.

In response, the judge ruled that Nicholas did have a right to reasonable care and safety but went on to conclude that because judges are not trained in psychology or psychiatry, they are not in a position to determine what treatment is most effective for various patients. Therefore, the judge ruled that decisions concerning what treatment is appropriate should be left to professionals (*Youngberg* v. *Romeo*, 1981). That seems reasonable, but by allowing professionals to determine what is appropriate, the court opened the door to a wide variety and possibly low levels of treatment because standards may differ from one professional or hospital to another.

Justification for Confinement. When Kenneth Donaldson was 49 years old, he was committed to the Florida state hospital at Chattahoochee on his father's allegation that he was delusional. After a brief hearing before a county judge, Donaldson was found to be suffering from paranoid schizophrenia and was committed to the hospital for "care, maintenance, and treatment." A progress note written in his hospital file shortly after he was hospitalized indicated that he was "in remission," which meant that he was no longer showing the symptoms of his disorder. Despite that, he was not released from the hospital. After Donaldson had been hospitalized against his will for almost 20 years, he petitioned for release. He argued that he should be released because (a) he was not dangerous or mentally ill, (b) he was not receiving treatment, and (c) there were people in the community who were willing to take him in and give him a job. In responding, the Supreme Court ruled that "a State cannot constitutionally confine . . . a nondangerous individual who is capable of surviving safely in freedom by himself or with the help of willing and responsible family members or friends" (*O'Connor* v. *Donaldson*, 1975). With this ruling, the Court said that individuals who are not dangerous and who can live effectively outside of a hospital cannot be held in hospitals against their will.

The Donaldson case received a lot of attention, but it is important to recognize that in this case, the Court did not address the question of whether patients who are not being treated have a right to be released; it simply said that *nondangerous patients cannot be kept in the hospital if they can function outside the hospital.* The question of whether untreated patients must be released was avoided because the Supreme Court will rarely go further than what is necessary to rectify the wrong in the case that is being heard, and in the case of Donaldson, the Court could order his release because he was not dangerous and thereby solve his problem. With this case, then, the issue of patients' right to treatment did not move forward or backward. That point is often misunderstood, and consequently, *O'Connor* v. *Donaldson* is often erroneously mentioned in discussions of the right to treatment when in fact it is only relevant to the question of whether patients who can function outside may be kept in the hospital.

In the four cases I have discussed, the Court (a) recognized that hospitalized mental patients have a right to treatment, (b) set the minimum number of staff members that must be available to treat patients, (c) said that it was the responsibility of professionals to determine what type and how much treatment was appropriate, and (d) declared that nondangerous individuals cannot be confined if they are able to function independently outside the hospital. Stated another way, the Court originally moved into the important but murky area of treatment when it established the right to treatment and specified the personnel necessary to provide minimal treatment, but then it backed away when it came to specifying what procedures constituted appropriate treatment. Little has changed since the Donaldson decision, but the law is a dynamic body that changes when new cases are brought up, and it is likely that sooner or later we will see a further evolution of the right to treatment.

The court rulings that I have discussed here specify what should be done with regard to the commitment, treatment, and release of hospitalized patients, but there is often a considerable difference between what the law requires and what in fact occurs. Unfortunately, most mental patients are not in a good position to defend their rights because they usually do not know their rights and therefore simply accept what seems to be their fate. In an attempt to make sure that patients know their rights with regard to treatment, it is now required that a statement of their rights be posted prominently in hospitals. That statement is presented in Figure 20.1.

Posting a notice of a patient's right to treatment is a step in the right direction, but it is a small and rather passive step, and its impact is questionable. Patients may not see the notice, and even if they do, they may not understand it. It should also be noted that in many

NOTICE TO PATIENTS

The United States Supreme Court recently ruled that a mental patient who has been involuntarily hospitalized, who is not dangerous to himself or others, who is receiving only custodial care, and who is capable of living safely in the community has a constitutional right to liberty—that is, has a right to be released from the hospital. The Supreme Court's opinion is available for patients to read.

If you think that the Supreme Court ruling may have a bearing on your present status, please feel free to discuss the matter with your hospital staff. In addition, if you wish to talk with an attorney about the meaning of the Supreme Court decision and how it may apply to you, the Superintendent has a list of legal organizations that may be of assistance. The staff will be glad to aid anyone who wishes to contact a lawyer.

FIGURE 20.1 This notice of mental patients' rights must be posted in hospitals.
Source: National Institutes of Mental Health.

cases, the hospital (or state) is not required to provide an attorney to help patients. That is in sharp contrast to the case of prisoners, who are guaranteed legal counsel. In other words, criminals are treated better than hospitalized mental patients. Furthermore, if patients believe that their rights are being violated and complain, there is often no one to listen, or if people do listen, they do not take the patients seriously. Why should they? The patients are "crazy"—if they were not crazy, they would not be in the hospital. It is a catch-22, so the patients and their rights are often ignored, and the patients languish in hospitals untreated.

Most of our discussion so far has focused on the legal principles involved in the right to treatment; no attention has been given to the practical implications associated with the implementation of those principles. Under a mandate to treat all hospitalized patients, states face a potentially overwhelming financial burden. What is to be done when there are not sufficient financial resources to treat all of the hospitalized patients? Should disturbed patients whom we cannot afford to treat be released from the hospitals to fend for themselves in the community? Will the professionals who have the responsibility for defining treatment redefine as "adequate" whatever can be afforded and thereby again turn hospitals into holding bins, human warehouses, or prisons? These practical issues are as important as the principles, and we will consider them in some detail in the next chapter when we consider deinstitutionalization and community care.

Right to Refuse Treatment

It is clear that patients have the right to be treated, but do they also have the right to refuse treatment? For example, if you were hospitalized, would you have the right to refuse psychotherapy? Would you have the right to refuse psychosurgery if it were recommended?

In our society, individuals are generally free to decide what is best for them, and this implies that patients have the right to refuse treatment if they do not think that the treatment is appropriate. However, there are three situations in which mental patients may *not* have the right to refuse treatment (Slovenko, 1992). First, they may not have the right to refuse treatment if they are declared *incompetent*. The notion is that the incompetent individual is unable to understand or evaluate what is going to be done and is therefore unable to make an informed judgment about whether the treatment is appropriate. If an individual is declared incompetent, the power to make the decision about treatment may be shifted to a parent or guardian, but in most cases, whoever is empowered to make the decision simply accepts the recommendation of the psychiatrist or psychologist in charge.

Second, individuals may not have the right to refuse treatment if they are *involuntarily committed* to a hospital. For example, depressed individuals who are suicidal and have been committed may not have the right to refuse antidepressant medication, and paranoid individuals who have been committed because they are dangerous to others who they think are plotting against them may not have the right to refuse neuroleptic (antipsychotic) medication. In those cases, the necessity to protect the individual or society takes precedence over the individual's right to refuse treatment.

Third, even a competent and voluntarily committed individual may not have the right to refuse treatment if the refusal results in *increased costs* for the community. For example, an individual may not have the right to refuse group psychotherapy or medication if the only option is more expensive individual psychotherapy.

However, there are two situations in which patients do have the right to refuse treatment. First, patients have the right to refuse treatment if the treatment *violates their religious beliefs*. This was affirmed when a circuit court ruled in favor of a patient who objected to taking drugs because she was a Christian Scientist (*Winters* v. *Miller*, 1971). The ruling was based on the First Amendment, which guarantees the right to the free expression of religion. However, it is noteworthy that if a patient refuses a treatment that would facilitate his or her release from the hospital, the patient cannot then demand to be released from the hospital because treatment is inadequate (*Rennie* v. *Klein*, 1983).

Second, an individual has the right to refuse a particular treatment if another *equally effective but less intru-*

sive treatment is available. For example, if it could be demonstrated that for a given patient psychotherapy was as effective as electroconvulsive therapy, the patient could refuse the electroconvulsive therapy.

To sum up, patients may not refuse treatment if (a) they are not competent to make the decision, (b) the refusal puts them or others at increased risk, or (c) the refusal increases the expenses of the state. However, those reasons can be set aside for religious reasons or if there is another equally effective treatment available.

Some of the problems posed by the courts' decision to grant patients the right to refuse treatment are illustrated in Case Study 20.3. The case involves a patient with the bipolar disorder who was in a private hospital and who refused medication. (For background on treatment of the bipolar disorder, see Chapter 10.)

Other Rights

The rights to receive and refuse treatment are certainly important because they may determine what is done for patients and how long patients stay in the hospital,

but a number of other rights must be protected as well so that the patients' stay in the hospital will not be unduly uncomfortable.

Physical Environment. With regard to the physical environment, it has been ruled, for example, that for each patient there should be at least 40 sq ft in the day room and 10 sq ft in the dining room. Patients must also be provided with curtains or screens in their sleeping quarters to ensure privacy, and there must be one toilet for every eight patients (*Wyatt* v. *Stickney*, 1971, 1972).

Personal Clothing. It has also been ruled that a patient has the right to wear his or her own clothing unless the clothing is determined to be dangerous or otherwise inappropriate in terms of the treatment program. Some patients who are likely to try to escape from an open ward are required to wear hospital gowns so that they can be easily spotted if they try to leave, and patients who are suicidal may not be allowed to wear belts or other articles of clothing that they could use to hang themselves. A patient who thinks he is Superman would probably not be allowed to go

CASE STUDY 20.3
Delay of Effective Treatment and Increased Cost of Care

Ms. A was a 55-year-old woman who was admitted for her fifth hospitalization to a private psychiatric hospital. She was diagnosed as suffering from a manic episode of the bipolar disorder. Ms. A was held in an intensive treatment ward but was frequently placed in seclusion because of outbursts in which she hit others and burned herself with cigarettes. During the first week of hospitalization, Ms. A was started on lithium, but the treatment was discontinued because she refused it. No attempt was made to force her to take the medication because of potential legal implications, and consequently she remained unmedicated for 19 days. After 37 days in the hospital, a hearing was held in which the court authorized an involuntary commitment. Once Ms. A was involuntarily committed, she was no longer able to refuse treatment, and so she was immediately given lithium. Within a month, she showed significant improvement, and two weeks later, she was discharged.

Ms. A's hospital bill was $25,137. Because of the delay in getting effective treatment started, it was estimated that the cost was $11,550 higher than it

would have been if she had accepted the lithium immediately. (Because only 80% of Ms. A's hospital expenses were paid by an insurance company, much of the expense that was associated with her refusal to take medication was borne by the public.) The family also incurred additional costs of $1,017 for legal fees and the consultation of an independent psychiatrist. In addition to these financial costs, there was also the cost to other patients of having a highly disturbed and disruptive patient on the ward and the emotional cost to the family of the prolonged illness of a loved one.

Because of cases such as this, the hospital in which Ms. A was hospitalized established a policy whereby if a potentially dangerous patient refuses treatment and, if after outside legal consultation, the family concurs with the patient's decision, the patient is sent to a public mental hospital. In other words, this hospital will no longer take responsibility for patients who refuse effective treatments.

Source: Adapted from Perr (1981).

around the hospital in a red-and-blue cape because that would condone his delusion. Furthermore, believing that he can fly with his cape on, the patient might jump off a high wall.

Patient Labor. The question of whether patients should be forced to work in the hospital is a difficult one. On the one hand, being involved in productive work can provide a much-needed boost in self-concept, and work done in the hospital may reduce the cost of running the hospital. On the other hand, if patients are committed involuntarily and then compelled to work, that is essentially slavery (involuntary servitude), which is prohibited by the 13th Amendment to the Constitution.

Two important decisions have been passed down by the courts in an attempt to strike a balance between work and slavery. First, it was ruled that mental patients may be required to do work that contributes to the operation of the institution *so long as the work has some therapeutic value.* The problem is in defining what work is therapeutic. It could be argued that forcing patients to scrub floors is inappropriate, but it can also be argued that scrubbing floors is a normal and necessary activity and that in doing so, patients learn to take responsibility and may even develop a sense of accomplishment and pride.

The question of whether a patient should be forced to work in a hospital is difficult. Being involved in productive work can boost self-esteem. However, a patient who has been involuntarily committed and then forced to work is essentially being subjected to involuntary servitude, a violation of the 13th Amendment to the Constitution.

Second, a more recent court decision placed a serious limitation on patient work programs when it was ruled that patients may not perform work "for which the hospital is under contract with an outside organization" (*Wyatt* v. *Stickney,* 1971). This means that if a hospital has contracted with an outside company to do maintenance work or prepare food, patients cannot participate in those activities even if doing so is therapeutic. It appears that this ruling was designed for the economic benefit of commercial firms that do business with the hospital rather than the psychological benefit of the patients who are confined in the hospital. The ruling has had some unfortunate consequences. For example, in one hospital in a rural area, the patients grew all of their own food, a practice that filled their days, gave them considerable self-satisfaction, and substantially offset the expense of their hospitalization. However, a local grocery company brought considerable political pressure to bear and got a contract to supply the hospital with food. Today the patients sit idly on benches and watch others plow the fields, and hospital costs have soared. Clearly, numerous pressures and concerns must be weighed and a delicate balance must be achieved if patient work is to be effective.

Civil Rights. The protection of civil rights is very important in our society, and simply being hospitalized as a mental patient *cannot be used as grounds for the restriction of civil rights.* For example, patients have the right to manage their personal and financial affairs, make contracts, marry, divorce, vote, and make a will (*Wyatt* v. *Stickney,* 1971, 1972). However, those rights can be restricted if the individual is judged incompetent, and in those cases, a court-appointed guardian will take responsibility for looking after the welfare of the individual.

THE PUBLIC'S RIGHT TO PROTECTION

The Tarasoff Ruling and the Duty to Protect

Most of the attention in this chapter has been focused on the rights of patients, but other people's right to safety must not be ignored. The right to safety was discussed briefly when I pointed out that one of the reasons for involuntary hospitalization of patients was the protection of others (police powers of the state). However, the right to safety has been extended to include *the right to be protected from patients who are not hospitalized.* That right grew out of a case in California in which a young male student told his therapist about his fantasies about killing a young woman named Tanya Tarasoff who had rejected his advances. The therapist was concerned, and he informed the campus police, who questioned the young man but then released him when he promised that he would stay away from Ms. Tarasoff. However, the therapist did not inform Ms. Tarasoff of the potential danger. A few weeks later, the young man stabbed Ms. Tarasoff to death. Her parents filed suit, alleging that the therapist was negligent for not warning their daughter about the danger. In what has come to be known as the **Tarasoff ruling,** the Supreme Court of California concluded that when a therapist *knows* or *should know* that a patient presents a serious risk of violence, the therapist "incurs an obligation to use reasonable care to protect the intended victim against such danger" (*Tarasoff* v. *Regents,* 1976, supra note 8). To discharge that obligation, the therapist must (a) warn the intended victim or others who are likely to warn the intended victim, (b) notify the police, or (c) take other reasonable steps to protect the intended victim. This is often called the "duty to warn" principle, but in fact the court ruled only that a therapist take reasonable care to protect individuals, and reasonable care may or may not involve warning. Therefore, this is more accurately referred to as the **"duty to protect" principle.**

This principle continues to evolve as new cases are brought to the courts, and there are a number of ambiguities and inconsistencies from state to state. One inconsistency involves the question of whether the patient must name a specific person in the threat. For example, when John Hinckley Jr. attempted to assassinate President Reagan, he seriously harmed some of the people with the president, and they sued Hinckley's therapist, alleging that he should have known that Hinckley was dangerous. However, their suits were dismissed because no specific threats were made against specific persons. In contrast, there is a case in which a former patient with a history of violent behavior began shooting people at random with a shotgun. A woman who was blinded in the attack and whose husband was killed filed suit against the man's therapist, and the court ruled in her favor because the history of violence supposedly made the future violence foreseeable despite the fact that the patient did not make a specific threat.

The duty to protect usually does not extend to cases of suicide. For example, when a young woman named Tammy committed suicide and her parents sued her therapist for not doing something to protect Tammy from herself, the court ruled against the suit. However, there are cases in which the duty to protect has been extended to property. For example, in one case, a patient told his therapist that he wanted to burn down his father's barn and in fact later did so. When the father filed suit, the court concluded that the therapist was in fact liable because he had not warned the father. Obviously, there is a need for increased clarity and consistency in the application of the duty to protect.

Problems Posed by the Duty to Protect

The duty to protect raises problems about the confidentiality of what patients tell therapists (Kagle & Kopels, 1994). For example, if patients are not assured of confidentiality, they might not feel free to talk openly with their therapists, and that might impede progress in therapy. Questions about confidentiality can also pose problems for therapists who could be sued for breaches of confidentiality but could also be sued for failure to protect if they do not breach confidentiality (Monahan, 1993). Therapists then may be "damned if they do and damned if they don't" breach confidentiality. Court rulings have been inconsistent with regard to whether a patient has grounds for suit if a therapist discloses information about the threat posed by the patient, but the code of ethics of the American Psychological Association is clear: *Protection of others takes precedence over the right to confidentiality.*

SUMMARY

- The legal issues that are associated with abnormal behavior are important because they reflect on the protection that is given to disturbed individuals and on the protection from disturbed individuals that is given to other members of society.
- Competence to stand trial refers to an individual's ability to understand the legal proceedings and participate in his or her defense. Being declared incompetent to stand trial does not relieve the individual of responsibility; it only postpones the trial until the individual is competent.
- Insanity refers to the notion that individuals who cannot control their behavior because of a mental disorder should not be held responsible for their behavior

and therefore should not be punished. An individual who is found to be insane is not punished but is sent to a hospital for treatment.

■ *Insanity* is a legal term, not a psychological or medical one. Different jurisdictions use different definitions for insanity, and there are differences of opinion concerning how insanity should be defined and whether there should even be an insanity defense.

■ The M'Naghten rule is based on the knowledge of right versus wrong; that is, an individual is deemed insane if at the time of the criminal act, the individual did not know that what he or she was doing was wrong. In some states, an irresistible impulse ("elbow rule") was also accepted as the basis for insanity. Critics argue that the M'Naghten rule does not make allowances for hallucinations or delusions.

■ The American Law Institute rule says that an individual is insane if at the time of the criminal act the individual was suffering from a mental disease or defect that either interfered with the ability to understand right versus wrong or caused cognitive (hallucinations, delusions) or emotional problems (irresistible impulses) that led to the criminal act. This rule excludes repeated criminal behavior as evidence for a mental disease or defect, and it is more liberal than the M'Naghten rule.

■ Practical problems with the insanity defense include the following: (a) Jurors must make decisions concerning insanity, but they may not have the necessary technical knowledge to make the decisions; (b) jurors must make decisions over which experts disagree; (c) decisions must be made about insanity at the time the criminal act was committed, but that may have been months or years earlier; (d) there is concern that an individual who is found to have been only temporarily insane and who is then released will become insane again and commit another crime; (e) individuals who are found to be insane may be incarcerated for treatment for longer periods of time than they would be imprisoned for the crime; and (f) in most states, the individual is presumed sane until proven insane.

■ After John Hinckley Jr. attempted to assassinate President Reagan but was found to be insane, (a) some states abolished the insanity defense; (b) other states gave up using the American Law Institute rule and returned to using the M'Naghten rule; and (c) some states introduced the "guilty but mentally ill" rule, which would lead to an individual's being treated for the disorder and then punished for the crime.

■ In cases of voluntary hospitalization, an individual who feels in need of help may sign into a hospital, but if the staff later concludes that the individual continues to need help, the individual may not be allowed to leave the hospital voluntarily.

■ Individuals can be hospitalized involuntarily for their own protection *(parens patriae)* or for the protection of others (police power of the state). Concerns about equal treatment arise because we do not confine (hospitalize) medical patients for their protection and because we do not confine other individuals (suspected criminals) whom we suspect of being dangerous to others.

■ Hospitalized patients have the right to (a) live in the least restrictive alternative; (b) receive treatment; and (c) refuse treatment unless they are judged to be incompetent, are involuntarily committed to the hospital because they are a danger to themselves or others, or their refusal increases the cost of their treatment to the state. Those reasons may be set aside if the individual refuses for religious reasons or if an equally effective alternative treatment is available.

■ Mental patients also have the right to (a) have a reasonable amount of living space; (b) wear their own clothes unless doing so is dangerous or inappropriate, (c) refuse having work forced on them (slavery) unless the work has some therapeutic value (and they cannot be made to perform work for which the hospital is under contract with an outside organization, even if the work *is* therapeutic); and (d) exercise their civil rights (e.g., make contracts, marry, divorce, vote) unless they have been declared incompetent.

■ Under the Tarasoff ruling, mental health workers have the duty to warn or otherwise protect individuals who may be endangered by individuals with mental disorders. If the duty to protect conflicts with a patient's right to confidentiality, the duty to protect takes precedence.

KEY TERMS, CONCEPTS, AND NAMES

In reviewing and testing yourself on what you have learned from this chapter, you should be able to identify and discuss each of the following.

American Law Institute rule	incompetent to stand trial	M'Naghten rule
"duty to protect" principle	insanity defense	*parens patriae*
elbow rule	involuntary commitment	police power of the state
emergency (involuntary) hospitalization	involuntary outpatient commitment	right to equal protection
"guilty but mentally ill" rule	irresistible impulse	Tarasoff ruling
	least restrictive alternative	voluntary admission

CHAPTER TWENTY-ONE
HOSPITALIZATION, COMMUNITY CARE, and PREVENTION

OUTLINE

Mark is 49 years old. He is diagnosed as having schizophrenia, and he has been in and out of hospitals for the past 20 years. His last hospitalization lasted 7 years and ended not because he had shown improvement but because of a new program designed to get patients out of the hospital and treat them in the community. Because of Mark's "crazy" behavior, neither his parents nor his sisters will let him live in their homes, so he now lives on welfare in a barren one-room apartment in a run-down part of the city. Treatment consists of going to a nearby clinic once a week to get medication that he is supposed to take four times a day. Frequently, however, he gets confused or forgets to take his medication, and then he becomes disoriented. When that happens, he is usually picked up by the police, who take him to the hospital, where he is given a high dose of medication, held for a few hours, and then released. Because he cannot care for himself adequately, Mark is underweight and at serious risk for disease. Mark has not committed suicide and has not been rehospitalized, so he is considered to be a "success."

■ ■ ■

Linda has been in the hospital for almost two years. Originally, she did not like being hospitalized and wanted to be released. However, when the possibility of being discharged came up about a year ago, she became very anxious about "making it on the outside," and her symptoms became worse. She was not discharged. Since then, she has begun "settling in" and "blending into the woodwork." She has become a "good patient"; her personal grooming has deteriorated somewhat, but she is compliant, and her behavior rarely attracts attention. Each time she is given a brief examination, she demonstrates enough symptoms to justify keeping her in the hospital, but not so much as to require any additional attention or a change in wards.

■ ■ ■

Christine is a psychologist in a community mental health center. Her primary responsibility is doing psychotherapy with individuals who live in the surrounding area. Most of her clients come to the clinic for help before their problems become so serious that hospitalization is necessary. When problems do become serious, clients at the center can be hospitalized for intensive care during the day, but they are sent home at night. Christine's goal is to help the clients at whatever stage they are, but to do so without breaking their contacts with their friends and families in the community. In addition to seeing clients, Christine also runs workshops for various community and business groups in which she talks about the early signs of mental health problems, teaches stress management techniques, and informs people about the various free services that are available such as support groups and crisis centers. With these workshops, Christine helps people not only with early detection but also with the prevention of mental health problems.

■ ■ ■

The state legislature faced a problem last term. Costs of education had gone up drastically, and numerous roads needed to be repaired or completely rebuilt, but tax income was flat, and funds from the federal government's revenue-sharing program had been reduced. One possible means of cutting costs was to reduce the number of patients in the state mental hospitals. Each patient was costing the state tens of thousands of dollars per year, so considerable yearly savings could be achieved. The legislators argued that the cutback in funds for the hospital system was not simply an economic strategy. Instead, getting patients out of the old hospitals and treating them in the community was a step in the direction of modern mental health practices. This was humane progress, not just economics. At the end of the legislative session, one other relevant bill was passed. It gave cities the right to pass zoning ordinances prohibiting the establishment of "halfway houses" in residential areas. Most cities immediately adopted the protective ordinances. A month later, a discharged patient stood on the front steps of a hospital and asked, "But where do I go?" No one heard because the door to the hospital was already closed, and no one was waiting in the community.

■ ■ ■

For many years disturbed individuals were thought of as patients; little was done for them until their problems became serious, and then they were treated in large hospitals. To some extent, that is still true, but in the late 1960s, a program was begun that was designed to (a) prevent the development of psychiatric disorders, (b) diagnose disorders sooner, (c) treat individuals in the community while they lived at home, and (d) get hospitalized individuals out of the hospitals and treat them in the community. In this chapter I will first describe the traditional mental hospital and discuss what a patient's life is like in such a hospital. Then I will explain the deinstitutionalization movement, which is designed to get patients out of the hospitals. Next I will review the types of care that are available for disturbed individuals who are living in the community, and finally I will consider the programs that have been established to prevent the development of abnormal behavior.

TRADITIONAL MENTAL HOSPITALS

Here we will consider important personal and practical questions such as, what is life like in mental hospitals, how do patients adjust to life in mental hospitals, and are mental hospitals effective places for treating abnormal behavior?

At the outset it should be recognized that psychiatric patients are hospitalized in a wide variety of facilities, ranging from huge mental hospitals with thousands of patients to small psychiatric wards in general medical hospitals. Some facilities are very pleasant, but most are rather unpleasant, and many are simply deplorable. Some hospitals have homelike qualities, and others are like college dormitories, but far too many have the characteristics of prisons. Because of the diversity in facilities, it is difficult to characterize the "typical" mental hospital, but I will try to convey some idea of what psychiatric hospitals are like and the effects they have on patients.

Physical Setting

Most psychiatric hospitals are organized by wards. Each ward usually has its own day room, nursing station, isolation room, sleeping facilities, and staff. There are generally between 20 and 100 patients on a ward.

Wards often differ in the types of patients they have or the functions they serve. For example, in a large hospital there may be an **admitting ward,** where new patients live while they are being diagnosed, and **intensive treatment wards,** where patients are given all that the hospital has to offer in an attempt to get them out before their problems become chronic. Large hospitals may also have separate wards for chronic patients who have not responded to treatment and who will probably never recover. A ward like that is often called a **domiciliary** (DOM-uh-SIL-ē-er-ē) or "back ward." Essentially, no

Hospitalized patients spend most of their waking time in a day room.

treatment other than medication is attempted on those wards; the patients are simply maintained ("warehoused") there until they die.

Wards are also usually organized by age so that children and adolescents are separated from adults, and some wards are devoted to only one type of patient, such as those with eating disorders (anorexia, bulimia) or substance abuse problems (alcoholism, drug addiction). In the case of a small psychiatric unit that is part of a general hospital, there are not enough patients or facilities for specialized wards, so all patients are grouped together on one ward.

Less disturbed patients and those who are not likely to escape are often assigned to **open wards,** where the doors are not locked and the patients are free to go to other parts of the hospital whenever they wish. More disturbed patients are assigned to **closed wards,** where the doors are locked and may be guarded by an attendant.

The **day room** is probably the most important part of any ward because it is where the patients spend most of their waking hours. By law, the day room must be large enough so that each patient has a space at least $6\frac{1}{2}$ ft by $6\frac{1}{2}$ ft. Day rooms are generally rather barren, drab, and utilitarian, with a minimum of furniture. Patients spend most of their time in the day room simply sitting or watching endless hours of television.

Another important part of the ward is the **nurses' station,** which is usually a glass-enclosed office where the nurses spend most of their time and where patients' records and medications are kept. The nurses supervise the patients from the station, and in some hospitals it is comparable to the guard tower in a prison.

Most wards also have an **isolation room** (often referred to as the "quiet room") in which patients can be confined temporarily if they become upset, agitated, destructive, or abusive (W. A. Fisher, 1994). Most isola-

tion rooms are cell-like rooms that contain only a mattress so that patients will not have anything with which to hurt themselves. In most cases, patients are forcibly confined to the isolation room when they are being disruptive or self-destructive, but sometimes patients will voluntarily use it as a retreat.

Adjoining the day room are the patients' sleeping rooms, each housing one to five patients. In most cases patients are not allowed to go to their sleeping rooms during the day, so they often sleep or nap in the day room.

Other important hospital facilities include a dining room (usually a cafeteria), often a snack bar (or at least

Most wards have an isolation room in which patients can be temporarily confined if they become agitated, destructive, or abusive.

an area with vending machines for candy), and an area for occupational, art, or music therapy. The hospital may also have recreational areas and work areas to which the patients can go or be taken. Finally, somewhere near the ward are the offices of the psychologists, psychiatrists, social workers, and various administrators who are responsible for the treatment and care of the patients. Unfortunately, in most hospitals, the offices of the treatment staff are some distance from the ward, a factor that symbolically separates treatment from daily living and separates the treatment staff from the patients.

Before concluding this discussion of hospital facilities, a comment should be made about **day** or **night hospitalization** versus full-time hospitalization. Most patients live in the hospital on a 24-hour-a-day basis, but some are admitted for only the daytime or the nighttime. With this approach, patients who have a place to go during the day are admitted to the night program. They come in at about dinnertime, receive treatment during the evening, spend the evening, sleep in the hospital, and leave in the morning. These people use the hospital like most people use their homes. In contrast, patients who have a supportive environment in which they can spend the night participate in the day hospital program. They come to the hospital in the morning, receive treatment during the day, and go home in the late afternoon or early evening. They go to the hospital like most people go to work.

The day or night hospital procedure has two advantages: First, patients can maintain better contact with the outside world if they are not hospitalized all the time, and second, the hospital can serve twice as many patients. Unfortunately, despite the fact that the day or night procedure is less expensive and has been consistently shown to be at least as effective as full-time hospitalization, the day or night procedure is not widely used.

The atmosphere in most hospitals is bleak and lonely at best. The physical facilities are usually gloomy, and although there may be many patients, they are often emotionally isolated from one another and hence alone in the crowd. Furthermore, patients are usually strictly segregated from staff, which increases the feelings of separation and abandonment among patients. Indeed, many staff members walk past patients as if they were inanimate objects rather than human beings who are overwhelmed with problems.

Staff

Every mental hospital has a variety of staff members with different responsibilities. **Psychologists** do individual and group therapy and often play a prominent role in diagnosing specific disorders and formulating treatment plans. **Psychiatrists** also do individual psychotherapy and sometimes group therapy. Because psychia-

trists are trained in medicine, they also take responsibility for the various physical treatments such as drugs and electroconvulsive (shock) therapy.

Because psychologists and psychiatrists spend most of their time in their offices dealing with individual patients, they are rarely on the ward, and therefore the day-to-day running of the ward is primarily in the hands of **psychiatric nurses.** Nurses become extremely important and powerful individuals in patients' lives because it is usually the nurses' reports that determine what happens to the patients. For example, if a nurse reports that a patient is agitated, the patient may be given a sedative, sent to the isolation room, or confined to the ward. In contrast, positive reports from a nurse can result in movement to a better ward, home visits, and other privileges.

There are numerous stories about head nurses such as Nurse Ratched in the book and movie *One Flew over the Cuckoo's Nest* (Kesey, 1962) who rule their wards like monarchs rule kingdoms, and there is more than a grain of truth in the stories about their legendary power. However, it is important to recognize that of all the professionals who deal with the patients in the hospital, the nurses are probably in the best position to know and evaluate the patients. The psychiatrists and psychologists may see the patients for an hour or two each week and talk with them about their innermost feelings, but the nurses must deal with the patients on a daily basis when they are tired, hungry, frustrated, unable to sleep at night, and rejected by their peers and families.

Although nurses have more contact with the patients than other professionals, that should not be taken to mean that they necessarily have a lot of contact. One study revealed that nurses came out of the nurses' station an average of only 11.5 times in an 8-hour shift, and that included the times they came out to leave the ward (Rosenhan, 1973). In that study it was impossible to determine the amount of time the nurses actually spent with the patients because the contacts were too brief.

The members of the hospital staff who have the most contact with the patients are the **psychological technicians** (formerly called *ward attendants*), who actually spend most of their time on the ward rather than in offices or at nursing stations. The technicians are important because they are often the patients' only ongoing contacts with normal individuals. Also, because the technicians are not professional staff, the patients can often relate to them better, and they sometimes become friends. In some circumstances the contact between attendants and patients can be very intense. This is especially true if the patient is put on "suicide watch" because then the technician must stay within a few feet of the patient on a 24-hour-a-day basis regardless of what the patient is doing.

Concerning the relationship between patients and technicians, one patient commented:

Psychological technicians (formerly called ward attendants) have more contact with patients than other hospital staff.

Mike is the only real friend I have left. He's the only guy I can talk to. The nurses, hell, they just come out to yell at me. The only time they know I'm alive is when I'm doing something wrong or when it's time to shove more medicine down me. The goddamned doctors just play useless word games in their offices and try to screw my head around. They don't know what's going on. How could they? They almost never see me. Mike knows me and keeps me straight.

Although the technicians are low on the power hierarchy, they do have considerable power because their reports about patients' behavior often provide the basis for the impressions that are formed by the nurses, psychologists, and psychiatrists who ultimately make the decisions about the patients. In the war against mental disorders, then, the psychiatrists and psychologists are the generals, the nurses are the lieutenants, and the psychological technicians are the foot soldiers on the front line.

Social workers also play important roles for hospitalized patients because they maintain the link between the patient and his or her family. The social worker also plays a crucial role in helping with the transitions into and out of the hospital and often works closely with the patient during the posthospitalization period when the patient is struggling with practical problems like finding a place to live, getting a job, paying bills, and gaining custody of children. In some cases, social workers also do group and individual psychotherapy.

Finally, various activity therapists, including **occupational therapists, art therapists,** and **music therapists,** often work with hospitalized patients. It is not expected that knitting a potholder, finger painting, or learning to play a musical instrument will cure schizophrenia. However, it is hoped that the social interaction associated with the activities will provide the opportunity to talk about problems, try out new social roles, and increase contact with reality. In other words, the activi-

ties themselves are not a cure, but they may be a medium in which more normal behavior can be developed.

It should now be clear that on the ward there is often very little contact between patients and the professional staff. The question then arises, what happens when there is contact? In one study, individuals who were pretending to be patients (pseudopatients) approached staff members with questions like "Could you tell me when I will be eligible for grounds privileges?" "Could you tell me when I will be presented at the staff meeting?" or "Could you tell me when I am likely to be discharged?" (Rosenhan, 1973). The results indicated that the staff members stopped to talk only 2% to 4% of the time. Fully 71% of the time, psychiatrists simply looked away and walked past. Those results are summarized in Table 21.1.

Furthermore, when staff members did respond to the questions asked by patients, the answers they gave were often not really answers. For example:

Pseudopatient: Pardon me, Doctor. Could you tell me when I'm eligible for grounds privileges?

TABLE 21.1 Psychiatric Ward Staff Avoided Responding to Questions Asked by Pseudopatients

	Frequency of Response (%)	
Type of Response	**Psychiatrist**	**Nurse or Attendant**
Moved on, head averted	71	88
Made eye contact	23	10
Paused to chat	2	2
Stopped to chat	4	<1

Source: Data from Rosenhan (1973), p. 255, tab. 1.

Physician: Good morning, Dave. How are you today? *(moves off without waiting for a response)*

If a patient responded that way to a question from a staff member, the response would be considered "inappropriate" and taken as evidence that the patient was out of contact with reality and needed continued hospitalization.

The nature of the contact (or lack thereof) between the professional staff and the patients in mental hospitals is unfortunate, but it should not be concluded that the behavior of the staff necessarily reflects a lack of concern or commitment. In most cases, the lack of contact between staff and patients stems from the fact that the staff is overworked. Furthermore, it is personally stressful and threatening to work with disturbed individuals on a daily basis. As the old saying goes, "There but for the grace of God go I," and that can be very threatening. It may be that the interpersonal distance that the staff maintains is to some extent a defensive strategy. Just as surgeons cover their patients' faces when they operate to separate "the person" from "the operation," so staff members in mental hospitals may place emotional screens between themselves and patients.

Patienthood

Mental hospitals differ from general medical hospitals in that they provide a total community in which individuals can live for long periods. Researchers who study social institutions point out that mental hospitals are more like the military or prisons than they are like other hospitals, and they refer to these types of organizations as **total institutions** (Goffman, 1961). Before I go on to discuss the research on how patients adjust to hospitalization, it might be helpful to consider the experience of hospitalization from the patient's point of view. Case Study 21.1 was written by a student of mine who was admitted to a psychiatric ward of a general medical hospital after she attempted suicide by taking an overdose of sleeping medication. Her comments are particularly interesting because they reflect changes in her attitudes about hospitalization and her ambivalence about the experience.

An important feature of total institutions is that the individuals inside the institution are rigidly stratified, and those at the bottom (enlisted persons, prisoners, mental patients) have no power. Individuals at the bottom of the hierarchy are told what to wear, with whom they may talk, when they may eat, and exactly how they will behave. In mental hospitals, they are even told *what is real* and *what to feel*. Finally, the staff in a mental hospital is especially powerful because the staff determines when or even if the individual will be released.

At first many patients reject the control of the staff and do not accept the role of "mental patient." New patients often make comments like "I'm just here for a couple of days of rest because I was under a lot of stress. I'm not a mental patient like the other people here." However, in time, patients come to accept their role—for better or for worse. For some patients hospitalization is an opportunity to get help, a positive experience. For many, however, it is not positive. Their self-confidence is eroded, they recognize that they are completely dependent on the staff for everything, and they accept the "mental patient" role. They realize that they are patients, and to behave otherwise would only provide the staff with more justification for concluding that they are out of contact with reality and holding them in the hospital longer.

The development of dependence in patients makes them much easier to deal with (which is why some institutions implicitly foster the dependence), but dependence results in some unwanted side effects. As patients become more dependent on the hospital, they become less competent socially and vocationally, and they experience a general loss in self-esteem. These factors decrease the patients' ability to function independently and reduce the likelihood that they will be able to leave the institution. Not only do the patients become *less able* to leave, but after some time, they become *less willing* to leave because they no longer have confidence that they can survive on the outside. This personal deterioration is due not to the patients' disorders but to their experience of being institutionalized. This surrendering of personal control and acceptance of dependence on the hospital is referred to as the **institutionalization syndrome,** and it can be as debilitating as the disorder that originally brought the patient to the hospital. So the experience of hospitalization can have a negative effect on patients that is independent of their disorders. If we want individuals to become self-assured and independent, confinement in a mental hospital may not be the best place to begin.

Patients are powerless in the institution, but they do learn to manipulate the system and thereby gain some indirect control over their circumstances. For example, if they want attention, they may act disturbed because the disturbed patients get more attention from the staff. Alternatively, if better-adjusted patients are getting privileges, they may act less disturbed. This method of gaining some control is referred to as **impression management,** and its effects were clearly demonstrated in a study in which "newcomers" (patients who had been in the hospital for less than 3 months) and "old-timers" (patients who had been in the hospital for more than 3 months) were asked to fill out a questionnaire about symptoms (Braginsky et al., 1966). For half of the patients, the questionnaire was labeled as a test of "mental illness," and the patients were told that those who got high scores would probably have to stay in the hospital. For the other half of the patients, the same questionnaire was labeled as a test of

CASE STUDY 21.1

Psychiatric Hospitalization After a Suicide Attempt: A College Junior Talks About Her Experience

"The first thing I remember was being in the emergency room of the hospital. All I could do was lie there. I wanted to tell them that I was all right, that everything would be fine if they would just let me die, but Mom and Dad were talking to a nurse, and I couldn't make myself move. They told me later that I rocked back and forth and moaned a lot, but I don't remember.

"A few hours later, a male nurse from the psychiatric ward came to my room and asked if I would sign a form to enter myself into the hospital voluntarily. I remember that it took me several minutes to figure out that I was supposed to sign my name—or at least it seemed like several minutes. My next thought was that later I was going to be really sorry that I signed myself in.

"When I awoke in the morning, I was in a hospital room in a regular medical ward, and they were getting ready to take me up to the psychiatric ward. When I realized what was going on, I pleaded with my parents to take me home. The thought of spending time on a psychiatric ward was scary!

"When the nurse took me up to the ward to show me around, I was really worried. I was worried that they would make me stay there, which they did. The psychiatric ward was different from the rest of the hospital. People walked around in street clothes, and adults sat in the lounge watching TV and playing games. I kept waiting for someone to start screaming or for someone to appear in a straitjacket.

"They assigned me to a room by myself, but first they took away everything I had. I found out later that they removed anything with which I could hurt myself. It took two days for me to get back my curling iron and my contact cooker. I wasn't allowed a razor, and they looked through everything that anyone brought me.

"They gave me a phone only on the condition that I promise not to try to hurt myself. They said that if I did try to hurt myself, they would put me in a hospital where they'd tie me down and keep me that way. I decided on the phone. I was so embarrassed when they told me that it would be a while before they would trust me to eat with the other patients in the cafeteria or to do anything by myself. Because I was a suicide risk, I was put on 'special observation,' which meant that someone sat right next to me *at all times*. Also, when I was in the bathroom, they knocked on the door every few seconds and made me answer.

"I told Mom not to tell my [college] roommates or anyone where I was. I was afraid they wouldn't want to know or, worse yet, wouldn't care. Mom told them anyway, but I was visited only twice by my roommates. I can understand that; it's hard to talk to someone who is not allowed to have sharp objects around and who you think is crazy. I suppose it was also frightening for them to be on the ward.

"The first few days were bad. I felt out of touch and like a person who was stuck someplace he wasn't

"self-insight," and the patients were told that those who got high scores would probably be released soon.

The results are very interesting: The old-timers responded so that they would have to stay in the hospital (high "mental illness" and low "self-insight"), but newcomers responded so that they would be released (low "mental illness" and high "self-insight"). These findings have two important implications. First, old-timers did not want to leave the hospital, a finding that reflects the institutionalization syndrome. Second, both old-timers and newcomers manipulated the impressions others received in an attempt to achieve what they wanted (continuance in the hospital or release).

Some patients are so good at impression management that they can even fool highly trained professionals. In one experiment, patients with schizophrenia who had been in a hospital for two years or more were assigned to a "discharge" condition or to an "open ward" condition (Braginsky & Braginsky, 1967). Patients in the discharge condition were told that they were going to be interviewed by an individual who "is interested in examining patients to see whether they might be ready for discharge." In contrast, patients in the open-ward condition were told that the interviewer "is interested in examining patients to see whether they should be in open or closed wards." The interviews were tape-recorded and later scored by three psychia-

supposed to be but couldn't convince anyone of it. When I was escorted around the halls for a walk, I looked at the other patients and wondered what it was like to be a psychiatric patient. It was scary and embarrassing to realize that I was one.

"My boyfriend came to visit me every day and always called. I don't think I could have maintained contact without him. He was the only person, except for the people on the floor, who saw me as an individual with problems, not as a *social disease*. My parents were uncomfortable at first. They stumbled when they talked and wouldn't look at me. I hated myself for putting them through it, but I blamed them for letting me live. Gradually, though, I was glad I was there. My mom was terrific. She was cheerful and optimistic. She told me not to worry about school, that I deserved a break. She sympathized with me and made me feel like it was OK to admit I had problems. My dad didn't handle it as easily. He wouldn't come to see me alone because the one time he did, we had nothing to say. He wouldn't talk about what was wrong, why I was there, or what help I was getting. I think he kind of tried to see it as a normal hospital stay.

"I was on the ward for about a week when they finally took me off 'special observation' and put me in a double room and allowed me to eat with the others. They told me that I was expected to mingle and talk with others on the ward, in group meetings, and with my counselors. I didn't want to talk. I didn't see the use of telling my problems to people who were already mentally ill. What good was that going to do anyone? Also, I was ashamed. Normal people do not lose control. Every time I tried to talk in group therapy, all I could do was cry. I just lost control, and I hated myself and them for making me do it.

"After about two weeks in the hospital, I begged my doctor to let me out. He did on Thanksgiving Day. Sometimes I wish that he'd made me stay longer, but I can't ask to go back because asking to go in is worse than being put there because then you're admitting you have a problem. It's even harder for people to understand when a person admits that he has a problem. Then they say he's begging for attention. I'm not so sure that's wrong, either. I don't know.

"When I got back to school, I felt like everyone was looking at me, saying, 'Look, I can tell she's been in a mental hospital.' I was scared to come back. I didn't want to be put into a group of people who were singled out for the rest of their lives. I still get nervous every time someone says, 'What were you doing last semester?' I don't want to talk about it or think about it. I still wish it had never happened. I needed to go to the hospital, and it helped, but I wish it had never happened."

trists in terms of the amount of abnormality the patients showed and the amount of hospital control the patients needed. The results indicated that the patients in the discharge condition led the psychiatrists to believe that they had high levels of abnormality and high needs for hospital control. Patients in the open-ward condition led the psychiatrists to believe that they had low levels of abnormality and low needs for hospital control. Those results are summarized in Figure 21.1. In other words, the long-term patients could manipulate the impressions of highly trained experts so that the patients could get what they wanted (stay in the hospital but on a good ward). The individuals may have been patients, but they were not stupid.

Another important factor to consider is how patients get "lost" in the hospital. In Chapter 20 I pointed out instances in which individuals had been admitted to a hospital and were then somehow overlooked for as long as 42 years (McGarry & Bendt, 1969). It is usually assumed that patients get lost in the system because there are so many patients and so few staff members. However, it also appears that some patients intentionally keep a low profile so as to lose themselves in the system (Braginsky et al., 1969). These have been called "invisible patients," and studies of them have shown that they are not necessarily more or less disturbed than other patients. Instead, it appears that they have accepted their role as mental patients,

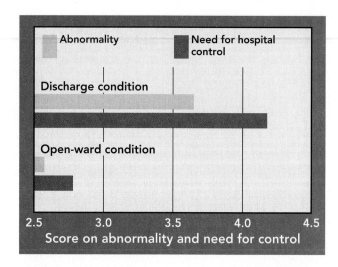

FIGURE 21.1 Long-term patients were able to influence psychiatrists' ratings so they could stay in the hospital or on an open ward.
Source: Data from Braginsky and Braginsky (1967).

decided that the hospital is a good and safe place to be, and adopted a lifestyle that does not give them much exposure to the staff. Their notion seems to be "out of sight, less likely to be discharged." Evidence for the fact that this strategy works comes from the finding that invisible patients are not more disturbed than other patients but are less likely to be discharged.

In this discussion of hospitalization, two seemingly contradictory views have been presented. On the one hand, I pointed out that most mental hospitals are distinctly unpleasant places in which to live. The physical facilities are drab, patients are restricted and powerless, and life is monotonous and dehumanizing. On the other hand, the evidence suggests that many mental patients want to stay in the hospital. Patients present themselves as sicker than they are so as not to be discharged, and the results of numerous surveys indicate that as many as 80% of mental patients have favorable attitudes about hospitals, sometimes seeing them as desirable or even liberating places in which to live (Brady et al., 1959; Imre, 1962; Imre & Wolf, 1962; Rosenblatt & Mayer, 1974; Shiloh, 1968).

The difference between the views of hospitals held by outsiders and those held by patients can be accounted for in terms of the reference points of the two groups. For many patients the hospital may provide better living conditions or a more psychologically secure environment than they face outside, whereas outsiders probably have better alternatives, making the hospital seem relatively unattractive (Mayer & Rosenblatt, 1974). It is important to recognize this difference and take the patients' perspective when attempting to understand their behavior. For example, you might assume that patients would work to get out of hospitals, but that is not necessarily so. In fact, there is evidence

that some patients' preference for living in the hospital leads them to stay longer and to return sooner (Drake & Wallach, 1979).

When struggling with the question of whether he should leave the hospital, one patient wrote a poem using a cave as a metaphor for the hospital (Hayward & Taylor, 1956):

Yes, I want the cave,
There, I know here I am.
I can grope, in the dark, and feel the cave walls.
And the people, there, know I'm there, and they step on me, by
*   mistake, —*
I think, I hope.
But outside —
Where am I?

Effectiveness of Hospitalization

The negative effects of hospitalization (the institutionalization syndrome) have been known for many years. However, it was generally assumed that the positive effects of hospitalization outweighed the negative effects and that patients who were treated in hospitals were more likely to improve than patients who were treated elsewhere. Those assumptions have been seriously challenged, and we need to consider carefully the question of whether hospitalization is in fact better than treatment elsewhere (Kiesler, 1982a, 1982b; Kiesler & Sibulkin, 1988).

In 10 experiments, disturbed individuals were randomly assigned to hospital treatment or to some alternative care—day care, drugs with outpatient psychotherapy, or adequate housing without any specific treatment (see Kiesler, 1982a). The results of these experiments are startling: *In no case was hospitalization found to be more effective than the alternative care, and in almost every case, the alternative care had more positive effects.* For example, in one experiment, first-admission patients who were diagnosed as suffering from schizophrenia were randomly assigned either to a good mental hospital where they received traditional treatment including psychotherapy, drugs, occupational therapy, and ward meetings or to a small, homelike facility run by a nonprofessional staff where the patients and staff shared the responsibility for maintenance and food preparation (Mosher et al., 1975; Mosher & Menn, 1978). Follow-up evaluations of the patients after 1 year and 2 years revealed that those who had been assigned to the homelike facility were less disturbed and more likely to be employed. Among patients who were discharged, those from the homelike facility were more likely to be living alone or with peers, whereas those from the hospital were more likely to be living with parents or relatives. Furthermore, the patients from the homelike facility were 20% less likely to be rehospitalized.

In another experiment, patients with acute schizophrenia were assigned to either regular inpatient treatment or outpatient treatment in which they received drug therapy and counseling (Levenson et al., 1977). There were no dramatic differences between the success rates of the two groups, but the patients who received the outpatient treatment tended to do better, and their treatment cost only *one-sixth* what the inpatient treatment cost. In summary, the 10 experiments on this question indicated that alternative care outside a hospital was at least as effective as treatment in a hospital—and it cost less. The results of these experiments raise serious questions about the use of hospitals for treating abnormal behavior. So let us examine two alternatives to hospitalization: deinstitutionalization and community care.

DEINSTITUTIONALIZATION

Some years ago, the superintendent of a large state mental hospital told me that one of his major goals was to "build more flower gardens." When I looked surprised, he explained that the hospital had embarked on an ambitious program of returning patients to the community for care and that as the hospital population became smaller, the buildings that had once housed patients were torn down. The foundations of the demolished buildings were then filled with earth, flowers, trees, and shrubs. Indeed, when I looked out his office window, I saw a series of large rectangular gardens, each surrounded by a low wall formed by the top of the foundation of the original building. Where patients once languished, petunias now flourished. However, as you will see, in some cases the bulldozing of buildings and planting of petunias may have been premature.

Not all former hospital buildings are being turned into flower beds, but the **deinstitutionalization** of mental patients has been widespread. The number of patients in hospitals was reduced by over 80% between 1950 and 1990, and the numbers continue to decline. The trend in the patient population of state and county mental hospitals during those years is presented graphically in Figure 21.2. Two changes in the curve are notable. First, the curve begins to flatten out and then decline slightly in the late 1950s and early 1960s. That change was due to the introduction of antipsychotic medication (neuroleptic drugs) that reduced the symptoms of many disturbed individuals and enabled them to live in the community. Second, in the late 1960s, the curve goes into a steep decline such that the total number of patients declines by over 25,000 per year, a change that reflects the deinstitutionalization movement. The number of patients is still dropping, but the decline has slowed recently, probably because we may

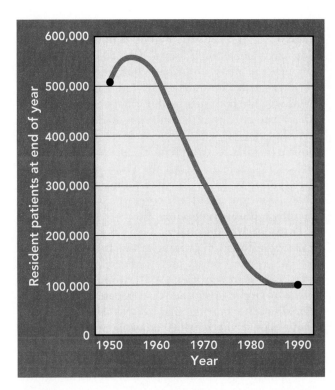

FIGURE 21.2 The number of patients in mental hospitals declined dramatically between 1950 and 1990.

be getting down to the "hard core" of chronic patients who are extremely difficult to release.

The reduction of the number of patients in hospitals is certainly striking, but it is even more dramatic when you realize that the reduction has occurred while the general population was increasing. The success of the deinstitutionalization movement is reflected in the fact that a feasibility study conducted in the state of Vermont led to the recommendation that the state hospital be abolished (Carling et al., 1987). In other words, it was recommended that Vermont have a state mental health system with *no state hospital.*

There are three major reasons behind the movement to treat individuals in the community rather than in hospitals: (a) to avoid the negative aspects of hospitals, (b) to capitalize on the positive aspects of communities, and (c) to cut costs. We will consider each of these reasons and then examine the problems posed by deinstitutionalization.

Negative Aspects of Hospitals

The first reason that is usually given for deinstitutionalization can be summarized with the statement "You can't make a normal adjustment in an abnormal environment." The notion is that the major goal of treatment is to help disturbed individuals make a better adjustment, but the concept of adjustment implies *adjustment to something.* In most cases we adjust to the standards or models around us, but the hospital environment does not provide a good standard for adjustment. That being the case, a hospital would be the worst place to make a normal adjustment because the individuals with whom patients interact most are other people who are behaving in abnormal ways. It is unlikely that a patient who was attempting to deal with his or her own problems would be able to make a good adjustment when surrounded by people who thought they were Napoleon, heard the voice of God in the bathroom, or believed they had radioactive saliva and whose behaviors included constant pacing, suicide attempts, and urinating on the floor.

Furthermore, hospitalization is not conducive to normal adjustment because it fosters the surrender of personal responsibility and undermines self-confidence. That is so because in most hospitals, things are done *to* or *for* patients rather than *by* patients. The institutionalization syndrome that I discussed earlier is due in large part to the patients' adjustment to the norms and standards of the hospital. Thus because hospitals have negative effects on patients, it seems reasonable to get the patients out of the hospital. However, as you will soon see, in some cases the circumstances into which we are releasing the patients may be worse than the hospitals.

Positive Aspects of Communities

The second reason for moving patients out of the hospital and into the community is the belief that patients can be cared for more effectively in the community. Most notable in this regard is that if individuals are treated in the community rather than at some distant hospital, it is not necessary for them to be separated from their friends, family, and coworkers, from whom they can obtain valuable social support. Furthermore, if they are treated while living in the community, the patients can work actively to overcome sources of stress rather than being isolated from them and only talking about them. In addition, if patients are treated in the community, they can avoid the difficult transition from the hospital back to the community. That transition usually comes at a time when the patients' adjustment is still fragile; they are unsure about their ability to function in the outside world (which is, after all, where they "broke down"), and the stress of the transition can result in a relapse.

Economics

The third factor behind the deinstitutionalization movement is simple economics. Mental hospitals are very expensive to operate. In addition to the direct costs of treatment (therapists and medication), there are numerous indirect costs such as food, building construction, building maintenance, and extensive support staffs that include everyone from nurses to groundskeepers. The indirect costs of hospitalization easily exceed the costs of treatment, but by treating patients in the community, all indirect costs can be eliminated and considerable savings can be achieved. It could also be argued that treating patients in the community might also result in greater savings later because treatment in the community is more effective for reducing relapses, therefore reducing the cost of rehospitalization.

Unfortunately, the savings achieved by deinstitutionalization are not always as great as they appear at first. That is because very disturbed individuals who are discharged from state hospitals often go to other facilities such as privately operated nursing homes. The costs of institutionalizing the patients in those facilities are usually higher and are usually paid for by private insurance companies or by the federal government through the Medicare program. In other words, the costs are not saved but simply *shifted* from state governments to private industry and the federal government.

Problems with Deinstitutionalization

When the deinstitutionalization movement began in the mid-1960s, the motivating factor was improved care of disturbed individuals. It was believed that patients could be served better in the community than in the hospital. However, when the boom economy of the 1960s slowed down and budget deficits began to appear, priorities changed, and the cost-cutting value of deinstitutionalization became more important. Unfortunately, not only did financially pressed legislatures take the savings created by closing hospitals, but they also attempted to save money by cutting back or stopping the funding for community-based treatment programs. As a result, many deinstitutionalized patients were left stranded. It was bad enough that the door to the hospital been closed behind them, but now the door to community care was also shut.

The closing of mental hospitals is usually presented as a "progressive, modern movement" toward more humane treatment of patients in communities, and few people stop to ask what happens to the patients after they are released. Ignored is the fact that getting patients out of the hospital is only half of the deinstitutionalization program, and if alternative care is not provided outside of the hospital, we are probably being more inhumane than humane. In many cases deinstitutionalized patients end up living on welfare in run-down areas of the cities that have become known as "psychiatric ghettos." Other former patients join the ranks of the homeless and live on the streets. In an attempt to avoid or hide such problems in their areas, some officials have given discharged patients one-way bus tickets to distant cities in other states.

It should also be noted that the failure to link community care with the closing of hospitals posed problems not only for former patients who were turned out but also for potential patients who were never able to get in when the need first arose and for whom community care was not available.

The existence of psychiatric ghettos and increasing numbers of disturbed individuals living on the streets caused a backlash against deinstitutionalization, and some efforts were made to reinstitutionalize patients, such as the program in New York City that resulted in the institutionalization of Joyce Brown, the woman who burned money (see Case Study 20.2). However, because of the high costs of hospitalization, those attempts have been tokens at best. The program in New York City involved setting aside only 28 beds for a city with nearly 9 million people! Furthermore, reinstitutionalization does not solve the problem; it just reintroduces the problems that deinstitutionalization was designed to overcome.

Do not conclude that community care is entirely unavailable, because that is not the case. Care is available, but there does not appear to be enough care or the right type of care to meet the need. Let us consider the types of community care that are available.

COMMUNITY CARE

The release of patients from the mental hospitals does not necessarily imply that the patients are cured or even completely treated. Thus an important component of deinstitutionalization involves providing adequate treatment programs in the community, known as **community care.** The idea of systematically treating disturbed individuals in the community is not new. It can be traced back to the town of Gheel in Flanders (modern-day Belgium) in the 13th century (Earle, 1851/1994). As legend has it, in A.D. 600 a pagan king decapitated his beautiful daughter, Dymphna, when she refused to marry him. The townspeople thought that the king was mentally ill and that his behavior was the work of the Devil. Because Dymphna had been able to resist the Devil, it was assumed that God had granted her special powers to fight the evil forces that led to mental illness. When her story spread, people who were struggling with mental disorders came to Gheel in the hope of being inspired to fight the Devil more effectively and be cured. A number of miraculous cures were documented, and Dymphna was canonized by the Catholic church in 1247. (Dymphna is still the patroness of individuals with epilepsy and mental illness.)

In 600 in the town of Gheel, in Flanders, a pagan king executed his daughter, Dymphna, for refusing to marry him. The townspeople thought that the king was mentally ill and that his behavior was the work of the Devil. Because his daughter had resisted the Devil, people thought that she had special powers to fight the evil forces that caused mental illness. Disturbed individuals flocked to the town of Gheel, and the community developed a tradition of caring for them.

Due to the publicity, hundreds of disturbed individuals began coming to Gheel seeking cures, and in 1430, a small hospital was built. However, because so many people came and because many who were not cured stayed on, the number of disturbed individuals quickly swelled beyond the capacity of the hospital. In an attempt to accommodate all of the disturbed people, the townspeople began taking them into their homes. The church initially administered the program, but in 1852 responsibility was shifted to the government of

Belgium, which then "certified" families as qualified to provide housing and care. Being certified became a matter of pride, social standing, and tradition that was handed down for generations.

Through the years Gheel has provided a model of community tolerance and care for disturbed individuals. It is interesting that the tradition of community care in Gheel grew from necessity when facilities and funds were not sufficient for institutional care. Similar limitations in facilities and funds also play important roles in the current movement toward community care, but today the disturbed individuals are not being welcomed with the same compassion and enthusiasm as they were in Gheel.

Community treatment programs revolve around *outpatient clinics, community mental health centers, halfway houses,* and *home care visits.* When reading about the facilities and programs for community care, keep in mind that they are designed both for former patients who have been discharged from hospitals and for other disturbed individuals who do not yet need hospitalization.

Community mental health centers are usually effective for short-term inpatient treatment, outpatient care, and crisis intervention.

Outpatient Clinics

As the name implies, **outpatient clinics** are nonresidential treatment facilities to which patients go for therapy while living in the community. Outpatient clinics have long been an important part of mental hospitals. After a hospitalized patient has improved enough to be released, treatment is continued in the outpatient clinic. However, the problem with outpatient clinics is that they are usually located in large hospitals, and because those hospitals often serve large areas, the clinics are not conveniently located for many patients. Patients who have to travel a great distance to get to an outpatient clinic once or twice a week are likely to drop out of treatment. That is unfortunate because treatment and support during the transitional period when patients are moving back into the community are crucial. Without such aftercare, gains made in the hospital may be lost, and the patients may have to be rehospitalized. Thus outpatient clinics play an important role in community care, but their role is often limited by practical problems.

Community Mental Health Centers

Community mental health centers were designed to overcome the location problem of hospital-based outpatient clinics. As the name implies, they are smaller clinics that are conveniently located in the communities in which potential users live. However, community mental health centers were designed to be much more than just convenient, and their development stemmed from what in the 1960s was a new approach to mental

illness. A brief review of the legislative history that led to the development of community mental health centers will help you understand the goals they were designed to meet.

In 1955 Congress established the Joint Commission on Mental Illness and Health to examine the treatment of mental patients in the United States. After 6 years of study, the commission concluded that patients in large mental hospitals were more likely to receive *custodial care* than *treatment* and that even when treatment was provided, it was *not readily available* to many individuals who needed it because the hospitals were located too far from where the patients lived. The commission also recommended that more attention be devoted to the *prevention* of mental illness.

In response to the commission's report, President Kennedy sent to Congress the Community Mental Health Centers Act, proposing that the large, centrally located state and federal mental hospitals be phased out and replaced by many community mental health centers. These centers were to be designed to serve four functions:

1. *Outpatient therapy with day hospitalization.* Patients could come in once or twice a week for treatment and, when necessary, stay at the centers during the day but return home at night. The hope was that by making treatment readily available near where the individuals lived, disturbed individuals would be more likely to come in for help before their problems became so serious that full-time hospitalization was necessary.

2. *Short-term inpatient hospitalization in emergency cases.* By hospitalizing the patients near where they lived, social support from friends and relatives could be maintained, and the difficult transition from a distant hospital back to the community could be avoided. The community mental health centers were not designed to have their own inpatient facilities; instead, they were to use the facilities of local general hospitals that had small psychiatric wards. Only as a last resort were individuals who required long-term care to be sent to large central hospitals.

3. *Round-the-clock emergency services.* People would be able to get help immediately over the phone or on a walk-in basis whenever it was necessary. When an individual is in the middle of a crisis, it does not help much to say, "Well, we can see you a week from Tuesday at 2:30." People in crisis need help *immediately,* and early intervention may keep the problem from getting worse. Essentially, the concept of the medical emergency room was applied to the treatment of psychological problems.

4. *Educational and consultation services.* The goal of these services, offered to both individuals and other agencies in the community, was not treatment but *prevention.* For example, in the community in which I live, the staff of the local community mental health center routinely provides lectures and seminars for various companies on topics such as stress management and the early identification of personal problems. Also, staff members are quick to step in to provide help when potential problems arise. Once when a firefighter was killed while battling a fire, the staff of the community mental health center immediately set up group and individual counseling sessions for all of the members of the fire department to help them deal with the stresses associated with the death of their comrade.

Thus the goals of the community mental health centers are summed up in their name: They provide help in the individuals' *community* and promote *mental health* by using the resources in the community, catching problems early, and working toward prevention.

Another potential value of community mental health centers is that they may be more "culturally sensitive" than the large hospital-based treatment facilities (Rogler et al., 1987). Traditionally, the mental health services that are provided by large hospitals are aimed at the middle class and are based on a middle-class lifestyle. In many cases, however, *Roseanne* might be a better model than *The Brady Bunch* for understanding the life of a client, and because community mental health centers are "where the clients are," the centers may be more sensitive to the problems of the populations they serve. With that sensitivity, they may also be more attractive to members of minority groups and therefore will be used more effectively than traditional facilities.

The community mental health center program has met with mixed success. On the positive side, the centers are located in the neighborhoods where their clients live and they do make outpatient treatment, day hospitalization, short-term inpatient treatment, and 24-hour crisis intervention readily available to members of the community. In addition to being physically accessible, the centers are also financially accessible because fees are based on a sliding scale that takes the family's income and expenses into account. On the negative side, the success of the program has been limited because there are not enough centers to meet the need. When President Kennedy originally proposed them, he suggested that there be one center for every 100,000 persons. With today's population, that would mean 2,415 centers, but more than 30 years later, only about 1,000 have been established. Furthermore, in many centers the staff are so busy providing primary care for disturbed individuals that they have very little time to devote to the problem of prevention. In other words, they are so busy bailing out the psychological boat that they do not have time to solve the problem by fixing the cracks in the hull. Even so, community mental health centers have had a significant impact on the delivery of mental health services, and there is no doubt that they will continue to play an important role.

Halfway Houses

It should be clear by now that some patients need to be in a hospital and others do not. However, many patients fall in between—they do not require the intensive care provided by hospitals, but they do need a semistructured environment in which to live. Other patients may need a supportive environment in which to live while making the transition from hospital to community life. As the name implies, **halfway houses** provide places for patients to live that are halfway between hospitalization and independent life in the community.

A halfway house is usually a large older home that has been converted into a number of small living units. Cooking and eating are usually done as a group so that costs can be kept low, work can be shared, and residents do not become socially isolated. Halfway houses are usually staffed by paraprofessionals, often a married couple who manage the house and supervise the residents in exchange for rent and possibly a small wage. Like the other residents, the paraprofessionals usually have other jobs.

Most halfway houses are not designed for long-term use by residents. Rather, they serve only as transitional living and care facilities while the residents are readjusting to life in the community. While living in the halfway house, the residents get settled into jobs and social groups before moving out on their own. In the halfway house, the residents can get support from the paraprofessionals and the other residents. Residents

CASE STUDY 21.2

Taking Help to the Homeless Mentally Ill: The Example of COSTAR

In Baltimore, it was recognized that many individuals are too disturbed to come in for treatment. One scenario runs as follows: A disturbed individual is hospitalized temporarily, put on a maintenance dosage of medication that enables him or her to function in the community, and is then released with the expectation that he or she will return to the hospital (or outpatient clinic) for medication as needed. However, for some reason, the patient stops taking the medication and consequently relapses. Once relapsed, the patient becomes too disoriented to return to the hospital. Then the disturbed patient is likely to wind up on the street because he or she cannot pay the rent, is rejected by his or her family, or is so disoriented that he or she cannot coexist with others in a normal environment.

In an attempt to reach out and treat such individuals, the Johns Hopkins Hospital and the city of Baltimore established the Community Support, Treatment, and Rehabilitation (COSTAR) program, in which psychiatric nurses work with the patients in the community—on the streets and in their homes. This program differs from most other programs in that it relies primarily on psychiatric nurses rather than social workers, and therefore patients can be given medical attention in addition to psychological treatment.

The case of a 41-year-old woman named Sinora provides a good example of the kinds of problems that the patients have and the kinds of treatments that are used. Sinora was diagnosed as suffering from chronic schizophrenia, and she must take her antipsychotic medication every day or her condition will seriously deteriorate. However, living on the streets as she did, she often forgot her medication, so she became very disoriented and eventually had to be rehospitalized. To circumvent this problem, every day Sinora is visited by a nurse who gives her the medication and makes sure she takes it, but that is not all the nurse does. When Sinora was first found, she was unable to take care of herself, and the nurse had to begin by helping her eat and even bathing her because Sinora frequently soiled herself. The nurse explains, "You start right where they are. . . . Often they'll stumble and go back down, but we all do. Everybody has the right to do that." Over the course of two years, the nurse has kept Sinora on her medication, helped her find housing, taught her good grooming and hygiene, taught her how to keep house and shop economically, and helped her budget her money, and she is now taking Sinora to a job-training center. This is real progress, progress that could not be made without daily contact. The

who have been out of the hospital longer can serve as models for newer residents, and later the newer residents will take on those responsibilities when the older residents move out.

Home Care

All of the treatment programs that I have discussed so far in this chapter require that the client go to the treatment facility, but some programs are now being established in which the caregivers go to the client. Going to the client is sometimes necessary because the client is too disturbed to come in for treatment. This approach is not unique to the care of psychologically disturbed individuals; for years, visiting nurse programs have served medical patients who were not sick enough for full-time hospitalization but too sick or otherwise unable to go to the hospital for outpatient care. Psychological and medical house calls may be somewhat expensive, but they are cheaper than hospitalizing patients, and if the patients are not going to be hospi-

talized, house calls may be the only way some patients will get treatment.

Many (but not all) of the individuals who are helped by these programs are homeless and living on the streets, so the mental health teams meet and work with them on the streets. Unlike the program in New York that was discussed earlier in which the goal was to get the people off the streets and into hospitals, the goal of these programs is to treat the people where they are. With these programs, it is hoped that in time the homeless will move off the streets, but into homes, not hospitals. Case Study 21.2 highlights a community program in Baltimore called COSTAR in which psychiatric nurses work in the community providing medical, psychological, and social support for disturbed individuals.

Public Acceptance of Patients in the Community

Most people agree that whenever possible, it is preferable to treat nondangerous patients in the community

nurse commented, "By seeing Sinora every morning for 15 or 20 minutes or maybe a half hour, she and I can sit down and plan her day, see what problems have come up, and solve them before they get to be big problems."

By seeing Sinora every day and doing things like having a meal with her in a fast-food restaurant, the nurse can consistently monitor Sinora's emotional state so that the medication can be adjusted if necessary. The nurse is also able to observe Sinora's behavior in the reality of day-to-day living so that real problems can be identified and solved. This is more effective than trying to work with a patient in the artificial environment of a hospital, where you can only talk about what goes on.

COSTAR even handles Sinora's welfare checks, budgeting the funds carefully over each month. This can be difficult because initially the client may not trust the nurse or understand what is being done. However, with assisted budgeting, as with other aspects of the program, the clients are encouraged to participate in treatment; the treatment is not forced on them from the outside.

Is the COSTAR program successful? The answer depends on how you measure success. It is unlikely that clients like Sinora will ever be completely "nor-mal," and they will probably always require a visit once a week or every other week if not every day. However, their ability to function on their own has been greatly increased, and with some assistance, many clients do very well. For example, recall that Sinora is now living in stable housing and is getting job training, so eventually she may be at least somewhat self-supporting. That is a long way from being a disoriented schizophrenic living on the street. An initial evaluation of the program revealed that in the year following admission to the COSTAR program, patients were much less likely to require hospitalization than they were in the preceding year when they were not in the program. Apart from the human benefit in terms of quality of life, keeping clients out of the hospital results in a substantial financial saving that more than offsets the costs of the labor-intensive visiting program.

Does Sinora think the program is successful? When asked about COSTAR, Sinora said, "I'm glad COSTAR found me so they could give me my right medicines. I don't never want to be put away no more, Mister. I'm tired of it."

Source: Giansante (1988).

rather than in hospitals. However, a problem arises when people have to face the possibility of having mental patients live in *their* communities. Numerous surveys have indicated that most people have negative attitudes about or are afraid of mentally ill individuals, and it has been estimated that as many as half of all psychiatric facilities that were planned for residential areas were blocked by community opposition (Piasecki, 1975). In one city in New York, the residents went so far as to pass a law making it illegal for mental patients to live within the city limits. (A mental patient was defined as anyone who was taking antipsychotic medication.)

People have negative attitudes about mental patients and oppose their presence in the community, but the question arises whether the presence of patients in a community is even noticeable. To answer that question, one group of investigators conducted a survey of 180 individuals living in 12 residential neighborhoods in New York City (Rabkin et al., 1984). Six of the neighborhoods contained a treatment facility such as a large outpatient clinic, a halfway house, or a single-room-occupancy hotel known to attract former mental patients. The community residents who were surveyed in those areas lived within one block of the treatment facility. The other six neighborhoods were comparable in all respects but did not contain a treatment facility; residents in those areas were used as controls.

The results revealed two interesting findings. First, when residents were asked to rate problems in their community (e.g., burglary, unemployment, and "crazy people in the street"), there were no differences between the responses of residents in the treatment and control areas. In other words, the presence of patients in the neighborhood did not influence the residents' perception of the quality of life in the neighborhood. Second, when residents were asked about the presence of treatment facilities in their neighborhoods, 77% of the residents in the treatment areas were unaware of the presence of the facility despite the fact that they lived within one block of it. Of the residents living near a facility, 23% reported being aware of it—but 13% of the residents living in the control areas incorrectly reported the presence of a treatment facility in their neighborhood. If 13% is taken as the error rate (the percentage of people with erroneous beliefs about the existence of a facility in their neighborhood), it could be concluded that only 10% of the individuals living within one block of a large psychiatric treatment facility were aware of its existence.

These results do not offer any evidence that the presence of a treatment facility for mental patients has a negative impact on the quality of a community, and they reveal that only very few people even become aware of such facilities in their communities. Unfortunately, facts like these do little to change people's emotionally based attitudes. Would you be in favor of having a mental patient treatment facility in your neighborhood?

It is interesting that some of the stigma associated with treatment facilities is related to the names we give the facilities. "Mental hospital" and "hospital for the criminally insane" certainly sound ominous to both the public and patients. In one state mental hospital in which I worked that was labeled a "mental health center," nurses often threatened disruptive patients by saying, "If you keep acting that way, we are going to transfer you from this *mental health center* to a *mental hospital!*" The patients quickly complied with whatever the nurse wanted. The effects of labels on the public's response to treatment facilities was documented when the name of one mental hospital was changed to the Madison Center. Immediately after the name change, the local residents passed a bond issue to provide additional funding, and children began walking on the sidewalk in front of the building rather than crossing the street to avoid coming near it (Roberts & Roberts, 1985).

As was the case in Gheel 500 years ago, today economic necessity is once again giving birth to the community care of disturbed individuals. However, unlike Gheel, in many cases the community care is given grudgingly at best, and often people want the care to be given in someone else's community.

The Need for Asylums

Community care is a laudable idea, and in many respects it is very successful. When it is not successful, the shortcomings often stem from problems of implementation rather than from flaws in the ideas. However, even if community care were operating at the optimal level that could be realistically expected, there would probably still be a need for mental hospitals. The reason is that individuals who are in great crisis or who are suffering from absolutely overwhelming symptoms (e.g., hideous hallucinations or dangerous delusions) may briefly need a place of refuge, a place to recoup before taking up the battle again. This was demonstrated during times of war when soldiers broke down under great stress. If they were given a few days away from the battle, they were able to recoup and return to

the front line. For some individuals, the same may be true during some of life's battles.

What may be needed in some cases is best described by the term **asylum.** The use of that term may seem somewhat paradoxical because it is usually associated with the early institutions for mentally ill individuals, institutions that were characterized by chaos and bedlam (see Chapter 1). Technically, however, the term refers to "a place of refuge and protection," and synonyms include *sanctuary, shelter,* and *refuge.* It was that sort of environment that the early mental health workers were trying to establish and that they thought would cure mental illness. Our mental health forebears may have been incorrect in their belief that asylums were effective for *curing* mental illness, but an asylum in the true sense of the word may be an important brief initial step in the process of treatment and recovery. In our enthusiasm for getting individuals out of impersonal and often deleterious large mental hospitals and keeping them in the community, it is important that we not forget that individuals who are under great stress can sometimes benefit from a brief respite—an *asylum.*

COST OF TREATMENT

An issue that recurs throughout this chapter is the *cost of treatment,* so at this point it will be helpful if I review some of the figures and financial issues associated with psychiatric care.

Cost

It is difficult to provide overall figures concerning costs because different disorders entail different costs, costs can vary with the quality of treatment, and there are regional differences in costs. However, the following figures will provide you with some rough estimates of costs.

Inpatient Hospitalization. The typical cost of hospitalization in private hospitals is often as high as $1,000 a day, and in many cases that figure may not include such "extras" as psychological testing, psychotherapy, physical exams, medication, laboratory work, other treatments such as ECT, or the services of other professionals such as social workers. Those additional costs can easily add hundreds of dollars a day. In many cases the cost of psychiatric hospitalization is comparable to medical or surgical hospitalization, but there is one very important difference between the two: Whereas medical or surgical hospitalization usually lasts for a few days or a week, *psychiatric hospitalization can last for months.* Being in a psychiatric hospital for one month could easily cost well over $40,000, so it is clear that the cost of psychiatric hospitalization can be overwhelming.

When attempting to understand these high costs, it is essential to recognize that the private hospitals are usually run to make a profit, and because there is relatively little competition in the area, there is little necessity to keep costs down and considerable incentive to keep them high. State hospitals do not provide an alternative to private hospitalization because the state hospitals are being phased out.

In some instances, hospitalization is essential for the welfare of the patient and the community, but in many cases, individuals are hospitalized to keep beds full and profits up. Indeed, one recent study revealed that nearly 40% of psychiatric hospital care days were unnecessary and that about 75% of the admissions for substance abuse were unnecessary (American Psychological Association, 1993). At one hospital I know of, patients who are being treated for eating disorders are usually discharged after 58 or 59 days. Why not earlier or later? The answer is that patients' insurance benefits run out after 60 days! In other words, it appears that in many cases patients are kept in the hospital or released not as a function of their mental condition but as a function of their financial condition. Such abuse is possible because patients and family members are frightened by psychiatric disorders, and they are not in a position to judge what treatment or how much treatment is necessary. Unfortunately, individuals rarely get second opinions concerning the treatment of psychiatric disorders.

Day Hospitalization and Outpatient Treatment. Day hospitalization rates can run $200 to $300 a day—still high, but a considerable saving compared to staying overnight, when little treatment would be provided anyway. Of course, all of the extras like therapy must be added to the base figure. Outpatient treatment is probably the most cost-effective. Psychotherapy outside of the hospital usually costs between $75 and $125 an hour. In addition to psychotherapy, many patients now receive other treatments such as electroconvulsive therapy on an outpatient basis.

Drugs. In most cases drugs are a relatively inexpensive mode of treatment. For example, a month's supply of Valium costs about $30 (generic form: $9), and Prozac, which is one of the most expensive antidepressants, costs about $70 a month. Many patients rely on Haldol to control the symptoms of their schizophrenia, and it costs about $260 a month (generic form: $60). However, some drugs are very expensive. For example, Clozaril (along with the necessary weekly blood tests) can cost over $800 per month. Of course, to the cost of drugs we must add the expense of regular consultations with a physician during which the effectiveness of the drug can be evaluated and dosage levels changed if necessary.

Drugs cost less than most other treatments, but we ought not conclude that drugs should be used simply because they are less expensive. Treatments should be chosen on the basis of their effectiveness for the disorder in question.

Insurance and Cost Control

The cost of treatment is usually covered by health insurance, but because those costs are simply passed on to the consumer in the form of higher premiums, there is now a strong movement to cut costs. One means of cutting costs is called **managed health care,** and that usually involves **health maintenance organizations (HMOs).** In those programs you buy a policy for all of your health care needs (physical and psychological) from one organization, and then whenever you have a problem, you see a **primary-care physician** who is responsible for deciding whether you need treatment. If this physician decides that you need treatment, you are referred to one of the specialists in the organization. Costs are reduced in HMOs because there is an emphasis on prevention and early detection (note *health maintenance* in the name), which is less expensive than treatment after a problem has developed. Costs are also controlled because the primary-care physician who evaluates your needs will not refer you for unnecessary treatments.

Some psychologists and psychiatrists have raised concerns about the role of psychiatric treatment in managed-care programs. They suggest that in attempts to reduce costs, some psychiatric disorders may not be covered by the insurance policies, patients may be less likely to be referred for benefits that do exist, and the amount of treatment that is budgeted may not be sufficient to overcome the problem. One of my colleagues complained that primary-care physicians underestimate the seriousness of many psychiatric problems, so the physicians do not refer the individuals for treatment, and when the physicians do refer individuals for treatment, they approve only a few weeks of treatment when adequate treatment may in fact take years.

There is no doubt that there have been serious abuses of the psychiatric component of the health care system and that there is a real need to overcome those problems and reduce costs in general. The challenge is to screen potential patients carefully and to identify the most cost-effective treatment. However, even the most cost-effective treatment can be very expensive. Case Study 21.3 illustrates the very high cost of drug treatment for Betty, about whom you read earlier.

PREVENTION OF ABNORMAL BEHAVIOR

We will never have enough mental health professionals to treat all disturbed individuals, and therefore our only real hope for eradicating abnormal behavior is to

CASE STUDY 21.3
The Cost of Betty's Drugs: $353 a Week

This case study is based on Betty, the woman who suffers from schizophrenia whom I discussed in Case Studies 11.2 and 13.4. You will recall that Betty has suffered from a very severe case of schizophrenia for about 20 years and that she has been hospitalized numerous times. However, Betty is now taking a number of drugs that are effective for reducing many of her symptoms. Those drugs, plus a good deal of social support from friends and the staff at a local mental health center, make it possible for Betty to live outside of the hospital.

Unfortunately, the drugs do not eliminate the symptoms, and she is still plagued by a variety of delusions (that the police are after her) and hallucinations (monks and demons telling her to kill herself, rats on the floor, people dissolving into blobs of blood). Struggling with her symptoms poses one serious problem for Betty, but she faces another—paying for her drugs. Here is a list of the drugs and treatments that Betty must take, along with the weekly costs.

Drug or Treatment	Weekly Cost ($)
Clozaril (antipsychotic)	220
Zoloft (antidepressant)	14
Oxybutynin chloride (antispasmodic for bladder control, to counter a side effect of the other drugs)	7
Ativan (antianxiolytic)	13
Klonopin (antianxiolytic)	28
Chloral hydrate (sleeping pill)	1
Blood test for agranulocytosis	20
Psychiatric consultation (to monitor symptoms, drugs)	50
Total	353

The cost of Betty's treatment comes to $18,356 a year. How does Betty pay for this? Betty is a very bright woman with a graduate degree in library science who once had a career as a librarian, but because of her symptoms, she is unable to work. Therefore, Betty must live on Social Security disability benefits of $160 a week, which is *less than half of her weekly medical bill.* Fortunately, Betty qualifies for Medicaid assistance, which will pay her medical bills *after she pays the annual deductible of $2,321.* Spread over the year, the deductible comes to $45 a week, so Betty has $115 a week to cover *all* of her expenses (rent, utilities, food, clothing, etc.). Sometimes Betty is simply not able to pay the deductible fee for the drugs, in which case she cannot get the drugs. Usually her pharmacist will give her credit and let her go into debt, but there are limits. One time Betty had no money and was within two days of running out of Clozaril. Without the drug, Betty's condition would immediately deteriorate, she would not be able to function in the community, and she would have to be placed in a state hospital (assuming that a space could be found). Hospitalization in the state hospital would cost the government about $40,000 per year, so the cost of the Clozaril is a bargain, but with deficits mounting, the government may not be able to afford either. Then what will happen? Clearly, the cost of treatment can be an overwhelming financial burden both for the individual and for the government. And remember, in many cases, this is a lifelong burden. What would you do if you faced this situation?

Note: The costs described here do not include those of the mental health service that provides a case manager who helps Betty deal with daily problems.

---

establish effective prevention programs. Actually, it may be more efficient, cheaper, and more humane to focus more efforts on prevention than treatment. In this section I will describe the problems, programs, and progress associated with our attempts at prevention.

Before discussing specific prevention programs, two obvious but often overlooked issues should be mentioned. First, when working to prevent abnormal behavior, we must concentrate on the factors that we think cause the abnormal behavior. That is probably obvious, but what may be missed is the fact that for any one disorder there are usually many suspected causes (psychodynamic, learning, cognitive, and physiological). The question then arises, on which suspected cause should

we focus? Do we attempt to develop defenses against intrapsychic conflicts, reduce stress, change learned thought patterns, or eliminate specific genes?

Most intervention programs revolve around stress reduction. The implicit notion is that stress leads to abnormal behavior or that stress will be most likely to trigger abnormal behavior in individuals who are predisposed to such behavior (the diathesis-stress hypothesis). That seems reasonable, but it should be recognized that in focusing on stress reduction, we have ignored a variety of other potential causes. Therefore, if our attempts at prevention are not completely successful, it may be that the program was focused on the wrong cause. For example, programs that are focused on stress reduction will not be successful in preventing disorders that are due to strictly physiological problems.

The second issue that should be noted is that regardless of what we think causes abnormal behavior, there are practical, technical, and ethical limits on what we can actually do to prevent it. For example, we may believe that abnormal behavior results from intrapsychic conflict, but it is not feasible to give every child intensive psychotherapy so that he or she can develop defenses against such conflict. Or we may believe that abnormal behavior is due to genetic problems, but it is neither ethical nor technically possible to use selective mating or surgery to eliminate specific genes. Therefore, when we design intervention programs, we must focus on the *possible,* and insofar as our prevention programs are constrained by practical, technical, and ethical factors, we must expect limitations on the effectiveness of the programs. In summary, when developing prevention programs, we must give careful attention to the questions of what causes abnormal behavior and how or whether we can intervene in the causal chain. Having recognized these issues and limitations, we can go on to consider the various types of intervention programs that have been tried.

There are three types of prevention, and each type is associated with a different phase of the development of abnormal behavior:

1. *Primary prevention* is aimed at *eliminating the causes* of abnormal behavior.

2. *Secondary prevention* is designed to *catch problems early* so that they do not become serious.

3. *Tertiary prevention* is focused on *reducing relapses* in recovered clients.

Now we can examine the programs and problems that are associated with these three types of prevention.

Primary Prevention

Primary prevention is designed to *eliminate the causes* of abnormal behavior. Attempts at primary prevention include such things as improved prenatal and postnatal care, day care for children and the elderly, educational programs to reduce substance abuse, reductions in environmental poisons (e.g., lead in paint and exhaust fumes), improvements in diet, increases in exercise, prevention of head injuries with better athletic helmets and greater use of seat belts, improved housing that allows for privacy and reduces stress, and the reduction of poverty in an attempt to reduce the stress it brings. Sometimes these programs are not thought of as mental health programs because they have other, more immediate physical health and safety benefits. However, the programs do have important "downstream" effects on mental health because they reduce brain damage and stress that lead to abnormal behavior.

One primary prevention program was designed to provide poor, young, unmarried pregnant women with better prenatal care and preparation for motherhood (Olds, 1982). These women usually get very poor prenatal care and give birth to babies who are underweight and suffer from neurological difficulties that lead to serious problems later. In addition, these women are likely to neglect or abuse their babies, causing additional problems for the children. The intervention program involved having a nurse visit the women to teach them proper diet and to help them obtain medical and financial assistance available in the community. The nurse also provided social support for the women and helped them establish relationships with others in the community so that they would have someone to turn to when problems arose. Visits by the nurse continued after the babies were born so that the mothers could be taught about infant development, care, and safety.

An evaluation of the effects of the program revealed that compared to mothers who were not visited, mothers who were visited made better use of community services, gave birth to heavier babies, were less likely to neglect or abuse their babies, and provided their babies with more appropriate playthings. In addition, the visited unmarried mothers were less likely to get pregnant again and were more likely to hold a job. These immediate effects are impressive, but it is likely that we can expect even more important effects in the future because the children of visited mothers will probably show fewer serious adjustment problems in adolescence and adulthood. A long-term follow-up will be necessary to verify that possibility, but it is clear that the children of visited mothers got a better start.

The implementation of primary prevention programs that focus on problems like air pollution, poverty, and safety is often more within the domain of politics than psychology, but psychologists are actively involved in the development and administration of the programs. Indeed, since the mid-1960s psychology has had a subspecialty known as **community psychology.** Practitioners in that area often work in governments rather than clinics and direct their efforts toward changing communities rather than changing clients.

The establishment of primary prevention programs is encouraging, but unfortunately many of the problems on which the programs are focused have proved to be very difficult to solve, and consequently successes have been limited. For example, despite massive federal programs, we have not been able to eliminate poverty. Also, advances that were being made were reduced by changes in budgetary priorities. For example, prenatal and postnatal care is crucial for warding off brain damage and various behavior problems, but funds for such care were cut in the face of the need to balance the federal budget. Advocates of prenatal and postnatal care argued that in the long run, cutting the programs

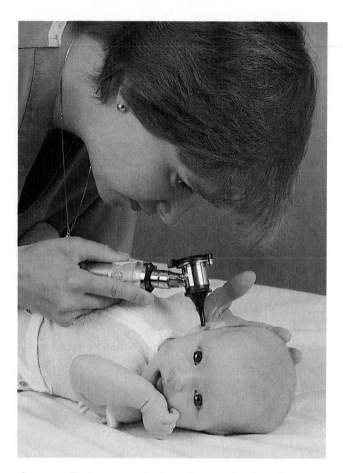

One very effective means of primary intervention is good postnatal care. The goal is to help improve the health of the newborn and provide support for the mother, thus reducing many of the physical complications and emotional stresses that can lead to abnormal behavior.

would lead to higher costs because the expense of supporting a mentally retarded individual for a lifetime is much higher than the cost of providing prenatal and postnatal care. In essence, they argued that we can pay *hundreds* of dollars for prenatal care now or pay *hundreds of thousands* of dollars for institutionalization later. Thus, because some problems proved difficult to solve and because of reductions in funding, much of the early optimism about the effects of primary prevention has faded. This is not to deny that great strides have been made, but the dream of a Camelot of mental health has turned out to be as elusive as the mythical kingdom itself.

Secondary Prevention

Because primary prevention has not been completely successful, we must fall back onto a second line of defense. That defense is known as **secondary prevention,** and it is aimed at *solving problems in their early stages so that they will not lead to more serious problems.* With sec-

ondary prevention, we identify individuals who are at high risk for developing disorders and then attempt to provide them with coping strategies and support that will reduce the impact of the disorder-causing factors. In other words, rather than eliminating the causes of abnormal behavior, the strategy is to build up the defenses of individuals who are most likely to be exposed to the causes. This is similar to vaccination in medicine: Since we cannot kill all of the germs that cause an illness, we inoculate the individuals who are most likely to be exposed to the germs. Our efforts are focused on high-risk individuals because our resources are limited and because for most diseases it is neither feasible nor necessary to inoculate everyone.

Efforts at secondary prevention include training programs for young children who are at high risk for developing abnormal behavior, support groups for individuals facing particular problems, and crisis intervention programs for individuals going through potentially overwhelming stresses.

Early Childhood Interventions. Many theorists believe that the development of abnormal behavior can be reduced if children who are at high risk are provided with warm, supportive emotional environments and are taught effective strategies for coping with problems. This approach makes intuitive sense, but three impediments must be recognized. First is the problem of identifying high-risk children. Probably the best strategy for doing that is to use family history. Throughout this book, it has been pointed out that the children of disturbed parents are at higher risk than other children. However, for most disorders, the risk rate for individuals with a family history of the disorder is only about 10% higher than for individuals who do not have a family history of the disorder. In other words, family history may be our best predictor of risk, but it is not a particularly good predictor. In the absence of a good risk predictor, we will miss treating many children who might benefit from the help.

A second problem revolves around compliance with the treatment program. When programs are provided for high-risk children, the dropout rate is often as high as 80%. In view of the difficulty we have in getting people to wear automobile seat belts, it is not surprising that we have difficulty getting them to wear "psychological seat belts" when the benefits are less clear and the effort required is greater.

A third problem stems from the fact that with many disorders, we do not know exactly what causes the problem (or there is disagreement over what causes the problem), and hence it is not clear what a prevention program should include. What would you do for an individual who was at high risk for the development of schizophrenia? The problems of identification, compliance, and nature of treatment make the development of effective prevention programs difficult—but not impossible, and we will now examine programs that have been developed for schizophrenia and school behavior problems.

In a number of places, children who were at high risk for schizophrenia were identified and then provided with a preventive program (e.g., Schulsinger et al., 1975). However, so far there are no reports concerning the long-term effects of the programs. This does not necessarily mean that the programs have been ineffective. It may simply be that because schizophrenia does not develop until early or middle adulthood, not enough time has gone by for the effects to appear. But some evidence suggests that early intervention programs may *not* be effective for reducing serious disorders such as depression and schizophrenia. For example, you may recall that adoption studies revealed that the children of disturbed parents who were adopted and raised by normal parents had about the same rates of abnormal behavior as the children who were not adopted and were raised by the disturbed parents. In other words, those results suggest that at least for the disorders that have a strong genetic basis, moving the children to a better psychological environment may not substantially reduce the likelihood of the disorder.

However, not all problems are due to genetic factors, and intervention programs might be effective for disorders that are due to other factors. Furthermore, it could be argued that the early intervention programs are more effective than simply a "normal" family environment. In summary, we do not yet have a conclusive answer to the question of whether early intervention programs are effective for reducing disorders such as schizophrenia in children who are at high risk.

In contrast to the case with schizophrenia, data suggest that early interventions can be effective for reducing less serious troubles such as school behavior problems (e.g., Durlak, 1980; Kirschenbaum et al., 1980; Yu et al., 1986). School behavior problems are of concern themselves, but they are also of interest because in some cases, they are thought to be early signs of more serious problems that will appear later. The notion is that if we can overcome the school problems, we will be able to avoid the more serious problems later.

In one prevention project, 119 first, second, and third graders with school behavior problems were assigned to one of three conditions: (a) a *behavioral* treatment condition in which assistants in the classroom gave the children tokens (candy or small toys) and praise for appropriate target behaviors, (b) a *relationship* treatment condition in which assistants developed warm and trusting nondirective therapeutic relationships with the children and helped the children express feelings and conflicts, and (c) a *no-treatment* control condition (Durlak, 1980). Before and after the

10-week program, teachers rated the children on behaviors such as acting out and shyness or withdrawal. A comparison of those ratings indicated that the children in the behavioral treatment condition showed substantial reductions in problem behaviors, while the children in the relationship and no-treatment conditions showed minimal or no improvement. These changes are presented in Figure 21.3.

Results indicating that we can reduce school behavior problems are encouraging, but we must be cautious in making interpretations concerning the long-term prevention of more serious problems. Programs like the one discussed here can reduce relatively minor current problems, and that is important, but so far there is no evidence that the programs reduce the incidence of more serious problems later. Long-term follow-up evaluations of the treated children are necessary, but none has yet been reported. At present, then, we do not have any evidence that early intervention programs for children at high risk are effective in terms of secondary prevention.

Support Groups. Another approach to secondary prevention involves the use of **support groups** for individuals who are facing specific stressful problems that could lead to abnormal behavior. Support groups are small groups of people who share a common problem (e.g., bereavement, being a single parent, illness) and meet

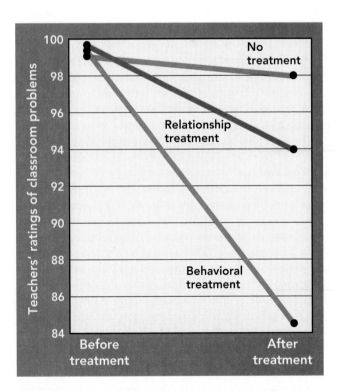

FIGURE 21.3 Behavioral treatment was more effective than relationship-based treatment or no treatment for reducing classroom behavior problems.
Source: Data from Durlak (1980), p. 333, tab. 1.

Support groups are often helpful to individuals who face specific stressful problems. Participants can benefit by sharing their experiences with others who face similar problems.

to share their experiences and to help one another deal with the problem.

Support groups are very popular today. In fact, in one university town of approximately 60,000 people, there were almost 60 different active support groups, and it is estimated that nationally, 12 million people participate in roughly 500,000 support groups. Name your problem, and there is probably a group for you; in fact, there is now a national self-help clearinghouse to help you find your group. Probably the best known of the support groups is Alcoholics Anonymous. Case Study 21.4 reflects the experiences of people who are in a support group for individuals with muscular dystrophy.

Support groups seem to derive their value from four factors. The first is *emotional support.* In the midst of a crisis, someone is there to hold you, figuratively and sometimes literally. The parents of a child who has just died unexpectedly are likely to be emotionally devastated and not believe that they will ever get through the experience. However, others in a support group who have "been there" can provide much-needed emotional support during the crisis. Similarly, a member of Alcoholics Anonymous will sit through the night with a struggling alcoholic who is fighting the urge to drink.

Second, support groups demonstrate to members that they are *not alone* in having the problem. Knowing that someone is there to help is important, but knowing that you are not the only person with the problem also helps. One member of Alcoholics Anonymous who had not had a drink in two years said that the first thing she learned was that

> I was not alone, that there was a roomful of people working toward what I was working toward. . . . AA showed me that I wasn't so different. I had always thought I was dropped here by aliens. Until AA, nobody understood

how I felt at 3 A.M. sitting by myself with a bottle. (Hurley, 1988, p. 67)

Third, support groups can provide good *role models.* New members can see that "you do get through it" and "there is a life after this experience."

Finally, support groups provide *information.* Members tell one another about other sources of help and how to cope with various problems. They also warn one another about what to expect in the future so as not to be caught off guard by a new phase of the problem.

Most support groups do not involve professionals or even paraprofessionals. Professionals such as physicians, psychologists, social workers, and child care specialists might be called on occasionally to talk about a particular problem, but for the most part, support groups involve *peers helping peers.* That is important because not only do peers provide good role models, but reliance on peers also greatly reduces the cost of support groups. Indeed, support groups usually operate free of charge. Sometimes support groups are referred to as "self-help groups," but in many respects that is a misnomer because in the group, individuals help one another. Probably better names would be *mutual-help groups* or *help and information groups.* Whatever they are called, the groups provide emotional support for the present, a sense of belonging, hope for the future, role models, and valuable information. As such, these groups probably do a lot to reduce stress and limit the development of abnormal behavior.

Crisis Intervention. Support groups are designed to provide prolonged help for relatively chronic problems. However, sometimes acute crises arise that require immediate short-term help. Examples of such crises include the death of a loved one, rape, suicide

CASE STUDY 21.4

A Support Group for Individuals with Muscular Dystrophy: Comments of Group Members

Muscular dystrophy (MD) is an inherited disease that involves the progressive deterioration of the muscles. During the early phases, individuals with the disorder may lose the ability to walk and have to rely on a wheelchair. Later they may lose all muscle control and even go blind. Because the consequences of MD are so dire and because there is no treatment for the disorder, having MD can be a very stressful experience.

In my community, there is a support group for individuals with MD. Eight or 10 people get together once a week at the home of one of them. The group was originally organized by a professor who has MD, but everyone shares in the leadership. Members include students, professionals, and blue-collar workers. Here are some of their responses when I asked about what the group meant to them.

> For me, the most important thing the group does is let me feel and express really strong emotions that I couldn't express anywhere else. Knowing that you've got MD and knowing what might happen to you can be really frightening. It can also make you angry—why me? In the group, it's OK to have strong feelings and to express them. Others do it too. It's good to get those feelings out, especially with other people who understand what you are going through. Our support group is strong because we cry together—and because we curse together!

The group helps me maintain my self-esteem. It's really hard to maintain your self-esteem when you are losing control of your body, have to live in a wheelchair, and may be going blind. It's easy to see yourself as "one down," not as good as others, or not having a future. But group members constantly tell you, "You're important to us," "We need you," "We care about you," "You're important in our lives," and "You have a contribution to make." With that boost from the group, I get the guts to go on. Without the group, I would have given up on myself long ago.

We don't share only bad things. It's important to get the bad things out, but it's also important to share some laughs. We have a thing we call "Laugh Together." Group members videotape or tape-record things that make them laugh and feel really good, and then we play the tapes at the meetings. We also share "take-home laugh tapes." You have to balance the crying with a little laughing, and we share and help each other with both.

I learn a lot from the people in the group. I learn what to expect if my disease progresses, and I learn practical ways of dealing with the problems. People with MD can tell you more about the disease and how to cope than your doctor can. They're living with it on a daily basis. With the tips they give me and with them showing me that they can live with this thing, I think I'll make it.

attempts, and financial problems. In those situations, many individuals turn to **crisis intervention centers** that provide services like telephone hot lines and 24-hour-a-day walk-in counseling.

The nature of a typical crisis center is reflected in Case Study 21.5. This case study was written by an undergraduate student of mine who is a volunteer worker in the crisis center.

Tertiary Prevention

Unfortunately, we are often unable to eliminate the causes of abnormal behavior, and we sometimes fail in our attempts to head off the development of such behavior. When those preventive strategies fail, individuals develop various disorders that must be treated, and that gives rise to tertiary prevention, the third line

of defense against abnormal behavior. **Tertiary** (TUR-shē-er-e) **prevention** involves working to *prevent relapses* in individuals who have had disorders. (The word *tertiary* simply means "third type.")

Because treatment is usually focused on correcting the problem that led to the disorder, most treatments are designed both to eliminate current symptoms and to prevent relapses. Therefore, most of our discussions of treatment so far have implicitly involved tertiary prevention. For example, if through treatment we resolve conflicts, improve the individual's ability to cope with stress, or correct chemical imbalances, we not only reduce current symptoms but also, it is hoped, prevent their return. A frequently used measure of the effectiveness of treatment is *relapse rate* (the length of time an individual can remain symptom-free or at least out of treatment after therapy has ended).

CASE STUDY 21.5

An Undergraduate Talks About Her Experiences Working at a Crisis Center

"When most people think about a phone-in crisis center, they probably think immediately about suicide calls, but that is only a very small part of what goes on. The crises come in all shapes and sizes and at all times of the day and night. Sometimes the work at our center is pretty intense, but at other times it can be fairly laid-back. People call to talk about relationships, loneliness, frustrations at work, and just about everything else. Our job is not to tell them how to handle these problems; we give them information and help them sort things out. The idea is to enable them to help themselves.

"The center in which I work as a volunteer is in a large old three-story house that's located between the university campus and the downtown area of the city. The first floor of the house has a room with three phones and two old couches, and it is here that the volunteers spend most of their time. Most night shifts are busy until about 2 or 3 in the morning, and then those couches come in really handy to crash on. Of course, there are some nights when you can kiss sleep good-bye completely. There are rooms on both the first and second floors where we can go with people who come in and want to talk. The second and third floors have sleeping accommodations for 10 or 12 people, but those are used only for emergencies, not for long-term stays.

"People volunteer to work at the center for a lot of different reasons. Some have had crises and want to return the help they received during those times, and others, like me, are just interested in what goes on at such a center. Regardless of what originally drew us to the center, we all share one motivation: We care about people and want to be able to express that in an active way.

"Before starting work, the 15 people in my training group took part in over 60 hours of training. We were taught about community services and resources so that we could make effective referrals, and we were given a lot of training in counseling skills. Most of that came through role playing and watching experienced staff members while they worked. We also spent a lot of time hashing through information and our own feelings about issues such as drug use, sexuality, suicide, and rape. Through those discussions, I learned a lot about the topics and myself. As for my skills as a counselor, I'm certainly no professional, but I know a lot more about how to find and give help than I did before.

"Nights in the center can be really hectic. One night not long ago, I came in the back door at about 20 before midnight and found the two staff members on the phone and the front doorbell ringing. I answered the door and found a family of five who'd just driven into town from Texas. They'd been driving all day and, having no money, needed a place to stay for a few days. I explained that we offer only emergency housing and that they would have to start looking for other accommodations the next day. (We don't encourage or allow people to stay for more than a few days. Independence is the goal, not dependence.) After explaining a few guidelines— smoking is permitted only on the first floor, short cleanup chores were expected in the morning in exchange for staying—I showed them to a bedroom.

"When I got downstairs, one of the phones was ringing. The caller was a young woman wanting to know the effects of some pills she'd found. I looked up the drug in one of the reference books we have and told her that the drug was an antihistamine with slight sedative effects. She thanked me and then went on to tell me that she'd found the pills on her roommate's dresser. She wanted to know what they were because her roommate had been acting funny lately and she was worried about her. We talked for another half hour or so about her relationship with her roommate and the frustration and sadness connected with the whole situation. She'd called for the drug info, but I think that the real issue was something different. It often seems to work that way.

"I had only a few minutes to record the call in the log, say hello to my shift partner, and say good-bye to the two departing staffers from the previous shift before the next call came in. It was from a man who started off by saying, 'Life's really slowing down for me.' His sleepy voice seemed to echo his sentiments, and he told me that he'd now been unemployed for about three months and he and his wife had separated. He missed his kids. I recognized this caller as someone who'd called before, depressed. We talked for a few minutes about his feelings of loneliness and worthlessness, and then I ventured a question about his sleepy voice. He admitted that he'd been drinking heavily and that he'd taken a few pills too. I told him that I was concerned about the effects of both the alcohol and the pills, and he replied that he thought it was OK, especially because he wouldn't mind not waking up in the morning. We then talked about his suicidal feelings, and he expressed a lot of his hurt and depression, but at the same time, he said he didn't really want to die. Because he was sounding sleepier and sleepier, I asked him if he would feel comfortable calling a friend to take him to the emergency room to make sure the alcohol and pills weren't doing permanent damage. He was fairly open to both my concern and his ambivalence about suicide and agreed to call a friend. I encouraged him to call back the next day and let us know how he was doing. It's rare that we do a 'crisis outreach' (driving to the person), even for suicide calls. This call is an example of how we encourage people to use their own resources such as friends to help them.

"Our next caller was a police officer requesting that we send a rape counselor to the hospital. Paul, my shift partner, called one of the staffers who is specially trained in rape counseling and asked her to go to the hospital.

"The call immediately following that was from a woman at the Women's Transition Center, a shelter mainly for abused women. She was calling to let us know that one of their volunteers was coming to meet a woman who'd been beaten up by her husband earlier in the evening. Our place serves as a neutral meeting ground for the shelter's volunteers to meet with women in transition (leaving an abusive situation, divorce, etc.) before taking them to the shelter's secret location. (The location of the Women's Transition Center is kept under wraps so that angry husbands and others cannot find the women.)

"While we were waiting for the staff member from the shelter, Paul got a call from a 'regular' (a person who calls us a lot). Some of these folks are trying to work through frustrating situations, but usually the reason they call is loneliness. While Paul talked with the regular, I took a call from a person wanting to know where he could get a free blood test. It turned out that the blood test he really wanted was for HIV antibodies, so I looked up the information in our files under "AIDS" and recommended that he contact the Health Department for the cheapest, most confidential setting. Then we talked for a while about some of the AIDS myths that are floating around and about the pressures he felt because he is gay.

"It was then about 2:30, and as I was finishing up the call about AIDS, Paul answered a knock at the front door. He expected it to be the volunteer from

the women's shelter, but it turned out to be two men and a woman, all rather inebriated. When I arrived in the entry hall, our late-night visitors were trying to convince Paul to let the woman spend the night at the center to 'sleep it off.' Paul was explaining to them that we generally don't serve as a flophouse, but they were in an argumentative mood and couldn't understand why we were refusing them a place to stay. While this was going on, the woman who had been beaten up by her husband arrived to meet the person from the women's shelter. It was a bit tricky for a moment because the woman was kind of skittish, having just left a violent situation. Walking in on a group of drunk people who were talking angrily couldn't have helped her much, so I took her off to another part of the house. Paul soon convinced the three drunken characters to leave, and as they were going out the front door, there was a knock at the back door. It was a relief to find it was just the staff member from the women's shelter.

"Paul and I spent the next hour talking through the various calls and visitors and writing up our log reports. Talking over what goes on with my shift partner helps me work through contacts that were disturbing or that I feel I didn't handle well. It also gives me a chance to offer support for what my partner is doing. Because everything is kept confidential within the center, we really rely on each other for encouragement and support.

"The two women left for the women's shelter around 3:45, and then Paul and I slept on the couches until about 7:30, when I was awakened by a phone call. The caller wanted to talk about what she was going to do that day and needed a listening ear and some support as she made plans to continue her job search and write some letters. I recognized this woman as someone who'd recently been released from the state hospital and who was reentering community life. She apologized for waking me up, and we laughed a little about her escapades earlier in the kitchen as she'd tried to make an omelet. I told her before she hung up that it was good to talk with her, and I meant it. Working at this center has given me a real sense of what's important when working with people: Whatever type of crisis they're in—whether it's suicide or a burned omelet—let them know that they're understood and that someone cares. It's that kind of human contact that makes this work so fulfilling."

Because most of the discussions of treatment have involved strategies for tertiary prevention, little else needs to be said here other than to highlight the fact that although causes of disorders may be eliminated through treatment, this does not necessarily mean that the causes will not return. In too many cases, individuals who have been effectively treated (even cured) think they can go back to their old ways, but that is not the case. Just as the individual who has been effectively treated for pneumonia must continue to avoid germs, so the individual who has been effectively treated for a psychological problem must be sensitive to the factors that brought on the problem (e.g., conflict, stress, physiological factors). In other words, in working with clients, we must avoid letting them think that once a problem is solved, they can ignore it in the future. Instead, in many cases, we must build cautions about the future into our initial treatments, and we must provide follow-up treatment programs for recovered clients.

SUMMARY

- There are wide differences among mental hospitals, but they often have some of the following characteristics: admitting wards, treatment wards, open wards, closed wards, day rooms, nurses' stations, and isolation rooms. Some large hospitals may also have domiciliaries where patients who do not respond to treatment are held. Many patients live in the hospital on a 24-hour basis, but some come for either day or night hospitalization.

- The staff includes psychologists, psychiatrists, psychiatric nurses, psychological technicians (ward attendants), social workers, occupational therapists, and possibly art and music therapists. There is often little contact between patients and the professional staff.

- Hospitalized patients may initially reject but later come to accept the role of "sick and dependent patient," and once they do, they give up control and are often hesitant to leave the hospital. In fact, some patients may behave in such a way as to ensure that they will be kept in the hospital; they show symptoms or get "lost" in the system.

- There is no reliable evidence that hospitalization is more effective for reducing symptoms than alternative care outside of the hospital (outpatient treatment or living in halfway houses), which is much less expensive.

- Deinstitutionalization involves moving patients out of hospitals and into treatment in the community, and this has resulted in a drastic reduction in the number of hospitalized patients. Deinstitutionalization is designed to (a) avoid the negative aspects of hospitals ("you can't make a normal adjustment in an abnormal environment"), (b) capitalize on the positive aspects of the community (keep patients in touch with their families and social support), and (c) reduce costs. Deinstitutionalization leads to problems when adequate treatment is not provided in the community.

- Community care involves (a) outpatient clinics in large hospitals; (b) community mental health centers, which are small, conveniently located facilities that focus on outpatient treatment and day hospitalization, short-term emergency hospitalization, 24-hour-a-day emergency services, and educational and consultation services that are designed to prevent the development of disorders; (c) halfway houses, where patients can live while making the transition from a hospital to the community; and (d) home care, in which mental health workers work with patients in their homes or on the streets.

- The public is often resistant to having former mental patients living in their communities, and there may be a need for "asylums" to provide a place of refuge and protection for individuals during periods of great stress.

- The cost of treatment can be very high, often more than $1,000 a day in hospitals. In attempts to control costs, insurance companies are turning to managed health care (e.g., health maintenance organizations) in which there is an emphasis on prevention and early detection, but concern has been expressed over the possibility that treatment may be withheld in attempts to control costs.

■ Attempts at prevention are hampered by our lack of understanding of what causes some disorders and by practical, technical, and ethical problems that may limit what we are able to do. There are three types of prevention: (a) primary prevention is aimed at eliminating the causes of abnormal behavior, and it includes things such as prenatal and postnatal care, day care for children and elderly, better health care, and stress reduction; (b) secondary prevention is designed to catch problems early before they become serious, and it often involves support groups, crisis intervention programs, and training programs for individuals who are at high risk; and (c) tertiary prevention is focused on reducing relapses, and it can involve helping patients stay on their treatment programs and avoid the problems that triggered their disorders.

KEY TERMS, CONCEPTS, AND NAMES

In reviewing and testing yourself on what you have learned from this chapter, you should be able to identify and discuss each of the following.

admitting ward
art therapist
asylum
closed ward
community care
community mental health center
community psychology
crisis intervention center
day hospitalization
day room
deinstitutionalization
domiciliary
halfway house

health maintenance organization
  (HMO)
impression management
institutionalization syndrome
intensive treatment ward
isolation room
managed health care
music therapist
night hospitalization
nurses' station
occupational therapist
open ward
outpatient clinic

primary-care physician
primary prevention
psychiatric nurse
psychiatrist
psychological technician
psychologist
secondary prevention
social worker
support group
tertiary prevention
total institution

GLOSSARY

abuse (drug) Use of a drug leading to clinically significant impairment or distress.

active phase The phase in the course of schizophrenia when the symptoms are clearest and most pronounced.

acute stress disorder An anxiety disorder lasting from several days to a month that is triggered by a stressor. Of interest because it may provide the basis for a later posttraumatic stress disorder.

Adler, Alfred A neo-Freudian who believed that stress and anxiety stemmed from feelings of inferiority.

admitting ward The ward of a mental hospital to which new patients are admitted while diagnoses and treatment plans are being made.

adoptee studies (in genetics) A method by which the genetic contribution to a disorder is measured by comparing the prevalence of the disorder among biological children of people with the disorder who are raised by their biological parents with that of those raised by adoptive parents who do not have the disorder.

aerobic exercise Exercise—including jogging, swimming, cycling, and others—that elevates heart rate to 70% of its maximum for at least 20 minutes.

aerobic fitness A measure of physical fitness based on the efficiency with which the body processes oxygen.

agitated depression Depression characterized by high levels of aimless activity such as pacing.

agoraphobia A disorder characterized by fear of being in situations in which escape might be difficult if symptoms of panic occurred.

agranulocytosis A disease involving the immune system that is sometimes a side effect of taking Clozaril.

AIDS (acquired immune deficiency syndrome). See **HIV.**

akathisia The inability to sit still, a side effect of some drugs.

alcohol A major depressant developed through fermentation of sugar in fruit or grains.

all-or-none principle The principle whereby stimulation of a nerve cell either does or does not cause it to fire.

Alzheimer's disease A type of dementia in which the major symptom is the loss of short-term memory followed by the loss of long-term memory.

amenorrhea Cessation of menstruation, often associated with anorexia.

American Law Institute rule A somewhat flexible rule for defining insanity.

amine hypothesis A hypothesis suggesting that a disorder (e.g., depression) is caused by a problem with a neurotransmitter (e.g., a catecholamine).

amines A class of neurotransmitters.

amnesia disorders Disorders in which the major symptom is a problem with memory; either the individual cannot recall previously known things or cannot put new information into memory.

amok A disorder in which an individual (usually male) broods for a brief period, goes into what appears to be an uncontrolled frenzy and indiscriminately kills people, and then usually kills himself.

amphetamine psychoses Abnormal behavior (usually revolving around delusions) resulting from high doses of amphetamines.

amphetamines A class of stimulants.

amygdala An area of the brain, responsible for aggression; part of the limbic system.

Anafranil (clomipramine) An antidepressant that is often used successfully for treating the obsessive-compulsive disorder.

analogue research Research in which variables or populations similar but not identical to those of interest are studied. Often done to avoid technical or ethical problems.

anal stage The second of Freud's stages of psychosexual development; important for the development of needs for cleanliness, order, and other habits.

analyst A psychotherapist who is trained in and uses the technique of psychoanalysis.

androgens Hormones that result in male characteristics.

aneurysm A weak spot in an artery that bursts, causing a heart attack or stroke.

anger turned inward One of Freud's explanations for depression.

angina Pain around the heart and left shoulder caused by reduced blood supply to the heart muscle.

angioplasty A surgical procedure in which a flexible tube with a balloon on the end is inserted into an artery that has been narrowed by the buildup of plaque. The balloon is inflated to compress the plaque against the sides of the artery in order to permit greater blood flow.

Anna O. A patient of Josef Breuer's whose treatment played an important role in Freud's early theorizing about abnormal behavior.

anorexia nervosa An eating disorder, the major symptom of which is the refusal to eat enough to maintain appropriate body weight.

anoxia Lack of oxygen; if it occurs during birth, brain damage can result.

anterograde amnesia The inability to put new information into memory.

antiandrogens Drugs that suppress androgens and are sometimes used in the treatment of sexual disorders. The best known is Depo-Provera.

anticonvulsive drugs A class of drugs sometimes used to treat the bipolar disorder.

antidepressant Medication used to treat depression. Types include bicyclics, tricyclics, and MAO inhibitors.

antigens "Foreign" substances in the body that result in increased activity of the immune system.

antisocial personality disorder (APD) A personality disorder in which the individual lacks anxiety (or a conscience) and consequently engages in antisocial behavior.

anxiety An emotional response characterized by apprehension, tension, physiological arousal (e.g., elevated heart rate, blood pressure, and muscular tension), and restlessness.

anxiety disorders A group of disorders including agoraphobia, social phobia, specific phobias, generalized anxiety disorder, panic disorder, obsessive-compulsive disorder, posttraumatic stress disorder, and acute stress disorder.

anxiety states Disorders in which anxiety is excessively high, diffused, and not limited to specific situations. (Contrast with **phobic disorders.**)

aphasia An inability to recall names or words.

apnea A brief cessation of breathing that results in oxygen deprivation and will awaken a sleeping individual; often the cause of a sleep disorder.

arousal disorder A sexual dysfunction in which the individual cannot achieve or maintain sexual arousal despite the presence of sexual desire.

arousal transference The idea that arousal can be transferred across different emotions, for example, from fear to sexual arousal.

arteriosclerosis The process by which arteries lose their elasticity ("hardening of the arteries").

arthritis A disorder characterized by pain in the joints that is caused by the destruction of the membrane that covers the joints.

art therapist An individual who works with patients, using art as a medium for interacting and relating.

Asperger's disorder A disorder with many of the symptoms of autism, but not involving problems with communication or delays in language development; the problems with motor behavior are often characterized as a general clumsiness.

associative intrusions Inappropriate associations that interfere with normal thought processes (see, for example, **clang associations**). Believed to be important in the thought disorders associated with schizophrenia.

associative network theory of memory The theory that related memories are stored in networks and that the stimulation of a network will result in the recall of the memories in that network.

asylum A place of refuge. The term was once used to refer to a mental hospital.

atherosclerosis A cardiovascular disease characterized by the buildup of fats on the walls of blood vessels, which reduces blood flow.

atrophy A loss or deterioration of nerve cells, often seen in the brains of individuals suffering from schizophrenia.

attention-deficit/hyperactivity disorder (ADHD) A disorder of childhood in which the major symptoms are a high level of activity and the inability to maintain attention.

atypical neuroleptics Drugs used to treat schizophrenia that are selective in the blocking of dopamine receptors sites and that increase the level of serotonin at synapses.

autistic disorder A developmental disorder of infancy and childhood that appears shortly after birth and involves a lack of responsiveness to others, impairment in verbal and nonverbal skills, and a greatly restricted repertory of activities and interests.

autoerotic asphyxiation Accidental death that occurs when an individual attempts to achieve sexual arousal by depriving himself or herself of oxygen.

autonomic division A division of the peripheral nervous system involving connections to glands and organs.

aversion therapy Treatment based on classical conditioning in which unpleasant consequences (shock, nausea) are paired with a stimulus or an activity (fetish object, drinking) so that eventually the stimulus or activity will elicit anxiety and be avoided.

aversive procedures See **aversion therapy.**

avoidance conditioning A procedure whereby a stimulus is paired with negative consequences; through a combination of classical and operant conditioning, the individual learns to avoid the stimulus.

avoidant personality disorder A personality disorder in which the individual is especially sensitive to social rejection and humiliation and therefore avoids other people.

avoidant thinking A strategy by which a person avoids anxiety by intentionally not thinking about an anxiety-provoking object or situation.

Axis I: Clinical Syndromes A diagnostic category used to identify the major disorders (e.g., anxiety state, schizophrenia).

Axis II: Personality Disorders and Mental Retardation A diagnostic category used to identify disorders of personality and mental retardation.

Axis III: General Medical Conditions A diagnostic category used to indicate whether there are any medical conditions that might influence a disorder.

Axis IV: Psychosocial and Environmental Problems A diagnostic category used to indicate whether there are any social or environmental stressors that might influence a disorder.

Axis V: Global Assessment of Functioning A diagnostic category rating current level of functioning and highest level of functioning in the past year so that potential for improvement can be assessed.

axon The arm of a nerve cell, down which the impulse travels.

barbiturate A type of depressant drug; an early form of tranquilizer.

baroreceptors Stretch-sensitive receptors around arteries coming from the heart that detect increases in blood pressure. Important in the development of hypertension.

basal ganglia Structures in the midbrain that control motor movements.

Beck, Aaron A theorist who developed cognitive therapy.

behavior modification An approach to changing behaviors that is based on conditioning.

behavioral contagion A process by which inhibitions related to certain behaviors are reduced by observing another person perform the behavior without negative consequences.

behavior therapy The use of the principles of learning to change behavior, such as rewarding individuals for normal behavior.

behaviorism An explanation for behavior developed by John B. Watson, based on classical and operant conditioning, in which attention is given only to observable factors.

bell-and-pad procedure A procedure for treating enuresis. A moisture-sensitive pad is placed on the mattress, and when a child urinates during sleep, the pad detects the urine and sets off a bell, which awakens the child.

benzodiazepines A class of drugs used to reduce anxiety by increasing levels of GABA activity. The best-known drug of this type is Valium.

beta blockers A class of drugs used to reduce heart rate.

bicyclics A type of antidepressant drug, the chemical structure of which has the form of two circles (see also **Prozac**).

Binet, Alfred The developer of one of the first tests of intelligence, used to predict academic performance.

binge type of alcoholism A drinking pattern characterized by relatively short periods of uncontrolled high levels of drinking separated by periods of nondrinking. (Contrast with **persistent type of alcoholism.**)

biofeedback training A procedure in which an individual is given immediate feedback about changes in some physiological response (e.g., heart rate, blood pressure, muscle tension) so that the person can learn to control the response.

biological traumas Prenatal and perinatal complications that can lead to abnormal conditions such as schizophrenia.

bipolar disorder A mood disorder in which mood fluctuates between mania and depression. Formerly called *manic-depressive disorder.*

Bleuler, Eugen The theorist who coined the term *schizophrenia* and suggested that the disorder stemmed from a breakdown in mental associations.

blocking agents Drugs that have their effect (reducing neural transmission) by blocking the receptor sites on the postsynaptic neuron so that the neuron cannot be stimulated.

blocking approach to (drug) treatment The use of a drug (e.g., naloxone) to block the positive effects of drugs that are being abused.

body dysmorphic disorder A somatoform disorder in which the individual is preoccupied with some imagined defect in his or her appearance.

borderline personality disorder A personality disorder characterized by serious instability. The diversity of symptoms seen in this disorder suggests that it borders on or overlaps with numerous other disorders.

brain stem A part of the brain, situated at its base, that controls basic physiological functions and generates arousal.

breathing-related sleep disorder See **apnea.**

Breuer, Josef An early colleague of Sigmund Freud. Probably best known because of his patient Anna O.

brief psychotic disorder A disorder usually involving florid symptoms of schizophrenia and sometimes stemming from overwhelming stress; the symptoms remit anywhere from a few hours to 4 weeks after onset.

bulimia nervosa An eating disorder, the major symptom of which is binge eating followed by self-induced purges (e.g., vomiting or excessive use of laxatives).

bundling A practice of "packaging" two treatments or procedures together, as in pairing Clozapine with blood tests for immune system functioning.

burned-out phase A stage of schizophrenia in which persons who have suffered for many years no longer show the major symptoms of the disorder but show great personal deterioration, due perhaps in part to their institutionalization and social isolation.

caffeine A stimulant, the strongest in a group known as methylxanthines.

cannabinoids The active ingredients in cannabis (marijuana).

cannabis   A mild hallucinogen; marijuana.

Cannon-Bard theory of emotion   A theory suggesting that emotions lead to physiological responses. (Contrast with **James-Lange theory of emotion.**)

case study research   Research based on the intensive study of one individual. In case study research, generalizations and conclusions concerning cause cannot be made.

catabolism   A process by which enzymes destroy neurotransmitters.

catatonic schizophrenia   A rare type of schizophrenia usually characterized by lack of motor movement or "waxy flexibility."

catecholamines   A class of neurotransmitters that includes norepinephrine and dopamine.

catecholamine hypothesis (of depression)   The hypothesis that depression is due to low levels of neurotransmitters of the catecholamine type.

catharsis   A release of tension, often by talking about a problem.

caudate nucleus   An area of the brain that plays a role in motor functions and the obsessive-compulsive disorder.

central apnea   Cessations in breathing (leading to a sleeper's awakening) caused by problems in the central nervous system. (Contrast with **obstructive apnea.**)

central nervous system   A division of the nervous system comprising the brain and spinal cord.

cerebral infarction   Death of brain cells due to lack of blood supply. Some forms of dementia in elderly persons are due to multiple cerebral infarctions. Also known as *stroke.*

cerebrum   The upper area of the brain that contains the cortex and where thinking is done.

Charcot, Jean-Martin   A 19th-century physician who thought that somatoform (hysterical) disorders were due to a weak nervous system and who treated them with suggestion (hypnosis).

Charles Bonnet syndrome   A disorder involving problems in the visual pathway in the brain which lead to vivid hallucinations in the absence of other psychiatric symptoms.

checklists of symptoms   An alternative to using diagnostic labels for describing persons.

Children's Apperception Test (CAT)   A projective test like the TAT designed especially for children.

cholesterol   Fats which at high levels can lead to coronary artery disease and which at low levels can lead to suicide because they are linked to low levels of serotonin.

cingulate gyrus   An area of the brain that is sometimes operated upon in very serious cases of the obsessive-compulsive disorder (OCD).

cingulotomy   An operation in which the cingulate gyrus is removed.

circadian rhythm   The normal daily pattern of wakefulness and sleep.

circadian rhythm sleep disorder   A disorder involving a mismatch between the timing of an individual's natural sleep-wake cycle and the demands made on the individual by the circumstances in which he or she lives.

clang associations   Associations based on a rhyme (*bug, dug; clown, frown*) that can result in the intrusion of new thoughts. Clang associations are thought to influence the thought disorders of persons with schizophrenia.

classical conditioning   Conditioning in which a neutral stimulus (e.g., a bell) is consistently paired with a particular response (e.g., salivation) so that in time the previously neutral stimulus will elicit the response. The process was originally identified by Ivan Pavlov.

client-centered psychotherapy   A form of psychotherapy, derived from a humanistic position, in which the goal is to establish a nurturant environment in which the client can grow personally.

clinical psychologist   A person with advanced training (PhD, PsyD) in the care and treatment of persons with mental disorders.

clinical significance   The practical significance of a research finding. (Contrast with **statistical significance.**)

clitoral shaft   A female sex structure containing erectile tissue that, during sexual excitement, fills with blood, causing swelling and increasing the sensitivity of the clitoris.

clitoris   A highly sensitive body of tissues located above a woman's vaginal opening. Its stimulation is important for reaching orgasm.

closed ward   A ward of a mental hospital reserved for highly disturbed patients who are not allowed to leave the ward.

Clozaril (clozapine)   An atypical neuroleptic that relieves negative as well as positive symptoms with fewer side effects than other neuroleptics.

cocaine (cocaine hydrochloride)   A stimulant derived from the leaves of the coca plant. It can reduce pain by blocking nerve impulses down the axon, and it causes a "high" by reducing the reuptake of neurotransmitters.

codeine   One of the active ingredients in opium; less powerful than morphine.

cognitive abulia   Inability to hold a memory long enough to transform it into purposeful action; seen in Alzheimer's disease.

cognitive anxiety   Symptoms of anxiety associated with arousing thoughts rather than somatic arousal.

cognitive diathesis-stress explanation   The notion that negative cognitions in combination with stress lead to depression.

cognitive disorders   Problems in cognitive functioning that are due to underlying physiological problems.

cognitive explanation   The view that abnormal behavior results from erroneous beliefs and from disruptions of thought processes.

cognitive flooding   A technique for treating anxiety in which the person is directed to think about the objects or situations that elicit anxiety. When the thoughts are not followed by the expected dire consequences, it is believed that the anxiety response will extinguish.

cognitive rigidity   Failure to consider alternatives, often seen in persons who are suicidal.

cognitive therapy   An approach to treatment in which an attempt is made to change the way a person thinks about situations (i.e., change cognitive sets) and thereby change behavior.

community care   An arrangement whereby persons suffering from abnormal behavior are treated in the community on an outpatient basis rather than in a hospital.

community mental health center   A small, conveniently located, usually nonresidential treatment center. Its goal is to provide early, easily accessible care and prevention programs.

community psychology   The branch of clinical psychology concerned with changing communities as a means of preventing abnormal behavior.

comorbidity   The co-occurrence of two or more disorders in an individual at one time.

compensation   A defense mechanism in which the individual works especially hard to overcome a weakness that provokes anxiety.

compulsion   An irresistible impulse to engage repeatedly in some act, usually maladaptive.

computerized axial tomography (CT scan)   A type of X-ray of the brain showing successive "slices" of the brain.

concordance rate   The rate of co-occurrence of a disorder in specific pairs of persons, usually monozygotic or dizygotic twins.

conditioned stimulus   A previously neutral stimulus that after classical conditioning occurs is able to elicit the conditioned response.

conduct disorders   A group of disorders involving extreme misbehavior; should be differentiated from the antisocial personality disorder.

confounding   The changing of more than one independent variable in an experiment so that it cannot be determined which variable is responsible for changes in the dependent variable.

conscious mind   One of the levels of consciousness, according to Freud. (Contrast with **unconscious** and **preconscious.**)

control condition   The condition in an experiment in which everything is identical to the experimental condition except that the independent variable is not manipulated.

controlled experimental research   Research involving experimental and control conditions. Conclusions concerning cause can be drawn from this type of research.

conversion disorder   A disorder in which the individual has one or more major physical symptoms for which an organic basis cannot be found. The symptoms usually impair functioning.

coping   A constructive means of dealing with stress, as compared to using defense mechanisms.

coping strategies   Constructive, adaptive means of dealing with stress.

coprolalia   The speaking or yelling of obscenities that sometimes occurs as part of Tourette's disorder.

coronary artery disease   A disease process in which blood flow to the muscles of the heart is reduced due to buildup of plaque (cholesterol) on the walls of the arteries.

coronary bypass surgery Surgery in which a piece of artery is grafted onto another artery so that blood flow can bypass an occluded area.

correction approach to (drug) treatment Treatment designed to overcome the underlying psychological problem that leads to drug abuse.

correlational research Research based on correlations. Conclusions concerning causation cannot be drawn from this type of research.

correlation coefficient (*r*) A statistic that reflects the degree to which two variables covary (increase or decrease together).

cortex A thin layer of cells in the cerebrum in which high functions such as thinking are done.

cortical atrophy Deterioration of the cortex of the brain.

cortisol A hormone produced by the adrenal gland during stress that in turn causes an increase in the productions of glucose.

counterconditioning See **systematic desensitization.**

covert suicide Suicide disguised to appear as an accident or natural death.

craft palsies Term once used to refer to conversion disorders that interfered with occupational functioning.

cretinism (hypothyroidism) Slowed metabolism and development, usually due to a recessive gene that interferes with the production of thyroxin. Symptoms include short stature and mental retardation.

crisis intervention center A health care center offering programs designed to reduce stress during crises and thereby prevent the development of abnormal behavior.

cross-dressing Dressing in the clothes of the opposite sex to gain sexual gratification.

cross-tolerance Development of tolerance for one drug resulting in tolerance for another drug in the same class.

current self The current level of functioning, according to humanists. Contrast with **ideal self.**

cycle of sleep The progression from Stage 1 through Stage 4 sleep and then a return from Stage 4 to Stage 1.

cyclothymic disorder A less severe form of the bipolar disorder.

dancing manias Mass psychogenic illnesses involving jerking movements, most frequently noted in 15th and 16th centuries.

day hospitalization An arrangement whereby patients are treated in the hospital during the day but sent home at night.

day room A room in a hospital where patients spend their days, usually watching television.

death instinct Freud's proposed counterbalance to the life instinct; the term is sometimes used to explain suicide.

decision tree In the DSM, a step-by-step guide to making a diagnosis.

defense mechanisms Strategies (e.g., repression, displacement) by which persons reduce anxiety without dealing with the cause of the anxiety.

deficit in classical conditioning The idea that persons with the antisocial personality disorder are limited in their ability to develop classically conditioned responses and therefore do not develop anxiety.

deinstitutionalization A movement begun in the late 1960s to move patients out of hospitals and treat them in the community.

delayed development The idea that mild mental retardation is due to slowed development rather than to a mental defect.

delayed neurological development The idea that the low level of cortical arousal in persons with the antisocial personality disorder (which is similar to that seen in young children) is due to a delay in development.

delirium disorders Disorders characterized by disturbances in consciousness and resulting in problems with awareness, attention, memory, language, and perception.

delirium tremens A disorder occurring when alcohol is withdrawn from a person used to high levels of it. Symptoms include delirium and uncontrollable muscle tremors.

delusion A bizarre belief that is held despite strong evidence to the contrary; a symptom often seen in schizophrenia.

delusional disorder A disorder in which the only symptom is a delusion, usually of persecution; formerly called *paranoid disorder.*

demand characteristics The pressures in a situation to behave in a specific way (e.g., to behave like a patient while in a hospital).

dementia disorders Disorders in which the symptoms revolve primarily around problems with memory.

dementia praecox A term once used to describe schizophrenia, referring to an early deterioration of cognitive abilities.

demonology The traditional belief that abnormal behavior is due to possession by demons.

dendrite A treelike structure that radiates outward from the body of a nerve cell.

denial A defense mechanism in which the person reinterprets an anxiety-provoking situation by redefining it as nonthreatening.

dependence The need to take a drug to avoid withdrawal symptoms.

dependent personality disorder A personality disorder in which the individual allows other persons to make decisions for him or her.

dependent variable The variable in an experiment that is influenced by the independent variable.

depersonalization disorder A dissociative disorder in which for brief periods individuals experience distortions of the self (e.g., feeling as if their extremities have changed in size or as if they are out of their bodies).

Depo-Provera An antiandrogen drug used to reduce sexual desire.

depressants A class of drugs, including alcohol, barbiturates, and benzodiazepines, the major effect of which is to reduce neurological activity.

depression An emotional response characterized by feelings of hopelessness and sadness, low self-esteem, pessimism, reduced motivation, slowed thought processes, psychomotor retardation or agitation, and disturbances of sleep, appetite, and sexual arousal.

depression with postpartum onset Depression that occurs shortly after a woman gives birth.

depression with seasonal pattern The diagnostic label for the *seasonal affective disorder (SAD).*

depressive disorder A mood disorder characterized by depression.

desire disorder A sexual dysfunction characterized by a lack of sexual desire; if stimulated sufficiently, however, the individual can achieve sexual arousal.

developmental approach to personality The idea that persons go through stages of psychosexual development (oral, anal, phallic, latency, genital).

developmental disorders A group of disorders beginning in infancy or childhood, including the pervasive disorder of autism and specific developmental disorders (language, academic, and motor skills).

deviance from cultural norms One of the factors that is sometimes used to define abnormal behavior.

dexamethasone suppression test (DST) A test used to determine whether depression is endogenous or exogenous.

Dexedrine (dextroamphetamine) A stimulant; sometimes used to treat the attention-deficit/hyperactivity disorder.

dhat A disorder occurring primarily in India that involves numerous somatic complaints—such as a decline in semen production, weakness, and fatigue—and the belief that the symptoms are due to a decline of a vital fluid (*sukra*) in the body.

diagnostic system The symptoms and procedures used for making psychiatric diagnoses contained in the DSM.

diastolic blood pressure The level of pressure in the circulatory system between beats of the heart; usually 80 mm Hg.

diathesis A predisposition, usually thought to be physiological.

diathesis-stress hypothesis The idea that a person may be predisposed to develop a disorder and that the disorder will become manifest when the person is exposed to a triggering stress.

diazepam (Valium) A benzodiazepine that is widely used to treat anxiety.

disability One of the factors that is sometimes used to define abnormal behavior.

disorganization A type of positive symptom in schizophrenia that consists of thought disorders, bizarre behaviors, and inappropriate affect.

disorganized schizophrenia The type of schizophrenia showing the most psychological disorganization and lacking a systematic set of delusions.

displacement A defense mechanism with two forms. In *object displacement,* an emotion is transferred from one object to another because the expression of the emotion with the original object is threatening. In *drive displacement,* an unacceptable drive is converted into an acceptable one.

disrupted cognitive processes Problems with thinking, in contrast to distortions in cognitive content.

disruptive behavior disorders A group of disorders of infancy, childhood, and adolescence including the attention-deficit/hyperactivity disorder and the conduct disorders.

dissociative amnesia A dissociative disorder involving a loss of memory due to psychological stress.

dissociative disorders A group of disorders involving a disturbance of the integrative functions of memory, identity, and consciousness. Disorders include dissociative amnesia, dissociative fugue, dissociative identity disorder, and depersonalization. Questions have been raised about the existence of dissociative disorders as they are traditionally described.

dissociative fugue A dissociative disorder in which the individual does not recall his or her previous experiences and forms a new identity.

dissociative identity disorder The diagnostic label that has replaced *multiple personality disorder.*

distortions of memories The alteration of memories by subsequent events.

distraction A strategy for reducing anxiety by diverting attention away from the anxiety-provoking factor; also a process thought to be responsible for the thought disturbance in schizophrenia.

distress One of the factors that is sometimes used to define abnormal behavior.

disturbed sleep A symptom often associated with depression and usually involving early morning awakening.

diuretic A drug given to reduce blood pressure by reducing the volume of bodily fluids.

Dix, Dorothea A 19th-century reformer who worked to raise funds for mental hospitals.

dizygotic (fraternal) twins Nonidentical twins who do not have identical sets of genes.

domiciliaries Wards in psychiatric hospitals that are used simply to hold patients who do not respond to treatment.

dopamine A neurotransmitter. High levels of dopamine activity are associated with schizophrenia; low levels are associated with Parkinson's disease.

dopamine explanation for schizophrenia The notion that schizophrenia is due to excessive levels of dopamine activity.

dose-dependent Having different effects at different dose levels.

dose-response relationship The fact that a drug can have different effects at different dosage levels.

double-bind hypothesis A hypothesis suggesting that schizophrenia stems from childhood experiences in which persons receive contradictory messages and then give irrelevant responses to avoid giving wrong responses.

double-blind procedure A procedure used in experimental research in which neither the subject nor the experimenter knows whether the subject has been exposed to the experimental procedure or the control procedure. This approach reduces bias.

Down syndrome Mental retardation caused by an extra number 21 chromosome.

Draw-A-Person Test A projective test in which personality interpretations are based on the client's drawing of persons.

dream interpretation A technique used in psychoanalysis to uncover unconscious material, involving analysis of the latent and manifest content of dreams.

drive displacement A process (sometimes a defense) by which an individual converts one drive into another.

drug prophylaxis The practice of keeping a patient on a maintenance dose of a drug to prevent relapse.

DSM-IV The fourth edition of the *Diagnostic and Statistical Manual of Mental Disorders,* published by the American Psychiatric Association in 1994.

duodenal ulcers Holes in the lining of the duodenum (first part of small intestine) caused by high levels of gastric acid.

"duty to protect" principle A rule stating that therapists have the duty to warn individuals if they are in danger from a person in therapy.

dyssomnias Disorders that involve problems with the amount, quality, or timing of sleep.

dysthymic disorder A less severe version of the depressive disorder.

echolalia A symptom of infantile autism in which the child repeats whatever is said to him or her.

ego The executive or mediating component in Freud's structural approach to personality.

ego psychology A revision of Freud's theory, suggested by his followers, that emphasizes cognitive processes over drives.

elbow rule A standard used to identify crimes that result from an irresistible impulse: Would the person have committed the crime if a police officer had been standing at his or her elbow?

Electra complex Freud's term for the attraction a young girl feels toward her father.

electroconvulsive therapy (ECT) A treatment for depression in which an electrical charge is passed through the brain, causing convulsions.

electroencephalograph (EEG) A device for measuring the electrical activity of the brain.

electromyographic (EMG) biofeedback training A procedure in which persons are given feedback concerning muscle activity and then use the feedback to learn to relax muscles or regain control of muscles after a stroke or an accident.

embolism A clot that blocks blood flow through an artery.

emergency (involuntary) hospitalization The hospitalization of a person thought to be a danger to him- or herself or to others.

encopresis An elimination disorder in which the symptom is the inability to control bowel movements.

endogenous depression Depression due to physiological factors.

endorphins Opiatelike substances produced by the body that serve to reduce synaptic transmission and reduce pain.

enlarged ventricles A widening of the ventricles (ducts through the brain) that is often associated with schizophrenia, particularly in patients with negative symptoms.

enuresis An elimination disorder in which the symptom is the inability to achieve bladder control.

epinephrine A circulating catecholamine. Also called *adrenaline.*

erectile tissue Tissue in the penis and clitoris that fills with blood during sexual arousal.

erroneous beliefs Inaccurate beliefs (e.g., "All spiders are dangerous"; "I am a bad person") that can lead to abnormal behaviors.

erroneous expectations Inaccurate expectations (e.g., "I will always fail") that can lead to abnormal behaviors.

essential hypertension High blood pressure due to psychological factors. Also known as *primary hypertension.*

exhibitionism A paraphilia in which sexual gratification is derived from exposing the genitals.

exogenous depression Depression due to psychosocial factors.

experimental condition The condition in an experiment in which the independent variable is manipulated.

experimental manipulation The changing of the independent variable to see if it influences the dependent variable.

experimental research A research strategy in which an independent variable is manipulated in an experimental condition but not the control condition, and consequent effects on the dependent variable are measured.

exposure with response prevention A cognitive approach to the treatment of the obsessive-compulsive disorder in which the individual is prevented from performing his or her ritual.

extinction Elimination of a classically conditioned response by the repeated presentation of the conditioned stimulus without the unconditioned stimulus, or elimination of an operantly conditioned response by no longer presenting the reward after the response.

extrapyramidal symptoms Motor behaviors such as twitches that are sometimes side effects of neuroleptic drugs.

factitious disorder Faking symptoms for some personal reason.

false memories Memories that are not true but have been implanted by suggestion, are thought to be true, and sometimes influence behavior.

family studies (in genetics) A means of determining the genetic contribution to a disorder by studying the degree to which biologically related relatives (as contrasted with nonbiologically related relatives) have the disorder.

family system explanation The notion that abnormal behavior is due to problems with how the family interacts.

family therapy A treatment strategy whereby an attempt is made to overcome problems in the family (e.g., stress) that contribute to disorders.

feelings of inferiority An factor believed by Alfred Adler to be important in the understanding of stress and anxiety.

fetal alcohol syndrome (FAS) Mental retardation that results from the mother's drinking alcohol while pregnant.

fetishism A paraphilia in which sexual gratification is derived from a nonhuman object (e.g., a shoe).

filter mechanism A hypothetical mechanism that is responsible for screening out stimulation; thought not to be operating in schizophrenia.

fixated Remaining at one stage of psychosexual development, and consequently showing abnormal behavior for one's age.

flashback Recurrence of an LSD experience without current ingestion of the drug; occurs in persons who have taken LSD repeatedly on previous occasions.

flooding A technique for treating anxiety in which the individual is asked to imagine a fear-provoking (phobic) stimulus. Negative consequences do not follow, thus permitting the fear response to extinguish.

free association A technique in which an individual talks about whatever comes to mind without censoring thoughts; developed by Freud and used in psychoanalysis to expose unconscious thoughts.

Freud, Anna The daughter of Sigmund Freud, who carried on her father's work but emphasized the role of the ego and defenses.

Freud, Sigmund The founder of the psychoanalytic approach to personality and abnormal behavior.

frontal lobes Areas of the brain in which integration of thoughts and feelings takes place. High and low levels of activity in the frontal lobes can lead to symptoms of schizophrenia.

frotteurism A paraphilia in which sexual gratification is derived from rubbing against another person.

GABA A neurotransmitter (gamma-aminobutyric acid) that is important for the functioning of inhibitory neurons. Low levels of GABA activity are associated with high levels of anxiety.

gastric ulcers Holes in the lining of the stomach due to low levels of protective mucus.

gender identity disorder A disorder in which the individual has a strong cross-gender identification, accompanied by persistent and intense distress about his or her physiological sex.

generalization The phenomenon whereby once classical conditioning has occurred, a stimulus similar to the conditioned stimulus can elicit the response.

generalized anxiety disorder A disorder in which the individual is anxious regardless of the stimulus situation; the anxiety is said to be "free-floating."

genital stage The last of Freud's stages of psychosexual development.

German measles See **rubella.**

glans The tip of the clitoris.

glove anesthesia A conversion disorder in which the person loses feeling in the hand.

glucose A sugar that is used for energy throughout the body.

glucose metabolism The use of glucose for cell activity, the measurement of which can be used for diagnostic purposes.

gonadotropins Hormones released by the pituitary gland that stimulate the testes to produce testosterone, resulting in sexual arousal.

granulovacuolar degeneration A condition involving small holes in the bodies of nerves that result in a general deterioration. Seen in persons with Alzheimer's disease.

group psychotherapy An approach to treatment in which several clients are seen simultaneously by one therapist.

G spot An area in the vagina that is allegedly highly sensitive to stimulation.

"guilty but mentally ill" rule A court ruling under which a defendant is found to be mentally ill and is treated; once treatment is completed, the defendant is punished for the crime that was committed while he or she was disturbed.

habit strength intrusions Thought intrusions based on sets of words that are frequently used together (e.g., "When it rains, it pours"), which may trigger inappropriate new thoughts.

Haldol (haloperidol) A widely used neuroleptic.

half-life The amount of time it takes for half of a drug to be eliminated from the body.

halfway house A small residential facility in which persons live while making the transition from hospital to community.

hallucinations Sensory experiences (e.g., sounds, feelings, or smells) that have no basis in reality.

hallucinogens Drugs, such as LSD, that cause perceptual distortions.

Halstead-Reitan Neuropsychology Battery A test used to identify the extent and nature of impairment due to brain damage.

hashish The dried resin from the top of the female marijuana plant. Has stronger effects than marijuana.

hash oil A concentrated form of hashish.

HDL (high-density lipoprotein) The "good" type of cholesterol, which carries LDL (low-density lipoprotein) away before it can occlude an artery.

health maintenance organization (HMO) An insurance organization from which you buy coverage for physical and psychological health problems; patients are treated by members of the organization, and the emphasis is on preventive care.

health psychology An area of psychology devoted to the influence of psychological factors on health and illness.

helper cells Cells in the immune system that identify antigens and signal the lymph nodes to produce killer cells.

hemispheric dominance An explanation for the finding that conversion symptoms tend to be on the left side of the body.

heroin A semisynthetic narcotic based on opium; it is rapidly delivered to the brain, where it is changed into morphine.

high-functioning individuals (with autism) Those individuals with mild cases of autism who are able to function in the community.

high-potency neuroleptics Neuroleptic drugs that are very effective for blocking dopamine but can cause serious side effects.

hippocampus An area of the brain that is crucial for processing information and that may be damaged in schizophrenia; part of the limbic system.

Hippocrates An early Greek physician who suggested that abnormal behavior stemmed from an imbalance of humors (fluids) in the body.

histrionic personality disorder A disorder characterized by seductiveness, need for attention, and emotional shallowness.

HIV The human immunodeficiency virus that causes AIDS; the virus kills lymphocytes instead of being killed by them.

hopelessness An attitude of despair that is symptomatic of depression and may lead to suicide.

hormones Fluids secreted by glands into the bloodstream that influence behavior, usually through stimulation.

Horney, Karen A neo-Freudian who emphasized interactions with other people as the cause of stress and anxiety.

hostility The important factor in the Type A behavior pattern in terms of the development of coronary artery disease.

House-Tree-Person Test A projective test in which inferences about personality are based on how a person draws a house, a tree, and a person.

humane care An approach to dealing with individuals with mental disorders that originated in the 16th century and involved treating people with such disorders as patients who needed help.

humanistic explanation An explanation for abnormal behavior that is based on the notion that the behavior of human beings is due to conscious choices and motivated by a desire to achieve enhanced levels of personal fulfillment.

humors (bodily fluids) In medieval psychology and physiology, four fluids in the body, the proportions of which were thought to determine a person's behavior, temperament, and health.

hypertension High blood pressure, usually defined as systolic pressure over 140 mm Hg or diastolic pressure over 90 mm Hg.

hyperventilation Rapid, shallow breathing that can lead to feelings of light-headedness and anxiety.

hypnotics Drugs that are used to help individuals sleep.

hypoactive sexual desire disorder A disorder involving reduced sexual desire.

hypochondriasis A somatoform disorder characterized by excessive concern over minor physical ills.

hypofrontality hypothesis The hypothesis that the negative symptoms of schizophrenia are due to low levels of activity in the frontal lobes of the brain.

hypotension Low blood pressure.

hypothalamus An area of the brain responsible for bodily processes such as eating, drinking, sleeping, and sexual behavior.

hysterical disorders (hysteria) An earlier term for what today are referred to as somatoform and dissociative disorders.

iatrogenic disorders Disorders that are introduced inadvertently in the course of treatment for other disorders.

ICD-10 The *International Classification of Disease,* 10th Edition.

id In Freud's structural approach to personality, the source of all energy and drives.

ideal self The self toward which the humanists believe all people strive; self-actualization.

identification A defense mechanism in which an individual takes on the characteristics of another person so as to be like that person.

immune system The bodily system that fights disease. Psychological stress can suppress its operation.

immunocompetence The degree of responsiveness of the immune system.

impression management Methods used by hospitalized patients to gain some control over their circumstances.

impulse control disorders A group of personality disorders that includes kleptomania, pyromania, and pathological gambling.

incompetent to stand trial A court ruling that an individual cannot understand the charges or cannot effectively participate in his or her own defense. The trial is then postponed until the person is judged competent.

Incomplete Sentences Test A projective test in which inferences about personality are based on how a person completes sentences (e.g., "What I hate most is . . .").

independent variable The variable that is manipulated and whose effects are studied in an experiment.

information processing The process by which the sensory memory, short-term memory, long-term memory, and memory networks influence the storage and retrieval of information.

inhibitory neurons Neurons the firing of which inhibits the firing of other neurons. Low levels of inhibitory neuron activity are associated with anxiety.

insanity defense A legal defense claiming the defendant is not responsible for a criminal act for psychological reasons.

institutionalization syndrome A set of behaviors (usually asocial) associated with long-term residence in an institution rather than with a disorder per se.

intellectualization A defense mechanism that reduces stress by focusing on objective, nonemotional aspects of a threatening situation.

intensive treatment ward A hospital ward to which new patients may be assigned for intensive treatment before their disorders become chronic.

intermittent explosive disorder A type of impulse control disorder involving a loss of control of aggressive impulses that cannot be attributed to other disorders.

intermittent schedule of reward A schedule whereby rewards for correct responses are given less than 100% of the time. This increases resistance to extinction.

intoxication Reversible symptoms such as belligerence, changes in mood, impaired judgment, and impaired functioning that stem from the recent ingestion of a drug that influences the central nervous system.

in vitro exposure Imagined exposure to a feared stimulus during desensitization therapy. (Contrast with **in vivo exposure.**)

in vivo exposure Actual exposure to a feared stimulus during therapy (see also **flooding**). (Contrast with **in vitro exposure.**)

involuntary commitment Commitment to a mental hospital against the patient's will because the patient is considered a danger to him- or herself or to others.

involuntary outpatient commitment A court judgment whereby a person may be required to participate in outpatient treatment as an alternative to involuntary hospitalization.

involutional depression Depression associated with old age; no longer considered a formal diagnostic condition separate from other depressions.

irresistible impulse A basis for an insanity plea. See also **elbow rule.**

isolation room A room in a hospital to which a patient can go for quiet or to which a disputive patient can be sent.

James-Lange theory of emotion The theory that physiological arousal leads to emotions. (Contrast with **Cannon-Bard theory of emotion.**)

killer cells Lymphocytes that break down antigens.

kleptomania The inability to resist the impulse to steal.

Klinefelter's syndrome Mental retardation in men resulting from the presence of one or more extra X (female) chromosomes.

koro A disorder occurring primarily in Asia that involves panic-like symptoms stemming from the belief that the genitalia are retracting into the abdomen and that the process will result in death.

Kraepelin, Emil Theorist who suggested in the late 19th century that schizophrenia had an early onset, consisted of progressive and irreversible intellectual deterioration, and was caused by physiological factors; coined the term *dementia praecox.*

latency stage The fourth of Freud's stages of psychosexual development.

LDL (low-density lipoprotein) The "bad" type of cholesterol that occludes arteries.

L-dopa A drug that increases dopamine levels and is used to treat Parkinson's disease but that can also bring on symptoms of schizophrenia.

learned helplessness The idea that when one cannot control outcomes, one develops feelings of helplessness, which lead to depression.

learning, communication, and motor skills disorders Disorders such as the reading disorder, the expressive language disorder, and the developmental coordination disorder.

learning explanation The view that abnormal behavior is learned from classical and operant conditioning.

least restrictive alternative A legal ruling requiring that mental patients not be subjected to greater restrictions during treatment than absolutely necessary.

leukocytes White blood cells, the major component of the immune system.

levels of retardation Four categories describing the degree of mental retardation: mild, moderate, severe, and profound.

limbic system A group of structures in the midbrain that are responsible primarily for arousal (e.g., mood, appetite, sex, sleep, aggression).

lithium carbonate A drug that is effective for treatment of the bipolar disorder, and in some cases the depressive disorder.

Little Albert A young child in whom John Watson classically conditioned a fear of furry objects.

long-term memory The part of the information-processing system where memories are stored for long periods in networks.

loss According to Freud, a crucial factor in the development of depression.

loss of libido A term referring to a loss of sexual motivation; often associated with depression.

low-potency neuroleptics Early antipsychotic drugs that are somewhat less effective for blocking dopamine activity than more recent drugs. (Contrast with **high-potency neuroleptics** and **atypical neuroleptics.**)

LSD (lysergic acid) A hallucinogen.

Luria-Nebraska A widely used neuropsychological test.

lymphocytes A group of leukocytes that includes B cells and T (killer, helper, and suppressor) cells.

magnetic resonance imaging (MRI) A technique for obtaining images of internal organs such as the brain.

maintenance approach to (drug) treatment Giving individuals a relatively harmless substitute (e.g., methadone) for the substance on which they are dependent.

major depressive disorder A mood disorder in which the major symptom is depression. Diagnostic criteria involve two or more depressive episodes, symptoms not explained by another disorder, and the absence of mania.

malignant neuroleptic syndrome A potentially fatal side effect of neuroleptics.

malingering Faking symptoms to avoid responsibility.

managed health care An insurance program in which the individual contracts with a group of specialists for treatment but is screened for treatment by a primary-care physician.

mania Excessive activity, flight of thought, and grandiosity, seen in one phase of the bipolar disorder.

manic-depressive disorder Earlier name for what is now referred to as the *bipolar disorder.*

mantra A nonsense word that is repeated or chanted as part of meditation.

MAO inhibitors (MAOIs) A class of antidepressant drugs that increase the levels of neurotransmitters by inhibiting the activity of chemical agents (monoamine oxidizers) that would destroy the neurotransmitters.

marginal disorders Personality disorders that are similar to more serious disorders such as schizophrenia and paranoia.

marijuana Cannabis.

Maslow, Abraham A humanistic theorist who suggested that people strive for self-actualization.

mass psychogenic illness Occurrence of a somatoform disorder (e.g., fainting, nausea) in a large number of people at one time; formerly called *mass hysteria.*

maternity blues A mild, transient depression that afflicts many women shortly after they give birth.

MD degree A degree in medicine earned by physicians and psychiatrists.

meditation A strategy for relaxation based primarily on distraction through the use of a mantra.

melatonin A hormone that has been implicated in the seasonal affective disorder (SAD).

menopausal depression Depression associated with menopause; not recognized as a type of depression in the DSM.

mental defect The theory that mental retardation is due to a defect in the brain rather than to delayed development.

mental retardation A disorder involving significantly subaverage intellectual functioning and deficits or impairments in adaptive behavior that begin before age 18.

mescaline A hallucinogen.

Mesmer, Franz Anton A physician who treated persons with somatoform disorders through suggestion; considered the father of hypnosis.

mesmerism The original term for hypnosis.

metabolites The end products of metabolism.

methadone A drug that can forestall the withdrawal symptoms of heroin dependence and can reduce the effects of heroin. Used in the treatment of heroin dependence.

methylxanthines A group of stimulants, among which the strongest is caffeine; found in coffee, tea, and chocolate.

MHPG A metabolite of norepinephrine. Changing levels in the urine are associated with changes in mood.

midbrain A second layer in the brain that controls homeostasis and emotion.

migraine headache A severe headache caused by dilatation of the extracranial arteries, which places pressure on surrounding pain-sensitive nerves.

milieu therapy Activities such as art, music, crafts, and discussion conducted in a hospital.

Minnesota Multiphasic Personality Inventory, Second Edition (MMPI-2) A widely used objective personality test containing more than 500 questions.

mitral valve prolapse Incomplete closing of the heart valve between the left ventricle and the left atrium, permitting some backflow of blood when the heart beats. Sometimes associated with anxiety, but the causal relationship is not clear.

M'Naghten rule A rule for determining insanity based on the defendant's knowledge of right versus wrong.

modeling Learning by observing and imitating others.

monoamine oxidase (MAO) An enzyme that destroys neurotransmitters.

monozygotic (identical) twins Twins who have identical gene structures.

mood disorder with psychotic features A disorder that involves both serious problems with mood (depression or mania) and delusions.

mood disorders A group of disorders that includes the depressive, dysthymic, bipolar, and cyclothymic disorders.

moral insanity Obsolete name for the *antisocial personality disorder.*

morphine One of the active ingredients in opium. Also extracted and used as a narcotic itself.

MPA See **Depo-Provera.**

multi-infarct dementia Dementia that results from many small cerebral infarcts (strokes).

multiple-baseline experimental research A research technique in which treatments for one group are introduced and then withdrawn a number of times, with changes in behavior noted, as opposed to research in which one group receives the treatment and another does not and then the behavior of the two groups is compared.

multiple personality disorder A dissociative disorder in which the individual has two or more separate personalities, usually sharply contrasting. Officially called the *dissociative identity disorder.*

muscle contraction headache A headache caused by the prolonged contraction of the muscles in the neck extending to the head. Also called *tension headache.*

music therapist An individual who works with patients, using music as a medium for interacting and relating.

myocardial infarction (MI) Death of heart muscle due to insufficient blood supply; also called *heart attack.*

myth of mental illness The notion that, rather than reflecting an illness, abnormal behavior is simply a different, wrong, or reasonable response to an unreasonable environment.

narcissistic personality disorder A disorder in which the person has a grandiose sense of importance and is preoccupied with fantasies about success, power, or beauty.

narcolepsy Irresistible attacks of sleep.

narcotics A class of drugs derived from opium, including opium, morphine, and heroin, that have the effect of numbing the senses.

negative cognitive sets Thought structures reflecting the tendency to see things in a bad light and to expect the worst. Cognitive theorists assume that these sets are related to the development of depression.

negative symptoms Symptoms such as poverty of speech, flat affect, inability to experience pleasure, and lack of motivation that are seen in schizophrenia and are thought to be due to structural problems in the brain or low levels of activity in the frontal lobes. (Contrast with **positive symptoms.**)

neo-Freudian theories Theories based on modifications of Freud's theories.

nerve fiber A group of nerve cells that all serve the same function.

nerve impulse An electrical impulse that travels down a nerve.

neural migration The process by which neurons move from one part of the brain to another and make connections with other neurons; thought to be disturbed in schizophrenia.

neurofibrillary tangling A tangling of nerves in the brain associated with Alzheimer's disease.

neuroleptics Drugs used to treat psychotic disorders.

neuron A nerve cell.

neuropsychological testing Testing to determine the nature, extent, and sometimes the location of brain damage.

neurotransmitters Chemicals (e.g., norepinephrine, dopamine, serotonin) released by presynaptic neurons that travel across the synapse and stimulate postsynaptic neurons. High or low levels influence the levels of neurological activity and can result in abnormal behavior.

nicotine A stimulant found primarily in tobacco. Use results in strong dependence.

night hospitalization An arrangement whereby patients spend their nights in a hospital where they receive treatment but spend their days in the community or at work.

nightmare disorder A disorder associated with nightmares that disrupt sleep.

nitroglycerin A drug taken to reduce angina.

nocturnal panic attacks Panic attacks that occur at night, usually during Stage 4 sleep.

nocturnal penile tumescence Erections that occur during sleep. Their occurrence is used to rule out physiological factors as a cause of arousal disorders in men.

nonspecific (common) factor explanation An explanation for the finding that most therapies are effective, the notion being that all of the therapies share a factor that contributes to improvement.

nootropic drugs "Mind-acting" drugs (e.g., Piracetam, Oxiracetam) once thought to help with the memory problems of Alzheimer's disease.

norepinephrine A neurotransmitter that plays a role in depression.

normalization The principle that retarded individuals would be more likely to develop more normal behavior patterns if they were exposed to normal living conditions.

nurses' station An office in a hospital ward, often enclosed in glass, where nurses remain when not attending to patients.

object displacement A defense in which the individual shifts the feelings for or responses to one object (person) to another.

objective personality tests Tests of personality that can be scored objectively (e.g., true or false, multiple choice). The Minnesota Multiphasic Personality Inventory is often used for objective testing. (Contrast with **projective personality tests.**)

observational learning Learning based on observing the behavior of others; see also **modeling.**

obsession The repeated, uncontrollable thinking of a thought.

obsessive-compulsive disorder A disorder characterized by obsessions, compulsions, or both.

obstructive apnea The obstruction of the airway to the lungs so the individual is briefly deprived of oxygen, often leading to problems with sleep. (Contrast with **central apnea.**)

occupational therapist An individual who works with patients, usually teaching them skills necessary for work activities after hospitalization.

Ondine's curse A disorder in which the individual is insensitive to a lack of oxygen and may suffocate.

Oedipus complex Freud's term for the attraction a young boy feels toward his mother.

open ward A ward where patients are free to come and go at will (though they may not necessarily leave the hospital).

operant conditioning Learning based on rewards for desired responses and punishment for undesired responses.

operantly conditioned avoidance of anxiety Learning to avoid anxiety by operant conditioning; a possible explanation of the secondary form of the antisocial personality disorder.

opiate antagonist A drug (e.g., naloxone) that blocks the effects of an opiate, thereby eliminating the pleasure it can induce.

opiates A group of drugs derived from opium; examples include opium, morphine, and heroin. Also called *narcotics.*

opium A narcotic that is also the basis for morphine and heroin.

oppositional defiant disorder A disorder of childhood in which the child or adolescent is negativistic, defiant, argumentative, hostile, and generally resistant to others.

oral stage The first of the stages of psychosexual development identified by Freud. Pleasure is associated with the mouth, and the infant has no sense of separateness from the external world.

orbitofrontal area An area of the brain through which nerves pass that connect the frontal lobes to other parts of the brain and which can be involved in the obsessive-compulsive disorder.

orgasmic disorder A sexual dysfunction involving the failure to achieve orgasm by women and premature ejaculation by men.

outpatient clinic A facility in which patients are treated while living in the community.

oxygen debt A lack of sufficient oxygen that in some individuals can trigger a panic attack.

pain disorder A somatoform disorder, the major symptom of which is pain that has no physiological basis.

panic disorder An anxiety disorder, the major symptom of which is intense periods of anxiety.

panic disorder with agoraphobia A disorder in which the individual develops agoraphobia as a result of having experienced panic attacks outside the home.

paranoid personality disorder A disorder characterized by unwarranted suspiciousness and mistrust of people; differs from delusion disorder (paranoia) in its absence of clearly formed delusions.

paranoid schizophrenia Schizophrenia characterized by delusions of persecution.

paraphilias Sexual disorders that involve deviant means of achieving sexual arousal. Examples include masochism, fetishism, and exhibitionism.

paraprofessionals Persons who do not have professional training or degrees in psychotherapy but treat (often successfully) individuals suffering from psychological disorders.

parasomnias Disorders such as the nightmare disorder and the sleepwalking disorder that involve abnormal behaviors that are associated with sleep.

parasympathetic branch The branch of the autonomic nervous system responsible for reducing arousal.

parens patriae The principle that the state has the right and responsibility to protect and provide for the well-being of its citizens; the basis for involuntary hospitalization.

Parkinson's disease A disease characterized by loss of muscle control (early or mild forms involve frequent twitches) resulting from low levels of dopamine. Treatment with L-dopa can be effective but may provoke symptoms of schizophrenia.

pathological gambling A type of impulse control disorder.

Pavlov, Ivan The Russian physiologist who first identified classical conditioning.

pedophilia A paraphilia in which the individual gains sexual gratification from sexual activities with children.

peptic ulcers Breaks in the lining of the digestive tract.

performance intelligence An intelligence test score based on the ability to perform various tasks such as putting a puzzle together and arranging colored blocks to create a design.

perinatal complications Problems during birth (e.g., lack of oxygen) that cause brain damage and lead to abnormal behavior.

peripheral nervous system Components of the nervous system outside the brain and spinal cord. Branches include the autonomic and the somatic.

persistent type of alcoholism A drinking pattern characterized by continued low levels of drinking; thought to be due to low levels of arousal that might be normalized by small amounts of alcohol. (Contrast with **binge type of alcoholism.**)

personality disorders Disorders involving behaviors that are less deviant than most of the behaviors associated with many other disorders. Examples include the antisocial, obsessive-compulsive, dependent, narcissistic, paranoid, and borderline personality disorders.

phallic stage The third stage of psychosexual development described by Freud. Most notable during this phase are Oedipal or Electra attractions.

PhD degree A graduate degree in psychology earned by clinical psychologists that is focused on both treatment and research.

phenylalanine An amino acid that if not broken down forms phenylpyruvic acid, which destroys the brain in infants and results in a type of mental retardation known as phenylketonuria (PKU).

phenylketonuria (PKU) Mental retardation due to high levels of phenylpyruvic acid, which destroys the brain.

phenylpyruvic acid See **phenylalanine.**

phobic disorder An anxiety disorder in which the individual has an inappropriate fear of a specific object or situation.

physiological explanation The view that abnormal behavior is the result of problems with synaptic transmission, brain structure, and hormones.

physiological sex identification An individual's objective knowledge (based on genitalia) of being male or female. (Contrast with **psychological gender identity.**)

pica An eating disorder characterized by the persistent ingestion of nonnutritive substances such as dirt, hair, or cloth.

Pinel, Philippe French reformer who in 1792 directed that mental patients in his hospital be taken out of their chains.

pituitary gland A structure in the brain that, among other things, secretes hormones known as gonadotropins that are essential for sexual arousal.

placebo effect A phenomenon whereby the expectation that a treatment will have a specific effect may produce the effect even if the treatment is technically inactive.

plaques Patches of deterioration in the brains of people with Alzheimer's disease.

pleasure principle Freud's notion that one of the factors underlying behavior is the desire for pleasure, which in most cases involves the reduction of drives.

police power of the state The principle that the state has the right to protect citizens from individuals who are dangerous; used as a basis for involuntary hospitalization of persons believed to be dangerous to others.

positive spiking Sudden abnormal bursts of EEG activity, often seen in persons with the antisocial personality disorder and suspected to be associated with outbursts of aggression.

positive symptoms Symptoms such as hallucinations, delusions, and disturbances of thought that are seen in schizophrenia and are believed to be due to problems with neural transmission. (Contrast with **negative symptoms.**)

positron emission tomography (PET scan) A means of graphically portraying chemical processes in the brain. Radioactive agents bind to chemicals (e.g., glucose), permitting the location of the chemicals to be tracked by measuring the radioactivity in various areas of the brain.

postamphetamine depression Depression resulting when a person ceases taking amphetamines.

postpartum depression See **depression with postpartum onset.**

postsynaptic neuron A neuron that is stimulated when a nerve impulse is transmitted across a synapse.

posttest A measurement of the dependent variable after the experimental manipulation.

posttraumatic stress disorder An anxiety disorder, the major symptom of which is the reexperiencing of feelings associated with an earlier traumatic event (e.g., war, natural disaster, physical attack).

preconscious One of the levels of consciousness, according to Freud; it involves memories of which one is not usually aware but which can be brought to awareness with some effort (e.g., names of friends from long ago). (Contrast with **conscious mind** and **unconscious.**)

prefrontal lobotomy An operation in which the frontal lobes of the brain are removed or separated from the rest of the brain.

premature ejaculation The orgasm disorder in men that involves reaching orgasm too soon.

premenstrual dysphoric disorder A mood disorder that involves excessive depression and stress prior to the onset of menstruation. It is not officially recognized in DSM-IV.

prenatal complications Problems during fetal development (e.g., the mother's illness, exposure to hormones) that affect brain development and lead to abnormal behavior.

presenile dementia A deterioration of cognitive functioning that occurs before the age of 65. (Contrast with **senile dementia.**)

presynaptic neuron A neuron that fires and then releases a neurotransmitter into the synapse so that the next (postsynaptic) nerve can be stimulated.

pretest A measurement of the dependent variable before the experimental manipulation.

primary-care physician A physician in a managed health care program who screens patients to determine whether they need the attention of a specialist and who attends to their general medical needs.

primary dementia Deterioration of cognitive functioning due to an organic disorder of the brain (e.g., damage due to strokes).

primary depression Depression that is not the result of another disorder, drug, or treatment. (Contrast with **secondary depression.**)

primary hypersomnia Excessive sleep.

primary insomnia A disorder that involves difficulty getting to sleep, difficulty staying asleep long enough, or difficulty getting sleep that is restful and in which the symptoms are not the result of another disorder.

primary orgasmic disorder A disorder in which a woman never experiences an orgasm through any means. (Contrast with **secondary organsmic disorder.**)

primary prevention Attempting to prevent disorders by eliminating their causes.

primary process According to Freud, fantasies used to satisfy needs.

primary sleep disorders Sleep disorders that are caused by physiological problems in the process that leads to sleep. Includes dyssomnias and parasomnias.

primary type of the APD A form of the antisocial personality disorder in which the individual seems incapable of developing anxiety as opposed to being effective at avoiding anxiety. (Contrast with **secondary type of the APD.**)

priming The notion that a memory network can be activated by using a thought or feeling in that network and thereby increase the likelihood that other memories or feelings in the network will be activated.

prodromal phase The phase of a disorder before the major symptoms become apparent.

prodromal symptoms Symptoms that precede the onset of a disorder. Prodromal symptoms of a classic migraine include visual problems, dizziness, and sometimes abdominal pain.

progesterone A hormone associated with feminine characteristics.

progressive muscle relaxation A procedure in which a person is taught to relax muscles, usually beginning with the head and working down to the feet.

projection A defense mechanism whereby a person attributes his or her undesirable traits to others; also the basis of projective tests.

projective personality tests Tests in which clients are shown ambiguous stimuli (e.g., inkblots, pictures of people) and asked to talk about them. (Contrast with **objective personality tests.**)

pronoun reversal A speech characteristic seen in children with autism in which they reverse genders of pronouns.

Prozac (fluoxetine) A bicyclic antidepressant drug that blocks the reuptake of serotonin and is effective for treating depression and the obsessive-compulsive disorder.

pseudocyesis A conversion disorder involving symptoms of pregnancy; formerly called *hysterical pregnancy.*

psilocybin A hallucinogen.

psychiatric nurse A nurse with specific training in the care and treatment of persons with mental disorders.

psychiatrist A physician (MD) with advanced training in the care and treatment of persons with mental disorders.

psychoactive drug Any substance that alters mood, awareness of the external environment, or awareness of the internal environment.

psychoanalysis A treatment developed by Freud that focuses primarily on identifying unconscious causes of abnormal behavior through the use of such techniques as free association.

psychoanalytic (Freudian) theory A theory of human behavior developed primarily by Freud.

psychodynamic explanation The view that abnormal behavior is the result of unconscious conflicts.

psychoeducation A strategy often used in treating schizophrenia in which the patient and the patient's family are taught about the disorder and how to cope with it.

psychological gender identity The subjective feeling of being male or female. If in conflict with one's physiological sex identification, a gender identity disorder results.

psychological technician An individual who supervises patients (formerly called a *ward attendant*).

psychologist An individual with a PhD degree in psychology or a PsyD degree who has passed a qualifying examination.

psychomotor agitation Increased motor activity such as pacing that is sometimes associated with depression.

psychomotor retardation Reduced motor activity that is often associated with depression.

psychomotor stimulants Drugs that increase the production of neurotransmitters and thereby elevate mood and increase activity. Depression may result when these drugs are withdrawn, so they are rarely used to treat depression.

psychopath Still widely used term for a person with what is now called the *antisocial personality disorder;* the term often implies a physiological basis for the disorder.

psychosomatic disorders A term once used to describe physical disorders (e.g., ulcers) that were caused by psychological factors.

psychosurgery A procedure in which parts of the brain are removed or destroyed in an attempt to treat mental disorders. (See also **prefrontal lobotomy.**)

psychotherapy A treatment for mental disorders that explores causes and solutions by having the client talk about them.

psychoticism A type of positive symptom in schizophrenia consisting of hallucinations and delusions.

PsyD degree A graduate degree earned by some clinical psychologists that is focused on treatment alone rather than both research and treatment.

punishment Words or actions that can lead to the reduced use of a behavior and/or to stress.

purge The use of self-induced vomiting, laxatives, and enemas to get rid of the food, usually after a binge.

pyromania An impulse control disorder in which the individual cannot resist setting fires.

quasi-experimental research Research in which, rather than manipulating the independent variable, the investigator uses naturally occurring situations in which there are differences in the independent variable (e.g., studying persons in stressful jobs rather than creating stress for persons). Often used to avoid ethical problems in research.

quasi-psychotic thought disturbance A thought disorder occuring in the borderline personality disorder that is less serious than that seen in schizophrenia.

random assignment A procedure in which experimental research subjects are assigned to conditions on a nonsystematic basis.

rapid cycling The tendency to go thorough the phases of the bipolar disorder quickly.

rapid eye movement (REM) sleep Stage 1 sleep in which the eyes move rapidly and during which dreams usually occur.

rational-emotive therapy Cognitive therapy in which the client is forced to reexamine erroneous beliefs and develop new, more appropriate ones.

rationalization A defense in which the individual gives a good reason but not the real reason for a behavior, thereby avoiding anxiety.

Rayner, Rosalie An early behaviorist who worked with John Watson on the conditioning of Little Albert.

reaction formation A defense in which the individual does or feels the opposite of what is expected and thereby avoids anxiety.

rebound effect Increased sleeplessness when an individual ceases taking hypnotics.

receptor sites Areas on a postsynaptic neuron that when stimulated by neurotransmitters cause the neuron to fire.

recidivism Relapse; a return to former patterns of behavior.

regression A defense mechanism characterized by a retreat to an earlier stage of development.

relaxation response A type of meditation.

releasing hormone (RH) A hormone released by the hypothalamus during sexual arousal that stimulates the pituitary gland.

reliability The extent to which test results or research findings obtained at one time can be found again at another time or by another tester or investigator.

repression A defense mechanism whereby threatening memories are stored in the unconscious.

residual phase The phase in the course of schizophrenia following the active phase, in which symptoms have diminished and become less marked.

residual schizophrenia A mild disorder that occurs after at least one schizophrenic episode and is characterized by some of the symptoms of schizophrenia, which are generally muted.

resistance Blocking or talking about trivial issues in psychotherapy (or analysis) when the client is faced with anxiety-provoking material. Can be used as a sign that an important issue has been encountered.

respiratory control center An area in the brain stem that monitors oxygen levels in the blood; if overly sensitive, it can trigger a panic attack.

response stereotypy Abnormal repetitive behaviors that result when persons with the attention-deficit/hyperactivity disorder are given too high a dose of stimulant medication.

retarded depression Depression characterized by slowed movements and thoughts. (Contrast with **agitated depression.**)

reticular activating system A network of nerves that carry arousal from the brain stem to higher areas of the brain.

retrograde amnesia Loss of memory for recent events that extends progressively to more distant events. Sometimes associated with electroconvulsive therapy.

reuptake Absorption of neurotransmitters by the presynaptic neurons. The process is inhibited by bicyclic and tricyclic drugs.

reversed cerebral asymmetry The fact that in some persons with schizophrenia, the right side of the brain (in right-handed persons) is heavier than the left side of the brain. The opposite is usually true in persons who do not suffer from schizophrenia.

rewards Words or actions that can be used to reinforce a behavior.

rheumatoid arthritis See **arthritis.**

right to equal protection Constitutional right under the Fourteenth Amendment that may be violated with mental patients (as when they are hospitalized involuntarily).

Risperidal (risperidone) An atypical neuroleptic drug.

Ritalin (methylphenidate) A stimulant used to treat the attention-deficit/hyperactivity disorder.

Rorschach test A projective test consisting of 10 cards, each with one inkblot.

rubella An infectious disease that if experienced by a woman during pregnancy can cause an inflammation of the brain of the fetus, which can in turn lead to degeneration of the brain and mental retardation.

rumination disorder An eating disorder of childhood involving repeated regurgitation of food.

Rush, Benjamin An early reformer in the area of mental disorders; known as the "father of American psychiatry."

schizoaffective disorder A disorder involving the symptoms of both schizophrenia and depression.

schizoid personality disorder A personality disorder characterized by a lack of interest in other people and little emotion. Lack of hallucinations, delusions, or problems with thought processes distinguish this from schizophrenia.

schizophrenia A serious disorder involving a decline in functioning, along with hallucinations, delusions, and/or disturbed thought processes. Symptoms must persist for at least 6 months.

schizophrenic deficit The impairment in intellectual functioning seen in schizophrenia, due to a disturbance in thought processes.

schizophreniform disorder A disorder involving the symptoms of schizophrenia that lasts only 1 to 6 months.

schizophrenogenic mother A mother who is both attentive and rejecting, once thought to contribute to the development of schizophrenia in her child.

schizotypal personality disorder A disorder involving many of the symptoms of schizophrenia, but not severe enough to result in a diagnosis of schizophrenia (e.g., the patient says, "I feel as if I am hearing voices," not "I am hearing voices").

scientist-practitioner model An approach to the training of psychologists in which they are trained to be both scientists who do research and practitioners who treat disturbed individuals.

seasonal affective disorder (SAD) A mood disorder characterized by depression during periods of less daylight and sometimes by mania during periods of increased daylight. Officially called *depression with seasonal pattern.*

season-of-birth effect The fact that individuals who later develop schizophrenia are more likely to be born in late winter.

secondary dementia Dementia as a side effect of some other disorder (e.g., depression) rather than due to an organic disorder.

secondary depression Depression as a side effect of medication or another disorder.

secondary hypertension High blood pressure that results from some known physical cause.

secondary mania Mania as a side effect of medication or another disorder.

secondary orgasmic disorder A sexual dysfunction in which a woman is able to achieve orgasm through masturbation but not through intercourse.

secondary prevention Attempting to solve problems at an early stage before they result in serious disorders.

secondary process Freud's term for thinking and problem solving.

secondary type of the APD A form of the antisocial personality disorder in which the individual is capable of experiencing anxiety but has learned to avoid it. (Contrast with **primary type of the APD.**)

selective attention The process in which individuals focus attention on what they believe is most important, thereby possibly missing other important material.

selective recall The influencing of recall by factors such as priming and mood, thereby possibly distorting what is recalled.

selective serotonin reuptake inhibitors (SSRIs) Antidepressant drugs such as Zoloft that block the reuptake of serotonin.

self-actualization A state of development defined by humanists as that in which individuals rise above their own needs and can freely give of themselves.

self-control approach to (drug) treatment Using moral persuasion and social support to help the individual avoid the use of drugs; Alcoholics Anonymous is an example.

self-efficacy An attitude reflecting self-confidence and positive expectancies.

self-fulfilling prophecy A result that occurs largely because the individual expects it (e.g., failure because of the expectancy of failure).

self-instruction A procedure used with children with the attention-deficit/hyperactivity disorder that is designed to help them focus their attention and improve self-control.

self-medication hypothesis The notion that individuals take drugs in an attempt to normalize their levels of arousal.

semantic intrusions Associative intrusions involving words with multiple meanings (e.g., hearing the word *date* in a conversation about fruits, the disturbed person takes it to refer to an interpersonal relationship).

senile dementia Dementia that begins after the age of 65.

sensory deprivation The limitation of all sensory inputs (sound, sight, touch, smell), once thought to be a cause of schizophrenia. The psychological effects of sensory deprivation are now known to be due in large part to demand characteristics.

sensory memory The component of the information-processing system in which incoming stimuli are first registered before some are sent to the short-term memory.

serotonin A neurotransmitter, low levels of which result in depression, aggression, or both.

sex reassignment surgery The procedure whereby an individual with the gender identity disorder is surgically altered to have the appearance and some of the functions of the opposite sex.

sexual aversion disorder An extreme aversion to sexual activities.

sexual dysfunctions A group of sex-related disorders including the desire, arousal, and orgasmic disorders.

sexual masochism A paraphilia in which the individual gains sexual gratification from pain.

sexual predator laws Laws that make it possible to confine an individual who is considered likely to commit a sexual crime.

sexual sadism A paraphilia in which the individual gains sexual gratification from hurting another person.

shared psychotic disorder A delusional disorder that develops in a second person as a consequence of his or her association with a person who has a delusional disorder. Formerly called *folie à deux*.

short-term memory The component of the information-processing system in which thinking is done and information is processed for storage in the long-term memory.

side effects Additional, unintended effects of a treatment (e.g., dry mouth from the use of antidepressants).

situation redefinition Reconceptualization of a threatening situation as nonthreatening (e.g., a test is regarded as an opportunity for learning). Also called *denial*.

Skinner, B. F. American scientist who contributed to the understanding and use of operant conditioning.

sleep terror disorder A disorder in which the individual wakes in a state of terror and is usually briefly disorientated.

sleepwalking disorder A disorder characterized by sleepwalking; most common in children.

slow-wave activity Brain-wave activity found primarily in the temporal lobes of persons with the antisocial personality disorder.

social phobia A disorder characterized by fear of behaving in an embarrassing way and of being criticized, resulting in avoidance of other people.

social support Emotional support from others, which has been shown to reduce the effects of stress.

social worker A professional who works with patients and their families, often with the goal of facilitating the patients' return and readjustment to the community.

sociocultural explanation The idea that abnormal behavior is due to social and cultural factors.

sociopath Obsolete term for a person with what is now called the *antisocial personality disorder*. Implicit in the term is the belief that the disorder stems from social factors (e.g., child rearing).

sodium lactate A substance that can set off a panic attack if injected into persons with a history of naturally occurring panic attacks.

soft signs (of brain damage) Problems with muscular or visual coordination that may reflect diffuse or minimal brain damage often not otherwise detectable.

somatic anxiety Anxiety reflected primarily in physiological symptoms such as rapid heartbeat, sweating, and rapid breathing.

somatic division The part of the peripheral nervous system involving connections with the muscles and skin.

somatization disorder A somatoform disorder involving complaints of a large number of physical symptoms for which no physical cause can be found.

somatoform disorders A class of disorders, including the somatization, hypochondriasis, conversion, idiopathic pain, and dysmorphic disorders.

specific patient-symptom explanation An explanation for the finding that all therapies appear to be somewhat effective because different therapies are effective for different patients.

specific phobia Any phobia other than agoraphobia or social phobia.

spectrum of schizophrenia disorders A group of disorders (e.g., delusional, schizoaffective, and induced psychotic disorders) that share symptoms with schizophrenia but may differ in severity.

sphygmomanometer A device used to measure blood pressure.

spontaneous recovery Spontaneous remission of symptoms or the spontaneous return of a classically conditioned response after extinction procedures.

spontaneous remission Disappearance of a disorder without treatment; often seen with depression.

stages of psychosexual development The oral, anal, phallic, latency, and genital stages suggested by Freud.

stages of sleep Four stages involving progressively deeper levels of sleep.

Stanford-Binet An individual intelligence test administered to schoolchildren.

start-squeeze technique An effective technique for treating premature ejaculation.

start-stop technique An effective technique for treating premature ejaculation.

state anxiety Anxiety that is limited to one particular situation (e.g., a test) as opposed to being continually present. (Contrast with **trait anxiety.**)

statistical significance The reliability of a research finding. (Contrast with **clinical significance.**)

statistical tests Tests used to determine whether research findings are significant.

stimulants A group of substances, including amphetamines, cocaine, caffeine, and nicotine, that have the effect of increasing neurotransmission.

stimulus overload In schizophrenia, the experience of being overwhelmed by external and internal stimulation, which contributes to problems with thought processes.

strategic eating disorders Eating disorders that stem from a goal such as losing weight for a particular event rather than from a more serious or pervasive problem.

stress The psychological and physiological response to overtaxing changes; results in responses such as anxiety, depression, and elevated physiological arousal.

stress management training Procedures for teaching persons to deal with stress, such as muscle relaxation, coping strategies, and time management.

stressor A factor that elicits the stress response.

stroke See **cerebral infarction.**

structural abnormalities of the brain Factors such as enlarged ventricles, cortical atrophy, and subcortical entropy that are associated with schizophrenia.

structural approach to personality Freud's description of personality in terms of the id, ego, and superego.

structured interview An interview that is limited to a specific set of questions. (Contrast with **unstructured interview.**)

subcortical atrophy The deterioration of tissues or structures such as the hippocampus deep in the brain; often seen in patients with schizophrenia, particularly those with negative symptoms.

substantia nigra A large, dark-colored area of the midbrain responsible for motor activity. Destruction of the substantia nigra and the associated drop in the production of dopamine are responsible for the motor symptoms of Parkinson's disease.

suicide The voluntary ending of one's own life.

suicide gestures Behaviors that are intended to look like attempts of a person to take his or her own life but are actually designed to communicate distress or to manipulate others.

superego In Freud's structural approach to personality, the conscience or moral arm of society, developed by identification with the parent.

support group A group of persons with similar problems who meet to give one another social support and exchange information and coping strategies.

suppression A defense mechanism consisting of conscious attempts to stop or avoid thinking about a threat.

suppressor cells Lymphocytes that reduce the activity of the immune system in the absence of antigens.

sympathetic branch The branch of the autonomic nervous system responsible for increases in arousal.

synapse The gap between neurons, crossed by neurotransmitters in the process of neural transmission.

systematic desensitization A treatment procedure in which a relaxation response is paired with an anxiety-provoking stimulus in an attempt at counterconditioning.

systolic blood pressure The high level of blood pressure that occurs immediately after each beat of the heart; usually around 120 mm Hg.

Tarasoff ruling A legal decision that therapists have a duty to protect people if a client poses a danger to those people.

tardive dyskinesia A disorder involving involuntary muscle contractions (initially of the face and head) due to long-term use of high levels of neuroleptic drugs.

temporal lobe epilepsy A disorder involving erratic firing of neurons in the temporal lobe that can bring on seizures. The episodes are sometimes preceded by hallucinations.

temporal lobes Areas of the brain where memories for visual and auditory experiences are stored; stimulation of the temporal lobes can result in hallucinations.

tension headache See **muscle contraction headache.**

terminal button A vessel at the end of the axon from which neurotransmitters are released.

tertiary prevention Attempting to prevent relapses in persons who have responded successfully to treatment.

testosterone A hormone produced by the testes (when stimulated by gonadotropins), responsible for sexual desire in males.

testosterone replacement therapy The administration of testosterone as a treatment for the desire disorder in males.

thalamus An area of the brain where incoming stimuli are initially processed; atrophied in some patients with schizophrenia.

Thematic Apperception Test (TAT) A projective test consisting primarily of drawings of people. Clients are asked to make up stories about what is going on in the pictures.

Thorazine (chlorpromazine) An early neuroleptic that is still widely used in the treatment of schizophrenia.

Thorndike, Edward L. An American scientist who studied operant conditioning.

thought content intrusions The inclusion of new and irrelevant thoughts, contributing to the disturbed thought processes seen in schizophrenia.

three-stage theory of memory processing The idea that memories move through the sensory, short-term, and long-term memories.

thrombus A clot that blocks the blood flow through an artery.

thyroxin A hormone produced by the thyroid gland, the underproduction of which leads to cretinism (hypothyroidism).

tic disorders Disorders involving recurrent and involuntary contractions of muscles resulting in jerking of the body or face. Includes Tourette's disorder, which often involves vocal tics.

time-limited psychotherapy Psychotherapy intended to last only a specified number of sessions.

token economy A treatment approach in which patients are rewarded with tokens when they show appropriate behaviors. Tokens can later be exchanged for food, improved living conditions, or privileges.

tolerance The phenomenon whereby a specific dose level of a drug has less effect after repeated administrations.

total institution An institution such as the military, a prison, or a mental hospital that can control all aspects of a person's life.

Tourette's disorder A tic disorder involving involuntary movements of large muscles; often includes vocal tics such as grunts, yelps, barks, and words (sometimes obscenities).

trait anxiety Anxiety that is a pervasive personality trait rather than a response to a specific situation. (Contrast with **state anxiety.**)

trait disorders A group of personality disorders that revolve around a trait that interferes with personal functioning or causes distress. Examples include the obsessive-compulsive, dependent, histrionic, and narcissistic disorders.

transcendental meditation A widely practiced form of meditation in which the individual allegedly transcends normal consciousness.

transference The process in psychotherapy (or analysis) in which the client redirects toward the therapist feelings about someone else in the client's life.

transorbital lobotomy Psychosurgery during which a knife is inserted into the frontal lobes through the eye socket and then swung back and forth.

transvestic fetishism A paraphilia in which the individual gains sexual pleasure from dressing in the clothes of the opposite sex.

trichotillomania An impulse control disorder in which the individual cannot resist the urge to pull out his or her hair.

tricyclics A group of drugs widely used to treat depression.

trisomy 21 The possession of an extra number 21 chromosome; the condition results in Down syndrome.

tryptophan An amino acid that can be converted into serotonin; low levels can lead to depression and eating disorders.

Tuke, William An English Quaker who opened a retreat for mental patients in the late 18th century.

Turner's syndrome (gonadal dysgenesis) A disorder limited to women that sometimes results in mental retardation, associated primarily with space-form relationships; caused by the absence of one female (X) chromosome.

twin studies (in genetics) A technique in which the concordance rate of a disorder is compared in monozygotic and dizygotic twins in an effort to determine the degree to which effects are genetic or environmental.

Type A behavior pattern Behavior characterized by urgency, competitiveness, overcommitment, and hostility.

Type I bipolar disorder The bipolar disorder that involves mania and depression.

Type II bipolar disorder The bipolar disorder that involves hypomania (a milder form of mania) and depression.

tyramine A substance that interacts with MAOIs to cause a hypertensive crisis.

unconditioned stimulus A stimulus that can elicit a response without prior conditioning (e.g., meat elicits salivation).

unconscious One of the levels of mind, according to Freud; it is where threatening memories that are not retrievable are stored (repressed). (Contrast with **conscious mind** and **preconscious.**)

undifferentiated schizophrenia A catchall category for all persons with schizophrenia who do not fit into other categories.

unstructured interview An interview in which the interviewer does not follow a specific set of questions. (Contrast with **structured interview.**)

validity The degree to which a test measures what it is supposed to measure.

vascular accidents Ruptures of arteries. Ruptured arteries that deprive the brain of blood are called *cerebral infarctions,* or *strokes.*

vasodilators Drugs that cause the dilation of blood vessels and thereby reduce blood pressure.

ventricles Cavities in the brain.

verbal conditioning The process whereby the use of particular words or statements can be increased by following them with rewards (attention). Suggested as a process that might occur in psychotherapy.

verbal intelligence Intelligence based on a person's ability to define words, provide information, explain similarities, do arithmetic problems, and remember lists of numbers.

vicarious conditioning Conditioning that occurs when one individual observes another being conditioned.

vocal tics Grunts, noises, and sometimes words that are produced by uncontrollable urges.

voluntary admission Self-admission to a hospital, which carries with it the right to leave after appropriate notice unless admission status is changed to involuntary commitment.

voyeurism   A paraphilia in which an individual gains sexual gratification from looking at others who are nude or disrobing.

Watson, John B.   An American scientist who pioneered the idea that conditioning provided the basis of fears. His most famous case was Little Albert.

waxy flexibility   A symptom of catatonic schizophrenia.

Wechsler Adult Intelligence Scale, Revised (WAIS-R)   An individual intelligence test for adolescents and adults.

Wechsler Intelligence Scale for Children, Third Edition (WISC-III)   An individual intelligence test for school-age children.

Wechsler Preschool-Primary Scale of Intelligence (WPPSI)   An individual intelligence test for preschool children.

white blood cells   See **leukocytes.**

withdrawal symptoms   A group of symptoms such as nausea and vomiting that may occur when a person stops taking a drug.

word salad   Jumbled words uttered by some persons with schizophrenia.

Zoloft (sertraline)   An antidepressant that works primarily by blocking the reuptake of serotonin.

REFERENCES

Aas, H., Klepp, K. I., Laberg, J. C. & Edvard, L. (1995). Predicting adolescents' intentions to drink alcohol: Outcome expectancies and self-efficacy. *Journal of Studies on Alcohol, 156*, 193–199.

Abbey, K. J., Madsen, C. H., & Polland, R. (1989). Short-term suicide awareness curriculum. *Suicide and Life Threatening Behavior, 19*, 216–227.

Abel, J. L. (1993). Exposure with response prevention and sertonergic antidepressants in the treatment of obsessive disorder: A review and implications for interdisciplinary treatment. *Behaviour Research and Therapy, 31*, 463–478.

Abikoff, H., & Gittelman, R. (1985). Hyperactive children treated with stimulants. *Archives of General Psychiatry, 42*, 953–961.

Able, E. L. (1990). *Fetal alcohol syndrome.* New York: Plenum.

Abou-Saleh, M. (1992). Lithium. In E. S. Paykel (Ed.), *Handbook of affective disorders* (2nd ed.). New York: Guilford Press.

Abraham, H. D., & Aldridge, A. M. (1993). Adverse consequences of lysergic acid diethylamide. *Addiction, 88*, 1327–1334.

Abraham, S. F., & Beumont, P. J. (1982). How patients describe bulimia or binge eating. *Psychological Medicine, 12*, 625–635.

Abramowitz, S. I. (1986). Psychosocial outcomes of sex reassignment surgery. *Journal of Consulting and Clinical Psychology, 54*, 183–189.

Abramson, L. Y., & Sackeim, H. A. (1977). A paradox in depression: Uncontrollability and self-blame. *Psychological Bulletin, 84*, 838–851.

Abramson, L. Y., Seligman, M. E. P., & Teasdale, J. D. (1978). Learned helplessness in humans: Critique and reformulation. *Journal of Abnormal Psychology, 87*, 49–74.

Acierno, R., Donohue, B., & Kogan, E. (1994). Psychological intervention for drug abuse: A critique and summation of controlled studies. *Clinical Psychology Review, 14*, 417–442.

Adams, J., McIntosh, E., & Weade, B. L. (1973). Ethnic background, measured intelligence, and adaptive behavior scores in mentally retarded children. *American Journal of Mental Deficiency, 78*, 1–6.

Adams, W. R., Kiefer, S. W., and Badia-Elder, N. (1995). Tryptophan deficiency and alcohol consumption in rats as a model for disadvantaged human populations: A preliminary study. *Medical Anthropology, 16*, 175–191.

Addiego, F., Belzer, E. G., Comolli, J., Moger, W., Perry, J. D., & Wipple, B. (1981). Female ejaculation: A case study. *Journal of Sex Research, 17*, 13–21.

Addonizio, G. (1991). The pharmacologic basis of neuroleptic malignant syndrome. *Psychiatric Annals, 21*, 152–156.

Adeniran, R.A., & Jones, J.R. (1994). Koro: Culture-bound disorder or universal symptom? *British Journal of Psychiatry, 164*, 559–561.

Adler, A. (1927). *The practice and theory of individual psychology.* New York: Harcourt Brace.

Agren, H. (1982). Depressive symptom patterns and urinary MHPG excretion. *Psychiatry and Research, 6*, 185–196.

Akbarian, S., Bunney, W. E., Jr., Potkin, S. G., Wigal, S. B., Hagman, J. O., Sandman, C. A., & Jones, E. G. (1993). Altered distribution of nicotinamide-adenine dinucleotide phosphate-diaphorase cells in frontal lobe schizophrenics implies disturbances of cortical development. *Archives of General Psychiatry, 50*, 169–177.

Akbarian, S., Vinuela, A., Kim, J. J., Potkin, S. G., Bunney, W. E., Jr., & Jones, E. G. (1993). Distorted distribution of nicotinamide-adenine dinucleotide phosphate-diaphorase neurons in temporal lobe of schizophrenics implies anomalous cortical development. *Archives of General Psychiatry, 50*, 178–187.

Akiskal, H. S., Maser, J. D., Zeller, P. J., Endicott, J., Coryell, W., Keller, M., Warshaw, M., Clayton, P., & Goodwin, F. (1995). Switching from "unipolar" to bipolar II: An 11-year prospective study of clinical and temperamental predictors in 559 patients. *Archives of General Psychiatry, 52*, 114–123.

Alessi, N. E., Naylor, M. W., Ghaziuddin, M., & Zubieta, J. K. (1994). Update on lithium carbonate therapy in children and adolescents. *Journal of the American Academy of Child and Adolescent Psychiatry, 33*, 291–304.

Alexander, B. K., & Hadaway, P. F. (1982). Opiate addiction: The case for an adaptive orientation. *Psychological Bulletin, 92*, 367–381.

Alexander, B. K., Beyerstein, B. L., Hadaway, P. F., & Coambs, R. B. (1981). The effect of early and later colony housing on oral ingestion of morphine in rats. *Pharmacology, Biochemistry, and Behavior, 15*, 571–576.

Alexander, B. K., Coambs, R. B., & Hadaway, P. F. (1978). The effect of housing and gender on morphine self-administration in rats. *Psychopharmacology, 58*, 175–179.

Alexander, J., Holtzworth-Monroe, A., & Jameson, P. (1994). Process and outcome of marital and family therapy: Research review and evaluation. In A. E. Bergin & S. L. Garfield (Eds.), *Handbook of psychotherapy and behavior change* (4th ed.). New York: Wiley.

Alexander, L. (1953). *Treatment of mental disorder.* Philadelphia: Saunders.

Alford, B. A., & Correia, C. J. (1994). Cognitive therapy of schizophrenia: Theory and empirical status. *Behavior Therapy, 25*, 17–34.

Allison, R. B. (1984). Difficulties diagnosing the multiple personality syndrome in a death penalty case. *International Journal of Clinical and Experimental Hypnosis, 32*, 102–117.

Allison, R. B., & Schwartz, T. (1980). *Minds in many pieces: The making of a very special doctor.* New York: Rawson, Wade.

Alloy, L. B. (1982). The role of perceptions and attributions for response-outcome noncontingency in learned helplessness: A commentary and discussion. *Journal of Personality, 50*, 441–479.

Alloy, L. B., & Abramson, L. Y. (1979). Judgment of contingency in depressed and nondepressed students: Sadder but wiser? *Journal of Experimental Psychology: General, 108*, 441–485.

Altamura, A. C., Percudani, M., Guercetti, G., & Invernizzi, G. (1989). Efficacy and tolerability of fluoxetine in the elderly: A double-blind study versus amitryptiline. *International Journal of Psychopharmacology, 4*, 103–106.

Altshuler, L. L., Post, R. M., Leverich, G. S., Mikalauskas, K., Rosoff, A., & Acherman, L. (1995). Antidepressant-induced mania and cycle acceleration: A controversy revisited. *American Journal of Psychiatry, 152*, 1130–1138.

Alzate, H., & Hoch, Z. (1986). The "G spot" and "female ejaculation": A current appraisal. *Journal of Sex and Marital Therapy, 12*, 211–220.

Amenson, C. S., & Lewinsohn, P. M. (1981). An investigation into the observed sex differences in prevalence of unipolar depression. *Journal of Abnormal Psychology, 90*, 1–13.

American Psychiatric Association. (1990). *The practice of electroconvulsive therapy: Recommendations for treatment, training, and privileging.* Washington, DC: Author.

American Psychiatric Association. (1980). *Diagnostic and statistical manual of mental disorders* (3rd ed.). Washington, DC: Author.

American Psychiatric Association. (1987). *Diagnostic and statistical manual of mental disorders* (3rd ed., rev.). Washington, DC: Author.

American Psychiatric Association. (1994). *Diagnostic and statistical manual of mental disorders* (4th ed.). Washington, DC: Author.

American Psychological Association Task Force on Laboratory Tests in Psychiatry. (1987). The dexamethasone suppression test: An overview of its current status in psychiatry. *American Journal of Psychology, 144,* 1253–1262.

American Psychological Association. (1993). Evidence grows of abuse by psychiatric hospitals. *APA Monitor, 24*(1), 20.

Anand, B. K., & Brobeck, J. R. (1951a). Hypothalamic control of food intake in rats and cats. *Yale Journal of Biology and Medicine, 24,* 123.

Anand, B. K., & Brobeck, J. R. (1951b). Localization of a feeding center in the hypothalamus of the rat. *Proceedings of the Society for Experimental Biology and Medicine, 77,* 323–324.

Anand, B. K., Dua, S., & Schoenberg, K. (1955). Hypothalamic control of food intake in rats and monkeys. *Journal of Physiology (London), 127,* 143–152.

Andersen, B. L., Kiecolt-Glaser, J. K., & Glaser, R. (l994). A biobehavioral model of cancer stress and disease course. *American Psychologist, 49,* 389–404.

Anderson, K. O., Bradley, L. D., Young, L. D., & McDaniel, L. K. (1985). Rheumatoid arthritis: Review of psychological factors related to etiology, effects, and treatment. *Psychological Bulletin, 98,* 358–387.

Anderson, L. T., Campbell, M., Grega, D. M., Perry, R., Small, A. M., & Green, W. H. (1984). Haloperidol in the treatment of infantile autism: Effects on learning and behavior symptoms. *American Journal of Psychiatry, 141,* 1195–1202.

Anderson, S., & Rizzo, M. (1994). Hallucinations following occipital lobe damage: The pathological activation of visual representations. *Journal of Clinical and Experimental Neuropsychology, 16,* 651–663.

Andreasen, N. (l987). Creativity and mental illness: Prevalence rate in writers and their first-degree relatives. *American Journal of Psychiatry, 144,* 1288–1292.

Andreasen, N. C. (1982). Negative symptoms in schizophrenia: Definition and reliability. *Archives of General Psychiatry, 39,* 784–788.

Andreasen, N. C. (1988). Brain imaging: Applications in psychiatry. *Science, 239,* 1381–1388.

Andreasen, N. C., & Olsen, S. C. (1982). Negative v. positive schizophrenia: Definition and validation. *Archives of General Psychiatry, 39,* 789–794.

Andreasen, N. C., Arndt, S. V., Alliger, R., Miller, D., & Flaum, M. (1995). Symptoms of schizophrenia. *Archives of General Psychiatry, 52,* 341–551.

Andreasen, N. C., Nasrallah, H. A., Dunn, V., Olsen, S. C., Grove, W. M., Ehrhardt, J. C., Coffman, J. A., & Crossett, J. H. (1986). Structural abnormalities in the frontal system in schizophrenia. *Archives of General Psychiatry, 43,* 136–144.

Andreasen, N. C., Rezai, K., Alliger, R., Swayze, V. W., Flaum, M., Kirchner, P., Cohen, G., & O'Leary, D. S. (1992). Hypofrontality in neuroleptic-naive patients and in patients with chronic schizophrenia: Assessment with xenon 133 single-photon emission computed tomography and the Tower of London. *Archives of General Psychiatry, 49,* 943–958.

Andreasen, N. C., Smith, M. R., Jacoby, C. G., Kennert, J. W., & Olsen, S. C. (1982). Ventricular enlargement in schizophrenia: Definition and prevalence. *American Journal of Psychiatry, 139,* 292–296.

Andrews, G., Tennant, C., Hewson, D., & Vaillant, G. (1978). Life event stress, social support, coping style, and risk of psychological impairment. *Journal of Nervous and Mental Disease, 166,* 307–316.

Angrist, B. M., & Gershon, S. (1970). The phenomenology of experimentally induced amphetamine psychosis: Preliminary observations. *Biological Psychiatry, 2,* 97–107.

Angrist, B. M., Lee, H. K., & Gershon, S. (1974). The antagonism of amphetamine-induced symptomatology by a neuroleptic. *American Journal of Psychiatry, 131,* 817–819.

Angrist, B. M., Sathananthan, G., & Gershon, S. (1973). Behavioral effects of L-dopa in schizophrenic patients. *Psychopharmacologica, 31,* 1–12.

Anisman, H. (1978). Aversively motivated behavior as a tool in psychopharmacological analysis. In H. Anisman & G. Binami (Eds.), *Psychopharmacology of aversively motivated behavior.* New York: Plenum.

Ansbacher, H. L., & Ansbacher, R. R. (1956). *The individual-psychology of Alfred Adler.* New York: Basic Books.

Appelbaum, P. S., Jick, R. Z., Grisso, T., Givelber, D., Silver, E., & Steadman, H. J. (1993). Use of posttraumatic stress disorder to support an insanity defense. *American Journal of Psychiatry, 150,* 229–234.

Appleby, I. L., Klein, D. F., Schar, E. J., & Levitt, M. (1981). Biochemical indices of lactate-induced panic: A preliminary report. In D. F. Klein & K. Rabkin (Eds.), *Anxiety: New research and changing concepts.* New York: Raven Press.

Ardlie, N. G., Glew, G., & Schwartz, C. J. (1966). Influence of catecholamines on nucleotide-induced platelet aggregation. *Nature, 212,* 415–417.

Arieti, S. (1974). An overview of schizophrenia from a predominantly psychological approach. *American Journal of Psychiatry, 131,* 241–249.

Arndt, S. V., Andreasen, N. C., Flaum, M., Miller, D., & Nopoulos, P. (1995). A longitudinal study of symptom dimensions in schizophrenia. *Archives of General Psychiatry, 52,* 352–360.

Arnold, S. E., Franz, B. R., Gur, R. C., Gur, R. E., Shapiro, R. M., Moberg, P. J., & Trojanowski, J. Q. (1995). Smaller neuron size in schizophrenia in hippocampal subfields that mediate cortical hippocampal interactions. *American Journal of Psychiatry, 152,* 738–748.

Asberg, M., Träskman, L., & Thoren, P. (1976). 5-HIAA in the cerebrospinal fluid: A biochemical suicide predictor? *Archives of General Psychiatry, 33,* 1193–1197.

Asmundson, G. J., & Stein, M. B. (1994). Triggering the false suffocation alarm in panic disorder patients by using a voluntary breath-holding procedure. *American Journal of Psychiatry, 151,* 264–266.

Asscheman, H., & Gooren, L. J. (1992). Hormone treatment in transsexuals. *Journal of Psychology and Human Sexuality, 5,* 39–54.

Attar, B. K., Guerra, N. G., & Tolan, P. H. (1994). Neighborhood disadvantage, stressful life events, and adjustment in urban elementary-school children. *Journal of Clinical Child Psychology, 23,* 391–400.

August, G. J., & Stewart, M. A. (1982). Is there a syndrome of pure hyperactivity? *British Journal of Psychiatry, 140,* 305–311.

August, G. J., Stewart, M. A., & Tsai, L. (1981). The incidence of cognitive disabilities in the siblings of autistic children. *British Journal of Psychiatry, 138,* 416–422.

Avery, D. H., Bolte, M. A., Dager, S. R., Wilson, L. G., Weyer, M., Cox, G. B., & Dunner, D. L. (1993). Dawn simulation treatment of winter depression: A controlled study. *American Journal of Psychiatry, 150,* 113–117.

Avery, D. H., & Lubrano, A. (1979). Depression treated with imipramine and ECT: The De Carolis study reconsidered. *American Journal of Psychiatry, 136,* 559–562.

Ayllon, T. (1963). Intensive treatment of psychotic behavior by stimulus satiation and food reinforcement. *Behaviour Research and Therapy, 1,* 53–61.

Azerrad, J., & Stafford, R. L. (1969). Restorative eating behavior in anorexia nervosa through operant conditioning and environmental manipulation. *Behaviour Research and Therapy, 7,* 165–171.

Baastrup, P. C., Paulsen, J. C., Schou, M., Thomsen, K., & Amdisen, A. (1970). Prophylactic lithium: Double-blind discontinuation in manic depressive and recurrent depressive disorders. *Lancet, 2,* 326–330.

Backman, L., & Forsell, Y. (1994). Episodic memory functioning in a community-based sample of older adults with major depression: Utilization of cognitive support. *Journal of Abnormal Psychology, 103,* 361–370.

Baer, L., & Minichiello, W. E. (1990). Behavior therapy for obsessive-compulsive disorder. In M. A. Jenike, L. Baer, & W. Minichiello (Eds.), *Obsessive-compulsive disorders: Theory and management.* Chicago: Year Book.

Baer, L., Rauch, S. L., Ballantine, T., Martuza, R., Cosgrove, R., Cassem, E., Girunas, I., Manzo, P. A., Dimino, C., & Jenike, M. A. (1995). Cingulotomy for intractable obsessive-compulsive disorder: Prospective long-term follow-up of 18 patients. *Archives of General Psychiatry, 52,* 384–392.

Baer, L., Ricciardi, J., Keuthen, N., & Pettit, A. (1994). Discontinuing obsessive-compulsive disorder medication with behavior therapy. *American Journal of Psychiatry, 151,* 1842.

Bagatell, C. J., & Bremner, W. J. (1996). Androgens in men: Issues and abuses. *New England Journal of Medicine, 334,* 707–714.

Baghurst, P. A., McMichael, A. J., Wigg, N. R., Vimpani, G. V., Robertson, E. F., Roberts, R. J., & Tong, S. (1992). Environmental exposure to lead and children's intelligence at the age of seven years. *New England Journal of Medicine, 327,* 1279–1284.

Bak, R. C., & Stewart, W. A. (1974). Fetishism, transvestism, and voyeurism: A psychoanalytic approach. In S. Arieti (Ed.), *American handbook of psychiatry* (Vol. 3). New York: Basic Books.

Baker, B. L. (1969). Symptom treatment and symptom substitution in enuresis. *Journal of Abnormal Psychology, 74,* 42–49.

Baker, F. M. (1991). Cocaine psychosis. *Journal of the National Medical Association, 81,* 987–1000.

Baker, F. M., Espino, D. V., Robinson, B. H., & Stewart, B. (1993). Assessing depressive symptoms in African American and Mexican American elders. *Clinical Gerontologist, 14,* 15–29.

Baker, G. H. (1982). Life events before the onset of rheumatoid arthritis. *Psychotherapy and Psychosomatics, 38,* 173–177.

Bakwin, H. (1971). Enuresis in twins. *American Journal of Diseases in Children, 121,* 221–225.

Baldessarini, R. J., Kando, J. C., & Centorrino, F. (1995). Hospital use of antipsychotic agents in 1989 and 1993: Stable dosing with decreased length of stay. *American Journal of Psychiatry, 152,* 1038–1044.

Baldessarini, R. J., & Viguera, A. C. (1995). Neuroleptic withdrawal in schizophrenic patients. *Archives of General Psychiatry, 52,* 189–192.

Baller, W. R. (1975). *Bed-wetting: Origin and treatment.* Elmsford, NY: Pergamon Press.

Bancroft, J. (1970). Disorders of sexual potency. In O. Hill (Ed.), *Modern trends in psychosomatic medicine.* Norwalk, CT: Appleton & Lange.

Bancroft, J. (1984a). Hormones and human sexual behavior. *Journal of Sex and Marital Therapy, 10,* 3–22.

Bancroft, J. (1984b). Testosterone therapy for low sexual interest and erectile dysfunction in men: A controlled study. *British Journal of Psychiatry, 14,* 146–151.

Bancroft, J., & Wu, F. C. (1983). Changes in erectile responsiveness during androgen therapy. *Archives of Sexual Behavior, 12,* 59–66.

Bandura, A. (1969). *Principles of behavior modification.* New York: Holt, Rinehart and Winston.

Bandura, A. (1977). Self-efficacy: Toward a unifying theory of behavioral change. *Psychological Review, 84,* 191–215.

Bandura, A. (1983). Psychosocial mechanisms of aggression. In R. G. Geen & E. I. Donnerstein (Eds.), *Aggression: Theoretical and empirical reviews, Vol. 1: Theoretical and methodological issues.* New York: Academic Press.

Bandura, A., & Rosenthal, T. (1966). Vicarious classical conditioning as a function of arousal level. *Journal of Personality and Social Psychology, 3,* 54–62.

Bandura, A., & Walters, R. H. (1963). *Social learning and personality development.* New York: Ronald Press.

Barbee, E. L. (1992). African-American women and depression: A review and critique of the literature. *Archives of Psychiatric Nursing, 6,* 257–265.

Barefoot, J. C., Dahlstrom, W. G., & Williams, R. B. (1983). Hostility, CHD incidence, and total mortality: A 25-year follow-up study of 255 physicians. *Psychosomatic Medicine, 45,* 59–63.

Barker, J. C. (1965). Behavior therapy for transvestism: A comparison of pharmacological and electrical aversion techniques. *British Medical Journal, 111,* 268–276.

Barlow, D. H. (1986). Causes of sexual dysfunction: The role of anxiety and cognitive interference. *Journal of Consulting and Clinical Psychology, 54,* 140–148.

Barlow, D. H. (1988). *Anxiety and its disorders: The nature and treatment of anxiety and panic.* New York: Guilford Press.

Barr, C. E., Mednick, S. A., & Munk-Jorgensen, P. (1990). Exposure to influenza epidemics during gestation and adult schizophrenia. *Archives of General Psychiatry, 47,* 869–874.

Barsky, A. J. (1992). Psychiatric comorbidity in DSM-III-R hypochondriasis. *Archives of General Psychiatry, 49,* 101–108.

Barsky, A. J. (1993). The diagnosis and management of hypochondriachal concerns in the elderly. *Journal of Geriatric Psychiatry, 26,* 129–141.

Bartak, L., Rutter, M., & Cox, A. (1975). A comparative study of infantile autism and specific developmental receptive language disorders: 1. The children. *British Journal of Psychiatry, 126,* 127–145.

Barthell, C. N., & Holmes, D. S. (1968). High school yearbooks: A nonreactive measure of social isolation in graduates who later became schizophrenic. *Journal of Abnormal Psychology, 73,* 313–316.

Bartholomew, R. E. (1994). The social psychology of "epidemic" koro. *International Journal of Social Psychiatry, 40,* 46–60.

Barton, J. L., Mehta, S., & Snaith, R. P. (1973). The prophylactic value of extra ECT in depressive illness. *Acta Psychiatrica Scandinavica, 49,* 386–392.

Bartrop, R., Luckhurst, E., Lazarus, L., Kiloh, L., & Penney, R. (1977). Depressed lymphocyte function after bereavement. *Lancet, 1,* 834–836.

Bartus, R. T. (1990). Drugs to treat age-related neurodegenerative problems. *Journal of the American Geriatrics Society, 38,* 680–695.

Basic Behavioral Science Task Force of the National Advisory Mental Health Council. (1996). Basic behavioral science research for mental health; Thought and communication. *American Psychologist, 51,* 181–189.

Basoglu, M., Paker, M., Ozmen, E., Tasdemir, O., & Sahin, D. (1994). Factors related to long-term traumatic stress responses in survivors of torture in Turkey. *Journal of the American Medical Association, 272,* 357–363.

Bassuk, E. L., & Schoonover, S. C. (1977). *The practitioner's guide to psychoactive drugs.* New York: Plenum.

Bateson, G., Jackson, D. D., Haley, J., & Weakland, J. (1956). Toward a theory of schizophrenia. *Behavioral Science, 1,* 251–264.

Battle, E. S., & Rotter, J. B. (1963). Children's feelings of personal control as related to social class and ethnic group. *Journal of Personality, 31,* 482–490.

Bauer, M. S., Calabrese, J. R., Dunner, P. L., & Post, R. (1994). Multisite data reanalysis of the validity of rapid cycling as a course modifier for bipolar disorder in DSM-IV. *American Journal of Psychiatry, 151,* 506–515.

Bauer, M. S., Kurtz, J. W., Rubin, L. B., & Marcus, J. G. (1994). Mood and behavioral effects of four-week light treatment in winter depressives and controls. *Journal of Psychiatric Research, 28,* 135–145.

Bauer, R. B., Stevens, C., Reveno, W. S., & Rosenbaum, H. (1982). L-dopa treatment of Parkinson's disease: A ten-year follow-up study. *Journal of the American Geriatrics Society, 30,* 322–325.

Baum, A., Gatchel, R. J., & Schaeffer, M. A. (1983). Emotional, behavioral, and physiological effects of chronic stress at Three Mile Island. *Journal of Consulting and Clinical Psychology, 51,* 565–572.

Baxter, L. R., Phelps, M. E., Mazziotta, J. C., Guze, B. H., Schwartz, J. M., & Selin, C. E. (1987). Local cerebral glucose metabolic rates in obsessive-compulsive disorder. *Archives of General Psychiatry, 44,* 211–218.

Baxter, L. R., Phelps, M. E., Mazziotta, J. C., Schwartz, J. M., Gerner, R. H., Selin, C. E., & Sumida, R. M. (1985). Cerebral metabolic rates for glucose in mood disorders. *Archives of General Psychiatry, 42,* 441–447.

Baxter, L. R., Schwartz, J. M., Bergman, K. S., Szuba, M. P., Guze, B. H., Mazziotta, J. C., Alazraki, A., Selin, C. E., Ferng, H. K., Munford, P., & Phelps, M. E. (1992). Caudate glucose metabolic rate changes with both drug and behavior therapy for obsessive-compulsive disorder. *Archives of General Psychiatry, 49,* 681–689.

Bearden, C. (1994). The nightmare: Biological and psychological origins. *Dreaming, 4,* 139–152.

Beasley, C. M., Dornseif, B. E., Bosomworth, J. C., Sayler, M. E., Rampey, A. H., Heiligenstein, J. H., Thompson, V. L., Murphy, D. J., & Masica, D. N. (1991). Fluoxetine and suicide: A meta-analysis of controlled trials of treatment for depression. *British Medical Journal, 303,* 685–692.

Beck, A. T. (1967). *Depression: Clinical, experimental, and theoretical aspects.* New York: Harper & Row.

Beck, A. T. (1976). *Cognitive therapy and the emotional disorders.* New York: International Universities Press.

Beck, A. T., Brown, G., Berchick, R. J., Stewart, B. L., & Steer, R. (1990). Relationship between hopelessness and ultimate suicide: A replication with psychiatric outpatients. *American Journal of Psychiatry, 147,* 190–195.

Beck, A. T., & Emery, G. (1985). *Anxiety disorders and phobias: A cognitive perspective.* New York: Basic Books.

Beck, A. T., Rush, A. J., Shaw, B. F., & Emery, G. (1979). *Cognitive therapy of depression.* New York: Guilford Press.

Beck, A. T., Steer, R., Kovacs, M., & Garrison, B. (1985). Hopelessness and eventual suicide: A 10-year prospective study of patients hospitalized with suicidal ideation. *American Journal of Psychiatry, 142,* 559–563.

Beck, A. T., Ward, C. H., Mendelson, M., Mock, J. E., & Erbaugh, J. K. (1961). An inventory for measuring depression. *Archives of General Psychology, 4,* 561–571.

Beck, A. T., Ward, C. H., Mendelson, M., Mock, J. E., & Erbaugh, J. K. (1962). Reliability of psychiatric diagnosis: 2. A study of consistency of clinical judgments and ratings. *American Journal of Psychiatry, 119,* 351–357.

Beck, A. T., Weissman, A., Lester, D., & Trexler, L. (1974). The measurement of pessimism: The Hopelessness Scale. *Journal of Consulting and Clinical Psychology, 42,* 861–865.

Becker, E., Pinck, M., & Margraf, J. (1994). Memory bias in panic disorder. *Journal of Abnormal Psychology, 103,* 296–399.

Becker, J. V., & Kavoussi, R. J. (1994). Sexual and gender identity disorders. In R. E. Hales, S. C. Yudofsky, & J. A. Talbott (Eds.), *American Psychiatric Press textbook of psychiatry,* (2nd ed.). Washington, DC: American Psychiatric Press.

Beckman, H., & Goodwin, F. K. (1980). Urinary MHPG in subgroups of depressed patients and normal controls. *Neuropsychobiology, 6,* 91–100.

Bedau, H. A., & Radelet, M. L. (1987). Miscarriages of justice in potentially capital cases. *Stanford Law Review, 40,* 21–179.

Bednar, R., & Kaul, T. (1994). Experimental group research. In A. E. Bergin & S. L. Garfield (Eds.), *Handbook of psychotherapy and behavior change* (4th ed.). New York: Wiley.

Beere, P. A., Glagov, S., & Zarins, C. K. (1984). Retarding effect of lowered heart rate on coronary atherosclerosis. *Science, 226,* 180–182.

Beidel, D. C., Turner, M. W., & Trager, K. N. (1994). Test anxiety and childhood anxiety disorders in African American and White school children, *Journal of Anxiety Disorders, 8,* 169–179.

Beiser, M., Cargo, M., & Woodbury, M. A. (1994). A comparison of psychiatric disorders in different cultures: Depressive typologies in Southeast Asian refugees and resident Canadians. *International Journal of Methods in Psychiatric Research, 4,* 157–172.

Bell, I. R. (1994). Somatization disorder: Health care costs in the decade of the brain. *Biological Psychiatry, 35,* 81–83.

Bell, R. A. (1968). A reinterpretation of the direction of effects in studies of socialization. *Psychological Review, 75,* 81–95.

Bellak, L. (1954). *The Thematic Apperception Test and the Children's Apperception Test in clinical use.* Philadelphia: Grune & Stratton.

Belsher, G., & Costello, C. G. (1991). Do confidants of depressed women provide less social support than confidants of nondepressed women? *Journal of Abnormal Psychology, 100,* 516–525.

Benkelfat, C., Ellenbogen M. A., Dean, P., Palmour, R. M., & Young, S. N. (1994). Mood-lowering effect of tryptophan depletion: Enhanced susceptibility in young men at genetic risk for major affective disorder. *Archives of General Psychiatry, 51,* 687–697.

Bennett, D., & Holmes, D. S. (1975). Influence of denial (situation redefinition) and projection on anxiety associated with threat to self-esteem. *Journal of Personality and Social Psychology, 32,* 915–921.

Bennett, D., Holmes, D. S., & Frost, R. O. (1978). Effects of instructions, biofeedback, cognitive mediation, and reward on the control of heart rate and the application of that control in a stressful situation. *Journal of Research in Personality, 12,* 416–430.

Benson, H. (1975). *The relaxation response.* New York: Morrow.

Bentall, R. P. (1990). The illusion of reality: A review and integration of psychological research on hallucinations. *Psychological Bulletin, 107,* 82–95.

Bentall, R. P., Haddock, G., & Slade, P. D. (1994). Cognitive behavior therapy for persistent auditory hallucinations: From theory to therapy. *Behavior Therapy, 25,* 51–66.

Berg, G., Laberg, J. C., Skutle, A., & Ohman, A. (1981). Instructed versus pharmacological effects of alcohol in alcoholics and social drinkers. *Behaviour Research and Therapy, 19,* 55–66.

Bergin, A. E., & Garfield, S. L. (1994). *Handbook of psychotherapy and behavior change* (4th ed.). New York: Wiley.

Berkowitz, L. (1989). Frustration-aggression hypothesis: Examination and reformulation. *Psychological Bulletin, 106,* 59–73.

Berlin, F. S. (1989). The paraphilias and Depo-Provera: Some medical, ethical, and legal considerations. *Bulletin of the American Academy of Psychiatry and the Law, 17,* 233–239.

Berlin, F. S., & Krout, E. (1986). Pedophilia: Diagnostic concepts, treatment, and ethical considerations. *American Journal of Forensic Psychiatry, 7,* 13–30.

Berlin, F. S., & Meinecke, C. (1981). Treatment of sex offenders with antiandrogenic medication: Conceptualization, review of treatment modalities, and preliminary findings. *American Journal of Psychiatry, 138,* 601–607.

Berman, K. F., Torrey, E. F., Daniel, D. G., & Weinberger, D. R. (1992). Regional cerebral blood flow in monozygotic twins discordant and concordant for schizophrenia. *Archives of General Psychiatry, 49,* 927–934.

Berry, H. K., Sutherland, B. S., Umbarger, B., & O'Grady, D. (1967). Treatment of phenylketonuria. *American Journal of Diseases of Childhood, 113,* 2–5.

Berscheid, E., & Walster, E. (1974). A little bit about love. In T. Huston (Ed.), *Foundations of interpersonal attraction.* New York: Academic Press.

Bertelsen, A. (1979). A Danish twin study of manic-depressive disorders. In M. Schou & E. Stromgren (Eds.), *Origin, prevention and treatment of affective disorder.* London: Academic Press.

Bertelsen, A., Havald, B., & Hauge, M. (1977). A Danish twin study of manic-depressive disorders. *British Journal of Psychiatry, 130,* 330–351.

Bettelheim, B. (1967). *The empty fortress.* New York: Free Press.

Beutler, L. E. (1991). Have all won and must all have prizes? Revisiting Luborsky et al.'s verdict. *Journal of Consulting and Clinical Psychology, 59,* 226–232.

Beutler, L. E., Machado, P., & Neufeldt, S. (1994). Therapist variables. In A. E. Bergin & S. L. Garfield (Eds.), *Handbook of psychotherapy and behavior change* (4th ed.). New York: Wiley.

Bexton, W. H., Heron, W., & Scott, T. (1954). Effects of decreased variation in sensory environment. *Canadian Journal of Psychology, 8,* 70–77.

Bianchi, G. N. (1973). Patterns of hypochondriasis: A principal components analysis. *British Journal of Psychiatry, 122,* 541–548.

Bieber, I. (1974). Sadism and masochism: Phenomenology and psychodynamics. In S. Arieti (Ed.), *American handbook of psychiatry* (Vol. 3). New York: Basic Books.

Biederman, J., Faraone, S. V., Mick, E., Spencer, T., Wilens, T., Kiely, K., Guite, J., Ablon, J. S., Reed, E., & Warburton, R. (1995). High risk for attention-deficit hyperactivity disorder among children of parents with childhood onset of the disorder: A pilot study. *American Journal of Psychiatry, 152,* 431–435.

Bihari, K., Pato, M. T., Hill, J. L., & Murphy, D. L. (1991). Neurologic soft signs in obsessive-compulsive disorder. *Archives of General Psychiatry, 48,* 278.

Billings, A. G., & Moos, R. H. (1981). The role of coping responses and social resources in attenuating the impact of stressful life events. *Journal of Behavioral Medicine, 4,* 139–157.

Billings, A. G., Cronkite, R. C., & Moos, R. H. (1983). Social-environmental factors in unipolar depression: Comparisons of depressed patients and nondepressed controls. *Journal of Abnormal Psychology, 92,* 119–133.

Biran, M., & Wilson, G. T. (1981). Treatment of phobic disorders using cognitive and exposure methods: A self-efficacy analysis. *Journal of Consulting and Clinical Psychology, 49,* 886–899.

Black, D. W., & Andreasen, N. C. (1994). Schizophrenia, schizophreniform disorder, and delusional (paranoid) disorder. In R. E., Hales, S. C. Yudofsky, & J. A. Talbott (Eds.), *American Psychiatric Press textbook of psychiatry* (2nd ed.). Washington, DC: American Psychiatric Press.

Blair, C. D., & Lanyon, R. I. (1981). Exhibitionism: Etiology and treatment. *Psychological Bulletin, 89,* 439–463.

Bland, S. H., Krogh, V., Winkelstein, W., & Trevisan, M. (1991). Social network and blood pressure: A population study. *Psychosomatic Medicine, 53,* 598–607.

Blaney, P. H. (1977). Contemporary theories of depression. *Journal of Abnormal Psychology, 86,* 203–233.

Blaney, P. H. (1986). Affect and memory: A review. *Psychological Bulletin, 99,* 229–246.

Blaser, M. J. (1996, February). The bacteria behind ulcers. *Scientific American, 274* (February) 104–107.

Bleuler, E. (1936). *Textbook of psychiatry* (A. Brill, Trans.). New York: Macmillan.

Bleuler, E. (1950). *Dementia praecox* (J. Zinkin, Trans.). New York: International Universities Press.

Bliss, E. L. (1980). Multiple personality. *Archives of General Psychiatry, 37,* 1388–1397.

Bliss, E. L. (1984). A symptom profile of patients with multiple personalities, including MMPI results. *Journal of Nervous and Mental Disease, 171,* 197–202.

Blom, B. E., & Moore, M. C. (1978). *Mental health audit criteria series: Psychotropic drug therapies.* Chicago: Interqual.

Bloom, B. L. (1992). Computer-assisted psychological intervention: A review and commentary. *Clinical Psychology Review, 12,* 169–197.

Bloom, F. E. (1993). Advancing a neurodevelopmental origin of schizophrenia. *Archives of General Psychiatry, 50,* 224–227.

Bloom, L., Houston, B. K., Holmes, D. S., & Burish, T. G. (1977). The effectiveness of attentional diversion and situation redefinition for reducing stress due to a nonambiguous threat. *Journal of Personality and Social Psychology, 11,* 83–94.

Bock, R. D., & Kolakowski, D. (1973). Further evidence of sex-linked major-gene influence on human spatial visualizing ability. *American Journal of Genetics, 25,* 1–14.

Bohman, M., Cloninger, C. R., Sigvardsson, S., & Knorring, A. von. (1982). Predisposition to petty criminality in Swedish adoptees: 1: Genetic and environmental heterogeneity. *Archives of General Psychiatry, 39,* 1233–1241.

Bollen, K. A., & Phillips, D. P. (1981). Suicidal motor vehicle fatalities in Detroit: A replication. *American Journal of Sociology, 81,* 404–412.

Bollen, K. A., & Phillips, D. P. (1982). Imitative suicides: A national study of the effects of television news stories. *American Sociological Review, 47,* 802–809.

Bond, I. K., & Hutchinson, H. C. (1960). Application of reciprocal inhibition therapy to exhibitionism. *Canadian Medical Association Journal, 83,* 23–25.

Bond, P. A., Jenner, J. A., & Sampson, D. A. (1972). Daily variation of the urine content of 3-methoxy-4-hydroxyphenylglycol in two manic-depressive patients. *Psychological Medicine, 2,* 81–85.

Boring, E. G. (1940). Was this analysis a success? *Journal of Abnormal and Social Psychology, 35,* 4–10.

Borison, R. L. (1995). Clinical efficacy of serotonin-dopamine antagonists relative to classic neuroleptics. *Journal of Clinical Psychopharmacology, 15,* 24S–29S.

Borison, R. L., Pathiraja, A. P., Diamond, B. I., & Meibach, R. C. (1992). Risperidone: Clinical safety and efficacy in schizophrenia. *Psychopharmacology Bulletin, 28,* 213–217.

Borkovec, T., & Sides, K. (1979). Critical procedural variables related to the physiological effects of progressive relaxation: A review. *Behaviour Research and Therapy, 17,* 119–126.

Bornstein, P. E., Clayton, P. J., Halikas, J. A., Maurice, W. L., & Robins, E. (1973). The depression of widowhood after thirteen months. *British Journal of Psychiatry, 122,* 561–566.

Bostock, T., & Williams, C. L. (1975). Attempted suicide: An operant formulation. *Australian and New Zealand Journal of Psychiatry, 9,* 107–110.

Bovim, G., Naess, P., Helle, J., & Sand, T. (1995). Caffeine influence on the motor steadiness battery in neuropsychological tests. *Journal of Clinical and Experimental Neuropsychology, 17,* 472–476.

Bower, E. M., Shellhamer, T. A., & Daily, J. M. (1960). School characteristics of male adolescents who later became schizophrenic. *American Journal of Orthopsychiatry, 30,* 712–729.

Bower, G. H. (1981). Mood and memory. *American Psychologist, 36,* 129–148.

Bower, G. H. (1987). Commentary on mood and memory. *Behaviour Research and Therapy, 25,* 443–455.

Bowlby, J. (1952). *Maternal care and mental health.* Geneva: World Health Organization.

Boyle, R. G., Jensen, J., Hatsukami, D. K., & Severson, H. H. (1995). Measuring dependence in smokeless tobacco users. *Addictive Behaviors, 20,* 443–450.

Bradbury, T. N., & Miller, G. A. (1985). Season of birth in schizophrenia: A review of evidence, methodology, and etiology. *Psychological Bulletin, 98,* 569–594.

Braden, W., Stillman, R. C., & Wyatt, R. J. (1974). Effects of marijuana on contingent negative variation and reaction times. *Archives of General Psychiatry, 31,* 537–541.

Brady, E. U., & Kendall, P. C. (1992). Comorbidity of anxiety and depression in children. *Psychological Bulletin, 111,* 244–255.

Brady, J. P., Zeller, W. W., & Reznikoff, M. (1959). Attitudinal factors influencing outcome of treatment of hospitalized psychiatric patients. *Journal of Clinical and Experimental Psychopathology, 20,* 326–334.

Braff, D. L., Grillon, C., & Geyer, M. A. (1992). Gating and habituation of the startle reflex in schizophrenic patients. *Archives of General Psychiatry, 49,* 206–215.

Braginsky, B. M., & Braginsky, D. D. (1967). Schizophrenic patients in the psychiatric interview: An experimental study of their effectiveness at manipulation. *Journal of Consulting Psychology, 21,* 543–547.

Braginsky, B. M., Braginsky, D. D., & Ring, K. (1969). *Methods of madness: The mental hospital as a last resort.* New York: Holt, Rinehart and Winston.

Braginsky, B. M., Grosse, M., & Ring, K. (1966). Controlling outcomes through impression management: An experimental study of the manipulative tactics of mental patients. *Journal of Consulting Psychology, 30,* 295–300.

Bramel, D., Bell, J., & Margulis, S. (1965). Attributing danger as a means of explaining one's fear. *Journal of Experimental Social Psychology, 1,* 267–281.

Brancato, V., Barbini, B., Regazzetti, M. G., Colombo, C., et al. (1994). Negative symptoms in schizophrenia: An open study of placebo-fluvoxamine treatment added to neuroleptics. *New Trends in Experimental and Clinical Psychiatry, 10,* 21–24.

Brandsma, J. M., & Ludwig, A. M. (1974). A case of multiple personality: Diagnosis and treatment. *International Journal of Clinical and Experimental Hypnosis, 22,* 216–233.

Braucht, G. (1979). Interactional analysis of suicidal behavior. *Journal of Consulting and Clinical Psychology, 47,* 653–669.

Braun, B. G. (1983a). Neurophysiologic changes in multiple personality due to integration: A preliminary report. *American Journal of Clinical Hypnosis, 26,* 84–92.

Braun, B. G. (1983b). Psychophysiologic phenomena in multiple personality and hypnosis. *American Journal of Clinical Hypnosis, 26,* 124–137.

Braun, B. G. (1984). Hypnosis creates multiple personality: Myth or reality? *International Journal of Clinical and Experimental Hypnosis, 32,* 191–197.

Breggin, P. R. (1979). *Electroshock: Its brain-disabling effects.* New York: Springer.

Brehm, S. S., & Smith, T. W. (1986). Social psychological approaches to psychotherapy and behavior change. In S. L. Garfield & A. E. Bergin (Eds.), *Handbook of psychotherapy and behavior change* (3rd ed.). New York: Wiley.

Breier, A. (1995). Serotonin, schizophrenia, and antipsychotic drug action. *Schizophrenia Research, 14,* 187–202.

Breier, A., & Astrachan, B. M. (1984). Characterization of schizophrenic patients who commit suicide. *American Journal of Psychiatry, 141,* 206–209.

Breier, A., Buchanan, R. W., Elkashef, A., Munson, R. C., Kirkpatrick, B., & Gellad, F. (1992). Brain morphology and schizophrenia: A magnetic resonance imaging study of limbic, prefrontal cortex, and caudate structures. *Archives of General Psychiatry, 49,* 921–926.

Breier, A., Buchanan, R. W., Kirkpatrick, B., Davis, O. R., Irish, D., Summerfelt, A., & Carpenter, W. T. (1994). Effects of clozapine on positive and negative symptoms in outpatients with schizophrenia. *American Journal of Psychiatry, 151,* 20–26.

Brenesova, V., Oswald, I., & Loudon, J. (1975). Two types of insomnia: Too much waking or not enough sleep. *British Journal of Psychiatry, 126,* 439–445.

Brennan, P. A., & Mednick S. A. (1994). Learning theory approach to the deterrence of criminal recidivism. *Journal of Abnormal Psychology, 103,* 430–440.

Breslau, N., Davis, G. C., Andreski, P., & Peterson, E. (1991). Traumatic events and posttraumatic stress disorder in an urban population of young adults. *Archives of General Psychiatry, 48,* 216–222.

Breslau, N., Kilbey, M. M., & Andreski, P. (1992). Nicotine withdrawal symptoms and psychiatric disorders: Findings from an epidemiological study of young adults. *American Journal of Psychiatry, 149,* 464–469.

Breslau, N., Kilbey, M. M., & Andreski, P. (1993). Nicotine dependence and major depression: New evidence from a prospective investigation. *Archives of General Psychiatry, 50,* 31–35.

Brewin, C. R. (1985). Depression and causal attributions: What is their relation? *Psychological Bulletin, 98,* 297–309.

Bromberg, W. (1959). *The mind of man: A history of psychotherapy and psychoanalysis.* New York: HarperCollins.

Brooks-Gunn, J., & Petersen, A. C. (1991). Studying the emergence of depression and depressive symptoms during adolescence. *Journal of Youth and Adolescence, 20,* 115–119.

Brotman, A. W., & Stern, T. A. (1983). Case study of cardiovascular abnormalities in anorexia nervosa. *American Journal of Psychiatry, 140,* 1227–1228.

Broughton, R. J., Billings, R., Cartwright, R., Doucette, D., Orchard, B., Hill, R., & Turnell, G. Edmeads, J., Edwards, M., Ervin, F., (1994). Homicidal somnambulism: A case report. *Sleep, 17,* 253–264.

Brown, D. R., Ahmed, F., Gary, L. E., & Milburn, N. G. (1995). Major depression in a community sample of African Americans. *American Journal of Psychiatry, 152,* 373–378.

Brown, G. L., & Goodwin, F. K. (1986). Human aggression and suicide. *Suicide and Life-Threatening Behavior, 16,* 223–240.

Brown, G. L., Goodwin, F. K., Ballenger, J. C., et al. (1979). Aggression in humans correlates with cerebrospinal fluid amine metabolites. *Psychiatry Research, 1,* 131–139.

Brown, G. W., & Birley, J. L. T. (1968). Crises and life changes and the onset of schizophrenia. *Journal of Health and Social Behavior, 9,* 203–214.

Brown, G. W., & Harris, T. O. (1978). *Social origins of depression: A study of psychiatric disorders in women.* New York: Free Press.

Brown, R. T., Wayne, M. E., & Medenis, R. (1985). Methylphenidate and cognitive therapy: A comparison of treatment with hyperactive boys. *Journal of Abnormal Child Psychology, 13,* 69–88.

Brown, T. A., Barlow, D. H., & Liebowtiz, M. R. (1994). The empirical basis of generalized anxiety disorder. *American Journal of Psychiatry, 151,* 1272–1280.

Bruce, T. J., Spiegel, D. A., Gregg, S. F., & Nuzzarello, A. (1995). Predictors of alpraxolam discontinuation with and without cognitive behavior therapy in panic disorder. *American Journal of Psychiatry, 152,* 1156–1160.

Bruch, H. (1982). Anorexia nervosa: Therapy and theory. *American Journal of Psychiatry, 139,* 1531–1538.

Buchsbaum, M. S., Haier, R. J., Potkin, S. G., Nuechterlein, K., Bracha, H. S., Katz, M., Lohr, J., Wu, J., Lottengerg, S., Jerabek, P. A., Trenary, M., Tafalla, R., Reynolds, C., & Bunney, W. E., Jr. (1992). Frontostriatal disorder of cerebral metabolism in never-medicated schizophrenics. *Archives of General Psychiatry, 49,* 935–942.

Buck, J. N. (1948). The H-P-T test. *Journal of Clinical Psychology, 4,* 151–158.

Buhrich, N., Theile, H., Yaw, A., & Crawford, A. (1979). Plasma testosterone, serum FSH, and serum LH levels in transvestism. *Archives of Sexual Behavior, 8,* 49–53.

Bumby, K. M. (1993). Reviewing the guilty but mentally ill alternative: A case of the blind "pleading" the blind. *Journal of Psychiatry and Law, 21,* 191–220.

Bunch, J. (1972). Recent bereavement in relation to suicide. *Journal of Psychosomatic Research, 16,* 361–366.

Bunney, W. E., Jr., & Murphy, D. L. (1976). Neurobiological considerations on the mode of action of lithium carbonate in the treatment of affective disorders. *Pharmacopsychiatry, 9,* 142–147.

Burckhardt, G. (1891). Über Rindenexcisionen als Beitrag zur operativen Therapie die Psychosen. *Algemeine Zeitschrift für Psychiatrie, 47,* 463–468.

Burish, T. G. (1981). EMG biofeedback in the treatment of stress-related disorders. In C. K. Prokop & L. A. Bradley (Eds.), *Medical psychology: Contributions to behavioral medicine.* New York: Academic Press.

Burrows, G. D., Davies, B., Fail, L., Poynton, C., & Stevenson, H. (1976). A placebo-controlled trial of diazepam and oxprenolol for anxiety. *Psychopharmacology, 50,* 177–179.

Burt, D. B., Zembar, M. J., & Niedershe, G. (1995). Depression and memory impairment: A meta-analysis of the association, its pattern, and specificity. *Psychological Bulletin, 117,* 285–305.

Buss, A. H., & Lang, P. J. (1965). Psychological deficit in schizophrenia: 1. Affect, reinforcement, and concept attainment. *Journal of Abnormal Psychology, 70,* 2–24.

Busto, U., Sellers, E. M., Naranjo, C. A., Cappell, H., Sanchez-Craig, M., & Sykora, K. (1986). Withdrawal reaction after long-term therapeutic use of benzodiazepines. *New England Journal of Medicine, 315,* 854–859.

Butler, G., & Mathews, A. (1983). Cognitive processes in anxiety. *Advances in Behaviour Research and Therapy, 5,* 51–62.

Bystritsky, A., & Waikar, S. (1994). Inert placebo versus active medication: Patient blindability in clinical pharmacological trials. *Journal of Nervous and Mental Disease, 182,* 475–485.

Cade, J. F. (1949). Lithium salts in the treatment of psychotic excitement. *Medical Journal of Australia, 2,* 349–352.

Cadoret, R. J. (1978a). Evidence of genetic inheritance of primary affective disorder in adoptees. *American Journal of Psychiatry, 135,* 463–466.

Cadoret, R. J. (1978b). Psychopathology in adopted-away offspring of biologic parents with antisocial behavior. *Archives of General Psychiatry, 35,* 176–184.

Cadoret, R. J., & Cain, C. (1980). Sex differences in predictors of antisocial behavior in adoptees. *Archives of General Psychiatry, 37,* 1171–1175.

Cadoret, R. J., Troughton, E., O'Gorman, T. W., & Heywood, E. (1986). An adoption study of genetic and environmental factors in drug abuse. *Archives of General Psychiatry, 43,* 1131–1136.

Cadoret, R. J., Troughton, E., & Widmer, R. (1984). Clinical differences between antisocial and primary alcoholics. *Comprehensive Psychiatry, 25,* 1–8.

Calev, A., Nigal, D., Shapira, B., Tubi, N., Chazan, S., Ben-Yehuda, Y., Kugelmass, S., & Lerer, B. (1991). Early and long-term effects of electroconvulsive therapy and depression on memory and other cognitive functions. *Journal of Nervous and Mental Disease, 179,* 526–533.

Campbell, D., & Beets, J. (1978). Lunacy and the moon. *Psychological Bulletin, 85,* 1123–1129.

Campbell, D. T., & Stanley, J. C. (1963). Experimental and quasi-experimental designs for research and teaching. In N. L. Gage (Ed.), *Handbook of research on teaching.* Chicago: Rand McNally.

Campinha-Bacote, J. (1992). Voodoo illness. *Perspectives in Psychiatric Care, 28,* 11–17.

Cannon, T. D., Mednick, S. A., & Parnas, J. (1989). Genetic and perinatal determinants of structural brain deficits in schizophrenia. *Archives of General Psychiatry, 46,* 883–889.

Cannon, T. D., Mednick, S. A., Parnas, J., Schulsinger, F., Praestholm, J., & Vestergaard, A. (1993). Developmental brain abnormalities in the offspring of schizophrenic mothers. *Archives of General Psychiatry, 50,* 551–564.

Cannon, T. D., Mednick, S. A., Parnas, J., Schulsinger, F., Praestholm, J., & Vestergaard, A. (1995). Developmental brain abnormalities in the offspring of schizophrenic mothers: 2. Structural brain characteristics of schizophrenia and schizotypal personality disorder. *Archives of General Psychiatry, 51,* 955–962.

Cannon, T. D., Zorrilla, L. E., Shatasel, D., Gur, R. E., Gur, R. C., Marco, E. J., Moberg, P., & Price, R. A. (1994). Neuropsychological functioning in siblings discordant for schizophrenia and healthy volunteers. *Archives of General Psychiatry, 51,* 651–661.

Cantwell, D. P. (1972). Psychiatric illness in the families of hyperactive children. *Archives of General Psychiatry, 27,* 414–417.

Caplan, L. (1984). *The insanity defense and the trial of John W. Hinckley, Jr.* Boston: Godine.

Carey, G., & Di Lalla, D. L. (1994). Personality and psychopathology: Genetic perspectives. *Journal of Abnormal Psychology, 103,* 32–43.

Carey, G., & Gottesman, I. I. (1981). Twin and family studies of anxiety, phobic, and obsessive disorders. In D. F. Klein & J. G. Rabkin (Eds.), *Anxiety: New research and changing concepts.* New York: Raven Press.

Carlat, D. J., & Camargo, C. A. (1991). Review of bulimia nervosa in males. *American Journal of Psychiatry, 148,* 831–843.

Carling, P. J., Miller, S., Daniels, L., & Randolph, F. L. (1987). A state mental health system with no state hospital: The Vermont feasibility study. *Hospital and Community Psychiatry, 38,* 617–619.

Carlson, E. B., & Rosser-Hogan, R. (1994). Cross-cultural response to trauma: A study of traumatic experiences and posttraumatic symptoms in Cambodian refugees. *Journal of Traumatic Stress, 7,* 43–58.

Carlson, G. A., Kotin, J., Davenport, Y. B., & Adland, M. (1974). Follow-up of 53 bipolar manic-depressive patients. *British Journal of Psychiatry, 124,* 134–139.

Carlsson, A. (1978). Antipsychotic drugs, neurotransmitters, and schizophrenia. *American Journal of Psychiatry, 135,* 164–172.

Caroff, S. N., Man, S. C., Lazarus, A., Sullivan, K., & MacFadden, W. (1991). Neuroleptic malignant syndrome: Diagnostic issues. *Psychiatric Annals, 21,* 147.

Carpenter, W. T. (1995). Serotonin-dopamine antagonists and treatment of negative symptoms. *Journal of Clinical Psychopharmacology, 15,* 30S–35S.

Carpenter, W. T., & Tamminga, C. A. (1995). Why neuroleptic withdrawal in schizophrenia? *Archives of General Psychiatry, 52,* 192–193.

Carrasco, J. L., Saiz-Ruiz, J., Hollander, E., Cesar, J., et al. (1994). Low platelet monoamine oxidase activity in pathological gambling. *Acta Psychiatrica Scandinavica, 90,* 427–431.

Carrington, P. J., & Moyer, S. (1994). Gun availability and suicide in Canada: Testing the displacement hypothesis. *Studies on Crime and Crime Prevention, 3,* 168–178.

Carroll, B. J. (1982). The dexamethasone suppression test for melancholia. *British Journal of Psychiatry, 140,* 292–304.

Carter, C. H. (Ed.). (1975). *Handbook of mental retardation syndromes.* Springfield, IL: Thomas.

Carter, M. M., Hollon, S. D., Carson, R., & Shelton, R. C. (1995). Effects of a safe person on induced distress following a biological challenge in panic disorder with agoraphobia. *Journal of Abnormal Psychology, 104,* 156–163.

Cartwright, R. D., Ristanovic, R., Diaz, F., Caldarelli, D., & Adler, G. (1991). A comparative study of treatments for positional sleep apnea. *Sleep, 14,* 546–522.

Carver, C. S., & Ganellen, R. J. (1983). Depression and components of self-punitiveness: High standards, self-criticism, and overgeneralization. *Journal of Abnormal Psychology, 92,* 330–337.

Carver, C. S., Coleman, A. E., & Glass, D. C. (1976). The coronary-prone behavior pattern and the suppression of fatigue on a treadmill test. *Journal of Personality and Social Psychology, 33,* 460–466.

Casper, R. C., Redmond, E., Katz, M. M., Schaffer, C. B., Davis, J. M., & Koslow, S. H. (1985). Somatic symptoms in primary affective disorder. *Archives of General Psychiatry, 42,* 1098–1104.

Cassiday, K. L., McNally, R. J., & Zeitlin, S. B. (1992). Cognitive processing of trauma cues in rape victims with posttraumatic stress disorder. *Cognitive Therapy and Research, 16,* 283–295.

Castaneda, R., & Franco, H. (1985). Sex and ethnic distribution of borderline personality disorder in an inpatient sample. *American Journal of Psychiatry, 142,* 1202–1203.

Ceci, S. J., Huffman, M. L. C., and Smith, E. (1995). Repeatedly thinking about a non-event: Source misattributions among preschoolers. The recovered memory/false memory debate [Special issue]. *Consciousness and Cognition: An International Journal, 3,* 388–407.

Centers for Disease Control. (1986). *Youth suicide surveillance.* Washington, DC: U.S. Public Health Service.

Cepeda-Benito, A. (1993). Meta-analytical review of the efficacy of nicotine chewing gum in smoking treatment programs. *Journal of Consulting and Clinical Psychology, 61,* 822–830.

Cerletti, U., & Bini, L. (1938). L'elettroshock. *Archivio Generale di Neurologia Psichiatria e Psicoanalisi, 19,* 266–268.

Cerny, J. A. (1978). Biofeedback and the voluntary control of sexual arousal in women. *Behavior Therapy, 9,* 847–855.

Chadwick, P. D., Lowe, C. F., Horne, P. J., & Higson, P. J. (1994). Modifying delusions: The role of empirical testing. *Behavior Therapy, 25,* 35–50.

Chang-Liang, R., & Denney, D. R. (1976). Applied relaxation training in self-control. *Journal of Counseling Psychology, 23,* 183–189.

Chapman, L. J., Chapman, J. P., & Miller, G. A. (1964). A theory of verbal behavior in schizophrenia. In B. A. Maher (Ed.), *Progress in experimental personality research* (Vol. 1). New York: Academic Press.

Chapman, L. J., Chapman, J. P., & Miller, G. A. (1984). A theory of verbal behavior in schizophrenia: Postscript. In B. A. Maher (Ed.), *Contributions to the psychopathology of schizophrenia.* New York: Academic Press.

Charney, D. S., Deutch, A. Y., Krystal, J. H., Southwick, S. M., & David, M. (1993). Psychobiologic mechanisms of posttraumatic stress disorder. *Archives of General Psychiatry, 50,* 294–305.

Chaturvedi, S. K. (1993). Neurosis across cultures. *International Review of Psychiatry, 5,* 179–191.

Checkley, A. A., Murphy, D. G. M., Abbas, M., Marks, M., Winton, F., Palazidov, E., Murphy, D., Franey, C., & Arendt, J. (1993). Melatonin rhythms in seasonal affective disorder. *British Journal of Psychiatry, 163,* 332–337.

Chesney, M. A., Eagleston, J. R., & Rosenman, R. H. (1981). Type A behavior: Assessment and interventions. In C. K. Prokop & L. A. Bradley (Eds.), *Medical psychology: Contributions to behavioral medicine.* New York: Academic Press.

Chesney, M. A., & Rosenman, R. H. (1985). *Anger and hostility in cardiovascular and behavioral disorders.* Washington, DC: Hemisphere.

Chesno, F., & Kilmann, P. R. (1975). Effects of stimulation intensity on sociopathic avoidance learning. *Journal of Abnormal Psychology, 84,* 144–150.

Chew, P. K., Phoon, W. H., & Mae-Lim, H. A. (1976). Epidemic hysteria among some factory workers in Singapore. *Singapore Medical Journal, 17,* 10–15.

Christiansen, K. O. (1968). Threshold of tolerance in various population groups illustrated by results from the Danish criminologic twin study. In A. V. S. de Reuck & R. Poter (Eds.), *The mentally abnormal offender.* Boston: Little, Brown.

Clark, D. M., & Teasdale, J. D. (1985). Constraints on the effects of mood on memory. *Journal of Personality and Social Psychology, 48,* 1595–1608.

Clarke, R. V., & Lester, D. (1989). *Suicide: Closing the exits.* New York: Springer.

Clayton, P., Desmarais, L., & Winokur, G. (1968). A study of normal bereavement. *American Journal of Psychiatry, 125,* 168–178.

Cleckley, J. (1941). *The mask of sanity.* St. Louis, MO: Mosby.

Cleckley, J. (1976). *The mask of sanity* (5th ed.). St. Louis, MO: Mosby.

Clomipramine Collaborative Study Group. (1991). Clomipramine in the treatment of patients with obsessive-compulsive disorder. *Archives of General Psychiatry, 48,* 730–738.

Cloninger, C. R. (1987). Neurogenetic adaptive mechanisms in alcoholism. *Science, 236,* 410–416.

Clum, G. A., Clum, G. A., & Surls, R. (1993). A meta-analysis of treatments for panic disorder. *Journal of Consulting and Clinical Psychology, 61,* 317–326.

Clum, G. A., & Knowles, S. L. (1991). Why do some people with panic disorders become avoidant? A review. *Clinical Psychology Review, 11,* 295–313.

Cobb, S., & Rose, R. M. (1973). Hypertension, peptic ulcer, and diabetes in air traffic controllers. *Journal of the American Medical Association, 224,* 489–492.

Coccaro, E. F., & Kavoussi, R. J. (1991). Biological and pharmacological aspects of borderline personality disorder. *Hospital and Community Psychiatry, 42,* 1029–1033.

Cochrane, R., & Robertson, A. (1975). Stress in the lives of parasuicides. *Social Psychiatry, 10,* 161–172.

Cohen, A., Barlow, D. H., & Blanchard, E. (1985). Psychophysiology of relaxation-associated panic attacks. *Journal of Abnormal Psychology, 94,* 96–101.

Cohen, C. I., & Thompson, K. S. (1992). Homeless mentally ill or mentally ill homeless? *American of Journal of Psychiatry, 149,* 816–823.

Cohen, J. (1995). New Alzheimer's gene found. *Reseach News, 268,* 1845–1846.

Cohen, J. D., & Servan-Schreiber, D. (1992). Introduction to neural network models in psychiatry. *Psychiatric Annals, 22,* 113–118.

Cohen, L., Delahanty, D. L., Schmitz, J. B., Jenkins, F. J., & Baum, A. (1993). The effects of stress on natural killer cell activity in healthy men. *Journal of Applied Biobehavioral Research, 1,* 120–132.

Cohen, N. J., Sullivan, S., Minde, K. K., Novak, C., & Helwig, C. (1981). Evaluation of the relative effectiveness of methylphenidate and cognitive behavior modification in the treatment of kindergarten-aged hyperactive children. *Journal of Abnormal Child Psychology, 9,* 43–54.

Cohen, S. L., & Fiedler, J. E. (1974). Content analysis of multiple messages in suicide notes. *Suicide and Life-Threatening Behavior, 4,* 75–95.

Cohen-Kettenis, P. T., & Gooren, L. J. (1992). The influence of hormone treatment on psychological functioning of transsexuals. *Journal of Psychology and Human Sexuality, 5,* 55–67.

Cole, J. O. (1982). Antipsychotic drugs: Is more better? *McLean Hospital Journal, 7,* 61–87.

Cole, J. O., Goldberg, S. C., & Davis, J. M. (1966). Drugs in the treatment of psychosis: Controlled studies. In P. Solomon (Ed.), *Psychiatric drugs*. Philadelphia: Grune & Stratton.

Cole, J. O., Goldberg, S. C., & Klerman, G. L. (1964). Phenothiazine treatment in acute schizophrenia. *Archives of General Psychiatry, 10*, 246–261.

Coleman, R. E. (1975). Manipulation of self-esteem as a determinant of mood of elated and depressed women. *Journal of Abnormal Psychology, 84*, 693–700.

Collaer, M. L., & Hines, M. (1995). Human behavioral sex differences: A role of gonadal hormones during early development? *Psychological Bulletin, 118*, 55–107.

Colligan, M. J., Pennebaker, J. W., & Murphy, L. R. (1982). *Mass psychogenic illness: A social psychological analysis*. Hillsdale, NJ: Erlbaum.

Collins, A. M., & Loftus, E. F. (1975). A spreading-activation theory of semantic processing. *Psychological Bulletin, 82*, 407–428.

Collins, R. L. (1993). Sociocultural aspects of alcohol use and abuse: Ethnicity and gender. *Drugs and Society, 8*, 89–116.

Collyer, F. (1994). Sex-change surgery: An "unacceptable innovation?" *Australian and New Zealand Journal of Sociology, 30*, 3–19.

Colvin, C. R., & Block, J. (1994). Do positive illusions foster mental health? An examination of the Taylor and Brown formulation. *Psychological Bulletin, 116*, 3–20.

Comings, D. E. (1990). *Tourette's syndrome and human behavior*. Duarte, CA: Hope Press.

Comings, D. E., & Comings, B. G. (1990). A controlled family history study of Tourette's syndrome: 1. Attention-deficit hyperactivity disorder and learning disorders. *Journal of Clinical Psychiatry, 51*, 275–280.

Congdon, M. H., Hain, J., & Stevenson, I. (1961). A case of multiple personality illustrating the transition from role playing. *Journal of Nervous and Mental Disease, 132*, 497–504.

Conger, J. J. (1951). The effects of alcohol on conflict between behavior in the albino rat. *Quarterly Journal of Studies on Alcohol, 12*, 1–29.

Conners, C. K., (1980). *Food additives and hyperactive children*. New York: Plenum.

Conte, H. R. (1986). Multivariate assessment of sexual dysfunction. *Journal of Consulting and Clinical Psychology, 54*, 149–157.

Conte, J. R., & Berliner, L. (1981). Sexual abuse of children: Implications for practice. *Social Casework, 62*, 601–606.

Cook, M., Mineka, S., Wolkenstein, B., & Laitsch, K. (1985). Observational conditioning of snake fear in unrelated rhesus monkeys. *Journal of Abnormal Psychology, 94*, 591–610.

Cook, T. D., & Campbell, D. T. (1979). *Quasi-experimentation: Design and analysis issues for field settings*. Chicago: Rand McNally.

Cools, J., Schotte, D. E., & McNally, R. J. (1992). Emotional arousal and overeating in restrained eaters. *Journal of Abnormal Psychology, 101*, 348–351.

Coons, P. M. (1988). Psychophysiological aspects of multiple personality disorder. *Dissociation, 1*, 47–53.

Coons, P. M., Milstein, V., & Marley, C. (1982). EEG studies of two multiple personalities and a control. *Archives of General Psychiatry, 39*, 823–825.

Cooper, A. J. (1964). A case of fetishism and impotence treated by behavior therapy. *British Journal of Psychiatry, 109*, 649–652.

Cooper, M. L., Russell, M., Skinner, J. B., Frone, M. R., & Mudar, P. (1992). Stress and alcohol use: Moderating effects of gender, coping, and alcohol expectancies. *Journal of Abnormal Psychology, 101*, 139–152.

Corrigan, P. W., Wallace, C. J., Schade, M. L., & Green, M. F. (1994). Learning medication self-management skills in schizophrenia: Relationships with cognitive deficits and psychiatric symptoms. *Behavior Therapy, 25*, 5–15.

Coryell, W., Endicott, J., & Keller, M. (1991). Major depression in a nonclinical sample. *Archives of General Psychiatry, 49*, 117–125.

Coryell, W., Endicott, J., & Keller, M. (1992). Rapidly cycling affective disorder: Demographics, diagnosis, family history, and course. *Archives of General Psychiatry, 49*, 126–131.

Coryell, W., Endicott, J., Winokur, G., Akiskal, H., Solomon, D., Leon, A., Mueller, T., & Shea, T. (1995). Characteristics and significance of untreated major depressive disorder. *American Journal of Psychiatry, 152*, 1124–1129.

Costello, C. G. (1982). Fears and phobias in women: A community study. *Journal of Abnormal Psychology, 91*, 280–286.

Couchells, S. M., Johnson, S. B., Carter, R., & Walker, D. (1981). Behavioral and environmental characteristics of treated and untreated enuretic children and matched nonenuretic controls. *Journal of Pediatrics, 99*, 812–816.

Cournos, F. Faulkner, L. R., Fitzgerald, L., Griffith, E. Muntez, M. R., & Winick, B. (1993). Report of the Task Force on Consent to Voluntary Hospitalization. *Bulletin of the American Academy of Psychiatry and the Law, 21*, 293–307.

Covi, L., Lipman, R., Derogatis, L. R., Smith, J. E., & Pattison, J. H. (1974). Drugs and group psychotherapy in neurotic depression. *American Journal of Psychiatry, 131*, 191–198.

Covington v. Harris, 419 F.2d 617 (D.C. Cir. 1969).

Coward, D. M., Imperato, A., Urwyler, S., & White, T. G. (1989). Biochemical and behavioral properties of clozapine. *Psychopharmacology, 99*, S6–S12.

Cox, J. L. (1992). Depression after childbirth. In E. S. Paykel (Ed.), *Handbook of affective disorders* (2nd ed.). New York: Guilford Press.

Coyne, J. C., Aldwin, C., & Lazarus, R. S. (1981). Depression and coping in stressful episodes. *Journal of Abnormal Psychology, 90*, 439–447.

Coyne, J. C., & Gotlib, I. H. (1983). The role of cognition in depression: A critical appraisal. *Psychological Bulletin, 94*, 472–505.

Coyne, J. C., & Whiffen, V. E. (1995). Issues in personality as diathesis for depression: The case of sociotropy-dependency and autonomy–self-criticism. *Psychological Bulletin, 118*, 358–376.

Craft, M. J. (1969). The natural history of psychopathic disorder. *British Journal of Psychiatry, 115*, 39–44.

Craig, R. J. (1995). The role of personality in understanding substance abuse. *Alcoholism Treatment Quarterly, 13*, 17–27.

Craighead, L. W., & Agras, W. S. (1991). Mechanisms of action in cognitive-behavioral and pharmacological interventions for obesity and bulimia nervosa. *Journal of Consulting and Clinical Psychology, 59*, 115–125.

Craske, M. G., & Barlow, D. H. (1989). Nocturnal panic. *Journal of Nervous and Mental Disease, 177*, 160–167.

Creese, I. (1985). Dopamine and antipsychotic medications. In R. E. Hales & A. J. Frances (Eds.), *Psychiatry update: The American Psychiatric Association annual review* (Vol. 4). Washington, DC: American Psychiatric Press.

Crick, N. R., & Dodge, K. A. (1994). A review and reformulation of social information-processing mechanisms in children's social adjustment. *Psychological Bulletin, 115*, 74–101.

Crisp, A. H. (1967). The possible significance of some behavioral correlates of weight and carbohydrate intake. *Journal of Psychosomatic Research, 11*, 117–131.

Crowe, R. R. (1974). An adoption study of antisocial personality. *Archives of General Psychiatry, 31*, 785–791.

Crowley, P. H., Hayden, T. L., & Gulitai, D. K. (1982). Etiology of Down syndrome. In S. M. Pueschel & J. E. Rynders (Eds.), *Down syndrome: Advances in biomedicine and the behavioral sciences*. Cambridge, MA: Ware Press.

Cutrona, C. (1983). Causal attributions and perinatal depression. *Journal of Abnormal Psychology, 92*, 161–172.

Da Costa, J. M. (1871). On irritable heart. *American Journal of Medical Science, 61*, 17–52.

Dager, S. R., Saai, A. K., Comess, K. A., & Dunner, D. L. (1988). Mitral valve prolapse and the anxiety disorders. *Hospital and Community Psychiatry, 39*, 517–527.

Dager, S. R., Strauss, W. L., Marro, K. I., Richards, T. L., Metzger, G. D., & Artru, A. A. (1995). Proton magnetic resonance spectroscopy investigation of hyperventilation in subjects with panic disorder and comparison subjects. *American Journal of Psychiatry, 152*, 666–672.

Dalgaard, O. S., & Kringlen, E. (1976). A Norwegian twin study of criminality. *British Journal of Criminology, 16*, 213–232.

Dalton, K. (1971). Prospective study into puerperal depression. *British Journal of Psychiatry, 118*, 689–692.

Damasio, A. R. (1994). *Descartes' error: Emotion, reason, and the human brain*. New York: Putnam.

Danker-Brown, P., & Baucom, D. H. (1982). Cognitive influences on the development of learned helplessness. *Journal of Personality and Social Psychology, 43*, 793–801.

Darkes, J., & Goldman, M. S. (1993). Expectancy challenge and drinking reduction: Experimental evidence for a mediational process. *Journal of Consulting and Clinical Psychology, 61*, 344–353.

Dasgupta, K., & Hoover, C. E. (1990). Additional cases of suicidal ideation associated with fluoxetine. *American Journal of Psychiatry, 147,* 1570–1571.

David, O. J., Clark, J., & Voeller, K. (1979). Lead and hyperactivity. *Lancet, 2,* 900–903.

Davidson, J. M. (1984). Response to "Hormones and human sexual behavior" by John Bancroft, MD. *Journal of Sex and Marital Therapy, 10,* 23–27.

Davidson, J. M., Camargo, C. A., & Smith, E. R. (1979). Effects of androgens on sexual behavior in hypogonadal men. *Journal of Clinical Endocrinology and Metabolism, 48,* 955–958.

Davidson, J. R. (1992). Monoamine oxidase inhibitors. In E. S. Paykel (Ed.), *Handbook of affective disorders* (2d ed.). New York: Guilford Press.

Davidson, J. R., Hughes, D. C., George, L. K., & Blazer, D. G. (1994). The boundary of social phobia: Exploring the threshold. *Archives of General Psychiatry, 51,* 975–983.

Davidson, M., Harvey, P. D., Powchik, P., Parrella, M., White, L., Knobler, H. Y., Losonczy, M. F., Keefe, R. S., Katz, S., & Frecska, E. (1995). Severity of symptoms in chronically institutionalized geriatric schizophrenic patients. *American Journal of Psychiatry, 152,* 197–207.

Davies, E., & Furham, A. (1986). The dieting and body shape concerns of adolescent females. *Journal of Child Psychology and Psychiatry, 27,* 417–428.

Davis, H., & Unruh, W. R. (1981). The development of the self-schema in adult depression. *Journal of Abnormal Psychology, 90,* 125–133.

Davis, J. M., Schaffer, C. B., Killian, G. A., Kinard, C., & Chan, C. (1980). Important issues in the drug treatment of schizophrenia. *Schizophrenia Bulletin, 6,* 70–87.

Davis, K. (1947). Final note on a case of extreme isolation. *American Journal of Sociology, 57,* 432–457.

Davis, K. L., Kahn, R. S., Ko, G., & Davidson, M. (1991). Dopamine and schizophrenia: A review and reconceptualization. *American Journal of Psychiatry, 148,* 1474–1486.

Dawes, R. M. (1994). *House of cards.* New York: Free Press.

Dawes, R. M., Faust, D., & Meehl, P. E. (1989). Clinical versus actuarial judgment. *Science, 243,* 1668–1674.

Deary, I. J., Fowkes, F. G. R., Donnan, P. T., & Housle, E. (1994). Hostile personality and risks of peripheral arterial disease in the general population. *Psychosomatic Medicine, 56,* 197–202.

de Beurs, E., van Balkom, A. J., Lange, A., Koele, P., & van Dyck, R. (1995). Treatment of panic disorder with agoraphobia: Comparison of fluvoxamine, placebo, and psychological panic management combined with exposure and of exposure in vivo alone. *American Journal of Psychiatry, 152,* 683–691.

Degreef, G., Ashari, M., Bogerts, B., Bilder, R. M., Jody, D. N., Alvir, J. M. J., & Lieberman, J. A. (1992). Volumes of ventricular system subdivisions measured from magnetic resonance images in first-episode schizophrenic patients. *Archives of General Psychiatry, 49,* 531–537.

de Jong, P. J., Merckelbach, H., & Arntz, A. (1995). Covariation bias in phobic women: The relationship between a priori expectancy, on-line expectancy, autonomic responding, and a posteriori contingency judgment. *Journal of Abnormal Psychology, 104,* 55–62.

DeLeon, P. H., & Wiggins, J. G. (1996). Prescription privileges for psychologists. *American Psychologist, 51,* 225–229.

De Leon–Jones, F., Maas, J. W., Dekirmenjian, H., & Sanchez, J. (1975). Diagnostic subgroups of affective disorders and their urinary excretion of catecholamine metabolites. *American Journal of Psychiatry, 132,* 1141–1148.

Delgado, P. L., Price, L. H., Heninger, G. R., & Charney, D. S. (1992). Neurochemistry. In E. S. Paykel (Ed.), *Handbook of affective disorders* (2nd ed.). New York: Guilford Press.

Delgado, P. L., Price, L. H., Miller, H. L., Salomon, R. M., Aghajanian, G. K., Heninger, G. R., & Charney, D. S. (1994). Serotonin and the neurobiology of depression: Effects of tryptophan depletion in drug-free depressed patients. *Archives of General Psychiatry, 51,* 865–874.

d'Elia, G., & Raotma, H. (1975). Is unilateral ECT less effective than bilateral ECT? *British Journal of Psychiatry, 126,* 83–89.

De Myer, M. K., Hingtgen, J. N., & Jackson, R. K. (1981). Infantile autism reviewed: A decade of research. *Schizophrenia Bulletin, 7,* 388–451.

DeNelsky, G. Y. (1996). The case against prescription privileges for psychologists. *American Psychologist, 51,* 207–212.

Denney, D. R., Stephenson, L. A., Penick, E., & Weller, R. (1988). Lymphocyte subclasses and depression. *Journal of Abnormal Psychology, 97,* 499–502.

Derogatis, L. R. (1993). *The symptom checklist series.* Minneapolis: NSC Assessments.

De Rubeis, R. J., Evans, M. D., Hollon, S. D., Garvey, M. J., Grove, W. M., & Tuason, V. B. (1990). How does cognitive therapy work? Cognitive change and symptoms change in cognitive therapy and pharmacotherapy for depression. *Journal of Consulting and Clinical Psychology, 58,* 862–869.

Detera-Wadleigh, S. D., Berrettini, W. H., Goldin, L. R., Boorman, D., Anderson, S., & Gershon, E. S. (1987). Close linkage of c-Harvey-ras-1 and the insulin gene to affective disorder is ruled out in three North American pedigrees. *Nature, 325,* 808–809.

Deutsch, M. (1967). *The disadvantaged child.* New York: Basic Books.

Devanand, D. P., Dwork, A. J., Hutchingson, E. R., Bolwig, T. G., & Sackeim. H. A. (1994). Does ECT alter brain structure? *American Journal of Psychiatry, 151,* 957–970.

Devanand, D. P., Verma, A. K., Tirumalasetti, F., & Sackeim, H. A. (1991). Absence of cognitive impairment after more than 100 lifetime ECT treatments. *American Journal of Psychiatry, 148,* 929–932.

DeVeaugh-Geiss, J., Moroz, G., Biederman, J., Cantwell, D., Fontaine, R., Greist, J. H., Reichler, R., Katz, R., & Landau, P. (1992). Clomipramine hydrocholoride in childhood and adolescent obsessive-compulsive disorder: A multicenter trial. *Journal of the American Academy of Child and Adolescent Psychiatry, 31,* 45–49.

Devor, E. J. (1990). Untying the Gordian knot: The genetics of Tourette's syndrome. *Journal of Nervous and Mental Disease, 178,* 669–679.

Diamond, B. L. (1974). Psychiatric prediction of dangerousness. *University of Pennsylvania Law Review, 123,* 439–452.

Diekstra, R. F. (1990). Suicide and attempted suicide: An international perspective. *Acta Psychiatrica Scandinavica, 80,* Suppl. 354, 1–24.

Dietz, P. E., Hazelwood, R. R., & Warren, J. (1990). The sexually sadistic criminal and his offenses. *Bulletin of the American Academy of Psychiatry and the Law, 18,* 163–178.

Dilsaver, S. C., Chen, Y. W., Swann, A. C., Shoaib, A. M., & Krajewski, K. J. (1994). Suicidality in patients with pure and depressive mania. *American Journal of Psychiatry, 151,* 1312–1315.

Dilsaver, S. C., Del Medico, V. J., Quadri, A., & Jaeckle, R. S. (1990). Pharmacological responsiveness of winter depression. *Psychopharmacology Bulletin, 26,* 303–309.

Di Mascio, A., Weissman, M. M., Prusoff, B. A., Neu, C., Zwilling, M., & Klerman, G. L. (1979). Differential symptom reduction by drugs and psychotherapy in acute depression. *Archives of General Psychiatry, 36,* 1450–1456.

Di Nardo, P. A., Moras, K., Barlow, D. H., Rapee, R. M., & Brown, T. A. (1993). Reliability of DSM-III-R anxiety disorder categories. *Archives of General Psychiatry, 50,* 251–256.

Doane, J. A., Falloon, R. H., Goldstein, M. J., & Mintz, J. (1985). Parental affective style and the treatment of schizophrenia. *Archives of General Psychiatry, 42,* 34–42.

Docherty, N. M. (1994). Cognitive characteristics of the parents of schizophrenic patients. *Journal of Nervous and Mental Disease, 182,* 443–451.

Dodge K. A., & Tomlin, A. M. (1987). Utilization of self-schemas as a mechanism of interpretational bias in children. *Social Cognition, 5,* 280–300.

Dodge, K. A., & Coie, J. D. (1987). Social-information-processing factors in reactive and proactive aggression in children's peer groups. *Journal of Personality and Social Psychology, 53,* 1146–1158.

Dodge, K. A., & Somberg, D. R. (1987). Hostile attributional biases among aggressive boys are exacerbated under conditions of threats to the self. *Child Development, 58,* 213–224.

Dohrenwend, B. P., & Egri, G. (1981). Recent stressful life events and episodes of schizophrenia. *Schizophrenia Bulletin, 7,* 12–23.

Dohrenwend, B. P., Levav, I., Shrout, P. E., Schwartz, S., Haveh, G., Link, B. G., Skodol, A. E., & Stueve, A. (1992). Socioeconomic status and psychiatric disorders: The causation-selection issue. *Science, 255,* 946–952.

Dohrenwend, B. S., & Dohrenwend, B. P. (1974). *Stressful life events.* New York: Wiley.

Doleys, D. M. (1977). Behavioral treatments for nocturnal enuresis in children: A review of the recent literature. *Psychological Bulletin, 84,* 30–54.

Dollard, J., Doob, L., Miller, N., Mower, O., & Sears, R. (1939). *Frustration and aggression.* New Haven, CT: Yale University Press.

Domino, G., & Takahashi, Y. (1991). Attitudes toward suicide in Japanese and American medical students. *Suicide and Life-Threatening Behavior, 21,* 345–359.

Douglas, J. W. (1973). Early disturbing events and later enuresis. In I. Kolvin, R. C., MacKeith, & S. Meadow (Eds.), *Bladder control and enuresis.* Philadelphia: Lippincott.

Downey, K. K., & Kilbey, M. M. (1995). Relationship between nicotine and alcohol expectancies and substance dependence. *Experimental and Clinical Psychopharmacology, 3,* 174–182.

Drake, R. E., & Wallach, M. A. (1979). Will mental patients stay in the community? A social psychological perspective. *Journal of Consulting and Clinical Psychology, 47,* 285–294.

Dressler, W. W. (1991). Social support, lifestyle incongruity, and arterial blood pressure in a southern black community. *Psychosomatic Medicine, 53,* 608–620.

Dreyfuss, F., & Czaczkes, J. W. (1959). Blood cholesterol and uric acid of healthy medical students under stress of an examination. *Archives of Internal Medicine, 103,* 708–711.

Dubbert, P. M. (1995). Behavioral (life-style) modification in the prevention and treatment of hypertension. *Clinical Psychology Review, 15,* 187–216.

Duckworth, J. C., & Anderson, W. P. (1995). *MMPI-1 and MMPI-2 interpretation manual for counselors and clinicians* (4th ed.). Bristol, PA: Accelerated Development.

Duggan, J. P., & Booth, D. A. (1986). Obesity, overeating, and rapid gastric emptying in rats with ventromedial hypothalamic lesions. *Science, 231,* 609–611.

Dulit, R. A., Fyer, M. R., Lenon, A. C., Brodsky, B. S., & Frances, A. J. (1994). Clinical correlates of self-mutilation in borderline personality disorder. *American Journal of Psychiatry, 151,* 1305–1311.

Durham v. United States, 214 F. 2nd 862 (D.C. Cir. 1954).

Durkheim, E. (1951). *Suicide* (J. A. Spaulding & G. Simpson, Trans.). New York: Free Press. (Originally published 1897)

Durlak, J. A. (1980). Comparative effectiveness of behavioral and relationship group treatment in the secondary prevention of school maladjustment. *American Journal of Community Psychology, 8,* 327–339.

Dusky v. United States, 362 U.S. 402 (1960).

Dutton, D. G., & Aron, A. P. (1974). Some evidence for heightened sexual attraction under conditions of high anxiety. *Journal of Personality and Social Psychology, 30,* 510–517.

Duvoisin, R. C. (1984). *Parkinson's disease.* New York: Raven Press.

Dyck, M. J. (1991). Positive and negative attitudes mediating suicide ideation. *Suicide and Life-Threatening Behavior, 21,* 360–373.

Earle, P. (1994). Gheel. *American Journal of Psychiatry, 151,* 16-19. (Originally published 1851)

Easton, W. W., Thara, R., Federman, B., Melton, B., & Liang, K. (1995). Structure and course of positive and negative symptoms in schizophrenia. *Archives of General Psychiatry, 52,* 127–134.

Eaves, G., & Rehm, A. J. (1984). Cognitive patterns in symptomatic and remitted unipolar major depression. *Journal of Abnormal Psychology, 93,* 31–40.

Eaves, L. C., Ho, H. H., & Eaves, D. M. (1994). Subtypes of autism by cluster analysis. *Journal of Autism and Developmental Disorders, 24,* 3–22.

Edelbrock, C. (no date). The child attention/activity profile. Unpublished manuscript, Pennsylvania State University.

Edgerton, R. B., & Cohen, A. (1994). Culture and schizophrenia: The DOSM challenge. *British Journal of Psychiatry, 164,* 222–231.

Edwards, A. J., Bacon, T. H., Elms, C. A., Verardi, R., Felder, M., & Knight, S. C. (1984). Changes in the populations of lymphoid cells in human peripheral blood following physical exercise. *Clinical and Experimental Immunology, 58,* 420–427.

Egeland, J. A., Gerhard, D. S., Pauls, D. L., Sussex, J. N., Kidd, K. K., Allen, C. R., Hostetter, A. M., & Housman, D. E. (1987). Bipolar affective disorders linked to DNA markers on chromosome 11. *Nature, 325,* 783–787.

Ehlers, S. & Gillberg, C. (1993). The epidemiology of Asperger syndrome: A total population study. *Journal of Child Psychology and Psychiatry and Allied Disciplines, 34,* 1327–1350.

Ehrenkranz, J., Bliss, E., & Sheard, M. (1974). Plasma testosterone: Correlations with aggressive behavior and social dominance. *Psychosomatic Medicine, 36,* 469–476.

Ehrhardt, A., Epstein, R., & Money, J. (1968). Fetal androgens and female gender identity in the early-treated andrenogenital syndrome. *Johns Hopkins Medical Journal, 122,* 160–167.

Ehrhardt, A., & Money, J. (1967). Progestin-induced hermaphroditism: IQ and psychosexual identity in a study of ten girls. *Journal of Sex Research, 3,* 53–100.

Eisenberg, L., & Kanner, L. (1956). Early infantile autism, 1943–1955. *American Journal of Orthopsychiatry, 26,* 556–566.

Eisendrath, S. J., & Valan, M. N. (1994). Psychiatric predictors of pseudoepileptic seizures in patients with refractory seizures. *Journal of Neuropsychiatry and Clinical Neurosciences, 6,* 257–260.

Ekselius, L. Lindstrom, E. Knorring, L., von, Bodlund, O. et al. (1994). Comorbidity among the personality disorders in DMS-III-R. *Personality and Individual Differences, 17,* 155–160.

Elashoff, J. D., & Snow, R. E. (1971). *Pygmalion reconsidered.* Worthington, OH: Jones.

El-Islam, M. (1991). Transcultural aspects of schizophrenia and ICD-10. *Psychiatria Danubina, 3,* 485–494.

Elkin, I., Parloff, M. B., Hadley, S. W., & Autry, J. H. (1985). NIMH Treatment of Depression Collaborative Research Program: Background and research plan. *Archives of General Psychiatry, 42,* 305–316.

Elkin, I., Shea, M. T., Watkins, J. T., Imber, S. D., Sotsky, S. M., Collins, J. F., Glass, D. R., Pilkonis, P. A., Leber, W. R., Kocherty, J. P., Fiester, S. J., & Parloff, M. B. (1989). National Institute of Mental Health Treatment of Depression Collaborative Research Program. *Archives of General Psychiatry, 46,* 971–982.

Elkins, R. (1991). An appraisal of chemical aversion (emetic therapy) approaches to alcoholism treatment. *Behaviour Research and Therapy, 29,* 387–411.

Ellicott, A., Hammen, C., Gitlin, M., Brown, G., & Jamison, K. (1990). Life events and the course of bipolar disorder. *American Journal of Psychiatry, 147,* 1194–1198.

Ellis, A. (1962). *Reason and emotion in psychotherapy.* Secaucus, NJ: Lyle Stuart.

Ellis, A., & Grieger, R. (1977). *Handbook of rational emotive therapy* (Vol. 1). New York: Springer.

Ellis, A., & Grieger, R. (1986). *Handbook of rational emotive therapy* (Vol. 2). New York: Springer.

Emmelkamp, P. M. (1994). Behavior therapy with adults. In A. E. Bergin & S. L. Garfield (Eds.), *Handbook of psychotherapy and behavior change* (4th ed.). New York: Wiley.

Ennis, B. J., & Litwack, T. R. (1974). Psychiatry and the presumption of expertise: Flipping coins in the courtroom. *California Law Review, 62,* 693–752.

Erickson, J. D., & Bjerkedal, T. O. (1981). Down syndrome associated with father's age in Norway. *Journal of Medical Genetics, 18,* 22–28.

Eriksson, E., & Humble, M. (1990). Serotonin and psychiatric pathophysiology: A review of data from experimental and clinical research. In R. Pohl & S. Gershon (Eds.), The biological basis of psychiatric treatment: *Progress in basic and clinical pharmacology.* Basel, Switzerland: Karger.

Eslinger, P. J., & Damasio, A. R. (1985). Severe disturbance of higher cognition after bilateral frontal lobe ablation: Patient EVR. *Neurology, 35,* 1731–1741.

Estes, W. K. (1991). Cognitive architectures from the standpoint of an experimental psychologist. *Annual Review of Psychology, 42,* 1–28.

Etzel, B. C., Hineline, P. N., Iwata, B. A., Johnston, J. M., Lindsley, O. R., McGrale, J. E., Morris, E. K., & Pennypacker, H. S. (1987). The ABA Humanitarian Awards for outstanding achievement in pursuit of the right to effective treatment. *Behavior Analyst, 10,* 235–237.

Etzersdorfer, E., Sonneck, G., & Nagel-Fuess, S. (1992). Newspaper reports and suicide. *New England Journal of Medicine, 327,* 502–550.

Evans, D. M. & Dunn, N. J. (1995). Alcohol expectancies, coping responses, and self-efficacy judgments: A replication and extension of Cooper et al.'s 1988 study in a college sample. *Journal of Studies on Alcohol, 56,* 186–193.

Evans, R. L. (1981). New drug evaluations: Alprazolam. *Drug Intelligence and Clinical Pharmacy, 15,* 633–637.

Exner, J. E. (1993). *The Rorschach: A comprehensive system: Vol. 1 Basic foundations* (3rd ed.). New York: Wiley.

Eysenck, H. J. (1961). The effects of psychotherapy. In H. J. Eysenck (Ed.), *Handbook of abnormal psychology.* New York: Basic Books.

Eysenck, M. W., Mogg, K., May, J., Richards, A., & Mathews, A. (1991). Bias in interpretation of ambiguous sentences related to threat in anxiety. *Journal of Abnormal Psychology, 100,* 144–150.

Fabrega, H., Mulsant, B. N., Rifai, A. H., Sweet, Robert A., et al. (1994). Ethnicity and psychopathology in an aging hospital-based population: A comparison of African-American and Anglo-European patients. *Journal of Nervous and Mental Disease, 182,* 136–144.

Faedda, G. L., Tondo, L., Teicher, M. H., Baldessarini, R. J., Gelbard, H. A., & Floris, G. F. (1993). Seasonal mood disorders: Patterns of seasonal recurrence in mania and depression. *Archives of General Psychiatry, 50,* 17–23.

Fahy, T. A. (1988). The diagnosis of multiple personality disorder: A critical review. *British Journal of Psychiatry, 153,* 597–606.

Fairburn, C. G., Agras, W. S., & Wilson, G. T. (1992). The research on the treatment of bulimia nervosa: Practical and theoretical implications. In G. Anderson & S. Kennedy (Eds.), *Biology of feast and famine: Relevance to eating disorders.* New York: Academic Press.

Fairburn, C. G., Jones, R., Peveler, R. C., Hope, R. A., & O'Connor, M. (1993). Psychotherapy and bulimia nervosa: Longer-term effects of interpersonal psychotherapy, behavior therapy, and cognitive therapy. *Archives of General Psychiatry, 50,* 419–428.

Falconer, D. S. (1960). *Introduction to quantitative genetics.* New York: Ronald Press.

Falk, B., Hersen, M., & Van Hasselt, V. B. (1994). Assessment of post-traumatic stress disorder in older adults: A critical review. *Clinical Psychology Review, 14,* 359–381.

Fallon, B. A., Klein, B. W., & Liebowitz, M. R. (1993). Hypochondriasis: Treatment strategies. *Psychiatric Annals, 23,* 374–381.

Falloon, I. R., Boyd, J. L., McGill, C. W., Williamson, M., Razani, J., Moss, H. B., Gilderman, A. M., & Simpson, G. M. (1985). Family management in the prevention of morbidity of schizophrenia. *Archives of General Psychiatry, 42,* 887–896.

Faraone, S. V., Kremen, W. S., & Tsuang, M. T. (1990). Genetic transmission of major affective disorders: Quantitative models and linkage analyses. *Psychological Bulletin, 108,* 109–127.

Farberow, N. L., & Litman, R. E. (1970). *A comprehensive suicide prevention program. Suicide Prevention Center of Los Angeles,* 1958–1969. Unpublished final report (DHEW NIMH Grants No. HM 14946 & MH 00128), Los Angeles.

Farberow, N. L., & Shneidman, E. S. (1961). *The cry for help.* New York: McGraw-Hill.

Farberow, N. L., & Simon, M. D. (1969). Suicide in Los Angeles and Vienna: An intercultural study of two cities. *Public Health Reports, 84,* 389–403.

Farberow, N. L., & Simon, M. D. (1975). Suicide in Los Angeles and Vienna. In N. L. Farberow (Ed.), *Suicide in different cultures.* Baltimore: University Park Press.

Farde, L., Wiesel, F., Halldin, C., & Sedvall, G. (1988). Central D2 dopamine receptor occupancy in schizophrenic patients treated with antipsychotic drugs. *Archives of General Psychiatry, 45,* 71–76.

Faris, R. (1934). Cultural isolation and the schizophrenic personality. *American Journal of Sociology, 40,* 155–169.

Farmer, J. E., & Peterson, L. (1995). Injury risk factors in children with Attention Deficit Hperactivity Disorder. *Health Psychology, 14,* 325–332.

Farmer, J. E., & Peterson, L. (1995). Injury risk factors in children with Attention Deficit Hperactivity Disorder. *Health Psychology, 14,* 325–332.

Fava, M., & Rosenbaum, J. F. (1991). Suicidality and fluoxetine: Is there a relationship? *Journal of Clinical Psychiatry, 52,* 108–111.

Fava, M., Rosenbaum, J. F., McGrath, P. J., Stewart, J. W., Amsterdam, J. D., & Quitkin, F. M. (1994). Lithium and tricyclic augmentation of fluoxetine treatment for resistant major depression: A double-blind controlled study. *American Journal of Psychiatry, 151,* 1372–1372.

Feingold, B. F. (1975). *Why your child is hyperactive.* New York: Random House.

Feingold, B. F. (1976). Hyperkinesis and learning disabilities linked to the ingestion of artificial food colors and flavors. *Journal of Learning Disabilities, 9,* 551–559.

Femina, D. D., Yeager, C. A., & Lewis, D. O. (1990). Child abuse: Adolescent records v. adult recall. *Child Abuse and Neglect, 145,* 227–231.

Fenichel, O. (1945). *The psychoanalytic theory of neuroses.* New York: Norton.

Fenton, W., Wyatt, R. J., & McGlashan, T. H. (1994). Risk factors for spontaneous dyskinesia in schizophrenia. *Archives of General Psychiatry, 51,* 643–650.

Ferdinand, R. F., & Verhulst, F. C. (1995). Psychopathology from adolescence into young adulthood: An 8-year follow-up study. *American Journal of Psychiatry, 152,* 1586–1594.

Ferster, C. B. (1961). Positive reinforcement and behavioral deficits of autistic children. *Child Development, 32,* 437–456.

Ferster, C. B. (1973). A functional analysis of depression. *American Psychologist, 28,* 857–870.

Fillmore, M. T., and Vogel-Sprott, M. (1995). Expectanices about alcohol-induced motor impairment predict individual differences in responses to alcohol and placebo. *Journal of Studies on Alcohol, 56,* 90–98.

Finegan, J., & Quarrington, B. (1979). Pre-, peri-, and neonatal factors and infantile autism. *Journal of Child Psychology and Psychiatry, 20,* 119–128.

Fink, M. (1979). *Convulsive therapy: Theory and practice.* New York: Raven Press.

Fink, M. (1992). Electroconvulsive therapy. In E. S. Paykel (Ed.), *Handbook of affective disorders* (2nd ed.). New York: Guilford Press.

Fink, M., Taylor, M. A., & Volavka, J. (1970). Anxiety precipitated by lactate. *New England Journal of Medicine, 281,* 1429.

Finn, P. R., Zeitouni, N. C., & Pihl, R. O. (1990). Effects of alcohol on psychophysiological hyperreactivity to nonaversive and aversive stimuli in men at high risk for alcoholism. *Journal of Abnormal Psychology, 99,* 79–85.

Fiore, M. C., Jorenby, D. E., Baker, T. B., & Kenford, S. L. (1992). Tobacco dependence and the nicotine patch. *Journal of the American Medical Association, 268,* 2687–2694.

Fischer, M. (1971). Psychoses in the offspring of schizophrenic monozygotic twins and their normal co-twins. *British Journal of Psychiatry, 118,* 43–52.

Fischer, M. (1973). Genetic and environmental factors in schizophrenia: A study of schizophrenic twins and their families. *Acta Psychiatrica Scandinavica,* Suppl. 238.

Fischer, M., Barkley, R. A., Edelbrock, C. S., & Smallish, L. (1990). The adolescent outcome of hyperactive children diagnosed by research criteria: 2. Academic, attentional, and neuropsychological status. *Journal of Consulting and Clinical Psychology, 58,* 580–588.

Fish, B., & Ritvo, E. R. (1979). Psychoses of childhood. In J. D. Noshpitz (Ed.), *Basic handbook of child psychiatry.* New York: Basic Books.

Fishbain, D. A. (1991). "Koro: Proposed classification for DSM-IV": Comment. *American Journal of Psychiatry, 148,* 1765–1766.

Fisher, C., Schiavi, R. C., Edwards, A., Davis, D. M., Reitman, M., & Fine, J. (1979). Evaluation of nocturnal penile tumescence in the differential diagnosis of sexual impotence. *Archives of General Psychiatry, 36,* 431–437.

Fisher, S. (1994). Identifying video game addiction in children and adolescents. *Addictive Behaviors, 19,* 545–553.

Fisher, W. A. (1994). Restraint and seclusion: A review of the literature. *American Journal of Psychiatry, 151,* 1584–1591.

Flaum, M., Swayze, V. W., O'Leary, D. S., Yuh, W. T., Ehrhardt, J. C., Arndt, S. V., & Andreasen, N. C. (1995). Effects of diagnosis, laterality, and gender on brain morphology in schizophrenia. *American Journal of Psychiatry, 152,* 704–714.

Fluoxetine Bulimia Nervosa Collaborative Study Group. (1992). Fluoxetine in the treatment of bulimia nervosa. *Archives of General Psychiatry, 49,* 139–147.

Folkman, S., & Lazarus, R. S. (1980). Coping in an adequately functioning middle-aged population. *Journal of Health and Social Behavior, 19,* 219–239.

Folland, S. S. (1975). *Suspected toluene exposure at a boot factory.* Internal report. Nashville: Tennessee Department of Health.

Folstein, S. E. (1991). Etiology of autism: Genetic influences. *Journal of Child Psychology and Psychiatry, 31,* 99–119.

Folstein, S. E., & Rutter, M. (1977). Infantile autism: A genetic study of 21 twin pairs. *Journal of Child Psychology and Psychiatry, 18,* 297–321.

Fonda, J. (1981). *Jane Fonda's workout book.* New York: Simon & Schuster.

Fontana, A. F., Kerns, R. D., Rosenberg, R. L., & Colonese, K. L. (1989). Support, stress, and recovery from coronary heart disease: A longitudinal causal model. *Health Psychology, 8,* 175–193.

Forssman, H. (1970). Klinefelter's syndrome. *British Journal of Psychiatry, 117,* 35–37.

Fortmann, S. P., & Killen, J. D. (1995). Nicotine gum and self-help behavioral treatment for smoking relapse prevention: Results from a trial using population-based recruitment. *Journal of Consulting and Clinical Psychology, 63,* 460–468.

Fowler, J. S., Volkow, N. D., Wang, G. J., Pappas, N., Logan, J., MacGregor, R., Alexoff, D., Shea, C., Schyler, D., Wolf, A. P., Warner, D. Zezulkova, I., & Cilento, R. (1996). Inhibition of monoamine oxidase B in the brains of smokers. *Nature, 379,* 733–736.

Franco, K. S., Campbell, N. Tamburrion, M. B., and Evans, C. (1993). Rumination: The eating disorder of infancy. *Child Psychiatry and Human Development, 24,* 91–97.

Frank, E. (1991). Interpersonal psychotherapy as a maintenance treatment for patients with recurrent depression. *Psychotherapy, 28,* 259–266.

Frank, E., Anderson, B., Reynolds, C. F., Ritenour, A., & Kupfer, D. J. (1994). Life events and the research diagnostic criteria endogenous subtype. *Archives of General Psychiatry, 51,* 519–524.

Frank, E., Kupfer, D. J., & Perel, J. M. (1989). Early recurrence in unipolar depression. *Archives of General Psychiatry, 46,* 771–775.

Frank, E., Kupfer, D. J., Perel, J. M., Cornes, C. L., Jarrett, D. J., Mallinger, A., Tase, M. E., McEachran, A. B., & Grochocini, V. J. (1990). Three-year outcomes for maintenance therapies in recurrent depression. *Archives of General Psychiatry, 47,* 1093–1099.

Frank, E., Kupfer, D. J., Wanger, E. F., McEachran, A. B., & Cornes, C. L. (1991). Efficacy in interpersonal psychotherapy as a maintenance treatment for recurrent depression: Contribution factors. *Archives of General Psychiatry, 48,* 1053–1059.

Frank, E., & Spanier, C. (1995). Interpersonal psychotherapy for depression: Overview, clinical efficacy, and future directions. *Clinical Psychology Science and Practice, 2,* 349–369.

Frank, J. D. (1982). Therapeutic components shared by all psychotherapies. In J. H. Harvey & M. M. Parks (Eds.), *Psychotherapy research and behavior change* (Vol. 1). Washington, DC: American Psychological Association.

Frederick, B. P., & Olmi, D. J. (1994). Children with attention-deficit hyperactivity disorder: A review of the literature on social skills deficits. *Psychology in the Schools, 31,* 288–296.

Freed, E. X. (1971). Anxiety and conflict: Role of drug-dependent learning in the rat. *Quarterly Journal of Studies on Alcohol, 32,* 13–29.

Freedman, B. J. (1974). The subjective experience of perceptual and cognitive disturbances in schizophrenia. *Archives of General Psychiatry, 30,* 333–340.

Freedman, B. J., & Chapman, L. J. (1973). Early subjective experience in schizophrenic episodes. *Journal of Abnormal Psychology, 82,* 46–54.

Freeman, Hugh. (1994). Schizophrenia and city residence. *British Journal of Psychiatry, 164,* 39–50.

Freeman, T. (1971). Observations on mania. *International Journal of Psychoanalysis, 52,* 479–486.

Freinkel, A., Koopman, C., & Spiegel, D. (1994). Dissociative symptoms in media eyewitnesses of an execution. *American Journal of Psychiatry, 151,* 1335–1339.

Freud, S. (1953). Three essays on the theory of sexuality. In J. Strachey & A. Freud (Eds.), *The standard edition of the complete psychological works of Sigmund Freud* (Vol. 7.). London: Hogarth Press. (Originally published 1905)

Freud, S. (1955). Beyond the pleasure principle. In J. Strachey & A. Freud (Eds.), *The standard edition of the complete psychological works of Sigmund Freud* (Vol. 18). London: Hogarth Press. (Originally published 1920)

Freud, S. (1955). A child is being beaten. In J. Strachey & A. Freud (Eds.), *The standard edition of the complete psychological works of Sigmund Freud* (Vol. 17). London: Hogarth Press. (Originally published 1919)

Freud, S. (1955). The economic problems of masochism. In J. Strachey & A. Freud (Eds.), *The standard edition of the complete psycho-*

logical works of Sigmund Freud (Vol. 19). London: Hogarth Press. (Originally published 1925)

Freud, S. (1955). Instincts and their vicissitudes. In J. Strachey & A. Freud (Eds.), *The standard edition of the complete psychological work of Sigmund Freud* (Vol. 14). London: Hogarth Press. (Originally published 1915)

Freud, S. (1955). Mourning and melancholia. In J. Strachey & A. Freud (Eds.), *The standard edition of the complete psychological works of Sigmund Freud* (Vol. 14). London: Hogarth Press. (Originally published 1911)

Freud, S. (1957). The interpretation of dreams. In J. Strachey & A. Freud (Eds.), *The standard edition of the complete psychological works of Sigmund Freud* (Vol. 4). London: Hogarth Press. (Originally published 1900)

Freud, S. (1959). Inhibitions, symptoms and anxiety. In J. Strachey & A. Freud (Eds.), *The standard edition of the complete psychological works of Sigmund Freud* (Vol. 20). London: Hogarth Press. (Originally published 1926)

Frick, P. J., Lahey, B. B., Loeber, R., Stouthamer-Lober, M., Christ, M. A., & Hanson, K. (1992). Familial risk factors to oppositional defiant disorder and conduct disorder: Parental psychopathology and maternal parenting. *Journal of Consulting and Clinical Psychology, 60,* 49–55.

Frick, P. J., O'Brien, B. S., Wootton, J. M., & McBurnett, K. (1994). Psychopathy and conduct problems in children. *Journal of Abnormal Psychology, 103,* 700–707.

Frieberg, J. (1975, August). Electroshock therapy: Let's stop blasting the brain. *Psychology Today,* pp. 18–23.

Friedman, A. S. (1975). Interaction of drug therapy with marital therapy in depressed patients. *Archives of General Psychiatry, 32,* 619–637.

Friedman, M., & Rosenman, R. H. (1959). Association of specific overt behavior pattern with blood and cardiovascular findings: Blood cholesterol level, blood clotting time, incidence of arcus senilis and clinical coronary artery disease. *Journal of the American Medical Association, 169,* 1286–1296.

Friedman, M., & Rosenman, R. H. (1974). *Type A behavior and your heart.* New York: Knopf.

Friedman, M., Rosenman, R. H., & Carroll, V. (1958). Changes in the serum cholesterol and blood clotting time in men subjected to cyclic variation of occupational stress. *Circulation, 17,* 852–861.

Friedman, M., Thoresen, C. E., Gill, J. J., Powell, L. H., Ulmer, D., Thompson, L., Price, V. A., Rabin, D. D., Breall, W. S., Dixon, T., Levy, R., & Bourg, E. (1984). Alteration of Type A behavior and reduction in cardiac recurrences in postmyocardial infarction patients. *American Heart Journal, 108,* 237–248.

Friedman, M., & Ulmer, D. (1984). *Treating Type A behavior and your heart.* New York: Knopf.

Friedman, S., Hatch, M., Paradis, C. M., Poplin, M., & Shalita, A. R. (1993). Obsessive-compulsive disorder in two black ethnic groups: Incidence in an urban dermatology clinic. *Journal of Anxiety Disorders, 7,* 343–348.

Friedman, S., Paradis, C. M., & Hatch, M. (1994). Characteristics of African–American and White patients with panic disorder and agoraphobia. *Hospital and Community Psychiatry, 45,* 798–803.

Friman, P. C., & Vollmer, D. (1995). Successful use of the nocturnal urine alarm for diurnal enuresis. *Journal of Applied Behavior Analysis, 28,* 89–90.

Frost, R. O., Goolkasian, G., Elv, R., & Blanchard, F. (1982). Depression, restraint and eating behaviour. *Behaviour Research and Therapy, 20,* 113–122.

Frost, R. O., Graf, M., & Becket, J. (1979). Self-devaluation and depressed mood. *Journal of Consulting and Clinical Psychology, 47,* 958–962.

Frost, R. O., & Green, M. (1982). Velten Mood Induction Procedure effects: Duration and post-experimental removal. *Personality and Social Psychology Bulletin, 8,* 341–348.

Frost, R. O., Morgenthau, J. E., Riessman, C. K., & Whalen, M. (1986). Somatic response to stress, physical symptoms and health service use. *Behaviour Research and Therapy, 24,* 569–576.

Fry, P. (1989). Mediators of perceptions of stress among community-based elders. *Psychological Reports, 65,* 307–314.

Fuchs, C. Z., & Rehm, L. P. (1977). A self-control behavior therapy program for depression. *Journal of Consulting and Clinical Psychology, 45,* 206–215.

Fuller, B. (1986, August 7). *Parents sue agency head for $15 million* [Press release]. United Press International.

Fullerton, D. T., Neff, S. and Carl, J. (1992). Persistent functional vomiting. *International Journal of Eating Disorders, 12,* 229–233.

Furby, L., Weinrott, M. R., & Blackshaw, L. (1989). Sex offender recidivism: A review. *Psychological Bulletin, 105,* 3–30.

Furst, S. S., & Ostow, M. (1979). The psychodynamics of suicide. In L. D. Hankoff & B. Einsidler (Eds.), *Suicide: Theory and clinical aspects.* Acton, MA: Publishing Sciences Group.

Gaist, P. A., Obarzanek, E., Skwerer, R., Duncan, G., Connie, C., Shultz, P. M., & Rosenthal, N. E. (1990). Effects of bright light on resting metabolic rate in patients with seasonal affective disorder and control subjects. *Biological Psychiatry, 28,* 989–996.

Galin, D., Diamond, R., & Braff, D. (1977). Lateralization of conversion symptoms: More frequent on the left. *American Journal of Psychiatry, 134,* 578–580.

Gallant, D. M. (1990). The Type 2 primary alcoholic? *Alcoholism Clinical and Experimental Research, 14,* 631.

Gaminde, I., Uria, M., Padro, D., Querejeta, I., & Ozamiz, A. (1993). Depression in three populations in the Basque country: A comparison with Britain. *Social Psychiatry and Psychiatric Epidemiology, 28,* 243–251.

Gange, P. (1981). Treatment of sex offenders with MPA. *American Journal of Psychiatry, 138,* 644–646.

Ganzini, L., McFarland, B. H., & Cutler, D. (1990). Prevalence of mental disorders after catastrophic financial loss. *Journal of Nervous and Mental Disease, 178,* 680–685.

Garb, H. N. (1985). The incremental validity of information used in personality assessment. *Clinical Psychology Review, 4,* 641–655.

Gardner, D. L., & Cowdry, R. W. (1985). Alprazolam-induced dyscontrol in borderline personality disorder. *American Journal of Psychiatry, 142,* 98–100.

Gardner, E. L., & Lowinson, J. H. (1991). Marijuana's interaction with brain reward systems: Update 1991. *Pharmacology Biochemistry, and Behavior, 40,* 571–580.

Gardos, G., Casey, D. E., Cole, J. O., Perenyi, A., Kocsis, E., Arato, M., Samson, J. A., & Conley, C. (1994). Ten-year outcome of tardive dyskinesia. *American Journal of Psychiatry, 151,* 836–841.

Garfield, S. L. (1994). Research on client variables. In A. E. Bergin & S. L. Garfield (Eds.), *Handbook of psychotherapy and behavior change* (4th ed.). New York: Wiley.

Garland, A. F., & Zigler, E. (1993). Adolescent suicide prevention: Current research and social policy implications. *American Psychologist, 48,* 169–182.

Garner, D. M., Garfinkel, P. E., Schwartz, D., & Thompson, M. (1980). Cultural expectations of thinness in women. *Psychological Reports, 47,* 483–491.

Garretson, D. J. (1993). Psychological misdiagnosis of African Americans. *Journal of Multicultural Counseling and Development, 21,* 119–126.

Gaw, A. C., & Bernstein, R. L. (1992). Classification of amok in DSM-IV. *Hospital and Community Psychiatry, 43,* 789–793.

Gawin, F. H. (1991). Cocaine addiction: Psychology and neurophysiology. *Science, 251,* 1580–1586.

Geekie, K. M., & Brown, H. P. (1995). Treating substance abuse in the multidisabled: An overview. *Alcoholism Treatment Quarterly, 12,* 87–95.

Geen, R. G. (1990). *Human aggression.* Pacific Grove, CA: Brooks/Cole.

Geer, J. H., & Fuhr, R. (1976). Cognitive factors in sexual arousal: The role of distraction. *Journal of Consulting and Clinical Psychology, 44,* 238–243.

Gelernter, C. S., Uhde, T. W., Cimbolic, P., Arnkoff, D. B., Vittone, B. J., Tancer, M. E., & Bartko, J. J. (1991). Cognitive-behavioral and pharmacological treatments of social phobia. *Archives of General Psychiatry, 48,* 938–945.

Geller, M. I., Kelly, J. A., Traxler, W. T., & Marone, I. J. (1978). Behavioral treatment of an adolescent female's bulimic anorexia: Modification of immediate consequences and antecedent conditions. *Journal of Clinical Child Psychology, 14,* 138–141.

George, M. S., Ketter, T. A., Parekh, P. I., Horwitz, B., Herscovitch, P., & Post, R. M. (1995). Brain activity during transient sadness and happiness in healthy women. *American Journal of Psychiatry, 152,* 341–351.

Gerardi, R. J., Kean, T. M., Cahoon, B. J., & Wlauminzer, G. W. (1994). An in vivo assessment of physiological arousal in posttraumatic stress disorder. *Journal of Abnormal Psychology, 103,* 825–827.

Gerin, W., Pieper, C., Levy, R., & Pickering, T. G. (1992). Social support in social interaction: A moderator of cardiovascular reactivity. *Psychosomatic Medicine, 54,* 324–336.

Gerner, R. H., & Hare, T. A. (1981). CSF GABA in normal subjects and patients with depression, schizophrenia, mania, and anorexia nervosa. *American Journal of Psychiatry, 137,* 1098–1101.

Ghaziuddin, N., & Alessi, N. E. (1992). An open clinical trial of trazodone in aggressive children. *Journal of Child and Adolescent Psychopharmacology, 2,* 291–297.

Giansante, L. (1988, February 5). *The Morning Show,* National Public Radio.

Gibbens, T. C., Pond, D. A., & Stafford–Clark, D. (1955). A follow-up study of criminal psychopaths. *British Journal of Delinquency, 5,* 126–136.

Gilbert, D. G., & Gilbert, B. O. (1995). Personality, psychopathology, and nicotine response as mediators of the genetics of smoking. *Behavior Genetics, 25,* 133–147.

Gilbert, P. L., Harris, M. J., McAdams, L. A., & Jeste, D. V. (1995). Neuroleptic withdrawal in schizophrenic patients. *Archives of General Psychiatry, 52,* 173–188.

Gillberg, C. (1991). Outcome in autism and autistic-like conditions. *Journal of the American Academy of Child and Adolescent Psychiatry, 30,* 375–382.

Gillberg, C. (1993). Asperger syndrome and clumsiness. *Journal of Autism and Developmental Disorders, 23,* 686–687.

Gillberg, C. Gillberg, I. C. & Steffenburg, S. (1992). Siblings and parents of children with autism: A controlled population-based study. *Developmental Medicine and Child Neurology, 34,* 389–398.

Gillberg, C., & Schaumann, H. (1982). Social class and infantile autism. *Journal of Autism and Developmental Disorders, 12,* 223–228.

Gillin, J. C., Rapoport, J. L., Mikkelsen, E. J., Langer, D., Vansleiver, C., & Mendelson, W. (1982). EEG sleep patterns in enuresis: A further analysis and comparison with controls. *Biological Psychiatry, 17,* 947–953.

Gilmore, J. V. (1991). Murdering while asleep: Clinical and forensic issues. *Forensic Reports, 4,* 455–459.

Ginsberg, H. (1972). *The myth of the deprived child.* Englewood Cliffs, NJ: Prentice Hall.

Gist, R., & Welch, Q. B. (1989). Certification change versus actual behavior change in teenage suicide rates, 1955–1979. *Suicide and Life-Threatening Behavior, 19,* 277–288.

Gitlin, M. J., Swendsen, J., Heller, T. L., & Mammenen, C. (1995). Relapse and impairment in bipolar disorder. *American Journal of Psychiatry, 152,* 1635–1640.

Gittelman, R., & Kanner, A. (1986). Psychopharmacotherapy. In H. C. Quay & J. S. Werry (Eds.), *Psychopathological disorders of childhood* (3rd ed). New York: Wiley.

Gittelman-Klein, R., Klein, D. F., Abikoff, H., Katz, S., Gloisten, A., & Kates, W. (1976). Relative efficacy of methylphenidate and behavior modification in hyperactive children: An interim report. *Journal of Abnormal Child Psychology, 4,* 461–472.

Gladis, M. M., Levinson, D. F., & Mowry, B. J. (1994). Delusions in schizophrenia spectrum disorders: Diagnostic issues. *Schizophrenic Bulletin, 20,* 747–754.

Glass, D. C. (1977). *Behavior patterns, stress, and coronary disease.* Hillsdale, NJ: Erlbaum.

Glazer, H. I., & Weiss, J. M. (1976). Long-term interference effect: An alternative to "learned helplessness." *Journal of Experimental Psychology: Animal Behavioral Processes, 2,* 202–213.

Goetz, K., & Price, T. R. (1994). The case of koro: Treatment response and implications for diagnostic classification. *Journal of Nervous and Mental Disease, 182,* 590–591.

Goetz, R. R., Klein, D. F., Gully, R., Kahn, J., Liebowitz, M. R., Fyer, A. J., & Gorman, J. M. (1993). Panic attacks during placebo procedures in the laboratory. *Archives of General Psychiatry, 50,* 280–285.

Goffman, E. (1961). *Asylums: Essays on the social situation of mental patients and other inmates.* Garden City, NY: Doubleday.

Gold, B. I., Bowers, M. B., Roth, R. H., & Sweeney, D. W. (1980). GABA levels in CSF of patients with psychiatric disorders. *American Journal of Psychiatry, 137,* 362–364.

Gold, M. S. (1994). The epidemiology, attitudes, and pharmacology of LSD use in the 1990s. *Psychiatric Annals, 24,* 124–126.

Goldberg, J. F., Harrow, M., & Grossman, L. S. (1995). Course and outcome in bipolar affective disorder: A longitudinal follow-up study. *American Journal of Psychiatry, 152,* 379–384.

Goldberg, D. C., Whipple, B., Fishkin, R. E., Waxman, H., & Fink, P. J. (1983). The Grafenberg spot and female ejaculation: A review of initial hypotheses. *Journal of Sex and Marital Therapy, 9,* 27–37.

Goldfried, M. R., & Trier, C. S. (1974). Effectiveness of relaxation as an active coping skill. *Journal of Abnormal Psychology, 83,* 348–355.

Goldgaber, D., Lerman, M., McBride, O., Saffiotti, U., & Gajdusek, D. (1987). Characterization and chromosomal localization of a cDNA encoding brain amyloid of Alzheimer's disease. *Science, 235,* 877–880.

Golding, J. M., Smith, R., & Kashner, M. (1991). Does somatization disorder occur in men? *Archives of General Psychiatry, 48,* 321–235.

Goldman, M. J. (1992). Kleptomania: An overview. *Psychiatric Annals, 22,* 68–71.

Goldman, M. S., Brown, S. A., Christiansen, B. A., & Smith, G. T. (1991). Alcoholism and memory: Broadening the scope of alcohol-expectancy research. *Psychological Bulletin, 110,* 137–146.

Goldstein, M. J. (1980). Family therapy during the aftercare treatment of acute schizophrenia. In J. S. Strauss, M. Bowers, T. W. Dowey, S. Fleck, S. Jackson, & I. Levine (Eds.), *The psychotherapy of schizophrenia.* New York: Plenum.

Goldstein, M. J., & Rodnick, E. H. (1975). The family's contribution to the etiology of schizophrenia: Current status. *Schizophrenia Bulletin, 14,* 48–63.

Goldstein, R. B., Weissman, M. M., Adams, P. B., Horwath, E., Lish, J. D., Charney, D. S., Woods, S. W., Sobin, C., & Wickramaratne, P. J. (1994). Psychiatric disorders in relatives of probands with panic disorder and/or major depression. *Archives of General Psychiatry, 51,* 383–394.

Golomb, M., Fava, M., Abraham, M., & Rosenbaum, J. F. (1995). Gender differences in personality disorders. *American Journal of Psychiatry, 152,* 579–582.

Good, B. J. (1992). Culture, diagnosis, and comorbidity. *Culture, Medicine and Psychiatry, 16,* 427–446.

Goodman, S. H., & Emory, E. K. (1992). Perinatal complications in births to low socioeconomic status schizophrenic and depressed women. *Journal of Abnormal Psychology, 101,* 225–229.

Goodwin, A., & Williams, J. (1982). Mood-induction research: Its implications for clinical depression. *Behaviour Research and Therapy, 20,* 373–382.

Goodwin, D. W. (1985a). Alcoholism and genetics. *Archives of General Psychiatry, 42,* 171–174.

Goodwin, D. W. (1985b). Genetic determinants of alcoholism. In J. H. Mendelson & N. K. Mello (Eds.), *The diagnosis and treatment of alcoholism.* New York: McGraw-Hill.

Goodwin, F. K., & Jamison, K. R. (1990). *Manic-depressive illness.* New York: Oxford University Press.

Goodwin, G. M. (1992). Tricyclic and newer antidepressants. In E. S. Paykel (Ed.), *Handbook of affective disorders,* (2nd ed.). New York: Guilford Press.

Goodwin, J. (1980). The etiology of combat-related post-traumatic stress disorders. In T. Williams (Ed.), *Post-traumatic stress disorders of the Vietnam veteran.* Cincinnati, OH: Disabled American Veterans.

Gordon, C. T., State, R. C., Nelson, J. E., Hamburger, S. D., & Rapoport, J. (1993). A double-blind comparison of clomipramine, desipramine, and placebo in the treatment of autistic disorder. *Archives of General Psychiatry, 50,* 441–447.

Gorenstein, E. E. (1991). A cognitive perspective on antisocial personality. In P. A. Magaro (Ed.), *Annual review of psychopathology:* Vol. 1. *Cognitive basis of mental disorders.* London: Sage.

Gorman, J. M. (1984). The biology of anxiety. In L. Grinspoon (Ed.), *Psychiatry update: The American Psychiatric Association annual review* (Vol. 3). Washington, DC: American Psychiatric Association.

Gorman, J. M., Goetz, R. R., Fyer, M., King, D. L., Fyer, A. J., Liebowitz, M. R., & Klein, D. F. (1988). The mitral valve prolapse–panic disorder connection. *Psychosomatic Medicine, 50,* 114–122.

Gorman, J. M., Papp, L. A., Coplan, J. D., Martinez, J. M., Lennon, S., Goetz, R. R., Ross, D., & Klein, D. F. (1994). Anxiogenic effects of CO_2 and hyperventilation in patients with panic disorder. *American Journal of Psychiatry, 151,* 547–553.

Gorwood, P., Leboyer, M., Jay, M., Payan, C., & Feingold, J. (1995). Gender and age at onset in schizophrenia: Impact of family history. *American Journal of Psychiatry, 152,* 208–212.

Gotlib, I. H., & Robinson, L. A. (1982). Responses to depressed individuals: Discrepancies between self-report and observer-rated behavior. *Journal of Abnormal Psychology, 91,* 231–240.

Gotlib, I. H., Whiffen, V. E., Wallace, P. M., & Mount, J. H. (1991). Prospective investigation of postpartum depression: Factors involved in onset and recovery. *Journal of Abnormal Psychology, 100,* 122–132.

Gottesman, I. I. (1991). *Schizophrenia genesis.* New York: Freeman.

Gottesman, I. I., & Shields, J. (1972). *Schizophrenia and genetics: A twin study vantage point.* New York: Academic Press.

Gould, M. S., Wallenstein, S., & Davidson, L. (1989). Suicide clusters: A critical review. *Suicide and Life-Threatening Behaviors, 19,* 17–29.

Graham, J. R. (1990). *MMPI-2: Assessing personality and psychopathology.* New York: Oxford University Press.

Gray, P. (1988). *Freud: A life for our time.* New York: Norton.

Greden, J. F., Fontaine, P., Lubetsky, M., & Chamberlin, K. (1978). Anxiety and depression associated with caffeinism among psychiatric inpatients. *American Journal of Psychiatry, 135,* 963–966.

Greden, J. F., & Tandon, R. (1995). Long-term treatment for lifetime disorders? *Archives of General Psychiatry, 52,* 197–200.

Green, R. (1974). *Sexual identity conflict in children and adults.* New York: Basic Books.

Green, R. (1976). One hundred ten feminine and masculine boys: Behavioral contrasts and demographic similarities. *Archives of Sexual Behavior, 5,* 425–446.

Green, R. (1985). Gender identity in childhood and later sexual orientation: Follow-up of 78 males. *American Journal of Psychiatry, 142,* 339–341.

Greenberg, R. P., Bornstein, R. F., Zborowski, M. J., Fisher, S., & Greenberg, M. D. (1994). A meta-analysis of fluoxetine outcome in the treatment of depression. *Journal of Nervous and Mental Disease, 182,* 547–551.

Greenblatt, D. J., Harmatz, J. S., Shapiro, L., Engelhardt, N., Gouthro, T. A., & Shader, R. I. (1991). Sensitivity to triazolam in the elderly. *New England Journal of Medicine, 324,* 1691–1698.

Greenblatt, D. J., & Shader, R. I. (1974). *Benzodiazepines in clinical practice.* New York: Raven Press.

Greenblatt, D. J., & Shader, R. I. (1978). Pharmacotherapy of anxiety with benzodiazepines and B-adrenergic blockers. In M. Lipton, A. Di Mascio, & K. Killam (Eds.), *Psychopharmacology: A generation of progress.* New York: Raven Press.

Greenblatt, M., Grosser, G. H., & Wechsler, H. (1964). Differential response of hospitalized depressed patients to somatic therapy. *American Journal of Psychiatry, 120,* 935–943.

Greeno, C. G., & Wing, R. R. (1994). Stress-induced eating. *Psychological Bulletin, 115,* 444–464.

Greenspan, J., Schildkraut, J. J., Gordon, E. K., Baer, L., Arnoff, M. S., & Durell, J. (1970). Catecholamine metabolism in affective disorders: 3. MHPG and other catecholamine metabolites in patients treated with lithium carbonate. *Journal of Psychiatric Research, 7,* 171–183.

Greist, J. H., Jefferson, J. W., Kobak, K. A., Katzelnick, D. J., & Serlin, R. C. (1995). Efficacy and tolerability of serotonin transport inhibitors in obsessive-compulsive disorder: A meta-analysis. *Archives of General Psychiatry, 52,* 53–60.

Grella, C. E., Anglin, M. D., & Wugalter, S. E. (1995). Cocaine and crack use and HIV risk behaviors among high-risk methadone maintenance clients. *Drug and Alcohol Dependence, 37,* 15–21.

Griffith, E. E., & Gonzales, C. A. (1994). Essentials of cultural psychiatry. In R. Hales, S. Yudofsky, & J. Talbott (Eds.), *American Psychiatric Press textbook of psychiatry.* Washington, DC: American Psychiatric Press.

Griffith, J., Cavanaugh, J., Held, J., & Oates, J. (1972). Dextroamphetamine: Evaluation of psychomimetic properties in man. *Archives of General Psychiatry, 26,* 97–100.

Grinspoon, L. (1977). *Marijuana reconsidered.* Cambridge, MA: Harvard University Press.

Grinspoon, L., Ewalt, J., & Shader, R. I. (1968). Psychotherapy and pharmacotherapy in chronic schizophrenia. *American Journal of Psychiatry, 124,* 67–75.

Grinspoon, L., Ewalt, J., & Shader, R. I. (1972). *Schizophrenia: Pharmacotherapy and psychotherapy.* Baltimore: Williams & Wilkins.

Grisso, T. (1992). Five-year research update (1986–1990): Evaluations for competence to stand trial. *Behavioral Sciences and the Law, 10,* 353–369.

Gross, M. (1979). Pseudoepilepsy: A study in adolescent hysteria. *American Journal of Psychiatry, 136,* 210–213.

Gross, M. D. (1995). Origin of stimulant use for treatment of attention deficit disorder. *American Journal of Psychiatry, 152,* 298–299.

Groth, A. N., & Birnbaum, H. J. (1978). Adult sexual orientation and attraction to underage persons. *Archives of Sexual Behavior, 7,* 175–181.

Groth, A. N., Hobson, W. F., & Gary, T. S. (1982). The child molester: Clinical observations. In J. Conte & D. A. Shore (Eds.), *Social work and child sexual abuse.* New York: Haworth Press.

Grube, J. W., Chen, M. J., Madden, P., & Morgan, M. (1995). Predicting adolescent drinking from alcohol expectancy values: A comparison of addictive, interactive, and nonlinear models. *Journal of Applied Social Psycholgy, 25,* 839–857.

Gruenewald, D. (1971). Hypnotic techniques without hypnosis in the treatment of a dual personality. *Journal of Nervous and Mental Disease, 153,* 41–46.

Gualtieri, T., Adams, A., Shen, D., & Loiselle, D. (1982). Minor physical anomalies in alcoholic and schizophrenic adults and hyperactive and autistic children. *American Journal of Psychiatry, 139,* 640–642.

Guess, D., Hemstetter, E., Turnbull, H. R., & Knowlton, S. (1987). Use of aversive procedures with persons who are disabled: A historical review and critical analysis. *Monograph for the Association for Persons with Severe Handicaps* (Whole No. 2).

Gupta, S., Andreasen, N. C., Arndt, S. V., Flaum, M., Schultz, S., Hubbard, W. C., & Smith, M. R. (1995). Neurological soft signs in neuroleptic-naive and neuroleptic-treated schizophrenic patients and in normal comparison subjects. *American Journal of Psychiatry, 152,* 191–196.

Guttmacher, L. B., Murphy, D. L., & Insel, T. R. (1983). Pharmacologic models of anxiety. *Comprehensive Psychiatry, 24,* 312–326.

Haaga, D. A. F., Dyck, M. J., & Ernst, D. (1991). Empirical status of cognitive theory of depression. *Psychological Bulletin, 110,* 215–236.

Hadaway, P. F., Alexander, B. K., Coambs, R. B., & Beyerstein, B. (1979). The effect of housing and gender on preference for morphine-sucrose solutions in rats. *Psychopharmacology, 66,* 87–91.

Haddad, G. G., Mazza, N. M., Defendini, R., Blanc, W. A., Driscoll, J. M., Epstein, M A., Epstein, R. A., & Mellins, R. B. (1978). Congenital failure of automatic control of ventilation, gastrointestinal motility, and heart rate. *Medicine, 57,* 517–526.

Hagnell, O., Lanke, J., Rorsman, B., & Ojesjo, L. (1982). Are we entering an age of melancholy? Depressive illnesses in a prospective epidemiological study over 25 years: The Lundby Study, Sweden. *Psychological Medicine, 12,* 279–289.

Hale, W. D., & Strickland, B. R. (1976). Induction of mood states and their effect on cognitive and social behaviors. *Journal of Consulting and Clinical Psychology, 44,* 155.

Hales, R., Yudofsky, S., & Talbott, J. (Eds.) (1994). *American Psychiatric Press textbook of psychiatry.* Washington, DC: American Psychiatric Press.

Halford, W. K., & Hayes, R. (1991). Psychological rehabilitation of chronic schizophrenic patients: Recent findings on social skills training and family psychoeducation. *Clinical Psychology Review, 11,* 23–44.

Halleck, S. (1981). The ethics of antiandrogen therapy. *American Journal of Psychiatry, 138,* 642–643.

Halmi, K. A., Powers, P., & Cunningham, S. (1975). Treatment of anorexia nervosa with behavior modification. *Archives of General Psychiatry, 32,* 92–96.

Halperin, J. M., Sharma,V., Siever, L. J., Schwartz, S. T., Matier, K., Wornell, G., & Newcorn, J. H. (1994). Serotonergic function in aggressive and nonaggressive boys with attention deficit hyperactivity disorder. *American Journal of Psychiatry, 151,* 243–248.

Hambrecht, M., Riecher-Rossler, A., Fatkenheuer, B., Louza, M. R., & Hafner, H. (1994). Higher morbidity risk for schizophrenia in males: Fact or fiction? *Comprehensive Psychiatry, 35,* 39–49.

Hamburger, C., Sturup, G. K., & Kahl-Iversen, E. (1953). Transvestism: Hormonal, psychiatric, and surgical treatment. *Journal of the American Medical Association, 152,* 391–396.

Hamilton, E. W., & Abramson, L. Y. (1983). Cognitive patterns and major depressive disorder: A longitudinal study in a hospital setting. *Journal of Abnormal Psychology, 92,* 173–184.

Hammen, C. L. (1991). Generation of stress in the course of unipolar depression. *Journal of Abnormal Psychology, 100,* 555–561.

Hanback, J. W., & Revelle, W. (1978). Arousal and perceptual sensitivity in hypochondriacs. *Journal of Abnormal Psychology, 87,* 523–530.

Hanksworth, H., & Schwarz, T. (1977). *The five of me.* New York: Pocket Books.

Hanson, D. R., & Gottesman, I. I. (1976). The genetics, if any, of infantile autism and childhood schizophrenia. *Journal of Autism and Childhood Schizophrenia, 6,* 209–234.

Hanson, R. K., Steffy, R. A., & Gauthier, R. (1993). Long-term recidivism of child molesters. *Journal of Consulting and Clinical Psychology, 61,* 646–652.

Hare, R. D. (1965a). Acquisition and generalization of a conditioned-fear response in psychopathic and non-psychopathic criminals. *Journal of Psychology, 59,* 367–370.

Hare, R. D. (1965b). Temporal gradient of fear arousal in psychopaths. *Journal of Abnormal Psychology, 70,* 442–445.

Hare, R. D., & Craigen, D. (1974). Psychopathy and physiological activity in a mixed-motive game situation. *Psychophysiology, 11,* 197–203.

Hare, R. D., Hart, S. D., & Harpur, T. J. (1991). Psychopathy and the DSM-IV criteria for antisocial personality disorder. *Journal of Abnormal Psychology, 100,* 391–398.

Hare, R. D., McPherson, L. M., & Forth, A. E. (1988). Male psychopaths and their criminal careers. *Journal of Consulting and Clinical Psychology, 56,* 710–714.

Hare, R. D., & Quinn, M. J. (1971). Psychopathy and autonomic conditioning. *Journal of Abnormal Psychology, 77,* 223–235.

Harlow, H. F. (1959). Love in infant monkeys. *Scientific American, 54,* 244–272.

Harpur, T. J., & Hare, R. D. (1994). Assessment of psychopathy as a function of age. *Journal of Abnormal Psychology, 103,* 604–609.

Harpur, T. J., Hart, S. D., & Hare, R. D. (1994). The personality of the psychopath. In P. T. Costa & T. A. Widiger (Eds.), *Personality disorders and the five-factor model of personality.* Washington, DC: American Psychological Association.

Harris, B. (1979). Whatever happened to Little Albert? *American Psychologist, 34,* 151–160.

Hartel, D. M., Schoenbaum, E. E., Selwyn, P. A., Kline, J., & Friedland, G. H. (1995). Heroin use during methadone maintenance treatment: The importance of methadone dose and cocaine use. *American Journal of Public Health, 85,* 83–88.

Hartmann, H. (1958). *Ego psychology and the problem of adaptation.* New York: International Universities Press.

Hartmann, H. (1964). *Essays on ego psychology: Selected problems in psychoanalytic theory.* New York: International Universities Press.

Haslam, N., & Beck, A. T. (1994). Subtyping major depression: A taxometric analysis. *Journal of Abnormal Psychology, 103,* 686–692.

Hatsukami, D., Skoog, K., Allen, S., & Bliss, R. (1995). Gender and the effects of different doses of nicotine gum on tobacco withdrawal symptoms. *Experimental and Clinical Psychopharmacology, 3,* 163–173.

Hawk, A. B., Carpenter, W. T., & Strauss, J. S. (1975). Diagnostic criteria and five-year outcome in schizophrenia. *Archives of General Psychiatry, 32,* 343–347.

Hawton, K. (1992). Suicide and attempted suicide. In E. S. Paykel (Ed.), *Handbook of affective disorders,* (2nd ed.) New York: Guilford Press.

Hay, P., Sachdev, P., Cumming, S., Smith, J. S., Lee, T., Kitchener, P., & Matheson, J. (1993). Treatment of obsessive-compulsive disorder by psychosurgery. *Acta Psychiatrica Scandinavica, 87,* 197–207.

Hayes, S. C. & Heibly, E. (1996). Psychology's drug problem: Do we need a fix or should we just say no? *American Psychologist, 51,* 198–206.

Haynes, S. G., Levine, S., Scotch, N., Feinleib, M., & Kannel, W. B. (1978). The relationship of psychosocial factors to coronary heart disease in the Framingham Study: 1. Methods and risk factors. *American Journal of Epidemiology, 107,* 362–383.

Hays, R. D., Wells, K. B., Sherbourne, C. D., Rogers, W., & Spritzer, K. (1995). Functioning and well-being outcomes of patients with depression compared with chronic general medical illnesses. *Archives of General Psychiatry, 52,* 11–19.

Hayward, M. L., & Taylor, J. E. (1956). A schizophrenic patient describes the action of intensive psychotherapy. *Psychiatry Quarterly, 30,* 211–248.

Heath, A. C., Madden, P. A. F., Slutske, W. S., & Martin, N. G. (1995). Personality and the inheritance of smoking behavior: A genetic perspective. *Behavior Genetics, 25,* 103–117.

Heath, E. S., Adams, A., & Wakeling, P. L. (1964). Short courses of ECT and simulated ECT in chronic schizophrenia. *British Journal of Psychiatry, 110,* 800–807.

Heatherton, T. F., & Baumeister, R. F. (1991). Binge eating as escape from self-awareness. *Psychological Bulletin, 110,* 86–108.

Heatherton, T. F., Herman, C. P., & Polivy, J. (1991). Effects of physical threat and ego threat on eating behavior. *Journal of Personality and Social Psychology, 60,* 138–143.

Heatherton, T. F., Nichols, P., Mahamedi, F., & Keel, P. (1995). Body weight, dieting, and eating disorder symptoms among college students, 1982–1992. *American Journal of Psychiatry, 152,* 1623–1629.

Heaton, R., Paulsen, J. S., McAdams, L., Kuck, J., Zissok, S., Braff, D., Harris, M. J., & Jeste, D. V. (1994). Neuropsychological deficits in schizophrenics. Archives of General Psychiatry, 51, 469–476.

Hebb, D. O. (1949). *Organization of behavior.* New York: Wiley.

Hedfors, E., Holm, G., Ivansen, M., & Wahren, J. (1983). Physiological variation of blood lymphocyte reactivity: T-cell subsets, immunoglobulin production, and mixed-lymphocyte reactivity. *Clinical Immunology and Immunopathology, 27,* 9–14.

Hefez, A. (1985). The role of the press and the medical community in the epidemic of "mysterious gas poisoning" in the Jordan West Bank. *American Journal of Psychiatry, 142,* 833–837.

Hegarty, J. D., Baldessarini, R. J., Tohen, M., Waternaux, C., & Oepen, G. (1994). One hundred years of schizophrenia: A meta-analysis of the outcome literature. *American Journal of Psychiatry, 151,* 1409–1416.

Heim, N. (1981). Sexual behavior of castrated sex offenders. *Archives of Sexual Behavior, 10,* 11–19.

Heimberg, R. G., Dodge, C. S., Hope, D. A., Kennedy, C. R., & Zollo, L. J. (1990). Cognitive behavioral group treatment for social phobia: Comparison with a credible placebo control. *Cognitive Therapy and Research, 14,* 1–23.

Helmes, E., & Reddon, J. R. (1993). A perspective on developments in assessing psychopathology: A critical review of the MMPI and MMPI-2. *Psychological Bulletin, 113,* 453–471.

Henderson, D. J., Boyd, C. J., & Whitmarsh, J. (1995). Women and illicit drugs: Sexuality and crack cocaine. *Health Care for Women International, 16,* 113–124.

Henderson, J. L., & Moore, M. M. (1944). The psychoneuroses of war. *New England Journal of Medicine, 230,* 273–278.

Henson, D. E., & Rubin, H. B. (1971). Voluntary control of eroticism. *Journal of Applied Behavior Analysis, 4,* 37–44.

Herbert, T. B., & Cohen, S. (1993). Depression and immunity: A meta-analytic review. *Psychological Bulletin, 113,* 472–486.

Herrington, R. N., & Lader, M. H. (1981). Lithium. In H. Van Praag, M. H. Lader, O. Rafaelsen, & E. Sachar (Eds.), *Handbook of biological psychiatry: Vol. 5., Drug treatment in psychiatry: Psychotropic drugs.* New York: Dekker.

Heston, L. L. (1966). Psychiatric disorders in foster-home-reared children of schizophrenic mothers. *British Journal of Psychiatry, 112,* 819–825.

Hietala, J., Syvalahti, E., Vuorio, K., Nagren, K., Lehikoinen, P., Ruotsalainen, U., Rakkolaien, V., Lehtinen, V., & Wegelius, U. (1994). Striatal D2 dopamine receptor characteristics in neuroleptic-naive schizophrenic patients studied with positron emission tomography. *Archives of General Psychiatry, 51,* 116–123.

Higgins, S. T., Budney, A. J., Bickel, W. K., Foerg, F. E., Donham, R., & Badger, G. J. (1994). Incentives improve outcome in outpatient behavioral treatment of cocaine dependence. *Archives of General Psychiatry, 51,* 568–576.

Higley, J. D., Mehlman, P. T., Taub, D. M., Higley, S. B., Suomi, S. J., Linnoila, M., & Vickers, J. H. (1992). Cerebrospinal fluid monoamine and adrenal correlates of aggression in free-ranging rhesus monkeys. *Archives of General Psychiatry, 49,* 436–441.

Higley, J. D., Thompson, W. W., Champoux, M., Goldman, D., Hasert, M. F., Kraemer, G. W., Scanlan, J. M., Suomi, S. J., & Linnoila, M. (1993). Parental and maternal genetic and environmental contributions to cerebrospinal fluid monoamine metabolites in rhe-

sus monkeys *(Macaca mulatta). Archives of General Psychiatry, 50,* 615–623.

Hilgard, E. R., & Marquis, D. G. (1961). *Conditioning and learning* (rev. ed.). Norwalk, CT: Appleton & Lange.

Hill, D. (1952). EEG in episodic psychotic and psychopathic behavior: A classification of data. *Electroencephalography and Clinical Neurophysiology, 4,* 419–442.

Hill, D., & Watterson, D. (1942). Electroencephalographic studies of psychopathic personalities. *Journal of Neurology and Psychiatry, 5,* 47–65.

Hinshaw, S. P. (1991). Stimulant medication and the treatment of aggression in children with attention deficits. *Journal of Clinical Child Psychology, 20,* 301–312.

Hinshaw, S. P., Heller, T., & McHale, J. P. (1992). Covert antisocial behavior in boys with attention-deficit hyperactivity disorder: Validation and effects of methylphenidate. *Journal of Consulting and Clinical Psychology, 60,* 274–281.

Hinshaw, S. P., Henker, B., & Whalen, C. K. (1984a). Cognitive-behavioral and pharmacologic interventions for hyperactive boys: Comparative and combined effects. *Journal of Consulting and Clinical Psychology, 52,* 739–749.

Hinshaw, S. P., Henker, B., & Whalen, C. K. (1984b). Self-control in hyperactive boys in anger-inducing situations: Effects of cognitive-behavioral training and of methylphenidate. *Journal of Abnormal Child Psychology, 12,* 55–77.

Hiroto, D. S. (1974). Locus of control and learned helplessness. *Journal of Experimental Psychology, 102,* 187–193.

Hiroto, D. S., & Seligman, M. E. P. (1975). Generality of learned helplessness in man. *Journal of Personality and Social Psychology, 31,* 311–327.

Hirsch, S. R., & Leff, J. P. (1975). *Abnormalities in parents of schizophrenics.* London: Oxford University Press.

Hirschfeld, R. M., & Shea, M. T. (1992). Personality. In E. S. Paykel (Ed.), *Handbook of affective disorders* (2nd ed.). New York: Guilford Press.

Hirst, W. (1982). The amnesic syndrome: Descriptions and explanations. *Psychological Bulletin, 91,* 435–460.

Hiss, H., Foa, E., & Kozak, M. J. (1994). Relapse prevention program for treatment of obsessive-compulsive disorder. *Journal of Consulting and Clinical Psychology, 62,* 801–808.

Hitchcock, P. B. & Mathews, A. (1992). Interpretation of bodily symptoms in hypochondriasis. *Behaviour Research and Therapy, 31,* 223–234.

Hittner, J. B. (1995). Tension-reduction expectancies and alcoholic beverage preferences revisited: Associations to drinking frequency and gender. *International Journal of the Addictions, 30,* 323–336.

Hobson, J. A. (1988). *The dreaming brain.* New York: Basic Books.

Hodgkinson, S., Sherrington, R., Gurling, H., Marchbanks, R., Reeders, S., Mallet, J., McInnis, M., Petursson, H., & Brynjolfsson, J. (1987). Molecular genetic evidence for heterogeneity in manic depression. *Nature, 325,* 805–806.

Hoffman, R. E. (1992). Attractor neural networks and psychotic disorders. *Psychiatric Annals, 22,* 119–124.

Hofmann, S. G., Newman, M. G., Ehlers, A., & Roth, W. T. (1995). Psychophysiological differences between subgroups of social phobia. *Journal of Abnormal Psychology, 104,* 224–231.

Hogarty, G. E., Anderson, C. M., Reiss, D. J., Kornblith, S. J., Greenwald, D. P., Javna, C. D., & Madonia, M. J. (1986). Family psychoeducation, social skills training, and maintenance chemotherapy in the aftercare treatment of schizophrenia. *Archives of General Psychiatry, 43,* 633–642.

Hogarty, G. E., Anderson, C. M., Reiss, D. J., Kornblith, S. J., Greenwald, D. P., Ulrich, R. F., & Carter, M. (1991). Family psychoeducation, social skills training, and maintenance chemotherapy in the aftercare treatment of schizophrenia: 2. Two-year effects of a controlled study on relapse and adjustment. *Archives of General Psychiatry, 48,* 340–347.

Hoge, S. K. (1994). On being "too crazy" to sign into a mental hospital: The issue of consent to psychiatric hospitalization. *Bulletin of the American Academy of Psychiatry and the Law, 22,* 431–451.

Holahan, C. K., Holahan, C. J., & Belk, S. S. (1984). Adjustment in aging: The roles of life stress, hassles, and self-efficacy. *Health Psychology, 3,* 315–328.

Hollander, E., DeCaria, C. M., Nitescu, A., Gully, R., Suckow, R., Cooper, T. B., Gorman, J., Klein, D. F., & Liebowitz, M. (1994).

Serotonergic function in obsessive-compulsive disorder: Behavioral and neuroendocrine responses to oral m-chlorophenylpiperazine and flenluramine in patients and healthy volunteers. *Archives of General Psychiatry, 49,* 21–28.

Hollander, E., Liebowitz, M. R., & Gorman, J. M. (1988). Anxiety disorders. In J. A. Talbott, R. E. Hales, & J. M. Gorman (Eds.), *American Psychiatric Press textbook of psychiatry.* Washington, DC: American Psychiatric Press.

Hollander, E., Schiffman, E., Cohen, B., Rivera-Stein, M. A., Rosen, W., Gorman, J. M., Fyer, A. J., Papp, L., & Liebowitz, M. R. (1990). Signs of central nervous system dysfunction in obsessive-compulsive disorder. *Archives of General Psychiatry, 47,* 27–32.

Hollander, E., Simeon, D., & Gorman, J. M. (1994). Anxiety disorders. In R. E. Hales, S. C. Yudofsky, & J. A. Talbott (Eds.), *American Psychiatric Press textbook of psychiatry* (2nd ed.). Washington, D.C.: American Psychiatric Press.

Hollingshead, A. B., & Redlich, F. C. (1958). *Social class and mental illness.* New York: Wiley.

Hollister, J. M., Mednick, S. A., Brennan, P., & Cannon, T. D. (1994). Impaired autonomic nervous system habituation in those at genetic risk for schizophrenia. *Archives of General Psychiatry, 51,* 552–558.

Hollon, S. D., & Beck, A. T. (1979). Cognitive therapy of depression. In P. C. Kendall & S. D. Hollon (Eds.), *Cognitive-behavioral interventions: Theory, research, and procedures.* New York: Academic Press.

Hollon, S. D., Shelton, R. C., & Loosen, P. T. (1991). Cognitive therapy and pharmacotherapy for depression. *Journal of Consulting and Clinical Psychology, 59,* 88–99.

Holmes, D. S. (1967). Verbal conditioning or problem solving and cooperation? *Journal of Experimental Research in Personality, 2,* 289–295.

Holmes, D. S. (1968). Dimensions of projection. *Psychological Bulletin, 69,* 248–268.

Holmes, D. S. (1971). The conscious self-appraisal of achievement motivation: The self-peer rank method revisited. *Journal of Consulting and Clinical Psychology, 36,* 23–26.

Holmes, D. S. (1974). Investigations of repression: Differential recall of material experimentally or naturally associated with ego threat. *Psychological Bulletin, 81,* 632–653.

Holmes, D. S. (1978). Projection as a defense mechanism. *Psychological Bulletin, 85,* 677–688.

Holmes, D. S. (1981). Existence of classical projection and the stress-reducing function of attributive projection: A reply to Sherwood. *Psychological Bulletin, 90,* 460–466.

Holmes, D. S. (1983). An alternative perspective concerning the differential physiological responsivity of persons with Type A and Type B behavior patterns. *Journal of Research in Personality, 17,* 40–47.

Holmes, D. S. (1984a). Defense mechanisms. In R. J. Corsini (Ed.), *Encyclopedia of psychology.* New York: Wiley.

Holmes, D. S. (1984b). Meditation and somatic arousal: A review of the experimental evidence. *American Psychologist, 39,* 1–10.

Holmes, D. S. (1985). Self-control of somatic arousal: An examination of meditation and biofeedback. *American Behavioral Scientist, 28,* 486–496.

Holmes, D. S. (1987). The influence of meditation versus rest on physiological arousal: A second examination. In M. A. West (Ed.), *The psychology of meditation.* Oxford: Oxford University Press.

Holmes, D. S. (1990). The evidence for repression: An examination of sixty years of research. In J. L. Singer (Ed.), *Repression and dissociation.* Chicago: University of Chicago Press.

Holmes, D. S. (1991). *Abnormal psychology.* New York: HarperCollins.

Holmes, D. S. (1993). Aerobic fitness and the response to psychological stress. In P. Seraganian (Ed.), *Exercise psychology: The influence of physical exercise on psychological processes.* New York: Wiley.

Holmes, D. S., & Burish, T. G. (1984). Effectiveness of biofeedback for treating migraine and tension headaches: A review of the evidence. *Journal of Psychosomatic Research, 27,* 515–532.

Holmes, D. S., & Houston, B. K. (1974). Effectiveness of situation redefinition and affective isolation for reducing stress. *Journal of Personality and Social Psychology, 29,* 212–218.

Holmes, D. S., & McCaul, K. D. (1989). Laboratory research on defense mechanisms. In R. Neufeld (Ed.), *Advances in investigation of psychological stress.* New York: Wiley.

Holmes, D. S., & McGilley, B. M. (1987). Influence of a brief aerobic training program on heart rate and subjective response to stress. *Psychosomatic Medicine, 49,* 366–374.

Holmes, D. S., McGilley, B. M., & Houston, B. K. (1984). Task-related arousal of Type A and Type B persons: Level of challenge and response specificity. *Journal of Personality and Social Psychology, 46,* 1322–1327.

Holmes, D. S., & Roth, D. L. (1985). Association of aerobic fitness with pulse rate and subjective responses to psychological stress. *Psychophysiology, 22,* 525–529.

Holmes, D. S., & Roth, D. L. (1989). *The measurement of cognitive and somatic anxiety.* Unpublished manuscript, University of Kansas at Lawrence.

Holmes, D. S., & Tyler, J. (1968). Direct versus projective measurement of achievement motivation. *Journal of Consulting and Clinical Psychology, 32,* 712–717.

Holroyd, K. A., and Penzien, D. B. (1994). Psychosocial interventions in the management of recurrent headache disorders: 1. Overview and effectiveness. *Behavioral Medicine, 20,* 53–63.

Holt, C. S., Heimberg, R. G., & Hope, D. A. (1992). Avoidant personality disorder and the generalized subtype of social phobia. *Journal of Abnormal Psychology, 101,* 318–325.

Honigfeld, G., & Patin, J. (1990). A two-year clinical and economic follow-up of patients on clozapine. *Hospital and Community Psychiatry, 41,* 882–885.

Hook, E. B. (1982). Epidemiology of Down syndrome. In S. M. Pueschel & J. E. Rynders (Eds.), *Down syndrome: Advances in biomedicine and the behavioral sciences.* Cambridge, MA: Ware Press.

Hook, E. B., & Chambers, G. M. (1977). Estimated rates of Down's syndrome in live births by one-year maternal age intervals for mothers aged 20 to 49 in a New York State study. In D. Bergsma, R. B. Lowry, B. K. Trimble, & M. Feingold (Eds.), *Numerical taxonomy of birth defects and polygenic disorders* (pp. 123–141). New York: Liss.

Hook, E. B., & Fabia, J. J. (1978). Frequency of Down syndrome by single-year maternal age interval: Results of a Massachusetts study. *Teratology, 17,* 223–228.

Hook, E. B., & Lindsjo, A. (1978). Down syndrome in live births by single-year maternal age interval in a Swedish study: Comparison with results from a New York study. *American Journal of Human Genetics, 30,* 19–27.

Hooley, J. M., & Teasdale, J. D. (1989). Predictors of relapse in unipolar depressives: Expressed emotion, marital distress, and perceived criticism. *Journal of Abnormal Psychology, 98,* 229–235.

Hopkins, J., Marcus, M., & Campbell, S. B. (1984). Postpartum depression: A critical review. *Psychological Bulletin, 95,* 498–515.

Hopper, J. L. (1994). Genetic factors in alcohol use: A genetic epidemiological perspective. *Drug and Alcohol Review, 13,* 375–384.

Horenstein, D., Houston, B. K., & Holmes, D. S. (1973). Relationship between clients', therapists', and judges' evaluations of the progress of psychotherapy. *Journal of Counseling Psychology, 20,* 149–153.

Horn, A. S., & Snyder, S. H. (1971). Chlorpromazine and dopamine: Conformational similarities that correlate with antischizophrenic activity of phenothiazine drugs. *Proceedings of the National Academy of Sciences, 68,* 2325–2328.

Horn, W. F., Chatoor, I., & Conners, C. K. (1983). Additive effects of Dexedrine and self-control training: A multiple assessment. *Behavior Modification, 7,* 383–402.

Horney, K. (1937). *Neurotic personality of our times.* New York: Norton.

Horney, K. (1939). *New ways in psychoanalysis.* New York: Norton.

Horney, K. (1945). *Our inner conflicts.* New York: Norton.

Horney, K. (1967). *Feminine psychology.* New York: Norton.

Houser, V. P. (1978). The effects of drugs on behavior controlled by aversive stimuli. In D. E. Blackman & D. J. Sanger (Eds.), *Contemporary research in behavioral psychopharmacology.* New York: Plenum.

Houston, B. K. (1972). Control over stress, locus of control, and response to stress. *Journal of Personality and Social Psychology, 21,* 249–255.

Houston, B. K. (1983). Psychophysiological responsivity and the Type A behavior pattern. *Journal of Research in Personality, 17,* 22–39.

Houston, B. K., Chesney, M. A., Black, G. W., Cates, D. S., & Hecker, M. H. (1992). Behavioral clusters and coronary heart disease risk. *Psychosomatic Medicine, 54,* 447–461.

Houston, B. K., & Holmes, D. S. (1974). Effectiveness of avoidant thinking and reappraisal in coping with threat involving temporal uncertainty. *Journal of Personality and Social Psychology, 30,* 382–388.

Houts, A. C., Berman, J. S., & Abramson, H. (1994). Effectiveness of psychological and pharmacological treatments for nocturnal enuresis. *Journal of Consulting and Clinical Psychology, 62,* 737–745.

Howells, K. (1981). Adult sexual interest in children: Considerations relevant to theories of etiology. In M. Cook & K. Howells (Eds.), *Adult sexual interest in children.* London: Academic Press.

Hucker, S. J. & Blanchard, R. (1992). Death scene characteristics in 118 fatal cases of autoerotic asphyxia compared with suicidal asphyxia. *Behavioral Sciences and the Law, 10,* 509–523.

Hucker, S. J., Langevin, R., Dickey, R., & Handy, L. (1988). Cerebral damage and dysfunction in sexually aggressive men. *Annals of Sex Reserach, 1,* 33–47.

Hughes, J. R., Gust, S. W., Skoog, K., Kenan, R. M., & Fenwick, J. W. (1991). Symptoms of tobacco withdrawal: A replication and extension. *Archives of General Psychiatry, 48,* 52–59.

Hughes, P. L., Wells, L. A., Cunningham, C. J., & Ilstrup, D. M. (1986). Treating bulimia with desipramine. *Archives of General Psychiatry, 43,* 182–186.

Hullin, R. P., MacDonald, R., & Allsop, M. N. (1972). Prophylactic lithium in recurrent affective disorders. *Lancet, 2,* 1044–1047.

Humphrey v. *Cady,* 405 U.S. 504 (1972).

Humphreys, K. (1996). Clinical psychologists as psychotherapists: History, future, and alternatives. *American Psychologist, 51,* 190–197.

Humphry, D. (1991). *Final exit.* Secaucus, NJ: Hemlock Society.

Humphry, D. (1992). Rational suicide among the elderly. *Suicide and Life-Threatening Behavior, 22,* 125–129.

Hurley, D. (1988, January). Getting help from helping. *Psychology Today,* 63–67.

Hurt, R. D., Offord, K. P., Lauger, G. G., Marusic, Z. Fagerström, K., Enright, P. L., & Scanlo, P. D. (1995). Cessation of long-term nicotine gum use: A prospective, randomized trial. *Addiction, 90,* 407–413.

Hutchings, B., & Mednick, S. A. (1974). Registered criminality in the adoptive and biological parents of registered male criminal adoptees. In R. R. Fieve, D. Rosenthal, & H. Brill (Eds.), *Genetic research in psychiatry.* Baltimore: Johns Hopkins University Press.

Hutt, C., & Ounsted, C. (1966). The biological significance of gaze aversion with particular reference to the syndrome of infantile autism. *Behavioral Science, 11,* 346–361.

Huttunen, M. O. (1995). The evolution of the serotonin-dopamine antagonist concept. *Journal of Clinical Psychopharmacology, 15,* 4S–10S.

Hyde, T. M., & Weinberger, D. R. (1995). Tourette's syndrome: A model neuropsychiatric disorder. *Journal of the American Medical Association, 273,* 498–501.

Hyman, I., Husband, T. H., & Billings, F. J. (1995). False memories of childhood experiences. *Applied Cognitive Psychology, 9,* 181–107.

Iacono, W. G., & Beiser, M. (1992). Are males more likely than females to develop schizophrenia? *American Journal of Psychiatry, 149,* 1070–1074.

Iga, M. (1993). Japanese suicide. In A. A. Leenaars (Ed.), *Suicidology.* Northvale, NJ: Aronson.

Ikuta, N., Zanarini, M. C., Minakawa, K., Miyake, Y., et al. (1994). Comparison of American and Japanese outpatients with borderline personality disorder. *Comprehensive Psychiatry, 35,* 382–385.

Iller, D. D., Perry, P. J., Cadoret, R. J., & Andreasen, N. C. (1994). Clozapine's effect on negative symptoms in treatment-refractory schizophrenics. *Comprehensive Psychiatry, 35,* 8–15.

Imber, S. D., Pilkonis, P. A., Sotsky, S. M., Elkin, I., Watkins, J. T., Collins, J. F., Shea, M. T., Leber, W. R., & Glass, D. R. (1990). Mode-specific effects among three treatments for depression. *Journal of Consulting and Clinical Psychology, 58,* 352–359.

Imre, P. D. (1962). Attitudes of volunteers toward mental hospitals compared to patients and personnel. *Journal of Clinical Psychology, 18,* 516.

Imre, P. D., & Wolf, S. (1962). Attitudes of patients and personnel toward mental hospitals. *Journal of Clinical Psychology, 18,* 232–234.

Ingram, R. E. (1984). Toward an information-processing analysis of depression. *Cognitive Therapy and Research, 8,* 443–478.

Ingram, R. E., & Kendall, P. C. (1987). The cognitive side of anxiety. *Cognitive Therapy and Research, 11,* 523–536.

Insanity Defense Work Group. (1983). American Psychiatric Association statement on the insanity defense. *American Journal of Psychiatry, 140,* 681–688.

Insel, T. R. (1993). Toward a neuroanatomy of obsessive-compulsive disorder. *Archives of General Psychiatry, 49,* 739–744.

Ironside, R., & Batchelor, I. R. (1945). The ocular manifestations of hysteria in relation to flying. *British Journal of Ophthalmology, 29,* 88–98.

Isen, A., & Gorgoglione, J. (1983). Some specific effects of four affect-induction procedures. *Personality and Social Psychology Bulletin, 9,* 136–143.

Isen, A., Shalker, T., Clark, M., & Karp, L. (1978). Affect, accessibility of material in memory, and behavior: A cognitive loop? *Journal of Personality and Social Psychology, 36,* 1–12.

Ivanoff, A., & Jang, S. J. (1991). The role of hopelessness and social desirability in predicting suicidal behavior: A study of prison inmates. *Journal of Consulting and Clinical Psychology, 59,* 394–399.

Jackson v. *Indiana,* 406 U.S. 715 (1972).

Jacob, H. E. (1935). *Coffee: The epic of a commodity.* New York: Viking Penguin.

Jacob, T. (1975). Family interaction in disturbed and normal families: A methodological and substantive review. *Psychological Bulletin, 82,* 33–65.

Jacobs, B. L. (1987). How hallucinogenic drugs work. *American Scientist, 75,* 386–391.

Jacobsen, C. F., Wolfe, J. B., & Jackson, T. A. (1935). An experimental analysis of the functions of the frontal association areas in primates. *Journal of Nervous and Mental Disease, 82,* 1–14.

Jacobson, E. (1938). *Progressive relaxation.* Chicago: University of Chicago Press.

Jacobson, N. S. (Ed.). (1988). Defining clinically significant change [Special issue]. *Behavioral Assessment, 10*(2).

Jacobson, N. S., & Truax, P. (1991). Clinical significance: A statistical approach to defining meaningful change in psychotherapy. *Journal of Consulting and Clinical Psychology, 59,* 12–19.

Jaffe, J. H. (1995). Pharmacological treatment of opioid dependence: Current techniques and new findings. *Psychiatric Annals, 25,* 369–375.

Jakob, H., & Beckmann, H. (1986). Prenatal developmental disturbances in the limbic allocortex in schizophrenics. *Journal of Neural Transmission, 65,* 303–326.

Jamison, K. K. (1992). Suicide and manic-depressive illness in artists and writers. *National Forum, 73,* 28–30.

Jamison, K. K. (1993). *Touched by fire: Manic-depressive illness and the artistic temperament.* New York: Free Press.

Jamison, K. K. (1995a). *An unquiet mind.* New York: Random House.

Jamison, K. K. (1995b). Manic-depressive illness and creativity. *Scientific American. 272,* 62–67.

Jamison, K. K., & Akiskal, H. S. (1983). Medication compliance in patients with bipolar disorder. *Psychiatric Clinics of North America, 6,* 175–192.

Janca, A., Isaac., M., Bennett, L. A., & Tacchini, G. (1995). Somatoform disorders in different cultures: A mail questionnaire survey. *Social Psychiatry and Psychiatric Epidemiology, 30,* 44–48.

Janicak, P. G., Davis, J. M., Gibbons, R. D., Ericksen, S., Chang, S., & Gallagher, P. (1985). Efficacy of ECT: A meta-analysis. *American Journal of Psychiatry, 143,* 297–302.

Janowsky, D. S., El-Yousef, M. K., Davis, J. M., & Sekerke, J. (1973). Provocation of schizophrenic symptoms by intravenous administration of methylphenidate. *Archives of General Psychiatry, 28,* 185–191.

Jansen, M. A., Arntz, A., Merckelbach, H. & Mersch, P. P. (1994). Personality disorders and features in social phobia and panic disorder. *Journal of Abnormal Psychology, 103,* 391–395.

Jarey, M. L., & Stewart, M. A. (1985). Psychiatric disorder in the parents of adopted children with aggressive conduct disorder. *Neuropsychobiology, 13,* 7–11.

Jarvis, G. K., Boldt, M., & Butt, J. (1991). Medical examiners and manner of death. *Suicide and Life-Threatening Behavior, 21,* 115–133.

Jeans, R. F. (1976). Independently validated case of multiple personality. *Journal of Abnormal Psychology, 85,* 249–255.

Jemmott, J. B., Borysenko, J. Z., Borysenko, M., McClelland, D. C., Chapman, R., Meyer, D., & Benson, H. (1983). Academic stress, power motivation, and decrease in secretion rate of salivary secretory immunoglobulin A. *Lancet, 1,* 1400–1402.

Jemmott, J. B., & Locke, S. E. (1984). Psychosocial factors, immunologic mediation, and human susceptibility to infectious diseases: How much do we know? *Psychological Bulletin, 95,* 78–108.

Jenike, M. A., Baer, L., Ballantine, H. T., Martuza, R. L., Tynes, S., Giriunas, I., Buttolph, M. L., & Cassem, N. H. (1991). Cingulotomy for refractory obsessive-compulsive disorder: A long-term follow-up of 33 patients. *Archives of General Psychiatry, 48,* 548–555.

Jenner, P., Sheehy, M., & Marsden, C. D. (1983). Noradrenaline and 5-hydroxytryptamine modulation of brain dopamine function: Implications for the treatment of Parkinson's disease. *British Journal of Clinical Pharmacology, 15* (Suppl.), 277S–289S.

Jervis, G. A. (1939). The genetics of phenylpyruvic oligophrenia. *Journal of Mental Science, 85,* 719–762.

Jervis, G. A. (1947). Studies of phenylpyruvic oligophrenia: The position of the metabolic error. *Journal of Biological Chemistry, 169,* 651–656.

Jeste, D. V., Gilbert, P. L., McAdams, L. A., & Harris, M. J. (1995). Considering neuroleptic maintenance and taper on a continuum: Need for individual rather than dogmatic approach. *Archives of General Psychiatry, 52,* 209–212.

Jeste, D. V., Harris, M. J., Krull, A., Kuck, J., McAdams, L. A., & Heaton, R. (1995). Clinical and neuropsychological characteristics of patients with late-onset schizophrenia. *American Journal of Psychiatry, 152,* 722–730.

Jimerson, D. C., Lesem, M. D., Kay, W. H., & Brewerton, T. D. (1992). Low serotonin and dopamine metabolite concentrations in cerebrospinal fluid from bulimic patients with frequent binge episodes. *Archives of General Psychiatry, 49,* 132–138.

Joffe, R. T., Singer, W., Levitt, A. J., & MacDonald, C. (1993). A placebo-controlled comparison of lithium and triiodothyronine augmentation of tricyclic antidepressants in unipolar refractory depression. *Archives of General Psychiatry, 50,* 387–393.

Johnson, D. (1994). Stress, depression, substance abuse, and racism. *American-Indian and Alaska Native Mental Health Research, 6,* 29–33.

Johnson, J. G., & Bornstein, R. F. (1991). Does daily stress independently predict psychopathology? *Journal of Social and Clinical Psychology, 10,* 58–74.

Johnson, M. H., & Magaro, P. A. (1987). Effects of mood and severity on memory processes in depression and mania. *Psychological Bulletin, 101,* 28–40.

Johnson, P. B. (1994). Alcohol expectancies and reaction expectancies: Their impact on student drinking. *Journal of Alcohol and Drug Education, 40,* 57–68.

Johnson, S. L., & Roberts, J. E. (1995). Life events and bipolar disorder: Implications from biological theories. *Psychological Bulletin, 117,* 434–449.

Johnstone, E. C., Crow, T. J., Firth, C. D., Husband, J., & Kreel, L. (1976). Cerebral ventricular size and cognitive impairment in chronic schizophrenia. *Lancet, 2,* 924–926.

Jones, B. T., & McMahon, J. (1994). Negative alcohol expectancy predicts posttreatment abstinence survivorship: The whether, when, and why of relapse to a first drink. *Addiction, 89,* 1653–1665.

Jones, F. D., Maas, F. J., Dekirmenjian, H., & Fawcett, J. A. (1973). Urinary catecholamine metabolites during behavioral changes in a patient with manic-depressive cycles. *Science, 179,* 300–302.

Jones, M. C. (1924). The elimination of children's fears. *Journal of Experimental Psychology, 7,* 382–390.

Jones, R., Peveler, R. C., Hope, R. A., & Fairburn, C. G. (1993). Changes during treatment for bulimia nervosa: A comparison of three psychological treatments. *Behaviour Research and Therapy, 31,* 479–485.

Jones, S. H., Gray, J. A., & Hemsley, D. (1990). The Kamin blocking effect, incidental learning and psychoticism. *British Journal of Psychology, 81,* 95–109.

Jones, S. H., Gray, J. A., & Hemsley, D. (1992). Loss of the Kamin blocking effect in acute but not chronic schizophrenics. *Biological Psychiatry, 32,* 739–755.

Judd, L. L., McAdams, L., Budnick, B., & Braff, D. L. (1992). Sensory gating deficits in schizophrenia. *American Journal of Psychiatry, 149,* 488–493.

Junginger, J., Barker, S., & Coe, D. (1992). Mood theme and bizarreness of delusions in schizophrenia and mood psychosis. *Journal of Abnormal Psychology, 101,* 287–292.

Kagan, V. (1981). Nonprocess autism in children: A comparative etiopathogenic study. *Soviet Neurology and Psychiatry, 14,* 25–30.

Kagle, J. D., & Kopels, S. (1994). Confidentiality after Tarasoff. *Health and Social Work, 19,* 217–222.

Kamin, L. J. (1969). Predictability, surprise, attention, and conditioning. In B. A. Campbell & R. M. Church (Eds.), *Punishment and aversive behavior.* New York: Appleton-Century-Crofts.

Kane, J. M. (1983). Low-dose medication strategies in the maintenance treatment of schizophrenia. *Schizophrenia Bulletin, 9,* 528–532.

Kane, J. M., Honigfeld, G., Singer, J., & Meltzer, H. (1988). Clozapine for the treatment-resistant schizophrenic. *Archives of General Psychiatry, 45,* 789–796.

Kane, J. M., Honigfeld, G., Singer, J., & Meltzer, H. (1989). Clozapine for the treatment-resistant schizophrenic: Results of a U.S. multicenter trial. *Psychopharmacology, 99,* S60–S63.

Kanfer, R., & Zeiss, A. M. (1983). Depression, interpersonal standard setting, and judgments of self-efficacy. *Journal of Abnormal Psychology, 92,* 319–329.

Kanner, A. D., Coyne, J. C., Schaefer, C., & Lazarus, R. S. (1981). Comparison of two modes of stress management: Daily hassles and uplifts versus major life events. *Journal of Behavioral Medicine, 4,* 1–40.

Kanner, L. (1943). Autistic disturbances of affective content. *Nervous Child, 2,* 217–240.

Kanofsky, J. D., Sandyk, R., & Kay, S. R. (1990). Anatomical abnormalities in the brains of monozygotic twins discordant for schizophrenia. *New England Journal of Medicine, 323,* 547.

Kaplan, H. S. (1981). *The new sex therapy: Active treatment of sexual dysfunctions.* New York: Brunner/Mazel.

Kaplan, J. R., Manuck, S. B., & Shively, C. A. (1991). The effects of cholesterol on social behavior in monkeys. *Psychosomatic Medicine, 53,* 634–642.

Karlsson, J. L. (1966). *The biologic basis of schizophrenia.* Springfield, IL: Thomas.

Kasa, K., Otsuki, S., Yamamoto, M., Sato, M., Kuroda, H., & Ogawa, N. (1982). Cerebrospinal fluid, aminobutyric acid and homovanillic acid, in depressive disorders. *Biological Psychiatry, 17,* 877–883.

Kassin, S. M., & Wrightsman, L. S. (1993). Confession evidence. In S. M. Kassin & L. S. Wrightsman (Eds.), *The psychology of evidence and trial procedure.* Newbury Park, CA: Sage.

Kaya, N., Moore, C., & Karacan, I. (1979). Nocturnal penile tumescence and its role in impotence. *Psychiatric Annals, 9,* 426–431.

Keck, P. E., McElroy, S. L., & Pope, H. G. (1991). Epidemiology of neuroleptic malignant syndrome. *Psychiatric Annals, 21,* 148–151.

Kellermann, A. L., Rivara, F. P., Somes, G., Reay, D. T., Francisco, J., Banton, J. B., Prodzinski, J., Fligner, C., & Hackman, B. B. (1992). Suicide in the home in relation to gun ownership. *New England Journal of Medicine, 327,* 467–472.

Kellner, R. (1992). The case for reassurance. *International Review of Psychiatry, 4,* 71–75.

Kellner, R., Uhlenhuth, E. H., & Glass, R. (1978). Clinical evaluation of antianxiety agents: Subject-own-control designs. In M. Lipton, A. Di Mascio, & K. Killam (Eds.), *Psychopharmacology: A generation of progress.* New York: Raven Press.

Kelly, D., Mitchell-Heggs, N., & Sherman, D. (1971). Anxiety and the effects of sodium lactate assessed clinically and psychologically. *British Journal of Psychiatry, 119,* 129–141.

Kenardy, J., Evans, L., & Oei, T. P. (1992). The latent structure of anxiety symptoms in anxiety disorders. *American Journal of Psychiatry, 149,* 1058–1061.

Kendall, P. C. (1984). Cognitive-behavioral self-control therapy for children. *Journal of Child Psychology and Psychiatry, 25,* 173–179.

Kendall, P. C. (Ed.). (1992). Comorbidity and treatment implications. *Journal of Consulting and Clinical Psychology, 60,* 833–908.

Kendler, K. S. (1993). Twin studies of psychiatric illness. *Archives of General Psychiatry, 50,* 905–915.

Kendler, K. S., Gruenberg, A. M., & Strauss, J. S. (1982). An independent analysis of the Copenhagen sample of the Danish adoption study of schizophrenia: The relationship between childhood withdrawal and adult schizophrenia. *Archives of General Psychiatry, 39,* 1257–1261.

Kendler, K. S., Heath, A. C., Neale, M. C., Kessler, R. C., & Eaves, L. J. (1992). A population-based twin study of alcoholism in women. *Journal of the American Medical Association, 268,* 1877–1882.

Kendler, K. S., Heath, A. C., Neale, M. C., Kessler, R. & Eaves, L. J. C., (1993). Alcoholism and major depression in women: A twin study of the causes of comorbidity. *Archives of General Psychiatry, 50,* 690–698.

Kendler, K. S., McGuire, M., Gruenberg, A. M., O'Hare, A., Spellman, M., & Walsh, D. (1993a). The Roscommon Family Study: 3. Schizophrenia-related personality disorders in relatives. *Archives of General Psychiatry, 50,* 781–788.

Kendler, K. S., McGuire, M., Gruenberg, A. M., O'Hare, A., Spellman, M., Walsh, D. (1993b). The Roscommon Family Study: 4. Affective illness, anxiety disorders, and alcoholism in relatives. *Archives of General Psychiatry, 50,* 952–960.

Kendler, K. S., Neale, M. C., Heath, A. C., Kessler, R. C. & Linton, J. E. (1994). A twin-family study of alcoholism in women. *American Journal of Psychiatry, 151,* 707–715.

Kendler, K. S., Neale, M. C., Kessler, R. C., Heath, A. C., & Eaves, L. J. (1992a). Generalized anxiety disorder in women: A population-based twin study. *Archives of General Psychiatry, 49,* 267–272.

Kendler, K. S., Neale, M. C., Kessler, R. C., Heath, A. C., & Eaves, L. J. (1992b). A population-based twin study of major depression in women. *Archives of General Psychiatry, 49,* 257–266.

Kendler, K. S., Neale, M. C., Kessler, R. C., Heath, A. C., & Eaves, L. J. (1993a). The lifetime history of major depression in women: Reliability of diagnosis and heritability. *Archives of General Psychiatry, 50,* 863–870.

Kendler, K. S., Neale, M. C., Kessler, R. C., Heath, A. C., & Eaves, L. J. (1993b). A longitudinal twin study of 1-year prevalence of major depression in women. *Archives of General Psychiatry, 50,* 843–852.

Kendler, K. S., Neale, M. C., Kessler, R. C., Heath, A. C., & Eaves, L. J. (1993c). A twin study of recent life events and difficulties. *Archives of General Psychiatry, 50,* 789–796.

Kendler, K. S., Neale, M. C., MacLean, C. J., Heath, A. C., Eaves, L. J., & Kessler, R. C. (1993). Smoking and major depression. *Archives of General Psychiatry, 50,* 36–43.

Kendler, K. S., Neale, M. C., & Walsh, D. (1995). Evaluating the spectrum concept of schizophrenia in the Roscommon Family Study. *American Journal of Psychiatry, 152,* 749–754.

Kendler, K. S., Pedersen, N., Johnson, L., Neale, M. C., & Mathe, A.. S. (1993). A pilot Swedish twin study of affective illness, including hospital- and population-ascertained samples. *Archives of General Psychiatry, 50,* 699–706.

Kendler, K. S., Walters, E. E., Neale, M. C., Kessler, R. C., Heath, A. C., & Eaves, L. J. (1995). The structure of the genetic and environmental risk factors for six major psychiatric disorders in women: Phobia, generalized anxiety disorder, panic disorder, bulimia, major depression, and alcoholism. *Archives of General Psychiatry, 52,* 374–383.

Kendler, K. S., Walters, E. E., Truett, K. R., Heath, A. C., Neale, M. C., Martin, N. G., & Eaves, L. J. (1994). Sources of individual differences in depressive symptoms: Analysis of two samples of twins and their families. *American Journal of Psychiatry, 151,* 1605–1614.

Kennedy, J. L., Giuffra, L. A., Moises, H. W., Cavalli-Sforza, L. L., Pakstis, A. J., Kidd, J. R., Castiglione, C. M., Sjogren, B., Wetterberg, L., & Kidd, K. K. (1988). Evidence against linkage of schizophrenia to markers on chromosome 5 in a northern Swedish pedigree. *Nature, 336,* 167–170.

Kent, H., & Rosanoff, A. J. (1910). A study of association in insanity. *American Journal of Insanity, 67,* 317–390.

Kerbeshian, J., & Burd, L., (1994). Tourette's syndrome: A developmental psychobiologic view. *Journal of Developmental and Physical Disabilities, 6,* 203–218.

Kerwin, R. W. (1994). The new atypical antipsychotics. *British Jounal of Psychiatry, 164,* 141–148.

Kesey, K. (1962). *One flew over the cuckoo's nest.* New York: Viking Penguin.

Kessler, R. C., Foster, C. L., Saunder, W. B., & Stang, P. E. (1995). Social consequences of psychiatric disorders: 1. Educational attainment. *American Journal of Psychiatry, 152,* 1026–1032.

Kessler, R. C., McGonagle, K. A., Zhao, S., Nelson, C. B., Hughes, M., Eshleman, S., Wittchen, H., & Kendler, K. S. (1994). Lifetime and 12-month prevalence of DSM-III-R psychiatric disorders in the United States. *Archives of General Psychiatry, 51,* 8–19.

Kety, S. S., Rosenthal, D., Wender, P. H., Schulsinger, F., & Jacobsen, B. (1975). Mental illness in the biological and adoptive families of adopted individuals who have become schizophrenic: A preliminary report based on psychiatric interviews. In R. R. Fieve, D. Rosenthal, & H. Brill (Eds.), *Genetic research in psychiatry.* Baltimore: Johns Hopkins University Press.

Kety, S. S., Wender, P. H., Jacobsen, B., Ingraham, L., Jansson, L., Faber, b., & Kinney, D. K. (1994). Mental illness in the biological and adoptive relatives of schizophrenic adoptees. *Archives of General Psychiatry, 51,* 442–455.

Keyes, D. (1981). *The minds of Billy Milligan.* New York: Bantam, Books.

Khantzian, E. J. (1985). Self-medication hypothesis of addictive disorders. *American Journal of Psychiatry, 142,* 1259–1263.

Khot, V., & Wyatt, R. J. (1991). Not all that moves is tardive dyskinesia. *American Journal of Psychiatry, 148,* 661–666.

Kidorf, M., Sherman, M. F., & Johnson, J. G. (1995). Alcohol expectancies and changes in beer consumption of first-year college students. *Addictive Behaviors, 20,* 225–231.

Kiecolt-Glaser, J. K., Garner, W., Speicher, C., Penn, G. M., Holliday, J., & Glaser, R. (1984). Psychosocial modifiers of immunocompetence in medical students. *Psychosomatic Medicine, 46,* 7–14.

Kiecolt-Glaser, J. K., Glaser, R., Williger, D., Stout, J., Messick, G., Sheppard, S., Ricker, D., Romisher, S. C., Briner, W., Bonnell, G., & Donnerberg, R. (1985). Psychosocial enhancement of immunocompetence in a geriatric population. *Health Psychology, 4,* 25–41.

Kiernan, C. (1988). Child abuse: A case of change? *British Journal of Special Education, 15,* 140–142.

Kiersch, T. A. (1962). Amnesia: A clinical study of ninety-eight cases. *American Journal of Psychiatry, 119,* 57–60.

Kiersch, T. A. (1990). Treatment of sex offenders with Depo-Provera. *Bulletin of the American Academy of Psychiatry and the Law, 18,* 179–187.

Kiesler, C. A. (1982a). Mental hospitals and alternative care: Noninstitutionalization as potential public policy for mental patients. *American Psychologist, 37,* 349–360.

Kiesler, C. A. (1982b). Public and professional myths about mental hospitalization: An empirical reassessment of policy-related beliefs. *American Psychologist, 37,* 1323–1340.

Kiesler, C. A., & Sibulkin, A. E. (1988). *Mental hospitalization: Myths and facts about a national crisis.* Newbury Park, CA: Sage.

Killen, J. D., Fortmann, S. P., Newman, B., & Varady, A. (1990). Evaluation of a treatment approach combining nicotine gum with self-guided behavioral treatments for smoking relapse prevention. *Journal of Consulting and Clinical Psychology, 58,* 85–92.

Kilmann, P. R., & Auerbach, R. (1979). Treatments of premature ejaculation and psychogenic impotence: A critical review of the literature. *Archives of Sexual Behavior, 8,* 81–100.

King, K. B., Reis, H. T., Porter, L. A., & Norsen, L. H. (1993). Social support and long-term recovery from coronary artery surgery: Effects on patients and spouses. *Health Psychology, 12,* 56–63.

King, R. A., Riddle, M. A., Chappell, P. B., Hardin, M. T., Anderson, G. M., Lombroso, P., & Scahill, L. (1991). Emergence of self-destructive phenomena in children and adolescents during fluoxetine treatment. *Journal of the American Academy of Child and Adolescent Psychiatry, 30,* 179–186.

Kinzl, J. F., Traweger, C., Guenther, V., & Biebl, W. (1994). Family background and sexual abuse associated with eating disorders. *American Journal of Psychiatry, 151,* 1127–1131.

Kirschenbaum, D. S., De Voge, J. B., Marsh, M. E., & Steffen, J. J. (1980). Multimodal evaluation of therapy versus consultation components in a large inner-city intervention program. *American Journal of Community Psychology, 8,* 587–692.

Kirsling, R. A. (1986). Review of suicide among elderly persons. *Psychological Reports, 59,* 359–366.

Kittrie, N. N. (1960). Compulsory mental treatment and the requirements of "due process." *Ohio State Law Journal, 21,* 28–51.

Klein, D. F. (1982). Medication in the treatment of panic attacks and phobic states. *Psychopharmacology Bulletin, 18,* 85–90.

Klein, D. F. (1993) False suffocation alarms, spontaneous panics, and related conditions: An integrative hypothesis. *Archives of General Psychiatry, 50,* 306–317.

Klein, D. F. (1994). "Klein's suffocation theory of panic": Reply. *Archives of General Psychiatry, 51,* 506.

Klein, D. N. (1990). Depressive personality: Reliability, validity, and relation to dysthymia. *Journal of Abnormal Psychology, 99,* 412–421.

Klein, R. G. (1996). Comments on expanding the clinical role of psychologists. *American Psychologist, 51,* 216–218.

Klein, R. G., Landa, B., Mattes, J. A., & Klein, D. F. (1988). Methylphenidate and growth in hyperactive children: A controlled withdrawal study. *Archives of General Psychiatry, 45,* 1127–1130.

Klein, S. B. (1987). *Learning.* New York: McGraw-Hill.

Klerman, G. L. (1979). The age of melancholy. *Psychology Today,* pp. 36–42, 88.

Klerman, G. L. (1990). Treatment of recurrent unipolar major depressive disorder. *Archives of General Psychiatry, 47,* 1158–1162.

Klerman, G. L., & Barrett, J. E. (1973). The affective disorders: Clinical and epidemiological aspects. In S. Gershon & B. Shopsin (Eds.), *Lithium: Its role in psychiatric research and treatment.* New York: Plenum.

Klerman, G. L., Di Mascio, A., Weissman, M., Prusoff, B. A. & Paykel, E. S. (1974). Treatment of depression by drugs and psychotherapy. *American Journal of Psychiatry, 131,* 186–191.

Klerman, G. L., & Schechter, G. (1982). Drugs and psychotherapy. In E. S. Paykel (Ed.), *Handbook of affective disorders.* New York: Guilford Press.

Klerman, G. L., & Weissman, M. M. (1989). Increasing rates of depression. *Journal of the American Medical Association, 261,* 2229–2235.

Klopfer, B. (1962). *The Rorschach technique: An introductory manual.* New York: Harcourt Brace.

Klorman, R., Brumaghim, J. T., Fitzpatrick, P. A., Borgstedt, A. D., & Strauss, J. (1994). Clinical and cognitive effects of methylphenidate on children with attention deficit disorder as a function of aggression/oppositionality and age. *Journal of Abnormal Psychology, 103,* 206–221.

Klosko, J. S., Barlow, D., Tassinari, R., & Cerny, J. A. (1990). A comparison of of alprazolam and behavior therapy in treatment of panic disorder. *Journal of Consulting and Clinical Psychology, 58,* 77–84.

Kluft, R. P. (1982). Varieties of hypnotic interventions in the treatment of multiple personality. *American Journal of Clinical Hypnosis, 24,* 230–240.

Kluft, R. P. (1993). The treatment of dissociative disorder patients: An overview of discoveries, successes, and failures. *Dissociation Progress in the Dissociative Disorders, 6,* 87–101.

Koch, J. L. (1891). *Die psychopathischen Minderwertigkeiten.* Ravensburg, Germany: Maier.

Kocsis, J. H., & Stokes, P. (1979). Lithium maintenance: Factors affecting outcome. *American Journal of Psychiatry, 136,* 563–566.

Kohn, M. L. (1973). Social class and schizophrenia: A critical review and reformation. *Schizophrenia Bulletin, 1,* 60–79.

Kohn, M. L., & Clausen, J. A. (1955). Social isolation and schizophrenia. *American Sociological Review, 20,* 265–273.

Kolb, L. C. (1973). *Modern clinical psychiatry.* Philadelphia: Saunders.

Kormos, H. R. (1978). The nature of combat stress. In C. R. Figley (Ed.), *Stress disorders among Vietnam veterans.* New York: Brunner/Mazel.

Korn, M. L., Brown, S., Apter, A., & Van Praag, H. M. (1990). Serotonin and suicide: A functional/dimensional viewpoint. In D. Lester (Ed.), *Current concepts in suicide.* Philadelphia: Charles Press.

Kornfeld, A. D. (1989). Mary Cover Jones and the Peter case: Social learning versus conditioning. *Journal of Anxiety Disorders, 3,* 187–195.

Kornitzer, M., Boutsen, M., Dramaix, M., Thijs, J., & Gustavsson, G. (1995). Combined use of nicotine patch and gum in smoking cessation: A placebo-controlled clinical trial. *Preventive Medicine, 24,* 41–47.

Koss, M., & Shiang, J. (1994). Research on brief psychotherapy. In A. E. Bergin & S. L. Garfield (Eds.), *Handbook of psychotherapy and behavior change* (4th ed.). New York: Wiley.

Kosten, T. A., & Kosten, T. R. (1991). Pharmacological blocking agents for treating substance abuse. *Journal of Nervous and Mental Disease, 179,* 583–592.

Kovacs, M., Akiskal, H. S., Gatsonis, C., & Parrone, P. L. (1994). Childhood-onset dysthymic disorder. *Archives of General Psychiatry, 51,* 365–374.

Kozol, H., Boucher, R., & Garofalo, R. (1972). The diagnosis and treatment of dangerousness. *Crime and Delinquency, 18,* 371–392.

Kraepelin, E. (1971). *Dementia praecox and paraphrenia* (R. M. Barclay & G. M. Robertson, Trans.). New York: Krieger. (Originally published 1919)

Kraft, D. P., & Babigian, H. M. (1976). Suicide by persons with and without psychiatric contacts. *Archives of General Psychiatry, 33,* 209–215.

Kramer, B. A. (1985). Use of ECT in California. *American Journal of Psychiatry, 142,* 1190–1192.

Kramer, M. A. (1957). A discussion of the concepts of incidence and prevalence as related to epidemiologic studies of mental disorders. *American Journal of Public Health, 47,* 826–840.

Kramer, P. D. (1993). *Listening to Prozac.* New York: Viking.

Krauthammer, C., & Klerman, G. L. (1979). The epidemiology of mania. In B. Shopsin (Ed.), *Manic illness.* New York: Raven Press.

Kreuz, L. E., Rose, R. M., & Jennings, J. R. (1972). Suppression of plasma testosterone levels and psychological stress: A longitudinal study of young men in officer candidate school. *Archives of General Psychiatry, 26,* 479–482.

Kringlen, E. (1967). Heredity and social factors in schizophrenic twins: An epidemiological-clinical study. In J. Romano (Ed.), *The origins of schizophrenia.* New York: Excerpta Medica Foundation.

Kringlen, E. (1968). An epidemiological-clinical twin study on schizophrenia. In D. Rosenthal & S. S. Kety (Eds.), *The transmission of schizophrenia.* Elmsford, NY: Pergamon Press.

Kristal-Boneh, E., Melamed, S., Bernheim, J., Peled, I., & Green, M. S. (1995). Reduced ambulatory heart rate response to physical work and complaints of fatigue among hypertensive males treated with beta-blockers. *Journal of Behavioral Medicine, 18,* 113–126.

Kronfol, Z., Silva, J., Greden, J., Deminski, S., Gardner, R., & Carroll, B. (1983). Impaired lymphocyte function in depressive illness. *Life Sciences, 33,* 241–247.

Kronig, M. H., Munne, R. A., Szymanski, S., Safferman, A. Z., Pollack, S., Cooper, T., Kane, J. M., & Lieberman, J. A. (1995). Plasma clozapine levels and clinical response for treatment-refractory schizophrenic patients. *American Journal of Psychiatry, 152,* 179–182.

Kruesi, M. J., Hibbs, E. D., Zahn, T. P., Keysor, C. S., Hamburger, S. D., Bartko, J. J., & Rapoport, J. L. (1992). A 2-year prospective follow-up study of children and adolescents with disruptive behavior disorders. *Archives of General Psychiatry, 49,* 429–435.

Kulhanek, F., Linde, O. K., & Meisenberg, G. (1979). Precipitation of antipsychotic drugs in interaction with coffee or tea. *Lancet, 2,* 1130.

Kulik, J. A., & Mahler, H. I. (1989). Social support and recovery from surgery. *Health Psychology, 8,* 221–238.

Kurlan, R. (1989). Tourette's syndrome: Current concepts. *Neurology, 39,* 1625–1630.

Kushner, M. (1965). The reduction of a long-standing fetish by means of aversive conditioning. In L. P. Ulmann & L. Krasner (Eds.), *Case studies in behavior modification.* New York: Holt, Rinehart and Winston.

Kushner, M. G., Sher, K. J., Wood, M. D., & Wood, P. K. (1994). Anxiety and drinking behavior: Moderating effects of tension-reduction alcohol outcome expectancies. *Alcoholism Clinical and Experimental Research, 18,* 852–860.

Kwan, M., Greenleaf, W. J., Mann, J., Crapo, L., & Davidson, J. M. (1983). The nature of androgen action on male sexuality: A combined laboratory–self-report study on hypogonadal men. *Journal of Clinical Endocrinology and Metabolism, 57,* 557–562.

Kwon, S., & Oel, T. P. S. (1992). Differential causal roles of dysfunctional attitudes and automatic thoughts in depression. *Cognitive Therapy and Research, 16,* 309–328.

Lacey, J. I. (1950). Individual differences in somatic response patterns. *Journal of Comparative and Physiological Psychology, 43,* 599–604.

Lacey, J. I. (1967). Somatic response patterning and stress: Some revisions of activation theory. In M. H. Appley & R. Trumball (Eds.), *Psychological stress.* New York: McGraw-Hill.

Ladas, A. K., Whipple, B., & Perry, J. D. (1982). *The G spot.* New York: Holt, Rinehart and Winston.

Lahey, B. B., Hart, E. L., Pliszka, S., Applegate, B., & McBurnett, K. (1993). Neurophysiological correlates of conduct disorder: A rationale and a review of research. *Journal of Clinical Child Psychology, 22,* 141–153.

Lahey, B. B., Loeber, R., Hart, E., L., Frick, P. J., Applegate, B., Zhang, Q., Green, S. M., & Russo, M. F. (1995). Four-year longitudinal study of conduct disorder in boys: Patterns and predictors of persistence. *Journal of Abnormal Psychology, 104,* 83–93.

Laing, R. D. (1964). Is schizophrenia a disease? *International Journal of Social Psychiatry, 10,* 184–193.

Laird, J. D., Wagener, J., Halal, M., & Szegda, M. (1982). Remembering what you feel: Effects of emotion on memory. *Journal of Personality and Social Psychology, 42,* 81–89.

Lake v. Cameron, 364 F.2d 657 (D.C. Cir. 1966).

Lam, R. W., Gorman, C. P., Michalon, M., Steiner, M., Levitt, A. J., Corral, M. R., Watson, G. D., Morehouse, R. L., Tam, W., & Joffe, R. T. (1995). Multicenter, placebo-controlled study of fluoxetine in seasonal affective disorder. *American Journal of Psychiatry, 152,* 1765–1770.

Lam, Raymond W. (1994). Morning light therapy for winter depression: Predictors of response. *Acta Psychiatrica Scandinavica, 89,* 97–101.

Lambert, M. J., & Bergin, A. E. (1994). The effectiveness of psychotherapy. In A. E. Bergin & S. L. Garfield (Eds.), *Handbook of psychotherapy and behavior change* (4th ed.). New York: Wiley.

Land, W., & Salzman, C. (1994). Risperidone: A novel antipsychotic medication. *Hospital and Community Psychiatry, 45,* 434–435.

Lander, E. S., & Schork, N. J. (1994). Genetic dissection of complex traits. *Science, 265,* 2037–2048.

Landesman, S., & Butterfield, E. C. (1987). Normalization and deinstitutionalization of mentally retarded individuals. *American Psychologist, 42,* 809–816.

Landmann, R. M., Muller, F. B., Perini, C., Wesp, M., Erne, P., & Buhler, R. R. (1984). Changes of immunoregulatory cells induced by psychological and physical stress: Relationship to plasma catecholamines. *Clinical and Experimental Immunology, 58,* 127–135.

Lang, A. R., Goechner, D. J., Adressor, V. J., & Marlatt, G. A. (1975). Effects of alcohol on aggression in male social drinkers. *Journal of Abnormal Psychology, 84,* 508–518.

Lang, P. J. (1995). The motivational organization of emotion: Affect-reflex connections. In S. Van Goozen, N. E. Van de Poll, & J. A. Sergeant (Eds.), *The emotions: Essays on emotional theory.* Hillsdale, NJ: Erlbaum.

Lang, P. J., & Buss, A. H. (1965). Psychological deficit in schizophrenia: 2. Interference and activation. *Journal of Abnormal Psychology, 70,* 77–106.

Lang, P. J., & Luoto, K. (1962). Mediation and associative facilitation in neurotic, psychotic, and normal subjects. *Journal of Abnormal and Social Psychology, 64,* 113–120.

Langevin, R., Bain, J., Wortzman, G., & Hucker, S. J. (1988). Sexual sadism: Brain, blood, and behavior. *Annals of the New York Academy of Sciences, 528,* 163–171.

Langevin, R., Paitich, D., Hucker, S. J., Newman, S., Ramsay, G., Pope, S., Geller, G., & Anderson, C. (1979). The effect of assertiveness training, Provera, and sex of therapist in the treatment of genital exhibitionism. *Journal of Behavioral and Experimental Psychiatry, 10,* 275–282.

Lanyon, R. I. (1986). Theory and treatment of child molestation. *Journal of Consulting and Clinical Psychology, 54,* 176–182.

Largen, J. W., Mathew, R. J., Dobbins, K., Meyer, J. S., & Claghorn, J. L. (1978). Skin temperature self-regulation and noninvasive regional cerebral blood flow. *Headache, 18,* 203–210.

Larmore, K., Ludwig, A. M., & Cain, R. L. (1977). Multiple personality: An objective case study. *British Journal of Psychiatry, 131,* 35–40.

Last, C. G., & Perrin, S. (1993). Anxiety disorders in African-American and White children. *Journal of Abnormal Child Psychology, 21,* 153–164.

Lavigna, G., & Donnellan, A. (1986). *Alternatives to punishment: Solving behavior problems with nonaversive strategies.* New York: Irvington.

Laws, D. R., & Rubin, H. B. (1969). Instructional control of an autonomic sexual response. *Journal of Applied Behavioral Analysis, 2,* 93–99.

Lawson, J. S., McGhie, A., & Chapman, J. (1967). Distractibility in schizophrenia and organic cerebral disease. *British Journal of Psychiatry, 113,* 527–535.

Lazarus, A. A. (1968). Learning theory and the treatment of depression. *Behaviour Research and Therapy, 6,* 83–89.

Lazarus, R. S., & Folkman, S. (1984). *Stress, appraisal, and coping.* New York: Springer.

Le Doux, J. E. (1992). Brain mechanisms of emotion and emotional learning. *Current Opinion in Neurobiology, 2,* 191–197.

Le Doux, J. E. (1994). Emotion, memory, and the brain. *Scientific American, 270* (6), 50–57.

Leershen, C. (1984, January 9). John Madden on a roll. *Newsweek,* 66–67.

Leff, J. P. (1976). Schizophrenia and sensitivity to the family environment. *Schizophrenia Bulletin, 2,* 566–574.

Leff, J. P. (1992). Transcultural aspects. In E. S. Paykel (Ed.), *Handbook of affective disorders,* (2nd ed.). New York: Guilford Press.

Lefkovitch, Y., Weiser, M., & Levy, A. (1993). Involuntary outpatient commitment: Ethics and problems. *Medicine and Law, 12,* 213–220.

Leibenluft, E., Fiero, P. L., Bartko, J. J., Moul, D. E., & Rosenthal, N. E. (1993). Depressive symptoms and the self-reported use of alcohol, caffeine, and carbohydrates in normal volunteers and four groups of psychiatric outpatients. *American Journal of Psychiatry, 150,* 294–301.

Leigh, B. C. (1989). In search of the Seven Dwarves: Issues of measurement and meaning in alcohol expectancy research. *Psychological Bulletin, 105,* 361–373.

Leppig, M., Bosch, B., Naber, D., & Hippius, H. (1989). Clozapine in the treatment of 121 out-patients. *Psychopharmacology, 99,* 77–79.

Lerer, B., Shapira, B., Calev, A., Tubi, N., Drexler, H., Kindler, Lidsky, D., & Schwartz, J. E. (1995). Antidepressant and cognitive effects of twice- versus three-times-weekly ECT. *American Journal of Psychiatry, 152,* 564–570.

Lerer, B., Weiner, R. D., & Belmaker, R. (1984). *ECT: Basic mechanisms.* Washington, DC: American Psychiatric Association.

Lerner, Y., Lwow, E., Leviton, A., & Belmaker, R. (1979). Acute high-dose parenteral haloperidol treatment of psychosis. *American Journal of Psychiatry, 136,* 1061–1064.

Lesage, A., Boyer, R., Grunberg, F., Vanier, C., Morissette, R., Menard-Buteau, C., & Loyer, M. (1994). Suicide and mental disorders: A case-control study of young men. *American Journal of Psychiatry, 151,* 1063–1068.

Lessard v. Schmidt, 349 F. Supp. 1078 (E.D. Wis. 1972); 94 S.Ct. 713 (1974).

Lester, D. (1988). *The biochemical basis of suicide.* Springfield, IL: Thomas.

Lester, D. (1989). *Can we prevent suicide?* New York: AMS Press.

Lester, D. (1990). The effects of the detoxification of domestic gas in Switzerland on the suicide rate. *Acta Psychiatrica Scandinavica, 82,* 383–384.

Lester, D. (1991a). Do suicide prevention centers prevent suicide? *Homeostasis in Health and Disease, 33,* 190–194.

Lester, D. (1991b). Suicide across the life span: A look at international trends. In A. A. Leenaars (Ed.), *Life span perspectives of suicide.* New York: Plenum.

Lester, D. (1992). State initiatives in addressing youth suicide: Evidence for their effectiveness. *Social Psychiatry and Psychiatric Epidemiology, 27,* 75–77.

Lester, D. (1993). The effectiveness of suicide prevention centers. *Suicide and Life-Threatening Behavior, 23,* 263–267.

Lester, D. (1995). The concentration of neurotransmitter metabolites in the cerebrospinal fluid of suicidal individuals: A meta-analysis. *Pharmacopsychiatry, 28,* 45–50.

Lester, D., & Anderson, D. (1992). Depression and suicidal ideation in African-American and Hispanic American high school students. *Psychological Reports, 71,* 618.

Levenson, A. J., Lord, C. J., Sermas, C. E., Thornby, J. I., Sullender, W., & Comstock, B. A. (1977). Acute schizophrenia: An efficacious outpatient treatment approach as an alternative to full-time hospitalization. *Diseases of the Nervous System, 38,* 242–245.

Levin, A. P., Schneier, F. R., & Liebowitz, M. R. (1989). Social phobia: Biology and pharmacology. *Clinical Psychology Review, 9,* 129–140.

Lewin, B. (1951). *The psycho-analysis of elation.* London: Hogarth.

Lewinsohn, P. M. (1974). A behavioral approach to depression. In R. J. Friedman & M. M. Katz (Eds.), *The psychology of depression: Contemporary theory and research.* Washington, DC: Winston/Wiley.

Lewinsohn, P. M., Duncan, E. M., Stanton, A. K., & Hautzinger, M. (1986). Age at first onset for nonbipolar depression. *Journal of Abnormal Psychology, 95,* 378–383.

Lewinsohn, P. M., Mischel, W., Chaplin, W., & Barton, R. (1980). Social competence and depression: The role of illusory self-perceptions. *Journal of Abnormal Psychology, 89,* 203–212.

Lewinsohn, P. M., Roberts, R. E., Seeley, J. R., Rohde, P. D. Gotlib, I. H., & Hops, H. (1994). Adolescent psychopathology: 2. Psychosocial risk factors for depression. *Journal of Abnormal Psychology, 103,* 302–315.

Lewinsohn, P. M., Rohde, P. D., Seeley, J. R., & Fischer, S. A. (1993). Age-cohort changes in the lifetime occurrence of depression and other mental disorders. *Journal of Abnormal Psychology, 102,* 110–120.

Lewinsohn, P. M., Rohde, P. D., Seeley, J. R., & Hops, H. (1991). Comorbidity of unipolar depression: 1. Major depression with dysthymia. *Journal of Abnormal Psychology, 100,* 205–213.

Lewinsohn, P. M., Steinmetz, J. L., Larson, D. W., & Franklin, J. (1981). Depression-related cognitions: Antecedent or consequence? *Journal of Abnormal Psychology, 90,* 213–219.

Lewinsohn, P. M., Zeiss, A. M., & Duncan, E. M. (1989). Probability of relapse after recovery from an episode of depression. *Journal of Abnormal Psychology, 98,* 107–116.

Lewis-Fernandez, R., & Kleinman, A. (1994). Culture, personality, and psychopathology. *Journal of Abnormal Psychology, 103,* 67–71.

Li, G., Silverman, J. M., Smith, C. J., Zaccario, M. L., Schmeidler, J., Mohs, R. C., & Davis, K. L. (1995). Age at onset and familial risk in Alzheimer's disease. *American Journal of Psychiatry, 152,* 424–430.

Liberman, R. P., Van Putten, T., Marshall, B. D., Mintz, J, Bowen, L., Kuehnel, T. G., Aravagiri, M., & Marder, S. R. (1994). Optimal drug and behavior therapy for treatment-refractory schizophrenic patients. *American Journal of Psychiatry, 151,* 756–759.

Lidren, D. M., Watkins, P. L., Gould, R. A., Clum, G. A., Asterino, M., & Tulloch, H. (1994). A comparison of bibliotherapy and group therapy in the treatment of panic disorder. *Journal of Consulting and Clinical Psychology, 62,* 865–869.

Lieberman, J., Jody, D., Geisler, S., Alvir, J., Loebel, A., Szymanski, S., Woener, M., & Borenstein, M. (1993). Time course and biologic correlates of treatment response in first-episode schizophrenia. *Archives of General Psychiatry, 50,* 369–376.

Lieberman, J. A., Safferman, A. Z., Pollack, S., Szymanski, S., Johns, C., Howard, A., Kronig, M., Bookstein, P., & Kane, J. M. (1994). Clinical effects of clozapine in chronic schizophrenia: Responses to treatment and predictors of outcome. *American Journal of Psychiatry, 151,* 1744–1752.

Liebowitz, M. R., Schneier, F., Campeas, R., Hollander, E., Hatterer, J., Fyer, A. J., Gorman, J. M., Papp, L., Davies, S. O., Gully, R., & Klein, D. F. (1992). Plenelzine vs. Atenolol in social phobia. *Archives of General Psychiatry, 49,* 290–300.

Lief, H., & Hubscham, L. (1993). Orgasm in the postoperative transsexual. *Archives of Sexual Behavior, 22,* 145–155.

Liem, J. H. (1980). Family study of schizophrenia: An update. *Schizophrenia Bulletin, 6,* 429–455.

Light, K. C., Dolan, C. A., Davis, M. R., & Sherwood, A. (1992). Cardiovascular responses to an active coping challenge as predictors of blood pressure patterns 10 to 15 years later. *Psychosomatic Medicine, 54,* 217–230.

Lilienfeld, S. O., & Waldman, I. D. (1990). The relation between childhood attention-deficit hyperactivity disorder and adult antisocial behavior reexamined: The problem of heterogeneity. *Clinical Psychology Review, 10,* 699–725.

Lin, K.-M., Lau, J. K., Yamamoto, J., Zheng, Y., Kim. H., Cho, K., & Nakaski, G. (1992). Hwa-byung: A community study of Korean Americans. *Journal of Nervous and Mental Disease, 180,* 386–391.

Lindner, R. (1944). *Rebel without a cause: The hypnoanalysis of a criminal psychopath.* Philadelphia: Grune & Stratton.

Lindstrom, L. H. (1989). A retrospective study on the long-term efficacy of clozapine in 96 schizophrenic and schizoaffective patients during a 13-year period. *Psychopharmacology, 99,* 84–86.

Linehan, M. M., Goodstein, J. L., Nielsen, S. L., & Chiles, J. A. (1983). Reasons for staying alive when you are thinking of killing yourself: The Reasons for Living Inventory. *Journal of Consulting and Clinical Psychology, 51,* 276–286.

Linehan, M. M., Tutek, D. A., Heard, H. L., & Armstrong, H. E. (1994). Interpersonal outcome of cognitive behavioral treatment for chronically suicidal borderline patients. *American Journal of Psychiatry, 151,* 1771–1776.

Linn, B., Linn, M., & Jensen, J. (1982). Degree of depression and immune responsiveness. *Psychosomatic Medicine, 44,* 128–129.

Linszen, D. H., Kingemans, P. M., & Lenior, M. E. (1994). Cannabis abuse and the course of recent-onset schizophrenic disorders. *Archives of General Psychiatry, 51,* 273–279.

Lipinski, J. F., Mallya, G., Zimmerman, P., & Pope, H. (1989). Fluoxetine-induced akathisias: Clinical and theoretical implications. *Journal of Clinical Psychiatry, 50,* 339–342.

Lishman, W. A. (1978). *The psychological consequences of cerebral disorder.* Oxford: Blackwell.

Litz, B. T. (1992). Emotional numbing in combat-related posttraumatic stress disorder: A critical review and reformulation. *Clinical Psychology Review, 12,* 417–432.

Litz, B. T., & Keane, T. M. (1989). Information processing in anxiety disorders: Application to the understanding of posttraumatic stress disorder. *Clinical Psychology Review, 9,* 243–257.

Livingston, R. (1993). Children of people with somatization disorder. *Journal of the American Academy of Child and Adolescent Psychiatry, 32,* 536–544.

Livingston, R., Witt, A., & Smith, G. R. (1995). Families who somatize. *Journal of Developmental and Behavioral Pediatrics, 16,* 42–46.

Lloyd, C., Zisook, S., Click, M., Jr., & Jaffe, K. E. (1981). Life events and response to antidepressants. *Journal of Human Stress, 7,* 2–15.

Lo Piccolo, J. (1983). The prevention of sexual problems in men. In G. Albee, S. Gordon, & H. Leitenberg (Eds.), *Promoting sexual responsibility and preventing sexual problems.* Burlington, VT: University Press of New England.

Lo Piccolo, J., & Stock, W. E. (1986). Treatment of sexual dysfunction. *Journal of Consulting and Clinical Psychology, 54,* 158–167.

Lobitz, W. C., & Post, R. D. (1979). Parameters of self-reinforcement and depression. *Journal of Abnormal Psychology, 88,* 33–41.

Lochman, J. E., & Dodge, K. A. (1994). Social-cognitive processes of severely violent, moderately aggressive, and nonaggressive boys. *Journal of Consulting and Clinical Psychology, 62,* 366–374.

Loeb, J., & Mednick, S. A. (1976). Asocial behavior and electrodermal response patterns. In K. O. Christiansen & S. A. Mednick (Eds.), *Crime, society, and biology: A new look.* New York: Gardner Press.

Loehlin, J. C., & Nichols, R. C. (1976). *Heredity, environment, and personality.* Austin: University of Texas Press.

Loewenstein, R. J. (1994). Diagnosis, epidemiology, clinical course, treatment, and cost effectiveness of treatment for dissociative disorders and MPD: Report submitted to the Clinton Administration Task Force on Health Care Financing Reform. *Dissociation Progress in the Dissociative Disorders, 7,* 3–11.

Loftus, E. F. (1992). *The reality of repressed memories.* Psi Chi Lowell Lewis Distinguished Lecture, American Psychological Association, Washington, DC.

Loftus, E. F., & Palmer, J. C. (1974). Reconstruction of automobile destruction: An example of the interaction between language and memory. *Journal of Verbal Learning and Verbal Behavior, 13,* 585–589.

Loftus, E. F., Polonsky, S., & Fullilove, M. T. (1994). Memories of childhood sexual abuse: Remembering and repressing. *Psychology of Women Quarterly, 18,* 67–84.

Lombroso, C. (1911). *Crime: Its causes and remedies.* Boston: Little, Brown.

Lombroso, P. J., Pauls, D. L., & Leckman, J. F. (1994). Genetic mechanisms in childhood psychiatric disorders. *Journal of the American Academy of Child and Adolescent Psychiatry, 33,* 921–932.

Loranger, A. W. (1984). Sex difference in age at onset of schizophrenia. *Archives of General Psychiatry, 41,* 157–161.

Loranger, A. W., & Levine, P. M. (1978). Age at onset of bipolar affective illness. *Archives of General Psychiatry, 35,* 1345–1348.

Lord, C. G., Ross, L., & Leeper, M. R. (1979). Biased assimilation and attitude polarization: The effects of prior theories on subsequently considered evidence. *Journal of Personality and Social Psychology, 37,* 2098–2109.

Lorion, R. P. (1996). Applying our medicine to the psychopharmacology debate. *American Psychologist, 51,* 219–224.

Lorist, M. M., Snel, J., Kok, A., & Mulder, G. (1994). Influence of caffeine on selective attention in well-rested and fatigued subjects. *Psychophysiology, 31,* 525–534.

Lotter, V. (1978). Follow-up studies. In M. Rutter & E. Schopler (Eds.), *Autism: Reappraisal of concepts and treatment.* New York: Plenum.

Lovaas, O. I. (1969). *Behavior modification: Teaching language to psychotic children* [Film]. Norwalk, CT: Appleton & Lange.

Lovaas, O. I. (1987). Behavioral treatment and normal educational and intellectual functioning in young autistic children. *Journal of Consulting and Clinical Psychology, 55,* 3–9.

Lovaas, O. I. (1993). The development of a treatment-research project for developmentally disabled and autistic children. *Journal of Applied Behavior Analysis, 26,* 617–630.

Lovaas, O. I., Berberich, J. P., Perloff, B. F., & Schaeffer, B. (1966). Acquisition of imitative speech in schizophrenic children. *Science, 151,* 705–707.

Lovaas, O. I., Koegel, R. L., Simmons, J. Q., & Long, J. S. (1973). Some generalizations and follow-up measures on autistic children in behavior therapy. *Journal of Applied Behavior Analysis, 6,* 131–165.

Lovaas, O. I., Schaeffer, B., & Simmons, J. Q. (1965). Experimental studies in childhood schizophrenia: Building social behaviors by use of electric shock. *Journal of Experimental Studies in Personality, 1,* 99–109.

Lovaas, O. I., & Simmons, J. Q. (1969). Manipulation of self-destruction in three retarded children. *Journal of Applied Behavior Analysis, 2,* 143–157.

Lovaas, O. I., & Smith, T. (1989). A comprehensive behavioral theory of autistic children: Paradigm for research and treatment. *Journal of Behavior Therapy and Experimental Psychiatry, 20,* 17–29.

Lovaas, O. I., Smith, T., & McEachin, J. J. (1989). Clarifying comments on the Young Autism Study: Reply to Schopler, Short, and Mesibov. *Journal of Consulting and Clinical Psychology, 57,* 165–167.

Lovibond, S. H. (1963). The mechanism of conditioning treatment of enuresis. *Behaviour Research and Therapy, 1,* 17–24.

Lovibond, S. H., & Coote, M. (1969). Enuresis. In C. G. Costello (Ed.), *Symptoms of psychopathology.* New York: Wiley.

Luborsky, L., Singer, B., & Luborsky, L. (1975). Comparative studies of psychotherapies: Is it true that "everyone has won and all must have prizes"? *Archives of General Psychiatry, 32,* 995–1008.

Lucas, A. R., Beard, C. M., O'Fallon, W. M., & Kurland, L. T. (1991). 50-year trends in the incidence of anorexia nervosa in Rochester, Minn.: A population-based study. *American Journal of Psychiatry, 148,* 917–922.

Lucio, E., Reyes-Lagunes, I., & Scott, R. (1994). MMPI-2 for Mexico: Translation and adaptation. *Journal of Personality Assessment, 63,* 105–116.

Ludwig, A. M. (1994). Mental illness and creative activity in female writers. *American Journal of Psychiatry, 151,* 1650–1656.

Ludwig, A. M., Brandsma, J. M., Wilbur, C. B., Benfeldt, F., & Jameson, D. H. (1972). The objective study of a multiple personality, or are four heads better than one? *Archives of General Psychiatry, 26,* 298–310.

Luntz, B. K., & Widom, C. S. (1994). Antisocial personality disorder in abused and neglected children grown up. *American Journal of Psychiatry, 151,* 670–674.

Luria, Z., & Osgood, C. E. (1976). A postscript to "The three faces of Evelyn." *Journal of Abnormal Psychology, 85,* 276–285.

Lykken, D. T. (1957). A study of anxiety in the sociopathic personality. *Journal of Abnormal and Social Psychology, 55,* 6–10.

Lyness, S. A. (1993). Predictors of differences between Type A and B individuals in heart rate and blood pressure reactivity. *Psychological Bulletin, 114,* 266–295.

Lyons, M. J., Kremen, W. S., Tsuang, M. T., & Faraone, S. V. (1989). Investigating putative genetic and environmental forms of schizophrenia: Methods and findings. *International Review of Psychiatry, 1,* 259–275.

Maas, J. W. (1975). Catecholamines and depression: A further specification of the catecholamine hypothesis of the affective disorders. In A. J. Friedhoff (Ed.), *Catecholamines and behavior.* New York: Plenum.

Maas, J. W., Fawcett, J. A., & Dekirmenjian, H. (1972). Catecholamine metabolism, depressive illness, and drug response. *Archives of General Psychiatry, 26,* 246–262.

MacCoun, R. J. (1993). Drugs and the law: A psychological analysis of drug prohibition. *Psychological Bulletin, 113,* 497–512.

MacCrimmon, D., Cleghorn, J., Asarnow, R., & Steffy, R. (1980). Children at risk for schizophrenia. *Archives of General Psychiatry, 37,* 671–674.

MacDougal, J. M., Dembroski, T. M., Dimsdale, J. E., & Hackett, T. P. (1985). Components of Type A, hostility, and anger-in: Further relationships to angiographic findings. *Health Psychology, 4,* 137–152.

Machon, R. A., Mednick, S. A., & Schulsinger, F. A. (1987). Seasonality, birth complications and schizophrenia. *British Journal of Psychiatry, 151,* 122–124.

Machover, K. (1949). *Personality projection in the drawing of the human figure.* Springfield, IL: Thomas.

MacLeod, C., & Cohen, L. (1993). Anxiety and the interpretation of ambiguity: A text comprehension study. *Journal of Abnormal Psychology, 102,* 238–247.

MacLeod, C., & Mathews, A. (1988). Anxiety and the allocation of attention to threat. *Quarterly Journal of Experimental Psychology, 40A,* 653–670.

MacLeod, C., Mathews, A., & Tata, P. (1986). Attentional bias in emotional disorders. *Journal of Abnormal Psychology, 95,* 15–20.

MacMahon, B., & Pugh, T. (1965). Suicide in the widowed. *American Journal of Epidemiology, 81,* 23–31.

Maddocks, P. D. (1970). A five-year follow-up of untreated psychopaths. *British Journal of Psychiatry, 116,* 511–515.

Madigan, R. J., & Bollenbach, A. (1982). Effects of induced mood in retrieval of personal episodic and semantic memories. *Psychological Reports, 50,* 147–157.

Magni, G., Borgherini, G., Zennaro, A. & Muscara, A. (1994). The role of stressful life events in duodenal ulcer recurrence: A prospective study. *Journal of Clinical Psychology, 50,* 711–714.

Maher, B. A. (1966). *Principles of psychopathology: An experimental approach.* New York: McGraw-Hill.

Maher, B. A. (1968). The shattered language of schizophrenia. *Psychology Today.* pp. 30–33, 60.

Maher, B. A. (1972). The language of schizophrenia: A review and interpretation. *British Journal of Psychiatry, 120,* 4–17.

Maher, B. A. (1983). A tentative theory of schizophrenic utterance. In B. A. Maher & W. Maher (Eds.), *Progress in experimental personality research* (Vol. 12). New York: Academic Press.

Maher, B. A. (1988a). Anomalous experience and delusional thinking: The logic of explanations. In T. F. Oltmanns & B. A. Maher (Eds.), *Delusional beliefs.* New York: Wiley.

Maher, B. A. (1988b). Delusions as the product of normal cognitions. In T. F. Oltmanns & B. A. Maher (Eds.), *Delusional beliefs.* New York: Wiley.

Mahesh Yogi, M. (1963). *The science of being and art of living.* London: Allen & Unwin.

Maier, S. F., & Seligman, M. E. P. (1976). Learned helplessness: Theory and evidence. *Journal of Experimental Psychology: General, 103,* 3–46.

Maier, S. F., Seligman, M. E. P., & Solomon, R. (1969). Pavlovian fear conditioning and learned helplessness: Effects on escape and avoidance behavior of the CS-US contingency and voluntary responding. In B. Campbell & R. Church (Eds.), *Punishment and aversive behavior.* Norwalk, CT: Appleton & Lange.

Maier, S. F., Watkins, L. R., & Fleshner, M. (1994). Psychoneuroimmunology; The interface between behavior, brain, and immunity. *American Psychologist, 49,* 1004–1017.

Maier, W., Lichtermann, D., Minges, J., & Heun, R. (1994). Personality disorders among the relatives of schizophrenia patients. *Schizophrenia Bulletin, 20,* 481–493.

Maldonado, G., & Kraus, J. F. (1991). Variation in suicide occurrence by time of day, day of week, and lunar phase. *Suicide and Life-Threatening Behavior, 21,* 174–187.

Males, M. (1991a). Reply to Kim Smith, PhD, on "Teen suicide and changing cause-of-death certification, 1953–1987." *Suicide and Life-Threatening Behavior, 21,* 402–405.

Males, M. (1991b). Teen suicide and changing cause-of-death certification, 1953–1987. *Suicide and Life-Threatening Behavior, 21,* 245–259.

Malmquist, C. P. (1986). Children who witness parental murder: Posttraumatic aspects. *Journal of the American Academy of Child Psychiatry, 25,* 320–325.

Manji, H. K., Hsiao, J. K., Risby, E. D., Oliver, J., Rudorfer, M. V., & Potter, W. Z. (1991). The mechanisms of action of lithium: 1. Effects of serotoninergic and noradrenergic systems in normal subjects. *Archives of General Psychiatry, 48,* 505–512.

Manjiviona, J., & Prior, M. (1995). Comparison of Asperger syndrome and high-functioning autistic children on a test of motor impairment. *Journal of Autism and Developmental Disorders, 25,* 23–39.

Manley, P. C., McMahon, R. J., Bradley, C. F., & Davidson, P. O. (1982). Depressive attributional style and depression following childbirth. *Journal of Abnormal Psychology, 91,* 245–254.

Mann, J. J., & Kapur, S. (1991). The emergence of suicidal ideation and behavior during antidepressant pharmacotherapy. *Archives of General Psychiatry, 48,* 1027–1033.

Mann, J. J., McBride, P. A., Brown, R. P., Linnoila, M., Leon, A. C., De Meo, M., Mieczkowski, T., Myers, J. E., & Stanley, M. (1992). Relationship between central and peripheral serotonin indexes in depressed and suicidal psychiatric in-patients. *Archives of General Psychiatry, 49,* 442–446.

Mannuzza, S., Klein, R. G., Bessler, A., Malloy, P., & La Padula, M. (1993). Adult outcome of hyperactive boys. *Archives of General Psychiatry, 50,* 565–576.

Mannuzza, S., Klein, R. G., Bonagura, N., Malloy, P., Giampino, T. L., & Adilli, K. A. (1991). Hyperactive boys almost grown up. *Archives of General Psychiatry, 48,* 77–83.

Manuck, S. B., Harvey, S. H., Lechleiter, S. L., & Neal, K. (1978). Effects of coping on blood pressure responses to threat of aversive stimulation. *Psychophysiology, 15,* 544–549.

Marcus, D. K., & Nardone, M. E. (1992). Depression and interpersonal rejection. *Clinical Psychology Review, 12,* 433–449.

Marcus, M. D., Wing, R. R., Ewing, L., Kern, E., McDermott, M., & Gooding, W. (1990). A double-blind, placebo-controlled trial of fluoxetine plus behavior modification in the treatment of obese binge-eaters and non-binge-eaters. *American Journal of Psychiatry, 147,* 876–881.

Marder, S. R., & Meibach, R. C. (1994). Risperidone in the treatment of schizophrenia. *American Journal of Psychiatry, 151,* 825–835.

Marder, S. R., Wirshing, W. C., Van Putten, T., Mintz, J., McKenzie, J., Johnston-Cronk, K., Labell, M., & Liberman, R. P. (1994). Fluphenazine vs placebo supplementation for prodromal signs of relapse in schizophrenia. *Archives of General Psychiatry, 51,* 280–287.

Margraf, J., Barlow, D. H., Clark, D. M., & Telch, M. J. (1994). Psychological treatment of panic: Work in progress on outcome, active ingredients, and follow-up. *Behaviour Research and Therapy, 31,* 1–8.

Margraf, J., Ehlers, A., & Roth, W. T. (1988). Mitral valve prolapse and panic disorder: A review of their relationship. *Psychosomatic Medicine, 50,* 93–113.

Markowitz, J., Brown, R., Sweeney, J., & Mann, J. J. (1987). Reduced length and cost of hospital stay for major depression in patients treated with ECT. *American Journal of Psychiatry, 144,* 1025–1029.

Marks, I. M. (1981). Review of behavioral psychotherapy: 2. Sexual disorders. *American Journal of Psychiatry, 138,* 750–756.

Marks, I. M., & Gelder, M. G. (1967). Transvestism and fetishism: Clinical and psychological changes during faradic aversion. *British Journal of Psychiatry, 113,* 711–729.

Marks, I. M., Gelder, M. G., & Bancroft, J. (1970). Sexual deviants two years after electric aversion. *British Journal of Psychiatry, 117,* 173–185.

Marlatt, G. A. (1978). Craving for alcohol, loss of control, and relapse: A cognitive-behavioral analysis. In P. E. Nathan, G. A. Marlatt, & T. Loberg (Eds.), *Alcoholism: New directions in behavior research and treatment.* New York: Plenum.

Marlowe, M., Cossairt, A., Moon, C., Errera, J., McNeel, A., Peak, R., Ray, J., & Schroeder, C. (1985). Main and interaction effects of metallic toxins on classroom behavior. *Journal of Abnormal Child Psychology, 13,* 185–198.

Marshall, P. (1989). Attention deficit disorder and allergy: A neurochemical model of the relation between the illnesses. *Psychological Bulletin, 106,* 434–446.

Marshall, W. L., Jones, R., Ward, T., Johnston, P., & Barbaree, H. E. (1991). Treatment outcome with sex offenders. *Clinical Psychology Review, 11,* 465–485.

Martin R. L., & Yutzy, S. H. (1994). Somatoform disorders. In R. E. Hales, S. C. Yudofsky, & J. A. Talbott (Eds.), *American Psychiatric Press textbook of psychiatry* (2nd ed.). Washington, DC: American Psychiatric Press.

Martin, A. (1923). History of dancing mania. *American Journal of Clinical Medicine, 30,* 265–271.

Martinez-Arevalo, M. J., Calcedo-Ordonez, A., & Varo-Prieto, J. R. (1994). Cannabis consumption as a prognostic factor in schizophrenia. *British Journal of Psychiatry, 164,* 679–681.

Marx, E. M., Williams, J. M. G., & Claridge, G. C. (1992). Depression and social problem solving. *Journal of Abnormal Psychology, 101,* 78–86.

Marzuk, P. M., Leon, A. C., Tardiff, K., Morgan, E. B., Stajic, M., & Mann, J. J. (1992). The effect of access to lethal methods of injury on suicide rates. *Archives of General Psychiatry, 49,* 451–458.

Masand, P., Gupta, S., & Dewan, M. (1991). Suicidal ideation related to fluoxetine treatment. *New England Journal of Medicine, 324,* 420.

Mason, M. A., & Gibbs, J. T. (1992). Patterns of adolescent psychiatric hospitalization: Implications for social policy. *American Journal of Orthopsychiatry, 62,* 447–457.

Masson, J. M. (1984). *The assault on truth: Freud's suppression of the seduction theory.* Harmondsworth, England: Penguin.

Masters, W., & Johnson, V. (1970). *Human sexual inadequacy.* Boston: Little, Brown.

Matarazzo, J. D. (1986). Computerized clinical psychological test interpretations. *American Psychologist, 41,* 14–24.

Mathews, A. (1990). Why worry? The cognitive function of anxiety. *Behaviour Research and Therapy, 28,* 455–568.

Mathews, A., May, J., Mogg, K., & Eysenck, M. W. (1990). Attentional bias in anxiety: Selective search or defective filtering? *Journal of Abnormal Psychology, 99,* 166–173.

Matthews, G. R., & Antes, J. R. (1992). Visual attention and depression: Cognitive biases in the eye fixations of dysphoric and the nondepressed. *Cognitive Therapy and Research, 16,* 359–371.

Matthews, K. A. (1982). Psychological perspectives on the Type A behavior pattern. *Psychological Bulletin, 91,* 293–323.

Matthews, K. A. (1988). Coronary heart disease and Type A behaviors: Update on and alternative to the Booth-Kewley and Friedman (1987) quantitative review. *Psychological Bulletin, 104,* 373–380.

Matthews, K. A., Glass, D. C., Rosenman, R. H., & Bortner, R. W. (1977). Competitive drive, pattern A, and coronary heart disease: A further analysis of some data from the Western Collaborative Group Study. *Journal of Chronic Diseases, 30,* 489–498.

Matthews, K. A., Wing, R. R., Kuller, L. H., Meilahn, E. N., Kelsey, S. F., Costello, E. J., & Caggiula, A. W. (1990). Influences of natural menopause on psychological characteristics and symptoms of middle-aged healthy women. *Journal of Consulting and Clinical Psychology, 58,* 345–351.

Mattick, R. P., Andrews, G., Hadzi-Pavlovic, D., & Christensen, H. (1990). Treatment of panic and agoraphobia: An integrative review. *Journal of Nervous and Mental Disease, 178,* 567–576.

Mavissakalian, M. R., & Michelson, L. (1983). Self-directed in vivo exposure practice in behavioral and pharmacological treatments of agoraphobia. *Behavior Therapy, 14,* 506–519.

Mavissakalian, M. R., & Perel, J. M. (1989). Imipramine dose-response relationship in panic disorder with agoraphobia. *Archives of General Psychiatry, 46,* 127–131.

Mavissakalian, M. R., & Perel, J. M. (1992a). Clinical experiments in maintenance and discontinuation of imipramine therapy in panic disorder with agoraphobia. *Archives of General Psychiatry, 49,* 318–323.

Mavissakalian, M. R., & Perel, J. M. (1992b). Protective effects of imipramine maintenance treatment in panic disorder with agoraphobia. *American Journal of Psychiatry, 149,* 1053–1057.

Mavissakalian, M. R., & Perel, J. M. (1995). Imipramine treatment of panic disorder with agrophobia: Dose ranging and plasma level-response relationships. *American Journal of Psychiatry, 152,* 673–682.

May, P. R. (1968). *Treatment of schizophrenia.* New York: Science House.

Mayer, J. E., & Rosenblatt, A. (1974). Clash in perspective between mental patients and staff. *American Journal of Orthopsychiatry, 44,* 432–441.

Mayes, S. D., Crites, D. L., Bixler, E. O., Humphrey, F. J., & Mattison, R. E. (1994). Methylphenidate and ADHD: Influence of age, IQ and neurodevelopmental status. *Developmental Medicine and Child Neurology, 36,* 1099–1107.

Maynert, E. W., & Levi, R. (1964). Stress-induced release of brain norepinephrine and its inhibition by drugs. *Journal of Pharmacology and Experimental Therapeutics, 143,* 90–95.

McCafferty, G., & Dooley, J. (1990). Involuntary outpatient commitment: An update. *Mental and Physical Disability Law Reporter, 14,* 277–287.

McCann, I. L., & Holmes, D. S. (1984). Influence of aerobic exercise on depression. *Journal of Personality and Social Psychology, 46,* 1142–1147.

McCarley, R. W. Shenton, M. E., O'Donnell, B. F., & Nestor, P. G., (1994). Neural circuits in schizophrenia. *Archives of General Psychiatry, 51,* 515.

McCord, W., & McCord, J. (1964). *The psychopath.* New York: Van Nostrand.

McCrady, B. S. (1994). Alcoholics Anonymous and behavior therapy: Can habits be treated as diseases? Can diseases be treated as habits? *Journal of Consulting and Clinical Psychology, 62,* 1159–1166.

McDaniel, J. S., Musselman, D. L., Porter, M. R., Reed, D. A., & Nemeroff, C. B. (1995). Depression in patients with cancer. *Archives of General Psychiatry, 52,* 89–99.

McDougle, C. J., Goodman, W. K., & Price, L. H. (1994). Dopamine antagonists in tic-related and psychotic spectrum obsessive compulsive disorder. *Journal of Clinical Psychiatry, 55,* 24–31.

McEachin, J. J., Smith, T., & Lovaas, O. I. (1993). Long-term outcome for children with autism who received early intensive behavioral treatment. *American Journal on Mental Retardation, 97,* 359–372.

McElroy, S. L., Hudson, J. I., Pope, H. G., & Keck, P. E.. (1991). Kleptomania: Clinical characteristics and associated psychopathology. *Psychological Medicine, 21,* 93–108.

McElroy, S. L., Hudson, J. I., Pope, H. G., Keck, P. E., & Aizley, H. G., (1992). The DSM-III-R impulse control disorders not elsewhere classified: Clinical characteristics and relationship to other psychiatric disorders. *American Journal of Psychiatry, 149,* 318–327.

McElroy, S. L., Keck, P. E., Pope, H., G. & Hudson, J. I. (1989). Pharmacological treatment of kleptomania and bulimia nervosa. *Journal of Clinical Psychopharmacology, 9,* 358–360.

McFarlane, W. R., Lukens, E., Link, B., Dushay, R., Deakins, S. A., Newmark, M., Dunne, E. J., & Toran, J. (1995). Multiple-family groups and psychoeducation in the treatment of schizophrenia. *Archives of General Psychiatry, 52,* 679–687.

McGarry, A. L., & Bendt, R. H. (1969). Criminal vs. civil commitment of psychotic offenders: A seven-year follow-up. *American Journal of Psychiatry, 125,* 1387–1394.

McGaugh, J. L. (1989). Involvement of hormonal and neuromodulatory systems in the regulation of memory storage. *Annual Review of Neuroscience, 2,* 255–287.

McGaugh, J. L. (1990). Significance and remembrance: The role of neuromodulatory systems. *Psychological Science, 1,* 15–25.

McGhie, A., & Chapman, J. (1961). Disorders of attention and perception in early schizophrenia. *British Journal of Medical Psychology, 34,* 103–116.

McGilley, B. M., & Holmes, D. S. (1988). Aerobic fitness and response to psychological stress. *Journal of Research in Personality, 22,* 129–139.

McGilley, B. M., Holmes, D. S., & Holmsten, R. D. (1993). *Influence of exercise rehabilitation on coronary patients: A six-year follow-up.* Unpublished manuscript. University of Kansas at Lawrence.

McGlashan, T. H., & Fenton, W. S. (1992). The positive-negative distinction in schizophrenia. *Archives of General Psychiatry, 49,* 63–72.

McGreevy, M. A., Steadman, H. J., & Callahan, L. A. (1991). The negligible effects of California's 1982 reform of the insanity defense test. *American Journal of Psychiatry, 148,* 744–750.

McGue, M., Pickens, R. W., & Svikis, D. S. (1992). Sex and age effects on the inheritance of alcohol problem: A twin study. *Journal of Abnormal Psychology, 101,* 3–17.

McHugh, P. R., & Goodell, H. (1971). Suicidal behavior: A distinction in patients with sedative poisoning seen in a general hospital. *Archives of General Psychiatry, 25,* 456–464.

McIntosh, J. L. (1992). Epidemiology of suicide in the elderly. *Suicide and Life-Threatening Behavior, 22,* 15–35.

McKim, W. A. (1986). *Drugs and behavior.* Englewood Cliffs, NJ: Prentice Hall.

McLean, P. D., & Hakstian, A. R. (1979). Clinical depression: Comparative efficacy of outpatient treatments. *Journal of Consulting and Clinical Psychology, 47,* 818–836.

McLean, P. D., & Hakstian, A. R. (1990). Relative endurance of unipolar depression treatment effects: Longitudinal follow-up. *Journal of Consulting and Clinical Psychology, 58,* 482–488.

McLeod, J. D., Kessler, R. C., & Landis, K. R. (1992). Speed of recovery from major depressive episodes in a community sample of married men and women. *Journal of Abnormal Psychology, 101,* 277–286.

McNally, R. J. (1990). Psychological approaches to panic disorder: A review. *Psychological Bulletin, 108,* 403–419.

McNally, R. J. (1994). Introduction to the special series: Innovations in cogitive-behavioral approaches to schizophrenia. *Behavior Therapy, 25,* 1–4.

McNally, R. J., & Foa, E. B. (1987). Cognition and agoraphobia: Bias in the interpretation of threat. *Cognitive Therapy and Research, 11,* 567–581.

McNally, R. J., Riemann, B. C., & Kim, E. (1990). Selective processing of threat cues in panic disorder. *Behaviour Research and Therapy, 28,* 407–412.

Mednick, S. A. (1958). A learning theory approach to research in schizophrenia. *Psychological Bulletin, 55,* 316–327.

Mednick, S. A., Cudeck, R., Griffith, J. J., Talovic, S. A., & Schulsinger, F. A. (1984). The Danish High-Risk Project: Recent methods and findings. In N. F. Watt, E. J. Anthony, L. C. Wynne, & J. E. Rolf (Eds.), *Children at risk for schizophrenia.* Cambridge: Cambridge University Press.

Mednick, S. A., Gabrielli, W. F., & Hutchings, B. (1984). Genetic influences in criminal convictions: Evidence from an adoption cohort. *Science, 224,* 891–894.

Mednick, S. A., Machon, R. A., & Huttunen, M. O. (1990). An update on the Helsinki influenza project. *Archives of General Psychiatry, 47,* 292.

Mednick, S. A., Machon, R. A., Huttunen, M. O., & Bonett, D. (1988). Adult schizophrenia following prenatal exposure to an influenza epidemic. *Archives of General Psychiatry, 45,* 189–192.

Mednick, S. A., Parnas, J., & Schulsinger, F. A. (1987). The Copenhagen High-Risk Project, 1962–86. *Schizophrenia Bulletin, 13,* 485–495.

Mednick, S. A., & Schulsinger, F. A. (1968). Some premorbid characteristics related to breakdown in children with schizophrenic mothers. In D. Rosenthal & S. S. Kety (Eds.), *The transmission of schizophrenia.* Elmsford, NY: Pergamon.

Meduna, L. von. (1935). Die Konvolsionstherapie der Schizophrenie. *Psychiatrisch-Neurologische Wochenschrift, 37,* 317–319.

Meduna, L. von. (1938). General discussion of the cardiazol therapy. *American Journal of Psychiatry, 94* (Suppl.), 46.

Meehan, P., Lamb, J. A., Saltzman, L. E., & O'Carroll, P. W. (1992). Attempted suicide among young adults: Progress toward a meaningful estimate of prevalence. *American Journal of Psychiatry, 149,* 41–44.

Meesters, C. M. G., & Smulders, J. (1994). Hostility and myocardial infarction in men. *Journal of Psychosomatic Research, 38,* 727–734.

Mehlum, L., Friis, S., Vaglum, P., & Karterud, S. (1994). The longitudinal pattern of suicidal behaviour in borderline personality disorder: A prospective follow-up study. *Acta Psychiatrica Scandinavica, 90,* 124–130.

Meichenbaum, D. (1972). Cognitive modification of test-anxious college students. *Journal of Consulting and Clinical Psychology, 39,* 370–379.

Meichenbaum, D., & Goodman, J. (1971). Training impulsive children to talk to themselves: A means for developing self-control. *Journal of Abnormal Psychology, 77,* 115–126.

Meisch, R. A. (1991). Studies of drug self-administration. *Psychiatric Annals, 21,* 196–205.

Melella, J. T., Travin, S., & Cullen, K. (1989). Legal and ethical issues in the use of antiandrogens in treating sexual offenders. *Bulletin of the American Academy of Psychiatry and the Law, 17,* 223–232.

Melia, P. I. (1970). Prophylactic lithium: A double-blind trial in recurrent affective disorders. *British Journal of Psychiatry, 116,* 621–624.

Mellman, T. A., & Uhde, T. W. (1989). Electroencephalographic sleep in panic disorder. *Archives of General Psychiatry, 46,* 178–184.

Meltzer, H. Y. (1995a). Neuroleptic withdrawal in schizophrenic patients: An idea whose time has come. *Archives of General Psychiatry, 52,* 200–202.

Meltzer, H. Y. (1995b). The role of serotonin in schizophrenia and the place of serotonin-dopamine antagonist antipsychotics. *Journal of Clinical Psychopharmacology, 15* 2S–3S.

Meltzer, H. Y., Bastani, B., Kwon, K. Y., Ramirez, L. F., Burnett, S., & Sharpe, J. (1989). A prospective study of clozapine in treatment-resistant schizophrenic patients. *Psychopharmacology, 99,* S68–S72.

Meltzer, H. Y., Bastani, B., Ramirez, L. F., & Matsubara, S. (1989). Clozapine: New research on efficacy and mechanism of action. *European Archives of Psychiatry and Neurological Sciences, 238,* 332–339.

Meltzer, H. Y., & Okayli, G. (1995). Reduction of suicidality during clozapine treatment of neuroleptic-resistant schizophrenia:

Impact on risk-benefit assessment. *American Journal of Psychiatry, 152,* 183–190.

Mendlewicz, J., & Rainer, J. D. (1977). Adoption study supporting genetic transmission in manic-depressive illness. *Nature, 268,* 327–329.

Menninger, K. A. (1938). *Man against himself.* New York: Harcourt Brace.

Merikangas, K. R., & Weissman, M. M. (1986). Epidemiology of DSM-III Axis II personality disorders. In A. J. Frances & R. E. Hales (Eds.), *The American Psychiatric Association annual review.* Washington, DC: American Psychiatric Press.

Messiha, F. S., & Carlson, J. C. (1983). Behavioral and clinical profiles of Tourette's disease: A comprehensive overview. *Brain Research Bulletin, 11,* 195–204.

Metalsky, G., Joiner, T. E., Hardin, T. S., & Abramson, L. Y. (1993). Depressive reactions to failure in a naturalistic setting: A test of the hopelessness and self-esteem theories of depression. *Journal of Abnormal Psychology, 102,* 101–109.

Mete, L., Schnurr, P. P., Rosenberg, S. D., & Oxman, T. E. (1993). Language content and schizophrenia in acute phase Turkish patients. *Social Psychiatry and Psychiatric Epidemiology, 28,* 275–280.

Metz, P., & Mathiesen, F. R. (1979). External iliac "steal syndrome" leading to a defect in penile erection and impotence. *Vascular Surgery, 13,* 70–72.

Meyer, J., & Reter, D. (1979). Sex reassignment: Follow-up. *Archives of General Psychiatry, 36,* 1010–1015.

Michal, V., Kramar, R., Pospichal, J., & Hejhal, L. (1977). Arterial epigastricocavernous anastomosis for the treatment of sexual impotence. *World Journal of Surgery, 1,* 515–524.

Michelson, L. K., & Marchione, K. (1991). Behavioral, cognitive, and pharmacological treatments of panic disorder with agoraphobia: Critique and synthesis. *Journal of Consulting and Clinical Psychology, 59,* 100–114.

Michelson, L. K., Marchione, K., Greenwald, M., Glanz, L., Testa, S., & Marchione, N. (1990). Panic disorder; Cognitive-behavioral treatment. *Behaviour Research and Therapy, 28,* 141–153.

Mikkelsen, M., & Stene, J. (1970). Genetic counseling in Down's syndrome. *Human Heredity, 20,* 457–464.

Miles, J. E., McLean, P. D., & Maurice, W. L. (1976). The medical student therapist: Treatment outcome. *Canadian Psychiatric Association Journal, 21,* 467–472.

Milgram, N. A. (1969). The rational and irrational in Zigler's motivational approach to mental retardation. *American Journal of Mental Deficiency, 73,* 527–532.

Miller, A. (1949). *Death of a salesman.* New York: Viking Penguin.

Miller, D. D., Perry, P. J., Cadoret, R. J., & Andreasen, N. C. Clozapine's effect on negative symptoms in treatment-refractory schizophrenics. *Comprehensive Psychiatry, 35,* 8–15.

Miller, D. H., Clancy, J., & Cummings, E. (1953). A comparison between unidirectional current, non-convulsive electrical stimulation given with Reiter's machine, standard alternating current electroshock (Cerletti method), and pentothal in chronic schizophrenia. *American Journal of Psychiatry, 109,* 617–620.

Miller, I. W., & Norman, W. H. (1979). Learned helplessness in humans: A review and attributional theory model. *Psychological Bulletin, 86,* 93–118.

Miller, M. P., Murphy, P. J., & Miller, T. P. (1978). Comparison of electromyographic feedback and progressive relaxation training in treating circumscribed anxiety-stress reactions. *Journal of Consulting and Clinical Psychology, 46,* 1291–1298.

Miller, P., & Ingham, J. G. (1976). Friends, confidants, and symptoms. *Social Psychiatry, 11,* 51–58.

Miller, R. D. (1994). The U.S. Supreme Court looks at voluntariness and consent. *International Journal of Law and Psychiatry, 17,* 239–252.

Miller, R. R., Barnet, R. C., & Grahame, N. J. (1995). Assessment of the Rescorla-Wagner Model. *Psychological Bulletin, 117,* 363–386.

Miller, S. D., & Triggiano, P. J. (1992). The psychophysiological investigation of multiple personality disorder: Review and update. *American Journal of Clinical Hypnosis, 35,* 47–61.

Miller, S. Glick. (1994). Borderline personality disorder from the patient's perspective. *Hospital and Community Psychiatry, 45,* 1215–1219.

Miller, T. Q., Smith, T. W., Turner, C. W., Guijarro, M. L., & Hallet, A. J. (1996). A meta-analytic review of research on hostility and physical health. *Psychological Bulletin, 119,* 322–348.

Milner, B. R. (1970). Memory and medial temporal regions of the brain. In K. H. Pribram & D. E. Broadbent (Eds.), *Biology of memory.* New York: Academic Press.

Mindham, R. H. S. (1973). An evaluation of continuation therapy with tricyclic antidepressants in depressive illness. *Psychological Medicine, 3,* 5–17.

Mindham, R. H. S. (1982). Tricyclic antidepressants and amine precursors. In E. S. Paykel (Ed.), *Handbook of affective disorders.* New York: Guilford Press.

Mineka, S., Davidson, M., Cook, M., & Keir, R. (1984). Observational conditioning of snake fear in rhesus monkeys. *Journal of Abnormal Psychology, 93,* 355–372.

Miniszek, N. A. (1983). Development of Alzheimer's disease in Down syndrome individuals. *American Journal of Mental Deficiency, 87,* 377–385.

Minkoff, K., Bergman, E., Beck, A. T., & Beck, R. (1973). Hopelessness, depression, and attempted suicide. *American Journal of Psychiatry, 130,* 455–459.

Minton, J., Campbell, M., Green, W., Jennings, S., & Samit, C. (1982). Cognitive assessment of siblings of autistic children. *Journal of the American Academy of Child Psychiatry, 21,* 256–261.

Mischel, W. (1990). Personality dispositions revisited and revised: A view after three decades. In L. A. Pervin (Ed.), *Handbook of personality: Theory and research.* New York: Guilford Press.

Mishara, Brian L., & Daigle, Marc. (1992). The effectiveness of telephone interventions by suicide prevention centres. *Canada's Mental Health, 40,* 24–29.

Mishler, E. G., & Waxler, N. E. (1968a). *Family processes and schizophrenia: Theory and selected experimental studies.* New York: Science House.

Mishler, E. G., & Waxler, N. E. (1968b). *Interaction in families: An experimental study of family processes and schizophrenia.* New York: Wiley.

Mitchell, J. E., & Groat, R. (1984). A placebo-controlled, double-blind trial of amitriptyline in bulimia. *Journal of Clinical Psychopharmacology, 4,* 186–193.

Mitler, M. M., & Hajdukovic, R. (1991). Relative efficacy of drugs for the treatment of sleepiness in narcolepsy. *Sleep, 14,* 218–220.

Mittelmann, B., Wolff, H. G., & Scharf, M. (1942). Emotions in gastroduodenal functions. *Psychosomatic Medicine, 4,* 5–61.

Mizes, J. S., & Lohr, J. M. (1983). The treatment of bulimia (binge-eating and self-induced vomiting): A quasi-experimental investigation of the effects of stimulus narrowing, self-reinforcement and self-control relaxation. *International Journal of Eating Disorders, 2,* 59–65.

Mohr, D. C. (1995). Negative outcome in psychotherapy: A critical review. *Clinical Psychology: Science and Practice, 2,* 1–27.

Monahan, J. (1973). The psychiatrization of criminal behavior. *Hospital and Community Psychiatry, 24,* 105–107.

Monahan, J. (1976). The prevention of violence. In J. Monahan (Ed.), *Community mental health and the criminal justice system.* Elmsford, NY: Pergamon Press.

Monahan, J. (1978). Prediction research and the emergency commitment of dangerous mentally ill persons: A reconsideration. *American Journal of Psychiatry, 135,* 198–201.

Monahan, J. (1984). The prediction of violent behavior: Toward a second generation of theory and policy. *American Journal of Psychiatry, 141,* 10–15.

Monahan, J. (1992). Mental disorder and violent behavior: Perceptions and evidence. *American Psychologist, 47,* 511–521.

Monahan, J. (1993). Limiting therapist exposure to Tarasoff liability. *American Psychologist, 48,* 242–250.

Monnelly, E. P., Woodruff, R. A., & Robins, L. N. (1974). Manic depressive illness and social achievement in a public hospital sample. *Acta Psychiatrica Scandinavica, 50,* 318–325.

Monroe, S. M., Imhoff, D. F., Wise, B. D., & Harris, J. E. (1983). Prediction of psychosocial symptoms under high-risk psychosocial circumstances: Life events, social support, and symptom specificity. *Journal of Abnormal Psychology, 92,* 338–350.

Monroe, S. M., & Simons, A. D. (1991). Diathesis-stress theories in the context of life stress research: Implications for the depressive disorders. *Psychological Bulletin, 110,* 406–425.

Moran, L. J. (1953). Vocabulary knowledge and usage among normal and schizophrenic subjects. *Psychological Monographs, 67* (370).

Moran, L. J., Mefford, R. B., Jr., & Kimble, J. P. (1964). Idiodynamic sets in word association. *Psychological Monographs, 78* (579).

Morgan, R. T., & Young, G. C. (1972). The conditioning treatment of childhood enuresis. *British Journal of Social Work, 2,* 503–509.

Morin, C. M., Culbert, J. P., & Schwartz, S. M. (1994). Nonpharmacological interventions for insomnia: A meta-analysis of treatment efficacy. *American Journal of Psychiatry, 151,* 1172–1180.

Morokoff, P. J., Baum, A., McKinnon, W. R., & Gilliland, R. (1987). Effects of chronic unemployment and acute psychological stress on sexual arousal in men. *Health Psychology, 6,* 545–560.

Morokoff, P. J., & Gilliland, R. (1993). Stress, sexual functioning, and marital satisfaction. *Journal of Sex Research, 30,* 43–53.

Morokoff, P. J., & Heinman, J. R. (1980). Effects of erotic stimuli on sexually functional and dysfunctional women: Multiple measures before and after therapy. *Behaviour Research and Therapy, 18,* 127–137.

Morrison, J. R., & Stewart, M. A. (1971). A family study of the hyperactive child syndrome. *Biological Psychiatry, 3,* 189–195.

Mosher, L. R., & Keith, S. J. (1980). Psychosocial treatment: Individual, family, and community support approaches. *Schizophrenia Bulletin, 6,* 10–41.

Mosher, L. R., & Menn, A. Z. (1978). Community residential treatment for schizophrenia: Two-year follow-up. *Hospital and Community Psychiatry, 29,* 715–723.

Mosher, L. R., Menn, A. Z., & Matthews, S. M. (1975). Soteria: Evaluation of a home-based treatment for schizophrenia. *American Journal of Orthopsychiatry, 45,* 455–467.

Motto, J. A. (1977). Estimation of suicidal risk by the use of clinical models. *Suicide and Life-Threatening Behavior, 74,* 237–245.

Motto, J. A., Heilbron, D. C., & Juster, R. P. (1985). Development of a clinical instrument to estimate suicide risk. *Archives of General Psychiatry, 42,* 680–686.

Mowrer, O. H. (1950). *Learning theory and personality dynamics.* New York: Ronald Press.

Mowrer, O. H., & Mowrer, W. A. (1938). Enuresis: A method for its study and treatment. *American Journal of Orthopsychiatry, 8,* 436–447.

Mucha, T. F., & Reinhardt, R. F. (1970). Conversion reactions in student aviators. *American Journal of Psychiatry, 127,* 493–497.

Muehlbach, M. J., & Walsh, J. K. (1995). The effects of caffeine on simulated night-shift work and subsequent daytime sleep. *Sleep, 18,* 22–29.

Muijen, M., Silverstone, T., Mehmet, A., & Christie, M. (1988). A comparative clinical trial of fluoxetine, mianserin and placebo in depressed outpatients. *Acta Psychiatrica Scandinavica, 78,* 384–390.

Mukherjee, S. (1993). ECT-lithium combination. *Convulsive Therapy, 9,* 274–284.

Mukherjee, S., Sackeim, H. A., & Schnur, D. B. (1994). Electroconvulsive therapy of acute manic episodes: A review of 50 years' experience. *American Journal of Psychiatry, 151,* 169–176.

Muldoon, M. F., Manuck, S. B., & Mann, J. J. (1992). Effects of a low-fat diet on brain serotoninergic responsivity in cynomolgus monkeys. *Biological Psychiatry, 31,* 739–742.

Mullinix, J. M., Norton, B. J., Hack, S., & Fishman, M. (1978). Skin temperature biofeedback and migraine. *Headache, 17,* 242–244.

Mulvey, E. P., Geller, J. L., & Roth, L. H. (1987). The promise and peril of involuntary outpatient commitment. *American Psychologist, 42,* 571–584.

Murphy, D. G. M., Murphy, D. M., Abbas, M., Palazidou, E., Binnie, C., Arendt, J., Costa, D., & Checkley, S. (1993). Seasonal affective disorder: Response to light as measured by electroencephalogram, melatonin suppression, and cerebral blood flow. *British Journal of Psychiatry, 163,* 327–331.

Murphy, E., & Macdonald, A. (1992). Affective disorders in old age. In E. S. Paykel (Ed.), *Handbook of affective disorders* (2nd ed.). New York: Guilford Press.

Murphy, G. (1923). Types of word-associations in dementia praecox, manic-depressives, and normal persons. *American Journal of Psychiatry, 2,* 539–571.

Murphy, G. E., Simons, A. D., Wetzel, R. D., & Lustman, P. J. (1984). Cognitive therapy and pharmacotherapy: Singly and together in the treatment of depression. *Archives of General Psychiatry, 41,* 33–41.

Murphy, J. (1976). Psychiatric labeling in cross-cultural perspective. *Science, 191,* 1019–1028.

Murray, H. A. (1943). *Thematic Apperception Test.* Cambridge, MA: Harvard University Press.

Murray, J. B. (1992). Kleptomania: A review of the research. *Journal of Psychology, 126,* 131–137.

Murrell, J., Farlow, M., Ghetti, B., & Benson, M. D. (1991). A mutation in the amyloid precursor protein associated with hereditary Alzheimer's disease. *Science, 254,* 97–99.

Murtagh, D. R., & Greenwood, K. M. (1995). Identifying effective psychological treatments for insomnia: A meta-analysis. *Journal of Consulting and Clinical Psychology, 63,* 79–89.

Muscettola, G., Potter, W. Z., Pickar, D., & Goodwin, F. (1984). Urinary 3-methoxy-4-hydroxyphenylglycol and affective disorders. *Archives of General Psychiatry, 41,* 337–342.

Myerson, A. (1940). Review of mental disorders in urban areas: An ecological study of schizophrenia and other psychoses. *American Journal of Psychiatry, 96,* 995–997.

Nakazawa, Y., Sakamoto, T., Yasutake, R., Yamaga, K., Kotorii, T., Miyahara, Y., Ariyoshi, Y., & Kameyama, T. (1992). Treatment of sleep apnea with prosthetic mandibular advancement (PMA). *Sleep, 15,* 499–504.

Narrow, W. E., Rae, D. S., Moscicki, E. K., Locke, B. Z., & Regier, D. A. (1990). Depression among Cuban Americans: The Hispanic Health and Nutrition Examination Survey. *Social Psychiatry and Psychiatric Epidemiology, 25,* 260–268.

Natale, M. (1977). Effects of induced elation-depression on speech in the initial interview. *Journal of Consulting and Clinical Psychology, 45,* 45–52.

Natale, M., & Hantas, M. (1982). Effect of temporary mood states on selective memory about the self. *Journal of Personality and Social Psychology, 42,* 927–934.

Nathan, P. E. (1988). The addictive personality is the behavior of the addict. *Journal of Consulting and Clinical Psychology, 56,* 183–188.

Nathan, S. G. (1986). The epidemiology of the DSM-III psychosexual dysfunctions. *Journal of Sex and Marital Therapy, 12,* 267–281.

National Institute of Mental Health. (1976, April 20). Rising suicide rate linked to economy. *Los Angeles Times,* sec. 8, pp. 2, 5.

Neal, A. M., & Turner, S. M. (1991). Anxiety disorders research with African Americans: Current status. *Psychological Bulletin, 109,* 400–410.

Neale, J. M. (1971). Perceptual span in schizophrenia. *Journal of Abnormal Psychology, 77,* 196–204.

Neale, J. M., & Oltmanns, T. F. (1980). *Schizophrenia.* New York: Wiley.

Needleman, H. L., Gunnoe, C., Leviton, A., Reed, R., Peresie, H., Maher, C., & Barrett, P. (1979). Deficits in psychologic and classroom performance of children with elevated dentine lead levels. *New England Journal of Medicine, 300,* 689–695.

Neimeyer, R. A. & Pfeiffer, A. M. (1994). Evaluation of suicide intervention effectiveness. *Death Studies, 18,* 131–166.

Nelson, K. B. (1991). Prenatal and perinatal factors in the etiology of autism. *Pediatrics, 87,* 761–766.

Nelson, R. E., & Craighead, W. E. (1977). Selective recall of positive and negative feedback, self-control behaviors, and depression. *Journal of Abnormal Psychology, 86,* 379–388.

Nelson, R. E., & Craighead, W. E. (1981). Tests of a self-control model of depression. *Behavior Therapy, 12,* 123–129.

Nemeroff, C. B., Knight, D. L., Franks, J., Craighead, W. E., & Krishan, R. (1994). Further studies on platelet serotonin transporter binding in depression. *American Journal of Psychiatry, 151,* 1623–1625.

Newman, S. C., & Bland, R. C. (1994). Life events and the 1-year prevalence of major depressive episode, generalized anxiety disorder, and panic disorder in a community sample. *Comprehensive Psychiatry, 35,* 76–82.

Neylan, T. C., Reynolds, C. F., & Kupfer, D. J. (1994). Sleep disorders. In R. E. Hales, S. C. Yudofsky, & J. A. Talbott (Eds.), *American Psychiatric Press textbook of psychiatry* (2nd ed.). Washington, DC: American Psychiatric Press.

Niccols, G. A. (1994). Fetal alcohol syndrome: Implications for psychologists. *Clinical Psychology Review, 14,* 91–111.

Nicholson, R. A., & Kugler, K. E. (1991). Competent and incompetent criminal defendants: A quantitative review of comparative research. *Psychological Bulletin, 109,* 355–370.

Nielsen, D. A., Goldman, D., Virkunnen, M., Tokola, R., Rawlings, R., Linnoila, M. (1994). Suicidality and 5-hydroxyindoleacetic acid concentrations associated with a tryptophan hydroxylase polymorphism. *Archives of General Psychiatry, 51,* 34–38.

Nigg, J. T., & Goldsmith, H. H. (1994). Genetics of personality disorders: Perspectives from personality and psychopathology research. *Psychological Bulletin, 115,* 346–380.

Nobler, M. S., Sackheim, H. A., Prohovik, I., Moeller, J. R., Mukherjee, S., Schnur, D. B., Prudic, J., & Devanand, D. P. (1994). Regional cerebral blood flow in mood disorders: 3. Treatment and clinical response. *Archives of General Psychiatry, 51,* 884–897.

Nolen-Hoeksema, S. (1991). Responses to depression and their effects on the duration of depressive episodes. *Journal of Abnormal Psychology, 100,* 569–582.

Nolen-Hoeksema, S., & Girgus, J. S. (1994). The emergence of gender differences in depression during adolescence. *Psychological Bulletin, 115,* 424–443.

Nowlin, N. S. (1983). Anorexia nervosa in twins: Case report and review. *Journal of Clinical Psychiatry, 44,* 101–105.

Noyes, R., Clarkson, C., Crowe, R. R., Yates, W. R., & McChesney, C. M. (1987). A family study of generalized anxiety disorder. *American Journal of Psychiatry, 144,* 1019–1024.

Noyes, R., Kathol, R. G., Fisher, M. M., Phillips, B. M., Suelzer, M. T., & Woodman, C. L. (1994). Psychiatric comorbidity among patients with hypochondriasis. *General Hospital Psychiatry, 16,* 78–87.

Nurnberger, J. I., & Gershon, E. S. (1992). Genetics. In E. S. Paykel (Ed.), *Handbook of affective disorders* (2nd ed.) New York: Guilford Press.

Oakes, W. F. (1982). Learned helplessness and defensive strategies: A rejoinder. *Journal of Personality, 50,* 515–525.

Oakes, W. F., & Curtis, N. (1982). Learned helplessness: Not dependent upon cognitions, attributions, or other such phenomenal experiences. *Journal of Personality, 50,* 387–408.

O'Carroll, R. (1991). Sexual desire disorders: A review of controlled treatment studies. *Journal of Sexual Research, 28,* 607–624.

O'Connor v. Donaldson, 493 F.2d 507 (5th Cir. 1974); 422 U.S. 563 (1975).

Ödegård, O. (1972). The multifactorial theory of inheritance in predisposition of schizophrenia. In A. K. Kaplan (Ed.), *Genetic factors in schizophrenia.* Springfield, IL: Thomas.

Offir, C. W. (1982). *Human sexuality.* New York: Harcourt Brace.

Ofshe, R., & Watters, E. (1994). *Making monsters: False memories, psychotherapy, and sexual hysteria.* New York: Scribner.

Ogles, B. M., Lambert, M. J., & Sawyer, J. D. (1995). Clinical significance of the National Institute of Mental Health Treatment of Depression Collaborative Research Program data. *Journal of Consulting and Clinical Psychology, 63,* 321–326.

O'Halloran, R. L., & Dietz, P. E. (1993). Autoerotic fatalities with power hydraulics. *Journal of Forensic Sciences, 38,* 359–364.

O'Hara, M. W., Schlechte, J. A., Lewis, D. A., & Varner, M. W. (1991). Controlled prospective study of postpartum mood disorders: Psychological, environmental, and hormonal variables. *Journal of Abnormal Psychology, 100,* 63–73.

O'Hara, M. W., Schlechte, J. A., Lewis, D. A., & Wright, E. J. (1991). Prospective study of postpartum blues. *Archives of General Psychiatry, 48,* 801–806.

O'Hara, M. W., Zekoski, E. M., Philipps, L. H. C., & Wright, E. J. (1990). Controlled prospective study of postpartum mood disorders: Comparison of childbearing and nonchildbearing women. *Journal of Abnormal Psychology, 99,* 3–15.

O'Hare, T. (1995). Differences in Asian and White drinking: Consumption level, drinking contexts, and expectancies. *Addictive Behaviors, 20,* 261–266.

Ohman, A., & Soares, J. F. (1993). On the automatic nature of phobic fear: Conditioned electrodermal responses to masked fear–relevant stimuli. *Journal of Abnormal Psychology, 102,* 121–132.

Olds, D. (1982). The Prenatal/Early Infancy Project: An ecological approach to prevention of developmental difficulties. In J. Belsky (Ed.), *In the beginning.* New York: Columbia University Press.

Olinger, L. J., Kuiper, N. A., & Shaw, B. F. (1987). Dysfunctional attitudes and stressful life events: An interactive model of depression. *Cognitive Therapy and Research, 11,* 25–40.

Olney, J. W., & Farber, N. B. (1995). Glutamate receptor dysfunction and schizophrenia. *Archives of General Psychiatry, 52,* 998–1007.

Olsson, S., Jansson, I., & Moller, A. (1995). A critical view on male-to-female sex reassignment surgical and hormonal treatment: An analysis of follow-up studies. *Norkisk-Sexologi, 13,* 14–35.

Oltmanns, T. F., & Maher, B. A. (1988). *Delusional beliefs.* New York: Wiley.

O'Malley, S., Jaffe, A. J., Chang, G., & Schottenfeld, R. S. (1996). Six-month follow-up of Naltrexone and psychotherapy for alcohol dependence. *Archives of General Psychiatry, 53,* 217–224.

O'Malley, S. S., Jaffee, A. J., Chang, G., Schottenfeld, R. S., Meyer, R. E., & Rounsaville, B. (1992). Naltrexone and coping skills therapy for alcohol dependence: A controlled study. *Archives of General Psychiatry, 49,* 881–887.

Opler, L. A., Albert, D., & Ramirez, P. M. (1994). Psychopharmacologic treatment of negative schizophrenic symptoms. *Comprehensive Psychiatry, 35,* 16–28.

Opler, L. A., Kay, S. R., Rosado, V., & Lindenmayer, J. P. (1984). Positive and negative syndromes in chronic schizophrenic inpatients. *Journal of Nervous and Mental Disease, 172,* 317–325.

Orbach, I., & Bar-Joseph, H. (1993). The impact of a suicide prevention program for adolescents on suicidal tendencies, hopelessness, ego identity, and coping. *Suicide and Life-Threatening Behavior, 23,* 120–129.

Orbach, I., Bar-Joseph, H., & Dror, N. (1990). Styles of problem solving in suicidal individuals. *Suicide and Life-Threatening Behavior, 20,* 56–64.

Oren, D. A., Moul, D. E., Schwartz, P. J., Brown, C., Yamada, E. M., & Rosenthal, N. E. (1994). Exposure to ambient light in patients with seasonal affective disorder. *American Journal of Psychiatry, 151,* 591–592.

Oren, D. A., & Rosenthal, N. E. (1992). Seasonal affective disorders. In E. S. Paykel (Ed.), *Handbook of affective disorders* (2nd ed.). New York: Guilford Press.

Orlinsky, D. E., Grawe, K., & Parks, B. (1994). Process and outcome in psychotherapy: *Noch einmal.* In A. E. Bergin & S. L. Garfield (Eds.), *Handbook of psychotherapy and behavior change* (4th ed.). New York: Wiley.

Orne, M. T. (1962). On the social psychology of the psychological experiment: With particular reference to demand characteristics and their implications. *American Psychologist, 17,* 776–783.

Orne, M. T., Dinges, D. F., & Orne, E. C. (1984). On the differential diagnosis of multiple personality in the forensic context. *International Journal of Clinical and Experimental Hypnosis, 32,* 118–169.

Orne, M. T., & Scheibe, K. E. (1964). The contribution of nondeprivation factors in the production of sensory deprivation effects: The psychology of the panic button. *Journal of Abnormal and Social Psychology, 68,* 3–12.

Osgood, C. E., & Luria, Z. (1954). A blind analysis of a case of multiple personality using the semantic differential. *Journal of Abnormal and Social Psychology, 49,* 579–591.

Osgood, C. E., Luria, Z., & Smith, S. W. (1976). A blind analysis of another case of multiple personality using the semantic differential technique. *Journal of Abnormal Psychology, 85,* 256–270.

Osler, W. (1892). *Lectures on angina and allied states.* Norwalk, CT: Appleton & Lange.

O'Sullivan, C. S., & Durso, F. T. (1984). Effect of schema–incongruent information on memory for stereotypical attributes. *Journal of Personality and Social Psychology, 49,* 55–70.

Overholser, J., Evans, S., & Spirito, A. (1990). Sex differences and their relevance to primary prevention of adolescent suicide. *Death Studies, 14,* 391–402.

Pachman, J. S. (1996). The dawn of a revolution in mental health. *American Psychologist, 51,* 213–215.

Palmer, R. L. (1981). *Electroconvulsive therapy: An appraisal.* New York: Oxford University Press.

Paradis, C. M., Hatch, M., & Friedman, S. (1994). Anxiety disorders in African Americans: An update. *Journal of the National Medical Association, 86,* 609–612.

Paris, J. (1992). Dhat: The semen loss anxiety syndrome. *Transcultural Psychiatric Research Review, 29,* 109–118.

Park, S., Holzman, P. S., & Goldman–Rakic, P. S. (1995). Spatial working memory deficits in the relatives of schizophrenic patients. *Archives of General Psychiatry, 52,* 821–828.

Parnas, J., Cannon, T. D., Jacobsen, B., Schulsinger, H., Schulsinger, F. A., & Mednick S. A. (1993). Lifetime DSM-III-R diagnostic outcomes in the offspring of schizophrenic mothers. *Archives of General Psychiatry, 50,* 707–714.

Pate v. *Robinson,* 384 U.S. 375 (1966).

Patel, C. (1994). Identifying psychosocial and other risk factors in Whitehall II study. [2nd International Congress of Behavioral Medicine CIANS-ISBM satellite conference]. *Homeostasis in Health and Disease, 35,* 71–83.

Patrick, C. J., Bradley, M. M., & Lang, P. J. (1993). Emotion in the criminal psychopath: Startle reflex modulation. *Journal of Abnormal Psychology, 102,* 82–92.

Patrick, C. J., Cuthbert, B. N., & Lang, P. J. (1994). Emotion in the criminal psychopath: Fear image processing. *Journal of Abnormal Psychology, 103,* 523–534.

Patsiokas, A., Clum, G., & Luscomb, R. (1979). Cognitive characteristics of suicide attempters. *Journal of Consulting and Clinical Psychology, 47,* 478–484.

Paul, G. L., & Lentz, R. J. (1977). *Psychosocial treatment of chronic mental patients.* Cambridge, MA: Harvard University Press.

Paul, S. M., Marangos, P. J., Goodwin, F. K., & Slotnick, P. (1980). Brain–specific benzodiazepine receptors and putative endogenous benzodiazepine–like compounds. *Biological Psychiatry, 15,* 407–428.

Pauls, D. L., Alsobrook, J. P., Goodman, W., Rasmussen, S., & Leckman, J. F. (1995). A family study of obsessive-compulsive disorder. *American Journal of Psychiatry, 152,* 76–84.

Pauls, D. L., Bucher, K., Crowe, R. R., & Noyes, R. (1980). A genetic study of panic disorder pedigrees. *American Journal of Human Genetics, 32,* 639–644.

Pauls, D. L., Kruger, S. D., Leckman, J. F., Cohen, D. J., & Kidd, K. K. (1984). The risk of Tourette's syndrome and chronic multiple tics among relatives of Tourette's syndrome patients obtained by direct interview. *Journal of the American Academy of Child Psychiatry, 23,* 134–137.

Pavy, D. (1968). Verbal behavior in schizophrenia: A review of recent studies. *Psychological Bulletin, 70,* 164–178.

Paykel, E. S., & Cooper, Z. (1992). Life events and social stress. In E. S. Paykel (Ed.), *Handbook of affective disorders* (2nd ed.). New York: Guilford Press.

Paykel, E. S., Prusoff, B. A., & Myers, J. K. (1975). Suicide attempts and recent life events: A controlled comparison. *Archives of General Psychiatry, 32,* 327–333.

Paykel, E. S., & Tanner, J. (1976). Life events, depressive relapse, and maintenance treatment. *Psychological Medicine, 6,* 481–485.

Payne, R. W. (1962). An object classification test as a measure of over–inclusive thinking in schizophrenic patients. *British Journal of Social and Clinical Psychology, 1,* 213–221.

Payne, R. W., & Friedlander, A. (1962). A short battery of simple tests for measuring overinclusive thinking. *Journal of Mental Science, 108,* 362–367.

Pearlin, L., & Schooler, C. (1978). The structure of coping. *Journal of Health and Social Behavior, 19,* 2–21.

Pearlson, G. D., Kim, W. S., Kubos, K., Moberg, P., Jayaram, G., Bascom, M., Chase, G., Goldfinger, A., & Tune, L. (1989). Ventricle–brain ratio, computed tomographic density, and brain area in 50 schizophrenics. *Archives of General Psychiatry, 46,* 690–697.

Pelham, W. E., Bender, M. E., Caddel, J., Booth, S., & Moorer, S. H. (1985). Methylphenidate and children with attention deficit disorder. *Archives of General Psychiatry, 42,* 948–952.

Pelham, W. E., Carlson, C., Sams, S. E., Vallano, G., Dixon, M. J., & Hoza, B. (1993). Separate and combined effects of methylphenidate and behavior modification on boys with attention-deficit hyperactivity disorder in the classroom. *Journal of Consulting and Clinical Psychology, 61,* 506–515.

Pelham, W. E., Schnedler, R. W., Bologna, N., & Contreras, A. (1980). Behavioral and stimulant treatment of hyperactive children: A therapy study with methylphenidate probes in a within-subject design. *Journal of Applied Behavior Analysis, 13,* 221–236.

Pelham, W. E., Schnedler, R. W., Miller, J., Ronnei, M., Paluchowski, C., Burdow, M., Marks, D., Nilsson, D., & Bender, M. E. (1986). The combination of behavior therapy and psychostimulant medication in the treatment of hyperactive children: A therapy outcome study. In L. Bloomingdale (Ed.), *Attention deficit disorders.* Jamaica, NY: Spectrum.

Penfield, W. (1955). The permanent record of the stream of consciousness. *Acta Psychologica, 11,* 47–69.

Penfield, W., & Perot, P. (1963). The brain's record of auditory and visual experience. *Brain, 86,* 595–696.

Penick, E. C., Powell, B. J., Nickel, E. J., Read, M. R., et al. (1990). Examination of Cloninger's Type I and Type II alcoholism with a sample of men alcoholics in treatment. *Alcoholism Clinical and Experimental Research, 14,* 623–629.

Pennebaker, J. W. (1982). *The psychology of physical symptoms.* New York: Springer-Verlag.

Pennebaker, J. W. (1990). *Opening up: The healing power of confiding in others.* New York: Morrow.

Pennebaker, J. W. (1993). Nonverbal and verbal emotional expression and health. *Psychotherapy and Psychosomatics, 59,* 11–19.

People v. *Buono,* Calif. 81-A354231 (1983).

Perna, G., Bertani, A., Arancio, C., Ronchi, P., & Bellodi, L. (1995). Laboratory response of patients with panic and obsessive–compulsive disorder to 35% CO_2 challenges. *American Journal of Psychiatry, 152,* 85–89.

Perna, G., Cocchi, S., Bertani, A., Arancio, C., & Bellodi, L. (1995). Sensitivity to 35% CO_2 in healthy first-degree relatives of patients with panic disorder. *American Journal of Psychiatry, 152,* 623–625.

Perr, I. N. (1981). Effects of the Rennie decision on private hospitalization in New Jersey: Two case reports. *American Journal of Psychiatry, 138,* 774–778.

Perris, C. (1992). Bipolar–unipolar distinction. In E. S. Paykel (Ed.), *Handbook of affective disorders* (2d ed.). New York: Guilford Press.

Perry, J. D., & Whipple, B. (1981). Pelvic muscle strength of female ejaculators: Evidence in support of a new theory of orgasm. *Journal of Sex Research, 17,* 22–39.

Petersen, M. E., & Dickey, R. (1995). Surgical sex reassignment: A comparative survey of international centers. *Archives of Sexual Behavior, 24,* 135–156.

Peterson, C., Schwartz, S. M., & Seligman, M. E. P. (1981). Self-blame and depressive symptoms. *Journal of Personality and Social Psychology, 41,* 253–259.

Peterson, C., & Seligman, M. E. P. (1984). Causal explanations as a risk factor for depression: Theory and evidence. *Psychological Review, 91,* 347–374.

Petraitis, J., Flay, B. R., & Miller, T. Q. (1995). Reviewing theories of adolescent substance abuse: Organizing pieces in the puzzle. *Psychological Bulletin, 117,* 67–86.

Petty, F., & Sherman, A. D. (1984). Plasma GABA levels in psychiatric illness. *Journal of Affective Disorders, 6,* 131–138.

Petty, R. G., Barta, P. E., Pearlson, G. D., McGilchrist, I. K., Lewis, R. W., Tien, A. Y., Pulver, A., Vaughn, D. D., Casanova, M. F., & Powers, R. E. (1995). Reversal of asymmetry of the planum temporale in schizophrenia. *American Journal of Psychiatry, 152,* 715–721.

Pfafflin, F. (1992). Regrets after sex reassignment surgery. *Journal of Psychology and Human Sexuality, 5,* 69–85.

Philipps, L. H. C., & O'Hara, M. W. (1991). Prospective study of postpartum depression: 4½-year follow-up of women and children. *Journal of Abnormal Psychology, 100,* 151–155.

Philipsborn, J. T. (1990). Assessing competence to stand trial: Rethinking roles and definitions. *American Journal of Forensic Psychology, 8,* 47–59.

Phillips, D. P. (1974). The influence of suggestion on suicide: Substantive and theoretical implications of the Werther effect. *American Sociological Review, 39,* 340–354.

Phillips, D. P. (1977). Motor vehicle fatalities increase just after publicized suicide stories. *Science, 196,* 1464–1465.

Phillips, D. P. (1979). Suicide, motor vehicle fatalities, and the mass media: Evidence toward a theory of suggestion. *American Journal of Sociology, 84,* 1150–1174.

Phillips, K. A. (1991). Body dysmorphic disorder: The distress of imagined ugliness. *American Journal of Psychiatry, 148,* 1138–1149.

Phillips, K. A., & Gunderson, J. G. (1994). Personality disorders. In R. E. Hales, S. C. Yudofsky, & J. A. Talbott (Eds.), *American Psychiatric Press textbook of psychiatry* (2nd ed.). Washington, DC: American Psychiatric Press.

Phillips, K. A., Gunderson, J. G., Hirschfeld, R. M., & Smith, L. E. (1990). A review of the depressive personality. *American Journal of Psychiatry, 147,* 830–837.

Pianta, R. C., & Egeland, B. (1994). Relation between depressive symptoms and stressful life events in a sample of disadvantaged mothers. *Journal of Consulting and Clinical Psychology, 62,* 1229–1234.

Piasecki, J. (1975). *Community response to residential services for the psychosocially disabled.* Paper presented at the first annual conference of the International Association for Psychosocial Rehabilitation Services, Horizon House Institute, Philadelphia.

Pickar, D., Owen, R. R., & Litman, R. E. (1991). New developments in the pharmacotherapy of schizophrenia. In A. Tasman & S. Goldfinger (Eds.), *American Psychiatric Press review of psychiatry* (Vol. 10). Washington, DC: American Psychiatric Press.

Pickar, D., Owen, R. R., Litman, R. E., Konicki, E., Gutierrez, R., & Rapaport, M. H. (1992). Clinical and biologic response to clozapine in patients with schizophrenia. *Archives of General Psychiatry, 49,* 345–353.

Pickar, D., Sweeney, D. R., Maas, J. W., & Heninger, G. R. (1978). Primary affective disorder, clinical state change, and MHPG excretion: A longitudinal study. *Archives of General Psychiatry, 35,* 1378–1383.

Pickens, R. W., Svikis, D. S., McGue, M., Lykken, D. T., Heston, L. L., & Clayton, P. J. (1991). Heterogeneity in the inheritance of alcoholism. *Archives of General Psychiatry, 48,* 19–28.

Pigott, T., Pato, M. T., Bernstein, S. E., Grover, G. N., Hill, J. L., Tolliver, T. J., & Murphy, D. L. (1990). Controlled comparisons of clomipramine and fluoxetine and the treatment of obsessive–compulsive disorder. *Archives of General Psychiatry, 47,* 926–932.

Pihl, R. O., Peterson, J., & Finn, P. (1990). Inherited predisposition to alcoholism: Characteristics of sons of male alcoholics. *Journal of Abnormal Psychology, 99,* 291–301.

Pinel, P. (1806). *A treatise on insanity* (D. Davis, Trans.). New York: Hafner.

Pitman, R. K. (1989). Posttraumatic stress disorder, hormones, and memory. *Biological Psychiatry, 26,* 221–223.

Pitt, B. (1968). "Atypical" depression following childbirth. *British Journal of Psychiatry, 114,* 1325–1335.

Pitt, B. (1973). Maternity blues. *British Journal of Psychiatry, 122,* 431–433.

Pitts, F. N., & Allen, R. E. (1979). Biochemical induction of anxiety. In W. E. Fann, I. Karacan, A. D. Pokorny, & R. L. Williams (Eds.), *Phenomenology and treatment of anxiety.* Englewood Cliffs, NJ: Prentice Hall.

Pitts, F. N., & McClure, J. N. (1967). Lactate metabolism in anxiety neurosis. *New England Journal of Medicine, 277,* 1328–1336.

Piven, J., Arndt, S. V., Bailey, J., Havercamp, S., Andreasen, N. C., & Palmer, P. (1995). An MRI study of brain size in autism. *American Journal of Psychiatry, 152,* 1145–1149.

Plomin, R., De Fries, J. C., & McClearn, G. E. (1990). *Behavioral genetics: A primer.* New York: Freeman.

Plomin, R., Lichtenstein, P., Pedersen, N., McClearn, G. E., & Nesselroade, J. R. (1990). Genetic influences on life events during the last half of the life span. *Psychology of Aging, 5,* 25–30.

Pokorny, A. D. (1968). Myths about suicide. In H. Resnik (Ed.), *Suicidal behaviors.* Boston: Little, Brown.

Pomerleau, O. F. (1995). Individual differences in sensitivity to nicotine: Implications of genetic research on nicotine dependence. *Behavior Genetics, 25,* 161–177.

Pope, H. G., Aizley, H. G., Keck, P. E., & McElroy, S. L. (1991). Neuroleptic malignant syndrome: Long-up follow-up of 20 cases. *Journal of Clinical Psychiatry, 52,* 208–212.

Pope, H. G., Champoux, R. F., & Hudson, J. I. (1987). Eating disorders and socioeconomic class: Anorexia nervosa and bulimia in nine communities. *Journal of Nervous and Mental Disease, 175,* 620–623.

Pope, H. G., & Hudson, J. I. (1982). Treatment of bulimia with antidepressants. *Psychopharmacology, 78,* 176–179.

Pope, H. G., & Hudson, J. I. (1984). *New hope for binge eaters: Advances in the understanding and treatment of bulimia.* New York: Harper & Row.

Pope, H. G., & Hudson, J. I. (1992). Is childhood sexual abuse a risk factor for bulimia nervosa? *American Journal of Psychiatry, 149,* 455–463.

Pope, H. G., & Hudson, J. I. (1995). Can memories of childhood sexual abuse be repressed? *Psychological Medicine, 25,* 121–126.

Pope, H. G., Hudson, J. I., Jonas, J. M., & Yurgelun-Todd, D. (1983). Bulimia treated with imipramine: A placebo-controlled double-blind study. *American Journal of Psychiatry, 140,* 554–558.

Pope, H. G., Hudson, J. I., Jonas, J. M., & Yurgelun-Todd, D. (1985). Antidepressant treatment of bulimia: A two-year follow-up study. *Journal of Clinical Psychopharmacology, 5,* 320–327.

Pope, H. G., Mangweth, B., Negrao, A., B., Hudson, J. I. et al (1994). Childhood sexual abuse and bulimia nervosa: A comparison of American, Austrian, and Brazilian women. *American Journal of Psychiatry, 151,* 732–737.

Popper, C. W., & Steingard, R. J. (1994). Disorders usually first diagnosed in infancy, childhood, and adolescence. In R. E. Hales, S. C. Yudofsky, & J. A. Talbott (Eds.), *American Psychiatric Press textbook of psychiatry* (2nd ed.). Washington, DC: American Psychiatric Press.

Post, F. (1982). Affective disorders in old age. In E. S. Paykel (Ed.), *Handbook of affective disorders* (pp. 393–402). New York: Guilford Press.

Post, L. L. (1994). Sexual side effects of psychiatric medications in women. *American Journal of Psychiatry, 151,* 1247.

Price, L. H., & Heninger, G. R. (1994). Lithium in the treatment of mood disorders. *New England Journal of Medicine, 331,* 591–598.

Prichard, J. C. (1835). *A treatise on insanity.* London: Sherwood, Gilbert & Piper.

Prien, R. F., Klett, C. J., & Caffey, E. M. (1974). Lithium prophylaxis in recurrent affective illness. *American Journal of Psychiatry, 131,* 198–203.

Prince, M. (1908). *The dissociation of personality.* New York: Longman.

Prince, V., & Bentler, P. M. (1972). Survey of 504 cases of transvestism. *Psychological Reports, 31,* 903–917.

Prior, M., & Sanson, A. (1986). Attention deficit disorder with hyperactivity: A critique. *Journal of Child Psychology and Psychiatry, 27,* 307–319.

Pueschel, S. M., & Goldstein, A. (1983). Genetic counseling. In J. L. Matson & J. A. Mulick (Eds.), *Handbook of mental retardation.* Elmsford, NY: Pergamon.

Pueschel, S. M., & Thuline, H. C. (1983). Chromosome disorders. In J. L. Matson & J. A. Mulick (Eds.), *Handbook of mental retardation.* Elmsford, NY: Pergamon.

Putnam, F. W. (1989). *Diagnosis and treatment of multiple personality disorder.* New York: Guilford Press.

Putnam, F. W., Guroff, J. J., Silberman, E. K., Barban, L., & Post, R. M. (1986). The clinical phenomenology of multiple personality disorder: Review of 100 recent cases. *Journal of Clinical Psychiatry, 47,* 285–293.

Quay, H. C. (1986). Conduct disorders. In H. C. Quay & J. S. Werry (Eds.), *Psychopathological disorders of childhood* (3rd ed.). New York: Wiley.

Quitkin, F., Rabkin, J. G., Ross, D., & McGrath, P. J. (1984). Duration of antidepressant drug treatment. *Archives of General Psychiatry, 41,* 238–245.

Rabkin, J. G., Muhlin, G., & Cohen, P. W. (1984). What neighbors think: Community attitudes toward local psychiatric facilities. *Community Mental Health Journal, 20,* 304–312.

Rackman, S. (1966). Sexual fetishism: An experimental analogue. *Psychological Record, 16,* 293–296.

Rackman, S., & Hodgson, S. (1968). Experimentally induced "sexual fetishism": Replication and development. *Psychological Record, 18,* 25–27.

Radloff, L. S. (1975). Sex differences in depression: The effects of occupational and marital status. *Sex Roles, 1,* 249–265.

Radloff, L. S., & Rae, D. S. (1979). Susceptibility and precipitating factors in depression: Sex differences and similarities. *Journal of Abnormal Psychology, 88,* 174–181.

Rahe, R. H., Mahan, J. L., & Arthur, R. J. (1970). Prediction of near–future health change from subjects' preceding life changes. *Journal of Psychosomatic Research, 14,* 401–406.

Raine, A., Venables, P. H., & Williams, M. (1990). Relationship between central and autonomic measures of arousal at age 15 years and criminality at age 24 years. *Archives of General Psychiatry, 47,* 1003–1007.

Raine, A., Venables, P. H., & Williams, M. (1995). High autonomic arousal and electrodermal orienting at age 15 years as protective factors against criminal behavior at age 29 years. *Archives of General Psychiatry, 152,* 1595–1600.

Raleigh, M. J., McGuire, M. T., Brammer, G. L., & Yuwiler, A. (1984). Social and environmental influences on blood serotonin concentrations in monkeys. *Archives of General Psychiatry, 47,* 405–410.

Rapoport, J. L. (1994). Clozapine and child psychiatry. *Journal of Child and Adolescent Psychopharmacology, 4,* 1–3.

Rapoport, J. L., Ryland, D. H., & Kriete, M. (1992). Drug treatment of canine acral lick: An animal model of obsessive–compulsive disorder. *Archives of General Psychiatry, 49,* 517–521.

Rapoport, S. I., Pettigrew, K. D., & Schapiro, M. B. (1991). Discordance and concordance of dementia of the Alzheimer type

(DAT) in monozygotic twins indicate heritable and sporadic form of Alzheimer's disease. *Neurology, 41,* 1549–1553.

Raymond, M. J., & O'Keefe, K. (1965). A case of pin–up fetishism treated by aversion conditioning. *British Journal of Psychiatry, 111,* 579–581.

Raz, S., & Raz, N. (1990). Structural brain abnormalities in the major psychoses: A quantitative review of the evidence from computerized imaging. *Psychological Bulletin, 108,* 93–108.

"A Recovering Patient." (1986). "Can we talk?" The schizophrenic patient in psychotherapy. *American Journal of Psychiatry, 143,* 68–70.

Redmond, D., Kosten, T., & Peiser, M. (1982). Spontaneous ejaculation associated with anxiety: Psychophysiological considerations. *American Journal of Psychiatry, 140,* 1163–1166.

Regal, R. R., Cross, P. K., Lamson, S. H., & Hook, E. B. (1980). A search for evidence for a paternal age effect independent of a maternal age in birth certificate reports of Down's syndrome in New York State. *American Journal of Epidemiology, 112,* 650–655.

Rehm, L. P. (1977). A self–control model of depression. *Behavior Therapy, 8,* 787–804.

Reid, C. M., Murphy, B., Murphy, M., Maher, T., et al. (1994). Prescribing medication versus promoting behavioural change: A trial of the use of lifestyle management to replace drug treatment of hypertension in general practice. *Behaviour Change, 11,* 177–185.

Reisner, A. D. (1994). Multiple personality disorder diagnosis: A house of cards? *American Journal of Psychiatry, 151,* 629.

Reiss, D., Plomin, R., & Hetherington, M. (1991). Genetics and psychiatry: An unheralded window on the environment. *American Journal of Psychiatry, 148,* 283–291.

Rennie v. Klein, No. 77-2624 (N.J. Sept. 14, 1979); 720 F.2d 266 (3rd Cir. 1983).

Rescorla, R. A. (1988). Pavlovian conditioning: It's not what you think it is. *American Psychologist, 43,* 151–160.

Revelle, W., Amaral, P., & Turriff, S. (1976). Introversion/extroversion, time stress, and caffeine: Effect on verbal performance. *Science, 192,* 149–150.

Rice, E. H., Sombrotto, L., B., Markowitz, J. C., & Leon, A. C. (1994). Cardiovasuclar morbidity in high–risk patients during ECT. *American Journal of Psychiatry, 15,* 1637–1641.

Rice, M. E., & Harris, G. T. (1991). Firesetters admitted to a maximum security psychiatric institution: Offenders and offenses. *Journal of Interpersonal Violence, 6,* 461–475.

Rice, M. E., Quinsey, V. L., & Harris, G. T. (1991). Sexual recidivism among child molesters released from a maximum security psychiatric institution. *Journal of Consulting and Clinical Psychology, 59,* 381–386.

Richardson, J. W., Fredrickson, P. A., & Siong-Chi, L. (1990). Narcolepsy update. *Mayo Clinic Proceedings, 65,* 991–998.

Richman, J. (1992). A rational approach to rational suicide. *Suicide and Life-Threatening Behavior, 22,* 130–141.

Rickels, K., Case, W. G., Schweizer, E., Garcia–Espana, F., & Fridman, R. (1991). Long–term benzodiazepine users 3 years after participation in a discontinuation program. *American Journal of Psychiatry, 148,* 757–761.

Rieber, I., & Sigusch, V. (1979). Psychosurgery on sex offenders and sexual "deviants" in West Germany. *Archives of Sexual Behavior, 8,* 523–528.

Rieder, R. O., Kaufmann, C. A., & Knowles, J. A. (1994). Genetics. In R. E. Hales, S. C. Yudofsky, & J. A. Talbott (Eds.), *American Psychiatric Press textbook of psychiatry,* (2nd ed.) Washington, DC: American Psychiatric Press.

Rifai, A. H. George, C. J. Stack, J. A., Mann, J. J., Reynolds, C. F. (1994). Hopelessness in suicide attempters after acute treatment of major depression in late life. *American Journal of Psychiatry, 151,* 1687–1690.

Rifai, A. H., Reynolds, C. F., & Mann, J. J. (1992). Biology of elderly suicide. *Suicide and Life-Threatening Behavior, 22,* 48–61.

Rifkin, A., Klein, D. F., Dillon, D., & Levitt, M. (1981). Blockade by imipramine or desipramine of panic induced by sodium lactate. *American Journal of Psychiatry, 138,* 676–677.

Rimon, R., & Laakso, R. (1985). Life stress and rheumatoid arthritis. *Psychotherapy and Psychosomatics, 43,* 38–43.

Risby, E. D., Hsiao, J. K., Manji, H. K., Bitran, J., Moses, F., Zhou, D. F., & Potter, W. Z. (1991). The mechanisms of action of lithium: 2. Effects of adenylate cyclase activity and beta-adrenergic receptor

binding in normal subjects. *Archives of General Psychiatry, 48,* 513–524.

Rist, R. C. (1970). Student social class and teacher expectations: The self-fulfilling prophecy in ghetto education. *Harvard Educational Review, 40,* 411–451.

Ritter, E., & Holmes, D. S. (1968). Behavioral contagion: Its occurrence as a function of differential restraint reduction. *Journal of Experimental Research in Personality, 3,* 242–246.

Ritvo, E. R., Mason–Brothers, A., Freeman, B. J., Pingree, C., Jenson, W. R., McMahon, W. M., Petersen, P. B., Jorde, L. B., Mo, A., & Ritvo, A. (1990). The UCLA–University of Utah epidemiologic survey of autism: The etiologic role of rare diseases. *American Journal of Psychiatry, 147,* 1614–1621.

Ritvo, E. R., Ritvo, A., & Brothers, A. (1982). Genetic and immunohematologic factors in autism. *Journal of Autism and Developmental Disorders, 12,* 109–114.

Roback, H. B., & Lothstein, L. M. (1986). The female midlife sex change applicant: A comparison with younger transsexuals and older male sex change applicants. *Archives of Sexual Behavior, 15,* 401–415.

Robbins, L. (1994). Precipitating factors in migraine: A retrospective review of 494 patients. *Headache, 34,* 214–216.

Roberts, A. H. (1985). Biofeedback: Research, training, and clinical roles. *American Psychologist, 40,* 938–941.

Roberts, J., & Roberts, T. (1985). Taking the center to market. *Community Mental Health Journal, 21,* 264–281.

Roberts, T. G., Fournet, G. P., and Penland, E. (1995). A comparison of the attitudes toward alcohol and drug use and school support by grade level, gender, and ethnicity. *Journal of Alcohol and Drug Education, 40,* 112–127.

Robertson, A. J., Ramesar, K. C., Potts, R. C., Hibbs, J. H., Browning, M. C., Brown, R. A., Hayes, P. C., & Beck, J. S. (1981). The effect of strenuous physical exercise on circulating blood lymphocytes and serum cortisol levels. *Journal of Clinical and Laboratory Immunology, 5,* 53–57.

Robins, C. J., & Block, P. (1989). Cognitive theories of depression viewed from a diathesis-stress perspective: Evaluations of the models of Beck and of Abramson, Seligman, and Teasdale. *Cognitive Therapy and Research, 13,* 297–313.

Robins, E., & Guze, S. B. (1972). Classification of affective disorders: The primary-secondary, the endogenous-reactive, and the neurotic-psychotic concepts. In T. A. Williams, M. M. Katz, & J. A. Shields (Eds.), *Recent advances in the psychobiology of the depressive illnesses.* Washington, DC: U.S. Government Printing Office.

Robins, L. N. (1966). *Deviant children grown up.* Baltimore: Williams & Wilkins.

Robins, L. N., Davis, D. H., & Nurco, D. N. (1974). How permanent was Viet Nam drug addiction? In M. H. Green & R. L. Du Pont (Eds.), *The epidemiology of drug abuse* (NIDA Journal Suppl., Pt. N, Vol. 64). Washington, DC: U.S. Government Printing Office.

Robins, L. N., Helzer, J. E., & Davis, D. H. (1975). Narcotic use in Southeast Asia and afterwards. *Archives of General Psychiatry, 32,* 955–961.

Robins, L. N., Helzer, J. E., Weissman, M. M., Orvaschel, H., Gruenberg, E., Burke, J. D., & Reigier, D. A. (1984). Lifetime prevalence of specific psychiatric disorders in three sites. *Archives of General Psychiatry, 41,* 949–958.

Robinson, D., Wu, H., Munne, R. A., Ashtari, M., Alvir, M. J., Lerner, G., Koreen, A., Cole, K., & Bogerts, B. (1995). Reduced caudate nucleus volume in obsessive-compulsive disorder. *Archives of General Psychiatry, 52,* 393–398.

Robinson, L. A., Berman, J. S., & Neimeyer, R. A. (1990). Psychotherapy for the treatment of depression: A comprehensive review of controlled-outcome research. *Psychological Bulletin, 108,* 30–49.

Robinson, N. M., & Robinson, H. B. (1976). *The mentally retarded child.* New York: McGraw-Hill.

Roff, M. (1974). Childhood antecedents of adult neurosis, severe bad conduct, and psychological health. In D. Ricks, A. Thomas, and M. Roff (Eds.), *Life history research in psychopathology* (Vol. 3). Minneapolis: University of Minnesota Press.

Rofman, E. S., Askinazi, C., & Fant, E. (1980). The prediction of dangerous behavior in emergency commitment. *American Journal of Psychiatry, 137,* 1061–1064.

Rogeness, G. A., Javors, M. A., & Pliszka, S. R. (1992). Neurochemistry and child and adolescent psychiatry. *Journal of the American Academy of Child and Adolescent Psychiatry, 31,* 765–781.

Rogeness, G., Javors, M., & Pliszka, S. (1993). Neurochemistry and child and adolescent psychiatry. *Annual Progress in Child Psychiatry and Child Development,* 305–343.

Rogers, C. R. (1951). *Client-centered therapy.* Boston: Houghton Mifflin.

Rogler, L. H., Malgady, R. G., Costantino, G., & Blumenthal, R. (1987). What do culturally sensitive mental health services mean? *American Psychologist, 42,* 565–570.

Rohde, P. D., Lewinsohn, P. M., & Seeley, J. R. (1991). Comorbidity of unipolar depression: 2. Comorbidity with other mental disorders in adolescents and adults. *Journal of Abnormal Psychology, 100,* 214–222.

Rokeach, M. (1964). *The three Christs of Ypsilanti.* New York: Knopf.

Rollnick, S., & Heather, N. (1982). The application of Bandura's self-efficacy theory to abstinence-oriented alcoholism treatment. *Addictive Behaviors, 7,* 243–250.

Rorschach, H. (1942). *Psychodiagnostics: A diagnostic test based on perception* (P. Lemkau & B. Kronenberg, Trans.). Philadelphia: Grune & Stratton.

Rorty, M., Yager, J., & Rossotto, E. (1994). Childhood sexual, physical, and psychological abuse in bulimia nervosa. *American Journal of Psychiatry, 151,* 1122–1126.

Rose, R. J., Bourne, P. G., Poe, R. O., Mougey, E. H., Collins, D. R., & Mason, J. W. (1969). Androgen responses to stress: 2. Excretion of testosterone, epitestosterone, androsterone, and etiochoanolone during basic combat training and under threat of attack. *Psychosomatic Medicine, 31,* 418–436.

Rosen, A., & Schalling, D. (1971). Probability learning in psychopathic and non-psychopathic criminals. *Journal of Experimental Research in Personality, 5,* 191–198.

Rosenbaum, M. (1980). The role of the term *schizophrenia* in the decline of diagnoses of multiple personality. *Archives of General Psychiatry, 37,* 1383–1385.

Rosenbaum, M. (1995). The demedicalization of methadone maintenance. *Journal of Psychoactive Drugs, 27,* 145–149.

Rosenberg, D., & Leland, J. (1995, July 10). "Generation depressed": Suicide attempts rock a New England town. *Newsweek,* p. 63.

Rosenblatt, A., & Mayer, J. E. (1974). Patients who return: A consideration of some neglected influences. *Journal of the Bronx State Hospital, 2,* 71–81.

Rosenhan, D. L. (1973). On being sane in insane places. *Science, 179,* 250–258.

Rosenman, R. H. (1978). The interview method of assessment of the coronary-prone behavior pattern. In T. M. Dembroski, S. M. Weiss, J. L. Shields, S. G. Haynes, & M. Feinleib (Eds.), *Coronary-prone behavior.* New York: Springer.

Rosenman, R. H., Brand, R. J., Jenkins, C. D., Friedman, M., Straus, R., & Wurm, M. (1975). Coronary heart disease in the Western Collaborative Group Study: Final follow-up experience of 8½ years. *Journal of the American Medical Association, 233,* 872–877.

Rosenman, R. H., Brand, R. J., Sholtz, R. I., & Friedman, M. (1976). Multivariate prediction of coronary heart disease during 8.5-year follow-up in the Western Collaborative Group Study. *American Journal of Cardiology, 37,* 903–910.

Rosenthal, D. (1961). Sex distribution and the severity of illness among samples of schizophrenic twins. *Journal of Psychiatric Research, 1,* 26–36.

Rosenthal, D. (1970). *Genetic theory and abnormal behavior.* New York: McGraw–Hill.

Rosenthal, D., Wender, P. H., Kety, S. S., Schulsinger, F. A., Weiner, J., & Ostergaard, L. (1968). Schizophrenics' offspring reared in adoptive homes. In D. Rosenthal & S. S. Kety (Eds.), *The transmission of schizophrenia.* Elmsford, NY: Pergamon.

Rosenthal, D., Wender, P. H., Kety, S. S., Welner, J., & Schulsinger, F. A. (1971). The adopted-away offspring of schizophrenics. *American Journal of Psychiatry, 128,* 307–311.

Rosenthal, N. E., Joseph-Vanderpool, J. R., Levendosky, A. A., Johnston, S. H., Allen, R., Kelley, K., Souetre, E., Schultz, P., & Starz, K. (1990). Phase-shifting effects of bright morning light as treatment for delayed sleep phase syndrome. *Sleep, 13,* 354–361.

Rosenthal, N. E., Sack, D. A., Gillin, J. C., Lewy, A. J., Goodwin, F. K., Davenport, Y., Mueller, P. S., Newsome, D. A., & Wehr, T. A. (1984). Seasonal affective disorder: A description of the syndrome and preliminary findings with light therapy. *Archives of General Psychiatry, 41,* 72–80.

Rosenthal, R., & Jacobson, L. (1968). *Pygmalion in the classroom.* New York: Holt, Rinehart and Winston.

Ross, C. A. (1989). *Multiple personality disorder: Diagnosis, clinical features, and treatment.* New York: Wiley.

Ross, C. A., Joshi, S., & Currie, R. (1990). Dissociative experiences in the general population. *American Journal of Psychiatry, 147,* 1547–1552.

Ross, C. A., Miller, S. D., Reagor, P., Bjornson, L., Fraser, G. A., & Anderson, G. (1990). Structured interview data on 102 cases of multiple personality disorder from four centers. *American Journal of Psychiatry, 147,* 596–601.

Ross, C. A., Norton R., & Wozney, K. (1989). Multiple personality disorder: An analysis of 236 cases. *Canadian Journal of Psychiatry, 34,* 413–418.

Ross, J. L. (1977). Anorexia nervosa: An overview. *Bulletin of the Menninger Clinic, 41,* 418–436.

Roth, D. L., & Holmes, D. S. (1985). Influence of physical fitness in determining the impact of stressful life events on physical and psychological health. *Psychosomatic Medicine, 47,* 164–173.

Roth, D. L., & Holmes, D. S. (1987). Influence of aerobic exercise training and relaxation training on physical and psychological health following stressful life events. *Psychosomatic Medicine, 49,* 355–365.

Roth, S. (1979). A revised model of learned helplessness in humans. *Journal of Personality, 48,* 103–133.

Roth, W. T., Margraf, J., Ehlers, A., Taylor, C. B., Maddock, R. J., Davies, S., & Agras, W. S. (1992). Stress reactivity in panic disorder. *Archives of General Psychiatry, 49,* 301–310.

Rotter, J. B., & Rafferty, J. E. (1950). *Manual for the Rotter Incomplete Sentences Blank, College Form.* New York: Psychological Corporation.

Rouillon, F., Phillips, R., Serrurier, D., Ansart, E., & Gérard, M. J. (1989). Rechutes de dépression unipolaire et efficacité de la maprotiline. *Encéphale, 15,* 527–534.

Rouse v. Cameron, 373 F.2d 451 (D.C. Cir. 1966).

Roviaro, S., & Holmes, D. S. (1980). Arousal transference: The influence of fear arousal on subsequent sexual arousal for subjects with high and low sex guilt. *Journal of Research in Personality, 14,* 307–320.

Roviaro, S., Holmes, D. S., & Holmsten, D. (1984). Influence of a cardiac rehabilitation program on the cardiovascular, psychological, and social functioning of cardiac patients. *Journal of Behavioral Medicine, 7,* 61–81.

Rovner, B. W., German, P. S., Brant, L. J., Clark, R., Burton, L., & Folstein, M. F. (1991). Depression and mortality in nursing homes. *Journal of the American Medical Association, 265,* 993–996.

Roy, A. (1978). Vulnerability factors and depression in women. *British Journal of Psychiatry, 113,* 106–110.

Roy, A. (1982). Risk factors for suicide in psychiatric patients. *Archives of General Psychiatry, 39,* 1089–1095.

Roy, A. (1983). Family history of suicide. *Archives of General Psychiatry, 40,* 971–974.

Roy, A. (1990). Possible biologic determinants of suicide. In D. Lester (Ed.), *Current concepts of suicide.* Philadelphia: Charles Press.

Roy, A., Pickar, D., Linnoila, M., Doran, A. R., & Paul, S. M. (1986). Cerebrospinal fluid monoamine and monamine metabolite levels and the dexamethasone suppression test in depression: Relationship to life events. *Archives of General Psychiatry, 43,* 356–360.

Roy, A., Segal, N., Centerwall, B., & Robinette, D. (1991). Suicide in twins. *Archives of General Psychiatry, 48,* 29–32.

Rozensky, R. H., Rehm, L. P., Pry, G., & Roth, D. (1977). Depression and self-reinforcement behavior in hospitalized patients. *Journal of Behavior Therapy and Experimental Psychiatry, 8,* 35–38.

Ruan, F., & Bullough, V. L. (1992). Lesbianism in China. *Academy of Chinese Culture and Health Sciences, 21,* 217–226.

Rubin, E. H., Kincherf, D. A., Grant, E. A., & Storandt, M. (1991). The influence of major depression on clinical psychometric assessment of senile dementia of the Alzheimer type. *American Journal of Psychiatry, 148,* 1164–1171.

Rubinstein, M., Yeager, C. A., Goodstein, C., & Lewis, D. O. (1993). Sexually assaultive male juveniles: A follow-up. *American Journal of Psychiatry, 150,* 262–265.

Rudd, M. D. (1989). The prevalence of suicidal ideation among college students. *Suicide and Life-Threatening Behavior, 19,* 173–183.

Rudestam, K. E. (1971). Stockholm and Los Angeles: A cross–cultural study of the communication of suicidal intent. *Journal of Consulting and Clinical Psychology, 36*, 82–90.

Ruff, G. A. (1985). Premature ejaculation: Past research progress, future directions. *Clinical Psychology Review, 5*, 627–639.

Rush, A. J., Beck, A. T., Kovacs, M., & Hollon, S. D. (1977). Comparative efficacy of cognitive therapy and imipramine in the treatment of depressed patients. *Cognitive Therapy and Research, 1*, 17–37.

Rush, B. (1812). *Medical inquiries and observations upon the diseases of the mind.* Philadelphia: Kimber & Richardson.

Russo, J., Vitaliano, P. P., Brewer, D. D., Katon, W., & Becker, J. (1995). Psychiatric disorders in spouse caregivers of care recipients with Alzheimer's disease and matched controls: A diathesis-stress model of psychopathology. *Journal of Abnormal Psychology, 104*, 197–204.

Rutter, M. (1967). Psychotic disorders in early childhood. *British Journal of Psychiatry* (Special Publ. No. 1), 133–158.

Rutter, M., Bartak, L., & Newman, S. (1971). Autism: A central disorder of cognition and language? In M. Rutter (Ed.), *Infantile autism: Concepts, characteristics and treatment.* London: Churchill–Livingstone.

Rutter, M., & Lockyer, L. (1967). A five to fifteen year follow-up study of infantile psychosis: 1. Description of sample. *British Journal of Psychiatry, 113*, 1169–1182.

Sacchetti, E., Vita, A., Guarneri, L., & Cornarccchia, M. (1991). The effectiveness of fluoxetine, clomipramine, nortriptyline and desipramine in major depressives with suicidal behavior: Preliminary findings. In G. Cassano & H. S. Akiskal (Eds.), *Serotonin-related psychiatric syndromes: Clinical and therapeutic links.* London: Royal Society of Medicine Services.

Sachdev, P., & Kruk, J. (1994). Clinical characterisitcs and predisposing factors in acute drug-induced akathisia. *Archives of General Psychiatry, 51*, 963–974.

Sackeim, H. A. (1985, June), The case for ECT. *Psychology Today*, pp. 37–40.

Sacks, H. (1940). Was this analysis a success? Comment. *Journal of Abnormal and Social Psychology, 35*, 11–16.

Saint George–Hyslop, P., Tanzi, R. E., Polinksy, R., Haines, J., Nee, L., Watkins, P. C., Myers, R., Feldman, R., Pollen, D., Drachman, D., Growdon, J., Bruni, A., Foncin, J., Salmon, D., Frommelt, P., Amaducci, L., Sorbi, S., Piacentini, S., Stewart, G., Hobbs, W., Conneally, P., & Gusella, J. F. (1987). The genetic defect causing familial Alzheimer's disease maps on chromosome 21. *Science, 235*, 885–890.

Sakheim, D. K., Barlow, D. H., Beck, J. G., & Abrahamson, D. J. (1984). The effects of an increased awareness of erectile cues on sexual arousal. *Behaviour Research and Therapy, 22*, 151–158.

Sammons, M. T., Sexton, J. L., & Meredith, J. M. (1996). Basic science training in psychopharmacology. *American Psychologist, 51*, 230–234.

Sanders, R. D., Keshavan, M. S., & Schooler, N. R. (1994). Neurological examination abnormalities in neuroleptic-naive patients with first-break schizophrenia: Preliminary results. *American Journal of Psychiatry, 151*, 1231–1233.

Sanderson, W. C., Di Nardo, P. A., Rapee, R. M., & Barlow, D. H. (1990). Syndrome comorbidity in patients diagnosed with a DSM-III-R anxiety disorder. *Journal of Abnormal Psychology, 99*, 308–312.

Sanderson, W. C., Wetzler, S., & Asnis, G. M. (1994). Alprazolam blockade of CO_2-provoked panic in patients with panic disorder. *American Journal of Psychiatry, 151*, 1220–1222.

Sanger, D. J., & Blackman, D. E. (1976). Effects of chlordiazepoxide, ripazepam, and d-amphetamine on conditioned acceleration timing behavior in rats. *Psychopharmacology, 48*, 209–215.

Sanger, D. J., & Blackman, D. E. (1981). Rate dependence and the effects of benzodiazepines. In T. Thompson, P. Dews, & W. A. McKim (Eds.), *Advances in behavioral pharmacology* (Vol. 3). New York: Academic Press.

Sarason, I. G. (1980). Introduction to the study of test anxiety. In I. G. Sarason (Ed.), *Test anxiety: Theory, research, and applications.* Hillsdale, NJ: Erlbaum.

Satel, S., & Edell, W. S. (1991). Cocaine–induced paranoia and psychosis proneness. *American Journal of Psychiatry, 148,* 1708–1711.

Satel, S., Southwick, S. M., & Gawin, F. H. (1991). Clinical features of cocaine-induced paranoia. *American Journal of Psychiatry, 148*, 495–498.

Satterfield, J. H., & Cantwell, D. P. (1975). Psychopharmacology in the prevention of antisocial and delinquent behavior. *International Journal of Mental Health, 4*, 277–335.

Schaar, K. (1974). Suicide rate high among women psychologists. *APA Monitor, 5*, 1, 10.

Schachter, S. (1964). The interaction of cognitive and physiological determinants of emotional state. In L. Berkowitz (Ed.), *Advances in experimental social psychology* (Vol. 1). New York: Academic Press.

Schachter, S., & Latané, B. (1964). Crime, cognition and the autonomic nervous system. In M. R. Jones (Ed.), *Nebraska symposium on motivation.* Lincoln: University of Nebraska Press.

Schachter, S., & Singer, J. E. (1962). Cognitive, psychological, and physiological determinants of emotional state. *Psychological Review, 69*, 379–399.

Schepank, H. G. (1981). Anorexia nervosa: Zwillings Kasuistik über ein seltens Krankheitsbild. In A. Heigl-Evers & H. G. Schepank (Eds.), *Ursprunge seelisch bedingter Krankheiten* (Vol. 2.). Göttingen, Germany: Verlag für Medizinische Psychologie/Vandenhoeck und Ruprecht.

Schiavi, R. C., Schreiner–Engel, P., Mandeli, J., Schanzer, H., & Cohen, E. (1990). Healthy aging and male sexual function. *American Journal of Psychiatry, 147*, 766–771.

Schiavi, R. C., Schreiner–Engel, P., White, B. S., & Mandeli, J. (1991). The relationship between pituitary-gonadal function and sexual behavior in healthy aging men. *Psychosomatic Medicine, 53*, 363–374.

Schildkraut, J. J., Hirshfeld, A., Murphy, J. M. (1994). Mind and mood in modern art: II. Depressive disorders, spirituality, and early deaths in the abstract expressionist artists of the New York School. *American Journal of Psychiatry, 151*, 482–488.

Schildkraut, J. J., Keeler, B. A., Grab, E. L., Kantrowich, J., & Hartmann, E. (1973). MHPG excretion and clinical classification in depressive disorders. *Lancet, 1*, 1251–1252.

Schildkraut, J. J., Orsulak, P. J., Schatzberg, A. F., Gudeman, J. E., Cole, J. O., Rohde, W. A., & La Brie, R. A. (1978). Toward a biochemical classification of depressive disorders: 1. Differences in urinary excretion of MHPG and other catecholamine metabolites in clinically defined subtypes of depression. *Archives of General Psychiatry, 35*, 1427–1433.

Schinka, J. A., Curtiss, G. & Mulloy, J. M. (1994). Personality variables and self-medication in substance abuse. *Journal of Personality Assessment, 63*, 413–422.

Schlaepfer, T. E., Harris, G. J., Tien, A. Y., Peng, L. W., Lee, S., Federman, E. B., Chase, G. A., Barta, P., & Pearlson, G. D. (1994). Decreased regional cortical gray matter in schizophrenia. *American Journal of Psychiatry, 151*, 842–848.

Schleifer, S. J., Keller, S. E., Meyerson, A. T., Raskin, M. J., Davis, K. L., & Stein, M. (1984). Lymphocyte function in major depressive disorder. *Archives of General Psychiatry, 41*, 484–486.

Schmauk, F. J. (1970). Punishment, arousal, and avoidance learning in sociopaths. *Journal of Abnormal Psychology, 76*, 325–335.

Schmidt, A. J. M., Wolfs-Takens, D. J., Oosterlaan, J. & van den Hout, M. A. (1994). Psychological mechanisms in hypochondriasis: Attention-induced physical symptoms without sensory stimulation. *Psychotherapy and Psychosomatics, 61*, 117–120.

Schmidt, G., & Schorsch, E. (1981). Psychosurgery of sexually deviant patients: Review and analysis of new empirical findings. *Archives of Sexual Behavior, 10*, 301–323.

Schmidt, P. J., & Rubinow, D. R. (1991). Menopause-related affective disorders: A justification for further study. *American Journal of Psychiatry, 148*, 844–852.

Schnarch, B. (1992). Neither man nor woman: Berdache—a case for non-dichotomous gender construction. *Anthropologica, 34*, 105–121.

Schofield, W. (1964). *Psychotherapy: The purchase of friendship.* Englewood Cliffs, NJ: Prentice Hall.

Schofield, W., & Balian, L. A. (1959). A comparative study of the personal histories of schizophrenic and nonpsychiatric patients. *Journal of Abnormal and Social Psychology, 59*, 216–225.

Schooler, C., & Spohn, H. E. (1982). Social dysfunction and treatment failure in schizophrenia. *Schizophrenia Bulletin, 8*, 85–98.

Schopler, E., Short, A., & Mesibov, G. (1989). Relation of behavioral treatment to "normal functioning": Comments on Lovaas. *Journal of Consulting and Clinical Psychology, 57,* 162–164.

Schotte, D. E., & Clum, G. (1982). Suicide ideation in a college population: A test of a model. *Journal of Consulting and Clinical Psychology, 50,* 690–696.

Schotte, D. E., & Clum, G. (1987). Problem-solving skills in suicidal psychiatric patients. *Journal of Consulting and Clinical Psychology, 55,* 49–54.

Schotte, D. E., Cools, J., & McNally, R. J. (1990). Film-induced negative affect triggers overeating in restrained eaters. *Journal of Abnormal Psychology, 99,* 317–320.

Schotte, D. E., Cools, J., & Payvar, S. (1990). Problem-solving deficits in suicidal patients: Trait vulnerability or state phenomenon? *Journal of Consulting and Clinical Psychology, 58,* 562–564.

Schou, M., Mellerup, E. T., & Rafaelsen, O. J. (1981). Mode of action of lithium. In H. M. Van Praag, M. H. Lader, O. J. Rafaelsen, & E. Sachar (Eds.), *Handbook of biological psychiatry: Vol. 4. Brain mechanisms and abnormal behavior.* New York: Dekker.

Schreiber, F. R. (1973). *Sybil.* New York: Warner Books.

Schreiner-Engel, P., Schiavi, R. C., White, D., & Ghizzani, A. (1989). Low sexual desire in women: The role of reproductive hormones. *Hormones and Behavior, 23,* 221–234.

Schroeder, S. R., Lewis, M. H., & Lipton, M. A. (1983). Interactions of pharmacotherapy and behavior therapy among children with learning and behavioral disorders. In K. Gadlow & I. Bialer (Eds.), *Advances in learning and behavioral disabilities* (Vol. 2). Greenwich, CT: JAI Press.

Schulsinger, F. A. (1972). Psychopathy, heredity and environment. *International Journal of Mental Health, 1,* 190–206.

Schulsinger, F. A., Kety, S. S., Rosenthal, D., & Wender, P. H. (1979). A family study of suicide. In M. Schou & E. Stromgren (Eds.), *Origin, prevention and treatment of affective disorders.* London: Academic Press.

Schulsinger, F. A., Mednick, S. A., Venables, P. H., Ramon, A. C., & Bell, B. (1975). Early detection and prevention of mental illness: The Mauritius project. *Neuropsychobiology, 1,* 166–179.

Schultz, E. (1974). Prevalence of behavioral symptoms in rural elementary school children. *Journal of Abnormal Child Psychology, 2,* 17–24.

Schultz, R., Braun, B. G., & Kluft, R. P. (1989). Multiple personality disorder: Phenomenology of selected variables in comparison to major depression. *Dissociation, 2,* 45–51.

Schwartz, G. E., Davidson, R. J., & Goldman, D. (1978). Patterning of cognitive and somatic processes in the self-regulation of anxiety. *Psychosomatic Medicine, 40,* 321–328.

Schwartz, S. M., Gramling, S. E. & Mancini, T. (1994). The influence of life stress, personality, and learning history on illness behavior. *Journal of Behavior Therapy and Experimental Psychiatry, 25,* 135–142.

Schwarz, J. R. (1981). *The hillside strangler: A murderer's mind.* New York: New American Library.

Scott, T., Bexton, W. H., & Doane, B. (1959). Cognitive effects of perceptual isolation. *Canadian Journal of Psychology, 13,* 200–209.

Scovern, A. W., & Kilmann, P. R. (1980). Status of electroconvulsive therapy: Review of the outcome literature. *Psychological Bulletin, 87,* 260–303.

Scoville, W. B., & Milner, B. R. (1957). Loss of recent memory after bilateral hippocampal lesions. *Journal of Neurology, Neurosurgery, and Psychiatry, 20,* 11–21.

Searles, J. S. (1988). The role of genetics in the pathogenesis of alcoholism. *Journal of Abnormal Psychology, 97,* 153–167.

Sears, R. R., Maccoby, E. E., & Levin, H. (1957). *Patterns of child rearing.* Evanston, IL: Row & Peterson.

Seeman, M. V., & Lang, M. (1990). The role of estrogens in schizophrenia gender differences. *Schizophrenia Bulletin, 16,* 185–194.

Segal, Z. V., Shaw, B. F., Vella, D. D., & Katz, R. (1992). Cognitive and life stress predictors of relapse in remitted unipolar depressed patients: A test of the congruency hypothesis. *Journal of Abnormal Psychology, 101,* 26–36.

Segrin, C., & Abramson, L. Y. (1994). Negative reactions to depressive behaviors: A communication theories analysis. *Journal of Abnormal Psychology, 103,* 655–668.

Seidman, L. J. (1983). Schizophrenia and brain dysfunction: An integration of recent neurodiagnostic findings. *Psychological Bulletin, 94,* 195–238.

Selemon, L. D., Rajkowska, G., & Goldman-Rakic, P. S. (1995). Abnormally high neuronal density in the schizophrenic cortex. *Archives of General Psychiatry, 52,* 805–818.

Seligman, M. E. P. (1968). Chronic fear produced by unpredictable shock. *Journal of Comparative and Physiological Psychology, 66,* 402–411.

Seligman, M. E. P. (1975). *Helplessness: On depression, development, and death.* New York: Freeman.

Seligman, M. E. P. (1994). *What you can change and what you can't.* New York: Knopf.

Selkoe, D. J., Bell, D. S., Podlisny, M. B., Price, D. L., & Cork, L. C. (1987). Conservation of brain amyloid proteins in aged mammals and humans with Alzheimer's disease. *Science, 235,* 873–877.

Serban, G. (1992). Multiple personality: An issue for forensic psychiatry. *American Journal of Psychotherapy, 46,* 269–280.

Shadish, W. R., Montgomery, L. M., Wilson, P., Wilson, M. R., Bright, I., & Okwumabua, T. (1993). Effects of family and marital psychotherapies: A meta-analysis. *Journal of Consulting and Clinical Psychology, 61,* 992–1002.

Shaffer, D. (1973). The association between enuresis and emotional disorder: A review of the literature. In I. Kolvin, R. MacKeith, & S. Meadow (Eds.), *Bladder control in enuresis.* London: Heinemann.

Shaffer, D. (1994). Attention-deficit hyperactivity disorder in adults. *American Journal of Psychiatry, 151,* 633–638.

Shakow, D. (1963). Psychological deficit in schizophrenia. *Behavioral Science, 8,* 275–305.

Shakow, D., & Jellinek, E. M. (1965). Composite index of the Kent-Rosanoff free association test. *Journal of Abnormal Psychology, 70,* 403–404.

Shapiro, A. (1980). A contribution to a history of the placebo effect. *Behavioral Science, 5,* 109–131.

Shapiro, A., & Morris, L. (1978). Placebo effects in medical and psychological therapies. In S. L. Garfield & A. E. Bergin (Eds.), *Handbook of psychotherapy and behavior change.* New York: Wiley.

Shapiro, D. A., & Shapiro, D. (1982). Meta-analysis of comparative therapy outcome studies: A replication and refinement. *Psychological Bulletin, 92,* 581–604.

Shapiro, D. H. (1980). *Meditation.* Chicago: Aldine.

Shaw, E. D., Stokes, P. E., Mann, J. J., & Manevitz, A. Z. (1987). Effects of lithium carbonate on the memory and motor speed of bipolar outpatients. *Journal of Abnormal Psychology, 96,* 64–69.

Shea, M. T., Widiger, T. A., & Klein, M. H. (1992). Comorbidity of personality disorders and depression: Implications for treatment. *Journal of Consulting and Clinical Psychology, 60,* 857–868.

Shear, M. K., Fyer, A. J., Ball, G., Josephson, S., Fitzpatrick, M., Gorman, J., Liebowitz, M., Klein, D. F., & Francis, A. J. (1991). Vulnerability to sodium lactate in panic disorder patients given cognitive-behavior therapy. *American Journal of Psychiatry, 148,* 795–797.

Shear, M. K., Pilkonis, P. A., Cloitre, M., & Leon, A. C. (1994). Cognitive behavioral treatment compared with nonprescriptive treatment of panic disorder. *Archives of General Psychiatry, 51,* 395–401.

Shearer, S. L. (1994). Phenomenology of self-injury among inpatient women with borderline personality disorder. *Journal of Nervous and Mental Disease, 182,* 524–526.

Shelton v. Tucker, 364 U.S. 479 (1960).

Sher, K. J., & Levenson, R. W. (1982). Risk for alcoholism and individual differences in the stress-response-dampening effect of alcohol. *Journal of Abnormal Psychology, 91,* 350–367.

Sher, K. J., & Trull, T. J. (1994). Personality and disinhibitory psychopathology: Alcoholism and antisocial personality disorder. *Journal of Abnormal Psychology, 103,* 92–102.

Sherrington, R., Bynjolfsson, J., Petursson, H., Potter, M., Dudleston, K., Barraclough, B., Wasmuth, J., Dobbs, M., & Gurling, H. (1988). Localization of a susceptibility locus for schizophrenia on chromosome 5. *Nature, 336,* 164–167.

Shiloh, A. (1968). Sanctuary or prison? Responses to life in a mental hospital. *Trans-Action, 6,* 28.

Shneidman, E. S. (1979). An overview: Personality, motivation, and behavior theories. In L. D. Hankoff & B. Einsidler (Eds.), *Suicide: Theory and clinical aspects.* Acton, MA: Publishing Sciences Group.

Shneidman, E. S., & Farberow, N. L. (Eds.). (1957). *Clues to suicide.* New York: McGraw-Hill.

Shoham-Salomon, V., & Hannah, M. T. (1991). Client-treatment interaction in the study of differential change processes. *Journal of Consulting and Clinical Psychology, 59,* 217–225.

Shorter, E. (1992). *From paralysis to fatigue: A history of psychosomatic medicine in the modern era.* New York: Free Press.

Siever, L. J., & Davis, K. L. (1985). Overview: Toward a dysregulation hypothesis of depression. *American Journal of Psychiatry, 142,* 1017–1031.

Siever, L. J., Silverman, J. M., Horvath, T. B., & Klar, H. M. (1990). Increased morbid risk for schizophrenia-related disorders in relatives of schizotypal personality disordered patients. *Archive of General Psychiatry, 47,* 634–640.

Silberstein, S. D. (1994). Tension-type headaches. *Headache, 34,* S2–S7.

Silbersweig, D. A., Stern, E., Frith, C., & Cahill, C. (1995). A functional neuroanatomy of hallucinations in schizophrenia. *Nature, 378,* 176–179.

Silver, J. M., Yudofsky, S. C., & Hurowitz, G. I. (1994). Psychopharmacology and electroconvulsive therapy. In R. E. Hales, S. C. Yudofsky, & J. A. Talbott (Eds.), *American Psychiatric Press textbook of psychiatry* (2d ed.). Washington, DC: American Psychiatric Press.

Silver, R. L., Wortman, C. B., & Klos, D. S. (1982). Cognitions, affect, and behavior following uncontrollable outcomes: A response to current human helplessness research. *Journal of Personality, 50,* 480–514.

Silverman, J. M., Li, G., Zaccario, M. L., Smith, C. J., Schmeidler, J., Mohs, R. C., & Davis, K. L. (1994). Patterns of risk in first-degree relatives of patients with Alzheimer's disease. *Archives of General Psychiatry, 51,* 577–586.

Silverstone, T., & Hunt, N. (1992). Symptoms and assessment of mania. In E. S. Paykel (Ed.), *Handbook of affective disorders* (2nd ed.) New York: Guilford Press.

Simon, G. E., Katon, W. J., & Sparks, P. J. (1990). Allergic to life: Psychological factors in environmental illness. *American Journal of Psychiatry 147,* 901–906.

Simons, A. D., Garfield, S. L., & Murphy, G. E. (1984). The processes of change in cognitive therapy and pharmacotherapy for depression: Changes in mood and cognition. *Archives of General Psychiatry, 41,* 45–51.

Sinyor, D., Schwartz, S. G., Peronnet, F., Brisson, G., & Seraganian, P. (1983). Aerobic fitness level and reactivity to psychosocial stress: Physiological, biochemical, and subjective measures. *Psychosomatic Medicine, 45,* 205–217.

Siris, S. G., Bermanzohn, P. C., Mason, S. E., & Shuwall, M. A. (1994). Maintenance imipramine therapy for secondary depression in schizophrenia. *Archives of General Psychiatry, 51,* 109–115.

Sirois, F. (1982). Perspectives in epidemic hysteria. In M. J. Colligan, J. W. Pennebaker, & L. R. Murphy (Eds.), *Mass psychogenic illness.* Hillsdale, NJ: Erlbaum.

Sizemore, C. C., & Pittillo, E. S. (1977). *I'm Eve.* Garden City, NY: Doubleday.

Skinner, B. F. (1953). *Science and human behavior.* New York: Macmillan.

Slater, E., & Glithero, E. (1965). A follow-up of patients diagnosed as suffering from hysteria. *Journal of Psychosomatic Research, 9,* 9–13.

Slater, J., & Depue, R. A. (1981). The contribution of environmental events and social support to serious suicide attempts in primary depressive disorder. *Journal of Abnormal Psychology, 90,* 275-285.

Slovenko, R. (1992). The right of the mentally ill to refuse treatment revisited. *Journal of Psychiatry and Law, 20,* 407–434.

Slovenko, R. (1995). Assessing competency to stand trial. *Psychiatric Annals, 25,* 392–397.

Small, G. W., & Nicholi, A. (1982). Mass hysteria among schoolchildren. *Archives of General Psychiatry, 39,* 721–724.

Small, G. W., Propper, M. W., Randolph, E. T., & Spencer, E. (1991). Mass hysteria among student performers: Social relationship as a symptom predictor. *American Journal of Psychiatry, 148,* 1200–1205.

Smalley, S. L., Asarnow, R. F., & Spence, A. (1988). Autism and genetics: A decade of research. *Archives of General Psychiatry, 45,* 953–961.

Smith v. United States, 148 F.2d 665 (1929).

Smith, A., & Weissman, M. M. (1992). Epidemiology. In E. S. Paykel (Ed.), *Handbook of affective disorders,* (2nd ed.). New York: Guilford Press.

Smith, B., & Sechrest, L. (1991). Treatment of aptitude × treatment interactions. *Journal of Consulting and Clinical Psychology, 59,* 233–244.

Smith, D. E., & Seymour, R. B. (1994). LSD: History and toxicity. *Psychiatric Annals, 24,* 145–147.

Smith, D. W., & Wilson, A. A. (1973). *The child with Down's syndrome (mongolism).* Philadelphia: Saunders.

Smith, G. R. (1994). The course of somatization and its effects on utilization of health care resources. Special series: Consultation-liaison outcome studies. *Psychomatics, 35,* 263–267.

Smith, G. R., Rost, K., & Kashner, T. M. (1995). A trial of the effect of a standardized psychiatric consultation on health outcomes and costs in somatizating patients. *Archives of General Psychiatry, 52,* 238–243.

Smith, G. T., Goldman, M. S., Greenbaum, P. E., & Christiansen, B. A. (1995). Expectancy for social facilitation from drinking: The divergent paths of high-expectancy and low-expectancy adolescents. *Journal of Abnormal Psychology, 104,* 32–40.

Smith, J. C. (1976). Psychotherapeutic effects of transcendental meditation with controls for expectation of relief and daily sitting. *Journal of Consulting and Clinical Psychology, 44,* 630–637.

Smith, T., McEachin, J. J., & Lovaas, O. I. (1993). Comments on replication and evaluation of outcome. *American Journal on Mental Retardation, 97,* 385–391.

Smith, T. W. (1992). Hostility and health: Current status of a psychosomatic hypothesis. *Health Psychology, 11,* 139–150.

Smith, T. W., & Leon, A. S. (1993). *Coronary heart disease: A behavioral perspective.* Champaign, IL: Research Press.

Snaith, P., Tarsh, M., & Reid, R. W. (1993). Sex reassignment surgery: A study of 141 Dutch transsexuals. *British Journal of Psychiatry, 162,* 681–685.

Snow, R. E. (1991). Aptitude-treatment interaction as a framework for research on individual differences in psychotherapy. *Journal of Consulting and Clinical Psychology, 59,* 205–216.

Snyder, M., & White, P. (1982). Moods and memories: Elation, depression, and the remembering of events of one's life. *Journal of Personality and Social Psychology, 50,* 149–167.

Snyder, S. H. (1976). The dopamine hypothesis of schizophrenia. *American Journal of Psychiatry, 133,* 197–202.

Sobin, C., Sackeim, H. A., Prudic, J., Devanand, D. P., Moody, B. J., & McElhiney, M. C. (1995). Predictors of retrograde amnesia following ECT. *American Journal of Psychiatry, 152,* 995–1001.

Solanto, M. V., & Conners, C. K. (1982). A dose-response and time-action analysis of autonomic and behavioral effects of methylphenidate in attention deficit disorder with hyperactivity. *Psychophysiology, 19,* 658–667.

Soloff, P. H. (1994). Is there any drug treatment of choice for the borderline patient? *Acta Psychiatrica Scandinavica, 89,* 50–55.

Soloff, P. H., George, A., Nathan, R. S., Schulz, P. M., & Perel, J. M. (1987). Behavioral dyscontrol in borderline patients treated with amitriptyline. *Psychopharmacological Bulletin, 23,* 177–181.

Soloff, P. H., Lis, J. A., Kelly, T., Cornelius, J., & Ulrich, R. (1994). Risk factors for suicidal behavior in borderline personality disorder. *American Journal of Psychiatry, 151,* 1316–1323.

Solomon, S. (1994). Migraine diagnosis and clinical symptomatology. *Headache, 34,* S8–S12.

Solomon, S., Holmes, D. S., & McCaul, K. D. (1980). Behavioral control over aversive events: Does control that requires effort reduce anxiety and physiological arousal? *Journal of Personality and Social Psychology, 39,* 729–736.

Sotsky, S. M., Glass, D. R., Shea, M. T., Pilkonis, P. A., Collins, J. F., Elkin, I., Watkins, J. T., Imber, S. D., Leber, W. R., Moyer, J., & Oliveri, M. E. (1991). Patient predictor of response to psychotherapy and pharmacotherapy: Findings in the NIMH Treatment of Depression Collaborative Research Program. *American Journal of Psychiatry, 148,* 997–1008.

Soubie, P. (1986). Reconciling the role of central serotonin neurons in human and animal behavior. *Behavioral and Brain Sciences, 9,* 319–364.

Southwick, S. M., Krystal, J. H., Morgan, C. A., Johnson, D., Nagy, L. M., Nicolaou, A. L., Heninger, G. R., & Charney, D. S. (1993). Abnormal noradrenergic function in posttraumatic stress disorder. *Archives of General Psychiatry, 50,* 266–274.

Southwick, S. M., Morgan, C. A., Darnell, A., Bremner, D., Nicolaou, A. L., Nagy, L. M., & Charney, D. S. (1995). Trauma-related symptoms in veterans of Operation Desert Storm: A 2-year follow-up. *American Journal of Psychiatry, 152,* 1150–1155.

Spanos, N. P. (1986). Hypnosis, nonvolitional responding, and multiple personality: A social psychological perspective. In B. A. Maher & W. Maher (Eds.), *Progress in experimental personality research* (Vol. 14). New York: Academic Press.

Spanos, N. P. (1994). Multiple identity enactments and multiple personality disorder: A sociocognitive perspective. *Psychological Bulletin, 116,* 143–165.

Spanos, N. P., Cross, P. A., Dickson, K., & Dubreuil, S. C. (1993). Close encounters: An examination of UFO experiences. *Journal of Abnormal Psychology, 102,* 624–632.

Spanos, N. P., Weekes, J. R., & Bertrand, L. D. (1985). Multiple personality: A social psychological perspective. *Journal of Abnormal Psychology, 94,* 362–367.

Spector, I. P., & Carey, M. P. (1990). Incidence and prevalence of the sexual dysfunctions: A critical review of the empirical literature. *Archives of Sexual Behavior, 19,* 389–408.

Speer, D. C. (1992). Clinically significant change: Jacobson and Truax (1991) revisited. *Journal of Consulting and Clinical Psychology, 60,* 402–408.

Spencer, T., Wilens, T., Biederman, J., Faraone, S. V., Ablon, S., & Lapey, K. (1995). A double-blind, crossover comparison of methylphenidate and placebo in adults with childhood-onset attention-deficit hyperactivity disorder. *Archives of General Psychiatry, 52,* 434–443.

Spiegel, D. A. (1994). Dissociative disorders. In R. E. Hales, S. C. Yudofsky, & J. A. Talbott (Eds.), *American Psychiatric Press handbook of psychiatry* (2nd ed.). Washington, DC: American Psychiatric Press.

Spiegel, D. A., Bruce, T. J., Gregg, S. F., & Nuzzarello, A. (1994). Does cognitive behavior therapy assist slow-taper alprazolam discontinuation in panic disorder? *American Journal of Psychiatry, 151,* 876–881.

Spielberger, C. D. (1971). Anxiety as an emotional state. In C. D. Spielberger (Ed.), *Anxiety: Current trends in theory and research.* New York: Academic Press.

Spoont, M. R. (1992). Modulatory role of serotonin in neural information processing: Implications for human psychopathology. *Psychological Bulletin, 112,* 330–350.

Squire, L. R. (1986). Mechanisms of memory. *Science, 232,* 1612–1619.

Stack, S. (1990). Media impacts on suicide. In D. Lester (Ed.), *Current concepts of suicide.* Philadelphia: Charles Press.

Stahl, S. M., & Lebedun, M. (1974). Mystery gas: An analysis of mass hysteria. *Journal of Health and Social Behavior, 15,* 44–50.

Stanley, M. A., & Stanley, B. (1989). Biochemical studies in suicide victims: Current findings and future implications. *Suicide and Life-Threatening Behavior, 19,* 30–42.

Stanley, M. A., & Turner, S. M. (1995). Current status of pharmacological and behavioral treatment of obsessive-compulsive disorder. *Behavior Therapy, 26,* 163–186.

Starcevic, V. (1992). Comorbidity models of panic disorder/agoraphobia and personality disturbance. *Journal of Personality Disorders, 6,* 213–225.

Starfield, B. (1972). Enuresis: Its pathogenesis and management. *Clinical Pediatrics, 11,* 343–350.

Steadman, H. J. (1973). Follow-up on Baxstrom patients returned to hospitals for the criminally insane. *American Journal of Psychiatry, 3,* 317–319.

Steadman, H. J., & Keveles, G. (1972). The community adjustment and criminal activity of Baxstrom patients, 1966–1970. *American Journal of Psychiatry, 129,* 304–310.

Steadman, H. J., & Keveles, G. (1978). The community adjustment and criminal activity of Baxstrom patients. *American Journal of Psychiatry, 135,* 1218–1220.

Steele, C. M., & Josephs, R. A. (1988). Drinking your troubles away: 2. An attention-allocation model of alcohol's effect on psychological stress. *Journal of Abnormal Psychology, 95,* 196–205.

Steele, C. M., Southwick, L., & Pagano, R. (1986). Drinking your troubles away: The role of activity in mediating alcohol's reduction of psychological stress. *Journal of Abnormal Psychology, 95,* 173–180.

Stehbens, J. A. (1970). Enuresis in schoolchildren. *Journal of School Psychology, 8,* 145–151.

Stein, D. J., Hollander, E., & Liebowitz, M. R. (1993). Neurobiology of impulsivity and the impulse control disorders. *Journal of Neuropsychiatry and Clinical Neurosciences, 5,* 9–17.

Stein, M. B., Millar, T. W., Larsen, D. K., & Kryger, M. H. (1995). Irregular breathing during sleep in patients with panic disorder. *American Journal of Psychiatry, 152,* 1168–1173.

Steinberg, M., Bancroft, J., & Buchanan, J. (1993). Multiple personality disorder in criminal law. *Bulletin of the American Academy of Psychiatry and the Law, 21,* 345–356.

Steiner, M., Steinberg, S., Stewart, D., Carter, D., Berger, C., Ried, R., Grover, D., & Steiner, D. (1995). Fluoxetine in the treatment of premenstrual dysphoria. *New England Journal of Medicine, 332,* 1529–1534.

Stengel, E. (1964). *Suicide and attempted suicide.* New York: Viking Penguin.

Stephens, J. H., & Kamp, M. (1962). On some aspects of hysteria: A clinical study. *Journal of Nervous and Mental Disease, 134,* 305–315.

Stephens, M. W., & Delys, P. (1973). External control expectancies among disadvantaged children at preschool age. *Child Development, 44,* 670–674.

Stern, D. B. (1977). Handedness and the lateral distribution of conversion reactions. *Journal of Nervous and Mental Disease, 164,* 122–128.

Stewart, M. W., Knight, R. G., Palmer, D. G., & Highton, J. (1994). Differential relationships between stress and disease activity for immunologically distinct subgroups of people with rheumatoid arthritis. *Journal of Abnormal Psychology, 103,* 251–258.

Stice, E., Neuberg-Schupak, E., Shaw, H. E., & Stein, R. I. (1994). Relation of media exposure to eating disorder symptomatology: An examination of mediating mechanisms. *Journal of Abnormal Psychology, 103,* 836–840.

Stiles, W. B., Shapiro, D. A., & Elliott, R. (1986). "Are all psychotherapies equivalent?" *American Psychologist, 41,* 165–180.

Stine, J. J. (1994). Psychosocial and psychodynamic issues affecting noncompliance with psychostimulant treatment. *Journal of Child and Adolescent Psychopharmacology, 4,* 75–86.

Stodolsky, S., & Lesser, G. (1967). Learning patterns in the disadvantaged. *Harvard Educational Review, 37,* 546–593.

Stolerman, I. P., & Jarvis, M. J. (1995). The scientific case that nicotine is addictive. *Psychopharmacology, 117,* 2–10.

Stoll, A. L., Tohen, M., & Baldessarini, R. J. (1992). Increasing frequency of the diagnosis of obsessive-compulsive disorder. *American Journal of Psychiatry, 149,* 638–640.

Stone, A. A. (1975). *Mental health and law: A system in transition.* Rockville, MD: Center for Studies of Crime and Delinquency, National Institute of Mental Health.

Stone, E. A. (1975). Stress and catecholamines. In A. J. Friedhoff (Ed.), *Catecholamines and behavior.* New York: Plenum.

Strassman, R. J. (1995). Hallucinogenic drugs in psychiatric research and treatment: Perspectives and prospects. *Journal of Nervous and Mental Disease, 183,* 127–138.

Strauss, J. S., & Carpenter, W. T. (1972). The prediction of outcome in schizophrenia: 1. Characteristics of outcome. *Archives of General Psychiatry, 27,* 739–746.

Strauss, J. S., Carpenter, W. T., & Bartko, J. J. (1974). The diagnosis and understanding of schizophrenia: 2. Speculations on the processes that underlie schizophrenic symptoms and signs. *Schizophrenia Bulletin, 11,* 61–76.

Strauss, J. S., Kokes, F. R., Ritzler, B. A., Harder, D. W., & Van Ord, A. (1978). Patterns of disorder in first-admission psychiatric patients. *Journal of Nervous and Mental Disease, 166,* 611–623.

Stravynski, A., Belisle, M., & Marcouiller, M. (1994). The treatment of avoidant personality disorder by social skills training in the clinic or in real-life setting. *Canadian Journal of Psychiatry, 39,* 377–383.

Streissguth, A. P., Herman, C. S., & Smith, D. W. (1978). Intelligence, behavior, and dysmorphogenesis in the fetal alcohol syndrome: A report on 20 patients. *Journal of Pediatrics, 92,* 363–368.

Strickland, B. R., Hale, W. D., & Anderson, L. K. (1975). Effect of induced mood states on activity and self-reported affect. *Journal of Consulting and Clinical Psychology, 43,* 587.

Strollo, P. J., & Rogers, R. M. (1996). Obstructive sleep apnea. *New England Journal of Medicine, 334,* 99–104.

Strom, A., Refsum, S. B., Eitinger, L., Gronvik, O., Lonnum, A., Engeset, A., & Rogan, B. (1962). Examination of Norwegian ex–concentration camp prisoners. *Journal of Neuropsychiatry, 4,* 43–62.

Sud, A., & Sharma, H. (1989). Test anxiety, intrusive thoughts, and attentional process. *Journal of Personality and Clinical Studies, 5,* 139–145.

Suddath, R. L., Christison, G. W., Torrey, E. F., Casanova, M. F., & Weinberger, D. R. (1990). Anatomical abnormalities in the brains of monozygotic twins discordant for schizophrenia. *New England Journal of Medicine, 322,* 789–794.

Suedfeld, P., & Landon, P. B. (1978). Approaches to treatment. In R. D. Hare & D. Schalling (Eds.), *Psychopathic behavior: Approaches to research.* New York: Wiley.

Sullivan, H. S. (1962). *Schizophrenia as a human process.* New York: Norton.

Sullivan, J. L., Baenziger, J. C., Wagner, D. L., Rauscher, F. P., Nurnberger, J. I., & Holmes, J. S. (1990). Platelet MAO in subtypes of alcoholism. *Biological Psychiatry, 27,* 911–922.

Suppes, T., Baldessarini, R. J., Faedda, G. L., & Tohen, M. (1991). Risk of recurrence following discontinuation of lithium treatment in bipolar disorder. *Archives of General Psychiatry, 48,* 1082–1088.

Suryani, L., & Jensen, G. (1992). Psychiatrist, traditional healer, and culture integrated in clinical practice in Bali. *Medical Anthropology, 13,* 301–314.

Susser, E. S., & Lin, S. P. (1992). Schizophrenia after prenatal exposure to the Dutch hunger winter of 1944–1945. *Archives of General Psychiatry, 49,* 983–989.

Susser, E., Fennig, S., Jandorf, L., Amador, X., & Bromet, E. (1995). Epidemiology, diagnosis, and course of brief psychoses. *American Journal of Psychiatry, 152,* 1743–1748.

Sutcliffe, J. P., & Jones, J. (1962). Personal identity, multiple personality and hypnosis. *International Journal of Clinical and Experimental Hypnosis, 39,* 281–300.

Sutker, P. B., & Allain, A. N. (1988). Issues in personality conceptualization of addictive behaviors. *Journal of Consulting and Clinical Psychology, 56,* 172–182.

Svartberg, M., & Stiles, T. C. (1991). Comparative effects of short-term psychodynamic psychotherapy: A meta-analysis. *Journal of Consulting and Clinical Psychology, 59,* 704–714.

Swann, W. B., Wenzlaff, R. M., Krull, D. S., & Pelham, B. W. (1992). Allure of negative feedback: Self-verification strivings among depressed persons. *Journal of Abnormal Psychology, 101,* 293–306.

Swayze, V. W. (1995). Frontal leukotomy and related psychosurgical procedures in the era before antipsychotics (1935–1954): A historical overview. *American Journal of Psychiatry, 152,* 505–515.

Swedo, S. E., Leonard, H. L., Kruesi, M. J. P., Rettew, D. C., Listwak, S. J., Berrettini, W., Sipetic, M., Hamburger, S., Gold, P. W., Potter, W. Z., & Rapoport, J. L. (1992). Cerebrospinal fluid neurochemistry in children and adolescents with obsessive-compulsive disorder. *Archives of General Psychiatry, 49,* 29–36.

Sweeney, P. D., & Gruber, K. L. (1984). Selective exposure: Voter information preferences and the Watergate affair. *Journal of Personality and Social Psychology, 46,* 1208–1221.

Sweet, R. A., Mulsant, B. H., Gupta, B., Fifai, A. H., Pasternak, R. E., McEachran, A., & Zubenko, G. S. (1995). Duration of neuroleptic treatment and prevalence of tardive dyskinesia in late life. *Archives of General Psychiatry, 52,* 478–486.

Swift, R. M., Whilihan, W., Kuznetsov, O., Buongiorno, G., & Husing, H. (1994). Naltrexone-induced alterations in human ethanol intoxication. *American Journal of Psychiatry, 151,* 1463–1467.

Szasz, T. S. (1961). *The myth of mental illness.* New York: HarperCollins.

Szasz, T. S. (1970). *The manufacture of madness.* New York: Macmillan.

Szatmari, P. (1992). The validity of autistic spectrum disorders: A literature review. *Journal of Autism and Developmental Disorders, 22,* 583–600.

Szymanski, S., Lieberman, J. A., Alvir, J. M., Mayerhoff, D., Loebel, A., Geisler, S., Chakos, M., Koreen, A., Jody, D., Kane, J., Woener, M., & Cooper, T. (1995). Gender differences in onset of illness, treatment response, course, and biologic indexes in first-episode schizophrenic patients. *American Journal of Psychiatry, 152,* 698–703.

Takei, N., Sham, P., O'Callaghan, E., Murray, G. K., Glover, G., & Murray, R. M. (1994). Prenatal exposure to influenza and the development of schizophrenia: Is the effect confined to females? *American Journal of Psychiatry, 151,* 117–119.

Tanzi, R. E., Gusella, J. F., Watkins, P. C., Burns, G. A., Saint George–Hyslop, P., Van Keuren, M. L., Patterson, D., Pagan, S., Kurnit, D. M., & Neve, R. L. (1987). Amyloid B protein gene: cDNA, mRNA distribution, and genetic linkage near the Alzheimer locus. *Science, 235,* 880–884.

Tarasoff v. *Regents of the University of California,* 551 P.2d 334 (1976).

Tate, J. C., Stanton, A. L, Green, S. B., Schmitz, J. M., et al. (1994). Experimental analysis of the role of expectancy in nicotine withdrawal. *Psychology of Addictive Behaviors, 8,* 169–178.

Taylor, A. (1993). Night terrors. *Journal of Contemporary Psychotherapy, 23,* 121–125.

Taylor, S. (1994). Klein's suffocation theory of panic. *Archives of General Psychiatry, 51,* 505–506.

Taylor, S. E., & Brown, J. D. (1988). Illusion and well-being: A social psychological perspective on mental health. *Psychological Bulletin, 103,* 193–210.

Taylor, S. E., & Brown, J. D. (1994). Positive illusions and well-being revisited: Separating fact from fiction. *Psychological Bulletin, 116,* 21–27.

Teasdale, J. D. (1988). Cognitive vulnerability to persistent depression. *Cognition and Emotion, 2,* 247–274.

Teasdale, J. D., & Bancroft, J. (1977). Manipulation of thought content as a determinant of mood and corrugator electromyographic activity in depressed patients. *Journal of Abnormal Psychology, 86,* 235–241.

Teasdale, J. D., & Fogarty, S. J. (1979). Differential effects of induced mood on retrieval of pleasant and unpleasant events from episodic memory. *Journal of Abnormal Psychology, 88,* 248–257.

Teicher, M. H., & Gold, C. A. (1989). Pharmacotherapy of patients with borderline personality disorder. *Hospital and Community Psychiatry, 40,* 887–889.

Teicher, M. H., Gold, C. A., & Cole, J. O. (1990). Emergence of intense suicidal preoccupation during fluoxetine treatment. *American Journal of Psychiatry, 147,* 207–210.

Teicher, M. H., Gold, C. A., Oren, D. A., Schwartz, P. J., Luetke, C., Brown, C., & Rosenthal, N. E. (1995). The phototherapy light visor: More to it than meets the eye. *American Journal of Psychiatry, 152,* 1197–1202.

Teitelbaum, P., & Steller, E. (1954). Recovery from the failure to eat produced by hypothalamic lesions. *Science, 120,* 894–895.

Telch, C. F., Agras, W. S., Rossiter, E. M., Wilfrey, D., & Kenardy, J. (1990). Group cognitive-behavioral treatment for the nonpurging bulimic: An initial evaluation. *Journal of Consulting and Clinical Psychology, 58,* 629–635.

Telch, M. J., Lucas, J. A., & Nelson, P. (1989). Nonclinical panic in college students: An investigation of prevalence and symptomology. *Journal of Abnormal Psychology, 98,* 300–306.

Tellegen, A., Lykken, D. T., Bouchard, T. J., Wilcox, K., Segal, N., & Rich, S. (1988). Personality similarity in twins reared apart and together. *Journal of Personality and Social Psychology, 54,* 1031–1039.

Tennant, C., & Babbington, P. (1978). The social causation of depression: A critique of the work of Brown and his colleagues. *Psychological Medicine, 8,* 565–575.

Tennen, H. (1982). A review of cognitive mediators in learned helplessness. *Journal of Personality, 50,* 526–541.

Tennen, H., Drum, P. E., Gillen, R., & Stanton, A. (1982). Learned helplessness and the detection of contingency: A direct test. *Journal of Personality, 50,* 426–442.

Tennen, H., Gillen, R., & Drum, P. E. (1982). The debilitating effect of exposure to noncontingent escape: A test of the learned helplessness model. *Journal of Personality, 50,* 409–425.

Teplin, L. A., Abram, K. M., & McClelland, G. M. (1994). Does psychiatric disorder predict violent crime among released jail detainees? *American Psychologist, 49,* 335–342.

Termal, M., Termal, J. S., Quitkin, F. M., McGrath, P. J., et al. (1989). Light therapy for seasonal affective disorder: A review of efficacy. *Neuropsychopharmacology, 2,* 1–22.

Terr, L. C. (1979). Children of Chowchilla. *Psychoanalytic Study of the Child, 34,* 547–623.

Terr, L. C. (1983). Chowchilla revisited: The effects of psychic trauma four years after a school-bus kidnapping. *American Journal of Psychiatry, 140,* 1543–1550.

Terr, L. C. (1994). *Unchained memories.* New York: HarperCollins.

Teunisse, R. J., Zitman, F. G., & Raes, D. C. (1994). Clinical evaluation of 14 patients with Charles Bonnet syndrome (isolated visual hallucinations). *Comprehensive Psychiatry, 35,* 70–75.

Thackwray, D. E., Smith, M. C., Bodfish, J. W., & Meyers, A. W. (1993). A comparison of behavioral and cognitive-behavioral interventions for bulimia nervosa. *Journal of Consulting and Clinical Psychology, 61,* 639–645.

Thapar, A., & McGuffin, P. (1993). Is personality disorder inherited? An overview of the evidence. *Journal of Psychopathology and Behavioral Assessment, 15,* 325–345.

Thau, K., Meszaros, K., & Simhandl, C. A. (1993). The use of high dosage lithium carbonate in the treatment of acute mania: A review. *Lithium, 4,* 149–159.

Thiel, A., Broocks, A., Ohlmeier, M., Jacoby, G. E., & Schubler, G. (1995). Obsessive-compulsive disorder among patients with anorexia nervosa and bulimia. *American Journal of Psychiatry, 152,* 72–75.

Thigpen, C. H., & Cleckley, H. M. (1954). A case of multiple personality. *Journal of Abnormal and Social Psychology, 49,* 139–151.

Thigpen, C. H., & Cleckley, H. M. (1957). *The three faces of Eve.* New York: Fawcett.

Thomasson, H. R., and Li, T. K. (1993). How alcohol and aldehyde dehydrogenase genes modify alcohol drinking, alcohol flushing, and the risk for alcoholism. *Alcohol Health and Research World, 17,* 167–172.

Thompson, J., Weiner, R. D., & Myers, C. P. (1994). Use of ECT in the United States in 1975, 1980, and 1986. *American Journal of Psychiatry, 151,* 1657–1661.

Timbrook, R. E., & Graham, J. R. (1994). Ethnic differences on the MMPI-2. *Psychological Assessment, 6,* 212–217.

Tohen, M., Waternaux, C. M., & Tsuang, M. T. (1990). Outcome in mania. *Archives of General Psychiatry, 47,* 1106–1111.

Tollefson, G. D., Rampey, A. H., Potvin, J. H., Jenike, M. A., Rush, A. J., Dominguez, R. A., Koran, L. M., Shear, M. K., Goodman, W., & Genuso, L. A. (1994). A multicenter investigation of fixed-dose fluoxetine in the treatment of obsessive-compulsive disorder. *Archives of General Psychiatry, 51,* 559–567.

Torgersen, S. (1979). The nature and origin of common phobic fears. *British Journal of Psychiatry, 119,* 343–351.

Torgersen, S. (1983). Genetic factors in anxiety disorders. *Archives of General Psychiatry, 40,* 1085–1089.

Torrey, E. F., Hersh, S. P., & McCabe, K. D. (1975). Early childhood psychosis and bleeding during pregnancy. *Journal of Autism and Childhood Schizophrenia, 5,* 287–297.

Torrey, E. F., Rawlings, R., & Waldman, I. N. (1988). Schizophrenic births and viral diseases in two states. *Schizophrenia Research, 1,* 73–77.

Toufexis, A. (1988, June 20). Why mothers kill their babies. *Time,* pp. 81–82.

Tough, S., Butt, J. C., & Sanders, G. L. (1994). Autoerotic asphyxial deaths: Analysis of nineteen fatalities in Alberta, 1978–1989. *Canadian Journal of Psychiatry, 39,* 157–160.

Towbin, A. (1978). Cerebral dysfunctions related to perinatal organic damage: Clinical-neuropathologic correlates. *Journal of Abnormal Psychology, 87,* 617–635.

Tredgold, A. F., & Soddy, K. (1970). *Tredgold's mental retardation.* Baltimore: Williams & Wilkins.

Troup, C. W., & Hodgson, N. B. (1971). Nocturnal functional bladder capacity in enuretic children. *Journal of Urology, 105,* 129–132.

Troutman, B. R., & Cutrona, C. E. (1990). Nonpsychotic postpartum depression among adolescent mothers. *Journal of Abnormal Psychology, 99,* 69–78.

True, W. R., Rice, J., Eisen, S. A., Heath, A. C., Goldberg, J., Lyons, M. J., & Nowak, J. (1993). A twin study of genetic and environmental contributions to liability for posttraumatic stress symptoms. *Archives of General Psychiatry, 50,* 257–264.

Tsai, L., & Stewart, M. (1983). Etiological implications of maternal age and birth order in infantile autism. *Journal of Autism and Developmental Disorders, 13,* 57–65.

Tsai, L., Stewart, M., Faust, M., & Shook, S. (1982). Social class distribution of fathers of children enrolled in the Iowa Autistic Program. *Journal of Autism and Developmental Disorders, 12,* 211–221.

Tu, G. C. and Israel, Y. (1995). Alcohol consumption by Orientals in North America is predicted largely by a single gene. *Behavior Genetics, 25,* 59–65.

Tuckman, J., Kleiner, R., & Lavell, M. (1959). Emotional content of suicide notes. *American Journal of Psychiatry, 116,* 59–63.

Turner, R. J., & Wagonfeld, M. O. (1967). Occupational mobility and schizophrenia: An assessment of the social causation and social selection hypothesis. *American Sociological Review, 32,* 104–113.

Turner, S. M., Beidel, D. C., & Stanley, M. A. (1992). Are obsessional thoughts and worry different cognitive phenomena? *Clinical Psychology Review, 12,* 257–270.

Tye, N. C., Iversen, S. D., & Green, A. R. (1979). The effects of benzodiazepines and serotonergic manipulations on punished responding. *Neuropharmacology, 18,* 689–654.

Tyrer, P., Lee, I., & Alexander, J. (1980). Awareness of cardiac function in anxious, phobic, and hypochondriacal patients. *Psychological Medicine, 10,* 171–174.

Ullman, L. P., & Krasner, L. (1969). *A psychological approach to abnormal behavior.* Englewood Cliffs, NJ: Prentice Hall.

Unden, A., Orth-Gomer, K., & Elofsson, S. (1991). Cardiovascular effects of social support in the workplace: Twenty-four-hour ECG monitoring of men and women. *Psychosomatic Medicine, 53,* 50–60.

United States v. *Brawner,* 471 F.2d 969 (D.C. 1972).

Vaillant, G. E. (1963). Twins discordant for early infantile autism. *Archives of General Psychiatry, 9,* 163–167.

Vaillant, G. E. (1994). Ego mechanisms of defense and personality psychopathology. *Journal of Abnormal Psychology, 103,* 44–50.

Valenstein, E. S. (Ed.). (1980). *The psychosurgery debate.* New York: Freeman.

van Blakom, A. J., van Oppen, P., Vermeulen A. W., van Dyck, R., Nauta, M. C., & Vorst, H. C. (1994). A meta-analysis on the treatment of obsessive compulsive disorder: A comparison of antidepressants, behavior, and cognitive therapy. *Clinical Psychology Review, 14,* 359–381.

Vandereycken, W., & Lowenkopf, E. L. (1990). Anorexia nervosa in 19th-century America. *Journal of Nervous and Mental Disease, 178,* 531–535.

van Oppen, P., & Arntz, A. (1994). Cognitive therapy for obsessive-compulsive disorder. *Behaviour Research and Therapy, 32,* 79–87.

Van Praag, H. M. (1986). Affective disorders and aggression disorders: Evidence for a common biological mechanism. *Suicide and Life-Threatening Behavior, 16,* 103–132.

Van Putten, T. (1975). Why do patients with manic-depressive illness stop their lithium? *Comprehensive Psychiatry, 16,* 179–183.

Van Putten, T., & May, P. (1976). Milieu treatment for schizophrenics. In L. West & D. Flinn (Eds.), *Treatment of schizophrenia.* Philadelphia: Grune & Stratton.

Vaughn, C. E., & Leff, J. P. (1976). The influence of family and social factors on the course of psychiatric illness: A comparison of schizophrenic and depressed neurotic patients. *British Journal of Psychiatry, 129,* 125–137.

Vaughn, C. E., Snyder, K. S., Jones, S., Freeman, W. B., & Falloon, R. H. (1984). Family factors in schizophrenic relapse: Replication in California of British research on expressed emotion. *Archives of General Psychiatry, 41,* 1169–1177.

Veith, I. (1965). *Hysteria: The history of a disease.* Chicago: University of Chicago Press.

Venables, P. H. (1964). Input dysfunction in schizophrenia. In B. A. Maher (Ed.), *Progress in experimental personality research* (Vol. 1). New York: Academic Press.

Virkkunen, M., De Jong, J., Barthko, J., Goodwin, F. K., & Linnoila, M. (1989). Relationship of psychobiological variables to recidivism in violent offenders and impulsive fire setters: A follow-up study. *Archives of General Psychiatry, 46,* 600–603.

Virkkunen, M., Rawling, R., Tokola, R., Poland, R. E., Guidotti, A., Nemeroff, C., Bissette, G., Kalogeras, K., Karnen, S., & Linnoila, M. (1994). CSF biochemistries, glucose metabolism, and diurnal activity rhythms in alcoholics, violent offenders, fire setters, and healthy volunteers. *Archives of General Psychiatry, 51,* 20–27.

Visser, S., & Bouman, T. K. (1992). Cognitive-behavioural approaches in the treatment of hypochondriasis: Six single case cross-over studies. *Behaviour Research and Therapy, 30,* 301–306.

Vitousek, K., & Manke, F. (1994). Personality variables and disorders in anorexia nervosa and bulimina nervosa. *Journal of Abnormal Psychology, 103,* 137–147.

Volavka, J., Cooper, T., Czobor, P., Bitter, I., Meisner, M., Laska, E., Gastanaga, P., Krakowski, M., Chow, J., Growner, M., & Douyon, R. (1992). Haloperidol blood levels and clinical effects. *Archives of General Psychiatry, 49,* 354–361.

Volavka, J., Czobor, P., Goodwin, D. W., Gabrielli, W. F., Penick, E., Mednick, S. A., Jensen, P., Knop, J., & Schulsinger, F. (1996). The electroencephalogram after alcohol administration in high-risk men and the development of alcohol use disorders 10 years later. *Archives of General Psychiatry, 53,* 258–263.

Volkow, N. J., Ding, Y., Fowler, J. S., Wang, G., Logan, J., Gatley, J. S., Dewey, S., Ashby, C., Liebermann, J., Hitzemann, R., & Wolf, A. P. (1995). Is methylphenidate like cocaine? *Archives of General Psychiatry, 52,* 456–463.

Volpicelli, J. R., Alterman, A. I., Hayashida, M., & O'Brien, C. P. (1992). Naltrexone in the treatment of alcohol dependence. *Archives of General Psychiatry, 49,* 876–880.

Vonnegut, M. (1975). *The Eden express.* New York: Praeger.

Waddington, J. L., Weller, M. P. I., Crow, T. J., & Hirsch, S. R. (1992). Schizophrenia, genetic retrenchment, and epidemiologic renaissance. *Archives of General Psychiatry, 49,* 990–994.

Wagner, E. E., & Heise, M. R. (1974). A comparison of Rorschach records of three multiple personalities. *Journal of Personality Assessment, 38,* 308–331.

Waldinger, M. D., Hengeveld, M. W., & Zwinderman, A. H. (1994). Paroxetine treatment of premature ejaculation: A double-blind, placebo-controlled study. *American Journal of Psychiatry, 151,* 1377–1379.

Wall, T. L., Thomasson, H. R., Schuckit, M. A., & Ehlers, C. L. (1992). Subjective feelings of alcohol intoxication in Asians with genetic variations of ALDH 2 alleles. *Alcoholism Clinical and Experimental Research, 16,* 991–995.

Walsh, B. T., Hadigan, C. M., Devlin, M. J., Gladis, M., & Roose, S. P. (1991). Long-term outcome of antidepressant treatment for bulimia nervosa. *American Journal of Psychiatry, 148,* 1206–1212.

Walsh, B. T., Stewart, J. W., Roose, S. P., Gladis, M., & Glassman, A. H. (1984). Treatment of bulimia with phenelzine. *Archives of General Psychiatry, 41,* 1105–1109.

Walsh, B. T., Stewart, J. W., Wright, L., Harrison, W., Roose, S. P., & Glassman, A. H. (1982). Treatment of bulimia with monoamine oxidase inhibitors. *American Journal of Psychiatry, 139,* 1629–1630.

Walters, E. E., & Kendler, K. S. (1995). Anorexia nervosa and anorexia-like syndromes in a population-based female twin sample. *American Jounal of Psychiatry, 152,* 64–71.

Ward, C. H., Beck, A. T., Mendelson, M., Mock, J. E., & Erbaugh, J. K. (1962). The psychiatric nomenclature: Reasons for diagnostic disagreement. *Archives of General Psychiatry, 7,* 198–205.

Ward, J., Mattick, R. P., & Hall, W. (1994). The effectiveness of methadone maintenance treatment: An overview. *Drug and Alcohol Review, 13,* 327–336.

Warren, L. W., & McEachren, L. (1983). Psychosocial correlates of depressive symptomatology in adult women. *Journal of Abnormal Psychology, 92,* 151–160.

Watkins, J. G. (1984). The Bianchi (L.A. Hillside Strangler) case: Sociopath or multiple personality? *International Journal of Clinical and Experimental Hypnosis, 32,* 67–101.

Watkins, J. T., Leber, W. R., Imber, S. D., Collins, J. F., Elkin, I., Pikonis, P. A., Sotsky, S. M., Shea, M. T., & Glass, D. R. (1993). Temporal course of change of depression. *Journal of Consulting and Clinical Psychology, 61,* 858–864.

Watson, C. G., Tilleskjor, C., Kucala, T., & Jacobs, L. (1984). The birth seasonality effect in nonschizophrenic psychiatric patients. *Journal of Clinical Psychology, 40,* 884–888.

Watson, J. B., & Rayner, R. (1920). Conditioned emotional reactions. *Journal of Experimental Psychology, 3,* 1–14.

Watt, N. (1978). Patterns of childhood social development in adult schizophrenics. *Archives of General Psychiatry, 35,* 160–165.

Watt, N., Stolorow, R., Lubensky, A., & McClelland, D. (1970). School adjustment and behavior of children hospitalized as schizophrenic as adults. *American Journal of Orthopsychiatry, 40,* 637–657.

Webb, C. T., & Levinson, D. F. (1993). Schizotypal and paranoid personality disorder in the relatives of patients with schizophrenia and affective disorders: A review. *Schizophrenia Research, 11,* 81–92.

Wedell, K., Welton, J., Evans, B., & Goacher, A. (1987). Policy and provision under the 1981 act. *British Journal of Special Education, 14,* 50–53.

Wegner, J. T., Catalano, F., Gibralter, J., & Kane, J. M. (1985). Schizophrenics with tardive dyskinesia. *Archives of General Psychiatry, 42,* 860–865.

Wehr, T. A., & Rosenthal, N. E. (1989). Seasonality and affective illness. *American Journal of Psychiatry, 146,* 829–839.

Wehr, T. A., Sack, D. A., Rosenthal, N. E., & Cowdry, R. W. (1988). Rapid cycling affective disorder: Contribution factors and treatment responses in 51 patients. *American Journal of Psychiatry, 145,* 179–184.

Weinberg, M. S., Williams, C. J., & Calham, C. (1994). Homosexual foot fetishism. *Archives of Sexual Behavior, 23,* 611–620.

Weinberger, D. R. (1987). Implications of normal brain development for the pathogenesis of schizophrenia. *Archives of General Psychiatry, 44,* 660–669.

Weinberger, J. (1993). Common factors in psychotherapy. In J. Gold & G. Stricker (Eds.), *Handbook of psychotherapy integration.* New York: Plenum.

Weinberger, J. (1995). Common factors aren't so common: The common factors dilemma. *Clinical Psychology: Science and Practice, 2,* 45–69.

Weiner, H. (1991). From simplicity to complexity (1950–1990): The case of peptic ulceration: 1. Human studies. *Psychosomatic Medicine, 53,* 467–490.

Weiner, H., Thaler, M., Reiser, M. F., & Mirsky, I. A. (1957). Etiology of duodenal ulcer: 1. Relation of specific psychological characteristics to rate of gastric secretion. *Psychosomatic Medicine, 17,* 1–10.

Weiner, R. (1982). Another look at an old controversy. *Contemporary Psychiatry, 1,* 61–62.

Weiss, B., & Laties, V. G. (1962). Enhancement of human performance by caffeine and the amphetamines. *Pharmacological Review, 14,* 1–36.

Weiss, J. M. (1968). Effects of coping responses on stress. *Journal of Comparative and Physiological Psychology, 24,* 409–414.

Weiss, J. M. (1970). Somatic effects of predictable and unpredictable shock. *Psychosomatic Medicine, 32,* 397–408.

Weiss, J. M. (1973). The natural history of antisocial attitudes: What happens to psychopaths? *Journal of Geriatric Psychiatry, 6,* 236–242.

Weiss, J. M., Glazer, H. I., & Pohoresky, L. A. (1976). Coping behavior and neurochemical change in rats: An alternative explanation for the original "learned helplessness" experiments. In G. Serban & A. King (Eds.), *Animal models in human psychobiology.* New York: Plenum.

Weisse, C. S. (1992). Depression and immunocompetence: A review of the literature. *Psychological Bulletin, 111,* 475–489.

Weissman, M. M., (1974). The epidemiology of suicide attempts, 1969–1971. *Archives of General Psychiatry, 30,* 737–746.

Weissman, M. M. (1979). The psychological treatment of depression: Research evidence for the efficacy of psychotherapy alone, in comparison and in combination with pharmacotherapy. *Archives of General Psychiatry, 36,* 1261–1269.

Weissman, M. M., Bruce, M. L., Leaf, P. J., Florio, L. P. & Holzer, C. (1991). Affective disorders. In L. Robins and K. Regier (Eds.), *The Epidemiologic Catchment Area Study.*

Weissman, M. M., & Klerman, G. L. (1992). Interpersonal psychotherapy. In E. S. Paykel (Ed.), *Handbook of affective disorders.* (2nd ed.). New York: Guilford Press.

Weissman, M. M., & Markowitz, J. C. (1994). Interpersonal psychotherapy: Current status. *Archives of General Psychiatry, 51,* 599–606.

Weissman, M. M., & Myers, J. K. (1978). Affective disorders in a United States urban community: The use of research diagnostic criteria in an epidemiologic survey. *Archives of General Psychiatry, 35,* 1304–1311.

Weissman, M. M., Prusoff, B. A., Di Mascio, A., Neu, C., Goklaney, M., & Klerman, G. L. (1979). The efficacy of drugs and psychotherapy in the treatment of acute depressive episodes. *American Journal of Psychiatry, 136,* 555–558.

Weisz, J. R., Weiss, B., Han, S. S., Granger, D. A., & Morton, T. (1995). Effects of psychotherapy with children and adolescents revisited: A meta-analysis of treatment outcome studies. *Psychological Bulletin, 117,* 450–468.

Wekstein, L. (1979). *Handbook of suicidology: Principles, problems, and practice.* New York: Brunner/Mazel.

Welch, S. L., & Fairburn, C. G. (1994). Sexual abuse and bulimia nervosa: Three integrated case control comparisons. *American Journal of Psychiatry, 151,* 402–407.

Welsch v. Litkins, 373 F. Supp. 487 (D. Minn. 1974).

Weltzin, T. E., Fernstrom, M. H., Fernstrom, J. D., Neuberger, S. K., & Kaye, W. H. (1995). Acute tryptophan depletion and increased food intake and irritability in bulimia nervosa. *American Journal of Psychiatry, 152,* 1668–1671.

Wender, P. H. (1971). *Minimal brain dysfunction in children.* New York: Wiley-Interscience.

Wender, P. H., Rosenthal, D., Kety, S. S., Schulsinger, F. A., & Weiner, J. (1974). Cross-fostering: A research strategy for clarifying the role of genetic and experiential factors in the etiology of schizophrenia. *Archives of General Psychiatry, 30,* 121–128.

Werner, M. J., Walker, L. S., & Greene, J. W. (1995). Relationship of alcohol expectancies to problem drinking among college women. *Journal of Adolescent Health, 16,* 191–199.

Werry, J. S. (1967). Enuresis nocturna. *Medical Times, 95,* 985–991.

Werry, J. S., & Quay, H. C. (1971). The prevalence of behavior symptoms in younger elementary school children. *American Journal of Orthopsychiatry, 41,* 136–143.

Wesson, D. R., & Smith, D. E. (1977). *Barbiturates: Their use, misuse, and abuse.* New York: Human Science Press.

West, M. A. (1987). *The psychology of meditation.* Oxford: Oxford University Press.

West, S. A., McElroy, S. L., Strakowski, S. M., Keck, P. E., & McConville, B. J. (1995). Attention-deficit hyperactivity disorder in adolescent mania. *American Journal of Psychiatry, 152,* 271–273.

Westermeyer, J. F., Harrow, M., & Marengo, J. T. (1991). Risk of suicide in schizophrenia and other psychotic and nonpsychotic disorders. *Journal of Nervous and Mental Disease, 179,* 259–266.

Wetter, M. W., Baer, R. A., Berry, D. T., & Reynolds, S. K. (1994). The effect of symptom information on faking on the MMPI-2. *Assessment, 1,* 199–207.

Wettstein, R. M., Mulvey, E. P., & Rogers, R. (1991). A prospective comparison of four insanity defense standards. *American Journal of Psychiatry, 148,* 21–27.

Wetzel, R. (1977). Factor structure of Beck's Suicide Intent Scales. *Psychological Reports, 40,* 295–302.

Wheeler, J., & Carlson, C. L. (1994). The social functioning of children with ADD with hyperactivity and ADD without hyperactivity: A comparison of their peer relations and social deficits. *Journal of Emotional and Behavioral Disorders, 2,* 2–12.

Wheeler, L. (1966). Toward a theory of behavioral contagion. *Psychological Review, 73,* 179–192.

Whiffen, V. E. (1992). Is postpartum depression a distinct diagnosis? *Clinical Psychology Review, 12,* 485–508.

Whiffen, V. E., & Gotlib, I. H. (1993). Comparison of postpartum and nonpostpartum depression: Clinical presentation, psychiatric history, and psychosocial functioning. *Journal of Consulting and Clinical Psychology, 61,* 485–494.

Whisman, M. A. (1993). Mediators and moderators of change in cognitive therapy of depression. *Psychological Bulletin, 114,* 248–265.

White, G. L., Fishbein, S., & Rutstein, J. (1981). Passionate love: The misattribution of arousal. *Journal of Personality and Social Psychology, 41,* 56–62.

White, J. L., Moffitt, T. E., Caspi, A., Bartusch, D. J., Needles, D. J., & Loeber-Stouthamer, M. (1994). Measuring impulsivity and examining its relationship to delinquency. *Journal of Abnormal Psychology, 103,* 192–205.

Whitlock, F. A. (1967). The aetiology of hysteria. *Acta Psychiatrica Scandinavica, 43,* 144–162.

Widiger, T. A. (1992). Generalized social phobia versus avoidant personality disorder: A commentary on three studies. *Journal of Abnormal Psychology, 101,* 340–343.

Widiger, T. A., Frances, A. J., Harris, M., Jacobsberg, L. B., Fyer, M. R., & Manning, D. (1991). Comorbidity among Axis II disorders. In J. M. Oldham (Ed.), *Personality disorders: New perspectives on diagnostic validity.* Washington, DC: American Psychiatric Press.

Wilcox, J. A. (1986). Perinatal distress and infectious disease as risk factors for catatonia. *Psychopathology, 19,* 196–199.

Wilcox, J. A., & Nasrallah, H. A. (1987a). Perinatal distress and prognosis of psychotic illness. *Neuropsychobiology, 17,* 173–175.

Wilcox, J. A., & Nasrallah, H. A. (1987b). Perinatal insult as a risk factor in paranoid and nonparanoid schizophrenia. *Psychopathology, 20,* 285–287.

Wilhelmsen, I., Tanger-Haug, T., Ursin, H., & Berstad, A. (1994). Effect of short-term cognitive psychotherapy on recurrence of duodenal ulcer: A prospective randomized trial. *Psychosomatic Medicine, 56,* 440–448.

Willerman, L. (1973). Activity level and hyperactivity in twins. *Child Development, 44,* 288–293.

Williams, C., & House, A. (1994). Reducing the costs of chronic somatisation. *Irish Journal of Psychological Medicine, 11,* 79–82.

Williams, L. M. (1992). Adult memories of child sexual abuse: Preliminary findings from a longitudinal study. *American Journal for Prevention of Child Abuse Advisor, 5,* 19–20.

Williams, L. M. (1994). Recall of childhood trauma: A prospective study of women's memories of child sexual abuse. *Journal of Consulting and Clinical Psychology, 62,* 1167–1176.

Williams, R. B., Haney, T. L., Lee, K. L., Kong, Y., Blumenthal, J. A., & Whalen, R. E. (1980). Type A behavior, hostility, and coronary atherosclerosis. *Psychosomatic Medicine, 42,* 539–549.

Williams, S. L., & Rappoport, A. (1983). Cognitive treatment in the natural environment for agoraphobics. *Behavior Therapy, 14,* 299–313.

Wilson, A. A. (1903). A case of double consciousness. *Journal of Mental Service, 49,* 640–658.

Wilson, G. T. (1987). Cognitive studies in alcoholism. *Journal of Consulting and Clinical Psychology, 55,* 325–331.

Wilson, G. T., & Abrams, D. (1977). Effects of alcohol on social anxiety and physiological arousal: Cognitive versus pharmacological processes. *Cognitive Therapy and Research, 1,* 195–210.

Wilson, G. T., & Fairburn, C. G. (1993). Cognitive treatments for eating disorders. *Journal of Consulting and Clinical Psychology, 61,* 261–269.

Wilson, G. T., & Lawson, D. M. (1976). The effects of alcohol on sexual arousal in women. *Journal of Abnormal Psychology, 85,* 489–497.

Winchel, R. M., & Stanley, M. A. (1991). Self-injurious behavior: A review of the behavior and biology of self-mutilation. *American Journal of Psychiatry, 148,* 306–317.

Wincze, J., Bansal, S., & Malamud, M. (1986). Effects of MPA on subjective arousal, arousal to erotic stimulation, and nocturnal penile tumescence in male sex offenders. *Archives of Sexual Behavior, 15,* 293–305.

Winefield, H. R. (1987). Psychotherapy and social support: Parallels and differences in the helping process. *Clinical Psychology Review, 7,* 631–644.

Wing, J. K. (1975). Impairment in schizophrenia: A rational basis for social treatment. In R. Wirt, G. Winokur, & M. Roff (Eds.), *Life history research in psychopathology.* Minneapolis: University of Minnesota Press.

Winick, B. J. (1991). Voluntary hospitalization after *Zinermon* v. *Burch. Psychiatric Annals, 21,* 584–589.

Winokur, A., Clayton, P., & Reich, T. (1969). *Manic depressive illness.* St. Louis, MO: Mosby.

Winokur, G., Morrison, J., Clancy, J., & Crowe, R. R. (1972). The Iowa 500: 2. A blind family history comparison of mania, depression, and schizophrenia. *Archives of General Psychiatry, 27,* 462–464.

Winters v. *Miller,* 446 F.2d 65, 71 (2d Cir. 1971).

Wirz-Justice, A., Graw, P., Krauchi, K., Gisin, B., Jochum, A., Arendt, J., Fisch, H., Buddeberg, C., & Poldinger, W. (1993). Light therapy in seasonal affective disorder is independent of time of day or circadian phase. *Archives of General Psychiatry, 50,* 929–936.

Wise, M. G., & Gray, K. F. (1994). Delirium, dementia, and amnesitic disorders. In R. E. Hales, S. C. Yudofsky, & J. A. Talbott (Eds.), *American Psychiatric Press textbook of psychiatry* (2nd ed.). Washington, DC: American Psychiatric Press.

Wittchen, H., Zhoa, S., Kessler, R. C., & Eaton, W. W. (1994). DSM-III-R generalized anxiety disorder in the National Comorbidity Survey. *Archives of General Psychiatry, 51,* 355–364.

Wittenborn, J. R. (1951). Symptom patterns in a group of mental hospital patients. *Journal of Consulting Psychology, 15,* 290–302.

Wittenborn, J. R. (1962). The dimensions of psychosis. *Journal of Nervous and Mental Disease, 134,* 117–128.

Wolf, M., Risley, T., Johnston, M., Harris, F., & Allen, E. (1967). Application of operant conditioning procedures to the behaviour problems of an autistic child: A follow-up and extension. *Behaviour Research and Therapy, 5,* 103–112.

Wolf, T. M., Elston, R. C., & Kissling, G. E. (1989). Relationship of hassles, uplifts, and life events to psychological well-being of freshman medical students. *Behavioral Medicine, 15,* 37–45.

Wolkin, A., Sanfilipo, M., Wolf, A. P., Angrist, B., Brodie, J. D., & Rotrosen, J. (1992). Negative symptoms and hypofrontality in chronic schizophrenia. *Archives of General Psychiatry, 49,* 959–965.

Wolpe, J. (1958). *Psychotherapy by reciprocal inhibition.* Stanford, CA: Stanford University Press.

Wolpert, E. A., Goldberg, J. F., & Harrow, M. (1990). Rapid cycling in unipolar and bipolar affective disorders. *American Journal of Psychiatry, 147,* 725–728.

Wolraich, M., Drummond, T., Salomon, M., O'Brien, M., & Sivage, C. (1978). Effects of methylphenidate alone and in combination with behavioral modification procedures on the behavior and academic performance of hyperactive children. *Journal of Abnormal Child Psychology, 6,* 149–161.

Wong, D. F., Wagner, H. N., Dannals, R. F., Links, J. M., Frost, J. J., Ravert, H. T., Wilson, A. A., Rosenbaum, A. E., Gjedde, A., Douglass, K. H., Petronis, J. D., Folstein, M. F., Toung, J. K. T., Burns, H. D., & Kuhar, M. J. (1984). Effects of age on dopamine and serotonin receptors measured by positron tomography in the living human brain. *Science, 226,* 1393–1396.

Wong, D. F., Wagner, H. N., Tune, L. E., Dannals, R. F., Pearlson, G. D., Links, J. M., Tamminga, C. A., Broussolle, E. P., Ravert, H. T., Wilson A. A., Toung, J. K. T., Malat, J., Williams, J. A., O'Tuma, L. A., Snyder, S. H., Kuhar, M. J., & Gjedde, A. (1986). Positron emission tomography reveals elevated D2 dopamine receptors in drug-naive schizophrenics. *Science, 234,* 1558–1563.

Woodruff, R. A., Robins, L. N., Winokur, G., & Reich, T. (1971). Manic depressive illness and social achievement. *Acta Psychiatrica Scandinavica, 47,* 237–249.

Wooten, V. (1992). Sleep disorders in geriatric patients. *Clinical Geriatric Medicine, 8,* 427–439.

Wright, J. H., & Beck, A. T. (1994). Cognitive therapy. In R. E. Hales, S. C. Yudofsky, & J. A. Talbott (Eds.), *American Psychiatric Press textbook of psychiatry,* (2nd ed.). Washington, DC: American Psychiatric Press.

Wright, J. M. von, Pekanmaki, L., & Malin, S. (1971). Effects of conflict and stress on alcohol intake in rats. *Journal of Studies on Alcohol, 32,* 420–441.

Wright, P., Takei, N., Rifkin, L., & Murray, R. M. (1995). Maternal influenza, obstetric complications, and schizophrenia. *American Journal of Psychiatry, 152,* 1714–1720.

Wyatt v. Stickney, 325 F. Supp. 781 (M.D. Ala. 1971); 344 F. Supp. 343 (M.D. Ala. 1972).

Wynne, L. C., Tookey, M. L., & Doane, J. (1979). Family studies. In L. Bellak (Ed.), *Disorders of the schizophrenic syndrome.* New York: Basic Books.

Xavier, F. A., Flaum, M., Andreasen, N. C., Strauss, D. H., Yale, S. A., Clark, S. C., & Gorman, J. M. (1994). Awareness of illness in schizophrenia and schizoaffective and mood disorders. *Archives of General Psychiatry, 51,* 826–836.

Yalom, I. D., Green, R., & Fish, N. (1973). Prenatal exposure to female hormones. *Archives of General Psychiatry, 28,* 554–561.

Yalom, I. D., Lunde, D. T., Moos, R. H., & Hamburg, D. A. (1968). "Postpartum blues" syndrome: A description and related variables. *Archives of General Psychiatry, 18,* 16–27.

Yankofsky, L., Wilson, G. T., Adler, J., Hay, W., & Vrana, S. (1986). The effect of alcohol on self-evaluation, awareness of negative interpersonal feedback, and perceptions of control and power. *Journal of Studies on Alcohol, 47,* 26–33.

Yates, A. J. (1975). *Theory and practice in behavior therapy.* New York: Wiley.

Yirmiya, N., & Sigman, M., (1991). High-functioning individuals with autism: Diagnosis, empirical findings, and theoretical issues. *Clinical Psychology Review, 11,* 669–683.

Yokoyama, T., Copeland, N. G., Jenkins, N. A., Montgomery, C. A. Elder, F. F., & Overbeek, P. A. (1993). Reversal of left-right asymmetry: A situs inversus mutation. *Science, 260,* 679–682.

Yonker, K. A., Kando, J. C., Cole, J. O., & Blumenthal, S. (1992). Gender differences in pharmacokinetics and pharmacodynamics of psychotropic medication. *American Journal of Psychiatry, 149,* 587–595.

Yoshikawa, H. (1994). Prevention as cumulative protection: Effects of early family support and education on chronic delinquency and its risks. *Psychological Bulletin, 115,* 28–54.

Young, R. C., & Klerman, G. L. (1992). Mania in late life: Focus on age at onset. *American Journal of Psychiatry, 149,* 867–878.

Young, W. C., Goy, R. W., & Phoenix, C. H. (1964). Hormones and sexual behavior. *Science, 143,* 212–218.

Youngberg v. Romeo, 457 U.S. 307 (1981).

Yu, P., Harris, G. E., Solovitz, B. L., & Franklin, J. L. (1986). A social problem-solving intervention for children at high risk for later psychopathology. *Journal of Clinical Child Psychology, 15,* 30–40.

Zametkin, A. J., Nordahl, T. E., Gross, M., King, A. C., Stemple, W. E., Rumsey, J., Hamburger, S., & Cohen, R. M. (1990). Cerebral glucose metabolism in adults with hyperactivity of childhood onset. *New England Journal of Medicine, 323,* 1361–1366.

Zamula, E. (1988). Taming Tourette's tics and twitches. *FDA Consumer Report, 22,* 104–110.

Zanarini, M. C., Gunderson, J. G., & Frankenburg, F. R. (1990). Cognitive features of the borderline personality disorder. *American Journal of Psychiatry, 147,* 57–63.

Zanarini, M. C., Gunderson, J. G., Frankenburg, F. R., & Chauncey, D. L. (1990). Discriminating borderline personality disorder from other Axis II disorders. *American Journal of Psychiatry, 147,* 161–167.

Zautra, A. J., Burleson, M. H., Matt, K. S., Roth, S., & Burrows, L. (1994). Interpersonal stress, depression, and disease activity in rheumatoid arthritis and osteoarthritis patients. *Health Psychology, 13,* 139–148.

Zeisset, R. M. (1968). Desensitization and relaxation in the modification of psychiatric patients' interview behavior. *Journal of Abnormal Psychology, 73,* 13–24.

Zerbin-Rudin, E. (1972). Genetic research and the theory of schizophrenia. *International Journal of Mental Health, 1,* 42–62.

Ziegler, F. J., Imboden, J. B., & Meyer, E. (1960). Contemporary conversion reactions: A clinical study. *American Journal of Psychiatry, 116,* 901–909.

Zigler, E. (1969). Development versus difference theories of mental retardation and the problem of motivation. *American Journal of Mental Deficiency, 73,* 536–555.

Zigler, E., & Balla, D. (1982). *Mental retardation: The developmental-difference controversy.* Hillsdale, NJ: Erlbaum.

Zigler, E., & Phillips, L. (1961). Psychiatric diagnosis: A critique. *Journal of Abnormal and Social Psychology, 3,* 607–618.

Zilbovicius, M., Garreau, B., Samson, Y., Remy, P., Beathelemy, C., Syrota, A., & Lelord, G. (1995). Delayed maturation of the frontal cortex in childhood autism. *American Journal of Psychiatry, 152,* 248–252.

Zillmann, D. (1983). Transfer of excitation in emotional behavior. In J. T. Cacioppo & R. E. Petty (Eds.), *Social psychophysiology: A sourcebook.* New York: Guilford Press.

Zillmann, D., Schweitzer, K. J., & Mundorf, N. (1994). Menstrual cycle variation of women's interest in erotica. *Archives of Sexual Behavior, 23,* 579–594.

Zimmerman, A., Frye, V., & Potter, N. (1993). Immunological aspects of autism. *International Pediatrics, 8,* 199–204.

Zinermon v. Burch, 110 S.Ct. 975 (1990).

Zipursky, R. B., Lim, K. O., Sullivan, E. V., Brown, B. W., & Pfefferbaum, A. (1992). Widespread cerebral gray matter volume deficits in schizophrenia. *Archives of General Psychiatry, 49,* 195–205.

Zis, A. P., & Goodwin, F. K. (1982). The amine hypothesis. In E. S. Paykel (Ed.), *Handbook of affective disorders.* New York: Guilford Press.

Zotter, D. L., & Crowther, J. H. (1991). The role of cognitions in bulimia nervosa. *Cognitive Therapy and Research, 15,* 413–426.

Zubenko, G. S., George, A. W., Soloff, P. H., & Schulz, P. (1987). Sexual practices among patients with borderline personality disorder. *American Journal of Psychiatry, 144,* 748–752.

Zubieta, J. K., & Alessi, N. E. (1993). Is there a role of serotonin in the disruptive behavior disorders? A literature review. *Journal of Child and Adolescent Psychopharmacology, 3,* 11–35.

Zucker, R., & Gomberg, E. (1986). Etiology of alcoholism reconsidered: The case for a biopsychosocial process. *American Psychologist, 41,* 783–793.

PHOTO CREDITS

NAME INDEX

SUBJECT INDEX

Abbott, Jim, 25
Abuse, 472. *See also* Substance dependence
   and abuse
Acrophobia, 95
Active phase, of schizophrenia, 294
Acute stress disorder, characteristics of, 92,
   102
Addictive personality, 488
Adler, Alfred, 25–26
Admitting wards, 587
Adolescence
   antisocial behavior and impulsivity in, 488
   attention-deficit/hyperactivity disorder
     in, 405–411
   conduct disorder in, 411–413
   depression in, 196
   eating disorders in, 433
   elimination disorders in, 422–423
   hospitalization during, 588
   Minnesota Multiphasic Personality Inven-
     tory for adolescents (MMPI-A), 64
   social isolation in, 318–319
   suicide in, 211, 213–214, 246
   tic disorders in, 423–425
Adoptee studies, 81
   alcoholism and, 491
   antisocial personality disorder and, 387
   bipolar disorder and, 243
   depression and, 238
   schizophrenia and, 339–340
   suicide and, 251
Aerobic exercise
   cardiovascular disorders and, 455–456
   depression and, 226
   immunological disorders and, 462
Age
   and antisocial personality disorder,
     379–381, 388
   and anxiety disorders, 104, 106, 155
   and bipolar disorder, 207
   and depression, 196, 199, 200–201
   and eating disorders, 433
   hospital wards based on, 588
   and schizophrenia, 304
   and suicide, 210
Aggression
   antisocial personality disorder and,
     379
   conduct disorder and, 412
   serotonin and, 266
   suicide and, 250
Agitated depression, 188
Agoraphobia, 72, 92, 94, 97, 152–154
Agranulocytosis, 364
Akathisia, 269, 365
Alcohol, 471–475, 490–491, 539
Alcohol abuse, 4
Alcoholics Anonymous, 493, 608
Alcoholism, 4
   binge type of, 489
   delirium disorders in, 475, 539

family influences on, 488
and fetal alcohol syndrome (FAS),
   547–548
persistent type of, 488–489
physiological explanations for, 491–492
primary, 491
secondary (psychopathic), 491
sociocultural factors in, 492
treatment of, 495
Algophobia, 95
All-or-none principle, 42
Alprazolam (Xanax), 151, 475–476
Alzheimer's disease, 531, 532–534, 535–537,
   544
Amenorrhea, 432
American Law Institute rule, 562–563
American Medical Association, 15
American Psychiatric Association, 56
American Psychological Association, 46
Amine hypothesis, 43
Amines, 43
Amitriptyline (Elavil), 275–276
Amnesia
   anterograde, 540
   dissociative, 171–172
   retrograde, 271–272, 540
   transient, 540
Amnesia disorders, 539–540
Amok, 46–47
Amphetamine psychoses, 479
Amphetamines, 268, 478–479
Amygdala, 40, 337
Anafranil (clomipramine), 47, 124, 151,
   152, 166, 421
Analogue research, 78
Anal stage, 21–22
Analysts, 9–10
Androgens, 524
Anesthesia, 162, 163
Aneurysm, 538
Anger turned inward, depression as,
   223–224
Angina, 449
Angioplasty, 454
Animal research, 77–78
   classical conditioning in, 10, 29, 31, 114,
     115
   on gender identity disorder, 524
   on learned helplessness, 233
Anna O. (case), 8, 29
Anorexia, 165, 431–441
Anoxia, 408
Antabuse (disulfiram), 495
Antagonistic reactions, 507
Anterograde amnesia, 540
Antiandrogens, 520–521
Anticonvulsive drugs, 278
Antidepressant drugs, 263–268
   for autistic disorder, 421
   for obsessive-compulsive disorder, 124,
     150, 151–152, 153

for orgasmic disorders, 511
for panic disorder, 123–124, 150, 152–154
serotonin and, 123, 124–125, 151, 152,
   263–265, 511
side effects of, 208
for sleep disorders, 444
Antigens, 460
Antihistamines, 11
Antipsychotic drugs, 11–12, 444
Antisocial personality disorder, 377–389
   age and, 379–381, 388
   causes of, 381–387
   cognitive perspective on, 385
   diagnosis of, 377
   historical background, 381
   issues concerning, 379–381
   learning-based perspective on, 382–385,
     488
   physiological perspective on, 385–387,
     488
   prevalence of, 379–381
   primary versus secondary, 381
   psychodynamic perspective on, 381–382
   substance dependence and, 488, 489
   symptoms of, 377–379, 388
   treatment of, 387–389
Anxiety. *See also* Stress
   alcohol in reduction of, 489–490
   and arousal disorders, 505–508
   blocking of, 142, 145–146
   cognitive versus somatic, 106–107
   and defense mechanisms, 23–25, 28
   eating disorders and, 437
   extinction of, 141–143
   fear versus, 105–106
   inhibition of, 142, 144–145
   lack of, 378
   normal versus abnormal, 102–103
   sources of, 25–26
   trait versus state, 106
Anxiety disorders, 90–156. *See also* Anxiety
     states; Phobic disorders
   anxiety states, 92, 96–102
   causes of, 110–128
   cognitive perspective on, 91, 116–121,
     128, 142, 146–150
   diagnosis of, 57, 91, 102–107
   issues concerning, 102–107
   learning-based perspective on, 113–116,
     128, 141–146
   phobic disorders, 92–96
   physiological perspective on, 91, 121–128,
     150–156
   prevalence of, 104
   psychodynamic perspective on, 91,
     111–113, 128, 132–141
   sociocultural perspective on, 104–105,
     155
   symptoms of, 91, 102–104, 106–107
   treatment of, 123–124, 132–156
   types of, 92–102

Negative Symptoms)/Episodic With No Interepisode Residual Symptoms/ Continuous (specify if: With Prominent Negative Symptoms)
Single Episode In Partial Remission (specify if: With Prominent Negative Symptoms)/ Single Episode In Full Remission
Other or Unspecified Pattern
.30   Paranoid Type
.10   Disorganized Type
.20   Catatonic Type
.90   Undifferentiated Type
.60   Residual Type
295.40   Schizophreniform Disorder
Specify if: Without Good Prognostic Features/With Good Prognostic Features
295.70   Schizoaffective Disorder
Specify type: Bipolar Type/ Depressive Type
297.1   Delusional Disorder
Specify type: Erotomanic Type/ Grandiose Type/Jealous Type/ Persecutory Type/Somatic Type/ Mixed Type/Unspecified Type
298.8   Brief Psychotic Disorder
Specify if: With Marked Stressor(s)/ Without Marked Stressor(s)/With Postpartum Onset
297.3   Shared Psychotic Disorder
293.xx   Psychotic Disorder Due to . . . *[Indicate the General Medical Condition]*
.81   With Delusions
.82   With Hallucinations
——.—   Substance-Induced Psychotic Disorder *(refer to Substance-Related Disorders for substance-specific codes)*
Specify if: With Onset During Intoxication/With Onset During Withdrawal
298.9   Psychotic Disorder NOS

MOOD DISORDERS (317)

Code current state of Major Depressive Disorder or Bipolar I Disorder in fifth digit:
1 = Mild
2 = Moderate
3 = Severe Without Psychotic Features
4 = Severe With Psychotic Features
    Specify: Mood-Congruent Psychotic Features/Mood-Incongruent Psychotic Features
5 = In Partial Remission
6 = In Full Remission
0 = Unspecified
The following specifiers apply (for current or most recent episode) to Mood Disorders as noted:
[a]Severity/Psychotic/Remission Specifiers/ [b]Chronic/[c]With Catatonic Features/[d]With Melancholic Features/[e]With Atypical Features/[f]With Postpartum Onset
The following specifiers apply to Mood Disorders as noted:
[g]With or Without Full Interepisode Recovery/ [h]With Seasonal Pattern/[i]with Rapid Cycling
Depressive Disorders
296.xx   Major Depressive Disorder
.2x   Single Episode[a,b,c,d,e,f]
.3x   Recurrent[a,b,c,d,e,f,g,h]
300.4   Dysthymic Disorder
Specify if: Early Onset/Late Onset
Specify: With Atypical Features
311   Depressive Disorder NOS

Bipolar Disorders
296.xx   Bipolar I Disorder
.0x   Single Manic Episode[a,c,f]
    Specify if: Mixed
.40   Most Recent Episode Hypomanic[g,h,i]
.4x   Most Recent Episode Manic[a,c,f,g,h,i]
.6x   Most Recent Episode Mixed[a,c,f,g,h,i]
.5x   Most Recent Episode Depressed[a,b,c,d,e,f,g,h,i]
.7   Most Recent Episode Unspecified[g,h,i]
296.89   Bipolar II Disorder[a,b,c,d,e,f,g,h,i]
Specify (current or most recent episode): Hypomanic/Depressed
301.13   Cyclothymic Disorder
296.80   Bipolar Disorder NOS
293.83   Mood Disorder Due to . . . *[Indicate the General Medical Condition]*
Specify type: With Depressive Features/With Major Depressive-Like Episode/With Manic Features/ With Mixed Features
——.—   Substance-Induced Mood Disorder *(refer to Substance-Related Disorders for substance-specific codes)*
Specify type: With Depressive Features/With Manic Features/With Mixed Features
Specify type: With Onset During Intoxication/With Onset During Withdrawal
296.90   Mood Disorder NOS

Anxiety Disorder (393)

300.01   Panic Disorder Without Agoraphobia
300.21   Panic Disorder With Agoraphobia
300.22   Agoraphobia Without History of Panic Disorder
300.29   Specific Phobia
Specify type: Animal Type/Natural Environment Type/Blood-Injection-Injury Type/Situational Type/Other Type
300.23   Social Phobia
Specify if: Generalized
300.3   Obsessive-Compulsive Disorder
Specify if: With Poor Insight
309.81   Posttraumatic Stress Disorder
Specify if: Acute/Chronic
Specify if: With Delayed Onset
308.3   Acute Stress Disorder
300.02   Generalized Anxiety Disorder
293.89   Anxiety Disorder Due to . . . *[Indicate the General Medical Condition]*
Specify if: With Generalized Anxiety/ With Panic Attacks/With Obsessive-Compulsive Symptoms
——.—   Substance-Induced Anxiety Disorder *(refer to Substance-Related Disorders for substance-specific codes)*
Specify if: With Generalized Anxiety/ With Panic Attacks/With Obsessive-Compulsive Symptoms/With Phobic Symptoms
Specify if: With Onset During Intoxication/With Onset During Withdrawal
300.00   Anxiety Disorder NOS

SOMATOFORM DISORDERS (445)

300.81   Somatization Disorder
300.81   Undifferentiated Somatoform Disorder

300.11   Conversion Disorder
Specify type: With Motor Symptom or Deficit/With Sensory Symptom or Deficit/With Seizures or Convulsions/With Mixed Presentation
307.xx   Pain Disorder
.80   Associated With Psychological Factors
.89   Associated With Both Psychological Factors and a General Medical Condition
Specify if: Acute/Chronic
300.7   Hypochondriasis
Specify if: With Poor Insight
300.7   Body Dysmorphic Disorder
300.81   Somatoform Disorder NOS

FACTITIOUS DISORDERS (471)

300.xx   Factitious Disorder
.16   With Predominantly Psychological Signs and Symptoms
.19   With Predominantly Physical Signs and Symptoms
.19   With Combined Psychological and Physical Signs and Symptoms
300.19   Factitious Disorder NOS

DISSOCIATIVE DISORDERS (477)

300.12   Dissociative Amnesia
300.13   Dissociative Fugue
300.14   Dissociative Identity Disorder
300.6   Depersonalization Disorder
300.15   Dissociative Disorder NOS

SEXUAL AND GENDER IDENTITY DISORDERS (493)

Sexual Dysfunctions
The following specifiers apply to all primary Sexual Dysfunctions:
Lifelong Type/Acquired Type
Generalized Type/Situational Type
Due to Psychological Factors/Due to Combined Factors
Sexual Desire Disorders
302.71   Hypoactive Sexual Desire Disorder
302.79   Sexual Aversion Disorder
Sexual Arousal Disorders
302.72   Female Sexual Arousal Disorder
302.72   Male Erectile Disorder
Orgasmic Disorders
302.73   Female Orgasmic Disorder
302.74   Male Orgasmic Disorder
302.75   Premature Ejaculation
Sexual Pain Disorders
302.76   Dyspareunia (Not Due to a General Medical Condition)
306.51   Vaginismus (Not Due to a General Medical Condition)
Sexual Dysfunction Due to a General Medical Condition
625.8   Female Hypoactive Sexual Desire Disorder Due to . . . *[Indicate the General Medical Condition]*
608.89   Male Hypoactive Sexual Desire Disorder Due to . . . *[Indicate the General Medical Condition]*
607.84   Male Erectile Disorder Due to . . . *[Indicate the General Medical Condition]*
625.0   Female Dyspareunia Due to . . . *[Indicate the General Medical Condition]*
608.89   Male Dyspareunia Due to . . . *[Indicate the General Medical Condition]*